KU-449-662

THE ENCYCLOPEDIA OF SHIPS

THE ENCYCLOPEDIA OF SHIPS

GENERAL EDITOR: TONY GIBBONS

FOREWORD BY REAR ADMIRAL ROY CLARE
DIRECTOR OF NATIONAL MARITIME MUSEUM, GREENWICH

Published by Silverdale Books
an imprint of Bookmart Ltd
Registered number 2372865
Trading as Bookmart Ltd
Blaby Road
Wigston
Leicester LE18 4SE

Reprinted 2002, 2003, 2004

ISBN: 1-85605-591-4

Editorial and design by
Amber Books Ltd
Bradleys Close
74-77 White Lion Street
London
N1 9PF

Authors: Roger Ford, Tony Gibbons, Rob Hewson, Bob Jackson, David Ross
Editors: Helen Wilson, Naomi Waters
Designer: Jeremy Williams
Illustrations: Tony Gibbons, Guy Smith

Printed in Singapore

Contents

The British ship *Royal George* is a fine example of an 18th century first-rate.

Foreword

Fewer people now earn their living afloat than at any time in the past 100 years, so it could be imagined that interest in maritime issues is ebbing. Indeed, it has been said that Britain and other countries have turned their back on the sea.

Yet there is proof to the contrary. Some 80 per cent of the world's population live within a day's journey of the coast, where a single tall ship alongside a quay attracts comments from passers by; a few together may cause a small crowd to point and stare; add more and people are likely to celebrate. This is the philosophy of organisers of International Festivals of the Sea and it is the experience of spectators at a parade of sail or the start of a major sailing event.

Now, this distinguished book adds to an armada of evidence that mankind's awareness of the sea is proportional to the scale and quality of effort devoted to projecting and interpreting it. An authoritative publication like this, an accessible exhibition at a museum like the National Maritime Museum, a vivid documentary, a graphic explanation, these are the ingredients of better understanding and insight and correspondingly greater support for the sea and sea affairs. Inescapably, the sea is the life support system for planet earth; it is also a farmyard, sometimes a battleground, and often an adventure park.

Above all, it is a trading highway, the life-giving arteries of international economies. Ships are the means by which wealth is delivered, exchanged and exported and their crews are the hard working enablers, who help to create conditions for successful trade. Individually, these men and women carry awesome responsibility; a typical, large container ship and her cargo can represent investment on a billion-dollar scale. Travelling swiftly between ports, these crews experience such risks of the sea as might intimidate faint hearts, yet seafarers bear these challenges with traditional professionalism. Countless millions of cargo and passenger miles are accomplished without incident; a statistical few reach the headlines and carry severe environmental and safety consequences, highlighting the fine judgement and skill this profession demands each day.

So this handsome celebration of ships is more than a beautiful book, packed with information, stylishly illustrated, loaded with facts and featuring every conceivable type of vessel – even some of my own commands, including the aircraft carrier HMS *Invincible*. It is also a reminder of the nature of the sea and her unforgiving ways, and a commemoration of her essential contribution to sustaining life itself and to creating wealth. It is a tribute to those who serve at sea and on its fringes and it is evidence of the diversity of technologies afloat. Best of all, it is a feast for those with a passion for the sea.

For these reasons and many more, I commend the researchers, authors, illustrators and publishers of the comprehensive work and congratulate them on a fine product. I am certain that you, dear reader, will enjoy navigating its pages.

Rear Admiral Roy Clare
Director, National Maritime Museum, Greenwich

The USS *Iowa* at sunset. From 1952 to 1958 she served with the US Atlantic Fleet, forming an important component of NATO's naval forces.

Introduction

For centuries mankind has travelled the oceans in search of commerce or to extend his own frontiers. This extensive book is a factual and pictorial record of those achievements set out in a clear format divided up into sections that breakdown the real progress in mercantile history as well as naval development.

Many advances have occurred gradually as new methods of shipbuilding and available materials dictated development as well as the areas of operation for ships of many nations ranging from small inshore rafts to vessels able to cross the oceans of the world.

Long before the Iron Age with its simple plank boats of Northern Europe, the Pharaohs were building sophisticated ships able to negotiate the Mediterranean. From this period distinct types of ships evolved with cargo vessels possessing uniquely different hull forms designed for great carrying capacity whilst the warship developed as fast, manoeuvrable fighting platforms able to mount and use a wide range of weapons.

The vessels of the Bronze Age were limited in their ability but by about 700BC the Greeks derived from

the Phoenicians fast-oared fighting ships with several banks of oars. This was typical of the type of fighting ship that fought at Salamis and remained the standard type for a considerable time after the Peloponnesian War. Manned by large crews sailors were able to propel these agile vessels at high speed under favourable conditions. Such speeds were not reached by sailing ships until several centuries later. Battle tactics were developed in this period notably by the Greek admiral Phormio in 400BC enabling him to defeat superior forces.

The launch of the *Lexington* on 3 October 1925. She and her sistership *Saratoga* were commissioned in late 1927. Both served with distinction in the Pacific during World War II.

Though Roman merchant ships had sailed the Mediterranean since the beginning of the third century BC the development of a fighting navy had been neglected. Carthage, originally a colony of the Phoenicians, possessed a strong navy because of the necessity to seek their livelihood on the Mediterranean. When commercial rivalry finally caused a war between Rome and Carthage in 264BC Romans soon saw the need to develop their navy and modelled their warships upon those captured from Carthage. Although the Romans were originally defeated they soon perfected their tactics developing the boarding bridge which enabled their soldiers to storm onto the decks of the Carthaginian vessels.

For several centuries there was little development in shipbuilding in the Mediterranean where the lateen rig held sway. This had been copied from the Gulf and Indian Ocean, where it was used by Arab traders because it had good sailing qualities especially in coastal waters. Such a rig, however, was not suitable for long ocean voyages where the fore and aft rig gave a better performance.

***Henry Grace à Dieu*, or the 'Great Harry', was a sistership to the *Mary Rose*, and was Henry VIII's flagship when he visited France at the Field of the Cloth of Gold in 1520.**

With the end of Roman seapower in the Mediterranean the development of shipbuilding underwent further changes especially in northern waters. Here the exploits of the Scandinavians began to have an effect upon surrounding countries who had no navies of any importance but relied mostly upon their armies for defence.

In northern Europe the warship began to develop upon distinct lives of its own. By 1300AD high castles were added to the ends of the vessel to give bowmen a distinct height advantage in battle. Over the next 300 years or so these castles grew in size but as the gun became the main weapon, housed in the hull for better stability, so the castles were reduced to a low poop and forecastle.

As the fore and aft rig gained predominance so the galleys with their banks of oars fell from favour. The need to have the hull sides left clear for the many rowers meant that only the extreme ends could carry

Los Angeles is the lead boat of a class of no less than 62 nuclear attack submarines, built for the US Navy in the last three decades of the 20th century.

guns making these lightly built vessels no match even for the lightly-armed frigates.

From 1400 warships and merchant vessels continued to develop along different lines. Ships would no longer need to carry a single mast but two- and later three-masted vessels were built which proved reliable on long voyages. The early practice of steering with a single large oar at the stern gave way to the rudder right aft on the centre line of the vessel so giving more positive control on the steering. Other detailed improvements in technology occurred, notably the compass and the hour glass and these, combined with the log which measured speed, made navigation by dead reckoning possible. Exploration of unknown seas and trade with far off countries was now possible.

By 1800 the sailing ship had reached the peak of its development. Over the proceeding few hundred years many countries developed their navies to a high degree with England, Spain, France and Holland leading the way and all with an expanding mercantile marine. Indeed, one of the prime factors in the development of these countries' naval forces was the need to protect the merchant ships trading in their far-flung colonies. By about 1800 America was also in the forefront of technology producing some of the world's finest sailing frigates.

Vessels were still built of wood and carried ever greater spreads of sails but by the end of the 17th century the first experiments were being made with steam propulsion, a method that would free ships from being reliant on the wind and eventually, once the steam engine reached a degree of perfection, enable ships to make faster passages along more direct routes. The industrial revolution ushered in other changes such as the use of iron, and later steel, in shipbuilding. In the 50 years between 1800 and 1850 there were more changes in ship construction than there had been in the proceeding 500 years.

In spite of these dramatic developments the sailing ship continued to play a major role in world commerce. In the 1860s the fast clipper ship appeared intended for service in the tea, wool and grain trade. The general cargo sailing vessel amongst the burgeoning steamship fleets to such an extent that in 1900 well over one third of all merchant ships, 10M tons out of 24M tons worldwide, were sailing ships. By 1932 there were still nearly 3000 sailing merchant ships over 100 tons still in regular service.

By the mid 1800s steam became more dominant and this, coupled with the growth in manufacturing, accelerated warship development although early attempts to build iron hulled warships were not successful. Up to 1860 major warships were still built of wood, some of these steam powered carried over 120 guns on three decks but in the late 1850s a major change took place with the laying down of Dupuy de Lôme's splendid creation *Gloire* which, although it had a wooden hull, was completely covered in iron armour able to resist the guns of the period.

With the introduction of the ironclad warship a completely new era of naval development opened up which, at one stroke, consigned the world's wooden battle fleets to the scrap heap. Progress in the development of warships now accelerated with the constant conflict between guns and armouring first giving advantage to one and then the other. A whole new range of warships also grew out of new found technology ranging from cruisers to submarines with a wide range of new weapons being introduced such as mines and torpedoes, all needed to fight a modern war. This trend has continued right up to the present day with the aircraft carrier now the main battle fleet unit with nuclear powered missile submarines able to patrol the world's oceans submerged without detection for months on end.

So too with merchant shipping. Progress here since 1900 has been tremendous with various new types of ships being introduced. Older styles of cargo boats have almost disappeared with bulk cargo carriers and container ships taking their place. Ocean liners once fashionable in the 1920s and 1930s became unfashionable in the 1950s as a result of expanding air travel but now there are cruise ships sailing the oceans; some of these huge floating hotels are amongst the largest vessels in the world.

All this is laid before the reader in the following pages; I hope you find it informative and instructive but above all enjoyable.

Voyager of the Seas **is a typical example of the enormous 'floaty hotel' concept that has dominated passenger-ship construction in recent years.**

THE AGE OF SAIL

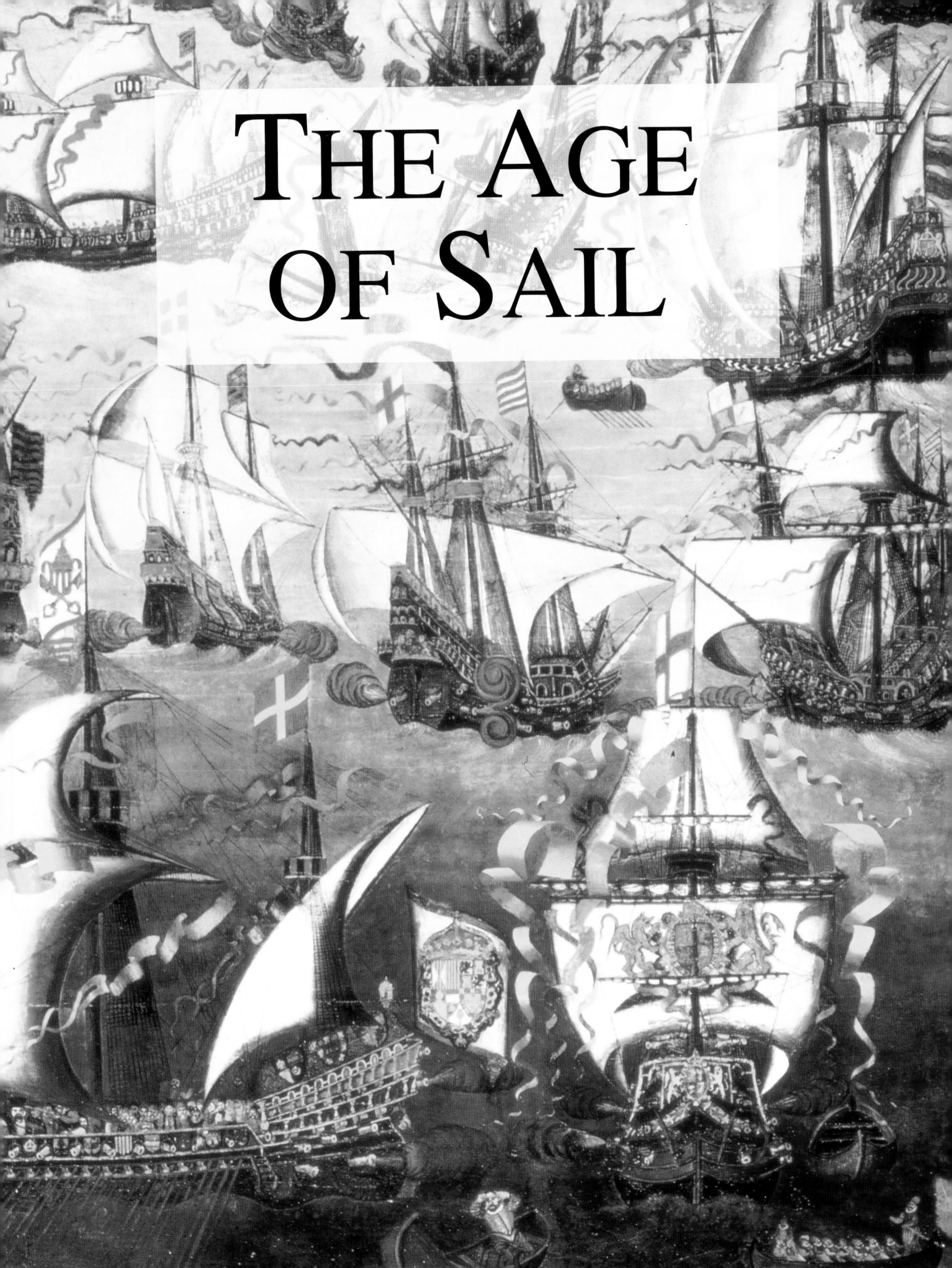

CHAPTER ONE

EARLY SHIPS UNTIL 1450

The greatest inventions in the history of ship construction took place long before any historical record exists. They were the hollowed-out – and later the assembled – hull; the paddle, the mast, the sail and the steering oar. With these, the human race had powered craft at its disposal from very early times. Right up to the introduction of steam power, new developments simply built on these basic features.

During the period of the Old Kingdom (*c*2680BC to *c*2180BC) models of reed boats were placed in tombs; higher up the Nile, wooden boats were built. The Egyptians' earlier vessels were chiefly for use on the Nile and its canals. Other races, however, were using sea-going boats. The windswept Orkney Islands, north of Scotland, were colonised by a seaborne people at a time before the Pyramids were built. On the coasts, rivers and lakes of ancient China, boats were used for trade and war.

Left: A contemporary painting of a fleet of sailing vessels employed to carry Isabella of Hainault from France to England, to wed Edward II.

In terms of later developments, the great cradle of early shipping was the eastern Mediterranean Sea. Round its coasts, a succession of resourceful trading and colonising peoples – Cretans, Greeks, Phoenicians, Romans – built increasingly specialised vessels for many different uses, although the main purpose was always fishing and cargo carrying. Passengers were an extra, accommodated on deck and in cramped cabin space below. The protection of trade routes and colonies brought about the need for warships. It was the building of these that helped to speed up the development of marine technology in the classical world: the fastest, best-armed, most manoeuvrable ships were the battle winners. Maritime states expended much of their resources in maintaining and improving their war fleets. From the 6th century BC on, naval battles were a regular aspect of warfare.

Roman rule developed the trading routes, and the fall of the empire did not stop trade. Eventually, new states emerged, some, like the Vikings, with innovative ships. By the 13th century the Mediterranean and Nordic traditions were merging, although each kept distinctive features.

EGYPTIAN REED BOAT

EGYPT: 3200BC

Evidence of reed boats from Egypt and South America has led us to assume that these were among the earliest boat types developed. Depictions of boats made from papyrus reeds go back to around 3200BC. In the Nile Delta, where timber was scarce and water everywhere, papyrus made a natural material for boatbuilding. Although the life of each vessel was only a few months, the supply of reeds was endless. Small reed boats are still constructed today.

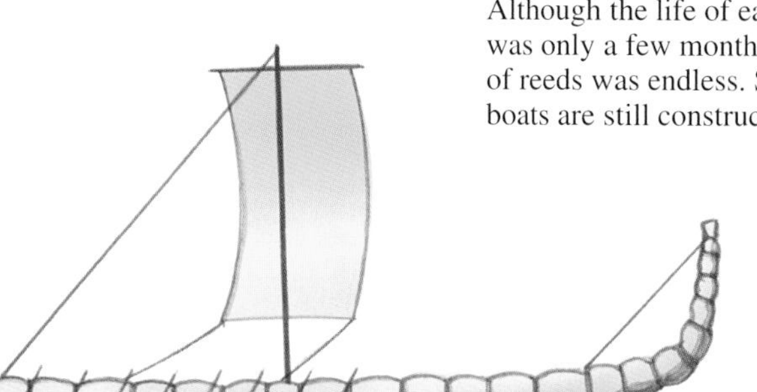

Length: 54ft (16.5m)
Beam: 9ft (2.7m)
Depth: 5ft (1.5m)
Displacement: not known
Rigging: none
Complement: not known
Main routes: Nile Delta
Cargo: fish, reeds, grain

In the Ra I and Ra II expeditions, the explorer Thor Heyerdahl deomonstrated that a reed vessel was capable of crossing the Atlantic.

CHEOPS SHIP

EGYPT: 2500BC

The Cheops ship, the oldest preserved ship from antiquity, was found in 1954 close to the Great Pyramid in Egypt. It is built almost entirely of imported cedar. Its 'shell-first' design shows that the hull was shaped before the internal members were added. It has no keel, and the side planking is lashed with rope for security. Two cabins stand on deck, the two-roomed main one covered by a canopy for added coolness. The ship is equipped with oars plus steering oars.

The Cheops ship was clearly a ceremonial vessel, yet compression marks of rope show that it was definitely used in the water.

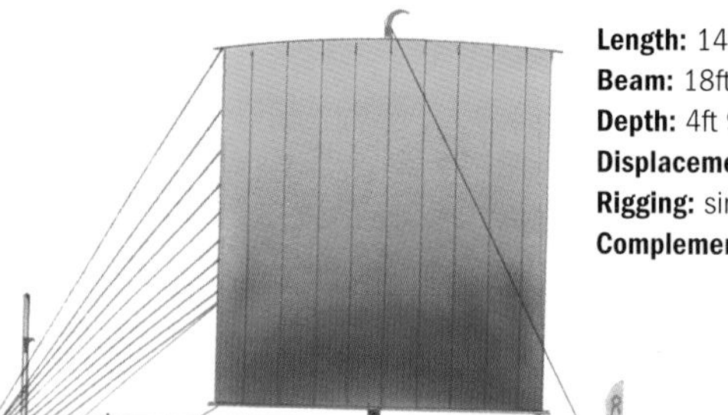

Length: 143ft (43.6m)
Beam: 18ft 7in (5.7m)
Depth: 4ft 9in (1.45m)
Displacement: 94t
Rigging: single mast
Complement: 12 plus officers

EGYPTIAN WARSHIP

EGYPT: *c*2500BC

Length: 70ft (21.3m)
Beam: 25ft (7.6m)
Depth: 6ft (1.8m)
Displacement: not known
Rigging: bipod mast; square sail
Armament: not known
Complement: not known

The squadron sent by Pharaoh Sahure in *c*2500BC to harry the Phoenician coast may have consisted of armed merchant ships rather than warships. Made of wooden blocks secured to one another by pegs, they had neither keel nor frame – a strong rope stretched above the deck from stem to stern helped to maintain rigidity; other ropes helped secure the sides. The mast was a bipod which could be dismounted in a contrary wind, when rowers took over.

By this time, a form of rowlock had been developed, and oars rather than paddles were used against the wind.

EGYPTIAN RIVER VESSEL

EGYPT: 2400BC

Length: 52ft (15.8m)
Beam: 12ft (3.7m)
Depth: 5ft (1.5m)
Displacement: 20t
Rigging: single dismountable mast; square sail
Complement: not known
Main routes: Nile River and Delta
Cargo: grain, foodstuffs, manufactured goods

The tomb of the 11th-dynasty chancellor Meket-ra has preserved a wide range of model river craft, including sporting boats.A variety of craft operated on the Nile, many of them reed boats. By around 2400BC, the newer wood-built designs had hulls built on to frames, and had a single dismountable mast instead of the older tripod or bipod. A single steering oar was fixed to the stern, and from six to nine oarsmen worked on each side. A deckhouse was fitted in the case of official vessels which was often quite elaborate. Cargo was carried on deck and sometimes beneath it.

EGYPTIAN BARGE

EGYPT: 1550BC

A massive obelisk barge was built for Queen Hatshepsut (ruled 1478–1458BC), and depicted in the rock temple of Deir-el-Bahri.

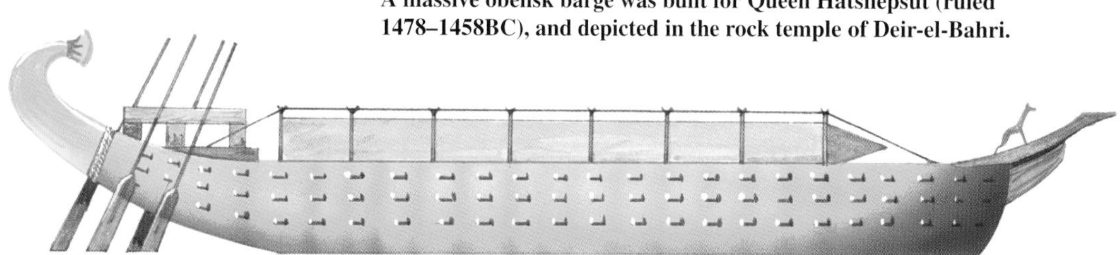

Length: 195ft (59.4m)
Beam: 70ft (21.3m)
Depth: 7ft (2.1m)
Displacement: 1500t loaded
Rigging: none
Complement: 900 including auxiliary crews
Main route: River Nile
Cargo: obelisks

The great temple obelisks were hewn from granite at Aswan, and floated down the Nile to Luxor and Heliopolis. Designed to hold two obelisks side by side, total weight 700t, this was the largest ship yet built. Unpowered, but fitted with a pair of steering oars at each side of the stern, it was prevented from hogging by a set of ropes secured at the bow, and wound round a windlass at the stern. The giant was towed by 27 small oared vessels, with a total manpower of around 900.

PHOENICIAN CARGO SHIP

PHOENICIA: 1500BC

The Phoenicians were a great trading nation and practical seafarers. Our evidence for this vessel comes from now-destroyed Egyptian tomb murals dating back to around 1500BC. Similar to Queen Hatshepsut's ships, it is the first to show such features as a masthead rope ladder and lookout point. The horse-head prow may have been a standard motif. There is no suggestion of rope bracing, implying that the vessel, even without a keel, had sufficient rigidity to withstand the sea. The wicker fencing was probably to separate deck cargo from the oarsmen. Timber was an important cargo, and one ancient relief, although from almost 700 years later, shows timber being towed. The Egyptian source showed a very large amphora attached to the prow – possibly for cargo, possibly for the crew's water or wine. Much of the detail on these ships is conjectural. Ships at this time possessed no metallic fixings at all. Ships at this time possessed no metallic fixings at all. The means of iron-making had not yet been discovered. Everything else would be of wood, rope or cloth, apart from pottery utensils.

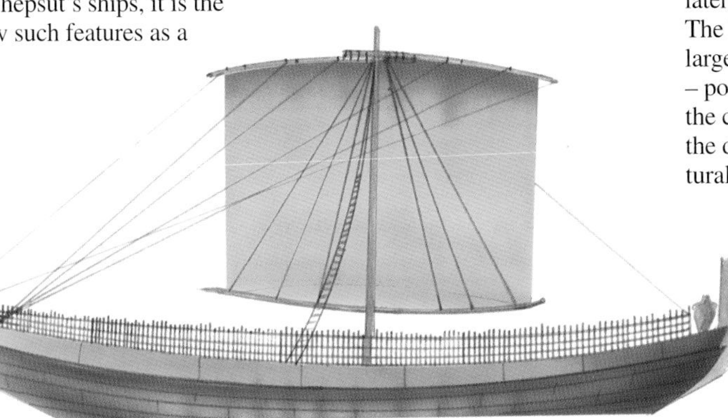

Length: 55ft (16.8m)
Beam: 12ft (3.7m)
Depth: 5ft (1.5m)
Displacement: not known
Rigging: single mast stayed fore and aft; square sail with upper and lower yards
Complement: 8–12
Main routes: eastern Mediterranean
Cargo: timber, grain, fish, metals

In ships like these, Solomon imported Lebanese timber to build his temple in Jerusalem.

EGYPTIAN CARGO SHIP

EGYPT: 1450BC

Length: 85ft (25.9m)
Beam: 18ft (5.5m)
Depth: 4ft (1.2m)
Displacement: not known
Rigging: single mast stayed fore and aft; square sail
Complement: 20
Main routes: Red Sea
Cargo: spices, tropical goods

Around 1450BC, Queen Hatshepsut sent a trading mission to the land of Punt, south of Nubia. The ships, of which this was one, sailed from a Red Sea port to the Somali coast. Although still rope-braced, this ship has a keel plank, projected into the lotus-shaped stern; and the lower yard, with its many lifts, shows that the sail has been made adaptable to varying winds. This is a ship designed to display and use 'state-of-the-art' technology.

Oarsmen were still essential, and short benches were built to accommodate them. The steering oars are mounted forward of the commander's platform.

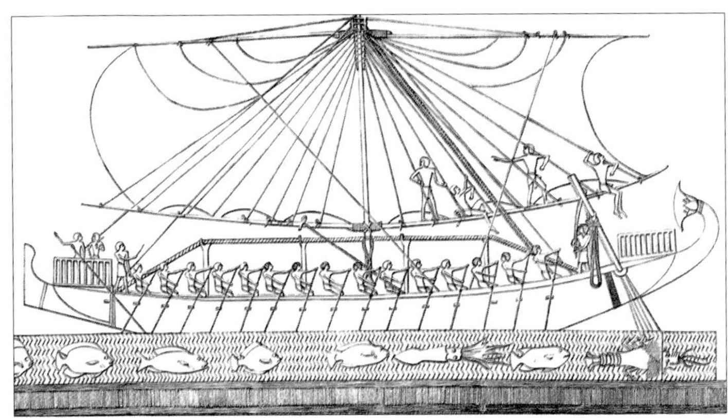

EGYPTIAN WAR GALLEY

EGYPT: 1180BC

Rameses III ruled Egypt from 1186 to 1154BC and constructed a fleet to repel the invasion of the 'People of the Sea'. The battle, fought off the Nile Delta, is graphically depicted in his tomb at Medinet Habu. The Pharaoh's ships show that the Egyptians, ultra-conservative in many ways, had learned much from their neighbours and enemies about shipbuilding. Rameses' galleys were assembled on a keel and equipped with rams, and with protective bulwarks for the oarsmen. They have fighting platforms fore and aft, side-screens and a crow's nest for a sharpshooter or lookout. The square sail could be readily furled by brailing up, instead of by the more laborious process of lowering the yard. These ships were 'state of the art', but after this period, Egyptian naval technology ceased to advance, and mastery of the seas passed to other nations.

Length: 75ft (22.9m)
Beam: 14ft (4.3m)
Depth: 5ft (1.5m)
Displacement: not known
Rigging: single mast stayed fore and aft; square sail on two-piece yard, loose-footed
Armament: ram; archers, spearmen
Complement: 24 oarsmen, steersman, plus deckhands and officers

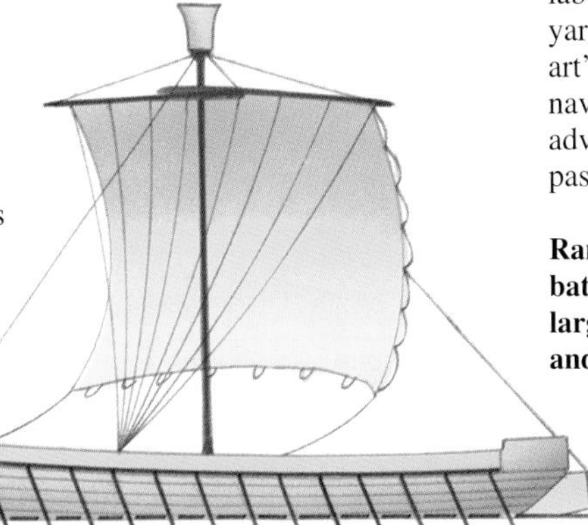

Rameses' victory is the first naval battle to be depicted. Fighting was largely hand-to-hand or with bows and arrows.

PHOENICIAN WAR GALLEY (BIREME) — PHOENICIA: *c*700BC

The appearance of this bireme, revolutionary at the time, signalled the beginning of Phoenician sea power. Mounted on a massive hollowed-out trunk, with thwarts built out to provide deck space for the outer set of double-banked oarsmen, the vessel also had a light, gallery-like upper deck to hold armed men. The bow terminated in a spiked ram, and the stern curved up in typical Mediterranean fashion. Some writers have doubted the dugout hull, although the original depictions seem to support it.

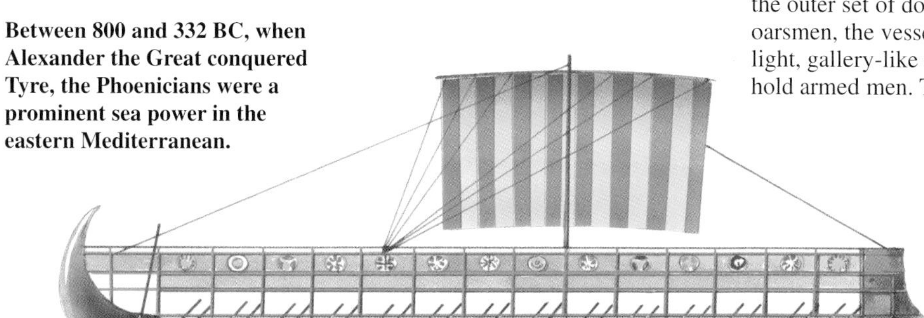

Between 800 and 332 BC, when Alexander the Great conquered Tyre, the Phoenicians were a prominent sea power in the eastern Mediterranean.

Length: 90ft (27.4m)
Beam: 14ft (4.3m)
Depth: 6ft (1.8m)
Displacement: not known
Rigging: single mast; square sail
Armament: ram; archers and spearmen on upper deck
Complement: *c*57 plus military

GREEK CARGO SHIP — GREEK CITY STATES: 500BC

At this time, there was little distinction between merchant ships and small warships; with war and piracy as constant factors, even a merchantman had to carry arms, and might well mount a ram at the prow. In emergencies, a city could commandeer its merchant fleet as warships. These pine-hulled vessels were light and manoeuvrable; sail technique was improving, and while oars were still carried, they were used only in calm or confined places.

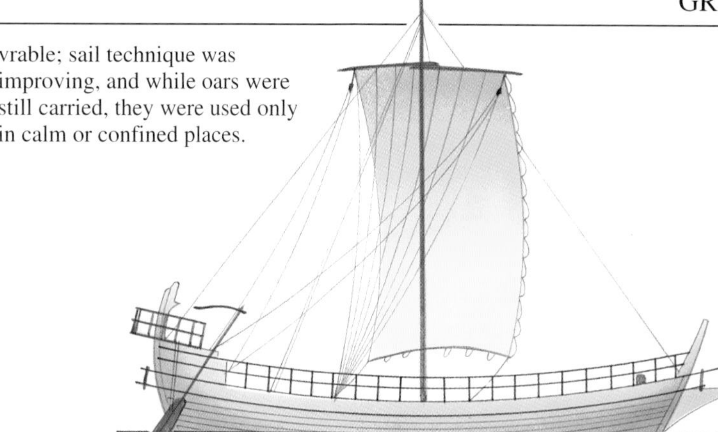

Wine and oil were frequent cargoes, carried in clay jars (amphorae); numerous wrecks of wine carriers have been located.

Length: 50ft (15.2m)
Beam: 14ft (4.3m)
Depth: 6ft (1.8m)
Displacement: not known
Rigging: single mast stayed fore and aft; furlable square sail
Complement: about 8
Main routes: Black Sea, Aegean and Ionian Seas
Cargo: wine, timber, grain, wool, hides

GREEK WAR GALLEY (BIREME) — GREEK STATES: 500BC

Length: 80ft (24.4m)
Beam: 10ft 6in (3.2m)
Depth: 5ft (1.5m)
Displacement: not known
Rigging: single mast stayed fore and aft, with two-piece yard; square sail
Armament: ram, flame pots; archers, spearmen
Complement: about 55 plus military

The standard Greek galley for hundreds of years before 700BC was the *pentecontor*, or 50-oared ship, with 25 oarsmen to a side in a single row. The two-tiered galley first appeared in the eastern Mediterranean around 700BC, and became the prime ship of war of that time. Evidence for its design comes mainly from paintings on contemporary Greek pottery. By 500BC, the bireme had been replaced for heavy duty by the trireme, but it continued to be widely used on account of its relative cheapness to build and its lightness. It was an ideal vessel for interception duties, and it could be hauled up stern-first on a suitable beach for an overnight bivouac, its paired steering oars pivoting up out of the way. Longitudinal strength was provided by the keel, and was reinforced by the 'catwalk' that ran the length of the vessel. The hull was assembled on ribs, a technique apparently first worked out in Corinth. The rowers were in two banks, the lower bank placed towards the centre, their oars resting on the rail; the upper placed further out, their oars resting on the outrigger framework that ran from the prow to the steering platform. The mast and single square sail were used only when the ship was running before the wind, and mast and yard could be dismounted when rowing into the wind. A large bireme mustered 50 oarsmen to a side, and could attain a ramming speed of over 10 knots. Like all Greek warships, biremes were kept hauled up out of the water in special shiphouses in ports such as Piraeus, and launched only for training and active service. Slave labour was not used in these vessels – the rowers were citizens liable for military service.

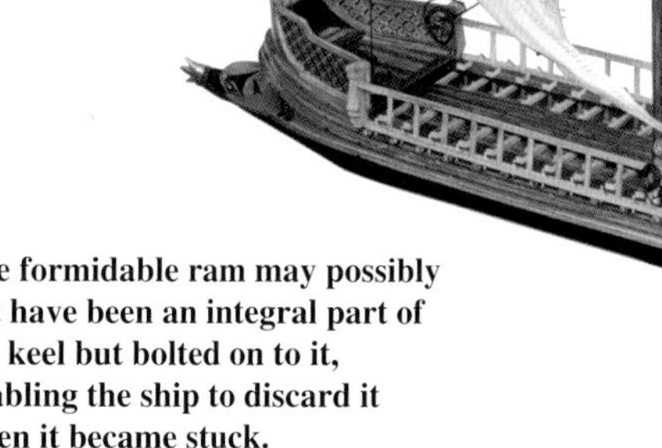

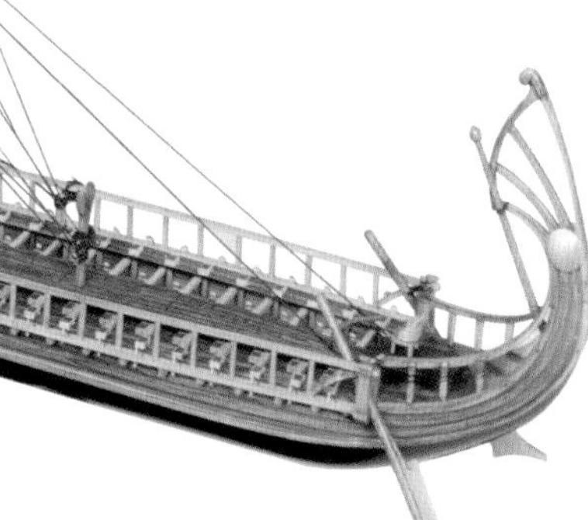

The formidable ram may possibly not have been an integral part of the keel but bolted on to it, enabling the ship to discard it when it became stuck.

GREEK WAR GALLEY (TRIREME)

GREEK CITY STATES: 500BC

The trireme was the heavy battleship of the classical world, representing the point at which weight, speed, and turning circle combined to form an optimum for the operation of an oared vessel. It has been likened to 'a giant spear, 50t in weight'. The rowers sat in three banks, one man to each oar. The type appears to have originated in the Greek city of Corinth around 650BC, and was quickly copied by other maritime states. Remarkably few details of the design survive, and there has been much controversy about how the trireme was laid out and rowed. The essence of the first trireme design was to incorporate an extra bank of oarsmen without making the ship much longer or heavier; better use was simply made of the hull space. The result was 170 oars powering the ship, 31 in the uppermost bank ('thranites') and 27 in each of the lower two ('thalamists' and 'zygians'). The zygian bank was close to the waterline, and sleeves were used to prevent water from entering the oar-ports. A platform deck ran from bow to stern above the top bank, and two dismountable masts were fitted – a short foremast and a mainmast – both carrying a square sail for use with a following wind. An open-decked Athenian trireme could travel 184 nautical miles (341km) in 24 hours, and attain a ramming speed 11.5 knots. The battle of Salamis in 479BC, in which a Greek fleet defeated a numerically far superior Persian-Phoenician fleet, was essentially a trireme battle, won by tactics and superb ship-handling. Later triremes were more massively built and broader in beam. They were slower but able to carry more marines and to fire projectiles.

Length: 106ft 7in (32.5m)
Beam: 15ft (4.6m)
Depth: 3ft 6in (1.1m)
Displacement: 50t
Rigging: two masts; square sails
Armament: ram; archers, marines
Complement: 170 rowers

In 1987, a replica Greek trireme was built at Piraeus and demonstrated convincingly that its pace and handling were everything classical authors had claimed.

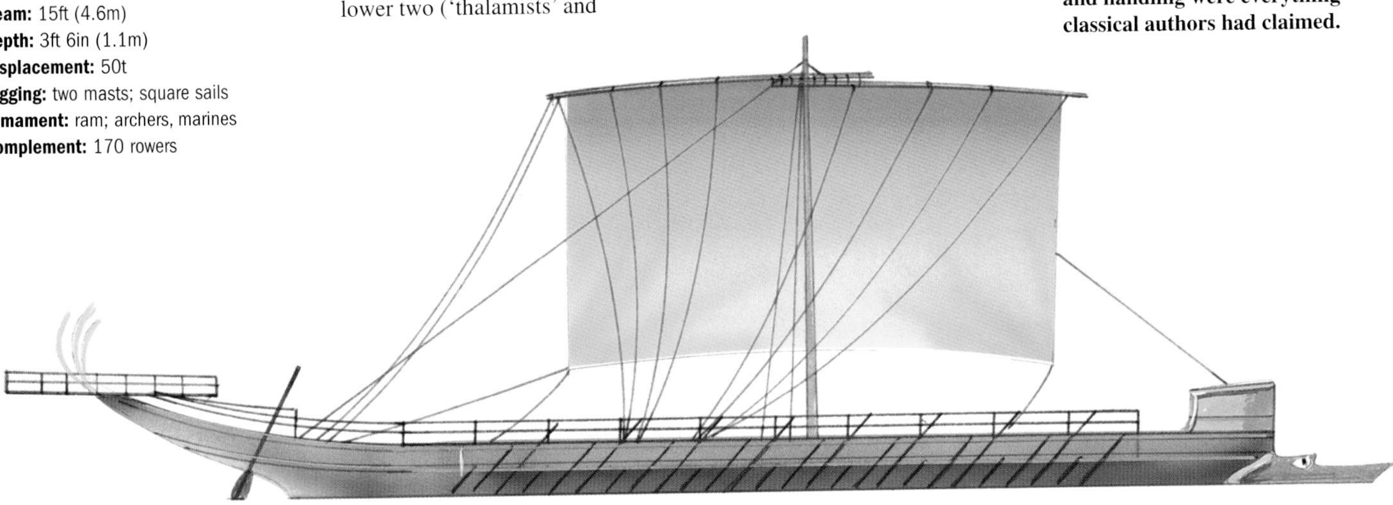

ROMAN WAR GALLEY (QUINQUEREME)

ROME: 350BC

Quinqueremes are referred to from as early as the 4th century BC and remained a powerful element in naval warfare for several centuries. Naval historians prefer the term 'fives', the name referring to the number of rowers in each file. Thus on a three-banked ship, rowers were two to an oar on the two lower levels; one to an oar on the upper level. There is no evidence of more than three levels. Some ships were 'sixes', with two men to an oar also on the topmost level (these vessels were normally flagships), and even larger ships were built, with three or four men to an oar on the lower banks. Fives and sixes fought by coming together and boarding. Broad-beamed ships had the advantage of being good platforms for catapults and for carrying marines, but their lack of manoeuvrability must always have been a disadvantage, as was their heavy expense and upkeep compared with smaller warships.

The largest ancient warship was a twin-hulled 'forty' of King Ptolemy IV Philopator (*c*200BC), which was over 55ft (16.8m) wide, for prestige rather than practicality.

Length: not known
Beam: 16ft 4in (5m)
Depth: not known
Displacement: not known
Rigging: single dismountable mast; square sail
Armament: catapults; marines
Complement: 300 oarsmen, 120 marines

GREEK CARGO SHIP

GREEK STATES: 300BC

Length: 55ft (16.8m)
Beam: 15ft (4.6m)
Depth: 7ft (2.1m)
Displacement: 70t
Rigging: single mast stayed fore and aft, tackles on shrouds and stays; square sail with upper yardarm only
Complement: about 8
Main routes: Black Sea, Aegean and Ionian Seas
Cargo: wine, oil, stone, hides, grain, military stores

In depictions of ancient ships, it is often hard to distinguish between a cutwater and a ram. However, it is likely that any long-distance trader had to be armed against pirates, and this armament could include a reinforced stem. Built to carry as much cargo as possible, this vessel has built-up bulwarks and a kind of bridge (like a 20th-century tanker) between bow and steering position. Crew accommodation was clearly a minor consideration; they slept on deck using the sail as an awning.

Like all Mediterranean vessels, this ship has the 'seeing eye' painted on its prow, as a sign of good guidance.

MEDITERRANEAN CARGO SHIP

CYPRUS OR A LEVANT PORT: *c*300BC

The Kyrenia ship was lead-sheathed below the waterline, as were other ancient merchant ships, for protection and perhaps as a form of ballast.

Length: 39ft 4in (12m)
Beam: 16ft 4in (5m)
Depth: c4ft 6in (1.4m)
Displacement: not known
Rigging: single mast; square sail
Complement: not known
Main routes: Mediterranean routes, Bay of Biscay and Cornwall
Cargo: grain, wine, wood, ores

The salvaged remains of a wreck from Kyrenia, Cyprus, dating from the 4th century BC, give some guidance to the form and build of the typical 'round ship' that carried cargo at this time. Unlike a warship, it was built to stay at sea for days at a time, and had a keel – at this point probably a recent feature – and edge-joined planking. With one open deck, it was of 'shell-first' construction, with the frame members added once the hull was assembled. It was a seaworthy design as long as the vessel's head was kept to the wind; if she broached to, she might fill with water and sink rapidly.

ROMAN WAR GALLEY (TRIREME)

ROME: *c*200BC

In the long war with Carthage which began in 264BC, the Romans built heavy triremes, armed with reinforced rams and with reinforced wooden sides. These vessels also possessed a tower, perhaps from which to direct attacks. One innovation was the *corvus*, a boarding plank 30 feet (9.1m) long and four feet (1.2m) wide with a spike at one end. As two ships came alongside one another, the *corvus* was dropped and lodged on the enemy's deck, permitting a rush attack to be made. Grappling irons were also employed.

The formidable Roman triremes, were originally based upon Carthaginian triremes captured in battle, carried ballistae (catapults) to hurl stone shot or incendiary material at enemy craft.

Length: 115ft (35m)
Beam: 15ft (4.6m)
Depth: 5ft (1.5m)
Displacement: 70t
Rigging: single mast; square sail (some had an *artemon* - bowsprit - with a small square sail)
Armament: ram, catapult, fire pots; marines, archers
Complement: 190

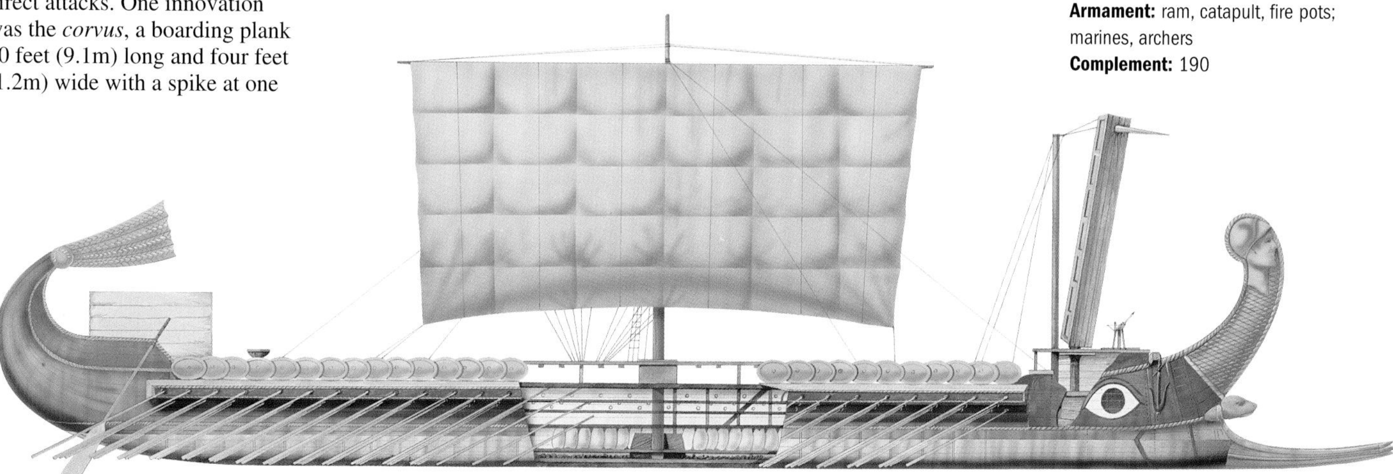

ROMAN CARGO SHIP

ROME: *c*300AD

This is the ship that sustained Rome's far-flung empire – it is capacious, sturdy and with a built-up stern; the steering oars were already more like rudders, partly housed within the built-out bulwarks. It is decked, with a hold below and relatively substantial crew and passenger space aft. The sternpost is formed into a swan neck; the bow is businesslike, with a bowsprit (*artemon*) carrying a yard with a small square sail. The basic form, improved in details, existed from around 100-400AD.

Length: 80ft (24.4m)
Beam: 20ft (6.1m)
Depth: 8ft (2.4m)
Displacement: 80-90t
Rigging: single mast stayed fore and aft; halyard blocks now in use; square mainsail can be brailed up
Complement: 8-10
Main routes: trans-Mediterranean, Black Sea, Atlantic coast of Europe
Cargo: grain, wine, military stores, firewood, mass-produced goods

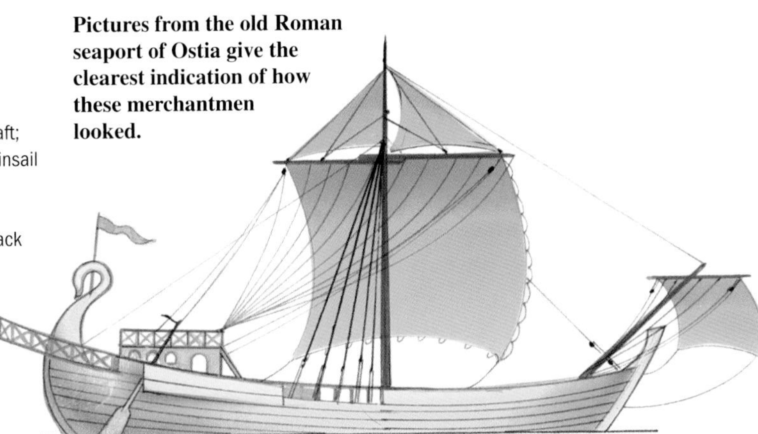

Pictures from the old Roman seaport of Ostia give the clearest indication of how these merchantmen looked.

MEDITERRANEAN CARGO SHIP

ROME: *c*800AD

Vessels of this type plied the waters of the Mediterranean around the 9th century AD. Although the basic hull is that of the old Roman cargo ship, its look above the freeboard is very different. The steering oars are still brought within an extension of the upper hull, but the stern and prow arrangements are far simpler; the bowsprit has gone completely. The mast, stayed by shrouds, has a forward tilt to accommodate the double-sparred yard of a lateen sail.

The lateen sail that could be trimmed to the wind was an innovation of this time, probably from Arab craft.

Length: 80ft (24.4m)
Beam: 25ft (7.6m)
Depth: 9ft (2.7m)
Displacement: not known
Rigging: single mast stayed laterally; lateen rig
Complement: 5-8
Main routes: trans-Mediterranean, Atlantic coast of Europe
Cargo: wine, grain, wood, hides, oil

NORWEGIAN CARGO SHIP

NORWAY: *c*800AD

In the 8th and 9th centuries, Scandinavian coast-dwellers developed shipbuilding skills of a high order, with the clinker-built hull as standard. Sea-going ships were the key to their territorial expansion, and vessels like this one may have been part of the Viking fleet that reached America. Undecked, and with a single mast stepped to the keel, its thwarts acted both as stiffeners to the hull and seats for oarsmen.

Length: 55ft (16.8m)
Beam: 15ft (4.6m)
Depth: 4ft (1.2m)
Displacement: not known
Rigging: single mast stayed fore and aft; square sail reinforced in a diaper pattern
Complement: 4-8
Main routes: western Scandinavian seaways, North Sea
Cargo: sheep, grain, amber, hides, timber

Rounder and shorter than the longships, this type became known as the *knorr*; its oars were mainly for work in harbours or rivers.

SCANDINAVIAN LONGSHIP

NORWAY, DENMARK: 1000AD

The celebrated 10th-century Gokstad ship preserved at Oslo, although shorter than a true longship, nevertheless shows the constructional style of these vessels. They were clinker-built of oak on a strong keel, and directed by a steering oar set at the starboard side. The most usual size was a 40-oared vessel (20 a side), but some were larger. The mast-stock rested directly on the keel, but the mast itself could be dismounted, and the yardarm, made of a single spar, supported a homespun square sail, strengthened by a diaper pattern of stout linen or leather. Early depictions show this pattern continued in a tracery of rigging, but this had been abandoned by the 10th century. The preserved ships of the period do not have thwarts or benches for the oarsmen; these features were not built in to the structure. Square holes were cut in the bulwarks as shield-fixings, purely for display purposes, and the dragon head mounted on the stem was always removed in home waters. Other names for larger longships were *skeid* or *drakkar*.

Using longships, the Vikings were able to raid, invade, and colonise great tracts of Britain, Ireland, and northern France in the ninth and 10th centuries, and to voyage as far as Constantinople in the 11th. A replica of the Gokstad ship made a 28-day voyage from Norway to America in 1893. There was no covered accommodation for the crew, and when possible, they spent the night on shore, with the boat hauled up on the beach. The longships were fine sea boats, and the Vikings who sailed them appreciated their qualities. There are many references in the Sagas to the excellence of individual ships.

Length: 120ft (36.6m)
Beam: 20ft (6.1m)
Depth: 3ft 6in (1.1m)
Displacement: not known
Rigging: single mast; square sail
Armament: armed men
Complement: 50
Main routes: North Sea and Baltic Sea; North Atlantic to Faroe Islands and Iceland

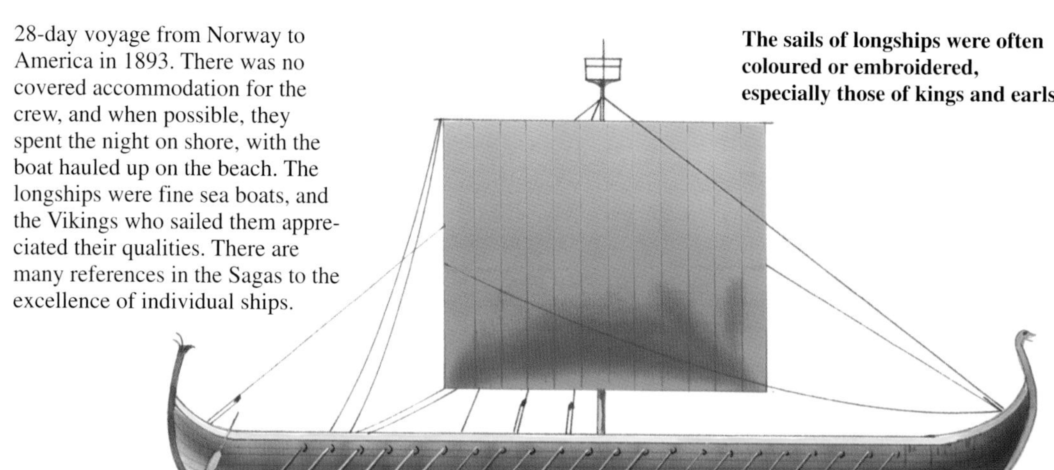

The sails of longships were often coloured or embroidered, especially those of kings and earls.

ITALIAN CARGO SHIP

ITALIAN PORTS: *c*1200AD

Length: 70ft (21.3m)
Beam: 25ft (7.6m)
Depth: 9ft (2.7m)
Displacement: 75t
Rigging: Lateen rig, with tackles on shrouds and backstay to allow for trimming
Complement: 6–10
Main routes: Genoa to North Africa, the Bosporus, and the eastern Mediterranean
Cargo: grain, wine, timber, cloth, oil

Mediterranean vessels were carvel-built, with the hull planking laid edge to edge. The three solid mooring bitts at the bow are traditional.

The lateen (Latin) sail so characteristic of medieval shipping in the Mediterranean was well established by now. Most craft were probably single-masted, but larger vessels might have two masts; the foremast set right in the bow, like a vertical bowsprit. Contemporary depictions show a hooked top to the masts, intended to keep the halyard forward of the mast. The masts are pitched slightly forward, as forestays could not be used with the rig. Little is known about the internal structure.

SWEDISH CARGO SHIP

SWEDEN: *c*1200AD

During 1932–34 a range of ship remains were found in the mud of Kalmar Bay, Sweden. The oldest were of this 13th-century coasting vessel. The vessel is clinker-built and part-decked at bow and stern, with cross-beams protruding through the planking, secured on the inside by angular wooden 'knees'. The mast mounted a square sail, and a small foresail could be rigged on the stubby bowsprit. These craft were fitted with a windlass, which could raise a net as well as the anchor.

The Kalmar boat has a stern rudder rather than a steering oar. In the late 12th century, this was an innovation.

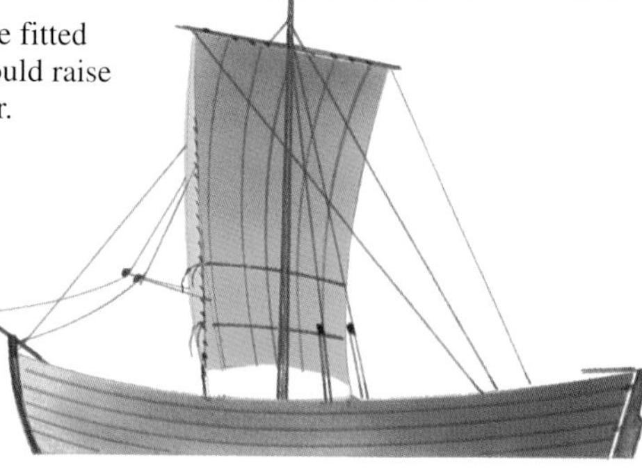

Length: 36ft 6in (11.1m)
Beam: 15ft (4.6m)
Depth: 3ft 6in (1.1m)
Displacement: 20t
Rigging: single dismountable mast stayed fore and aft; square mainsail; short bowsprit for a small staysail.
Complement: 4
Main routes: inshore Baltic routes
Cargo: dried fish, hides, timber, barrels

HANSEATIC COG

BREMEN, GERMANY: 1239AD

Length: 78ft 9in (24m)
Beam: 26ft 3in (8m)
Depth: 10ft (3m)
Displacement: 120t
Rigging: single mast; square sail, sometimes fitted with a bonnet, sometimes with reefpoints.
Complement: 6
Main routes: North Sea, southern Baltic
Cargo: wood, coal, hides, wine

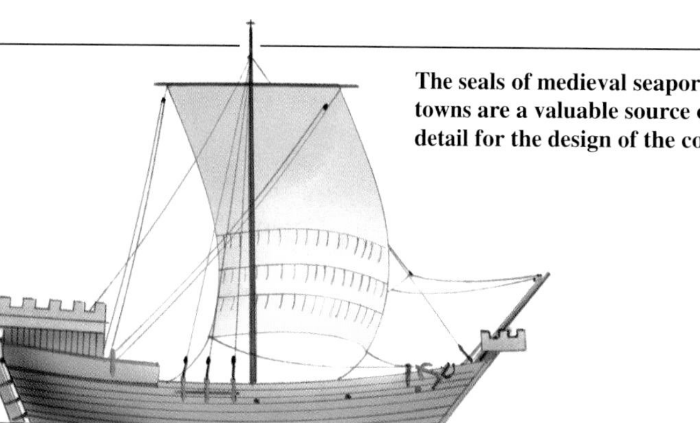

The seals of medieval seaport towns are a valuable source of detail for the design of the cog.

In 1962, a well-preserved ship was found in the River Weser at Bremen, Germany. It is a fine example of the cog, mainstay of trade between the Hanseatic ports of the North Sea. The lowest part of the hull was flush-built, the upper parts clinker-built, and the hull was rounded out between a pointed stem and stern to maximise carrying capacity. A rudder was fitted, with the tiller housed below the built-out stern platform.

ITALIAN CARGO SHIP

ITALIAN MARITIME REPUBLICS: *c*1250AD

Length: 70ft (21.3m)
Beam: 22ft (6.7m)
Depth: 10ft (3m)
Displacement: 70t
Rigging: two masts; lateen rig
Complement: not known
Main routes: trans-Mediterranean
Cargo: grain, wine, oil, metals, wood, dried fish, cloth, luxury goods

Ships of this type ran the extensive trade of the Italian maritime republics. Decked, and with a hatch to the storage space below, the basic hull, with its transverse beams, still resembles the old Roman one. Innovations include the wings built up from the afterdeck extensions, providing a support for the lowered yard, and the forecastle, which provides some shelter at the bow. This type of vessel remained in use for some 200 years. The average life of a ship was probably short, perhaps five or 10 years. Fire, shipwreck, marine worms, and warfare all took their toll.

BYZANTINE WAR GALLEY (DROMON)

BYZANTINE EMPIRE: *c*1250AD

Dromon means 'runner' in Greek, and the term has been applied to Byzantine galleys from their first appearance in the 11th century until the fall of Byzantium in 1453. No doubt these were intended to be swift ships. There is very little information on early dromons, but they are clearly based on the traditional Greek form of the bireme, or double-banked galley. The oldest (11th- and 12th-century) depictions give no indication of mast or rigging. The numbers of oars on each side may have varied between 21 and 50. Contemporary drawings show a pair of up-curved wings at the stern, in some cases joined by a brace. On a rigged ship, this would form a support for the lowered yard. A notable feature is that the ram has been raised from the waterline to a higher position, perhaps with the aim of ripping through oar blades rather than holing – and perhaps locking on to – an enemy vessel. By the late 12th century, the dromon possessed a lateen rig, with up to two masts although a three-masted Saracen vessel of this type was encountered by Crusaders in 1191.

The dromon was armed with a catapult, or ballista, and also with 'Greek fire', an early type of flame-thrower.

Length: 135ft (41.1m)
Beam: 25ft (7.6m)
Depth: 4ft (1.2m)
Displacement: not known
Rigging: two masts, with crow's nest on mainmast; lateen rig
Armament: 'Greek fire' projector, catapult
Complement: up to 230

VENETIAN CRUSADE SHIP

VENICE: *c*1268AD

Length: 84ft 6in (25.8m)
Beam: 21ft (6.4m)
Depth: 11 ft (3.4m)
Displacement: c120t
Rigging: two masts; lateen rig; ratlined shrouds or rope ladders for access to tops
Complement: not known
Main routes: western Mediterranean to Sicily, Cyprus, and the Holy Land
Cargo: soldiers, horses, military stores, grain, fodder, wine, oil

The spars of the lateen rig have become immensely long, longer than the ship itself. Despite this, they could be handled adeptly by a small crew.

In 1268, Louis IX of France ordered ships for a Crusade. Those built in Venice were substantial two-deckers – the projecting beam ends can be seen; they were two-masted, with lateen rig, and their purpose was to carry both men and materials. The aftercastle is quite substantial, to accommodate high-ranking officers. Although single rudders were in use further north, these ships retained paired side-rudders. Both masts have crow's nests fitted to the after sides.

ENGLISH WARSHIP

ENGLAND: 1300AD

The English Cinque Port towns maintained a fleet of vessels like this – clinker-built with fore- and aftercastles for fighting purposes, and a wide, clear deck. The steering oar is still employed, but the mast is stayed laterally by shrouds, kept taut by deadeyes and lanyards. The decorative prow has also now become a functional bowsprit, the sheets attached to it helping to hold the sail to the wind. Such ships are shown in many town seals and manuscripts.

Length: 42ft (12.8m)
Beam: 12ft (3.7m)
Depth: 7ft (2.1m)
Displacement: 180t
Rigging: single mast stayed fore and aft, port and starboard; square sail with bowlines attached to bowsprit
Armament: machines to project arrows and stones; archers, marines
Complement: 6

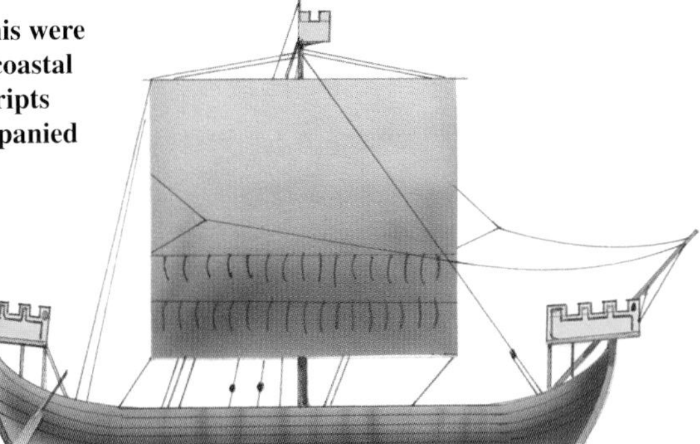

Vessels such as this were not only used in coastal defence. Manuscripts show they accompanied crusading forces to Palestine.

Christopher

ENGLAND: 1338AD

The later addition of the 'Of The Tower' added to English warships was the contemporary equivalent of 'HMS': the Tower of London ws the main royal armoury and the designation indicated a kings' ship.

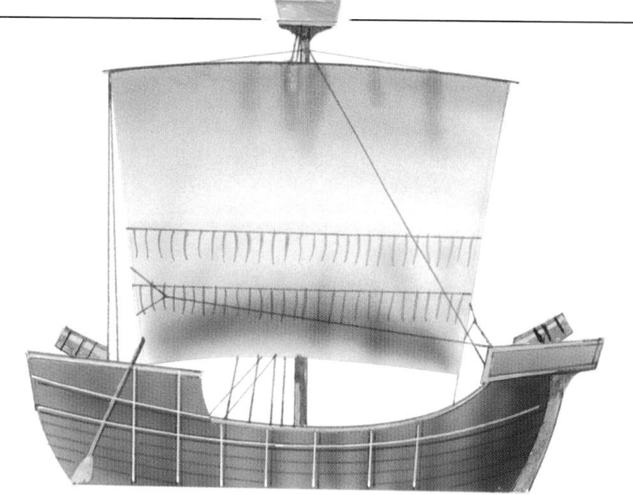

The first known ship to have carried guns was the *Christopher*, a cog armed with three iron guns plus a hand gun. These were still relatively light, designed to kill men rather than pierce hulls, and mounted on the upper deck on the raised 'castles' at each end of the ship. Records show the guns to have five chambers, (possibly breech-loaders), although many guns of the period were cast.

Christopher was captured by the French in 1339 and recaptured by the English at the Battle of Sluys in 1340 in which the English had 180 ships with 16,000 troops and bowmen plus crew. It was not until 1406 in another English ship called *Christopher of the Tower* that guns were properly mounted for shipboard use.

Displacement: 300t
Rigging: two masts; square sail on foremast and small lateen mizzen
Armament: four guns; bowmen, spearmen

Chinese junk

CHINA: *c*1350AD

First described to Westerners by Marco Polo in 1298, the junk, in its various guises, has had a long career. The 13th-century product is clearly the result of a centuries-long history of Chinese ship design, of which little is known. The junk was not so much a type as a family, and various types and sizes could be built, for purposes ranging from warfare to cargo-carrying to transporting imperial embassies. As in other sciences, ancient China made many discoveries in shipbuilding techniques which came much later in the West. Notable features include a single stern rudder and a pontoon-type hull-divided into as many as 20 watertight compartments, with the deck built up above its arched top. The planking was flush, with heavy rubbing strakes, and the vessel's bottom was flat, enabling it to sit level if beached. A series of hatches gave access to the watertight compartments. Up to four or even five masts were fitted, two being dismountable. A 16th-century depiction of a three-masted fighting junk shows a fighting top on the mainmast, reached by rope or bamboo-runged ladder (but by then this could have been borrowed from a Western ship). The sails were of fibre matting, woven in an interlocking pattern, and strengthened by lateral bamboo battens. The masts were not stayed, and a system of crow's feet (multiple lines spreading from the sheets to the edges of the sails) enabled what was probably a small crew to reef sail rapidly. Crew accommodation was under the built-up quarterdeck. This could be quite substantial, as it seems many junks carried teams of merchants or traders, who may have been owners or lessees of the ship. Most larger junks carried one or more sampans on board. These may have been used for towing when necessary, as well as for gaining access to shallow-water ports.

The dimensions of junks varied widely, although from Marco Polo it seems that four masts were common. The dimensions given are based on a four-masted vessel.

Length: 180ft (54.9m)
Beam: 30ft (9.1m)
Depth: 18ft (5.5m)
Displacement: not known
Rigging: four unstayed masts; lugsail-type rig, reefed from top downwards
Complement: 8-10 seamen
Main routes: coast and main rivers of China
Cargo: timber, rice, metals, cloth, foodstuffs

English warship

ENGLAND: 1370AD

Showing considerable advances on the Cinque Ports ship, this vessel has a built-in aftercastle – although it was probably still open to the deck – and a hull design that owes much to the cog, including a somewhat rounded stern with a fixed rudder. There is a substantial fighting top, but no ratlines yet to help access; the rigging remains much as before. The bowsprit has not yet acquired a sail. Heraldic art would be depicted on the sail and pennants.

Although the long aftercastle designates it as a warship, this vessel could have carried cargo in a hold beneath the deck.

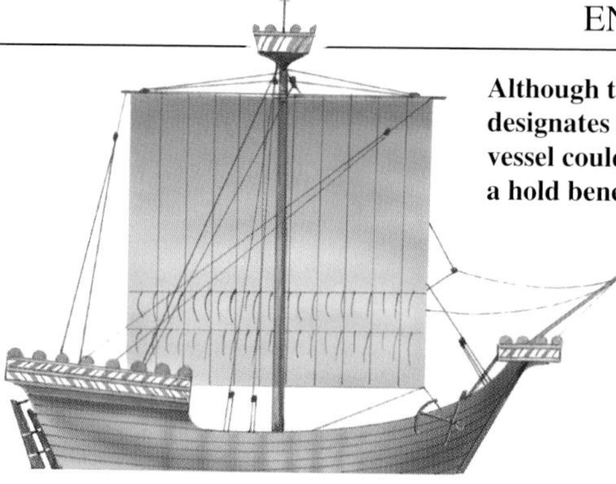

Length: 75ft (22.9m)
Beam: 22ft (6.7m)
Depth: 6ft 6in (2m)
Displacement: perhaps 120t
Rigging: single mast; square sail
Armament: projectile equipment; archers, marines
Complement: 6-12 seamen

DANISH WARSHIP

DENMARK: *c*1390AD

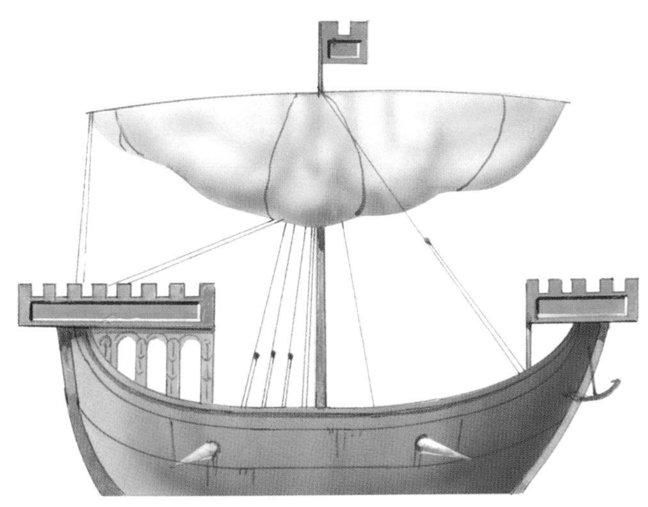

The varicoloured planking of the Skamstrup ship indicates a vessel intended for warfare.

Two ship paintings were made on the ceiling of the church at Skamstrup, Denmark, around the end of the 14th century. These are of interest as they reveal the changing style of Nordic ship design. Whilst the basic long warship hull has changed little, a rudder has been fixed to the sternpost; there is also a little forecastle round the dragon-head prow, and a long aftercastle abaft the mast. Both of these features look uncomfortably grafted on when compared with the Gdansk ship. They show a response to a style of naval fighting in which ships came together in each one's effort to 'board' and capture the other; the positioning of fighting men assumed prime importance. It was far easier to board an opponent from above than below.

Length: 100ft (30.5m)
Beam: 20ft (6.1m)
Depth: 5ft (1.5m)
Displacement: not known
Rigging: single mast; square sail from yard mounted on parrel truck
Armament: archers, marines
Complement: 6 plus military

POLISH CARGO SHIP

POLAND: *c*1450AD

Length: 53ft 6in (16.3m)
Beam: c19ft 6in (5.9m)
Depth: not known
Displacement: not known
Rigging: not known
Complement: not known
Main routes: Baltic, Scandinavian, and North Sea ports
Cargo: wood; casks of pitch, tar, resin and wax; iron ore and bars; copper ingots

In 1975, a 15th-century wreck was raised from the seabed off Gdansk, Poland. It appears to have been a trading vessel which foundered on her outward-bound journey. In construction it represents a developed form of the cog. Clinker-built throughout, it is constructed on a keel of oak 53ft 6in (16.3m) long. Its shape is more rounded to increase its cargo capacity, and it may have been referred to as a hulk. Among other items, an anchor over 6ft (1.8m) in length was retrieved with the vessel.

Piracy was rife in the northern seas, and the Gdansk ship had stone shot, crossbow bolts, and other defensive armament.

SPANISH WARSHIP

SPAIN: 1450AD

The Mataró ship, now in the Rotterdam maritime museum, is a unique surviving model of a mid-15th-century ship. It reveals the very substantial developments made around the end of the 14th century. Its Spanish name of *nao* simply means ship (as distinct from a caravel), and perhaps the most striking detail is the additional mast set up on the long quarterdeck, which has replaced the sterncastle (an attenuated form of which still rises on the poop). This vessel was lateen-rigged, perhaps modelled on the Mediterranean two-masted vessel. The forecastle has been integrated with the hull in a rounded, clinker-built structure, with the railed deck placed on top, perhaps to ease the process of weighing anchor. In this period the bowsprit, already at a steep angle, was raised to become a foremast in many vessels, and the forecastle beak was extended to replace it.

This two-decked vessel, with its high freeboard, was the prototype of the carrack and indeed of subsequent ship types.

Length: 65ft (19.8m)
Beam: 22ft (6.7m)
Depth: 6ft 6in (2m)
Displacement: 150t
Rigging: two masts; mainmast with bonneted square sail and rope ladder to fighting-top, mizzen with lateen sail
Armament: projectile equipment; archers, marines
Complement: 10–20

CHAPTER TWO

THE AGE OF EXPLORATION 1451–1729

Exploration of unknown seas and trade with far-off countries were not new developments in the 15th century. Warfare at sea also had a long tradition. But between the 15th and 18th centuries, all these human activities became more efficient and systematic and far more intensive – all driven by the improvement and specialisation of ship design. This was not a steady process; it took place in spurts, in different places at different times, and was largely accomplished by the end of the 16th century. The most significant step was the building of the three-masted ship which provided mariners with a vessel which was reliable on long voyages. The single-pole mast was replaced by the composite mast of two, or even three, joined spars.

Left: A Venetian argosy, a large merchant vessel from the 1500s. Venice was a powerful republic at this time, controlling trade to the Levant and ruling parts of the Mediterranean.

By the end of the period, warship and merchant ship were two very different kinds of vessel. Improvements in detail technology accompanied the increase in size, notably the invention of the whipstaff to ease the clumsy business of steering a big ship by tiller. The compass had been known since the 12th century and the hour-glass came into use in the 15th century; these developments, combined with the log to measure speed, made navigation by dead reckoning possible. Maps and charts came into regular use. By the end of the period, the big sailing ship was a complex wind-driven machine far removed from the vessels of the 14th century.

Nao

PORTUGAL: 1450

Length: 72ft (21.9m)
Beam: 20ft (6m)
Depth: 12ft (3.6m)
Displacement: 65t
Rigging: two masts; square sail on main, lateen-mizzen
Complement: 10-20
Routes: Iberian coast, north-west Africa
Cargo: wine, grain, manufactured goods, baled and barrelled goods

The yard is supported by topping lifts, a feature of the square-rig not found in north-European ships for almost another century.

The Portuguese for ship is *nao*, a generic word, like the Italian *nave*, to describe a larger seagoing vessel. Today, it would be classed as a carrack, of an early sort with two masts. The type was soon to be developed and enlarged, Portugal at this time led the world in ship-building. Although a quarter deck has replaced the aftercastle, the deck beam ends still protrude from the sides, as in much earlier ships.

Caravel

PORTUGAL: 1470

The caravel lacked the top-hamper of larger ships of the time. The lower hull made it easier to steer and more weatherly in handling.

The caravel emerged from the basic form of a 13th-century Iberian fishing boat, enlarged, decked, and fitted first with two, and later three, masts. It was a ship that could undertake oceanic voyages of unprecedented length. With the encouragement of the Portuguese Prince Henry the Navigator, the progress of the type was driven rather than evolutionary. The caravel was originally lateen-rigged. It was in a caravel that Bartholomew Diaz rounded the Cape of Good Hope in 1487.

Length: 75ft (22.8m)
Beam: 25ft (7.6m)
Depth: 10ft (3m)
Displacement: 60t
Rigging: three masts, lateen-rig
Complement: 12-20
Routes: African coast
Cargo: tropical products, bulk goods

Caravel Redonda

SPAIN, PORTUGAL: 1470

Length: 75ft (22.8m)
Beam: 25ft (7.6m)
Depth: 10ft (3m)
Displacement: 60t
Rigging: three masts; square sail on fore and main; lateen-mizzen
Complement: 12-20
Routes: African coast; Atlantic after 1492
Cargo: trading goods, bullion, timber, ores

The three-masted caravel was the finest sailing ship of its time. Its capacity, sailing qualities, and weatherliness gave captains the confidence to undertake long voyages in unknown waters.

Many caravels were converted (*redonda*) to square-rig on the foremast and mainmast, notably *Pinta* and *Niña*, the ships in which Christopher Columbus sailed to the New World. He chose a caravel to take advantage of the prevailing trade and westerly winds on the voyage out and back.

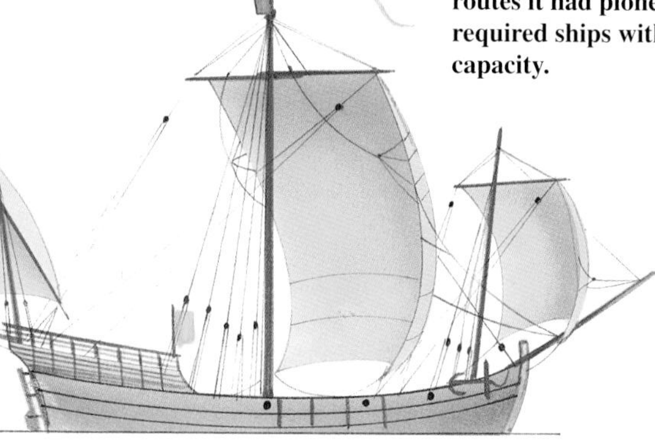

The limited size of the caravel was, over time, to reduce its use. The routes it had pioneered soon required ships with greater capacity.

Carrack

THE NETHERLANDS: 1470

Around 1470, a Flemish artist made an engraving of a *Kraeck*, or carrack, one of the earliest detailed drawings of a ship.

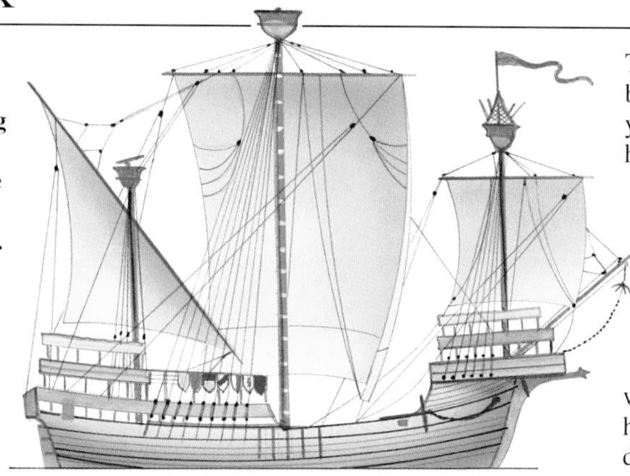

The three-masted ship began to be built in Europe from the early years of the 15th century. Genoa has been suggested as the most likely port to begin the type, as it specialized in bulk cargoes like timber, alum, and ore.

The name is a puzzle: though apparently from the Italian *caracca*, the Italians simply called it *nave* ('ship'). The design was a radical change from what had gone before, and ship sizes doubled within a few years.

Length: 112ft (34.1m)
Beam: 33ft (10m)
Depth: 17ft (5.18m)
Displacement: 180t
Rigging: three masts; square sail on fore and main; lateen-mizzen
Complement: 20
Routes: long-distance trading routes
Cargo: hides, oil, ore, wine, iron

NIÑA

SPAIN: *c*1491

Length: c60ft (18.3m)
Beam: c18ft (5.5m)
Depth: c7ft (2.1m)
Displacement: c75t
Rigging: three masts; square-rigged on fore and main; lateen-mizzen (final form)
Complement: 24

Officially named *Santa Clara*, the name *Niña* came from her owner, Juan Niño de Moguer. She made at least five transatlantic voyages, including the historic first one under the command of Christopher Columbus, accompanied by the *Santa Maria* and the *Pinta*. Originally built as a *caravela latina* (lateen-rigged caravel), the rig was altered to that of a *caravela redonda*, with a new mast stepped in the bows. In this form, *Niña* was the fastest of Columbus's three vessels, and his favourite. After making the historic landfall in the Bahamas on 12 October 1492, *Niña* sailed along the Cuban coast, where she was fitted with a new mizzen mast. On 25 December, *Santa Maria* having grounded, the admiral shifted his flag to *Niña* and set sail for home. Having weathered two major storms, *Niña* was first to reach Las Palos, a few hours ahead of *Pinta*. In 1493, Columbus included *Niña* in his second fleet to America, returning to Spain in 1496. After an interlude in which she was briefly captured by Sardinian corsairs, *Niña* made a further Atlantic voyage in January 1498. It is believed that she spent the rest of her career in the Caribbean.

***Niña* was a lucky ship for Columbus. When a hurricane hit his ships at Hispaniola in June 1495, she was the only one to survive.**

SANTA MARIA

SPAIN: 1492

One sideline of the first voyage Columbus made was that his sailors introduced the hammock, which they found in use in the Caribbean. It rapidly became a basic feature of crew accommodation on European ships. This view shows a reproduction ship fitted out minus a foremast.

Christopher Columbus used the Spanish town of Los Palos de la Frontera as the base for his first Atlantic voyage of 1492. Here he hired *Santa Maria*, a merchant ship from Spanish Galicia. This origin gave her the by-name of *La Gallega* ('the Galician'). Her owner, Juan de la Cosa, came on the voyage as sailing master. *Santa Maria*, the largest of the three ships on the voyage, was classified as a *nao* ('ship'), meaning a square-rigged vessel larger than a caravel; in fact, a carrack. No contemporary depiction of her has survived, though many models and three full-size replicas have been built at different times. Her carrying capacity was 100t – equivalent to 100 double hogsheads of wine. The rig was standard for a *nao*: three masts, with a lateen sail on the mizzen, square main course (mainsail), with a small topsail on the mainmast, and a small squaresail on the foremast. A further square spritsail was fitted to the bowsprit. The course, with two bonnets to give more sail area, was by far the main source of drive power, but Columbus could rely on running before consistent winds for much of the voyage, the trade winds on the outward leg and the westerlies on the return. He was not impressed by *Santa Maria*, regarding her as too deep in draught, and insufficiently weatherly compared to the caravels. Some light guns were carried but the ship was not equipped for battle. From the main truck, Queen Isabella of Spain's royal pennant was flown along with the castles of Castile and the lions of Léon and other heraldry decorated the sails. Columbus was Captain General, next in rank were the *pilot* (deep-sea navigator), the *escribano* (captain's secretary), and the master, responsible for the working

Length: c77-85ft (23.4-25.9m)
Beam: c23ft (7m)
Depth: c10ft (3m)
Displacement: c110t
Rigging: three masts; square-rigged on fore and main, with topsail on main; lateen-mizzen; spritsail
Complement: 40

of the ship. A doctor-surgeon was also carried. At 2 a.m. on 10 October 1492 the ship's lookout sighted land, identified as the Caribbean island of Guanahani (San Salvador). For two months *Santa Maria* sailed among the islands, along the coast of Cuba, and on to Hispaniola (Haiti). At midnight on Christmas Day, with de la Cosa asleep and apparently only a boy at the tiller, *Santa Maria* grounded on a coral reef. There were no fatalities, but the ship was immovable. That was the end of her. Everything that could be salvaged was removed. Her timbers were taken to build a fort, La Navidad, as the two remaining vessels were too small to hold all the men. Some of the crew volunteered to remain until another ship should come for them from Spain – none survived to greet their rescuers.

Santa Maria's chief navigational aid was the dry compass, a calibrated card with a magnet under the north point. It was set on a pin and mounted on gimbals in a binnacle. Time was measured by a half-hour glass, turned by a ship's boy.

MATTHEW

ENGLAND: 1493

In 1996, a replica of *Matthew*, necessarily somewhat conjectural as so little is known about the actual ship, was sailed from Bristol to Newfoundland to mark the 500th anniversary of Cabot's voyage.

Four years after the epic voyage of Christopher Columbus to the New World, King Henry VII of England granted letters patent to another Italian to make a westward voyage to the Orient. The Italian, his name anglicised to John Cabot, planned to assemble a fleet of five ships, but could raise neither interest in nor funds for the voyage. However, on 20 May 1497, Cabot and his son Sebastian set out in the solitary *Matthew*, described at the time as a *navicula* ('little ship') with a capacity reckoned at only 50 tuns of wine (wine was the main commodity handled through Bristol at the time). Though *Matthew* was even smaller than Columbus's ship *Niña*, and most probably caravel-rigged, she was an excellent ship, and her eleven-week round voyage was unbeaten for another 100 years. On 24 June 1497, *Matthew* made landfall off Newfoundland, very close to where the Vikings had landed in AD1001. Cabot traced the eastern coast of the great island to its extreme south at Cape Race, returned north to his first landing point, then sailed back to Bristol believing he had reached the coast of China. Though not used on Cabot's second expedition (on which he was lost), *Matthew* continued to work as a trading vessel from Bristol on more workaday trips to Ireland, France, and Spain. Her ultimate fate is unknown.

Length: 73ft (22.2m)
Beam: 20ft 6in (6.25m)
Depth: 7ft (2.1m)
Displacement: 85t
Rigging: three masts; square-rigged on fore and main; lateen-mizzen
Complement: 18

SÃO GABRIEL

PORTUGAL: 1497

The thrust of Portuguese exploration and exploitation was down the west coast of Africa, and *São Gabriel* was built specifically to extend exploration beyond the Cape of Good Hope. She was a *nao* and the flagship of the aristocrat Vasco da Gama, in a four-ship flotilla. The epic voyage lasted from 8 June 1497 to late July 1499. When *São Gabriel* docked at Lisbon, she had found the sea route to India, and so instigated a major change in the pattern of East-West trading across the world. It can be reliably assumed that she was a three-masted, square-rigged ship, since this had become the standard for a long-distance voyage of exploration; at the time, Portugal was at the forefront of maritime science and technology. Compared to the *Santa Maria*, the *São Gabriel* was quite heavily armed, with 20 guns. This reflected the belligerent approach of the Portuguese to peoples they encountered on these journeys of exploration.

Length: c70ft (21.3m)
Beam: c23ft (7m)
Depth: c9ft (2.7m)
Displacement: c100t burthen
Rigging: three masts; square-rigged on fore and main; lateen-mizzen
Complement: 60

Vasco da Gama made a second voyage to the Indies in 1502, but the further history of the *São Gabriel* is not known.

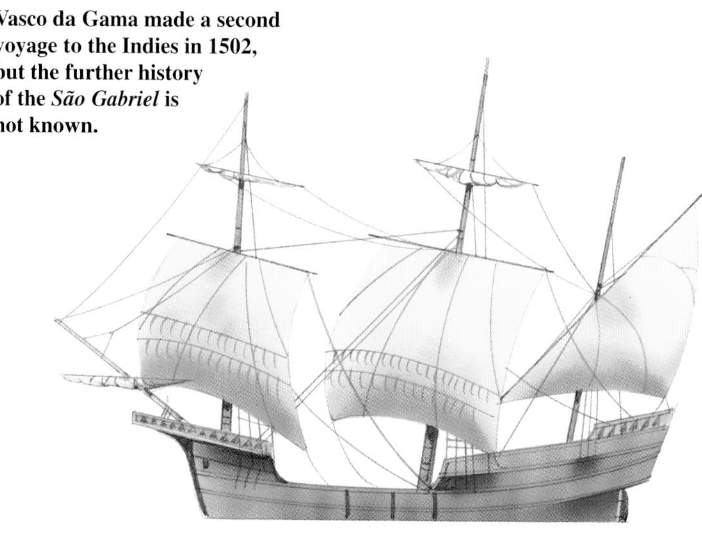

CARRACK

VENICE: 1500

Thirty years on from the previous one, this carrack shows four masts, with a bonaventure-mizzen mounted right on the stern, with an outligger to stay it. It has ratlines fitted to the shrouds, and carries a short topsail yard above the top. If not a warship, it is definitely an armed vessel, with around 56 guns, mostly lightweight. Considering its size, capital cost and load capacity, it would need a formidable defence against pirate attacks.

This ship has a full-length covered deck above the hold space, with a two-deck forecastle and a long quarter deck.

Length: 115ft (35m)
Beam: 34ft (10.3m)
Depth: 20ft (6m)
Displacement: 200t
Rigging: four masts; square-rigged on fore and main with topsail on main; lateen-mizzens, spritsail on bowsprit
Complement: 22
Routes: long-distance routes in Mediterranean, Black Sea; and to northern Europe
Cargo: wine, oil, ores, wood, military equipment

MARY ROSE

ENGLAND: 1510

Length: 105ft (32m)
Beam: 38ft 3in (11.6m)
Depth: 15ft 1in (4.6m)
Displacement: 600t
Rigging: four masts; square-rigged with lateen-mizzen
Armament: 78 guns (91 after 1536)
Complement: 415

One of England's first purpose-built warships, the *Mary Rose* was a carrack whose structure (and fate) demonstrate the progress and attendant perils of the art of warship construction. By the early-16th century, naval guns had been developed to the point where they could make a serious contribution to a battle, not simply by killing men, but by holing an enemy vessel at the waterline. At the same time, the watertight gunport was devised, so that heavy guns could be safely set low in the waist of the vessel, with the ports open only for action. Ships of the time still also retained the lofty structures of forecastle and after-castle, providing both accommodation and high-level platforms from which fighting men could fire on to hostile craft in the close-quarters struggle which formed the conventional naval battle until the 16th century. *Mary Rose*, named for Henry VIII's sister, was built in the naval dockyard at Portsmouth and fitted out at London. She won praise, both for the splendour of her appearance and for her handling: Admiral Sir Edward Howard declared that a 100t ship could not go about any faster than the 600t *Mary Rose*. She saw much active service in Henry's French and Scottish wars and, in 1536, was given a complete refit; her armament was increased to 91 guns, and 100t added to her

'Mary Rose represents a day in the life of Tudor England. You cannot get that sort of information from libraries, you cannot get it from excavating a land site . . . a four- or five-storey structure complete with everything it contained on that day in 1545.' Alexander McKee, founder of Project Solent Ships.

weight. In 1545, the French sent a large and well-armed invasion force against England; the English fleet was hastily mobilized to repel the threat. *Mary Rose* was in the forefront, under the command of Vice Admiral Sir George Carew. Carew was new to the ship, and the crew appears to have been a scratch assembly. On 18 July, as the English ships advanced on the French galleys in choppy conditions, the guns on *Mary Rose* were not secured nor were the gunports closed. In the northerly wind, the ship heeled over and instantly took in water through the ports; she flooded and sank. Only 35 of the crew were saved. In 1970, the position of the wreck was pinpointed, and a programme of careful excavation and preservation ensued. In 1982, a substantial portion of the hull was raised along with many other artefacts, which now form the focal point of a museum in Portsmouth.

Despite the fate of the *Mary Rose*, the low positioning of gunports remained a problem with British men-of-war. Even in the 18th century, it frequently happened that the lowest tier of guns in a multiple-decked ship could not be brought into use, whilst the higher-sided French or Spanish vessels could fire a full broadside.

HENRY GRACE À DIEU (GREAT HARRY) ENGLAND: 1514

Length: c190ft (57.9m)
Beam: c50ft (15.2m)
Depth: not known
Displacement: c1500t
Rigging: four masts; square-rigged on fore and main; lateen-rigged mizzens
Armament: 43 heavy guns, 141 light pieces
Complement: 700

In the reign of Henry VIII there began the process of English warship design that culminated in the highly effective ships of his daughter, Elizabeth I. 'Great Harry', launched in 1514, was Henry's flagship or 'admiral'. Up to now, English warships had been converted merchantmen, with all the difficulties involved in the hiring and refitting of them in time of war. *Henry Grace à Dieu*, a large carrack, was purpose-built as a warship, as were her sister ships, the ill-fated *Mary Rose* (1505) and the *Great Galley* (1513). Very heavily armed, she carried the heavier guns in the waist, which assisted both her stability and the penetrative power of the shot. The smaller guns, set high in the forecastle and aftercastle, were intended to sweep the decks of enemy vessels. Grapnels were hung from the ends of the mainyard as well as the bowsprit. The superstructure was high, with a four-deck forecastle and probably six decks aft of the mainmast. The aftercastle undoubtedly included royal accommodation, since Henry used this ship (with simulated gold sails) for his 1520 visit to France and the 'Field of the Cloth of Gold'. In 1536–39, the 'Great Harry' was rebuilt and fitted with 21 heavy bronze guns and 130 lighter iron guns. On the accession of Edward VI in 1547, she was renamed *Edward*, and was based at the Woolwich Arsenal on the Thames. She was destroyed there, by fire, on 23 August 1553.

The 'Great Harry' was a king's ship in every way. A gunnery officer, Anthony Anthony, depicted the, by then refitted, vessel in 1545 along with other ships of Henry VIII's navy. Beflagged and pennanted, she was intended to display the power and splendour of the monarch.

LA DAUPHINE FRANCE: 1519

Built in the royal dockyard of Le Havre, *La Dauphine* was named after the Dauphin, or crown prince, of France. The ship was selected to sail for North America in 1523 under the command of the Italian navigator Giovanni da Verrazzano, with the aim of finding a westward passage to China for the benefit of French trade. Landfall was made at Cape Fear, North Carolina, and Verrazzano explored the coast to the south for 225 miles before turning north and making a thorough investigation of the bays and inlets of New Jersey and 'Orumbega', later called New England. The Verrazzano Narrows of New York Bay commemorate his search. Although he failed to find a route to China, Verrazzano's journey established that North America was not an extension of the Asian continent. *La Dauphine* returned to Dieppe on 8 July 1524. Her subsequent history is not known; on a later voyage, Verrazzano was captured and eaten by Carib Indians.

A contemporary depiction of *La Dauphine*, showing a two-masted caravel-type ship, is found on the Vatican's 'Verrazzano Map'.

Length: 80ft (24.5m)
Beam: 19ft (5.8m)
Depth: 15ft (4.6m)
Displacement: 100t burthen
Rigging: two masts; square-rigged
Complement: 50

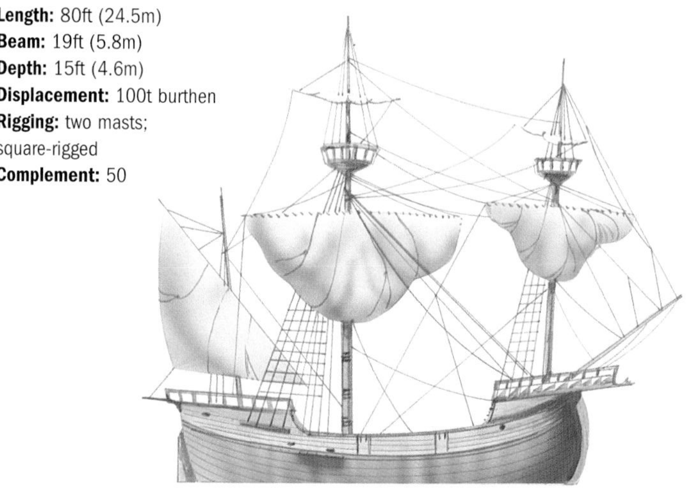

VICTORIA

SPAIN: *c*1519

Length: not known
Beam: not known
Depth: not known
Displacement: 85t
Rigging: three masts; square-rigged on fore and main; lateen-mizzen
Complement: 60

A small Spanish carrack, *Victoria* was the first ship to circumnavigate the globe. She was one of five ships under the command of Fernão de Magalhaes (Magellan), the other ships being *Concepcion, San Antonio, Santiago,* and Magellan's flagship, *Trinidad.* The fleet sailed from Sanlucar, on the Guadalquivir River, on 20 September 1519. The mission, backed by the Emperor Charles V, was to succeed where Columbus was now known to have failed, in finding a sea route westwards to the Indies. Magellan was Portuguese, and some of his Spanish officers plotted against him, including *Victoria*'s captain, Luis de Mendoza, who was killed in a scuffle in the admiral's cabin. The fleet was down to three ships by the time they had found the strait near the tip of South America, which now bears Magellan's name. On 28 November 1520, they completed the passage of the strait, passed Cape Desire and entered the Pacific. Beset by starvation and scurvy, they reached the Mariana Islands on 6 March 1521. On 27 April, Magellan was killed in a skirmish on the Philippine island of Cebu. Command of *Victoria* was taken over by the master of the *Concepcion*, Juan del Cano. The depleted Spanish burned *Concepcion* and proceeded in *Trinidad* and *Victoria*. In November 1521, the two ships were in the Moluccas and traded whatever goods they had for cloves, cinnamon, sandalwood, mace, and nutmeg. It was with this valuable cargo that they set sail to return to Spain by the established South African route, but *Trinidad* was forced to turn back and *Victoria* continued on alone. It was a difficult passage and it took 12 weeks for *Victoria* to double the Cape of Good Hope, during which time the foremast was lost in one of many storms. On 22 September 1522, she finally moored in the Guadalquivir after three years' travel. *Victoria*, alone of the original five ships, had survived the entire voyage. Of the crew, 29 of the 47 Europeans and 10 out of 13 East Indians had died on the return voyage. *Victoria* must have been in poor condition by this time yet, as a much-renewed vessel with scraped and probably patched hull, she went on to make two transatlantic voyages to Hispaniola (Haiti). On the return leg of the second voyage, she sank in mid-Atlantic, with the loss of all her crew.

By 1519, the 85t *Victoria* was a relatively small vessel, similar in size to a caravel. She was in fact the second smallest of Magellan's fleet. By comparison, the largest vessel was the *San Antonio* at 120t.

SANTA CATERINA DO MONTE SINAI

PORTUGAL: 1520

Length: c90ft (27.4m)
Beam: c30ft (9.1m)
Depth: c17ft (5.1m)
Displacement: c400t
Rigging: four masts; fore and main square-rigged with topsails; lateen-mizzens; spritsail
Armament: 140 guns, mostly small
Complement: c400

The large Portuguese ship *Santa Caterina do Monte Sinai* represents the final form of the carrack before the galleon superseded it. The high forecastle still extends beyond the bow, and the stern is rounded. The after-castle is notably high, making the ship a six-decker. Three tiers of guns are set abaft the mainmast, and two in the forecastle, but this ship is chiefly equipped for the classic closing and boarding form of naval warfare. Most of the guns, with a total estimated to be over 140, would be lightweight pieces, intended for raking a deck packed with armed men. Boarding nets would be mounted in the waist to prevent her own deck being stormed. Both forecastle and after-castle could be battened up to deny access, while archery and musketry were directed into the waist from above, including from the wide fighting tops on the foremast and main mast. The rig is square-sailed, apart from the two mizzens, both with a lateen sail; that on the bonaventure-mizzen secured to a stern boom or outligger. The topgallant sail has not yet appeared, but the foremast has a topsail, which was a new development at the time. The mainsail is of notably vast dimensions, cut in such a way as to billow out, and with a bonnet, in order both to increase sail area and to assist in rapid reduction of sail. Martinets, or crowsfeet tackle, are attached to the upper edges of the big sails to give further control. The collar-like parrel tackles also allow vertical movement of the yards.

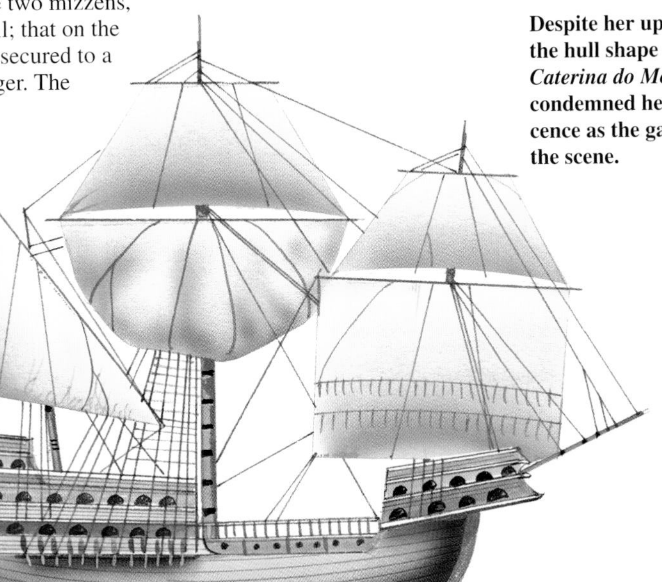

Despite her up-to-date features, the hull shape of the *Santa Caterina do Monte Sinai* condemned her to early obsolescence as the galleon appeared on the scene.

La Grande Hermine

FRANCE: *c*1534

In 1535, Jacques Cartier had already made one voyage to North America when the French king, François I, commissioned him to lead a flotilla to explore beyond Newfoundland. The exploration was in the hope of finding a route to China. *La Grande Hermine* was Cartier's flagship; the other vessels were the 60t *La Petite Hermine,* and the pinnace, *L'Emerillon*. On 10 August 1535, St Lawrence's day, Cartier named a small bay after the saint, then sailed up what he called 'la grande rivière' (now the St Lawrence) and into Quebec. Cartier returned to France in early 1536 but in 1541 he sailed to Canada, again in *La Grande Hermine* which the king had presented to him. This new expedition was intended to set up a permanent colony, but after trouble with the Indians, Cartier returned to France with the mission unaccomplished.

Few details of *La Grande Hermine* survive, but a full-size model, on early galleon lines, was built in 1967, and is preserved in Quebec.

Length: 78ft 8in (23.9m)
Beam: 25ft (7.6m)
Depth: 12ft (3.6m)
Displacement: 120t
Rigging: three masts; fore and main square-rigged; lateen-mizzen; spritsail
Armament: 12 guns
Complement: 112

Jesus of Lübeck

HANSEATIC PORT OF LÜBECK (REBUILT ENGLAND): *c*1544

Length: 135ft (41.2m)
Beam: 30ft (8.9m)
Depth: 20ft (6.1m)
Displacement: 700t
Rigging: four masts; fore and main square-rigged, lateen-mizzens
Armament: 26 guns
Complement: 300

In the course of her career, the carrack *Jesus of Lübeck* saw some varied action. Built some time before 1544 (perhaps at Lübeck in Germany) and intended as a Hanseatic trading ship, she had a lofty forecastle and aftercastle and was not a good sailer. Bought by Henry VIII of England in 1544, she was converted to a warship. Later, in 1564, she was leased as an armed slave-ship to Captain John Hawkins, who used her for that purpose during the next four years. Hawkins cut down the upperworks, which may have inspired the trim and weatherly design of English galleons of the 1580s. In September 1568, at San Juan de Ulloa on the Gulf of Mexico, Hawkins and his flotilla were trapped by the Spanish; in an armistice-breaking attack, the *Jesus of Lübeck* was sunk, though not before she had destroyed two Spanish ships.

The only known drawing of the *Jesus of Lübeck* shows a lateen topsail on the mizzen mast, but this, if used at all, was only for display.

Bull

ENGLAND: 1546

On conversion, the gun deck was moved down to the former rowing deck, a configuration that anticipated the frigate.

English naval records from 1546 show that combined sailing and oared vessels were still being built, although smaller than earlier versions. The *Bull* was originally a galleass of around 200t, with four masts, a gun deck set above the rowers' deck, and 22 oars a side shipped. The extent to which the oars were used is unknown and may have been very limited. A report to the Venetian government in 1551, penned by a Venetian observer, states that the English did not use 'galleys' – a term which would at that time embrace a galleass if the latter was regularly propelled by oars. With four masts, the fore and main being square-rigged with courses and topsails, and lateens on the mizzens, there was fairly considerable sail power available.

Though it is likely that the *Bull* and her three sister ships were intended for defensive use in the Thames estuary, in 1588 she fought in the Armada battles. Records show that the *Bull* (converted to sail only) survived until 1603.

Length: 120ft (36.5m)
Beam: 22ft (6.7m)
Depth: 11ft (3.3m)
Displacement: 200t
Rigging: four masts; fore and main square-rigged with topsails; lateen-mizzens; spritsail
Armament: 18 guns
Complement: 84 seamen-oarsmen, 16 gunners, 20 soldiers

TIGER

ENGLAND: 1546

Length: 115ft (35m)
Beam: 22ft (6.7m)
Depth: 11ft (3.3m)
Displacement: 200t
Rigging: (as ship) three masts; square-rigged on fore and main; lateen-mizzen
Armament: 20 guns
Complement: 80 seamen-oarsmen, 12 gunners, 8 soldiers

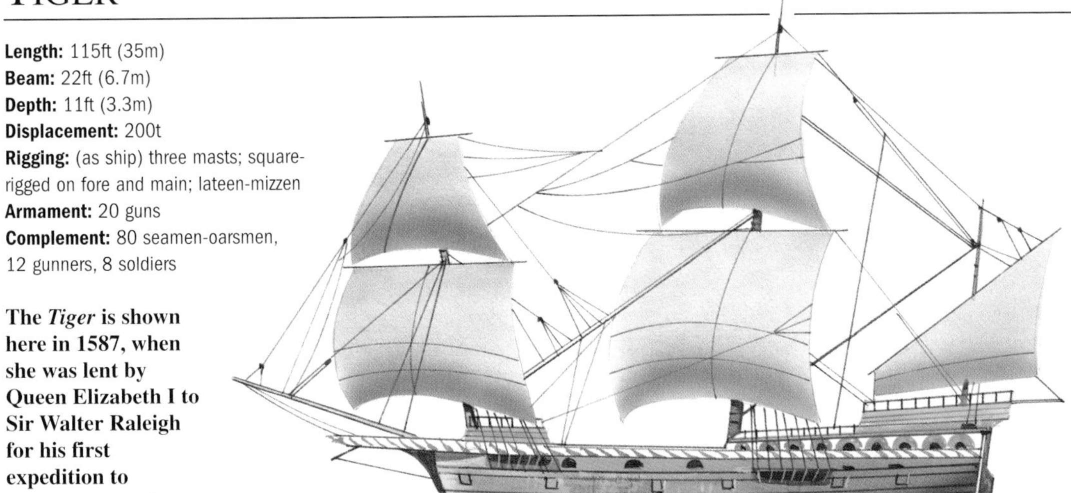

The *Tiger* is shown here in 1587, when she was lent by Queen Elizabeth I to Sir Walter Raleigh for his first expedition to Virginia in 1587.

Built as a galleass in Henry VIII's reign, *Tiger* was later converted to standard ship form. She joined in the bombardment of a Spanish outpost at Smerwick, Ireland, in 1580. *Tiger* was home in time to participate in the Armada battles of 1588, and was then sent to Edinburgh to encourage the Scots to give up their Armada refugees. She was broken up in 1603.

Tiger was a name kept for galleass-type vessels. The illustration shown her in converted form. A new *Tiger*, sweep-propelled, was built in 1684 to fight the galleasses of the Barbary corsairs.

GALLEASS

VENICE: 1550

Representing an attempt to combine the qualities of a sailing ship and an oared vessel, the galleass was introduced in the 16th century. Though associated mostly with Spain and Venice, it was also tried out in Sweden and in England. Four galleasses sailed in the Spanish Armada of 1588. The design was based on the big Venetian merchant galley; three-masted, lateen-rigged, and with a square sail mounted on the bowsprit to help in steering, it was a formidable but somewhat ponderous vessel. Interestingly, a Sienese painting of around 1510 shows a galleass – presumably Italian – with a square-rigged mainmast. The galleasses used in Northern waters were also square-rigged. Heavy guns were mounted in the bows, but the presence of the oarsmen – up to seven on each oar – made it extremely difficult to fit any but the lightest artillery on the sides.

Length: 130ft (39.6m)
Beam: 27ft (8.2m)
Depth: 11ft (3.3m)
Displacement: not known
Rigging: three masts; lateen-rigged
Armament: 14 guns
Complement: 260 oarsmen, 40 gunners, 30 seamen, plus soldiers

Six large galleasses took part in the Battle of Lepanto in 1571. They were towed into fighting position. This painting shows the typical lateen rig on all three masts.

GALLEON

SPAIN: *c*1550

Brueghel was one of the most distinguished of many artists to represent contemporary ships in paintings and engravings. This is a valuable aid to naval historians, since almost no technical drawings survive from before the 17th century.

As so often, the origin of the name 'galleon' is obscure. It is first found in English use in 1529, and it is likely that the first ships of galleon type were built in Spain. However, in the early 16th century, there was a general trend towards a longer, narrower hull than that of the carrack and, by the 1530s, galleons were being built by all the maritime powers of Europe.

The crucial new feature was the hull shape: the somewhat greater length in relation to beam helped in sailing to windward but, more significant, was the complete re-design of the forecastle. This no longer projected over the bow, as in the carrack, but was pulled back, lightening and raising the bows, and making control of the ship's head easier. The ship illustrated, based on a Pieter Brueghel engraving of around 1550, seems to be earlier than that date; compared to the galleon proper, it has an incompletely developed beak, and is of smaller dimensions.

Length: 126ft (38.4m)
Beam: 33ft (10m)
Depth: 16ft (4.8m)
Displacement: 250t
Rigging: four masts; square-rig with topsails of fore and main; lateen-mizzens; spritsail
Complement: 30–40
Routes: deep-sea
Cargo: wood, spices, ore, bullion, military stores

GALLEY

TURKEY: 1560

Length: 120ft (36.5m)
Beam: 18ft (5.5m)
Depth: 9ft (2.7m)
Displacement: not known
Rigging: one-three masts; lateen-rigged
Armament: up to five, bow-mounted, cannon
Complement: 240 oarsmen, 20-40 seamen, 8 gunners, plus soldiers

An important change in Mediterranean galley propulsion took place at the start of the 16th century. Previously, oars and oarsmen had been grouped in sets of two or three, one man to each oar. Now the oars, typically 24 to a side, were spaced evenly along the sides, with each one drawn by a team of up to seven men – the unfortunate galley slaves. Around the same time, galleys began to mount guns, sometimes a single heavy gun firing forward from the bows. These superseded the ram, which was mounted well above the waterline, and was used more as a boarding bridge. Although galleys were used throughout the Mediterranean, it seems likely that the innovations came from Italy, specifically Venice. The traditional lateen rig was unchanged; some galleys had three masts, the majority only one. This illustration shows two.

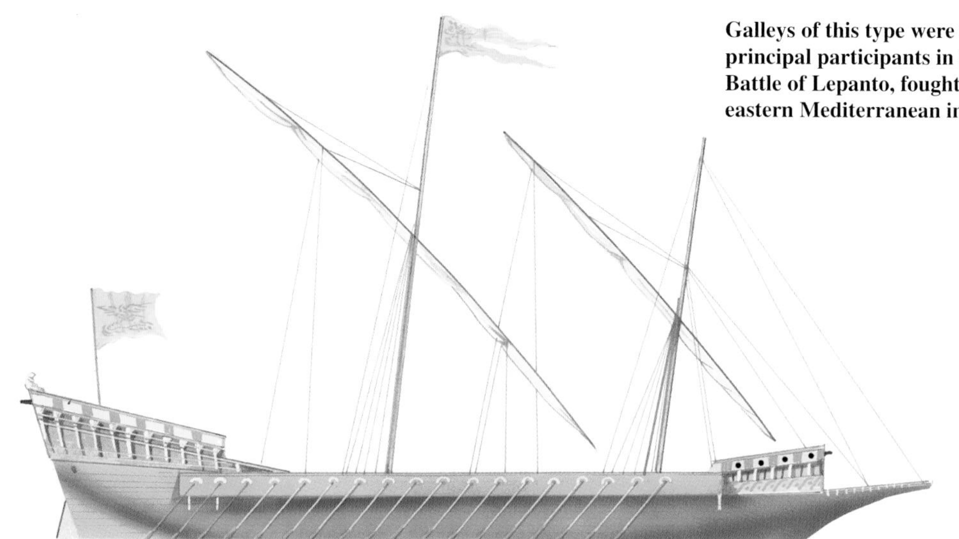

Galleys of this type were the principal participants in the great Battle of Lepanto, fought in the eastern Mediterranean in 1571.

MERCHANT SHIP

THE NETHERLANDS: 1564

A small galleon of the mid-16th century, intended as a cargo vessel. However, with piracy still a hazard in the North Sea, it is quite well armed, with gunports along the main deck and quarter deck. The stern below the counter is rounded, suggesting that this Dutch-built ship may represent a transitional phase between the galleon and the fluyt, which appeared at the end of the 16th century. The shallow draft enabled these vessels to operate along the comparitively shallow inshore waters with safety. All had excellent carrying capacity for ships of this size. There were over 30 guns for self defence.

The illustration is based on a Brueghel engraving dated 1565.

Length: 91ft (27.7m)
Beam: 26ft (7.92m)
Depth: 13ft (3.96m)
Displacement: not known
Rigging: three masts; square-rigged on fore and main; lateen-mizzen; spritsail
Complement: 30-40
Routes: deep-sea

BOIER (BOEJER)

THE NETHERLANDS: 1565

Length: 70ft (21.3m)
Beam: 20ft (6m)
Depth: 9ft (2.7m)
Displacement: 100t
Rigging: two masts; mainmast with spritsail, square topsail and jib; lateen-mizzen; spritsail
Complement: 4-6
Routes: Dutch and north German coasts
Cargo: baled and barrelled goods

In the 16th and 17th centuries, the Dutch excelled in building the 'bulk carriers' of their day. The boier (or boejer) was one such vessel, widely in use by 1575, and an effective short-sea merchant ship. The foresail, not attached to the bowsprit, is a very early example on a seagoing ship. The original rig, with topsail and lateen on the mizzen, gave way over the next 100 years to a single-masted spritsail rig, and a simpler hull with no quarterdeck.

The big spritsail was unwieldy, and in time gave way to the more manageable gaffrig found on later versions of the boier.

San Juan

SPAIN: 1565

Length: c65ft (19.8m)
Beam: c19ft (5.8m)
Depth: not known
Displacement: c280t
Rigging: three masts; square-rigged on fore and main; lateen-mizzen
Complement: 75
Routes: from Basque coast to Labrador whaling grounds
Cargo: whale oil and other whale by-products

A ship of galleon construction, *San Juan* was a whaler from the Basque coast. As blubber boiling, processing and barrelling were done at a shore station, she was more a mother ship and oil transporter than a factory ship. The whalers' hunting area was the Strait of Belle Isle, between Labrador and Newfoundland, and it was here that *San Juan* was wrecked at Red Bay, Labrador, in 1565. Much of her structure was recovered between 1979–84.

Whaling was a considerable industry for Basque towns. For example, in Bilbao, an estimated 30 vessels were engaged in the industry in the mid-16th century.

Armed Hoy

THE NETHERLANDS: 1570

Here a Dutch *hoy* has been transformed into a gunboat. A small cannon is mounted in the bows, two more on each side and, just abaft of the single mast, a kind of fortification has been installed to give protection against gunfire. The cause for such a vessel was the Dutch war against Spanish rule (since the Low countries were then a province of the Habsburg Empire), which went on through the 1570s and 1580s. The hoop-supported awning over the stern may have been to conceal armed men.

Length: 48ft (14.6m)
Beam: 14ft (4.26m)
Depth: 5ft (1.5m)
Displacement: 30t
Rigging: single mast; gaff-rig with small jib
Armament: three cannon
Complement: 2, plus military
Routes: Dutch inshore, and inland waterways

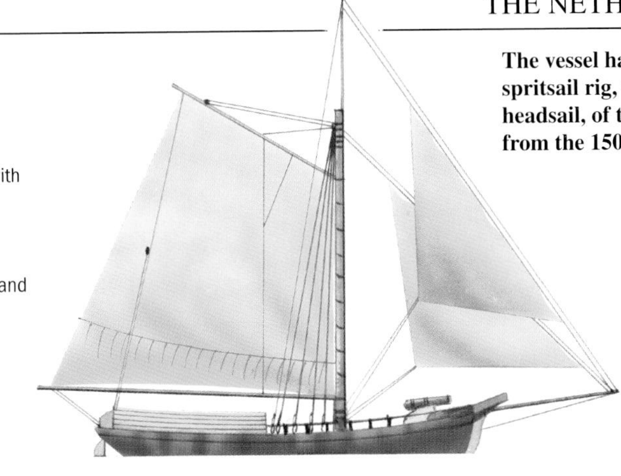

The vessel has the typical gaff and spritsail rig, with triangular headsail, of the Dutch *hoy*, known from the 1500s onwards.

Golden Hind

ENGLAND: 1576

According to one authority, the *Golden Hind* was built in France and bought by the English West Country Hawkins family; another source says that she was launched in Plymouth in 1576. First named as the *Pelican*, she was renamed by her captain, Francis Drake, in August 1578 at the mouth of the Magellan Strait. She was the emblem of his voyage's chief patron, Sir Christopher Hatton and flagship of a five-ship squadron which left London in December 1577. The purpose of the voyage was to navigate the Magellan Strait, explore the western coast of South America and plunder the Spanish ports, and then return to England via the North west Passage. All except the last were triumphantly achieved; instead the *Golden Hind* became the first English vessel to circumnavigate the globe, reaching Plymouth in September 1580. She was a ship of galleon type. The hull was double-sheathed with a layer of tarred horsehair between inner and outer planking in an effort to prevent the boring teredo worm. Her 18 guns were mounted on two decks, and the gunports could be sealed up in heavy weather. Under the forecastle, Drake had a forge installed. After Drake's epic voyage, the *Golden Hind* crossed to Labrador and back with Sir Humphrey Gilbert's expedition of 1583. Queen Elizabeth I ordered that she should be kept in preservation at Deptford, London, but the shed to house the ship was never built. By 1660, the *Golden Hind* had rotted away.

A modern replica of the *Golden Hind* is docked close by Tower Bridge, London.

Length: 70ft (21.3m)
Beam: 19ft (5.8m)
Depth: 9ft (2.7m)
Displacement: c150t burthen
Rigging: three masts; square-rigged on fore and main; lateen-mizzen; spritsail
Armament: 18 guns
Complement: 80–85

REVENGE

ENGLAND: 1577

Revenge was one of the first of the new-style galleons developed in England around 1580 by Sir John Hawkins and the shipwright Matthew Baker. Typified by a narrower length-to-beam ratio than the normal galleon, by a low freeboard, and by substantially reduced forecastle and aftercastle, these new-style galleons also embodied a new concept in naval warfare: that of firing heavy shot, low down, from a distance, rather than grappling with an enemy and relying on manpower and light guns. *Revenge*, commanded by Sir Francis Drake, played an active role in the war with Spain. In 1590, she was the flagship of Sir Martin Frobisher, in his attempt to intercept the Spanish treasure fleet, and she formed part of a similar expedition in 1591 under Lord Thomas Howard. In the Azores, encircled and outnumbered by a Spanish fleet at Flores, Howard extricated his ships, but his vice-admiral, Sir Richard Grenville, on *Revenge*, chose to stay on. The ensuing action lasted 14 hours, the English fighting against impossible odds. Two Spanish ships were sunk and another heavily damaged, but Grenville was killed. The battered *Revenge* was taken as a prize, but she sank, with many other vessels, in a heavy storm on the way to Spain.

Her long-range cannon were an important part of the advantage *Revenge* had over her opponents; she could engage the enemy from 300 yards.

Length: 92ft (28m)
Beam: 32ft (9.75m)
Depth: 16ft (4.8m)
Displacement: 500t
Rigging: three masts; square-rigged except lateen-mizzen
Armament: 36 guns
Complement: 150 sailors, 24 gunners, 76 soldiers

SAN MARTIN

PORTUGAL/SPAIN: *c*1579

Length: 122ft 3in (37.3m)
Beam: 30ft 5in (9.3m)
Depth: not known
Displacement: 1000t
Rigging: three masts; square-rigged on fore and main; lateen-mizzen
Armament: 48 guns
Complement: 350 seamen and gunners, plus soldiers

Apart from seamen, the *San Martin* embarked 202 arquebusiers and 100 musketeers, disposed mostly on the forecastle and after-castle and in the fighting tops on the foremast and mainmast.

The flagship of the Spanish Armada in 1588, the *San Martin* was built as a Portuguese galleon, and taken into Spanish ownership when Portugal was annexed in 1580. Two years later, she was flagship of the fleet that defeated the French at the Battle of Terceiro in the Azores. Like other Iberian galleons, she was built high for more effective grappling and close-quarters fighting, though among her guns were some 30pdrs. As Armada leader, the *San Martin* was heavily engaged in the skirmishes and fights as the fleet moved up-Channel, including the rescue of Martinez de Recalde's cut-off rearguard vessels. Her involvement culminated in the battle off Gravelines on 8 August 1588, a close-range contest in which she took over 200 hits and was only saved by two divers who plugged the shot-holes at the waterline. *San Martin* was one of the 67 ships to return safely to Spain, though with the loss of 180 men.

THE BLACK PINNACE

ENGLAND: *c*1580

Length: c75 ft (22.8m)
Beam: c17ft (5.2m)
Depth: c8ft (2.4m)
Displacement: c75t
Rigging: three masts; square-rigged with topsails on fore and main; lateen-mizzen; spritsail
Complement: 20
Routes: North Sea and English Channel trade
Cargo: perishable goods, valuable low-bulk items

The *Black Pinnace* brought the body of Sir Philip Sidney, a popular Elizabethan courtier, from Zutphen to England in 1586. The pinnace, as a small full-rigged ship, may be the caravel continued under a new name. It had an updated hull and upperworks, with a beak prow, low forecastle, and stern lines that rose to a short quarterdeck. The pinnace was used both as a merchantman and as a small warship. By the 1650s, the type had grown to 90ft (27m) long, and was virtually a frigate.

The word 'pinnace', confusingly, can also mean a large, about 32ft (9.75m), boat. It is carried inboard or towed and is always oared, but usually also with a single mast.

TRIUMPH

ENGLAND: *c*1580

Frobisher's reputation is chiefly that of an explorer. In 1576–78, he made three determined but unsuccessful voyages in the attempt to penetrate the Northwest Passage.

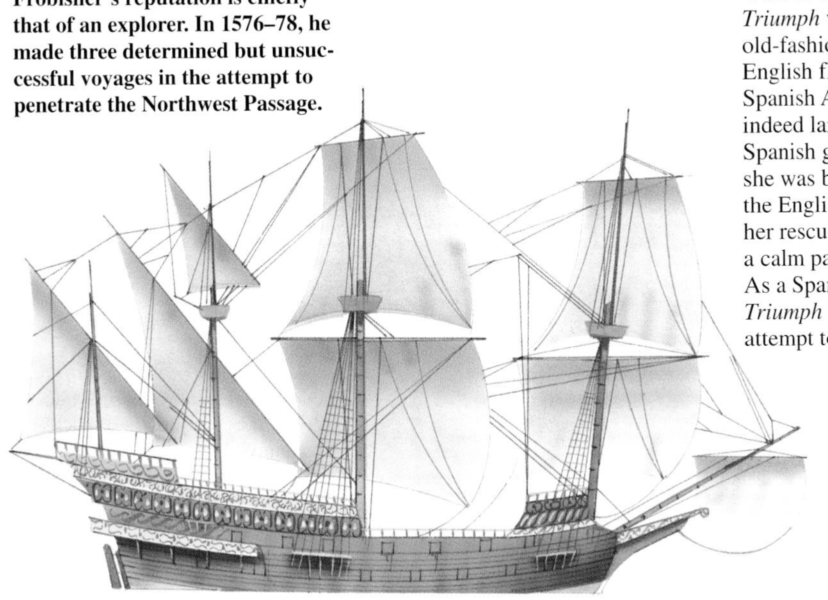

With an armament of 60 guns, *Triumph* was the largest and most old-fashioned galleon in the English fleet which opposed the Spanish Armada in 1588, and indeed larger than any of the Spanish galleons. Despite her size, she was built on the racier lines of the English galleon. This came to her rescue when she was caught in a calm patch off the Isle of Wight. As a Spanish squadron advanced, *Triumph* lowered her boats in an attempt to tow herself out of trouble, but a sudden gust of wind got her quickly on the move, enabling her to escape. Her captain was Martin Frobisher, a seaman of great experience who knew every trick of ship handling. *Triumph* was heavily engaged in other fighting, including a sharp conflict with four galleasses off Portland Bill in which she shattered their oars. For his distinguished service, Frobisher was knighted at sea by Howard, the Lord Admiral.

Length: 210ft (64m)
Beam: 51ft (155.5m)
Depth: 21ft (6.4m)
Displacement: 1100t
Rigging: four masts; square-rigged on fore and mainmasts; lateen-mizzens
Armament: 60 guns
Complement: 300 sailors, 40 gunners, 160 soldiers

SQUIRREL

ENGLAND: 1583

Length: 42ft (12.2m)
Beam: 12ft 6in (3.8m)
Depth: 5ft (1.5m)
Displacement: c45t
Rigging: three masts; square-rigged fore and main with lateen-mizzen
Armament: not known
Complement: 11

Sir Humphrey Gilbert (*c*1539–83), half-brother of Sir Walter Raleigh, claimed Newfoundland for England in 1583. His expedition consisted of five ships of which *Squirrel*, apparently his own property, was much the smallest. For the outward journey to Newfoundland, Gilbert had sailed in *Delight*, which was wrecked later in the expedition. He chose *Squirrel* for the return journey to England but she was lost, with all hands, somewhere in the Atlantic, having last been seen from the *Golden Hind* on 9 September 1583.

The small size of *Squirrel* indicates the difficulty which explorers had in assembling a squadron for voyages of uncertain outcome.

ARK ROYAL

ENGLAND: 1587

Built for defence, *Ark Royal* and her sister ships were more manoeuvrable than Spanish warships because they were not loaded down with stores for a long voyage.

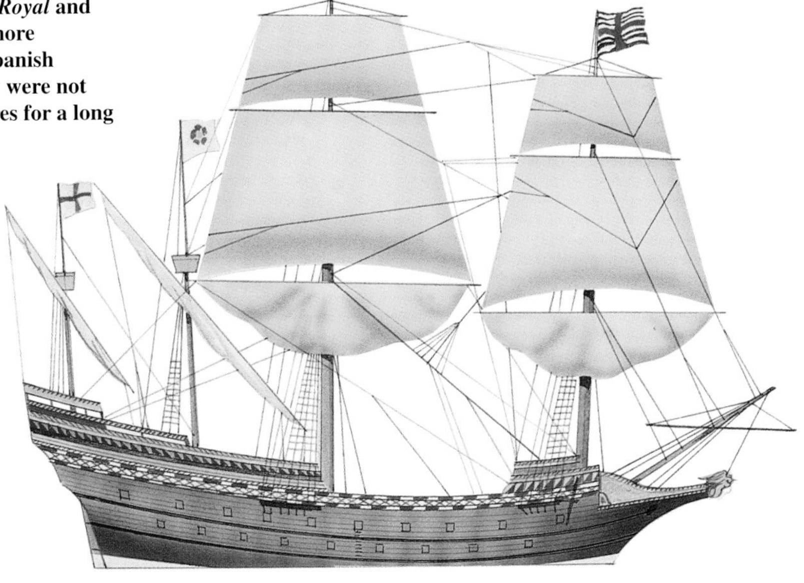

Length: 140ft (42.6m)
Beam: 37ft (11.2m)
Depth: 15ft (4.5m)
Displacement: 690t
Rigging: four masts; square-rigged apart from lateen-mizzens
Armament: 38 guns, plus 17 small pieces
Complement: 270 sailors, 34 gunners, 126 soldiers

Initially intended for Sir Walter Raleigh, the English galleon *Ark Raleigh* was taken over while building by the government of Queen Elizabeth 1. She was launched at Deptford and renamed *Ark Royal*. As the flagship of the English fleet under Lord Howard of Effingham, she sailed to meet the Spanish Armada on 30 July 1588, and was the first ship to engage the enemy. At that time,

English ship design was perhaps the best in Europe. The English 'race-built' galleon had four points of superiority over its rivals: fine underwater lines helped both speed and handling; the solidly-built forecastle and aftercastle, less towering than on Continental vessels, improved stability; the armament was carefully thought out – English galleons of 1588 and later carried fewer guns, to more effect, than their predecessors had done; and the sails were cut to be taut and responsive. *Ark Royal* had one old-fashioned feature, the bonaventure-mizzen at her stern being perhaps more for effect than performance. Three tiers of sail were carried on the fore and main masts. Howard wrote: 'I think her the odd [only] ship in the world for all conditions.' *Ark Royal* participated in the attack on Cadiz in 1596. In 1608, she was rebuilt and renamed, after James I's queen, *Anne Royal*. In 1636, she sank at Tilbury on the Thames.

CARRACK (SLAVE SHIP)

PORTUGAL: 1590

Length: 120ft (36m)
Beam: 27ft 6in (8.4m)
Depth: not known
Displacement: 400t
Rigging: four masts; square-rigged on foremast, others lateen-rigged
Complement: not known
Routes: West Africa to the West Indies and Central America
Cargo: slaves

In the 16th century the Portugese, with their large Brazilian possessions, dominated the transatlantic slave trade.

Slave ships would moor in creeks on the West African coast in order to rendezvous with their agents in the grim trade. Speed at sea was essential since the mortality rate in the slave hold was very high. At this time there was no ban on slaving, but official licences were needed; many captains did without them, since they were expensive to procure. This fast carrack was typical, longer and slimmer in line than a conventional cargo ship.

MAYFLOWER

ENGLAND: *c*1606

A replica of the *Mayflower*, based on the few known details of the ship and much knowledge of the type, was built in 1956 and sailed across the Atlantic. The route taken was from Plymouth, England, to Plymouth, Massachusetts, where the replica is still exhibited.

Length: c90ft (27.4m)
Beam: c26ft (7.92m)
Depth: c11ft (3.3m)
Displacement: 180t
Rigging: three masts; square-rigged with lateen-mizzen
Complement: c20 crew, 101 passengers
Routes: normally England to eastern France
Cargo: baled wool, wine

The *Mayflower* plied from London and English south coast ports with such export items as wool and hides, and returned from Bordeaux or Nantes with wine and brandy. She was an entirely typical ship of the galleon type; there were hundreds like her. Her home port was probably Southampton, but the first definite mention of *Mayflower* is in London port papers of 1606, with one Christopher Jones noted as master and co-owner. In 1620, a more momentous voyage was proposed. The *Mayflower* was chartered by a group of people who wished to emigrate from England to North America, where they could count on freedom to practise their Puritan form of religion, which was forbidden in England. They were picked up by *Mayflower* at Southampton and sailed on to Plymouth, their last English port. On 6 September 1620, they set out for Virginia, but landed some 200 miles to the north, at Truro, Cape Cod. *Mayflower* wintered at the Massachusetts harbour which was already, by coincidence, called Plymouth. Half her crew died, but she returned safely to England in May 1621. The future of the passengers, the Pilgrim Fathers, was to be well documented, that of the *Mayflower* somewhat less so. She seems to have resumed the cross-channel trade she was originally built for, being last heard of in 1624, when she was surveyed at Rotherhithe, London, and valued at £128 8s 4d.

D'HALVE MAEN

THE NETHERLANDS: 1608

Length: 65ft (19.8m)
Beam: 17ft 3in (5.25m)
Depth: 8ft (2.4m)
Displacement: 80t burthen
Rigging: three masts; square-rigged on fore and main with topsails; lateen-mizzen; bowsprit
Complement: 17-20
Routes: deep-sea trading routes
Cargo: sandalwood, spices, ores

A *vlieboot* built at Amsterdam in 1608 for the Dutch East India Company, the *D'Halve Maen* ('Half-moon') had four guns mounted as two ports to each side. The guns were chiefly for show as she was essentially a merchant vessel. In 1609, the English explorer Henry Hudson crossed the North Atlantic in the *D'Halve Maen,* and sailed for 147 miles up the river which now bears his name. The voyage was by no means prompted by idle curiosity. Hudson made land claims on behalf of both the Dutch (who were sponsors of his expedition) and the English. On his return to England, he docked at Dartmouth where he left the ship. It was returned to the Dutch the following year and sailed to the East Indies. According to one report, *D'Halve Maen* was wrecked off Mauritius in 1611; other reports claim that she was either wrecked off Sumatra in 1616, or burned there by the English in 1618.

A *vlieboot* was a somewhat flat-bottomed design. The name is connected with the Dutch island of Vlieland, and is often rendered into English as 'flyboat'.

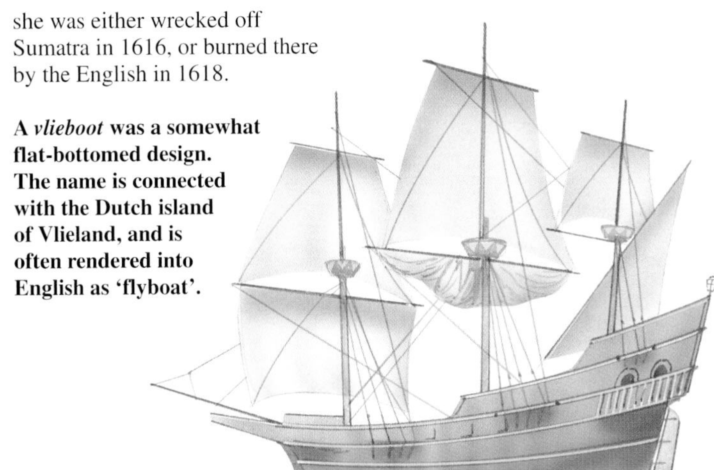

BRIG

THE NETHERLANDS: 1610

From this early Dutch example, the brig evolved in different ways, both as a merchant vessel and as a 14-gun warship.

'Brig' and 'brigantine' are tricky words; brigantine is the older and may originally have meant pirate ship. But by 1695, brigantine indicated a two-masted ship with the foremast square-rigged and the mainmast fore-and-aft rigged. The brig evolved from this design as being square-rigged on both masts, but with a fore-and-aft sail rigged on gaff, and boom abaft the mainmast. However, both terms were used later on to refer to vessels with differing kinds of two-masted rig.

Length: 65ft (18.9m)
Beam: 20ft (6m)
Depth: 10ft (3m)
Displacement: 160t
Rigging: two masts, square-rigged with course and topsail
Complement: 12
Routes: North Sea coastal routes
Cargo: timber, ore, general goods

PRINCE ROYAL

ENGLAND: 1610

Length: 111ft (33.8m) (keel)
Beam: 43ft (13.1m)
Depth: 18ft (5.4m)
Displacement: 1200t
Rigging: four masts; square-rigged on fore and main with topgallant on main; lateen-mizzens with square topsails; spritsail and bowsprit topsail
Armament: 56 guns
Complement: c400

The largest warship of her time, *Prince Royal* was one of the first to mount three complete gun decks. Named in honour of Prince Henry, and fitted with sumptuous staterooms that made her Armada-beating and smaller predecessors look austere indeed, she was used for royal visits abroad. The accounts of cost for her carvings, gilding, and decoration still survive: a total of £1309 7s, a huge sum for the time. The builder was Phineas Pett, a master shipbuilder of great renown and expertise but who – perhaps through bribery – used unseasoned timber in the construction, which was to cause early decay. *Prince Royal* was regarded as a poor sailer and, in 1641, was comprehensively rebuilt. A further rebuild followed, by which time her original armament of 56 guns had been increased to 90. Like the other major warships of the early-17th century, *Prince Royal* carried four masts, and her original bonaventure mizzen mast was additionally rigged with a square topsail; in the course of their service careers, not only this sail, but the fourth mast, tended to disappear from these ships. From mid-century on, three masts were regarded as adequate to drive even the largest of warships. Steering a ship of this size was aided by the whipstaff, a recently devised vertical lever attached to the inboard end of the tiller; it enabled the steersman to work on the deck above (the tiller came in on the lower gun deck).

***Prince Royal* was one of the first ships with a spritsail topmast, which was rigged only in summer conditions.**

EENDRACHT

THE NETHERLANDS: 1614

Length: not known
Beam: not known
Depth: not known
Displacement: 360t
Rigging: three masts; square-rigged on fore and main; lateen-mizzen; spritsail
Armament: 19 guns, 12 swivel cannon
Complement: 87
Routes: deep-sea trading and exploratory
Cargo: tropical products

Isaac Le Maire was a Dutch merchant who had broken with the East India Company, and was barred from using the Straits of Magellan because of the company's monopoly. Undeterred, he set about financing his own route to the Spice Islands. *Eendracht* was flagship of a two-ship expedition. Under Isaac's son, Jacques, and Willem Cornelis Schouten, she became the first ship to navigate the open sea south of Cape Horn, passing from the South Atlantic into the South Pacific on 29 January 1516. On arrival at Bantam in the Dutch East Indies, the ship and her cargo were confiscated, and the captain's story ridiculed. It took more than two years for recognition and restitution to be made. *Eendracht* was well provided in every way, and was prepared with utmost care for what was, despite its unfortunate end, a model voyage of discovery.

An exceptional arrangement was that *Eendracht* carried four boats: a sailing pinnace, a smaller oared pinnace, a launch, and a dinghy.

D'BATAVIASE EEUW

THE NETHERLANDS: 1620

The Dutch East India Company built stout and substantial ships. They were of a variety of types, reflecting the company's long-range and highly profitable trade with the Spice Islands, via the Cape of Good Hope. In form, ships like the *D'Bataviase Eeuw* anticipated the frigate; they had a single complete gun deck, and they could be chartered as ships of war, but their principal function was to carry cargo. Reliability, rather than speed, was the aim behind their design.

The East India Company's own yard at Amsterdam was capable of building three large ships a year, and was one of the most advanced in Europe.

Length: 121ft 6in (37m)
Beam: 33ft 6in (10m)
Depth: c12ft (3.6m)
Displacement: 700t
Rigging: three masts; square-rigged with topgallants on fore and main; lateen-mizzen with square topsail; spritsail and bowsprit topsail
Complement: not known
Routes: Dutch ports to Batavia and other ports in the Indonesian archipelago
Cargo: tropical woods, spices

NUESTRA SEÑORA DE BEGONIA

SPAIN: 1625

In 1625, aware of the vulnerability of their treasure ships, the Spanish government contracted with the Basque shipbuilder, Don Martin de Arana, for six galleons to carry silver bullion. One of the six was the *Nuestra Señora de Begonia*. Strict guidelines for construction were laid down, and she and her sister ships, smaller and faster than the usual galleon and normally sailing in convoy formation, all fulfilled their purpose successfully.

The reduction in their size enabled the treasure ships to use harbours which were beginning to silt up, following more than a century of Spanish exploitation.

Length: 80ft 8in (24.59m)
Beam: 31ft 2in (9.53m)
Depth: 14ft 8in (4.47m)
Displacement: 450t
Rigging: three masts; square-rigged on fore and main, with lateen-mizzen
Complement: not known
Routes: from American harbours to Seville and other Spanish ports
Cargo: silver, gold, other ores, field and forest products

SAINT LOUIS

FRANCE (BUILT IN THE NETHERLANDS): 1626

Length: *c*120 ft (36.5m)
Beam: *c*42ft (12.8m)
Depth: not known
Displacement: 1000t
Rigging: three masts; square-rigged with topgallants on fore and main; lateen-mizzen with square topsail; spritsail and bowsprit topsail
Armament: 60 guns
Complement: 700

In the second quarter of the 17th century, the French, conscious of their lack of seapower, set about establishing a fleet to rival those of the Dutch and English. The first ships were built in Dutch yards, including the *Saint Louis*. She was a galleon with around 60 guns on two gun decks. Other European powers had responded to English developments by building ships of similar type, and the *Saint Louis* shows a much-reduced superstructure profile compared with European galleons of a previous generation. She has a square stern, with partly covered-in gallery, and three masts, with square topsail on the mizzen, and a spritsail topmast and topsail. Protective gratings were built over the open main deck; the gratings were removable to allow for stowage of boats, supplies, and the internal arrangements would have included a whipstaff to ease steering, as well as hand-powered bilge pumps.

***Saint Louis* has the Continental 'square tuck' or transom stern, rather than the rounded stern planking of an English ship.**

WASA

SWEDEN: 1628

Length: 180ft (54.8m)
Beam: 38ft 3in (11.6m)
Depth: 15ft 4in (4.6m)
Displacement: 1300t
Rigging: three masts; square-rigged with topgallants on fore and mainmasts; topsail and lateen on mizzen; spritsail and square sail on bowsprit mast
Armament: 64 guns
Complement: 145 seamen, 300 soldiers

***Wasa* lay at a depth of 115ft (35m), gradually settling into the muddy floor, which helped to preserve much of her contents. In 1959, naval divers made six tunnels under the wreck to allow slings to be laid for an eventual lifting operation.**

The pride of the Swedish Navy, the 1300t *Wasa* most embarrassingly sank in the first minutes of her maiden voyage on 10 April 1628. The cause of the disaster, as with the English *Mary Rose* 93 years earlier, was the entry of water through open gunports when the ship heeled. About 50 of the 250 people on board were drowned. *Wasa*'s builder was an experienced Dutchman, Henrik Hyberson de Groot and, though the Swedish authorities attempted to blame his design, it is clear that there was something of a festival atmosphere about the maiden cruise. There were women and children on board, and neglecting to close the gunports as the ship reached open water was a fatal lapse. The salvaged *Wasa* shows us a ship of the line from the second quarter of the 17th century, though, as it was a 'royal ship' built for display, it may have possessed features that were not typical of other ships. From a low forecastle and level main deck, the decks rake steeply in five steps to the lofty poop. The distinct aft rake of the mainmast is also untypical. As in English ships of equivalent size, the bowsprit and foremast were socketed together, with the foremast stepped in the keel. There were two gun decks, with 48 24pdrs as the main armament. *Wasa* was not built purely for show. Europe was in turmoil, and Swedish armies were engaged in action deep in the continent, fighting the Austrians in the Thirty Years' War. All maritime powers were building new ships and Sweden, with a fleet blockading the great Polish harbour of Gdansk, also needed to keep control of the Sound and the Baltic Sea. Salvage operations began soon after the ship sank and 53 guns were removed in 1663–64. Then the *Wasa* was largely forgotten until the 20th century, when she was again located. A careful salvage operation first extracted the wreck from the mud, and then brought it to the surface on 24 April 1960. With a host of artefacts that reveal much about daily life on board, the conserved hull of the *Wasa* is now the central feature in Stockholm's Maritime History Museum.

BEZAAN YACHT

THE NETHERLANDS: 1630

Length: 15ft (4.5m)
Beam: 6ft (1.8m)
Depth: 2ft 6in (0.75m)
Displacement: not known
Rigging: single mast; gaff-rig with jib and staysail
Complement: 2
Routes: inshore; broad inland waterways

Bezaan **was the name of a yacht presented to King Charles II by the Dutch East India Company, but based on the later 'admiralty yacht'.**

During the 17th century, The Netherlands was both prosperous in trade and imperial in ambition. It also had highly competent and inventive shipbuilders who, living with a long coastline, intricate coastal waterways, and an inland sea, were to develop a range of small craft, mostly for trade and fishing, but also, for the first time since the classical era, for pleasure sailing. In Dutch, *bezaan* means 'mizzen' and the fore-and-aft sail of this craft was rigged on the single mast, between a short gaff and a long boom extending almost to the sternpost. A jib-boom (which could be brought inboard when not in use) enabled a jib to be set in front of the foresail – completing a simple rig which two men, or even one man, could control. The shallow-draught boat was fitted with a leeboard, which pivoted from the top, and could be lowered to give additional keel and so help in tacking. The predecessor of the bezaan yacht was a two-masted craft, with two bezaan sails but no foresails; a later derivative was a schooner-like vessel built on a similar, but somewhat larger, hull and mounting two bezaan sails, foresail and jib. With its much-lengthened gaff and clew-lines attached to the mainsail, this little *bezaan jacht* was the ancestor of a substantial family of small craft, cutters, despatch boats, admiralty barges, and so on, which were to evolve into the many different kinds of leisure and racing 'yachts' of today.

AEMELIA

THE NETHERLANDS: 1637

Built at Rotterdam in 1637, this was the flagship of Admiral Tromp when, with 100 assorted ships, he destroyed a 70-vessel Spanish fleet, bound for The Netherlands, in the Downs, off Kent, on 21 October 1639. The neutral English navy stood by, although the careful Tromp placed a detachment to watch them. The battle was a vital one for Dutch independence and made Holland dominant in Northern waters. It was some years before her position could be challenged, and with England engaged in Civil War, it was the chance for Holland to extend her power and wealth.

Aemilia **was lost or sunk before 1646, when a new 28-gun ship of the same name joined the Dutch fleet.**

Length: not known
Beam: not known
Depth: not known
Displacement: not known
Rigging: three masts; square-rigged
Armament: 56 guns
Complement: not known
Routes: not applicable

SOVEREIGN OF THE SEAS

ENGLAND: 1637

Length: 232ft (70.7m)
Beam: 46ft 6in (14.2m)
Depth: 23ft 6in (7.1m)
Displacement: 1141 t
Rigging: three masts; square-rigged fore and main, with topgallants; lateen-mizzen with topsail; spritsail and bowsprit topsail
Armament: 102 guns
Complement: 250 sailors, plus gunners and soldiers

It was at the direct command of King Charles I that *Sovereign of the Seas* was built. She was a great vessel, the masterwork of the shipwright Phineas Pett. Charles intended to display the naval might of England and the prestige of the English-Scottish king. On a larger scale than *Prince Royal*, she had three complete gun decks, and was the first man-of-war to carry 100 heavy guns. Setting a trend for subsequent English ships, she had a round stern, squared some 10ft (3m) above the waterline for the galleried cabins. In her original form, she appears to have been the first ship to both carry royals above the topgallants (though the royal yards were removed on rebuilding), and to have a topgallant set above the mizzen topsail. Despite the number of sails carried, she was sluggish and unable to keep up with the rest of the fleet. An important consideration was how to stop and hold a ship of this unprecedented size, and a description of the time stated that she carried 11 anchors. The cost of construction and

***Sovereign of the Seas* was the most lavishly decorated vessel ever to sail in the Royal Navy. The king's favourite artist, Van Dyck, is believed to have prepared the designs of her many carvings, statues and decorations.**

decoration came to over £65,500 – a staggering sum that required a special and deeply unpopular tax, 'ship-money'. Trinity House, the pilotage authority founded in 1514, protested that the ship would be too large for English waters. However, *Sovereign of the Seas* saw considerable action, much of it fairly close offshore. In 1649, under the Commonwealth, she was renamed *Sovereign* and, in 1651, her upperworks were reduced. This improved her handling, though her reputation was always that of a poor sailer. A complete rebuild was undertaken in 1660, when with the monarchy restored, she was renamed *Royal Sovereign*. A final rebuild was carried out in 1685. In the three Anglo-Dutch wars between 1652 and 1674, this great ship saw action at the Battles of Kentish Knock (1652), Orfordness (1666), Sole Bay (1672), Schoonveld (1673), and the Texel (1673). The Dutch called the gilded monster 'the golden devil'. She was also involved in actions against the French off Beachy Head (1690) and Barfleur (1692). Her long career finally came to an end in 1703, when a fire, started by a candle, resulted in her destruction as she lay at Chatham. Ahead of her time both in size and rig, *Sovereign of the Seas* was a true forerunner of the first-raters of the later 18th century.

The stern was constructed in round form, squared to provide maximum cabin space from about 10ft (3m) above the waterline. The built-out galleries are clearly visible, as are the gun-parts for 'stern chaser' cannon. This lofty stern construction was later reduced to lighten her weight.

SKUTA

SWEDEN: 1640

The name goes right back to the age of the Icelandic saga, but is chiefly identified with the clinker-built boats with homespun sails used for 200 years by the Åland islanders to carry firewood and lime on the 120-mile (195km) run to Stockholm. Small *skutor* were single-masted; the bigger ones had two. It was in the nature of their work to carry deck cargo, and it seems to have been usual for them to be steered from the cabin roof. In the 19th century, they went over to *galeas* rig.

Length: 60ft (18.3m)
Beam: 24ft (7.3m)
Depth: 3ft 4in (1m)
Displacement: c60t
Rigging: two masts; square-rigged with square topsail on mainmast
Complement: 2
Routes: Åland Islands-Stockholm
Cargo: firewood, lime, some passengers

From the later 18th century on, three-masted *skutor* were also built as shown in this illustration. The dimensions given above are for a two-masted craft.

THAMES SAILING BARGE

ENGLAND: 1640

Length: 65ft (19.8m)
Beam: 17ft (5.2m)
Depth: 6ft (1.8m)
Displacement: 50t
Rigging: single dismountable mast; with square sail
Complement: 2–4
Routes: Thames river and estuary
Cargo: trans-shipped goods, farm produce, general goods of all kinds

The Thames barge survived until well into the 20th century, although later forms were gaffrigged.

Navigation of the lower Thames was assisted by the tide. Ships lay below London Bridge and trans-shipped their cargoes into flat-bottomed barges. Similar barges brought goods down from the country, including baled straw and hay for the huge number of animals kept in the city. The 17th-century barge was little more than a lighter fitted with a single square sail, often set well forward; the cut-back stem was known as a 'swimhead'. The mast could be lowered in order for the barge to make the tricky passage under the old London Bridge, whose many arches created a form of weir when the tide was running.

CURRAGH

IRELAND: 1650

The Celtic nations were not great sailors, despite some celebrated early voyages. On the west coast of Celtic Ireland, boatbuilding techniques changed little from the 5th century to the 19th century. The basic boat, used for fishing and for the transport of goods and people, was the curragh. It consisted of a framework formed of thin, strong laths covered with stretched and sewn hides. By the 19th century the hides were replaced by tarred canvas.

Length: 30ft (9.1m)
Beam: 5ft (1.5m)
Depth: 2ft (0.6m)
Displacement: not known
Rigging: dismountable mast; with square sail
Complement: 4–8
Routes: west coast of Ireland
Cargo: animals, fish, hides

The larger curraghs had a light dismountable mast with a square sail. The film *Man of Aran*, from the 1930s, shows curraghs still in daily use.

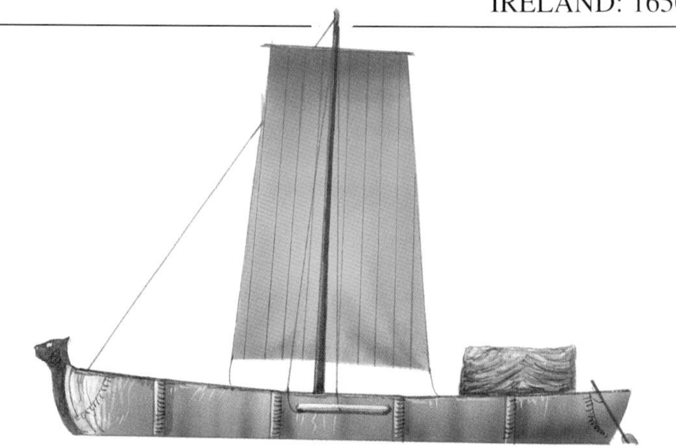

FLUYT

THE NETHERLANDS: 1650

The bulging sides and narrow deck of the fluyt minimised the taxable dimensions, for example, this made less toll payable passing through in the Sound between Denmark and Sweden.

Accountancy and economics have always had an effect on merchant shipping. Greater capacity, simpler operation, less crew, faster sailing times – all are sought today as they were two thousand years ago. The *fluyt* was a 17th-century accountant's dream-ship. The first vessel definitely of the type was built in 1595, at Hoorn in Holland. Long in relation to beam, with a vast hold beneath a single deck, and almost vertical stem and stern, the low prow reduced her exposure to the wind. The rounded stern (an innovation, since ships had had square sterns ever since the cog) helped to maintain the course. Intended to sail in peaceful waters, the fluyt was lightly built and unarmed, factors which reduced the cost of building and maintenance. The masts were often on the short side, and the sail area no more than adequate.

Length: 105ft (32m)
Beam: 28ft (8.5m)
Depth: 14ft (4.26m)
Displacement: 300t
Rigging: three masts; square-rigged on fore and main; lateen-mizzen
Complement: 20–30
Routes: North Sea and Baltic trading routes
Cargo: timber, ore, baled and barrelled goods

GALLEASS

VENICE, TURKEY: 1650

Over a period of 100 years the galleass altered very little. The North Sea countries had abandoned their experiments with its larger form, but persisted with smaller versions. In 1627, 10 smaller English vessels, known as 'lion's whelps', were launched; powered by both sail and oar, they do not appear to have been successful. Nonetheless, England retained a handful of galleasses into the 18th century, and the Venetians and Turks persisted with it, largely because, though ineffective against sailing ships which could mount more and heavier guns, it had some value in fighting galleys which had lighter armament. As the light winds and calms of the Mediterranean favoured galleys, they were still being built in substantial numbers into the 17th and 18th centuries. However, the Mediterranean galleass was rapidly becoming obsolescent; it is unlikely that any were built after 1700, though the bucintoro (1728), the Venetian ducal barge, had many resemblances.

Length: 160ft (48.7m)
Beam: 30ft (9.1m)
Depth: 12ft (3.6m)
Displacement:
Rigging: three masts; lateen-rigged
Armament: 20 guns, plus 20-30 light swivel cannon
Complement: 350 oarsmen, 40 gunners, 30 seamen, plus soldiers

Oars were never wholly abandoned; even large men-of-war in the 19th century carried long sweeps, to turn the vessel in a calm.

DUTCH PINNACE

THE NETHERLANDS: 1650

The example illustrated carries a light ship rig with no upper foresail and a flush deck with no after cabin. The light armament of six small guns was only sufficient for self defence.

The name 'pinnace' was applied to various types of ship, or boat, at the same time. During the late Elizabethan era, a pinnace was either a small ship, used for scouting and courier work during time of war, and trading in peace, or it could be a large boat, carried on the deck of a large ship and used as a ship's boat. As either type might carry oars, the confusion could be considerable.

Length: 75ft (22.8m)
Beam: 17ft (5m)
Depth: 8ft (2.4m)
Displacement: 70t
Rigging: not available
Armament: not available
Complement: not available

HERRING BUSS

THE NETHERLANDS: 1650

The herring *buss* was the typical larger Dutch fishing boat of North Sea waters. Its length to beam ratio of 4:1 was unusually great, giving it the strength in the water to hold a long driftnet. Both foremast and mainmast were usually lowered whilst fishing, with the square mizzen keeping a slow headway on the taut net cable. The buss reached its maximum size in the mid-16th century, and then smaller versions were built, perhaps because other types replaced it as a cargo carrier.

By the mid-18th century, the characteristic buss-rig had been largely superseded by a version of the hooker-rig.

Length: 65ft (19.8m)
Beam: 16ft (4.8m)
Depth: 8ft (2.4m)
Displacement: 100t
Rigging: three masts; each with single square sail
Complement: 6-8
Routes: North Sea fishing grounds
Cargo: herring

Schooner Yacht

THE NETHERLANDS: 1650

The Dutch word *jacht* originally implied a hunting vessel, and there is little doubt that it developed as a fishing craft. Early on, it also acquired an association with speed, and by the 17th century was used for pleasure (the *speeljacht*), as well as for commercial and naval purposes. This vessel, found from around 1650, had an early kind of schooner-rig, with two gaff-rigged masts but no foresails.

This rig does not appear to have led to any advance, and the larger single gaff-sail became the standard rig.

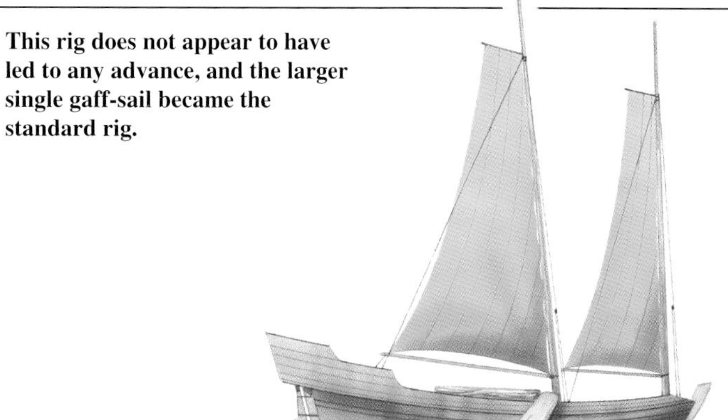

Length: 42ft (12.8m)
Beam: 15ft (4.5m)
Depth: 7ft (2.1m)
Displacement: not known
Rigging: two masts; gaff-rigged
Complement: 3–5

Dauphin Royal

FRANCE: 1658

Built in a French yard and named for the crown prince, *Dauphin Royal* followed traditional French construction principles. She was a *vaisseau*, a first-rate ship of the line, and represented the next generation of French warships after that of the *Saint Louis*. In relation to length, French ships of the line were wider than their English counterparts, carried fewer guns for their size, and had a shallower draught. This made for greater stability and, because their lower gunports were higher above the waterline, they could fire a full broadside in conditions which forced English ships to keep their lower gunports sealed. *Dauphin Royal* had two complete gun decks, and further guns on the upper deck; she also rigged studding sails on the mainmast, as Dutch ships of the line had also done from about 1625. She saw action after war was declared on England in 1666, being part of the French fleet outmanoeuvred off Beachy Head by a smaller Anglo-Dutch fleet, which succeeded in doubling the French line and pounding the French warships from both sides. A *vaisseau* required a very large crew: in action, for example, the large cannon needed seven men apiece, the culverins four, and the sakers three. In all, some 480 men serviced the guns, including the supply of powder and shot, and a further 110 men fired handguns, 120 manned the sails, and 50 men were in the boats and tops.

***Dauphin Royal* may have been one of the first vessels fitted with stay-sails, an innovation of around 1660.**

Length: 144ft (44m)
Beam: 40ft (12.2m)
Depth: not known
Displacement: 1060t
Rigging: three masts; square-rigged, with studding sails to mainmast; topgallant to lateen-mizzen; spritsail and bowsprit topsail
Armament: 104 guns
Complement: 760

Admiralty Yacht

THE NETHERLANDS: 1660

Length: 52ft (15.8m)
Beam: 14ft (4.2m)
Depth: 6ft (1.8m)
Displacement: 35t
Rigging: single mast, gaff-rigged with jib and staysail
Complement: 4–6 seamen

The Dutch term for small, swift boats is *jacht*. In the 1600s, great numbers of them were built for the wealthy. The *admiralty* kind was a larger version, intended as a state vessel which could be used to convey dignitaries, or for use as a fast despatch ship, or as a survey ship. Of shallow draught, it carried a leeboard to reduce the tendency to drift to leeward. Originally spritsail-rigged, by the 1630s these vessels were gaff-rigged, with staysails, and often a topsail.

Vessels of this type had luxurous quarters aft which were highly decorated inside and out with the usual lavish gilding of the period. A few light cannons were carried for saluting purposes. The type soon became popular in the UK where the first yacht club was opened in 1729 to cater for the newly introduced sport of yachting and yacht racing.

Two yachts, *Bezaan* and *Mary*, were presented by the Dutch East India Company to King Charles II of England in 1660.

BEURTMANN

THE NETHERLANDS: 1660

One of the many types of Dutch inshore vessel, *beurtmann* craft were designed to transport cargoes along sheltered waterways. They were built from the 17th century to the late-19th century; there was some development to the basic spritsail rig, with the stump-mast replaced by a taller mast with a topsail yard, and a jib-boom also fitted. Speed was not vital; ease of handling by a small crew was of importance.

Length: 42ft (12.8m)
Beam: 12ft (3.6m)
Depth: 5ft (1.5m)
Displacement: 60t
Rigging: single mast; gaff-rigged with jib
Complement: 3
Routes: inshore; inland waterways
Cargo: baled and barrelled goods

The hatch was built up above deck level to increase cargo capacity and to prevent water entering.

DOGGER

THE NETHERLANDS: 1660

North Sea fishing was dominated by the Dutch, who often spread their nets far from their own coastal waters. The name dogger was current between the 14th and 17th centuries, and the vessel itself was among a range of vessels used for fishing. In its early form, the dogger appears to have been two-masted, with a raised poop deck, and it was often used on naval duties. The Dogger Bank in the North Sea is a memorial to this unassuming but useful craft. The *dogger* appears never to have progressed from square sail to the hoy-rig with gaff, so typical of other small Dutch craft.

Length: 40ft (12.2m)
Beam: 14ft (4.2m)
Depth: 5ft (1.5m)
Displacement: 20t
Rigging: single mast; with square sail
Complement: 2-6
Routes: Dutch coastal waters
Cargo: fish

FRIGATE

THE NETHERLANDS: 1660

This vessel was built in 1660, a few years before the second Anglo-Dutch war. It shows certain typical Dutch features, including the clinker-laid external upperworks. Dutch ships in general were not decorated in the elaborate manner favoured by the English, French and Spanish. Like so many other older ship terms, 'frigate' was not used with great precision: its conventional, 17th-century sense was a full-rigged warship with a single complete gun deck. Both the Dutch and English were building ships of this type from the mid-17th century. Usually armed with about 36 guns, the frigate was inferior to the lowest-rated ship of the line. Its role was not in the line of battle, however, but as an escort vessel or, more often, as a swift independent operator, the 'eyes and ears' of the fleet. Significantly, the first English frigate, the *Constant Warwick* of 1649, was built originally as a privateer for capturing merchantmen.

Length: 118ft (35.9m)
Beam: 25ft (7.6m)
Depth: 14ft (4.26m)
Displacement: 270t
Rigging: three masts; square-rigged; lateen-mizzen with square topsail; spritsail and bowsprit topsail
Armament: 30 guns
Complement: 135

The main armament of the frigate type at this time was the demi-culverin, of 4.5in (114mm) calibre, firing a 9lb shot.

De Zeven Provincien

THE NETHERLANDS: 1665

Launched at Delft in anticipation of the second Anglo-Dutch War, this two-decker became the flagship of Admiral de Ruyter. In 1665, she was engaged in confrontations with the English off the Downs, during the second of which she was dismasted. On 14 June 1666, she led the Dutch fleet to the Medway, where they burned more than 20 ships, and captured the 90-gun *Royal Charles. De Zeven Provincien* fought at Sole Bay and the Texel (1673) and at La Hogue (1692). She was finally broken up in 1694.

Length: 146ft 9in (44.7m)
Beam: 38ft 9in (11.8m)
Depth: 14ft 5in (4.4m)
Displacement: not known
Rigging: three masts; square-rigged
Complement: 450
Armament: 80 guns
Country: Netherlands

On 27 May 1674, she made a peaceful visit to Dover, England, where she received a tremendous welcome as a doughty ex-enemy.

Le Soleil Royal

FRANCE: 1669

***Le Soleil Royale* was one of the largest warships of King Louis XIV. She reflected the inordinate wealth of the French monarch; she never fired her guns in anger.**

Length: 122ft 3in (37.3m)
Beam: 30ft 5in (9.3m)
Depth: not known
Displacement: c1000t
Rigging: three masts; square-rigged on fore and main with topgallants; lateen-mizzen with topsail; spritsail and bowsprit topsail
Armament: 104 guns
Complement: c150 seamen, 120 gunners, 150 soldiers

As flagship of the navy of the 'Sun King', Louis XIV, *Le Soleil Royal*, classified as a *vaisseau*, equivalent to a first-rate, was one of the largest and most powerful warships of her time. Painted in royal blue and sumptuously decorated in gold, she must have been a spectacular sight. Launched at Brest in 1669, she was refitted in 1689. In the following year, at Bevéziers, she was the flagship of Admiral Count Tourville when the French triumphed over the English. She was engaged in another encounter with the English, in 1692 off Pointe de Barfleur, in which Tourville successfully evaded a much larger fleet. But she was severely damaged in this action, and the admiral moved his flag to *Ambitieux*. Running into Cherbourg Roads, *Le Soleil Royal* grounded and was destroyed, with 11 other vessels, by English fireships in the Battle of La Hogue.

Berlin

BRANDENBURG: 1674

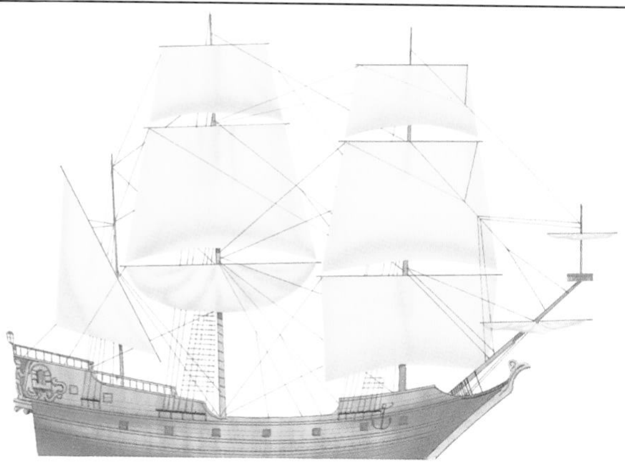

Most European frigates carried 30 guns, and later vessels carried even more. *Berlin*, with her 20 24pdr guns, was considered smaller than average.

In the 1670s, the north German state of Brandenburg was heavily involved in European war. New vessels were needed to protect shipping and the Baltic coastline. *Berlin* was Dutch-built and classed as a *leichte Fregatte* ('light frigate'). She served in the Baltic 1675–79, taking many prizes. In October 1687, she was sent on an expedition to the East Indies and was last heard of at Fida on 7 January 1688.

Length: 74ft 6in (22.7m)
Beam: 20ft 7in (6.3m)
Depth: unknown
Displacement: not known
Rigging: three masts; square-rigged on fore and main; lateen-mizzen with topsail; spritsail and bowsprit topsail
Armament: 24 guns
Complement: 72

CHEBECK

MOROCCO: 1679

Length: 103ft 9in (31)
Beam: 22ft (6.7m)
Depth: 8ft 2in (2.5m)
Displacement: 190t
Rigging: three masts; lateen-rigged
Armament: 12-15 guns
Complement: 24, plus fighting men

The *chebeck* (or *xebec*) originated in the western Mediterranean during the 17th century. The name stems from the Arabic *sabak*. This suggests that the Barbary pirates, who are closely associated with this vessel, may have developed it, borrowing both from the galley and the caravel traditions. The Spanish and French were quick to follow, if only to have a ship that could match the fine sailing qualities of the chebeck. Three-masted, and originally with full lateen-rig, it carried 18 oars to assure mobility during calms, and had a distinctive built-out stern platform, with outligger to stay the mizzen. Although of shallow draught, the chebeck was far from being tub-like, having fine underwater lines. It carried 12 to 15 guns, including four 12pdr guns mounted on the bow. The chebeck was designed to emerge from shallow harbours and appear at speed on a course to intercept a merchant vessel, which would be unable either to outrun or out-manoeuvre it.

From the mid-18th century, some French and Moroccan chebecks were fitted with square-rigging on the mainmast and a square topsail on the mizzen.

POLACCA

VENICE AND OTHER MEDITERRANEAN STATES: 1679

The name may refer to the 'pole-mast', a single-spar mast which appears to have been characteristic of this vessel.

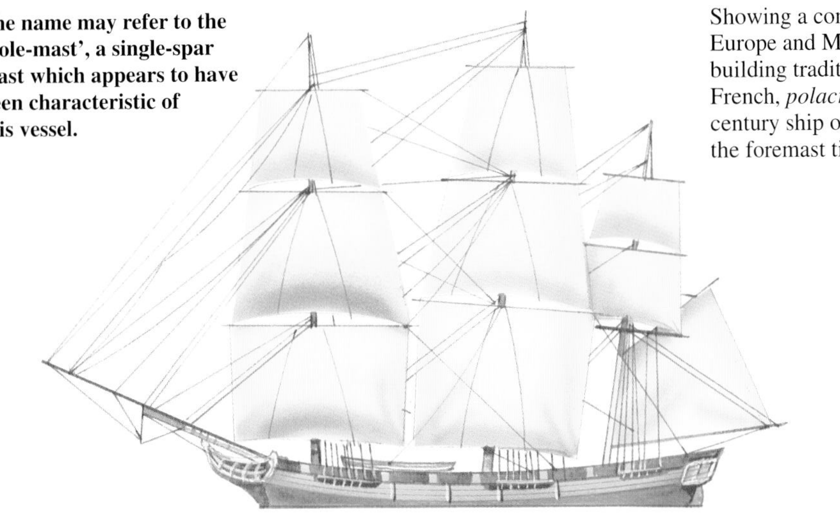

Showing a combination of northern Europe and Mediterranean ship-building traditions, the *polacca* (in French, *polacre*) was a 17th-century ship of three masts, with the foremast tilting forwards and rigged with a lateen sail. Mainmast and mizzen were square-rigged, though the mizzen had a lateen spar fitted. Such a vessel might also be referred to as a *barca* ('bark'), though this appellation had nothing to do with the later 'bark' or 'barque'-rig.

Length: c115ft (35m)
Beam: c20ft (6m)
Depth: c9ft (2.7m)
Displacement: c110t
Rigging: three masts; square topsail rig on main, lateen on foremast with jib; gaff-rigged mizzen with square topsail
Complement: 20–30
Routes: Mediterranean long-distance
Cargo: general

COLLIER BRIG

ENGLAND: 1680

Length: 80ft (24.4m)
Beam: 24ft (7.3m)
Depth: 12ft (3.65m)
Displacement: 180t
Rigging: two masts; foremast square-rigged with topsail and jib; mainsail fore-and-aft-rigged with square topsail
Complement: 8–10
Routes: English coast and short North Sea routes
Cargo: coal

This was probably the most numerous single type of merchant ship in the 17th and 18th centuries.

Collier brigs, and vessels like them, plied up and down the eastern coast of England and across the North Sea, carrying Newcastle coal. Many were brig-rigged on older cat-built hulls. The flat-bottomed ship could sit on a beach at low tide. Derricks were rigged between the masts and the coal, shovelled from the hold, was discharged by the bucket-load or chute into carts. Few seamen were required to man a collier brig, and it was notably short on comfort, even for the times.

JUNK

CHINA: 1680

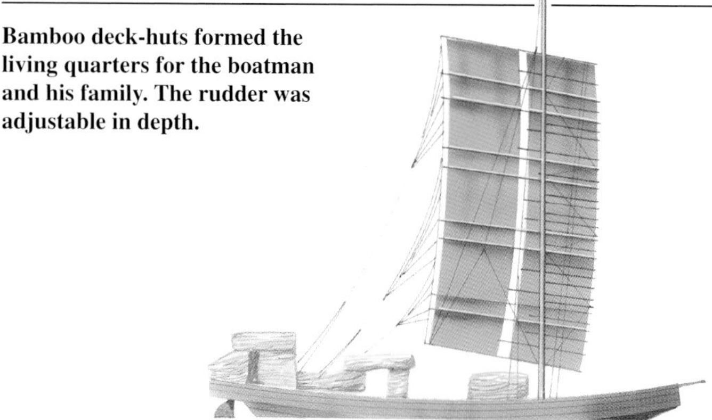

Bamboo deck-huts formed the living quarters for the boatman and his family. The rudder was adjustable in depth.

Built for work close inshore, or on the wide rivers of China, the shallow-draught junk shares some characteristics of the seagoing junk. These include a pontoon-type hull, divided into watertight compartments, with a flat bottom and squared-off bow and stern. A leeboard might be fitted. Such junks had up to three masts, rigged with the traditional square sail and crowsfeet rigging.

Length: 90ft (27.4m)
Beam: 24ft (7.3m)
Depth: 6ft (1.8m)
Displacement: 20t
Rigging: one to three masta; with lugsail-type rig
Complement: 2-6
Routes: rivers, and sheltered coasts
Cargo: rice, wood, hay, oil, farm produce

LA RÉALE

FRANCE: 1680

France had to maintain a naval presence on three coasts, with the Mediterranean fleet having a strong quotient of galleys. *La Réale* was the traditional name of the flagship of the galley fleet, and as such was the largest and most powerful vessel, as well as the most ornately-painted and decorated. She had 31 oars on each side, each manned by at least five men, requiring a very large crew, mostly slaves or prisoners-of-war. Her size and draught meant that there was considerable accommodation and storage beneath the rowing deck, which was set so low that the rowers were often in danger of being swamped. Nevertheless, the inevitable stench created by chained men and the impossibility of sleeping space meant that cruises were short. Heavy guns were mounted beneath the forecastle (a true fighting platform), including a 36pdr, mounted on the central gangway, or *course*.

Length: 200ft (61m)
Beam: 21ft (6.4m)
Depth: 10ft (3m)
Displacement: c 220t
Rigging: two masts; lateen-rigged
Armament: five guns, including one 36pdr, plus light swivel guns

***La Réale* had two boats which were both rowed by freemen: a *caique* which was used in raising anchor, and a smaller *canot*. They were normally towed but could be hoisted on board as necessary.**

BOMB KETCH

FRANCE: 1685

Warships had used mortars at sea from the 15th century. In 1682, France was the first nation to design a ship specifically for shore bombardment, the *galiote à bombes*. It carried large-calibre mortars, mounted on massive timbers bedded into the vessel's frame. The short barrels of the mortars, of some 10in–13in (254mm–330mm) calibre, fired explosive shells almost vertically up in the air, enabling them to fall behind the high walls of clifftop forts. Early examples of these 'bomb' vessels carried only a single mortar, but later ones carried two, plus from six to eight carronades. The ketch-rig, with mainmast and mizzen only, allowed a clear field of fire forwards – but some 18th-century British 'bombs' were ship-rigged. While most navies had bomb ketches, the number built was never large.

The crew found the bomb ketch to be a particularly cramped ship, due to its reinforced frame and heavy mortar mountings.

Length: 105ft (32m)
Beam: 26ft (7.9m)
Depth: 14ft (4.26m)
Displacement: 160t
Rigging: two masts; fore-and-aft-rigged with topsail and topgallant on mainmast, topsail on mizzen; staysail and jib
Armament: single (two in later craft) mortar, 10in-13in (254mm-330mm; six cannon
Complement: 36

CAT

ENGLAND: 1700

The North Country cat was essentially an enlarged version of the Dutch *fluyt*, many of which had been seized as English prizes in the wars between 1652 and 1674. Sturdy, blunt-bowed, a bulk carrier (chiefly for the coal trade), the cat had a flush deck and flat bottom. It was three-masted and could carry a considerable amount of sail. With the cat design, shipbuilders in the north-east of England seized the initiative from East Anglia, previously England's main shipbuilding region.

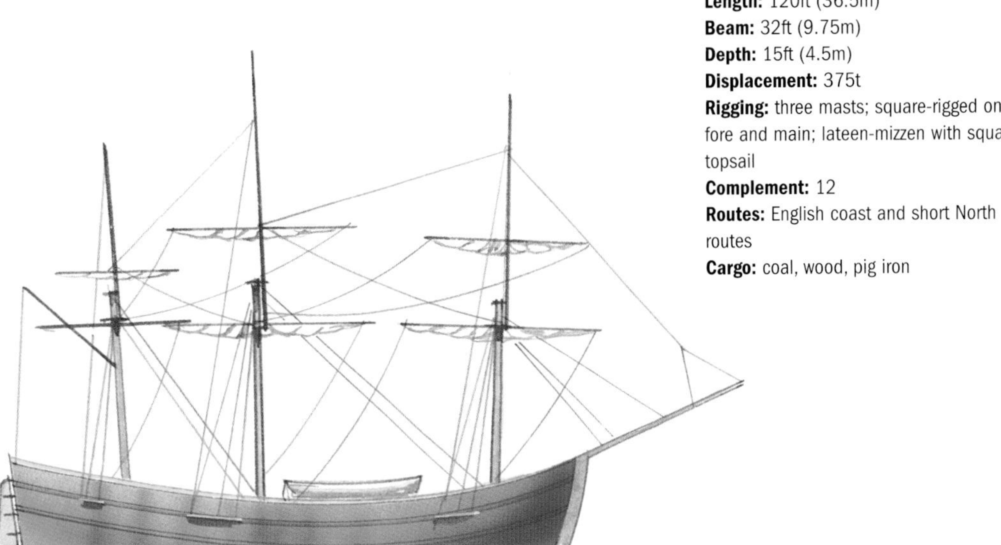

'Cat-built' referred to the blunt, unornamented stern and bow and boxy section of these hulls – many of which, re-rigged, survived over 100 years.

Length: 120ft (36.5m)
Beam: 32ft (9.75m)
Depth: 15ft (4.5m)
Displacement: 375t
Rigging: three masts; square-rigged on fore and main; lateen-mizzen with square topsail
Complement: 12
Routes: English coast and short North Sea routes
Cargo: coal, wood, pig iron

GALEAS

THE NETHERLANDS: 1700

Length: 65ft (19.8m)
Beam: 18ft (5.5m)
Depth: 9ft (2.7m)
Displacement: 85t
Rigging: two masts; fore-and-aft-rigged, with square topsail on main; staysail, jib and flying jib
Complement: 4-8
Routes: north European coast
Cargo: baled and barrelled goods

The Baltic *galeas* was a two-masted merchant vessel used in the North Sea and Baltic trades. A completely different type to the Mediterranean *galleass*, its original form was probably square-rigged, but by the early 1700s, it was rigged fore-and-aft, with only a square topsail and sometimes a topgallant remaining – a precursor of the ketch. With square stern and greater sheer than the *galiot*, the galeas was more suited to the open sea.

By 1700, the jib-boom had been greatly extended, to almost half the length of the vessel and accommodating a flying jib.

GALIOT

THE NETHERLANDS: 1700

Length: 65ft (19.8m)
Beam: 18ft (5.5m)
Depth: 9ft (2.7m)
Displacement: 85t
Rigging: two masts; fore-and-aft-rigged, with topsail and possible topgallant on main; staysail, jib and flying jib
Complement: 4-8
Routes: north European coasts
Cargo: baled and barrelled goods

The lengthy jib-boom, usually formed of two spars fished together, could be hinged up when not in use.

Similar in size to the *galeas*, and more typically Dutch with its rounded stem and stern, the *galiot* was in use far into the 19th century. With a tall mast for its shallow draught, it usually carried a leeboard as a supplementary keel. The rig was basically fore-and-aft, but a square topsail, and sometimes also a topgallant, were fitted to the mainmast.

PINK

ENGLAND: 1700

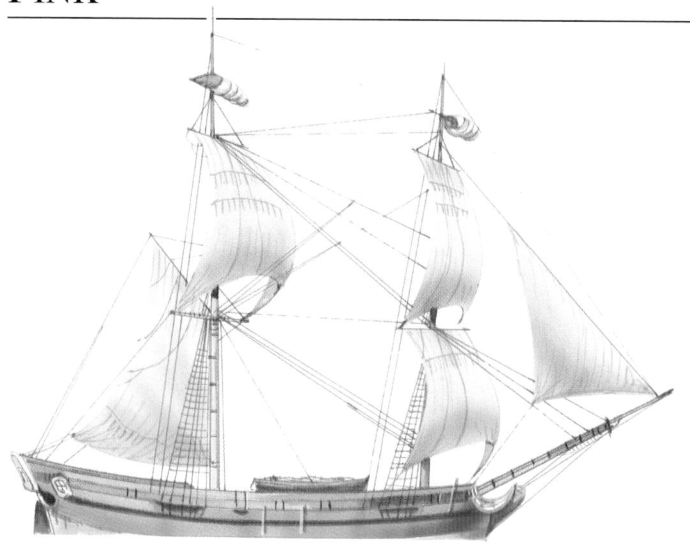

Use of the term 'pink' goes back at least to the 1470s, when it denoted a small, flat-bottomed, fishing-craft with a narrow stern. As with so many other terms, it could also mean something unrelated; for example, by the 18th century, pink referred to a square-rigged bulk-carrier with a distinctive high, rounded stern, an evolved form of the Dutch *fluyt*. As the term was a hull description, it applied to various rigs; in England, especially, pink was used to describe two-masted ships. The example shown here has the high-placed loading ports aft so that timber could more easily be loaded and stowed for transit.

English pinks were fast. Admiral George Anson used two, *Anna* and *Industry*, as store-ships during his world circumnavigation of 1740–44.

Length: 120ft (36.5m)
Beam: 33ft (10m)
Depth: 13ft (3.7m)
Displacement: 380t
Rigging: two masts; square-rigged
Complement: 104
Routes: North Atlantic and other long-distance
Cargo: timber, ores, stores

BILANDER

THE NETHERLANDS: 1710

Length: 80ft (24.38m)
Beam: 22ft (6.7m)
Depth: 10ft 3in (3.1m)
Displacement: 160t
Rigging: two masts; settee mainsail with square topsail; square sails on foremast; spritsail
Complement: 12-16
Routes: North Sea and English Channel
Cargo: baled and barrelled goods in bulk

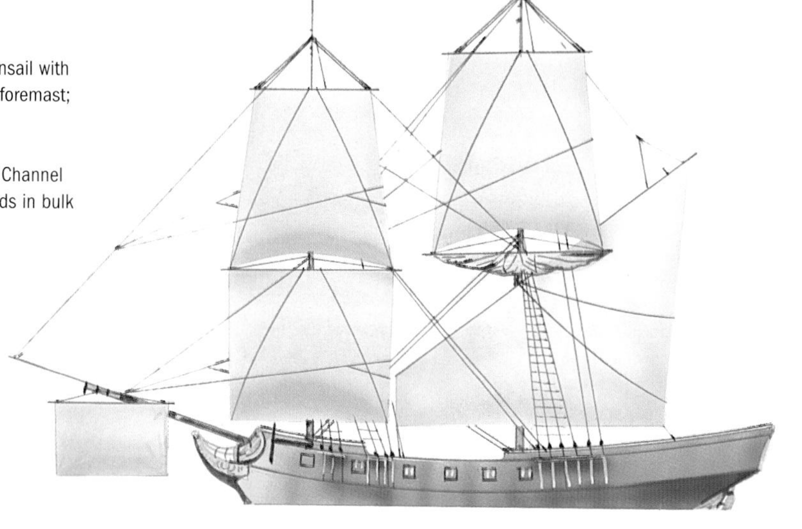

The name *bilander* probably means 'sailing by land', as opposed to ocean-going. Its origins are Dutch, though bilanders, large vessels intended for short-sea trading, were also built in England and other countries, with both square and rounded sterns. The most distinctive feature is the lateen-style settee (four-sided lateen) mainsail, which has a somehow experimental look; it is as though someone were trying to make a rig that would work in changeable wind conditions.

The bilander-rig seems to have become obsolescent soon after 1750, while brigs and snows continued to evolve.

CUTTER

GB: 1710

In 1791 an experimental cutter, *Cynthia*, with sliding or drop keels, designed by Captain John Schanks, RN, was successfully tested.

The name for the classic light British naval ship of the 18th century, 'cutter' was first used to describe its clinker-built hull – and later the rig, which was impressively large for a single-masted ship. The hull was quite broad and deep, and could mount 14 light cannon. Used in the Royal Navy as an inshore patrol and despatch boat, the cutter was also the prime vessel of the Revenue service, and used in the constant battle against smuggling.

There were vertical timbers on the outside of the bulwars which were used to support the swivel guns. The jib boom was four fifths of the length of the vessel and this large area of sail coupled with the long bowsprit which could hold large sails enabled speed to be maintained in a light breeze.

Length: 68ft (20.5m)
Beam: 20ft (6m)
Depth: 9ft (2.7m)
Displacement: 100t
Rigging: single mast; with square sail, fore-and-aft mainsail, topsail, staysail, jib
Armament: up to 14 light cannon
Complement: 20-30

FERRET

GB: 1711

Launched at Woolwich Dockyard, London, in 1711, Ferret was a two-masted sloop and may have been rigged as a ketch, as a brigantine or as a snow. In addition she was pierced to carry nine oars or sweeps on each side.

A numerous type, with many variants, the sloops were lightly armed and could fulfil a variety of functions as patrol ships and cruising vessels. Their light armament and construction made them eminently suitable for police-type duties.

Ferret may have begun life as a single-masted craft, but by 1716 she had the two-mast rig.

Displacement: 114t
Length: 65ft 7in (20m)
Beam: 20ft 10in (6.3m)
Depth: 9ft (2.7m)
Rigging: two masts; probably ketch rig
Armament: 10 3pdr guns
Complement: 50

HAGBOAT

SWEDEN: 1720

Length: c115ft (35m)
Beam: c25ft (7.6m)
Depth: c14ft (4.2m)
Displacement: c250t
Rigging: three masts; square-rigged
Complement: 30 (merchant ship)
Routes: European sea routes
Cargo: general

'Hagboat' or occasionally 'hag' is a descriptive term applied to a ship with a certain type of hull. In the *Architectura Navalis Mercatoria*, by the 18th-century Swedish shipwright and naval architect F. H. Chapman, the hagboat is one of five types. With a beaked prow and a single gun deck, its hull closely resembles that of a frigate. The stern planking was continued round to a beam just below the taffrail.

The hagboat's lines resemble that of a warship more than a merchant vessel, although it may have been readily convertible from the latter to the former.

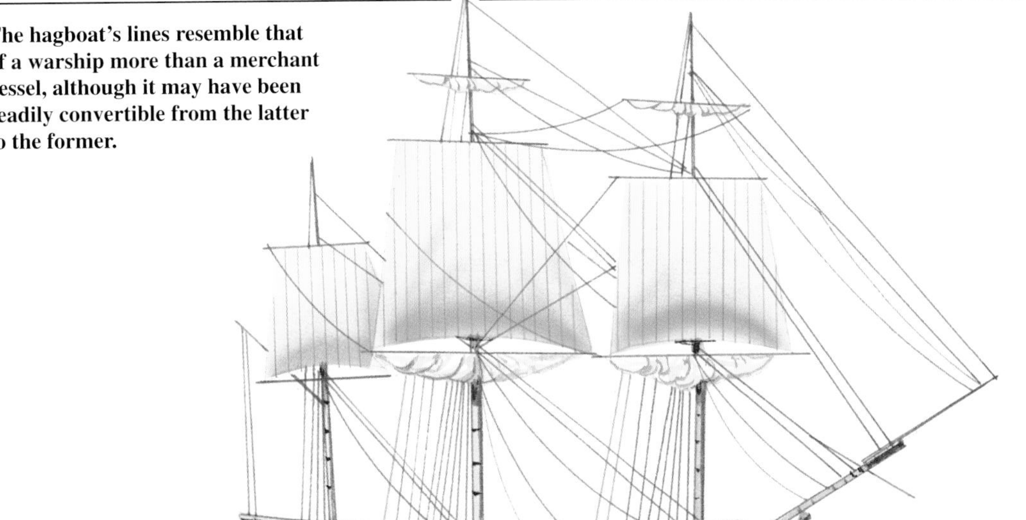

BUCINTORO

VENICE: 1728

The state barge of the Doge of Venice was used every year on Ascension Day in the re-enactment of Venice's symbolic marriage with the sea. A ring, blessed by the Patriarch of Venice, would be dropped into the waters of the Adriatic by the Doge, with the words: 'We wed you, Adriatic, as the sign of our true and perpetual dominion.' The ceremony probably goes back to the 12th century.
A succession of state barges bore the name *bucintoro*, which means 'man-ox', probably referring to the first craft's figurehead. The last of the series was launched at the Venice Arsenal in 1728 and was used until 1797; the French captured Venice, and the city's long career as 'bride of the sea' came to an end. At the orders of Napoleon, the ornamentation was stripped and destroyed; the hull was eventually used as a floating battery by the Austro-Hungarian navy and was finally broken up in 1824.

Length: 114ft (34.7m)
Beam: 23ft 9in (7.2m)
Depth: 7ft 6in (2.3m)
Rigging: one flagpole mast
Complement: 168 oarsmen

The archaic design preserved many features of its predecessors, but the basic form was that of a galleass.

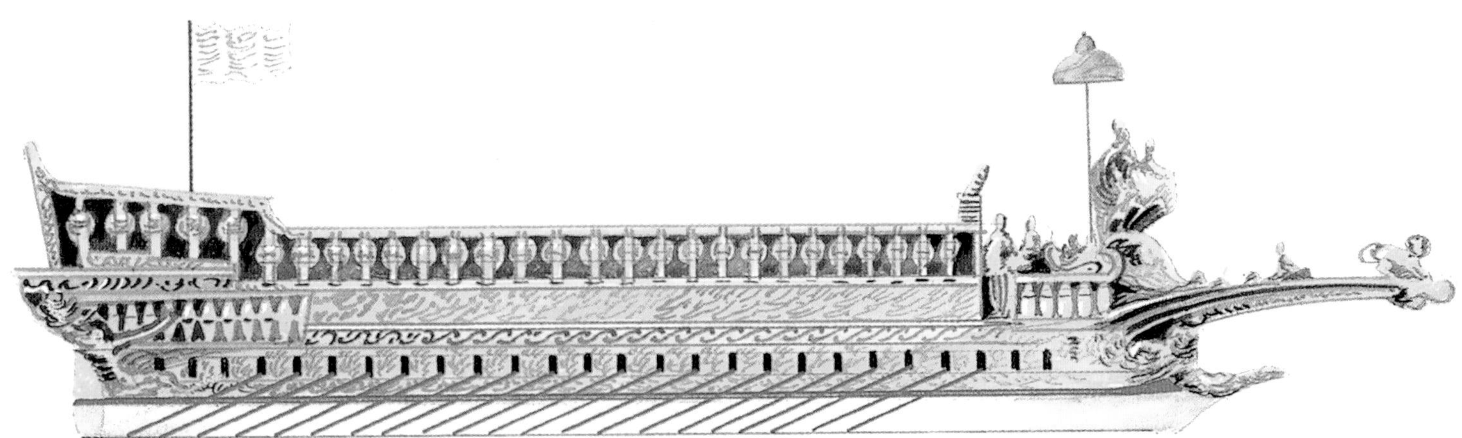

CHAPTER THREE

The End of Sail 1730–1859

By the beginning of the 18th century, only one vital improvement remained to be made to the sailing ship – the steering wheel, which was introduced in the very early years. Replacing the unwieldy and often dangerous whipstaff, it brought a dramatic improvement to the handling of large ships – and ships were getting larger year by year. The rest of the century saw the achievement of earlier periods brought to the highest standard of technique and performance for ships whose structure was still based almost entirely on wood and hemp. New and additional sails and bigger sail plans were devised.

But by the end of the century, the first experiments with steam-powered vessels were being made. Laughed off by the conservative-minded, not least those in high naval office, the smoky, clanking ships were taken up first by the merchant marine, concerned to make voyages last as little time as possible and to minimise crew numbers. The new steam propulsion, and the new materials provided by the industrial revolution, especially iron plate in mass quantities, wrought more change in the 50 years between 1800 and 1850 than all the developments of the previous 500 years. A flood of new inventions was prompted, as engineers explored the possibilities of the new machinery. Yet in the 1850s, a full-rigged ship with the wind behind her could still overtake the average packet steamer. At this time, harbours around the world might contain vessels ranging from the newest iron steamship to boats whose design went back into prehistory.

Left: A full wood colour engraving by jacques La Grande (1936) depicting *Sovereing of the Seas,* a Californian clipper ship of around 1852

CENTURION (SOMETIME EAGLE)

GB: 1733

This British fourth rate, built at Portsmouth Dockyard, was Commodore George Anson's flagship in a squadron of six warships and two supply pinks sent out in September 1740 to intercept the Spanish 'Manila Galleon' carrying gold from Mexico to the Philippines. With an insufficient and elderly crew, the squadron suffered extreme hardship at the tip of South America. Of the 961 men who embarked, 626 had died by the time the surviving ships entered the Pacific. Through 1741–42, they sailed on the west coast of South America, taking prizes and making shore raids. In August 1742, Anson was ashore with half his crew at Tinian when a typhoon blew *Centurion* out to sea; it was three weeks before she returned. Anson sailed to China and refitted the ship at Macao, then sailed for the Philippines in the hope of finding the treasure ship. On 20 June 1743, he caught it off Cape Espirito Santo. The 36-gun galleon *Nuestra Señora de la Covadonga* was carrying a treasure of coin and pure silver valued at more than half a million pounds in contemporary money. Even Drake had not brought back booty of such value. The only survivor of the squadron, *Centurion* saw further action in the Battle of Finisterre in May 1747 and was the 24-year-old Commodore Keppel's flagship in the Mediterranean in 1749. She then served in the Western Atlantic, at the capture of Louisburg in 1758, in Canada in 1759 and at the capture of Havana in 1762. She was broken up in 1769.

Length: 144ft (43.9m)
Beam: 40ft (12.2m)
Depth: 16ft 5in (5m)
Displacement: 1068t
Rigging: three masts; square rig
Armament: 50 guns
Complement: 400

In 1744–45, *Centurion* was briefly renamed *Eagle* before reacquiring her original name.

BOSTON

BRITISH AMERICAN COLONIES: 1748

Considering the lack of a naval building tradition in the North American colonies, the construction of *Boston* was a remarkable achievement. Many lessons were quickly learned.

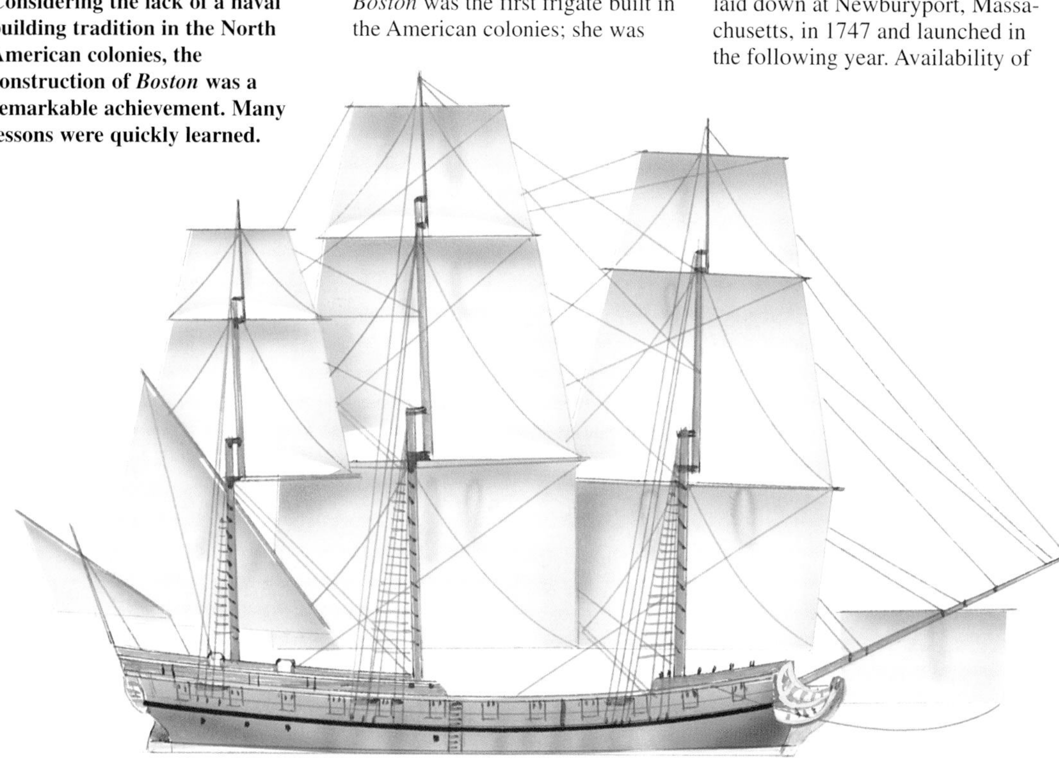

Boston was the first frigate built in the American colonies; she was laid down at Newburyport, Massachusetts, in 1747 and launched in the following year. Availability of cheap wood supplies led to rapid growth in the shipbuilding industry along the American coast, although prior to 1776 the products were chiefly merchant vessels. Although classified as a frigate, *Boston* was on the small side and probably lacked the speed of later American-built frigates, which were built with wider yards and carried a greater spread of sail; she was built for coastal patrol and convoy escort duties. *Boston*'s career was brief. In 1752, she was broken up, probably because she had been constructed of unseasoned wood, which led to extensive problems with leaks and rot. This 'built-in obsolescence' was not infrequent with ships constructed in America during the 18th century.

Length: 114ft 3in (34.8m)
Beam: 31ft 6in (9.6m)
Depth: 10ft 3in (3.1m)
Displacement: 514t
Rigging: three masts; square rig
Armament: 24 guns
Complement: c200

ROYAL GEORGE (EX-ROYAL ANNE) GB: 1756

Length: 178ft (54.3m)
Beam: 51ft 10in (15.8m)
Depth: 21ft 6in (6.6m)
Displacement: 2047t
Rigging: three masts; square rig
Armament: 28 42pdr, 28 24pdr, 28 12pdr, 16 6pdr guns
Complement: 850

One of the six first rates built for the Royal Navy between 1750 and 1790, *Royal George* was laid down as *Royal Anne* in 1746. Commissioned in 1756, at the start of the Seven Years' War, she spent virtually the whole period in the blockade of Brest. On 20 November 1759, she was Admiral Hawke's flagship when the British squadron, blown off station, returned from shelter in Torbay to encounter 21 French ships of the line under Vice-Admiral the Comte de Conflans. The French attempted to return to Brest, but Hawke followed them into Quiberon Bay and forced a battle. *Royal George* attacked the French flagship *Soleil Royal* and sank *Superbe* with one devastating broadside. Laid up after the war and recommissioned in 1778, she was in active service until 29 August 1782. On that day, whilst heeled slightly for repairs in Spithead, she rolled over and sank, drowning some 800 people.

Thirty guns were salvaged from the *Royal George*, but the wreck was blown up during the 1840s as a hazard to shipping.

HEMMEMA SWEDEN: 1760

Length: c90ft (27.4m)
Beam: c26ft (7.9m)
Depth: c7ft (2.1m)
Displacement: not known
Rigging: three masts; lateen rig
Armament: 24 36pdr, two 12pdr guns
Complement: c80

When the Swedish fleet defeated the Russians at Svensksund in 1790, the *hemmemas* were towed into position and used as floating batteries.

This was one of the earlier of the Swedish ship types specifically designed by F H af Chapman for use in the many shallow channels of the Finnish archipelago. Much reliance was placed on oars – 26 of them in this case – and the lateen-rigged vessel looks as if it would have been more at home in the Mediterranean than the Gulf of Finland. Its main disadvantage was its inability to fire a broadside while under oars, and the later gunsloops effectively replaced it.

ENDEAVOUR (EX-EARL OF PEMBROKE, LATER LA LIBERTÉ) GB: 1764

This is the first 'discovery ship' of which detailed descriptions are available. Launched at Whitby in 1764 as the cat-built collier barque *Earl of Pembroke*, she was purchased by the British Admiralty and fitted out for a scientific journey to the South Seas to observe the transit of Venus from Tahiti and ascertain whether a southern continent really existed. In command was Lieutenant James Cook. The expedition left Plymouth on 25 August 1768 and was to fill in substantial gaps in the world map, determining New Zealand to be two islands and exploring the eastern coast of Australia. She returned to England on 12 July 1771. *Endeavour* underwent a much-needed refit and was then used for three voyages to the Falkland Islands. In March 1775, sold by the Admiralty, she resumed her first occupation as a collier. From 1790, under French ownership and the name *La Liberté*, she was used as a whaler until she grounded off Newport, Rhode Island, in 1793 and was subsequently broken up.

A replica of *Endeavour* – built at Fremantle, Australia, in 1994 – was sailed to the United Kingdom.

Length: 97ft 8in (29.7m)
Beam: 29ft 4in (8.9m)
Depth: 11ft 3in (3.4m)
Displacement: 366t burthen
Rigging: three masts; square rig
Armament: six swivel guns
Complement: 85
Routes: South Seas

TRUELOVE

GB: 1764

Built at Philadelphia, the *Truelove* was captured by the British in the American War of Independence and sold to a British shipowner who used her as a transport with 12 guns. In 1784, the hull was strengthened and the vessel was used for many years as a whaler with brief periods as a transport. In 1849, *Truelove* was used to convey relief supplies to the Franklin expedition. She was very nearly lost on several occasions when trapped in pack ice which threatened to crush her. *Truelove* was broken up about 1888.

Length: 100ft (30.5m)
Beam: 30ft (9.1m)
Depth: 16ft (4.9m)
Displacement: 400t
Rigging: three masts; square rig
Complement: not known
Cargo: general cargo, whale oil

Truelove served several owners almost continuously for 144 years, her stout hull surviving many mishaps.

VILLE DE PARIS

FRANCE: 1764

Now 'owners' of the name, the British built a new _Ville de Paris_ in 1795, a two-decker of 80 guns, closely modelled on the new French two-deckers.

One of the first products of a massive building programme which saw the French fleet virtually doubled between 1763 and 1771, this three-decker, originally intended as *L'Impétueux* of 90 guns, was launched at Rochefort in 1764. She joined in the inconclusive battle off Ushant in July 1778, and in 1781 was the flagship of Admiral de Grasse escorting a military convoy to Martinique; further service in the Caribbean followed. In August-September 1781, *Ville de Paris* was off Chesapeake Bay in support of the United States. In April 1782, she collided with the 74-gun *Zélé*, dismasting her, an unfortunate prelude to the Battle of the Saints, against the British under Admirals Rodney and Hood, which took place on 12 April. *Ville de Paris* was in battle for the entire day, until at 6.30pm, having exhausted all her ammunition, she was obliged to surrender. Taken as a prize, she sank in a storm on the way to England in late September 1782, with only one survivor.

Length: 185ft 7in (56.5m)
Beam: 53ft 8in (16.33m)
Depth: 22ft 2in (6.7m)
Displacement: 2347t
Rigging: three masts; square rig
Armament: 100 guns
Complement: 850
Routes: not applicable

BONHOMME RICHARD (EX-DUC DE DURAS)

USA: 1765

Length: 145ft (47m)
Beam: 36ft 10in (11.9m)
Depth: 17ft 5in (5.7m)
Displacement: 700t
Rigging: three masts; square rig
Armament: six 18pdr, 28 12pdr, six 8pdr guns
Complement: 322

Although destroyed in the action, the *Bonhomme Richard* was the victor in one of the most celebrated ship-to-ship combats of history – with the frigate HMS *Serapis*, off Flamborough Head, northeast England, on the night of 23 September 1779. Under the command of the Scots-American John Paul Jones, she was cruising as flagship of a seven-vessel American squadron, looking for trouble off the British coasts. The two ships engaged at close quarters, and broadsides wreaked havoc on board each of them. Reduced to two guns, Jones made the famous reply to the British captain's request for his surrender: 'No, I'll sink, but I'm damned if I'll strike.' In fact it was the British vessel which surrendered. Jones moved his flag on to her, and *Bonhomme Richard*, holed and shattered, sank in deep water the following day. Her career had begun 14 years before, as the French East Indiaman *Duc de Duras*. After two voyages to China, she was taken over by the French government and used as a troopship, then sold to private owners. Repurchased by the government, she was presented to John Paul Jones in 1778 as a token of French support for American independence. Refitted and armed, although with comparatively light guns (her main armament was 28 12pdrs), her new name was the French form of 'Poor Richard', as in *Poor Richard's Almanac*.

Another of Jones's exploits was to threaten Edinburgh's port of Leith, causing some panic in the capital of his native country.

VICTORY

GB: 1765

A major restoration-conservation programme was commenced in 1921, at which time *Victory* was in a highly decrepit state. On 12 January 1922, she was carefully manoeuvred into Dry Dock No 2, at the Royal Naval Dockyard, Portsmouth.

Laid down in 1759 at Chatham Dockyard and launched in 1765, *Victory*, a first rate of 100 guns, was not put into commission until 1778, when France allied herself with the American colonists. For three years she was flagship of the Channel Fleet under Admiral Keppel, taking part in the indecisive fight off Ushant on 23 July 1779. In December 1781, she captured a French convoy in the same area. Under Admiral Lord Howe she was flagship when the British raised the siege of Gibraltar in 1782. With the end of the American War of Independence she was laid up until 1792, when to the relief of many officers ashore on half pay, the Royal Navy was readied for war again. *Victory* went to the Mediterranean as flagship, first to Admiral Hood, then in 1793 to the formidable Sir John Jervis, who drilled the fleet into order and won a crushing victory over the Spanish off Cape St Vincent on 14 February 1797, with *Victory* disabling the Spanish vice-flagship, *Principe de Asturias*. She returned to England in 1798 and was converted to a hospital ship, based at Chatham. Between 1800 and 1803, she was rebuilt, losing her old open stern galleries, and on 18 May 1803, ready to return to the Mediterranean under Captain Hardy, she hoisted the flag of Admiral Lord Nelson. Between 30 July 1803 and the Battle of Trafalgar, Nelson spent only 25 days off the ship. The task was to contain the French fleet at Toulon, but in January 1805 Admiral Villeneuve was able to slip past the British, return and leave port again on 30 March. Nelson's ships pursued him across the Atlantic and back again, but Villeneuve made Cadiz and remained there with the Spanish fleet, blockaded by the British. On 19 October, the combined fleet began to emerge from the anchorage, and on the morning of 21 October, off Cape Trafalgar, battle commenced. Nelson divided his fleet in two, with himself in *Victory* leading the weather squadron, and Vice-Admiral Collingwood in *Royal Sovereign* leading the lee squadron. Nelson's bold tactics exposed the *Victory* to hostile fire for 45 minutes before she broke through the French line, firing a devastating broadside into the stern of *Bucentaure*, Villeneuve's flagship. Coming alongside *Redoutable*, Nelson, in full-dress uniform on *Victory*'s quarterdeck, was shot by a musketeer from the mizzen fighting top and was carried below. By 2.30pm, *Victory* was out of the battle; two hours later, knowing he had won a conclusive victory, Nelson died. The battered *Victory* was towed to Gibraltar, then made her own way to England with Nelson's body, reaching Spithead on 5 December and Sheerness on the 22nd. She was refitted and saw further service in the Baltic as Admiral Saumarez' flagship, remaining there until 1812 apart from one convoy escort duty to Spain. In 1812, she was paid off but retained at the Royal Naval Dockyard at Portsmouth, where she remains in dry dock, as flagship of the Commander-in-Chief.

Length: 186ft (56.7m)
Beam: 51ft 10in (15.8m)
Depth: 21ft 6in (6.5m)
Displacement: 2162t burthen
Rigging: three masts; square rig
Armament: 100 guns
Complement: 850

***Victory* was the masterpiece of the leading English designer of 18th-century warships, Sir Thomas Slade, Surveyor of the Navy.**

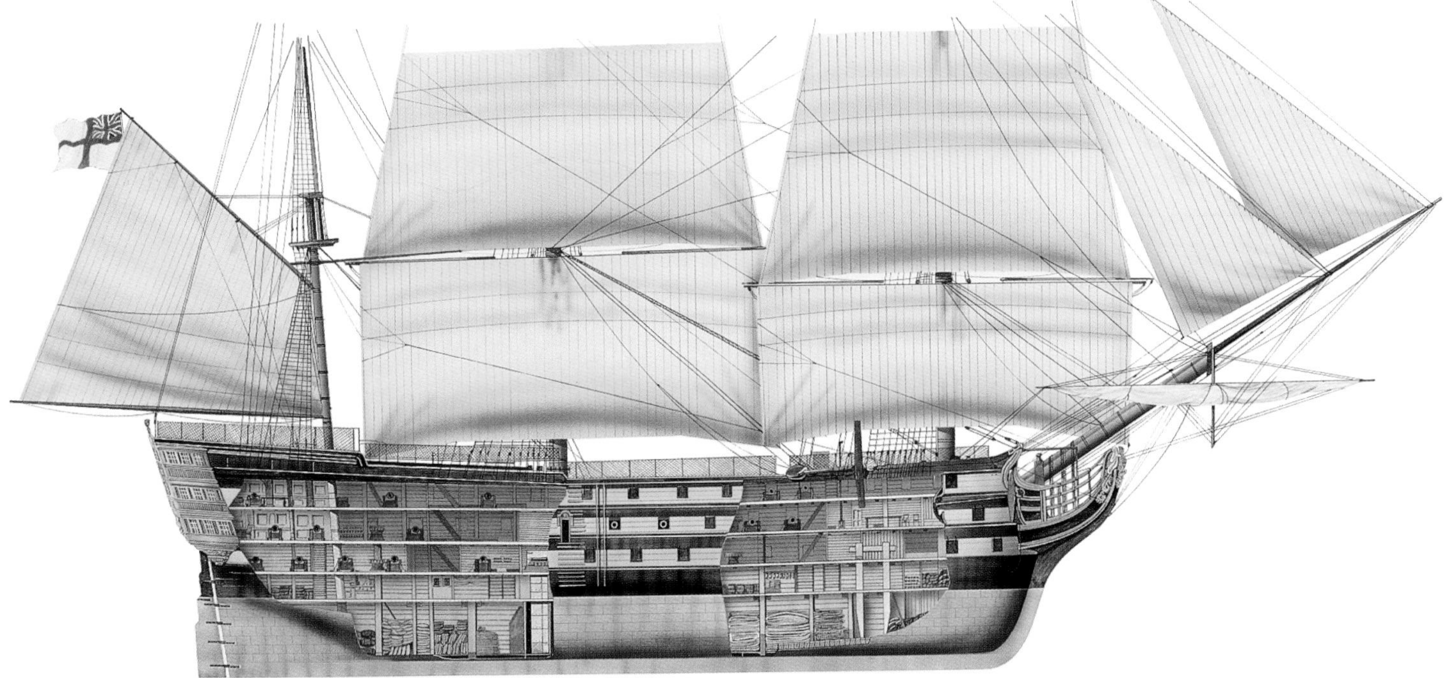

SANTISSIMA TRINIDAD

SPAIN: 1769

Built at Havana, *Santissima Trinidad* was the largest warship of the 18th century. She took part in the Battle of Cape St Vincent, when a daring manoeuvre by Nelson, then a commodore on HMS *Captain*, effectively detached her and two other first rates from the battle. Captain Saumarez in HMS *Orion* actually compelled her to strike her colours, but Admiral Jervis signalled to his fleet to wear and come to the wind, and *Santissima Trinidad* was able to break away. Her next fleet action was at Trafalgar on 21 October 1805, where she flew the flag of Rear-Admiral Cisneros; she was formed in the French-Spanish line just ahead of the flagship *Bucentaure* and was in the thick of the battle when the British ships broke through the line.

Length: 200ft (60.1m)
Beam: 62ft 9in (19.2m)
Depth: not known
Displacement: 4572t
Rigging: three masts; square rig
Armament: 130 guns
Complement: 950

Towards the close of the Battle of Trafalgar, *Santissima Trinidad*, dismasted and out of control, was boarded by HMS *Africa*, at 64 guns the smallest ship in Nelson's fleet. The boarders were informed that the ship was still in action and were politely sent back. She struck only after the battle was over, to HMS *Prince*.

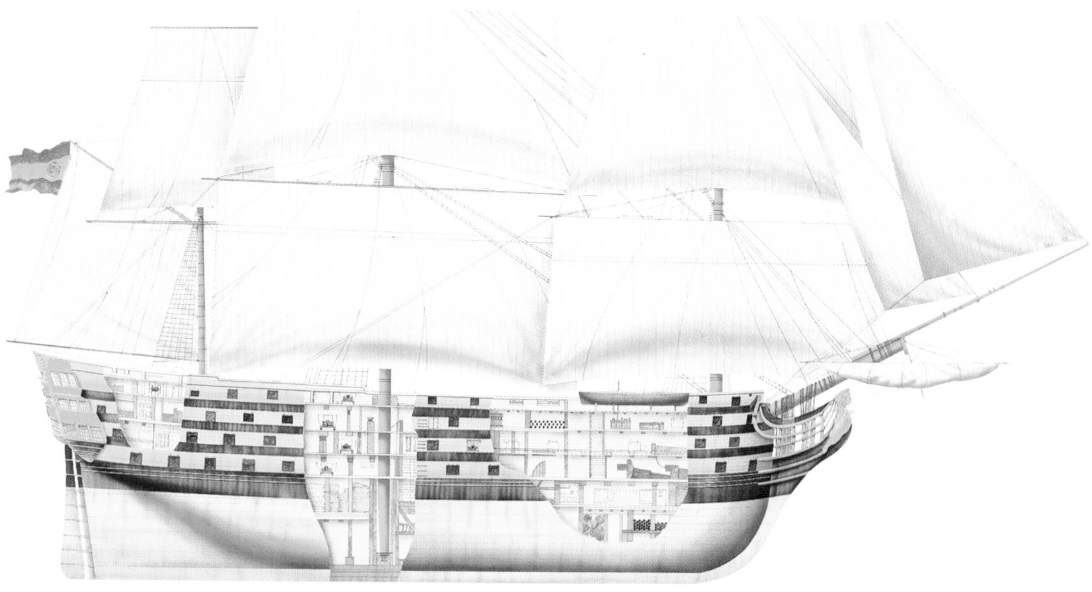

COLONIAL SCHOONER

BRITISH NORTH AMERICAN COLONIES: 1770

The modern schooner developed in the eastern states of America and quickly took varying forms. The classic schooner is, however, a two-masted ship with the aftermast as tall as, or taller than, the foremast; the vessel's rig is principally fore and aft. The name 'schooner' may originally have described the hull but later defined the rig. Such ships were used for several purposes, including fishing on the outer banks. Although Dutch vessels had a schooner rig in the 17th century, the first schooner as such is generally credited to Gloucester, Massachusetts, in 1713.

Length: 60ft (18.3m)
Beam: 17ft 6in (5.3m)
Depth: 7ft (2.1m)
Displacement: 80t
Rigging: two masts; fore-and-aft rig with gaff and boom; foresail to bowsprit
Complement: 6
Cargo: fish
Routes: New England coastal waters

HOOKER

FRANCE: 1770

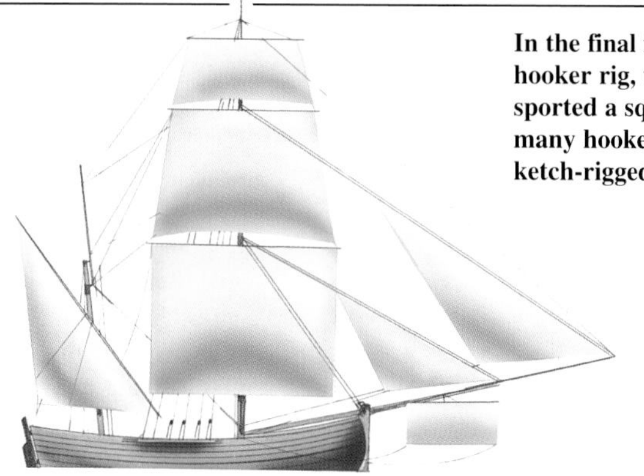

In the final form of hooker rig, the mizzen sported a square topsail; many hookers ended up ketch-rigged.

One of the most common of coastal vessels, the hooker was built in many countries, although it probably originated as a Dutch fishing craft in the late 15th century. By the later 18th century, it had a lofty mainmast (commonly a pole mast) with topgallant, staysail, jib and flying jib; these three attached to a very long boom fixed to the mainmast. It also had a driving spritsail. Hookers varied in size from around 50t to well over 200t.

Length: 87ft (26.5m)
Beam: 22ft (6.7m)
Depth: 9ft (2.7m)
Displacement: c115t
Rigging: two masts; square-rigged on mainmast with two jibs, fore-staysail and square spritsail; lateen mizzen
Complement: not known
Cargo: general freight
Routes: North Sea, British coasts, Baltic Sea

RESOLUTION (EX-DRAKE, MARQUIS OF GRANBY)

GB: 1770

Built at Whitby, Yorkshire, as the collier brig *Drake*, then renamed *Marquis of Granby*, this vessel's most famous name was bestowed by the Admiralty in 1772, when she was converted to a ship-rigged sloop, and, with her sister HMS *Adventure*, was despatched under Captain James Cook on a voyage to ascertain the existence of a continent in the Southern Ocean. Between 13 July 1772 and 29 July 1775, she explored the stormy and empty waters between South Africa, Australia, South America and the Antarctic, twice crossing the Antarctic Circle and making the furthest south navigation yet achieved. By making his crew eat sauerkraut and drink lemon juice, Cook successfully avoided the centuries-old plague of long voyages – scurvy; only one man died of illness in the course of the 70,000-mile (112,650km) cruise. A year later, Cook sailed again in *Resolution*, accompanied by HMS *Discovery*, this time under orders to explore around the top of Canada in search of the Northwest Passage from the Pacific into the North Atlantic. In April 1778, the ship was fitted with a new foremast, main topmast and mizzen at Nootka Sound, Alaska, then explored northwards into the Bering Strait but failed to find a way through. Cook sailed for Hawaii to wait out the Arctic winter and was killed there in a fracas with islanders on 14 February 1779. Captain Clerke of *Discovery* took command of *Resolution*, and a further unsuccessful attempt was made to find the Northwest Passage. Clerke died, and under Lieutenant John Gore, *Resolution* and *Discovery* returned to Chatham on 4 October 1780. *Resolution* was in use as a naval transport when captured by two French ships in the Indian Ocean on 10 June 1782; her history after 1783 is unknown.

Length: 110ft 8in (33.7m)
Beam: 30ft 5in (9.2m)
Depth: 13ft 1in (4m)
Displacement: 461t
Rigging: three masts; square rig
Armament: 12 6pdr guns
Complement: 110
Routes: Southern Ocean, North Pacific

This view of *Resolution* in a tropical anchorage shows her under bare poles, with the mizen topmast taken down for replacement.

CHARLES

FRANCE: 1776

Built for the Mediterranean fleet, this was a substantial frigate-hulled warship equipped with complete banks of oars on the lower deck, fifteen a side. The aim was to have a ship that would outgun a Barbary corsair, while being equally manoeuvrable under sail or oars. *Charles* proved satisfactory in action against the pirates, but it was a specialised design of limited utility, unsuitable for fleet action in northern waters.

Length: 15ft (45m)
Beam: 38ft (11m)
Depth: 14ft (4m)
Displacement: 1000t
Rigging: three masts; square-rigged
Machinery: single-screw steam engine
Armament: 40 guns
Complement: c300

This 'frigate-galley' represented a considerable advance on the older galley type as represented by *La Réale*.

HANCOCK (LATER IRIS)

USA: 1776

Thirteen frigates, of which *Hancock* was one, were ordered by the US Congress in 1775 to protect the new republic's coast and shipping from the Royal Navy in the War of Independence. The 34-gun *Hancock* was launched at Newburyport, Massachusetts, in the following year. Unusually – apart from royal ships – she, like some of her sisters, was named for a living man, John Hancock, President of the Continental Congress and first signatory of the Declaration of Independence. In May 1777, under Captain John Manley, she was cruising with the smaller USS *Boston* off the New England coast, where, on the 29th, they took a British merchantman. *Hancock* was pursued by the 64-gun HMS *Somerset* but escaped. One 21 June, *Hancock* and *Boston* received the surrender of HMS *Fox* (28 guns) and took her into their squadron. Two weeks later, the three ships were engaged by a British trio, the frigates HMSs *Rainbow* (44 guns) and *Flora* (32) and the 10-gun sloop *Victor*. On 7 July, *Hancock* was forced to strike her colours to *Rainbow*, and *Fox* was recaptured by the British. The next phase of *Hancock*'s career was as HMS *Iris*. Captured ships generally retained their names, but the Royal Navy was not going to preserve the name of John Hancock under the British flag! On 29 August 1781, she encountered her former sistership, the 30-gun USS *Trumbull*, which was already without her fore-topmast and topgallant mast after a storm, and obtained her surrender after a short battle. On 11 September, *Iris* participated in the Battle of the Virginia Capes and was captured by the French. Commissioned into the French fleet under the same name, she was eventually hulked at Toulon. In the British raid on Toulon of 18 December 1793, she was blown up.

Length: 136ft 6in (41.6m)
Beam: 35ft 6in (10.8m)
Depth: 11ft 6in (3.5m)
Displacement: 750t burthen
Rigging: three masts; square rig
Armament: 24 10pdr, 10 6pdr guns
Complement: 290

The US frigates of 1775, although relatively small, were fine sailing ships. *Hancock*, after capture by the British, was described by them in glowing terms as 'the finest and fastest frigate in the world'.

BRYNHILDA

SWEDEN: 1776

Length: 100ft (30.5m)
Beam: 26ft (7.9m)
Depth: not known
Displacement: not known
Rigging: two masts; square rig on mainmast with staysail and jib; gaff and boom rig on mizzen
Armament: four 24pdr guns on traversing carriages; 12 3pdr swivel guns
Complement: 46-50

The unsuitability of the Finnish coastline for naval operations under sail prompted the construction of this gunboat named *Brynhilda*, after a heroine of Nordic myth; the type name *pojama* is from a Finnish province. Of galley shape, long and slender, the vessel shipped 16 oars on each side. The heavy guns were in the stem and the stern, and swivel mountings gave them a wider degree of bearing than in the smaller Swedish gunboats.

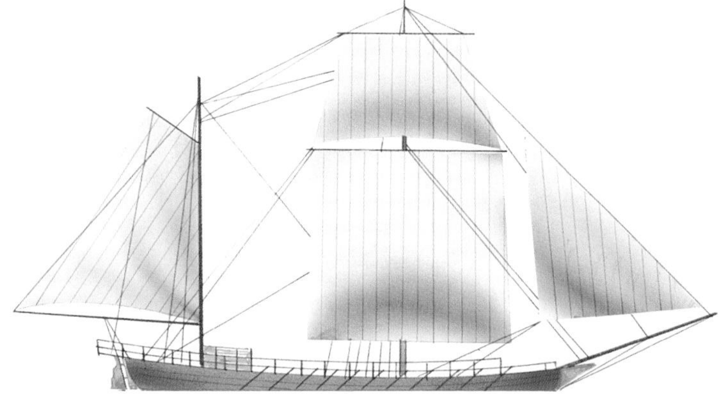

The *Brynhilda* had the usual sail-oar problems, and relatively few were built. They were probably towed into action positions.

LA BOUDEUSE

FRANCE: 1766

The round-the-world cruise of the Indret-built *La Boudeuse*, a 26-gun frigate, commanded by Louis Antoine de Bougainville, marked France's determination to share both in geographical and scientific discovery and its economic rewards. Departing Brest on 5 December 1766, escorted by the ship *Etoile*, *La Boudeuse*'s circumnavigation took two and a quarter years, in which only seven men were lost and more than 3000 botanical and zoological specimens brought back for further study.

Length: 134ft 6in (41m)
Beam: 35ft 1in (10.7m)
Depth: 17ft 7in (5.4m)
Displacement: 960t
Rigging: three masts; square rig
Armament: 26 8pdr guns
Complement: 214
Routes: circumnavigation

The hull of *La Boudeuse* was given a protective sheathing of flat-headed iron nails, forming a layer impermeable to the teredo worm.

PHILADELPHIA

USA: 1776

In 1935, the wreck of the *Philadelphia* was found and brought to the surface with many contemporary items. It is now in the Smithsonian Museum, Washington DC.

Philadelphia was one of a flotilla of gunboats and galleys hastily built by Benedict Arnold's men at Skenesborough in Upper New York State to counter the British during the American War of Independence. She was known as a *gundalow*, a flat-bottomed, oared vessel mounting three guns and propelled by 16 oars. The scratch flotilla met an English fleet on Lake Champlain on 11 October 1776, and *Philadelphia* was sunk by a single 24-pound shot.

Length: 53ft 4in (16.3m)
Beam: 15ft 6in (4.7m)
Depth: 3ft 10in (1.2m)
Displacement: not known
Rigging: one mast; two square sails
Armament: one 12pdr, two 9pdr guns
Complement: 45

SOUTH CAROLINA (EX-L'INDIEN)

USA: 1776

Built in Amsterdam in 1776 as *L'Indien*, this vessel was originally intended for French service. American purchasing agents, looking for ships in a hurry during the War of Independence, arranged to acquire her, but the French reclaimed her and sold her to the Grand Duke of Luxembourg (who had no coastline); he then lent her to the state of South Carolina in 1777. On 19 December 1782, she was captured by HMSS *Astrea* (32 guns), *Diomede* (44 guns) and *Quebec* (32 guns) after an 18-hour chase. *South Carolina*'s hull had hogged (sagged in the middle) as a consequence of the weight of her heavy guns, and she was not taken into service in the Royal Navy. The lesson was taken up by American warship builders, who put much more longitudinal strength into home-built frigates.

Length: 154ft (46.9m)
Beam: 40ft (12.2m)
Depth: 16ft 6in (5m)
Displacement: 1186t
Rigging: three masts; square rig
Armament: 28 36pdr, 12 12pdr guns
Complement: not known

***South Carolina* represented a considerable increase in dimensions on frigates of the Hancock class, and pointed the way toward the big US frigate.**

TURTLE

USA: 1776

Like 'two upper tortoise shells of equal size, joined together', her shape and underwater purpose explain the name of this early submersible, built by David and Ezra Bushnell at Saybrook, Connecticut in 1776. Intended to attack British shipping in the American War of Independence, *Turtle* had an offensive weapon, a mine packed with 150lb (68kg) of gunpowder that could be secured to a hostile ship by means of an auger operated from within the vessel. With George Washington's agreement, *Turtle* was tried in action off Staten Island by a volunteer, Ezra Lee. He failed to attach the mine to the British flagship, HMS *Eagle*, and abandoned the attempt. On returning to shore he was chased by a British cutter, but deterred it by releasing the mine, which duly exploded an hour later. Although no damage was done, the British fleet left the anchorage. *Turtle* made two further unsuccessful sorties and was destroyed to prevent the British capturing it.

***Turtle* was a well-conceived vessel, with a foot-pump to the bilge-tank, a hand-driven screw, watertight windows and a primitive type of snorkel valve.**

Length: 7ft 6in (2.3m)
Beam: not known
Depth: 6ft (1.8m)
Displacement: c2000lb (900kg)
Machinery: hand-cranked vertical and horizontal screws
Armament: one mine
Complement: 1

WASHINGTON

USA: 1776

Washington was one of four 'Continental galleys' built in haste at Skenesborough, New York, for General Arnold's Lake Champlain flotilla; all of them had a two-masted lateen rig and provision for seven oarsmen on each side, together with such guns as could be acquired, mostly 12pdrs and 9pdrs. *Washington* was captured by the British in the Battle of Valcour Island on 11 October 1776, and is believed to have been converted into a brig.

Length: 72ft 4in (22m)
Beam: 19ft 7in (5.9m)
Depth: 6ft 2in (1.9m)
Displacement: 123t
Rigging: two masts; lateen rig
Armament: not known
Complement: 40

The lateen rig may have been chosen for its simplicity in construction and handling, although it was also used in similar Swedish ships at this time.

KANONJOLLE

SWEDEN: 1778

Literally 'cannon yawl', the *kanonjolle* was the most numerous type of vessel in the Swedish fleet that patrolled the Gulf of Finland. Longitudinal bulkheads supported the single 24pdr cannon. The stern, cut away to the waterline, was pointed, enabling the boat to be rowed backwards to achieve the correct firing position. The rig, on two masts, was of very simple type. The *kanonjolle*, when facing an enemy vessel, presented a very narrow head-on target.

Length: 41ft (12.5m)
Beam: 10ft (3m)
Depth: c2ft 9in (0.8m)
Displacement: not known
Rigging: two masts; lugsail rig
Armament: one 24pdr gun
Complement: 18-25, including soldiers

Like the other Swedish sail-oar vessels of this period, the *kanonjolle* was designed by F H af Chapman.

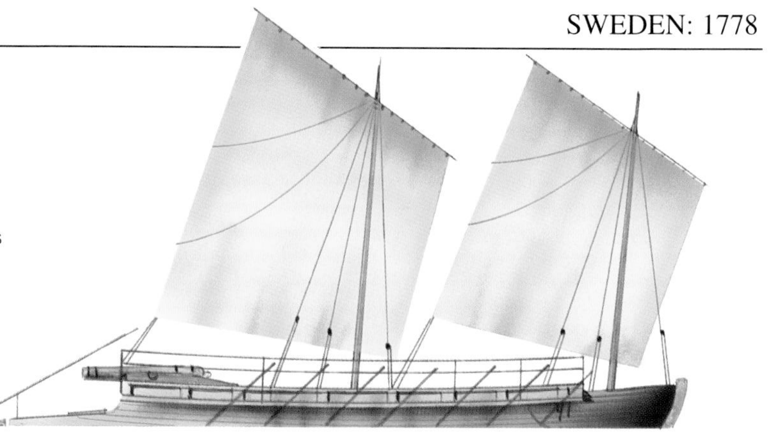

SHEBECK

RUSSIA: 1778

Length: 120ft (37m)
Beam: 30ft (9.1m)
Depth: not known
Displacement: not known
Rigging: three masts with topmasts fitted abaft; lateen rig; jib and fore-staysail
Armament: 18 18pdr guns
Complement: 42

It is unlikely that very many of these ships were built, and some of them may have been square-rigged on fore and main masts.

This type of 'oared frigate', built by the Russians in the late 18th century, was very like, perhaps a copy of, the Swedish *udema*, against which it fought in the Russian-Swedish War. The name clearly comes from the *chebeck* of the Mediterranean, with which there are similarities in the three-mast lateen rig and low hull profile, although the Russian vessel had more oars (28 in this case) and the hull looks much less finely lined.

BOMB VESSEL

SWEDEN: 1780

Length: 35ft (10.7m)
Beam: 12ft (3.7m)
Depth: 5ft (1.5m)
Displacement: c55t
Rigging: single mast; spritsail rig with foresail
Armament: one 13-15in (330-381mm) mortar plus light bow- and stern-chaser cannon
Complement: 18

Unusually in a ship of its size, this vessel appears to have had a square stern, perhaps to carry the small stern-chaser cannon.

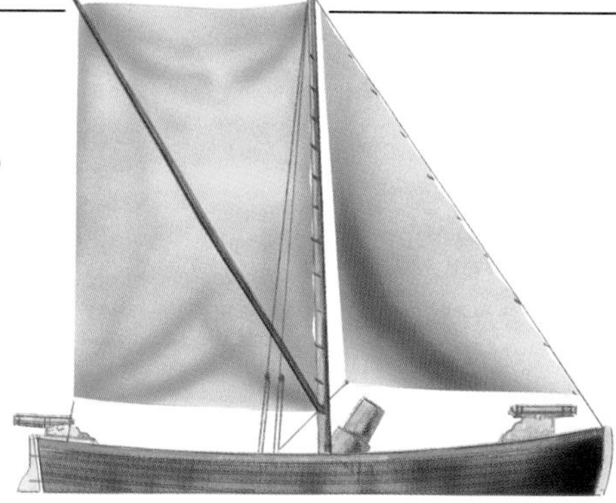

Much smaller than the bomb ketch, this was an adaptation of a small coasting vessel for bombarding landward targets. Like the later coastal ironclad monitor, which was designed for the same purpose, it had a single heavy weapon, in this case a large-calibre mortar. Whilst the angle of the mortar's trajectory could be varied, it was aimed by moving the boat to point in the appropriate direction, hence the oars.

Fishing Vessel

FRANCE: 1780

The depth of water on the Grand Banks is shallow enough to allow fishing vessels to anchor whilst fishing. Weather permitting, the vessel was kept beam on to the wind while the fishermen fished, using single lines, from a platform set up along the weather side of the ship protected from the wind. Other members of the crew were stationed at each end of the ship with nets to catch any fish that fell from the lines. The wooden hulled vessels were sturdily built, with a spacious hold to process the catch.

Length: 102ft (31m)
Beam: 27ft (8.3m)
Depth: 16ft (4.9m)
Displacement: 400t
Rigging: ship
Complement: not known
Cargo: fish
Routes: not known

This large Normandy fishing vessel of about 1780 was typical of the type seen in great numbers off the grand banks.

Friendship

GB: 1780

Four members of *Friendship*'s crew were flogged for excessive 'fraternization' with women convicts on board.

This ship, probably new in 1780, was chartered by the British government to transport convicts to Australia in the 'first fleet' of May 1787. She was intended to carry female convicts, but at the Cape Town stop these were transferred to other ships and *Friendship* was loaded with sheep for the new convict colony. On the return journey, she was scuttled in Macassar Strait on 28 October 1788, and her remaining crew transferred to *Alexander*.

Length: not known
Beam: not known
Depth: not known
Displacement: 278t
Rigging: three masts; square rig
Complement: not known
Cargo: convicts, sheep
Routes: Great Britain-Australia

Grampus

GB: 1780

Grampus was the first in a class of two 50-gun fourth rates. Launched at Liverpool in October 1782, her service life was relatively brief; she was broken up in 1794. The two-decker 50-gun ships, never very numerous in the Royal Navy, were cruising vessels with heavier firepower than frigates and greater speed than ships of the line. Convoy escort was a frequent duty. Outgunned by ships of the line and outmanouevured by frigates, ships of the *Grampus* type found little favour with seamen of the Royal Navy.

Following the 1799 decision to 'copper' the bigger ships of the Royal Navy, *Grampus* was one of the first to be launched with a copper-sheathed hull.

Length: 148ft (45m)
Beam: 40ft 6in (12.3m)
Depth: 17ft 9in (5.4m)
Displacement: 1062t
Rigging: three masts; square rig
Armament: 50 guns
Complement: 350

Hoy

GB: 1780

Described as a maid-of-all-work of the coastal trade, and of any size between 12 and 50t, the hoy was also the 'water bus' of the 18th century river. Single-masted, the hoy had a boomless gaff mainsail and a fore-staysail; the mainsail foot could be hoisted to give the steersman a view through congested traffic. Larger hoys carried a square topsail in addition. Hoys are referred to from the end of the 15th century.

Prospective passengers could hail hoys from shore, and from this practice the call 'Ahoy!' has been claimed to originate.

Length: 79ft (24m)
Beam: 21ft (6.4m)
Depth: 11ft (3.4m)
Displacement: 160t burthen
Rigging: single mast; fore-and-aft gaff rig with topsail and foresail
Complement: 4-6
Cargo: general goods, naval stores
Routes: coastal routes and anchorage roads

CHASSE-MAREE

FRANCE: 1781

The lugger, although known to all North Sea countries, was most fully exploited by France, and *La Gloire*, captured in 1781, was typical. Originally fishing boats, many of the type were used as privateers off the coast of Brittany in the late 18th and early 19th centuries. *La Gloire* had a decked hull which could mount up to 18 small cannon. With topsails on all three masts and a long jib, she was both very fast and excelled at sailing close to the wind.

In this example of a lugger in a 19th century painting, the topmasts are rigged abaft the lower masts on fore and main, a practice seen on very few other vessels.

Length: 70ft 2in (21.1m)
Beam: 18ft 10in (5.7m)
Depth: 7ft 10in (2.3m)
Displacement: 114t burthen
Rigging: three masts; with lugsails and lug-topsails, jib and fore-staysail
Armament: 16 carronades
Complement: 40

LA BOUSSOLE (EX-LE PORTEFAIX)

FRANCE: 1781

The name means 'compass', apt for an exploration vessel. She was the refitted and renamed fisheries store ship *Le Portefaix*, but now became flagship of the Comte de la Pérouse's geographic-scientific expedition to the South Pacific, which left Brest on 1 August 1785. Having cruised over a vast extent of the South and West Pacific, *La Boussole* and her sistership *L'Astrolabe* were wrecked on a coral reef near Ambi, New Caledonia.

Length: not known
Beam: not known
Depth: not known
Displacement: 450t
Rigging: three masts; square rig
Complement: 113
Routes: South Pacific
Role: exploration vessel

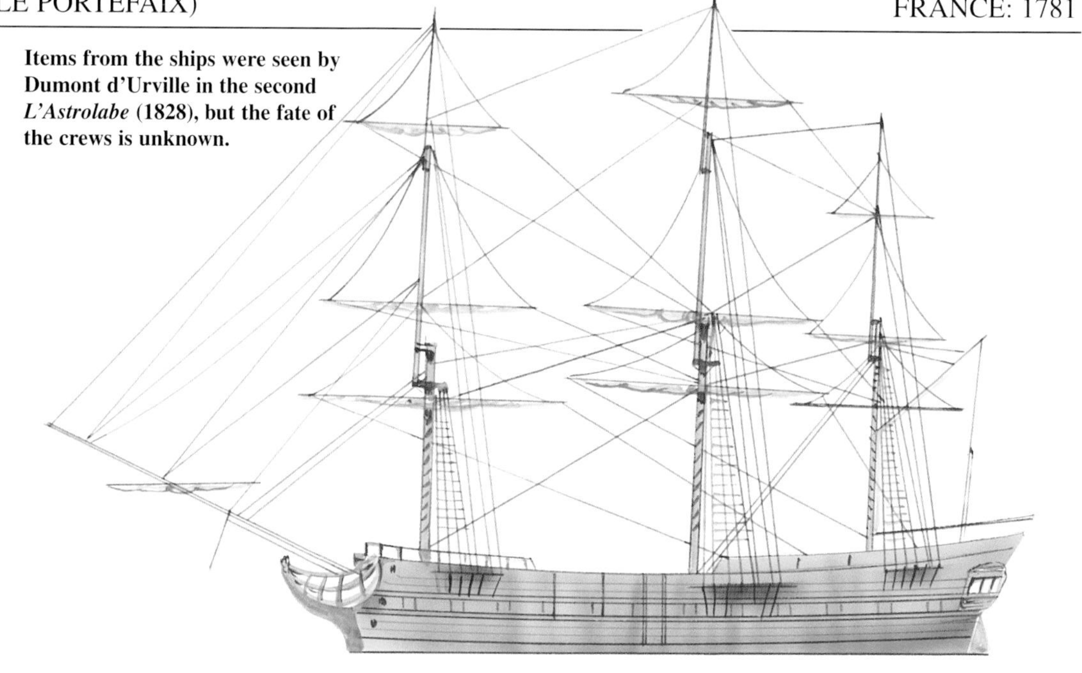

Items from the ships were seen by Dumont d'Urville in the second *L'Astrolabe* (1828), but the fate of the crews is unknown.

PYROSCAPHE

FRANCE: 1783

It was 1816 before Jouffroy built another steamboat, by which time other vessels had been built, including Fulton's ship in Paris.

Length: 148ft 6in (45.2m)
Beam: 14ft 10in (4.5m)
Depth: not known
Displacement: 163t
Rigging: not applicable
Machinery: sidewheels, double-acting
Complement: 3
Routes: Saône River

Literally 'fire boat' in ancient Greek, *Pyroscaphe* was the second steamship built by the Marquis de Jouffroy d'Abbans, and was one of the earliest experimental steam vessels to give a working demonstration. On 15 July 1783, *Pyroscaphe*'s horizontal double-acting engines drove her, via twin paddle wheels, up the Saône River for 15 minutes before failing. Jouffroy hoped for a French monopoly on steamboat-building, but his claim was turned down.

BOUNTY (EX-BETHIA)

GB: 1784

Bounty began as the merchant vessel *Bethia*, a ship-rigged craft of 220t, built in the port of Hull in 1784; three years later the Admiralty purchased her. English merchants had made vast investments in slave-tended plantations in the West Indies, and voyages to the South Pacific had shown that the breadfruit grown in the Society Islands could be the ideal food to keep slaves well nourished cheaply. Under her commander, Lieutenant William Bligh, *Bounty*'s task was to transport breadfruit plants from the South Pacific to the Caribbean. Ventilated with gratings and scuttles, she duly loaded at Tahiti, where her crew revelled in the easy-going life. On the way back, on 28 April 1789, the crew mutinied under the leadership of Fletcher Christian. The captain and the loyal men were set adrift in the ship's launch. *Bounty* was sailed by the mutineers to Pitcairn Island and burned with her thousand breadfruit plants.

Length: 91ft (27.7m)
Beam: 24ft 4in (7.5m)
Depth: 11ft 4in (3.5m)
Displacement: 220t
Rigging: three masts; square rig
Armament: four guns
Complement: 45
Routes: South Pacific-Caribbean

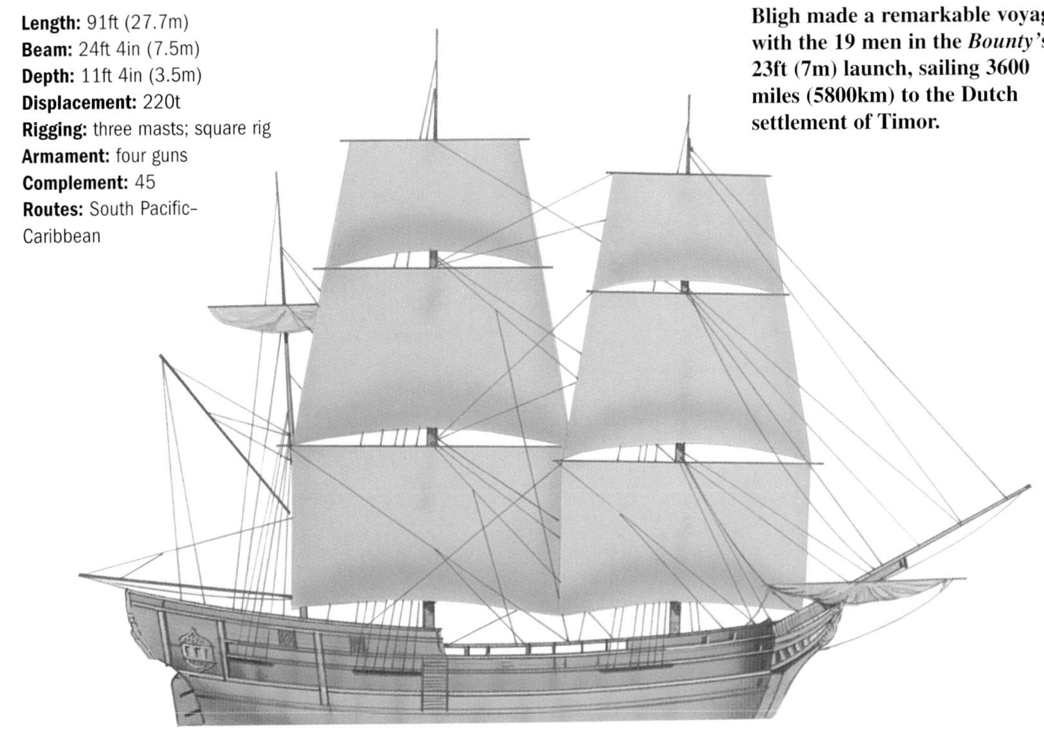

Bligh made a remarkable voyage with the 19 men in the *Bounty*'s 23ft (7m) launch, sailing 3600 miles (5800km) to the Dutch settlement of Timor.

RATTLESNAKE

USA: 1784

Early American privateers were hastily converted merchant vessels not entirely suitable. By 1776, specially built fast vessels started to enter service with *Rattlesnake*.

Rattlesnake was a splendid ship of the larger type built by Peck at Boston. Towards the end of both the War of Independence and the war of 1812 the size of American privateers increased, however, the largest privateers did not exceed 120ft (36m) in length due to the problem of finding sufficient crew members, this problem also had a serious effect upon the manning of the regular naval frigates. After a short career, *Rattlesnake* was captured by the British 44-gun frigate *Assurance* and taken into the Royal Navy.

Length: 120ft (36m)
Beam: 24ft (7.2m)
Depth: not known
Displacement: 310t
Rigging: three masts, square rigged
Armament: 20 guns
Complement: 85

ALEXANDER

GB: 1785

Length: 114ft (34.7m)
Beam: 31ft (9.4m)
Depth: not known
Displacement: 450t
Rigging: three masts; ship rig
Complement: not known
Cargo: convicts
Routes: England-Australia

On the fleet's arrival, Botany Bay was found to be unsuitable for landing, and in the search for a better site, Sydney harbour was discovered.

Built in 1783, *Alexander* was the largest of the convict transports in the 'first fleet' that carried criminals to found the colony at Botany Bay, Australia. There were five other transports, three store ships and two naval sloops which acted as escorts. Having left England on 12 May 1787, the fleet reached its destination on 20 January 1788. *Alexander* returned to England, picking up the crew of *Friendship* (1780) on the way. She was last heard of registered at Hull; she disappeared from the record in 1808.

AUDACIOUS

GB: 1785

The most numerous type of ship of the line, the 74-gunner was the backbone of the Royal Navy and other large fleets.

Launched in July 1785, *Audacious* was a third rate of 74 guns built at Rotherhithe on the Thames and one of 14 ships of the *Arrogant* class. Under Captain Gould, she was in Nelson's fleet at the Battle of the Nile on 1 August 1798 and was one of the ships that took the tricky inner channel to bombard the French from the landward side; she was again with Nelson at the Battle of Copenhagen on 1 April 1801. In December 1808-January 1809, she was one of the escort vessels to the transport convoy sent to relieve the British army at Corunna. She was broken up in 1815.

Length: 168ft (51.2m)
Beam: 46ft 9in (14.25m)
Depth: 19ft 9in (6m)
Displacement: 1604t
Rigging: three masts; square rig
Armament: 28 32pdr, 28 18pdr, 18 9pdr guns
Complement: 550

JOHN FITCH

USA: 1787

The American inventor John Fitch devised a form of steam propulsion consisting of two sets of three vertical oars mounted on each side of the boat's hull and driven by shafts connected to the engine by crank rods. This vessel made a number of short journeys under steam on the Delaware River in 1787 but could make only three knots. Fitch built improved stern-driven versions in 1788 and 1790, but they were not a commercial success.

Length: 60ft (18.3m)
Beam: 12ft (3.7m)
Depth: 3ft (0.9m)
Displacement: not known
Rigging: gantry to support mechanical oars
Machinery: vertical oars, steam
Complement: 2
Routes: Delaware River

Like Fulton, Fitch went to France, but during the revolution no one was interested in his proposals. He returned to the United States, where he died in poverty.

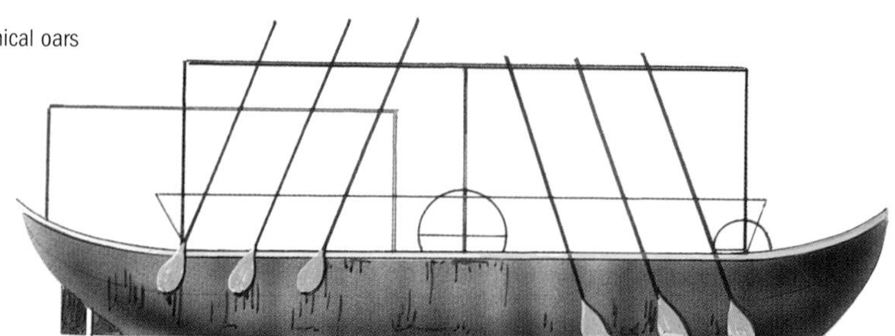

VANGUARD

GB: 1787

The many third rates were grouped in sub-classes representing the designer and the first ship of the sub-class. *Vanguard* belonged to the sub-class headed by HMS *Arrogant*, which contained 14 ships in all.

Launched at Deptford in 1787, *Vanguard*, as a third-rate ship of the line with 74 guns, was one of the most numerous class of big ships; her designer was Sir Thomas Slade. In 1796, she was in the Mediterranean as flagship of Rear-Admiral Nelson, under Lord St Vincent. Detailed to watch the movements of the French fleet at Toulon, *Vanguard* was totally dismasted and made for Sardinia for repairs, accomplished within four days. Meanwhile, the French sailed, and there followed a long chase, as Nelson, with 14 sail of the line but no frigates, sought to find them. Anticipating their destination as Alexandria, Egypt, he arrived before them, left, and then returned on 1 August 1798 with 11 ships to find 17 French warships, commanded by Admiral de Brueys, anchored in Aboukir Bay. Relying on the seamanship and drill of his captains – the 'band of brothers' – and crews, Nelson surprised his enemy by forcing a unique night action, placing his fleet on both sides of the French line. *Vanguard*, anchored on the seaward side, opened fire at sunset; before long the scene was lit by the blazing *L'Orient* (120 guns). *Vanguard*'s crew took more punishment than most of the other British ships, including the wound that almost cost Nelson his remaining eye. Ten French ships of the line were captured and one destroyed; only two escaped. In December 1798, *Vanguard* took the Bourbon royal family from Naples to safety in Sicily as the French approached by land. In June 1799, she ceased to be flagship and returned to England in the following year. Although she remained on active service, she saw no further action. In 1812, she was converted to a prison ship; in 1814, to a powder hulk. She was finally broken up in 1821.

Length: 168ft (51.2m)
Beam: 46ft 9in (14.25m)
Depth: 19ft 9in (6m)
Displacement: 1604t
Rigging: three masts; square rig
Armament: 28 32pdr, 28 18pdr, 18 9pdr guns
Complement: 550

GUNSLOOP

SWEDEN: 1789

The gun mountings could be slid down into the centre of the vessel in transit, giving the effect of ballast and reducing hull strain.

Designed by F H af Chapman and built by the Swedes for use amongst the Finnish islands, this 26-oared vessel had no mast, presenting a minimal target profile. Undecked, like the Viking ships of old it offered no shelter; the crew spent the night on land. In the bow was one large gun flanked by two smaller ones, with another big gun in the stern. These and other gunboat types were used in the Swedish-Russian War of 1788-90.

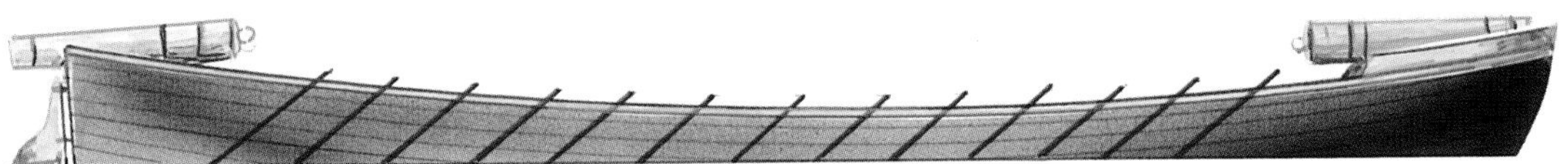

Length: 66ft 3in (20.2m)
Beam: 14ft 6in (4.4m)
Depth: 4ft (1.2m)
Displacement: not known
Rigging: not applicable
Armament: two 18pdr guns
Complement: 55

PANDORA

GB: 1789

Launched at Deptford on the Thames in 1779, the frigate *Pandora* was despatched by the Admiralty in November 1790 to track down the mutineers of HMS *Bounty*. Reaching Tahiti in March 1791, she arrested 14 of the *Bounty*'s crew, but on 27 August, while searching for others and the ship itself, she hit a reef in Endeavour Strait between Australia and New Guinea and sank. Four prisoners and 39 crew were drowned.

Length: 114ft 6in (34.9m)
Beam: 32ft (9.8m)
Depth: 16ft (4.9m)
Displacement: 520t
Rigging: three masts; square rig
Armament: 22 9pdr, two 3pdr guns
Complement: 160

After an arduous voyage in the ship's boats, the survivors of the *Pandora* reached Timor. Three of the surviving prisoners were eventually hanged in London.

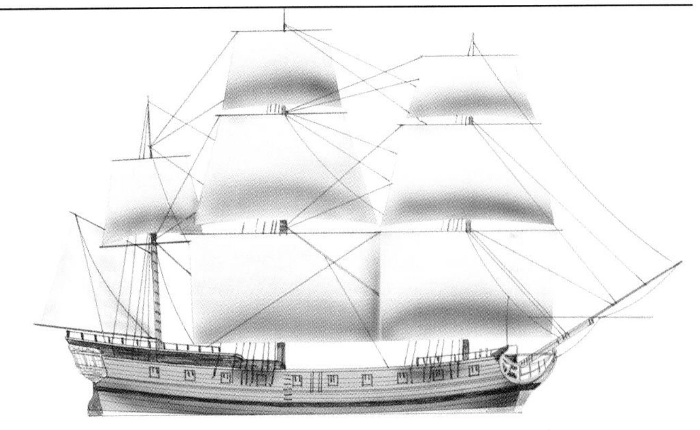

BEAULIEU

GB: 1790

Beaulieu was a 40-gun 'private venture' frigate, built as a speculation at a time when the Admiralty's need for such vessels was at its peak (no admiral ever admitted to having enough frigates). Built at Buckler's Hard, Beaulieu, Hampshire, and purchased by the Admiralty when on the stocks in 1790, she was launched in May 1791. *Beaulieu* served until 1806, when she was broken up.

Frigates of the period 1780-1799 carried the 18pdr gun and the carronade and had considerably greater firepower than their predecessors.

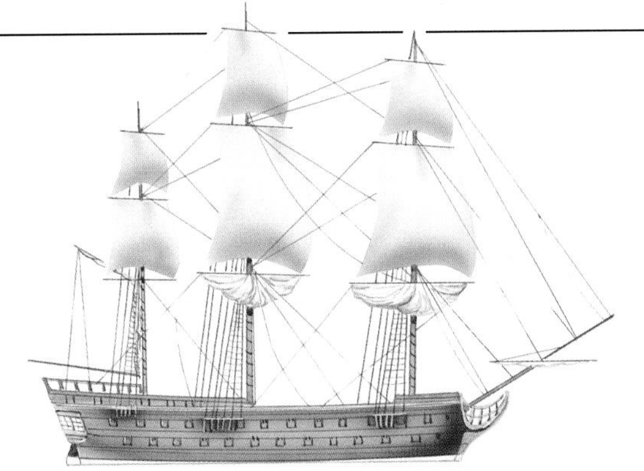

Length: 147ft 3in (44.9m)
Beam: 39ft 6in (12m)
Depth: 15ft 2in (4.6m)
Displacement: 1019t
Rigging: three masts; square rig
Armament: 28 18pdr, 12 9pdr guns
Complement: 280

LA RECHERCHE

FRANCE: 1790

Length: 124ft (37.8m)
Beam: 32ft (9.8m)
Depth: not known
Displacement: 500t
Rigging: square
Armament: 26 guns
Complement: not known
Routes: South Pacific
Role: exploration vessel

In September 1791, the Chevalier d'Entrecasteaux, governor of Mauritius and an experienced seaman, was sent in this store ship to look for any traces of La Pérouse's *Boussole* expedition of 1785. He failed to find anything but made significant explorations of the coasts of Tasmania and Australia. D'Entrecasteaux died of scurvy off Java in July 1793.

D'Entrecasteaux's voyage was dogged by disputes as to whether the expedition should sail under the white ensign of the monarchy or the tricolour of the Republic.

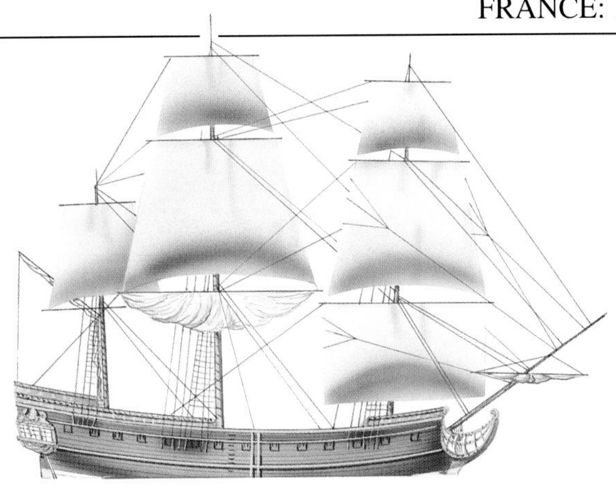

QUEEN CHARLOTTE

GB: 1790

A first rate of 100 guns, built at the Royal Naval Dockyard, Chatham, *Queen Charlotte* was the flagship of Admiral Lord Howe, when he was sent, with a large fleet of 32 sail of the line, to intercept a heavily escorted French grain convoy in May 1794. This action resulted in the battle of the Glorious First of June, in which six French warships were captured; *Queen Charlotte* lost her foretopmast in the engagement. She saw further action off Brest with Admiral Hood, but caught fire and sank off Livorno, Italy, on 17 March 1800.

Length: 190ft (57.9m) (gundeck)
Beam: 52ft 6in (16m)
Depth: 22ft 4in (6.8m)
Displacement: 2286t burthen
Rigging: three masts; square rig
Armament: 100 guns
Complement: 850

First rates – 100-gun ships – were the juggernauts of the sea, and there were never more than about six of them in service with the Royal Navy at any one time in the 18th century.

SNOW

GB: 1790

Length: 78ft (23.8m)
Beam: 23ft 1in (7m)
Depth: 15ft 11in (4.8m)
Displacement: 168t
Rigging: two masts; square-rigged with trysail mast on main carrying gaffsail; jib, fore-staysail, square spritsail on bowsprit
Complement: 6-10
Cargo: mixed and bulk freight
Routes: western Europe and Atlantic

Snows were also used in 18th-century naval fleets, primarily as despatch vessels.

The term goes back to the 1670s and possibly has a Dutch origin. A two-masted, square-rigged vessel, the snow was very like a brig except that a trysail mast was fitted abaft of the mainmast, and the driver sail, or spanker, was rigged to this. Although the type was very numerous throughout north Europe and North America, used for both passenger and cargo work, the term *snow* gradually dropped out of use in favour of *snowbrig* and then just *brig*.

CAESAR

GB: 1793

Length: 181ft (55.1m)
Beam: 50ft 3in (15.3m)
Depth: 22ft 11in (7m)
Displacement: 1991t
Rigging: three masts; square rig
Armament: 30 32pdr, 32 24pdr, 18 9pdr guns
Complement: 650

Designed in 1783 and launched in 1793, *Caesar* was the first two-decker of 80 guns since the 1690s and led the van in the Battle of the First of June in 1794. In September 1798, under Captain Sir James Saumarez, she was one of the ships which intercepted a French squadron off Killala Bay, Ireland. She was Admiral Strachan's flagship in 1806. In 1814, she was hulked as an army depot at Plymouth and broken up in 1821.

Captain Molloy of *Caesar* disputed Admiral Howe's account of the First of June and at a court martial was dismissed from his command.

CONSTITUTION

USA: 1797

One of a trio of exceptionally large and well-armed frigates, the Boston-built *Constitution*, with her sisters *President* and *United States*, although officially classed as 44-gun vessels, had virtually two gundecks and a total of 50 guns and carronades. They were much admired, and *Constitution* gave valuable service in the American confrontation with the Barbary States, where, as flagship of the Mediterranean Squadron, her speed and gunnery were more than a match for the corsairs' ships; from 1809, she served with the North Atlantic Squadron. In the British-American War of 1812, the American frigates outclassed their British counterparts. This was not immediately apparent to the British frigate captains, who issued confident challenges. Under the command of Isaac Hull, *Constitution* escaped from a British squadron in July 1812 after a three-day chase. On 19 August, she encountered HMS *Guerrière* on the Grand Banks and in a fierce, short action at close range left the British frigate dismasted and helpless, too battered to be taken as a prize. After this, *Constitution* acquired the nickname 'Old Ironsides'. In December 1812, now under Captain William Bainbridge and en route for the South Pacific, she made similarly short work of the 38-gun HMS *Java* off Brazil, then returned to Boston for repair. In February 1815, after the war had formally ended, she captured two smaller King's ships off Madeira – HMS *Cyane* and HMS *Levant*. Kept in ordinary for six years after the war, she served again in the Mediterranean between 1821 and 1828. In 1830, she was listed for breaking up, but a national outcry ensued, and Oliver Wendell Holmes wrote the famous poem 'Old Ironsides'. The ship was again refitted and went on to serve in the stations she had previously known. In 1844-46, *Constitution* went on a circumnavigation of the globe. During the Civil War, she was used as a training vessel and continued in this role after a rebuild until 1881, when, still on the Navy List, she became a receiving vessel for entrants to the service. It was 1897 before she ceased to be used, but by then there was no question of scrapping her and she was moved to Boston Harbor to be preserved as a national heirloom. Still a commissioned vessel in the US Navy, and by far the oldest such, *Constitution* makes an annual cruise each 4 July in Boston Harbor.

Length: 175ft (53.3m)
Beam: 43ft 6in (13.3m)
Depth: 22ft 6in (6.9m)
Displacement: 2200t
Rigging: three masts; square rig
Armament: 20 32pdr, 34 24pdr guns
Complement: 450

The US privateer *Decatur*, mistaking *Constitution* for a British ship, threw overboard 12 of her 14 guns in her haste to get out of the way of likely annihilation.

Essex

USA: 1799

Length: 140ft (42.7m)
Beam: 31ft (9.4m)
Depth: 12ft 4in (3.7m)
Displacement: 850t
Rigging: three masts; square rig
Armament: 40 32pdr, six 18pdr guns
Complement: 319

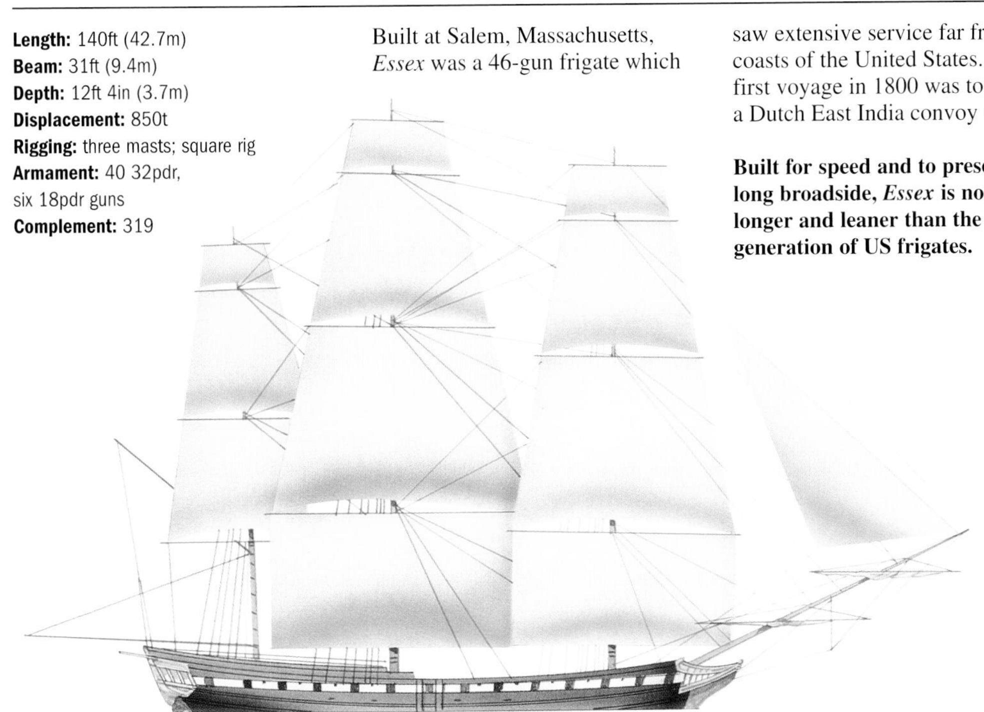

Built at Salem, Massachusetts, *Essex* was a 46-gun frigate which saw extensive service far from the coasts of the United States. Her first voyage in 1800 was to escort a Dutch East India convoy across the Indian Ocean; the following year she was in the Mediterranean Squadron which compelled the Barbary corsairs to cease their attacks on American shipping. Laid up between 1806 and 1809, she was refitted and had a distinguished career in the British-American War of 1812, on both the east and west coasts of America, under Captain David Porter. Between July and September 1812, she took 10 prizes, including the 18-gun vessel HMS *Alert*. At the beginning of 1813, *Essex* sailed for the Pacific, where, in a 'lone wolf' campaign, she raided British shipping. Fifteen prizes were taken in the course of the year, including the armed whaler *Atlantic*, which was taken into US service and renamed *Essex Junior*. In February 1814, the two were in the neutral port of Valparaiso, Chile, when two Royal Navy ships sent to intercept them,

Built for speed and to present a long broadside, *Essex* is notably longer and leaner than the first generation of US frigates.

the 36-gun frigate *Phoebe* and the 18-gun sloop *Cherub*, mounted a blockade. In trying to break out, on 28 March 1814, *Essex* lost her main topmast in a storm and was bombarded by *Phoebe*, whose cannon outranged *Essex*'s heavier carronades. After three hours of battle, and with more than half his crew dead or wounded, Porter struck his colours. *Essex* was taken into the Royal Navy. From 1823 to 1837, she was used as a ship to transport convicts to the colonies; her history after her sale in 1837 is unknown.

BUCENTAURE

FRANCE: 1800

Her name a reminder that the Emperor Napoleon had humbled the Republic of Venice, this French 80-gun vessel was the flagship of the combined French and Spanish fleet of 33 ships of the line, under Admiral Villeneuve, which sailed from Cadiz to encounter the Royal Navy off Cape Trafalgar on 21 October 1805. In many ways of more advanced design and construction than her British rivals, *Bucentaure* carried two decks of guns, well-spaced and with the lower gundeck well above the waterline. Better hull design gave the French ships of the line greater speed and more efficient handling than the British ships. Placed in the centre of the battle line, *Bucentaure* saw Nelson's flagship *Victory* cut across her stern, no more than 10 yards (9.1m) away, firing a murderous barrage of shot, gun by gun, through the stern windows and along the gundeck. In the battle, *Bucentaure*'s masts and bowsprit were all shot away and the guns on her upper deck all destroyed; more than half the crew were killed or wounded. At 1.45pm, the despairing Villeneuve was forced to strike her colours to HMS *Conqueror*, and the imperial eagle standard presented by Napoleon was thrown overboard to prevent its capture as a trophy. Villeneuve was taken aboard HMS *Mars* as a prisoner. He had ordered a boat to be towed behind *Bucentaure* so that he could shift his flag to another ship, but the boat was smashed by gunfire.

Length: c190ft (57.9m)
Beam: c52ft (15.8m)
Depth: c22ft (6.7m)
Displacement: c1900t
Rigging: three masts; square rig
Armament: 80 guns
Complement: 850

Some 4000 mature oak trees were required to build a ship of *Bucentaure*'s size.

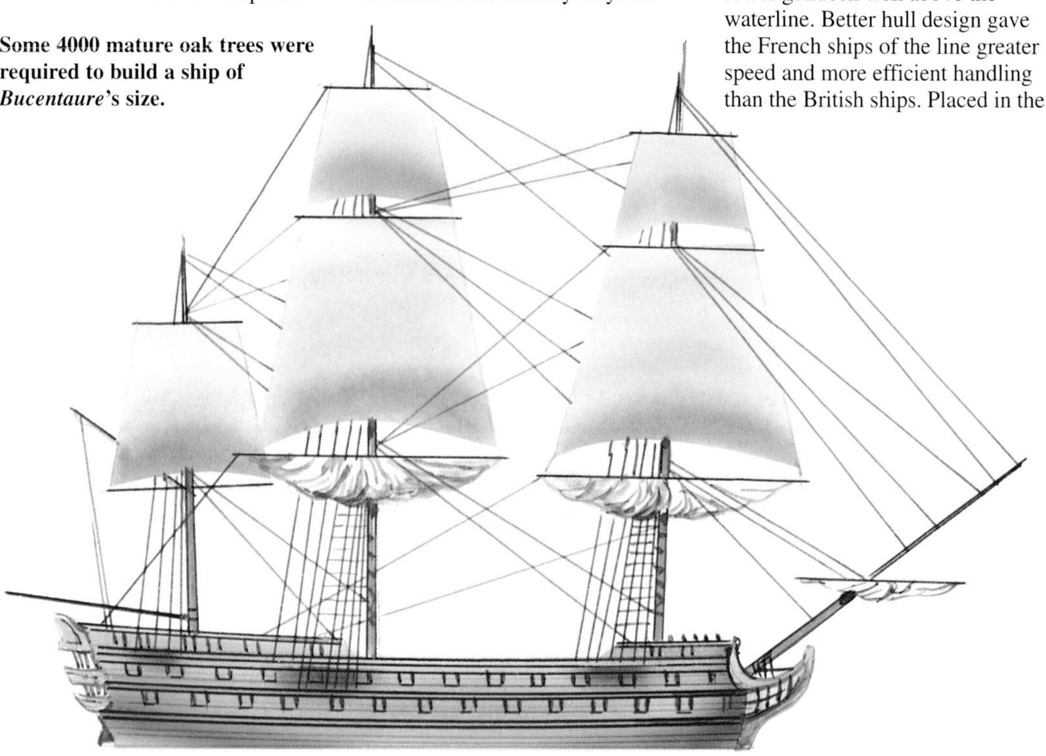

L'URANIE (EX-LA CIOTAT)

FRANCE: 1800

Launched as *La Ciotat*, a corvette of 20 guns, this vessel was renamed in 1816 and refitted for a scientific voyage to Australia and the South Seas, leaving Toulon on 17 September 1817. The voyage went successfully for over two years, until the ship, loaded with scientific specimens, ran hard aground at Berkeley Sound in the Falkland Islands on Christmas Day 1819; she had to be abandoned and left derelict. The captain, Louis-Claude de Freycinet, had brought his wife on the cruise, initially disguised as a midshipman; they returned safely.

Length: not known
Beam: not known
Depth: not known
Displacement: not known
Rigging: three masts; square rig
Armament: 20 guns
Complement: 126
Routes: Australia and South Seas

***L'Uranie* was the first ship to carry water supplies in tin drums rather than wooden barrels; she also had metal anchor chains.**

NJADEN

DENMARK: 1800

The Danish Navy extensively relied upon 74-gun ships, such as the *Njaden*, and by 1801 the type formed the main part of a fleet of 23 ships of the line.

During the 18th century, Denmark built up a substantial navy, with its ships based upon French and British designs. Rather than employing foreign shipwrights in their yards, the Danes sent their trainee shipwrights abroad for experience. Under chief constructor Hohlenberg there were some advanced designs, including the 74-gun ship *Njaden*, which was the first vessel to feature a new type of stern allowing for all-round fire. This feature was later incorporated by the British in some of their 74-gun ships.

Length: 180ft (54.8m)
Beam: 50ft (15.2m)
Depth: not known
Displacement: 1995t
Rigging: not known
Armament: 74 guns
Complement: not known

PHILADELPHIA

USA: 1800

Length: 157ft (47.9m)
Beam: 39ft (11.9m)
Depth: 13ft (4m)
Displacement: 1240t
Rigging: three masts; square rig
Armament: 26 long 18pdr guns; 16 32pdr carronades
Complement: 307

Regarded as one of the fastest frigates of her time, this vessel was built at Philadelphia, and in her first voyage captured five French ships and retook six American ships. In 1801, she joined in the blockade of Tripoli; she did so again in 1803, when she captured the 24-gun Moroccan ship *Mirboka* and reclaimed its American prize, *Celia*. On 31 October that same year, *Philadelphia* ran aground off Tripoli and, under the guns of its forts, was obliged to surrender.

In January 1804, Captain Stephen Decatur Jr slipped past the guardships and set the grounded *Philadelphia* ablaze to prevent her being refloated by the enemy.

WAKA TAUA

NEW ZEALAND: 1800

Waka is a Maori word meaning 'hollowed box'. The hull of this war canoe was a totara-wood dugout, with added washboard planking to give greater freeboard. The long, narrow craft was paddled by 30 or more men seated on gratings. It could also hoist a triangular fibre sail between a pair of bipod masts. The prow was carved with a symbolic bird or animal, but the main decoration was the lofty open-carved 'tail', which could reach up to 20ft (6.1m) above the open deck.

Length: 65ft (19.8m)
Beam: 5ft (1.5m)
Depth: 2ft (0.6m)
Displacement: not known
Rigging: two bipod masts; triangular sail
Complement: 20

The *waka taua* had to be paddled along the trough of the waves; to meet them head-on might break the vessel's back.

CHARLOTTE DUNDAS

GB: 1801

Length: 56ft (17.1m)
Beam: 18ft (5.5m)
Depth: 8ft (2.4m)
Machinery: sternwheel, horizontal steam
Complement: 4
Routes: Forth & Clyde Canal

Charlotte Dundas was the first practical steamship; she was built to tow barges along the Forth & Clyde Canal in Scotland. The vessel had a single sternwheel-type paddle, with the engine placed just ahead of it on the port side and the boiler to starboard. Although she proved effective in test, canal owners felt that her wash would erode the banks and she was not put into service. Left to rot, the ship was scrapped in 1861.

***Charlotte Dundas*'s paddle wheel was turned by a crank joined by a connecting rod to the piston; this became the standard drive system.**

DILIGENTE

FRANCE: 1801

Length: 110ft 11in (33.8m)
Beam: 27ft 9in (8.45m)
Depth: 15ft (4.6m)
Displacement: 472t
Rigging: three masts; square rig
Armament: 18 6pdr guns

The French effort to blockade Britain led to the construction of many smaller vessels, although the corvette itself was an enlargement of the earlier chaloupe type.

French corvettes were either ship- or brig-rigged and carried a substantial armament of carronades. *Diligente*, designed by Pierre Ozanne and built at Brest, was considered the fastest ship in the French Navy and was used as the model for a post 1815 corvette class.

By this period, the corvette bore little relationship to the oared sloops or chaloupes from which it was descended.

DREADNOUGHT

GB: 1801

Length: 185ft (56.4m)
Beam: 51ft (15.5m)
Depth: 21ft 6in (6.5m)
Displacement: 2110t
Rigging: three masts; square rig
Armament: 28 32pdr, 60 18pdr, 10 12pdr guns
Complement: 750

Laid down in 1788 and launched in June 1801 as a second rate of 98 guns, *Dreadnought* was later relisted as a first rate with 104 guns. She was Admiral Collingwood's flagship until just before Trafalgar (21 October 1805); in that battle she captured the Spanish *San Juan Nepomuceno*. In 1812, she was in the blockading squadron off Brest, and after 1825 she was decommissioned as a floating hospital at Pembroke, then moved to Greenwich. *Dreadnought* was broken up in 1857.

***Dreadnought*, in her role as a floating hospital, moored in the Thames at Greenwich.**

NAUTILUS

FRANCE: 1801

Hostility to the project among French naval officials prompted Fulton to dismantle the *Nautilus*. He found a similar reaction at the British Admiralty in 1804.

Length: 21ft 4in (6.5m)
Beam: 6ft 3in (1.9m)
Depth: not known
Displacement: not known
Rigging: collapsible mast; square sail
Machinery: hand-cranked screw
Armament: one mine
Complement: 4

The American engineer Robert Fulton appreciated the possibilities of the submarine as a hidden weapon. Living in Paris, he tried to interest the French government in the notion in 1797, and in 1800 began the building of *Nautilus*, which was launched at Paris in 1801. It was an effective working submarine, hand-cranked, able to make two knots under water; it was fitted with ballast tanks and with horizontal as well as vertical rudders. A collapsible mast with a sail drove it on the surface. The craft had a periscope, and Fulton made numerous improvements to it over the next two years, including adding a glass porthole. Its weapon was an auger, intended for drilling holes into enemy vessels, into which explosive charges could then be fixed. In 1801, *Nautilus* sailed on the surface from Paris to the mouth of the Seine and on to Cape La Hogue; she was at Brest the following year.

FULTON

FRANCE: 1803

The American entrepreneur-engineer Robert Fulton constructed two early sidewheel steamships in Paris. The first one sank, but the machinery was retrieved and installed in a stronger hull. Tried out on 9 August 1803, it caused a considerable sensation, towing two barges against the current. *Fulton*'s hull was long and narrow, with the engine installed on the deck.

Despite his success with this project, Fulton found little support in France or England. He returned to America in 1806 where he continued to build innovative ships.

Length: 90ft (27.4m)
Beam: 16ft (4.9m)
Depth: 5ft (1.5m)
Displacement: not known
Rigging: not applicable
Machinery: sidewheels, steam

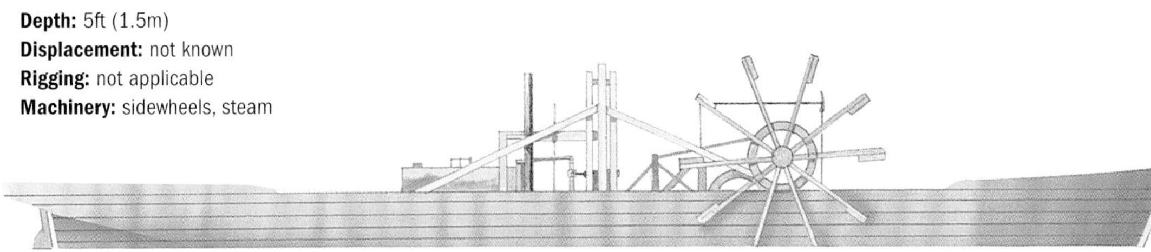

GUNBOAT

FRANCE: 1803

Several hundred three-gun vessels were built on the French and Dutch coasts around the early 1800s in anticipation of an invasion of Britain. The *chaloupe-cannonière* as built in Holland had a schooner-type rig, but was also equipped as a galley. It could potentially make the short crossing at some considerable speed, making two trips a day in favourable conditions and helping to convey large numbers of invading troops.

Length: 82ft (25m)
Beam: 18ft 4in (5.6m)
Depth: 6ft 6in (2m)
Displacement: not known
Rigging: two masts; fore-and-aft rig with gaff and boom; square topsails, two jibs and fore-staysail
Armament: three 24pdr, one 6pdr guns
Complement: not known

MUSKIN

FRANCE: 1803

The 'Boulogne Flotilla', built to transport and escort the projected French invasion of Britain in the early 1800s, contained very many ships, amongst them this light-weight version of the *chaloupe cannonière*, the *bateau cannonier*.

Whether these ships could have played the part both of landing craft and of bombarding craft effectively remains an open question.

Designed as a mixed-power sail-oar vessel, it borrowed various features from the Swedish gunboats of the time. With its shallow draught it was intended to play an amphibious role, coming right inshore.

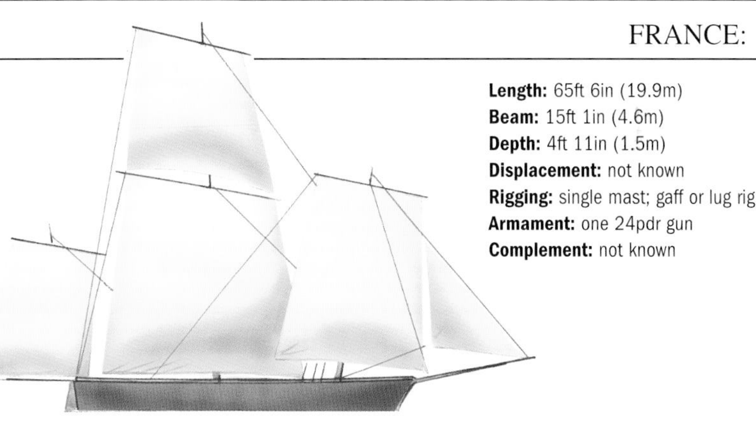

Length: 65ft 6in (19.9m)
Beam: 15ft 1in (4.6m)
Depth: 4ft 11in (1.5m)
Displacement: not known
Rigging: single mast; gaff or lug rig
Armament: one 24pdr gun
Complement: not known

PENICHE

FRANCE: 1803

Length: 75ft (23m)
Beam: 20ft (5.8m)
Depth: not known
Displacement: not known
Rigging: lug
Armament: one 24pdr
Complement: not known

The modern French Navy had its origins in the 1670s and for a time, with nearly 200 warships, it was the largest navy in the world. By 1800, and after numerous conflicts, France was once again at war with her greatest rival; Britain. Plans were ready for the invasion of Britain once it was safe to commence the attack using a wide variety of purpose-built boats including the *Peniche*, a small shallow draft vessel able to mount a few light guns, as well as carry troops.

The *Peniche* was one of over 10 different types of vessels intended to carry troops for the French invasion of Britain.

PRAME

FRANCE: 1803

Although known as early as 1759, it was as part of Napoleon's great scheme for the invasion of Britain that the *prame d'artillerie* came to prominence, when many were speedily built between Le Havre and Dunkerque. It was a tubby, small vessel designed to mount a single mortar for coastal bombardment to assist invasion troops in landing.

Vessels like this demonstrate the increased sophistication of wartime operations, with a range of specialised craft not seen before.

Length: 48ft (14.6m)
Beam: 14ft (4.3m)
Depth: 6ft 4in (1.9m)
Displacement: not known
Rigging: single mast; gaff or lug rig
Armament: one 10in (254mm) mortar
Complement: 6

GUNBOAT NO. 5

USA: 1806

The US gunboat fleet was built in an effort to provide a range of vessels for escort and offensive purposes that were cheaper than frigates or ships of the line. Some were rigged as cutters; others were oared. This model, No. 5, had a triangular fore-and-aft sail on a long sprit. The main weapon was carried in the bow, and the entire ship had to be pointed at the target to bring it to bear, suggesting that oars must also have been used.

Six gunboats were included in the US Mediterranean Squadron in 1806; they were used for bombarding shore targets.

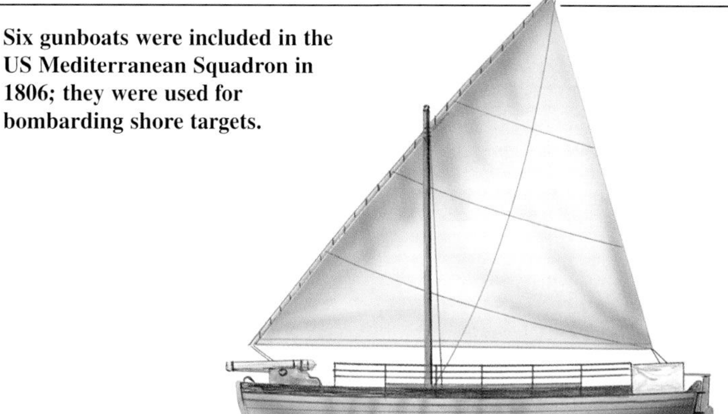

Length: 50ft (15.2m)
Beam: 17ft (5.2m)
Depth: 4ft (1.2m)
Displacement: 30t
Rigging: single mast; lateen or spritsail rig
Armament: one bow-mounted 18pdr gun; two 12pdr carronades
Complement: 6

LA LÉGÈRE

FRANCE: 1806

Length: 125ft (37.6m)
Beam: 32ft (9.8m)
Depth: not known
Displacement: not known
Rigging: ship
Armament: eight 24-pdr, 20 9-pdr
Complement: not known

La Légère was a French sixth rate 28-gun frigate and one of the most common versions of the type, first introduced in 1748. By 1793 it had started to fall from favour. Armament was mixed, comprising nine-pounder cannon and 24-pounder carronades, the latter on the poop and forecastle. There was no deck amidships in the hold and the cables were led directly over the barrels and stores. The action between *La Légère* and the British ship *Pilot* in 1815 was the last action fought in the long running wars between France and Britain.

By the 1790s, the smaller frigate such as *La Légère*, like the small two-decker battleships, started to fall from favour.

CLERMONT (SOMETIME STEAM BOAT, NORTH RIVER STEAMBOAT)

USA: 1807

Length: 133ft (40.5m)
Beam: 13ft (4m)
Depth: 7ft (2.1m)
Displacement: 100t
Rigging: two masts; square sail on main, gaff on mizzen
Complement: not known
Cargo: 90 passengers
Routes: Hudson River

Originally known as *Steam Boat*, then *North River Steamboat*, *Clermont* can claim to be the first steamship in regular service; she was built at Corlear's Hook, New York, in 1807 and designed by the prolific Robert Fulton. The engine was made by Boulton & Watt in England, and the vessel also had two masts – she was square-sailed on the main and had a gaff mizzen. Nicknamed 'Fulton's Folly', she actually operated very successfully between New York and Albany until 1814, when she was retired from service.

Outperforming both land coaches and river sloops, *Clermont* could carry up to 140 passengers; a second steamer joined her ranks in 1809.

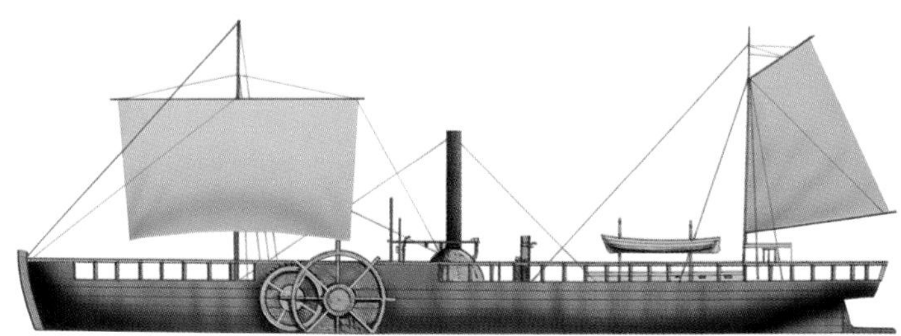

CALEDONIA (LATER DREADNOUGHT)

GB: 1808

Between 1790 and 1830, the sailing warship reached its ultimate state of development. Improvement was made to bow and stern design, increasing both seaworthiness and firing capacity from these positions. *Caledonia*, the Plymouth-built class leader of four three-decker 120-gun first rates, benefited from these advances. Hulked in 1856, she served as a hospital ship under the name of

Dreadnought until 1875, when she was broken up.

The most notable improvement in *Caledonia* was the disappearance of the old low beakhead bow that had characterized large warships for two centuries.

Length: 205ft (62.5m)
Beam: 53ft 6in (16.3m)
Depth: 23ft 2in (7.1m)
Displacement: 2602t burthen
Rigging: three masts; square rig
Armament: 32 32pdr, 34 24pdr, 34 18pdr, 20 12pdr guns
Complement: 875

Le Canot Impérial

FRANCE: 1810

Oared state barges have a long history, back to pre-classical times. Elaborately decorated and carved, they were used for conveying kings and dignitaries within harbours and anchorages and on rivers. This state barge was built at Antwerp in some haste for the conveyance of the Emperor Napoleon I, when he came to inspect his fleet in that city in 1810. A number of these state vessels have been preserved; this one now reposes at the Musée de la Marine in Paris.

Length: 56ft 5in (17.2m)
Beam: 11ft (3.4m)
Depth: 3ft 2in (0.9m)
Displacement: not known
Rigging: not applicable
Complement: 26 oarsmen plus officers
Routes: Antwerp harbour
Role: state barge

Sump

SWEDEN: 1810

Length: 40ft 6in (12.3m)
Beam: 14ft (4m)
Depth: not known
Displacement: 30t
Rigging: ketch
Complement: 2-3
Cargo: mixed
Routes: not known

In the 16th and 17th centuries trade in the Baltic continued to grow with a corresponding increase in the number of specialized vessels needed, ranging in size and capacity according to needs. The *Sump* was a relatively small single-masted wooden vessel suitable for the coastal trade, able to carry mixed cargo but with no deck covering to the cargo space. Aft was a small covered space for the crew of two or three. The type continued in service for many years.

The flat-roofed deck-house aft on the *Sump* acted as a deck for the helmsman.

L'Astrolabe (ex-Coquille)

FRANCE: 1811

Originally named *Coquille*, she was renamed in 1825 in memory of La Pérouse's frigate *L'Astrolabe*, lost on a voyage of exploration in the South Pacific in 1788.

The most notable of this corvette's three great voyages of exploration with the scientist Jules Dumont d'Urville was that to locate the South Magnetic Pole in 1837-40, which took her – although unarmoured against ice – to the Antarctic ice pack. She had already been twice to the South Seas and had brought back more data and specimens of natural history than any vessel before her. Her post-1840 history is unknown.

Length: not known
Beam: not known
Depth: not known
Displacement: 380t
Rigging: three masts; square rig
Complement: 79
Routes: South Seas; Antarctic
Role: exploration vessel

New Orleans

USA: 1811

Built at Pittsburgh by the innovator Robert Fulton, this sidewheel paddle steamer was the first steamboat to call at New Orleans, on 12 January 1812, having navigated the Ohio and picked up a cargo of cotton at Natchez. She then ran between New Orleans and Natchez for two years before hitting an underwater obstruction and sinking, near Baton Rouge, in July 1814.

New Orleans was almost certainly the first steamship on which a baby was born, to Mrs Livingston, wife of Fulton's partner, in April 1811.

Length: 116ft (35.4m)
Beam: 20ft (6.1m)
Depth: not known
Displacement: not known
Rigging: two masts
Machinery: sidewheels, steam
Complement: not known
Cargo: passengers, light freight
Routes: Mississippi River

Baltimore Clipper

USA: 1812

Built in 1812 at Baltimore, the *Chasseur* was the most famous of the 'Baltimore clippers' – fast, sharp-lined schooners carrying a very large amount of sail. As a US privateer, she took many prizes in 1812-15, including the 16-gun HMS *St Lawrence*. After a spell under brig rig, she was sold to the Spanish Navy as *Cazador*. Sold again in 1824, she may have become a slaver, but her subsequent career is uncertain.

Developed from the cutter, the typical Baltimore clipper was schooner-rigged with topsails and an extended driver on the mizzen.

Length: 85ft 9in (26.1m)
Beam: 26ft (7.9m)
Depth: 12ft 7in (3.8m)
Displacement: 356t
Rigging: two masts; fore-and-aft rig with square rig also on mainmast; stunsails, mizzen staysail, two jibs, fore-staysail
Armament: 16 12pdr guns
Complement: 115

Comet

GB: 1812

Length: 43ft 5in (13.3m)
Beam: 11ft 3in (3.4m)
Depth: 5ft 6in (1.7m)
Displacement: 23t
Rigging: square sail; yard mounted to funnel
Machinery: sidewheels, double-acting; 4hp
Complement: 6 (plus piper)
Cargo: 50 passengers
Routes: west coast of Scotland

The first European steamship in commercial service, *Comet* was launched in 1812. Her designer Henry Bell had her built as a speculative venture, and although her arrival stimulated the building of further steamships, *Comet* was not a commercial success, partly because the subsequent ships were able to improve on her design. She ran passengers on the west coast of Scotland and was wrecked in Argyll on 13 December 1820.

***Comet*'s engine, a vertical single-cylinder powerplant, is preserved at the Science Museum in London.**

Detroit

GB (NORTH AMERICAN COLONIES): 1813

The 19-gun sloop-of-war *Detroit* was flagship of the British squadron on Lake Erie in the British-American War of 1812; she was built at Amherstburg to support an invasion of the United States from the north. In a miniature but very real form of the traditional naval battle, with ships formed up in line, her squadron was defeated at Put-In Bay by the scratch-built US squadron of Commandant Oliver Perry. *Detroit* was taken as a prize along with the other five British vessels.

***Detroit*'s captain, Robert Barclay, was the first commander in British naval history to surrender an entire squadron.**

Length: 111ft 6in (34m)
Beam: 27ft 10in (8.5m)
Depth: 12ft (3.7m)
Displacement: 450t
Rigging: two masts; probably brig rig
Armament: 16 24pdr carronades, four 12pdr guns
Complement: not known

GENERAL PIKE

USA: 1813

Built in 1813 just 63 days by Henry Eckford at Sackett's Harbour, New Hampshire, and classed as a corvette, *General Pike* was in fact almost a small frigate. A flush-decked vessel of 26 guns, she served in the Lake Ontario Squadron, whose purpose was to hold the northeastern frontier of the United States against British invasion from Canada. She was one of the largest vessels in a fleet whose composition of light lake schooners and bigger ships proved difficult to manage tactically. *General Pike* survived the war but was not retained long in service, being sold some time prior to 1824.

Length: 145ft (44.1m)
Beam: 37ft (11.3m)
Depth: 15ft (4.6m)
Displacement: 900t
Rigging: three masts; square rig
Armament: 26 long 24pdr guns
Complement: not known

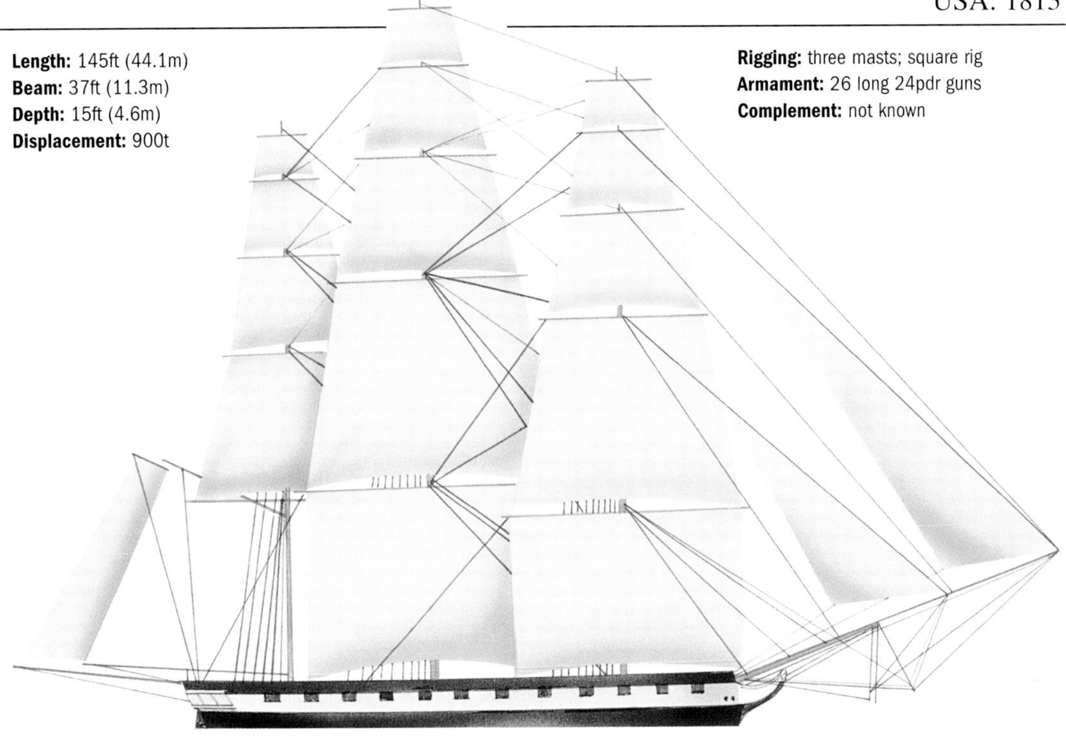

***General Pike* carried a very full suit of sails, including skysails on all three masts. Note also the extended mizen with its supported boom.**

JAVA

USA: 1813

Java and *Guerrière*, both built in 1813, were the largest frigates built by the United States; they were essentially improved versions of the *Constitution* design. The United States had played a leading part in the design of bigger frigates, but *Java* was not of significantly greater dimensions than her predecessors – at that time US ships had to clear numerous sandbanks and bars in the coastal anchorages. The gun arrangement was different, in that the spar deck, as the deck between forecastle and quarterdeck came to be called, carried no guns amidships; this was to avoid overstressing the hull. Thus *Java* was not fully 'double-banked', and this same layout was adopted in contemporary British frigates. In 1815, *Java* was sent to the Mediterranean under Captain Oliver Perry to ensure that the United States' treaty, against molestation of its merchant vessels, with the Barbary States was honoured. From 1817, she was kept in ordinary at Boston, but was recommissioned and returned to the Mediterranean in 1827. In 1831, she became receiving ship at Norfolk naval base, and served in that role until she was stricken from the list. She was broken up in 1842.

Length: 175ft (53.3m)
Beam: 44ft 6in (13.5m)
Depth: 22ft 6in (6.8m)
Displacement: 1511t
Rigging: three masts; square rig
Armament: 20 42pdr, 33 32pdr guns
Complement: 400

***Java*'s name was a reminder to the British of the fate of HMS *Java*, which had fallen victim to USS *Constitution* at the end of 1812.**

INDEPENDENCE

USA: 1814

Used as a receiving ship at San Francisco until 1914, the centenarian *Independence* was scrapped that same year.

Length: 190ft 8in (58.2m)
Beam: 54ft 6in (16.6m)
Depth: 24ft 3in (7.4m)
Displacement: 2257t
Rigging: three masts; square rig
Armament: 90 32pdr guns (later 54 guns)
Complement: 79

The first American ship of the line, the 74-gun *Independence* was one of three commissioned in 1814 to supplement the frigate fleet in the British-American War. The war was all but over on her completion, and she was briefly flagship of the Mediterranean Squadron in 1815. In 1835, she was converted to a 'razee frigate' of two decks and 54 guns and was much improved as a result, remaining in sea service until 1857.

NEWCASTLE

GB: 1813

The success of the big American frigates in the War of 1812 prompted the British Admiralty to build two even larger frigates in something of a hurry. These were *Newcastle* and *Leander*, each of 60 guns; they were the first 60-gun frigates in the Royal Navy. A third, HMS *Java*, followed in 1815. *Newcastle*, built of fir wood at Blackwall Yard, London, was 'double-banked', with two complete gundecks. Her dimensions were almost the same as those of USS *Constitution*. The soft-wood construction meant that she was not intended to last long; it also made her of lighter construction than the conventional man-of-war. In 1814, she was sent with *Leander* to join Commodore Collier's frigate squadron off New England and ran at 13 knots in pursuit of the US privateer *Neufchatel*, which was captured on 28 December 1814. *Newcastle* was hulked in 1824.

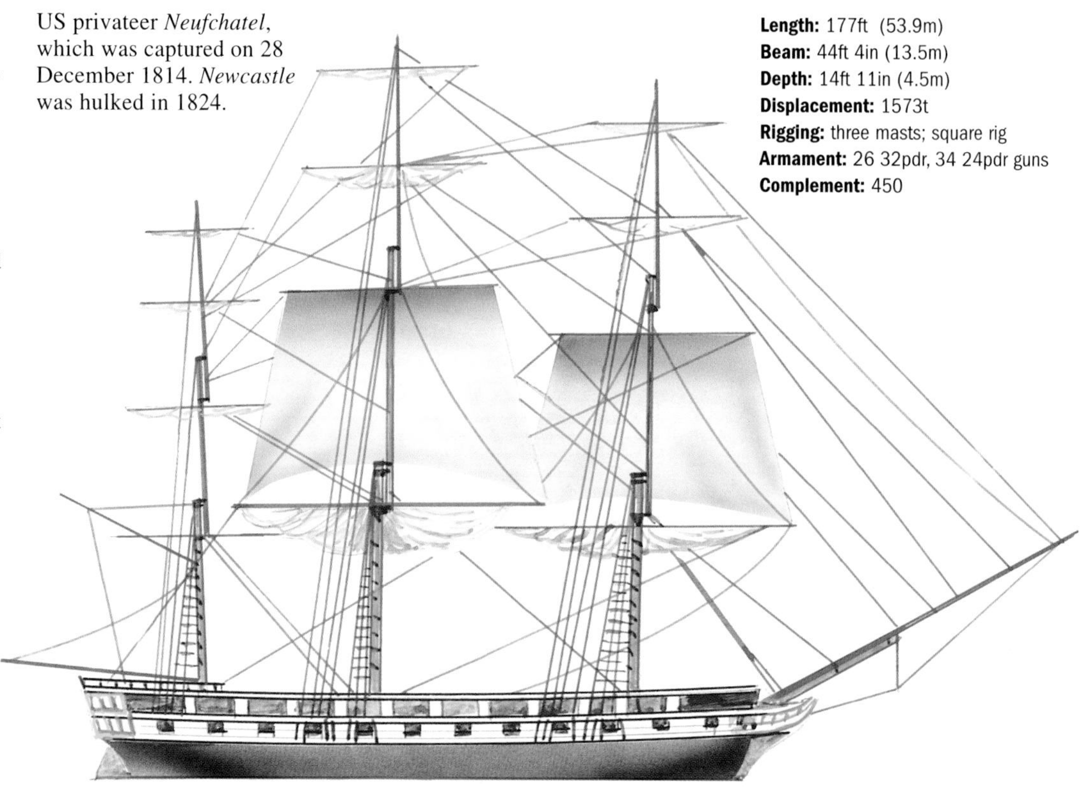

Ships of this kind were regarded as 'hostilities-only' vessels; they were not intended to form part of the peacetime establishment.

Length: 177ft (53.9m)
Beam: 44ft 4in (13.5m)
Depth: 14ft 11in (4.5m)
Displacement: 1573t
Rigging: three masts; square rig
Armament: 26 32pdr, 34 24pdr guns
Complement: 450

DEMOLOGOS

USA: 1815

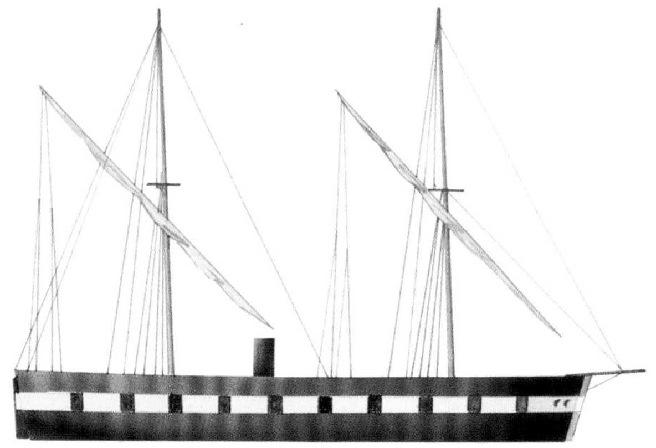

Length: 156ft (47.5m)
Beam: 56ft (17.1m)
Depth: 11ft (3.4m)
Displacement: 2475t
Rigging: steadying sails
Machinery: centre wheel, inclined
Armament: 24 32pdr guns
Complement: 200

The *Demologos* has also been recorded as 'Fulton the First'. She was the last ship designed by Robert Fulton.

The US Navy's first steamship has been variously described as a floating battery and a steam frigate. She was double-ended and double-ruddered, with a twin-pontoon hull and a single paddle wheel mounted between. Her wide gundeck supported 24 heavy guns, but she was completed after the 1812 War was over; although she was satisfactory on test she never saw action. The engine was removed in 1821. On 6 June 1829, she blew up at Brooklyn Navy Yard.

ELIZABETH

RUSSIA: 1815

Length: 72ft (21.9m)
Beam: 15ft 9in (4.8m)
Depth: 5ft 6in (1.7m)
Displacement: 38t
Rigging: not applicable
Machinery: sidewheels, side lever; 20hp
Complement: 3
Cargo: passengers, light freight
Routes: Neva Estuary

Charles Baird, a Scot living in St Petersburg, converted a wooden barge into Russia's first steamboat, the *Elizabeth*; she went into regular service on the Neva River between St Petersburg and its port of Kronstadt on the Gulf of Finland. Baird built a side-lever engine that could drive the sidewheels at up to six knots; the vessel had a brick 'funnel'. Other steam craft followed, since the wide rivers in Russia, as in the United States, were favourable operating areas for early steamboats.

This was the first paddle vessel to have self-feathering paddle blades, ensuring vertical entry into the water.

DELAWARE

USA: 1817

Built at Norfolk Navy Yard in 1817, *Delaware* was one of a class of six ships of the line with three decks of guns, intended to provide a heavyweight battleship element in what had been largely a frigate fleet. Expensive to keep in service, she saw little action during her career. On 20 April 1861, she was one of the ships destroyed by fire in the Confederate raid on the Norfolk Navy Yard.

Length: 196ft 3in (59.8m)
Beam: 53ft (16.2m)
Depth: 21ft 7in (6.5m)
Displacement: 2602t
Rigging: three masts; square rig
Armament: 90 guns
Complement: 820

In European terms she would have been classed as a second rate, with 90 guns; but *Delaware* was the largest US warship of her time.

IRIS

FRANCE: 1818

Iris was a French lugger successfully used in smuggling; she carried two lugsails for easy handling by a crew of four or five. The hold had false bulkheads plus an additional lining standing out from the hull, behind which was hidden contraband. More could be carried beneath a false bottom or beneath the ballast of stone or iron. Some luggers, including the *Iris*, were fast on a wind and could often leave the revenue cutter behind in a long chase, as they could change tack more easily. *Iris* was eventually captured in December 1819 after successfully landing a large cargo earlier in the day on the South Coast after a fast run from Boulogne.

At one time during the 1800s, 20,000 people were employed in smuggling in England, with ships like the *Iris* playing a prime role in the trade.

Length: 60ft (18.3m)
Beam: 5ft 6in (1.7m)
Depth: not known
Displacement: 50t
Rigging: two lugsails
Complement: 4-5
Cargo: contraband
Routes: France-England

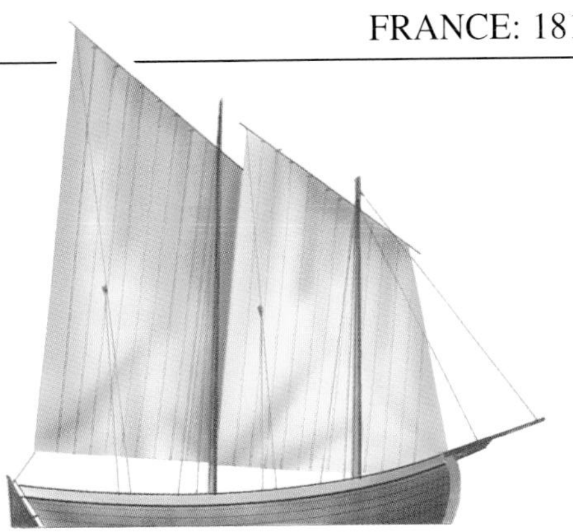

SAVANNAH

USA: 1818

Savannah was a full-rigged ship whose engine was essentially an auxiliary. However, although she did not use her steam power exclusively, she was certainly the first steam-powered ship to cross the Atlantic Ocean and also the first to navigate the Baltic Sea. The idea of a transatlantic steamer was conceived by Captain Moses Rogers, backed by the city of Savannah. Rogers purchased the ship on the stocks at Fickett & Crockett's yard, New York, and arranged for the engine to be installed. The first voyage was from New York to Savannah in March–April 1819. It proved difficult to get either cargo or passenger orders, and the Atlantic voyage was made without either. With Rogers as captain, she left Savannah on 22 May 1819 and sailed for Liverpool. Westbound ships observed her under steam, and indeed off Ireland her smoke was taken to mean she was on fire, and a revenue cutter was sent to her

This model clearly shows *Savannah's* distinctive angled funnel and lightweight paddle wheels.

Length: 109ft (33.2m)
Beam: 25ft 10in (7.9m)
Depth: 12ft (3.7m)
Displacement: 320t
Rigging: three masts; rig not known
Machinery: not known
Complement: 20
Cargo: general freight, 24 passengers
Routes: intended for Atlantic routes; served US east coast

aid. From Liverpool she proceeded to Helsingør and then Stockholm, where the enthusiastic King Charles XIV of Sweden offered to buy her in exchange for a cargo of hemp and iron, which Rogers declined. Rogers took *Savannah* on across the Baltic Sea to Kronstadt, the port of St Petersburg, but the Russians did not wish to buy her. By 30 November 1819, the vessel was back at Savannah. Efforts to interest the US government in buying the ship came to nothing; her owning company went bankrupt and she was bought in August 1820 by the New York captain Nathan Holdridge, who took out the engines and ran her as a sail packet between New York and Savannah. On 5 November 1821, she ran aground on Fire Island in New York Bay and became a total loss.

ANCHOR HOY

USA AND OTHERS: 1820

The anchor hoy was equipped with two capstans to share the weight of the heavy anchor.

Length: 61ft (18.6m)
Beam: 20ft (6.1m)
Depth: 8ft (2.4m)
Displacement: not known
Rigging: single mast with topmast and trysail mast; fore-and-aft rig
Complement: 4
Cargo: anchors
Routes: naval anchorages

Originally and mostly coastal traders, hoys found a specialized use as service vessels to big naval ships. The anchor hoy was used in naval anchorages to transport the massive anchors required by ships of the line. It could also be used to warp big ships from their moorings when they could not use their sails. The mainsail is mounted on a trysail mast, as the mainmast was fitted with tackle used in hoisting the anchors.

BEAGLE

GB: 1820

The *Beagle* belonged to the largest class of British sailing warships; her third mast and barque rig was unusual but not exceptional.

Launched at Woolwich Dockyard as a 10-gun brig of the Cherokee class, *Beagle* was converted almost immediately to barque rig, which she then retained. Although her name is always associated with that of Charles Darwin, the ship had already made a major voyage to South America in 1826-30 – and left her name on the Beagle Channel south of Tierra del Fuego – before the voyage of 1831-36 under Captain Fitzroy, on which the young Darwin was so often seasick and made such momentous discoveries. Survey work was one of the tasks of the class, and *Beagle* carried 22 chronometers and a range of equipment which Magellan could hardly have dreamed of. The circumnavigation took her up and down the South American coast, through the Strait of Magellan and up the west of South America to the Galápagos Islands, then across the Pacific to New Zealand and Australia and home via Cape Town and St Helena. Darwin's observations laid the foundation for his revolutionary treatise *The Origin of Species*, published in 1859. In 1837, the *Beagle* sailed again for Australia, surveying the west and southeastern coasts before moving to the north coast in 1839. In 1843, she returned to Britain and was paid off as a naval vessel in 1845. Acquired by the Revenue Service, she was deployed as a permanently moored anti-smuggling station, Beagle Watch Vessel, on the Essex coast. Her career came to an end in 1870, when she was broken up.

Length: 90ft (27.4m)
Beam: 24ft 6in (7.4m)
Depth: 11ft (3.4m)
Displacement: 235t
Rigging: three masts; barque rig, square sails on fore and main, spanker on mizzen
Armament: 10 guns (reduced to six as survey ship)
Complement: 70
Routes: various, including circumnavigation

AARON MANBY

FRANCE: 1821

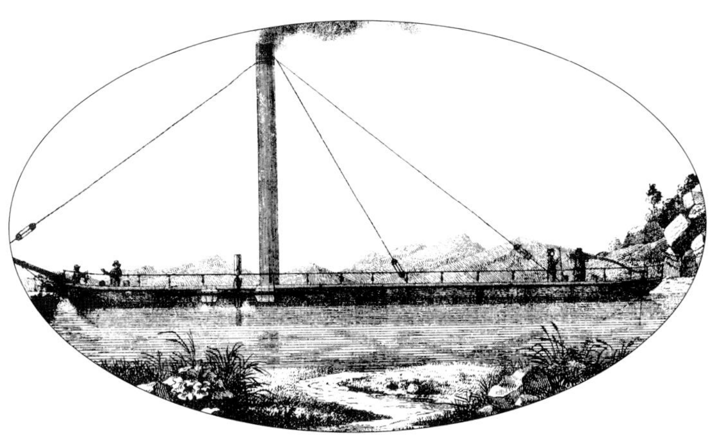

The first iron ship to venture into the open sea, she was built in sections at the Horseley Ironworks, Staffordshire, and assembled on the Thames; she steamed to Le Havre on 10 June 1822. She worked as a Seine River steamer for 10 years, then was sold and transferred to work on the Loire above Nantes. The hull was formed from iron plates .25in thick, fastened to iron ribs; her best speed was seven knots. She was finally broken up in 1855.

With a funnel 47ft (14.3m) tall, and paddle wheels 12ft (3.7m) across, *Aaron Manby* was a distinctive sight in 1821.

Length: 120ft (36.6m)
Beam: 17ft 3in (5.2m)
Depth: 3ft 6in (1.1m)
Displacement: 116t
Rigging: not applicable
Machinery: sidewheels, steam; 30hp
Complement: 4
Routes: Seine and Loire rivers, France

JAMES WATT

GB: 1821

Length: 104ft 11in (31.9m)
Beam: 25ft 6in (7.7m)
Depth: 16ft 5in (5m)
Displacement: 448t
Rigging: three masts; square-rigged on fore and main, gaffsail on mizzen
Machinery: sidewheels, steam; 100hp
Complement: not known
Cargo: passengers, light goods
Routes: Edinburgh-London

On her launch the largest steamship afloat, *James Watt* was built to serve the busy and competitive coastal route between Leith (for Edinburgh) and London, carrying passengers and cargo. In pre-railway days, ships were the swiftest way between the two cities, and this steamer was built with finely drawn bow lines to help her speed: this, plus reliability, attracted plenty of custom. The vessel's engines developed 100hp, and her paddle-wheel diameter was 18ft (5.5m).

***James Watt* was the first steamship to be entered in Lloyd's Register of Shipping, an indication that steam power was here to stay.**

MONTEBELLO

FRANCE: 1822

Designed by the eminent engineer Baron Sané, Inspector-General of the French Navy, and launched on 6 December 1822, *Montebello* was one of a class of three 120-gun ships built over a 20-year period; the others were *Souverain* (1819) and *Friedland* (1840). Her service was chiefly in the Mediterranean Fleet. In the Crimean campaign she was vice-flagship, participating in the bombardment of Fort Kinburn on 17 October 1855. She was stricken in 1867.

In 1852, a 140hp Indret auxiliary screw engine was fitted to the *Montebello*.

Length: 207ft 4in (62.2m)
Beam: 57ft 5in (17.5m)
Depth: not known
Displacement: 5005t
Rigging: three masts; square rig
Machinery: single screw, auxiliary steam; 140hp
Armament: 114 guns
Complement: not known

COLUMBUS

CANADA: 1823

Columbus was one of two great raft ships built in Quebec. They were packed solid with timber and designed to make the trip to Europe and there to be broken up for the timber from which they were built. When launched, *Columbus* already had 4000t of timber stowed and a further 2300t of timber was placed on board when the sailing rig was positioned; since the ship was also

to be dismantled for her timber, the estimated total was about 10,000t. *Columbus*'s midship hull section was rectangular, with the deck beams jutting out of the side. There was no sheer to the hull, and living accommodation for the crew of 60 was primitive. It was decided that the vessel would return for another lucrative cargo, but on the return journey she sank in heavy weather.

One of the most unusual vessels ever built, *Columbus* was a massive ship-shaped raft fitted with sails. By the time she reached the Thames there was 18ft (5.5m) of water in the hold and she was kept afloat only by her own cargo of timber.

Length: 301ft (91.7m)
Beam: 51ft 5in (15.6m)
Depth: not known
Displacement: 3690t
Rigging: not known
Complement: 60
Cargo: timber
Routes: Canada-Europe

ASIA

GB: 1824

Length: 196ft 1in (59.7m)
Beam: 51ft 5in (15.6m)
Depth: 22ft 6in (6.8m)
Displacement: 2279t
Rigging: three masts; square rig
Armament: 84 guns
Complement: 700

Asia was one of three two-decked ships of the line, with hulls of teak wood, built at Bombay Dockyard, India, between 1816 and 1828; they were classed as second/third rates and were based on a modified version of the design of HMS *Formidable* but ultimately on the captured French *Canopus*. *Asia* served as flagship to Admiral Codrington in the Mediterranean, and fought at the Battle of Navarino on 20 October 1827, at which the Turkish-Egyptian fleet was destroyed. She was hulked in 1859.

By this time, British ships benefited from design improvements, including the rounded stern, introduced by Sir Robert Seppings, Surveyor of the Navy from 1813 to 1832.

CARL XIV JOHAN

SWEDEN: 1824

Launched as a sailing man-of-war, this two-decker was converted to steam propulsion in the mid 1850s. Impressed by new British steam warships such as HMS *Agamemnon*, the Swedes based the conversion work on British models, but these were deeper-hulled and the rebuilt ship was not a success. *Carl XIV Johan* was scrapped in 1867.

The Baltic Sea's shallow waters and frequent ice-cover required ships of rounder and shallower underwater profile than other seas.

Length: 176ft 11in (54m)
Beam: 48ft 2in (14m)
Depth: c19ft (5.9m)
Displacement: 2600t
Rigging: three masts; square-rigged
Machinery: single-screw steam engine
Armament: 68 guns

KENT

GB: 1825

Built at the Blackwall Yard, London, and launched in 1819, *Kent* was amongst the largest of the British East Indiamen. Whilst transporting members of the 31st Regiment to India, including wives and children, someone dropped a lamp in the hold and the vessel caught fire. At the time she was sailing through in a storm in the Bay of Biscay and the fire could not be controlled; 547 people were rescued and 82 perished.

The fate of *Kent* was a popular subject for 19th century painters and lithographers.

Length: 171ft (52.1m)
Beam: 42ft 9in (13m)
Depth: 31ft 6in (9.6m) below upper deck
Displacement: 1315t
Rigging: three masts; square rig
Armament: 38 guns
Complement: 133
Cargo: general goods, military stores, Indian products
Routes: London-India

CURAÇAO (EX-CALPE)

THE NETHERLANDS: 1826

The first steamship to work the route from Europe to South America, *Curaçao* had a funnel almost as high as her mizzen mast. Launched at Dover, England, as *Calpe*, she was immediately sold to the Netherlands and became the warship *Curaçao*, her function being to run between Rotterdam and the Dutch Caribbean colony of Surinam. From 1829 to 1839, she was stationed in home waters but returned to the Caribbean from 1840 until 1846; she was scrapped in 1850.

***Curaçao* was the first steam-powered vessel in the Dutch Navy; lightly armed, she was a supply vessel rather than a true warship.**

Length: 130ft 6in (39.8m)
Beam: 26ft 9in (8.2m)
Depth: 13ft 6in (4.1m)
Displacement: 438t
Rigging: three masts; barque rig
Machinery: side lever; 100hp
Armament: two 12pdr carronades
Complement: 42
Routes: Netherlands-Surinam

EREBUS

GB: 1826

Launched at Pembroke Dockyard, Wales, as a mortar vessel, *Erebus* was refitted as a polar exploration ship, presumably because of her reinforced hull. On 30 September 1839, with HMS *Terror* and under the command of James Clark Ross, she sailed on a scientific voyage, chiefly to study the earth's magnetism and locate the South Magnetic Pole. Passing through pack ice, the expedition reached the Ross Sea and eventually the great Antarctic ice shelf. After wintering at Hobart, they returned to the Antarctic, suffering many perils in ice-filled and stormy waters; they eventually returned to England on 4 September 1843. In 1844, an auxiliary engine and screw propeller were fitted to both *Erebus* and *Terror*, and on 19 May 1845, under Sir John Franklin, they sailed in search of the Northwest Passage to the Pacific. They were last seen in August of that year. The ships became icebound and the entire expedition perished during 1847-48.

On 22 April 1848, the surviving crew of the stranded *Erebus* abandoned the vessel and attempted to march 600 miles (965km) overland to the nearest settlement.

Length: 105ft (32m)
Beam: 28ft 6in (8.7m)
Depth: 13ft 10in (4.2m)
Displacement: 372t
Rigging: three masts; square rig
Machinery: single screw, auxiliary steam; 20hp
Armament: one 13in (330mm), one 10in (254mm) mortars; eight 24 pdr, two 6pdr guns (removed on conversion)
Complement: 67
Routes: Antarctic; Arctic

UNION

USA: 1828

Length: 80ft 2in (24.4m)
Beam: 23ft 8in (7.1m)
Depth: 6ft 6in (2m)
Displacement: not known
Rigging: two masts; schooner rig with topsails
Armament: one pivot gun amidships; two carronades each side plus centrally mounted pivot gun
Complement: not known

In the 1820s, US designers put much more thought into schooner and other small-ship design than into frigate design, and the result was some very smart vessels. The plan for this adjustable-centre-board schooner was drawn in 1828, and *Union* was launched in the same year. Lightly armed, she was built for speed and manoeuvrability, with chasing and interception her prime duties.

The two centreboards were fixed to pivots for raising and lowering, one before and one abaft the mainmast.

DOS AMIGOS (LATER FAIR ROSAMOND)

USA: 1830

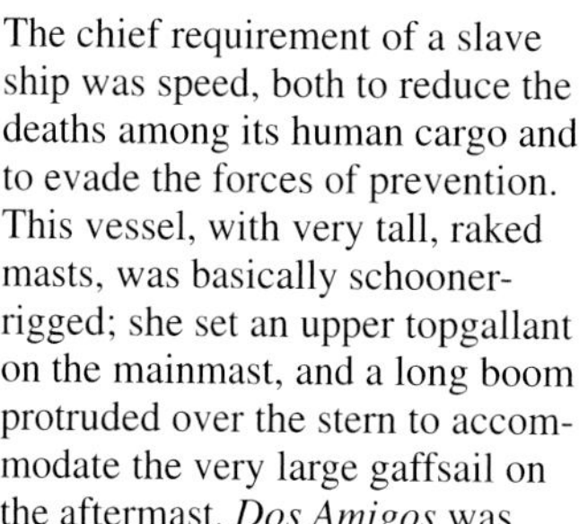

The chief requirement of a slave ship was speed, both to reduce the deaths among its human cargo and to evade the forces of prevention. This vessel, with very tall, raked masts, was basically schooner-rigged; she set an upper topgallant on the mainmast, and a long boom protruded over the stern to accommodate the very large gaffsail on the aftermast. *Dos Amigos* was captured by a British naval ship, renamed *Fair Rosamond* and used to combat the vicious trade in which she had participated.

Slave-ship diagrams show how designers worked to ensure that the human cargo was as closely packed as possible.

Length: 90ft (27.4m)
Beam: 23ft (7m)
Depth: 10ft 4in (3.1m)
Displacement: 172t
Rigging: two masts; topsail schooner rig
Complement: 10
Cargo: slaves
Routes: West Africa/West Indies-Southern USA

MORRIS

USA: 1830

A product of the New York Navy Yard in 1830, *Morris* was a very swift 'clipper schooner'. From the start of the 19th century, the Americans had a reputation for building the finest schooners, and much thought and planning went into her design to ensure that she was the best interception and chasing ship of her time. *Morris* was amongst the first US government vessels to be fitted with a geared steering wheel. As built, she was pierced to carry 14 guns, but as a cutter she carried only six. The design was a highly successful one, and *Morris* replaced earlier designs for US revenue cutters. However, subsequent cutters based on her lines had a straight stem rather than her curved naval-style stem.

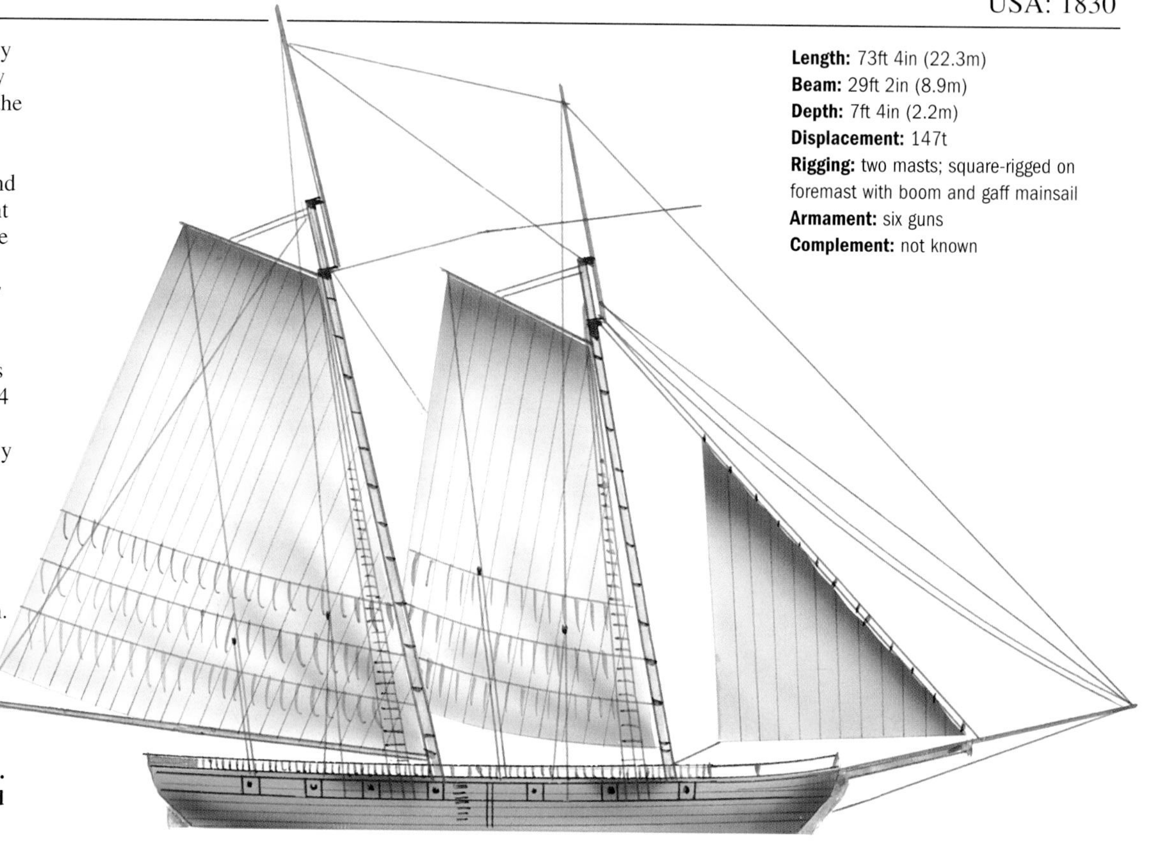

A game of 'hounds and hares' was played, for high stakes, between revenue cutters and contraband runners. But official technology produced the best ships.

Length: 73ft 4in (22.3m)
Beam: 29ft 2in (8.9m)
Depth: 7ft 4in (2.2m)
Displacement: 147t
Rigging: two masts; square-rigged on foremast with boom and gaff mainsail
Armament: six guns
Complement: not known

THAMES BARGE

GB: 1830

The Thames Estuary was always the busiest waterway in England, and any period picture shows a wide range of small shipping. Ever-present is the Thames barge, with its big spritsail. This example is more elaborately rigged than usual, with a square foresail and topsail; a staysail has been rigged between topmast and gaff. Most would have only the mainsail and mizzen spritsail.

A barge such as this would venture well beyond the Thames, sailing north to Ipswich and Yarmouth or south and east to the north Kent ports.

Length: 77ft (23.5m)
Beam: 16ft (4.9m)
Depth: 6ft (1.8m)
Displacement: 140t
Rigging: single mast with square sail and spritsail; short sternmast with spritsail
Complement: 2
Cargo: sand, lime, lumber, bulk goods
Routes: Thames Estuary and adjacent coast

ROYAL WILLIAM

GB: 1831

A wooden-hulled vessel built at Liverpool, England, by William & Thomas Wilson, *Royal William* was one of the first ships to be fitted with watertight bulkheads; they were four in number and made of iron. The ship went into service on the Liverpool-Canada run in 1833 and operated successfully. In a letter of 4 October 1835 to the London *Times*, following various marine disasters, C W Williams of Wilson's asserted the need for higher shipbuilding standards, noting of the watertight bulkheads: 'this division fell so well in with the business of the several parts of the vessel as to give it at once precedence'. In 1839, *Royal William* collided outside Liverpool with the steamer *Tagus*. One compartment flooded, but the vessel stayed afloat and was duly saved and repaired for service. She was broken up in 1888 at Dublin, Ireland, where she had been used as a storage hulk for some years.

Another *Royal William*, built at Quebec, had operated on the Canada run a year or two earlier. She was sold to the Spanish Navy as *Isabella Segunda* in 1834.

Length: 175ft (53.3m)
Beam: 27ft (8.2m)
Depth: 17ft 6in (5.3m)
Displacement: 564t
Rigging: three masts; barquentine rig
Machinery: single screw, steam; 200hp
Complement: not known
Cargo: general goods, passengers
Routes: Liverpool-Canada

RHADAMANTHUS

GB: 1832

Length: 175ft (53.3m)
Beam: 27ft 6in (8.4m)
Depth: not known
Displacement: 813t
Rigging: not applicable
Machinery: sidewheels, steam; 220hp
Armament: four guns
Complement: not known

Steam vessels were often used as tugs, in sheltered anchorages or becalmed situations.

Built at Devonport Naval Dockyard, this wooden-hulled paddle sloop, under the command of Commander George Evans, was the first British-built steamer to cross the Atlantic, stopping en route at the Azores to take on coal. She was also the first Royal Navy steamship to operate in the Americas, being based with the West Indian Squadron between 1832 and 1835. On her return, she joined the fleet in home waters; *Rhadamanthus* was broken up at Sheerness in February 1864.

BEAVER

GB: 1836

Length: 100ft 10in (30.75m)
Beam: 20ft (6.1m)
Depth: 8ft 6in (2.6m)
Displacement: 187t
Rigging: two masts; brigantine rig
Machinery: sidewheels, side lever
Cargo: timber, stores, baled furs
Armament: four brass cannon
Complement: 31
Routes: Pacific coast

Ordered by the Hudson's Bay Company in 1834, the London-built *Beaver* went under sail power across the Pacific to her operating base at Fort Vancouver (now Vancouver, Oregon), where her engine and paddle wheels were assembled and fitted. The first steamer in the North Pacific, she worked as a cargo boat, survey vessel and tugboat, up as far as Sitka, Alaska, for various owners until she was wrecked in 1888 in Burrard Inlet, Vancouver.

Efforts to salvage and preserve *Beaver* came to nothing, although some parts were recovered and the wreck has been mapped.

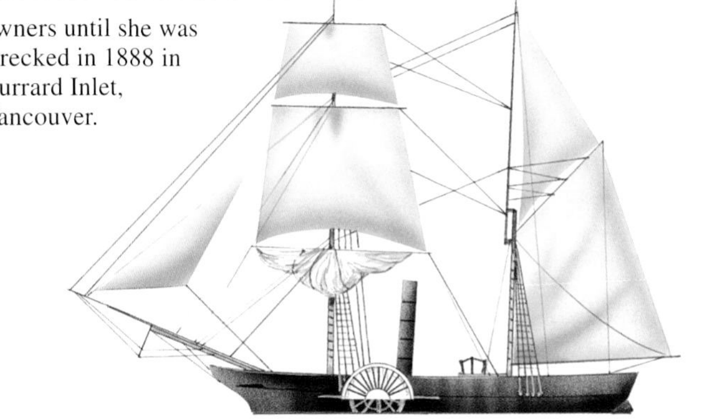

GREAT WESTERN

GB: 1837

I K Brunel's first steamer, Bristol-built, was in effect a maritime extension of the Great Western Railway, which he had engineered – fast train to Bristol and thence steamer, a combination that provided the fastest route between London and New York. *Great Western* also enshrined a crucial theoretical principle first enunciated by Brunel: the capacity of a ship is a factor of the cube of its dimensions, but the power required increases only as the square of those dimensions. This was to refute those who said that any large steamship would need all its capacity simply to carry its own coal. Flush-decked and with virtually no superstructure, *Great Western* was intended to carry 148 first-class passengers. The ship was engined in London and on her first voyage down the Thames, lack of insulation caused the deck above the boiler to catch fire. On 8 April 1838, she left Bristol for New York, crossing the Atlantic in 15 days with ample fuel reserves left. A further engine-room accident on arrival caused the death of the engineer, but *Great Western* went on to make almost 70 crossings. Her best time was 12 days and 9 hours eastbound. From 1846, now sold by the GWR to the Royal Steam Packet Company, she was on the Southampton-West Indies route. On the outbreak of the Crimean War, *Great Western* was requisitioned by the Admiralty as a troopship. By this time, despite her strength of hull, she was an old-fashioned vessel. She was broken up on the Thames in 1856-57.

Length: 236ft (71.9m)
Beam: 35ft 4in (10.7m)
Depth: 16ft 6in (5.1m)
Displacement: 2300t
Rigging: four masts; foremast square-rigged, remainder fore-and-aft-rigged
Complement: not known
Cargo: passengers, general cargo
Routes: transatlantic

The opportunism of Liverpool shipowners, who thrust the Irish steam packet *Sirius* into service, prevented *Great Western* from being the first regular Atlantic steamer.

PENNSYLVANIA

USA: 1837

Pennsylvania was the biggest sailing warship built by the United States. Her construction at Norfolk Navy Yard lasted from 1822 to 1837, and her designer was Samuel Humphreys. No US yard had built a first rate before, and Humphreys made use of plans from both Spain and Great Britain. This probably explains the archaic beakhead prow fitted to the ship, a feature no longer seen on new European warships by that time. The flush spar deck was, however, an American feature taken from frigate design. *Pennsylvania*'s great dimensions included a main mast 132ft (40.2m) high, with a main yard 110ft (33.5m) across. The intention behind *Pennsylvania* and her sisters was to possess ships that could outgun the standard line-of-battle 74s and act as blockade-busters in the event of war. It is likely that considerations of national prestige played a part as well. Despite her size, *Pennsylvania* had a considerable turn of speed when properly trimmed, but several officers expressed critical views, including one that she was 'cumbersome, leewardly and crank'. American officers, used to smaller and more dashing vessels, without the high freeboard and deep draught of a first rate, may not have made the most of the big ship's potential. In the event, *Pennsylvania* saw little in the way of active service. At the beginning of the American Civil War, she was lying in the Norfolk Navy Yard, and in the Confederate raid on 20 April 1861, she was set on fire and destroyed with a number of other ships.

Length: 210ft (64m)
Beam: 56ft 9in (17.3m)
Depth: 24ft 3in (7.4m)
Displacement: 3104t
Rigging: three masts; square rig
Armament: 104 32pdr guns; 16 8in (203mm) shell guns fitted 1840
Complement: 800

***Pennsylvania* was part of a programme of eight ships of the line, of which six were completed; the last of these, USS *Alabama*, was not launched until 1864.**

SIRIUS

GB: 1837

This Scottish-built paddle steamship, launched at Leith, was the first to cross the Atlantic under sustained steam power. Her engines had Samuel Hall's patent condensers fitted, preventing the boilers from caking up with sea salt, although these were only partially successful through lack of suitable lubrication. Although intended for work between the Irish city of Cork and London, she was chartered by a rival company to steal the thunder from Brunel's *Great Western* and snatch the honour of making the first all-steam Atlantic crossing. Having started in London, *Sirius* left Cork on 4 April 1838 and made New York in 18 days and 10 hours. Having departed three days later, *Great Western* arrived the day after *Sirius*. *Sirius* made one more transatlantic round voyage in July 1838, then returned to her short-sea routes. She was wrecked in Ballycotton Bay, off the south coast of Ireland, on 29 January 1847, whilst on the way from Glasgow to Cork.

Length: 208ft (63.4m)
Beam: 25ft 10in (7.9m)
Depth: 15ft (4.6m)
Displacement: 703t
Rigging: two masts; brig rig
Machinery: sidewheels, side lever
Complement: 35
Cargo: 60 passengers, light freight
Routes: transatlantic, Irish Sea routes

On the outward Atlantic run, *Sirius* made an average speed of 6.7 knots, compared with *Great Western*'s 8.8 knots.

MERLIN

GB: 1838

This small British survey ship, built at Pembroke Dock and classed as a 'paddle packet', was converted to a gunboat and despatched to the Black Sea during the Crimean War of 1853–56. In June 1855, she became the first ship ever to be hit by a floating mine. The mine was part of the Russian coastal defences, and although it did minimal damage the Admiralty was greatly concerned about this new weapon. *Merlin* returned safely and was sold in May 1863.

Numerous technical drawings were made of *Merlin*'s wooden hull and the effects of the mine upon it.

Length: 175ft (53.3m)
Beam: 33ft (10m)
Depth: not known
Displacement: 890t
Rigging: not applicable
Machinery: sidewheels, steam
Armament: one 50pdr gun
Complement: not known

ALECTO

GB: 1839

Length: 164ft (50m)
Beam: 32ft 9in (10m)
Depth: 12ft 6in (3.8m)
Displacement: 795t
Rigging: three masts; brigantine rig
Machinery: sidewheels, direct action; 280hp
Armament: not known
Complement: not known

Classed as a paddle sloop, the wooden-hulled, brigantine-rigged *Alecto* was built at Chatham Dockyard and served six years with the Mediterranean Fleet. In March and April 1845, she took part in a series of trials against HMS *Rattler*, a vessel of similar size and power but screw-driven, culminating in the famous 'tug-of-war' in which *Rattler* towed *Alecto* backwards at a speed of around 2.8 knots, demonstrating the superiority of screw propulsion and ensuring its future use.

***Alecto* went on to do 20 years of honourable service, mostly on the American and African stations, and was scrapped in 1865.**

NEMESIS

GB: 1839

Ordered by the British East India Company and launched at Birkenhead, *Nemesis* was a paddle-propelled gunboat intended for service on the Chinese coast and estuaries. Sailing for China in 1840, she was the first iron ship to round the Cape of Good Hope. In the Opium War of 1839–42, she was active in bombarding shore forts, sustaining little damage herself. From 1843 to 1852, she served in the Indian Ocean; she was sold in the latter year.

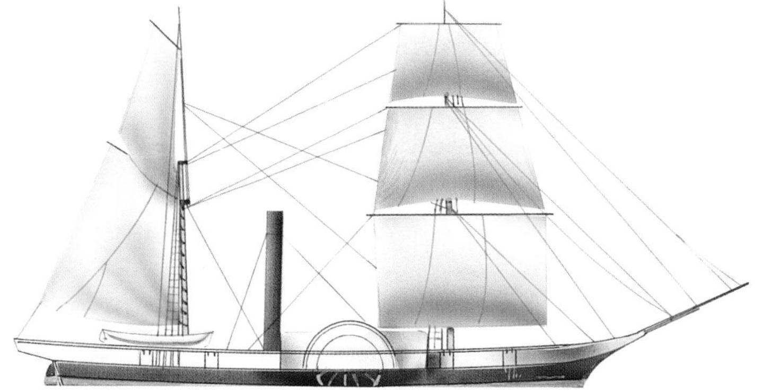

Length: 184ft (56m)
Beam: 29ft (8.8m)
Depth: 6ft (1.8m)
Displacement: 660t
Rigging: two masts; brig rig
Machinery: sidewheels, steam
Armament: two 32pdr, four 6pdr guns
Complement: 60

The first real iron warship, *Nemesis* was one of the first vessels to carry a compass corrected for the effect of her iron hull.

BRIGHTON HOG BOAT

GB: 1840

The hog boat's tiller presumably was made with an elbow to clear the mast, rather as those of some earlier ships had to clear the sternpost.

This was a type local to the south English ports of Brighton, Hove and Shoreham and was used for inshore fishing and freight traffic up the shallow tidal rivers of the region. Round and double-ended and fitted with a leeboard, the Brighton hog boat's typical features were the droopy bowsprit and short sprit-booms fitted some way up the masts, with an outrigger, or bumkin, to stay the stern-mounted mizzen. Another characteristic of the hog boat was its flat bottom, enabling it to settle on sand of level mud-flats at low water.

Length: 28ft (8.5m)
Beam: 12ft (3.7m)
Depth: 3ft (0.9m)
Displacement: 20t
Rigging: two masts; fore-and-aft spritsail rig
Complement: two
Cargo: fish
Routes: Sussex coast, England

BRITANNIA (LATER BARBAROSSA)

GB: 1840

One of the first ships built for the Cunard Line, Britannia was launched on the Clyde in 1840. She was the first steamer to carry the mail from Britain to the United States, making her first crossing in 12 days and 10 hours. In 1849, she was sold to Prussia, fitted with nine heavy 68pdr guns and renamed *Barbarossa*. Later used as a floating barracks and guardship, the vessel's final role was as a target ship, with engine removed. In 1880, she was sunk at Kiel but salvaged for scrap.

Length: 207ft (63m)
Beam: 34ft 6in (10.5m)
Depth: not known
Displacement: 1154t
Rigging: three masts; barque rig
Machinery: sidewheels, steam
Complement: not known
Cargo: passengers
Routes: transatlantic

Cunard's early disposal of *Britannia* reflects the speed of steamer development in the rapidly growing transatlantic passenger trade.

HUMBER KEEL

GB: 1840

A double-ended barge, its hull similar to that of the Thames barge, the Humber keel had a simple rig that required minimal crew and attention. The pole mast could be lowered, enabling the vessel to work up the Humber and into the rivers and canals of industrial Yorkshire. Leeboards were fitted to help it manoeuvre in the wider Humber. A topsail was also sometimes fitted.

Towing bitts were fitted in the bows to enable the Humber keel to negotiate the increasing number of narrow inland waterways where sails would be impracticable.

Length: 60ft (18.3m)
Beam: 15ft 6in (4.7m)
Depth: 7ft (2.1m)
Displacement: 100t
Rigging: pole mast; square sail
Complement: 2
Cargo: barrelled and baled goods, bricks, stone
Routes: Humber Estuary and adjacent canals

JANE GIFFORD

GB: 1840

From about 1840 the flow of migrants from the United Kingdom steadily increased being carried in small bluff-towed slow sailing ships that also carried general cargo to Australia and New Zealand. Amongst the first of the migrant ships was *Jane Gifford* which, after landing her human cargo, and because of a full return cargo that could not be obtained in the newly established colonies, would often sail on to the Far East or India to pick up a return cargo. By the 1860s and 1870s sufficient trade became available to set up regular lines serving Australia.

Jane Gifford in 1842. The hold carried the migrants plus cargo divided off. Officers were berthed aft with crew forward.

Length: 117ft (35m)
Beam: 31ft (9.4m)
Depth: not known
Displacement: 500t
Rigging: ship
Complement: not known
Cargo: migrants, mixed cargo

NORFOLK WHERRY

GB: 1840

Length: 65ft (19.8m)
Beam: 17ft 9in (5.4m)
Depth: 3ft (0.9m)
Displacement: 50t
Rigging: single mast; gaffsail
Complement: 2
Cargo: farm produce, wood, general cargo
Routes: Norfolk Broads

The word 'wherry' dates back to the 15th century, when it meant a small, oared passenger boat; by the 19th century it was largely restricted to the Norfolk wherry, which had become larger, with a single, large gaffsail, and was used mainly for cargo. Nevertheless, the vessel retained a more pointed and shapely hull than the barge. Loaded, it had virtually no freeboard at the waist; there was no leeboard, but it often had a false keel fitted for work in deeper water. Wherries were clinker built, but the only survivor of the type, *Albion* of 1898, has, uniquely, found little favour with seamen of the Royal Navy.

Special poles, known as quants, were used to move the wherry in very shallow water and for fending.

CHARLES W. MORGAN

USA: 1841

Length: 111ft (33.8m)
Beam: 27ft 7in (8.4m)
Depth: 13ft 7in (4.2m)
Displacement: 351t
Rigging: three masts; barque rig
Complement: 26
Routes: Southern Ocean

This New Bedford-built whaler survives to show what a vessel like *Pequod* of *Moby Dick* fame was really like. In a long active career, she made well over 30 lengthy voyages, each usually of more than three years' duration, seeking and killing whales, extracting the oil, melting the blubber, and storing it in barrels. A compact floating factory, she also had to be highly seaworthy and easily manageable in waters south of the capes Horn and Good Hope. In 1867, she was rigged as a barque and is preserved in this form. The peak of the New England whaling industry came around 1850, but her hard-worked hull was destined to continue for 70 years. In 1916, she sailed to South Georgia in search of elephant seals; she also featured in the silent film *Miss Petticoats* and appeared in two later films. Her last whaling voyage was in 1921. Laid up in 1935, she was preserved and has been on view at Mystic Harbor since 1941.

In 1850, the New England ports were home to 502 ships and 51 brigs or schooners engaged in the whaling industry.

CONGRESS

USA: 1841

By the 1840s, the United States was playing a part in global affairs, especially in the Americas, and its modest fleet was widely deployed. A product of the final US sailing frigate design, *Congress* saw service in the Mediterranean Sea and at the siege of Montevideo (1844), then sailed to become flagship of the Pacific Squadron. She was active in the Mexican War of 1846-48, then transferred again to the east, serving in the Atlantic and Mediterranean. On the outbreak of the American Civil War in 1861, she formed part of the squadron blockading the Confederate ports. On 8 March 1862, *Congress* was engaged by the newly completed Confederate ironclad ship *Virginia* (formerly USS *Merrimac*) in Hampton Roads. Run aground on the Union side of the Roads, under Signal Point, *Congress* was pounded by incendiary shells, and after some hours she blew up when her magazine was ignited.

Length: 164ft (50m)
Beam: 41ft (12.5m)
Depth: 13ft 4in (4.1m)
Displacement: 1867t
Rigging: three masts; square rig
Armament: 49 32pdr, four 8pdr guns
Complement: 480

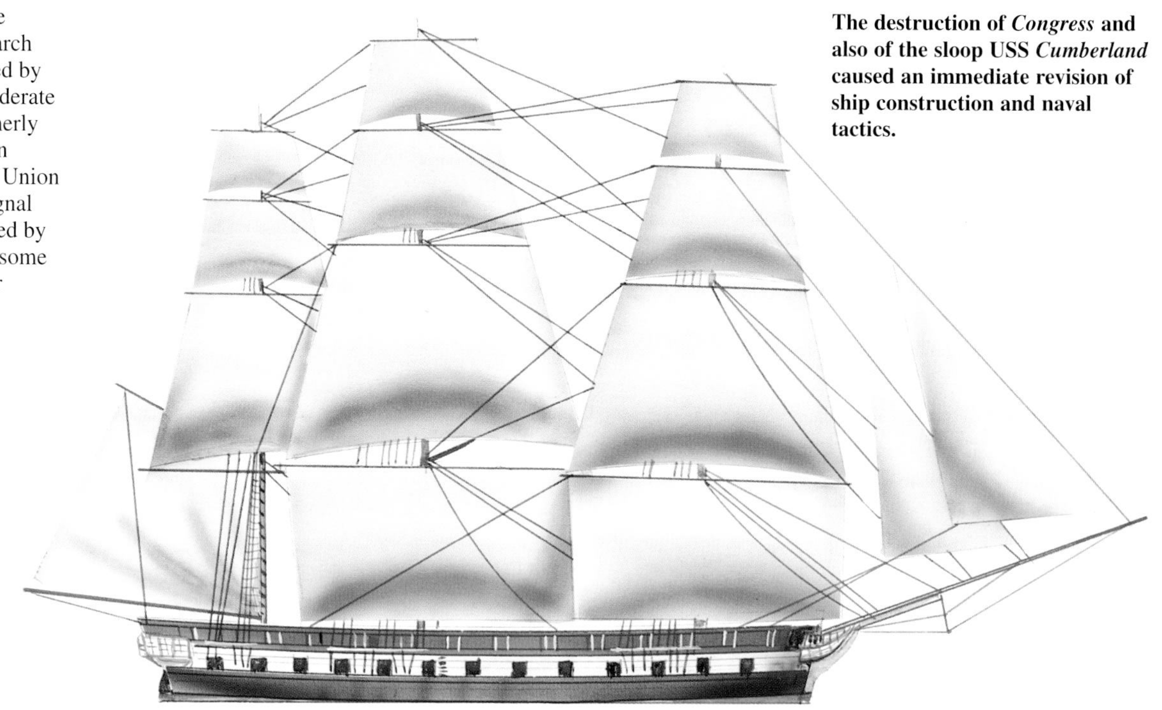

The destruction of *Congress* and also of the sloop USS *Cumberland* caused an immediate revision of ship construction and naval tactics.

MISSISSIPPI

USA: 1841

The paddle frigate as a type was hampered by the amount of side room occupied by the paddles and by their vulnerability to enemy fire.

Commodore Matthew Perry was a strong advocate of steam propulsion and he supervised construction of this paddle-wheel frigate at the Philadelphia Navy Yard. In 1845, she was his flagship in the West Indian Squadron, taking part in coastal operations of the Mexican War. After duty in the Mediterranean from 1849 to 1851, she was in the squadron under Perry which forced Japan to open its borders to foreign trade; with USS *Susquehanna*, she was the first steamship to visit Japan, in July 1852. *Mississippi* was Pacific-based until the Civil War began in 1861, when she was recalled and did blockade duty off Key West. In April 1863, she joined Farragut's fleet to attack New Orleans. In the river whose name she bore, she sank the Confederate ironclad *Manassas*, but a month later she grounded by Port Hudson, south of Vicksburg. Under devastating bombardment from Confederate guns, she was abandoned and set on fire.

Length: 229ft (69.8m)
Beam: 40ft (12.2m)
Depth: 21ft 8in (6.6m)
Displacement: 3220t
Rigging: three masts; barque rig
Machinery: sidewheels, side lever
Armament: two 10in (254mm), eight 8in (203mm) guns
Complement: 257

TRUXTON

USA: 1842

Length: 100ft (30.5m)
Beam: 27ft 4in (8.3m)
Depth: 13ft (4m)
Displacement: 355t
Rigging: two masts; square-rigged with gaff-and-boom mainsail
Armament: 10 guns
Complement: not known

Built in 1842 at Norfolk Navy Yard, *Truxton* was an exceptionally fast brig. She was also a very advanced ship in technical terms, heavily sparred, with a spencer (trysail mast) on the foremast as well as the main, and equipped with chain rigging. *Truxton* was a weatherly ship, but her unusual depth was her undoing. She grounded on Tuxpan Bar on the Mexican coast on 15 August 1846 and was burned to prevent her being taken by the Mexicans.

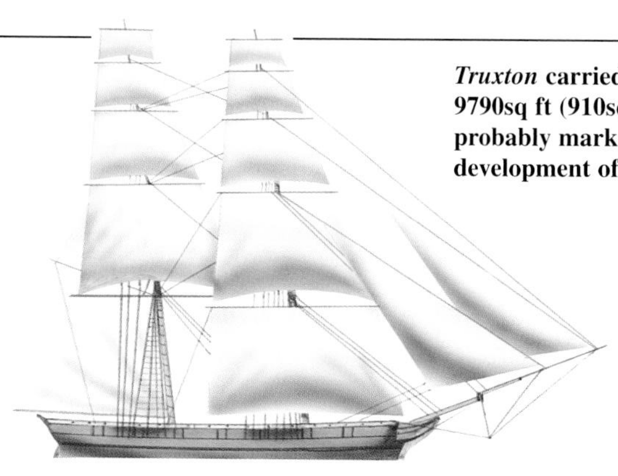

***Truxton* carried around 9790sq ft (910sq m) of sail and probably marked the peak of development of the naval brig.**

GREAT BRITAIN

GB: 1843

Length: 322ft (98.1m)
Beam: 50ft 6in (15.4m)
Depth: 16ft (4.9m)
Displacement: 3270t
Rigging: six masts; second mast square-rigged, all others fore-and-aft-rigged
Machinery: single screw; four cylinder engine
Complement: 350 passengers, 300 crew
Cargo: 260 passengers; general goods
Routes: transatlantic; GB-Australia, GB-San Francisco

In 1970, *Great Britain* was brought back to Bristol and restoration work began. She is now a museum ship, with replica engines.

Like all I K Brunel's ships, *Great Britain* was an epoch-making achievement: the biggest iron ship yet built; the first to be intended for deep-sea voyaging; the first to be driven by a screw propeller; and the first screw steamer to cross the Atlantic. Launched at Bristol in 1843, she embodied many features that would become standard in later steamships. Even when she grounded near Belfast Lough in September 1846, and remained there for nine months, she was towed off in repairable state; this was one of many events that confirmed the iron hull as the way forward. *Great Britain* was conceived as a paddle steamer, but Brunel changed his plans and this necessitated a change of engines. Ultimately she was driven by engines of four cylinders – each of which was 7ft 3in (2.2m) in diameter – which turned the shaft via a chain drive at 53rpm; the screw itself was six-bladed (later reduced to three blades) and was 15ft 6in (4.7m) in diameter. On trials the engines drove the vessel at nine knots. Nevertheless, *Great Britain* was still equipped with six masts bearing around 15,000sq ft (1400sq m) of sail; all masts had fore-and-aft rig apart from the second, which carried yards for course and topsail. On 26 July 1845, *Great Britain* made her first voyage – from Liverpool to New York, in 14 days and 21 hours. After the grounding, her owners, the Great Western Steamship Co, sold her; in 1852, following a three-year lay-up and now fitted with four masts, a three-blade screw and new engines, *Great Britain* was redirected to Australia. Herrig was reduced to three mastsin 1853, then in 1877 the engines were removed, the hull was sheathed in wood, and she worked as a sail bulk carrier between Britain and San Francisco. On the third outward run, she was condemned at Port Stanley, Falkland Islands, in February 1886 and converted to a storage hulk.

PRINCETON

USA: 1843

Built in the Philadelphia Navy Yard, *Princeton*, although short-lived, was the first steam screw warship; she was also an innovative ship in many other ways. Planned by John Ericsson and Robert F Stockton, she followed their principle, already tested in the *Robert F. Stockton*, of having the engine – Ericsson's 'pendulum' design – placed below the waterline and so out of conventional artillery shot. Her two 12in (305mm) shell-firing guns were also new designs; one exploded at an official demonstration on the Potomac River on 29 February 1844, killing some of the eminent guests. *Princeton* was on blockade duty in the Mexican Gulf during the Mexican War, then served in the Mediterranean during 1848-49. On return to Boston that year, she was decommissioned and broken up, although her engine and some other parts were incorporated in the new USS *Princeton* of 1851.

Length: 164ft (50m)
Beam: 31ft 6in (9.6m)
Depth: 17ft (5.2m)
Displacement: 954t
Rigging: three masts
Machinery: single screw, reciprocating
Armament: two 12in (304mm), 12 42pdr guns
Complement: 166

Driven by a single helicoidal screw, *Princeton* outsteamed the British screw merchant ship *Great Western* over a 21-mile (33.6km) course in 1843.

RATTLER

GB: 1843

More than 30 different types of screw propeller were tested on *Rattler*, which was ordered by the Admiralty in 1840 as Britain's first screw-driven warship and built at the Sheerness Dockyard; she was designated a screw sloop. Her engine was designed by I K Brunel, whose screw steamer *Great Britain* was launched in the same year, and in her first years *Rattler* was treated very much as a

floating test-bed. Most famously, she was matched against the paddle-driven HMS *Alecto*, of equal power rating, in a series of trials in March-April 1845. Some of these trials utilised steam and sail; others steam only. *Rattler* was the undoubted winner. In the climactic trial – more a stunt – the two ships engaged in a tug-of-war. *Alecto* began by pulling *Rattler* backwards before the latter's engines were engaged, but once *Rattler*'s screw began to turn, she gradually brought the other vessel to a halt, then, as *Alecto*'s paddles churned vainly, *Rattler* towed her backwards at 2.8 knots.

***Rattler* was not commissioned until 1849; after fleet service off Africa and China, she was broken up at Woolwich Dockyard in 1856.**

Length: 176ft 6in (53.8m)
Beam: 32ft 8in (10m)
Depth: 11ft 10in (3.6m)
Displacement: 1112t
Rigging: three masts; square-rigged on foremast, fore-and-aft rig on main and mizzen
Machinery: single screw, steam; 200hp
Armament: one 68pdr, four 32pdr carronades
Complement: not known

BERTHA

GB: 1844

Designed by I K Brunel and built by Lunel & Co in Bristol, this is the oldest steam vessel still afloat. Her long working life was spent scraping mud from Bridgwater docks in Somerset with a dozer blade fixed to the end of a long pole mounted aft. She was retired in 1968 when the docks closed and is now at Bristol as one of the 'core collection' of British heritage ships.

Length: 54ft (16.4m)
Beam: 13ft 9in (4.2m)
Depth: 3ft (0.9m)
Displacement: 64t
Rigging: not applicable
Machinery: single-acting
Complement: not known
Routes: River Parrett, England

***Bertha*'s official designation was that of a 'drag boat', since she hauled herself along on chains fixed to the quaysides.**

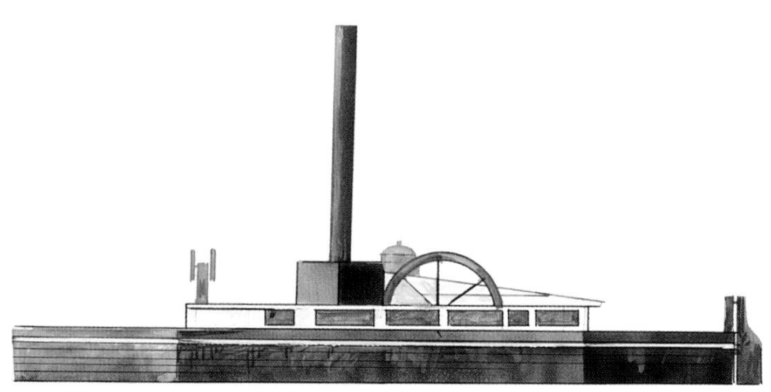

GLADIATOR

GB: 1844

Length: 190ft (57.9m)
Beam: 37ft 6in (11.4m)
Depth: not known
Displacement: 1190t
Rigging: three masts; square rig
Machinery: sidewheels, steam
Armament: two 110pdr, four 10in (254mm) guns
Complement: not known

Gladiator was a wooden-hulled paddle frigate built at Woolwich Dockyard, London. Her guns compensated for their small number with their huge calibre. At a period when broadside firing was the standard, the paddle ship was at a disadvantage – the space occupied by her motive system both inhibited the placing of her guns and was vulnerable to attack. *Gladiator* was broken up in March 1879.

Despite her 'modern' guns, two decades of rapid change were about to ensue, which would make *Gladiator*'s type obsolete.

RAINBOW

USA: 1845

Designed by John Griffiths in 1843 and built in New York by Smith & Dimon, *Rainbow* presaged the age of the clipper ship in terms of her hull, which was sharp and concave at the bow. Conventional wisdom said she would plough her bow down, but she sailed superbly. Going first into the China tea trade, she made New York-Canton in 92 days out, 84 back. She was lost between New York and Valparaiso in 1848.

The full-rounded bow for a big ship was regarded as a fact of life at this time; Griffiths' concave bow was revolutionary.

Length: 160ft 9in (49m)
Beam: 31ft 8in (9.6m)
Depth: 19ft 5in (5.9m)
Displacement: 1043t
Rigging: three masts; full-rigged ship
Complement: not known
Cargo: tea, bulk goods
Routes: New York-Canton, New York-San Francisco via Cape Horn

SIMOOM

GB: 1845

Length: not known
Beam: not known
Depth: not known
Displacement: not known
Rigging: three masts; rig not known
Machinery: single screw, steam; 250hp
Complement: not known
Cargo: troops, military stores
Routes: Great Britain to India and other colonies

In 1844, the British Admiralty undertook research on the ability of an iron hull to withstand shot by test-firing at the hull of a target ship. The results appeared to indicate that iron was less satisfactory than wood. It emerged later that the whole experiment had been botched, or rigged, by the use of a target whose 2in (5cm) plates had rusted to a half-inch (1.3cm) thickness. Meanwhile, iron construction was halted. Laid down as an iron-hulled frigate, *Simoom* was consequently altered during construction to become a troopship; her engine was given to the new battleship *Duke of Wellington* and a less powerful one provided for *Simoom*. In some ways the alteration was timely, as the Crimean War of 1853–56 required the movement of large numbers of men and stores from Britain to the Black Sea. After that, the requirements of imperial garrisons around the world, from Canada to the South Pacific and especially India, made for steady employment of troopships.

***Simoom*'s sister vessel, *Birkenhead*, became a legend of military discipline when she foundered in 1852. The troops remained on board; all women and children were saved.**

TERRIBLE

GB: 1845

***Terrible* was one of three ships which moved the Bermuda dry dock across the Atlantic in 1869.**

Laid down as *Simoom* but renamed *Terrible* for her launch at Deptford on the Thames in 1845, this vessel was bigger than a sailing 74-gunner and was the largest and most powerful British paddle frigate. She was also the first two-funnelled warship in the Royal Navy and in some ways anticipated the cruiser type to come; there was a considerable gap between the fore and main masts, for gunnery purposes. She saw service in the Baltic and Black Sea fleets during the Crimean War of 1853–56; in the Black Sea she played a major part in disabling the barbettes of Fort Constantine. Although she carried only eight (later 19) guns, they were all of very large calibre. Such armament showed that the 'floating battery' of grouped warships could be more than a match for coastal fortresses previously regarded as impregnable. *Terrible* was sold in 1879.

Length: 226ft 2in (68.9m)
Beam: 42ft 6in (12.9m)
Depth: 27ft 4in (8.32m)
Displacement: 1850t
Rigging: three masts; square rig
Machinery: sidewheels, steam
Armament: four 68pdr, four 56pdr guns
Complement: 250

WASHINGTON

USA: 1847

In 1846, when the US government subsidized the transatlantic mail service, American companies began to compete with the established British lines on the Atlantic run. The wooden-hulled paddle steamer *Washington*, launched at New York for the Ocean Steam Navigation Company, was the first American liner. She operated successfully until 1857, when Congress withdrew the mail subsidy and she was withdrawn from service.

Length: 230ft (70.1m)
Beam: 40ft (12.2m)
Depth: 31ft (9.4m)
Displacement: 1750t
Rigging: three masts, square rigged on forre and main; spanker on mizzen
Machinery: sidewheels, side lever
Complement: not known
Cargo: passengers, light freight, mails
Routes: New York-Bremen

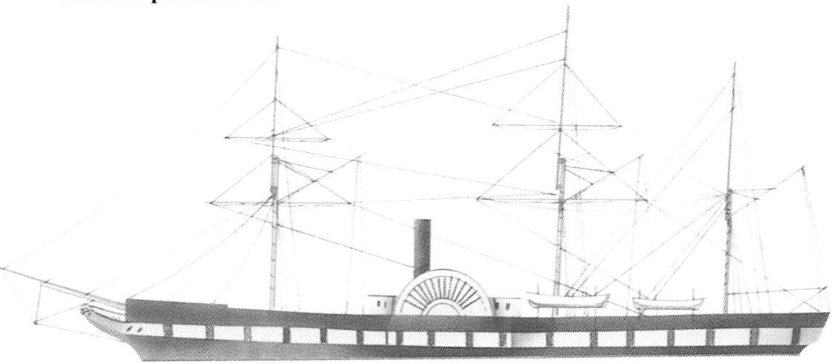

***Washington* and her sistership Herman ran a regular service between New York, Cowes on England's Isle of Wight and the German port of Bremen.**

WINE BARGE

PORTUGAL: 1847

A vessel of conservative style, with upswept prow and stern and a remarkably long steering oar fixed to the sternpost (one illustration shows three men wielding it), this barge carried hogsheads of wine up and down the Douro River at Oporto and out to cargo ships. A scaffolding along the deck acted as a barrel rack, and this was raised aft to make a gantry for the helmsman. A line was made to the middle of the square sail's foot to draw it up.

Substantial rowlocks towards the bow suggest that the vessel was often manoeuvred in the waterway using sweeps.

Length: c42ft (12.8m)
Beam: c16ft 6in (5.7m)
Depth: c3ft (0.9m)
Displacement: not known
Rigging: single mast; square sail
Complement: 3
Cargo: wine barrels
Routes: River Douro

CALIFORNIA

USA: 1848

Length: 200ft (60.1m)
Beam: 33ft (10m)
Depth: 22ft (6.7m)
Displacement: 1057t
Rigging: three masts; barque rig
Machinery: not known
Complement: 75
Cargo: general freight
Routes: Pacific coast, Panama-Oregon

Built in New York and destined for the Pacific coast mail trade between Oregon and Panama, the paddle steamer *California* was the third steamship to pass through the Strait of Magellan and the first to enter San Francisco Bay, on 28 February 1849, packed with a motley band of passengers, mostly gold-seeking 'forty-niners'. In 1875, her engine was removed and she sailed as a barque until she was wrecked on the Peruvian coast in 1895.

On her maiden voyage, *California*'s coal supply ran out, and spare rigging and even wooden furniture was burned to make steam.

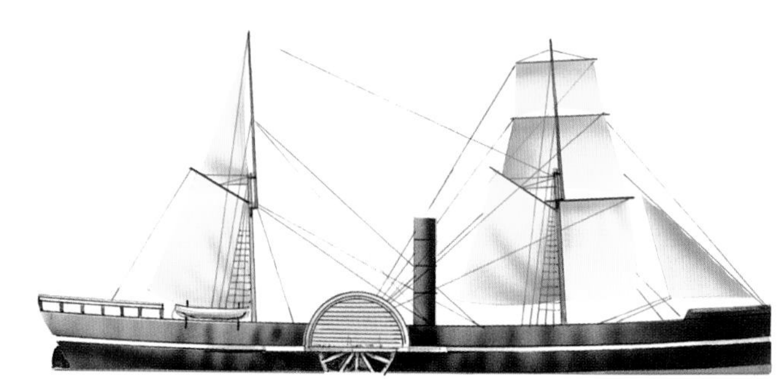

NEW ENGLAND

USA: 1849

Length: 166ft 10in (50.8m)
Beam: 34ft 7in (10.5m)
Depth: 17ft 4in (5.2m)
Displacement: 920t
Rigging: three masts; full-rigged ship
Complement: not known
Cargo: passengers, light freight
Routes: transatlantic

Many passengers still distrusted steamers at this time, preferring a ship that could not 'break down' and was not sooty and smoky.

Built by the firm of W V & O Moses at Bath, Maine, this was a purpose-built sailing packet ship with extensive deckhouse accommodation; the main deckhouse was joined to the forecastle, and the poop extended forward of the mainmast. Boats were carried not in the small well but on top of the cabin. Under Captain G W Edge, she was dismasted in an Atlantic storm but survived.

AAK

THE NETHERLANDS: 1850

This river and estuary barge, once common in Germany and the Netherlands, is defined by its 'swimhead' bow, where the planking is angled up from the flat bottom, with no stempost. It could sit on the bottom at low tide and carried a leeboard to help in tacking. In the 18th century, it was gaff-rigged, but by the 19th this had been superseded. Apart from the short mizzen mast, a large 19th-century *aak* was virtually schooner-rigged.

An *aak*-built vessel could vary in length from around 20ft (6.1m) to 130ft (40m); the term is often taken just to mean 'barge'.

Length: 128ft (39m)
Beam: 19ft (5.8m)
Depth: 5ft 11in (1.8m)
Displacement: 250t
Rigging: two masts; ketch rig
Complement: 4
Cargo: baled and barrelled goods
Routes: Rhine River, Rhine-Meuse estuaries

ARCTIC

USA: 1850

The fate of the *Arctic* led to much-needed reforms in maritime safety arrangements, including lifeboat provision and the establishment of Atlantic 'sea lanes'.

The New York-built, wooden-hulled *Arctic* was an elaborately decorated and furnished paddle-wheel mail steamer of the Collins Line. Sailing from Liverpool to New York, she collided in fog off Cape Race with an iron French ship, *Vesta*, on 27 September 1854 and sank, with the loss of 322 lives, including E K Collins's wife and children. There was no rescue drill and there were insufficient lifeboats for the number of passengers on board.

Length: 285ft (86.8m)
Beam: 45ft 11in (14m)
Depth: 22ft 11in (7m)
Displacement: 2856t
Rigging: two masts; square-rigged on foremast
Machinery: sidewheels, side lever
Complement: not known
Cargo: passengers, light freight, mails
Routes: transatlantic

BAGHLA

ARAB STATES: 1850

A deep-sea ship which plied the coasts of Arabia and East Africa and also crossed the Indian Ocean to trade with the subcontinent, the lateen-rigged *baghla* shows an intriguing resemblance in the shape of its stern and afterdecks to early 18th-century Western ships, although the long, sleek prow, free of any foremast, is an Eastern feature. The arched, five-windowed transom stern was usually finely carved.

Length: c70ft (21.3m)
Beam: c14ft (4.3m)
Depth: c5ft (1.5m)
Displacement: c135t
Rigging: two masts; lateen rig
Complement: not known
Cargo: general cargo
Routes: Red Sea, Persian Gulf

With other Arab vessels, this craft was usually referred to by Europeans as a *dhow*, a word unknown in Arabic.

BEZAANSCHUIT

THE NETHERLANDS: 1850

This was a small coastal vessel, perhaps used for fishing, as it appears to have had a small cabin to protect the crew from the elements; however, it was probably used chiefly for leisure sailing. With a single mast and a loose-footed mainsail on a standing gaff, it was easily handled. The hull, low in the water, had a canoe profile – rising at stem and stern – of somewhat archaic appearance.

Length: 30ft (9.1m)
Beam: 9ft (2.7m)
Depth: 4ft (1.2m)
Displacement: not known
Rigging: single pole mast; fore-and-aft rig with gaff mainsail
Complement: two
Cargo: light freight, fish
Routes: Dutch coastal waters

Vessels of this type abound in Dutch marine paintings of the 18th and 19th centuries.

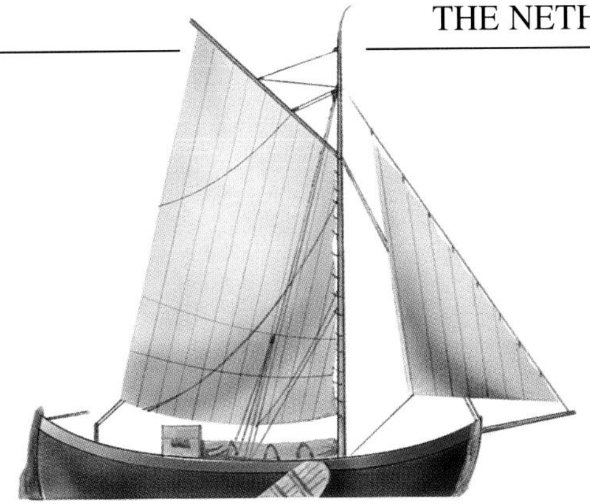

BOOM

ARAB STATES: 1850

It is likely that ships of this form had been built in the Persian Gulf region since the 16th century. Some still sailed in the late 20th century, with motor assistance.

Length: 100ft (30.5m)
Beam: 20ft (6.1m)
Depth: 7ft 6in (2.3m)
Displacement: c190t
Rigging: two masts; lateen rig with fore-staysail to bowsprit
Complement: 10
Cargo: animals, foodstuffs, bulk freight
Routes: Persian Gulf and Indian Ocean

One of the largest types of Arab sailing vessel, the *boom* traded across the Indian Ocean and down the African coast as far as Zanzibar. Fitted with the traditional lateen rig on two masts, it also had a massively built-up bow with a long sprit on which a kind of staysail was fastened. There is something reminiscent of the galley's shape and ram here, but the *boom* was not oared.

Calie

TONGA: 1850

A double-hulled vessel from Tonga in the South Pacific, the *calie* was composed of two hull elements of differing size, one being considerably longer and higher than the other. A booster framework on the smaller partner was needed to set the broad deck between the two on a level. It mounted a raked bipod mast with a broad sail. Although really an outrigger, the smaller hull also accommodated paddle-wielders.

With its open platform deck, the *calie* was more of a fishing vessel than a cargo carrier and was used for fish-spearing.

Length: *c*65ft (19.8m)
Beam: *c*15ft (4.6m)
Depth: not known
Displacement: not known
Rigging: bipod mast; two claw-shape bamboo-framed sails
Complement: not known
Role: fishing vessel
Routes: coastal

Cektirme

TURKEY: 1850

The name covers more than one type of hull and rig. A cektirme would have had a 'modern' sail plan seen on the 19th-century vessel, with jib and flying jib stayed to a lengthy bowsprit. Instead of the lateen sail which it undoubtedly would once have had, it had a triangular mainsail, attached at the foot to a long boom which extended over the stern. Due to the low freeboard, weather-cloths were fitted to keep some of the wet out.

Length: *c*36ft (11m)
Beam: *c*15ft (4.6m)
Depth: *c*4ft (1.2m)
Displacement: not known
Rigging: single mast; triangular gunter-rigged mainsail; two jibs and foresail
Complement: two to four
Cargo: foodstuffs, firewood
Routes: Sea of Marmara-Constantinople

City of Glasgow

GB: 1850

Length: 234ft (71.3m)
Beam: 34ft (10.4m)
Depth: 24ft (7.3m)
Displacement: 1609t
Rigging: three masts; barque rig
Machinery: geared overhead beam
Complement: not known
Cargo: passengers, light freight
Routes: transatlantic

Unsubsidized by mail contracts, this Clyde-built, iron-hulled liner showed how screw steamers could pay their way simply by speed, passenger capacity and efficiency. She could carry 400 steerage, 85 second-class, and 55 first-class passengers on the Glasgow-New York route and was the prototype for many similar ships.

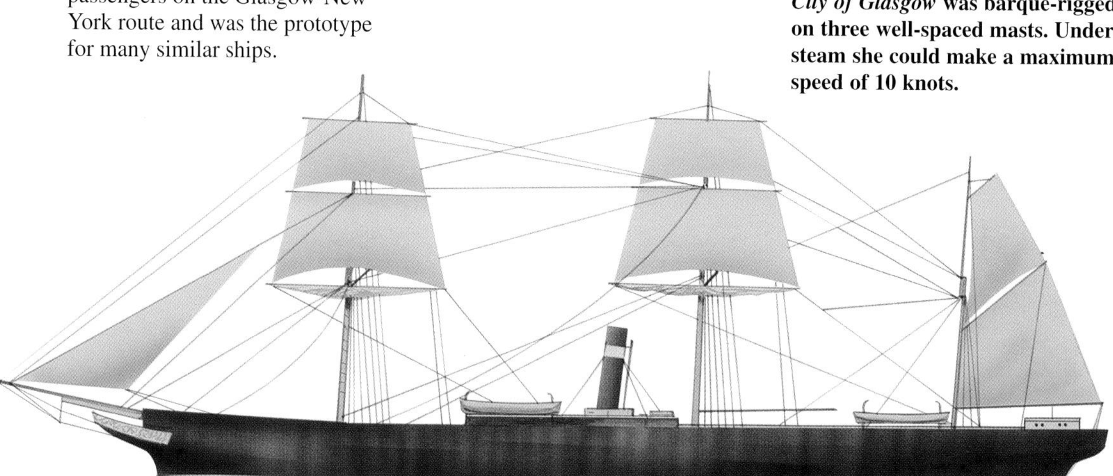

***City of Glasgow* was barque-rigged on three well-spaced masts. Under steam she could make a maximum speed of 10 knots.**

Dahabieh

EGYPT: 1850

***Dahabiehs* came in different sizes, but the two-mast rig, with the small mizzen lateen to help in steering, was typical.**

Passenger transport on the Nile and in the lagoons and channels of its delta was provided by vessels of this sort. The apparent quality of the cabin and its awning-covered roofdeck suggests that this could have been an official ship or the property of someone wealthy; ordinary passengers would have simply sat on deck and provided their own shade. But the dahabieh was always the 'luxury boat' of Nile passenger transport, right up to the advent of motor power in the twentieth century.

Length: 96ft (29.2m)
Beam: 18ft (5.5m)
Depth: 5ft (1.5m)
Displacement: not known
Rigging: two masts; lateen rig
Complement: four
Cargo: passengers
Routes: Nile River and Delta

DHOW

ARAB STATES: 1850

The term *dhow* is used only in English, to describe a variety of two- and three-masted lateen- or settee-rigged sailing ships, and even some much smaller craft. Such vessels are widely used in the Persian Gulf and all around the Arabian Sea, often venturing much further afield – to Zanzibar and Malaysia, for example. They are characterized by their rig and often have a high-set poop and an undercut transom.

Length: 110ft (33.5m)
Beam: 38ft (11.6m)
Depth: 16ft (4.9m)
Displacement: 280t
Rigging: two masts; lateen rig
Complement: not known
Cargo: general, timber, grain
Routes: Persian Gulf and beyond

DONI

INDIA: 1850

Of antique appearance, this Indian craft's construction embodied 'stitched planking'. Carvel-built, as almost all oriental vessels were, she then had ribs laid along the joins and stitched into the hull. At gunwale height, transverse beams strengthened the hull, and a light outrigger helped to give the vessel stability. A convex deck of bamboo was fitted, turning the space beneath into a hold or a low-roofed cabin.

The stitched-planking technique is found in some very ancient vessels, including the Cheops ship.

Length: c20ft (6.1m)
Beam: c8ft (2.4m) within hull
Depth: not known
Displacement: not known
Rigging: two masts; lugsail-type rig; jib and staysail set to bowsprit
Complement: not known
Cargo: general small cargo, fish
Routes: south Indian coasts

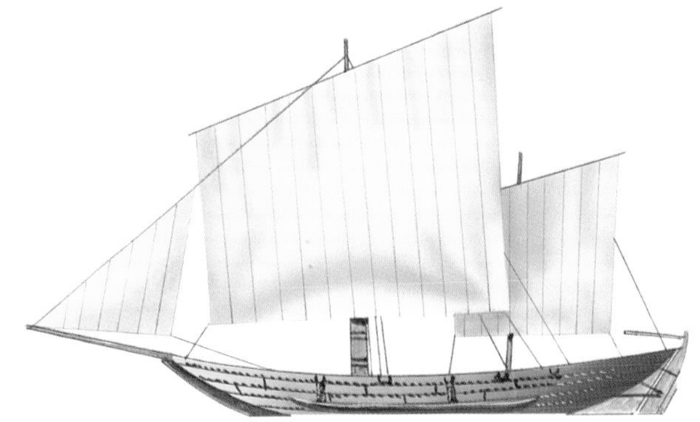

EVERT

GERMANY: 1850

Wide German rivers like the Rhine, Elbe and Oder are major traffic arteries; they have big seaports on the estuaries and river ports upstream and pass through intensively farmed and industrial countryside. In earlier centuries, as now, the rivers were heavily used for bulk goods transport. The *evert* was a two-masted, fore-and-aft-rigged barge used for trans-shipping cargo and for coastwise trading. In size and function, the *evert* was comparable to the large Dutch *aak* and the Thames barge.

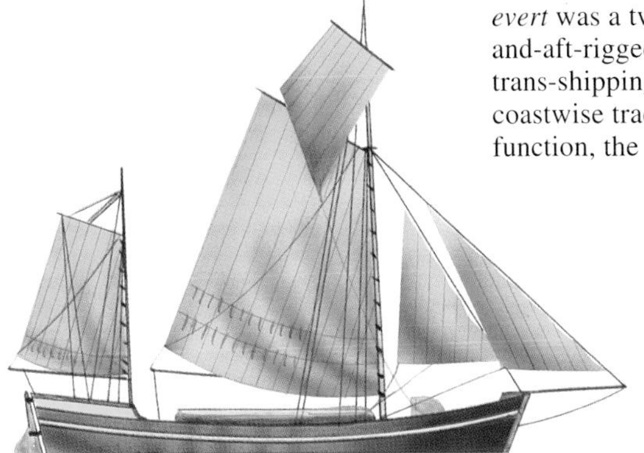

The high stem and raised cargo hatch both suggest this was a seagoing as well as a river craft.

Length: 95ft (29m)
Beam: 19ft (5.8m)
Depth: 4ft (1.2m)
Displacement: 180t
Rigging: two masts; fore-and-aft gaff rig with spritsail topsail on mainmast; jib and staysail
Complement: 4
Cargo: baled and barrelled goods
Routes: North German coast and estuaries

FELUCCA

SPAIN: 1850

Length: 58ft 6in (17.8m)
Beam: 16ft 11in (5.1m)
Depth: 6ft 6in (2m)
Displacement: 50t
Rigging: two masts; forward-raked mainmast with lateen mainsail and jib, lateen mizzen
Complement: 20
Cargo: light general cargo
Routes: Balearic Islands and Spanish coast

The racy lines of the *felucca* clearly display its Mediterranean descent from the galley, and forms of this craft were found everywhere between Gibraltar and the Levant. The forward-raked mainmast supports a lateen mainsail and a jib on a long boom; the raised afterdeck extends well out over the stern. With between eight and 20 oars to move it in calms, it was often used as a privateer or pirate ship. After the 18th century, few were built.

Known from the early 17th century, its name suggests an Arab origin for the craft.

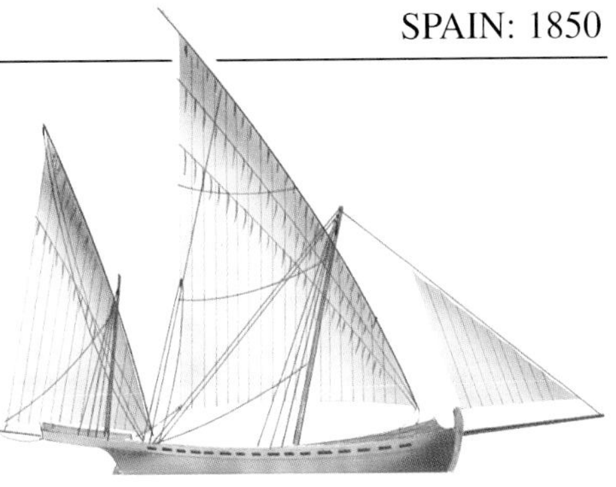

FRAGATA

PORTUGAL: 1850

This River Tagus vessel, designed to be easily manoeuvrable in cramped and crowded waterway conditions, preserved the square stern of the old caravel. With two stumpy masts and lateen rig, the *fragata* was easily handled; her prime purpose was most probably as a fishing boat. The size of these craft varied enormously, although the smaller versions were generally far more numerous. Some, perhaps chiefly for naval use, were rigged as brigantines.

Length: 72ft 3in (22m)
Beam: 20ft (6.1m)
Depth: 9ft 10in (3m)
Displacement: 100t
Rigging: two masts; lateen rig
Complement: 6
Cargo: light cargo, fish
Routes: Tagus Estuary

GAIASSA

EGYPT: 1850

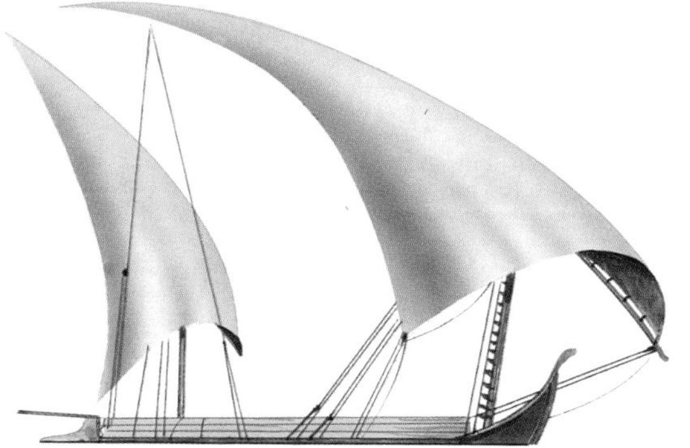

The *gaiassa* was a sailing barge used for Nile cargo transport, probably in a form little changed for centuries besides the provision of a tiller to replace a steering oar. According to size, the vessel was equipped with from one to three masts – most often two, placed well forward and aft in order to leave maximum loading space.

The high-raised prow, with an anchor slung from a block at the tip, has no apparent purpose and may be an archaic feature.

Length: 87ft (26.5m)
Beam: 18ft (5.5m)
Depth: 5ft 6in (1.6m)
Displacement: not known
Rigging: two masts; lateen rig
Complement: 2
Cargo: grain, papyrus, barrelled and baled goods
Routes: Nile River and Delta

GALEAS

SWEDEN: 1850

Often called the Swedish- or Baltic-rigged *galeas*, to avoid confusion with the completely different *galleass*, this was a merchant vessel, known around the northern European ports in the 17th and 18th centuries; it was a relative of the hooker. Its fore-and-aft rig was its main drive. The little topgallant and the topsail cut to clear the inner jibstay are remnants of an original full square rig.

F H af Chapman reproduced a *galeas* rig in his *Architectura Navalis Mercatoria* of 1766, in two versions – seagoing and lake/river-going.

Length: 65ft (19.8m)
Beam: 18ft (5.5m)
Depth: 9ft (2.7m)
Displacement: c90t
Rigging: two masts; both gaff-rigged with booms; topsail on main, two jibs and fore-staysail
Complement: 6-8
Cargo: grain, barrelled and baled goods, ore, timber
Routes: North Sea and Baltic trading routes

GHANJA

ARAB STATES: 1850

Length: c110ft (33.5m)
Beam: c22ft (6.7m)
Depth: 9ft (2.7m)
Displacement: not known
Rigging: three masts; lateen rig
Complement: not known
Cargo: passengers, light goods
Routes: Arabian coasts

Although some of its detail is conjectural, the *ghanja* appears to have been a three-masted vessel; its lines were longer and lower than the *sambuk* and it had the sort of extended stern platform, probably grating-decked, also seen on the Mediterranean *chebeck*. It may have been used more as a warship than as a trader; certainly it looks built for speed, although there is no evidence of its carrying guns. Her size and speed would also have made the ghanja a useful ship for piracy, coastal raids and smuggling on the long Red Sea and Gulf coasts.

Like the *baghla*, *boom* and *sambuk*, the *ghanja* would generally have been referred to by non-Arabs simply as a *dhow*.

GHE LUOI RUNG

KOREA: 1850

Shaped like a slice of melon, this Korean coastal craft has a very distinctive rig, its three masts including two small foremasts. All three masts are like trysail masts and are fitted with triangular sails in an oriental version of the gunter rig. With a 'seeing eye' painted on the bow and the yin-yang symbol on its side, the *ghe luoi rung* was protected against water hazards and demons.

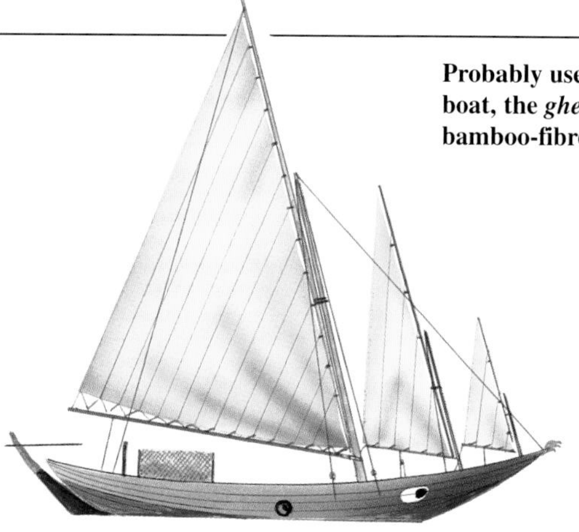

Probably used chiefly as a fishing boat, the *ghe luoi rung* had a small bamboo-fibre deck-shelter.

Length: c20ft (6.1m)
Beam: c6ft (1.8m)
Depth: c2ft (0.6m)
Displacement: not known
Rigging: three trysail masts; triangular fore-and-aft sails
Complement: not known
Cargo: fish
Routes: Korean coast

Greek Coaster

GREECE: 1850

Greek coastal sailing vessels had a variety of hulls and rigs and had type names with a confusing tendency to overlap. This is a form of the *bratsera*, a good-looking and also practical-looking craft. The rig is entirely fore and aft, although the lugsails are very old-fashioned and in a 19th-century vessel would usually be replaced by gaffsails, with a large spanker set on the mainmast. Topmasts and up to three levels of topsails could be fitted to the foremast.

Length: 60ft (18.3m)
Beam: 14ft (4.3m)
Depth: 5ft (1.5m)
Displacement: c40t
Rigging: two masts; lugsails with fore-staysail set to bowsprit
Complement: 3
Cargo: general goods, animals, oil, firewood, passengers
Routes: Greek western coasts and islands

The *bratsera* was a multi-purpose ship, but was used chiefly to carry inter-island cargoes in the Ionian Sea.

Hektjalk

THE NETHERLANDS: 1850

In the 17th century, these vessels were generally spritsail-rigged.

Built with a curved stempost and single-masted with fore-and-aft rig, the *hektjalk* was the most common form of the Dutch *tjalk*, or keel barge, although there were many regional variations in size and detail; the type had evolved over some 200 years. The mainsail was far wider at the foot than at the top, bent from a short gaff to a long boom that reached to the vessel's stern. Like most others of its kind, it was fitted with a leeboard on the starboard side.

Length: 64ft (19.5m)
Beam: 16ft (4.9m)
Depth: 7ft 3in (2.2m)
Displacement: 60-80t
Rigging: single mast; fore-and-aft rig with gaff, fore-staysail and jib
Complement: 2
Cargo: agricultural goods, beer, wood
Routes: Dutch inland waterways

Jagt

FINLAND: 1850

Length: c55ft (16.8m)
Beam: c14ft (4.3m)
Depth: c4ft 6in (1.3m)
Displacement: c45t
Rigging: single mast; spanker and gaff topsail; two jibs and fore-staysail
Complement: four
Cargo: passengers, light freight
Routes: Finnish coast and islands

Finland has a long coastline with innumerable tiny islands grouped in two main archipelagoes, and the Finnish *jagt*, used both for cargo and passenger services, was an elegant-looking ship with a clipper bow. The single mast carried considerable spread of sail, the driver being a very large fore-and-aft sail rigged to gaff and boom; a form of spritsail topsail, found also in some other Nordic *jagt* types, was rigged from a short gaff.

The name is a form of the Dutch *jacht*, and the lines suggest it to have been a speedy vessel.

Junk

JAPAN: 1850

Length: 32ft (9.8m)
Beam: 8ft (2.4m)
Depth: 4ft (1.2m)
Displacement: not known
Rigging: single mast with square sail; small bowsprit-type mast with square sail
Complement: 3
Cargo: general freight
Routes: Japanese coast

Decked and with protruding deck beams, this ship's fortuitous resemblance to a Roman vessel has often been commented on.

Quite a different vessel from the Chinese junk, this Japanese junk has a number of apparently archaic features, including the way in which the deck is built out in wings towards the stern, suggesting one-time steering-oar positions. Driven by a single square mainsail, with a small square foresail on what is more of a bowsprit than a foremast, it was a solid craft but with a reputation as a poor sailer.

KETCH

GB: 1850

Amongst the smallest of 18th-century square-rigged vessels was the ketch, which was widely used in the short-sea trade. The name refers to the rig, which, however, changed around the mid-19th century. It usually became wholly fore-and-aft in nature, with gaff topsails replacing a square topsail and topgallant on the mainmast, and a spanker replacing the lateen mizzen. This rig was simpler and cheaper for a vessel often manned by only a 'master and boy'.

The foremast of the English ketch was set well back from the bow, enabling it to mount two staysails, a jib and a flying jib.

Length: 58ft 6in (17.8m)
Beam: 21ft 4in (6.5m)
Depth: 9ft 4in (2.8m)
Displacement: 106t
Rigging: two masts; mainmast with gaffsail and boom, triangular topsail, two jibs, two staysails; mizzen with spanker and spritsail topsail
Complement: 3–4
Cargo: coal, china clay, grain, bricks etc
Routes: British coastal routes

KOF

NETHERLANDS: 1850

Length: 98ft (30m)
Beam: 24ft 7in (7.5m)
Depth: 5ft (1.5m)
Displacement: 250t
Rigging: two masts; mainmast square-rigged with gaffsail; two jibs, two staysails; mizzen with large spanker
Complement: 6
Cargo: general cargo
Routes: North Sea, Scandinavia

The *kof* and the ketch had much in common, both being coastal and short-sea cargo and passenger vessels. However, the Dutch *kof* – the word refers to the hull rather than the rig – was usually bigger and retained the old square rig on the mainmast. As with other types, the rig evolved in the 19th century. This *kof* had a large gaff as mainsail, rigged abaft the mainmast, and a spanker on the mizzen, with no topsail.

The *kof* typically had a rounded stern with a built-out straight sternpost to support the rudder.

LAKATOI

NEW GUINEA: 1850

Although the *lakatoi* had no hold, baled cargo such as attap leaves or copra could be carried, lashed to the deck for security.

A form of trimaran, this striking vessel from New Guinea consisted of three dugout hulls joined to one another by transverse beams and supporting a deck made of bamboo. Two masts, set close to each other in the midship area, carried the bamboo-framed 'crab-claw' sails also found on other ancient South Pacific vessels. With cabins built on the deck, this was certainly a ship intended for sea voyages.

Length: c40ft (12.2m)
Beam: c16ft (4.9m)
Depth: not known
Displacement: not known
Rigging: bipod mast; two claw-shape bamboo-framed sails
Complement: not known
Cargo: tropical produce
Routes: South Pacific islands

LE NAPOLÉON (EX-LE 24 FÉVRIER, PRÉSIDENT)

FRANCE: 1850

Length: 233ft (71m)
Beam: 53ft 2in (16.2m)
Depth: not known
Displacement: 5040t
Rigging: three masts; square rig
Machinery: single screw, steam; 900hp
Armament: 90 guns
Complement: not known

The French designer Stanislas Dupuy de Lôme was one of the most brilliant and inventive marine engineers of the 19th century. He succeeded in making the French naval authorities into early converts to the concept of screw-propelled steam warships. In 1847, they commissioned a Dupuy de Lôme two-funnelled two-decker of novel design. Destined to be leader of a class of nine, she was an epoch-making vessel. Laid down as *Le 24 février*, then renamed *Président*, her successive names reveal the shifting state of domestic politics. She was launched at the Toulon naval dockyard on 16 May 1850. From the beginning she was planned as a steamer, with sailing qualities sacrificed to enable her machinery to be used to best advantage. She could maintain a speed of almost 14 knots under steam and made many long passages under steam alone. *Napoléon* and her sister-vessels contributed a great sister-vessels contributed a great deal to French naval prestige, but they had little to do in the way of active service after the Crimean War of 1853-56, during which *Napoléon* took part in the bombardment of Russian shore fortresses. After the Crimean War, she made a large number of cruises to French dependencies and colonies on 'showing the flag' missions. She was stricken from the list in 1876.

***Le Napoléon* was designed as a vessel that relied on steam power, with sail as auxiliary. British practice was exactly the opposite.**

LORCHA

CHINA: 1850

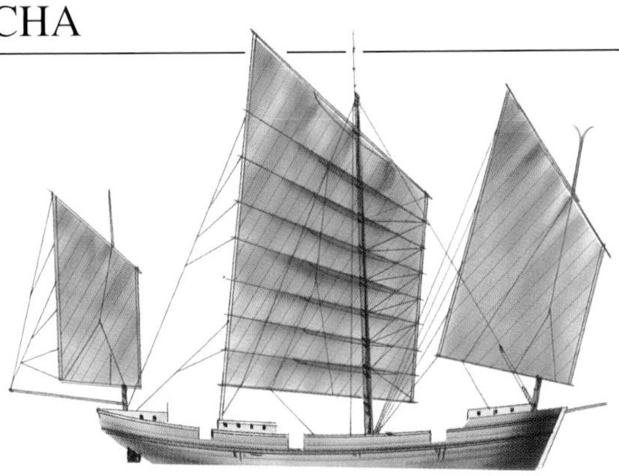

Length: 98ft (29.8m)
Beam: 22ft (6.7m)
Depth: 9ft (2.7m)
Displacement: not known
Rigging: three masts; lugsail rig with slatted fibre sails
Complement: 4
Cargo: rice, general cargo
Routes: South Chinese coast

The swift and manoeuvrable *lorcha* had a boat slung at the stem, ready for boarding operations.

The *lorcha* was a Chinese vessel in which the traditional style of lugsail junk rig was fitted to a hull built in the European style. The slightly raked stem had a short boom; there was a forecastle, a waist and a raised afterdeck. *Lorchas* were chiefly built in south China, around Canton and Hong Kong. Originally they may have been pirate hunters, their finer lines making them swifter than the pirate junks of the South China Sea.

MAHOVNA

TURKEY: 1850

Length: *c*28ft (8.5m)
Beam: *c*9ft (2.7m)
Depth: not known
Displacement: not known
Rigging: stump mast; spritsail gaff, short jib and staysail
Complement: 2
Cargo: hay, foodstuffs, wood, passengers
Routes: Bosporus

A smaller version of the *cektirme*, the Turkish *mahovna* would have been used to take off passengers from vessels moored in a seaway, as well as for trans-shipping the multifarious goods arriving at a great port. It had a very stumpy mast and a long sprit boom supporting a triangular sail. The purpose of this may have been to enable the vessel to pass under the low Galata Bridge at Constantinople (Istanbul) with the sprit lowered.

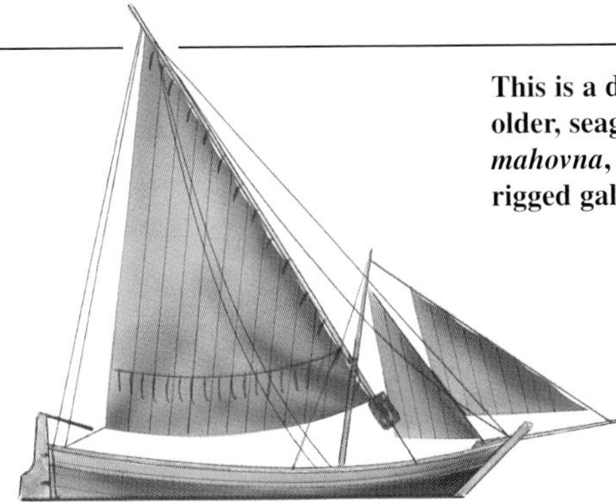

This is a different vessel from the older, seagoing *mahona*, or *mahovna*, which was a lateen-rigged galleass.

MOLICEIRO

PORTUGAL: 1850

Length: c25ft (7.6m)
Beam: c6ft (1.8m)
Depth: c2ft (0.6m)
Displacement: not known
Rigging: single mast; spritsail rig
Complement: 2
Cargo: barrels, farm produce
Routes: Portuguese river routes

A light barge with an extraordinary upswept prow somewhat resembling that of a Venetian gondola, this Portuguese craft preserved an antique appearance into the 19th century. The *moliceiro* was fitted with a small spritsail and was probably also equipped with oars, and her shallow draught enabled her to go a considerable way up rivers such as the Tagus and Douro, transporting casks and other material for the port wine producers.

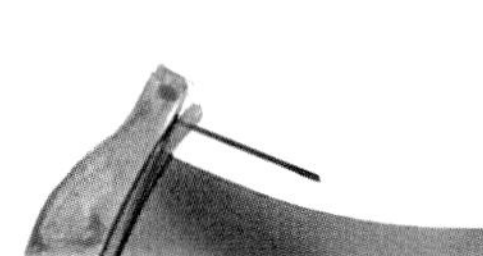

The *moliceiro* could be up to 50ft (15.2m) long.

NAVICELLO

ITALY: 1850

The *navicello* was used on Italy's Ligurian coast, from Livorno to west of Genoa, and on the island of Elba.

Length: 63ft 4in (19.3m)
Beam: 18ft (5.5m)
Depth: 7ft 6in (2.3m)
Displacement: not known
Rigging: two masts; fore-and-aft gaff rig with staysails and jib
Complement: 6–8
Cargo: general goods
Routes: Ligurian Sea

Racy-looking with its clipper-type bow, this coastal trading vessel shows an interesting combination of Mediterranean and 'international' features. The short foremast is angled forward as in older Mediterranean craft and supports a jib. A gaffsail is the main driver, with a triangular topsail; but between foremast and mainmast there is another gaffsail, without a spar, rigged to a line between the masts, and a staysail above it. The flush hull has a modern look.

JEKT

NORWAY: 1850

Length: 34ft 6in (10.5m)
Beam: 11ft (3.4m)
Depth: 3ft (0.9m)
Displacement: not known
Rigging: single pole mast; square sail, sometimes square topsail
Complement: 2
Cargo: farm produce
Routes: Norwegian fjords and inner coast

The Dutch word *jacht* was picked up by the Scandinavian countries and applied to a variety of smaller vessels, most of which did not come directly from the Dutch tradition. This Norwegian craft has a strong resemblance in the stem to the old Viking boat; it is clinker-built and has a single pole mast, but the hull is wider in relation to the relatively short length, and the square stern shows the influence of North Sea ships.

Light and flexible, the *jekt* was built to cope with the squalls and variable winds of the long Norwegian fjords.

PALLAR

INDIA: 1850

A small, useful vessel used for carrying passengers and light goods on the River Ganges in India, the *pallar* was clinker-built, as was the *patile*. Its single mast carried a square sail and sometimes a square topsail. The deck abaft the mast was largely covered by a bamboo cabin, on top of which perched the steersman, who was in charge of a side-rudder that was really an improved steering oar with a two-sided blade.

Length: c18ft (5.5m)
Beam: c6ft (1.8m)
Depth: c2ft (0.6m)
Displacement: not known
Rigging: single mast; square sail, small square topsail
Complement: 2
Cargo: passengers, light freight
Routes: River Ganges

PATILE

INDIA: 1850

Like the smaller *pallar*, this Ganges vessel, constructed as a cargo carrier, was clinker-built; this building technique evolved independently both here and in the far north of Europe. With a low prow and a high stern, the *patile* had a single deck, its beam ends showing between the strakes. The shallow draught was compensated for by a long pitch-roofed structure on the deck, built right out to the gunwales but with a catwalk along its length.

The single, wide square sail was cut to enable the helmsman, on top of the cabin, to see forward.

Length: c36ft (11m)
Beam: c12ft (3.7m)
Depth: c4ft (1.2m)
Displacement: not known
Rigging: single mast; square sail
Complement: not known
Cargo: general goods
Routes: River Ganges

PRAU

MALAY STATES: 1850

Length: c50ft (15.2m)
Beam: c13ft (4m)
Depth: not known
Displacement: not known
Rigging: two stump masts; lateen rig
Complement: not known
Cargo: tropical products, passengers
Routes: northeastern Java, around Surabaya and Madura

In Malay, *prau*, or *prahu*, simply means 'boat', and many types of *prau* were in use among the islands of the Indonesian archipelago, often dating back to very early times. Many were equipped with outriggers for greater stability, either single outriggers or, as with the *prau beduang*, double outriggers. The rig of the larger, single-hulled *prau mayang* was a lateen sail with a European-style foresail. The *Madura prau* shown here has a teak hull with no keel.

Larger *praus* were covered by a long bamboo and leaf roof to protect crews and cargo from rain and sun.

RASCONA

ITALY (VENICE): 1850

The deck-cabin suggests that the *rascona* might have gone on voyages beyond the lagoon, although it can only have been a slow sailer.

With a distinct resemblance to its passenger-carrying relative, the gondola, this two-masted sailing craft operated in and perhaps beyond the Venetian lagoon, carrying bulk supplies to and from the islands and coastal ports. It was fitted with a steering oar, not a rudder, and was lugsail-rigged. Often the *rascona* must have been poled along in shallow water on windless days by its two-man crew.

Length: c45ft (13.7m)
Beam: c16ft (4.9m)
Depth: c4ft (1.2m)
Displacement: not known
Rigging: two masts; lugsail rig
Complement: 2
Cargo: rice, grain, sand, wood, wine
Routes: Venice and northern Adriatic Sea

PISCATAQUA RIVER BARGE

USA: 1850

Also known as a gundalow, this barge, with a 'swimhead' type of stem rather than a blunt barge prow, had a very distinctive rig. A strong, stumpy mast supported a very long spar fitted with a triangular lateen-type sail. Attached very near its lower end, the boom was counter-weighted to allow rapid lowering as the vessel approached a bridge or overhanging building. The boom was stayed to the stern, but the vessel's tendency to yaw must have been considerable. This barge's draught appears to have been minimal, with cargo stacked on deck. Leeboards were fitted to help in tacking.

Length: 72ft (21.9m)
Beam: 19ft (5.8m)
Depth: 4ft (1.2m)
Displacement: not known
Rigging: stump mast; spritsail rig
Complement: 2
Cargo: farm produce, baled and barrelled goods
Routes: Piscataqua River, New England

ROSLAGSJAKT

SWEDEN: 1850

Of the various Scandinavian single-masted coastal craft whose names derive from the Dutch *jacht*, this sloop had one of the most simple rigs, with no bowsprit. Its form emerged from that of the *storbåt*, and it was a common carrier of passengers and cargo in the Stockholm archipelago during the 19th century. Able to operate with a minimal crew, it was economical to fit out and maintain.

A notable feature of the *roslagsjakt* was the lengthy boom extending well abaft the stern and secured by a strong stay to the mast.

Length: c30ft (9.1m)
Beam: c8ft (2.4m)
Depth: not known
Displacement: not known
Rigging: single mast; gaff-and-boom-rigged driver; foresail
Complement: 1–2
Cargo: passengers, light freight
Routes: Swedish islands around Stockholm

SACOLEVA

GREECE: 1850

Length: c55ft (16.8m)
Beam: c16ft (4.9m)
Depth: c7ft (2.1m)
Displacement: c100t
Rigging: two masts; square-rigged on mainmast with fore-and-aft gaffsail; spritsail mizzen, mizzen foresail; two jibs and fore-staysail
Complement: not known
Cargo: grain, wine, foodstuffs, general cargo
Routes: outer Greek islands

This was one of the larger Greek merchant vessels, able to take to the open sea and sail as far as Crete and Rhodes, although its one open deck did not offer much in the way of accommodation or shelter. Its rig is very advanced for the early 19th century, with a dolphin-striker stay fitted to the high-raked bowsprit and jib-boom.

Undoubtedly modelled on an older type of boat, the sacoleva shows the Greek seamen's capacity to adapt to and borrow new techniques.

SAMBUK

ARAB STATES: 1850

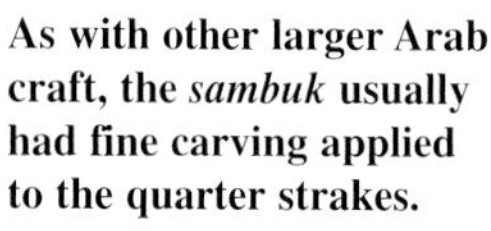

As with other larger Arab craft, the *sambuk* usually had fine carving applied to the quarter strakes.

One of the numerous craft known generally as *dhows*, the *sambuk* was a two-masted Arab trader of similar rig to the *baghla*, but longer and lower; more of a cargo carrier. The main distinguishing feature was the curved stemhead. Like the *baghla*, its lateen sails were four-sided; this was known as a settee rig.

Length: c55ft (16.8m)
Beam: 12ft (3.7m)
Depth: 5ft (1.5m)
Displacement: c100t
Rigging: two masts; lateen rig
Complement: not known
Cargo: foodstuffs, fish, general cargo
Routes: Arabian and East African ports

SCAPHO

GREECE: 1850

Scapho is Greek for 'boat', and this type of vessel sailed among the Aegean islands and the promontories of the mainland. Its unusual rig seems an adaptation of the spritsail, with the sprit rigged derrick-fashion and stayed to each gunwale close to the stern. The sail was mounted curtain-style, enabling it to be 'drawn' rapidly. Loose-footed, it could be hauled across the sheet to cope with changing winds or direction. There is no bowsprit, but the forestay is fixed to the extended stempost.

Length: 56ft (17.1m)
Beam: 14ft (4.3m)
Depth: 6ft (1.8m)
Displacement: not known
Rigging: single mast; derrick-type gaff and curtain-rig mainsail; fore-staysail
Complement: 2
Cargo: fish, foodstuffs, wine, water, firewood, animals
Routes: inner Aegean islands

This curtain-style rig is also seen in one or two Turkish ship types of similar size and function.

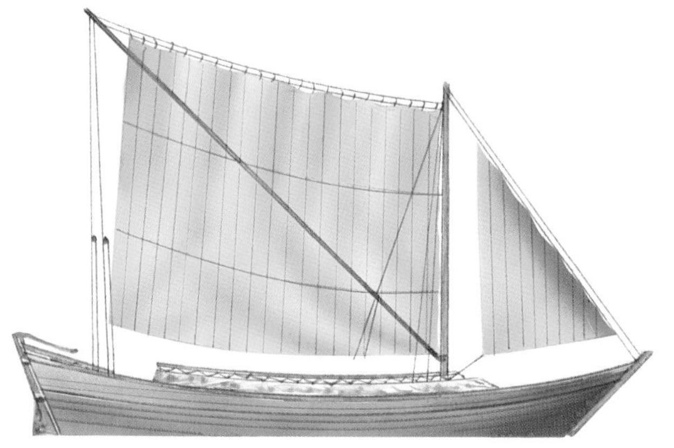

SOVEREIGN OF THE SEAS

USA: 1852

Length: 258ft 2in (78.7m)
Beam: 44ft (13.4m)
Depth: 21ft (6.4m)
Displacement: 2421t
Rigging: three masts; full-rigged ship
Complement: 45
Cargo: bulk freight, including tea, oil, wool
Routes: trans-oceanic routes

One of the longest clippers ever built, *Sovereign of the Seas* was constructed by Donald McKay and launched at his East Boston yard in 1852. She survived near-catastrophe west of Cape Horn on her maiden voyage when parts of her masts and spars were carried away. A superb sailer, her record run was 411 miles (661km) in 24 hours; her best speed 22 knots. Sold to the Liverpool Black Ball Line, then to Godeffroy of Hamburg, she ran aground on the China-Hamburg run and became a total loss.

Such was the Black Ball Line's confidence that they offered a rebate on the freight price if *Sovereign* did not beat the time of any steamer on the Australia run.

SPERONARA

MALTA: 1850

A number of archaic Mediterranean features can be detected in this Maltese craft, although it also sports a jib-boom and jib on a long stay in addition to its more traditional lateen sail. With numerous variants of rig, the *speronara* served as a small packet boat and general cargo boat. The hull was double-ended, mostly undecked, and with a low freeboard. The name refers to the vestigial *sperone*, or ram, and not to any specific rig or number of masts.

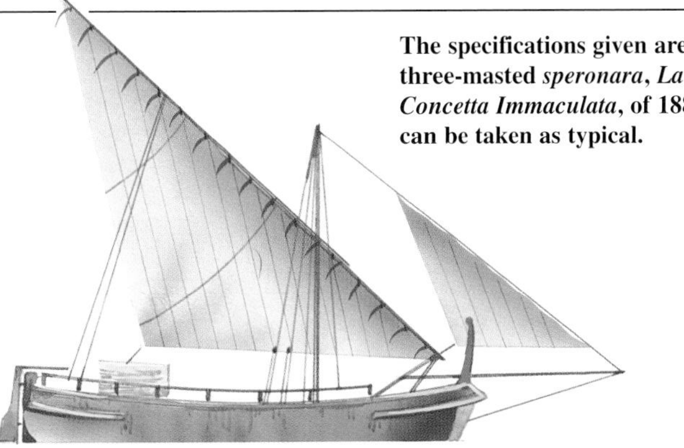

The specifications given are for a three-masted *speronara*, *La Concetta Immaculata*, of 1882 and can be taken as typical.

Length: 50ft 10in (15.5m)
Beam: 14ft 5in (4.4m)
Depth: 3ft 11in (1.2m)
Displacement: 17t
Rigging: three masts; lateen rig
Complement: 2
Cargo: general goods, passengers
Routes: Malta-Sicily, Malta-Italy

STAG HOUND

USA: 1850

Length: 215ft (65.5m)
Beam: 39ft 10in (12.1m)
Depth: 21ft (6.4m)
Displacement: 1534t
Rigging: three masts; full-rigged ship
Complement: 40
Cargo: bulk freight
Routes: New York-Cape Horn-San Francisco, Atlantic routes

An 'extreme clipper', so-called because of her size and vast 11,000sq ft (1000sq m) sail plan, *Stag Hound* was designed and built by Donald McKay at East Boston. Intended for the New York-San Francisco run, with a return via China, she was often logged at a speed of 17 knots. She was carrying English coal to San Francisco when the cargo caught fire off Recife, and on 12 October 1861 she was abandoned by her crew and burnt out.

Experts thought *Stag Hound* was too sharp for her lofty rig, but her fine sailing qualities belied this.

STORBÅT

SWEDEN: 1850

For at least 300 years up to the 19th century, the *storbåt*, 'big boat', was used by Swedish farmers to transport their produce to the markets of Stockholm, the Swedish capital. Usually two-masted, it was double-ended, clinker-built, with a small cabin built into the stern and a rounded plank-tiled roof, hence the name sometimes given of *kajutbåt*, 'cabin-boat'. The square sails were replaced by fore-and-aft rig in the course of the 19th century.

Vessels similar to the *storbåt* were used by coastal farms in other parts of Scandinavia.

Length: 30ft (9.1m)
Beam: 14ft (4.3m)
Depth: 2ft 3in (0.7m)
Displacement: not known
Rigging: two masts; one square-rig sail on each; headsail
Complement: 1-2
Cargo: hay, farm produce
Routes: Swedish coast and islands

TARTANA

SPAIN: 1850

Length: 66ft 10in (20.4m)
Beam: 21ft 11in (6.7m)
Depth: 8ft 8in (2.67m)
Displacement: c180t
Rigging: two masts; lateen rig with jib
Complement: 10
Cargo: general cargo, passengers
Routes: eastern Spain, Balearic Islands, southern France

Tartane, or *tartana*, is a name found across the Mediterranean and applied to different sorts of craft. In the Western Mediterranean, it has some resemblance to the Maltese *speronara* – a single-masted vessel with traditional lateen rig and with a jib-boom plainly added to a prow that was not designed for one. However, the Spanish vessel is less barge-like in its hull form. The single-masted *tartana* was a fishing boat; the larger cargo version had two masts.

The big *tartana* was one of the most common cargo vessels of the Western Mediterranean in the 17th and 18th centuries.

TRABACOLO

VENICE: 1850

A variant on the *trabacolo* was the *peligo*, with a topmast on the aftermast, a spanker and triangular topsail.

This was the most common type of Adriatic coasting ship, and working examples could be found far into the 20th century. It had a double-ended hull built on a keel, a long bowsprit, rounded bows curving slightly inwards, pole masts and big lugsails. A modified form of the rig fitted a topmast to the main pole, with a spanker and triangular topsail. *Trabacolos* were found as far down the Adriatic as Dubrovnik.

Length: 56ft 6in (17.2m)
Beam: 21ft 4in (6.5m)
Depth: 7ft 1in (2.2m)
Displacement: not known
Rigging: two masts; two lugsails; two jibs
Complement: 2–4
Cargo: foodstuffs, hay, wood, animals, general freight
Routes: Adriatic coastal routes

TREKANDIRI

GREECE: 1850

Length: c32ft (9.8m)
Beam: c9ft (2.7m)
Depth: c4ft (1.2m)
Displacement: not known
Rigging: two masts; main with sprit mainsail and topsail; square topsail, jib; lateen mizzen
Complement: not known
Cargo: general freight
Routes: Greek coast and islands

Low-slung in the waist, the *trekandiri* usually carried weatherboards to help provide shelter in that area of the vessel.

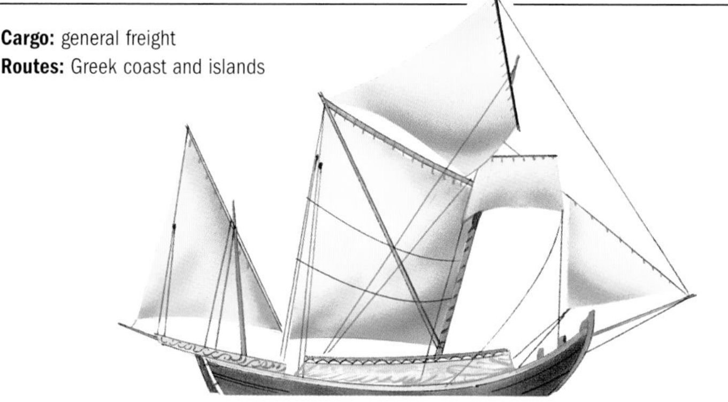

As coastal vessels go, this Greek cut more of a dash than most, with her double-ended hull upswept to stem and stern and a high stern platform built far out, with a bumkin pole beyond it to secure the corner of the lateen mizzen. She was similar to the *bratsera*, but her masts were not parallel, and she was normally smaller than the even more flamboyant *sacoleva*. By the 19th century, the *trekandiri* tended to have only a single mast.

TURKISH COASTER

TURKEY: 1850

Like the similar-sized Greek *sacoleva*, this ship mounts a varied rig on a single mast; square-rigged with course and topsail, there is also a staysail and jib. The derrick-rigged sprit supports not a spritsail but a curtain-like sail similar to that of the Greek *scapho*, suspended on rings and furled by being 'drawn' towards the mast. Ships thus rigged plied the Black Sea coast into the 20th century.

Length: 50ft (15.2m)
Beam: 13ft (4m)
Depth: 5ft (1.5m)
Displacement: c45t
Rigging: single mast with square sails and jib; fore-and-aft curtain mainsail from sprit
Complement: 4
Cargo: grain, rice, firewood, water, oil, animals
Routes: Black Sea coast, Bosporus

Turkish coastal transport was very much focused on supplying the needs of Constantinople (Istanbul) with food, fodder and fuel.

VINCO

PIEDMONT (ITALY): 1850

Genoa grew once again in importance as a port in the 19th century, and many ships traded from there, including this *vinco*, which appears to be a local type. She was three-masted, with a long, raised quarterdeck, and her rig was distinctive even for the Mediterranean with its combination of square-rigged foremast, lateen-rigged mainmast and lateen mizzen perched on the sternpost. Such a ship could have made rapid sail to Corsica or Elba.

The mixed rig again shows the versatility of the Mediterranean seaman, facing the highly variable wind conditions of the Ligurian Sea.

Length: c95ft (29m)
Beam: c25ft (7.6m)
Depth: c8ft (2.4m)
Displacement: c180t
Rigging: three masts; square-rigged with topmast on foremast; two jibs and foresail; lateen rig on mainmast and mizzen
Complement: not known
Cargo: farm products, industrial products, general cargo
Routes: Genoa to Tuscan coast, Elba and Corsica

YENG HE

CHINA: *c*1850

Length: 65ft 7in (20m)
Beam: 11ft 10in (3.6m)
Depth: not known
Displacement: not known
Rigging: not applicable
Machinery: sidewheels, steam
Complement: not known

Now located in the grounds of Beijing's Summer Palace, this iron-hulled paddle-wheel steam yacht was presented by the Japanese Emperor to the last Manchu Emperor of China on his accession in 1909. Its earlier history is obscure; it was probably British-built in the mid-19th century, shipped out in parts and assembled in Japan. Since the Chinese Empire came to an end in 1911, it was scarcely used. The hull remains intact.

The Summer Palace grounds also feature a stone-built pavilion designed to resemble a sidewheel river steamer.

ZARUK

SOUTH YEMEN: 1850

This small vessel, with a partially decked section at bow and stern, was used in the Red Sea around Aden and the coast of South Yemen. Probably shell-built and braced by lateral planks between the gunwales, it had a curious rudder, whose depth seems out of proportion to the ship; perhaps it also served as a sort of keel. Said to be used for slave-running and smuggling, the zaruk was probably a fishing boat in origin and, usually, in function.

Length: c36ft (11m)
Beam: c7ft (2.1m)
Depth: c1ft 6in (0.5m)
Displacement: not known
Rigging: single mast; lateen rig
Complement: 1–2
Cargo: fish, contraband
Routes: southern Arabian coast

AMERICA (SOMETIME CAMILLA, AMERICA)

USA: 1851

Length: 101ft 9in (31m)
Beam: 23ft (7m)
Depth: 11ft (3.4m)
Displacement: 180t
Rigging: two masts; schooner rig
Complement: 25
Role: yacht

Her name perpetuated in the America's Cup, this schooner yacht had a varied career over more than 90 years. Designed by George Steers and built in the yard of New York shipbuilder William H Brown, she was intended to be the fastest racing schooner of the day, and specifically to win honours from British yachts in British waters. This she triumphantly did by winning the Royal Yacht Squadron's Cup at Cowes, Isle of Wight, on 22 August 1851. The owning syndicate sold her that year and her new owner took her on a cruise to the Mediterranean.

Between 1853 and 1861, *America* had several owners. At Savannah, in 1861, she was renamed *Camilla* and crossed the Atlantic again. On her return she was sold to the Confederate government and used as a blockade runner in the Civil War because of her speed. Scuttled when the Union Army captured Jacksonville, Florida, she was refloated and commissioned as USS *America* to fight against the Confederacy. Refitted in 1863, she was used as a training ship by the US Navy and came fourth in the first America's Cup race of 1870. In 1873, she was sold to a private owner and raced for almost 30 years more, making her final appearance in 1901. After 15 years laid up, she was presented to the US Naval Academy, but neglect during World War II led to her deterioration, and she was broken up in 1945.

***America*'s Cowes victory in 1851 occasioned a vast outburst of national pride. 'America is first and there is no second!' declared Daniel Webster.**

ARABIA

GB: 1851

Length: not known
Beam: not known
Depth: not known
Displacement: 3900t
Rigging: two masts; square rig
Machinery: sidewheels, steam
Complement: not known
Cargo: passengers, light freight, mails
Routes: transatlantic

Arabia was a two-funnelled paddle steamer belonging to Samuel Cunard's British and North American Royal Mail Steam Packet Company; she was built in Govan, Scotland. In 1855, she was converted to carry 203 horses for Crimean War service, and in 1856 resumed the company's transatlantic sailings, which had begun in 1840. Her top service speed was 15 knots. In 1864, she was sold for conversion to a sailing vessel and was eventually broken up.

***Arabia* was the last wooden-hulled Cunard liner; she was followed by the iron-hulled *Persia* in the development of this premier Atlantic fleet.**

FLYING CLOUD

USA: 1851

For all her elegance of line, *Flying Cloud* was a big ship, twice the tonnage of the British racers like *Ariel* and *Cutty Sark*.

Designed by the Scots-Canadian Donald McKay and launched at East Boston, *Flying Cloud* was claimed to be the fastest American clipper, perhaps the fastest of all clippers. Her maiden voyage from New York to San Francisco was made in 89 days and 21 hours. In 1854, she clipped 13 hours from that time, a record beaten only once before 1888 and then by only four hours (by *Andrew Jackson* in 1860). Her best day's run was a remarkable 402 miles (647km). Built as a tea clipper, she made a risky voyage from Whampoa to New York in 1855 with a punctured hull, which required constant pumping. From 1859, she sailed between England, China and Australia, passing into British ownership in 1862. For almost 10 years, she ran immigrant passengers from England to Australia, returning with wool and vying with other high-speed clippers such as *Cutty Sark* and *Thermopylae* for the fastest journey times, since the earliest cargoes fetched the best auction prices. Sold again to Smith Edwards of South Shields, she went into service between Newcastle, England, and St John's, New Brunswick, with coal and pig iron on the outward leg and timber on the return. Her career ended when she grounded by Beacon Island and, although refloated, was broken-backed. In 1875, at St John's, she was stripped of her metalwork and all salvageable parts, and the hulk, with its fine underwater lines, was burned.

Length: 235ft (71.6m)
Beam: 40ft 9in (12.4m)
Depth: 21ft 4in (6.5m)
Displacement: 1782t
Rigging: three masts; full-rigged ship
Complement: not known
Cargo: tea, wool, cotton, nitrates
Routes: main oceanic trading routes

HUMBOLT

USA: 1851

In 1850, the New York and Havre Steam Navigation Company ordered two paddle steamships, *Humbolt* and *Franklin*, as mail steamers for the USA-Germany service; both had wooden hulls reinforced by iron strapping. *Humbolt* was launched in 1851, and from May of that year the two ships ran a regular service until *Humbolt*, under Captain David Lines, foundered in the Atlantic in December 1853.

The US Mail contract for Germany was worth $200,000 a year to the company that met the government's strict demands.

Length: 283ft (86.2m)
Beam: 40ft (12.2m)
Depth: 27ft 2in (8.2m)
Displacement: 2181t
Rigging: three masts; barque rig
Machinery: sidewheels, side lever
Complement: not known
Cargo: passengers, light freight, mail
Routes: USA-Le Havre, USA-Bremen

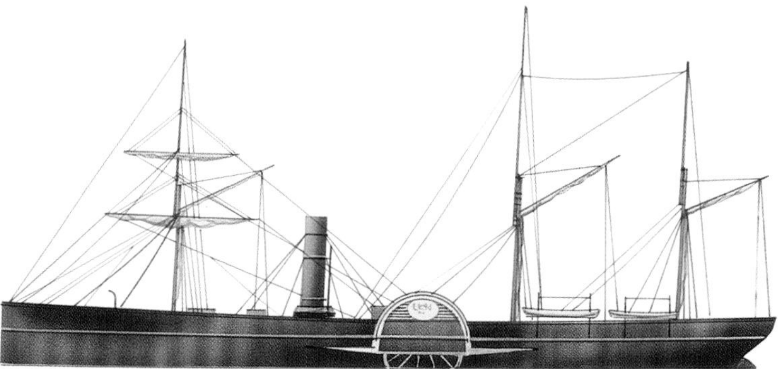

MARCO POLO

GB: 1851

Built at St John, New Brunswick, but sold early on to Liverpool owners, *Marco Polo* ran mostly in the Australian trade, carrying emigrants out and cargo back. Her first Liverpool-Melbourne run was accomplished in only 76 days, earning her for a time the title of fastest ship in the world. In 1874, rerigged as a barque, she became a cargo carrier and finally came under Norwegian ownership. After springing a leak, she was run ashore with a cargo of lumber on Prince Edward Island on 22 July 1883.

Length: 184ft 1in (56.1m)
Beam: 36ft 4in (11m)
Depth: 29ft 3in (8.9m)
Displacement: 1625t
Rigging: three masts; full-rigged ship
Complement: not known
Cargo: passengers; later bulk cargoes and timber
Routes: main trans-oceanic routes

Marco Polo was unusually deep, probably with cotton cargoes in mind. She also had bow ports to assist in loading timber.

VALOROUS

GB: 1851

Even in its conversion to steam, the British Admiralty remained conservative. Paddle wheels were held to be more reliable than the more powerful screw.

Length: 210ft (64m)
Beam: 26ft (7.9m)
Depth: not known
Displacement: 2300t
Rigging: three masts; square rig
Machinery: sidewheels, steam
Armament: 16 guns
Complement: not known

The famous *Rattler* versus *Alecto* trials of 1845 did not spell the immediate end of the British paddle-driven warship. This big wooden-hulled steam frigate, launched at Pembroke Dock in April 1851, was the last fighting paddle ship of the Royal Navy and remained on the list for 40 years. She was sold at Plymouth on 27 February 1891.

AGAMEMNON

GB: 1852

The first British warship built with screw propulsion, *Agamemnon* was launched at Woolwich Dockyard, London, in 1852. Her success in service made her the prototype for a generation of steam-powered warships. In the Crimean War, she was flagship of the British Black Sea Fleet, taking part in the shelling of Sevastopol in October 1854 and of Fort Kinburn at the mouth of the Dnieper River in 1855. In 1857, *Agamemnon* was loaded with 1250t of telegraph cable in the first attempt to lay a transatlantic cable. The attempt failed, but in the following year, she and USS *Niagara* met in mid-Atlantic, spliced their respective ends, then sailed back, laying the first trans-ocean telegraph link. *Agamemnon* returned to normal service in 1858 and did duty on the Caribbean and North American stations. She was paid off in 1862, lay unused, and was finally sold in 1870.

Length: 230ft 4in (70.2m)
Beam: 55ft 4in (16.9m)
Depth: 24ft 1in (7.3m)
Displacement: 5080t
Rigging: three masts; square rig
Machinery: single screw, trunk; 2268hp
Armament: 34 8in (203mm), 56 32pdr, one 68pdr guns
Complement: 860

Agamemnon shown upon completion. Her original design was drawn up in 1847 as a direct response to the French 90-gun _La Napoléon_. Later, when employed in 1858 to lay the Atlantic cable, the screw and rudder were protected by an outrigger. A large structure was added amidships to house the heavy cable.

CONNECTOR

GB: 1852

Length: 170ft (51.8m)
Beam: 30ft (9.1m)
Depth: not known
Displacement: 2000t
Rigging: three masts; schooner rig
Machinery: single screw, compound
Complement: not known
Cargo: coal
Routes: Tyne ports to London

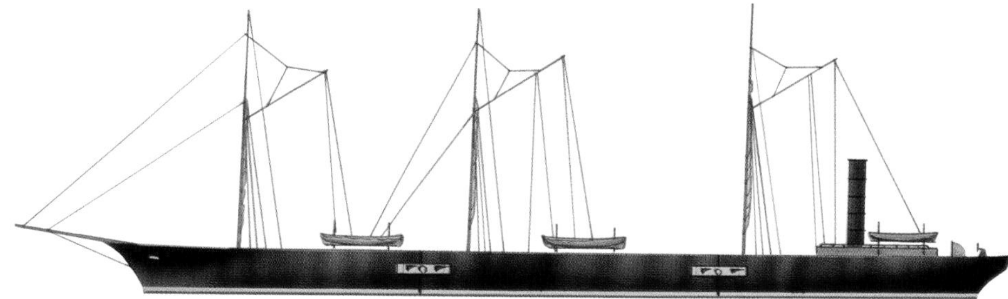

Launched in 1852, this experimental steamship was conceived on a similar principle to the articulated truck, with detachable hull sections enabling the aft motor section to be separated and used on another hull. Designed for the bulk coal trade, *Connector*'s hull was not rigid – its three self-contained sections, each with mast and sail, were hinged together. Unsurprisingly, the ship proved almost unworkable and was speedily scrapped.

The siting of the engine in the afterpart was a practice which would ultimately be followed in many bulk carriers.

DUKE OF WELLINGTON (EX-WINDSOR CASTLE)

GB: 1852

The engine put into *Duke of Wellington* had been destined for the iron frigate *Simoom* until that vessel was redesignated as a troopship.

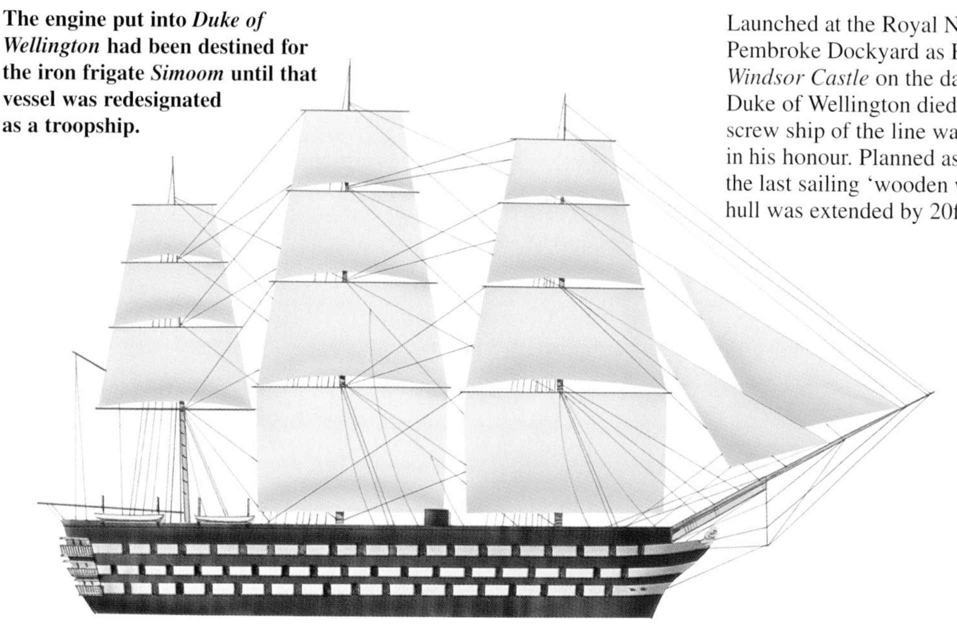

Launched at the Royal Navy's Pembroke Dockyard as HMS *Windsor Castle* on the day the Duke of Wellington died, this screw ship of the line was renamed in his honour. Planned as one of the last sailing 'wooden walls', her hull was extended by 20ft (6.1m) during building to accommodate an engine. In 1854, during the Crimean War, she was flagship of the Baltic Fleet under Vice-Admiral Sir Charles Napier. This was her only period of high-seas service. She became guardship at the Portsmouth Naval Base and for a time replaced HMS *Victory* as flagship there. Later she was converted to a depot ship and in 1904 she was sold off for breaking.

Length: 240ft (73m)
Beam: 60ft (18.3m)
Depth: 27ft (8.2m)
Displacement: 3771t
Rigging: three masts; square rig
Machinery: single screw, steam; 700hp
Armament: 16 8in (203mm), 113 32pdr and one 68pdr guns
Complement: 1100

POWHATAN

USA: 1852

Length: 253ft 10in (77.3m)
Beam: 45ft (13.7m)
Depth: 18ft 6in (5.6m)
Displacement: 3479t
Rigging: three masts; barque rig
Machinery: sidewheels, steam
Armament: one 11in (279mm), 10 9in (228mm), five 12pdr guns
Complement: 289

Powhatan was the largest of the US Navy's paddle-wheel frigates. She served as flagship to Commodore Perry in his second Japanese mission of 1854, and the trade treaty of Kanagawa was signed on her deck. During the American Civil War, she took part in blockades and coastal bombardments of the Confederate States. She then served in the Pacific and Atlantic until she was broken up in 1887.

The imposing sight of US steam-powered warships played its own part in the 'opening' of Japan to international trade in the 1850s.

SAN JACINTO

USA: 1852

Designated as a screw frigate, *San Jacinto* was launched at the Brooklyn Navy Yard in 1852. Her unreliable engines and propulsion system were replaced after the first year and from 1854 she was on active duty. The United States was extending its worldwide trading interests, and *San Jacinto* sailed to Thailand and Japan with official delegates; she also participated in the Second Opium War. In August

1860, she captured the slaver brig *Storm King*, releasing 616 slaves at Monrovia, Liberia. During the American Civil War she caused an international incident by stopping the British Royal Mail vessel *Trent* in the Atlantic and taking off two diplomats from the Confederacy. On blockade duty off the Southern coast, mostly with the East Gulf Squadron, she took four prizes. On 1 January 1865, she hit a reef close to Great Abaco Island in the Bahamas and was lost.

Length: 237ft (72.2m)
Beam: 37ft 10in (11.5m)
Depth: 17ft 3in (5.3m)
Displacement: 2150t
Rigging: three masts; square rig
Machinery: single screw, horizontal condensing
Armament: six 8in (203mm) guns
Complement: 235

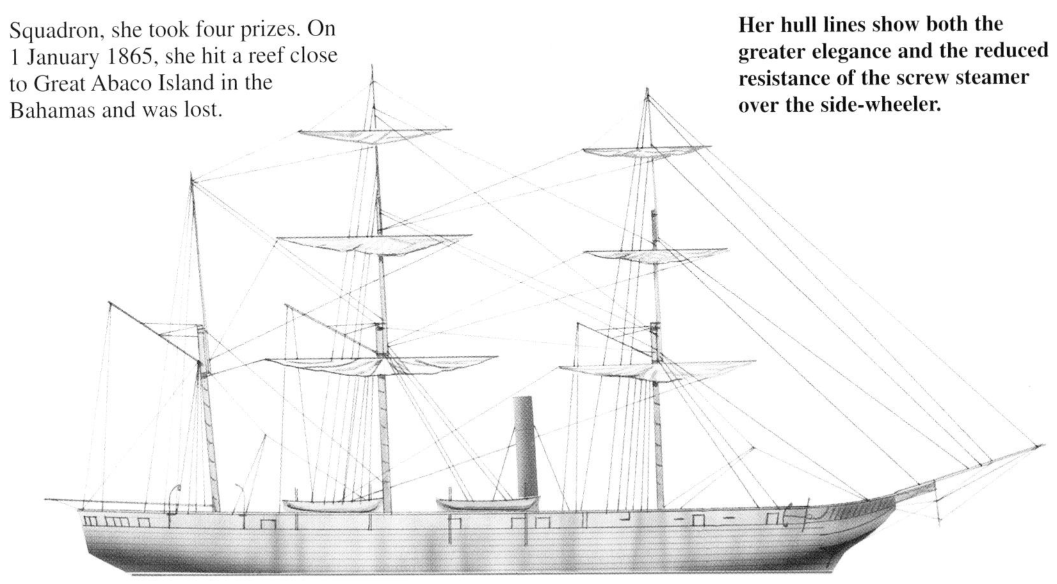

Her hull lines show both the greater elegance and the reduced resistance of the screw steamer over the side-wheeler.

EURYALUS GB: 1853

Classified as a screw frigate, *Euryalus* was built on a hull initially planned for a 60-gun sailing frigate and was launched at Chatham Royal Naval Dockyard. In 1854–55, she served with the Baltic Fleet under Vice-Admiral Napier. In 1860, she was fitted with the new large Armstrong screw gun and sent first to South Africa, then to the China station in 1862. During a period of hostilities between Britain and Japan in 1863-64, *Euryalus* was fired on by the Japanese fortress of Kagosima in August 1863 and encountered serious difficulties with her guns in returning fire, one of them exploding. During a land action against Japanese forces on 8 September 1864, Midshipman Duncan Boyes, bearing the British ensign, won the Victoria Cross for outstanding bravery. On her return to Britain, *Euryalus* was laid up for a short time, then sold off in 1867.

Length: 212ft (64.6m)
Beam: 50ft (15.2m)
Depth: 17ft (5.2m)
Displacement: 3125t
Rigging: three masts; square rig
Machinery: single screw, steam
Armament: 51 guns
Complement: 750

On the South African station, *Euryalus* had a royal midshipman, Prince Arthur. Queen Victoria paid a special allowance to the gunroom.

GREAT REPUBLIC (LATER DENMARK) USA: 1853

After the fire, *Great Republic*'s tonnage was reduced to 3357t and the sail plan cut back substantially from McKay's initial 15,653sq ft (1454sq m).

One of many notable ships designed by Donald McKay, *Great Republic*, built at East Boston, was the largest sailing vessel constructed in the USA and one of the largest wooden vessels ever built. Although her hull was drawn on clipper lines, she carried four masts – square-rigged on all but the mizzen, which was fore-and-aft-rigged – and was in effect the first four-masted barque. She was loading at New York for a maiden voyage to Liverpool when a bakery adjacent to the quay caught fire. Sparks from the burning building rapidly set the rigging ablaze, and the upperworks were severely burned. McKay sold her, and she was rebuilt in somewhat altered form internally, with three instead of four decks, and with her sail plan considerably reduced. Nevertheless, *Great Republic* was a fine sailer and handled beautifully. Her first captain, Joseph Limebourne, said: 'she steers like a boat in a pond'. In 1856, she made a record-breaking run from New York to the

Length: 320ft (92m)
Beam: 48.4ft (14.8m)
Depth: 29.2ft (8.9m)
Displacement: 4555t (later 3357t)
Rigging: four masts; fore-and-aft-rigged on mizzen, square-rigged on remainder
Complement: 130
Cargo: bulk freight
Routes: New York-Cape Horn-San Francisco; transatlantic

equator en route for San Francisco in 15 days and 19 hours. Prior to that she had been chartered to ship French troops to the Crimea in 1854. Until the American Civil War broke out in 1861, *Great Republic* continued in the California trade; during the war the federal government chartered her. In 1865, she returned to the east coast, under the ownership of a Nova Scotian company. This concern in turn sold her to the Liverpool Merchants' Trading Company, England, who renamed her *Denmark*. Still on the Nova Scotia-London route, she sprang a leak sailing eastbound; the crew had to abandon her, and she foundered off Bermuda on 5 March 1872.

HIMALAYA

GB: 1853

Planned as a paddle ship but eventually built as P&O Lines' first big screw steamer, the iron-hulled *Himalaya* was the biggest steamship in the world until the advent of the *Great Eastern*. She could manage 13.9 knots, but she proved rather heavy in fuel consumption and was speedily sold to the Admiralty as a troopship, remaining in that service until 1893, when her engines were taken out and she was turned into a coal hulk. Sunk in Portland harbour, England, by German bombs in 1940, her wreck remains.

During the Crimean War (1853-56), *Himalaya* carried 65,000 troops and 15,000 horses between Britain and the war zone.

Length: 315ft (96m)
Beam: 41ft 6in (12.6m)
Depth: 24ft 4in (7.4m)
Displacement: 5500t
Rigging: three masts; square-rigged on fore and main, spanker on mizzen
Machinery: single screw, trunk; 2500hp
Complement: not known
Cargo: passengers; troops

MONUMENTAL CITY

USA: 1853

Length: 235ft (72m)
Beam: 38ft (11.6m)
Depth: not known
Displacement: 768t
Rigging: not applicable
Machinery: not known
Complement: not known
Cargo: passengers
Routes: USA-Australia, Melbourne-Sydney

The gold discoveries in Australia attracted prospectors from America who travelled across the Pacific in sailing vessels. Seeing a good opportunity to open up a new and lucrative line Peter Stroebed purchased the steamer *Monumental City*. She left San Francisco on 17 February 1853, arriving at Sydney on 23 April. She proved a successful ship and was placed on the Melbourne-Sydney trade list on 15 May 1853. *Monumental City* ran aground on a small rocky island, becoming a total loss.

***Monumental City* was the first steamship to cross the Pacific. Her owner, Peter Stroebed, was one of those who died when she was wrecked.**

ARROW

GB: 1854

The outbreak of the Crimean War created demand for steam-powered shallow-draught gunboats for inshore work against shore batteries. Several types of such craft were built, of which *Arrow* was one. Flat-bottomed and slab-sided, she mounted a single heavy gun. In some ways these ships replaced the bomb ketch, although mortar vessels were also built, as guns from the *Arrow* type could not achieve the high trajectory of the mortar.

Length: 100ft (30.5m)
Beam: not known
Depth: 6ft 6in (2m)
Displacement: not known
Rigging: three masts; lugsail rig (later gaff-rigged)
Machinery: single screw, steam; 40hp
Armament: one 68pdr gun
Complement: not known

Gunboats went on to do service in most colonial stations of the Victorian Royal Navy, notably in China and Southeast Asia.

QUAKER CITY

USA: 1854

***Quaker City* was the only union privateer to operate during the Civil War. She captured four confederate vessels.**

Launched at Philadelphia in 1854, this sidewheel paddle steamer was first chartered, then bought by the US government in 1861. Fitted with nine guns, she became an effective blockading ship with the North Atlantic Squadron. She was able to make 13 knots and was used to chase Confederate raiders and blockade runners. Decommissioned on 18 May 1865 and sold in June that year, she was sold again to foreign owners in 1869.

Length: 244ft 8in (74.5m)
Beam: 36ft (11m)
Depth: 29ft 9in (9m)
Displacement: 1600t
Rigging: three masts, square-rigged on fore and main; spanker on mizzen
Machinery: sidewheels, steam
Armament: eight 32pdr, one 20pdr guns
Complement: 163

RADETZKY

AUSTRO-HUNGARIAN EMPIRE: 1854

Length: 231ft 8in (70.6m)
Beam: 42ft 10in (13m)
Depth: 18ft (5.5m)
Displacement: 2234t
Rigging: three masts; barque rig
Machinery: single screw, steam
Armament: six 60pdr shell guns; 40 30pdr guns; four 24pdr breech-loaders (from 1863)
Complement: 354

Name ship of a group of three screw frigates of the second class, *Radetzky* was built by Wigrams of London and launched in May 1854. She took part in the Austrian victory over the Italian fleet in the Battle of Lissa on 16 July 1866, and it was in the same location, on 2 February 1869, that she foundered after her powder magazine exploded, with the loss of 344 men.

The Austrian ships of this period retained obsolescent muzzle-loading guns, while other navies were installing rifled-barrelled breech-loaders.

BRETAGNE

FRANCE: 1855

Length: 265ft 8in (81m)
Beam: 59ft 4in (18.1m)
Depth: not known
Displacement: 6770t
Rigging: three masts; square rig
Machinery: single screw, steam; 1200hp
Armament: 130 guns
Complement: c900

Launched at Brest on 17 February 1855, this mighty steam-powered three-decker put France firmly in the lead for capital ship design; for the first time, sail was used as an auxiliary to steam in the largest class of warship. *Bretagne* was based with the Mediterranean Fleet at Toulon, and her active career was relatively short; she was converted to a training vessel in 1866.

***Bretagne* was greeted with concern by the British Admiralty, which speeded up its conversion to the notion of steam power.**

FOUDROYANTE

FRANCE: 1855

***Foudroyante* as a hulk at her last mooring.**

One of five 'screw floating batteries', *Foudroyante* was launched at Lorient in June 1855, too late to take part in the Crimean War. Double-ended, with flat sides and a distinct tumble-home and protected by 4in (10cm) of wrought iron armour over a 17in (43cm) wooden hull, she and her sisters were ungainly and slow vessels. Development of the turreted warship left them obsolete, and *Foudroyante* was condemned at Lorient in 1871.

Length: 173ft 9in (53m)
Beam: 43ft 9in (13.3m)
Depth: 8ft 9in (2.6m)
Displacement: 1674t
Rigging: three masts; 9520sq ft (885sq m) of sail
Machinery: single screw, steam; 150hp
Armament: 16 50pdr guns
Complement: 260

ADRIATIC

USA: 1856

Built at the Novelty Works, New York, this two-funnelled paddle steamer was the largest and last vessel of the Collins Line. The company was in severe difficulties caused by the loss of passenger confidence after the *Arctic* disaster, and *Adriatic* was almost immediately laid up, then sold to the Galway Line. After a boiler explosion in 1864, she was towed in to Liverpool. She ended her career as a store ship at Bonny, West Africa, she was broken up in 1885.

Length: 345ft (105.1m)
Beam: 50ft (15.2m)
Depth: not known
Displacement: 5888t
Rigging: two masts; brig rig
Machinery: sidewheels, side lever; 1350hp
Complement: not known
Cargo: passengers, light freight, mails
Routes: transatlantic

Among *Adriatic*'s new features was a calcium 'searchlight' on the foretopmast, with a four-mile (6.4km) beam.

ERZHERZOG FRIEDRICH

AUSTRO-HUNGARIAN EMPIRE: 1857

A steam corvette of the Imperial Austro-Hungarian Navy and built at the Venice Arsenal, *Erzherzog Friedrich* was in the second division under Commodore Petz in the Battle of Lissa in 1866. Later she made friendly visits to America, India, China and Japan. Having been regunned in 1866, she underwent a major refit from 1877 to 1880, during which she was fitted with topgallant forecastle and poop decks. Stricken from the list in August 1897, she was used for transporting boilers before being scrapped in 1899.

Length: 222ft 5in (67.8m)
Beam: 39ft 11in (12.1m)
Depth: 16ft 8in (5.1m)
Displacement: 1697t
Rigging: three masts; barque rig
Machinery: single screw, steam
Armament: four 60pdr shell guns; 17 30pdr, 14 8pdr guns
Complement: 294

Until its demise in 1918, the Austro-Hungarian Empire had a long Adriatic coastline and maintained a considerable fleet at Trieste and Pola.

GRILLE

PRUSSIA: 1857

Length: 186ft 4in (56.8m)
Beam: 24ft (7.3m)
Depth: 9ft (208m)
Displacement: 491t
Rigging: three masts; used for display of ensigns
Machinery: single screw; simple expansion steam engine
Complement: 30

By the 1850s, a steam yacht was part of the equipage of any up-to-date European monarch. King Wilhelm IV of Prussia, elder brother of Kaiser Wilhelm I, had *Grille* ('Grasshopper') built by a French yard. Maintained at the Kiel naval dockyard, she was a familiar visitor at the annual Cowes regatta in England. Replaced for royal duties in 1898 by a more up-to-date vessel, *Grille* was kept in service and converted in 1914 to a cadet training ship. She was scrapped in 1920.

The concept of the 'sailor-king' was a fashionable one in 19th century Europe, and monarchs often took the helm of their vessels.

HARRIET LANE (LATER LAVINIA, ELLIOTT RICHIE)

USA: 1857

Launched at New York as a revenue cutter, *Harriet Lane* fired the first shot of the Civil War on the night of 11/12 April 1861. Transferred to the US Navy, she served on the east coast and in the West Gulf Blockading Squadron. Taken by the Confederates when Galveston was recaptured, she was sold and used – renamed *Lavinia* – to run the blockade. Having sunk at Havana in January 1865, she was raised, refloated and given a ship rig as *Elliott Richie*, and sailed for almost another 20 years before being wrecked on the Brazilian coast in 1884.

The vessel's original name came from President Buchanan's niece, who acted as his 'First Lady', as he was unmarrie.d

Length: 180ft (54.9m)
Beam: 30ft (9.1m)
Depth: 12ft 6in (3.8m)
Displacement: 639t
Rigging: two masts; brigantine rig (later ship rig)
Armament: four 32pdr, one 20pdr, four 9in (228mm) guns
Complement: 130

ROANOKE

USA: 1857

Length: 263ft 8in (80.3m)
Beam: 52ft 6in (16m)
Depth: not known
Displacement: 4772t
Rigging: originally three masts; bark rig
Machinery: single screw, steam
Armament: two 10in (254mm), 28 9in (228mm), 14 8in (203mm) guns (as originally equipped)
Complement: 674

Launched in 1857 and classed as a screw frigate, and with a maximum speed of 11 knots, *Roanoke* became flagship of the Home Squadron on commissioning. She made a cruise to the West Indies, and on the outbreak of the Civil War in 1861 was put on duty in the North Atlantic Blockading Squadron. She took on 286 men from USSs *Congress* and *Cumberland* after the battle with the Confederate ironclad *Virginia* in Hampton Roads. During 1862-63, her superstructure was reconfigured, with three centre-line turrets. The alteration was not a success; the ship rolled to a dangerous degree in even a moderate sea. She was decommissioned at the New York Navy Yard on 20 June 1865, struck from the list in 1882 and sold for scrap in 1883.

***Roanoke* as she appeared after conversion into a turret ship.**

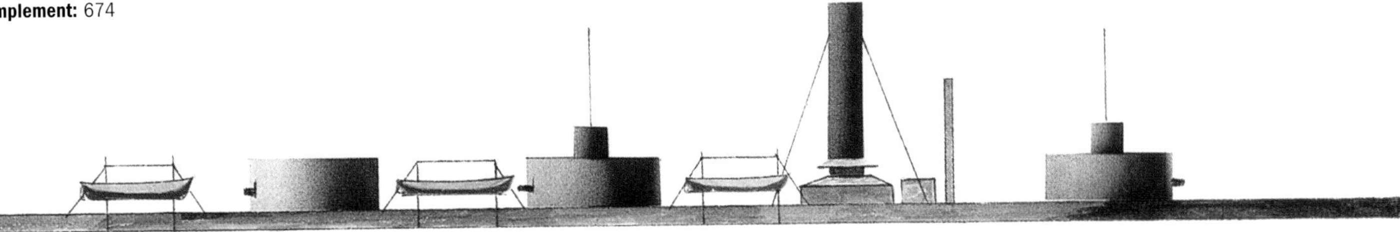

ROYAL SOVEREIGN

GB: 1857

Built at Portsmouth Dockyard and launched as a 121-gun three-decker, *Royal Sovereign* was converted between 1862 and 1864 to become the Royal Navy's first turret ship. Cut down to the lower deck, and with her hull massively armoured, she carried three turrets on the centre-line and was given screw propulsion. Coastal defence was the ship's chief role, despite her considerable draught. She was sold for breaking up in 1885.

***Royal Sovereign* in converted form was regarded as an experiment; it did not lead to further conversions of ships of the line.**

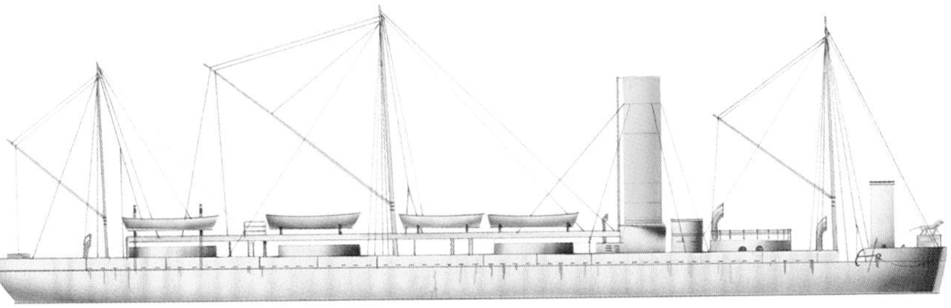

Length: 240ft 6in (73.3m)
Beam: 62ft (18.9m)
Depth: 23ft 3in (7m)
Displacement: 5080t
Rigging: three masts; fitted with gaffs
Machinery: single screw, return connecting rod
Armament: five 10.5in (266mm) guns (one double and two single turrets)
Complement: 300

BREMEN

GERMANY: 1858

Length: 318ft (96.9m)
Beam: 40ft (12.2m)
Depth: 26ft (7.9m)
Displacement: 2674t
Rigging: three masts; barque rig
Machinery: single screw, inverted direct drive
Complement: not known
Cargo: passengers, light freight, mails
Routes: Hamburg/Bremen-New York

Built at Greenock for Norddeutscher Lloyd, *Bremen* was iron-hulled with a single funnel and could make a speed of 13.1 knots; she and her sistership *New York* were the first German transatlantic liners. At this time steamships had scarcely more superstructure – funnel apart – than sailing vessels, mainly because they were still fully sparred with the consequent lack of clearance for construction on deck.

Mails figured largely in the economics of these ships; the majority of passengers were emigrants, most of them poor and looking for low-cost transport.

BROOKLYN

USA: 1858

Designated as a screw sloop, *Brooklyn* was commissioned in 1859, and in the Civil War was sent to join the West Gulf Blockading Squadron. She participated in attacks on Fort Jackson and other strongpoints and in the capture of New Orleans (1862); in August 1864, she was in the Battle of Mobile Bay. *Brooklyn* ended the Civil War in the North Atlantic Blockading Squadron, served on for more than 20 years and was decommissioned and sold in 1891.

It was to the commander of USS *Brooklyn*, at Mobile Bay, that Farragut uttered the words 'Damn the torpedoes – full speed ahead.'

Length: 233ft (71m)
Beam: 43ft (13.1m)
Depth: not known
Displacement: 2686t
Rigging: three masts; barque rig
Machinery: single screw, steam
Armament: one 10in (254mm), 20 9in (228mm) smooth-bore guns
Complement: 300

CHALLENGER

GB: 1858

The corvette was classed under the frigate and was intended for scouting and escort duties. *Challenger* was larger than 20th-century corvettes.

A screw corvette, *Challenger* was provided, with her crew, by the Royal Navy to undertake for the Royal Society (of London) the most extensive and intensive scientific cruise so far envisaged. The principal purpose was to investigate the Atlantic, Pacific and Indian oceans, and the ship was equipped to take soundings to a maximum depth of 6000 fathoms (36,000ft/11,000m). Other equipment was provided to take temperature readings, measure currents, and collect bottom samples from as far down as 4000 fathoms (24,000ft/7300m). *Challenger* departed Sheerness on 7 December 1872 and spent 10 months in the Atlantic. In the Antarctic summer, she went south as far as the ice in the Southern Ocean and reached Melbourne, Australia, in March 1874. The following year was spent in cruising the Pacific, where a number of important discoveries were made, including the presence of manganese nodules at great depth on the ocean floor. The greatest depth plumbed by the expedition was 4475 fathoms (26,850ft/8184m). The ship

Length: 200ft (60.1m)
Beam: 40ft 6in (12.3m)
Depth: not known
Displacement: 2306t
Rigging: three masts; barque rig
Machinery: single screw, compound; 1200hp
Complement: 243
Routes: Atlantic, Pacific and Indian oceans

returned to England via the Strait of Magellan and the Atlantic, anchoring in Portsmouth harbour on 24 May 1876, having travelled a total of 68,990 miles (111,025km). *Challenger* remained on active service until 1880, when her engines and equipment were removed; she was kept in Admiralty service as a hulk until 1921, when she was scrapped.

El Ictineo

SPAIN: 1858

Length: 30ft (9m)
Beam: not known
Depth: 7ft (2m)
Displacement: 30t
Machinery: single screw, steam
Complement: three

During the 19th century, work went on in several countries to construct a practicable submarine. This vessel, designed by the Spanish engineer Monturiol, had many innovative features. Its steam engine was intended to operate even when the vessel was submerged; it had a double hull and a compressed-air pump to empty the ballast tanks. Its large oxygen requirement was supplied by a chemical conversion plant.

El Ictineo's shape also anticipated later practice in submarine design, but the vessel's mechanisms were too experimental to be consistently reliable.

Great Eastern

GB: 1858

A long-lived but false maritime myth was that a riveter had been accidentally sealed into the vessel's double-skinned iron hull in the course of its construction.

Length: 692ft (210.9m)
Beam: 82ft 9in (25.2m)
Depth: 30ft (9.1m)
Displacement: 18,915t
Rigging: six masts; second and third square-rigged, remainder fore-and-aft-rigged
Complement: not known
Cargo: 4000 passengers, 6000t of cargo
Routes: transatlantic

A giant in her day, *Great Eastern* was designed by Isambard Kingdom Brunel, one of Britain's most versatile and inventive engineers, and built on the Isle of Dogs in the lower Thames. In every dimension and virtually every aspect she was a record-breaker, and she even had to be launched sideways into the tideway. The hull was double and was divided by bulkheads into 10 watertight compartments. She was the only ship to be fitted with both paddle-wheel and screw propulsion, with two 56ft (17m) sidewheels and a 24ft (7.3m) propeller; there were separate engines for each drive. The six masts could support more than 15,000sq ft (1400sq m) of sail. There was passenger accommodation for 4000, with 2000 in second class and 1200 in third, and she could also carry 6000t of cargo. Anticipating the later transatlantic liners in many ways, *Great Eastern*, like many ships built by visionaries, was ahead of her time and commercially a failure. Her engines were insufficiently powerful for her bulk, and despite her size she had a tendency to roll. Few harbours could accommodate her and she was too big for the tugboats to handle. Brunel died in December 1859 before fitting-out was complete and never made a voyage in the ship. Although Brunel had had the Australian route in mind, *Great Eastern* began on the North Atlantic and made 10 return voyages before being withdrawn.

Her greatest value was as a cable layer. The original transatlantic cable of 1858 (see HMS *Agamemnon*) had failed and between June 1865 and August 1866, *Great Eastern* laid two cables across the Atlantic; she went on to lay a further three, plus the trans-oceanic cable between Suez, Aden and Bombay. Sold in 1874 to a French company for passenger work again, *Great Eastern* made a single voyage between France and New York, then was laid up in Milford Haven, Wales, between 1875 and 1886. Used for two years as a floating exhibition site at Liverpool, she was broken up in 1888.

Port Fairy Lifeboat

AUSTRALIA: 1858

An excellent example of an early shore-based rescue craft, the Port Fairy (Victoria) Lifeboat stayed in continuous service from 1858 until 1941. Built of double-diagonal wooden planking on a wooden frame with an iron keel, she was generally propelled by oars (although she had a dipping lugsail for use in easier conditions). She was later preserved in the town where she was stationed, displayed in a boathouse built for her in 1861.

The Port Fairy Lifeboat is an excellent example of an oared rescue lifeboat of the mid-19th century and one of the oldest still in existence.

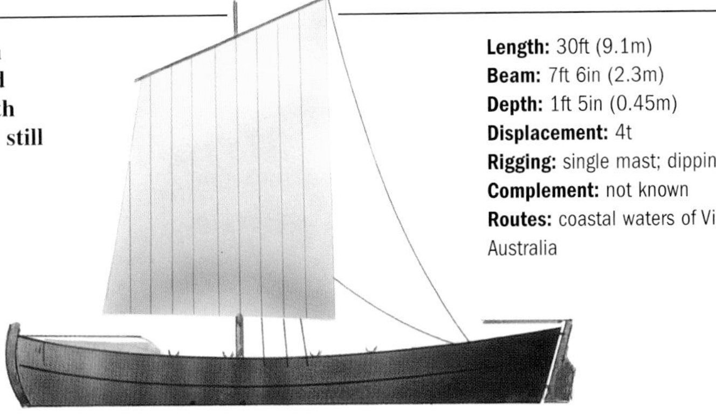

Length: 30ft (9.1m)
Beam: 7ft 6in (2.3m)
Depth: 1ft 5in (0.45m)
Displacement: 4t
Rigging: single mast; dipping lugsail
Complement: not known
Routes: coastal waters of Victoria, Australia

GALATEA

GB: 1859

Built at Woolwich Dockyard, London, *Galatea* was one of a class known as 'Walker's Big Frigates' – large screw-driven wooden-hulled frigates designed by Sir Benjamin Walker in response to the US Navy's new steam-driven vessels of 1854. Her chief characteristics were speed and firepower and she stands out as a transitional type between the sailing frigate and the steam-powered, turreted ironclad. *Galatea* was scrapped in 1882.

Galatea was amongst the slower vessels in her class, with a maximum speed of 11.8 knots; her faster sisters had shorter careers.

Length: 280ft (85.3m)
Beam: 50ft (15.2m)
Depth: 21ft 4in (6.5m)
Displacement: 4686t
Rigging: three masts, full square rig
Machinery: single screw, single expansion
Armament: 24 10in (254mm) muzzle-loader guns; two 68pdr guns
Complement: 450

HARTFORD

USA: 1859

A wooden-hulled, Boston-built 'screw sloop', USS *Hartford* saw much action in the course of the Civil War. One of the US Navy's largest ships, she served as flagship to the Philippines Squadron until recalled when the Civil War broke out in 1861. At the end of that year she was flagship of the blockading squadron in the western Gulf, under Admiral Farragut. The week-long naval attack on New Orleans was led by *Hartford*. It was a hard-fought campaign in which the Union vessels faced the obstacles of gunboats, fireships, shore batteries and the Confederate ironclad *Manassas*; *Hartford* grounded during the attack but was refloated. With New Orleans secure, Farragut took his force up the Mississippi past Vicksburg to link up with the Western Flotilla. In July 1862, *Hartford* underwent repairs at Pensacola before returning to the Mississippi to support General Grant's attack on Vicksburg in November. Vicksburg was taken on 4 July 1863, and *Hartford* spent the rest of the year on Gulf blockade duty. On 5 August 1864, she played a leading part in the Battle of Mobile Bay, in which Farragut took his ships through a minefield and forced the surrender of the ironclad CSS *Tennessee*. After the war, *Hartford* was flagship of the Asiatic Squadron from 1865 to 1868 and again from 1872–75; she was based in California as a training vessel from 1887 to 1890 and was used for training in Atlantic waters from 1899 to 1912. From 1912 to 1938, she was station ship at Charleston, South Carolina. Moved to Washington DC in 1938 and then to Norfolk Navy Yard, the now-venerable ship sank at her berth and was broken up.

In US Naval parlance, a sloop-of-war was a full-rigged three-masted ship of up to 20 guns; it was smaller than a frigate.

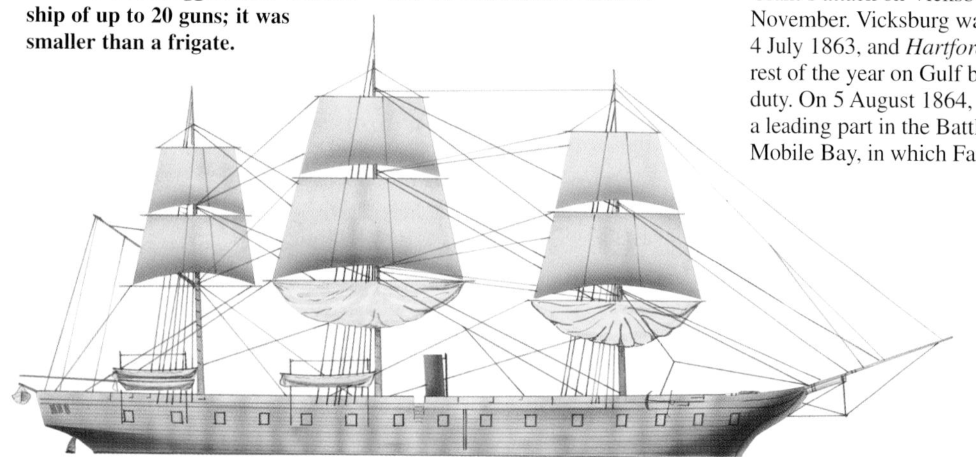

Length: 225ft (68.6m)
Beam: 44ft (13.4m)
Depth: 17ft 3in (5.2m)
Displacement: 2900t
Rigging: three masts; barque rig
Machinery: single screw, steam
Armament: 20 9in (228mm), 20 20pdr, two 12pdr guns
Complement: 310

KAISER (LATER BELLONA)

AUSTRO-HUNGARIAN EMPIRE: 1859

The Austro-Hungarian Empire maintained a fleet on its Adriatic coast, with Trieste as its headquarters, and on 20 July 1866, this fleet, under Admiral von Tegetthoff, fought that of Italy off the island of Lissa; it was the first open-sea fleet battle since Trafalgar. *Kaiser*, built in 1859 and leading the second division under Commodore Petz, was a relatively old-fashioned vessel, a two-decker, screw-driven steamship with a wooden hull. She had 91 cannon with unrifled barrels, ranged in broadside

Length: 255ft (77.75m)
Beam: 58ft 3in (17.8m)
Depth: 24ft 2in (7.4m)
Displacement: 5720t
Rigging: three masts; barquentine rig (until conversion)
Machinery: single screw, steam; 2786hp
Armament: 91 guns
Complement: 471

The Battle of Lissa reinforced the message about wooden hulls being obsolete for warships; it also encouraged a vogue for the ram bow.

formation. In the battle, Petz drove her obliquely against the Italian *Re di Portogallo*, tearing away armour plate and boats but laying *Kaiser* open to an Italian broadside which brought down her foremast and set the ship on fire. The Austrian ship was able to back off. She survived and in 1869–71 was converted to an ironclad with rifled guns. In 1902, her engines were removed and, renamed *Bellona*, she became an accommodation hulk. Her later history is unknown.

PAWNEE

USA: 1859

Length: 221ft 6in (67.5m)
Beam: 47ft (14.3m)
Depth: 10ft (3m)
Displacement: not known
Rigging: three masts; full square rig
Machinery: single screw, steam
Armament: eight 9in (228mm), two 12pdr guns
Complement: 181

Launched on 8 October 1859 at Philadelphia Navy Yard and classed as a screw sloop, *Pawnee* went into service with the Home Squadron. Her hull was designed to enable heavy guns to be mounted on a vessel of relatively shallow draught. This proved useful in the American Civil War, when on 20 April 1861, she towed USS *Cumberland* out of Gosport Yard, Norfolk. *Pawnee* did duty on the Potomac River, then joined first the Atlantic, then the South Atlantic Squadron. Decommissioned at the end of the Civil War in 1865, she was refitted in 1866. In 1869, her engines were removed and she was refitted as a sailing vessel and stationed at Key West, Florida, where she acted as a hospital and receiving ship. In 1882, she was decommissioned finally; she was sold to breakers at Great Neck, New York, on 3 May 1884.

Much larger than the old US frigates, Pawnee's designation as a screw sloop shows how mechanization affected the navy's perceptions, with a trend to greater size.

VICTORIA

GB: 1859

Laid down in 1855 but not launched until 12 November 1859, this screw ship of the line was prompted by the launch of the French steam three-decker *La Bretagne*. The French ship, *Victoria* and HMS *Howe* were the only ships of this type to be built. *Victoria* had unique machinery, with two sets of four boilers on each side and two funnels located to port and starboard respectively. Commissioned in the mid-19th century, when Britain was involved in no major sea wars, *Victoria* did not see much hostile action. In 1864, she was flagship of the Mediterranean Fleet. Manoeuvres, formal visits and considerable time spent within the anchorages of Gibraltar and Grand Harbour, Valletta, were the order of her day. *Victoria*'s latter service years were spent in home waters, and her last appearance was at the Spithead Naval Review of 1867. By this time advances in gunnery and hull design had made the ponderous three-decker virtually obsolete. *Victoria* was soon paid off, but she was not finally disposed of until 31 May 1893, when she was sold for breaking up.

Despite the warship-building rivalry between French and British, neither country was to go to war again with the other.

Length: 260ft (79.2m)
Beam: 60ft (18.3m)
Depth: 25ft 10in (7.8m)
Displacement: 6959t
Rigging: three masts; square rig
Machinery: single screw, steam; 1000hp
Armament: 62 8in (203mm), 58 32pdr, one 68pdr guns
Complement: 1000

THE AGE OF STEAM AND BEYOND

STATES LINES

CHAPTER FOUR

MERCHANT SHIPS 1860–2000

By the mid-1800s, the 'new technologies' of the industrial revolution had begun to pick up speed. Marine engineering, based on the twin innovations of the steam engine and metal construction, was one of its paradigms, and new developments in the field followed hard on each others' heels. More efficient machinery and stronger, lighter construction translated into faster ships.

Not that the transition from sail to steam was not instantaneous, or even that rapid. Even in 1900, well over a third of all merchant tonnage worldwide (10m tons out of a total of 26m) was still in sail, and small sailing ships in the general cargo trade only gave way definitively to steamers after World War I, and still had a role to play two decades later.

In more modern times, change was to come about more rapidly. With the development of jet aircraft, the long-distance point-to-point passenger trade, so important for so long, disappeared entirely, while freight operations were revolutionized in terms of both technology and methodology. Steam propulsion gave way to the more efficient diesel, and the resultant decline in the number of seafarers was multiplied by the development of automated ship-handling systems, while the introduction of containerization and the streamlining of bulk cargo handling changed the nature of port operation beyond recognition. Such changes were vital to accommodate the increase in worldwide trade, 90 percent of that still went by sea, and the world's mercantile fleet grew to keep pace with the demand, going from 130m tons in 1960 to over 500m tons in 2000 – a fifty-fold increase since the start of our period.

New York's West Side piers – widely known as 'Luxury Liner Row' – in mid-July 1956 with *Vulcania, Constitution, America, United States, Olympia* and *Queen Elizabeth*.

A J MEERWALD

USA: 1928

Like some former sailing workboats, the *A J Meerwald*, a schooner-rigged oyster dredger, was to have a second lease of life as a working feature of a maritime exhibition and as an occasional sail training vessel. She was originally constructed in Dorchester, New Jersey, near the mouth of the short Maurice River, which runs into Delaware Bay, at the time a prolific oyster fishery. The vessel ran the fresh-dredged shellfish to markets in nearby Wilmington, Philadelphia and Camden, up the Delaware River.

***A J Meerwald* was typical of the Delaware Bay oyster dredger schooners; she was substantially re-built after half a century, and put back into commission in her original form.**

Tonnage: 57 grt
Dimensions: 76ft 4in x 22ft 2in x 6ft 4in (23.25m x 6.75m x 1.9m)
Machinery: one-shaft, auxiliary diesel; 100hp
Service speed: not applicable
Role: oyster dredger
Route: Delaware River
Capacity: not applicable
Constructor: Charles H Stowman & Sons, Dorchester, NJ
Material: wood
Built for: A J Meerwald & Sons, South Dennis, NJ
Owner: Delaware Bay Schooner Project

ABA (EX-GLENAPP, LATER MATRONA)

GB: 1917

Tonnage: 7937 grt
Dimensions: 450ft 6in x 55ft 8in (137.2m x 17m)
Machinery: two shaft, diesels; 4800hp
Service speed: 14 knots
Role: passenger liner
Route: UK–West Africa
Capacity: 220 1st, 105 2nd, 35 3rd
Constructor: Barclay, Curle and Co Ltd, Clydeside
Material: steel
Built for: Russian government

Aba, the first passenger ship to be powered by diesel engines, was laid down for the Tsarist government of Russia, prior to the revolution, but work on her was stopped when the regime was toppled in 1917. She was launched and completed the following year, in time to be employed as a troop transport by the US Army, and was purchased, post-war, by the Elder Dempster Line to operate on its West Africa service as the MS *Glenapp*. At her service speed, her 750-t bunkerage was enough for a return voyage between London and Lagos, in Nigeria, with several intermediate stops. She was taken up as a hospital ship during World War II, renamed *Aba*, and at its end was sold to the Bantry Steamship Co, but sank in dock while being refitted, in 1947.

MS *Aba* as she appeared during World War II, in hospital ship livery. She survived the conflict, but sank soon after, during the course of refurbishment.

ACADIA

CANADA: 1913

Acadia was built by Swan, Hunter & Wigham Richardson in Newcastle upon Tyne for the Canadian government, and was one of the first vessels commissioned into the newly created Royal Canadian Navy. She was employed for many years as a hydrographic research ship, and at the end of her useful life was preserved, unchanged both internally and externally, at the Maritime Museum of the Atlantic in the port of Halifax, Nova Scotia.

The *Acadia* was one of the earliest purpose-built hydrographic survey ships and added much to our knowledge of the waters around Canada's east coast.

Tonnage: 846 grt
Dimensions: 170ft x 33ft 6in x 12ft (51.8m x 10.25m x 3.65m)
Machinery: one shaft, vertical triple expansion; about 1750hp
Service speed: not known
Role: hydrographic survey ship
Constructor: Swan, Hunter & Wigham Richardson, Wallsend
Material: steel
Built for: Government of Canada
Owner: Maritime Museum of the Atlantic

ADELAIDE

AUSTRALIA: 1866

Adelaide was believed to be the oldest wooden-hulled steamer still operating in 2000, 134 years after she was built in Echuca, Victoria, Australia. She was built for towing barges laden with wool up and down the Murray River, but worked for most of her life, from 1872 to 1957, hauling trains of barges laden with red gum logs to the Echuca sawmills. She was laid up ashore between 1963 and 1984, but was then entirely refurbished and refloated, to operate in conjunction with a restored barge, *D 26*.

Tonnage: 58 grt
Dimensions: 76ft 5in x 17ft x 2ft 4in (23.3m x 5.2m x 0.7m)
Machinery: sidewheels, two-cylinder double-acting; 36hp
Service speed: not known
Role: river tugboat
Route: Murray River
Capacity: not applicable
Constructor: G Link, Echuca, Victoria
Material: wood
Built for: J G Grassie, Echuca, Victoria
Owner: City of Echuca

The *Adelaide* still runs on the original engine, built by Fulton & Shaw in Melbourne; like most power units on Murray River vessels, it was wood-fired.

ALASKA (LATER MEGALLANES) — GB: 1881

The Liverpool & Great Western Steamship Co, better known as the Guion Line after its founder, ran its first transatlantic service, between Liverpool and New York, in 1866. In 1881, it put the liner *Alaska* into service, to operate alongside the *Arizona*; she was to prove a very fast ship, setting records in both directions in 1892 and 1894 at an average speed of a little over 17 knots. Somewhat surprisingly, she was built of iron, although innovations included electric lighting. She was scrapped in 1902.

Tonnage: 6932 grt
Dimensions: 500ft x 50ft (152.4m x 15.25m)
Machinery: one-shaft, triple expansion
Service speed: 16 knots
Role: passenger liner
Route: North Atlantic
Constructor: John Elder & Co, Glasgow
Material: iron
Built for: Liverpool & Great Western Steamship Co

SSs *Arizona* and *Alaska* were the first of the 'Atlantic greyhounds'; they were soon joined in service by the *Oregon*, which also took the Blue Riband. *Alaska* was sold to the Spanish Trasatlántica Line in 1897, and renamed *Megallanes*.

ALMA DOEPEL — AUSTRALIA: 1903

Tonnage: 151 grt
Dimensions: 116ft 2in x 26ft 6in x 7ft 6in (35.4m x 8.1m x 2.3m)
Machinery: one-shaft, auxiliary diesel
Service speed: not applicable
Role: general cargo vessel; sail training vessel
Route: east coast of Australia
Constructor: Frederick Doepel, Bellinger, NSW
Material: wood
Built for: Frederick Doepel, Bellinger, NSW
Owner: Sail & Adventure Ltd

Following her restoration, which was very extensive and took 12 years, the *Alma Doepel* became a familiar sight around Melbourne.

The topsail schooner *Alma Doepel* was constructed on the Bellinger River in New South Wales to trade between there, Sydney and Hobart, a task she carried out for 56 years, during which time she crossed the notorious Bass Strait 578 times. After a period laid up, followed by 14 years as a motorized barge, with her masts and rigging removed, she was restored to her original condition for use as a sail training vessel at a cost of A$3 million, being recommissioned in 1987.

AMERICA (LATER TRINACRIA) — GB: 1883

The National Line first began operations during the American Civil War, in 1863, and by the 1880s had become established on the Liverpool–Queenstown (Cork)–New York run. By then, however, the youngest member of its fleet was a decade old, and none of its ships had ever made a record-breaking crossing. In 1884, it tried to correct that situation, taking delivery of a new and very elegant ship, the *America*. She was to fail narrowly in her attempt to win the Blue Riband but posted a very satisfactory crossing – six days, 14 hours and 18 minutes from Sandy Hook to Queenstown (17.78 knots) – on her maiden voyage. She was briefly taken up by the Admiralty the following year, in a war scare which came to nothing, for conversion as an armed merchant cruiser. She was sold to the Italian Navy in 1887 and served as the *Trinacria* in a variety of roles, including that of royal yacht, until 1925, when she was scrapped.

Despite her relatively small size, the *America* was very expensive to operate; a single voyage Liverpool–New York consumed over 1250 tons of coal.

Tonnage: 5528 grt
Dimensions: 441ft 9in x 51ft 2in (134.65m x 15.6m)
Machinery: one-shaft, compound
Service speed: 17 knots
Role: passenger liner; armed merchant cruiser; royal yacht
Route: North Atlantic
Capacity: 300 1st, 700 st
Constructor: J&G Thompson, Glasgow
Material: steel
Built for: National Steamship Co Ltd

AMERICA (LATER WEST POINT, AUSTRALIS, ITALIS) — USA: 1939

Tonnage: 33,532 grt
Dimensions: 723ft x 93ft x 29ft (220.3m x 28.35m x 8.85m)
Machinery: two-shaft, geared turbines
Service speed: 22 knots
Role: passenger liner; cruise ship
Route: North Atlantic; Europe-Australia
Capacity: 516 1st, 371 cb, 159 tr; 2258 tr
Constructor: Newport News Shipbuilding & Dry Dock Co
Material: steel
Built for: United States Line

The second *America* was built for the United States Line by Newport News Shipbuilding and was launched on 31 August 1939. She wasn't employed on the North Atlantic run for which she had been designed, but instead went into service as a cruise ship. She was 'called up' in 1941, and served as the USS *West Point* until 1946, when, after a $6 million refit, she finally entered the New York – Southampton service in tandem with the *United States*. In 1960, she reverted to the cruise ship role in the winter, and in 1964 was sold to Greece, operating on the Europe–Australia run as the *Australis*. She returned to New York in 1978, still under Greek ownership, and made two disastrous short cruise voyages. The vessel then went back to Europe, as the *Italis*, until 1979, when she was laid up. Bound for Thailand as a hotel ship, she was wrecked in the Canary Islands on 18 January 1994.

The *America* was an excellent example of a passenger liner of the last period; her active life spanned four decades.

AMERIGO VESPUCCI — ITALY: 1930

The Italian Navy's principal sail training ship during much of the second half of the 20th century was the *Amerigo Vespucci*, purpose-built for the task from a design by Ing. Francesco Rotundi at the beginning of the 1930s with accommodation for a large crew (228 men) in addition to 170 cadets. Unlike other contemporary sail training ships, which were conventional merchant sailing ships, she was built to resemble a fourth- or fifth-rate ship of the line of an earlier period, with scuttles replacing gunports. However, the subterfuge was not complete – she had a modern rig with a total sail area of 30,140 square feet (2800 square metres) and a clipper bow. Somewhat unusually for a sail training ship, she had a fairly sophisticated diesel-electric powerplant. The *Amerigo Vespucci* was the second of two almost identical ships; the other, the *Cristoforo Colombo*, was transferred to the Soviet Union in reparation after the end of World War II but was eventually scrapped.

The *Amerigo Vespucci* was designed to resemble an early 19th-century frigate but was quite sophisticated, with a diesel-electric auxiliary powerplant.

Tonnage: 3545t displacement
Dimensions: 269ft x 50ft 9in x 21ft 6in (82m x 15.5m x 6.55m)
Machinery: one-shaft, auxiliary diesel-electric; 1900hp
Service speed: not applicable
Role: sail training ship
Constructor: Cantiere di Castellamare di Stabbia
Material: steel
Built for: Italian Navy
Owner: Italian Navy

ANASTASIS (EX-VICTORIA) — MALTA: 1953

Tonnage: 11,695 grt
Dimensions: 521ft 6in x 67ft 10in (159m x 20.7m)
Machinery: two-shaft, diesels; 16,100hp
Service speed: 19.5 knots
Role: passenger liner; cruise ship; hospital ship
Route: Genoa-Hong Kong; Trieste-Beirut
Capacity: 286 1st, 181 tr
Constructor: Cantieri Riuniti dell' Adriatico, Trieste
Material: steel
Built for: Lloyd Triestino Line
Owner: Mercy Ships

The *Anastasis* was the largest member of a small fleet of privately owned hospital ships. Built as the *Victoria,* a small passenger liner, for the Lloyd Triestino Line, to operate on the Far Eastern route, she was later converted to a cruise ship. In 1978 she was acquired by Mercy Ships, and in three years was converted to a hospital ship, with three operating tables, a 25-bed recovery ward, laboratories, radiology facilities, a large pharmacy and a dental surgery.

The hospital ship *Anastasis* was built as one of a pair of small passenger liners; her sistership, the *Asia*, also changed roles, becoming a livestock carrier.

ANDREA DORIA — ITALY: 1953

Tonnage: 29,082 grt
Dimensions: 630ft 1in x 79ft 9in x 30ft (192m x 24.3m x 9.15m)
Machinery: two-shaft, geared turbines
Service speed: 26 knots
Role: passenger liner
Route: Genoa–New York
Capacity: 218 1st, 320 cb, 703 tr
Constructor: Ansaldo, Genoa
Material: steel
Built for: Italia Line

The *Andrea Doria* was the first passenger liner built post-World War II for the Italia Line's North Atlantic service between Genoa and New York via Cannes and Naples; she operated in tandem with the *Cristoforo Colombo*. On 17 July 1956, she left Genoa on her 51st voyage and eight days later was rammed in the fog off Nantucket Sound by the Swedish-American Line's *Stockholm*. Forty-three people died in the collision, and the ship's integrity was breached. She sank the following morning, with no further loss of life.

The *Andrea Doria* was a modern, well-maintained ship, just three years old when she was lost; no satisfactory explanation was ever advanced as to the cause of the collision which sank her.

ANITA JACOBA (EX-RISICO, EMANUEL) — NETHERLANDS: 1892

Tonnage: 123 grt
Dimensions: 80ft x 17ft 9in x 4ft 4in (24m x 5.35m x 1.1m)
Machinery: not applicable
Service speed: not applicable
Role: general cargo vessel
Route: inland and coastal waters
Constructor: Ruitenberg, Waspik
Material: wood

During the 19th century, much of the commerce of the Netherlands was carried in shallow-draught vessels with leeboards to serve as a drop keel. These vessels were equally at home in inland waterways or in coastal regions and had a variety of names, depending on their size, form and origin; the *zeeuwse klipper*, of which the *Anita Jacoba* was a fine example, could be one- or two-masted and gaff-rigged as sloop or ketch; larger vessels traded as far away as Portugal.

Rigged as a 'bald-headed' gaff sloop (that is, without topsails), the *Anita Jacoba* proved a very handy craft. She was restored in 1971.

AP.1-88 — GB: 1982

In its original form, the commercial hovercraft was powered by very expensive gas turbine engines, but by the 1980s, advances in diesel engine technology enabled this much cheaper powerplant to be substituted, a fact which went a long way towards making the small hovercraft commercially viable. The Type AP.1-88 was the first to come to market, and it made a considerable impact, both as a freight carrier and as a passenger ferry. A militarized version, armed with Rarden cannon and SAM, was also available.

The AP.1-88 hovercraft were the first diesel-powered air cushion vehicles to enter service; they reduced operating costs of the type dramatically.

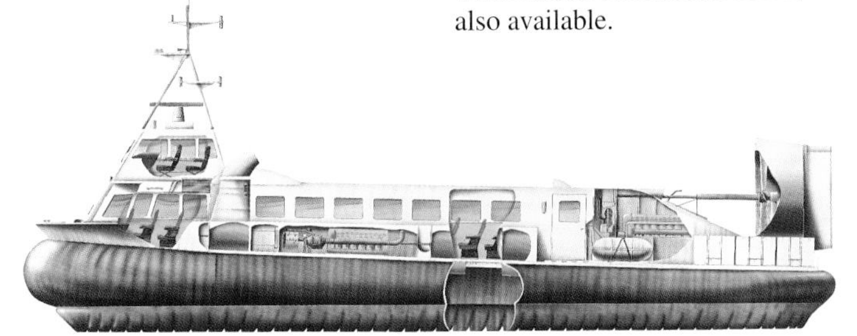

Maximum operating weight: 40t
Dimensions: 80ft 4in x 36ft (24.5m x 11m)
Machinery: four diesel engines; 1800hp
Service speed: 40 knots
Role: general cargo and passenger carrier
Route: not applicable
Capacity: 101 p, 12t
Constructor: British Hovercraft Corporation
Material: aluminium
Built for: not applicable

AQUITANIA

GB: 1913

Tonnage: 45,647 grt
Dimensions: 901ft x 97ft (274.6m x 29.6m)
Machinery: four-shaft, geared turbines
Service speed: 23 knots
Role: passenger liner; cruise ship
Route: North Atlantic; Mediterranean
Capacity: 618 1st, 614 2nd, 1998 3rd; 610 1st, 950 2nd, 640 tr
Constructor: John Brown & Co Ltd, Glasgow
Material: steel
Built for: Cunard Steam Ship Co Ltd

The *Aquitania* was regarded by many as the finest example of the 'four-stacker' and was to be the last in service. Constructed to operate in tandem with the *Lusitania* and *Mauretania*, she served in both world wars as a troopship and spent most of the rest of the time navigating the North Atlantic, with occasional Mediterranean cruises. She ended her days carrying war brides, returning servicemen, displaced persons and immigrants; refused a certificate in 1950, she was sold for scrap.

The Cunard Line's *Aquitania* was thought by many to be the most beautiful of all the North Atlantic 'greyhounds', her sheer-line, superstructure and four massive raked funnels all in perfect proportion.

ARABIA MARU

JAPAN: 1918

Amongst the world's shipbuilding nations, Japan was a latecomer, only expanding during World War I. Under a wartime agreement with America, Japan was supplied with steel in return for new merchant ships. Amongst the largest merchant ships built for home ownership was the *Arabia Maru*. She had three continuous decks with accommodation for 356 passengers plus 11,500t of cargo. Coal capacity was 2700t and she burnt 85t per day. *Arabia Maru* was sunk east of Manila by a US submarine in October 1944.

In the 1920s *Arabia Maru* was one of the major home-built merchant vessels in Japan's expanding mercantile fleet, which had for so many years relied upon foreign construction.

Tonnage: 9500 (later 9414) grt
Dimensions: 475ft x 61ft x 28ft (145m x 18.4m x 8.3m)
Machinery: two-shaft, triple expansion; 8153hp
Service speed: 16.2 knots
Role: passenger/cargo liner
Route: North Pacific; Japan–River Plate
Capacity: 42 1st, 314 (later 125) 3rd; 11,500t
Constructor: Mitsubishi Zosen Kaisha
Built for: Osaka Shosen Kaisha

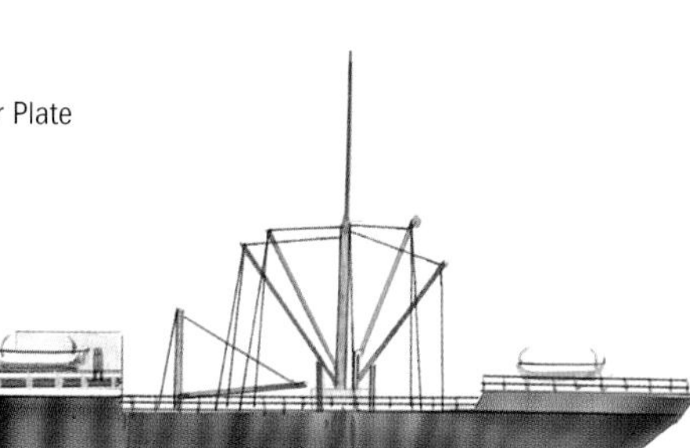

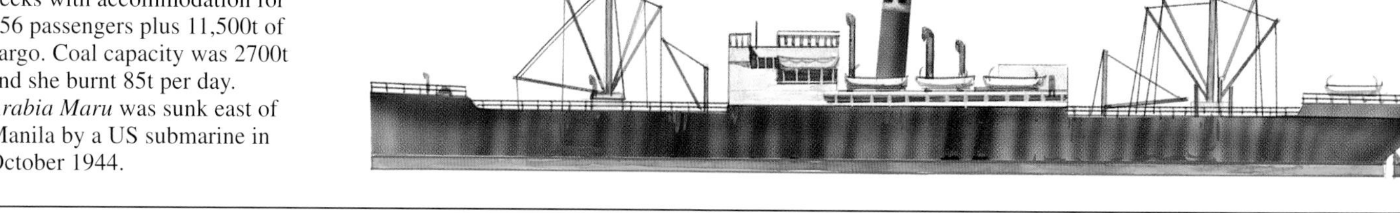

ARCHIBALD RUSSELL

GB: 1905

The four-masted barque *Archibald Russell* was the last square-rigger built on the Clyde and remained in commercial service until 1939.

The *Archibald Russell* was built for John Hardie & Sons, to work in the Pacific nitrate and wheat trade, returning to Falmouth from Australia in 93 days on her maiden voyage. She was the last square-rigged ship built on the Clyde, and one of very few fitted with bilge keels to reduce roll. She was later sold to Gustaf Erikson of Mariehamn, and continued to carry grain from Australia until the outbreak of World War II, when she was laid up. She was broken up in 1949.

Tonnage: 2385 grt
Dimensions: 291ft 5in x 43ft 2in x 24ft 1in (88.8m x 13.2m x 7.3m)
Role: nitrate/grain carrier
Route: Australia/Chile–Europe
Constructor: Scott's Shipbuilding & Engineering Co, Greenock
Material: steel
Built for: John Hardie & Co

ARETHUSA (EX-PEKING) USA: 1911

The four-masted barque *Peking* was built for the Flying 'P' Line, to carry nitrate from Chile to Europe via Cape Horn. In 1932 she was acquired by a British charity, the Shaftsbury Homes for Poor Boys, and converted into a school ship as the *Arethusa*, taking over from an ex-Royal Naval frigate of the same name. More recently, she was bought by New York's South Street Seaport Museum, and since 1975 has been open to the public.

The *Peking* was captured by the British during World War I, and was then laid up until she was acquired by Shaftsbury Homes for Poor Boys as a school ship.

Tonnage: 3100t grt
Dimensions: 321ft x 47ft x 15ft 4in (97.85m x 14.35m x 4.7m)
Role: nitrate/grain carrier; school ship
Route: Australia/Chile-Europe
Constructor: Blohm & Voss, Hamburg
Material: steel
Built for: Reederei Ferdinand Laeisz
Owner: South Street Seaport Museum

ARGONAUT USA: 1897

Tonnage: 60t standard displacement
Dimensions: 55ft 9in x 13ft 9in (17m x 4.2m)
Machinery: one-shaft/two wheels, petrol engine; 60hp
Service speed: 6 knots
Role: salvage craft
Constructor: Simon Lake
Material: steel
Built for: Simon Lake

The *Argonaut* was built by submarine pioneer Simon Lake, whose somewhat eccentric ideas caused him to lose out to John Holland in the race to become the US Navy's prime supplier. Lake's boats were designed to submerge on an even keel, and most, like the *Argonaut*, were fitted with wheels, to allow them to run along the seabed, and driven by both a single screw propeller and via the twin front wheels. Intended primarily for salvage work, the *Argonaut* was only marginally successful.

Some features of Lake's early submarine designs, notably the double hull and the trimming mechanism, were to find their way into later, more successful boats.

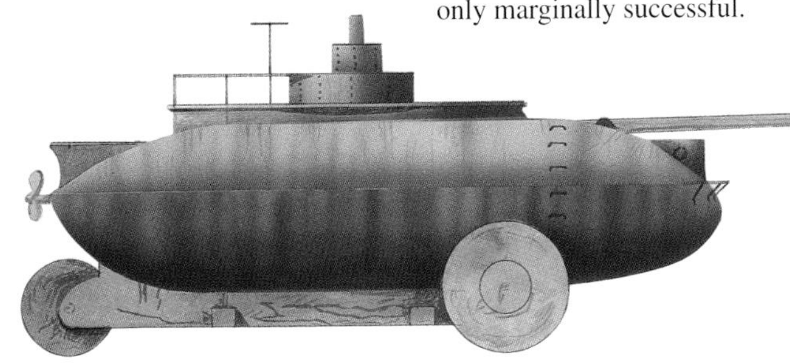

ARIEL GB: 1865

The 1860s saw the full-rigged, three-masted ship brought to its most refined – and most would say definitive – form in the composite wood-plank-on-iron-frame vessels built, the majority of them in Scotland, for the tea trade from China. One of the best of them was the *Ariel*, 'a perfect beauty to every nautical man who saw her', according to her first and most successful captain, John Keay. *Ariel* was one of a group of 16 ships, including the *Serica*, the *Sir Lancelot*, the *Taeping* and the *Titania*, built by Robert Steele & Co of Greenock, at the mouth of the River Clyde. Of those, only *Serica* was built entirely of wood, the rest were of composite construction. This building method was unknown before 1850 and by 1885 it had ceased to be used, having given way to all-metal construction, but in that short period it was used to produce ships capable of almost incredible performances, day in and day out. It must be said that these ships were almost anomalies, built for just one purpose – to be the first vessel to land the new season's China tea in London – and they were, in the words of James MacCunn, who owned three Steele-built ships, including *Sir Lancelot*, 'only yachts in disguise'. They were certainly expensive – *Ariel* cost £15,350 – but they lived up to the expectations placed upon them. On her third voyage, in 1868, *Ariel* left Foochow with 1,221,508lb (554,076kg) of tea plus 200t of extra ballast on 28 May and arrived in London on 2 September, a passage of just 97 days. She had a short career; in 1872 she was lost at sea on a passage from London to Sydney.

Some experts believed the *Ariel* to have been the fastest of all the China clippers, but others favoured her sistership *Sir Lancelot*. *Cutty Sark*, *Thermopylae* and *Titania* also had their supporters, as did *Leander* and *Spindrift*.

Tonnage: 853 grt
Dimensions: 197ft 5in x 33ft 10in x 21ft (60.2m x 10.3m x 6.4m)
Role: tea carrier
Route: Foochow-London
Constructor: Richard Steele & Co, Greenock
Material: composite, wood on iron
Built for: Shaw, Lowther & Maxton Ltd

ARIZONA (LATER HANCOCK)

GB: 1879

The Guion Line had no really fast ship until it took delivery of the *Arizona* from Elder's in 1879. On her second voyage eastbound she beat the *Britannic*'s best average speed by 0.02 knots with a passage of seven days, eight hours and 11 minutes to take the Blue Riband. On her fifth voyage back to Liverpool, she hit an iceberg at full speed, but the forward bulkhead held and the ship was able to make St John's for repairs under her own steam.

The *Arizona* was re-engined in 1898 and operated between San Francisco and China. She was bought by the US Navy in 1903.

Tonnage: 5147 grt
Dimensions: 450ft 2in x 45ft 5in (137.2m x 13.85m)
Machinery: one-shaft, compound (later three triple expansion)
Service speed: 15 knots
Role: passenger liner; receiving ship; troopship
Route: North Atlantic; San Francisco-China
Capacity: 140 1st, 70 2nd, 140 3rd, 1000 st; 40 1st, 1000 3rd
Constructor: John Elder & Co, Glasgow
Material: iron
Built for: Liverpool & Great Western Steamship Co

ARKTIKA (EX-LEONID BREZHNEV)

USSR; RUSSIA: 1974

Tonnage: 18,172 grt
Dimensions: 435ft 3in x 91ft 10in x 36ft 2in (148m x 28m x 11m)
Machinery: two-shaft, two PWR/turbo-electric; 75,000hp
Service speed: 18 knots
Role: ice-breaker
Route: Northeast Passage; Arctic Ocean
Constructor: Baltic Shipbuilding & Engineering Works, Leningrad (St Petersburg)
Material: steel
Built for: Murmansk Shipping Co

Arktika was the leader of a class of five nuclear-powered ice-breakers, considerably more powerful than the prototype, *Lenin*. Designed to lead winter convoys between Murmansk and Vladivostok through the Northeast Passage, she entered service in 1975, and on 17 August 1977 became the first surface ship ever to reach the North Pole. In November 1983, she led a flotilla of 12 ice-breakers which released a 51-ship convoy trapped north of Chukotka.

ARTIGLIO II

ITALY: 1931

The *Artiglio II* was built to the order of the Italian salvage firm Sorima in 1931 to act as the support ship for the operation aimed at recovering gold from the P&O liner *Egypt*, sunk in 70 fathoms (130m) of water off Ushant in 1922. The first *Artiglio* was destroyed by accident while divers were clearing the wreck of an ammunition ship at St Nazaire. Sorima eventually recovered bullion worth £1,183,000 from the wreck of the *Egypt*.

The *Artiglio II* was purpose-built as a diving support and salvage ship, and was well equipped with derricks and lifting gear.

Tonnage: 300 grt
Dimensions: 139ft 9in x 25ft x 7ft (42.6m x 7.6m x 2.1m)
Machinery: one-shaft, vertical triple expansion; about 400hp
Role: diving support ship
Material: steel
Built for: Sorima

ATLAND

SWEDEN: 1910

Tonnage: 5029 grt
Dimensions: 388ft 9in x 52ft 4in (116m x 16m)
Machinery: one-shaft, triple expansion; 2200hp
Service speed: 12.7 knots
Role: iron ore carrier
Capacity: 8000 dwt
Constructor: William Doxford and Sons, Sunderland
Built for: Tirfing SS Co Ltd

Of the various types of merchant ships built in the early part of the 20th century, the turret steamer was amongst the most revolutionary. Below the waterline the hull was of conventional shape, but above it it was only just over half the width. This design reduced the amount of steel used in construction but still gave added strength. Costs were reduced, since fees paid in harbour dues on deadweight were reduced, whilst the easy stowage of bulk cargoes saved time. *Atland* was designed by Doxford and Sons of Sunderland, who built 178 of the type between 1890 and 1911.

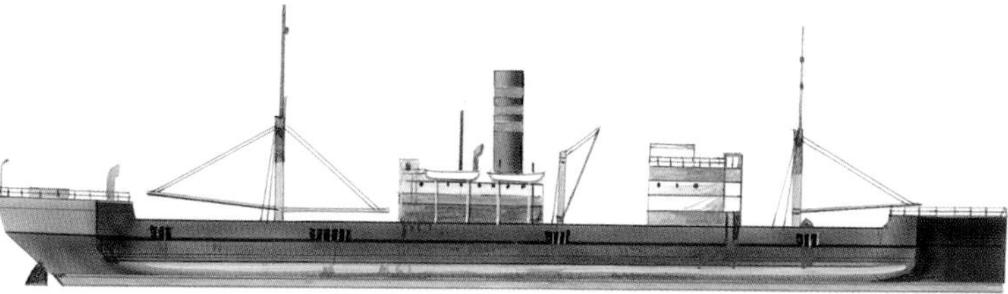

***Atland* was used in the iron ore trade with Northern Europe. She sank after colliding with another ship in a convoy in March 1943.**

ATLANTIC

USA: 1903

Tonnage: 303 grt
Dimensions: 185ft x 29ft 6in x 17ft 6in (56.4m x 9m x 5.3m)
Machinery: one-shaft, auxiliary triple expansion
Service speed: not applicable
Role: yacht
Route: New York–Lizard
Constructor: Townsend & Downey, Shooters Island, NY
Material: steel
Built for: Wilson Marshall

The three-masted topsail schooner *Atlantic* was one of 12 vessels which competed for the 1905 Emperor's Cup, a prize Kaiser Wilhelm put up for a race between New York and the Lizard, which *Atlantic* won in a time of 12 days and four hours; in one 24-hour period she ran 348 nautical miles (645km). She was taken up by the US Navy during both world wars and was later acquired by the US Coast Guard Academy.

Although the *Atlantic* was built to race, she had stateroom accommodation for seven people.

AUGUSTA VICTORIA (LATER AUGUSTE VICTORIA, KUBAN)

GERMANY: 1889

Tonnage: 7661 (later 8479) grt
Dimensions: 462ft 7in x 55ft 7in; later 520ft 9in x 55ft 7in (141m x 16.95m; later 158.75m x 16.95m)
Machinery: two-shaft, two vertical triple expansion
Service speed: 18 knots
Role: passenger liner; auxiliary cruiser
Route: Europe–New York
Capacity: 400 1st,120 2nd, 580 3rd
Constructor: AG Vulcan, Stettin (Szczecin)
Material: steel
Built for: Hamburg-Amerikanische Packetfahrt AG ('Hapag')

From 1894, the *Augusta Victoria* spent some of her time cruising, initially in the Mediterranean. She had actually been misnamed; the mistake was corrected when she was relaunched in 1897.

The *Augusta Victoria* was built for the Hamburg-Amerika Line by AG Vulcan in Stettin (Szczecin) and was the largest ship ever constructed in Germany until that time. She was destined for the company's principal route, from Hamburg to New York, but from 1894 her winter European terminus was Genoa. She was lengthened by 58ft (17.7m) in 1896-97 by Harland & Wolff. In 1904, she was sold to Russia and went into service as the auxiliary cruiser *Kuban*. She was scrapped in 1907.

AUGUSTUS

ITALY: 1927

The Navigazione Generale Italiana's *Augustus* was the biggest passenger motor ship of her day, with four German-built diesel engines producing 28,000bhp. She was constructed for the North Atlantic service, with extensive emigrant accommodation, but initially sailed to the River Plate, not switching to New York until 1928 and alternating thereafter. The *Augustus* was extensively rebuilt in 1934, largely to change the character of her passenger accommodation.

There were plans to convert her to an aircraft carrier during World War II, but they came to naught and she was eventually sunk as a blockship at Genoa.

Tonnage: 32,650 (later 30,418) grt
Dimensions: 711ft x 82ft 8in (216.6m x 25.2m)
Machinery: four-shaft, MAN diesels; 28,000hp
Service speed: 19 knots
Role: passenger liner
Route: Genoa–River Plate; Genoa–New York
Capacity: 302 1st, 504 2nd, 1404 3rd; 210 1st, 604 2nd, 454 tr, 766 3rd
Constructor: Ansaldo, Genoa
Material: steel
Built for: Navigazione Generale Italiana

AUSTRALIA II

AUSTRALIA: 1982

Tonnage: 21.8t displacement
Dimensions: 63ft 1in x 12ft x 8ft 6in (19.2m x 3.7m x 2.6m)
Role: racing yacht
Constructor: Steve Ward, Perth
Material: aluminium
Built for: Alan Bond
Owner: National Maritime Museum, Sydney

The America's Cup was finally wrested from the grasp of the New York Yacht Club in 1983, 132 years after the competition's inception, by the sloop *Australia II*. Considerable controversy surrounded the form of the challenger's keel, which had near-horizontal 'wings'. In fact they were only one innovative feature, and the fact that the vessel was built to the lower limit of the 12-metre rating rules, and had a comparatively small wetted area, was probably more significant.

The Ben Lexcen-designed *Australia II* was one of seven yachts to challenge for the America's Cup in 1983. She defeated *Liberty* to win the series 4–3.

BAIKAL

RUSSIA: 1900

Originally, the trains of the Trans-Siberian Railway, which was completed in 1901, crossed Lake Baikal, some 400 miles (645km) long and 60 miles (100km) wide, aboard a ferry named after the lake. The *Baikal* was constructed by Armstrong at Elswick on the Tyne and broken down into manageable pieces for a long overland journey, and was then reassembled. She had a strengthened hull and functioned as an ice-breaker in the winter. She remained in service until the railway was extended around the lake's southern tip.

The *Baikal* was one of the biggest vessels ever pre-fabricated, to be transported in sections and assembled on site.

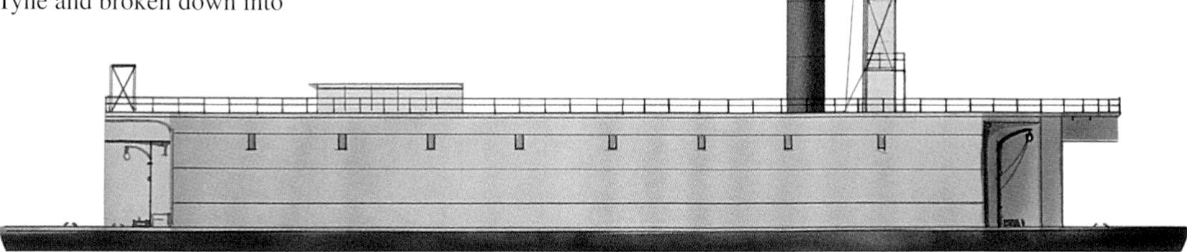

Tonnage: 2800 grt
Dimensions: 250ft x 63ft (76.2m x 19.2m)
Machinery: two-shaft, vertical triple expansion
Service speed: not known
Role: train ferry
Route: Lake Baikal
Constructor: Armstrong, Elswick
Material: steel
Built for: Trans-Siberian Railway Co

BALDER

NETHERLANDS: 1912

Tonnage: 105 grt
Dimensions: 78ft 1in x 21ft 8in x 10ft 2in (23.8m x 6.6m x 3.1m)
Role: fishery vessel
Route: North Sea
Constructor: de Jong, Vlaardingen
Material: steel
Built for: Visserij Mis, Vlaardingen
Owner: Ver Nederlandisch Scheepvart Museum

Sailing vessels of around a hundred tons gross were widely used in the North Sea fishery; those from Dutch ports, like the *Balder*, were known as *loggers* and were often rigged with loose-footed mainsails, an arrangement that was popular with fishermen because it was easy to handle. The *logger*'s loose-footed mainsail was the only point of similarity with the English lugger, which wore a four-sided sail similar to a gaff, but set on a boom which extended before the mast, rather than having its luff laced to it.

The ketch-rigged *Balder* was an interesting example of a late, steel-built Dutch *logger*, as used in the North Sea fishery, restored to original condition in Amsterdam.

BALLARAT

GB: 1920

Ships similar in size and character to the *Ballarat* were common between the wars – the P&O fleet alone had five – and were designed to give economical passenger/cargo service on the already-lucrative UK–Australia and UK–Far East routes, via Suez and the coaling station the company had established at Aden with intermediate stops at Bombay and other British possessions along the way. From the outset the ships were intended to be easily convertible to carry troops; they were 'no frills' vessels and had no first-class accommodation.

The *Ballarat* was one of five similar ships the P&O Line operated on its service between the UK and Australia in the 1920s and 1930s.

Tonnage: 15,000 grt
Dimensions: 537ft x 64ft 4in (163.7m x 19.6m)
Machinery: two-shaft, vertical triple expansion
Service speed: 13.5 knots
Role: passenger/cargo liner
Route: UK–Australia
Capacity: 500 3rd, 700 st
Material: steel
Built for: Peninsular & Oriental Steam Navigation Co

BALMORAL CASTLE

GB: 1909

The Union and Castle Lines were fierce rivals over the lucrative UK–South Africa routes, and when they merged they had a virtual monopoly. In 1909, Union-Castle took delivery of two new ships destined for this service, the *Edinburgh Castle* and the *Balmoral Castle*, which had quadruple-expansion engines to give them a service speed of 17 knots. Quadruple-expansion engines were developed at the same time as turbines and were soon superseded by them, both in warships and in passenger ships.

***Balmoral Castle* was transformed into a royal yacht during the celebrations which marked the creation of the Union of South Africa in 1910.**

Tonnage: 13,360 grt
Dimensions: 590ft 6in x 64ft 4in x 31ft 6in (180m x 19.6m x 9.6m)
Machinery: two-shaft, vertical quadruple expansion
Service speed: 17 knots
Role: passenger liner
Route: UK-South Africa
Capacity: 317 1st, 220 2nd, 268 3rd
Constructor: Harland & Wolff
Material: steel
Built for: Union-Castle Line

BALOERAN (LATER STRASSBURG) NETHERLANDS: 1930

Tonnage: 16,981 grt
Dimensions: 574ft x 70ft x 28ft (175m x 21.3m x 8.5m)
Machinery: two-shaft, Sulzer two-stroke diesel engines; 14,000hp
Service speed: 18 knots
Role: passenger/cargo liner
Route: Netherlands-East Indies
Capacity: 236 1st, 280 2nd, 70 3rd, 48 4th
Constructor: Wilton-Fijenoord Shipyard, Schiedam
Material: steel
Built for: Rotterdam-Lloyd Line

The Rotterdam-Lloyd Line operated between Rotterdam and Dutch possessions in the East Indies (now Indonesia). In 1930, it took delivery of a new diesel-powered ship, the *Baloeran*, designed specifically to operate in the tropics. The *Baloeran* was in her home port in May 1940, when the Netherlands fell to Germany, and was taken over by the Kriegsmarine, initially as a hospital ship, and renamed *Strassburg*. She sank after she struck a mine in the North Sea on 1 September 1943.

The *Baloeran* was one of the first passenger liners to be powered by diesel engines, in this case single-acting two-stroke units produced by the Sulzer brothers in Switzerland.

BALTIC GB/USA: 1903

By the early years of the 20th century, the White Star Line was challenging Cunard for domination of the UK–New York service, then operating from Liverpool but soon to switch to Southampton. By 1904, the twin liners *Celtic* and *Cedric* had proven themselves on the route and were joined by the slightly larger *Baltic* and later by the *Adriatic*. For a brief period, the *Baltic* was the largest ship afloat, but she was never a breaker of speed records, having been designed for economical operation.

Like many passenger liners, the *Baltic* was taken up for service as a troopship during World War I. She was scrapped in Japan in 1933.

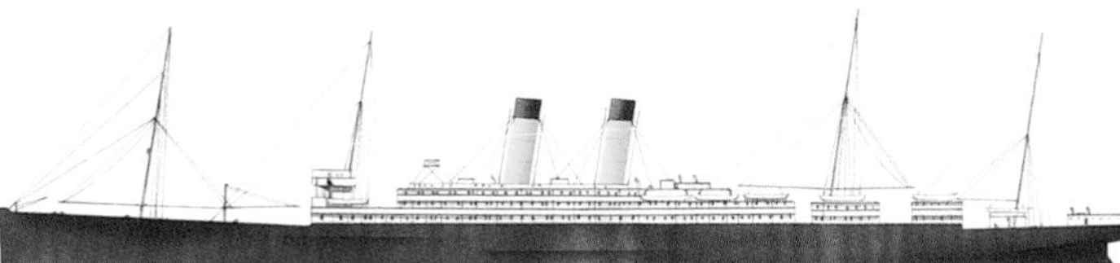

Tonnage: 23,876 grt
Dimensions: 709ft 2in x 75ft 6in (216.15m x 23.05m)
Machinery: two-shaft, two eight-cylinder quadruple expansion
Service speed: 17 knots
Role: passenger liner; troopship
Route: North Atlantic
Capacity: 425 1st, 450 2nd, 2000 st
Constructor: Harland & Wolff, Belfast
Material: steel
Built for: White Star Line

BANSHEE (LATER USS BANSHEE, J L SMALLWOOD, IRENE) CONFEDERATE STATES OF AMERICA: 1862

Tonnage: 325 grt
Dimensions: 214ft x 20ft 3in x 10ft (65.2m x 6.2m x 3m)
Machinery: sidewheels, two-cylinder oscillating; 120hp
Service speed: 12 knots
Role: cargo carrier (blockade runner)
Route: Bahamas-Eastern Seaboard
Capacity: not known
Constructor: Jones, Quiggin & Co, Liverpool
Material: steel on iron frames
Built for: John T Lawrence & Co

The paddle steamer *Banshee* was the first steel-built ship to cross the Atlantic, leaving Liverpool on 2 March 1863. She was built to operate out of Nassau in the Bahamas, running the blockade imposed by the Union Navy on the ports of the Confederacy, carrying in manufactured goods and munitions and carrying out cotton. By 21 November 1863, when she was captured by USS *Grand Gulf* near Cape Hatteras, bound for Wilmington, she had already made eight (some reports say 15) return trips.

Built for speed alone, the *Banshee* was less successful as a legitimate trader than as a blockade runner. She later carried cattle and fruit to and from Cuba.

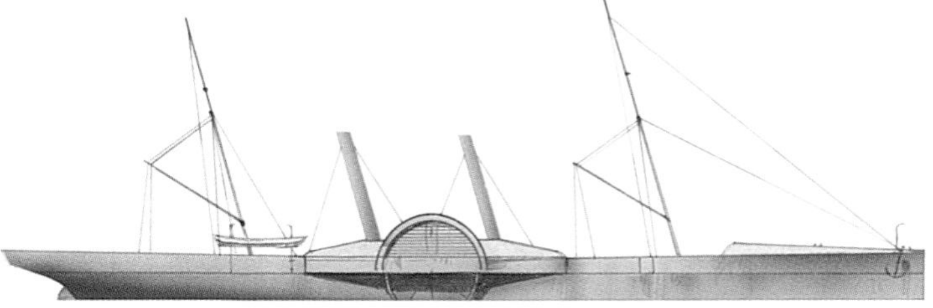

BARBARA — GERMANY: 1926

The Magnus Effect was discovered in 1852. In broad terms, it holds that a sphere or a cylinder rotating in an airstream generates a force at right angles to the direction of its flow. In 1920, physicist Anton Flettner, who was to do important work on the development of the helicopter from 1930, attempted to prove that the Magnus Effect had applications in marine engineering. He constructed twin rotor cylinders, 55ft (16.8m) high by 9ft (2.7m) in diameter, which he mounted aboard a stripped-down steel barquentine named the *Buckau*, driving them by means of 45hp motors. He tested her against her conventionally rigged sistership and proved his point handsomely. The Hamburg-Amerika Line later ordered 10 ships fitted with Flettner rotors to supplement their diesel engines, but only one, the *Barbara*, was ever built. She served commercially with the Sloman Line in this form in the Mediterranean and proved capable of attaining six knots under her rotors alone, but after only a few voyages the cylinders were removed.

The *Barbara* was the only merchant ship purpose-built to harness the Magnus Effect, and was distinctive in appearance, with her three giant funnel-like columns.

Tonnage: 2075 grt
Dimensions: 295ft 3in x 42ft 8in x 18ft 4in (90m x 13m x 5.6m)
Machinery: one-shaft, diesel engines plus Flettner cylinders
Service speed: 13 knots
Role: general cargo vessel
Route: Mediterranean
Material: steel
Built for: Hamburg-Amerika Line

BELGIC (LATER BELGENLAND, COLUMBIA) — USA/BELGIUM: 1914

Tonnage: 24,578 (later 27,132) grt
Dimensions: 670ft 4in x 78ft 4in (204.3m x 23.9m)
Machinery: three-shaft, two triple-expansion reciprocating plus one low-pressure steam turbine
Service speed: 17 knots
Role: cargo/troopship; passenger liner; cruise ship
Route: Antwerp–New York; Caribbean
Capacity: 500 1st, 600 2nd, 1500 3rd; 500 1st, 2000 tr
Constructor: Harland & Wolff, Belfast
Material: steel
Built for: International Mercantile Marine Co

The *Belgic* was ordered by the Belgian-American Red Star Line as the *Belgenland* and was launched under that name in 1914. She was eventually completed austerely in 1917, to be operated by the White Star Line as the *Belgic*, a cargo/troopship. She was largely rebuilt as a passenger liner for her original owners in 1922-23 and went back into service under her original name. She was laid up from 1933-35 and then sold to the Panama-Pacific Line as a cruise ship, but was scrapped the following year.

The 1922–23 rebuild saw the *Belgic* transformed – with two additional superstructure decks and three funnels instead of two – and named *Belgenland* once again.

BELRAY (LATER ARTIGAS) — NORWAY: 1926

One of the most important new merchant ship types to appear during the 1920s was the specialist ship designed to carry extra-large or extra-heavy loads. One such vessel was the motor ship *Belray*, built with wide, clear holds with a minimum number of bulkheads and large hatches with covers specially strengthened to allow them to support heavy loads; she boasted heavy winches and derricks able to lift 100t plus great inherent stability to prevent excessive listing during loading and unloading. The machinery was placed aft and the single deck was surmounted by a poop, bridge deck and forecastle.

***Belray* was designed to deliver heavy locomotives complete and ready to work after unloading. She was sold in 1960, becoming the *Artigas*, and was scrapped in 1970.**

Tonnage: 2888 grt
Dimensions: 328ft 9in x 46ft (69m x 14m)
Machinery: one-shaft, diesel; 1350hp
Service speed: 10 knots
Role: heavy cargo carrier
Capacity: 4280 dwt
Constructor: Armstrong, Whitworth and Co
Material: steel
Built for: Christian Smith

BENRINNES (LATER THORPENESS) GB: 1914

Tonnage: 4798 grt
Dimensions: 405ft x 51ft 5in x 23ft 10in (123.5m x 15.8m x 7.2m)
Machinery: one-shaft, triple expansion; 2150hp
Service speed: 12 knots
Role: general cargo vessel; blockade runner
Route: not applicable
Capacity: 7500 dwt
Constructor: Bartram and Sons, Sunderland
Material: steel
Built for: Ben Line Steamers Ltd, Edinburgh

SS *Benrinnes* was something of an anachronism, having an elegant but totally unnecessary clipper bow (a feature included in her design so that she would fit in with the other, older, ships of the Ben Line, for which she was constructed). She was otherwise a conventional three-island type, with two continuous decks, capable of loading 7500 tons of cargo, which was handled by 12 derricks, each with its own steam winch. She narrowly escaped a submarine torpedo attack during World War I and, renamed *Thorpeness*, was sunk by Nationalist aircraft whilst operating as a blockade runner during the Spanish Civil War.

SS *Benrinnes* was quite typical of the tens of thousands of 'three-island' cargo ships which carried the world's merchandise for a half-century and more.

BERMUDA (LATER GENERAL MEADE) CONFEDERATE STATES OF AMERICA: 1861

The Confederacy's blockade-running operation during the American Civil War was split into two parts: fast ships like the *Banshee* ran the blockade proper from bases in the Bahamas and Bermuda, while bigger, slower ships were used between there and (usually) Liverpool. The *Bermuda* was one of the latter, although in the first year of the war she ran the blockade herself on a number of occasions. She was taken by a Union gunboat in 1862 and sold to a Boston shipping line.

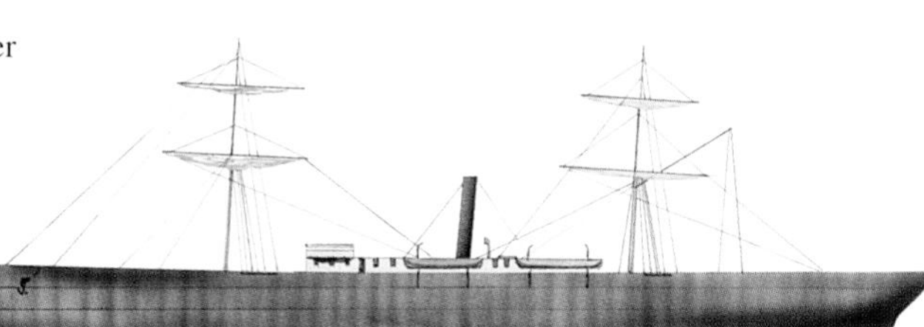

The *Bermuda* was a small, screw-driven auxiliary steamship, with machinery which was already somewhat old-fashioned by 1860.

Tonnage: 1005 grt
Dimensions: 211ft x 30ft (64m x 9m)
Machinery: one-shaft, vertical direct-acting
Service speed: 8 knots
Role: cargo carrier (blockade runner)
Route: Liverpool–Bermuda
Material: iron

BERNHARD OLENDORFF (EX-YEOMAN BURN) GERMANY: 1990

Tonnage: 43,332 grt
Dimensions: 830ft 9in x 105ft 8in x 46ft (245m x 32.2m x 14m)
Machinery: one-shaft, diesel; 12,520hp
Service speed: 13.5 knots
Role: bulk carrier
Route: not applicable
Capacity: 2,546,296 cubic feet (72,103 cubic metres) (grain)
Constructor: Daewoo
Material: steel

The *Bernhard Olendorff* was typical of the third-generation bulk carriers built during the 1990s. She was double-hulled throughout and divided into nine holds. She had her own machinery for loading and discharging cargo, which made her independent of port facilities. She was commonly used to transport raw materials for the steel industry but could also carry grain as and when required. Originally constructed for Norwegian interests for a 20-year-term charter to a British company, she was later transferred to German owners.

BIDEFORD POLACCA BRIGANTINE GB: 1860 ONWARDS

Tonnage: 80 grt
Dimensions: 82ft x 20ft x 9ft 6in (25m x 6.1m x 2.9m)
Role: general cargo vessel
Route: not applicable
Capacity: not applicable
Constructor: not applicable
Material: wood
Built for: not applicable

The Bideford polacca (or poleacre) was a variant of the standard brigantine, many of which were built in the North Devon town of that name, an important small ship-building centre. The genre had its origins in the Mediterranean, where a polacca was any vessel with one-piece masts, with no tops or crosstrees. The Bideford version (though they were also built elsewhere) had a pole foremast, and was instantly recognisable by it being notably shorter than the main, usually extending to only one topsail.

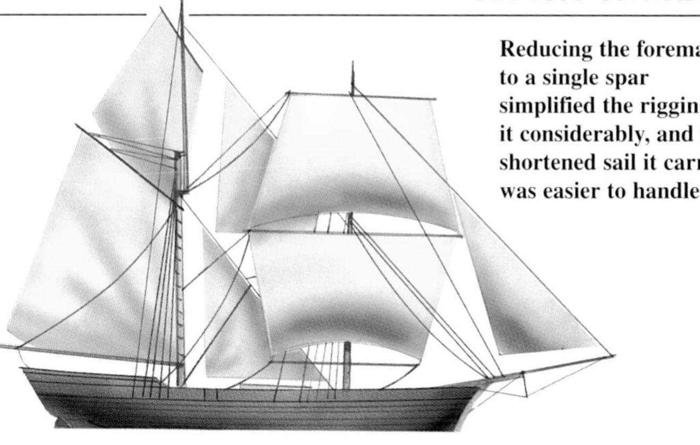

Reducing the foremast to a single spar simplified the rigging of it considerably, and the shortened sail it carried was easier to handle.

BLÜCHER (LATER LEOPOLDINA, SUFFREN) — GERMANY: 1901

Tonnage: 12,350 grt
Dimensions: 525ft 7in x 62ft 3in (160.2m x 19m)
Machinery: two-shaft, two eight-cylinder quadruple expansion
Service speed: 15 knots
Role: passenger liner
Route: North Atlantic
Capacity: 500 cb, 250 3rd
Constructor: Blohm & Voss, Hamburg
Material: steel
Built for: Hamburg-Amerika Line

The Hamburg-Amerika Line ordered a passenger liner, to be known as the *Blücher*, from Blohm & Voss in Hamburg in 1900. She was launched the following year and entered service between Hamburg and New York in 1902. In 1917, she was seized by the Brazilian government at Pernambuco and briefly put into service as the *Leopoldina*. Sold to the French Compagnie Générale Transatlantique and later renamed *Suffren*, she operated between Le Havre and New York until 1928 and was scrapped the following year.

The *Blücher* was one of a pair of German ships seized at Pernambuco, where they had taken refuge, when Brazil entered World War I on the side of the Allies in 1917.

BLUENOSE — CANADA: 1921

In 1963, the government of Nova Scotia commissioned the two-masted gaff topsail schooner *Bluenose II*, an exact replica of the original ship.

The Grand Banks fishing schooner *Bluenose* had a dual personality. When the fishing was over, in October, she raced for the International Trophy, put up by the Halifax *Herald* as a rival to the America's Cup. She was built specially for the competition and won it easily at her first attempt in 1921, again in 1922, in 1930 and in 1937, its final year. Sold to the West Indies Trading Company in 1942, she was wrecked off Haiti in 1946.

Tonnage: 285t displacement
Dimensions: 143ft x 27ft x 15ft 9in (43.6m x 8.2m x 4.8m)
Role: fishery vessel; general cargo vessel; yacht
Route: Grand Banks; Caribbean
Constructor: Smith & Rhuland, Lunenburg, Nova Scotia
Material: wood

BRILLIANT — GB/USA: 1901

Tonnage: 3609 nrt
Dimensions: not known
Role: cargo carrier
Route: North Atlantic
Constructor: Russel & Co, Port Glasgow
Material: steel
Built for: Anglo-American Oil Co

Brilliant was a four-masted barque of just over 3600t net displacement. By the time she was built in 1901, steel had taken over almost entirely from iron in vessels of this size, and her displacement was probably some 15-20 per cent less than that of a similar-sized vessel built 30 years earlier. Steel vessels were also considerably more robust, the metal being both stronger and more malleable than iron. *Brilliant* was constructed for the Anglo-American Oil Co, specifically for the 'case oil' trade, to carry lubricating and lamp oil across the Atlantic.

The *Brilliant* was one of the last square-riggers constructed on Clydeside.

BRITANNIA

GB: 1893

Tonnage: 221t TM
Dimensions: 100ft x 23ft 3in x 12ft 7in (30.5m x 7.1m x 3.8m)
Machinery: not applicable
Service speed: not applicable
Role: yacht
Route: not applicable
Capacity: not applicable
Constructor: D & W Henderson, Glasgow
Material: composite, wood on iron
Built for: HRH Prince of Wales

***Britannia* was placed first in 20 races in her first season, and over her entire career she took 231 first places and 129 seconds or thirds out of 635 starts.**

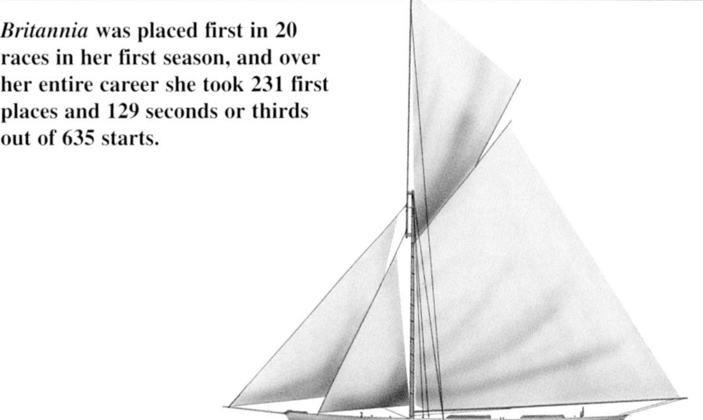

Built for King Edward VII while he was still Prince of Wales and later handed down to his son, King George V, the *Britannia* was initially one of the most successful racing yachts of her day, although in 1897 Edward sold her because rule changes had made her less competitive. He bought her back in 1902, however, and used her for cruising. His son raced her again, and in 1931 had her rerigged with a Bermuda mainsail; she had originally been a gaff cutter. On his death in 1935 she was sunk.

BRITANNIC

GB/USA: 1914

The White Star Line's second *Britannic* was destined never to sail, as intended, on the Southampton–New York route. Instead, she was requisitioned by the British government in November 1915 and commissioned as a hospital ship. In February 1916, after she had made five successful voyages to the Eastern Mediterranean and returned with a total of 15,000 British and Empire servicemen, she struck a mine and sank with the loss of 21 of her crew.

Tonnage: 48,158 grt
Dimensions: 903ft x 94ft (275.25m x 28.65m)
Machinery: three-shaft, two triple-expansion reciprocating engines plus one low-pressure steam turbine
Service speed: 21 knots
Role: hospital ship
Route: UK–Eastern Mediterranean
Capacity: 3109 patients, 489 medical staff
Constructor: Harland & Wolff, Belfast
Material: steel
Built for: White Star Line

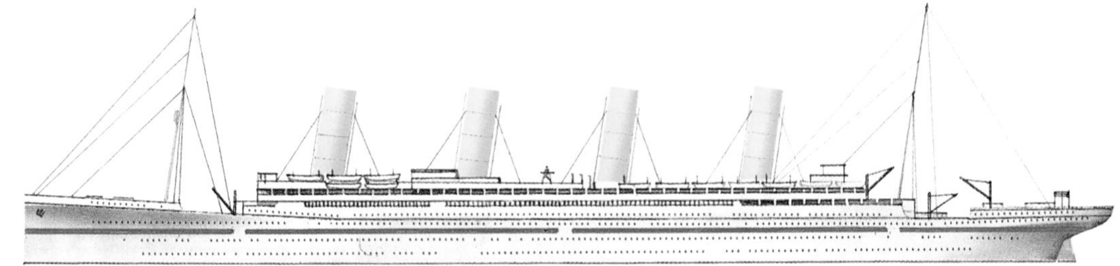

The ill-fated *Britannic* was an improved version of the *Titanic*; she was one of five White Star liners lost during World War I.

BRITANNIC

GB/USA: 1874

Tonnage: 5004 grt
Dimensions: 455ft x 45ft 2in (138.7m x 13.75m)
Machinery: one-shaft, four-cylinder compound
Service speed: 15 knots
Role: passenger liner; troopship
Route: North Atlantic; UK–South Africa
Capacity: 220 1st, 1500 3rd
Constructor: Harland & Wolff, Belfast
Material: steel
Built for: White Star Line

The *Britannic* and her sistership *Germanic* were improved versions of the first *Oceanic*. The two operated in tandem on the North Atlantic route, both holding the Blue Riband at times in their careers. In May 1887, the *Britannic* collided with the *Celtic* at full speed in fog, 300 miles (485km) off Sandy Hook. She made her last commercial voyage in 1899 and was then taken up as a troopship. Re-engining was contemplated in 1903 but proved uneconomical, and she was scrapped in Germany instead.

As completed, *Britannic* had her propeller mounted very low down to reduce the tendency to race as the ship pitched. The experiment was not a success, and she was soon altered to a normal configuration.

BRITISH SKILL

GB: 1990

BP Oil's medium-capacity crude oil-carrying tanker *British Skill* was one of the most efficient ships afloat when she entered service in the early 1990s, although by no means one of the biggest – many contemporaries had well over twice her 128,000t carrying capacity. Much of the running of the ship was entrusted to a computerized automatic pilot, and only when entering and leaving an anchorage was it necessary for the captain and pilots to assume manual control.

The medium crude carrier *British Skill* was representative of the smaller crude-oil carriers of the 1990s; most of her control systems were automated.

Tonnage: 66,034 grt
Dimensions: 856ft 3in x 131ft 3in x 53ft (261m x 40m x 16.2m)
Machinery: one-shaft, diesel; 16,250hp
Service speed: 13.5 knots
Role: crude-oil carrier
Capacity: 128,000t
Constructor: Harland & Wolff, Belfast
Material: steel
Built for: BP Shipping

CABOTIA (EX-WAR VIPER)

GB: 1917

Tonnage: 5160 grt
Dimensions: 411ft 7in x 50ft 8in x 25ft (125.5m x 15.5m x 7.7m)
Machinery: one-shaft, vertical triple expansion; 1800hp
Service speed: 10 knots
Role: general cargo tramp
Route: not applicable
Material: steel

From 1917 onwards, small general-purpose British merchant ships were built to a set of standard designs, chosen largely for ease and speed of construction. *Cabotia* was an A Type, 400ft (120m) long between perpendiculars, with a single internal deck. A Types were essentially three-island vessels (although *Cabotia* had a shelter deck between the poop and the bridge deck), with two cargo hatches forward of the bridge and two aft. They could carry around 8000t of cargo and fuel.

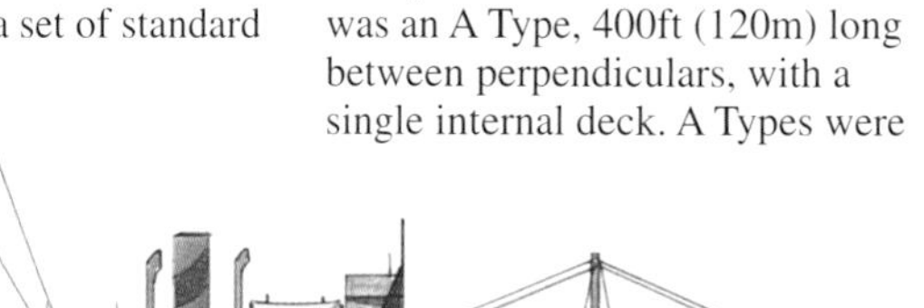

The *Cabotia* was one of many hundreds of small steamers built hurriedly to standard designs to replace war losses.

CALEDONIA (LATER SCOTSTOUN)

GB: 1925

Tonnage: 17,046 grt
Dimensions: 552ft x 72ft x 29ft (168.25m x 21.85m x 8.85m)
Machinery: two-shaft, geared turbines
Service speed: 16 knots
Role: passenger liner; armed merchant cruiser
Route: North Atlantic
Capacity: 205 1st, 403 2nd, 800 3rd
Constructor: Alexander Stephen & Sons, Glasgow
Material: steel
Built for: Anchor Line

When *Caledonia* was fitted out as an armed merchant cruiser, much of her internal space was packed with empty oil drums as a protection against torpedoes.

The *Caledonia* was built as a mixed passenger/cargo liner for the Anchor Line's Glasgow–New York service with accommodation for 1408 passengers in three classes plus two large cargo holds. She entered service in 1926 and proved popular. On the outbreak of war she was requisitioned by the Royal Navy and fitted out with eight obsolescent 6in (152mm) Mk VII guns and two 3in (76mm) AA guns to serve as the *Scotstoun*. She was sunk by *U 25* on 13 June 1940.

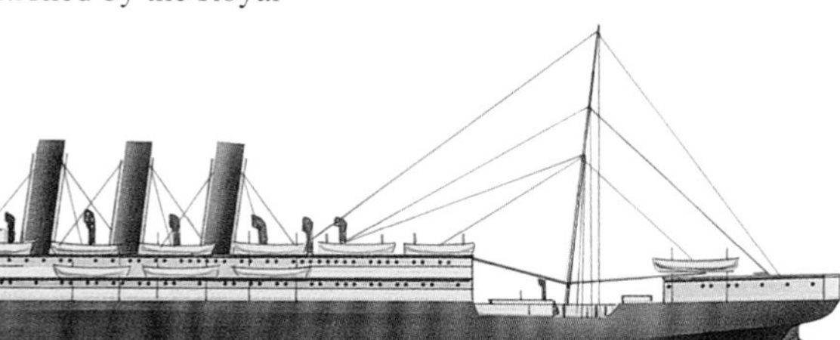

CALSHOT SPIT LIGHTVESSEL

GB: 1920

The history of lightships goes back to the end of the 18th century, and as recently as the 1970s ships built before or just after World War I, like the Calshot Spit Lightvessel, were still in widespread use around the British Isles. They were 'dumb' ships, constructed on small trawler hulls, with no propulsion units, permanently moored to mark shoals and obstructions. Their diesel engines were there only to generate power to run the light and the foghorn, and for the small crew's accommodation.

Lightvessels left their station only at infrequent intervals for major overhaul; the seven-man crews were changed monthly.

Tonnage: 210t standard displacement
Dimensions: 70ft x 17ft (21m x 5m)
Machinery: not applicable
Service speed: not applicable
Role: lightvessel
Route: Calshot Spit
Capacity: not applicable
Material: steel
Built for: Corporation of Trinity House

CALYPSO

FRANCE: 1911

Tonnage: 3t displacement
Dimensions: 41ft 3in x 7ft 10in x 5ft (12.6m x 2.4m x 1.55m)
Machinery: not applicable
Service speed: not applicable
Role: yacht
Route: not applicable
Capacity: not applicable
Constructor: Chantiers Guedon, Lormont
Material: wood
Built for: Pictet de Rochement
Owner: Musée de la Marine

***Calypso* was one of the classic Godinet yachts which cruised and raced on Lac Leman.**

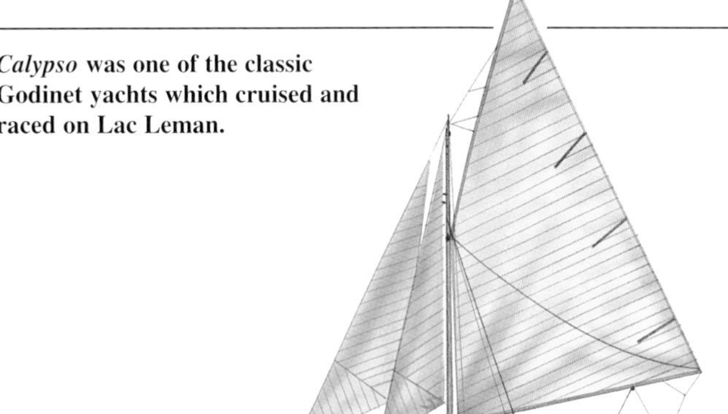

Lac Leman, which sits astride the Franco-Swiss border with two major cities on its banks, was home to many racing yachts, amongst them the classic shallow-draught Godinet cutters, with their extreme straight-leech gunter rig. *Calypso* was a superb example and is now owned by the French Musée de la Marine and displayed at Dives-sur-Mer in Normandy, having been restored to her original condition.

CAMPANIA (LATER HMS CAMPANIA)

GB: 1892

The *Campania* and her sistership *Lucania* were built for the Cunard Line's Liverpool–New York service; they were the first new construction for eight years and were an immediate success. In 1893, on her maiden return voyage, *Campania* took the eastbound Blue Riband and repeated the feat westbound the following year. The two sisters dominated the Europe–New York route until 1897, when *Kaiser Wilhelm der Grosse* entered service. In 1914, by which time she was largely worn out as well as obselescent, the *Campania* was transferred to the Anchor Line and made two voyages from Glasgow, and one from Liverpool in place of the *Aquitania*. Later that year she was sold for breaking up, but the Admiralty intervened and purchased her for conversion to an aircraft carrier. She was given a 120ft (37m) flight deck forward – later extended to 200ft (60m) – and hangars and workshops aft. She had an unremarkable career and in November 1918 foundered after colliding with the battleship HMS *Revenge* in the Firth of Forth.

***Campania* and *Lucania* were instrumental in restoring the Cunard Line's dominance on the North Atlantic service to New York.**

Tonnage: 12,950 grt (later 18,000t displacement)
Dimensions: 622ft x 65ft x 26ft (189.6m x 19.8m x 7.9m)
Machinery: two-shaft, two five-cylinder vertical triple expansion; 28,000hp
Service speed: 21 knots
Role: passenger liner; seaplane carrier
Route: North Atlantic
Capacity: 600 1st, 400 2nd, 1000 3rd
Constructor: Fairfield Co Ltd, Glasgow
Material: steel
Built for: Cunard Steam Ship Co Ltd

CANADA (EX-PANAMA)

FRANCE: 1866

In 1866, a sidewheel paddle steamer named the *Panama* was launched at St Nazaire for the Compagnie Générale Transatlantique. She operated between France and Central America. In 1876, she was converted to screw propulsion by Leslie on Tyneside, and was renamed *Canada*, for the North Atlantic service; she returned to the Central American service in 1886. Electric lighting was installed in 1888, and in 1892 she got triple-expansion engines to replace the Maudslay compound powerplant. *Canada* was scrapped in 1908.

The CGT constructed a number of paddle steamers. Between 1872 and 1876 all were converted to screw propulsion and most were lengthened in the process.

Tonnage: 3400 (later 4054) grt
Dimensions: 355ft 5in x 43ft 9in (108.3m x 13.35m)
Machinery: sidewheels, two side lever (later one-shaft, compound (later triple expansion)
Service speed: 12 knots
Role: passenger liner
Route: St Nazaire-Vera Cruz; Le Havre-New York; Le Havre-Panama
Constructor: Chantiers de Penhoët, St Nazaire (under supervision of Scott & Co, Greenock)
Material: iron
Built for: Compagnie Générale Transatlantique

CANBERRA — GB: 1961

Tonnage: 45,270 grt
Dimensions: 818ft x 102ft x 32ft (250m x 31m x 9.9m)
Machinery: two-shaft, turbo-electric; 88,000hp
Service speed: 27.5 knots
Role: passenger liner; cruise ship; troopship
Route: Southampton-Australia
Capacity: 556 1st, 1716 tr; 1737 tr
Constructor: Harland & Wolff, Belfast
Material: steel & aluminium
Built for: P&O Steam Navigation Co
Owner: P&O Line

Canberra, instantly recognizable then by her futuristic lines, was constructed in 1960 as a passenger liner to operate in the newly merged P&O-Orient Line's UK–Australia service alongside the *Oriana*. Within 10 years, air fares had reached a level with which she could not compete, and in 1973 she began year-round cruises. *Canberra* had just completed one in April 1982 when she was requisitioned by the British government to carry troops to the Falkland Islands. Despite operating close inshore, she was undamaged and later returned to the cruise trade.

The *Canberra* was one of the last purpose-built passenger liners, but the changing economic climate soon saw her converted to cruising.

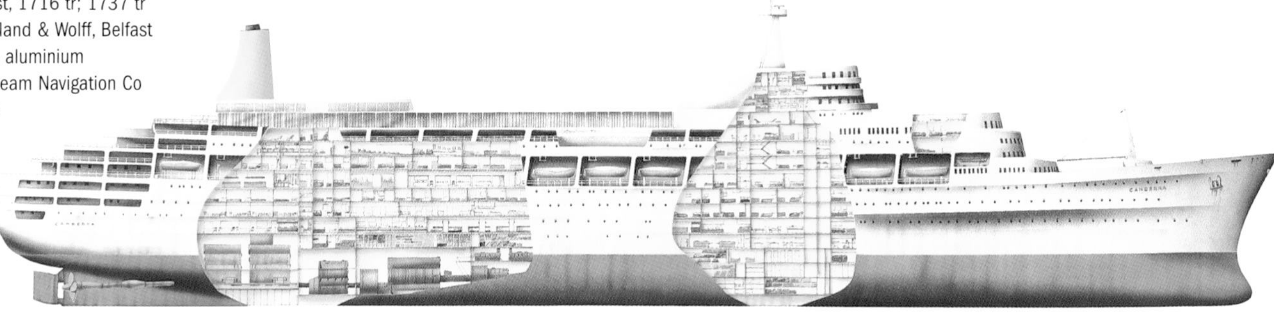

CANDIOPE (EX-WAR MINGAN) — GB: 1918

The *Candiope* was built in Canada in 1918 as the *War Mingan* to a standard pattern which was intended to ensure ease and speed of construction. Most unusually, she was built of wood to conserve steel stocks. She had not entered service by the time of the November 1918 Armistice and was sold the following year to an Italian bank, Credito Industriale di Venezia, and operated as a short-sea tramp steamer in the Mediterranean. She was broken up four years later.

The *Candiope* was one of a few standard small merchant steamships of wooden construction, steel being at a premium in 1918.

Tonnage: 3300 grt
Dimensions: 251ft x 43ft 6in (76.5m x 13.25m)
Machinery: one-shaft, vertical triple expansion; 1400hp
Service speed: 10 knots
Role: general cargo vessel
Route: not applicable
Constructor: not known
Material: wood

CANIS (EX-ANDREW WELCH, OLGA, SOPHUS MAGDALON) — NORWAY: 1918

Canis was originally the sailing ship *Andrew Welch* (launched in 1888) and was typical of the older sailing ships being given a new lease of life by conversion into steam- or diesel-powered vessels. She was converted in 1918, about half way through her life of 60 years, and was renamed *Olga*. She stranded badly but was repaired and sold to Sophus Kahrs as the *Sophus Magdalon*; in 1922 she was bought by the Bergen Steamship Co and plied the Norwegian coast as the *Canis*.

Tonnage: 934 grt
Dimensions: 185ft 6in x 36ft x 17ft 5in (56.4m x 11m x 5.2m)
Machinery: one-shaft, diesel; 520hp
Service speed: 10 knots
Role: general cargo vessel
Route: coastal waters, Norway
Capacity: 1450 dwt
Constructor: Russell and Co, Kingston Shipbuilding Yard
Material: not known
Built for: Captain Marston, San Francisco

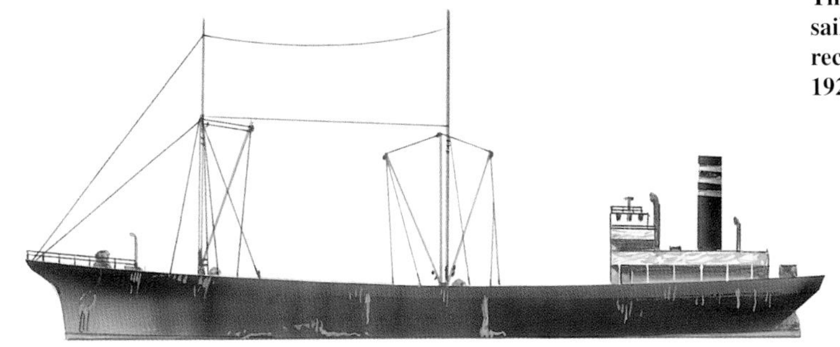

The graceful lines of the former sailing ship can still be seen in the reconstructed *Canis*, shown in 1922.

CAP TRAFALGAR

GERMANY: 1913

Thanks to the Imperial German Navy's decision to arm her as an auxiliary cruiser, the *Cap Trafalgar* had one of the shortest careers of any major steamship.

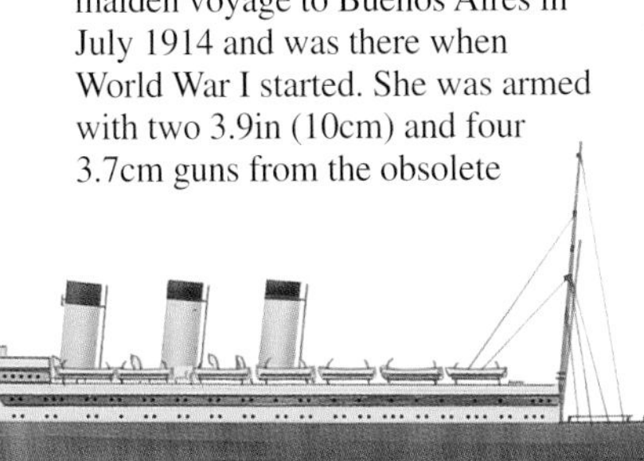

The Hamburg-Südamerika Line's *Cap Trafalgar* set out on her maiden voyage to Buenos Aires in July 1914 and was there when World War I started. She was armed with two 3.9in (10cm) and four 3.7cm guns from the obsolete gunboat *Eber* and commissioned on 31 August. Fourteen days later she was intercepted while coaling off Trinidade Island by the British armed merchant cruiser *Carmania*, which had considerably superior armament, and was sunk after a furious hour-long artillery duel, with the loss of 16 of her crew.

Tonnage: 18,805 grt
Dimensions: 610ft 3in x 71ft 10in x 27ft 3in (186m x 21.9m x 8.3m)
Machinery: three-shaft, two vertical triple expansion plus one low-pressure turbine
Service speed: 17 knots
Role: passenger liner; auxiliary cruiser
Route: Hamburg–Buenos Aires
Capacity: 400 1st, 275 2nd, 900 3rd
Constructor: AG Vulkan, Hamburg
Material: steel
Built for: Hamburg-Südamerikanischen Dampffschiffahrts Gesellschaft

CARELIA

FINLAND: 1921

Tonnage: 1123 grt
Dimensions: 217ft x 34ft 5in x 15ft (66m x 10.4m x 4.6m)
Machinery: one-shaft, triple expansion
Service speed: 8 knots
Role: timber carrier
Route: Baltic and North Sea
Capacity: not known
Constructor: Maskin and Brobygnade Aktiebolager, Helsinki
Material: steel
Built for: Atlantic Rederi A/B

In the 1920s, the Baltic and North Sea timber trade provided employment for a large number of small steamers. By placing the masts and winches at the ends of the bridge deck and on the forecastle and poop, the well decks between these structures were left clear for the easy stowage of a deck cargo of timber. These ships were mainly built in Scandinavian shipyards. In 1925, *Carelia* and three near-sisters were absorbed into Finland's largest shipping concern, Finland SS Co Ltd. *Carelia* was broken up in Holland in 1963.

Although relatively small, *Carelia* could stow a large cargo of timber, thanks to the positioning of masts and winches at the extreme ends of the vessel and centre structure.

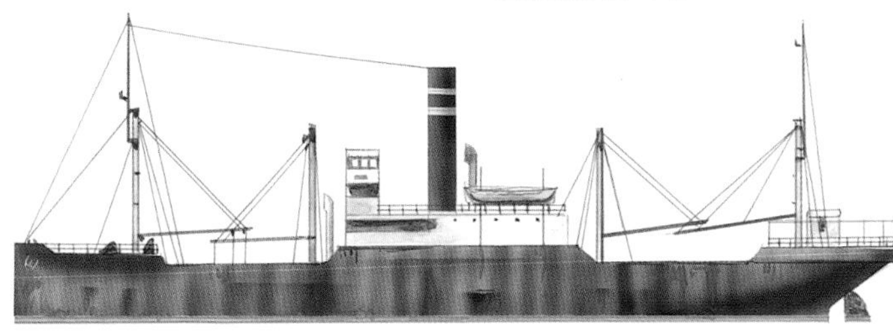

CARMANIA

GB: 1905

The *Carmania* was built for the Cunard Line's Liverpool–New York service. She was the company's first turbine-powered ship, operating alongside a reciprocating-engined sister vessel, the *Caronia*, for purposes of comparison; she proved to be superior in terms of speed. In 1914, she was taken up by the Royal Navy as an armed merchant cruiser, with eight 4.7in (119mm) guns, and sank the *Cap Trafalgar* on her first voyage. She later served as a troopship before being returned to Cunard. She was scrapped in 1932.

The superior performance of the *Carmania*'s turbine machinery led to the Cunard Line's specifying it for all its ships.

Tonnage: 19,524 grt
Dimensions: 674ft 10in x 72ft 2in (205.7m x 22m)
Machinery: three-shaft, direct-acting turbines; 32,000hp
Service speed: 18 knots
Role: passenger liner; armed merchant cruiser; troopship
Route: North Atlantic
Capacity: 300 1st, 350 2nd, 900 3rd, 1100 st
Constructor: John Brown & Co, Glasgow
Material: steel
Built for: Cunard Steam Ship Co Ltd

CARPATHIA

GB: 1903

The *Carpathia*, constructed to operate on the Cunard Line's mixed passenger/cargo Trieste–New York service, with only second- and third-class accommodation, was typical of the second-rate liners of the period. She briefly entered the spotlight when, bound for the Mediterranean, she was the first ship on the scene of the sinking of the *Titanic* in April 1912, rescuing some 706 survivors. She herself was sunk late in World War I, torpedoed about 120 nautical miles (195km) west of Queenstown (Cork) by *U 55*, with the loss of five lives.

The Cunard Line's *Carpathia* was briefly famous after she rescued 706 survivors of the *Titanic* disaster in April 1912.

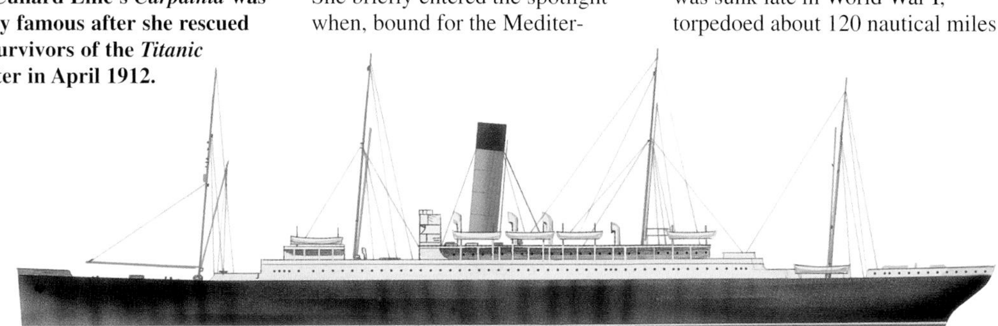

Tonnage: 13,555 grt
Dimensions: 558ft x 64ft 4in (170m x 20m)
Machinery: two-shaft, quadruple expansion
Service speed: 14 knots
Role: passenger liner
Route: Trieste–New York; Liverpool–Boston
Capacity: 204 2nd, 1500 3rd
Constructor: Swan, Hunter and Wigham Richardson Ltd, Wallsend
Material: steel
Built for: Cunard Steam Ship Co Ltd

CARTHAGE (EX-CANTON)

GB: 1931

Tonnage: 14,182 grt
Dimensions: 540ft x 71ft (165m x 22m)
Machinery: two-shaft, geared turbines
Service speed: 18 knots
Role: passenger liner; armed merchant cruiser; troopship
Route: Europe–Far East
Capacity: 175 1st, 196 2nd
Material: steel

The 14,200-t passenger liner *Carthage* was built as the *Canton* for service to the Far East, between London and Hong Kong, carrying first- and second-class passengers and mixed cargo. She was taken up by the Admiralty in 1940 and armed as a merchant cruiser, with eight 6in (152mm) guns. In 1943, she was stripped of her armament and operated as a troopship. She was refurbished after the war and returned to passenger service; she was broken up in 1961.

The *Carthage* was constructed for the Far Eastern service, where there was no emigrant traffic, and thus had only first- and second-class accommodation.

CASTALIA

GB: 1874

The *Castalia* consisted of two identical hulls joined at deck level by a simple platform which carried the bridge and upperworks.

The *Castalia* was the world's first catamaran ferry and briefly operated on the London, Chatham and Dover Railway's cross-channel service between the United Kingdom and France in the mid-1870s. She was the brainchild of a captain in the employ of the East India Company, who had encountered small double-hulled craft in the Far East. *Castalia*'s single paddle wheel, located between the hulls, proved vulnerable.

Tonnage: 1533 grt
Dimensions: 290ft x 50ft x 6ft (88.3m x 15.25m x 1.8m)
Machinery: sidewheels, side-lever
Service speed: 6 knots
Role: ferry
Route: Dover-Calais
Material: iron
Built for: London, Chatham and Dover Railway Co

CEPHEE

BELGIUM: 1937

Tonnage: not applicable
Dimensions: 126ft 5in x 16ft 7in x 6ft 7in (38.55m x 5.05m x 2m)
Machinery: not applicable
Service speed: not applicable
Role: canal barge
Route: canals, Belgium/France
Capacity: not known
Constructor: Pruvost Frères, Merville
Material: wood
Built for: Marcel Ruyffelaere
Owner: Rijn en binnenvaartmuseum, Antwerp

The canal barge *Cephee* was a late example of those used to transport goods from the industrial centres of Belgium and northern France to the port of Antwerp. The basic style of the barges in this region changed little over more than a century and a half, the canal system remaining in everyday use until after World War II. They were exclusively horse-drawn, usually by two teams.

'Dumb' horse-drawn barges like the *Cephee* were in widespread use over Belgium and northern France until after World War II.

CHINA (LATER THEODOR)

GB: 1862

Tonnage: 2550 grt
Dimensions: 326ft x 40ft x 27ft 6in (99.4m x 12.2m x 8.4m)
Machinery: one-shaft, oscillating (later compound); 2200hp
Service speed: 12 knots
Role: passenger liner
Route: North Atlantic
Capacity: 150 1st, 770 st; 1400t
Constructor: R Napier & Sons, Glasgow
Material: steel
Built for: British & North American Royal Mail Steam Packet Co (Cunard Line)

The screw-propelled *China* soon proved herself much superior to paddle-wheel-driven ships on the Liverpool–New York service.

The Cunarder *China* was the first screw-propelled ship the company constructed, although it had earlier chartered at least one. *China* was specifically for the all-important mail service from Liverpool to New York. She proved very successful, and her simple two-cylinder beam engine was later replaced by compound machinery. Twenty years after she entered service she was sold. Renamed *Theodor*, her machinery was removed and she was rigged as a four-masted barque. She was lost at sea in 1906.

CITY OF BERLIN (LATER BERLIN, MEADE)

GB: 1875

The Inman Line was one of the pioneers of steam on the North Atlantic route. Its *City of Berlin* entered service in May 1875 and was the biggest steamer on the route for some years. In 1887, the ship was re-engined with the newly developed triple-expansion machinery, from Laird Bros of Birkenhead, which proved to be an outstanding success. She was transferred to the American Line in 1893, but also made voyages for the Red Star Line. She was eventually scrapped in 1921.

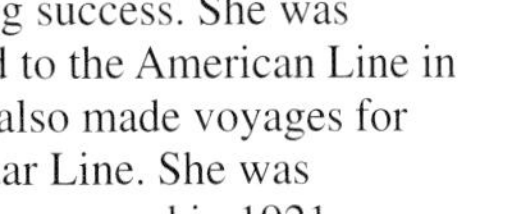

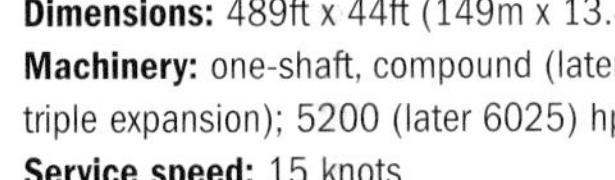

Tonnage: 5491 grt
Dimensions: 489ft x 44ft (149m x 13.4m)
Machinery: one-shaft, compound (later triple expansion); 5200 (later 6025) hp
Service speed: 15 knots
Role: passenger liner
Route: North Atlantic
Capacity: 202 cb, 1500 3rd
Constructor: not known
Material: steel
Built for: Inman Line

In the year in which she entered service, the *City of Berlin* briefly held the Blue Riband in both directions.

CITY OF BRUSSELS

GB: 1869

The Inman Line's *City of Brussels* was a notable success from the outset, taking the eastbound Blue Riband on her second voyage. She was the first North Atlantic liner to be constructed with steam-assisted steering gear. She received an additional promenade deck in 1872, and compound engines replaced her original horizontal trunk machinery in 1876. In December 1883, she sank after she was in collision with SS *Kirby Hall* at the mouth of the River Mersey, with the loss of 10 lives.

Builders Tod & McGregor were responsible for the 'City of' which prefixed the name of most of the Inman Line's vessels, having originally operated the first, *City of Glasgow*, on their own account.

Tonnage: 3081 (later 3747) grt
Dimensions: 390ft x 40ft 3in (118.85m x 12.3m)
Machinery: one-shaft, horizontal trunk (later compound)
Service speed: 14 knots
Role: passenger liner
Route: Liverpool–New York
Capacity: 200 1st, 600 3rd
Constructor: Tod & McGregor, Glasgow
Material: iron
Built for: Liverpool, New York & Philadelphia Steam Ship Co (Inman Line)

CITY OF NEW YORK (LATER NEW YORK, SOMETIME HARVARD, PLATTSBURG GB/USA: 1888

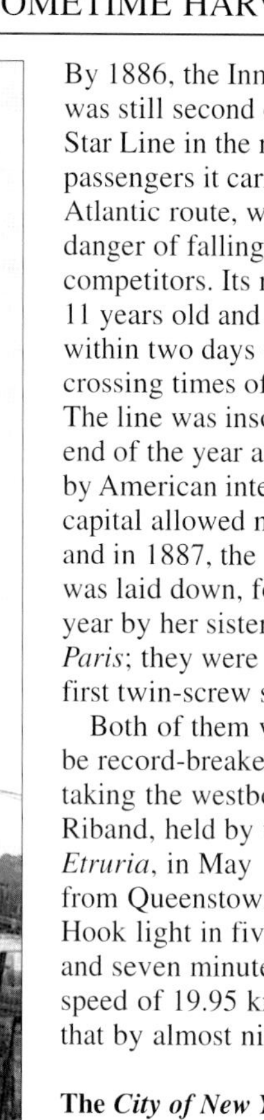

By 1886, the Inman Line, while it was still second only to the White Star Line in the number of passengers it carried on the North Atlantic route, was in grave danger of falling behind its competitors. Its newest ships were 11 years old and unable to come within two days of the average crossing times of Cunard's ships. The line was insolvent before the end of the year and was taken over by American interests. Extra capital allowed new construction and in 1887, the *City of New York* was laid down, followed the next year by her sistership, the *City of Paris*; they were the company's first twin-screw ships.

Both of them were destined to be record-breakers, *City of Paris* taking the westbound Blue Riband, held by the Cunarder *Etruria*, in May 1889, crossing from Queenstown to the Sandy Hook light in five days, 23 hours and seven minutes, at an average speed of 19.95 knots. She bettered that by almost nine hours when she took the record again in October 1892, by which time *City of New York* had also held the westbound record. Their success in this respect was short-lived, however, because even then the Cunard twins *Campania* and *Lucania* were nearing completion and would soon eclipse them. *City of New York* had a confused career thereafter. She passed to the associated US-flag American Line in 1893, was named *New York* and plied to Southampton with a newly awarded mail contract. She was taken up as an armed cruiser briefly in 1898, and again, also briefly, as a transport in 1918. She later went through four changes of ownership under the same name before being scrapped in 1923 in Genoa.

The *City of New York* was the first twin-screw liner on the North Atlantic route; as well as increasing her speed, this allowed the insertion of a longitudinal bulkhead the entire length of the ship.

Tonnage: 10,499 (later 10,798) grt
Dimensions: 527ft 6in x 63ft 2in (160.8m x 19.25m)
Machinery: two-shaft, vertical triple expansion
Service speed: 20 knots
Role: passenger liner; armed merchant cruiser; transport
Route: North Atlantic
Capacity: 540 1st, 200 2nd, 1000 3rd
Constructor: J&G Thomson, Glasgow
Material: steel
Built for: Inman & International Steamship Co Ltd (Inman Line)

CITY OF ROME GB: 1881

The *City of Rome* was the first ship the Inman Line had built outside Scotland. She was intended to be constructed of steel, but sufficient supplies were not available, and she was constructed of iron instead. She was widely held to be the most beautifully proportioned and most graceful vessel of her day, with a pronounced clipper bow and stern and equal angles of rake to her three funnels and four masts. She was ordered to meet competition from the Guion Line, and specifically to rival the *Arizona* and the *Alaska*, but she never came even near to doing so, with a maiden crossing of over nine and a half days; she was eventually handed back to her builders as unsatisfactory. She was transferred to the Anchor Line (which held a 50 per cent stake in Barrow Shipbuilding) in 1882 and remained in service for 20 more years, being scrapped in 1902.

The *City of Rome* was far and away the biggest ship the Inman Line had constructed by 1881, but the use of iron instead of steel upped her displacement by over 1500t and reduced her cargo capacity accordingly.

Tonnage: 8415 grt
Dimensions: 560ft 2in x 52ft 3in (170.75m x 15.95m)
Machinery: one-shaft, two three-cylinder compound
Service speed: 16 knots
Role: passenger liner
Route: North Atlantic
Capacity: 271 1st, 250 2nd, 810 3rd (later 75 1st, 250 2nd, 1000 3rd)
Constructor: Barrow Shipbuilding Co
Material: iron
Built for: Inman Steamship Co (Inman Line)

CLEOPATRA

GB: 1877

The *Cleopatra* is better considered as a lighter than as a true ship, since she had no machinery and only an (ineffectual) steadying sail. She was built around the 190-t granite obelisk known as Cleopatra's Needle, to transport it to London. Cylindrical in form, with her bow and stern crudely brought together on the vertical axis, the *Cleopatra* was the brainchild of Benjamin Baker and John Fowler, whose rather more significant achievements included building much of London's underground railway system and the magnificent railway bridge across the Firth of Forth. Towed by the steamer *Olga*, at the end of a 1200ft (370m) hawser, she got as far as the Bay of Biscay before weather conditions made the operation impossible, and she had to be cast loose and her small crew taken off. Later, in calmer conditions, she was taken in tow by the British steamer *Fitzmaurice* and lodged at El Ferrol. The following year she finished her journey to the Thames Embankment behind the tug *Anglia*.

The *Cleopatra*'s semi-cylindrical plates were prefabricated in the UK; they were then riveted together around the obelisk, and the whole ensemble rolled down to the sea.

Tonnage: 274t displacement
Dimensions: 92ft x 15ft 1in x 8ft (28m x 4.6m x 2.45m)
Role: artefact transport
Route: Alexandria-El Ferrol-London
Capacity: not applicable
Constructor: John & Wainman Dixon
Material: steel
Built for: British government

CLUB MED 1 (LATER WIND SURF)

FRANCE: 1989

Tonnage: 1600dwt
Dimensions: 613ft 6in x 65ft 6in x 16ft 5in (187m x 20m x 5m)
Machinery: two-shaft, auxiliary diesel-electric
Service speed: 12 knots
Role: cruise ship
Route: Mediterranean; Caribbean
Capacity: 410
Constructor: Ateliers et Chantiers du Havre, Le Havre
Material: steel
Built for: Club Med

The auxiliary five-masted staysail schooner *Club Med 1* was one of the first of a new generation of sailing cruise ships. Constructed by Ateliers et Chantiers du Havre, she entered service in 1990 with a month-long cruise the length of the Mediterranean from Cannes on the Côte d'Azur to Egypt and back, and then crossed the Atlantic. Sail-handling was motorized and under computer control, the auxiliary diesel engine being brought into operation as and when required. After 10 years' service with her original owners she was sold to Winstar Cruises, but continued to operate as before.

For ease of handling, *Club Med 1* carried only staysails save on the No 5 spanker mast, where she also carried a conventional Bermuda course.

COCKERILL

BELGIUM: 1901

The Belgian steamship *Cockerill* was constructed by the company of that name to carry perishables – mostly fruit and vegetables – between Antwerp and London. She was one of the earliest small steam cargo liners on the short-sea route and did much to set the standard for those which came after her. The light rig she carried was more in the way of steadying sails than to provide propulsive power.

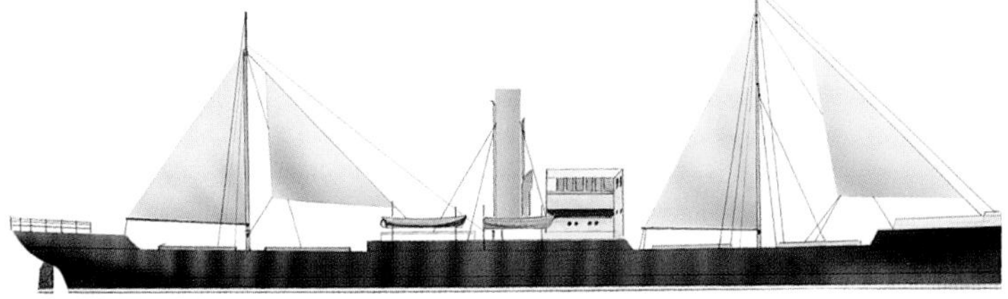

The *Cockerill* did much to establish the pattern for later small steam tramps and liners alike, and proved to be very economical to operate.

Tonnage: 2440 grt
Dimensions: 288ft 8in x 45ft (88m x 14m)
Machinery: one-shaft, vertical compound; 1200hp
Service speed: 8 knots
Role: general cargo vessel
Route: English Channel; coastal
Capacity: not known
Constructor: John Cockerill & Co, Hoboken
Material: steel
Built for: not known

COLUMBIA (SOMETIME COLUMBELLA, LATER MOREAS)

GB: 1902

The *Columbia* was built to replace the ageing *City of Rome* and was the first of four similar ships which did much to improve the Anchor Line's position (it was later taken over by Cunard). She was taken up as an armed merchant cruiser from 1914-1919 (as the *Columbella*) and then returned to her owners, who kept her in service until 1926, latterly converted to oil, when she was sold to Greek interests and made three runs between Piraeus and New York. She was scrapped in 1929.

Tonnage: 8292 grt
Dimensions: 485ft 6in x 56ft 3in (147.95m x 17.15m)
Machinery: two-shaft, vertical triple expansion
Service speed: 16 knots
Role: passenger liner; armed merchant cruiser
Route: North Atlantic; Piraeus–New York
Capacity: 345 1st, 218 2nd, 740 3rd (later 72 1st, 430 2nd, 378 3rd; later 492 1st, 420 3rd)
Constructor: D & W Henderson, Glasgow
Material: steel
Built for: Anchor Line

The *Columbia*'s three near-sisters – *Caledonia*, *California* and *Cameronia* – were all sunk by German submarines during World War I.

COLUMBUS (EX-HINDENBURG)

GERMANY: 1922

Tonnage: 32,354 grt
Dimensions: 749ft 7in x 83ft 1in (228.5m x 25.35m)
Machinery: two-shaft, two four-cylinder triple expansion (later two geared turbines)
Service speed: 19 (later 23) knots
Role: passenger liner
Route: Bremen–New York
Capacity: 478 1st, 644 2nd, 602 3rd
Constructor: F Schichau, Danzig (Gdansk)
Material: steel
Built for: Norddeutscher Lloyd Line

The Norddeutscher Lloyd Line's *Columbus* took the name of her sistership, which was seized by Britain and operated by the White Star Line as the *Homeric*.

A 34,000-t passenger liner was laid down for the Norddeutscher Lloyd Line in 1914 as the *Hindenburg*, but work on her was discontinued until 1920, and she was finally launched (with considerable difficulty) as the *Columbus*, in 1922. She made her maiden voyage from Bremen to New York in 1924. In 1929, she was re-engined with turbines. In December 1939, she was intercepted off Norfolk, Virginia, by HMS *Hyperion*, and her captain ordered her scuttled to avoid capture.

COMMANDANT DE ROSE

FRANCE: 1917

The *Commandant de Rose* and her sisterships were basically steam-powered, with gaff courses to act as steadying sails, rather than true auxiliary schooners.

The *Commandant de Rose* was one of a score of wooden auxiliary five-masted schooners ordered during World War I by the French from American East Coast yards, where a building tradition still flourished. They were not delivered until late in 1917 and thus never actually repaid the investment in them, even though freight charges had climbed to roughly 10 times 1914 levels by then. They were uneconomical to operate as soon as the world returned to normal and were scrapped in the early 1920s.

Tonnage: 4500 grt
Dimensions: 280ft x 45ft 6in x 23ft (85m x 14m x 7m)
Machinery: two-shaft, auxiliary vertical triple expansion
Service speed: 10 knots
Role: general cargo vessel
Route: North Atlantic
Material: wood

CONDOR EXPRESS

GB: 1997

Tonnage: 380 dwt
Dimensions: 282ft 10in x 85ft 3in x 11ft 6in (86.25m x 26m x 3.5m)
Machinery: four water jets, four Ruston 20-cylinder diesel; 37,950bhp
Service speed: 40 knots
Role: vehicle/passenger ferry
Route: Poole–St Malo
Capacity: 776 p, 200 v
Constructor: Incat, Hobart
Material: steel, aluminium
Built for: Condor Ferries

Condor Express was one of a pair of catamaran vehicle/passenger ferries linking Poole, on the south coast of England, with St Malo in Brittany via the Channel Islands. In optimum conditions, the journey took just four hours at speeds of up to 40 knots; the vessels could carry up to 776 passengers and 200 cars. Like the majority of catamaran ferries in service at the end of the 20th century, they were built by International Catamarans (Incat) in Hobart, Tasmania, and featured water-jet propulsion.

In trials, *Condor Express* achieved a top speed of 48.7 knots over a five-minute period and maintained over 45 knots at full displacement.

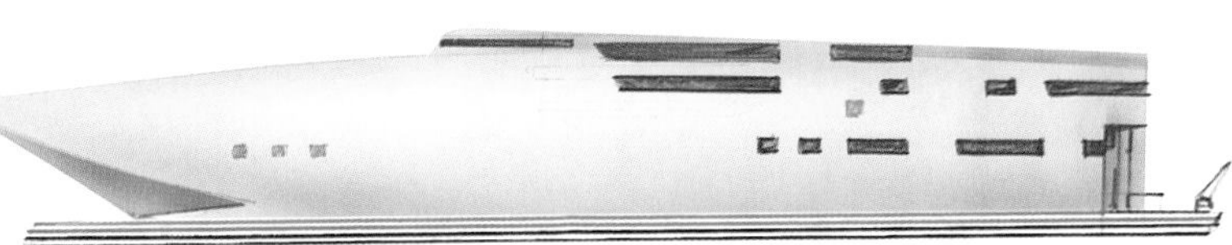

CONTE DI SAVOIA

ITALY: 1931

The orders for the *Rex* and the *Conte di Savoia* were announced almost simultaneously, but there was no rivalry between the two – *Rex* was built for speed, *Conte di Savoia* for style and grace. She was launched in October 1931 and began trials just over a year later, proving herself able to sustain 29 knots. With some trepidation (for the *Rex* had broken down on *her* maiden voyage), she was prepared to leave Genoa for New York on 30 November. All went well until, some 900 nautical miles (1450km) off her destination, an outlet valve stuck and blew a hole in her hull below the waterline. A superhuman effort saw it patched, and she continued on her way, her passengers unaware of how close they had come to disaster. Repaired, she continued in service until 1940 and was then laid up near Venice. She was sunk by Allied aircraft in September 1943, salvaged in 1945 and broken up five years later.

Tonnage: 48,502 grt
Dimensions: 814ft 8in x 96ft 2in (248.3m x 30m)
Machinery: four-shaft, geared turbines
Service speed: 27 knots
Role: passenger liner
Route: Genoa–New York
Capacity: 500 1st, 366 2nd, 412 tr, 922 3rd
Constructor: Cantieri Riuniti dell'Adriatico, Trieste
Material: steel
Built for: Lloyd Sabaudo Line

***Conte di Savoia* was known as 'the roll-less ship', having a new (and heavily publicized) system of gyroscopic stabilization; unfortunately, it could seldom be used.**

CONTE VERDE

ITALY: 1922

Tonnage: 18,765 grt
Dimensions: 559ft x 74ft (170.4m x 22.55m)
Machinery: two-shaft, geared turbines
Service speed: 18.5 knots
Role: passenger liner; troopship
Route: Genoa–South America; Genoa–Far East
Capacity: 230 1st, 290 2nd, 1880 3rd
Constructor: Wm Beardmore & Co, Glasgow
Material: steel
Built for: Lloyd Sabaudo Line

The Lloyd Sabaudo Line ordered a 19,000-t twin-screw turbine ship from Beardmore in Glasgow in 1921, to operate its service to the east coast of South America. The *Conte Verde* was transferred to the Far East route in 1931. She was laid up in Shanghai on Italy's entry into the war in 1940, and on the Italian armistice in September 1943 her crew scuttled her. She was raised by the Japanese and briefly employed as a troopship before being wrecked in an air raid in 1944.

The *Conte Verde* was originally built primarily to service the important emigration route between Italy and Argentina.

CORSICAN (LATER MARVALE)

GB/CANADA: 1907

The twin-screw *Corsican* was constructed for the long-established Allan Line in 1907 to replace the *Bavarian* on the route from Glasgow to St John, New Brunswick, and later to Quebec and Montreal – ice allowing. The Canadian Pacific Line secretly acquired the Allan Line in 1909, the fact not being made public until 1915, whereupon the *Corsican* officially changed hands. Her name was changed to *Marvale* in 1922, and in May the following year she was wrecked, with no loss of life, near Cape Race.

Tonnage: 11,419 grt
Dimensions: 500ft 3in x 61ft 2in (152.5m x 18.65m)
Machinery: two-shaft, vertical triple expansion
Service speed: 16 knots
Role: passenger liner
Route: UK–Canada
Capacity: 208 1st, 298 2nd, 1000 3rd
Constructor: Barclay, Curle & Co, Glasgow
Material: steel
Built for: Allan Line Steamship Co

During the months when the St Lawrence River was free of ice, the *Corsican*' s western terminus was Montreal. She hit an iceberg once, but was not badly damaged.

COUNTY OF PEEBLES (LATER MUÑOZ GAMERO)

GB: 1875

The *County of Peebles* was the first of a dozen iron four-masted ships built for R & J Craig of Dundee.

The *County of Peebles* was the first four-masted ship built of iron and was to be very influential indeed. She was constructed for the jute trade between Dundee and India and was later in the North Atlantic trade until 1898, when she was bought by the Chilean government and used as a coal hulk at Punta Arenas. She was sunk as a breakwater in the 1960s, but her living quarters, which remained above water, were preserved intact and furnished.

Tonnage: 1691 grt
Dimensions: 266ft 7in x 38ft 8in x 23ft 5in (81.3m x 11.8m x 7.1m)
Machinery: not applicable
Service speed: not applicable
Role: jute carrier; general cargo vessel; coal hulk
Route: Dundee–India; North Atlantic; Punta Arenas
Constructor: Barclay, Curle & Co, Glasgow
Material: iron
Built for: R & J Craig

CRETECABLE

GB: 1919

Tonnage: 262t standard displacement
Dimensions: 125ft x 27ft 6in x 13ft 4in (38m x 8.5m x 4m)
Machinery: one-shaft, vertical triple expansion
Service speed: 8 knots
Role: coastal tug
Route: coastal waters/harbours, UK
Capacity: not applicable
Material: ferro-cement; steel
Built for: Admiralty

The ferro-cement construction methods used during World War I were crude by later standards, but they produced serviceable, durable small ships.

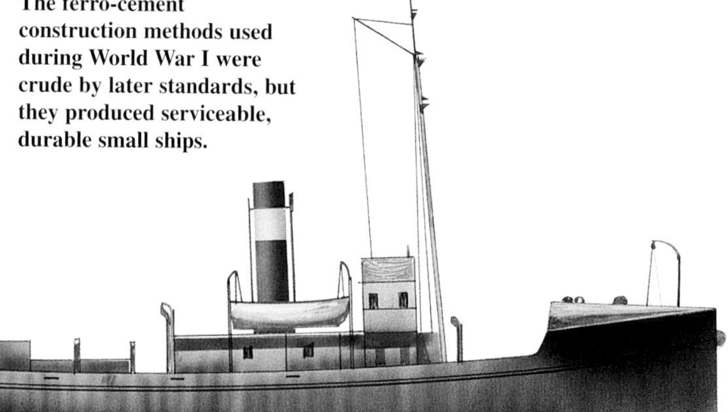

Considerable numbers of ferro-cement hulls were constructed during World War I for ships of up to around 1000t displacement; not only was it a more durable material than wood but it was far easier to work, and could be constructed away from traditional shipyards by largely unskilled labour. The *Cretecable* was built from one such hull; she was a single-screw steam tug for harbour and coastal operations. Her career was a brief one, for she was wrecked in October 1920 after less than 18 months in service.

CROISINE

FRANCE: 1936

Tonnage: 3900 grt
Dimensions: 308ft x 56ft x 24ft (92m x 17m x 7.2m)
Machinery: two-shaft, diesel
Service speed: 16 knots
Role: fruit carrier
Route: Mediterranean; France–West Indies
Material: steel

With her unusual curved superstructure, the French fruit carrier *Croisine* was a notably elegant vessel. Constructed at a time when fruit cultivation was strictly seasonal, she was designed to do double-duty as a carrier of either citrus fruit or bananas; her high freeboard betrays an unusually large number of decks for a freighter, and they were divided by as few bulkheads as possible, in order to create large open spaces and improve through draughts. Ventilators were grouped around the foremast, and fed air into 'cooler houses', where fans, which forced it through the fruit bins, were located.

Built in Sweden for the Mediterranean service, the *Croisine* is shown in the typical white hull colour scheme of fruit carriers.

CUAUHTEMOC

MEXICO: 1982

The three-masted barque *Cuauhtemoc* was almost identical to the Ecuadorian *Guayas* and the Venezuelan *Simon Bolivar*.

The *Cuauhtemoc* was purpose-built as a sail training ship by a Spanish yard which had earlier constructed two somewhat smaller but almost identical ships, the Ecuadorian *Guayas* and the Venezuelan *Simon Bolivar*. Like most of their kind, these were steel-hulled, three-masted barques; *Cuauhtemoc* had a plain sail area of 23,680 square feet (2200 square metres) and small auxiliary Detroit Diesel from General Motors, which propelled her at 11 knots. She could accommodate up to 90 officer and petty officer cadets.

Tonnage: 1200 grt
Dimensions: 297ft x 39ft 3in x 16ft 9in (90.5m x 12m x 5.1m)
Machinery: one-shaft, GM Detroit Diesel auxiliary; 750hp
Service speed: not applicable
Role: sail training ship
Constructor: Astilleros Talleres Celaya, Bilbao
Material: steel
Built for: Mexican Navy
Owner: Mexican Navy

CUNENE (EX-ADELAIDE)

PORTUGAL: 1911

Tonnage: 8825 grt
Dimensions: 450ft x 58ft x 25ft 3in (137m x 17.6m x 7.7m)
Machinery: one-shaft, triple expansion; about 4500hp
Service speed: 12 knots
Role: cargo/passenger liner
Route: Lisbon-Africa
Capacity: 12 cb
Constructor: not known
Material: steel
Built for: not known

Under the terms of the Treaty of Versailles, Germany forfeited all merchant ships of over 1600 grt, and they were distributed amongst the Allies in reparation for war losses. As a member of the alliance, Portugal benefited from this distribution. The 9000t *Adelaide* was handed over, renamed *Cunene*, and put into service between Lisbon and the African colonies of Angola and Mozambique. She was laid up from 1925 to 1930 and then reactivated, not being scrapped until 1955.

The *Cunene* was a typical cargo liner of the pre-World War I period, with accommodation for a dozen passengers. Her numerous derricks allowed her to handle her own cargo.

CUTTY SARK (SOMETIME FERREIRA, SOMETIME MARIA DO AMPARO)

GB: 1869

Cutty Sark's keel was laid at the Dumbarton yard of Scott, Linton & Co early in 1869, and the ship was launched in November of that year. Hercules Linton, who had designed her, drove his company into bankruptcy in obeying his client's instructions to build her of nothing but the finest materials, and she was taken over for completion by one of the other Clyde yards, William Denny and Brothers. Even as she was sliding down the ways, so was she sliding into obsolescence. On the 17th day of that same month the Suez Canal had opened, cutting the distance to the Far East by almost a third – but only for steamships – and dooming the clipper trade at a stroke. Nonetheless, on 15 February 1870, *Cutty Sark* left The Downs bound for China. She crossed the equator 25 days out and picked up the Shanghai pilot on 31 May, just 104 days after leaving the United Kingdom. After 25 days in the Chinese port, loading tea, she set sail for home, arriving on 13 October, after a passage of 110 days. In all, *Cutty Sark* had eight years in the tea trade, her best passage being in the second of them, when she made the voyage home in 107 days, pilot to pilot.

Cutty Sark's fame is due in no small part to the fact that she was preserved and returned to her original condition; she looks today exactly as she did in 1870, before setting out on her maiden voyage to Shanghai in ballast.

Most of the tea clippers dropped out of the trade over the next decade, unable to compete with fast steamships sailing a shorter route, and *Cutty Sark* was amongst them. After some years in general trade she found a new niche, carrying general cargo from Britain's factories out to Australia, and raw wool back, once making the trip in 69 days. Then, in 1895, she was sold to a Portuguese owner and operated under that country's flag (as the *Ferreira*, and later as the *Maria do Amparo*) for 27 years, most of them rigged as a barquentine.

In 1922, after refitting in London, *Cutty Sark* put in to

***Cutty Sark*'s name was taken from a poem by Robert Burns, 'Tam O'Shanter'. Tam, a Scottish farmer, was chased by the pretty young witch Nannie, who wore nothing but 'a cutty sark' – a short petticoat. It is the witch Nannie who appears as the ship's figurehead, her left arm outstretched, eternally reaching for the tail of Tam's grey mare.**

Falmouth to wait out a Channel gale; there she caught the eye of a retired windjammer skipper named Captain Wilfred Downman, who bought her for £3750. When he died, in 1936, his widow presented the vessel to the Thames Nautical Training College, and she was moored on the river at Greenhithe, not far from the spot where her greatest voyages had ended.

In 1949, no longer required as a training ship, she was retired, and public subscription eventually secured her preservation, in a specially built dry dock close to Britain's National Maritime Museum, at Greenwich. Fittingly, her nearest neighbour is *Gypsy Moth IV*, the boat Sir Francis Chichester sailed around the world single-handed to see if modern technology could produce a boat to emulate the old clipper ships' runs.

Tonnage: 963 grt
Dimensions: 212ft 6in x 36ft x 21ft (64.8m x 11m x 6.4m)
Machinery: not applicable
Service speed: not applicable
Role: tea carrier; general cargo vessel
Route: China–London; London–Australia–London
Constructor: Scott, Linton & Co, Dumbarton; Wm Denny & Bros, Glasgow
Material: composite, wood on iron
Built for: John Willis
Owner: Cutty Sark Maritime Trust

CZAR (LATER ESTONIA, PULASKI, EMPIRE PENRYN) — DENMARK: 1912

Tonnage: 6503 grt
Dimensions: 426ft x 53ft (130m x 16m)
Machinery: two-shaft, quadruple expansion
Service speed: 15 knots
Role: passenger/cargo liner
Route: Russia–New York
Capacity: 30 1st, 260 2nd, 1086 3rd/4th; 290 cb, 500 3rd; 110 cb, 180 tr, 500 3rd
Constructor: Barclay, Curle & Co, Glasgow
Material: steel
Built for: East Asiatic Co

The *Czar* operated with no less than six different companies in a career which spanned both world wars.

The 6500-t *Czar* was constructed, along with the *Czaritza*, for the Russian American Line to operate to New York. She remained in that service until the revolution broke out in Russia in 1917 and was then put under the management of the Cunard Line. She underwent four changes of ownership before she was finally scrapped in 1949, by which time she had spent many years in the South American service.

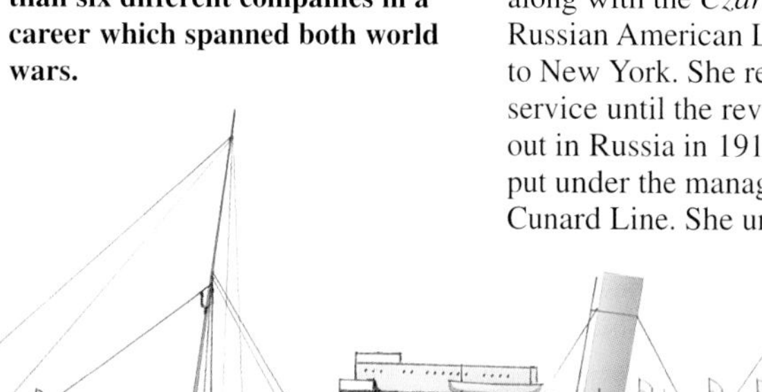

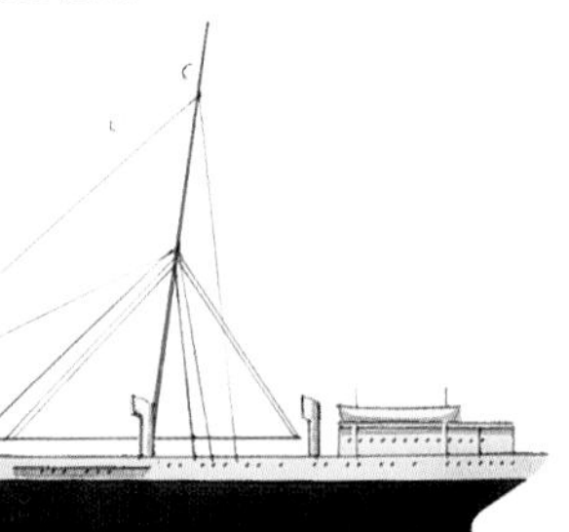

D 26 — AUSTRALIA: 1926

D 26, now preserved where she was built in 1926, was a very shallow draught outrigger barge constructed to carry red gum logs between the logging grounds and the sawmills on the Murray River in Victoria, Australia. She was built as part of a small fleet to operate with the paddle-steamer tug *Adelaide*, which was also restored to her original condition.

***D 26* was constructed to work with the paddle-wheel steam tug *Adelaide*, and is displayed alongside her.**

Tonnage: not applicable
Dimensions: 81ft 6in x 17ft x 1ft 4in (24.85m x 5.2m x 0.4m)
Machinery: not applicable
Service speed: not applicable
Role: timber barge
Route: Murray River
Constructor: C Felshaw, Echuca, Victoria
Material: wood; iron keel
Built for: Murray River Sawmills
Owner: City of Echuca

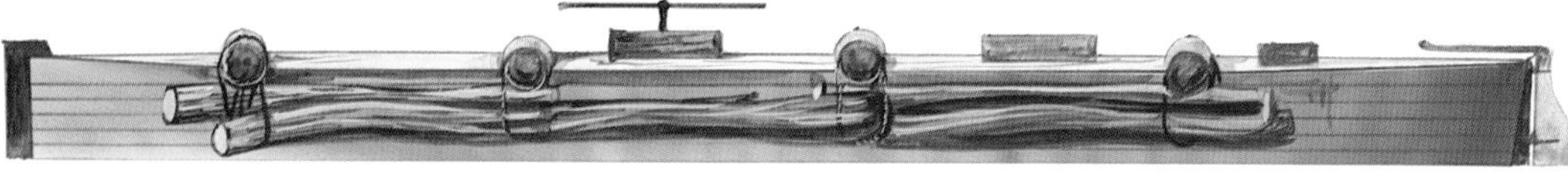

DANIEL GASTON

CANADA: 1860

The tern schooner's rounded lines made her sea-kindly rather than particularly fast; the design was well adapted to the North Atlantic.

The so-called tern schooner was one of the many variants of the basic pattern. It was invariably three-masted, with all masts being of equal height, and is said to have originated in Nova Scotia. Variations from the norm came in the form of the hull – the tern schooner had a rounded stern and forefoot and a greater degree of dead rise than other types, many other East Coast (of North America) designs being similar in this latter respect.

Tonnage: 125 grt
Dimensions: 100ft x 23ft x 10ft (30.4m x 7m x 3.1m)
Machinery: not applicable
Service speed: not applicable
Role: general cargo vessel
Route: not applicable
Capacity: not applicable
Constructor: not applicable
Material: wood
Built for: not applicable

DANNEBROG

DENMARK: 1931

Tonnage: 1070 grt
Dimensions: 207ft 2in x 34ft 1in x 11ft 8in (63.15m x 10.4m x 3.55m)
Machinery: two-shaft, Burmeister & Wain diesel engines
Service speed: not known
Role: royal yacht
Constructor: Royal Shipyard, Copenhagen
Material: steel; wood decks
Built for: Danish Royal Family
Owner: Danish Royal Family

Designed and built as a royal yacht for Denmark's ruling family, the *Dannebrog* was constructed at the Royal Dockyard in Copenhagen in a lull between building two classes of 290-t torpedo boats. Since then, she has been maintained in pristine condition, and seven decades after embarking on her maiden cruise was still in regular use.

The Danish royal yacht *Dannebrog* was one of the last of this class of vessels to remain in service.

DAR POMORZA (EX-PRINZESS EITEL FRIEDRICH, COLBERT)

POLAND: 1909

Tonnage: 1561 grt
Dimensions: 299ft x 41ft x 18ft 6in (91m x 12.6m x 5.7m)
Machinery: one-shaft, auxiliary diesel; 430hp
Service speed: not applicable
Role: sail training ship
Route: not applicable
Capacity: not applicable
Constructor: Blohm & Voss, Hamburg
Material: steel
Built for: German Training Ship Association
Owner: Merchant Marine Academy

During her 50-year career as the training ship of the *Wyzsza Szkola Morska*, *Dar Pomorza* trained 13,000 cadets and sailed half a million miles (800,000km).

Constructed to the order of the *Deutscher Schulschiff Verein* (German Training Ship Association), this vessel was launched as the *Prinzess Eitel Friedrich*. She was handed over to France and laid up as the *Colbert* after the end of World War I, then acquired by the Polish Merchant Navy Academy in 1929, becoming the *Dar Pomorza*. She was a member – one of the oldest – of the Tall Ships fleet from 1972, when she won the race, until she was retired to become a static museum exhibit at Gdynia in 1981.

DERBYSHIRE

GB: 1935

Tonnage: 11,650 grt
Dimensions: 502ft x 66ft 4in (153m x 20m)
Machinery: two-shaft, diesel
Service speed: 15 knots
Role: passenger/cargo liner; armed merchant cruiser; troopship
Route: Liverpool-Colombo-Rangoon
Capacity: 291 single class
Material: steel
Built for: Bibby Line

The motor ship *Derbyshire* was built for the Bibby Line's long-established service linking Liverpool with Colombo in Ceylon (Sri Lanka) and Rangoon in Burma (Myanmar). Her passengers were mostly expatriate civil servants and tradespeople. In 1939, she was taken up and armed as a merchant cruiser, with six 6in (152mm) guns; her armament was removed in 1942, when she became a troopship. Refurbished after the war, she went back into service until 1963.

The Bibby Line's passenger/cargo ships – the majority were named after English counties – were a mainstay of the British Empire in Asia.

DERWENT

GB: 1867

Tonnage: 599 nrt
Dimensions: 186ft 7in x 28ft 9in x 17ft 1in (56.85m x 8.8m x 5.2m)
Machinery: not applicable
Service speed: not applicable
Role: tea carrier
Route: China-London
Capacity: not known
Constructor: Barclay, Curle & Co
Material: iron
Built for: not known

The *Derwent* was one of the first iron ships built for the tea trade with China when it was at its most competitive. At just 599t net, she was rather smaller than her contemporaries, most of which were of composite construction. There was considerable controversy over *Derwent*'s fitness to carry this most delicate of cargoes – many felt that the iron would somehow have a deleterious effect on it – but *Derwent* proved this fear to be groundless, and in so doing, opened the way for more iron construction.

The *Derwent* had a greater length-to-beam ratio than the real flyers and her lines were almost as fine, but she was much cheaper to build.

DEUTSCHLAND (LATER VICTORIA LUISE, HANSA)

GERMANY: 1900

The *Deutschland* was built specifically to be the fastest ship across the Atlantic, to capture the Blue Riband from rival Norddeutscher Lloyd Line's *Kaiser Wilhelm de Grosse*. She accomplished that handsomely, taking the record in both directions on her maiden voyage between Hamburg and New York. She always suffered from excessive vibration and once lost her sternpost and rudder in mid-Atlantic as a result. She later became a cruise ship and, in 1920, an emigrant ship. She was scrapped in 1925.

The *Deutschland* was Albert Ballin's Hamburg-Amerika Line's only record-breaker; her best-ever Atlantic crossing was made at over 23.5 knots.

Tonnage: 16,502 (later 16,333) grt
Dimensions: 684ft x 67ft 4in (208.5m x 20.4m)
Machinery: two-shaft, two six-cylinder quadruple expansion; 37,800hp
Service speed: 22 knots
Role: passenger liner; cruise ship; emigrant ship
Route: Hamburg-New York
Capacity: 450 1st, 300 2nd, 350 3rd; 487 1st, 36 cb, 1350 3rd
Constructor: AG Vulcan, Stettin (Szczecin)
Material: steel

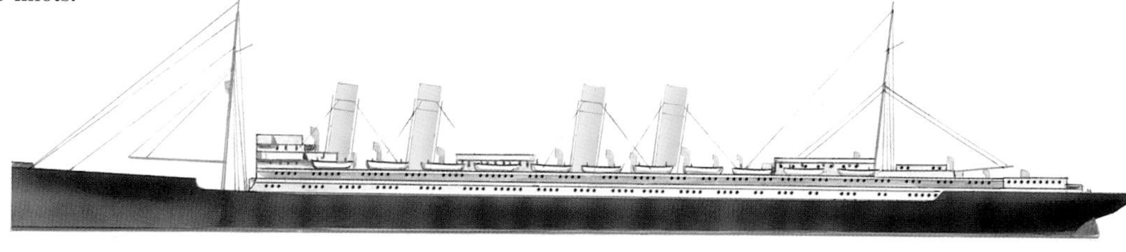

DIESBAR (EX-PILLNITZ)

GERMANY: 1884

The *Diesbar* was one of a group of very similar sidewheel paddle steamers built in Dresden for passenger service on the River Elbe, a surprising number of which were still operating well over a hundred years after they were constructed. Most were re-engined at some point in their long life and converted from coal- to oil-firing. The entire fleet was used to evacuate civilians from Dresden after the bombing raids which destroyed much of the city in February 1945.

The *Diesbar* was re-engined with the rebuilt powerplant from the original *Pillnitz*, which was constructed in 1857.

Tonnage: 230t displacement
Dimensions: 173ft x 33ft x 2ft 4in (52.75m x 10.05m x 0.75m)
Machinery: paddle wheels, compound; 140hp
Service speed: not known
Role: river ferry
Route: River Elbe
Constructor: Werft Blasewitz, Dresden
Material: steel
Owner: Sachsische Dampfschiffahrts, Dresden

DISCOVERY

GB: 1901

The *Discovery* was built in Dundee, then a major whaling port as well as a centre for the jute industry, in 1901. Her design was based on an earlier whaling ship of the same name, which had carried an 1875 expedition to the Arctic. She had a reinforced hull, and both screw and rudder could be lifted clear of the water to prevent ice damage; she was barque rigged. Her maiden voyage in 1901, under the command of Robert Falcon Scott, took her to the Ross Sea in Antarctica, where she was to remain until 1904, having been frozen into the ice. She broke free with the help of the supply ship *Morning* and the *Terra Nova*, both of them Dundee whalers; the latter was to carry Scott and his party back south for the fatal polar expedition of 1911-12. *Discovery* was sold on her return to the UK, to the Hudson's Bay Company, which used her on trading voyages to the bay itself. She was laid up from 1912-15, later making a series of voyages between Archangel and the Black Sea. In 1916, she was loaned to the British government to mount a mission to rescue Ernest Shackleton's party. In 1923, she was purchased by the Crown Agents for use as a research ship. She was laid up again from 1931-36, and was then acquired by the Sea Scouts as a training ship and hostel on the Thames in central London, a role she played until 1979, when she was transferred to the Maritime Trust. By 1986, she had been restored to her 1926 appearance and placed on permanent display in the city where she was built.

Tonnage: 1570t displacement
Dimensions: 171ft x 33ft 9in x 15ft 9in (52.1m x 10.3m x 4.8m)
Machinery: one-shaft, auxiliary triple expansion; 450hp
Service speed: 8 knots
Role: research ship; cargo carrier; training ship
Route: UK–Antarctica; UK–Hudson's Bay; Archangel–Black Sea; UK–Arctic
Capacity: not applicable
Constructor: Steven's Yard, Dundee Shipbuilders, Dundee
Material: wood
Built for: British National Antarctic Expedition
Owner: Dundee Heritage Trust

By virtue of the many years she spent moored alongside the Embankment on the Thames, between Blackfriars and Waterloo Bridges, RRS *Discovery* became familiar to millions.

DORIC — GB: 1923

For almost 10 years the *Doric* operated between Liverpool and the St Lawrence River, but from May 1932 she switched over to cruising.

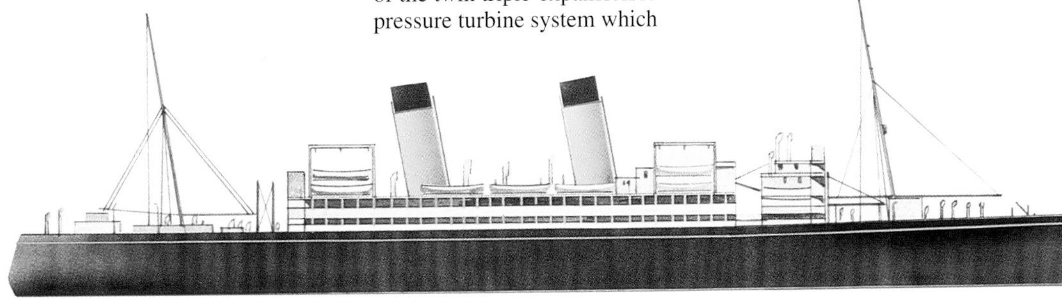

The White Star Line's *Doric* was essentially a sistership of the *Regina*, built some six years earlier for the Dominion Line, but with single-reduction turbines in place of the twin triple-expansion/low-pressure turbine system which Harland & Wolff employed for many years. She was employed initially in the Liverpool–Canada service and later became a cruise ship. She collided with the French SS *Formigny* in September 1935 and was patched up in Vigo, but was never repaired, and was scrapped a month later.

Tonnage: 16,484 grt
Dimensions: 575ft 6in x 67ft 10in (175.4m x 20.7m)
Machinery: two-shaft, single-reduction turbines
Service speed: 15 knots
Role: passenger liner; cruise ship
Route: Liverpool–Montreal
Capacity: 600 cb, 1700 3rd
Constructor: Harland & Wolff, Belfast
Material: steel
Built for: White Star Line

DUILIO — ITALY: 1916

Tonnage: 24,281 grt
Dimensions: 602ft 4in x 76ft 3in (183.6m x 23.25m)
Machinery: four-shaft, single-reduction turbines
Service speed: 19 knots
Role: passenger liner
Route: Genoa–New York; Genoa–Buenos Aires; Genoa–Durban
Capacity: 280 1st, 670 2nd, 600 3rd
Constructor: Ansaldo, Sestri Ponente
Material: steel
Built for: Navigazione Generale Italiana

In 1914, Ansaldo laid down what was to be the biggest ship yet built in Italy, the 24,000-t *Duilio*, for Navigazione Generale Italiana. She was not completed until 1923, when she was put into service to New York. Later her destination was changed to Buenos Aires and then, in Italia Line colours, to Durban. Transferred to the Lloyd Triestino Line in 1937, she was laid up in 1940. Briefly chartered to the International Red Cross in 1942, she was sunk by Allied bombers in 1944.

The *Duilio*, the biggest vessel built in an Italian yard up until that time, took nine years to complete, very little work being carried out during World War I.

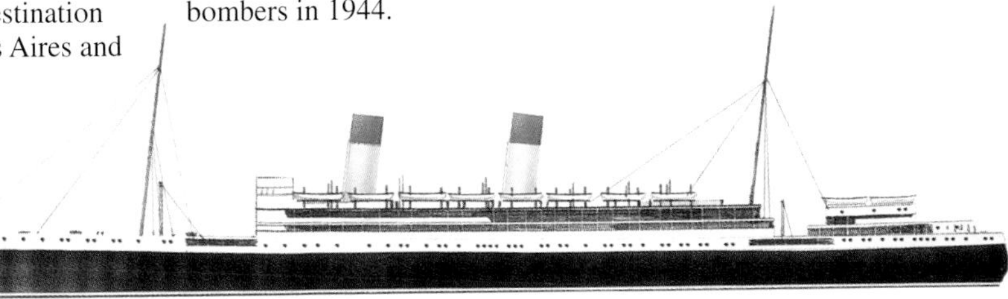

DUNQUERKUE

FRANCE: 1896

Between the mid-1870s and the outbreak of World War I, the distinctive hull colour scheme of French shipowners AD Bordes et fils of Dunquerkue graced no fewer than 68 sailing ships.

During the last two decades of the 19th century, the French government, intent on boosting domestic steel production, made a significant contribution – 65 francs per ton – to the cost of building ships in the material, and French shipowners were quick to take advantage of the offer. One of the most important amongst them was AD Bordes et fils of Dunquerkue, which took delivery, in February, 1897 of a new four-masted steel barque, the Dunquerkue, from Laporte et Cie of Rouen, to replace a similar Scottish-built ship of the same name, lost in mysterious circumstances on a voyage from Cardiff to Rio de Janeiro with coal, in June, 1891. She was destined for the Chilean nitrate trade, and remained in that service until 1924, when she was broken up in Italy. She came briefly to the public's attention when, in April, 1906, she rescued the (few) survivors from the Belgian sail training ship Comte de Smet de Naeyer, which had foundered in the Atlantic in fair weather.

Tonnage: 3338 grt
Dimensions: 327ft 8in x 45ft 6in x 25ft 6in (99.85m x 13.85m x 7.75m)
Role: bulk carrier
Route: Europe-Chile
Capacity: c4500 dwt
Constructor: Laporte et Cie
Material: steel
Built for: AD Bordes et fils

EAGLE (EX-HORST WESSEL)

USA: 1936

Tonnage: 1634t standard displacement
Dimensions: 266ft x 39ft x 16ft (82m x 12m x 4.8m)
Machinery: one-shaft, auxiliary diesel; 750hp
Service speed: not applicable
Role: sail training ship
Route: not applicable
Capacity: not applicable
Constructor: Blohm & Voss, Hamburg
Material: steel
Built for: German Navy
Owner: United States Coast Guard

Originally constructed by Blohm & Voss for the Kriegsmarine as the *Horst Wessel*, the *Eagle* was renamed when she was commissioned into the United States Coast Guard after being awarded to the USA as a war reparation in 1946. A sistership to the original *Gorch Fock* (later the Russian *Tovarich*) and the Portuguese Navy's *Sagres II* (originally *Albert Leo Schlageter*), *Eagle* was easily recognizable in her standard USCG livery of white hull with a broad diagonal red stripe forward.

***Eagle* was one of three identical sail training ships built by Blohm & Voss of Hamburg in the late 1930s.**

EGYPT

GB: 1871

When she was launched, the 4670-t *Egypt* was the biggest ship in the world save for the giant *Great Eastern* and was the last ship the National Line constructed until the *America*, 13 years later. She was built for the Liverpool–New York service, although at the very end of her life she made one and a half return passages from London, returning bound for her home port. She did not make harbour, but was destroyed by fire at sea, with no loss of life, in July 1890.

Tonnage: 4670 grt
Dimensions: 443ft x 44ft 4in (135m x 13.5m)
Machinery: one-shaft, two compound
Service speed: 13 knots
Role: passenger liner
Route: North Atlantic
Capacity: 120 1st, 1400 3rd
Constructor: Liverpool Shipbuilding Co, Liverpool
Material: iron
Built for: National Line

The *Egypt* was built primarily to service the emigrant trade; most of her accommodation was given over to third class.

EL HORRIA (EX-MAHROUSSA) — EGYPT: 1865

Despite her considerable age, *El Horria* sailed to New York in 1976 to take part in the International Naval Review in the bicentennial year.

El Horria was built as a royal yacht for the Khedive of Egypt by Samuda Brothers, in Poplar, East London, and continued in that role until the last King of Egypt, Farouk, was deposed in 1952. Still in everyday use as a school ship 135 years after she was built, she retained some vestiges of her 19th-century charm, even though she had twice been lengthened and had shed her side paddle wheels in favour of turbine-driven screw propellers.

Tonnage: 3762 grt
Dimensions (after lengthening): 478ft x 42ft 7in x 17ft 6in (145.7m x 13m x 5.35m)
Machinery: sidewheels, oscillating (later three-shaft, geared turbine)
Service speed: not known
Role: royal yacht; training ship
Route: not applicable
Capacity: not applicable
Constructor: Samuda Bros, Poplar
Material: iron
Built for: Khedive of Egypt
Owner: Egyptian government

EMPIRE FAITH — GB: 1936

Tonnage: 7061 grt
Dimensions: 432ft x 57ft 5in x 27ft 6in (131.65m x 17.5m x 8.4m)
Machinery: one-shaft, diesel
Service speed: not known
Role: catapult-armed merchantman
Route: not applicable
Armament: one Hawker Hurricane fighter aircraft

In 1940, merchant ships crossing the North Atlantic came under a new threat, from long-range Focke-Wulf Fw.200 Condor bombers, operating out of Bordeaux; between 1 August and 9 February 1941, they sank 363,000t of shipping. In reply, the Royal Navy began equipping selected merchant ships with catapults, allowing them to launch obsolete Hawker Hurricane fighters manned by RAF pilots from 804 Squadron. Ellerman Lines' *Empire Faith* was one of 35 so modified, of which 12 were lost.

The catapult-armed merchantmen's Hurricanes brought down five Condors and had a considerable effect on the morale of both sides.

EMPRESS OF BRITAIN (LATER MONTROYAL) — GB: 1906

The first *Empress of Britain* was built for Canadian Pacific Steamships by Fairfield in Glasgow just after the turn of the 20th century, to serve the Liverpool–St Lawrence River route. Emigration from Europe to Canada was increasing annually, and the ship had a considerable amount of third-class accommodation. Having done duty as a troopship right through World War I, she returned to CPS service in 1919; she had a major refit in 1924 and was renamed *Montroyal*, sailing from Antwerp. She was scrapped in 1930.

The first *Empress of Britain* carried immigrants to the Canadian east coast ports for over 20 years.

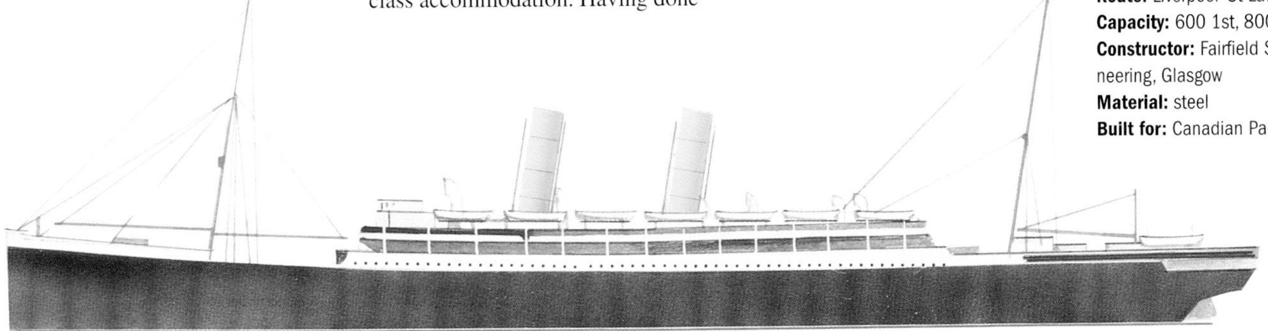

Tonnage: 14,189 (later 15,646) grt
Dimensions: 570ft x 65ft (173.75m x 19.8m)
Machinery: two-shaft, quadruple expansion
Service speed: 18 knots
Role: passenger liner; troopship
Route: Liverpool–St Lawrence River
Capacity: 600 1st, 800 3rd
Constructor: Fairfield Shipbuilding & Engineering, Glasgow
Material: steel
Built for: Canadian Pacific Steamships

EMPRESS OF BRITAIN — GB: 1931

The Canadian Pacific Line's second *Empress of Britain* was built by John Brown, with quadruple screws and geared turbines to give her a service speed of 24 knots. She operated between Southampton and Quebec, with a capacity of 1195 passengers. During World War II she was taken up as a troopship; she was attacked by German long-range bomber aircraft southwest of Ireland on 26 October 1940 and left crippled, to be sunk by the submarine *U 32* two days later, with the loss of 49 men.

The *Empress of Britain* was just one of 57 ships lost in the North Atlantic in October 1940; German losses amounted to one submarine.

Tonnage: 42,348 grt
Dimensions: 758ft x 97ft (231m x 29.55m)
Machinery: four-shaft, geared turbines
Service speed: 24 knots
Role: passenger liner; troopship
Route: Southampton–St Lawrence River
Capacity: 465 1st, 260 tr, 470 3rd
Constructor: John Brown & Co, Glasgow
Material: steel
Built for: Canadian Pacific Steamships

ENDURANCE (EX-ANITA DAN) — GB: 1956

Tonnage: 2641 grt
Dimensions: 302ft x 46ft x 18ft (93m x 14m x 5.5m)
Machinery: one-shaft, diesel; 3220hp
Service speed: 14 knots
Role: guardship; research vessel
Route: South Atlantic
Constructor: Krögerwerft, Rendsburg
Material: steel
Built for: J Lauritzen Lines
Owner: Royal Navy

HMS *Endurance* was constructed in Germany by Krögerwerft of Rendsburg, for J Lauritzen Lines of Copenhagen and was originally known as the *Anita Dan*. She was acquired by the Royal Navy in February 1967, renamed after Ernest Shackleton's ship and modified by Harland & Wolff. She was equipped with workshops and laboratories to allow her to carry out her secondary duties as a hydrographic and meteorological research ship, and two 20mm cannon for her primary role as regional guardship.

The decision (later reversed) to withdraw *Endurance* from service in 1981 encouraged the Argentine seizure of the Falkland Islands.

ERIDAN — FRANCE: 1928

The *Eridan* was employed latterly to preserve the link between France and Mahé and Pondicherry, her outposts in India, and was scrapped when France relinquished possession of them.

When she was launched in 1929, the *Eridan* was the biggest motor ship built in France; she had somewhat unusual styling, with her lifeboats double-tiered above the promenade deck. She was built for Messageries Maritime, to operate between Marseilles and New Caledonia via the Panama Canal. Captured by the Allies in 1942, she was used as a troopship, then returned to her owners in 1946 to be refitted and employed between Marseilles and the Indian Ocean. She was sold for breaking up in 1956.

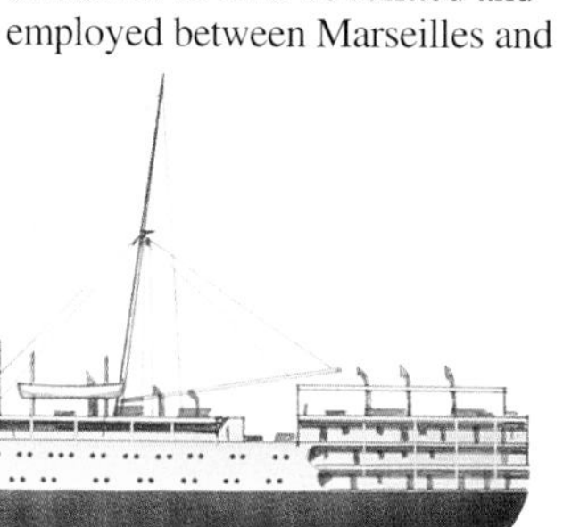

Tonnage: 9927 grt
Dimensions: 468ft 6in x 61ft (142.6m x 18.5m)
Machinery: two-shaft, diesel
Service speed: 15 knots
Role: passenger liner; troopship
Route: Marseilles–New Caledonia; Marseilles–Indian Ocean–India
Capacity: 60 1st, 91 2nd, 468 st
Constructor: La Ciotat
Material: steel
Built for: Société des Services Contractuels des Messageries Maritime

ERNESTINA (EX-EFFIE M MORRISSEY) — USA: 1894

The *Ernestina* was built as a fishing schooner, operating as far as the Grand Banks out of Gloucester, Massachusetts. She was later employed to carry expeditions to the Arctic and was subsequently converted to maintain a trade link between the small Cape Verdian community in New England and the islands themselves. After being rebuilt in Cape Verde at its government's expense over a six-year period, she returned to New Bedford, close to her original home port, in 1982, to be a training ship.

Strongly built and seaworthy, the *Ernestina*, a two-masted 'bald head' schooner, was equally at home in the Arctic or in the tropics.

Tonnage: 120 grt
Dimensions: 97ft x 23ft x 13ft (29.55m x 7m x 3.95m)
Machinery: one-shaft, auxiliary diesel
Service speed: not applicable
Role: fisheries vessel; exploration vessel; general cargo carrier; training ship
Route: USA–Arctic; USA–Cape Verde
Constructor: Tarr & James, Essex, Mass
Material: wood
Built for: John F Wonson & William E Morrissey
Owner: State of Massachusetts

ESSO MANCHESTER (EX-SANTIAGO) — USA: 1944

Tonnage: 10,448 grt
Dimensions: 523ft 6in x 68ft x 30ft 1in (159.6m x 20.75m x 9.15m)
Machinery: one-shaft, turbo-electric; 6000hp
Service speed: 14.5 knots
Role: tanker
Route: not applicable
Capacity: not known
Constructor: Sun Shipbuilding & Drydock Co, Chester, Pa
Material: steel
Built for: Maritime Service Commission

The *Esso Manchester* was one of the very successful 'T2-SE-A1' tankers, a standard design evolved in the United States in 1942, a total of 481 of which were produced in four yards. The T2s were widely held to have been one of the most successful merchant ship designs of the period, and many were to stay in service long after the war was over, often with new mid-sections and renewed powerplants, in a wide variety of different roles, including that of floating power station.

The *Esso Manchester* had a long career but remained substantially unmodified when she was scrapped in Scotland in 1963.

ETERNAL MARINER (EX-HYUNDAI NO 2) — KOREA: 1980

Eternal Mariner was one of the conglomerate car-maker Hyundai's purpose-built car carriers, a member of a fleet operating between the company's manufacturing plants and consumer countries. At 12,000t gross and with a capacity of 2400 cars, she was only half the size of some such vessels. Ships of this type had both stern and side doors to speed loading and unloading operations and 12 or more decks. They usually operated at around 19 knots.

Tonnage: 11,808 grt
Dimensions: 537ft 9in x 81ft x 26ft 6in (163.9m x 24.7m x 8.1m)
Machinery: one-shaft, Pielstick diesel; 11,700hp
Service speed: 17.5 knots
Role: car carrier (ro-ro)
Route: Korea–Europe
Capacity: 2400 cars
Constructor: Hyundai Heavy Industries, Ulsan
Material: steel
Built for: Hyundai Merchant Marine

ETRURIA — GB: 1884

The Cunard Line's *Etruria* was the last North Atlantic express liner to be powered by compound engines, and the last single-screw Cunarder. She was the second of a pair of ships, similar in character to the *Oregon* from the same builders (which Cunard took over from the Guion Line when the latter could not keep up the payments) but built in steel rather than iron. She soon proved herself to be a superior ship, taking the westbound Blue Riband on her second voyage, at an average speed of 18.87 knots, and breaking records again in 1887 and 1888. Both she and her sistership, the *Umbria*, got noticeably faster with age – an unusual (but by no means unique) occurrence. In company with her sistership and the *Campania* and *Lucania* she continued to operate on the prestige Liverpool–New York route, but her days were numbered when she lost her propeller in mid-Atlantic in 1902. She made her last crossing in 1908 and was scrapped the following year.

Despite her machinery being obsolescent, *Etruria* still managed to take the Blue Riband three times during the latter half of the 1880s.

Tonnage: 7718 grt
Dimensions: 501ft 7in x 57ft 2in (152.85m x 17.45m)
Machinery: one-shaft, compound
Service speed: 19 knots
Role: passenger liner
Route: Liverpool–New York
Capacity: 550 1st, 160 tr, 800 3rd
Constructor: John Elder & Co, Glasgow
Material: steel
Built for: Cunard Steam Ship Co

EULE (EX-MELPOMÈNE, CHRISTINA) — GERMANY: 1895

Tonnage: not known
Dimensions: 63ft 11in x 13ft 4in x 3ft 9in (19.55m x 4.05m x 1.15m)
Machinery: one-shaft, auxiliary diesel; 70hp
Service speed: not applicable
Role: general cargo vessel; yacht
Route: coastal, Germany
Capacity: not known
Constructor: Ernst Niemand, Boizenburg
Material: steel
Built for: not known

The steel, ketch-rigged 'besan ewer' *Eule* was constructed for the German coastal trade in 1895. The rather coarse lines of vessels of this type were determined by their owners' choice of carrying capacity rather than performance. At one point during her long career, the *Eule* lost her masts and was employed as a dumb cargo barge, but she was later returned to her original condition by an enthusiastic owner, who operated her as a private yacht.

The 'besan ewer' was able to carry a considerable cargo for its size; its shallow draught meant it could navigate far inland by river and canal.

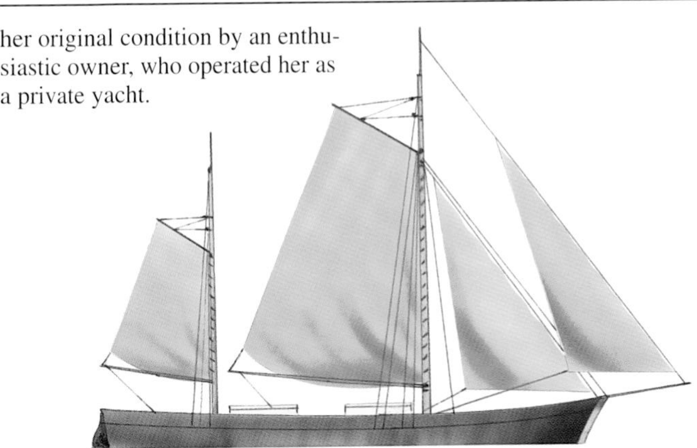

EUROPA (LATER LIBERTÉ)

GERMANY: 1928

The Norddeutscher Lloyd Line's *Europa* and her sistership, the *Bremen*, were launched on consecutive days, *Europa* first, on 15 August. She was to be many months late in completing, however, thanks to a serious fire. She was quite striking in her appearance, with tall superstructure dominated by two long, squat funnels. *Europa* took the westbound Blue Riband with an average speed of 27.91 knots in 1930, but the *Bremen* was always marginally the faster of the two. *Europa* spent World War II laid up in Germany, having been in port when it broke out. Allied air forces made a number of attempts to bomb her, but caused no more than light damage. She was seized by the victorious Allies in 1945 and made three voyages to New York, carrying a total of almost 19,000 returning servicemen. Awarded to France, she sank in harbour in 1946 but was extensively rebuilt between 1947 and 1950 and put into service between Le Havre and New York as the *Liberté*. She was scrapped in 1962.

The *Europa* emerged from World War II virtually unscathed and was able to leave Bremen for New York, laden with American troops, on 13 September 1945.

Tonnage: 49,746 (later 51,839) grt
Dimensions: 936ft 10in x 102ft 2in (285.55m x 31.1m)
Machinery: four-shaft, single reduction turbines
Service speed: 27 knots
Role: passenger liner
Route: Bremen–New York; Le Havre–New York
Capacity: 723 1st, 500 2nd, 300 tr, 600 3rd; 553 1st, 500 cb, 444 tr
Constructor: Blohm & Voss, Hamburg
Material: steel
Built for: Norddeutscher Lloyd Line

EUROPA

GERMANY: 1999

Tonnage: 28,400 grt
Dimensions: 644ft 6in x 78ft x 39ft (198.6m x 24m x 6m)
Machinery: two-shaft, diesel-electric
Service speed: 21 knots
Role: cruise ship
Route: not applicable
Capacity: 410
Constructor: Kavaerner-Masa, Helsinki
Material: steel
Built for: Hapag-Lloyd

The *Europa* was a distinctly unusual vessel. She was designed from the outset with passenger comfort very firmly in mind; in that she was by no means unique amongst cruise ships, but in her case, her constructors went so far as to mount the propulsion stage of her diesel-electric machinery in orientable outboard pods, to reduce noise and vibration aboard (which had the secondary effect of improving the ship's manoevrability). They also fitted 'tractor' rather than a 'pusher' propellers which, coupled with a very refined hull form, made her markedly more efficient than other ships with similar power-to-weight ratios. Aimed at the luxury end of the cruiseing market, there was space for only 410 passengers, with most cabins having their own private balcony; there was more space per person than aboard any other cruise ship of the period.

***Europa* incorporated many improvements in hull design which gave the vessel better performance.**

EXPLORATEUR GRANDIDIER

FRANCE: 1924

Completed in December 1925, *Explorateur Grandidier* was one of a pair of ships built to operate on the important trade route between France and Madagascar, then a major colony. She had a considerable cargo capacity and comfortable accommodation for her passengers, most of whom were French colonial civil servants and tradespeople. She was laid up in Marseilles for most of World War II, and was sunk as a blockship there when the Germans were driven out in 1944. She was soon raised and later broken up.

The *Explorateur Grandidier* was typical of the second-rate cargo liners of the between-the-wars period, carrying passengers and freight economically if not very quickly.

Tonnage: 10,268 grt
Dimensions: 475ft 9in x 60ft 8in (145m x 18.5m)
Machinery: two-shaft, triple expansion
Service speed: 14 knots
Role: passenger/cargo liner
Route: Marseilles–Madagascar
Capacity: 141 1st, 90 2nd, 68 3rd, 392 st
Constructor: Ateliers et Chantiers de l'Atlantique, St Nazaire
Material: steel
Built for: Société des Services Contractuels des Messageries Maritime

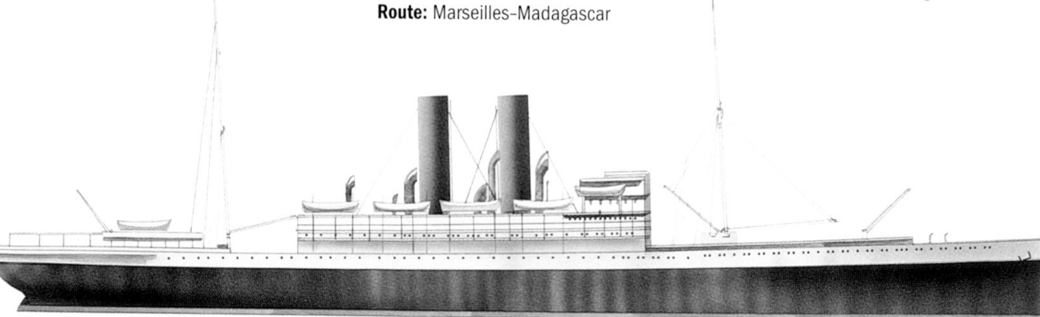

FERRY LAVENDER

JAPAN: 1991

Ferry Lavender, operated by Shin Nihonkai Ferry Co in Japan and put into service in 1991, was typical of third-generation fast ferries, able to carry around 800 passengers and up to 300 light vehicles. The stern ramp gave access to the two-storey car deck, wide enough to allow 'U-turn' drive-through loading and unloading, which simplifies docking procedures considerably.

Despite the growing number of submarine tunnels, by the end of the 20th century many fast, short-route passenger/vehicle ferries were still being built every year.

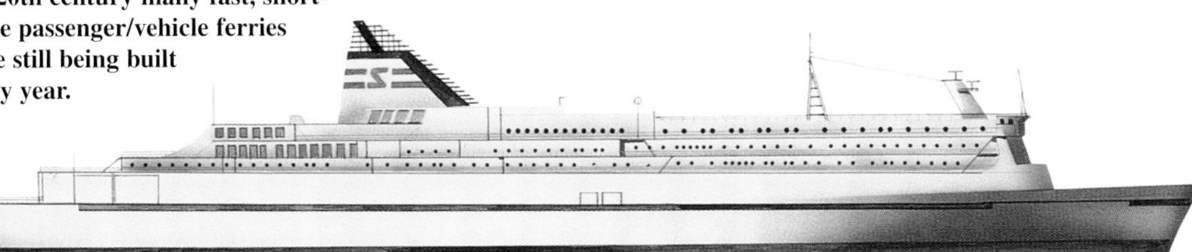

Tonnage: 19,905 grt
Dimensions: 632ft x 96ft 6in x 29ft 5in (193m x 29.4m x 9m)
Machinery: two-shaft, diesel; 23,600hp
Service speed: 21 knots
Role: passenger/vehicle ferry
Route: inter-island, Japan
Capacity: 880 p; 300 v
Constructor: IHI
Material: steel
Built for: Shin Nihonkai Ferry Co

FERRY SCOW

GERMANY: 1954

Tonnage: not applicable
Dimensions: 51ft 4in x 14ft 3in (15.65m x 4.35m)
Machinery: not applicable
Service speed: not applicable
Role: river ferry
Route: River Danube
Capacity: not known
Constructor: Josef Kainz, Niederalteich
Material: wood
Built for: not known
Owner: Deutsches Schiffahrtsmuseum

Even as late as the 1950s, wooden scows were still being constructed in much of central Europe. Scows are some of the simplest vessels of all. They have a little more form to their hull than a lighter but are generally flat-bottomed and usually have external propulsion and no machinery of their own (although some were rowed). Many were in use as vehicle ferries across major and minor inland waterways.

Small riverine craft like the ferry scows were unsophisticated and were built locally from locally available materials. Most had a very short lifespan.

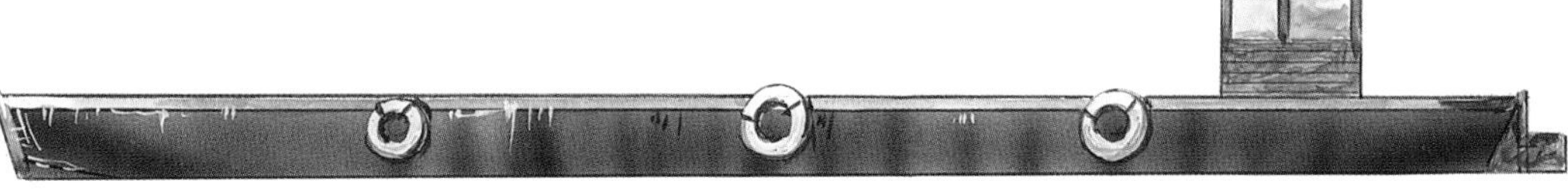

FINNJET

FINLAND: 1977

While gas-turbine machinery quickly became commonplace in warships, it was employed only very rarely in merchant ships, for it seldom made economic sense. One exception was the Baltic ferry *Finnjet*, which was built for the 600-nautical mile (965km) Helsinki–Travemünde service and covered the distance in 22 hours. This route proved to be viable in summer only, and after five years in service she was refitted to include auxiliary 16,000hp diesel-electric machinery for use on the shorter Helsinki–Tallinn route during the winter months.

The fast ferry *Finnjet* was one of the very few merchant ships in the world to be equiped with gas-turbine machinery.

Tonnage: 25,908 (later 32,940) grt
Dimensions: 698ft 7in x 80ft 2in x 21ft 3in (212.95m x 24.45m x 6.5m)
Machinery: two-shaft, gas turbines/diesel-electric; 73,900hp/16,000hp
Service speed: 30.5/18.5 knots
Role: passenger/vehicle ferry
Route: Baltic
Capacity: 1790 p, 380 v
Constructor: Wärtsilä
Material: steel
Built for: Finnlines

FORMBY

GB: 1863

Steel, thanks to its much-superior strength, was a much more satisfactory material for the construction of large ships than iron or wood, and with the widespread adoption of the Bessemer process, from the mid-1850s, it became much more realistically priced. In 1863, the shipbuilders Jones, Quiggin & Co of Liverpool built their first ship in the material. She was to be the first major steel ship – earlier efforts had been considerably less ambitious – and was an immediate success; though at £24,000 she cost perhaps 35 percent more than an iron ship of similar size, the premium was considered reasonable, given that she could load over 15 percent more cargo. Her crew was reduced, too, over similar contemporaries, thanks to the adoption of labour-saving devices such as Emerson & Walker's patent windlass.

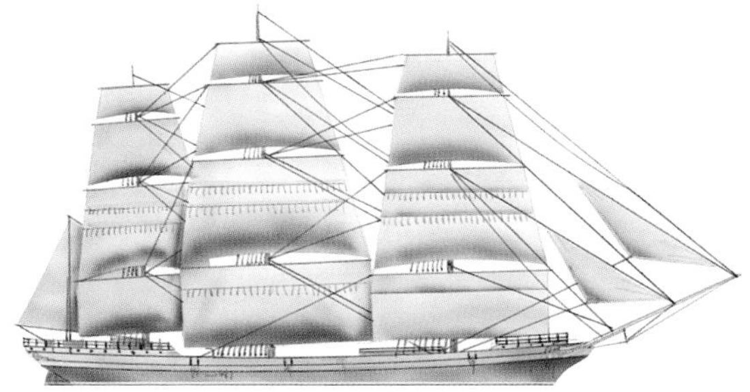

When the *Formby* entered service in 1864, she was immediately hailed as a success; constructors Jones, Quiggin and Co built at least three more ships to the same design.

Tonnage: 1271 grt
Dimensions: 209ft 5in x 36ft x 23ft 6in (63.85m x 10.95m x 7.15m)
Role: general cargo
Constructor: Jones, Quiggin and Co, Liverpool
Material: steel

FRAM

NORWAY: 1892

The *Fram*, Nansen told her designer, must be 'as round and slippery as an eel', so that the ice would not grip her but instead would tend to push her up and out as it tried to take hold. His theory worked perfectly.

When Fridtjof Nansen wanted a ship to take him as close as possible to the North Pole, he turned to the expatriate Briton Colin Archer to design and build her, and like most of Archer's creations she was double-ended and massively strongly built. Two balks of American elm, some 14 inches (36cm) square, made up her keel, and attached to them were frames of Italian oak, each grown to shape, which had been maturing in the Navy Yard at Horten for 30 years. Each frame timber was almost 20 inches (50cm) wide and was separated from its neighbour by only a little over an inch (3cm). Oak timbers some 51 inches (1.3m) square and tied together with juniper dowels made up the almost identical stem- and sternposts. Three layers of carvel planking covered the hull – first a layer of pitch pine 3.1 inches (8cm) thick, then a second layer of pitch pine 3.9 inches (10cm) thick, and then an outer layer of the South American laurel called greenheart, which is so dense it will not float by itself but is both tough and slippery. Inside went another 3.9-inch (10cm) layer of pitch pine, after the gaps between the frames had been filled with a mixture of coal tar, pitch and sawdust.

No less than 450 knees joined the framing timbers to the deck beams and the diagonal shoring. These knees were white pine, and each had been cut from the tree below ground level, where the trunk divides into the major roots, to obtain the correct angle without resorting to cross-grain cutting or bending. Finally, when all the timbers were in place, the bow and stern were bound with iron. The end result was exactly as Nansen had imagined it. *Fram* looked, as one commentator put it, like half a coconut shell, and was to prove just about as manageable, but she carried Nansen's expedition of 1893-96 home safely, and then took Amundsen south to conquer the Antarctic in 1911.

Tonnage: 402 grt
Dimensions: 127ft 9in x 34ft x 15ft (39m x 11m x 4.8m)
Machinery: one-shaft, auxiliary triple expansion; 220hp
Service speed: 6 knots
Role: exploration vessel
Route: Arctic; Antarctic
Capacity: not applicable
Constructor: Colin Archer, Larvik
Material: wood
Built for: Fridtjof Nansen
Owner: Norsk Sjøfartsmuseum

FRANCE

FRANCE: 1890

Tonnage: 3784 grt
Dimensions: 361ft x 48ft 9in x 25ft 10in (110m x 14.9m x 7.9m)
Role: nitrate carrier
Route: Europe-Chile
Capacity: 5500dwt
Constructor: D & W Henderson, Glasgow
Material: steel
Built for: AD Bordes et fils

The five-masted barque *France* was the biggest sailing ship in the world when she was launched – 361 feet (110m) long and able to load up to 5500t of bulk cargo. She was built for the Chilean nitrate trade and proved to be surprisingly fast, her best outward-bound passage being just 63 days. She was also comparatively easy to work, being equipped with steam winches used both for making sail and for cargo handling. She foundered off Brazil in March 1901.

In 1897, the *France* suffered a freak accident – she was run down in the dark by the British cruiser HMS *Blenheim*, which saw lights at bow and stern and made to steer between them.

FRANCE

FRANCE: 1910

The Compagnie Générale Transatlantique's second *France* was to have been called *La Picardie*. She made her maiden voyage from Le Havre to New York in 1912. At that time, she was the fastest liner in service save for the Cunard Line's twins *Lusitania* and *Mauretania*. A troopship and hospital ship from 1914-19, she then resumed service on the North Atlantic route. Converted to oil fuel and refitted in 1923-24, she stayed in service for a further eight years and was eventually scrapped in 1935.

With a nominal capacity of 2025 passengers, the *France* arrived in New York on 16 January 1921 with no less than 2591 people aboard, the most CGT ever carried on one trip.

Tonnage: 23,666 grt
Dimensions: 690ft 2in x 75ft 7in (210.35m x 23.05m)
Machinery: four-shaft, direct-acting turbines
Service speed: 24 knots
Role: passenger liner; troopship; hospital ship
Route: Le Havre–New York
Capacity: 535 1st, 440 2nd, 250 3rd, 800 st; 517 1st, 444 2nd, 660 3rd
Constructor: Chantiers et Ateliers de St Nazaire
Material: steel
Built for: Compagnie Générale Transatlantique

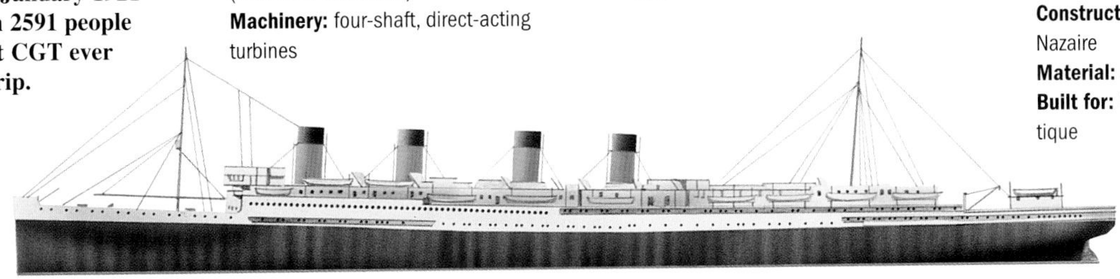

FRANCE (LATER NORWAY) — FRANCE: 1961

Tonnage: 66,348 grt
Dimensions: 1035ft 2in x 110ft 11in x 34ft (315.5m x 33.8m x 11.2m)
Machinery: four-shaft (later two-shaft), double-reduction turbines
Service speed: 30 (later 16) knots
Role: passenger liner; cruise ship
Route: Le Havre–New York
Capacity: 500 1st, 1550 tr; 2181 tr
Constructor: Chantiers de l'Atlantique
Material: steel
Built for: Compagnie Générale Transatlantique

The third *France* was, by design, the longest passenger ship in the world overall when she was launched. She was also the last of the true North Atlantic express liners, the later *Queen Elizabeth II* having been designed with cruising in mind (although the *France* too was later given over to cruising). Her maiden circumnavigation in 1972 took her round Cape Horn, for she was marginally too broad abeam to transit the Panama Canal. She was sold in 1979 to the Norwegian Caribbean Line and refitted as a cruise ship.

The refit which transformed the *France* into the *Norway* cost $80 million; two of her turbine sets were removed in the course of it, making her much more economical to run.

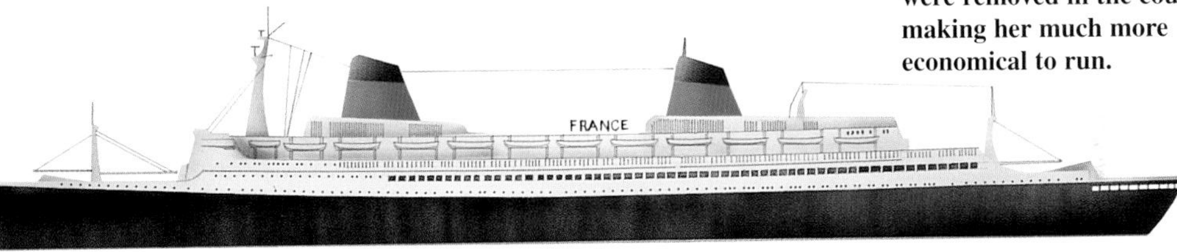

FRANCE I — FRANCE: 1958

For hundreds of years sailors were at the mercy of the elements as they lacked any prior warnings of bad weather and relied upon experience in judging the type of weather to be expected in certain regions at specific times of year. Not until the 20th century was any form of warning system set up on the North Atlantic with ice patrols providing merchant ships with information about the location of icebergs and other such hazards. It was an iceberg of course that sunk the *Titanic* in 1912, precipitating the introduction of the ice patrols. This service soon grew into a worldwide phenomenon with every country in the world possessing its own permanently-stationed weather reporting systems. *France I* was a late development of the type of merchant ship featuring state of the art weather-tracking equipment. The *France I* was constructed for the French government's meteorological service to act as a weather ship and ocean station vessel. As such, she had only very simple low-power machinery but very spacious and luxurious accommodation for her crew, who spent months at a time on board. She was stationed some 600 nautical miles (965km) west of Ushant, off the coast of France. In the early 1990s, after more than three decades in service in the North Atlantic, she was acquired by the Musée Maritime La Rochelle and put on display in her original condition.

Tonnage: 1886t standard displacement
Dimensions: 249ft 7in x 41ft 2in x 15ft 3in (76.1m x 12.55m x 4.65m)
Machinery: two-shaft, diesel; 932hp
Service speed: not known
Role: weather ship
Route: North Atlantic
Capacity: not applicable
Constructor: Forges et Chantiers de la Mediterranée, Graville
Material: steel
Built for: French National Meteorological Service
Owner: Musée Maritime de La Rochelle

FRANCONIA — GB: 1910

Tonnage: 18,150 grt
Dimensions: 600ft 3in x 71ft 3in (182.95m x 21.75m)
Machinery: two-shaft, quadruple expansion
Service speed: 17 knots
Role: passenger liner; troopship
Route: North Atlantic
Capacity: 300 1st, 350 2nd, 2200 3rd
Constructor: Swan, Hunter & Wigham Richardson, Wallsend
Material: steel
Built for: Cunard Steam Ship Co

The *Franconia* and the *Laconia* were built primarily for the Cunard Line's Liverpool–Boston service, although both occasionally operated to New York instead; at the time the company operated four different North Atlantic routes. However, they were clearly also constructed with an eye to Mediterranean cruising in the slack winter months, their first- and second-class accommodation being particularly well appointed. They were both ill fated – both were sunk by German submarines during World War I, *Franconia* in October 1916, southeast of Malta.

The *Franconia* and *Laconia* were very similar in character and appearance to the successful *Caronia*, and often operated in tandem with her and the *Carmania*.

FRONT DRIVER

SWEDEN/BERMUDA: 1991

The OBO carriers were built in an attempt to reduce the time that ships of this type spend in ballast by allowing them to carry different cargo in each direction, at least for some of the way.

The *Front Driver* was characteristic of a new breed of dual-purpose oil and bulk ore carriers first introduced during the 1970s, with cargo space which amounted to around a quarter of a million cubic metres (in this case, 169,146 dwt). She had nine separate holds with large oil- and gas-tight covers – all of which could accommodate either oil or ore – as well as wing tanks for oil products. The demand for vessels of this type was small. By 1995, only some 30 had been built.

Tonnage: 89,004 grt
Dimensions: 935ft x 147ft 8in x 60ft 8in (285m x 45m x 18.5m)
Machinery: one-shaft, diesel; 21,964hp
Service speed: 15 knots
Role: oil/bulk ore (OBO) carrier
Route: not applicable
Capacity: 169,146 dwt
Constructor: Hyundai Heavy Industries
Material: steel
Built for: Bonfield Shipping

FÜRST BISMARCK (LATER DON, MOSKVA, GAEA, SAN GIUSTO)

GERMANY: 1890

In 1891, the *Fürst Bismarck* entered service for the Hamburg-Amerika Line between Europe (Hamburg in summer, later Genoa in winter) and New York. She was sold to Russia in 1904 and transformed into the armed merchant cruiser *Don*. Disarmed in 1906, she became the *Moskva*, and in 1913 was sold to Austria to become a depot ship. She was seized in 1918 and largely rebuilt, and made one voyage to New York as the *San Giusto*. She was scrapped in 1924.

An enlarged version of the successful *Augusta Victoria*, the *Fürst Bismarck* was to sail under four different flags.

Tonnage: 8430 grt
Dimensions: 502ft 7in x 57ft 7in (153.2m x 17.55m)
Machinery: two-shaft, triple expansion
Service speed: 19 knots
Role: passenger liner; armed merchant cruiser; depot ship
Route: North Atlantic
Capacity: 420 1st, 172 2nd, 700 3rd
Constructor: AG Vulcan, Stettin (Szczecin)
Material: steel
Built for: Hamburg-Amerikanischen Packetfahrt AG ('Hapag')

FUTURA

FINLAND: 1992

The *Futura* was enormous by any standards save those of her own industry; able to carry 96,000t, she was less than a third the size of the real giants.

The environmental impact of the grounding of a supertanker is so devastating, and the public outcry so loud, that oil companies were forced to go to considerable lengths to improve the chances of an oil or petroleum products tanker surviving such an incident without releasing its cargo into the sea. The Dutch-owned Futura was built with a double hull, the space between the two hulls being empty save for pumping equipment and venting pipes.

Tonnage: 50,907 grt
Dimensions: 790ft 8in x 131ft 3in x 47ft 6in (241m x 40m x 14.5m)
Machinery: one-shaft, diesel; about 12,000hp
Service speed: 14 knots
Role: oil carrier
Route: not applicable
Capacity: 96,000t
Constructor: Wärtsilä
Material: steel
Built for: Fortum Oil & Gas

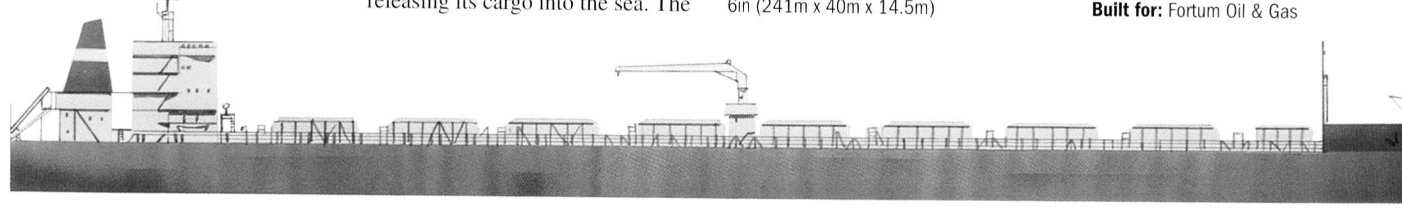

GABRIELLA (EX-FRANS SUELL)

SWEDEN: 1991

Some of the longest ferry routes in the world are those which criss-cross the Baltic, from east to west and north to south. By the 1980s, this service had been largely turned over to so-called 'super ferries', with accommodation which was almost up to cruise ship standards. All had two vehicle decks, with space for 400 and more cars, and passenger accommodation for over 2000, all with cabins. *Gabriella* was quite typical of the genre, but somewhat larger than most; the choice of twin 16,000hp diesels for her powerplant meant that she was rather slow but economical to run.

Tonnage: 35,000 grt
Dimensions: 556ft x 90ft 6in x 20ft 6in (169.4m x 27.6m x 6.25m)
Machinery: two-shaft, diesel; 32,280hp
Service speed: 21 knots
Role: passenger/vehicle ferry
Route: Baltic
Capacity: 2300 p, 462 v
Constructor: Brodosplit, Split
Material: steel
Built for: Viking Line

GALILEO GALILEI (LATER GALILEO, MERIDIAN, SUN VISTA)

ITALY: 1963

Built for the Lloyd Triestino Line's Italy–Australia service, *Galileo Galilei* was a victim of low-cost air travel. She was withdrawn from service in 1977 and laid up for two years, then became a cruise ship. Sold in 1983, she was refitted and became the *Galileo*. She was extensively rebuilt in 1989-90, increasing her gross tonnage from 28,000 to 30,500, to re-enter service as the *Meridian*, cruising in the Caribbean. She was sold in 1996 to a Singapore-based cruise line, Sun Cruises, and renamed *Sun Vista*. On the afternoon of 20 May 1999, while passing the Straits of Malacca on a voyage between Phuket Island and Singapore, a fire in the main engine room switchboard caused a complete power loss and a blackout. Inexplicably, the ship took on a heavy list, and, at 1.22

the next morning, sank. All the 1104 passengers and crew aboard were saved.

Tonnage: 27,907 (later 30,440) grt
Dimensions: 700ft 11in x 93ft 10in x 28ft 4in (213.65m x 28.6m x 8.65m)
Machinery: two-shaft, geared turbines; 44,000hp
Service speed: 24 knots
Role: passenger liner; cruise ship
Route: Italy–Australia; Caribbean; Far East
Capacity: 156 1st, 1594 tr; 1440 sc
Constructor: Cantieri Riuniti dell'Adriatico, Monfalcone
Material: steel
Built for: Lloyd Triestino Line

The loss of the *Sun Vista* after what started as a fairly minor incident caused great concern, even though no lives were lost.

GALLIA

GB: 1878

Tonnage: 4809 grt
Dimensions: 430ft 1in x 44ft 6in (131.1m x 13.6m)
Machinery: one-shaft, compound
Service speed: 13 knots
Role: passenger liner
Route: North Atlantic
Capacity: 300 1st, 1200 3rd
Constructor: J & G Thomson, Glasgow
Material: iron
Built for: Cunard Steam Ship Co

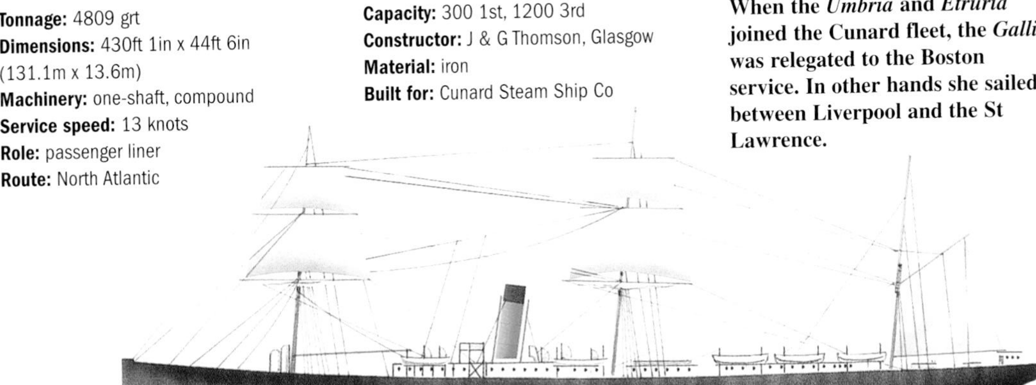

When the *Umbria* and *Etruria* joined the Cunard fleet, the *Gallia* was relegated to the Boston service. In other hands she sailed between Liverpool and the St Lawrence.

In the late 1870s, the Cunard Line was struggling to improve its position as a major player on the North Atlantic routes. In 1878, the company was recapitalized, and that allowed a major shipbuilding programme to go ahead. The first ship into service for the new Cunard Steam Ship Co was the *Gallia*, built for the Liverpool–New York route. She was switched to Boston in 1886, when newer, bigger and faster ships joined the fleet, and later changed ownership three times before going aground near Quebec.

GALWAY CASTLE

GB: 1911

The Union-Castle Line's *Galway Castle* was one of a class of smaller passenger/cargo liners, with less powerful machinery and reduced performance, built for the company's second-string service between Southampton and Cape Town. For all that they were slower than the mail carriers, the 'G Castles' had good accommodation and proved popular with pasengers. *Galway Castle* was taken up as a troopship during World War I; she was torpedoed and sunk near its end, in September 1918.

Tonnage: 7988 grt
Dimensions: 470ft x 56ft 3in x 27ft (143.3m x 17.1m x 8.2m)
Machinery: two-shaft, quadruple expansion
Service speed: 13 knots
Role: passenger/cargo liner; troopship
Route: Southampton–Cape Town
Capacity: 87 1st, 130 2nd, 195 3rd
Constructor: Harland & Wolff, Belfast
Material: steel
Built for: Union-Castle Line

As well as her 412 passengers, the *Galway Castle* also carried over 7000t of cargo in five holds.

GASCON

GB: 1896

Tonnage: 12,642 grt
Dimensions: 445ft x 52ft 2in x 26ft (135.6m x 15.9m x 7.9m)
Machinery: two-shaft, triple expansion
Service speed: 12 knots
Role: passenger/cargo liner; hospital ship
Route: UK–South Africa
Capacity: 80 1st, 118 2nd, 180 3rd
Constructor: not known
Material: steel
Built for: Union Line

The *Gascon* was the first of a class of three medium-sized passenger/cargo liners constructed for the Union Line's service from the UK to South Africa in the closing years of the 19th century. Smaller and slower – and thus cheaper – than the mail carriers, she had comfortable accommoda-tion which made her a favourite with her passengers. During World War I she was taken up to serve as a hospital ship but later returned to commercial service; she was scrapped in 1926.

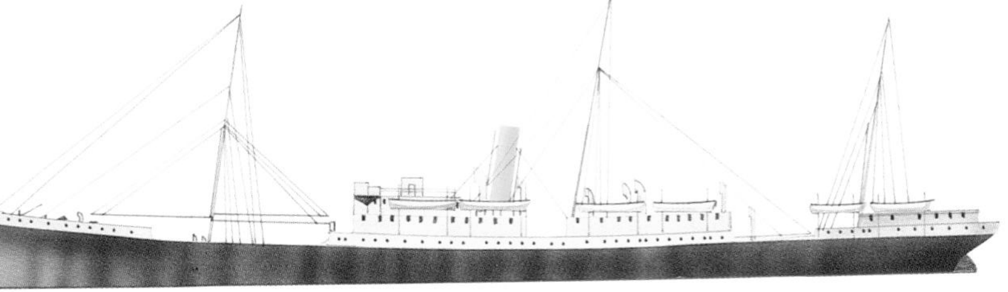

The Union Line's *Gascon* was typical of the second-class passenger/cargo liners which carried the majority of the world's travellers in the early 20th century.

GEORGE W WELLS

USA: 1900

Tonnage: 2970 grt
Dimensions: 319ft 3in x 48ft 6in x 23ft (97.3m x 14.8m x 7m)
Machinery: not applicable
Service speed: not applicable
Role: collier
Route: US East Coast
Capacity: 5000 dwt
Constructor: H M Bean, Camden, Me
Material: wood

The *George W Wells* was the first six-masted schooner ever built (in all, there were only ever 10). She carried coal from Philadelphia and Norfolk, Virginia, the closest ports to the Pennsylvania coalfield, north to the New England cities, as far as Portland, Maine, averaging perhaps 14 round trips per year. She was amongst the biggest wooden ships ever built and could carry 5000t of cargo.

The ownership of ships such as the *George W Wells* was customarily split up into 64 parts, spread among perhaps half as many individuals.

GEORGE WASHINGTON (LATER CATLIN)

GERMANY: 1908

Tonnage: 25,570 grt
Dimensions: 722ft 5in x 78ft 3in (220.2m x 23.85m)
Machinery: two-shaft, quadruple expansion
Service speed: 18 knots
Role: passenger liner; troopship
Route: North Atlantic
Capacity: 520 1st, 377 2nd, 2000 3rd
Constructor: AG Vulcan, Stettin (Szczecin)
Material: steel
Built for: Norddeutscher Lloyd Line

The Norddeutscher Lloyd Line's *George Washington* was the largest of the German-built passenger liners pre-World War I, marginally larger than the Hamburg-Amerika Line's Belfast-built *Amerika*, which was her main competitor. In New York at the outbreak of the war she was interned and was later seized and put into service as a troop transport. She subsequently made a number of commercial transatlantic crossings in the service of different American companies and was taken up again in 1940. She was laid up following a serious fire in 1947 and scrapped in 1951.

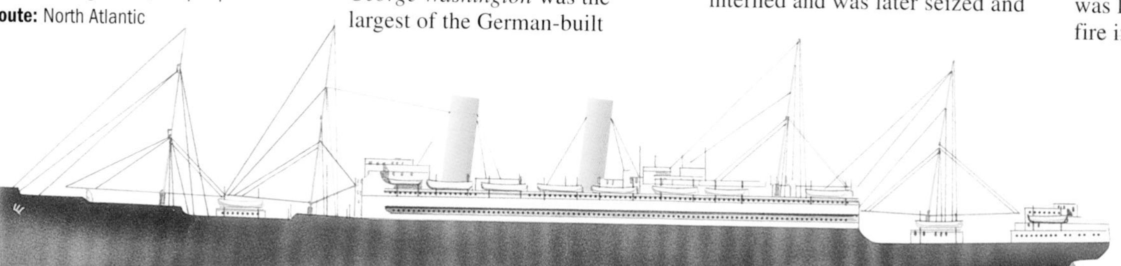

The *George Washington* and the smaller *Prinz Friedrich Wilhelm* together operated a second NDL service from Bremen to New York via Southampton and Cherbourg.

GEORGES PHILIPPAR

FRANCE: 1930

The Messageries Maritime Line's *Georges Philippar* had one of the shortest careers of any liner in peacetime service. Constructed at St Nazaire for the Marseilles–Indo-China service, she set out on her maiden voyage in February 1932. On her return trip, she caught fire on 16 May and sank in the Gulf of Aden three days later, with the loss of 54 lives. The blaze was caused by an electrical fault.

The *Georges Philippar* was one of the large fleet of motor ships operated out of Marseilles to serve French possessions in the eastern hemisphere.

Tonnage: 17,538 grt
Dimensions: 566ft 8in x 68ft 3in (172.7m x 20.8m)
Machinery: two-shaft, diesel
Service speed: 15 knots
Role: passenger/cargo liner
Route: Marseilles–Saigon
Capacity: 196 1st, 110 2nd, 89 3rd, 650 st
Constructor: Ateliers et Chantiers de l'Atlantique, St Nazaire
Material: steel
Built for: Société des Services Contractuels des Messageries Maritime

GIOVANNI PASCOLI

ITALY: 1936

The two-masted lugger *Giovanni Pascoli* was typical of the small coastal cargo vessels known as *trabaccoli*, which were used at the head of the Adriatic and in the Venetian lagoons from the 17th century. They could be single- or two-masted, and the rig varied according to personal choice; many had lateens or settees, but a conventional lug rig proved easier to handle. The last trading *trabaccoli* were taken out of service in the 1950s.

The *trabaccoli* were used at sea but also in the shallow waters of the lagoons and were thus of relatively shallow draught and wide in the beam.

Tonnage: 61 grt
Dimensions: 67ft 3in x 20ft 8in x 6ft 10in (20.5m x 6.3m x 2.1m)
Machinery: not applicable
Service speed: not applicable
Role: general cargo vessel
Route: Adriatic coast of Italy
Material: wood
Owner: Museo Maritimo, Cesenatico

GIPSY MOTH IV

GB: 1965

Gipsy Moth IV was built by Camper & Nicholson to a design drawn by John Illingworth and Angus Primrose, two partnerships which produced many fine yachts. She was basically a standard design but altered to the requirements of Francis Chichester, who bought her with the intention of sailing her single-handed around the world. He did so, with one stop in Sydney, in an overall time of 274 days. She was preserved next to *Cutty Sark*, one of the ships which inspired Chichester's odyssey.

On his return to the UK, Chichester sailed *Gipsy Moth IV* up the Thames to Greenwich, where he was knighted by HM Queen Elizabeth II with the sword her namesake used to knight Drake in 1581.

Tonnage: 18t TM
Dimensions: 54ft x 10ft 6in x 7ft (16.5m x 3.2m x 2.1m)
Machinery: one-shaft, auxiliary diesel; 40hp
Service speed: not applicable
Role: yacht
Route: circumnavigation
Capacity: not applicable
Constructor: Camper & Nicholson, Gosport
Material: wood
Built for: Francis Chichester
Owner: Cutty Sark Maritime Trust

GJØA

NORWAY: 1872

Tonnage: 67 grt
Dimensions: 70ft x 20ft 6in x 7ft 7in (21.3m x 6.3m x 2.3m)
Machinery: one-shaft, paraffin auxiliary; 13hp
Role: fishery vessel; exploration vessel
Route: Northwest Passage
Constructor: Kurt Johannesson, Hardanger
Material: wood
Built for: Asbjørn Sexe
Owner: Norsk Sjøfartsmuseum

The *Gjøa* was built as a fishing boat and served thus for 28 years before Roald Amundsen bought her in 1900, and made history by making the first ever northern passage between the Atlantic and Pacific Oceans in her. He reinforced her hull with three inches of oak, added iron strapping to the stem and a small parafin-fuelled engine, and together with his crew of six, left Oslo on 16 June 1903. They arrived at the western extremity of the Northwest Passage on 26 August 1905, too late to continue that year, and reached San Francisco in October 1906.

Amundsen was invited to inaugurate the Panama Canal, but he declined. The *Gjøa* remained for 68 years in San Francisco's Golden Gate Park.

GLOMAR EXPLORER (SOMETIME AG-193)

USA: 1973

The exploits of the *Glomar Explorer* were long shrouded in mystery; The US CIA is reported to have invested $550 million in the project.

Glomar Explorer was built for a single purpose – to raise at least portions of a Soviet *Golf* class ballistic-missile submarine, which sank 750 miles (1200km) northwest of Hawaii in 13,000 feet (4000m) of water. She was constructed ostensibly for Global Marine Development, Inc, but actually for the Central Intelligence Agency. She arrived on site on 4 July 1974 and over the next month raised the bow section of the submarine, together with the bodies of six of the boat's 88 crew members. The rest of the submarine, and its SS-N-5 missiles, was left on the seabed.

Tonnage: 63,300t displacement
Dimensions: 618ft 9in x 115ft 8in x 46ft 8in (188.8m x 35.3m x 14.2m)
Machinery: two-shaft, diesel-electric; 13,200hp
Service speed: 11 knots
Role: heavy lift ship
Route: Pacific Ocean
Constructor: Sun Shipbuilding & Dry Dock Co, Chester, Pa
Material: steel
Built for: Central Intelligence Agency/Global Marine Development, Inc

GOLIATH

GERMANY: 1941

Tonnage: 143 grt
Dimensions: 102ft 7in x 23ft 1in x 5ft 5in (31.25m x 7.05m x 1.65m)
Machinery: two-shaft, diesel; 940hp
Role: tug; salvage vessel
Route: port of Bremen
Capacity: not applicable
Constructor: Deschimag, Bremen
Material: steel
Built for: German Navy
Owner: Schiffergilde, Bremerhaven

The *Goliath* was typical of harbour tugs of the between-the-wars period, although she was somewhat unusual in having been equipped, perhaps at the end of the war, with a derrick forward for use in salvage operations. She was in daily use until the 1960s and then fell into disrepair but was later fully restored to working condition by an historic trust in Bremerhaven.

A port of any size, especially one like Bremen, which handled the biggest ships, had many dozens of tugboats like the *Goliath*.

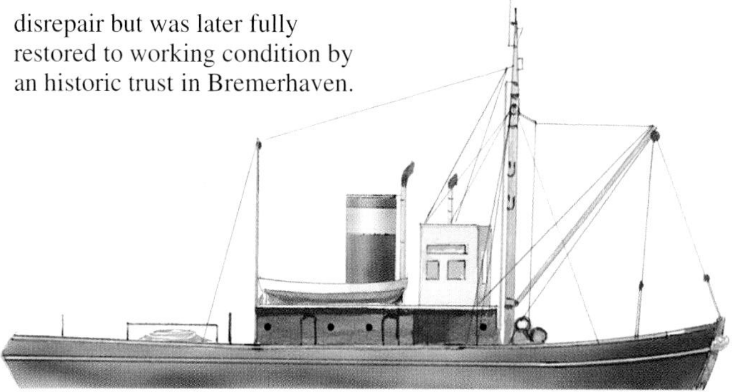

GORCH FOCK II

GERMANY: 1958

Built originally for the Federal German Navy, the *Gorch Fock II* was an anachronism – a steel-built barque, square-rigged on her fore and main masts and with fore-and-aft rig on her mizzen and setting over 21,500 square feet (2000 square metres) of sail but built half a century out of her time. She replaced a ship of the same name, taken over after World War II by the USSR as the *Tovarich*. Her permanent crew consisted of 12 officers and 65 men, and she accommodated 120 officer and petty officer cadets.

The *Gorch Fock II*, named after the poet Johann Kinau, who took the name Gorch Fock as his *nom de plume*, was specially built for the Federal German Navy in 1958.

Tonnage: 1740 grt
Dimensions: 295ft x 39ft x 15ft 6in (90m x 12m x 4.75m)
Machinery: one-shaft, auxiliary diesel; 1660hp
Service speed: not applicable
Role: sail training ship
Constructor: Blohm & Voss, Hamburg
Material: steel
Built for: Bundesmarine (Federal German Navy)
Owner: Bundesmarine

GOTHLAND (EX-GOTHIC)

BELGIUM (EX-GB): 1893

The 7755-t twin-screw *Gothland* was originally built for the White Star Line as the *Gothic*, to operate between the UK and New Zealand. She was sold to the Belgian Red Star Line in 1906 after her cargo of wool had caught fire and she had to be beached and flooded near Plymouth. She was converted into a one-class emigrant ship, to carry over 1800 in small four-berth cabins from Antwerp to New York and occasionally to Quebec. She was scrapped in 1926.

During much of World War I, the *Gothland* was chartered to the Belgian Relief Commission, carrying aid and supplies from New York to Rotterdam.

Tonnage: 7755 grt
Dimensions: 490ft 8in x 53ft 2in (149.55m x 16.2m)
Machinery: two-shaft, triple expansion
Service speed: 14 knots
Role: passenger/cargo liner; emigrant ship; transport
Route: UK-New Zealand; North Atlantic
Capacity: 1800 3rd
Constructor: Harland & Wolff, Belfast
Material: steel
Built for: White Star Line

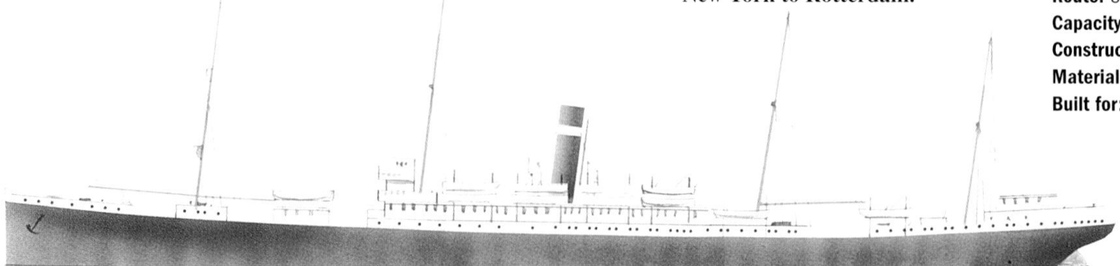

GRAMPIAN

GB: 1907

The 10,000-t *Grampian* and her sistership the *Hesperian* were built for the Allan Line's Glasgow–Canada service, operating to St John or Halifax in winter and into the St Lawrence River in the summer months. She made a number of voyages for the Canadian Pacific Line before passing into that company's ownership. She later operated out of London, Liverpool and occasionally Antwerp as well as her old home port, mostly carrying emigrants. She was gutted by fire during a refit in 1921 and subsequently scrapped.

The *Grampian* was built to carry travellers and emigrants from Europe to Canada and spent her whole life in that trade.

Tonnage: 10,187 grt
Dimensions: 485ft 8in x 60ft 3in (148.05m x 18.35m)
Machinery: two-shaft, triple expansion
Service speed: 15 knots
Role: passenger liner
Route: North Atlantic
Capacity: 210 1st, 250 2nd, 1000 3rd
Constructor: Alexander Stephen & Sons, Glasgow
Material: steel
Built for: Allan Line Steamship Co

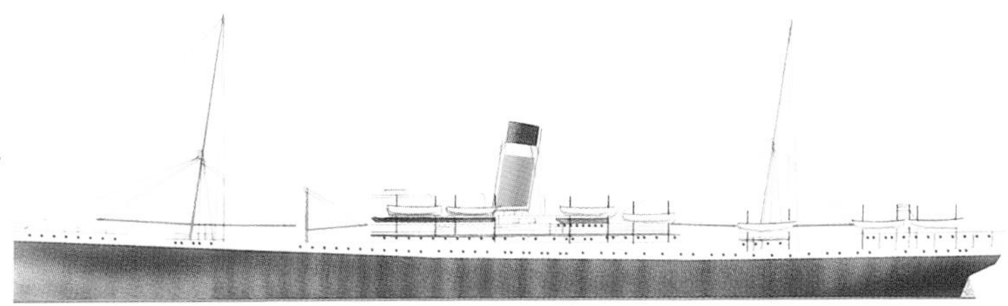

GRÖNLAND

GERMANY: 1867

Save for Roald Amundsen's *Gjøa*, the *Grönland* was the only single-masted polar expeditionary ship. She was built in Norway to carry the first German expedition to the Arctic in 1868. This group fell well short of its polar objective but returned relatively unharmed, and the *Grönland* subsequently operated in the coastal trade. She was later transferred to the maritime museum in Bremerhaven, where she was preserved in something very like her original condition.

The first German North Pole Expedition looked for its vessel to a Norwegian boatbuilder, who constructed the *Grönland* as a somewhat modified version of a local fishing boat.

Tonnage: 50 grt
Dimensions: 84ft 8in x 19ft 8in x 9ft 10in (25.8m x 6m x 3m)
Machinery: one-shaft, steam auxiliary
Service speed: not applicable
Role: expeditionary ship; general cargo vessel
Route: Arctic; coastal
Capacity: not known
Constructor: Tollef Tollefsen, Matre
Material: wood
Built for: German North Pole Expedition
Owner: Deutsches Schiffahrtmuseum

GROSSER KURFÜRST (LATER CITY OF LOS ANGELES)

GERMANY: 1899

While the *Grosser Kurfürst* was only marginally smaller than her livery companion the record-breaking *Kaiser Wilhelm der Grosse*, she was in an entirely different league, with a service speed some six knots slower.

Grosser Kurfürst was constructed for the Norddeutscher Lloyd Line's second-class North Atlantic service. In addition, between 1900 and 1912 she made nine return voyages between Germany and Australia. She was interned in New York in August 1914, and in 1917 was seized by the US government. In 1922, she was transferred to the Los Angeles Steam Ship Co and renamed *City of Los Angeles*. Refitted and re-engined with turbines, she operated as a cruise ship until 1933 and was scrapped four years later.

Tonnage: 13,182 grt
Dimensions: 560ft 6in x 62ft 4in (170.85m x 19m)
Machinery: two-shaft, quadruple expansion (later geared turbine)
Service speed: 16 knots
Role: passenger liner; cruise ship
Route: North Atlantic; Germany–Australia
Capacity: 424 1st, 176 2nd, 1211 3rd
Constructor: F Schichau, Danzig (Gdansk)
Material: steel
Built for: Norddeutscher Lloyd Line

HAKURYU MARU

JAPAN: 1991

Tonnage: 5195 grt
Dimensions: 377ft 4in x 59ft x 16ft 6in (115m x 18m x 5m)
Machinery: one-shaft, diesel
Service speed: 11.5 knots
Role: steel carrier
Route: coastal, Japan
Capacity: not known
Constructor: Kawasaki Heavy Industries
Material: steel
Built for: not known

The *Hakuryu Maru* was built for a single purpose – to carry coiled steel sheet from the steelworks at Fukuyama either to deep-sea ports for trans-shipment or to consumer plants. She was built with a total of almost 1400t of permanent ballast to minimise her movement while loading and unloading, and cargo stowage always adhered to the same plan. Loading and unloading was largely automated and utilised a large central platform mounted on hydraulic rams.

The designers of the *Hakuryu Maru* had the advantage of knowing that her cargo would always be in exactly the same form.

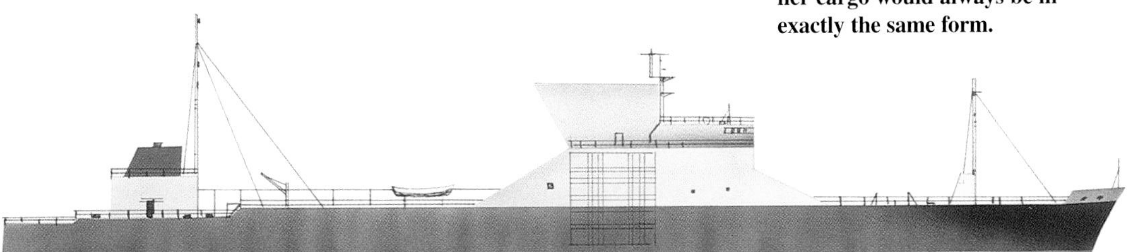

HALLA

KOREA: 1991

The carriage of cement in bulk has always been complicated by problems in discharging the cargo, which tends to compact in transit. Modern purpose-built cement carriers such as the *Halla* incorporated a pneumatic system, which blew air under pressure into the cargo from the floor of the hold, so that it could be picked up by a bucket chain conveyor. Loading was also automated – the arriving powder was placed in a central distribution hopper and transferred to the holds by four orientable 'air slides'.

By the end of the 20th century, there were hundreds of vessels afloat carrying Portland cement; some were converted bulk carriers, able to load almost 100,000t.

Tonnage: 10,427 grt
Dimensions: 367ft x 58ft 6in x 23ft (111.8m x 17.8m x 7m)
Machinery: one-shaft, diesel; about 10,000hp
Service speed: 12 knots
Role: bulk cement carrier
Route: not applicable
Material: steel

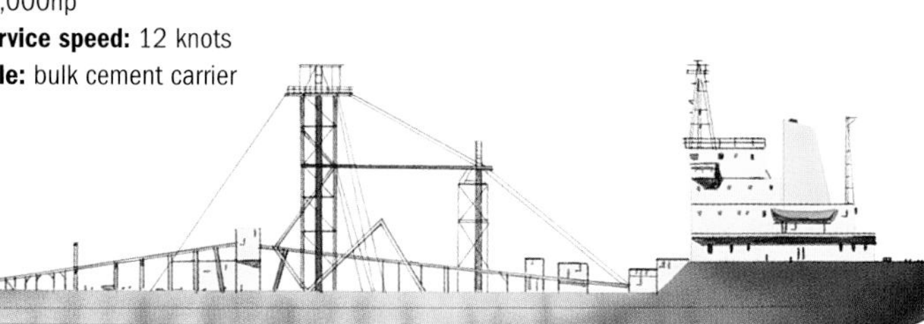

HANNOVER EXPRESS

GERMANY: 1990

A minority of the world's container ships, including some of the largest, were designed to operate at 24 knots, rather than the more common 20 knots; *Hannover Express* was one of a class of five such ships. By using a high proportion of high-tensile steel in the hull, carrying capacity was increased by 10 per cent over similar-sized 'conventional' ships, the containers stacked 11 high, rather than 10 high. Ships of this type were almost always built to the 'Panamax' limit of 106 feet (32.3m) breadth.

The *Hannover Express* was automated to such a degree that despite her size she required a crew of just 21.

Tonnage: 53,783 grt
Dimensions: 965ft 8in x 105ft 10in x 44ft 4in (294.3m x 32.25m x 13.5m)
Machinery: one-shaft, diesel; 48,240hp
Service speed: 24 knots
Role: general cargo vessel
Route: not applicable
Capacity: 4100 TEU
Constructor: Samsung Shipbuilding
Material: steel
Built for: Hapag-Lloyd Line

HANOVERIAN (LATER MAYFLOWER, CRETIC, DEVONIAN)

GB: 1902

Tonnage: 13,507 (later 12,153) grt
Dimensions: 582ft x 60ft 4in (177.4m x 18.4m)
Machinery: two-shaft, triple expansion
Service speed: 15 knots
Role: passenger/cargo liner; troopship
Route: North Atlantic
Capacity: 260 1st; 260 1st, 250 2nd, 1000 3rd
Constructor: R & W Hawthorn, Leslie & Co, Hebburn
Material: steel
Built for: Leyland Line

The 13,500-t *Hanoverian* was originally constructed for the Leyland Line and had only first-class accommodation. She was acquired by the Dominion Line before her maiden voyage and sent to Harland & Wolff to have additonal second- and third-class accommodation added; she entered service as the *Mayflower*. She was soon transferred to the White Star Line as the *Cretic*, and in 1923 she returned to her original owners as the *Devonian*. She was sold for breaking up in 1929.

As well as working for three commercial operators, the *Mayflower*, as she then was, spent four years as a troopship during World War I.

HANSEATIC (EX-SOCIETY ADVENTURER)

GERMANY: 1991

The Hapag-Lloyd Line's *Hanseatic* was constructed specially as an expedition cruise ship, designed to operate for up to eight weeks at a time in such diverse areas as the Antarctic, the River Amazon and the Great Barrier Reef. In the summer of 1997 she made a successful transit of the Northwest Passage, in just 14 days. Each of her 94 twin cabins had closed-circuit television, allowing passengers to monitor diving teams.

The *Hanseatic* was one of only a few cruise ships to have a strengthened hull so that she was able to navigate in ice.

Tonnage: 8200 grt
Dimensions: 402ft 8in x 59ft x 15ft 6in (122.8m x 18m x 4.7m)
Machinery: two-shaft, diesel; 4000hp
Service speed: 17 knots
Role: cruise ship
Route: not applicable
Capacity: 188 sc
Constructor: Rauma-Repola
Material: steel
Built for: Hapag-Lloyd

HANSTEEN (EX-IVAR ELIAS, HAAREK)

NORWAY: 1866

Tonnage: 114 grt
Dimensions: 101ft 6in x 16ft 4in x 7ft 5in (30.95m x 5m x 2.25m)
Machinery: one-shaft, steam auxiliary; 125hp
Service speed: not applicable
Role: survey ship; general cargo vessel
Route: coastal waters, Norway
Capacity: not applicable
Constructor: Nylands Verksted, Oslo
Material: iron
Built for: Norges Geografiske Opmaaling

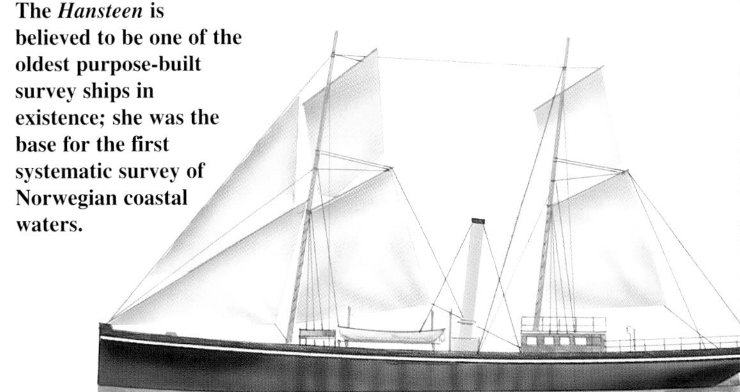

The *Hansteen* is believed to be one of the oldest purpose-built survey ships in existence; she was the base for the first systematic survey of Norwegian coastal waters.

The *Hansteen* was constructed in 1866 in Oslo for use as a hydrographic survey ship in Norwegian coastal waters. She was an auxiliary schooner, with the sort of enlarged four-sided lug topsails found on the Baltic *galeaser* of the period. She was later employed as a cargo carrier in the coastal trade. Late in her life she passed into the hands of a private owner in Oslo, who restored her to original condition.

HATHOR

GB: 1902

The Norfolk wherry was used extensively up until World War II to carry produce through the lakes and canals of the Broads from the hinterland of East Anglia to the feeder port of Yarmouth, returning with manufactured goods. The single mast, set very far forward, was stepped in a stout tabernacle, so it could be lowered to pass below bridges. In adverse wind conditions wherries were propelled by poling. By the end of the 20th century, only two authentic wherries remained in existence.

The 'bald headed' gaff sloop *Hathor* was built as a pleasure craft, for members of a wealthy Norwich family.

Tonnage: 23 grt
Dimensions: 56ft x 14ft 2in (17.05m x 4.35m)
Machinery: not applicable
Service speed: not applicable
Role: general cargo vessel; pleasure craft
Route: Norfolk Broads
Capacity: not known
Constructor: D S Hall, Reedham
Material: wood
Built for: E & H Colman
Owner: Wherry Yacht Charter

HAVEL (LATER METEORO, ALFONSO XII)

GERMANY: 1890

Tonnage: 6875 grt
Dimensions: 463ft x 51ft 10in (141.1m x 15.8m)
Machinery: one-shaft, triple expansion
Service speed: 18 knots
Role: passenger liner; armed merchant cruiser
Route: North Atlantic
Capacity: 244 1st, 122 2nd, 460 3rd
Constructor: AG Vulcan, Stettin (Szczecin)
Material: steel
Built for: Norddeutscher Lloyd Line

The Norddeutscher Lloyd Line's 6900-t *Havel* and *Spree* were the last single-screw liners built for the express service on the North Atlantic route. *Havel* operated on the Bremen–New York route from 1891 to 1898, when she was sold to the Spanish government and armed as an auxiliary cruiser; the following year she was transferred to the Compania Transatlántica Española and operated as the *Alfonso XII*, sailing between Bilbao and New York via Havana from 1916-18. She was scrapped in 1926.

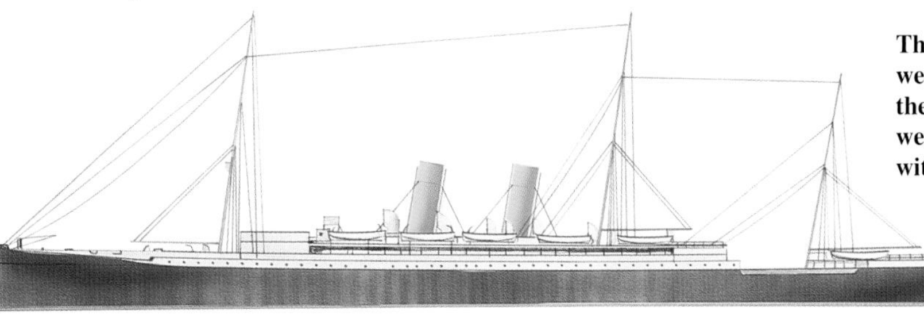

The *Havel* and the *Spree* were obsolete even before they were completed, and were unable to compete with twin-screw ships.

HD-4 (HYDRO-DOME IV)

CANADA: 1918

Alexander Graham Bell is perhaps best remembered for his pioneering work on the telephone, but he also had a lively interest in boats and was the first man to construct a true hydrofoil, although the development of the successful *Hydro-Dome IV* was actually financed by his wife, Mabel. Bell, together with F W Baldwin, came up with a design for a proto-hydrofoil as early as 1909 and constructed a towed model, but it was to be 1919 before a powered craft actually took shape. To a later eye, it looks decidedly ungainly, its foils being not the single 'wing-in-water' we have come to expect but 'ladders' of small foils, one at the bow and one on each beam. Power was provided by two aero-engines – initially 250hp Renault V-12s, later 350hp Liberty V-12s – driving airscrews, the solution to the problems of keeping a marine screw propeller at optimum depth having eluded Bell. The craft took the world water speed record at 70.86 mph (114.03 km/h) on 9 September 1919.

Bell attempted to interest the Royal and US Navies in the hydrofoil concept but failed; it was 44 years before one entered service.

Tonnage: not applicable
Dimensions: 60ft x 5ft 7in x 1ft 4in (18.3m x 1.75m x 0.4m)
Machinery: two airscrews, petrol; 350hp
Maximum speed: 70.86 mph (114.03 km/h)
Role: experimental vessel
Route: not applicable
Capacity: not applicable
Constructor: Bell & Baldwin
Material: wood and aluminium
Built for: Bell & Baldwin

HEALY

USA: 1997

The *Healy* was a combined ice-breaker and research ship, purpose-built for the US Coast Guard; she was not an improved version of existing designs but was drawn from scratch, work starting in 1994. She had five fully equipped interdisciplinary laboratories for 49 scientists, carried two helicopters and a six-t landing craft and could make three knots through ice 55 inches (1.4m) thick. Like most modern ships of the type she had a powerful (2000hp) bow thruster, but she lacked rolling tanks, which facilitate the release of a ship caught in encroaching ice.

Despite being considerably larger than the 'Polar' class ice-breakers, the *Healy* was much more economical, thanks to having diesel-electric and not CODLOG machinery.

Tonnage: 15,350t standard displacement
Dimensions: 420ft x 82ft x 28ft (128m x 25m x 8.54m)
Machinery: two-shaft plus bow thruster, diesel-electric; 30,000hp
Service speed: 12.5 knots
Role: ice-breaker; research ship
Constructor: Avondale Shipbuilding, New Orleans
Material: steel
Built for: US Coast Guard

HELENA

SWEDEN: 1990

Tonnage: 22,193 grt
Dimensions: 554ft 6in x 84ft x 23ft (169m x 25.6m x 7m)
Machinery: two-shaft, diesel; 6250hp
Service speed: 14.5 knots
Role: general cargo vessel
Route: Northern Europe
Constructor: Daewoo
Material: steel
Built for: MoDo Distribution

The 22,000-t *Helena* was a roll on-roll off (ro-ro) ship, access to her three lower cargo decks being by means of intermediate ramps from the level of the weather deck, which was itself accessed by a stern ramp. Based in Sweden, she was employed to carry vehicles and largely containerised cargo (but also paper products) between the Baltic ports and other locations, chiefly in Northern Europe.

***Helena* was one of the second-generation ro-ro ships; she could stow containers three-high on her weather deck.**

HELICE

NORWAY: 1990

The Norwegian-owned *Helice* was typical of late 20th-century mixed-cargo tankers. Her hull was divided into four holds, each of which contained free-standing tanks fabricated from corrosion-resistant steel, each of them quite separate from all the others. Each hold was equipped with two large-capacity cooling fans, those in the largest hold being capable of changing the air in it every eight minutes.

The *Helice* was capable of carrying a variety of separately-held liquid cargoes; an extensive venting/purging system was fitted to allow her to transport liquefied petroleum gas.

Tonnage: 34,974 grt
Dimensions: 672ft 6in x 105ft 8in x 42ft 8in (205m x 32.2m x 13m)
Machinery: one-shaft, diesel; c15,000hp
Service speed: 16 knots
Role: bulk liquid/LPG carrier
Route: not applicable
Capacity: c2 million cubic feet (57,000 cubic metres)
Constructor: Kvaerner, Govan
Material: steel
Built for: Bergesen dy

HERZOGIN CECILIE

GERMANY: 1902

Tonnage: 3242 grt
Dimensions: 310ft x 46ft x 24ft 8in (94.5m x 14m x 7.4m)
Machinery: not applicable
Service speed: not applicable
Role: general cargo vessel
Route: Europe–Australia/South America
Constructor: Rickmers Reismühlen Rederei und Schiffbau, Bremerhaven
Material: steel
Built for: Norddeutscher Lloyd Line

In 1903, the Norddeutscher Lloyd Line took delivery of a purpose-built sail training ship, named after the Herzogin Cecilie von Mecklenburg-Schwerin. She was to be manned by a mixed crew of experienced seamen and the company's officer cadets (experience under sail was still a

The *Herzogin Cecilie* was one of the last ships to trade under sail; her destruction – over a period of many weeks – made international news.

requirement, at the time, for an officer's 'ticket') and trade between Bremerhaven and Australia and South America, carrying mixed cargo outward bound and grain, nitrates and other bulk cargo on the homeward leg. She was a smart sailer and made some creditable passages.

She was interned in Chile from 1914 to 1920, and on her return to Europe was awarded in reparation to France, who sold her to Gustaf Erikson of Mariehamn in the Åland Islands. Homeward bound from Australia with 4295t of grain in April 1936, she ran aground near Bolt Head off the south coast of England. Much of her cargo and gear was offloaded and she was refloated, only to run aground again just outside Salcombe harbour, where she was wrecked.

HIBERNIAN GB: 1861

The *Hibernian* originally sailed between Liverpool and Montreal in summer, and to Portland, Maine, in the winter. Baltimore and Philadelphia were later destinations.

The 1900-t *Hibernian* was built for the Allan Line's Liverpool–Montreal service; it was a profitable but ill-fated route for the company, six ships being lost on it in a period of three and a half years. *Hibernian* was not amongst them, but her sistership *Norwegian* was, off Cape Breton in 1863. *Hibernian* was lengthened by over 70 feet (21.3m) in 1871 and rebuilt and re-engined in 1884. She made her last voyage, between Glasgow and Boston, in 1900 and was scrapped the following year.

Tonnage: 1888 (later 2752, later 3440) grt
Dimensions: 280ft x 37ft 8in (85.35m x 11.5m); later 351ft 2in x 37ft 8in (107.5m x 11.5m)
Machinery: one-shaft, inverted (later compound)
Service speed: 11 knots
Role: passenger liner
Route: North Atlantic
Capacity: 101 1st, 30 2nd, 324 3rd
Constructor: Wm Denny & Bros, Dumbarton
Material: iron
Built for: Allan Line

HIGHLAND CHIEFTAIN (LATER CALPEAN STAR) GB: 1928

Tonnage: 14,141 grt
Dimensions: 544ft 10in x 69ft 5in (166.05m x 21.15m)
Machinery: two-shaft, diesel; about 10,000hp
Service speed: 15 knots
Role: passenger/cargo liner; whaling factory ship
Route: London–Buenos Aires
Capacity: 150 1st, 70 2nd, 500 3rd
Constructor: Harland & Wolff, Belfast
Material: steel
Built for: Nelson Line

Speed was not of the essence in the passenger/general cargo service to Argentina, and the five 'Highlands' were built with economy in mind.

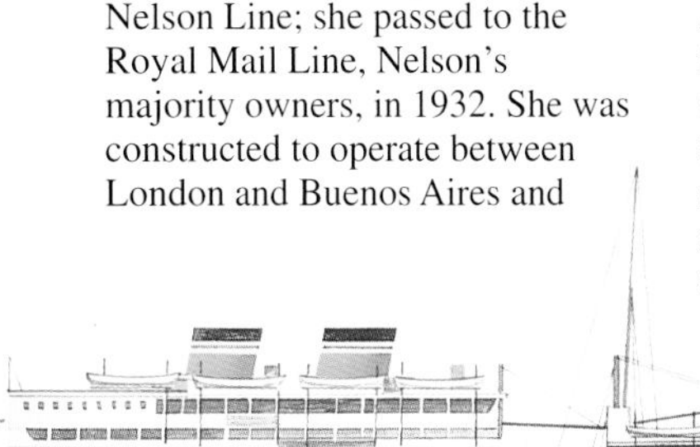

Highland Chieftain was the fourth of a class of five ships built for the Nelson Line; she passed to the Royal Mail Line, Nelson's majority owners, in 1932. She was constructed to operate between London and Buenos Aires and stayed in the South American service until she was sold in 1959. At that point she was transformed into a whaling factory ship as the *Calpean Star*. Leaving Montevideo for London on 1 June 1960, a seacock failed and flooded the engine room; she was abandoned and later scrapped.

HOPE (LATER SAVANNAH) CONFEDERATE STATES OF AMERICA: 1864

The paddle steamer *Hope* and her sistership the *Colonel Lamb* were constructed in Liverpool during the American Civil War as blockade runners for the Confederate Navy, to carry war materials from Nassau in the Bahamas to Charleston and return with a cargo of cotton, which would eventually be trans-shipped and make its way to Liverpool. The blockade runners were mostly steel-built to save weight and allow them to carry more cargo, and were some of the fastest ships in service at the time. On trial, *Colonel Lamb* achieved 16.7 knots, her two oscillating-cylinder engines producing an estimated 1300ihp. *Hope* had some initial success but was captured, supposedly by USS *Eolus* (ex-*Shawnee*, a shallow-draught monitor) in 1865. She was sold and became the SS *Savannah* that year, and was sold again the following year to Spain. She was broken up in 1885.

The PS *Hope* was one of the fastest, but certainly not the most successful, of the Confederacy's blockade runners.

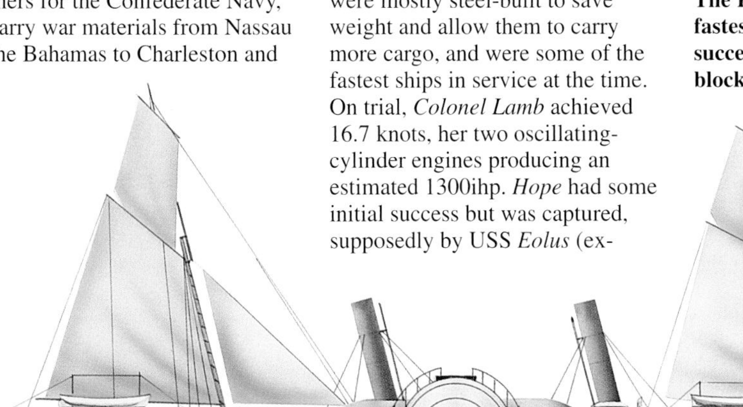

Tonnage: 113 grt
Dimensions: 296ft x 34ft 7in (on deck) x 11ft (90.2m x 10.55m x 3.35m)
Machinery: paddle wheels, oscillating; 1300hp
Service speed: 14 knots
Role: general cargo vessel (blockade runner)
Route: Nassau-Charleston
Capacity: 560t
Constructor: Jones, Quiggin & Co, Liverpool
Material: steel
Built for: not known

HUNTSMAN

GB: 1921

Despite having been constructed as late as 1921, the *Huntsman* was of somewhat antiquated appearance. She had four masts, although they served as anchor-posts for cargo derricks, and not for setting sail, in place of the by-then more common and considerably handier king posts. She was twin-decked and had considerable freeboard as a result, and her tall, unraked funnel, straight stem and counter stern added to the impression that she was perhaps from an earlier period. She was a victim of the German commerce raider *Admiral Graf Spee* in October 1939.

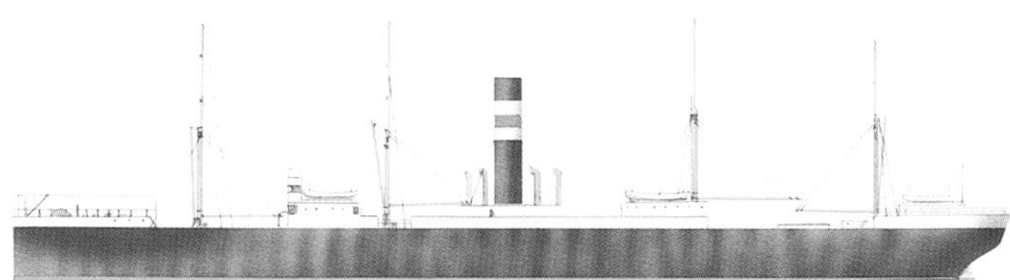

Her single-reduction turbine powerplant gave the somewhat upright-looking *Huntsman* a useful service speed of 13 knots.

Tonnage: 11,960 grt
Dimensions: 502ft x 58ft x 27ft 6in (153m x 17.6m x 8.4m)
Machinery: one-shaft, single-reduction turbine; c3200hp
Service speed: 13 knots
Role: general cargo vessel
Material: steel

ILE DE FRANCE (LATER 'CLARIDON')

FRANCE: 1927

The first major passenger liner to be constructed after World War I, the *Ile de France* set new standards of elegence in her accomodation, and her designers can be said to have invented the 'ocean liner' style; her public rooms included a restaurant three decks high. She made her maiden voyage in June 1927, and proved to be enormously popular. From 1928 to 1930, the *Ile de France* carried a catapult-launched seaplane, used to land mail and passengers in a great hurry. In New York at the outbreak of war, she was briefly laid up and then chartered to the British government, who officially seized her (in Singapore) in June 1940, and converted her to carry 9700 soldiers. She served as a troopship until she was handed back to her owners in 1947; a rebuild took two years, and she re-entered the North Atlantic service in July 1949, cruising to the Caribbean in the winter.

She stayed in the service for which she had been built until 1959 (and achieved new fame when she rescued 750 survivors from the *Andrea Dora* after she collided with the *Stockholm* in July 1956), and was then sold to Japan for scrap, a process which involved her being sunk in the Inland Sea during the making of a disaster film called *The Last Voyage*.

The *Ile de France* set new standards of luxury and elegance when she entered service in 1927; her bar – there was prohibition in the USA at the time – was the longest in any passenger ship.

Tonnage: 43,153 (later 44,356) grt
Dimensions: 792ft 10in x 91ft 9in (241.7m x 28m)
Machinery: four-shaft, geared turbines; 60,000hp
Service speed: 23 knots
Role: passenger liner; troopship
Route: North Atlantic
Capacity: 537 1st, 603 2nd, 646 3rd; 541 1st, 577 cb, 277 tr
Constructor: AG Vulcan, Hamburg
Material: steel
Built for: Compagnie Générale Transatlantique

IMPERATOR (LATER BERENGARIA)

GERMANY: 1912

Planned as the *Europa*, she was to have been the pride of her age, surpassing the White Star Line's *Oceanic* in every respect. She was renamed *Imperator* before she was launched, in May 1912. Completed a year later, she set sail on her maiden voyage to New York in June 1913, but it was a dismal failure, thanks to her top-heaviness, and soon her three funnels were cut down by 10 feet (3m), all upper deck panels and fittings were replaced by those of a lighter material, and even the bronze imperial eagle which adorned her bow was removed; that, and the addition of hundreds of tons of cement ballast, reduced her sickening tendency to roll, and she re-entered service, but only until July 1914. She was laid up throughout World War I, and when the American authorities came to survey her in 1919, to put her into service as a troopship,

The *Imperator*, the *Vaterland* and the *Bismarck* were the biggest ships of their day; the smallest of them, *Imperator*, was equipped to carry a total of 4594 passengers between Germany and the USA.

Tonnage: 51,969 (later 52,226) grt
Dimensions: 919ft x 98ft x 35ft (280m x 29.85m x 10.65m)
Machinery: four-shaft, geared turbines
Service speed: 23 knots
Role: passenger liner
Route: North Atlantic
Capacity: 908 1st, 972 2nd, 942 3rd, 1772 st; 972 1st, 630 2nd, 606 3rd, 515 st
Constructor: AG Vulcan, Hamburg
Material: steel
Built for: Hamburg-Amerikanische Packetfahrt AG ('Hapag')

they found that she had deteriorated badly. Nonetheless, she made two and a half return voyages and was then laid up again in New York. In 1920, she was chartered to the Cunard Line and was later allocated to Britain in reparation, together with her sistership *Bismarck*, which became the White Star Line's *Majestic*. *Imperator* stayed in Cunard service as the *Berengaria*, on the Southampton–New York service, and indeed became the line's flagship. She was extensively modernised during the 1920s, but by the end of the decade she had become outmoded and by the mid-1930s positively dangerous, thanks to corroded wiring, which caused three serious fires. She was sent for scrapping in 1938, and the process was completed in 1946.

IMPERIAL STAR — GB: 1935

Tonnage: 10,670 grt
Dimensions: 516ft x 70ft (157.3m x 21.4m)
Machinery: two-shaft, diesel
Service speed: 15 knots
Role: refrigeration ship
Route: not applicable
Capacity: *c*500,000 cubic feet (14,150 cubic metres)
Constructor: not known
Material: not known
Built for: not known

The specially designed refrigeration ship *Imperial Star* had over half a million cubic feet (14,150 cubic metres) of cargo space.

When first introduced over 100 years ago, the refrigerated ship changed the lives of millions of people, especially those who lived in the crowded industrial countries of Europe. Over the years, the meat-carrying vessels continued to develop and by the 1930s had reached a high standard of reliability. *Imperial Star* had 29 cargo spaces insulated by granulated cork; a duplicate set of refrigeration plant consisting of a comprehensive layout of brine pipes closely packed together was able to operate at four temperature settings.

INDEPENDENCE (SOMETIME OCEANIC INDEPENDENCE, SOMETIME SEA LUCK 1) — USA: 1951

Tonnage: 30,293 grt
Dimensions: 683ft x 89ft x 30ft (208.15m x 27.1m x 9.15m)
Machinery: two-shaft, geared turbines
Service speed: 23 knots
Role: passenger liner; cruise ship
Route: New York–Mediterranean; Hawaiian Islands
Capacity: 295 1st, 375 cb, 330 tr
Constructor: Bethlehem Steel Co, Quincy
Material: steel
Built for: American Export Lines

The *Independence* was built for American Export Lines' New York–Mediterranean service in 1951; the emphasis was upon high-quality tourist accommodation, in an attempt to entice holiday travellers away from the North Atlantic route. By the late 1960s, that traffic had largely disappeared and she was laid up for five years. She was sold to Hong Kong interests, then bought for use as a casino ship, but the venture failed. She eventually returned to the American flag as a cruise ship, under her original name, in 1980.

Despite occasional lay-ups, the *Independence* was to have a long career, and was still operating as a cruise ship some 50 years after her launch.

INDUSTRY

AUSTRALIA: 1911

The shallow-draught sidewheel paddle steamer *Industry* was built for the State of South Australia to keep the channels of the Murray River free of obstructions and clear for navigation. She was variously employed as a snag boat to remove floating logs, as a bucket dredger and as a floating workshop for lock repair. She stayed in active service until 1969 and was eventually restored to original condition and put on display at Renmark.

The *Industry*, with shallow draught and low freeboard and equipped with a sizeable derrick, was typical of small ships employed to maintain navigation channels in rivers.

Tonnage: 91 grt
Dimensions: 112ft x 18ft 6in x 3ft 1in (34.15m x 5.65m x 0.94m)
Machinery: sidewheels, steam; 30hp
Role: navigation maintenance ship
Route: Murray River
Constructor: A J Inches, Goolwa
Material: wood; iron frames
Built for: Government of South Australia
Owner: Renmark Corporation

INFANTA BEATRIZ (LATER CIUDAD DE SEVILLA)

SPAIN: 1928

Tonnage: 6279 grt
Dimensions: 410ft x 52ft x 21ft 6in (125m x 15.8m x 6.4m)
Machinery: two-shaft, diesel; 4340hp
Service speed: 14 knots
Role: passenger/cargo liner
Route: Germany–Canary Islands
Capacity: 134 1st, 38 2nd, 60 3rd; 5200 dwt
Constructor: Krupp AG (Germaniawerft), Kiel
Built for: Cia Trasmediterranea

Infanta Beatriz was the first motor passenger ship built for Spain. She was built by Krupp of Kiel, with the design following closely two successful motor ships built for a major German shipping firm.

Infanta Beatriz was a major addition to a fleet of over 60 vessels, many of them older and smaller. Passenger accommodation was to a high standard, with an unusually large number of single cabins. Cargo holds were fitted out for the banana trade, since she was intended for service between Germany and the Canary Islands. Cargo capacity was 5200 dwt.

Whilst alongside at Barcelona in January 1939, during the Spanish Civil War, *Ciudad de Sevilla*, as she had recently become, was bombed and sunk. She was later raised and repaired, and served until the 1960s.

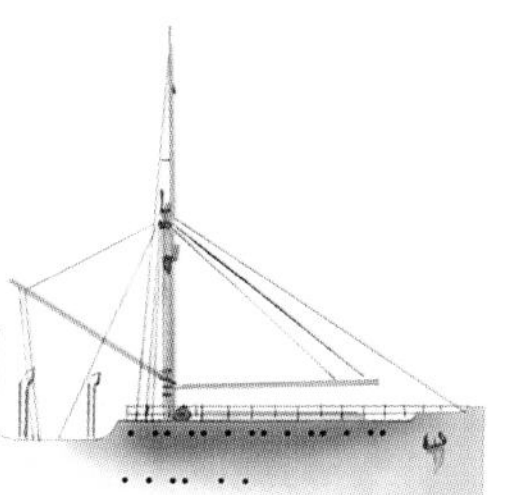

INVERLAGO

NETHERLANDS: 1925

Inverlago was the first of a small fleet of crude oil carriers constructed for use on Venezuela's Lake Maracaibo, an important oilfield but one where local conditions were unique. On a draught of only just over 13 feet (4m) she was able to carry over 3150t of cargo. As the channel into the lake was progressively deepened, larger ships came into service, and by 1953 the need for these shallow-draught vessels had disappeared.

Royal Dutch Shell originally solved the problem of navigating the shallow waters of Lake Maracaibo by converting ex-Royal Navy coastal monitors as tankers.

Tonnage: c2600 grt
Dimensions: 305ft x 38ft x 13ft 3in (92.95m x 11.6m x 4.05m)
Machinery: one-shaft, triple expansion; c1400hp
Service speed: 10 knots
Role: crude oil carrier
Route: Lake Maracaibo-Cardon
Capacity: 3156 dwt
Constructor: Harland & Wolff, Belfast
Material: steel
Built for: Royal Dutch Shell

ISAR (LATER STANROYAL, HURON, NECIP IPAR)

GERMANY: 1929

Tonnage: 9026 grt
Dimensions: 546ft 6in x 63ft 6in x 28ft (166m x 19.2m x 8m)
Machinery: one-shaft, triple expansion/geared turbine; 6500hp
Service speed: 14 knots
Role: cargo/passenger liner
Route: Germany–Far East; Baltic
Capacity: c12,000 dwt, 16 cb
Constructor: AG Vulcan, Hamburg
Material: steel
Built for: Norddeutscher Lloyd Line

Isar was one of the last in a group of successful cargo liners built for the German Norddeutscher Lloyd Line, all of which had a similar layout, with a short, raised forecastle, four tall masts and eight hatches. *Isar* differed from the group by having a modified hull form, with a stem that sloped back sharply, joining the keel beneath the foremast. This hull form gave reduced skin friction and easier waterflow, so giving better speed and fuel consumption. A turbine could be coupled up to the conventional reciprocating engine for economical steaming.

Isar was the first merchant ship to have the 'Maierform' hull, a design used on many later passenger/cargo ships.

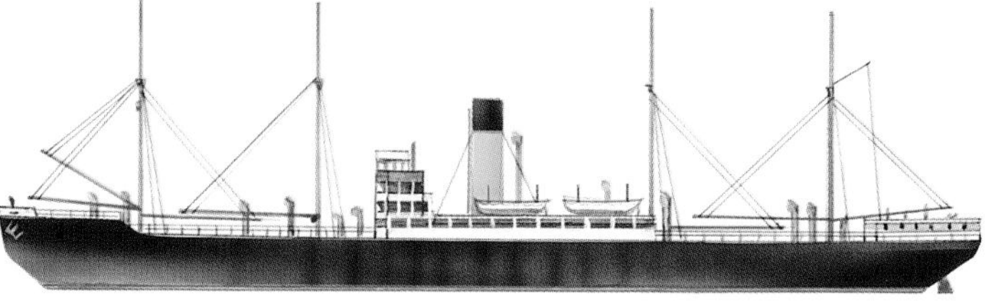

ISHIKARI

JAPAN: 1990

To many Japanese, ferries are an accepted part of the everyday way of life – 1990 figures showed that there were some 510 car ferries running on 260 routes around and between the islands. Competition is thus very severe, and the largest operators go to considerable lengths to outdo each other in terms of speed and passenger comfort. The *Ishikari* was a good example of a modern Japanese ferry, with accommodation for 850, plus 150 cars and 165 trucks.

Tonnage: 6936 grt
Dimensions: 631ft 6in x 88ft 7in x 22ft 8in (192.5m x 27m x 6.9m)
Machinery: two-shaft, diesel; about 12,000hp
Service speed: 21.5 knots
Role: passenger/vehicle ferry
Route: coastal waters, Japan
Capacity: 850 p; 315 v
Constructor: Mitsubishi Heavy Industries
Material: steel
Built for: Taiheiyo Ferries

The *Ishikari* had cabins and restaurants arranged in both western and Japanese styles.

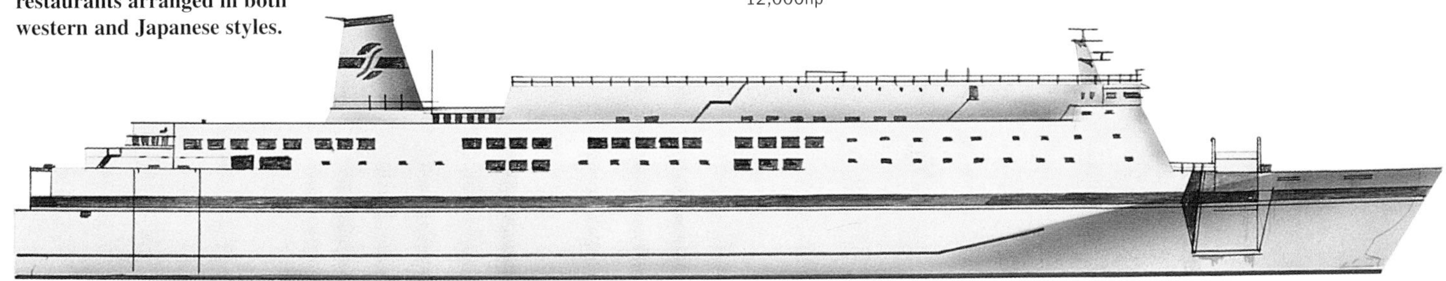

ISLAND BREEZE (EX-TRANSVAAL CASTLE, S A VAAL, FESTIVALE)

GREECE (EX-GB): 1962

Tonnage: 32,697 grt
Dimensions: 760ft x 90ft x 32ft (231.65m x 27.45m x 9.75m)
Machinery: two-shaft, geared turbines; 46,000hp
Service speed: 22.5 knots
Role: passenger liner; cruise ship
Route: Southampton–South Africa; Caribbean; Mediterranean
Capacity: 728 sc; 1432 sc
Constructor: John Brown & Co, Glasgow
Material: steel
Built for: Union-Castle Line

The career of the *Island Breeze* was typical of that of many smaller passenger/cargo liners of the 1960s.

Built for the Union-Castle Line's Southampton–South Africa service in the 1960s, *Transvaal Castle* later passed into South African ownership on the same route. By the mid-1970s, cheap air fares had made the passenger service uneconomical, and most freight was containerized, so she was sold again, to Carnival Cruise Lines, and rebuilt as a cruise ship to go into service as the *Festivale*. She later passed to Dolphin Hellas Shipping as the *Island Breeze*, operating chiefly in the Mediterranean.

JAKOB MAERSK

NETHERLANDS: 1991

The Dutch-owned *Jakob Maersk* was one of a class of small (by the standards of the time) multi-cargo tankers, constructed with independent free-standing tanks in her four holds, lined with polyurethane to a thickness of 4.7 inches (120mm) to minimise damage. She was equipped with an inert-gas generator and had forced-air systems incorporating dryers in each hold. Eight centrifugal pumps were fitted for cargo handling, and she had a bow thruster to improve her manoeuvrability.

Tonnage: 41,757 grt
Dimensions: 670ft x 90ft x 41ft (185m x 27.4m x 12.5m)
Machinery: one-shaft, diesel; 16,500hp
Service speed: 17 knots
Role: bulk liquid carrier
Route: not applicable
Capacity: not known
Constructor: not known
Material: steel
Built for: not known

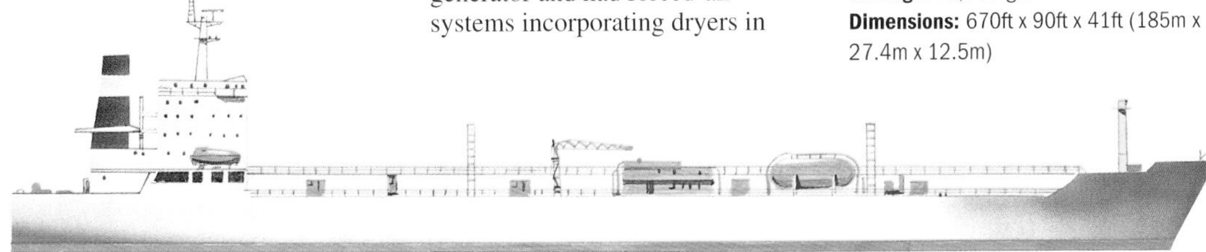

The *Jakob Maersk*, like most ships of her type, was highly automated and required a crew of just 23 to run her.

JAMES CLARK ROSS

GB: 1991

The *James Clark Ross*, as her name might suggest, was specially designed to carry out oceanographic surveys in the Antarctic. To that end, she had a reinforced hull and was able to break fresh ice, navigate in broken floe ice up to five feet (1.5m) thick, and in fragmented ice up to 10 feet (3m) thick. She was equipped with both specialist and generalist laboratories, with the ability to onload others in containerized form and locate them on the quarterdeck. She was able to remain at sea for 10 months at a time, should that prove necessary, but somewhat surprisingly, she did not carry a helicopter of her own.

The *James Clark Ross* was purpose-built for the British government's National Environmental Research Council to carry out oceanographic surveys in the Antarctic.

Tonnage: 5416 grt
Dimensions: 324ft 8in x 62ft x 21ft 4in (99m x 18.9m x 6.5m)
Machinery: one-shaft, diesel
Service speed: 15.5 knots
Role: oceanographic survey vessel
Route: Antarctica
Capacity: not applicable
Constructor: Swan Hunter, Wallsend-upon-Tyne
Material: steel
Built for: National Environmental Research Council

JEREMIAH O'BRIEN

USA: 1943

Tonnage: 7176 grt
Dimensions: 417ft 9in x 57ft x 27ft 9in (127.35m x 17.35m x 8.45m)
Machinery: one-shaft, triple expansion; 2500hp
Service speed: 11 knots
Role: general cargo vessel
Route: not applicable
Constructor: New England Shipbuilding Corp, Portland, Me
Material: steel
Built for: War Shipping Administration
Owner: Maritime National Historical Park, San Francisco, Ca

Jeremiah O'Brien was one of over 2500 merchant ships built to a standard design in the United States during World War II. They were known as the Liberty ships and all were named after men and women who had made a real contribution to achieving that. They were the mainstay of wartime commerce; almost all the survivors stayed in service post-war, but the *Jeremiah O'Brien* was one which was retained by the US government and lay idle in reserve from 1945. She was restored from 1978.

The Liberty ships were very basic vessels indeed, largely prefabricated and welded together. *Jeremiah O'Brien* was present during the Normandy landings.

JERVIS BAY

GB: 1922

Tonnage: 13,839 grt
Dimensions: 530ft 6in x 68ft 3in x 12ft 2in (161.7m x 20.8m x 3.9m)
Machinery: two-shaft, geared turbines; 9000hp
Service speed: 15 knots
Role: passenger/cargo liner; armed merchant cruiser
Route: London–Brisbane; North Atlantic
Capacity: 12 1st, 712 3rd
Constructor: Vickers Ltd, Barrow-in-Furness
Material: steel
Built for: Commonwealth Line

The *Jervis Bay* was one of a class of five ships constructed for the Australian Commonwealth Line's monthly passenger/cargo service between London and Brisbane, the passengers being mainly emigrants. On the outbreak of World War II, by now owned by a

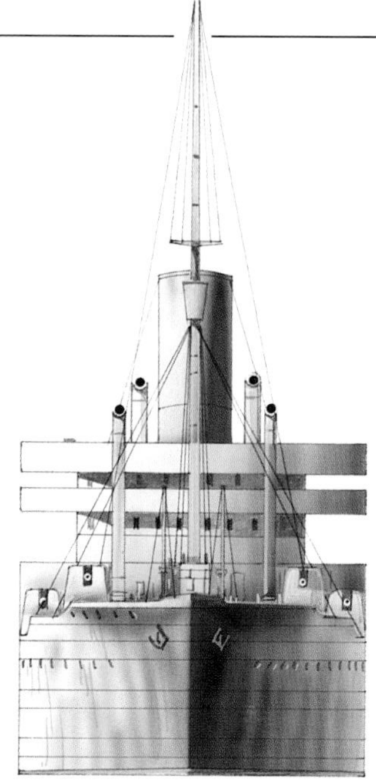

P&O subsidiary, the *Jervis Bay* was in London and was promptly requisitioned by the Admiralty for use as an armed merchant cruiser. She was armed with seven obsolete 6in (152mm) Mk VII guns of World War I vintage, which could elevate to only 20 degrees and had a maximum range of 14,200 yards (12,985m). She also received two 3in (76mm) AA guns and was assigned to duty in the North Atlantic, escorting convoys.

At about 3.00pm on 5 November 1940, roughly in mid-Atlantic, the convoy HX84, of 37 ships, eastbound from Halifax to Liverpool, which *Jervis Bay* alone was escorting, came under fire from the German 'pocket battleship' *Admiral Scheer*, armed with six 11in (280mm) guns which ranged out to 45,930 yards (42,000m). The armed merchantman's captain, S E Fogarty Fegen RN, turned to face the heavy cruiser and engaged her, in an heroic attempt to give his charges time to scatter. Within 15 minutes, his ship had been disabled; she sank, with the loss of 190 of her crew of 259, some four hours later. The sacrifice was not entirely in vain, however, for only five of the convoy fell victim to the *Admiral Scheer*. Fegen was awarded the Victoria Cross.

The *Jervis Bay* was one of three sisterships taken up and armed as merchant cruisers; *Esperance Bay* and *Moreton Bay* were later disarmed and served out the war as troopships.

JERVIS BAY

GB: 1992

Tonnage: 51,000 grt
Dimensions: 958ft 6in x 105ft 6in x 36ft 9in (292.15m x 32.2m x 11.2m)
Machinery: one-shaft, diesel; 46,800hp
Service speed: 23.5 knots
Role: general cargo vessel
Route: Europe–Far East
Capacity: 4038 TEU
Constructor: Ishikawajima-Harima Heavy Industries, Kure
Material: steel
Built for: P&O Containers

Despite her huge size, the *Jervis Bay* had a crew of just nine officers and 10 men. She was allowed just 24 hours to turn around at Southampton.

P&O-Nedlloyd's 50,000-t *Jervis Bay* was a fast container ship with a capacity of over 4000 20-ft equivalent units, some 240 of which could be refrigerated. While she and her six sisterships were constructed to be employed mainly in the Europe–Far East service (accomplishing a round trip from Southampton to Yokohama and back in 63 days), their beam measurement was marginally within the maximum able to pass through the locks of the Panama Canal.

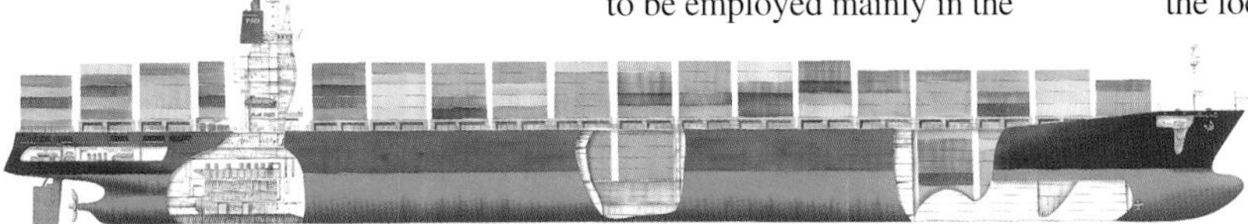

JFJ DE NUL

NETHERLANDS: 1992

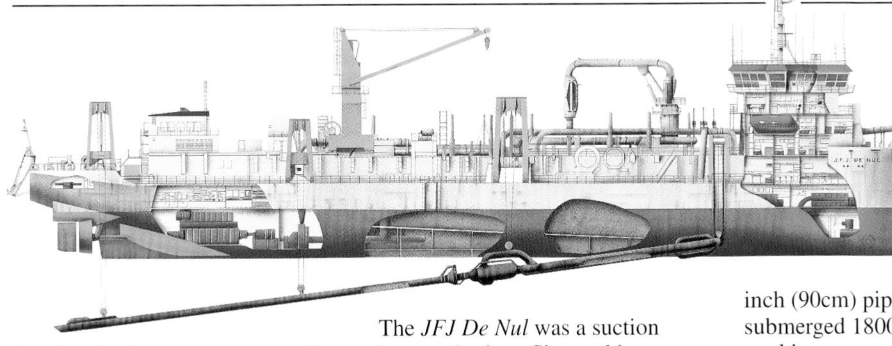

Tonnage: 11,985 grt
Dimensions: 472ft 5in x 83ft 8in x 26ft 3in (144m x 25.5m x 8m)
Machinery: two-shaft, diesels plus bow thruster; 15,800hp
Service speed: 15 knots
Role: suction dredger
Route: not applicable
Capacity: 414,948 cubic feet (11,750 cubic metres)
Constructor: Merwede, Giessendam
Material: steel
Built for: Ondernemingen Jan de Nul

Suction dredgers were commonly used either to recover material for building or so-called 'beach nourishment' or to keep navigation lanes clear.

The *JFJ De Nul* was a suction hopper dredger. She could recover material from depths of up to 150 feet (45.7m) via two 43-inch (110cm) diameter pipes or from twice that depth using a single 35-inch (90cm) pipe incorporating a submerged 1800kW pump. She could pump spoil up to five miles (8km) inland if required. The ship was air-conditioned throughout and could operate in temperatures from 50 degrees to minus 20 degrees Celsius; the bow and the forward section of the hull were strengthened for ice operation.

JO ALDER

ITALY: 1991

Tonnage: 7922 grt
Dimensions: 456ft x 69ft 9in x 26ft 5in (139m x 21.25m x 8m)
Machinery: one-shaft, diesel; 16,400hp
Service speed: 14 knots
Role: liquid products carrier
Route: not applicable
Capacity: 503,234 cubic feet (14,250 cubic metres)
Constructor: Società Esercizio Cantieri, Viareggio
Material: steel
Built for: Alta Italia

The multi-purpose products tanker *Jo Alder* was constructed specifically to carry a variety of bulk liquids, including food products, in 25 stainless steel tanks constructed in her holds. Each tank had its own entirely self-contained pump and pipeline system, so in theory as many different cargoes as there were tanks could be carried at one time without risk of cross-contamination. All cargo management operations were computer controlled, and the engine room was designed for unmanned operation.

The *Jo Alder* was typical of a new design of very versatile bulk liquid products carriers first introduced in the 1980s. She was double-hulled throughout.

JOHN LOUIS

AUSTRALIA: 1954

Even as late as the second half of the 20th century, wooden sailing vessels were still being constructed in many parts of the world, particularly where materials were plentiful and time and skill were in greater supply than money. The ketch-rigged pearling lugger *John Louis* was built in Western Australia in 1954 by entirely traditional methods to a traditional design, and to be worked in the traditional way (although she did have a small auxiliary diesel engine).

The area in which the *John Louis* operated has a considerable tidal difference, and she was constructed to withstand regular strandings.

Tonnage: 34 grt
Dimensions: 60ft x 14ft 5in x 5ft 8in (18.3m x 4.4m x 1.75m)
Machinery: one-shaft, auxiliary diesel
Service speed: not applicable
Role: pearl fishery vessel
Route: coastal, Western Australia
Capacity: not applicable
Constructor: Male & Co, Broome
Material: wood
Built for: L Placanico
Owner: Australian National Maritime Museum

KAISER FRANZ JOSEF I (LATER PRESIDENTE WILSON, GANGE, MARCO POLO) AUSTRIA: 1911

For a period until the end of World War I, Austria had an outlet to the sea and a minor shipping line, the Unione Austriaca, founded by the Cosiluch brothers in 1903. Its most important vessel by far was the *Kaiser Franz Josef I*. She was awarded to Italy in 1919 and handed to the Cosiluch Line, which operated her as the *Presidente Wilson*. She was later transferred first to Lloyd Triestino and then to Adriatica and was eventually scuttled at La Spezia in 1944.

The *Kaiser Franz Josef I* was built primarily to carry emigrants to the United States but also made one return voyage to South America.

Tonnage: 12,567 grt
Dimensions: 477ft 6in x 60ft 3in (145.55m x 18.35m)
Machinery: two-shaft, quadruple expansion; 12,500hp
Service speed: 17 knots
Role: passenger liner
Route: Trieste–New York
Capacity: 125 1st, 550 2nd, 1230 3rd
Constructor: Cantiere Navale Triestino, Monfalcone
Material: steel
Built for: Unione Austriaca

KAISER WILHELM DER GROSSE GERMANY: 1897

By the 1890s, Germany's merchant marine had reached a position where it was eager to challenge the British domination of the North Atlantic steamship traffic. To do so, the Norddeutscher Lloyd Line ordered the largest and most powerful ship ever built at the time. The *Kaiser Wilhelm der Grosse* was to achieve everything expected of her and more, for she was truly the first 'superliner'. She took the eastbound Blue Riband in September 1897 and added the westbound the following March. She narrowly escaped destruction in June 1900, when fire broke out at the company's piers in New York, and five years later she was rammed by the British freighter *Orinoco* off Cherbourg, with the loss of five lives. She was refitted to carry only emigrants early in 1914 and on the outbreak of war was taken up and armed as a merchant cruiser. Coaling in Rio de Oro (Spanish Sahara) on 21 August 1914, she was surprised by the British cruiser HMS *Highflyer* and scuttled to avoid capture.

The *Kaiser Wilhelm der Grosse* was not only the biggest and fastest liner of her day but the first to have four funnels and remotely actuated watertight doors.

Tonnage: 14,349 (later 13,952) grt
Dimensions: 627ft 5in x 66ft (191.2m x 20.1m)
Machinery: two-shaft, triple expansion; 14,000hp
Service speed: 22 knots
Role: passenger liner; armed merchant cruiser
Route: Bremen–New York
Capacity: 332 1st, 343 2nd, 1074 3rd
Constructor: AG Vulcan, Stettin (Szczecin)
Material: steel
Built for: Norddeutscher Lloyd Line

KALAKALA (EX-PERALTA) USA: 1927

Tonnage: 1417 grt
Dimensions: 265ft 2in x 53ft 5in (80.8m x 16.3m)
Machinery: one-shaft, diesel; 3000hp
Service speed: 17.5 knots
Role: passenger/vehicle ferry
Route: Seattle–Bremerton; Port Angeles–Victoria
Capacity: 2000 p, 100 v
Constructor: Moore Drydock Co, San Francisco; Lake Washington Shipyard, Seattle
Material: steel
Built for: Key Transit Co; Puget Sound Navigation Co
Owner: Kalakala Foundation

The passenger and vehicle ferry *Kalakala* was the world's first streamlined ship, designed by Boeing engineers. It was not always thus, for she was launched as the *Peralta*, an entirely conventional San Francisco Bay ferryboat and was rebuilt in her later form at Seattle in 1935 after a near-disastrous fire. She remained in service until 1967 and was then sold to become a shrimp processing plant in Alaska. She returned to Puget Sound in 1993, to be restored to her former glory.

In a poll of visitors to the Seattle World's Fair in 1963, *Kalakala* was ranked second only to the Space Needle as a visitor attraction.

KARIMOEN NETHERLANDS: 1911

Between 1920 and the late 1930s, it was usual for the average cargo ship to have only two masts because dock handling facilities provided all the lifting power needed. However, since some companies traded in the east, twin masts standing side by side were sometimes carried, especially on Dutch ships, so that cargo handling could be carried out in open roadsteads, with an array of local craft alongside, or in poorly equipped harbours. *Karimoen* had 22 derricks to handle the 9556t of cargo she could stow in her five holds. She was scrapped in 1934.

Tonnage: 14,500t displacement
Dimensions: 445ft 6in x 55ft x 28ft 4in (135m x 17m x 8.4m)
Machinery: one-shaft, triple expansion; 4500hp
Service speed: 16.5 knots
Role: passenger/cargo liner
Route: Netherlands–Dutch East Indies (Indonesia)
Capacity: 9556 dwt
Constructor: W Hamilton and Co Ltd, Port Glasgow
Material: not known
Built for: Nederland Line

***Karimoen* was used on the Dutch East Indies service and was fitted out to carry pilgrims to Jeddah; she was also used briefly on the Holland to Africa service.**

KDD OCEAN LINK

JAPAN: 1991

Even after the coming of satellite communications, there was still a very large demand for submarine cables (although by that time they were almost exclusively fibre optics rather than true cables). *KDD Ocean Link* was a fourth-generation cable ship (the *Great Eastern* was one of the earliest), with two full-length decks and three cable holds. The cable was laid over the stern and buried in one operation, the plough carrying both TV and forward-scanning sonar.

Tonnage: 9510 grt
Dimensions: 436ft 10in x 64ft 4in x 24ft 3in (133.15m x 19.6m x 7.4m)
Machinery: two-shaft, diesel; 8800hp
Service speed: 15 knots
Role: deep-sea cable layer
Route: North Pacific
Constructor: Mitsubishi Heavy Industries
Material: steel
Built for: Kokusai Cable Ships

***KDD Ocean Link* was constructed to operate in the North Pacific and to endure the severest weather conditions.**

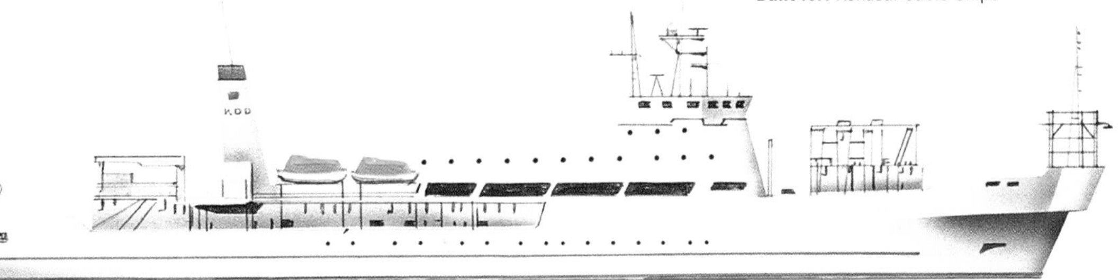

KIAUTSCHOU (LATER PRINCESS ALICE, CITY OF HONOLULU)

GERMANY: 1900

Tonnage: 10,911 (later 10,421) grt
Dimensions: 523ft 6in x 60ft 2in (159.55m x 18.3m)
Machinery: two-shaft, quadruple expansion
Service speed: 15 knots
Role: passenger/cargo liner
Route: Germany–Far East; North Atlantic; USA–Mediterranean; Pacific
Capacity: 255 1st, 115 2nd, 1666 3rd; 350 cb, 500 3rd
Constructor: AG Vulcan, Stettin (Szczecin)
Material: steel
Built for: Hamburg-Amerikanische Packetfahrt AG

The *Kaiutschou* was entirely typical of the sort of passenger/cargo liners built around the turn of the century to service the lucrative Europe–Asia trade.

The *Kiautschou* was ordered for Hapag's Hamburg–Far East service. She was soon sold to the rival Norddeutscher Lloyd Line, renamed *Princess Alice* and operated to New York and the Far East alternately. She operated on behalf of the US government, then was sold to the America Palestine Line in 1925. Later that same year she became the Los Angeles Steam Ship Co's *City of Honolulu*. She was damaged by fire in 1930 and scrapped three years later.

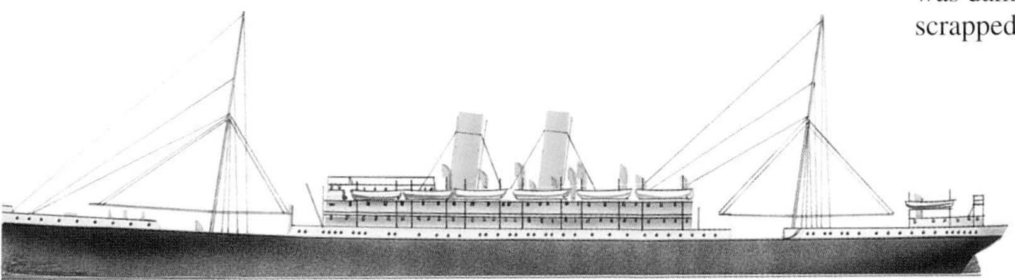

KONING WILLEM II (LATER ATENE)

NETHERLANDS: 1899

Koning Willem II was constructed to carry mail, passengers and cargo between the Netherlands and its considerable colonies in the Far East, as one of a fleet large enough to operate a weekly service. Her passenger accommodation was limited to first- and second-class, and there was no provision for emigrants, although she did have relatively austere accommodation for a small number of troops. She was sold to Italian interests in 1913 and renamed *Atene*.

The *Koning Willem II* and her sisterships maintained the all-important link between Amsterdam and the Dutch colonies in what is now Indonesia.

Tonnage: 4293 grt
Dimensions: 408ft x 45ft x 23ft 3in (124.4m x 13.7m x 7m)
Machinery: one-shaft, quadruple expansion; 4000hp
Service speed: 11 knots
Role: passenger/cargo liner
Route: Netherlands–Indonesia
Capacity: 70 1st, 30 2nd
Constructor: not known
Material: steel
Built for: Koninklijke Nederlandsche Stoomboot Maatschappij

KOTA WIJAYA

SINGAPORE: 1991

The Singapore-registered *Kota Wijaya* was a container ship with a capacity of just 1160 20-ft equivalent units – barely a quarter of that of the real giants of the trade. As a result, she was considerably more economical to operate; in particular she could be loaded and unloaded very quickly indeed. She was double-hulled and carried her fuel in wing tanks; a heeling tank, to be filled with water as ballast, was fitted to starboard to assist in loading/unloading operations.

Tonnage: 16,730 grt
Dimensions: 605ft 4in x 90ft 6in x 29ft 6in (184.5m x 27.6m x 9m)
Machinery: one-shaft, diesel; 14,400hp
Service speed: 19 knots
Role: general cargo vessel
Route: not applicable
Capacity: 1160 TEU
Constructor: Kanasashi
Material: steel
Built for: Pacific International Lines

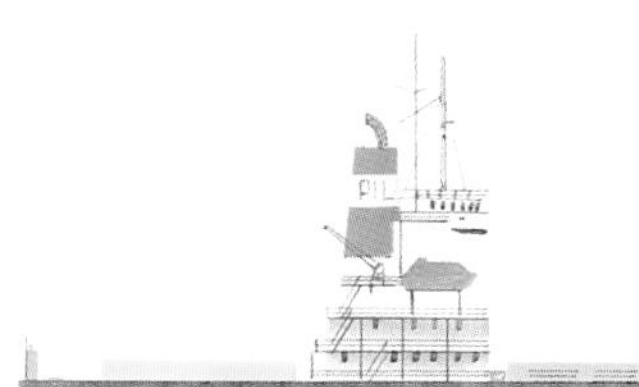

The *Kota Wijaya* was typical of smaller container ships; she could accommodate both 20- and 40-ft containers, up to 120 of which could be refrigerated.

KRASNOGRAD (LATER NORDANA SURVEYOR)

RUSSIA: 1992

The *Krasnograd* was typical of smaller con-bulkers. Electric cranes and derricks allowed her own crew to handle her cargo, an advantage in out-of-the-way ports.

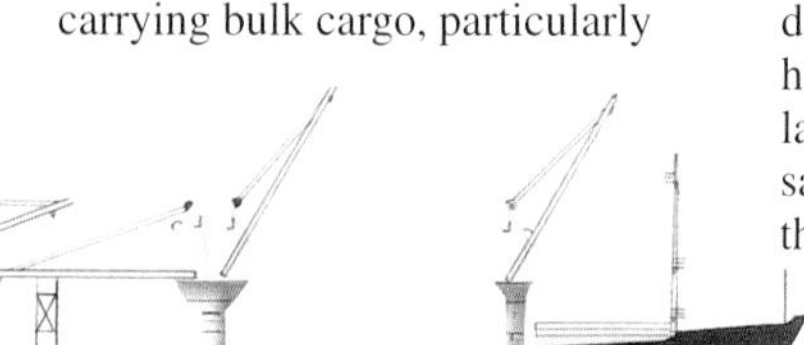

The *Krasnograd* was one of many modern ships built for the Russian merchant marine at a foreign yard. She was a multi-role 'con-bulker', carrying bulk cargo, particularly grain, in four holds and general cargo in containers on two through-decks. She had five electric cranes and two 25-t derricks to allow her crew to handle cargo themselves. She was later sold to Greek interests and sailed under Maltese registration as the *Nordana Surveyor*.

Tonnage: 16,075 grt
Dimensions: 569ft 3in x 75ft 6in x 33ft (173.5m x 23.05m x 10m)
Machinery: one-shaft, diesel; 12,960hp
Service speed: 18 knots
Role: general cargo and bulk carrier
Route: not applicable
Capacity: 717,277 cubic feet (20,311 cubic metres) (grain); 1136 TEU
Constructor: Neptun Industrie, Rostock
Material: steel
Built for: Murmansk Shipping Co

KRONPRINZ WILHELM (LATER VON STEUBEN)

GERMANY: 1901

Tonnage: 14,908 grt
Dimensions: 637ft 4in x 66ft 4in (194.25m x 20.2m)
Machinery: two-shaft, quadruple expansion
Service speed: 22 knots
Role: passenger liner; auxiliary cruiser; troopship
Route: North Atlantic
Capacity: 367 1st, 340 2nd, 1054 3rd
Constructor: AG Vulcan, Stettin (Szczecin)
Material: steel
Built for: Norddeutscher Lloyd Line

The *Kronprinz Wilhelm* took the westbound Blue Riband from the rival Hapag liner *Deutschland* in September 1902 at an average speed of 23.09 knots, but lost it back to her a year later.

Kronprinz Wilhelm was built as a consort for *Kaiser Wilhelm der Grosse*. She made a hasty exit from New York on 3 August 1914 to be armed (at sea) as an auxiliary cruiser; over the next nine months she captured 15 Allied ships but then ran out of supplies and was interned at Newport News. On the US entry into the war she was seized and operated as a troopship under the name *Von Steuben*. She was scrapped in 1923.

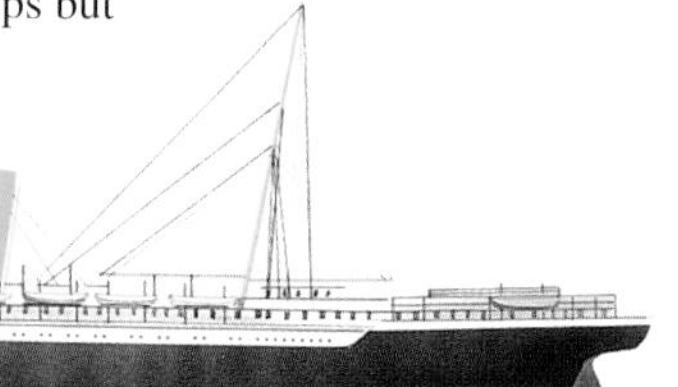

KRUZENSTERN (EX-PADUA)

ESTONIA: 1926

The *Kruzenstern* was employed as an oceanographic survey vessel before being converted to a training ship at Sevastopol in 1967-71.

The four-masted barque *Kruzenstern* was originally constructed for one of Germany's great shipping concerns, Ferdinand Laeisz's Flying 'P' Line, as the *Padua* (all Laeisz's ships had names beginning with P). She was one of 16 similar vessels, most from the same yard, carrying nitrates from Chile and later wool from Australia, and was one of the last in commercial sail. She was acquired by the Soviet Union after World War II and was much modified below decks. Ownership passed to Estonia in the early 1990s.

Tonnage: 3064 grt
Dimensions: 376ft x 46ft x 22ft 6in (114.5m x 14m x 6.85m)
Machinery: two-shaft, auxiliary diesels; 1600hp
Service speed: not applicable
Role: nitrate carrier; wool carrier; survey vessel; sail training ship
Route: Chile–Europe; Australia–Europe
Constructor: J C Tecklenborg, Bremerhaven-Geestemünde
Material: steel
Built for: Reederei Ferdinand Laeisz
Owner: Ministry of Fisheries

LA CHAMPAGNE

FRANCE: 1886

Tonnage: 7087 grt
Dimensions: 493ft 6in x 51ft 9in (150.4m x 15.8m)
Machinery: one-shaft, triple expansion (later quadruple expansion)
Service speed: 17 knots
Role: passenger liner
Route: North Atlantic; France-Central America
Capacity: 390 1st, 65 2nd, 600 3rd
Constructor: Chantiers et Ateliers de l'Atlantique, St Nazaire
Material: steel
Built for: Compagnie Générale Transatlantique

The quartet of *La Bourgogne*, *La Bretagne*, *La Champagne* and *La Gascogne* were modelled on *La Normandie*, France's first luxury express liner, which was built in Britain.

La Champagne was one of a quartet of near-sisterships built in pairs, two of steel and two of steel on iron, in the mid-1880s. Six months after entering service in the North Atlantic, she was seriously damaged in a collision with the *Ville de Rio Janeiro* near Le Havre and sank; she was salvaged, re-engined and put back into service. She later operated to Mexico and Panama. In 1913, she stranded (while at anchor) at St Nazaire, broke her back and was scrapped.

LADY HOPETOUN

AUSTRALIA: 1902

The *Lady Hopetoun* was constructed for Sydney's Maritime Services Board ostensibly as an inspection vessel, for use in Sydney Harbour; she was very well appointed, as befitted the personal transportation of the Board's senior officials. She had a long active career during the course of which she inevitably deteriorated and was acquired for restoration and preservation as an operating museum exhibit in 1967. Restoration was completed in 1991.

The *Lady Hopetoun* was an excellent example of a turn-of-the-century steam pinnace, many of which were in service throughout the British Empire.

Tonnage: 38 grt
Dimensions: 70ft x 13ft 9in x 6ft 9in (23.45m x 4.2m x 2.05m)
Machinery: one-shaft, triple expansion
Role: harbour inspection and VIP transport
Route: Sydney Harbour
Capacity: not applicable
Constructor: Watty Ford, Sydney
Material: wood
Built for: Sydney Maritime Services Board
Owner: Sydney Maritime Museum

LAFAYETTE (EX-ILE DE CUBA, LATER MÉXIQUE)

FRANCE: 1914

Tonnage: 11,953 grt
Dimensions: 546ft 8in x 64ft (166.6m x 19.5m)
Machinery: four-shaft, compound plus low-pressure turbine
Service speed: 16 knots
Role: passenger liner; hospital ship
Route: North Atlantic; Le Havre-Caribbean
Capacity: 500 1st, 350 2nd, 1500 3rd
Constructor: Chantiers Et Ateliers de Provence, Port de Bouc
Material: steel
Built for: Compagnie Générale Transatlantique

The *Lafayette* was the last passenger liner built for the Compagnie Générale Transatlantique before World War I. She was launched as the *Ile de Cuba*, but her name was changed before she was completed. She made nine return voyages between Bordeaux and New York and was then taken up as a hospital ship, returning to service in 1919. From 1924, she sailed to the Antilles, and later, as the *Méxique*, to Vera Cruz.

While she carried a large number of emigrants, *Lafayette*'s first-class accommodation was very well appointed.

LAKE CHAMPLAIN (LATER RUTHENIA, KING GEORGE V, CHORAN MARU)

GB: 1900

The *Lake Champlain*, built for Elder Dempster's Beaver Line, had the most varied of careers. From 1901 to 1913, she operated on the North Atlantic route to Canada, latterly from Trieste and then London as the *Ruthenia*. During the war, she was first disguised as the battleship HMS *King George V*, then became a store ship, then an oiler. After the war she became an oil hulk at Singapore, was

Tonnage: 7392 grt
Dimensions: 460ft x 52ft (140m x 15.8m)
Machinery: two-shaft, triple expansion
Service speed: 13 knots
Role: passenger/cargo liner; decoy; cistern ship; oil hulk
Route: North Atlantic
Capacity: 100 1st, 80 2nd, 500 3rd; 150 2nd, 1000 3rd
Constructor: Barclay, Curle & Co, Glasgow
Material: steel
Built for: Canadian Pacific Steamship Co

captured by the Japanese in 1942, and recaptured in 1945. She was scrapped in 1949.

The *Lake Champlain* was the first liner on the North Atlantic route to carry a useful radio; earlier sets had been used only to announce impending arrival.

LANCASHIRE — GB: 1917

The Bibby Line's *Lancashire*, launched in 1917, was the second ship of the name, a passenger/cargo vessel built for the company's regular service between the UK and the Indian subcontinent, including Ceylon (Sri Lanka) and Burma (Myanmar). The majority of her passengers were civil servants or service personnel and their families. In 1930, she was taken up as a troopship for the Indian service and she continued to operate in this role throughout World War II, which she survived, being broken up in 1956.

The Bibby Line's *Lancashire* was typical of the ships the company operated to the Indian subcontinent until after World War II.

Tonnage: 9552 grt
Dimensions: 500ft x 57ft 3in x 28ft (152.4m x 17.4m x 8.5m)
Machinery: two-shaft, quadruple expansion
Service speed: 15 knots
Role: passenger/cargo liner; troopship
Route: UK–India–Burma
Material: steel
Built for: Bibby Line

LANDSORT (LATER CRUDEGULF) — SWEDEN: 1991

Tonnage: 81,135 grt
Dimensions: 899ft x 157ft 6in x 55ft 9in (274m x 48m x 17m)
Machinery: one-shaft, diesel; 19,200hp
Service speed: 14 knots
Role: crude oil and oil products carrier
Route: not applicable
Capacity: 5,888,620 cubic feet (166,747 cubic metres)
Constructor: Daewoo Shipbuilding & Heavy Machinery Co, Koje
Material: steel

With a deadweight capacity of almost 150,000t, the *Landsort* was not the biggest crude oil and oil products carrier of her day by any means, but she was the first built to conform to new International Maritime Organisation rules laid down after the grounding of the *Exxon Valdez*. She was double-hulled throughout, with wing tanks filled with water ballast. Her cargo space was divided into nine self-contained tanks, each one with its own discharge pump capable of delivering some 53,000 cubic feet (1500 cubic metres) per hour.

The new hull layout pioneered by the *Landsort* was intended to reduce the risk of cargo loss should the vessel take the ground.

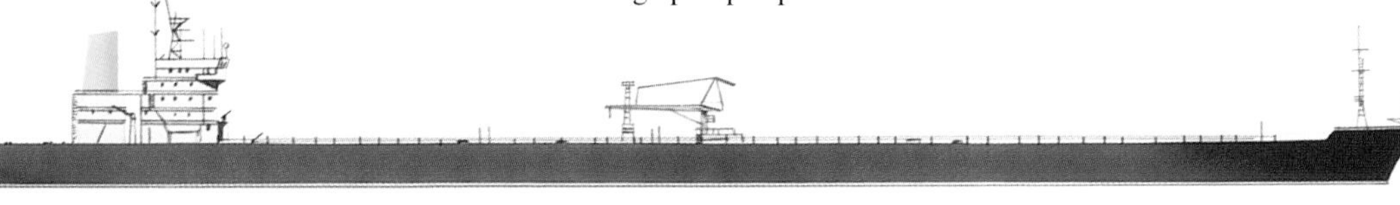

LAWHILL — GB: 1892

The *Lawhill* was built for the jute trade but was too late to succeed in it and was given over to general cargo. In 1900, she was sold to the Anglo-American Oil Co to carry case oil (kerosene) to the Far East and passed into Finnish ownership in 1914. Gustaf Erikson bought her in 1917, and she sailed under his flag until 1941, when she was seized in South Africa. *Lawhill* was later sold to Portuguese interests but never went to sea again. She was scrapped in 1958.

In the course of an active career which spanned over half a century, the four-masted barque *Lawhill* made a total of 50 voyages, not including coastal passages.

Tonnage: 2816 grt
Dimensions: 317ft 4in x 45ft x 25ft 2in (96.7m x 13.7m x 7.6m)
Machinery: not applicable
Service speed: not applicable
Role: general cargo vessel; case oil carrier; grain carrier; nitrate carrier
Route: not applicable
Constructor: W B Thompson, Dundee
Material: steel
Built for: Charles Barrie

LEONARDO DA VINCI — ITALY: 1960

The liner *Leonardo da Vinci* was built as a replacement for the *Andrea Doria*. She operated on the Genoa–New York route from 1960, and from Naples to New York from 1965 until 1976, latterly spending part of the year cruising. She was then taken over by the Costa Line for full-time cruising. She proved uneconomical to run and was laid up at La Spezia in 1978. In July 1980, fire broke out aboard and she was scuttled, to be raised and scrapped the following year.

Despite heavy subsidies from the Italian government in the last decade she spent in service, the *Leonardo da Vinci* could not compete with airliners.

Tonnage: 33,340 grt
Dimensions: 767ft x 92ft 2in x 30ft (233.9m x 28.1m x 9.15m)
Machinery: two-shaft, geared turbines; 52,000hp
Service speed: 23 knots
Role: passenger liner; cruise ship
Route: Italy–New York
Capacity: 413 1st, 342 cb, 571 tr
Constructor: Ansaldo, Genoa
Material: steel
Built for: Italia Line

LIEMBA (EX-GRAF VON GOETZEN) — TANZANIA: 1914

The *Liemba* was one of a considerable number of lake steamers which were prefabricated for transportation and then assembled where they were to operate. In this case, she was constructed in Papenburg on the River Ems, shipped to East Africa and then carried overland to Kigoma, on Lake Tanganyika. To prevent her capture by the British, she was scuttled in 1916 after all her working parts had been heavily greased. She was recovered in 1924, refurbished, renamed, and put back into service.

The *Liemba* was one of four ships on Lake Tanganyika; they inspired C S Forester's novel *The African Queen* which was turned into a film of the same name.

Tonnage: 1575t displacement
Dimensions: 232ft x 33ft x 9ft (70.7m x 10.05m x 2.75m)
Machinery: two-shaft, triple expansion (later diesel); 500hp
Service speed: 10 knots
Role: passenger/cargo vessel
Route: Kigoma-Mpulungu (Lake Tanganyika)
Capacity: 18 1st, 16 2nd, 350 3rd
Constructor: Jos L Meyer, Papenburg
Material: steel
Built for: German government
Owner: Tanzania Railways

LOUIS S ST LAURENT — CANADA: 1966

Tonnage: 10,908 grt
Dimensions: 366ft 6in x 80ft 3in x 29ft 6in (111.7m x 24.45m x 9m)
Machinery: three-shaft, turbo-electric (later diesel-electric); 27,000hp
Service speed: 16 knots
Role: ice-breaker
Route: coastal waters, Canada
Capacity: not applicable
Constructor: Canadian Vickers, Montreal
Material: steel
Built for: Canadian Coast Guard

The Canadian Coast Guard's ice-breaker *Louis S St Laurent* was that organisation's most important vessel. She proved her worth in 1976 when she negotiated the Northwest Passage, in company with the oil exploration vessel *Canmar Explorer*, even though she lacked modern systems such as waterflushing, waterline air injection and forward propellers.

The *Louis S St Laurent* carried two helicopters and two landing craft; she received a reprofiled bow during a 1988 rebuild.

In 1988, she was re-engined with a diesel-electric powerplant comprising five generator sets and three electric motors.

LUDGATE HILL (LATER LIVONIAN) GB: 1881

The *Ludgate Hill* was one of the first twin-screw liners to see service on the North Atlantic route. She ran first between London and New York and later to Boston and Montreal. In 1897, the Allan Line bought her, renamed her *Livonian* and put her into service between Glasgow and the River Plate; she was re-engined in 1900. In 1914, she was sunk as a blockship in Dover harbour; she was not salvaged and scrapped until 1933.

Although the *Ludgate Hill* was built by a small yard of little note, she proved a very successful ship and was in service almost without a break for over 30 years.

Tonnage: 4162 grt
Dimensions: 420ft 4in x 47ft (128.1m x 14.3m)
Machinery: two-shaft, compound (later triple expansion)
Service speed: 12 knots
Role: passenger liner
Route: North Atlantic; UK-South America
Capacity: 40 1st, 3rd not known
Constructor: Dobie & Co, Glasgow
Material: steel
Built for: Twin Screw Line

LUSITANIA GB: 1906

Tonnage: 31,550 grt
Dimensions: 762ft 3in x 87ft 9in x 33ft 6in (232.3m x 26.75m x 10.2m)
Machinery: four-shaft, direct-drive turbines; 68,000hp
Service speed: 24 knots
Role: passenger liner
Route: Liverpool-New York
Capacity: 563 1st, 464 2nd, 1138 3rd
Constructor: John Brown & Co, Glasgow
Material: steel
Built for: Cunard Steam Ship Co.

During October 1907, the Cunard Line's 31,500-t *Lusitania*, the biggest ship in the world at that time, and the most luxuriously appointed, held both eastbound and westbound Blue Ribands simultaneously; she eventually posted an average speed, westbound, of 25.65 knots over 2890 nautical miles (5352km). For all that she excelled as a ship, however, it is probably the manner of her passing which defined the *Lusitania*. On 7 May 1915, she was sunk without warning by a torpedo from the German submarine *U 20* off the Old Head of Kinsale on the south coast of Ireland, with the loss of 1198 (some reports say 1201) men, women and children. Among the dead were 127 (possibly 128) American citizens, and it was long held that their deaths were a factor in the United States' eventual entry into World War I. One factor in the *Lusitania*'s destruction was the inexplicable failure of her master to obey orders to zig-zag at maximum speed. Her sistership the *Mauretania* was marginally faster when she took the Blue Ribands from her.

The *Lusitania* cost £1.75 million – almost exactly the same as the mould-breaking monocalibre battleship HMS *Dreadnought*, constructed the same year.

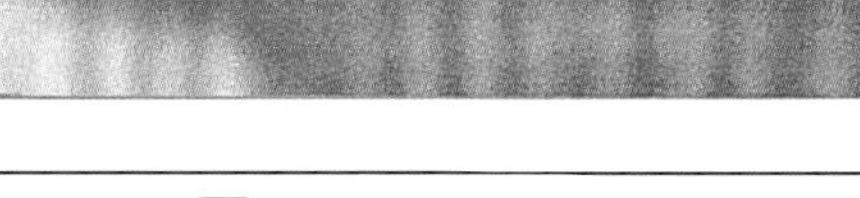

LYDIA EVE (EX-WATCHMOOR) GB: 1930

The steam drifter *Lydia Eve* was typical of the boats engaged in the North Sea herring fishery during the first half of the 20th century. These boats were very little changed outwardly from earlier designs, the modification being limited to the addition of a wheelhouse, and they still carried a reduced sailing rig, although increasingly they were built of steel rather than wood. They used the same fishing method, streaming a curtain net, two nautical miles (3.2km) in length, before them as they lay head-to-wind.

Although they were beamy boats, the herring drifters were graceful, with considerable sheer and a clean run aft.

Tonnage: 138 grt
Dimensions: 95ft x 20ft 6in x 9ft 8in (28.95m x 6.25m x 2.95m)
Machinery: one-shaft, triple expansion; 120shp
Role: fishery vessel
Route: North Sea
Constructor: Kings Lynn Slipway, Kings Lynn
Material: steel
Built for: Harry Eastick
Owner: Lydia Eve & Mincarlo Charitable Trust, Lowestoft

MAGDALENA

GB: 1889

The *Magdalena* was the second of a quartet of small ships constructed for the Royal Mail Line's east coast of South America service. They were somewhat anachronistic in appearance, having clipper bows and bowsprits, but were otherwise quite modern, with triple-expansion machinery. *Magdalena*'s first public appearance came at the annual Naval Revue at Spithead in August 1889; she had an unremarkable career and was scrapped in 1921, having spent some years as a troopship.

Tonnage: 5373 grt
Dimensions: 421ft 2in x 50ft (128.35m x 15.25m)
Machinery: one-shaft, triple expansion
Service speed: 15 knots
Role: passenger liner; troopship
Route: Southampton-Brazil-River Plate
Capacity: 174 1st, 44 2nd, 330 3rd
Constructor: R Napier & Sons, Glasgow
Material: steel
Built for: Royal Mail Steam Packet Co

Together with the *Thames* and the *Clyde*, *Magdalena* operated a regular service terminating at Buenos Aires, her sistership *Atrato* having been switched over to the West Indies.

MAGELLAN

FRANCE: 1955

The cargo liner *Magellan* was typical of the many such ships built in the 1950s and '60s, well-supplied with derricks and winches to make her independent of port facilities and enable her crew to handle cargo themselves, an essential in the French South Pacific territories which were her usual destination. She offered a high standard of accomodation to both passengers and crew, who were all housed aft of the bridge, in an extended superstructure which had the single funnel at its after end.

Ships like the *Magellan* were commonplace after World War II; they were designed specifically to operate to locations without well-developed port facilities.

Tonnage: 7200 grt
Dimensions: 490ft 6in x 61ft 7in x 27ft (148.5m x 18.6m x 8.2m)
Machinery: one-shaft, diesel
Service speed: 12 knots
Role: passenger/cargo liner
Route: South Pacific

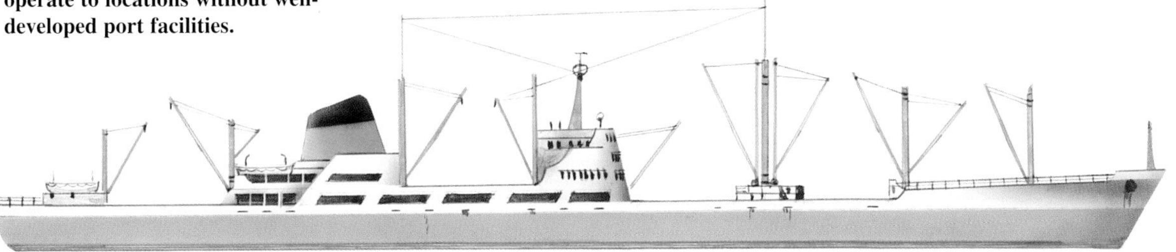

MAJESTY OF THE SEAS

NORWAY: 1992

Majesty of the Seas was the third of a trio of almost identical cruise ships constructed in France for Norway's Royal Caribbean Cruise Lines. They were purpose-built for one-week duration Caribbean cruises, and each one could accommodate some 2350 passengers, in small double staterooms, the emphasis being on public areas. When her sistership *Monarch of the Seas* hit a shoal off the island of St Maarten and had to be beached, in December 1998, repairs cost $41 million.

Tonnage: 73,941 grt
Dimensions: 874ft x 106ft x 25ft (266.4m x 32.3m x 7.6m)
Machinery: one-shaft, diesel; 27,840hp
Service speed: 21 knots
Role: cruise ship
Route: Caribbean
Capacity: 2350 sc
Constructor: Chantiers de l'Atlantique (Alsthom)
Material: steel
Built for: Royal Caribbean Cruise Lines

Designed very specifically for one-week Caribbean cruising, *Majesty of the Seas* generated around $3 million in revenue per voyage at the height of the season.

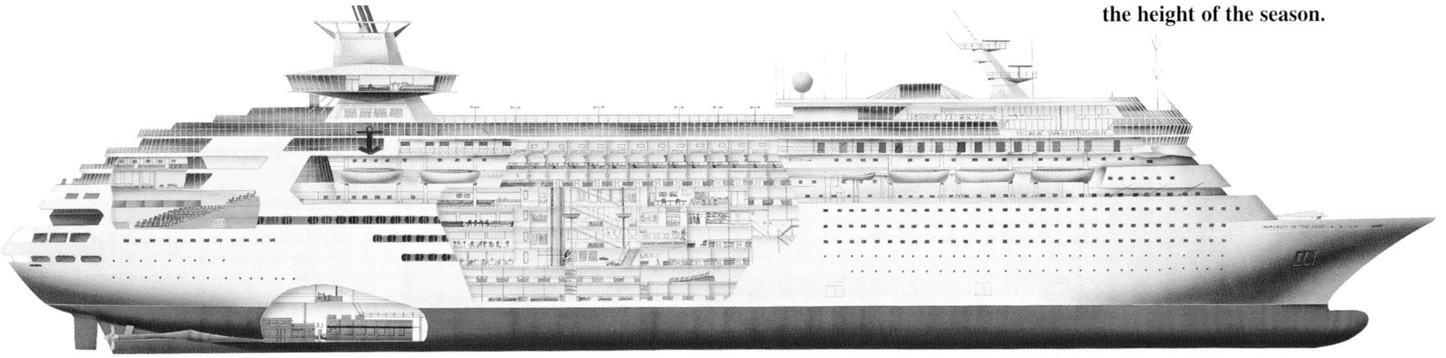

MARIE SOPHIE

GB: 1879

Marie Sophie was a brig – a two-masted vessel carrying conventional square sail – usually a course, a single topsail, a single topgallant and a royal – on both masts, with an additional four-sided gaff spanker on the main mast. Sometimes the last sail was laced to a short independent mast stepped immediately abaft the main, in which case the vessel was properly known as a snow. In a very real sense, a brig was a full-rigged ship reduced to two masts. While this rig was more expensive than that of the brigantine, it was more flexible.

Two-masted sailing vessels were commonly used in the coastal and short-sea trades; the brig rig was more flexible than that of the brigantine or the schooner.

Tonnage: 190 grt
Dimensions: 112ft x 26ft 6in x 11ft 3in (34.1m x 8.1m x 3.4m)
Service speed: not applicable
Role: general cargo vessel
Material: wood

MARINOR

GB: 1993

Marinor was designed for a specific purpose – to transport raw materials for the paper-making industry, including china clay slurry and sulphuric acid. She was double-hulled for safety but had relatively low-powered machinery, there being no urgency in her schedule. She had 12 cargo tanks – half for china clay, the rest for a variety of chemicals – along her centre line, all of them lined with stainless steel; they were connected in pairs and all were heated.

Tonnage: 4600 grt
Dimensions: 368ft 1in x 59ft x 24ft 7in (112.2m x 18m x 7.5m)
Machinery: one-shaft, diesel; 6120hp
Service speed: 14 knots
Role: chemical carrier
Route: North America–Caribbean
Capacity: 300,175 cubic feet (8500 cubic metres)
Constructor: Welgelegen, Netherlands
Material: steel
Built for: Bibby Line

Like the *Marinor*, many late 20th-century products carriers were built for a very precise purpose; this specialisation ensured that they would be as economic as possible to operate.

MARY MURRAY

USA: 1938

Mary Murray was one of the famous passenger and vehicle ferries which linked Staten Island with Manhattan. These were some of the simplest ships, with a large unencumbered vehicle deck surmounted by open-sided passenger accommodation, atop which sat a pilot house giving an all-round view – a very necessary attribute in what was one of the world's busiest waterways. She retired from service in the 1960s, and there were plans, unrealised, to turn her into a floating restaurant.

Tonnage: 2126 grt
Dimensions: 252ft 6in x 47ft 9in (76.95m x 14.55m)
Machinery: two-shaft, compound; 4000hp
Service speed: not known
Role: passenger/vehicle ferry
Route: Staten Island–Manhattan (New York Harbour)
Capacity: not known
Constructor: United Shipyards, Staten Island, NY
Material: steel
Built for: City of New York

The Staten Island ferries take 20-30 minutes to make the 6.2-mile (10km) trip between St George's Terminal and the Whitehall terminal in Manhattan.

MATSONIA (LATER ETOLIN)

USA: 1913

Tonnage: 9728 grt
Dimensions: 480ft 6in x 58ft x 30ft 6in (146m x 17.5m x 9m)
Machinery: one-shaft, triple expansion; 9000hp
Service speed: 15 knots
Role: passenger/cargo liner; armed transport
Route: Hawaii–San Francisco
Capacity: 251 1st, 78 3rd; 9900 dwt
Constructor: Newport News Shipbuilding and Dry Dock Co
Built for: Matson Navigation Co

Matson Lines' *Matsonia* combined a large cargo capacity of 9900 dwt with accommodation for over 300 passengers. She was one of the first large passenger liners to carry the machinery aft. *Matsonia* was flush decked with a long superstructure which started well forward and continued unbroken almost to the stern. She was laid up from 1932 to 1937, when she was bought by the Alaska Packers Association, who owned her until 1940. She later passed to the US government; she was sold for scrapping in 1957.

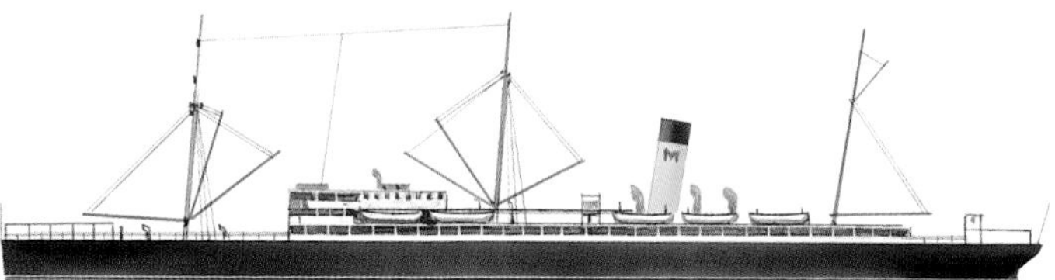

Matsonia was armed with four 6in (152mm) guns in World War I and was used by the US Army in World War II.

MEIJI MARU

JAPAN: 1874

The *Meiji Maru* had a very mixed career indeed; she was constructed in Glasgow as the imperial yacht and was subsequently taken over by the Japanese lighthouse service for use as a tender. Following that she was modified to carry a full ship's rig and became a sail training ship, operated by the Mercantile Marine University. When she began to deteriorate she was turned into a stationary drill ship, and more recently became a permanent onshore exhibit.

Although built as a steamship, *Meiji Maru* always carried auxiliary sail, so it was no difficult matter to rig her as a sail training ship.

Tonnage: 1038 grt
Dimensions: 249ft 4in x 28ft (76m x 8.55m)
Machinery: one-shaft, compound
Role: imperial yacht; lighthouse tender; sail training ship; drill ship
Route: not applicable
Capacity: not applicable
Constructor: R Napier & Sons, Glasgow
Material: iron
Built for: Japanese government
Owner: Mercantile Marine University, Tokyo

MICHELANGELO

ITALY: 1962

The *Michelangelo* and her sistership the *Raffaello* were once the biggest passenger ships in Italian service and were very distinctive in appearance, being dominated by lattice-cased funnels with enormous platform caps. By 1970, they were costing the Italian government $700 in subsidies for every passenger carried. In 1977, they were sold to the government of Iran for use as barrack ships; *Raffaello* was sunk by Iraqi missiles in 1983, and *Michelangelo* was scrapped in 1992.

Tonnage: 45,911 grt
Dimensions: 902ft x 102ft x 34ft (276.2m x 30.1m x 10.35m)
Machinery: two-shaft, geared turbines; 87,000hp
Service speed: 26.5 knots
Role: passenger liner; cruise ship; accommodation ship
Route: Genoa–New York
Capacity: 535 1st, 550 cb, 690 tr
Constructor: Ansaldo, Genoa
Material: steel
Built for: Italia Line

Part of the reason that the *Michelangelo* and the *Raffaello* were uneconomical was their very high performance; in 1966, with new propellers fitted, *Michelangelo* managed 31.59 knots.

MIGHTY SERVANT 3

NETHERLANDS: 1984

The *Mighty Servant 3* was a semi-submersible heavy-lift ship, specially designed for the transportation of very large objects up to 25,000t in weight. She could take on water ballast sufficient to allow her to be lowered by 33 feet (10m), permitting ships with up to 23 feet (7m) of draught to be loaded. In addition, she had a hold with a capacity of 423, 776 cubic feet (12,000 cubic metres), accessible by means of a large hatch and served by a 250-t-capacity crane.

Tonnage: 23,600 grt
Dimensions: 590ft 6in x 131ft 4in x 39ft 5in (180m x 40m x 12m)
Machinery: two-shaft, diesel-electric plus bow thrusters; 16,610hp
Service speed: 14 knots
Role: heavy-lift ship
Route: not applicable
Capacity: 24,800 dwt
Constructor: Oshima, Nagasaki
Material: steel
Built for: Wijsmuller Transport

Instead of using pumps to fill and void the ballast tanks, *Mighty Servant 3* used air compressors with a capacity of 423,776 cubic feet (12,000 cubic metres) per hour.

MINNEHAHA

GB: 1900

Built for service on the London–New York route with the small Atlantic Transport Line, the *Minnehaha* sank a tug in New York Harbour on her maiden voyage. Ten years later, she ran aground on the Scilly Isles; she was refloated, but it was six months before she was back in service. On 7 September 1917, she was torpedoed and sunk 12 nautical miles (19.3km) off the Fastnet Rock by the German submarine *U 48*, with the loss of 43 lives.

The Atlantic Transport Line's *Minnehaha* carried a mix of passengers and freight on the secondary North Atlantic route linking London with New York.

Tonnage: 13,443 grt
Dimensions: 600ft 8in x 65ft 6in (183.1m x 19.95m)
Machinery: two-shaft, quadruple expansion
Service speed: 16 knots
Role: passenger/cargo liner
Route: London–New York
Capacity: 250 1st, other classes not known
Constructor: Harland & Wolff, Belfast
Material: steel
Built for: Atlantic Transport Line

MINNEKAHDA

GB: 1917

Tonnage: 17,221 grt
Dimensions: 620ft 6in x 66ft 4in (189.1m x 20.25m)
Machinery: three-shaft, triple expansion plus turbine
Service speed: 15 knots
Role: troopship; passenger/cargo liner
Route: UK–Canada; New York–London; New York–Hamburg
Capacity: 2150 3rd
Constructor: Harland & Wolff, Belfast
Material: steel
Built for: Atlantic Transport Line

The *Minnekahda* was four years in the building, thanks to World War I, and when she entered service it was as a troopship, between the UK and Canada. She was returned to mercantile service, carrying cargo between London and New York, in 1920, and later that year was extensively rebuilt by Bethlehem Steel to provide third-class accommodation for 2150 people. After that, she operated mostly on the New York–Hamburg route under the American flag. She was laid up in New York in 1931 and scrapped five years later.

Like many ships built by Harland & Wolff, the *Minnekahda* had composite reciprocating and turbine machinery, 'exhaust' steam from the triple-expansion engines driving a low-pressure turbine.

MISSOURIAN (LATER GENOVA)

USA: 1922

Missourian was one of only two large US cargo liners fitted with diesel engines. She was sold, together with 90 other US cargo vessels, to the British Ministry of War Transport in 1940. In 1946, she was reconstructed for service between Genoa and the River Plate carrying labourers. Rebuilt again in 1955, she received increased superstructure and more lavish accommodation. Now renamed *Genova*, she changed roles and owners several times. During her 48 years of service, the vessel was owned by five different nations and had at least eight different trades.

***Missourian* as she appeared when she carried pilgrims to Jeddah, one of her many roles. She was scrapped in 1970.**

Tonnage: 16,500 grt
Dimensions: 461ft 8in x 59ft 10in x 28ft 7in (130.6m x 18.2m x 8.7m)
Machinery: two-shaft, diesel; 4500hp (later 7200hp)
Service speed: 14.5 knots
Role: general cargo vessel etc
Route: Genoa–River Plate etc

MOLLIETTE

GB: 1919

Tonnage: 293 dwt
Dimensions: 131ft x 25ft x 9ft 9in (40m x 7.6m x 3m)
Machinery: one-shaft, diesel; 120hp
Service speed: 7 knots
Role: sea-going barge
Route: not applicable
Material: concrete
Built for: B Oppenheimer

Reinforced concrete was adopted as a construction material in the shipbuilding industry in the United Kingdom towards the end of World War I, when the country

The concrete ship *Molliette* was an unusual shape, with its straight sides and lack of curves. Crew were berthed forward and officers aft in a wooden cabin.

was faced with an urgent need to replace merchant shipping losses but lacked both skilled labour and more conventional materials. Admiralty-sponsored construction programmes focussed on producing sea-going barges of up to 1000dwt, at sites not tradionally associated with shipbuilding and employing an unskilled workforce, and the first vessel produced was the *Molliette*.

MOUNT CLINTON

USA: 1921

After the end of World War I, thanks to late large-scale construction, there was a surfeit of merchant shipping, and it was some years before further new building re-commenced; *Mount Clinton* and her sistership, *Mount Carol*, were the first to be laid down for private owners in the USA, and were not launched until 1921. to meet the changing needs of the times both vessels were converted to carry a large number of emigrants, up to 1500 per trip. As the emigrant trade was from Europe to the US, the cabins, on two upper decks, were designed for quick assembly and removal, so that on the return trip to Europe the space could be used for cargo. She was sold to the Matson Line in 1925 and carried sugar and pineapples from Hawaii to the United States; she was sold on twice more before being scrapped in 1954.

Tonnage: 15,000 grt
Dimensions: 457ft x 57ft x 28ft 9in (139m x 17.2m x 8.8m)
Machinery: one-shaft, turbine; 4200hp
Service speed: 13 knots
Role: emigrant ship; sugar/fruit carrier
Route: New York-Hamburg; Hawaii-USA
Capacity: 1500 (later 585) st
Constructor: Merchant Shipbuilding Corporation
Built for: Shawncut Steamship Co Inc, NY

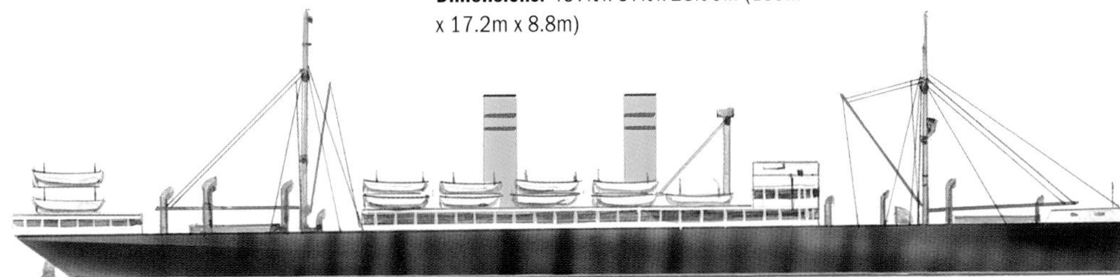

***Mount Clinton* as completed in 1922 had a continuous superstructure with double-stacked lifeboats to cater for the 1500 passengers plus crew.**

NALDERA

GB: 1917

The *Naldera* was one of many passenger/cargo liners in service with the P&O Line, which maintained an essential link between Britain and the Empire in the Far East for over a hundred years.

The P&O Line ordered the *Naldera* for use in its Far Eastern service in 1914, but the onset of World War I meant that work was delayed, and she was then taken up incomplete by the Admiralty, with the intention of arming her as a merchant cruiser. This work was not begun, however, and she was belatedly delivered to P&O at the war's end, to be completed as originally planned. She entered service in 1920 and was scrapped in 1938.

Tonnage: 23,000 grt
Dimensions: 600ft x 67ft 6in x 29ft 3in (182.8m x 20.6m x 8.9m)
Machinery: two-shaft, quadruple expansion
Service speed: 16 knots
Role: passenger/cargo liner
Route: UK-Far East
Material: steel
Built for: Peninsular & Oriental Steam Navigation Co

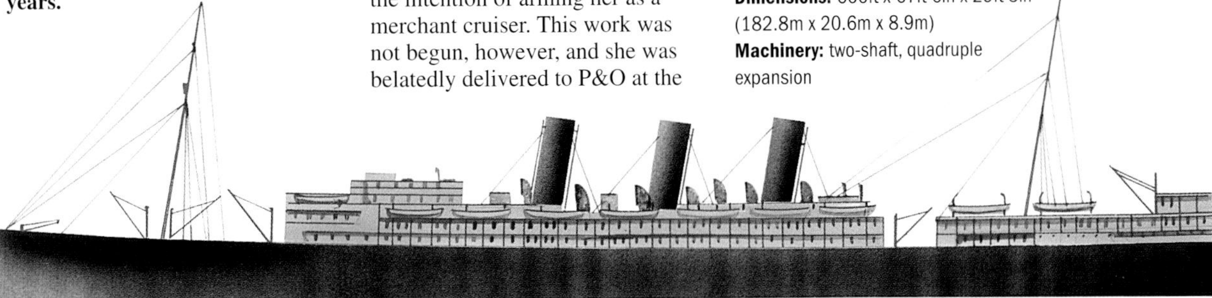

NATCHEZ

USA: 1869

Tonnage: 1547 grt
Dimensions: 301ft x 42ft 6in (91.7m x 13m)
Machinery: sidewheels, engine type not known
Service speed: 10 knots
Role: riverboat
Route: New Orleans-St Louis
Capacity: not known
Constructor: Cincinnati Marine Ways, Cincinnati, Oh
Material: wood
Built for: Thomas P Leathers

The *Natchez* of 1869 was the sixth of seven riverboats of the same name built for Thomas P Leathers. Said to be an ungainly-looking craft, she soon had a well-deserved reputation for speed; in 1870, she steamed the 1039 miles (1672km) from New Orleans to St Louis at an average of 11.17 knots, breaking a record which had stood for 25 years. She was perhaps best known for the celebrated (but inconclusive) race against the *Rob't E Lee* that same year. She remained in service until 1879.

Sidewheelers, such as the *Natchez* and the *Rob't E Lee*, were much more manoeuvrable and faster than sternwheel riverboats.

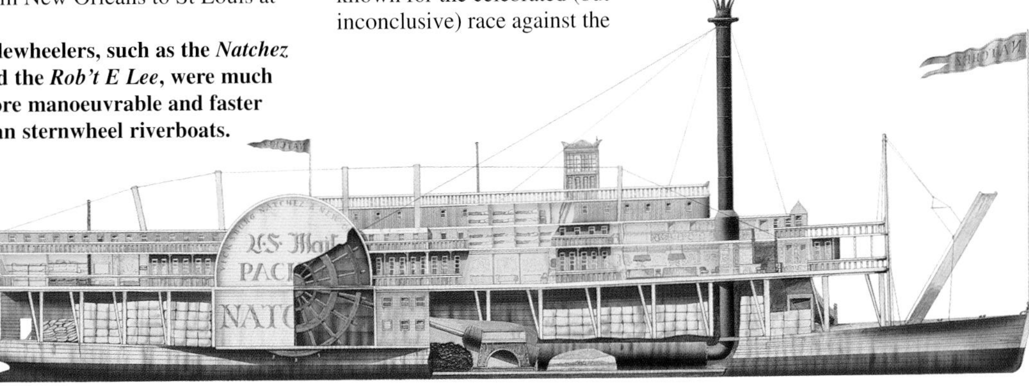

NEDLLOYD EUROPA

NETHERLANDS: 1991

Tonnage: 48,508 grt
Dimensions: 872ft 9in x 105ft 10in x 41ft (266m x 32.25m x 12.5m)
Machinery: one-shaft, diesel; 41,600hp
Service speed: 23.5 knots
Role: general cargo vessel
Route: NW Europe–Far East
Capacity: 3568 TEU
Constructor: Mitsubishi Heavy Industries, Kobe
Material: steel
Built for: P&O Nedlloyd

The container guide system used in the *Nedlloyd Europa* was less flexible than other methods, 20-ft and 40-ft containers not being interchangeable.

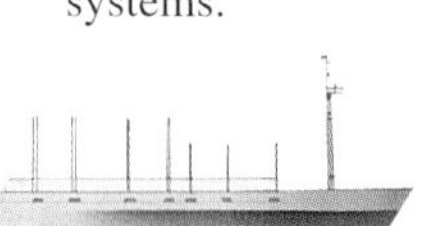

P&O Nedlloyd's fast container ship *Nedlloyd Europa* was the second of a class of five ships originally built for service between Europe and the Far East. They were the result of a development programme aimed at maximising carrying capacity on minimum gross tonnage; they dispensed with hatch covers, container stacks being aligned by guides which reached down to the hull sole. They were equipped with duplicated pumping and drainage systems.

NERISSA

GB: 1926

The *Nerissa*'s strengthened hull and stem profile allowed her to navigate in broken ice, an important asset when Halifax was a port of call.

The passenger/cargo liner *Nerissa* was built for the New York, Newfoundland & Halifax Steam Ship Co (the Red Cross Line), with a strengthened hull to allow her to navigate in ice. She passed to the Bermuda & West Indies Steamship Co (a subsidiary of Furness Withy) in 1929, and in 1939 was chartered to an associate, the Warren Line, for service between the UK and Canada. On 30 April 1941, she was torpedoed and sunk some 200 miles (320km) west of Ireland on an eastbound voyage from Halifax.

Tonnage: 5583 grt
Dimensions: 349ft 6in x 54ft 4in x 29ft 8in (106.5m x 16.55m x 6.3m)
Machinery: one-shaft, triple expansion
Service speed: 14 knots
Role: passenger/cargo liner
Route: Liverpool–New York; New York–Caribbean; Liverpool–Halifax
Capacity: 162 1st, 66 2nd
Constructor: W Hamilton & Co, Port Glasgow
Material: steel
Built for: New York, Newfoundland & Halifax Steam Ship Co

NIEUW AMSTERDAM

NETHERLANDS: 1937

The *Nieuw Amsterdam* was the second vessel of that name; like her predecessor, she operated on the Rotterdam–New York service. She made her last pre-war Atlantic crossing in September 1939 and then sailed as a cruise ship out of New York before converting to a troopship a year later. She returned to mercantile service in October 1947 after a refit, having sailed over half a million miles (800,000km) as a troopship. She was used for cruising from 1971 and was scrapped in 1974.

The *Nieuw Amsterdam* was designed and constructed with economy, rather than record breaking, in mind and enjoyed a long useful career as a result.

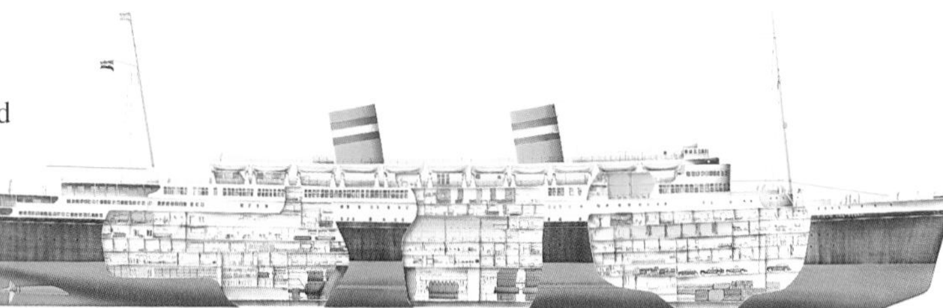

Tonnage: 36,287 grt
Dimensions: 758ft 6in x 88ft 4in (231.2m x 26.9m)
Machinery: two-shaft, geared turbines
Service speed: 20.5 knots
Role: passenger liner; troopship; cruise ship
Route: Rotterdam–New York
Capacity: 556 cb, 455 tr, 209 3rd; 552 1st, 426 cb, 209 tr
Constructor: Rotterdamsche Droogdok Mij, Rotterdam
Material: steel
Built for: Holland America Line

NORILSK

USSR: 1982

Tonnage: 14,000 grt
Dimensions: 570ft x 80ft 4in x 29ft 6in (174m x 24.5m x 9m)
Machinery: one-shaft, diesel; 21,000hp
Service speed: 12 knots
Role: general cargo vessel
Route: Arctic Ocean, North Pacific Ocean
Capacity: 576 TEU
Constructor: Wärtsilä, Helsinki
Material: steel
Built for: Murmansk Shipping Co

Many experts hold that the most significant advance in merchant shipping in the latter part of the 20th century was the opening up of the Arctic routes. Some of the most important vessels sailing those routes were the Russian SA-15-type, *Norilsk*-class ice-breaker/cargo ships, 18 of which were built in the mid-1980s by Wärtsilä and Valmet in Finland. These 20,000dwt ro-ro ships, able to carry 576 20-ft containers, could maintain way in ice up to 39 inches (1m) thick; their five cranes made them largely self-sufficient.

NORMAN

GB: 1894

When the Union Line and the Castle Packet Co merged in 1900, the former's *Norman* was the new undertaking's most important ship and had already made almost 50 voyages between Southampton and South Africa. She had luxurious accommodation for up to 250 in first class and also had limited third class accommodation for emigrants. She was a troopship during the Boer War and again in World War I. Laid up in 1925, she was demolished the following year.

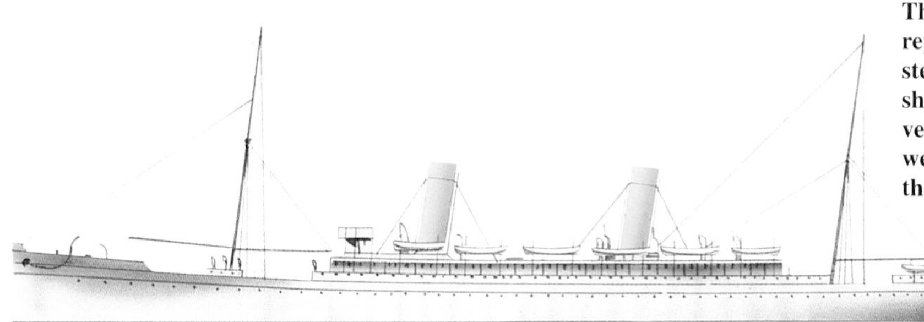

The *Norman* was representative of mail steamers of the period; she and eight other vessels maintained a weekly service between the UK and South Africa.

Tonnage: 13,400 grt
Dimensions: 507ft x 53ft 2in x 27ft 9in (154.5m x 16.2m x 8.5m)
Machinery: two-shaft, triple expansion
Service speed: 15 knots
Role: passenger liner; troopship
Route: Southampton–South Africa
Capacity: 250 1st, 100 3rd
Constructor: not known
Material: steel
Built for: Union Line

NORMANDIE (LATER USS LAFAYETTE) FRANCE: 1935

Tonnage: 79,280 (later 82,799, later 83,423) grt
Dimensions: 1029ft x 117ft 10in x 33ft 6in (313.6m x 35.7m x 10.2m)
Machinery: four-shaft, turbo-electric; 165,000hp
Service speed: 29 knots
Role: passenger liner
Route: Le Havre–New York
Capacity: 848 1st, 670 tr, 454 3rd
Constructor: Chantiers et Ateliers de l'Atlantique, St Nazaire
Material: steel
Built for: Compagnie Générale Transatlantique

The *Normandie*'s story is one of superlatives. She was the biggest liner of her day (and a new dry dock had to be built specially for her), the most expensive (at over $60 million, much of it contributed by the French government), the most powerful (with machinery developing 165,000hp), the fastest (and the only French ship ever to hold the Blue Riband), the most extravagantly decorated (by all the great names of the period)… Aesthetically she was superb, her three funnels raked and reducing in height, moving aft. (The third funnel was actually a ventilator; there were no others to be seen.) Mechanically she was less than perfect to begin with and was plagued by vibration which was cured only by substituting four-bladed for three-bladed propellers, but she certainly lived up to expectations concerning her performance, taking both westbound and eastbound Blue Ribands (the latter at an average speed of 30.3 knots) on her maiden voyage. She was to lose the record to the new Cunarder, the *Queen Mary*, and although she won it back again in March 1937, she lost it for good in August 1938. Laid up in New York in August 1939 and taken over by the US Navy as the USS *Lafayette* in December 1941, she was destroyed just days before she was due to enter service in February 1943, by a fire started in stored bedding by a careless welder; she capsized in New York Harbour as a result of all the water pumped into her in an attempt to extinguish the blaze. She was eventually sold for scrap for just $160,000.

The principal first-class accommodation aboard the *Normandie* consisted of a pair of suites on the Sun Deck; each had four double bedrooms (each with its own bath), a sitting room and a dining room with a serving pantry.

NORMANNIA

GB: 1911

The *Normannia* and her sistership the *Hantonia* were built to link Southampton and Le Havre and were the first merchant ships to be fitted with the single-reduction geared turbine machinery which Charles Parsons developed in 1910, and more economical than earlier direct-drive turbine machinery. The pair made three Channel crossings a day each for over a quarter of a century.

The success of the small turbine installation in the *Normannia* convinced shipping companies to make the switch away from reciprocating machinery even for quite small vessels.

Tonnage: 1567 grt
Dimensions: 290ft 3in x 36ft 1in x 12ft 3in (88.5m x 11m x 3.75m)
Machinery: two-shaft, geared turbine; 6000hp
Service speed: 19.5 knots
Role: passenger ferry
Route: Southampton–Le Havre
Constructor: Fairfield Shipbuilding & Engineering Co, Glasgow
Material: steel
Built for: London & South Western Railway Co

OCEANIC

GB: 1870

The first *Oceanic*, which entered service between Liverpool and New York in the spring of 1871, was the first White Star liner. She was innovative chiefly in her accommodation: her very spacious first-class quarters were amidships instead of aft, and for the first time there was a promenade deck. After four years on the Atlantic she was chartered to run between San Francisco and Hong Kong and spent the rest of her life in that service. She was scrapped in 1896.

Tonnage: 3707 grt
Dimensions: 420ft x 40ft 10in (128m x 12.45m)
Machinery: one-shaft, compound
Service speed: 14 knots
Role: passenger liner
Route: Liverpool–New York; San Francisco–Hong Kong
Capacity: 166 1st, 1000 3rd
Constructor: Harland & Wolff, Belfast
Material: iron
Built for: White Star Line

The *Oceanic* and her three near-sisters established the newcomer White Star Line as a serious rival to Cunard and Inman on the North Atlantic route.

OCEANIC

GB: 1899

The White Star Line's second *Oceanic* was probably intended originally to take the Blue Riband, which the line had last held in 1891, but by the time she was launched *Kaiser Wilhelm der Grosse* had taken the average speed to 22.35 knots, and the idea was abandoned. Instead, her designers concentrated

There is a lasting suspicion that the *Oceanic* was indeed meant to take the Blue Riband but that she fell short of the mark on trial and the attempt was never made.

Tonnage: 17,272 grt
Dimensions: 685ft 8in x 68ft 4in (209m x 20.85m)
Machinery: two-shaft, triple expansion
Service speed: 19 knots
Role: passenger liner; armed merchant cruiser
Route: Liverpool–New York; Southampton–New York
Capacity: 410 1st, 300 2nd, 1000 3rd
Constructor: Harland & Wolff, Belfast
Material: steel
Built for: White Star Line

on improving the standard of accommodation in all three classes. She marked a turning point in company policy in this respect, and it soon became clear that many seasoned travellers preferred to travel at a somewhat more leisurely pace in greater comfort. That is not to say that generally the competition for the Blue Riband became any less important, but the option was one which was to remain attractive; White Star never had another record-breaker while it remained independent. *Oceanic* was to be the biggest ship of her day and the first to exceed the dimensions (although not the tonnage) of the *Great Eastern*. On her maiden voyage to New York, she took a little over six days from Queenstown (Cork) to Sandy Hook, at an average speed of 19.57 knots, so she was no sluggard in real terms – the record at the time was only four and a half hours shorter. She continued to run between Liverpool and New York until 1907 and was then switched over to Southampton, which allowed her to call at Cherbourg. She remained in service until the outbreak of World War I, when she was taken up as an armed merchant cruiser, a role she had been designed to fulfil at need. She was wrecked in the Shetlands just weeks later.

OSCAR HUBER (EX-WILHELM VON OSWALD, FRITZ THYSSEN) GERMANY: 1922

The *Oscar Huber* was an example of the type of large sidewheel steam tug once common on the Rhine, where such vessels were used to pull strings of dumb barges. This particular craft was returned, on her retirement, to Duisburg, where she had been constructed, and preserved as a museum exhibit.

A notable feature of the Rhine sidewheel tugs was their shallow draught.

Tonnage: 200t displacement
Dimensions: 246ft x 67ft 10in x 5ft 1in (75m x 20.7m x 1.55m)
Machinery: sidewheels, triple expansion; 1550hp
Service speed: not known
Role: river tug
Route: River Rhine
Capacity: not applicable
Constructor: Ewald Berninghaus, Duisburg
Material: steel
Built for: not known
Owner: Museum für Deutsche Binnenschiffahrt

PARISIAN GB: 1880

The Allan Line's single-screw steamer *Parisian* was the first steel liner on the North Atlantic route and, temporarily at least, the largest; she was also the first to have bilge keels. In 1882, when the *Alaska* held the Blue Riband, having crossed from Sandy Hook to Queenstown (Cork) in six days and 22 hours, she made the passage from Rimouski, on the St Lawrence, to Moville, the port of Londonderry, in six days and 14 hours. In 1899, by which time she had made over 150 round-trip crossings, she was re-engined with triple-expansion machinery, her second funnel was removed and her sailing rig was reduced to pole masts. Until 1905, she operated out of Liverpool, to Quebec and Montreal in the summer months, when the St Lawrence was ice free, and to Halifax and St John, New Brunswick, with occasional extensions to Boston, in the winter. Later she was relegated to the second-class service from Glasgow. She rescued some survivors from the *Titanic*. She was scrapped in 1914.

Tonnage: 5359 grt
Dimensions: 440ft 9in x 46ft 2in (134.35m x 14.1m)
Machinery: one-shaft, compound (later triple-expansion)
Service speed: 14 knots
Role: passenger liner
Route: UK-Canada
Capacity: 150 1st, 100 2nd, 1000 3rd
Constructor: R Napier & Sons, Glasgow
Material: steel
Built for: Allan Line

The *Parisian* was an outstandingly successful ship, criss-crossing the North Atlantic for over three decades; the expense of re-engining her was well justified.

PARRAMATTA GB: 1866

The Blackwall frigates took their name from the Green and Wigram Yard on the Thames, where the first example, the *Seringapatam*, was constructed in 1837. They were built almost exclusively of teak from Burma.

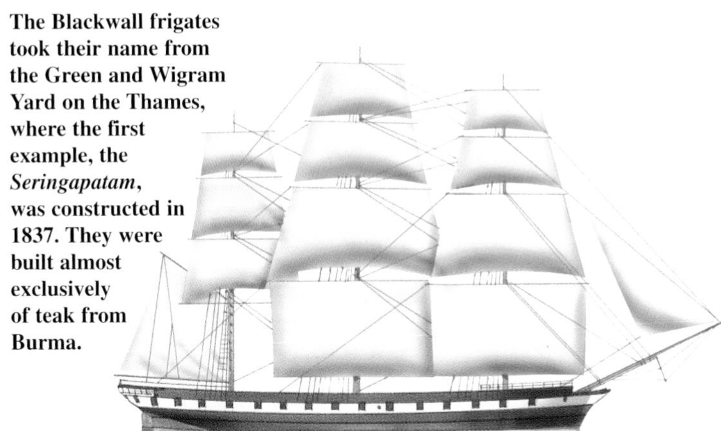

Though the change-over to iron construction for ocean-going ships began in earnest during the 1840s, relatively large vessels were still being built in wood even up to the early 1870s. A few, like the *Parramatta*, were so-called Blackwall frigates (the type originated in the 1830s at the Blackwall Yard on the Thames, hence the name; they were called frigates because they bore the same relationship to the other 'East Indiamen', alongside which they originally operated). *Parramatta* was the last major ship her builders, James Laing of Sunderland and was one of the largest wooden merchant ships ever launched. By the time she entered service the cost of iron construction was some 30 percent lower – around £14 per ton, as opposed to £20 – than that of a wooden ship.

Tonnage: 1521 grt
Dimensions: 185ft x 40ft (56m x 12m)
Role: passenger and wool carrier
Route: UK-Australia
Constructor: James Laing
Material: wood

PENANG (EX-ALBERT RICKMERS) GERMANY: 1905

The *Penang*, originally built for the constructor's own account for the rice trade, and launched as the *Albert Rickmers*, was sold to Ferdinand Laeisz in 1911, and renamed in keeping with the Flying 'P' Line's policy (she passed through other hands later, but was never renamed again). She was a three-masted barque, square-rigged on the fore and main and fore-and-aft rigged on the mizzen, and was one of the most famous, thanks to her having been acquired, like so many fine ships of the period, by Gustaf Erikson of Mariehamn, who kept her in service until 1940, when she was torpedoed, on 10 December, by a German submarine, *U140*, off the south coast of Ireland, with the loss of all hands. She was widely held to have been under-canvassed (though nonetheless she made many fast passages between Southern Hemisphere ports and Europe, carrying nitrates and grain), and was very unstable when imperfectly ballasted – she capsized in a gale in 1926, but was recovered, and almost did so again in 1931.

The three-masted barque was cheaper to fit out and man than a three-masted ship, and there was very little difference in performance between the two.

Tonnage: 2039 grt
Dimensions: 265ft 6in x 40ft x 24ft 6in (81m x 12.2m x 7.55m)
Role: nitrate and grain carrier
Route: Australia/Chile-Europe
Capacity: 3300 dwt
Constructor: Rickmers AG
Material: steel
Built for: Rickmers AG

PENNSYLVANIA (LATER NANSEMOND) GERMANY: 1896

Tonnage: 12,891 (later 13,333) grt
Dimensions: 557ft 6in x 62ft (169.9m x 18.9m)
Machinery: two-shaft, quadruple expansion
Service speed: 14 knots
Role: passenger liner
Route: Hamburg-New York
Capacity: 162 1st, 197 2nd, 2382 3rd; 404 2nd, 2200 3rd
Constructor: Harland & Wolff, Belfast
Material: steel
Built for: Hamburg-Amerikanische Packetfahrt AG

The Belfast-built *Pennsylvania* was the biggest ship the Hamburg American Line had put into service up to that point and was soon to be joined by three near-sisters. The emigrant trade was at its height, and each carried well in excess of 2000 third-class passengers between Hamburg and New York on a weekly sailing schedule. *Pennsylvania* was laid up in New York from 1914 and was taken over by the US government as the *Nansemond* in 1917. She was scrapped in 1924.

The *Pennsylvania* carried more on a single voyage than all the ships which Hapag had on its foundation, half a century earlier, could carry in a year.

POMMERN (SOMETIME MNEME) GERMANY: 1903

Tonnage: 2376 grt
Dimensions: 310ft 6in x 43ft 4in x 22ft (94.65m x 13.2m x 6.7m)
Machinery: not applicable
Service speed: not applicable
Role: general cargo vessel; bagged grain carrier
Route: Europe-Australia
Constructor: J Reid & Co, Greenock
Material: steel
Built for: B Wencke Sohn
Owner: City of Mariehamn

Built in Scotland for a Hamburg shipowner, the four-masted steel barque *Pommern* passed, like many of the last generation of 'windjammers', into the ownership of Gustaf Erikson of Mariehamn in the Finnish Åland Islands. He operated her alongside the *Herzogin Cecilie*, *Lawhill*, *Pamir* and *Peking*, to name but some. She was laid up at Mariehamn at the outbreak of World War II and was later given to the city, which maintains her as an exhibit afloat.

The *Pommern* is the last vessel of the large 20th-century Åland Islands sailing fleet to remain there; she is an exhibit at Mariehamn.

PORTLAND

USA: 1947

Tonnage: 928 grt
Dimensions: 186ft x 42ft x 7ft (56.7m x 12.8m x 2.15m)
Machinery: sternwheel, engine type not known; 1800hp
Service speed: not known
Role: river/harbour service craft
Route: Columbia River
Capacity: not applicable
Constructor: Northwest Marine Iron Works, Portland, OR
Material: steel
Built for: Port Authority of Portland
Owner: Port Authority of Portland

Although they were much less efficient than vessels with screw propellers, sternwheelers had important advantages as riverboats – they were of relatively shallow draught and offered good resistance to snagging. Small numbers were built in the United States even after World War II, and some remained in operation as service craft into the 1980s; the last remaining example on the Columbia River in the Pacific Northwest was the *Portland*, which was preserved in the city from which she took her name.

The *Portland* was one of the last of the sternwheel river steamers and is preserved in original working condition.

POTOMAC (EX-ELECTRA)

USA: 1934

The *Potomac* was built as a Coast Guard cutter, specifically to interdict rum-runners during the era of Prohibition, and was converted to become the official yacht of US President Franklin D Roosevelt in 1936. She remained in service until replaced by USS *Williamsburg* in 1946 and was transferred to the State of Maryland's Tidewater Fisheries Commission until 1960, when she passed into private hands. She was eventually purchased by the City of Oakland and restored.

Somewhat ironically, considering her original role, the *Potomac* fell back into US government hands when she was seized in a drugs raid.

Tonnage: 416t displacement
Dimensions: 165ft x 23ft 9in x 8ft 2in (42.6m x 9.5m x 2.5m)
Machinery: two-shaft, diesel
Service speed: 13 knots
Role: Coast Guard cutter; presidential yacht
Route: not applicable
Capacity: not applicable
Constructor: Manitowoc Ship Building Co, Manitowoc, WI
Material: steel
Built for: US Coast Guard
Owner: Port of Oakland, Oakland, CA

PRESIDENT HARDING (EX-LONE STAR STATE, LATER VILLE DE BRUGES)

USA: 1921

Tonnage: 14,187 grt
Dimensions: 535ft x 72ft x 30ft 6in (132.7m x 22m x 9m)
Machinery: two-shaft, turbines; 12,000hp
Service speed: 19 knots
Role: passenger/cargo liner
Route: North Atlantic
Capacity: 320 1st, 324 3rd; 13,000 dwt
Constructor: New York Shipbuilding, Camden, NY
Material: steel
Built for: United States Lines

Originally intended as a follow-on design from a previous class of passenger ship, *President Harding* and her sistership *President Roosevelt* were later redesigned as far more ambitious ships that served in a regular way on the North Atlantic from 1922 to 1939. They were the largest merchantmen built in the US during World War I, with accommodation for 644 passengers and a cargo capacity of 13,000 dwt. *President Harding* was transferred in 1940 to a Belgian subsidiary, the Antwerp Navigation Co, and renamed *Ville de Bruges*; she was bombed and sunk by German aircraft in May 1940 whilst about to leave for the US.

***President Harding* was a major advance in merchant ship design and proved to be one of the most successful vessels on the North Atlantic route.**

PRESIDENTE SARMIENTO

ARGENTINA: 1897

The full-rigged ship *Presidente Sarmiento* was one of the first purpose-built sail training ships, constructed by Laird Brothers for the Argentine Navy in 1897. She remained in full commission for over 40 years, making annual cruises (six of them circumnavigations), before being reduced to a static training ship; she was finally decommissioned to become a floating museum in

Tonnage: 2750t displacement
Dimensions: 265ft x 43ft x 18ft 6in (80.75m x 13.1m x 5.65m)
Machinery: one-shaft, auxiliary triple expansion; 1000hp
Service speed: not applicable
Role: sail training ship
Route: not applicable
Capacity: not applicable
Constructor: Laird Bros, Birkenhead
Material: steel
Built for: Argentine Navy
Owner: Argentine Navy

absolutely original condition, complete with her three-cylinder vertical triple-expansion steam auxiliary machinery, in Buenos Aires in 1961.

The *Presidente Sarmiento*, immaculately restored to her original condition and preserved in Buenos Aires, was the last survivor of the first generation of purpose-built sail training ships.

PREUSSEN

GERMANY: 1902

On her one indirect voyage to Chile, chartered by the Standard Oil Co to carry lamp oil from New York to Yokohama via the Cape of Good Hope, *Preussen* ran 3019 nautical miles (5591km) in 11 days, an average speed of over 11.4 knots.

The *Preussen* of 1902 was the second ship of the name built for Ferdinand Laeisz's Flying P Line; she was one of only four five-masted square-riggers ever built and the only one rigged as a ship (the others were all barques). She was also the largest vessel ever built without propulsive machinery of any sort, although she did have auxiliary power for winches, capstans and pumps in the shape of two deck-mounted steam engines. She set a total of 43 sails, with a total area of 59,848 square feet (5565.9 square metres). While the ship rig was more difficult to handle than the barque rig, and thus required a larger crew and was in turn more expensive, it offered a slight increase in speed, and the *Preussen* was very fast indeed. Between 1902 and 1910, she made 12 direct voyages to Chile (the other was by way of New York and Yokohama, carrying lamp oil) from Northern Europe in an average time of 65 days. Her 13 return voyages averaged 73 days, and her best westbound voyage, in 1903, took just 55 days, while her best return, in 1905, took just 57 days. The *Preussen* had but a short career. On her 14th voyage to Chile, in November 1910, she was run down by the *Brighton*, a Newhaven–Dieppe ferry, which misjudged her speed and struck her abreast the foremast at 17 knots in foggy conditions. She anchored off Dungeness, but the chains parted in a squall; she was then taken in tow, but the hawsers also parted. She ran aground in Crab Bay and broke up there.

Tonnage: 5081 grt
Dimensions: 407ft 8in x 53ft 6in x 27ft 1in (124.25m x 16.3m x 8.25m)
Machinery: not applicable
Service speed: not applicable
Role: nitrate carrier
Route: Europe–Chile
Capacity: c4790t
Constructor: John Tecklenburg, Geestemünde
Material: steel
Built for: Reederei F Laeisz

PRINCESSE ELISABETH

BELGIUM: 1904

Tonnage: 1767 grt
Dimensions: 300ft x 36ft (91.5m x 11m)
Machinery: three-shaft, turbines; 12,000hp
Service speed: 24 knots
Role: passenger ferry
Route: Dover–Ostend
Capacity: c900
Constructor: John Cockerill, Hoboken
Material: steel
Built for: Belgian Marine Administration

In the service between Ostend and Dover the changeover from paddle wheels to turbine came in 1904 with the introduction of the *Princesse Elisabeth*. She had a designed speed of 24 knots, but during her trials off Greenock, Scotland, she achieved 26.25 knots, which made her the fastest merchant ship afloat. As a result of her success two more ships of a similar design were built, entering service in 1910, with two more slightly smaller versions following on shortly afterwards. However, none of these were as successful as the *Princesse Elisabeth* and it was not until 1922 that a ship added to this service could match her performance.

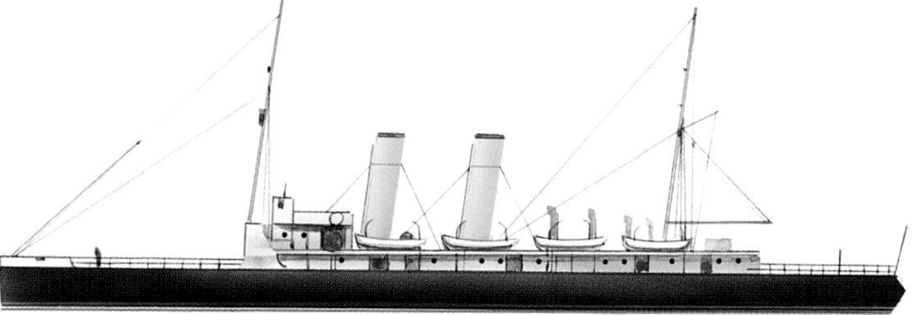

***Princesse Elisabeth* set a trend for fast ferry travel across the North Sea. She had a passenger capacity of over 900 and is shown as she looked in 1904.**

PRINCESS MARY

GB: 1929

Tonnage: 40 grt
Dimensions: 61ft x 15ft (18.6m x 4.6m)
Machinery: not known
Service speed: 9.5 knots
Role: rescue craft
Route: coastal waters, UK
Capacity: 130

The British lifeboat service was founded in 1824 by Colonel Sir William Hillary and has been responsible for the saving of many thousands of lives over the years. The *Princess Mary* was one of the best lifeboats afloat when first completed and showed a massive improvement over the earlier types that relied upon the crew to row out to a stricken vessel. The area around the engine room was packed with flotation boxes and the hull was built of two skins for added strength. The vessel could carry 130 people.

Stationed at north Cornwall, *Princess Mary* is shown with a light steadying rig in position.

QUEEN ELIZABETH (LATER ELIZABETH, SEAWISE UNIVERSITY)

GB: 1940

Built as a running mate for the *Queen Mary*, the *Queen Elizabeth* first saw service as a troopship. She entered commercial service between Southampton and New York in 1946. By the early 1960s, she was cruising in the winter months and was refitted for that role in 1965. Withdrawn three years later, she changed hands three times, ending up in Hong Kong, where she was converted to become an ocean-going university. Somewhat mysteriously she caught fire and capsized in 1972 and was scrapped in situ.

Tonnage: 83,673 (later 82,998) grt
Dimensions: 1030ft 6in x 118ft 6in (314.25m x 36.15m)
Machinery: four-shaft, geared turbines; 160,000hp
Service speed: 29 knots
Role: troopship; passenger liner; cruise ship; ocean-going university
Route: Indian Ocean; North Atlantic; Southampton–New York
Capacity: 5600 (later 15,000) troops; 823 1st, 662 cb, 798 tr
Constructor: John Brown & Co, Glasgow
Material: steel
Built for: Cunard-White Star Ltd

During her wartime service, *Queen Elizabeth* sailed alone, without escort, relying on her speed alone to keep her from harm.

QUEEN ELIZABETH 2

GB: 1967

Tonnage: 65,836 (later 67,107) grt
Dimensions: 963ft x 105ft x 32ft (293.5m x 32.1m x 9.75m)
Machinery: two-shaft, geared turbines (later diesel-electric); initial power figures not known (later 118,000 hp)
Service speed: 29 knots
Role: passenger liner; cruise ship; troopship
Route: Southampton–New York
Capacity: 564 1st, 1441 tr; 1820 sc
Constructor: John Brown & Co, Glasgow
Material: steel
Built for: Cunard Line

Anachronistic though she certainly was, the *QE 2*, as she was popularly known from the outset, was designed and built very much in the spirit of her predecessors, and did much to set the style for the giant cruise ships which came later.

The last Cunarder built for the transatlantic passenger service, *Queen Elizabeth 2* was an anachronism even before she was launched on 20 November 1967, for by then aircraft had long overtaken express liners as the preferred means of business and recreational travel from one point to another. From the outset she was plagued by mechanical problems – Cunard refused to accept her at first, and her maiden voyage was delayed by five months – and by 1971 she was said to be costing her owners £500,000 per year. During this phase of her career she was twice the subject of threats of terrorism.

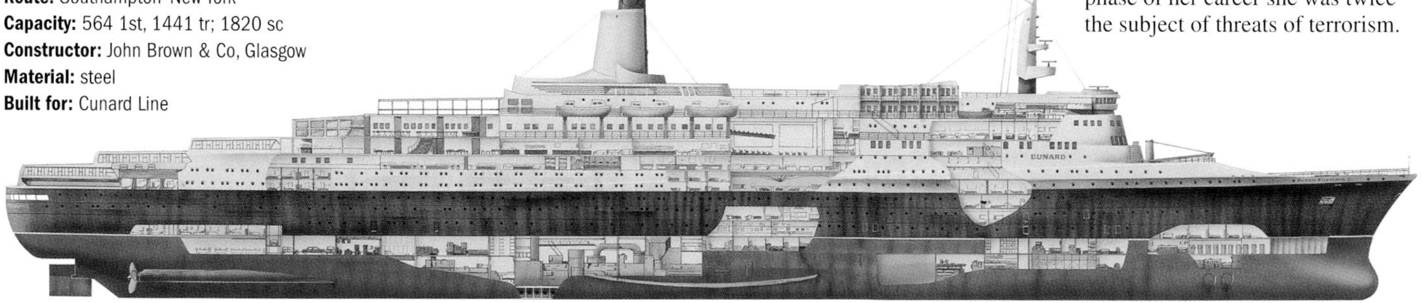

In 1972, the Royal Air Force delivered four bomb disposal experts to her in mid-Atlantic in response to what turned out to be a hoax aimed at extorting money. In 1973, while chartered for a cruise from New York to Israel to celebrate that country's 25th anniversary, she was targeted by Libya's President Gaddafi, who wanted her torpedoed; he was dissuaded from this course by the Egyptian president, Anwar Sadat. And that was not all – the following year she was left adrift off Bermuda after an engine failure; in 1975, she hit a coral reef off the Bahamas; and in 1976, she was partially crippled by an engine-room fire in the eastern Atlantic, which caused her to have to return to Southampton. In 1982, she redeemed herself in many eyes by her successful performance as a troopship during the Falklands War, and later, appropriately refitted and re-engined, she had an active career as a cruise ship. However, in 2000, she still made a number of scheduled North Atlantic crossings between Southampton and New York.

QUEEN MARY

GB: 1934

The *Queen Mary* was built to take the Blue Riband and was to hold the record, both ways, until 1952. Not that she was in any way an austere ship – she was a fitting successor to the *Aquitainia*, with which she operated pre-war. Wartime service as a troopship was marred by her colliding with and sinking the cruiser HMS *Curacoa* in October 1942; she was forbidden to stop to render assistance to the cruiser's crew, all but 26 of whom perished.

Tonnage: 80,744 (later 81,237) grt
Dimensions: 1019ft 6in x 118ft 7in (310.75m x 36.15m)
Machinery: four-shaft, geared turbines; 160,000hp
Service speed: 29 knots
Role: passenger liner; troopship
Route: Southampton-New York
Capacity: 776 cb, 784 tr, 579 3rd; 15,000 troops; 711 1st, 707 cb, 577 tr
Constructor: John Brown & Co, Glasgow
Material: steel
Built for: Cunard-White Star Line

The *Queen Mary* completed 1001 Atlantic crossings in mercantile service. She was sold to the City of Long Beach, California, as a museum and hotel in 1967. To reach her new home she had to round Cape Horn, being too wide – by 39 inches (1m) – to pass through the Panama Canal.

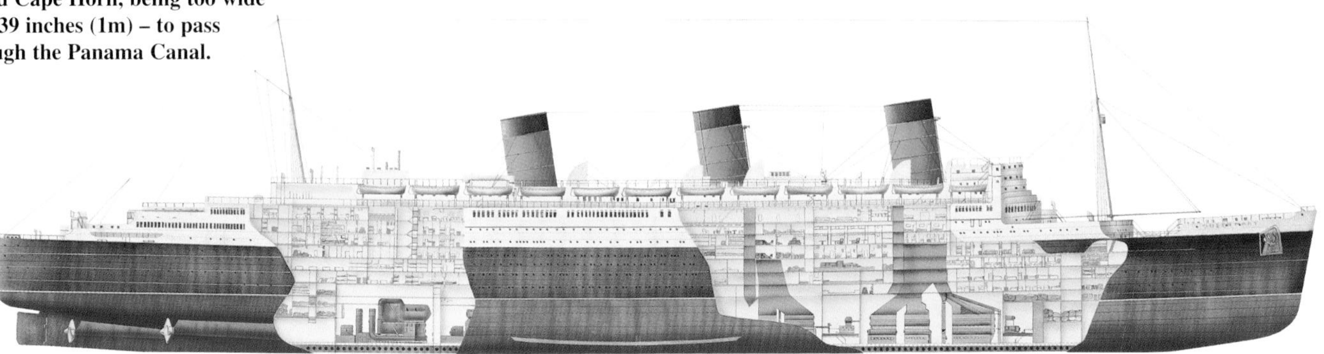

RADISSON DIAMOND

FINLAND: 1991

By the end of the 20th century, cruise ships were little more than enormous floating luxury hotels, but the *Radisson Diamond* was slightly different. Much smaller than most, she was based on a catamaran hull form and had a length to beam ratio of little more than 4:1, which both maximised the deck area and improved her seakeeping and manoeuvrability. Her machinery was located low down in each hull and thus was removed from the passenger areas, which made her very quiet indeed.

Amongst the *Radisson Diamond*'s more unusual attractions were a 295-yard (270m) jogging track and a hydraulic platform which could be lowered to the waterline between the hulls aft to act as a boat dock.

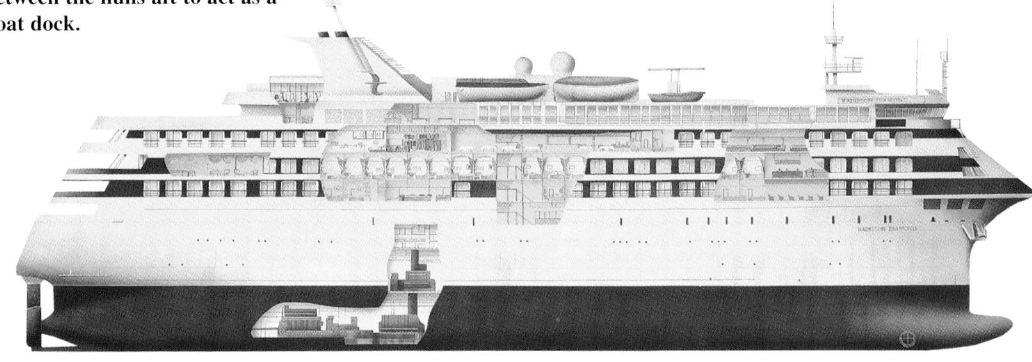

Tonnage: 18,400 grt
Dimensions: 423ft x 105ft (131m x 32m)
Machinery: two-shaft, diesel plus bow thrusters; 15,200hp plus 2650hp
Service speed: 12.5 knots
Role: cruise ship
Route: Caribbean; Mediterranean; Baltic
Capacity: 354 sc
Constructor: Finnyards OY, Rauma
Material: steel
Built for: Diamond Cruises

RAU IX

GERMANY: 1939

The whaling factory ships which came into widespread use in the early 20th century operated as mother ships for a fleet of catcher vessels. Despite their relatively small size, these latter vessels had to be able to withstand extreme weather conditions in the high latitudes. Boats of this type, like the *Rau IX* (which was smaller than the average), served as the model for small escorts and patrol craft for both sides in World War II. *Rau IX* is preserved at Bremerhaven.

Tonnage: 380 grt
Dimensions: 151ft 3in x 26ft 10in x 13ft 1in (46.1m x 8.2m x 4m)
Machinery: one-shaft, triple expansion; 1600hp
Service speed: 14 knots
Role: whale catcher
Capacity: not applicable
Constructor: Deschimag, Bremerhaven
Material: steel
Built for: Walfang AG
Owner: Deutsches Schiffarhtsmuseum, Bremerhaven

RAVEN

CANADA/GB: 1875

Raven was a brigantine, which as the name suggests, was a variant of the brig, with an even simpler sail plan – square sails on the foremast to the topgallant, a fore-and-aft gaff course and square topsail on the main. Relative to the spanker carried by ships and barques, the gaff course of the brigantine was larger and more important. When the brigantine's main topsail was replaced by a jib-headed sail, the result was known as a hermaphrodite brig, but this later became the accepted form for the brigantine.

Raven **was simple and straightforward to manage even short-handed and remained popular in the coastal and short-sea trades.**

Tonnage: 213 grt
Dimensions: 90ft 6in x 24ft 6in x 11ft (27.6m x 7.45m x 3.4m)
Machinery: not applicable
Service speed: not applicable
Role: general cargo vessel
Route: not applicable
Capacity: not applicable
Constructor: Keefe
Material: wood
Built for: JC Head

RESULT

GB: 1893

Tonnage: 122 grt
Dimensions: 122ft 2in x 21ft 9in x 9ft 1in (37.2m x 6.6m x 2.8m)
Service speed: not applicable
Role: general cargo vessel
Route: coastal waters, UK
Constructor: Robert Kent & Co, Carrick-fergus
Material: steel
Built for: Thomas Ashburner & Co, Barrow-in-Furness
Owner: Ulster Folk & Transport Museum

The *Result* has a secret history. During 1917, she was taken up and armed as a Q-ship, to decoy enemy submarines. She almost succeeded in sinking *U 45*.

There were comparatively few steel-hulled schooners built in the British Isles; one exception was the *Result*, a three-masted double-topsail schooner constructed in Ulster for a Barrow-in-Furness-based shipowner. The *Result* had a long career in the coastal trade, being fitted with an auxiliary engine and later stripped down to a ketch. She was eventually acquired by the Ulster Folk and Transport Museum, just across Belfast Lough from where she was built.

REX

ITALY: 1931

Tonnage: 51,062 grt
Dimensions: 879ft x 96ft in x 28ft (268m x 29.25m x 8.55m)
Machinery: four-shaft, geared turbines; 136,000hp
Service speed: 28 knots
Role: passenger liner
Route: Genoa–New York
Capacity: 604 1st, 378 2nd, 410 tr, 866 3rd
Constructor: Ansaldo, Genoa
Material: steel
Built for: Navigazione Generale Italiana

In 1927, Navigazione Generale Italiana ordered what was to be the biggest passenger liner ever built in Italy to supplement the *Roma* and *Augusta* on its Genoa–Cote d'Azur–New York service. As it happened, the rival Lloyd Sabaudo Line announced almost simultaneously that it, too, had ordered a major ship, the *Conte di Savoia*. In fact there was no real competition between the two, for the former was to be built primarily for speed and the latter as a showpiece of Italian style, and by the time they were ready to enter service the two lines had merged with Cosiluch to become the Italia Line. From the outset the *Rex*, as she eventually became, was meant to win the Blue Riband, until then the preserve of British and latterly German ships. Ultimately she succeeded, but it was to be a difficult process. On her maiden voyage, she developed a major problem with her geared turbine powerplant, limped to New York and was stuck there for months awaiting spare parts, and it was almost a year later before she captured the record, then held by the *Bremen*, at an average speed of 28.92 knots. She held it until the arrival on the scene of the *Normandie*. *Rex* was laid up in the spring of 1940 – just before Italy entered World War II – initially at Bari, later at Trieste, and there were reports that she was to be converted to an aircraft carrier. In the event she fell victim to air attack by the RAF in September 1944 and sank in the Gulf of Muggia. Salvage was economically impossible, and scrapping began in 1947.

The Italia Line worked hard to promote the advantages of the 'sunny southern route' to New York, but with only limited success. Despite the ship's taking the speed record, much of the *Rex*'s passenger list was made up of westbound emigrants.

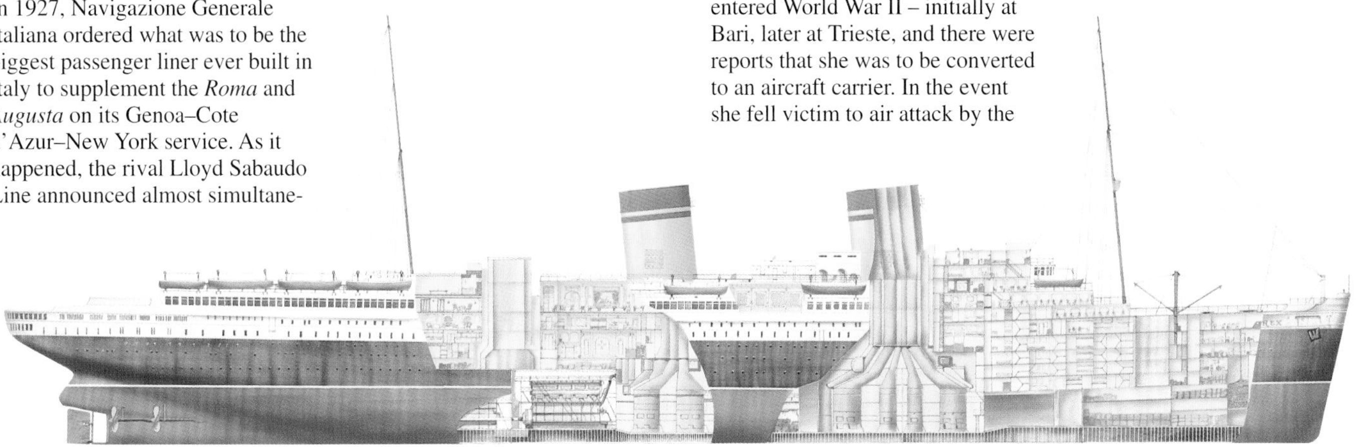

ROTTERDAM (LATER REMBRANDT) NETHERLANDS: 1958

The *Rotterdam*, launched in 1958, was the fifth vessel of that name built for the Holland-America Line and was its flagship. She was the first passenger ship of any real size to have exhaust uptakes, rather than the traditional funnels. She operated scheduled summer services between Rotterdam and New York from 1959 to 1969 and was then transferred to full-time cruising. She was sold to Premier Cruises in 1997 and continued in service as the *Rembrandt*; a new *Rotterdam* replaced her.

Tonnage: 38,645 grt
Dimensions: 748ft x 94ft 2in x 29ft (227.9m x 28.7m x 8.85m)
Machinery: two-shaft, geared turbines; 38,500hp
Service speed: 20.5 knots
Role: passenger liner; cruise ship
Route: Rotterdam–New York
Capacity: 655 1st, 801 tr; 401 tr, 1055 tr
Constructor: Rotterdamsche Droogdok Maatschappij
Material: steel
Built for: Holland-America Line

The *Rotterdam* was designed from the outset to operate as a cruise ship during the winter months; during her first season she offered a 75-day 'Four Continents' cruise for US$2400 and upwards.

SAN JERONIMO (LATER SOUTHERN EMPRESS) GB: 1914

When she entered service, just prior to the outbreak of World War I, *San Jeronimo* was one of the biggest oil tankers in existence; she was one of 10 built hurriedly for the Eagle Oil Co, a British firm with substantial interests in Mexico, and the fleet, when complete, accounted for 10 per cent of the world's tanker tonnage. Fourteen years later she was sold to Lever Brothers, which then had major whaling interests, and was converted to become a whaling factory ship, with the addition of a lofty superstructure linking the bridge with the machinery space, and a stern ramp. She was sunk by a German submarine in October 1944.

Tonnage: 12,030 (later 12,380) grt
Dimensions: 540ft x 66ft 6in x 28ft (164.6m x 20m x 8.5m)
Machinery: one-shaft, quadruple expansion
Service speed: 11.5 knots
Role: oil tanker; whaling factory ship
Route: UK–Mexico; Antarctica
Capacity: 15, 578 dwt
Constructor: William Doxford and Sons, Sunderland
Material: steel
Built for: Eagle Oil Co

In both her guises, *San Jeronimo/Southern Empress* was to play an important role. She was one of the biggest oil tankers initially, and later the biggest British-flagged whaling ship.

SANTA ROSA (LATER SAMOS SKY) USA: 1957

The *Santa Rosa* was one of a pair of passenger/cargo ships the American Grace Line had constructed for its New York–Central America service in the late 1950s. Twin-screwed with turbine machinery, they steamed at 20 knots and had first-class accommodation only. Nine months after entering service, the *Santa Rosa* collided with a tanker, the *Valchem*, 20 miles (37km) off Atlantic City, New Jersey; both ships were badly damaged. She was sold to the Vintero Corporation in 1976 and renamed *Samos Sky*.

Tonnage: 15,371 grt
Dimensions: 584ft x 84ft (177.9m x 25.6m)
Machinery: two-shaft, geared turbines; 22,000hp
Service speed: 20 knots
Role: passenger/cargo liner
Route: New York–Central America
Capacity: 300 1st
Constructor: Newport News Shipbuilding & Dry Dock Co
Material: steel
Built for: Grace Lines

The Grace Line's *Santa Rosa* and her sistership *Santa Paula* operated between New York and Central American ports.

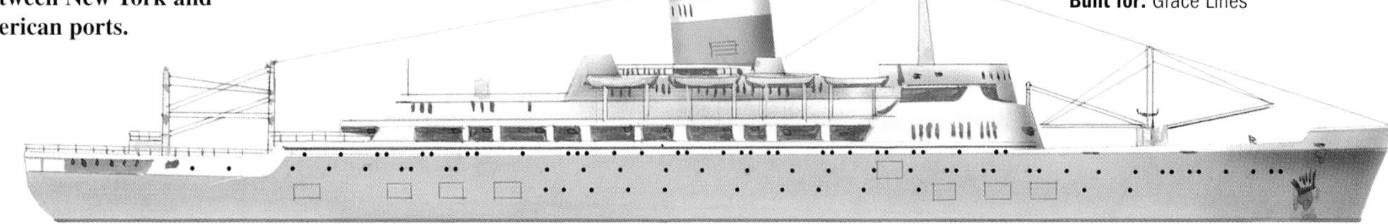

SAVANNAH

USA: 1959

Tonnage: 13,599 (later 15,585) grt
Dimensions: 595ft x 78ft 2in (181.5m x 23.8m)
Machinery: one-shaft, geared turbine; 22,000hp
Service speed: 21 knots
Role: passenger/cargo carrier
Route: USA–Mediterranean
Capacity: 60 sc
Constructor: New York Shipbuilders, Camden, NJ
Material: steel
Built for: US Dept of Commerce/States Marine Lines

The *Savannah* was built as an experiment to test the feasibility, both technical and economic, of fitting merchant ships with nuclear powerplants. As such, the first two years of her operational life were taken up with demonstration voyages. She then went into (heavily subsidised) service between the United States and Mediterranean ports, first with a small number of paying passengers, latterly with cargo only. Although she was the world's first nuclear-powered freighter, she was not the first nuclear-powered merchant ship; that honour went to the Soviet ice-breaker *Lenin*, which made her maiden voyage two months after the *Savannah* was launched. A second nuclear-powered freighter, the *Otto Hahn*, an ore carrier, was launched in Kiel in June 1964. The success of the *Savannah* experiment can perhaps be judged by the fact that she was laid up with the reserve fleet in 1972, by which time it had become clear that she was uneconomical.

The *Savannah*, named after the first steamship to cross the Atlantic, was the world's first nuclear-powered freighter.

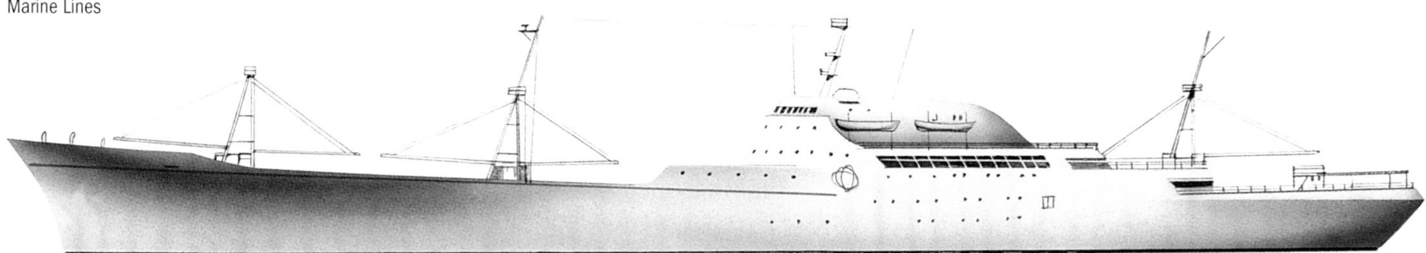

SAVARONA

USA: 1931

The *Savarona* was probably the biggest steam yacht ever built for a private individual, Mrs E R Cadwalader. The vessel eventually passed into the hands of the Turkish government and was, for a while, the presidential yacht. Later, after a very comprehensive refit, she was leased to private interests and went into the charter trade.

The *Savarona* was built at a time when a private steam yacht was the status symbol *par excellence*. There was no expense spared in her construction.

Tonnage: 4646 grt
Dimensions: 408ft 6in x 53ft x 20ft 6in (124.5m x 16.15m x 6.25m)
Machinery: two-shaft, geared turbines (later diesel); 7000hp
Service speed: 16 knots
Role: yacht
Route: not applicable
Capacity: not applicable
Constructor: Blohm & Voss, Hamburg
Material: steel and wood
Built for: Mrs E R Cadwalader

SCOTIA

GB: 1861

Tonnage: 3871 grt
Dimensions: 379ft 5in x 47ft 9in x 30ft 6in (115.6m x 14.6m x 9.3m)
Machinery: sidewheels, side-lever (later two-shaft, compound)
Service speed: 14 knots
Role: passenger liner; cable layer
Route: Liverpool–New York
Capacity: 573 1st
Constructor: R Napier & Sons, Glasgow
Material: iron
Built for: Cunard Line

The Cunard Line's *Scotia* was the company's last sidewheel paddle steamer in transatlantic service and the first ship to make the westbound passage in under nine days. She made her last North Atlantic voyage in 1876; she was subsequently re-engined with compound machinery driving twin screws and chartered to the Telegraph Construction and Maintenance Co as a cable ship. In 1896, her watertight bulkhead held when an unexplained explosion blew her bow off. She was wrecked off Guam in 1904.

In July 1863, the *Scotia* took the eastbound Blue Riband at an average speed of over 14.5 knots and added the westbound to it the following December. The westbound record stood for nine years.

SEA SPIDER

THE NETHERLANDS: 1999

Tonnage: 4008 grt
Dimensions: 285ft x 78ft x 15ft (86.1m x 24m x 4.5m)
Machinery: controllable pitch, diesel electric
Service speed: 9.5 knots
Role: cable layer
Route: Sweden–Poland
Capacity: 5000t

Sea Spider was a specialist ship for laying cables between Sweden and Poland; she was built in only nine months by a consortium of suppliers. Initially it was planned to convert an existing ship, but eventually a purpose-built vessel was constructed which was able to lay cable down to 8 feet (2.4m) deep and in waves 8 feet (2.4m) high. The 5000t of high voltage cable was carried on a carousel with a diameter of 78 feet (24m) and on a smaller 1600t cable basket. There were three cable engines with pick-up arms to handle the cable over the stern via a large A frame which also handled the trencher.

The long afterdeck of *Sea Spider* enables swift cable-laying in most sea conditions. A double bottom was installed for fuel and spares.

SELANDIA

DENMARK: 1912

The *Selandia* was the first of a trio of ships the Danish-owned East Asiatic Co put into service just prior to the outbreak of World War I to operate between Europe and Siam (Thailand). These were the first major ocean-going vessels to be powered by compression ignition (diesel) engines. She was an instant success, both for her owners and for her constructors, Burmeister & Wain, who had obtained a licence to build the new powerplant as early as 1896, just three years after Rudolf Diesel was granted his patent. By modern standards, the engines were very inefficient indeed and quite enormous, with eight separate cylinders, each with an exposed connecting rod and valve gear and standing some 20 feet (6.1m) high. In their construction and scale they had more in common with contemporary steam engines than with later internal-combustion engines.

Tonnage: 4964 grt
Dimensions: 386ft x 53ft 2in x 23ft (117.65m x 16.2m x 7m)
Machinery: two-shaft, diesel; 2500hp
Service speed: 11.25 knots
Role: cargo/passenger liner
Route: Copenhagen–Bangkok
Capacity: 26 p, 7400dwt
Constructor: Burmeister & Wain, Copenhagen
Material: steel
Built for: East Asiatic Co

The *Selandia*'s maiden voyage took her 22,000 miles (40,750km) and proved conclusively that diesel machinery was both more economical and more reliable than steam.

SEAWELL (EX-STENA SEAWELL)

GB: 1987

Tonnage: 11,935t displacement
Dimensions: 365ft 6in x 73ft 10in x 23ft 10in (111.4m x 22.5m x 7.25m)
Machinery: three-shaft, diesel plus bow thruster; 12,000hp plus 2000hp
Service speed: 13 knots
Role: multi-role offshore support ship
Route: not applicable
Capacity: not applicable
Constructor: North-east Shipbuilders, Sunderland
Material: steel
Built for: Stena Offshore

The *Seawell* was the most sophisticated multi-role offshore support vessel in the world when she entered service in 1988. She had accommodation for 147 and was certified as a stand-by and rescue ship; she had saturation diving chambers, a remotely operated unmanned submarine and two diving bells, a hospital, a large helicopter platform forwards and even a conference suite for clients. Her twin cranes could lift 140t when operating in tandem, and she was equipped as an anchor-handler, with a dynamic positioning system.

The *Seawell* was a good example of a third-generation offshore support ship, at home in any maritime oilfield in the world.

SHAMROCK V (SOMETIME QUADRIFOGLIO) GB: 1930

The cutter-rigged *Shamrock V*, like all her predecessors, was built for Sir Thomas Lipton to challenge for the America's Cup. She was built by Camper & Nicholson to J-class rules and lost out to the American *Resolute*. She was then sold to Tommy Sopwith, who used her as a trials boat for his two cup attempts, and later passed into Italian hands and was rerigged as a cruising ketch. In the 1980s, she was acquired by the Newport Museum of Yachting and was restored.

Only a handful of yachts were built to the J-class, or 'universal', rules, which permitted waterline length to vary between 75 feet (22.86m) and 87 feet (26.5m). They required a crew of 24.

Tonnage: 104 grt
Dimensions: 119ft 9in x 19ft 8in x 14ft 8in (36.5m x 6.8m x 4.5m)
Machinery: not applicable
Service speed: not applicable
Role: racing yacht
Route: not applicable
Capacity: not applicable
Constructor: Camper & Nicholson, Gosport
Material: composite, wood on steel
Built for: Sir Thomas Lipton
Owner: Museum of Yachting, Newport, Rhode Island

SHIN AITOKU MARU JAPAN: 1976

Tonnage: 1600 grt
Dimensions: 230ft x 43ft x 16ft 3in (70.1m x 13.1m x 4.95m)
Machinery: one-shaft, diesel; 1400hp
Service speed: 12 knots
Role: oil carrier
Route: not applicable
Capacity: not known
Constructor: Nippon Kokan
Material: steel
Built for: not known

In the mid-1970s, a Japanese shipbuilder, Nippon Kokan, constructed a small tanker, the *Shin Aitoku Maru*, fitted with roller-furling square sails on two masts. Unlike traditional square sails, these were unfurled on the vertical axis, and were stowed, rolled, within the mast when not in use. They were set and trimmed under computer control when the wind was in a favourable direction and sufficiently strong. The experiment resulted in a 10 per cent saving in fuel cost with no loss of performance.

SILJA SERENADE SWEDEN: 1991

In the early 1990s, the Swedish Silja Line introduced a pair of ships onto its Stockholm–Helsinki service which it described as 'cruise ferries'. The *Serenade* and the *Symphony* had accommodation for over 2500 people and 450 cars; they featured a ballroom big enough for 650, a five-storey atrium running three quarters the length of the ship, swimming pools and a 'show lounge', as well as the normal run of restaurants, discotheques and shops.

These Baltic 'cruise ferries' are some of the biggest and best appointed of their type in the world, finished to cruise ship standards.

Tonnage: 58,376 grt
Dimensions: 666ft 1in x 104ft 9in x 23ft 4in (203.05m x 31.95m x 7.1m)
Machinery: two-shaft, diesel; 44,300hp
Service speed: 21 knots
Role: passenger/vehicle ferry
Route: Stockholm–Helsinki
Capacity: 2656 p, 450 v
Constructor: Kvaerner Masa, Finland
Material: steel
Built for: Silja Line

SIR LANCELOT GB: 1865

Tonnage: 847 grt
Dimensions: 197ft 5in x 33ft 7in x 21ft (60.2m x 10.2m x 6.4m)
Machinery: not applicable
Service speed: not applicable
Role: tea carrier; general cargo vessel
Route: China–London
Capacity: not known
Constructor: Richard Steel & Co, Greenock
Material: composite, wood on iron
Built for: James MacCunn

The three-masted ship *Sir Lancelot* was virtually identical to *Ariel*, built the same year, and was another contender for the 'fastest clipper' title. On her first outward voyage to China she was dismasted off Ushant, and the delay meant she was two weeks late in arriving and had to go 440 nautical miles (815km) further north, to Shanghai, to load, but she arrived in London the same day as *Ariel*. She had a comparatively long career; downrigged to a barque by 1877, she was wrecked off Calcutta in 1895.

Owner James MacCunn wanted *Sir Lancelot* built 10 feet (3m) longer but was dissuaded by designer William Rennie. She proved to be one of the fastest ships of her day.

SLÄTTOPPARE

DENMARK, FINLAND SWEDEN: 1860 ONWARDS

Tonnage: 150 grt
Dimensions: 115ft x 25ft x 11ft (35m x 7.6m x 3.4m)
Machinery: not applicable
Service speed: not applicable
Role: general cargo vessel
Material: wood

The Baltic *slättoppare* was one of the many regional variations on the basic small schooner, with the addition of a square sail before the foremast.

The Baltic *slättoppare* was one of the many regional variations on the basic schooner rig. It was three-masted, generally with all masts of equal height (although a shortened mizzen was also quite common), and carried a square sail from a cross-jack (or crojack) yard before the foremast in place of the more normal fore-and-aft staysail. The rig proved enduringly popular in the region where it was developed, and many *slättopparer* made voyages to North America and the Mediterranean.

SMACK

NORTHERN EUROPE: 1860 ONWARDS

The smallest of all the Northern European commercial craft of the late 19th century, the smack was the maid-of-all-work of the coastal trade, equally at home hauling general cargo or as a fishing vessel. Single-masted, gaff-rigged and often with a jackstaff topsail, smacks were very easy to sail – often by no more than a man and a boy – and yet were capable of a surprising turn of speed under the right conditions. Smacks were still in everyday use in the west of England up until World War II.

Smacks were the smallest merchant vessels in use in Northern Europe in the late 19th century; they were equally home carrying general cargo or in the fisheries.

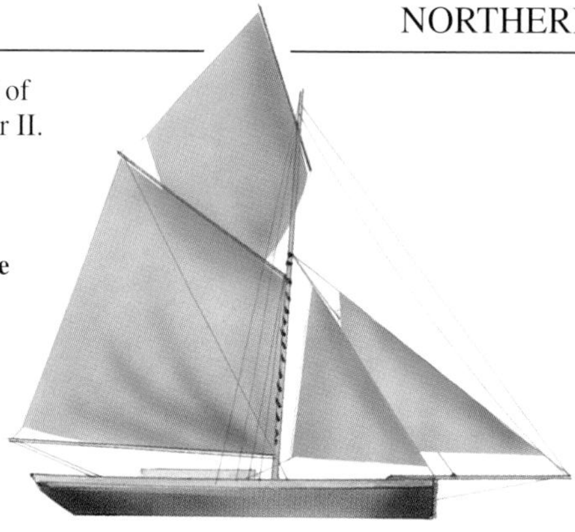

Tonnage: 25 grt
Dimensions: 50ft x 17ft 6in x 5ft 9in (15.25m x 6.35m x 1.75m)
Machinery: not applicable
Service speed: not applicable
Role: general cargo vessel; fishery vessel
Route: coastal
Capacity: not applicable
Constructor: not applicable
Material: wood

SOUTH STEYNE

AUSTRALIA: 1938

Built in Leith, Edinburgh, the *South Steyne* was delivered to her owners in Australia under her own power in just nine weeks – a very significant maiden voyage for a ship which would henceforth sail over a seven-mile (13km) route between Circular Quay and Manly in Sydney Harbour. She was a true double-ender, with two navigating bridges and propellers at each extremity connected to centrally mounted machinery. She remained in service until 1974 and was then extensively refurbished as an excursion steamer.

Tonnage: 1203 grt
Dimensions: 222ft 6in x 38ft 3in x 12ft 4in (67.8m x 11.65m x 3.8m)
Machinery: two-shaft (opposed), triple expansion; 3250hp
Service speed: 12 knots
Role: passenger ferry; excursion steamer
Route: Sydney Harbour
Capacity: 1780
Constructor: Henry Robb & Co, Leith
Material: steel
Built for: Port Jackson & Manly Steamship Co

The double-ended *South Steyne* was both the biggest and the last steam ferry operating in Sydney Harbour. She remained in service until 1974.

SOUTHERN CROSS (LATER CALYPSO)

GB: 1954

When she entered service with the Shaw, Savill Line in 1955, *Southern Cross* was seen as a mould-breaker – she was the first large passenger liner to be built with her machinery right aft, a feature later taken up almost universally, since it made it possible to optimise the way in which passenger space was used and allocated right through the midship area, down to the waterline and below. She was also – somewhat surprisingly – the first passenger liner to have no cargo space whatsoever, which cut out any risk of delays in port. She was destined for the Line's round-the-world service out of Southampton, via South Africa and Panama, and made four circumnavigations a year until 1973, when she was sold to Greek interests and re-fitted as a cruise ship.

Tonnage: 20,200 grt
Dimensions: 604ft x 78ft 10in x 26ft (184.1m x 23.4m x 8m)
Machinery: two-shaft, turbines; 20,000hp
Service speed: 20 knots
Role: passenger liner; cruise ship
Route: round-the-world
Capacity: 1160 tr
Constructor: Harland and Wolff, Belfast
Material: steel
Built for: Shaw, Savill and Albion Line

SPAARNDAM — THE NETHERLANDS: 1922

Tonnage: 8857 grt
Dimensions: 466ft x 58ft x 30ft (142m x 17.5m x 20.5m)
Machinery: one-shaft, turbines; 4200hp
Service speed: 13 knots
Role: general cargo vessel; emigrant ship
Route: Havana-Rotterdam service
Capacity: c1000
Material: steel
Built for: the Holland-America Line

At the time when the *Spaarndam* and her three sisters were ordered, Europe was still suffering the ravages of World War I, whilst America was experiencing a boom. The number of emigrants needing transport to the United States was growing daily, so it was decided to press these four vessels quickly into service. Unfortunately the boom was short lived, and in 1919, the ships were transferred to the route between the United States and Mexico when that was reopened. Alterations made beforehand included part of the superstructure being raised one deck for extra cabin space and an enlarged emigrant area being installed between decks, so enabling nearly 1000 passengers to be carried. She was sunk by a mine in the Thames Estuary on 14 December 1939.

***Spaarndam* and her sisters were originally designed as cargo carriers but underwent changes for emigrant service. The second funnel was a dummy.**

ST LOUIS (SOMETIME LOUISVILLE) — USA: 1894

The *St Louis* and her sistership the *St Paul* were the first American-built passenger liners with screw propulsion. They were constructed for the American Line's service between New York and Southampton, with accommodation in three classes. In 1898, the *St Louis* was briefly taken up by the US Navy and employed as an armed merchant cruiser during the Spanish-American War. She resumed service in October that year. In 1903, she was reboilered and had her two funnels raised in height. Just prior to the outbreak of World War I she was refitted, with second- and third-class passenger accommodation only, and was switched to the Liverpool service. She was taken up as the *Louisville* and operated as a troopship from late 1918 until 1920. She caught fire during the subsequent refit, and instead of joining her sistership on the Southampton service was sold as an exhibition ship. The transformation was never completed, and she was towed to Genoa and broken up in 1924.

Tonnage: 11,629 grt
Dimensions: 535ft 6in x 63ft (163.2m x 19.2m)
Machinery: two-shaft, triple expansion
Service speed: 19 knots
Role: passenger liner; armed merchant cruiser; troopship
Route: North Atlantic
Capacity: 350 1st, 220 2nd, 800 3rd
Constructor: W Cramp & Co, Philadelphia
Material: steel
Built for: American Line

Despite being built as late as 1894, the *St Louis* was the first screw passenger liner ever constructed in the United States.

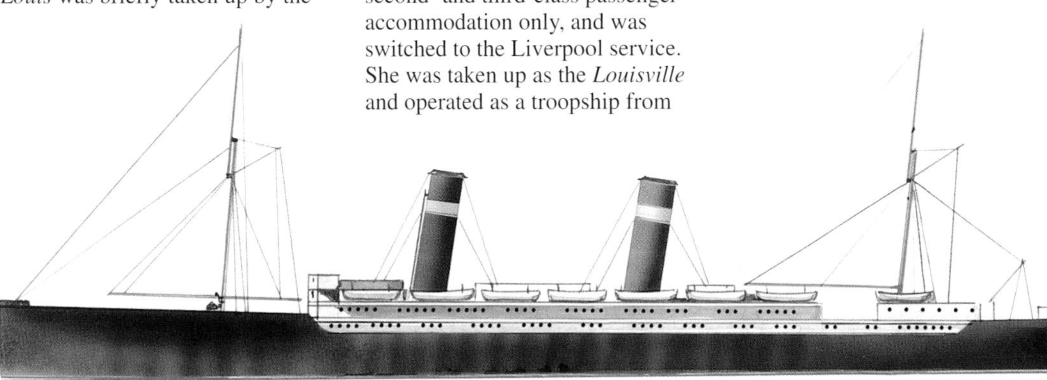

ST LUCIA

GB: 1993

As well as carrying bananas and other fruit from the Caribbean to European markets, the Geest ships also carry most of the Caribbean islands' imported goods.

The international trade in bananas and other exotic fruit has long been such that it was economical for trading companies to operate their own fleets of specialist ships. Geest took delivery of two new ships in 1993, the first of them being the *St Lucia*. By normal freight-carrier standards, they were fast; they were refrigerated throughout, divided into seven temperature zones independently controllable from –29 degrees to 13 degrees Celsius. On the outward journey they normally carried containerised general cargo.

Tonnage: 13,000 grt
Dimensions: 518ft 4in x 80ft x 32ft 9in (158m x 24.4m x 10m)
Machinery: one-shaft, diesel; 16,250hp
Service speed: 21 knots
Role: refrigerated fruit and produce carrier
Route: UK-Caribbean
Capacity: 13,981dwt
Constructor: Danyard, Frederikshavn
Material: steel
Built for: Geest Corporation

ST ROCH

CANADA: 1928

Tonnage: 323t displacement
Dimensions: 104ft 3in x 24ft 8in x 13ft (31.8m x 7.5m x 4m)
Machinery: one-shaft, auxiliary diesel; 150hp (later 300hp)
Service speed: not applicable
Role: Arctic patrol vessel
Route: Canadian Arctic
Capacity: not applicable
Constructor: Burrard Dry Dock Co, North Vancouver
Material: wood
Built for: Royal Canadian Mounted Police
Owner: Vancouver Maritime Museum

The Royal Canadian Mounted Police's auxiliary schooner *St Roch* was the first ship to transit the Northwest Passage from west to east, in 1941-42, and made the return journey, in a single season, in 1944. She was retired from service in Halifax in 1948 after yet another transit and was laid up. Public sentiment for bringing the vessel back to her home port of Vancouver was strong, and in 1954 she returned there to be preserved at the Maritime Museum, becoming the first ship to circumnavigate North America in the process.

The primary duty of the *St Roch* was to pay annual visits to isolated communities in the Canadian Western Arctic, returning to Vancouver every winter. She began life as a two-masted schooner, being later rerigged as a ketch.

SUN MARIA (EX-HUDSON REX)

NETHERLANDS: 1991

Designed to operate in places where port facilities are minimal or non-existent, the Bahamian-registered *Sun Maria* was a throwback to an earlier age, although entirely up to date for all that. Each of her eight holds, two of which were refrigerated, was served by a derrick, allowing her to onload and offload her own cargo onto the quayside or into lighters as required.

Tonnage: 9070 grt
Dimensions: 487ft 3in x 67ft 7in x 31ft (148.5m x 20.6m x 9.4m)
Machinery: one-shaft, diesel; 9600hp
Service speed: 19 knots
Role: partially refrigerated general cargo vessel
Route: not applicable
Capacity: not known
Constructor: Kanasashi
Material: steel
Built for: Vroom BV

SUOMEN JOUTSEN (EX-LAENNEC, OLDENBURG) FINLAND: 1902

At the end of the 19th century, the French government made large sums of money available to shipowners to finance the construction of steel-hulled sailing ships. Just one example of the type, the *Suomen Joutsen*, survives. Now an exhibit, she was originally a general cargo carrier under the French flag, then a training ship for a German merchant line and later the Finnish Navy's sail training ship.

Tonnage: 2260 grt
Dimensions: 262ft 6in x 40ft 4in x 17ft (80m x 12.3m x 5.2m)
Machinery: not applicable
Service speed: not applicable
Role: general cargo vessel; sail training ship
Route: not applicable
Capacity: not applicable
Constructor: Chantiers et Ateliers de St Nazaire, St Nazaire
Material: steel
Built for: Société des Armateurs Nantais
Owner: Merchant Navy Seaman's School, Abo

Suomen Joutsen **is a good example of the so-called 'bounty ships', built in significant numbers in France around the end of the 19th century with heavy government subsidies.**

SUWA MARU JAPAN: 1914

Suwa Maru and her sister *Fushimi Maru* were the largest Japanese merchant ships of the time to operate from Japan to European waters. During World War I, the route to European ports was transferred from the Suez Canal to the long route round Africa. There was accommodation for 170 passengers plus over 300 steerage, but the latter were usually carried only when in the East. There were six holds, two continuous decks and a third partial deck, with three of the holds having partial decks. Bunker capacity was 4000t, and the vessel burnt about 130t per day. *Suwa Maru* was sunk by a US submarine in March 1943 near Wake Island.

Tonnage: 21,020 grt
Dimensions: 516ft x 62ft 6in x 29ft (157.3m x 19m x 8.3m)
Machinery: two-shaft, triple expansion
Service speed: 15.5 knots
Role: passenger/cargo liner
Route: Japan-Europe
Capacity: 170, *c*300 st
Constructor: not known
Material: steel
Built for: Nippon Yusen Kaisha

Suwa Maru **of the Nippon Yusen Kaisha was the largest vessel used by the company on the European route and was one of the largest home-built vessels up to that time.**

TEUTONIC GB: 1889

Tonnage: 9984 grt
Dimensions: 565ft 9in x 57ft 9in (172.45m x 17.6m)
Machinery: two-shaft, triple expansion
Service speed: 19 knots
Role: passenger liner; armed merchant cruiser; troopship
Route: North Atlantic
Capacity: 300 1st, 190 2nd, 1000 3rd; 550 2nd, 1000 3rd
Constructor: Harland & Wolff, Belfast
Material: steel
Built for: White Star Line

The White Star liner *Teutonic* and her sistership, the *Majestic*, marked a departure for their owners. Built, like all the White Star ships, by Harland & Wolff, they were the first White Star passenger liners to have triple-expansion machinery. They were also the first in the world to dispense entirely with a sailing rig and the first to be built to incorporate Admiralty requirements to allow them to be transformed into armed merchant cruisers in time of war. They were built to compete with the Inman Line's *City of New York* and *City of Paris* and were similar in character although they were quite dissimilar in appearance. Both took the westbound Blue Riband.

The *Teutonic* was innovative in a number of ways – she was the first White Star passenger liner to be fitted with triple-expansion machinery and the first to rely entirely on that machinery, dispensing with sails.

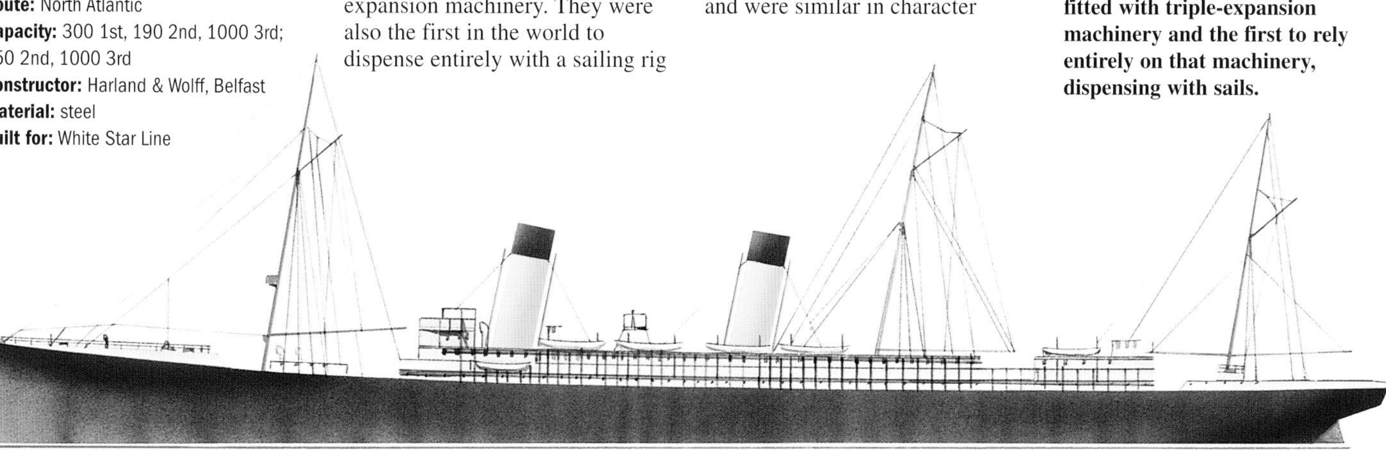

Majestic first and *Teutonic* two weeks later, in August 1891. *Teutonic*'s record, an average speed of 20.35 knots, stood for nearly a year.
Teutonic made her first public appearance at the 1889 Spithead Naval Review and seven days later made her maiden voyage from Liverpool to New York. She remained in that service until 1907, when she was switched over to Southampton. In 1911, she returned to Liverpool to operate alongside the *Laurentic*, the *Megantic* and the *Canada* in the joint White Star-Dominion Line service to Quebec and Montreal, with second- and third-class accommodation only. As had always been envisaged, she was taken up and armed in 1914, and was purchased by the British government in August 1915. She operated as a troopship from 1918 and was laid up three years later at Cowes. She was scrapped later in 1921 in Germany.

THEODORA

NETHERLANDS: 1991

The Netherlands-registered *Theodora* was one of a relatively small number of specialist chemical products tankers equipped to transport cargoes such as asphalt, bituminous coal and naphtha, which solidify – and become impossible to unload – on cooling. Her hull was fitted with nine flexibly mounted tanks, any or all of which could be heated as required. Since her cargo was usually classified as dangerous, she was double-hulled throughout and carried extensive firefighting equipment.

Like most chemical products carriers, *Theodora* operated to a schedule which was prepared months in advance and so she had no need of powerful machinery.

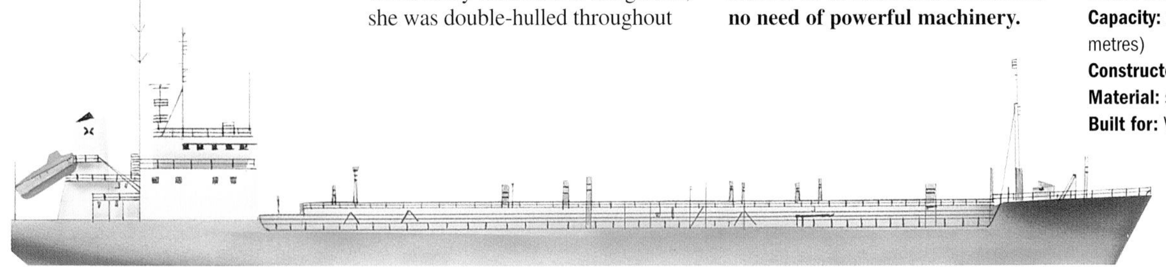

Tonnage: 5000 grt
Dimensions: 361ft 6in x 55ft 9in x 23ft in (110.2m x 17m x 7m)
Machinery: one-shaft, diesel; 3570hp
Service speed: 14 knots
Role: chemical products carrier
Route: not applicable
Capacity: 182,050 cubic feet (5155 cubic metres)
Constructor: Meuwede, Giessendam
Material: steel
Built for: Vopak Theodora Tankers

THERMOPYLAE

GB: 1868

***Thermopylae* was designed by the prodigal Bernard Waymouth, who produced many fast ships and went on to become Secretary of Lloyd's Register.**

Thermopylae was one of the best of the China clippers, built expressly to bring the tea crop from Foochow and Shanghai to London and New York. She was also amongst the fastest of them –

on her maiden outward-bound voyage she made Melbourne from London in 63 days, and her return from Foochow took 91 days. Homeward bound from Shanghai in 1873, she logged 2085 nautical miles (3861km) in seven days. She was always compared with *Cutty Sark*, and to this day no one can be sure which was the faster ship.

She was sold to Canadian interests in 1890 to operate in the rice trade between China and British Columbia, and two years later she was converted to carry lumber, cut down to a barque. In 1896, by now 28 years old, she was sold to the Portuguese Navy as a sail training ship, but a survey showed her to be in poor condition and she became a coal hulk instead. In 1907, she was towed out to sea with considerable ceremony and sunk.

Tonnage: 947 nrt
Dimensions: 212ft x 36ft x 20ft 10in (64.6m x 11m x 6.4 m)
Machinery: not applicable
Service speed: not applicable
Role: tea carrier; rice carrier; lumber carrier; coal hulk
Route: China-London/New York; China-British Columbia
Capacity: not known
Constructor: Walter Hood & Co, Aberdeen
Material: composite, wood on iron
Built for: George Thompson & Co

THOMAS F BAYARD (SOMETIME SANDHEADS NO. 16) CANADA: 1880

Tonnage: 70 grt
Dimensions: 86ft x 21ft 2in x 8ft 7in (26.2m x 6.4m x 2.6m)
Machinery: not applicable
Service speed: not applicable
Role: pilot cutter; general cargo vessel; sealer; lightship
Route: coastal waters, North America
Capacity: not known
Constructor: C & R Poillon, Brooklyn, New York
Material: wood
Built for: Captain Henry Virden, Lewes, Delaware
Owner: Thomas F Bayard Preservation Society

Thomas F Bayard was a Delaware Bay pilot schooner and was designed to the same sort of criteria as a racing yacht. She was sold to West Coast interests in 1887 to transport people and supplies north to the Alaska gold fields and was later used as a sealer. In 1913, now in poor condition, she was purchased by the Canadian government and became the first lightship on the Pacific coast. She was acquired by the Vancouver Maritime Museum in the mid-1970s for restoration.

***Thomas F Bayard* was designed by William Townsend, who also drew an America's Cup defender, the *Sappho*.**

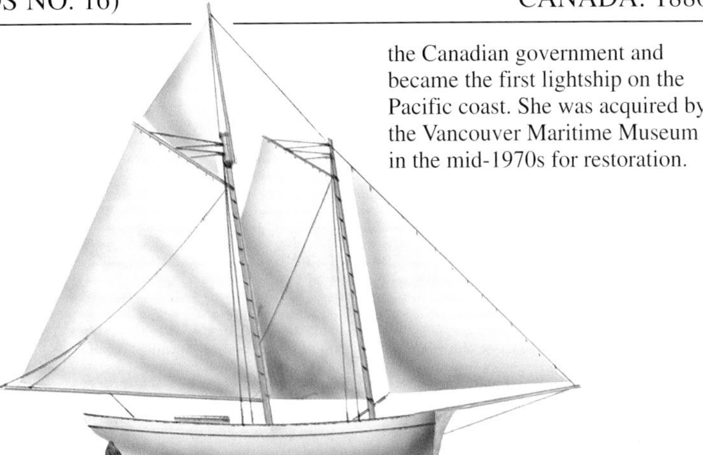

THOMAS W LAWSON USA: 1902

The *Thomas W Lawson* was the largest sailing schooner ever built, her seven 190-ft (58m) masts each carrying a course, a jib-headed topsail and a topmast staysail plus five headsails. She was built of steel by the Fore River Ship & Engine Building Company at Quincy, Massachusetts. Launched in 1902, she was employed in the coastal trade originally, carrying 11,000t of coal on each voyage. She was soon converted to carry oil in bulk from the Gulf of Mexico, her draught being too great for the coaling ports. Every halyard, topping lift and sheet aboard the 385-ft-long (117.3m) ship was led to one or other of two large steam winches, one forward, the other on the after deckhouse. As a result she needed a crew of just 16 men, but she was unhandy in anything but strong winds. She was lost in heavy weather off the Scilly Isles on 13 December 1907. Only her captain and one of her crewmen survived.

Basil Lubbock described the *Lawson* as being 'as sweet as a bathtub', but she was known to make 11 knots before the wind under bare poles. Her sails weighed a total of 18t when dry.

Tonnage: 5218 grt
Dimensions: 385ft x 50ft x 35ft (117.3m x 15.2m x 10.7m)
Machinery: not applicable
Service speed: not applicable
Role: coal/oil carrier
Route: coastal waters, USA; Atlantic
Capacity: 11,000t (coal)
Constructor: Fore River Ship & Engine Building Co, Quincy, MA
Material: steel
Built for: Coastwise Transportation Co

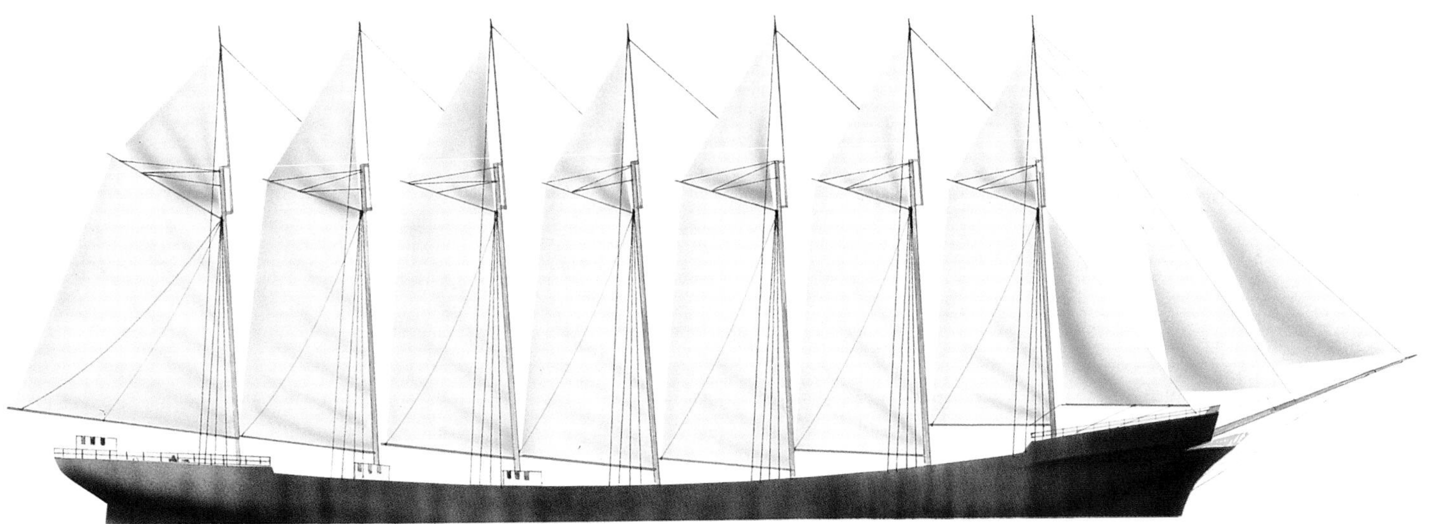

TITANIC

GB/USA: 1911

The *Titanic* was the second of a trio of ill-fated 45,000t ships constructed in Belfast for the White Star Line; she was preceded by the *Olympic*, which was involved in no less than four collisions in a 24-year career, and followed by the *Britannic*, which never saw mercantile service, being sunk by a German mine while serving as a hospital ship.

The *Titanic* was just a few tons larger than her elder sistership as she was completed, making her the biggest of her day. The fourth of her funnels was false and was added only for aesthetic purposes.

All three had double bottoms and no less than 15 transverse watertight bulkheads, with electrically operated doors, although these only extended to the lower deck. When the *Titanic*'s fateful collision came, breaching the integrity of the six foremost watertight compartments and flooding them so that the ship went down by the head, water poured over the remaining bulkheads one by one until she sank.

RMS *Titanic* left Southampton on her maiden voyage, bound for New York via Cherbourg and Queenstown (Cork), on 10 April 1912. Her departure itself almost ended in tragedy, as the suction created by her three propellers dragged the Inman Line's *City of New York* away from the quay, snapping her mooring lines. By the afternoon of 14 April she was some 600 nautical miles (1100km) east of Newfoundland. Her wireless operators received warnings of ice in her path, but her captain, Edward Smith, chose to ignore them and continued at an undiminished 22 knots. At 2340 a lookout reported ice ahead. The First Officer gave orders to leave it to starboard, but the ship grazed an underwater spur, buckling her port-side hull plates along the riveted seams. She sank, with the loss of 1503 of the 2223 people aboard, in less than two and a half hours. Much of the resulting scandal centred on the disproportionate number of lives lost (75 per cent) amongst third-class passengers.

Tonnage: 46,328 grt
Dimensions: 852ft 6in x 92ft 6in x 34ft (259.85m x 28.2m x 10.35m)
Machinery: three-shaft, triple expansion plus low-pressure turbine; 50,000hp
Service speed: 21 knots
Role: passenger liner
Route: Southampton–New York
Capacity: 1034 1st, 510 2nd, 1022 3rd
Constructor: Harland & Wolff, Belfast
Material: steel
Built for: White Star Line

TOPAZ

GB: 1920

Tonnage: 577 grt
Dimensions: 168ft x 27ft x 13ft (50m x 8m x 4m)
Machinery: one-shaft, triple expansion
Service speed: 8 knots
Role: general cargo vessel
Route: coastal waters, UK
Capacity: 770 dwt
Constructor: Lewis
Material: not known
Built for: W Robertson, Glasgow

Topaz was typical of the small coasters that thrived in the British coastal trade from 1900 to 1925. She was of simple design with a long quarterdeck extending half the length of the hull, a raised forecastle and a short well deck with a standard bridge at the end. Positioning of the derricks and handling gear varied with the needs of each ship. Aft was a bunker running across the width of the vessel with a capacity of sevens tons of coal. There was a small mizzen mast right aft for a steadying sail plus a main mast aft of the bridge and one forward, rising up from the forecastle; all were fitted with derricks.

Ships such as the coaster *Topaz* were once a common sight around the shores of the UK. *Topaz* was scrapped in 1956.

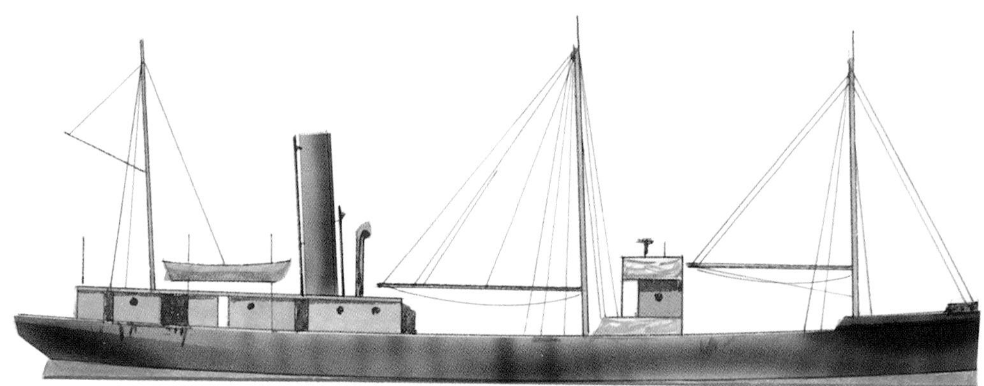

TRIESTE

USA: 1953

The bathyscaphe *Trieste* was designed and built by Auguste Piccard. It was a vessel in two parts. The upper was simply a tank containing 3745 cubic feet (106 cubic metres) of gasoline. Being of lower specific gravity than water, this provided a sufficient measure of buoyancy to return the craft to the surface when water ballast held in two small tanks at the extremities was

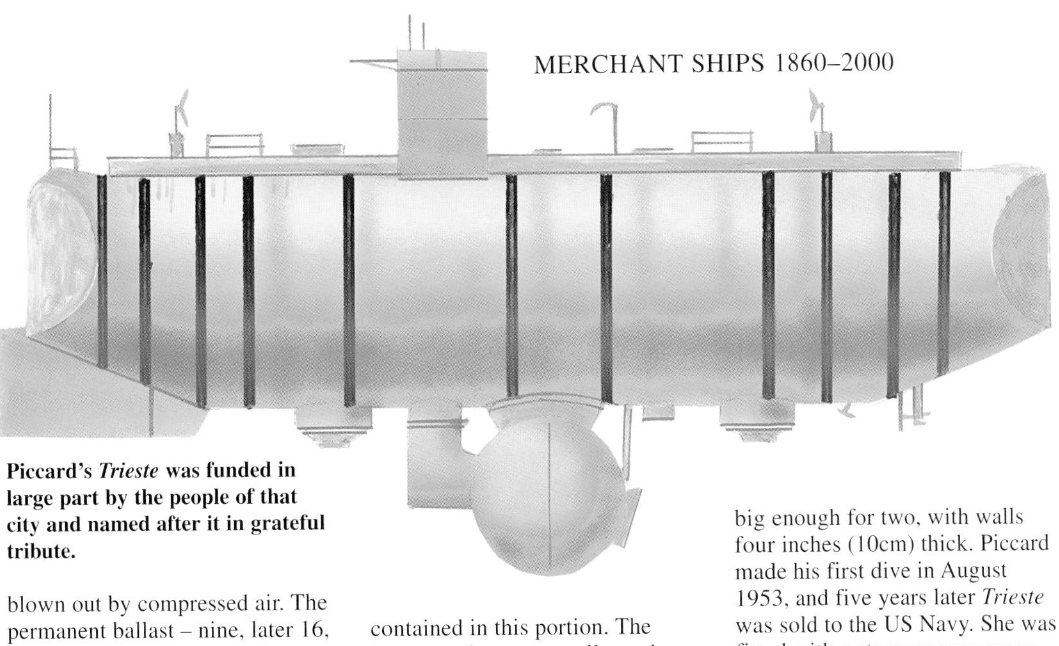

Piccard's *Trieste* was funded in large part by the people of that city and named after it in grateful tribute.

blown out by compressed air. The permanent ballast – nine, later 16, tons of iron pellets – was also contained in this portion. The lower section was an alloy sphere, big enough for two, with walls four inches (10cm) thick. Piccard made his first dive in August 1953, and five years later *Trieste* was sold to the US Navy. She was fitted with a stronger passenger sphere, and in January 1960, Piccard's son Jacques and Lieutenant Don Walsh USN descended to 35,800 feet (10,912m) in the Challenger Deep, southwest of Guam, then believed to be the deepest point on earth.

Tonnage: 50t displacement
Dimensions: 59ft 6in x 11ft 6in (18.1m x 3.5m)
Machinery: two-shaft, electric; 2hp
Service speed: 1 knot
Role: exploration vessel
Route: not applicable
Capacity: not applicable
Constructor: Navalmeccanica, Naples
Material: steel/steel alloy
Built for: Auguste Piccard
Owner: US Navy

TURBINIA

GB: 1894

Tonnage: 44t displacement
Dimensions: 103ft 4in x 9ft x 3ft (31.5m x 2.7m x 0.9m)
Machinery: three-shaft, direct-acting turbine; 2100hp
Service speed: 32 knots
Role: demonstrator
Route: not applicable
Capacity: not applicable
Constructor: Charles Parsons (Turbinia Works; Brown & Hood Ltd)
Material: steel
Built for: Charles Parsons
Owner: Tyne & Wear County Museum

The Hon (later Sir) Charles Parsons is regarded as the last of the great 19th-century engineers. When he died in 1931 he had some 300 patents to his name, but far and away his most important achievement was the invention of the steam turbine, which he first demonstrated in 1884. Initially, he intended the engines to be used to drive dynamos to produce electrical power, and in the first 20 years of their employment in this field, coal consumption was cut by 75 per cent, it is claimed. However, he soon saw that they could be utilised as marine powerplants, too. Parsons set up a separate company and built the 44t *Turbinia* to test his theories, arriving at the right combination of propeller shafts and propellers by trial and error. He first tried a single shaft with three propellers, and then switched to three-shafts, initially with three propellers each. He also exchanged the original radial-flow turbine for an axial-flow design of greater efficiency. Parsons demonstrated the effectiveness of his new powerplant publicly in a rather unorthodox but very effective manner. He made an unannounced and certainly uninvited appearance at the Diamond Jubilee Spithead Review in 1897 and sped through the serried ranks of warships and passenger liners at a speed of around 34 knots – six or seven knots faster than any of the assembled cast could manage. 'Her speed', reported *The Times*, 'was simply astonishing.' *Turbinia* was later exhibited at the 1900 Paris Exhibition and made her last voyage in 1907. In 1960, she was put on permanent display in a museum in Newcastle-upon-Tyne. Parsons subcontracted the construction of the first turbine-powered warship, HMS *Viper*, to Hawthorne, Leslie. She was commissioned in 1900.

Sir Charles Parsons' diminutive *Turbinia* made her debut public appearance, uninvited, at Queen Victoria's Diamond Jubilee Naval Review and astonished the gathering by speeding through the fleet at over 34 knots, leaving the pursuing guard boats in her wake.

TYCHO BRAHE

DENMARK: 1991

The train and vehicle ferry *Tycho Brahe*, named after the Danish astronomer, was built to operate across the 2.7-mile (5km) straits separating Helsingør in Denmark and Helsingborg in Sweden. She was the largest double-ended ferry in the world, with room for 260 trucks, 240 cars and nine railway passenger carriages. One of the *Tycho Brahe*'s most important features was her ability to accelerate to and decelerate from her 14-knot service speed in very short distances.

The *Tycho Brahe*'s double-ended construction ensured the fastest turnaround possible on what is one of the world's shortest international ferry routes.

Tonnage: 12,000 grt
Dimensions: 364ft 2in x 92ft 6in x 18ft 8in (111m x 28.2m x 5.7m
Machinery: four-shaft, diesel; 3350hp
Service speed: 14 knots
Role: passenger/train/vehicle ferry
Route: Ore Sund (Helsingør-Helsingborg)
Capacity: 1250 p, 500 v, 9 rc
Constructor: Langsten, Tomresfjord
Material: steel
Built for: Dansk Statsbaner

UNITED STATES

USA: 1952

The machinery of the *United States* was derived from warships. Her double-reduction turbines were designed for an aircraft carrier which was never built, while her oil-fired boilers were the same as those fitted to the *Iowa*-class battleships.

The SS *United States* was the most advanced passenger ship ever built when she entered service in 1952, and many have argued that she had not been surpassed half a century later in most respects but size. (Her designer utilised every artifice to increase her gross register tonnage, which is actually a measurement of internal volume. He used an antiquated measuring system to arrive at a figure of 53,329 grt, but a more accurate figure was probably 38,216 grt.) She was almost the personal creation of William Francis Gibbs, a self-taught naval architect, who drew up the first tentative design for the ship as early as 1916.

In terms of her machinery, and the technology embodied therein, the claims for the supremacy of the *United States* were undeniable. Her machinery, supplied by the Westinghouse Corporation, which was an early collaborator of Charles Parsons, inventor of the steam turbine, consisted of four 60,000hp double-reduction turbines, designed for the aborted aircraft carrier which was also to have been called the *United States*. On trial they actually produced a total of 241,758shp, for a sustained top speed of 38.32 knots and an unconfirmed (and, it must be said, almost incredible) burst speed of 43 knots.

By the time she was laid up, the *United States* had cost the US government over $100 million in subsidies. This was largely due to her never having the reputation for luxury which the Cunard *Queens* or the *DH* enjoyed.

The massive installed power – specified because he intended to make absolutely sure that she gained the transatlantic speed record – was exploited by Gibbs when it came to raising finance for the ship, and he established the case for her being largely US government funded on the grounds that she would be a national strategic asset as a high-speed troop carrier. He reinforced the illusion by locating the machinery in two quite separate engine rooms, stating that this was to ensure redundancy in the case of torpedo attack.

The *United States* naturally took the eastbound and westbound Blue Ribands on her maiden voyage, beating the records established by the *Queen Mary* 14 years earlier by around 12 per cent, with average speeds of 35.59 knots outward bound and 34.51 knots homeward bound against the prevailing westerly winds. She lost them – and the Hales Trophy – to a specially designed speedboat with just two 'paying passengers' aboard in the mid-1990s.

For all her performance – and she had all the amenities that went with it – the *United States* soon fell foul of cheap air transport. She was laid up after just 17 years in service, in 1969, and was acquired by the US Maritime Administration in 1973. She passed to Turkish interests in 1992 and was towed to the Eastern Mediterranean. Considerable sums were spent on bringing her up to more modern standards (including stripping out many tons of asbestos), but the attempt came to naught. She was returned to the USA in 1996 and became a static exhibit in Philadelphia.

Tonnage: 53,329 grt
Dimensions: 990ft x 101ft 7in x 31ft (301.8m x 31m x 9.4m)
Machinery: four-shaft, geared turbines; 240,000hp
Service speed: 34 knots
Role: passenger liner
Route: New York-Southampton
Capacity: 913 1st, 558 cb, 537 tr
Constructor: Newport News Shipbuilding & Dry Dock Co
Material: steel and aluminium
Built for: United States Lines
Owner: not known

VADERLAND (LATER GÉOGRAPHIQUE) — USA/BELGIUM: 1872

Tonnage: 2748 grt
Dimensions: 320ft 6in x 38ft 6in (97.7m x 11.75m)
Machinery: one-shaft, compound
Service speed: 13 knots
Role: passenger/cargo liner
Route: Antwerp-Philadelphia/New York
Capacity: 30 (later 70) 1st, 800 3rd
Constructor: Palmers Shipbuilding & Iron Co, Jarrow
Material: iron
Built for: International Navigation Co (Red Star Line)

The *Vaderland*, which entered service between Antwerp and Philadelphia in 1873, was the first ship constructed for the Red Star Line. She was actually designed as a dual-purpose ship and was intended to carry both passengers and petroleum in bulk. For this reason she was of distinctive appearance, with her machinery and accommodation aft. In fact she never did load petroleum, it being deemed too dangerous by the American authorities to combine its carriage with that of passengers.

The *Vaderland* was built as a dual-purpose petrol tanker/passenger liner; in practice her cargo consisted of bacon, bark, hides, lard and tobacco.

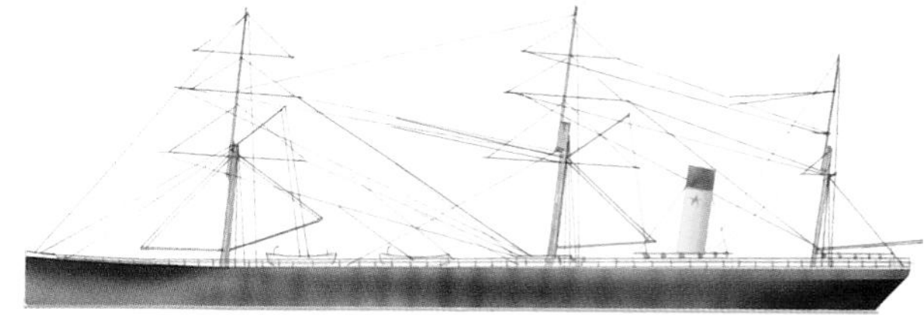

VICTORIAN (LATER MARLOCH) — GB: 1904

The Allan Line's *Victorian* represents an important landmark in passenger transport, for she was the first liner on the North Atlantic to be turbine-powered and the first with triple screws. She and her sistership *Virginian* were thus considerably faster than other ships of their size. *Victorian* was later re-engined with geared turbines and converted to oil-firing. She remained in service until 1928. Her sistership, similarly modified, had a very long career indeed, and was not scrapped until 1955.

The *Victorian* and *Virginian* had a main turbine, operating at high pressure, on the centre shaft and low pressure turbines attached to the wing shafts.

Tonnage: 10,635 grt
Dimensions: 540ft x 60ft 5in x 29ft 6in (164.6m x 18.4m x 9m)
Machinery: three-shaft, direct-acting (later geared) turbines; 15,000hp
Service speed: 18 knots
Role: passenger liner
Route: Europe-Canada
Capacity: 346 1st, 344 2nd, 1000 3rd; 418 cb, 566 3rd
Constructor: Workman, Clark & Co, Belfast
Material: steel

VOIMA

FINLAND: 1954

Tonnage: 3481 grt
Dimensions: 274ft x 63ft 9in x 22ft 2in (83.5m x 19.45m x 6.75m)
Machinery: four-shaft, diesel-electric; 10,500hp (later 17,460hp)
Service speed: 15 knots
Role: ice-breaker
Route: Gulf of Finland
Constructor: Wärtsilä, Helsinki
Material: steel
Built for: Finnish Board of Navigation

The ice-breaker *Voima*, constructed in 1954, was a marked improvement over earlier types, with twin propellers fore and aft, the latter drawing water from beneath the ice ahead of the vessel and passing it down the sides, thus reducing friction considerably. She was modernised and re-engined by her builders in 1977-78 but was written off in February 1994 after colliding with a German general cargo ship, the *Alita*, off Helsinki.

The *Voima* had heeling tanks, with high-speed pumps which could transfer 300t of water in 45 seconds, allowing her to break free from encroaching ice.

VOYAGER OF THE SEAS

NORWAY: 1999

Tonnage: 137,300 grt
Dimensions: 1020ft x 127ft (310.9m x 38.7m)
Machinery: three-shaft, diesel-electric; 101,340hp
Service speed: 22 knots
Role: cruise ship
Route: Caribbean
Capacity: 3880 sc
Constructor: Kvaerner, Helsinki
Material: steel
Built for: Royal Caribbean Cruises

At the close of the 20th century, Royal Caribbean Cruise's *Voyager of the Seas* was the world's biggest passenger ship, with a register tonnage of 137,300t gross. At 1020 feet (310.9m) overall, she was only marginally smaller than the longest of them all – the *Norway* (ex-*France*) and the Cunarder *Queens* – and with a beam of 127 feet (38.7m) she was too broad to pass through the Panama Canal. Naturally enough, her performance did not even come near to that of the last generation of 'ocean greyhounds', although by contemporary cruise ship standards it was quite high. Quite simply, the *Voyager of the Seas* set out to be all things to all people, with facilities which would not disgrace any terrestrial holiday resort, including an ice rink big enough for hockey

When she embarked on her maiden cruise in November 1999, the *Voyager of the Seas* was the biggest passenger ship the world had ever seen, with accommodation for 3880 people in double en suite cabins on 14 decks.

games, a putting course and driving range, a 16,150-square-ft (1500-square-metre) fitness centre, a climbing wall and even a wedding chapel, not to mention six restaurants and five bars. Technically, too, her specification read like a list of superlatives – 84 miles (135km) of pipework, 1864 miles (3000km) of electrical cabling, 101,340hp diesel engines powering generator sets producing 75.6MW of power to run the three electrical propulsion motors mounted in pods slung beneath the hull. She also had 2221 guest and crew staterooms and enormous public spaces on a total of 14 decks (with three others given over to ship's services) with a total of 690,000 square feet (64,000 square metres) of floor space. And all of it completed in just 57 weeks by a workforce which numbered 10,000. The ship herself needed a crew of 1180 to cater to the manifold needs of her 3880 passengers, each of whom expected the voyage of a lifetime during a week spent cruising the Caribbean out of Florida.

The facilities provided on the *Voyager of the Seas* are quite staggering – this shopping mall rivals any terrestrial holiday resort.

VULCANIA (LATER CARIBIA)

ITALY: 1926

The 24,000-t *Vulcania* and her sistership *Saturnia* were the biggest motor ships of their day, built for the Cosiluch Line to operate between Trieste and New York. She proved to be very durable indeed. During World War II she served as a troopship for both the Italian and US governments and was later returned to the service for which she had been constructed. She was sold to the SIOSA Line in 1965, carrying immigrants from the Caribbean to Europe, and was not finally retired until 1974.

Tonnage: 23,970 (later 24,469) grt
Dimensions: 631ft 4in x 79ft 9in (192.45m x 24.35m)
Machinery: two-shaft, diesel
Service speed: 19 (later 21) knots
Role: passenger liner; troopship
Route: Trieste–New York; Caribbean–Europe
Capacity: 310 1st, 460 2nd, 310 tr, 700 3rd; 240 1st, 270 cb, 860 tr
Constructor: Cantiere Navale Triestino, Monfalcone
Material: steel
Built for: Cosiluch Line

The *Vulcania* her sistership *Saturnia* were the biggest motor ships in the world when they were built for the Cosiluch Line's Trieste–New York service in the mid-1920s.

WATERWITCH

GB: 1872

Tonnage: 900 grt
Dimensions: 205ft x 35ft x 18ft 6in (62.5m x 10.65m x 5.65m)
Machinery: not applicable
Service speed: not applicable
Role: general cargo vessel
Route: not applicable
Capacity: not applicable
Constructor: not applicable
Material: iron or steel
Built for: not applicable

The barquentine was a vessel carrying three or more masts, square-rigged to topgallants on only the foremost of them. As it became possible to build longer and longer ships, so additional masts were carried, and this rig proved very popular – it was hardly less weatherly than the barque rig and was cheaper to construct and needed a smaller crew. It was to prove enduringly popular. Many of the late 20th-century sailing cruise ships adopted it, often with a modified arrangement of courses and staysails.

The barquentine had fore-and-aft sails on all but the foremost of its three or sometimes four masts; the rig proved to be easily manageable and economical.

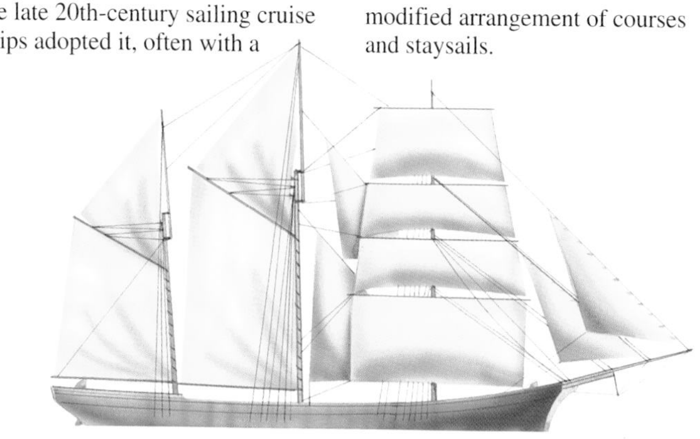

WERRA

GERMANY: 1882

Tonnage: 4817 grt
Dimensions: 433ft 2in x 45ft 10in (132m x 14m)
Machinery: one-shaft, compound
Service speed: 16 knots
Role: passenger liner
Route: Bremen–New York; Genoa–New York
Capacity: 125 1st, 130 2nd, 1000 3rd
Constructor: John Elder & Co, Glasgow
Material: iron
Built for: Norddeutscher Lloyd Line

Formed in 1858, the Norddeutscher Lloyd Line made rapid inroads into the migrant trade. By the early 1870s, it was carrying over 50,000 people a year to New York. There followed a five-year slump, but by 1880 the situation was profitable again, and the company began building more express steamers, starting with the *Elbe*. The *Werra* came next and was followed by another seven substantially similar ships, all Glasgow-built, with third-class accommodation for a thousand people.

The *Werra* operated between Bremen and New York for 10 years, and was then switched over to the Italian service.

WESTERNLAND

USA/BELGIUM: 1883

The *Westernland* was built to operate the American-Belgian Red Star Line's newly inaugurated weekly service from Antwerp to New York in tandem with the *Noordland* and three older ships. She was the line's first steel ship and was built by Lairds of Birkenhead, one of the pioneers of the material. In 1901, she was refitted, chartered to the American Line and operated between Liverpool and Philadelphia, although she later made three return trips in the original service. She was scrapped in 1912.

Tonnage: 5736 grt
Dimensions: 440ft x 47ft 3in (134.1m x 14.4m)
Machinery: one-shaft, compound
Service speed: 14 knots
Role: passenger liner
Route: Antwerp–New York; Liverpool–Philadelphia
Capacity: 80 1st, 60 2nd, 1200 3rd; 170 2nd, 1200 3rd
Constructor: Laird Bros, Birkenhead
Material: steel
Built for: Red Star Line

The Red Star Line went from strength to strength from 1885, thanks largely to its foresight in ordering the *Westernland* and the *Nordernland*.

WILLIAM G MATHER

USA: 1925

The *William G Mather* was typical of the bulk carriers built to operate on the North American Great Lakes, with the command position right forward and engines right aft. She was equally at home carrying grain from the prairies or iron ore. She had four holds, each of them served by four large hatches to speed loading and discharging. Built in 1925, she had a long career before being acquired as a floating museum exhibit.

Tonnage: 8662 grt
Dimensions: 601ft x 62ft x 18ft (183.2m x 18.9m x 55.5m)
Machinery: one-shaft, geared turbine; 5500hp
Service speed: 12 knots
Role: bulk carrier
Route: Great Lakes
Capacity: c10,000t
Constructor: Great Lakes Engineering Works, River Rouge, Michigan
Material: steel
Built for: Cleveland-Cliffs Steamship Co
Owner: Great Lakes Historical Society, Vermillion, Ohio

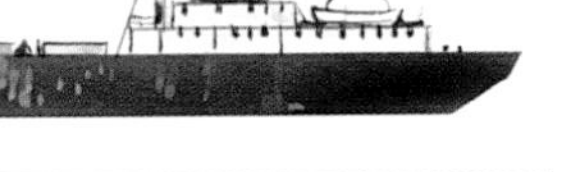

The Great Lakes bulk carriers of the 1920s incorporated many features later found in sea-going bulkers.

WISCONSIN

GB: 1870

The *Wisconsin*, commissioned in July 1870, was the seventh ship the Guion Line put into service on its very successful Liverpool–New York route. More importantly, perhaps, she was the first steamer designed for the North Atlantic to be fitted with compound machinery and set a standard for speed and reliability which other lines were forced to match or see their share of a fast-growing market erode. She remained in service for 22 years.

Tonnage: 3238 grt
Dimensions: 366ft x 43ft 3in (111.55m x 13.15m)
Machinery: one-shaft, compound
Service speed: 11 knots
Role: passenger liner
Route: Liverpool-New York
Capacity: 76 1st, 100 2nd, 800 3rd
Constructor: Palmer Bros & Co, Jarrow
Material: iron
Built for: Liverpool & Great Western Steamship Co

The *Wisconsin* was joined in service the following year by her sistership, the *Wyoming*, and both were successful. The next pair, *Montana* and *Dakota*, were both wrecked on Anglesey.

WYOMING

USA: 1909

The six-masted schooner *Wyoming*, one of only 10 such ships ever constructed, was probably the biggest wooden ship ever built. She was constructed in Bath, Maine, in 1909, by which time the coal trade between New England and the ports serving the Pennsylvania coalfield, for which she was built, had largely passed to steamships. She later made longer offshore voyages. In March 1924, she was en route from Norfolk to St John when she was overtaken by a storm and foundered with the loss of all 13 hands.

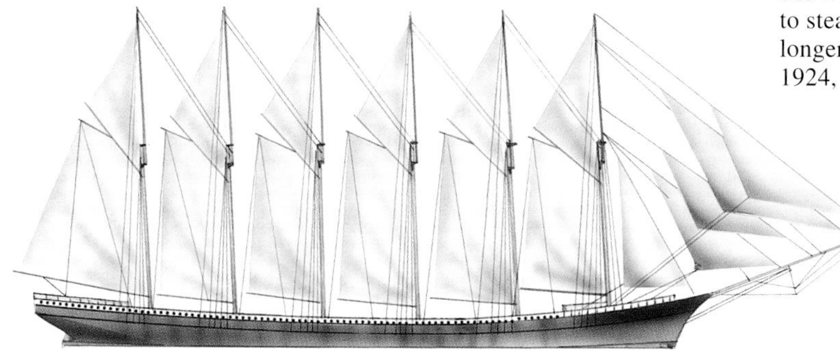

The *Wyoming* was sold in 1916 for $350,000; by 1 October 1919, she was reported to have already paid for herself twice over.

Tonnage: 3730 grt
Dimensions: 329ft 6in x 50ft x 30ft 4in (100.4m x 15.3m x 9.3m)
Machinery: not applicable
Service speed: not applicable
Role: collier
Route: Eastern Seaboard, USA
Capacity: c6500t
Constructor: Percy & Small, Bath, Maine
Material: wood
Built for: Percy & Small

YERMAK

RUSSIA; USSR: 1898

Tonnage: 8730t displacement
Dimensions: 320ft x 71ft 6in x 25ft (97.55m x 21.8m x 7.6m)
Machinery: three-shaft, triple expansion; 9390hp
Service speed: 12 knots
Role: ice-breaker
Route: Murmansk-Vladivostok
Capacity: not applicable
Constructor: Sir W G Armstrong, Whitworth & Co, Elswick
Material: steel
Built for: Imperial Russian Navy

The large and powerful ice-breaker *Yermak* was built by Armstrong-Whitworth at Elswick on the Tyne at the end of the 19th century and enjoyed a very lengthy career indeed, especially for a ship employed in such arduous duties, not being finally discarded until 1964. One of the earliest purpose-built ice-breakers, she served as a model for most later ships of the type, significant innovations not appearing until after World War II.

The *Yermak* was built for the Baltic, but spent most of her life in the Arctic, keeping the route between Murmansk and Vladivostok open for as long as possible.

CHAPTER FIVE

STEAM AND STEEL 1860–1905

The period 1860–1905 saw an unprecedented upsurge in warship development; with the introduction of the ironclad warship a new era dawned. Iron-hull construction enabled vessels to be built far larger than in the days of the wooden hull. After 1860, wooden-hulled warships would continue to be built, but mostly in the cruiser and lesser groups, until the 1880s when steel took over due to its relative lightness and strength.

In the 1860s, the broadside ironclad frigates replaced the wooden-hulled two- and three-decker line-of-battle ships. As guns became more powerful so armour grew thicker which, because of weight limitations, was restricted to protecting the vitals. Capital ships now carried a mixed armament of quick-firing guns increasing the number of rounds fired per minute.

Left: HMS *Formidable* was launched in November 1898 as the name ship of a class of three first-class battleships. She was torpedoed and sunk by *U24* off Portland on January 1 1915.

Machinery and boilers developed rapidly. As engines became more reliable and economical so sail power was dispensed with. Boiler power continued to increase leading to the triple expansion engine with its good economy. Liquid fuel began to be used in the 1890s and the turbine first appeared marking a major step in engineering that would develop further after 1900.

Mine warfare continued to develop also and by the 1890s it had become a permanent feature in naval defence. The locomotive torpedo was adopted by all navies. During this period the submarine slowly evolved, and with the development of the battery by 1900, became a practical weapon. Also by 1900 the battleship had reached its peak, but by 1906 the all-big gun *Dreadnought* was on the scene and, like the *Warrior* before her, immediately eclipsed existing capital ships, thus heralding another new era.

ABOUKIR

GB: 1902

By the end of the 1890s, great improvements in the manufacture of armour made it possible to protect large areas of the broadside with armour capable of resisting 6in (152mm) quick-firing guns, while keeping the size and cost of the ships within reasonable limits. Completed in April 1902, *Aboukir* had a Krupp steel belt 6in (152mm) thick, 231ft (70m) long by 11ft 6in (3.4m) deep; it extended from 5ft (1.5m) below the waterline up to the main deck, and was closed at the ends with 5in (127mm) bulkheads. A 2in belt continued to the bows. The 9.2in (234mm) guns were mounted in turrets, one at each end of the ship, with the 6in (152mm) guns sited in casemates. Total weight of the armour was 2100t. *Aboukir*, together with her sisters, *Hogue* and *Cressey*, were sunk on 22 September 1914 on patrol in the North Sea by the German submarine *U9*.

***Aboukir* and her five sisters were the first British armoured cruisers laid down since the 5000t *Orlando* class of 1886-87.**

Displacement: 12,000t
Dimensions: 472ft x 69ft 6in x 26ft (143.9m x 21.2m x 7.9m)
Machinery: twin screw, triple expansion, 30 boilers; 21,352hp
Armament: two 9.2in (234mm), 12 6in (152mm); two 18in (457mm) TT
Armour: belt 2-6in (51-152mm); turrets 6in (152mm); casemates 5in (127mm); deck 1-3in
Speed: 22.5 knots
Range: not known
Complement: 760

AFFONDATORE

ITALY: 1865

Displacement: 4307t
Dimensions: 307ft 9in x 40ft x 20ft 10in (93.8m x 12.2m x 6.3m)
Machinery: single screw, single expansion, eight boilers; 2717hp
Armament: two 9in (229mm)
Armour: hull 5in (127mm); turrets 5in (127mm); deck 2in
Speed: 12 knots
Range: 1650 miles at 10 knots
Complement: 309

Due to the worsening relations with Austria in the 1860s, Italy decided to acquire a turret ship, a type that was felt to be superior to the broadside ironclads then in service. Built in Britain, *Affondatore* was delivered incomplete and hurried away to Italy to avoid seizure on the outbreak of war between Italy and Austria in 1866. *Affondatore* was an iron-hulled schooner-rigged vessel with a full-length armoured belt extending from 7ft 3in (2.2m) above water to 4ft (1.2m) below. Upon arrival in Italy, *Affondatore* joined the fleet as Admiral Count Persano's flagship at the Battle of Lissa on 20 July 1866. *Affondatore* was rebuilt in 1885, receiving increased superstructure and modern guns.

***Affondatore* as completed in 1866, showing the relatively clear decks and the enormous ram bow, which was 26ft (7.9m) long.**

ALABAMA

CONFEDERATE STATES OF AMERICA: 1862

Displacement: 1050t
Dimensions: 220ft x 31ft 8in x 14ft (67m x 9.6m x 4.2m)
Machinery: single screw
Armament: one 6.4in (162mm), one 68 PDR, six 32 PDR
Speed: 13 knots
Range: not known
Complement: 145

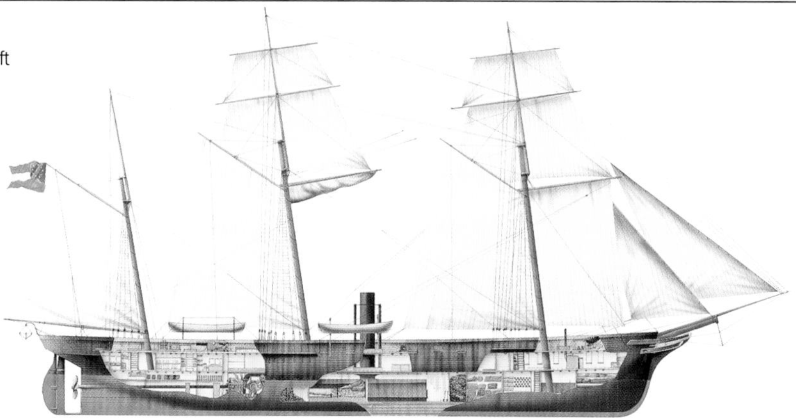

The barque-rigged sloop *Alabama* is probably one of the world's most famous raiders ever built. Her depreciations of northern merchant shipping, together with the exploits of the other Confederate raiders during the American Civil War of 1861–65, had a major effect upon the American merchant marine. By 1865, American import-export trade plunged to a mere fraction of its

***Alabama* was the most successful of the Confederate raiders.**

pre-civil war period, taking nearly 40 years for it to regain its former position of strength. Eventually Great Britain had to pay $15.5 million compensation to United States shipowners. She was ordered in 1862 by James Bullock, the special agent sent to Europe by the Confederate government to obtain much-needed ships as the South lacked suitable ship-construction facilities, and was built of wood which was easier to repair away from a regular dockyard, with extra space allowed for stores, and spares. Designed to sail for long periods while saving fuel, *Alabama* had a lifting screw, reducing the drag of the propellor, which took 15 minutes to raise. With steam and sail combined she made just over 13 knots. Known originally as 290, Raphael Semmes, her captain, took her to sea in August 1862 narrowly escaping seizure by British officials. Meeting up with her tender *Agrippina*, *Alabama* took on guns, ammunition, and stores prior to commencing a 22-month-long cruise covering 75,000 miles without once touching at a Southern port. During this time, *Alabama* destroyed or captured 66 vessels valued at over $6 million. Included was the auxiliary Union gunboat *Hatteras*, sunk off Galverston in January 1863.

By April 1864, after a successful cruise, *Alabama* was desperately in need of repair and Semmes headed for France, entering Cherbourg on 10th June, here to be blockaded by the US sloop *Kearsage*. Nine days later, *Alabama* emerged to face *Kearsage* but was sunk in the ensuing action.

ALMIRANTE COCHRANE

CHILE: 1874

Designed by Sir Edward Reed, *Almirante Cochrane* and her sister *Blanco Encalada* combined a powerful armament with good protection on a relatively small displacement. They were also very 'handy' ships, with a turning circle of only 300yd (274m). The main armament was concentrated in a central battery, part of which overhung the hull sides, thus enabling four guns to fire ahead and two astern; all could fire on the broadside. Iron-hulled, *Almirante Cochrane* had a double bottom beneath the engine room, stokehold, and magazines. The complete belt was 9in (229mm) thick amidships at the waterline, with a 6in (152mm) strake above and below, reducing to 4.5in (115mm) at the ends. In October 1879, *Almirante Cochrane* and *Blanco Encalada* fought and captured the Peruvian turret ship *Huascar* after a fierce action lasting nearly two hours. In 1891, a revolution broke out in Chile, and both ironclads joined the Congressional forces at war with President Balmaceda. *Blanco Encalada* was lying in Caldera Bay, where she was attacked at 3.30am on 23 April by two torpedo gunboats, *Almirante Lynch* and *Almirante Condell*. In poor light, both vessels fired torpedoes at the anchored ship, striking the ironclad amidships and causing her to sink in minutes.

Displacement: 3560t
Dimensions: 210ft x 45ft 9in x 21ft 10in (64m x 14m x 6.6m)
Machinery: twin screw, compound horizontal trunk, six boilers; 2920hp
Armament: six 9in (229mm)
Armour: belt 4.5-6-9in (115-152-229mm); battery 6-8in (152-203mm)
Speed: 12.7 knots
Range: 1900 miles at 10 knots
Complement: 300

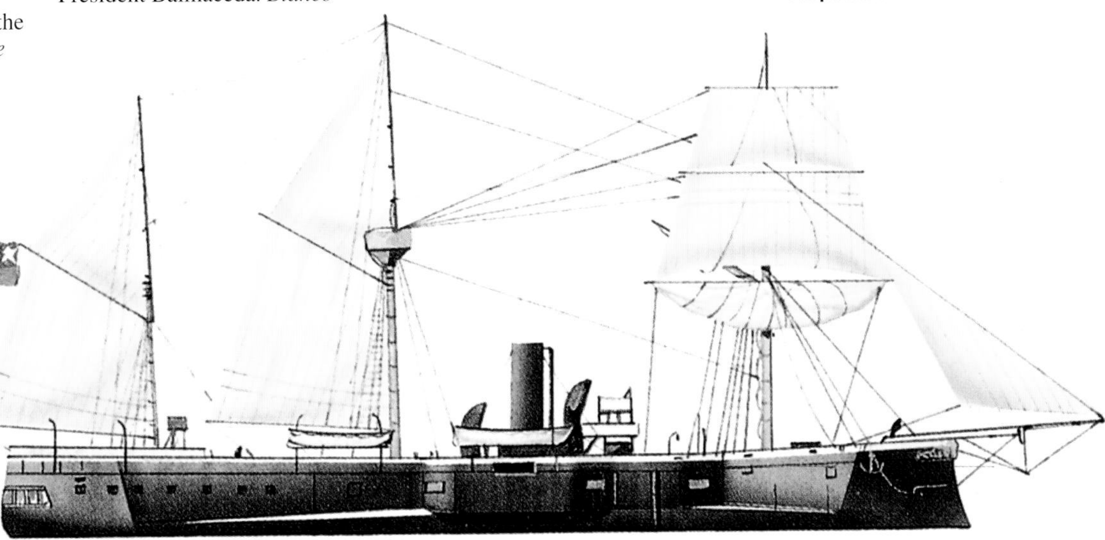

***Almirante Cochrane* upon completion in 1875 with barque rig. She was rearmed in 1889 with 8in (203mm) breech-loaders in place of the 9in (229mm) guns. She was scrapped in 1935.**

ALMIRANTE LYNCH

CHILE: 1890

Displacement: 713t
Dimensions: 230ft x 27ft 6in x 8ft 3in (70.1m x 8.4m x 2.5m)
Machinery: twin screw, triple expansion, four boilers; 4532hp
Armament: three 14pdr; five 14in (356mm) TT
Armour: 1in steel plating over boilers and engine room
Speed: 20.2 knots
Range: not known
Complement: 87

The steel-hulled torpedo gunboat *Almirante Lynch* and her sister *Almirante Condell* were built by Laird Bros and launched in 1890. They had a raised forecastle and poop, plus a ram bow. Two 14pdr guns were mounted *en échelon* on the forecastle, with the third one on the poop. One torpedo tube was mounted in the bow, and two trainable tubes were sited on each broadside. During the Chilean Civil War of 1891, *Almirante Lynch* and her sister attacked and sank the rebel ironclad *Blanco Encalada*. This was the first successful attack on a warship with locomotive torpedoes.

***Almirante Lynch* formed part of the small force of vessels available to Balmaceda in his struggle with Congressional forces in 1891.**

AMIRAL CECILLE

FRANCE: 1888

In the 1860s and 1870s, France made strenuous efforts to build up its armoured fleet but this was achieved at the expense of its cruiser force. Then, in 1878, specifications were approved for a group of 16-knot 3000t vessels for war against commerce. Instead, however, a group of wooden-hulled fully rigged cruisers were started. After protests, three far more advanced types were laid down, one of which was the steel-hulled *Amiral Cecille*. These three vessels comprised the entire French commerce-raiding fleet in 1885. Six of the 6.4in (163mm) guns were in sponsons on the upper deck, with another mounted in the bows firing right ahead over a pronounced ram bow; an eighth 6.4in (163mm) weapon was mounted right aft. The 5.5in (140mm) guns were carried on the broadside in the main deck battery. The protective deck ended 4ft 3in (1.3m) below the waterline.

Laid down in 1886 and completed in 1890, *Amiral Cecille* was, for several years, one of the major cruisers in the French Navy.

Displacement: 5839t
Dimensions: 379ft x 49ft x 22ft 4in (115.5m x 15m x 6.8m)
Machinery: twin screw, vertical compound, 12 boilers; 10,200hp
Armament: eight 6.4in (163mm), 10 5.5in (140mm); three 15in (381mm) TT
Armour: deck 2.2–4in (56–102mm)
Speed: 19.4 knots
Range: not known
Complement: 517

APOLLO

GB: 1891

Displacement: 3400t
Dimensions: 314ft x 43ft x 17ft 6in (95.7m x 13.1m x 5.6m)
Machinery: twin screw, triple expansion, five boilers; 9000hp
Armament: two 6in (152mm), six 4.7in (119mm); four 14in (356mm) TT
Armour: deck 1.5–2in (38–51mm); gunshields 4.5in (115mm)
Speed: 20 knots
Range: not known
Complement: 273

The chief object of building cruisers of this type was to protect or attack commerce, especially in the waters surrounding the British Isles. For this service, the large, costly first-class cruisers were unsuitable, and for a given expenditure, smaller ships could be had in greater numbers. *Apollo* and her 20 sisters were second-class cruisers forming part of the Naval Defence Act of 1889, which was a massive expansion programme for the Royal Navy. Their design followed the previous *Medea* class, but *Apollo* and her sisters were armed with quick-firing guns, instead of the earlier slower-firing breech-loaders as carried by the *Medea*. The 6in (152mm) weapons were mounted one forward and one aft, with the 4.7in (119mm) guns sited on the upper deck, three on each beam. The protective deck was complete with 5in (127mm) on the glacis protecting the engines, which were now positioned side by side with a bulkhead running between.

The *Apollo* group led to a whole series of second-class cruisers that steadily rose to 5600t in displacement with a corresponding increase in armament.

AQUIDABAN (SOMETIME VINTE QUATRO DE MAYO)

BRAZIL: 1885

When *Aquidaban* was completed in 1887, she was one of the most powerful warships in American waters and far more potent than any US warship. She a profound effect upon future US naval policy. *Aquidaban* was a steel-hulled turret ship, the compound armour belt was 7ft (2.1m) deep with a steel deck 2in thick covering the central redoubt, curving down at the ends. The two hydraulically operated turrets, each housing two 9.2in (234mm) guns, were placed *en échelon* on top of the redoubt. The narrow superstructure allowed the turret guns to fire ahead and astern, as well as on their own broadsides, with the gaps in the superstructure permitting 50-degree arcs of fire on the opposite beam. In the political upheaval of the newly established republic of Brazil, civil war broke out in 1893 and *Aquidaban* became the backbone of the insurgent forces. She was in action almost daily at Rio de Janeiro, but with the collapse of rebel forces in Rio in March, *Aquidaban* was left isolated. She was torpedoed and sunk by government torpedo boats. She was raised, repaired, and renamed *Vinte Quatro de Mayo*. In 1896–98, she was rebuilt and renamed *Aquidaban* once more. She blew up and sank in January 1906.

Displacement: 4921t
Dimensions: 280ft x 52ft x 18ft 4in (85.3m x 15.8m x 5.6m)
Machinery: twin screw, inverted compound, eight boilers; 6500hp
Armament: four 9.2in (234mm), four 5.5in (140mm); five 14in (356mm) TT
Armour: belt 7-11in (178-280mm); turrets 10in (254mm); deck 2in
Speed: 15.8 knots
Range: 4000 miles at 15 knots
Complement: 277

***Aquidaban* was built by Samuda Bros, London. Later the full-sail rig was replaced with two, then one, military masts.**

ARMIDE

FRANCE: 1867

Displacement: 3513t
Dimensions: 226ft x 45ft 9in x 20ft 6in (68.9m x 13.9m x 6.2m)
Machinery: single screw, horizontal compound return connecting rod, four boilers; 1580hp
Armament: six 7.6in (194mm), six 6.4in (163mm)
Armour: belt 6in (152mm); battery 4.7in (119mm)
Speed: 11 knots
Range: not known
Complement: 300

A wooden-hulled broadside ironclad, *Armide* was one of a class of seven designed for overseas service. They were cheap to build and economical to maintain, thus freeing up the larger more expensive ironclads for service in home waters. She had a complete waterline belt deep, with thin iron plating over the area not covered by the armour protecting the battery. This latter housed four of the 7.6in (194mm) guns; two more were mounted in open barbettes on the deck above, which jutted out several feet from the hull side, giving an improved angle of fire. This system was developed and used in later French casemate ships, and was the direct forerunner of the modern barbette system still in use in World War II.

The ships of this class were rigged as barques with 15,500sq ft (1440sq m) of canvas. They were extremely manoeuvrable, with a tactical diameter of only 360yd (329m).

ARMINIUS

GERMANY: 1864

Displacement: 1800t
Dimensions: 207ft 5in x 35ft 9in x 15ft (63.2m x 10.9m x 4.5m)
Machinery: single screw, horizontal single expansion; 1400hp
Armament: four 8.2in (208mm)
Armour: belt 4.5in (115mm); turret 4.5in (115mm)
Speed: 11.2 knots
Range: 2000 miles at 8 knots
Complement: 132

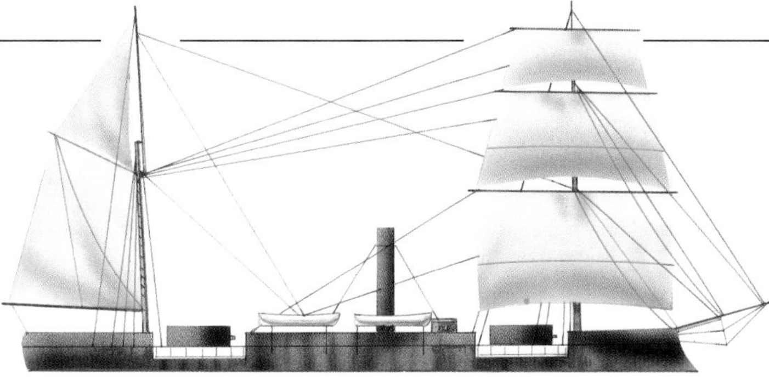

***Arminius* was completed in 1865. She was one of the first major warships in the fledgling German Navy.**

Arminius was an iron-hulled twin-turreted ironclad laid down in 1863. She was a private venture and was purchased on the stocks by the Prussians, who were anxious to create a navy to defend their Baltic coast against the Danes, but had no adequate facilities to build their own warships. Originally *Arminius* was to have carried two 72pdr bronze guns in each of the turrets, but eventually four 8.2in (208mm) weapons were substituted. The complete wrought-iron armour belt extended 2ft 9in (0.8m) below the waterline, and was 4.5in (115mm) thick amidships on a 9in (229mm) teak backing. *Arminius* served as a coast defence vessel in the Elbe during the Franco-Prussian War of 1870–71, and was one of only five ironclads in the Prussian Navy.

ASKOLD

RUSSIA: 1900

Until the 1890s, Russia was extremely weak in cruisers. The few built, however, such as the *Rurik* and *Rossia*, were amongst the largest and most powerful afloat. In 1898, efforts were made to increase cruiser numbers, and competitive designs for 6500t vessels were called for from Germany and America. One of these became the *Askold*, which was laid down in 1898. She had five tall, thin funnels and an extended superstructure forward, on which stood a single 6in (152mm) gun. The remaining 6in (152mm) weapons were mounted one aft and five on each beam at upper deck level behind shields. The protective deck ran the full length, with increased armour on the raised glacis covering the base of the funnels.

Displacement: 5905t
Dimensions: 437ft x 49ft 3in x 20ft 4in (133.2m x 15m x 6.2m)
Machinery: three screws, vertical triple expansion, nine boilers; 20,420hp
Armament: 12 6in (152mm); six 15in (381mm) TT
Armour: deck 2-3in (51-76mm)
Speed: 23.8 knots
Range: not known
Complement: 576

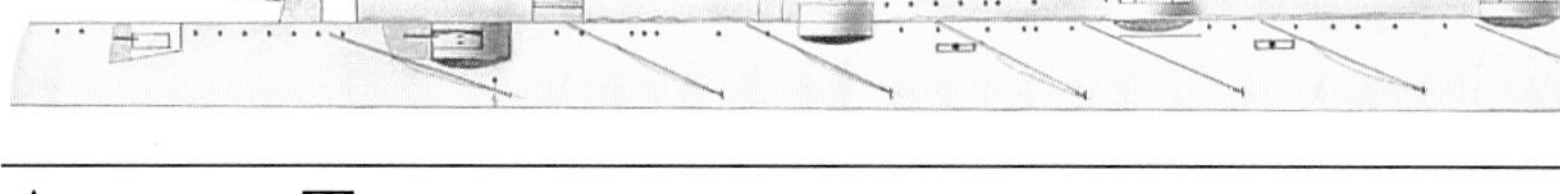

***Askold* served as flagship to the cruisers at Port Arthur in 1904 during the Russo-Japanese War.**

ASSARI TEWFIK

TURKEY: 1868

Displacement: 4687t
Dimensions: 272ft 4in x 52ft 6in x 21ft 4in (83m x 16m x 6.5m)
Machinery: single screw, compound, six boilers; 3560hp
Armament: eight 9in (229mm)
Armour: belt 3-8in (76-203mm)
Speed: 13 knots
Range: not known
Complement: 320

Launched at La Seyne, France, in 1868 and completed in 1870, *Assari Tewfik* was an iron-hulled barbette/battery ship with two 9in (229mm) muzzle-loaders in barbettes on the upper deck, and the remaining 9in (229mm) weapons concentrated in an armoured battery directly below. By 1891, these guns had been replaced with 8.3in (211mm) breech-loaders. In 1903-06, she was extensively modernized by Krupp, receiving new engines. During the Balkan War, while in action against Greek forces, *Assari Tewfik* ran aground on 11 February 1913 and became a total loss.

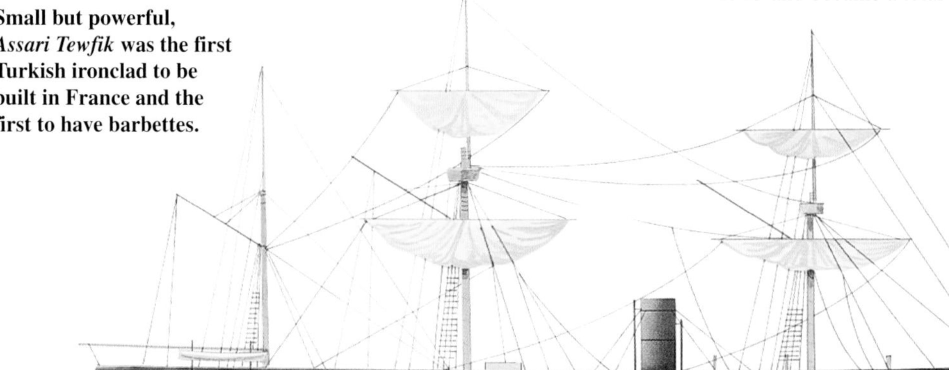

Small but powerful, *Assari Tewfik* was the first Turkish ironclad to be built in France and the first to have barbettes.

ATLANTA (EX-FINGAL)

USA: 1861

Displacement: 1006t
Dimensions: 204ft x 41ft x 17ft (62.5m x 12.8m x 5.2m)
Machinery: three screws, two vertical direct acting, one boiler
Armament: two 7in (178mm), two 6.4in (163mm); one spar torpedo
Armour: casemate 5in (127mm)
Speed: 8 knots
Range: not known
Complement: 145

The fast, iron-hulled blockade runner *Fingal* arrived at Savannah in November 1861 with a large cargo of war material. Unable to escape, she was converted into an ironclad and renamed *Atlanta*. She was cut down to the waterline, and an armoured deck projecting 6ft (1.8m) beyond the original hull was fitted; a casemate with sloping sides containing the guns was built up on the centre section, which itself was armoured with railroad iron which had formed part of the original cargo.

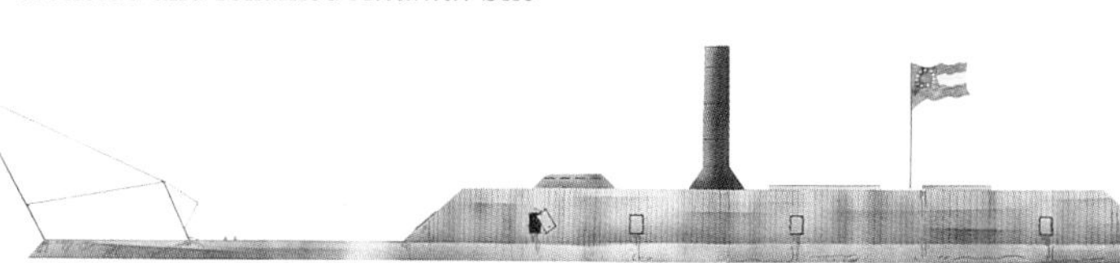

***Atlanta* was captured after running aground during an action with the US monitors *Weehawken* and *Nahant* on 17 June 1863.**

BAINBRIDGE

USA: 1901

Displacment: 420t
Dimensions: 250ft x 23ft 7in x 6ft 6in (76.2m x 7.2m x 2m)
Machinery: twin screw, vertical triple expansion, four boilers; 8000hp
Armament: two 3in (76mm); two 18in (457mm) TT
Speed: not known
Range: not known
Complement: 73

***Bainbridge* was listed as destroyer No 1 in the US Navy. By the end of World War II, numbers had reached 890.**

Bainbridge, laid down in August 1899 and completed in November 1902, was the lead ship in a class of five. This was the first group of destroyers to have a raised forecastle to provide better seakeeping qualities. They were also the first group built in relatively large numbers, previous destroyers having been built as single units. The four funnels were in two groups, with one torpedo tube between and a second tube right aft. All served most of their careers in the Philippines.

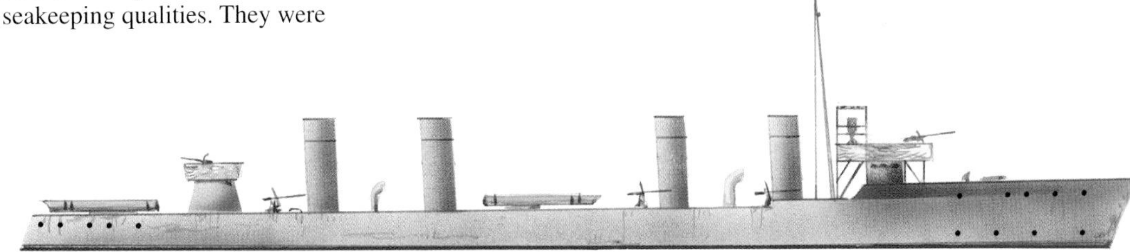

BALTIC

CONFEDERATE STATES OF AMERICA: 1860

Baltic was a wooden sidewheel steamer, built in 1860 and converted into an ironclad for service in Mobile Bay, which was then being blockaded by Union wooden gunboats. At one time *Baltic* was the only Confederate ironclad available for the defence of this sensitive area. The lower hull was strengthened, but due to a lack of space the crew slept on deck. The conditions on board were not ideal, and, on average, each member of the crew reported sick three times during the vessel's short career.

***Baltic* laid 180 mines in Mobile Bay, one of which sank the US monitor *Tecumseh*. *Baltic*'s armour was later removed and used to plate CSS *Nashville*.**

Displacement: 624t
Dimensions: 186ft x 38ft x 6ft 5in (56.7m x 11.6m x 1.95m)
Machinery: sidewheel, inclined
Armament: two 32pdr, two 12pdr howitzers
Armour: 2.5in
Speed: 5 knots
Range: not known
Complement: 86

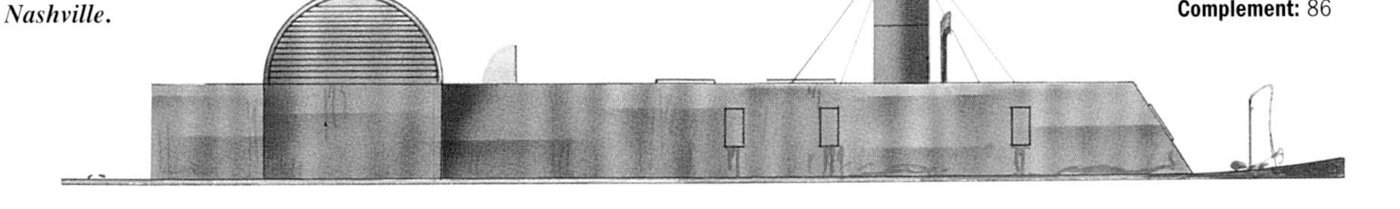

BALTIMORE

USA: 1888

The protected cruiser *Baltimore*, laid down in 1887, was based upon plans prepared by Elswick for the Spanish cruiser *Reina Regent*. The four 8in (203mm) guns were sponsoned out on the poop and forecastle, with the 6in (152mm) guns, also on sponsons, on the gundeck amidships behind light shields. The protective deck was 4in (102mm) thick on the slope, and 2in thick on the flat. Rearmed and reboilered in 1900–03, *Baltimore* was one of the first United States cruisers to dispense with sails.

Baltimore was possibly one of the best United States cruisers laid down in the 1880s. She compared favourably with contemporary European cruisers.

Displacement: 5436t full load
Dimensions: 335ft x 48ft 6in x 19ft 6in (102.1m x 14.8m x 5.9m)
Machinery: twin screw, horizontal triple expansion, four boilers; 10,750hp
Armament: four 8in (203mm), six 6in (152mm)
Armour: protective deck 4in (102mm) on slopes, 2in on flat
Speed: 19 knots
Range: not known
Complement: 386

BARROZO

BRAZIL: 1864

Displacement: 1354t
Dimensions: 186ft x 37ft x 8ft 10in (56.7m x 11.3m x 2.7m)
Machinery: single screw, single expansion; 420hp
Armament: two 7in (178mm), two 68pdr, three 32pdr
Armour: belt and battery 2.5-3.8in (64-97mm) with 25in (635mm) wood backing
Speed: 32 knots
Range: not known
Complement: 230

Barrozo, launched in 1864, was a wooden-hulled coast defence ship, with a raised battery amidships housing two 7in (178mm) Whitworth MLRs and two 68pdr guns. None of these weapons could fire ahead or astern. Armour covered the battery and machinery spaces amidships to the height of the main deck. In 1864, Paraguay declared war on Brazil, Argentina, and Uruguay. Of the participants, only Brazil had any semblance of a modern fleet. The conflict lasted six years, and was fought mainly on the rivers, where *Barrozo*'s shallow draft was a distinct advantage, and where she saw extensive service.

***Barrozo* was one of 11 small but powerful ironclads in the Brazilian Navy in the 1860s. She was scrapped about 1885.**

BASILEUS GEORGIOS

GREECE: 1867

In the 1860s, Greece had the smallest navy in Europe. It comprised two ironclads, *Basileus Georgios*, launched in December 1867, and the 2060t broadside ironclad *Basilissa Olga*, launched in 1869. *Basileus Georgios* was a small central battery ship designed by George Mackrow of the Thames Ironworks. The full-length iron belt extended from 3ft 6 in (1.1m) below the waterline to 6ft 6in (2m) above. The hexagonal-shaped battery was forward of the funnel, and had end ports, enabling the guns to fire almost directly ahead or astern. There were two 20pdr guns outside the battery.

For her size, *Basileus Georgios* had greater offensive/defensive power than any other ironclad. Her armour weighed 330t.

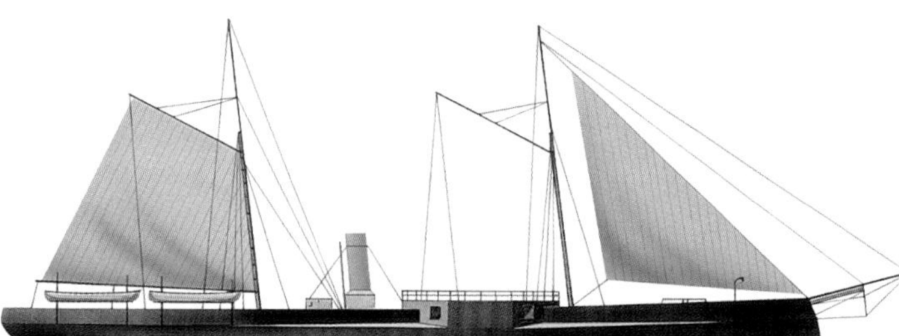

Displacement: 1774t
Dimensions: 200ft x 33ft x 16ft (61m x 10m x 4.9m)
Machinery: twin screw, compound; 2400hp
Armament: two 9in (229mm) MLR, two 20pdr
Armour: belt 7in (178mm) with 6in (152mm) ends; battery 6in (152mm); wood backing 9in (229mm)
Speed: 13 knots
Range: 1200 miles at 10 knots
Complement: 152

BAYAN

RUSSIA: 1900

Bayan, launched in June 1900, was an armoured cruiser built at La Seyne and designed by Lagane.

***Bayan* was an outstanding design, combining a good balance between offence and defence. *Bayan* was captured by the Japanese in January 1905.**

The two 8in (203mm) guns were in closed turrets fore and aft, protected by 7in (178mm) armour; the eight 6in (152mm) guns were carried four in a central redoubt and four in casemates, all protected by 3in armour. The belt ran from the bow to the aft turret, ending in a 7–8in (178–203mm) bulkhead. This belt had its lower edge 4ft (1.2m) below the waterline and its upper edge 2ft (0.6m) above; above the belt ran a second strake 3in thick. The protective deck was a uniform 2in. Eight of the 11pdr guns were behind armour in the central redoubt, with the rest sited on the upper deck behind shields. The lifeboats were made of steel to cut down the risk of fire in action. *Bayan* took part in most of the

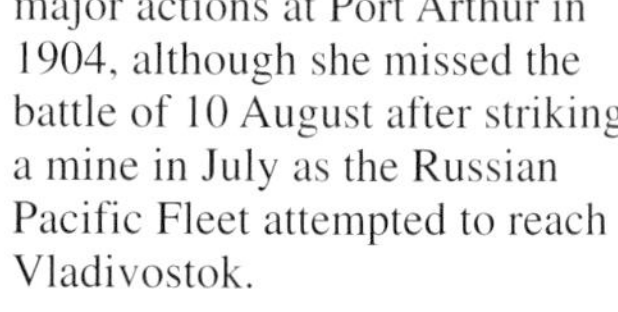

major actions at Port Arthur in 1904, although she missed the battle of 10 August after striking a mine in July as the Russian Pacific Fleet attempted to reach Vladivostok.

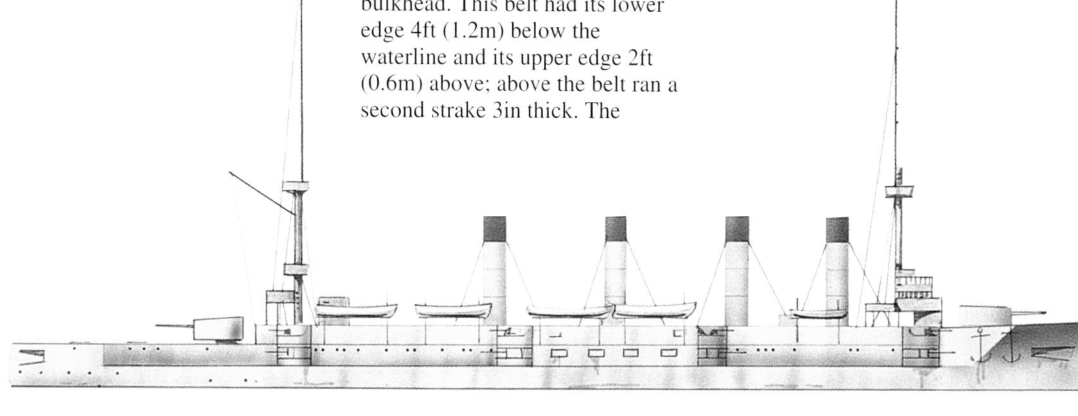

Displacement: 7775t
Dimensions: 449ft 7in x 57ft 6in x 21ft 3in (137m x 17.5m x 6.5m)
Machinery: twin screw, vertical triple expansion, 26 boilers; 17,400hp
Armament: two 8in (203mm), eight 6in (152mm), 20 11pdr; two 15in (381mm) TT
Armour: belt 3-8in (76-203mm); casemates and redoubt 3in (76mm)
Speed: 22 knots
Range: not known
Complement: 568

BENBOW

GB: 1885

***Benbow* was one of the six *Amiral*-class vessels that were the first battleships to have a mixed armament, and the first for many years to form a cohesive group.**

Displacement: 10,600t
Dimensions: 330ft x 68ft 6in x 27ft 10in (100.6m x 20.9m x 8.5m)
Machinery: twin screw, inverted compound, 12 boilers; 10,860hp
Armament: two 16.25in (412mm), 10 6in (152mm); five 14in (356mm) TT
Armour: belt 8-18in (203-457mm); barbettes 14in (356mm); bulkheads 7-16in (178-406mm)
Speed: 17.5 knots
Range: 7100 miles at 10 knots
Complement: 523

In 1880, the first of the *Admiral* class was laid down as a direct answer to the French *Amiral Duperré* type, which were armed with guns ranging up to 16.5in (418mm). *Benbow*, laid down in November 1882, was armed with two 16.25in (412mm) 100t Armstrong breech-loaders, because of delays in the delivery of the newly developed 13.5in (343mm) weapon. The 16.25in (412mm) guns fired one round about every five minutes, and were sited one at each end of the superstructure. The compound armour, 18in (457mm) thick, was concentrated amidships along the waterline, reducing to 8in (203mm) at the lower edge. The ends of the ship were divided up into small watertight compartments to reduce the risk of flooding in action.

BENTON — USA: 1861

Displacement: 633t
Dimensions: 202ft x 72ft x 9ft (60.8m x 21.8m x 2.8m)
Machinery: sternwheel, inclined, five boilers
Armament: two 9in (229mm), seven 42pdr, seven 32pdr
Armour: casemate 2.5in
Speed: 5.5 knots
Range: not known
Complement: 176

The sternwheel ironclad river gunboat *Benton* was originally the catamaran-hulled salvage vessel *Submarine no. 7*. She was rebuilt from designs by James Eades, and had the 20ft (6.1m) gap between the twin hulls planked over. A new bow was added plus a two-tier casemate, the front and first 60ft (18m) of which was plated over with 2.5in of iron attached to a wood backing 20in (508mm) thick. *Benton*'s armour weighed a total of 260t. Upon completion, she was the most powerful unit in the newly formed Mississippi Squadron.

Ordered by the army in 1861 as they pushed south down the Mississippi, *Benton* was transferred to the navy on 1 October 1862.

BLAKE — GB: 1889

In the late-19th century, British cruisers had to carry out extended ocean patrols which required a large coal supply. This requirement was in addition to the need for increased ammunition, brought about by the introduction of the quick-firing gun in the early 1890s. If displacement was to be kept within reasonable limits, then the combination of side armour with deck protection was not possible, and it was decided to develop the deck-protected cruiser to its full potential. In *Blake* and her sistership, *Blenheim*, the armoured deck rose 18in (457mm) above water, curving down at the sides to 6ft 6in (1.8m) below, and was able to withstand 12in (305mm) projectiles. The breechloaders were mounted one on the forecastle and one aft. Four of the 6in (152mm) quick-firing guns were on the main deck behind casemates with the rest on the upper deck behind shields. There were four engines in two engine rooms, with the aft one used for cruising only. Both ships were able to maintain 19 knots for many days under natural draught.

***Blake* became the pattern for future British protected cruisers. She was ideal for the protection of Britain's vast mercantile marine, which was estimated in 1890 to be worth £900 million.**

Displacement: 9150t
Dimensions: 399ft 9in x 65ft x 24ft (121.8m x 19.8m x 7.3m)
Machinery: twin screws, triple expansion, six boilers; 13,000hp
Armament: two 9.2in (234mm); 10 6in (152mm); four 14in (356mm) TT
Armour: deck 6-3in (152-76mm); casemates 6in (152mm)
Speed: 21.4 knots
Range: 10,000nm (18,520km) at 10 knots
Complement: 570

BOGATYR — RUSSIA: 1901

Displacement: 6750t
Dimensions: 416ft 9in x 54ft 6in x 20ft 9in (134m x 16.6m x 6.3m)
Machinery: twin screws, vertical triple expansion, 16 boilers; 20,250hp
Armament: 12 6in (152mm); 12 11pdr; two 15in (381mm) TT
Armour: not known
Speed: 23.46 knots
Range: not known
Complement: 576

***Bogatyr* was the lead ship in a class of four high-speed cruisers, with good protection and a powerful armament.**

At the end of the 1890s, Russia needed to increase her fleet of protected cruisers. These cruisers were intended primarily for commerce destruction and were built as a class of three: *Askold*, *Variag*, and the *Bogatyr*. A well-balanced design, *Bogatyr* had four 6in (152mm) guns in twin turrets fore and aft, with four more in casemates and four behind shields amidships. Protection was to a high level, and caused Britain to build the *Monmouth* class of armoured cruiser in response.

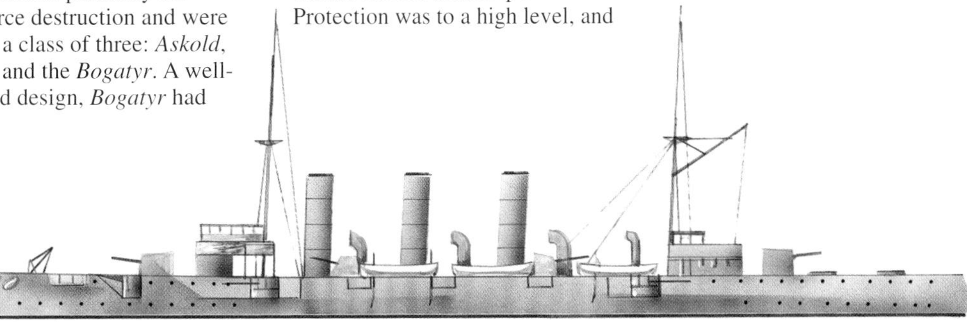

Boston

USA: 1884

By the late 1870s, it was obvious that United States naval development had been neglected. For nearly 20 years the Navy had stagnated, and at one point its effectiveness was well below that of many South American republics. Clearly, this situation could not continue, and the first few years of the 1880s marked the beginning of a new era. In 1883, Congress authorized the construction of four ships, including *Boston* and her sistership, *Atlanta*. These vessels had a partial protective deck extending over the machinery spaces. Two barbettes were positioned at each end of the superstructure, each housing a single 8in (203mm) gun and placed one echeloned to port forward and starboard aft, with a single 6in (152mm) gun in opposite corners to the 8in (203mm) weapons. The remaining 6in (152mm) guns were in the large superstructure amidships. During construction, the builder, John Roach, went bankrupt so the vessels were completed by the New York Naval Dockyard.

***Boston* was designed by Francis Bowles, who later became chief constructor in 1901. Through lack of experience, problems were encountered during construction. Even so, *Boston* and *Atlanta* were amongst the first vessels of the modern US Navy.**

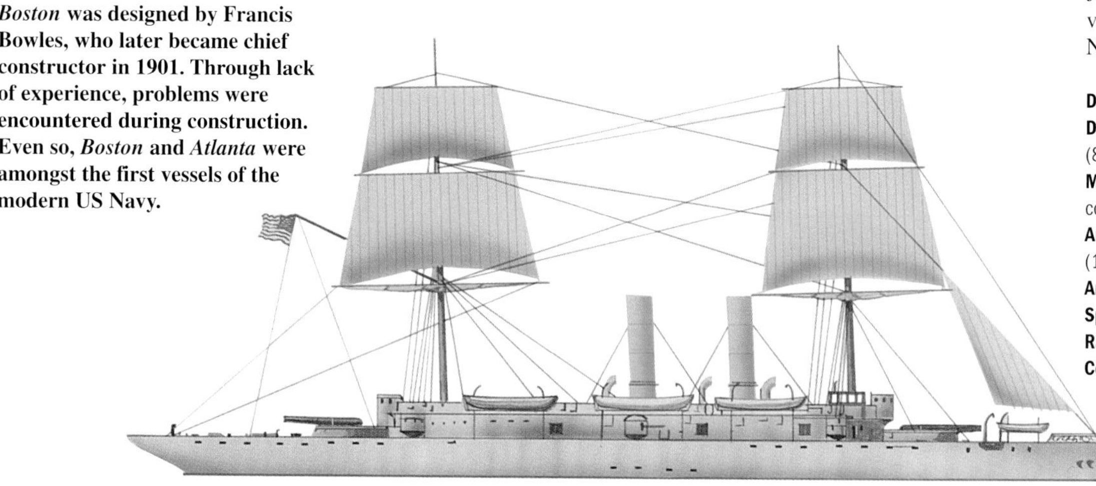

Displacement: 3189t
Dimensions: 283ft x 42ft x 17ft (86.2m x 12.8m x 5.2m)
Machinery: single screw, horizontal compound, eight boilers; 3500hp
Armament: two 8in (203mm); six 6in (152mm)
Armour: barbettes 2in; deck 1.5in
Speed: 16.3 knots
Range: 3390nm (6278km) at 10 knots
Complement: 284

Bouvet

FRANCE: 1896

Displacement: 12007t
Dimensions: 397ft x 70ft 2in x 27ft 6in (117.8m x 21.4m x 8.4m)
Machinery: triple screws, vertical triple expansion, 32 boilers; 14,000hp
Armament: two 12in (305mm), two 10.8in (276mm), eight 5.5in (140mm), four 18in (457mm) TT
Speed: 18.8 knots
Range: not known
Complement: 666

Bouvet was one of five battleships laid down in 1890–92. All adopted the lozenge gun layout, with the 12in (305mm) weapons in single balanced turrets fore and aft, and with the 10.8in (274mm) guns one on each beam. The 5.5in (140mm) guns were carried four in single turrets, and four more at each corner of the long superstructure.

***Bouvet* was an excellent steamer, burning only 11t of coal per hour at full power. She was sunk at the Dardanelles in March 1915.**

BRANDENBURG

GERMANY: 1891

Unlike earlier German battleships, which had their armour supplied from abroad, the four *Brandenburgs* were built from German materials.

With the accession of Kaiser Wilhelm II in 1888, a new era in the development of the German Navy commenced. By 1890, the construction of four large ocean-going battleships was started. With the main armament of six 11in (280mm) guns on the centreline, these units represented a step towards the 'all big gun' dreadnought that would not appear in its final form for another 15 years. The secondary armament was in a battery in the fore structure behind a strip of 4in (102mm) armour. Secondary batteries on subsequent German battleships would be greatly increased.

Displacement: 10501t
Dimensions: 379ft x 64ft x 26ft (121.6m x 20.5m x 8.3m)
Machinery: twin screws, triple expansion, 12 boilers; 10,000hp
Armament: six 11in (280mm); eight 4.1in (105mm); six 17.7in (450mm) TT
Armour: belt 15-12in (381-305mm); barbettes 12in (305mm); battery 3in (76mm)
Speed: 16.5 knots
Range: 4300 miles at 10 knots
Complement: 568

BRENNUS

FRANCE: 1891

Displacement: 11395t
Dimensions: 375ft x 65ft 6in x 27ft 6in (110.3m x 20.4m x 8.3m)
Machinery: twin screws, vertical triple expansion, 32 Bellville boilers; 13,900hp
Armament: three 13.4in (340mm); 10 6.4in (159mm); four 18in (457mm) TT
Armour: belt 18-12in (457-305mm); upper belt 4.5in (115mm); main turrets 18in (457mm); secondary turrets 4in (102mm); deck 4in (102mm)
Speed: 18 knots
Range: not known
Complement: 673

Brennus was a major advance in French battleship design. The lozenge arrangement of the previous *Magenta* class, with the heavy guns in vulnerable open barbettes, was replaced with well-protected closed turrets; this, in order to meet the dangers from the newly introduced quick-firing guns and high explosives being introduced by foreign navies. The 13.4in (340mm) guns were mounted in a twin turret forward and one in a turret aft.

***Brennus* was the first large ship fitted with Bellville water tube boilers, and the first battleship built without a ram.**

BROOKLYN

USA: 1895

Displacement: 10,068t
Dimensions: 402ft 7in x 64ft 8in x 24ft (122.7m x 19.7m x 7.3m)
Machinery: twin screws, vertical triple expansion, five boilers; 18,769hp
Armament: eight 8in (203mm); 12 5in (127mm); five 18in (457mm) TT
Armour: belt 6-3in (152-76mm); deck 2in; barbettes 8in (203mm)
Speed: 21.9 knots
Range: 5000 miles at 10 knots
Complement: 561

Brooklyn was the second armoured cruiser built for the US Navy. She had the characteristic features of French warships of the 1890s, with high sides and pronounced tumble-home, so enabling the beam 8in (203mm) guns to fire in line with the keel. The armoured belt was 267ft (82m) long and 8ft (2.4m) deep; protective deck armour was 6in (152mm) thick amidships, reducing to 3in (76mm) at the ends. Above this, and behind the belt, was a cellular layer. A twin 8in (203mm) gun turret stood on the raised forecastle with the midship 8in (203mm) gun turrets, one on each beam, with their armoured supports rising from the inward sloping side; the fourth turret was on the poop. Eight of the 5in (127mm) guns were on the main deck, with two placed in the forecastle, all behind 4in (102mm) armour. Comparative tests between steam and electric power

for working the gun turrets were conducted in the *Brooklyn*; the result was that electricity was introduced for this purpose in the US Navy. The twin engine rooms were in tandem; for full speed, both engines had to be coupled up, which could only be done when the ship was stationary. This caused major problems off Santiago de Cuba in July 1898, when Spanish warships emerged from the blockaded port in an attempt to escape to Havana. With only the aft cruising engine in use, *Brooklyn* managed 16 knots. During this action she was the flagship of Commodore Schley.

The unusual profile of *Brooklyn*. Her high sides and tall funnels stretched down 100ft (33m) to the grates, thereby providing massive draft to the furnaces.

CAIMAN

FRANCE: 1885

Displacement: 7530t
Dimensions: 271ft 6in x 59ft x 26ft 2in (87m x 18.9m x 8.4mm)
Machinery: twin screws, vertical compound, 12 boilers; 6500hp
Armament: two 16.5in (468mm); four 3.9in (100mm); four 14in (356mm) TT
Armour: belt 19.5-11.75in (495-300mm); deck 4in (102mm); turrets 10in (254mm)
Speed: 14.5 knots
Range: 3000 miles at 10 knots
Complement: 381

In 1878, France laid down the four *Caiman*-class coastal defence ships intended for service in the Baltic. They were armed with two massive 16.5in (420mm) guns – the largest ever in a French warship – mounted on the centreline in shallow barbettes of compound armour. The armour belt was continuous, with the protective deck resting flat on top. Compared to contemporary battleships, the *Caimans* were almost as fast and carried more armour for their size, 2670t on a 7200t displacement.

Following her defeat by Prussia in 1870, France concentrated on building a series of powerful battleships, one of which was the *Caiman*.

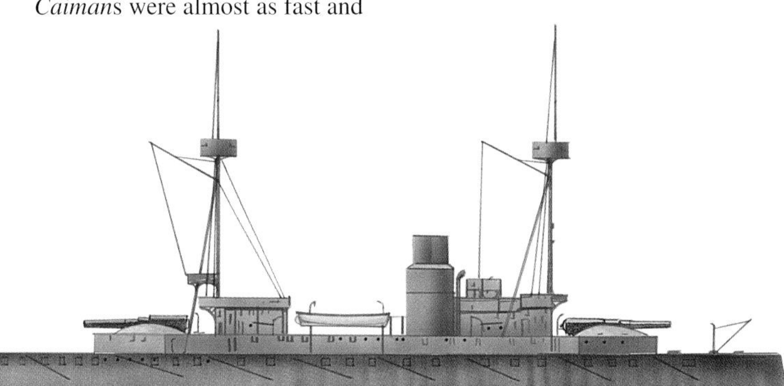

CAIRO

USA: 1862

On the outbreak of the US Civil War in 1861, plans were prepared for Union forces to push down the Mississippi from Cairo, Illinois, to join up with another powerful force fighting its way up the river from New Orleans. The intention was to split the Confederate forces in two, and to reduce further its power to continue what was already an unequal struggle. The Union army first converted two large wooden stern wheel steamers into armoured gunboats. As the upper Mississippi and Ohio rivers were well provided with shipyards and machine shops, and could be protected from raiding Confederate forces, the *Cairo* class of purpose-built ironclad gunboats were also laid down. Construction began in 1861 and was completed in January 1862; five ships were built, and they became the backbone of the Mississippi

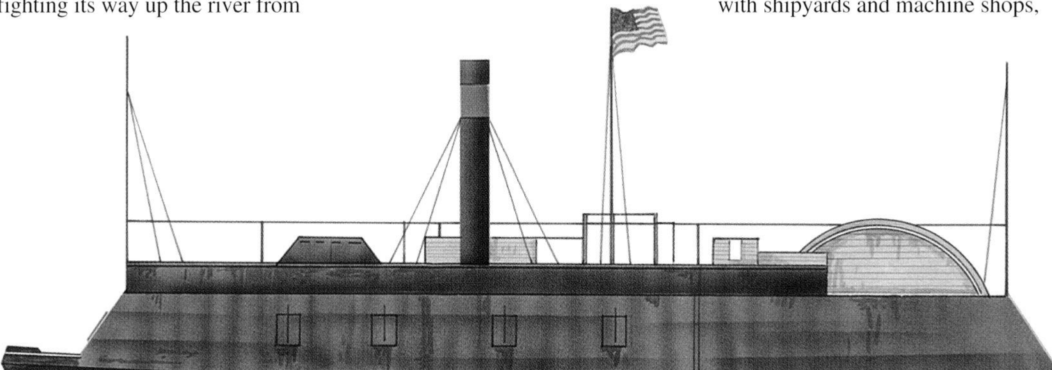

***Cairo* and her sisters saw extensive service in the American Civil War. At one stage during construction, Eades paid for materials and wages from his own funds to avoid delay in completion. *Cairo* was sunk by a mine in December 1862. She was then raised and is now on display at Vicksburg.**

squadron which was destined to fight on for five long years. James Eades prepared the final plans, which incorporated a flat-bottomed hull with an upward gentle curve to ease the flow of water onto the stern-mounted paddle wheel. The hull was built up of white oak and divided into small compartments for coal, stores, and so on, with the boilers and machinery kept low in the hold for protection. A tall, wide strongly-built superstructure ran for almost the full length of the vessel, and housed the powerful armament with three 8in (203mm) guns firing ahead, and a mix of 42pdr and 36pdr guns along the broadside. The casemate front was angled back 45 degrees, and the sides 35 degrees with 2.5in armour over 60ft (19.3m) which covered the boiler and machinery.

Displacement: 512t
Dimensions: 175ft x 51ft 2in x 6ft (54m x 15.7m x 1.8m)
Machinery: centre wheel, two horizontal high pressure, five boilers
Armament: three 8in (203mm) SB, four 42pdr, six 32pdr
Armour: casemate 2.5in
Range: not known
Speed: 8 knots
Complement: 251

CALIFORNIA

USA: 1904

Displacement: 13680t
Dimensions: 503ft 11in x 69ft 7in x 24ft (153.6m x 21.2m x 7.3m)
Machinery: twin screws, vertical triple expansion, 16 boilers; 23,000hp
Armament: four 8in (203mm); 14 6in (152mm); 18 3in (76mm); two 18in (457mm) TT
Armour: belt 6-5in (152-127mm); barbettes 6in (152mm); turrets 6.5in (166mm); secondary 5in (127mm); deck 4in (102mm)
Speed: 22.4 knots
Range: 6000 miles at 15 knots
Complement: 829

The Spanish-American war of 1898 made the United States a global power. She had interests in the Caribbean and across the Pacific, which now required ships with increased endurance. Eventually, a large group of armoured cruisers emerged, the equals of some foreign battleships which had been completed only a few years before. *California* and her five sisters were the same basic design as the contemporary battleships of the *Virginia* class; they had their main 8in (203mm) guns in twin turrets fore and aft, and a battery of 10 6in (152mm) in a citadel with four more in casemates.

In 1911, the first landing of an aircraft onto a ship was made on USS *Pennsylvania*, a sistership to *California*.

CALLIOPE

GB: 1884

Displacement: 2770t
Dimensions: 235ft x 44ft 6in x 19ft 11in (71.6m x 13.6m x 6m)
Machinery: single screw, horizontal compound, six boilers; 3000hp
Armament: four 6in (152mm); 12 5in (127mm)
Armour: deck 1.5in
Speed: 13.75 knots
Range: 4000 miles at 10 knots
Complement: 317

In 1889 a hurricane swept over Samoa destroying five warships; only *Calliope* was able to steam to safety.

Towards the end of the 1870s, better protection was needed for cruisers as neither the low position of the machinery nor coal bunkers could prevent vessels of this type from being put out of action. In the steel-hulled *Calliope*, a short protective deck, angled down at its outer lower edge, was provided instead of the usual flat deck. The 6in (152mm) guns were carried on sponsons, with the 5in (127mm) weapons mounted on the vessel's broadside.

CANONICUS

USA: 1863

Displacement: 2100t
Dimensions: 235ft x 43ft 8in x 13ft 6in (69m x 13m x 3.8m)
Machinery: single screw, vibrating lever, two boilers; 320hp
Armament: two 15in (381mm)
Armour: belt 5in (127mm); turret 11in (280mm); deck 1.5in
Speed: 8 knots
Range: not known
Complement: 85

Many shortcomings of the original *Monitor* and *Passaic* class were overcome in the *Canonicus* group of nine monitors. Lessons learnt from day-to-day operations of this unique type of warship were incorporated into their design, making them the best of their type. *Canonicus* had a double hull made up of an armoured raft resting on top of a lower hull, which contained machinery, boilers, coal, and crew quarters. Extra framing was worked into this hull to provide additional strength.

Due to improvements in gun manufacturing, *Canonicus* was armed with two 15in (381mm) smoothbores instead of the mix of guns mounted in the *Passaic*-class vessels.

CANOPUS

GB: 1897

Displacement: 14,300t
Dimensions: 421ft 6in x 74ft x 26ft 3in (128.3m x 22.5m x 8m)
Machinery: twin screws, three cylinder triple expansion, 20 boilers; 13700hp
Armament: four 12in (305mm), 12 6in (152mm), four 14in (356mm) TT
Armour: belt 6in (152mm); bulkheads 10-6in (254-152mm); barbettes 12in (305mm); gunhouses 8in (203mm); casemates 6in (152mm); main deck 2in
Speed: 18.3 knots
Range: not known
Complement: 682

The *Canopus*-class vessels were designed as reduced *Majestic*s and intended for service on the Pacific station as an answer to the expanding Japanese naval strength. By using improved armour (produced by Krupp in Germany), the thickness of the belt could be reduced to 6in (152mm) from the 9in (229mm) belt on the *Majestic*s. The belt ran for 195ft (59m) and was 14ft (4.27m) deep with 5ft (1.5m) of it below the waterline. Total armour weighed 3600t. The *Canopus* class were the first British battleships fitted with water tube boilers.

The *Canopus* class formed a group of fast battleships able to maintain 18 knots for lengthy periods.

CAPITAN PRAT

CHILE: 1890

Displacement: 6901t
Dimensions: 328ft x 60ft 8in x 22ft 10in (100m x 18.5m x 7m)
Machinery: twin screws, horizontal triple expansion, five cylindrical; 12,000hp
Armament: four 9.4in (240mm), eight 4.7in (119mm), four 18in (457mm) TT
Armour: belt 11.8in (300mm) - 4in (102mm) redoubts 4in (102mm) deck 3in (76mm) barbettes 10.5in (262mm)
Speed: 18.3 knots
Range: not known
Complement: 486

In 1887, Chile circulated to European shipbuilders a brief for construction of a battleship. Estimates were received from 12 shipbuilders, representing three countries, between them submitting a total of 19 designs. A French firm won the work, at a time when France was exceeding Britain in the supply of warships to foreign navies by over 2:1 in tonnage. The main guns of the *Capitan Prat* were mounted in a lozenge layout with one right forward, one aft, and one on each beam amidships, with the 4.7in (119mm) in twin turrets on the upper deck.

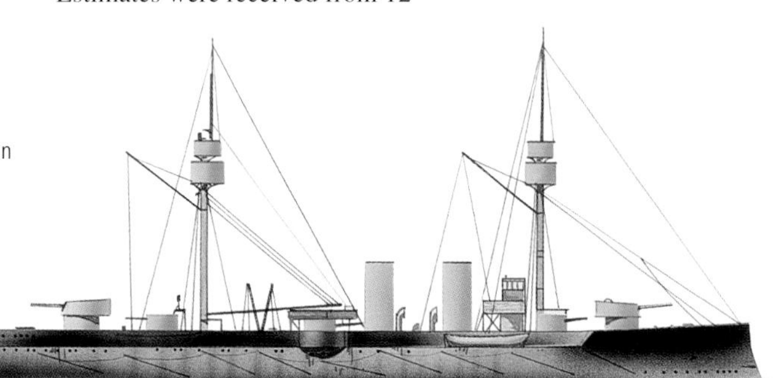

The small but powerful steel-hulled battleship *Capitan Prat* would remain Chile's most powerful warship until World War I.

CAPTAIN

GB: 1869

Captain was built as a result of popular demand. She incorporated the ideas of Captain Cowper Coles, to build an ocean-going battleship combining full sail power on a freeboard of only 8ft 6in (2.3m), and carrying the main guns in turrets (of Cole's design). This design departed widely from the standard, low freeboard, monitor type developed throughout the 1860s and the high-sided broadside and central battery ironclads then in service. Coles had previously criticized the Admiralty for its turret ship designs but was now authorized to produce a ship that would incorporate his ideas. However, he was to work in partnership with Lairds Shipbuilders and leave the basic design to them. Lairds added a forecastle, central superstructure, and poop to improve sea-keeping; all three structures were connected by a narrow bridge from which the sails were worked. Tripod masts were also fitted, so improving the arcs of fire of the turret guns now no longer hampered by standing rigging. *Captain* was the only two-decked, ocean-going battleship in the Royal Navy and consequently had the lowest freeboard of the type; the length to beam proportion of 10:1 was also the greatest in any capital ship for the next 35 years. There was a continuous armoured belt increasing in thickness at the areas abreast of the two widely-spaced turrets. The 25t guns in the turrets were only 2ft 3in (685mm) above the deck– which was awash in a moderate sea – but their handling was not affected. The two 7in (178mm) MLRs were positioned one forward and one aft, high above the waterline.

Displacement: 7767t
Dimensions: 320ft x 53ft 3in x 24ft 10in (97.5m x 16.2m x 7.6m)
Machinery: twin screws, horizontal trunk, eight boilers; 5400hp
Armament: four 12in (305mm); two 7in (178mm)
Armour: belt 8-4in (203-102mm); turrets 10in (254mm)
Speed: 15.3 knots
Range: not known
Complement: 500

***Captain* was the result of many years of hard work put in by Coles, her creator. Owing to poor stability, she capsized (with Captain Coles on board) during a violent storm on the night of 6/7 September 1870.**

CHAO YUNG

CHINA: 1880

The steel-hulled cruiser *Chao Yung* was designed by George Rendel and built by Mitchells for the Chinese Peiyang Squadron. It was a major advance in cruiser design, combining high speed and great offensive power on a small displacement. A single 10in (254mm) gun, the 25t Armstrong BL, was mounted at each end on a turntable in a fixed turret. These weapons were far more powerful than the massive MLR guns in the contemporary Italian *Duilo* and British *Inflexible*.

Displacement: 1542t
Dimensions: 210ft x 32ft x 15ft (64m x 10m x 4.5m)
Machinery: twin screws, horizontal compound, four boilers; 2887hp
Armament: two 10in (254mm); four 4.7in (119mm)
Armour: deck 27in (6mm); turret 1in
Speed: 16.8 knots
Range: 5380nm (9953km) at 8 knots
Complement: 177

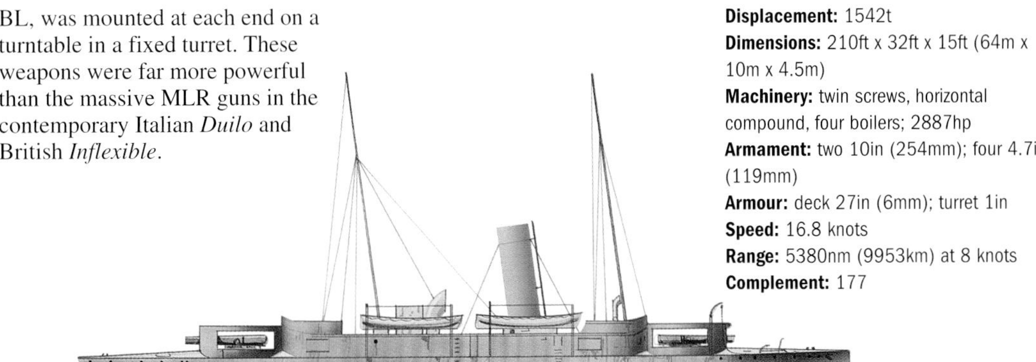

***Chao Yung* had a thin protective steel deck over the boiler and engine rooms.**

CHARLEMAGNE

FRANCE: 1895

Displacement: 11100t
Dimensions: 380ft 9in x 66ft 5in x 27ft 6in (114m x 20.2m x 8.4m)
Machinery: triple screws, vertical triple expansion, 20 boilers; 15,294hp
Armament: four 12in (305mm); 10 5.5in (140mm); eight 3.9in (100mm); four 17.7in (450mm) TT
Armour: belt 14.5-8in (368-203mm); upper belt 4in (102mm); turrets 15in (381mm)
Speed: 18.1 knots
Range: not known
Complement: 694

***Charlemagne* was an economical steamer burning less than 10t an hour at full power.**

In the arrangement of her armament, *Charlemagne* differed from previous French battleships. She followed British practice: four 12in (305mm) guns in twin centre pivot turrets at forecastle and upper-deck level, leaving room on the broadside amidships for the 5.5in (140mm) guns, eight in a long, lightly-armoured casemate, partly sponsoned out over the side, on the main deck with two more on top. Between the splinter deck and the protective deck was a cellular layer 7ft (2m) deep.

CHARLESTON

USA: 1888

In the United States during the mid-1880s there was a lull in the building of warships, to enable the erection of suitable steel-making plant and availability of sufficient work to make it profitable. Although several warships were authorized in 1885 and 1886, none were laid down until 1887, four years after the last class of cruisers had been started. Plans for the new cruisers were purchased in England, but all the materials used in their construction were to be of domestic manufacture.

The first of this group was the *Charleston*, a duplicate of the Japanese *Naniwana*, one of several successful cruisers that developed from the Chilean *Esmeralda* of 1884. Protective armour deck ran the full length of the ship, and between it and the berth deck above a cellular layer was fitted. The main deck was unbroken, and carried one 8in (203mm) gun at each end in a low 2in high-plated barbette. The secondary guns were also on this deck, three each side.

Displacement: 4200t
Dimensions: 320ft x 46ft x 18ft 6in (97.5m x 14m x 5.6m)
Machinery: twin screws, horizontal compound, six boilers; 7650hp
Armament: two 8in (203mm); six 6in (152mm)
Armour: deck 3-2in (76-54mm)
Speed: 18.9 knots
Range: 3000 miles at 10 knots
Complement: 300

Charleston was the first US Navy cruiser not to be fitted with sails. Completed in 1889, she was wrecked 10 years later.

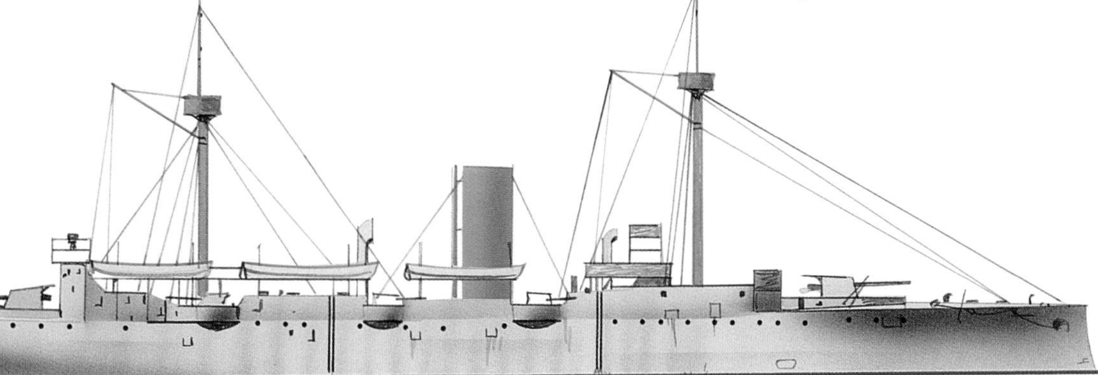

CHÂTEAURENAULT

FRANCE: 1898

Around half of the length of *Châteaurenault* was taken up with machinery. Her maximum speed was 24.5 knots.

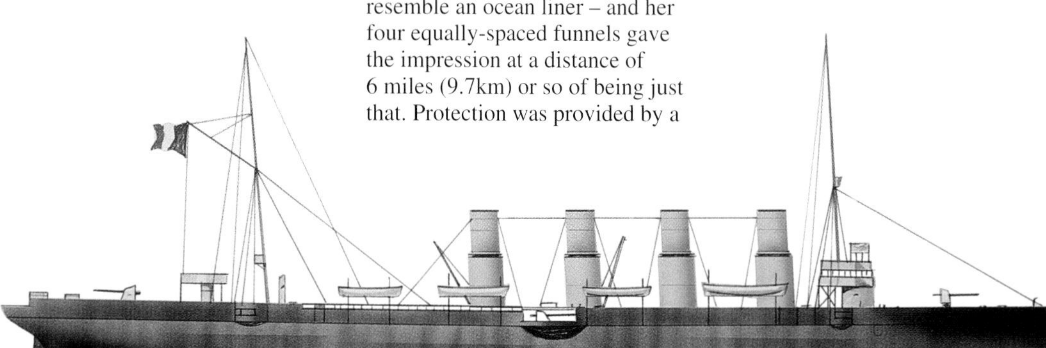

A purpose-built commerce raider, the *Châteaurenault* had a good range and great speed but was lightly armed. She was designed to resemble an ocean liner – and her four equally-spaced funnels gave the impression at a distance of 6 miles (9.7km) or so of being just that. Protection was provided by a full-length armoured deck, curving down at the ends and sides. Above this was a cellular layer. The 6.4in (165mm) guns were carried one on the foredeck and one aft, with three 5.5in (140mm) on each beam and four in the casemates.

Displacement: 7898t
Dimensions: 442ft 11in x 55ft 9in x 23ft 3in (135m x 17m x 7.4m)
Machinery: triple screws, vertical triple expansion, 14 boilers; 24,964hp
Armament: two 6.4in (165mm); six 5.5in (140mm)
Armour: deck 3in (76mm); casemates 1.5in
Speed: 24.5 knots
Range: not known
Complement: 604

CHEN YUAN

CHINA: 1882

Displacement: 7670t
Dimensions: 308ft x 59ft x 20ft (93.9m x 18m x 6.1m)
Machinery: twin screws, horizontal compound, eight boilers; 7500hp
Armament: four 12in (305mm); two 5.9in (150mm); three 14in (356mm) TT
Armour: belt 14in (356mm); barbettes 14-12in (356-305mm); deck 3in (76mm)
Speed: 15.7 knots
Range: not known
Complement: 350

By 1879, China had been forced to expand her navy, due to prolonged disputes with Western nations over their attempted seizures of her land. She began laying down in Germany two sister battleships, *Chen Yuan* and *Ting Yuan*. They were steel-hulled vessels, with the four 12in (305mm) guns in twin turrets on top of a 144ft (43.9m) long barbette forward of the centreline under the bridge, and with the conning tower between the two turrets. The barbette protected the magazines, boilers, and engine rooms. The 5.9in (150mm) guns were in single turrets fore and aft. In action against the Japanese fleet at the Battle of the Yalu in September 1894, both battleships were struck repeatedly by 6in and 4.7in (152mm and 119mm) shellfire, and received hits from heavier guns. Although struck more than 200 times each in the neighbourhood of the armoured waterline, the main guns and the vitals of both vessels remained intact. The *Chen Yuan* and *Ting Yuan* were the only battleships to serve in the Chinese Navy.

Prior to the Battle of Yalu, some of the *Chen Yuan*'s 12in (305mm) shells had been filled with coal dust! In early 1895, she was captured by the Japanese.

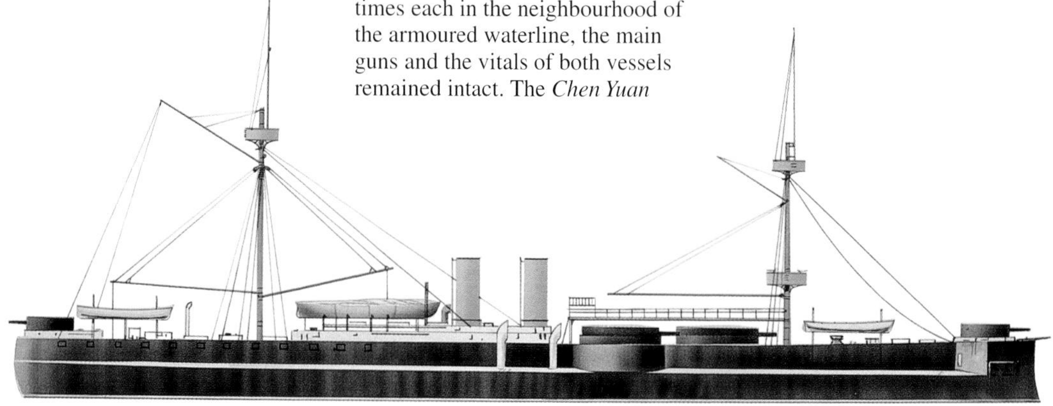

CHICAGO

USA: 1885

The cruiser *Chicago* was one of the quartet of steel-hulled warships that formed the foundation of the modern US Navy. Her deck was protected by armour 136ft (42m) long and 1.5in thick, reducing to only 0.75in over the magazines. The 8in (203mm) guns were on sponsons on the upper deck, with the secondary battery spread along the broadside one deck below. Later, her armour protection was increased. Completed in 1889, *Chicago* eventually became an accommodation ship. She foundered while under tow to the breakers in 1936.

Displacement: 4864t
Dimensions: 342ft 2in x 48ft 3in x 19ft (104.3m x 14.7m x 5.8m)
Machinery: twin screws, compound overhead beam, five boilers; 5000hp
Armament: four 8in (208mm); eight 6in (152mm); two 5in (127mm)
Armour: deck 1.5-0.75in (38-19mm)
Speed: 16.3 knots
Range: 4000 miles at 10 knots
Complement: 409

***Chicago* was the largest of the quartet known as the 'White Squadron', which included two more cruisers and a despatch boat.**

CHIYODA

JAPAN: 1890

Displacement: 2400t
Dimensions: 310ft x 42ft x 14ft (94.5m x 13m x 4.3m)
Machinery: twin screws, vertical triple expansion, eight boilers; 5600hp
Armament: 10 4.7in (119mm); three 14in (356mm) TT
Armour: belt 4.5in (115mm); deck 1.5-1in (38-25mm)
Speed: 19 knots
Range: not known
Complement: 350

***Chiyoda* was built as a replacement for the cruiser *Unebi*, lost on its delivery journey to Japan in a storm in 1887.**

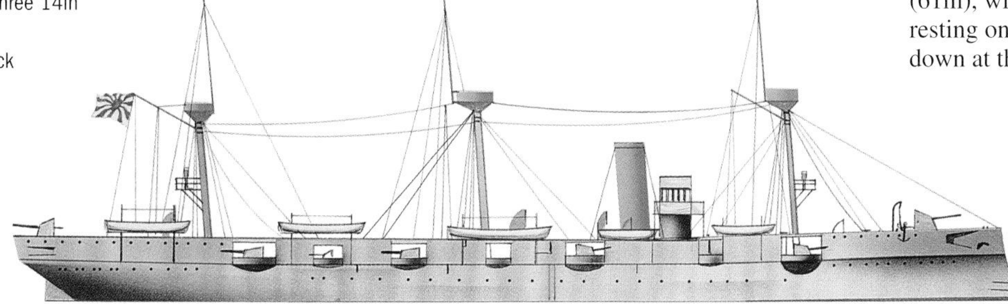

Chiyoda was Japan's first armoured cruiser. She was also the first to be armed with the new Elswick 4.7in (119mm) quick-firing gun – it had a 12-rounds-per minute rate of fire. One gun was on the forecastle with another right aft, and the rest on the main deck on sponsons. The shallow, chrome steel belt stretched for 200ft (61m), with the protective deck resting on top of it and curving down at the ends.

COLBERT

FRANCE: 1875

Displacement: 8750t
Dimensions: 317ft 9in x 57ft 3in x 29ft (96.9m x 17.5m x 8.8m)
Machinery: single screw, horizontal return connecting rod, eight boilers; 4600hp
Armament: eight 10.8in (274mm); one 9.4in (240mm); eight 5.5in (140mm)
Armour: belt 8.7-7in (221-178mm); battery 6.3in (160mm); bulkheads 4.7in (119mm)
Speed: 14 knots
Range: 3000 miles at 10 knots
Complement: 774

Colbert and her sistership *Trident* were the last French wooden-hulled battleships. Iron plating covered the timber hull above the full length belt, with a 6in (15mm) thick deck on top of the belt. Six 10.8in (274mm) guns were in the central battery, with two more above and forward in open barbettes. By 1880, two of the 5.5in (140mm) guns had been replaced with a single 9.4in (240mm) on the upper deck aft, and another 9.4in (240mm) gun was forward under the forecastle.

***Colbert* was laid down in 1870 and not completed until seven years later. A full sail rig of 23,000sq ft (2137sq m) was carried.**

COLLINGWOOD

GB: 1882

In 1880, the *Collingwood* was laid down for the Royal Navy. She was the first of the *Admiral* class of barbette-ship, designed to compete with the powerful French *Amiral Duperré* type. The class had a compound belt which was low and short, and with the ends of the hull constructed on the raft principle. Transverse bulkheads joined the belt at each end, covered with a flat horizontal armoured deck. Above the belt, between this deck and the main deck, coal bunkers 10ft (3m) deep were fitted to assist in maintaining stability should the unprotected sides become damaged. The underwater armoured deck at the ends curved slightly down. The barbettes, one at each end of the superstructure, were polygonal in shape with the sides sloping at 60 degrees; the bottom of the barbettes was protected by a floor of 3in (76mm) armour against shells exploding below. The main guns were about 20ft (6m) above water, with the secondary battery positioned in the superstructure amidships. *Collingwood* was the first British battleship to have a mixed armament.

The overall layout of the *Collingwood* fixed the pattern for future British battleship development, until the 'all big gun' *Dreadnought* of 1906.

Displacement: 9500t
Dimensions: 325ft x 68ft x 26ft 4in (99m x 20.7m x 8m)
Machinery: twin screws, inverted compound, 12 boilers; 9600hp
Armament: four 12in (305mm); six 6in (152mm); four 14in (356mm) TT
Armour: belt 18-8in (457-203mm); bulkheads 16-7in (406-178mm); barbettes 11.5-10in (292-254mm); deck 3in (76mm)
Speed: 16.8 knots
Range: 8500nm (15,742km) at 10 knots
Complement: 498

COSSACK

GB: 1886

Displacement: 1950t
Dimensions: 240ft x 36ft x 14ft 6in (73.2m x 11m x 4.4m)
Machinery: twin screws, horizontal direct acting compound, four boilers; 2500hp
Armament: six 6in (152mm); three 14in (356mm) TT
Armour: deck 0.37in (10mm)
Speed: 17.6 knots
Range: 7000 miles at 10 knots
Complement: 176

Cossack and her seven sisters formed part of a group of third-class cruisers. Their role was to cruise with the battlefleet, providing defence against torpedo attack, and also to carry out their own torpedo attacks on an enemy. Their 6in (152mm) guns were mounted one on each side of the forecastle and poop, with two more amidships. However, this weight of armament – each gun weighed 5t – proved too great for their displacement, making them roll and become 'wet' in heavy weather. The *Cossacks* were the last British cruisers to have horizontal engines.

Between 1884 and 1891, the Royal Navy received 18 cruisers of the *Cossack* type, all below 2000t. She was completed in 1889.

COURBET

FRANCE: 1882

The largest central battery ships ever built, *Courbet* and her sister *Dévastation* were modelled on *Redoubtable*. These three vessels were the French Navy's first capital ships built after the Franco-Prussian war of 1870. The four main 13.4in (340mm) guns were positioned in the corners of the central battery, the top of whose armour rose 19ft 6in (5.9m) above the waterline. The 9.25ft (2.8m) deep belt, 2.25ft (0.7m) of it above water, ran the length of the vessel, ending 28ft (8.5m) from the stern.

***Courbet*'s 13.4in (340mm) guns were the largest ever carried in a central battery ship.**

Displacement: 10450t
Dimensions: 311ft 6in x 69ft 9in x 27ft (95m x 21.2m x 8.2m)
Machinery: twin screws, vertical compound, 12 boilers; 8300hp
Armament: four 13.4in (340mm); four 10.8in (274mm); six 5.5in (140mm)
Armour: belt 15–7in (381–178mm); battery 9.5in (244mm)
Speed: 14.2 knots
Range: 3100 miles at 10 knots
Complement: 689

COURONNE

FRANCE: 1861

Couronne was the first iron-hulled capital ship to be laid down, but her completion was delayed by changes in design. Modelled on the *Gloire*, and a forerunner to the 10-strong wooden-hulled *Provence* class of 1863, *Couronne* was a typical broadside ironclad of the time with her hull totally protected by armour. There were 36 guns in the battery, and four 6.4in (163mm) weapons on the upper deck. She remained afloat for 70 years, not being disposed of until 1932.

Displacement: 5983t
Dimensions: 262ft 5in x 54ft 9in x 26ft 11in (80m x 16.7m x 8.2m)
Machinery: single screws, horizontal return connecting rod, eight boilers; 2900hp
Armament: 10 55pdr sb; 30 6.4in (163mm)
Armour: belt 5–3.2in (102–81mm)
Speed: 13 knots
Range: not known
Complement: 570

The hull of *Couronne* was extremely strong, being made up of 1.3in iron lattice work, backed by two layers of teak and the 0.8in thick iron-hull plating.

CRISTÓBAL COLÓN

SPAIN: 1896

Displacement: 6840t
Dimensions: 366ft 8in x 59ft 10in x 23ft 3in (111.7m x 18.3m x 7.1m)
Machinery: twin screws, vertical triple expansion, 24 boilers; 14700hp
Armament: 10 6in (152mm); six 4.7in (119mm); five 17.7in (450mm) TT
Speed: 19.8 knots
Range: not known
Complement: 567

The armoured cruiser *Cristóbal Colón* began as the *Guiseppe Garibaldi*, being purchased by Spain from Italy in 1896. Her belt was complete, and above this was a redoubt which extended to the main deck and housed a battery of 10 6in (152mm) guns on the second deck. On top of the redoubt she mounted six 4.7in (119mm) guns. The main armament of two 10in (254mm) guns was never carried. After the Battle of Santiago, in July 1898, *Cristóbal Colón* was run aground on a rocky ledge, later shipped off and sank in deep water.

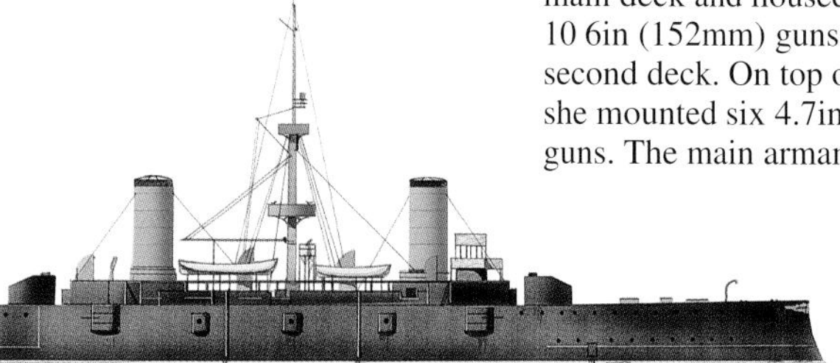

During the Battle of Santiago, *Cristóbal Colón* made 18 knots, but failed to escape when the good quality coal she was burning ran out, leaving only inferior local coal available.

CUSHING

USA: 1890

Cushing, listed as *TB1*, was a first-class torpedo-boat. She was built by Herreshoff and used initially for experimental work in order to develop torpedo tactics, the US Navy at that time being several years behind European navies in their adoption of these boats. Indeed, it was another seven years before the second torpedo-boat, the 120t *Ericsson*, would be commissioned. The *Cushing* was armed with two trainable torpedo tubes, one between the two widely spaced funnels, and one aft with the third in the bows.

Displacement: 116t
Dimensions: 140ft x 15ft 1in x 4ft 10in (42.7m x 4.6m x 1.5m)
Machinery: twin screws, vertical quadruple expansion, two boilers; 1600hp
Armament: two 6pdr; three 18in (457mm) TT
Speed: 23 knots
Range: not known
Complement: 22

Cushing saw considerable service in the Spanish-American war, acting as a despatch boat to the ill-fated _Maine_.

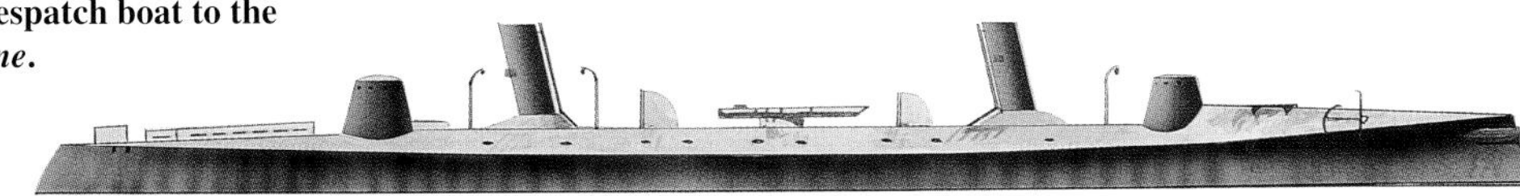

CUSTOZA

AUSTRIA: 1872

Displacement: 7609t
Dimensions: 311ft 9in x 58ft x 26ft (95m x 17.7m x 8m)
Machinery: single screw, horizontal engine, eight boilers; 4158hp
Armament: eight 10.2in (260mm); six 3.5in (90mm)
Armour: belt 9in (229mm); casemate 7in (178mm)
Speed: 13.75 knots
Range: not known
Complement: 548

Custoza was the first iron-hulled ship laid down for the Austrian Navy. Her battery of heavy guns was concentrated amidships on two levels, so they could bear forward when the ship was speeding up to ram the enemy. The design of *Custoza* and Austrian ironclads of this period emphasised protection, with fewer guns and less speed. This feature had developed out of the experience which had been gained from the Battle of Lissa in July 1866.

The sides of the hull forward on _Custoza_ were angled back to allow four guns to fire ahead as she bore down to ram the enemy.

D'ENTRECASTEAUX

FRANCE: 1896

A flush-decked protected cruiser, designed by Lagane and intended for service overseas, *D'Entrecasteaux* was one of two vessels planned. Eventually, the second unit emerged as the *Jeanne D'Arc*, the first modern armoured cruiser in the French Navy. The protective deck of the *D'Entrecasteaux* was nickel steel 2.2in on the flat and 4in (102mm) on the slope, where it curved down below the waterline. There was a second deck 0.8in thick above this, with a cofferdam at the sides between. Her 9.4in (240mm) guns were in single turrets fore and aft; eight of the 5.5in (140mm) were in casemates on the main deck, with four more behind shields one deck above. The hull sides had a tumble-home, so allowing better axial fire. Each of the secondary guns had an ammunition supply of 200 rounds with 75 rounds for each of the 9.4in (240mm). There were two boiler rooms: one forward, with four boilers, and one aft, with a single boiler. At full power, *D'Entrecasteaux* burnt 15.5t of coal every hour; she carried a maximum coal stock of 1000t. In 1922 she was presented to Belgium.

The distinctive outline of this powerful cruiser, with its widely-spaced funnels and prominent bow.

Displacement: 7995t
Dimensions: 383ft 10in x 58ft 6in x 24ft 7in (117m x 17.8m x 7.5m)
Machinery: twin screws, vertical triple expansion, five boilers; 14,500hp
Armament: two 9.4in (240mm); 12 5.5in (140mm); two 18in (457mm) TT
Armour: deck 4–2.2in (102–56mm); turrets 10in (254mm); casemates/shields 2.2in (56mm)
Speed: 19.2 knots
Range: 1200nm (2222km) at 19 knots
Complement: 559

DANMARK

CONFEDERATE STATES OF AMERICA: 1864

Lieutenant North of the Confederate States Navy was sent to Europe for the purpose of purchasing warships. He contracted with Thompsons of Glasgow for construction of the *Danmark*, a broadside ironclad which, had it been completed in time, would have been the most powerful vessel in the Confederate Navy. The iron armour was complete and backed by 18in

(457mm) of teak. With 700t of coal, *Danmark* was able to steam for 20 days. She was purchased in 1864 by Denmark, then at war with Prussia.

***Danmark* as completed. Later, more powerful 8in (203mm) guns were added and her stern was altered to give end fire.**

Displacement: 4747t
Dimensions: 270ft x 50ft x 19ft 6in (82.3m x 15.2m x 6m)
Machinery: single screw, single expansion, two boilers; 1000hp
Armament: 12 8in (203mm), 12 26pdr
Armour: 4.5in (115mm)
Speed: 8.5 knots
Range: 3000nm (5550km) at 6 knots
Complement: 530

DAVOUT

FRANCE: 1889

***Davout* as completed in 1891. Later, lighter masts were fitted. By 1900 she could still make 19.4 knots.**

After the two large cruisers *Tage* and *Amiral Cecille* were laid down in the mid-1880s, France commenced to build a series of much smaller cruisers. The first of this new type was the *Davout*. She was of striking appearance, with two widely-spaced funnels, a ram bow, and originally two heavy military masts. Her hull had a considerable tumblehome; one 6.4in (162mm) gun was mounted right forward with another aft, and four more were on sponsons on the upper deck. Above the protective deck was a 4ft (1.2m) wide cofferdam.

Displacement: 3031t
Dimensions: 288ft 9in x 39ft 4in x 21ft 7in (88m x 12m x 6.5m)
Machinery: twin screws, horizontal triple expansion, eight boilers; 9000hp
Armament: six 6.4in (162mm)
Armour: deck 4-2in (102-51mm)
Speed: 20.7 knots
Range: not known
Complement: 329

DEUTSCHLAND

GERMANY: 1874

Displacement: 8799t
Dimensions: 293ft 1in x 62ft 8in x 26ft (88.5m x 19m x 7.9m)
Machinery: single screw, horizontal single expansion, eight boilers; 5700hp
Armament: eight 10.2in (260mm)
Armour: belt 10-5in (254-127mm); casemate 8-7in (203-178mm); deck 2in
Speed: 14.5 knots
Range: 2470 miles at 10 knots
Complement: 656

Designed by Reed, the armoured frigates *Deutschland* and her sistership *Kaiser* were the last foreign-built ironclads ordered for the German Navy. Powerful cruising ships of this type were needed to maintain Germany's newly established empire. The complete waterline belt was reduced in depth ahead of the central battery, which housed the 10.2in (260mm) guns, four to a side at main deck level. The forward bulkhead to the battery ran down to the lower deck to give added protection to the engine room.

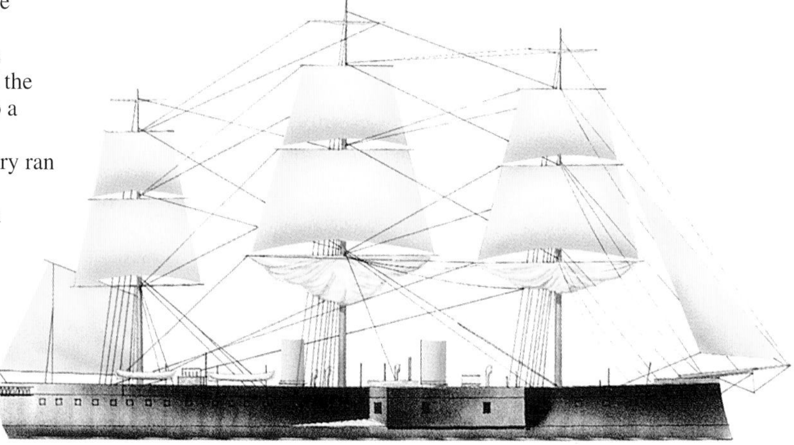

***Deutschland* was a good sea-boat. She carried 36,000sq ft (3345sq m) of sail, which helped increase her cruising range.**

DEVASTATION

GB: 1871

While the seagoing fully-rigged turret ship *Captain*, which incorporated the advanced ideas of Captain Cowper Coles RN, was under construction, Sir Edward Reed produced the first of a new type of seagoing mastless turret ship known as the 'breastwork monitor'. This vessel was named *Devastation* and was completed in 1873. The low hull had a greater freeboard than contemporary monitors and had a raised armoured redoubt, or breastwork, amidships on which the turrets were mounted, one at each end. The armoured freeboard provided stability, while the guns were placed considerably higher than in the monitor type; the turret-turning gear was also well protected. By dispensing with rigging, a far greater arc of fire was obtained, and the low freeboard could be used with greater safety. The breastwork did not at first extend the full width of the ship, and a passage was left on each side of the main deck. Later, a light superstructure was added, running from the bow to near the stern. A recess in the aft end of the superstructure allowed the rear turret to fire with maximum depression over the stern. The full-length armour belt ran from 5ft 6in (1.7m) below the waterline up to the main deck. The 14in (356mm) armour on the turrets was in two layers with oak between. Each steam-trained turret of 30ft 6in (9.3m) diameter housed two 12in (305mm) 35t guns. When first commissioned, *Devastation* carried the most powerful guns afloat. The extensive armour protection accounted for over 27 per cent of the displacement. *Devastation* was refitted in 1879, and again in 1891, receiving four 10in (254mm) breech-loading guns in place of the original muzzle-loaders.

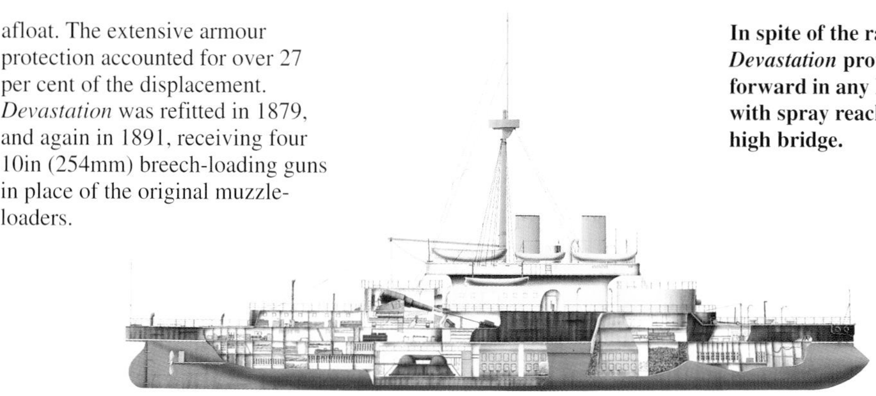

In spite of the raised freeboard, *Devastation* proved very wet forward in any kind of sea, often with spray reaching back over the high bridge.

Displacement: 9330t
Dimensions: 307ft x 62ft x 26ft 8in (93.6m x 19m x 8m)
Machinery: twin screws, horizontal direct acting, eight boilers; 6640hp
Armament: four 12in (305mm)
Armour: belt 8.5-12in (215-305mm); breastwork 10-12in (254-305mm); turrets 10-14in (254-356mm); deck 2-3in (51-76mm)
Speed: 13.8 knots
Range: 6000 miles at 10 knots
Complement: 358

Dogali — ITALY: 1885

Displacement: 2050t
Dimensions: 250ft x 37ft x 14ft 6in (76.2m x 11.3m x 4.4m)
Machinery: twin screws, triple expansion, four boilers; 5012hp
Armament: four 6in (152mm); four 14in (356mm) TT
Armour: deck 6-2in (152-52mm); shields 4.5in (115mm)
Speed: 19.7 knots
Complement: 224

Originally laid down as the *Salamis* by Greece, the Italian cruiser *Dogali* was the first warship to have triple expansion engines. When first completed, she carried a light fore and aft rig, but this was discarded in the 1890s. The 6in (152mm) guns were placed one on the forecastle, which had a slight turtle back deck, one aft, and one each side in the waist amidships. Designed by Sir William White, she was a good example of the Elswick cruiser although lightly built. Sold in 1908 to Uruguay, *Dogali* was discarded in 1914, but she was not scrapped until 1930.

On a displacement of only 2050t, *Dogali* combined high speed, good protection, and a powerful armament.

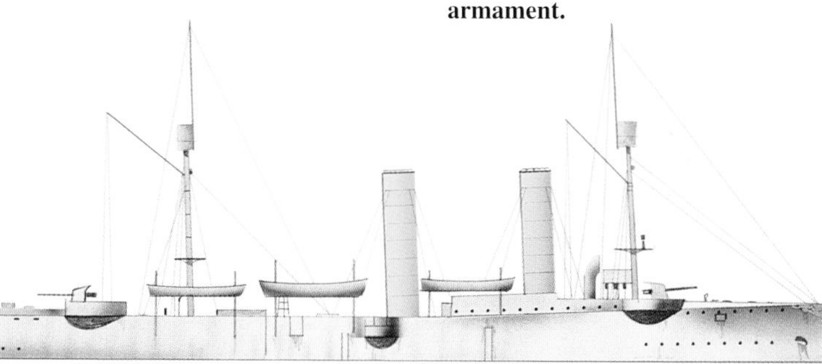

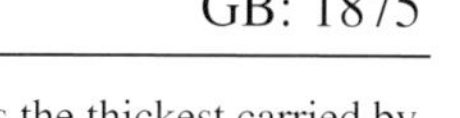

Dreadnought — GB: 1875

***Dreadnought* was an advanced design combining an almost ideal combination of armour and guns, which were hydraulically worked for the first time.**

The last pure breastwork monitor in the British Navy, *Dreadnought* was a contemporary of the fully-rigged casemate ironclad *Alexandra*. The breastwork in the *Dreadnought* extended the full width of the ship, providing improved stability over the earlier *Devastation* with the waterline belt running the full length and covering the hull between the main and upper deck, thus giving additional protection to the turret bases. Total armour carried equalled one third of her displacement and the 14in (356mm) iron belt was the thickest carried by a British warship up until then.

Displacement: 10886t
Dimensions: 343ft x 63ft 10in x 26ft 6in (104.5m x 19.5m x 8m)
Machinery: twin screws, vertical compound, 12 boilers; 8206hp
Armament: four 12.5in (317mm)
Armour: belt 14-8in (356-203mm); citadel 14-11in (356-280mm); decks 3-2in (76-52mm)
Speed: 14.5 knots
Complement: 369

Duguesclin — FRANCE: 1883

Displacement: 6112t
Dimensions: 265ft 9in x 57ft 3in x 25ft 3in (81m x 17.5m x 7.7m)
Machinery: twin screws, vertical compound, eight boilers; 4400hp
Armament: four 9.45in (240mm); one 7.6in (190mm); six 5.5in (140mm)
Armour: belt 10-6in (254-152mm); barbettes 8in (203mm)
Speed: 14 knots
Range: 2800 miles at 10 knots
Complement: 440

In the late 1870s, French naval building policy was concentrating on replacing the aged wooden warships of the 1863 to 1866 period. The particular need for cruising ironclads for service on overseas stations and *Duguesclin* and her sistership *Vauban* were the epitome of this type. They were built of steel instead of wood, as in the previous *Bayard* class, and mounted four 9.45in (240mm) guns in barbette towers, a 7.6in (190mm) in the bow, and six 5.5in (140mm) on the broadside. The iron waterline belt was complete with the protective deck resting on top.

***Duguesclin* had a brig rig with 23,200sq ft (2155sq m) of canvas. Later, this was replaced by two military masts.**

DUILIO

ITALY: 1876

Thanks to the combined efforts of the Italian Minister of Marine, Admiral de Saint Bon, and Benedotto Brin, *Duilio* and *Dandolo* were the most powerful vessels in the Mediterranean.

After the Battle of Lissa in 1866, the Italians were faced with the problem of being situated between two great nations, France and Austria, who both maintained powerful fleets. Italy needed to create a modern navy, now that her earlier broadside ironclads were becoming outdated. Designed by the brilliant Benedetto Brin, *Duilio* and her sistership *Dandolo* were a major step in the evolution of the battleship. *Duilio* was the first battleship built without sails, and the first with giant guns; the guns were in twin turrets, placed *en échelon* close together amidships in the short central redoubt, and protected by 17in (432mm) nickel steel. The main Creusot steel belt was longer and to the ends of the ship. Beyond the redoubt was an underwater armoured deck fitted level with the lower edge of the belt, the space between this deck and the one above being minutely sub-divided, forming a cellular raft. Originally, it was planned to fit 35t guns, and later 65t, but 100t guns were finally adopted as an answer to the British 80t gun. The 100t gun fired a 1905lb (866kg) shell every 15 minutes. The stern had a compartment for a 26.5t torpedo boat.

Displacement: 12071t
Dimensions: 358ft 2in x 64ft 9in x 27ft 3in (109.2m x 19.7m x 8.3m)
Machinery: twin screw, vertical, eight boilers; 7711hp
Armament: four 17.7in (450mm); three 14in (356mm) TT
Armour: side 20.5in (548mm); turrets/redoubt 17in (432mm); deck 2-1in
Speed: 15 knots
Range: 3760nm (6963km) at 10 knots
Complement: 420

DUPETIT-THOUARS

FRANCE: 1874

France constructed a number of wooden-hulled cruisers from the mid-1860s to the 1870s, when iron was becoming more readily available. All carried canvas and mounted most of their armament on the broadside, on a displacement of about 2000t. The *Dupetit-Thouars* was one of a class of four wooden-hulled vessels rigged as barques. On the short forecastle stood a 5.5in (140mm) gun for ahead fire with another aft; the rest of the 5.5in (140mm) guns were evenly spaced along the broadside on the upper deck.

Displacement: 2000t
Dimensions: 262ft x 35ft 9in x 18ft 9in (79.8m x 10.9m x 5.7m)
Machinery: single screw, vertical compound, four boilers; 2000hp
Armament: 10 5.5in (140mm)
Speed: 15 knots
Range: 4000 miles at 10 knots
Complement: 205

There were minor variations in the *Dupetit-Thouars* class with three units having straight stems and one with a clipper bow. Tripod masts were tried on one vessel but later removed.

DUPUY DE LÔME

FRANCE: 1892

Towards the end of the 1880s, France possessed a number of protected cruisers designed with the likely object of preying upon British commerce. However, the introduction of the high-explosive shell and the quick-firing gun meant that these vessels lost much of their value and, in order to meet these new dangers, it was thought necessary to armour the sides. After firing tests using the old ironclad *Belliquese*, it was decided to protect the entire hull with 4in (102mm) armour. In 1888, construction of the armoured cruiser *Dupuy De Lôme*, designed by De Bussy, was authorized. She was to be a very advanced vessel and the first armoured cruiser France possessed. The sides were completely protected by 4in (102mm) armour from the main deck, 13ft (4m) above the waterline to 3ft 9in (1.3m) below the waterline. A 1.5in curved protective deck joined the lower edge of the side armour, with a splinter deck worked in way of the machinery. The space between was filled with coal, while above the main deck there was a cellulose-filled cofferdam 3ft (0.9m) deep. The 7.6in (194mm) guns were one each side amidships, with the 6.4in (162mm) guns grouped together, three forward and three aft. *Dupuy De Lôme* was the first large vessel to have triple-screws, a practice carried on with all later French armoured cruisers.

The unique positioning of the armament of *Dupuy De Lôme* allowed five guns to fire ahead or astern.

Displacement: 6676t
Dimensions: 364ft 2in x 51ft 6in x 24ft 7in (111m x 15.7m x 7.5m)
Machinery: triple screw, triple expansion, 13 boilers; 13,000hp
Armament: two 7.6in (194mm); six 6.4in (162mm)
Armour: hull 4in (102mm); turrets 4in (102mm)
Speed: 19.7 knots
Range: not known
Complement: 526

EDGAR

GB: 1890

Edgar had a powerful armament and good protection provided by the thick protective deck.

Edgar was one of a group of nine first-class protected cruisers that formed part of the Naval Defence Act of 1889. France had started to develop the armoured cruiser at the end of the 1880s. With the added weight of side armour, it would not be possible to carry the large coal supply needed for extended ocean patrols, plus increased ammunition supply, and keep the displacement within acceptable limits. The 9.2in (234mm) guns were mounted one each end of the vessel, with four of the 6in (152mm) guns on the main deck and six on the upper deck.

Displacement: 7350t
Dimensions: 387ft 6in x 60ft x 23ft 9in (118.1m x 18.3m x 7.2m)
Machinery: twin screw, triple expansion, four boilers; 12,000hp
Armament: two 9.2in (234mm); 10 6in
Armour: deck 5-3in (127-76mm)
Speed: 20 knots
Range: 10,000nm at 10 knots
Complement: 544

EKATRINA II

RUSSIA: 1886

Displacement: 11,032t
Dimensions: 339ft 6in x 69ft x 28ft 9in (103.5m x 21m x 8.5m)
Machinery: twin screw, vertical compound, 14 boilers; 9100hp
Armament: six 12in (305mm); seven 6in (152mm)
Armour: belt 8-16in (203-406mm); redoubt 12in (305mm); deck 1.5in
Speed: 15 knots
Range: not known
Complement: 650

Ekatrina II and her four sisterships were of a unique design, featuring the 12in (305mm) guns at the corners of an amidships triangular-shaped redoubt. There was one twin mount on each corner, firing forward as well as on its own beam; a third twin mount was positioned aft on the centre line. All *Ekatrina II*'s 12in (305mm) guns were in hydraulic disappearing mounts, with light shields providing some protection. The 6in (152mm) guns were in unarmoured positions on the main deck. The main belt was complete; above this was a 102ft (30.5m) strake ending in bulkheads.

The _Ekatrina II_ class served in the Black Sea Fleet and were intended to fight head-on, with two thirds of their powerful armament concentrated forward.

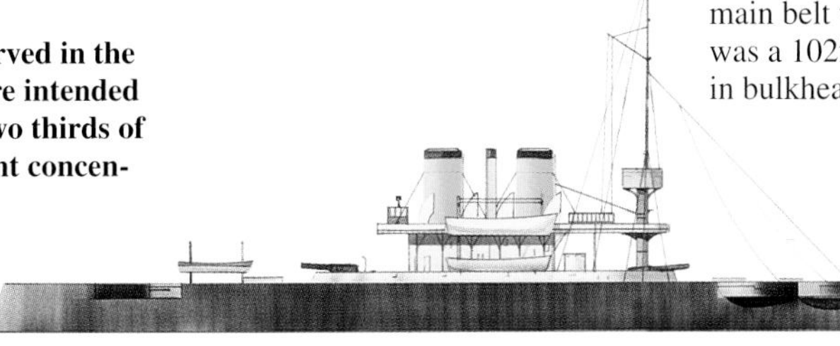

EMPERADOR CARLOS V

SPAIN: 1895

The armoured cruiser *Emperador Carlos V* was completed in 1898. The laminated belt was made up of 1in of Siemens and 1in of chrome steel, with the main protection being provided by a 6.5in (165mm) thick protective deck reducing to 2in at the ends. The two 11in (280mm) Hontoria guns were a powerful model and mounted one at each end; there were four of the 5.5in (140mm) guns on the main deck behind 2in armour, and the rest on the upper deck behind shields.

The imposing outline of _Emperador Carlos V_. She formed part of the aborted Spanish Squadron that was intended to retake the Philippines from the United States in 1898.

Displacement: 9090t
Dimensions: 380ft x 67ft x 25ft (115.8m x 20.4m x 7.6m)
Machinery: twin screw, vertical triple, 10 boilers; 18,500hp
Armament: two 11in (280mm); 10 5.5in (140mm)
Armour: belt 2in; deck 6.5-2in (165-50mm); battery 2in
Speed: 20 knots
Range: not known
Complement: 600

ERZHERZOG FERDINAND MAX

AUSTRIA: 1865

Displacement: 5130t
Dimensions: 274ft 9in x 52ft 4in x 23ft 9in (83.7m x 16m x 7.2m)
Machinery: single screw, horizontal; 2925hp
Armament: 16 48pdr
Armour: belt 5-3.5in (123-90mm)
Speed: 12.5 knots
Range: not known
Complement: 511

Erzherzog Ferdinand Max as she appeared at the Battle of Lissa in 1866. The use of the ram at Lissa meant that this mode of attack was perpetuated until the turn of the 20th century.

The Austrian *Erzherzog Ferdinand Max*, and her sistership *Habsburg*, were broadside ironclads designed by Joseph von Romako. They were hurried to completion in order to

take part in the war of 1866, in which Italy tried to reclaim Italian-speaking territories then under Austrian rule. Both ironclads were completely armoured, from the spar deck down to below the waterline, with wood backing nearly 28in (711mm) thick. Originally, it was intended to mount 32 48pdr smoothbore guns but, when *Erzherzog Ferdinand Max* was commissioned, this was reduced to 16 smoothbores firing a 55lb (25kg) steel ball. In 1867, the armament was changed to 14 7in (178mm) guns. Having been defeated on land at the Battle of Custoza, the Italians attacked the island of Lissa in July 1866, and it was here that the broadside ironclads built by Austria and Italy were put to the test; the iron armour kept out all shells, even from the heavy guns. During this battle, *Erzherzog Ferdinand Max*, Admiral Tegethoff's flagship, rammed the Italian *Re D'Italia* and sunk her.

ESMERALDA

CHILE: 1883

Displacement: 2950t
Dimensions: 270ft x 42ft x 18ft 6in (82.3m x 12.8m x 5.6m)
Machinery: twin screw, horizontal compound, four boilers; 6803hp
Armament: two 10in (254mm); six 6in (152mm)
Armour: deck 2–1in
Speed: 18.3 knots
Range: 2200nm at 10 knots
Complement: 296

The Chilean protected cruiser was a major advance in cruiser design, combining good protection, powerful armament, and high speed. Designed by George Rendel of Armstrong, many similar cruisers were built for numerous foreign navies. *Esmeralda* was a steel-hulled vessel with a ram bow and initially a light sail-rig. The 10in (254mm) breech loader 25t guns were mounted in barbettes fore and aft, with the 6in (152mm) guns carried in sponsons amidships. *Esmeralda* was sold to Japan in 1894.

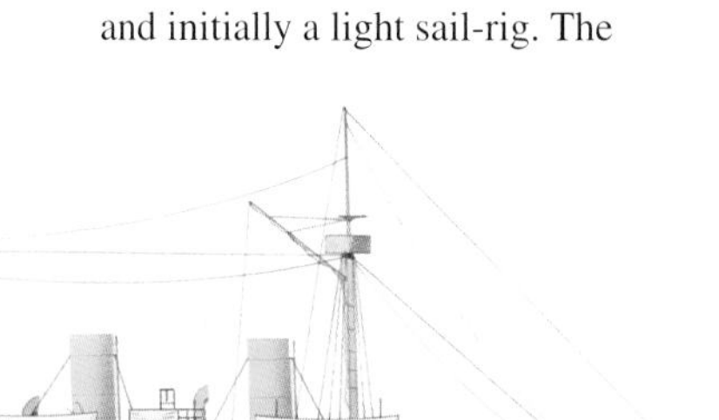

Protection on *Esmeralda* was increased with a 6ft- (2.1m-) deep cellular layer bordered by a cofferdam fitted with cork.

ESMERALDA

CHILE: 1894

The Chilean armoured cruiser *Esmeralda* was typical of the cruisers built by the British company, Armstrong. She combined high speed, great offensive powers, and good protection. The belt was 350ft (106m) long and 7ft (2.1m) deep. Behind this, the armoured deck sloped down at the sides connecting with the lower edge of the belt, as well as sloping down at the bow and stern. The immensely powerful armament comprised an 8in (203mm) gun forward and aft, each firing a 250lb (114kg) shell at the rate of four rounds in 62 seconds. In addition, the secondary battery spread along the sides behind shields, with a mix of smaller weapons filling the gaps between. It was calculated that if all the guns were fired simultaneously, the energy developed would be sufficient to lift the *Esmeralda*'s 7000t some 40ft (12m) into the air! A screen was positioned in front of the bridge and over the forecastle to deflect the blast from the forward firing guns. This was the first time such a device was fitted to a warship. This screen was used extensively on all later types of warships.

Esmeralda was one of many successful cruisers built by Armstrong, though their lighter scantlings were not favoured by the Royal Navy.

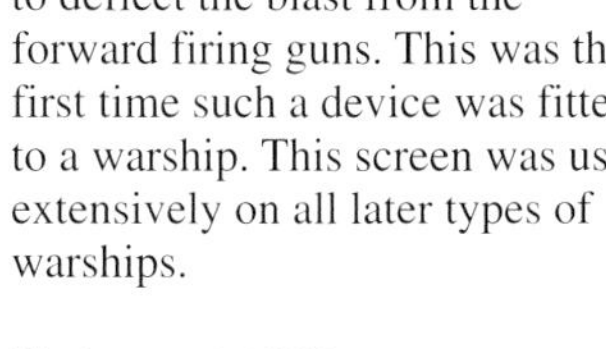

Displacement: 7000t
Dimensions: 436ft x 53ft x 20ft 3in (133m x 16.2m x 6.2m)
Machinery: twin screw, vertical triple expansion; 16,000hp
Armament: two 8in (203mm); 16 6in (152mm); three 18in (451mm) TT
Armour: belt 6in (152mm); deck 2–1.5in; shields 4.5in (115mm)
Speed: 22.25 knots
Range: not known
Complement: 500

FLANDRE

FRANCE: 1864

In the late-1850s, France planned an ironclad programme of 30 seagoing vessels. This proved to be beyond French financial and construction capabilities; additionally, the French iron industry had expended much of its resources in a large group of ironclad floating batteries. So the plan was amended to build 10 ironclads, nine of them with wooden hulls. The class was closely modelled on the *Gloire*, but had thicker armour on the waterline, and a 4.3in (109mm) strake above protecting the battery. *Heroine* had an iron hull and was scuttled at Dakar in 1901.

The *Flandre* class of 10 vessels was the largest single class of battleships built for the French Navy.

Displacement: 5700t
Dimensions: 262ft 5in x 55ft 9in x 27ft (80m x 17m x 18.8m)
Machinery: single screw, horizontal return connecting rod, nine boilers; 3100hp
Armament: 10 55pdr, 22 6.4in (162mm)
Armour: belt 6in (152mm); battery 4.3in
Speed: 13 knots
Range: 2500 miles at 8 knots
Complement: 579

FLORIDA

CONFEDERATE STATES OF AMERICA: 1862

Displacement: 700t
Dimensions: 191ft x 27ft 2in x 13ft (58.2m x 8.3m x 4m)
Machinery: single screw
Armament: two 7in (178mm); four 6.4in (162mm)
Speed: 9.5 knots
Range: not known
Complement: 146

When the US Civil War broke out in 1861, the hastily formed Confederate Navy desperately needed more warships. Initially, the best option was to purchase suitable existing ships or have them built in Europe. *Florida* was one of several vessels built in Britain. W. A. Miller and Sons of Liverpool were selected as the builders because of their experience in constructing wooden vessels for the Royal Navy, where the requirement for a heavy weight of armament was the norm. Wood was chosen instead of cheaper iron because a wooden hull was easier to repair without the aid of dockyard facilities. All the guns were carried on *Florida*'s spar deck, the 7in (178mm) Blakely RML were mounted on centre pivots, with the 6.4in (162mm) guns on the broadside. Speed under steam alone was 9.5 knots, but under steam and sail *Florida* made 12 knots. As the political situation worsened, *Florida* managed to slip to sea before being seized by the British authorities, and embarked on her career as one of the most successful of Confederate raiders. During her first cruise, which ended in August 1863, she captured 24 vessels; on her second cruise, from March to September 1864, *Florida* took 13 more captives and her sailing tenders took 23 more.

The graceful lines of *Florida*. Under Captain Newland Maffitt, she had her greatest success. She was seized by US forces at Bahia, Brazil in 1864 and later sunk.

FLORIDA

USA: 1864

When first completed (and named *Wampanoag*), the cruiser *Florida* was the fastest steamer afloat and a credit to her designers Delano and Isherwood.

In 1863, the US Secretary of the Navy realized the urgent need for a group of high speed cruisers constructed of wood able to hunt down enemy merchant vessels. This was at a time when war between Britain and the US seemed likely; as an answer, Britain built several large iron-hulled frigates that were amongst the fastest and most powerful cruisers afloat in the 1860s. *Florida*, formerly *Wampanoag*, was designed by Benjamin Delano. The engines, designed by B. F. Isherwood, were massive; each 8ft 4in (2.5m) long piston connected with two more rods which rotated nine gears, each of which were 10ft (3m) in diameter and 9ft (2.7m) long, connected in turn to 5ft (1.5m) long pinions mounted on the propeller shaft. The machinery took up half of the length of the vessel and 30 per cent of the displacement. Space was so tight aboard that coal was also stowed on the berth deck. Eight Martin water-tube boilers, plus four small superheating boilers, provided steam from a grate area of nearly four times that on the 4635t *Merrimack* of 10 years earlier. Though high speed was reached on trials, *Florida* and her four sister-ships were not considered a success. Even so, they were still a remarkable achievement in US naval development.

Displacement: 4215t
Dimensions: 335ft x 44ft x 18ft 6in (102.1m x 13.5m x 5.6m)
Machinery: single screw, horizontal direct acting geared, 12 boilers; 4100hp
Armament: 10 9in (229mm); three 60pdr
Speed: 17.7 knots
Range: not known
Complement: 330

FORBAN

FRANCE: 1895

Displacement: 150t
Dimensions: 144ft 6in x 15ft 3in x 4ft 5in (44m x 4.7m x 1.3m)
Machinery: twin screw, triple expansion, two boilers; 3260hp
Armament: two 37mm; two 14in (356mm) TT
Speed: 31 knots
Range: not known
Complement: 27

The early torpedo-boats were armed with spar torpedoes and were usually launches. By the 1870s, they had become specially-built light craft of high speed and small size and without any protection, relying upon surprise for a successful attack. In 1876, the US Navy ordered a large wooden launch from the Herreshoff Company with a speed of 17.5 knots. One year later, the first torpedo-boat arrived with the Locomotive Whitehead torpedo, the Lightning, also built by Thornycroft. As the type developed, so the French began to build them both for coast defence and use with the battle fleet. By 1895, the French Navy had entire flotillas of these nimble craft, totalling over 250 vessels. The French seagoing torpedo-boat *Forban* was launched in July 1895 from the yard of Normand. An improved *Filibustier*, and with more powerful engines, at her trials *Forban* achieved slightly over 31 knots making her the fastest vessel in the world at the time.

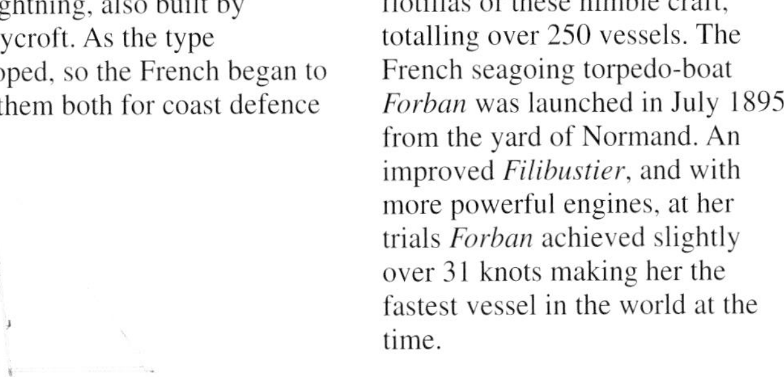

***Forban* caused great interest when she was the first vessel to exceed 30 knots at her trials in 1895.**

FORMIDABLE

ITALY: 1861

***Formidable* as completed in 1862 with a light rig. She is a good example of the early powerful broadside ironclads.**

In 1856, the leading Italian artillerist, Cavall, proposed three ironclad batteries. Originally planned as armoured batteries of 30 guns, and built in France, the ironclads eventually emerged as ocean-going corvettes armed with 20 guns, and the sides completely armoured. Both *Formidable* and her sistership, *Terrible*, took part in the Italian attack upon the island of Lissa in July 1866. *Formidable*, almost alone, fought several batteries at a range of only 900ft (274m), sustaining severe damage, but was expertly handled by her captain, Saint Bon.

Displacement: 2682t
Dimensions: 215ft 10in x 47ft 3in x 17ft 10in (65.8m x 14.4m x 5.4m)
Machinery: single screw, single expansion, six boilers; 1080hp
Armament: four 8in (203mm); 16 6.5in (164mm)
Armour: belt 4.3in (110mm); battery 4in (102mm)
Speed: 10 knots
Range: 1300nm (2408km) at 10 knots
Complement: 371

FORMIDABLE

FRANCE: 1885

Displacement: 11720t
Dimensions: 331ft 6in x 70ft x 27ft 9in (101m x 21.3m x 9m)
Machinery: twin screw, vertical compound, 12 boilers; 9700hp
Armament: three 14.6in (371mm); 12 5.5in (140mm)
Armour: belt 22-14in (560-356mm); deck 4-3in (102-76mm); barbettes 16in (406mm)
Speed: 16 knots
Range: not known
Complement: 625

The first French ocean-going battleships to dispense with sail power, *Formidable* and her sistership, *Admiral Baudin*, were powerful ships. Their design returned to the high freeboard barbette skip with a pronounced tumblehome, and the 14.6in (371mm) guns were mounted singly in barbettes, all on the centreline. The choice of these heavy guns was prompted by the rapid strides then being made in the resisting powers of armour. The steel belt was complete and 7ft 2in (2.2m) deep, but only 1ft (305mm) of this was above water.

The layout of the main guns carried by *Formidable* was not repeated, as it did not conform to the tactical thinking of the time.

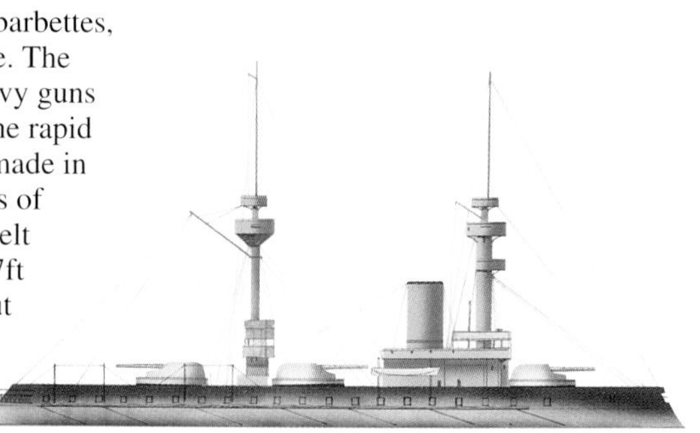

FORTH

GB: 1886

Forth and her three sisterships established the pattern for future British cruiser design. The main guns on the upper deck at each end had a good field of fire, and the secondary battery spread along each side. These were also the first cruisers not to have sails and the first to have an armoured conning tower. The armament was a heavy one on a 4000t displacement and, when combined with a 3in (76mm) thick sloping protective deck, made these cruisers effective. They were also good sea-boats and steady gun platforms.

***Forth* was one of the forerunners of the modern cruiser. She was eventually sold in 1921.**

Displacement: 4050t
Dimensions: 315ft x 46ft x 19ft 6in (96m x 14m x 6m)
Machinery: twin screw, horizontal direct acting compound, 12 boilers; 4500hp
Armament: two 8in (203mm); 10 6in (152mm); four 14in (356mm) TT
Armour: deck 3-2in (76-50mm)
Speed: 18.2 knots
Range: 7400nm at 10 knots
Complement: 300

FRANCESCO MOROSSINI

ITALY: 1885

Displacement: 11145t
Dimensions: 347ft 5in x 65ft x 27ft 6in (106m x 19.8m x 8.4m)
Machinery: twin screw, compound, eight boilers; 10,000hp
Armament: four 17in (432mm); two 6in (152mm); four 4.7in (119mm)
Armour: side 17.75in (452mm); citadel and barbettes 14.2in (362mm); deck 3in (76mm)
Speed: 16 knots
Range: not known
Complement: 507

Due to the opposition from the Minister of Marine to the building of such large ships as the *Lepanto* (launched in 1880), plans were drawn up by the Italian Navy for a scaled-down *Dandolo*. This vessel was to have better quality armour more evenly distributed, and breech-loading guns. It was hoped that such vessels would not take so long to build or cost so much. The result was the *Francesco Morossini* and her two sisterships; they had a high forecastle with the barbettes concentrated *en échelon* in the middle section of the vessel. The *Francesco Morossini* was sunk as a target in 1909.

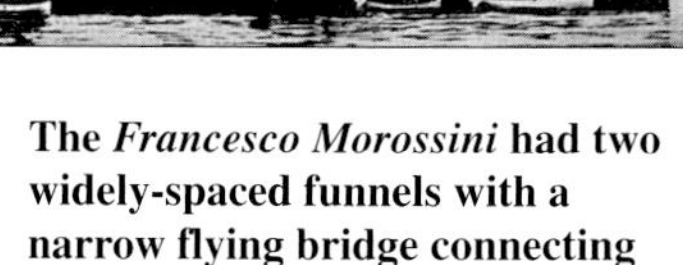

The *Francesco Morossini* had two widely-spaced funnels with a narrow flying bridge connecting the two bridge structures.

FRIEDRICH DER GROSSE

GERMANY: 1874

***Friedrich der Grosse*'s sistership, *Grosser Kurfurst*, was sunk in a collision only days after she had entered service.**

The battleship *Friedrich der Grosse* and her two sisterships were the first comprehensive class of battleships built for the German Navy. All the previous classes had been 'one-offs', laid down as central battery ships and then converted to turret ships. This change, coupled with problems experienced in iron construction resulted in a protracted period of time, some eight years, for the construction of the three *Friedrich der Grosse*-class battleships. Their two closely-spaced turrets were protected by a short length of armour, and their masts were hollow for added ventilation.

Displacement: 7596t
Dimensions: 316ft 10in x 53ft x 23ft 6in (96.6m x 16.3m x 7.2m)
Machinery: single screw, horizontal single expansion, six boilers; 5000hp
Armament: four 10.2in (259mm)
Armour: belt 9-4in (229-102mm); turrets and citadel 8in (203mm)
Speed: 14 knots
Range: 1690 miles at 10 knots
Complement: 500

FRIEDRICH KARL

GERMANY: 1867

Displacement: 6822t
Dimensions: 308ft 10in x 54ft 6in x 26ft 5in (94.1m x 16.6m x 8m)
Machinery: single screw, horizontal single expansion, six boilers; 3550hp
Armament: 16 8.2in (210mm)
Armour: belt 5-4.5in (127-115mm); battery 4.5in (115mm)
Speed: 13.5 knots
Range: 2210 miles at 10 knots
Complement: 531

The first major ironclad to join the German Navy was the *Friedrich Karl*, built in France and completed in 1867 – three years before the Franco-Prussian war. Even when the German ship-building industry did get underway, heavy forgings and machinery were still imported from Britain. The *Friedrich Karl* was a ship-rigged central battery ship, originally planned to carry 26 72pdr guns, all on the main gun deck. Her wrought iron armour had 15in (381mm) teak backing. She was a good sea-boat.

The *Friedrich Karl*, one of two central battery ironclads added to the expanding German Navy in 1867. The other was the British-built *Kronprinz*.

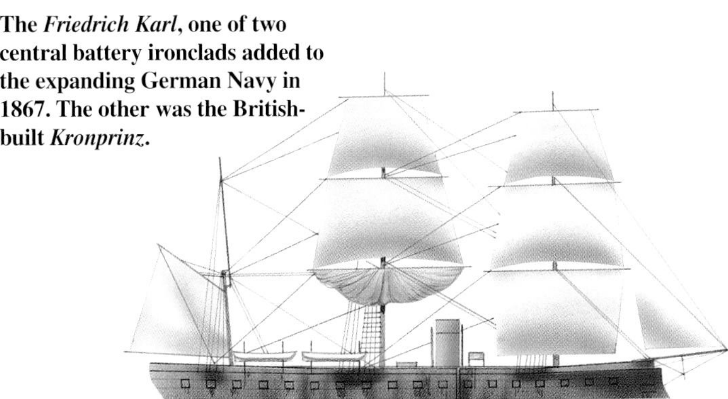

FU LUNG

CHINA: 1886

The Chinese *Fu Lung* was a large oceangoing steel-hulled torpedo-boat. Built by Schichau of Elbing, she was one of the best of its type. There were two torpedo tubes in the bows, three light pole masts for steadying sails, and the four 1pdr guns were placed two on pedestals and one on each beam. The coal supply was 15t. During the Battle of the Yalu, in September 1894, *Fu Lung* fired several torpedoes without success, but her very presence as night fell caused the Japanese fleet great concern, forcing them to hold off until daylight the next day.

Displacement: 120t
Dimensions: 140ft 3in x 16ft 5in x 7ft 6in (42.7m x 5m x 2.3m)
Machinery: single screw, triple expansion, one boiler; 1600hp
Armament: two 14in (356mm) TT
Speed: 24.2 knots
Range: not known
Complement: 20

***Fu Lung* belonged to the Chinese Peiyang Fleet, the best equipped of China's naval forces. She had two conning towers, one each side of the funnel.**

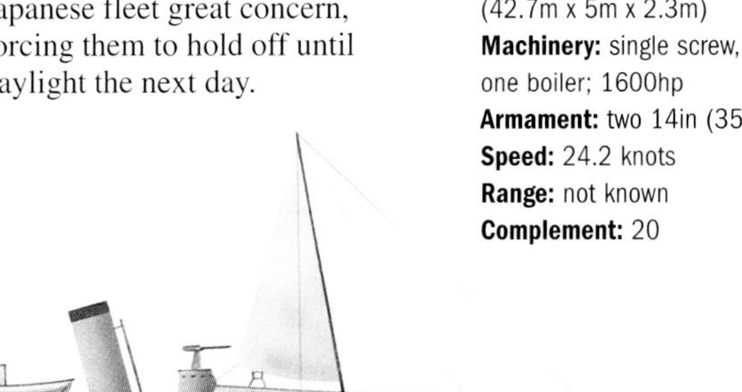

FUJI

JAPAN: 1896

In the early-1890s, Japan anticipated war with China, and was anxious to possess battleships capable of facing the powerful Chinese turret ships, *Ting Yuan* and *Chen Yuan*. Subsequently, Japan ordered from British yards her first major battleships, the first for 20 years. Built to an improved *Royal Sovereign* design, *Fuji* and her sistership *Yashima* saved weight by mounting the new 12in (305mm) wire-bound gun, which was just as powerful as a 13.5in (343mm). The weight saved was used to provide better protection to the main guns by fitting turrets and increasing barbette armour. The belt was 230ft (70m) long and 7ft 6in (2.3m) deep with the thickest part by the machinery spaces amidships, with bulkheads at each end. The deck rested flat on top, but curved down at the ends. Above the main belt was a 4in (102mm) thick strake of armour. The 12in (305mm) guns, placed in twin turrets on the centreline, one at each end, had a rate of fire, with end-on-loading, of one round every 80 seconds. Four of the 6in (152mm) guns were in casemates, with the rest on the upper deck behind shields. Delivered long after the 1894–95 war with China, *Fuji* played a major part in the later war with Russia. *Yashima* was sunk by a mine in May 1904.

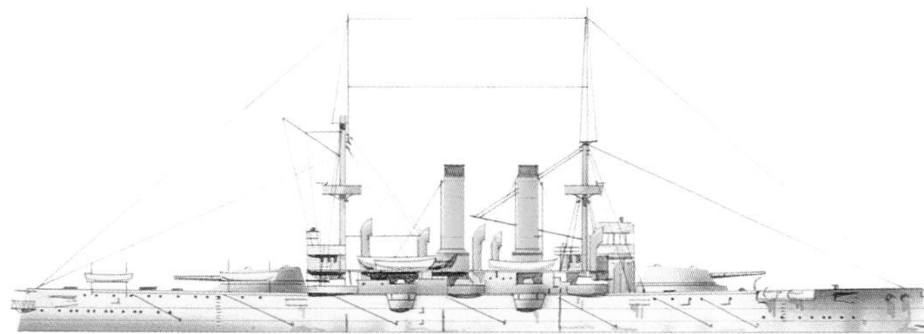

Displacement: 12,533t
Dimensions: 412ft x 73ft x 26ft 6in (118.8m x 22.2m x 8m)
Machinery: twin screw, vertical triple expansion, 10 boilers; 14,000hp

Designed by George Macrow of the Thames Ironworks, *Fuji* and her sistership *Yashima* set the trend for future Japanese battleships.

Armament: four 12in (305mm); 10 6in (152mm); five 18in (457mm) TT
Armour: belt 18-14in (457-356mm); upper belt 4in (102mm); deck 2.5in; barbettes 14-9in (356-229mm); casemates 6-2in (152-52mm)
Speed: 19.2 knots
Range: not known
Complement: 637

FÜRST BISMARK

GERMANY: 1897

Displacement: 11,281t
Dimensions: 417ft x 67ft x 27ft 9in (127m x 20.4m x 8.5m)
Machinery: twin screw, triple expansion, 12 boilers; 13,622hp
Armament: four 9.4in (240mm); 12 6in (152mm); six 17.7in (450mm) TT
Armour: belt 8-4in (203-102mm); turrets/barbettes 8in (203mm); battery 4in (102mm); deck 2in
Speed: 19 knots
Range: not known
Complement: 621

Germany was late in adopting the armoured cruiser, and it was not until 1896 that the *Fürst Bismark* was laid down. From this, the type grew in size to the 17,500t *Blücher* of 1908. Designed for overseas service, the *Fürst Bismark* had a 7ft 3in deep belt, thickest by the boiler and engine rooms and tapering to 4in at the ends, with the protective deck resting on top of the belt but tapering down at the ends. The 9.4in (240mm) guns, in well-protected twin turrets, were also used on contemporary German battleships; six of the 6in (152mm) guns were concentrated amidships, with four more forward and two aft.

The 9.4in (240mm) guns featured on *Fürst Bismark* were only carried by the next German armoured cruiser, *Prinz Heinrich*.

FUSO

JAPAN: 1877

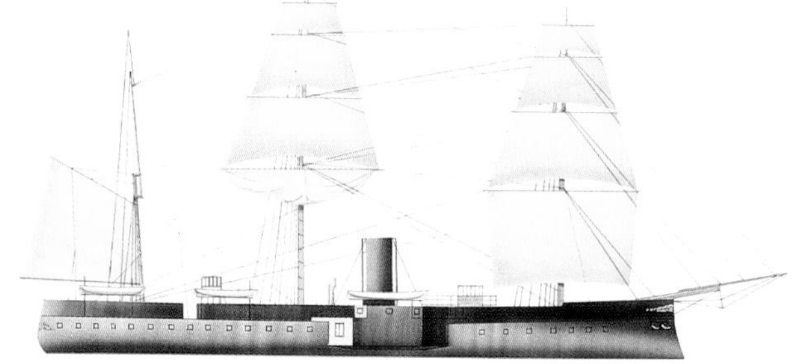

***Fuso* as she was first completed, with a barque-rig of 11,700sq ft (1087sq m) of canvas.**

As part of the naval expansion programme of 1875, Japan ordered the central battery ironclad *Fuso* and two armoured corvettes from British yards. The iron-hulled *Fuso* followed Reed's ideas on the battery concentrated amidships behind thick armour with good all-round fire; the total weight of the armour was 776t. With a length to beam ratio of 4.5:1, *Fuso* was very handy. In 1894, *Fuso* was rebuilt and took part in the China-Japan War of 1894–95. She was damaged at the Battle of the Yalu, in September 1894.

Displacement: 3717t
Dimensions: 220ft x 48ft x 18ft 4in (67m x 14.6m x 5.5m)
Machinery: twin screw, horizontal compound, eight boilers; 3932hp
Armament: four 9.4in (240mm); two 6.7in (162mm)
Armour: 9-4in (229-102mm); battery 8in (203mm)
Speed: 13.2 knots
Range: 4500nm (8333km) at 10 knots
Complement: 250

GALATEA

GB: 1887

Displacement: 5600t
Dimensions: 300ft x 56ft x 22ft 6in (91.5m x 17m x 7m)
Machinery: twin screw, triple expansion, four boilers; 5500hp
Armament: two 9.2in (234mm); 10 6in (152mm); six 18in (457mm) TT
Armour: belt 10in (254mm); bulkheads 16in (406mm); deck 3-2in (76-51mm)
Speed: 19 knots
Range: 10,000 miles at 10 knots
Complement: 484

The seven belted cruisers of the *Orlando* class, as initially planned, were a distinct advance on earlier British armoured cruisers. *Galatea* was one of them. The 10in (254mm) belt extended for two-thirds of the length amidships, but was very narrow and only 18in (457mm) above water on the designed draught. It was covered by a flat armoured deck which sloped down at the ends. Due to changes in design the draught was increased by 7in (178mm); when the full coal supply of 900t was on board, the top of the belt was 6in (152mm) below the water level. A detailed study was made between belted cruisers and protected cruisers, and the latter were found to be the superior type. The *Orlando* class were the last belted or armoured cruisers built for the Royal Navy

Designed to protect trade routes worldwide, *Galatea* and her sisterships had an estimated endurance of 10,000nm (18,520km) at 10 knots.

for a number of years. The main armament had shields, and was carried on the upper deck on the centreline, fore and aft, with the 6in (152mm) guns five each side amidships. Initially, 9.2in (234mm) guns, each weighing 18t, were planned but these were replaced by the improved 22t version. There was an increase in the weight of the 6in (152mm) guns, coupled with an increase in the coal supply, displacement increased from 5040t to 5600t. Yet, in spite of all these drawbacks, the *Orlandos* proved to be good sea-boats.

GENERAL ADMIRAL

RUSSIA: 1873

Displacement: 5031t
Dimensions: 285ft 10in x 48ft x 24ft 5in (87m x 14.6m x 7.3m)
Machinery: single screw, vertical compound, 12 boilers; 4470hp
Armament: six 8in (203mm); two 6in (152mm)
Armour: belt 6-5in (152-127mm)
Speed: 12.3 knots
Range: not known
Complement: 480

Laid down for the Russian Navy in 1870, the *General Admiral* was the world's first armoured cruiser and was completed several years before the appearance of deck-protected cruisers. *General Admiral* and her sistership, *Gerzog Edinburgski*, were iron-hulled, fully-rigged ships with a complete armoured belt which extended from 2ft (0.6m) above water to 5ft (2m) below. The 1in thick deck rested on top of the belt with a 6in (152mm) glacis 4ft 6in (1.8m) high round the engine room hatch. She was powerfully armed, with the 8in (203mm) guns on the upper deck amidships with the 6in (152mm) below the forecastle and poop. The armoured cruisers built for the Russian Navy steadily developed into formidable ships.

By 1900, Russia had completed 10 armoured cruisers, of which *General Admiral* was the first.

They were well able to deal with the small battleships usually stationed overseas by the European powers, and were ideal for commerce raiding, being able to deal with smaller cruisers patrolling trade routes. *General Admiral* carried 1000t of coal, giving her a good cruising range. She was not deleted from the Navy list until 1938.

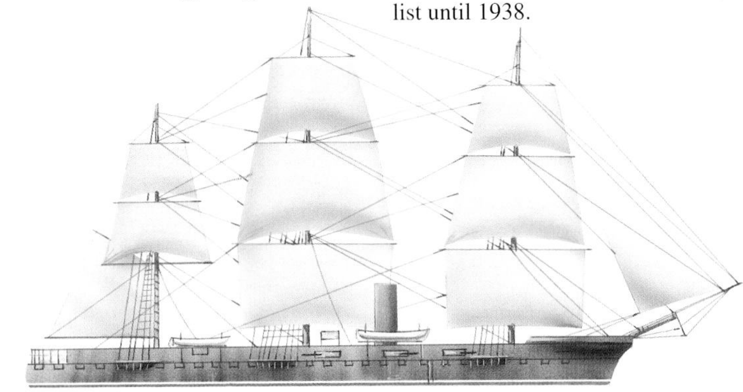

GIOVANNI BAUSAN

ITALY: 1883

Displacement: 3277t
Dimensions: 293ft x 42ft x 19ft 7in (89.3m x 12.8m x 6m)
Machinery: twin screw, double expansion, four boilers; 6470hp
Armament: two 10in (254mm); six 6in (152mm); two 14in (356mm) TT
Armour: deck 1.5in
Speed: 17.5 knots
Range: 5000nm (9260km) at 10 knots
Complement: 295

Italy's first modern protected cruiser was the *Giovanni Bausan*, designed by George Rendel and built by Armstrong. She was completed in 1885, a steel-hulled cruiser with a fore-and-aft rig. She was a forerunner of the successful Elswick cruisers that saw service in many navies. The 10in (254mm) 20 calibre guns weighed 25t each, and were positioned on the centreline, one forward and one aft; the 6in (152mm) guns were on the broadside, one amidships and four in sponsons. When completed, the *Giovanni Bausan* was the most effective of the small cruisers in the Italian Navy.

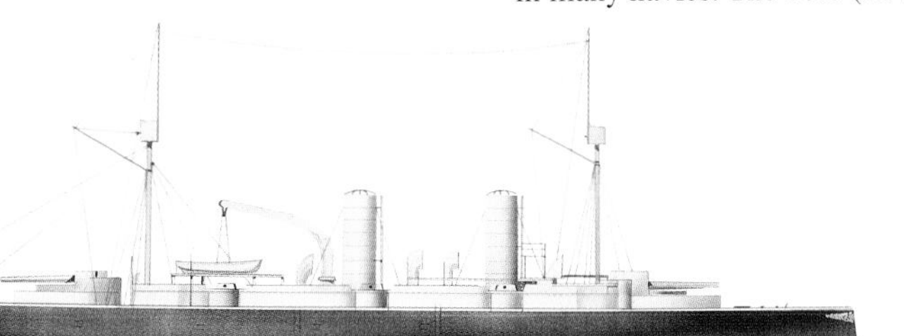

Of typical Armstrong design, with a well-proportioned layout, the *Giovanni Bausan* was eventually discarded in 1920.

GIUSEPPE GARIBALDI

ITALY: 1899

Displacement: 7972t
Dimensions: 366ft 8in x 60ft x 23ft (111.8m x 18.2m x 7m)
Machinery: twin screws, vertical triple expansion, 24 boilers; 14,713hp
Armament: one 10in (254mm); two 8in (203mm); 14 6in (152mm)
Armour: belt 8-4in (203-102mm); turrets 8-4in (203-102mm); deck 2in
Speed: 19.7 knots
Range: 4400nm (8149km) at 10 knots
Complement: 510

During 1870-90, Italy suffered severe financial restraint which set back the ambitious building programme she had embarked upon to replace the early broadside ironclads. Several unique warships were delayed in completion due to a lack of funds, and some had to be sold to foreign navies while still under construction. One such group of vessels comprised the powerful armoured cruisers; they were exceedingly well-protected for their size, and considered suitable to form in the line with battleships if need be. Their armament comprised one 10in (254mm) gun forward and two 8in (203mm) in barbettes, 10 6in (152mm) in a battery, and four more on the upper deck behind shields. Protection was afforded by a complete waterline belt of armour that rose amidships up to the battery deck, thinning out at the ends with 6in (152mm) armour on the battery. The protective deck sloped down at the sides to join the lower edge of the belt. These were extremely successful cruisers, and the four original ships in this class, launched 1895 to 1897, were sold to Argentina, with one more going to Spain where she became the *Cristóbal Colón*.

The distinctive outline of the *Giuseppe Garibaldi*. This group were formidable warships and equal to cruisers twice their size.

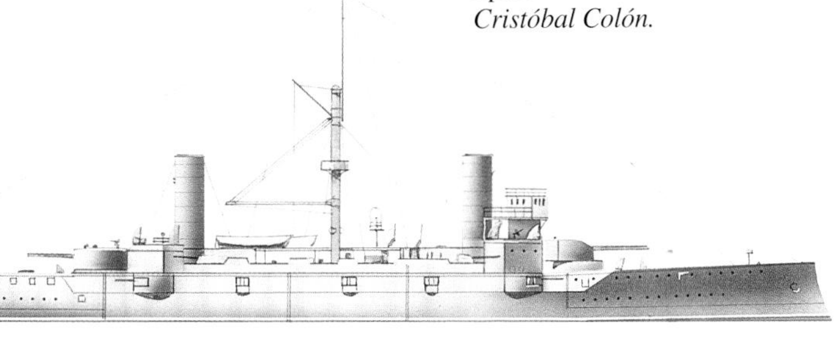

Gloire

FRANCE: 1860

Displacement: 5630t
Dimensions: 255ft 6in x 55ft 9in x 27ft 10in (77.9m x 17m x 8.5m)
Machinery: single screw, horizontal return connecting rod, eight boilers; 2500hp
Armament: 36 6.4in (162mm)
Armour: belt 4.7-4in (119-110mm)
Speed: 12.5 knots
Range: not known
Complement: 570

The success of French armoured batteries in the Crimean War, and the necessity for protecting vessels against shellfire (which had steadily increased in power and accuracy), soon brought about the permanent use of armour in warship construction. As early as 1845, the brilliant French naval architect, Dupuy De Lôme, submitted proposals for an armoured frigate built of iron instead of wood, so achieving a saving of 20 per cent in weight. He suggested that the saving could be utilized as an armoured belt over 6in (152mm) thick and 8ft (2.5m) deep. This plan was rejected as it was thought that iron plates were not shot proof. Nevertheless, it was decided to proceed with a seagoing ironclad that was well in advance of any ship then afloat. Dupuy De Lôme submitted further plans in November 1857; he believed that in an action between two ships with equal armour and armament, the smaller vessel would have a distinct advantage. The displacement was therefore fixed at 5620t, only 500t more than his earlier masterpiece, the wooden-hulled 92-gun screw line of battleship *Le Napoléon* which made nearly 14 knots. Dupuy De Lôme planned to reach a similar speed with the same horsepower by lengthening the hull of the new ship, retaining the same beam and draught, and also giving her finer lines, which reduced the immersed midship section. Construction started in March 1858 at Toulon and the vessel was named *Gloire*. Because of the greatly increased weight of the armour plating, which covered the entire hull, questions were asked regarding the strength of the vessel. This was solved by fitting a thick layer of sheet metal, nearly 10mm thick, beneath the upper wooden deck and securely fitting it to the hull side. This method also solved the problem of the lost strength that the upper deck gave to the ship, had it been fitted. In February 1859, tests were carried out on 4.75in (121mm) thick armour plates supplied by several companies; the plates submitted by Petit et Gaudet proved able to resist the fire of 68pdr smoothbores. It was now also possible to manufacture armour of a consistently high standard. The complete belt on *Gloire* extended from 6ft (1.8m) below the water to the upper deck level, with 26in (660mm) at the waterline. The backing formed the skin, framework, and hull, with the armour screwed in, as tests showed that bolts tended to fly out when the plates were struck. Original plans to arm *Gloire* with 6.4in (163mm) smoothbores were changed, and rifled versions were carried instead. With the introduction of the ironclad, Napoleon III at last saw a chance to rival Great Britain; *Gloire* and her two sisterships, *Normandie* and *Invincible*, were to form the basis of his powerful French fleet.

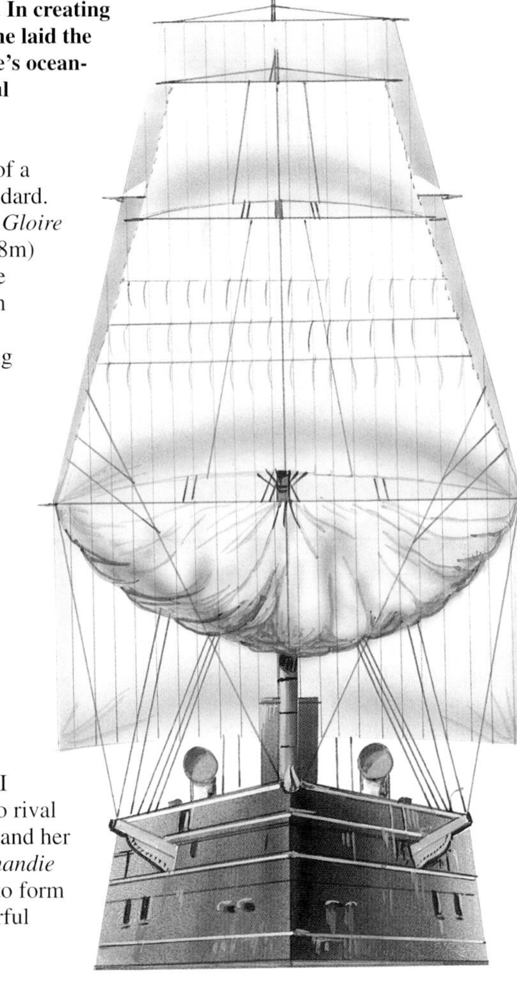

Bow view of *Gloire* showing the formidable appearance of the world's first ironclad. In creating *Gloire* Dupuy De Lôme laid the foundation for France's ocean-going fleet of powerful ironclads.

***Gloire* in 1860. Her sistership, *Normandie*, was the first ironclad to cross the Atlantic. Unfortunately, the lifespan of the French wooden-hulled ironclads was short, with *Gloire*'s two sisters lasting only about 10 years.**

GOUBET II

FRANCE: 1889

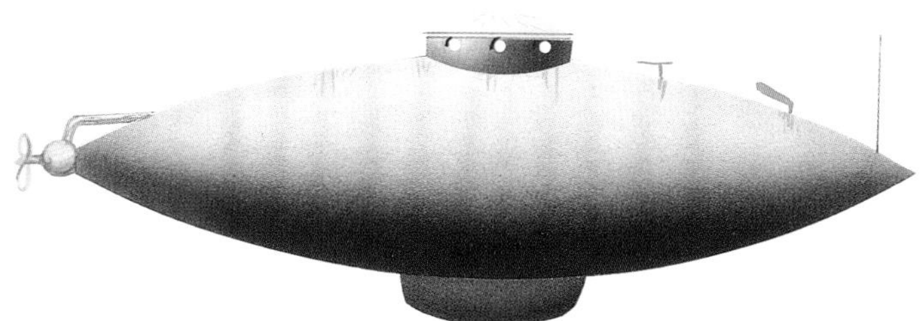

***Goubet II* had a 1in thick shell, cast in bronze in three pieces, flanged and bolted together. There was a 1.5t drop weight for safety.**

In France, Goubet had been experimenting with small submarines for a number of years. These boats were too small and too slow to be of any great military value, but their design was well-planned, ingenious, and well-detailed. A great deal of experience was gained from these experimental boats, especially one built in the late-1880s which featured a variable pitch propeller. A second boat had her trials in 1899–1900; she was driven by an electric motor, which derived its energy from a battery of the Laurent-Cely type. However, the naval authorities turned the idea down.

Displacement: 10t
Dimensions: 15ft x 6ft (4.6m x 1.8m)
Machinery: single screw, electric; 4hp
Speed: 3 knots
Complement: 3

GUSTAVE ZÉDÉ

FRANCE: 1893

Ordered in October 1890, *Gustave Zédé* was a single-hulled submarine. Roma bronze was used for the hull as it was a material less likely to suffer damage from seawater. The lead keel was detachable, for release in emergencies. Power was supplied by electric batteries comprising 720 cells; these caused problems because of excessive weight. Originally the engine developed 760hp, but this was greatly reduced after an accident. Additional hydroplanes were fitted to improve fore and aft control, and *Gustave Zédé* made over 2500 successful dives. She was the first submarine to be fitted with a periscope.

Displacement: 226t surfaced; 272t submerged
Dimensions: 159ft x 10ft 6in x 10ft 7in (48.5m x 3.2m x 3.2m)
Machinery: single screw, electric; 208hp
Armament: one 17.7in (450mm) TT
Speed: 9.2 knots surfaced; 6.5 knots submerged
Range: 2200nm(4074km) at 5.5 knots; 105nm (194km) at 4.5 knots
Complement: 19

In 1898, during trials, *Gustave Zédé* successfully 'torpedoed' the battleship *Magenta*, so setting alarm bells ringing in the British Admiralty about this new threat.

GUSTAVO SAMPAIO

BRAZIL: 1893

Built by Armstrong as a private venture and to keep skilled workmen available instead of laying them off, this steel-hulled torpedo gunboat had a raised forecastle, two masts, and a single funnel. Armstrong named the unit *Aurora*. There was a fixed torpedo tube in the bow, and two trainable tubes, one on each beam just aft of the break in the forecastle. The 4in (102mm) guns were mounted fore and aft. *Aurora* was purchased by Brazil in October 1893 and renamed *Gustavo Sampaio*. In April 1894, she led the torpedo attack against the battleship *Aquidaban*, then in revolt against the Brazilian authorities.

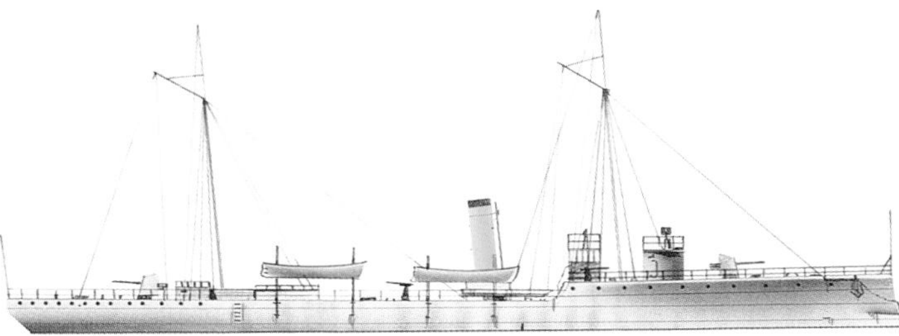

***Gustavo Sampaio* was one of the many fast torpedo gunboats of the 1880s and 1890s. The type was eventually to give way to the faster destroyers then entering service.**

Displacement: 480t
Dimensions: 196ft 9in x 20ft x 8ft 6in (60m x 6.1m x 2.6m)
Machinery: twin screw; 2000hp
Armament: two 4in (102mm); three 14in (356mm) TT
Speed: 18 knots
Range: not known
Complement: 60

GYMNÔTE

FRANCE: 1888

Displacement: 30t surfaced; 31t submerged
Dimensions: 58ft 5in x 6ft x 5ft 6in (17.8m x 1.8m x 1.7m)
Machinery: single screw, electric; 33.4hp/25hp
Armament: two 14in (356mm) TT
Speed: 7.3 knots surfaced; 4.3 knots submerged
Range: 65nm (120km)at 7.3 knots; 31nm (57km) at 5 knots
Complement: 5

A single-hull steel submarine designed by Gustave Zédé, *Gymnôte* was ordered in 1886 and proved to be a great success. Power was supplied from batteries made up of 204 cells and weighing nearly one-third of the displacement. Experiments with hydroplanes led to their being incorporated in the design of all subsequent submarines. The French were successful with several of their early submarines built during the late-1880s and 1890s, and *Gymnôte* was no exception, making about 2000 successful dives. The torpedoes were carried in drop collars, one on each beam. *Gymnôte* was modernized in 1898 and stricken in 1909.

***Gymnôte* had a raised conning tower added in 1898, so indicating the shape of submarines to come.**

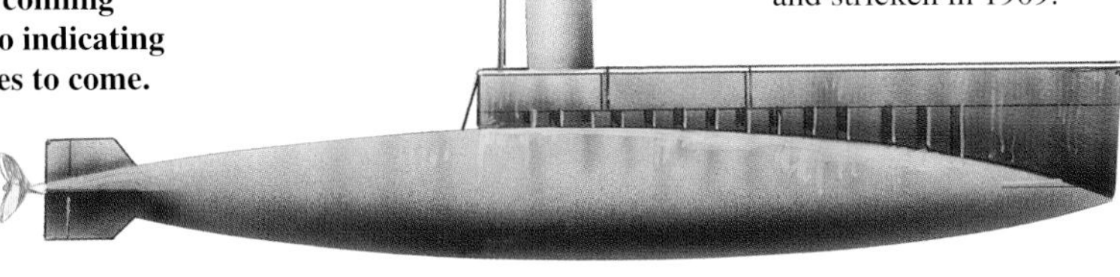

H L HUNLEY

CONFEDERATE STATES OF AMERICA: 1863

The submarine *Hunley* was built in 1863 at the workshops of Park and Lyons in Mobile from the designs of H. L. Hunley, James McClintock, and Baxter Watson. Two Confederate Army engineers, Lt. Alexander and Lt. Dixon, supervised the construction. The main section of the hull was fashioned from a cylindrical steam boiler which had tapered ends added. *Hunley* was powered by hand cranking a single screw which needed a crew of eight; a ninth person stood at the controls in the forward section. There were ballast tanks at each end, which worked by opening valves and were emptied by hand pumps. An iron keel was bolted to the base of the craft which could be unscrewed from the inside in case of any emergency. A compass was used to navigate under water, and depth of water was monitored via a mercury gauge. When slightly submerged, two pipes with stopcocks were raised to let in air. When on the surface, small glass windows in the walls of the manhole covers allowed the commander to see out. Taken to Charleston for use against the blockading Union Fleet, *Hunley* carried out trials but unfortunately several crews were lost in these tests. Eventually she did have some success, sinking the *Housatonic* in February 1864, but *Hunley* and her crew were all lost in doing so.

Displacement: not recorded
Dimensions: 40ft x 3ft 6in x 5ft (12m x 1m x 1.6m)
Machinery: single screw, hand-cranked
Armament: one spar torpedo
Speed: 5 knots surfaced; 3 knots submerged
Range: not known
Complement: 9

***H L Hunley* was a privately-built submarine, and armed with a spar torpedo with a charge of 90lb (41kg) of powder in a copper cylinder.**

HABSBURG

AUSTRIA: 1900

The *Habsburgs* were the world's smallest capital ships, with their main armament in a twin turret forward and a single turret aft, both on the centreline. The 5.9in (150mm) guns, carried in double storey casemates, were as powerful as battleships twice their size. The Krupp steel belt was 223ft (67.8m) long and 8ft (2.5m) deep, and the bow was reinforced with 2in plating 8ft (25m) high with nearly half above water. Above the main belt was a strake 4in (104mm) thick. Casemates had 5in (127mm) armoured fronts and 3in (76mm) backs.

A small fast battleship, the *Habsburg* had two sisterships, all later had the superstructure reduced to save excess top weight.

Displacement: 8823t
Dimensions: 375ft 10in x 65ft x 24ft 6in (114.6m x 19.9m x 7.5m)
Machinery: twin screw, vertical triple expansion, 16 boilers; 15,063hp
Armament: three 9.45in (240mm); 12 5.9in (150mm)
Armour: belt 8.5-7in (220-180mm); upper belt 4in (102mm); turrets/casemates 11-8.2in (280--210mm); deck 1.7in (40mm)
Speed: 19.6 knots
Range: 3700nm at 10 knots
Complement: 638

HATTERAS

USA: 1861

Displacement: 1152t
Dimensions: 215ft x 33ft 6in x 21ft 3in (66m x 10m x 6.3m)
Machinery: side wheels, side lever, two boilers; 240hp
Armament: eight 32pdr; one 20pdr
Speed: 12.5 knots
Range: not known
Complement: 120

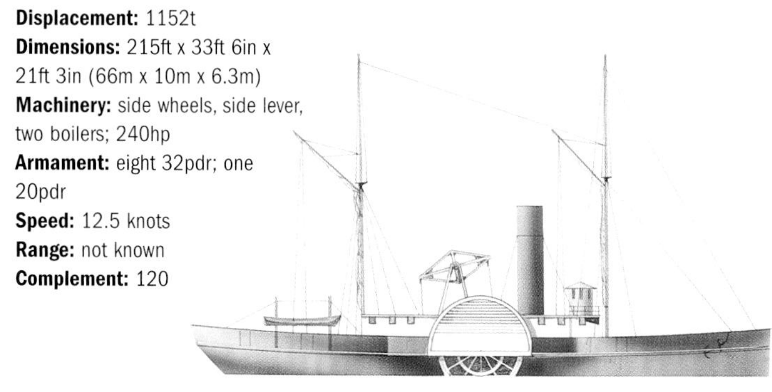

The iron-hulled, side wheel steamer ferry *St Mary's* was purchased in September 1861. Renamed the *Hatteras*, she was one of the many existing merchant vessels hastily acquired by the Union Navy to make up the serious shortfall of ships desperately needed to establish a blockade along the 3000 miles of Confederate coastline. On blockade duty off Galverston, recently recaptured by Confederate forces, *Hatteras* chased the raider *Alabama,* and after a short action with that vessel was sunk. *Hatteras* was the only Union warship to be sunk by a Confederate raider.

***Hatteras* was typical of the early makeshift Union Navy; merchant ships costing many thousands of dollars were sold off at the end of the Civil War at a fraction of their original cost.**

HAVOCK

GB: 1893

Displacement: 275t
Dimensions: 185ft x 18ft 6in x 7ft 6in (56.4m x 5.6m x 2.2m)
Machinery: twin screws, triple expansion; 3400hp
Armament: one 3in (76mm); three 6pdr; three 14in (356mm) TT
Speed: 26.7 knots
Range: 1000 miles at 10 knots
Complement: 43

In the early 1890s, considerable concern was felt in the British Admiralty regarding the rapid growth in size and numbers of French torpedo-boats. Speeds of 25 knots were being attained, and the leading French torpedo-boat builder, Normand, was planning a boat of 30 knots. This prototype vessel eventually became the *Forban*. Britain's existing torpedo gun-boats were unable to cope with these torpedo-boats, but in early 1892, Yarrow put forward plans for a super torpedo-boat that would eventually be called a destroyer. Two designs were submitted and four vessels were ordered: steel-hulled, lightly built, with a turtle back deck forward, and armed with one 3in (76mm) gun mounted on a raised platform, and three 6pdrs (one aft and one on each beam). They also carried one bow torpedo tube and two trainable deck tubes.

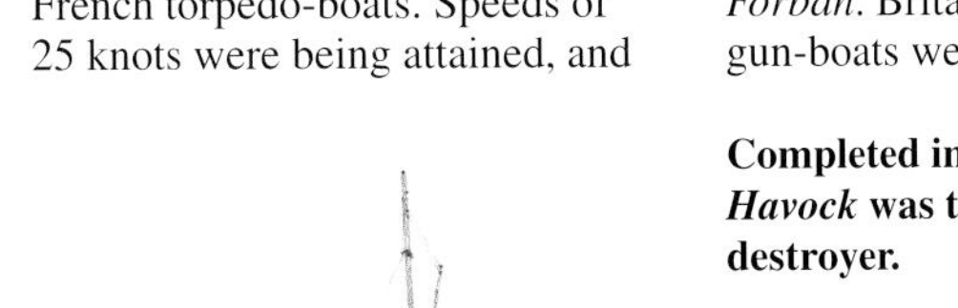

Completed in January 1894, *Havock* was the world's first destroyer.

HELGOLAND

DENMARK: 1878

Laid down in 1876 and completed in 1879, *Helgoland* was Denmark's largest warship for many years. She had the armament and protection of a true battleship, with a 12in (305mm) full-length iron belt amidships at the waterline, and 10in (254mm) on the casemate. The latter housed four 10.2in (259mm) guns firing one from each corner, with the hull sides recessed back to allow some end-on fire. Forward and above the battery was a single 12in (305mm) gun, mounted in a barbette. *Helgoland* had two masts with a small sail area.

Displacement: 5332t
Dimensions: 259ft 7in x 59ft x 19ft 4in (79.1m x 18m x 5.9m)
Machinery: twin screw; 4000hp
Armament: one 12in (305mm); four 10.2in (259mm); five 4.7in (119mm)
Armour: belt 12-8in (305-230mm); battery/barbette 10in (254mm); deck 1.5in
Speed: 13.7 knots
Range: 1070nm (1982km) at 10 knots
Complement: 331

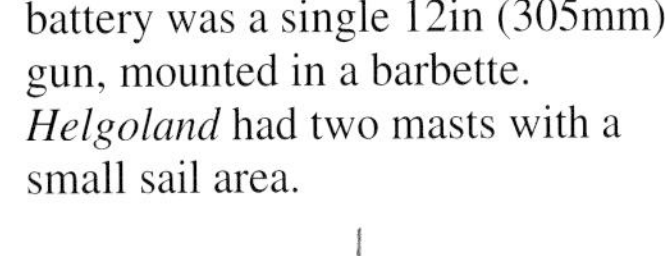

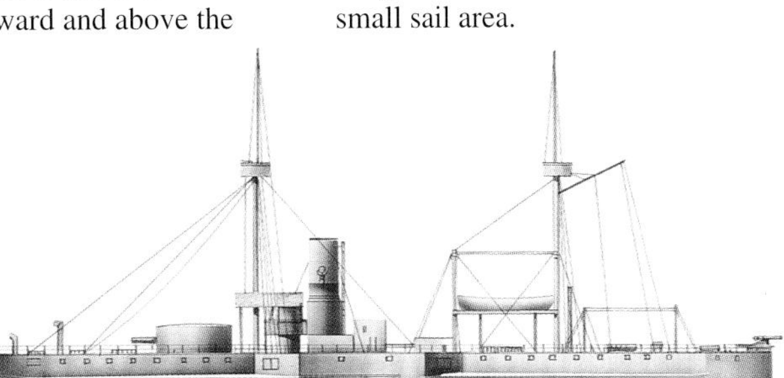

The iron-hulled *Helgoland*, with her 11ft (3.35m) freeboard, was a good sea-boat. She was in service for more than 30 years.

HERCULES

GB: 1868

Displacement: 8830t
Dimensions: 325ft x 59ft x 25ft 4in (99m x 18m x 7.7m)
Machinery: single screw, horizontal compound, nine boilers; 7178hp
Armament: eight 10in (254mm); two 9in (229mm); four 7in (178mm)
Armour: belt 9-6in (229-152mm); bulkheads 6-5in (152-127mm); battery 8-6in (203-152mm)
Speed: 14.7 knots
Range: 1760 miles at 10 knots
Complement: 638

In a report made in 1866, the gunnery expert Captain Cooper Key stressed the need for all-round fire in ironclads. Reed, the chief designer, responded, providing end-on fire in the *Hercules* by adding embrasures at each end of the battery amidships to house the new and more powerful 10in (254mm) guns. In addition, two 7in (178mm) guns were carried at each end of the upper deck, with a single 9in (229mm) gun immediately below firing ahead, and one aft. Improved hull lines, better boilers, and more efficient engines gave a speed of nearly 15 knots, the fastest yet in any ironclad. *Hercules* was one of the best central battery ships produced. Her hull was not sold until 1932.

HOCHE

FRANCE: 1886

Displacement: 10,820t
Dimensions: 336ft 7in x 66ft 4in x 27ft (102.6m x 20.2m x 8.3m)
Machinery: twin screws, vertical compound, eight boilers; 12,000hp
Armament: two 13.4in (340mm); two 10.8in (274mm); 18 5.5in (140mm); three 15in (381mm) TT
Armour: belt 18-10in (457-254mm); upper belt 3.2in (81mm); turrets/barbettes 16in (406mm)
Speed: 16.5 knots
Range: 3500 miles at 11 knots
Complement: 611

The designers of the *Hoche* moved away from the French trend of four main gun turrets in a lozenge layout by adopting barbettes for the 10.8in (274mm) broadside guns. These were sponsoned out beyond the marked tumblehome, so giving them good axial fire. The 13.4in (340mm) guns were mounted in canet hydraulically operated turrets fore and aft. Seven 5.5in (140mm) unprotected guns were also carried at the base of the large superstructure, with four more, also unprotected, carried two decks above. A thick but narrow complete compound belt extended only 24in (609mm) above water. Above this there was a thin steel belt and a cellulose-filled cofferdam.

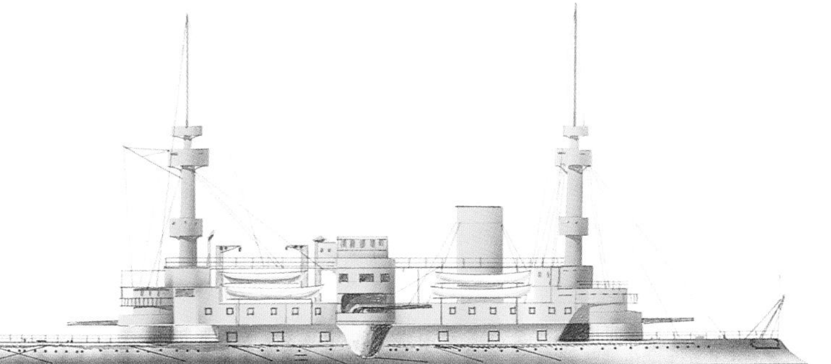

The imposing outline of *Hoche* when completed in 1890. Later the superstructure was reduced.

HOLLAND

USA: 1897

In 1887, the US Navy invited designs for a submarine. The specification was a tough one, and several designs were submitted before two were accepted. One of these, by John P. Holland, used horizontal rudders to incline the axis as the boat submerged or rose to the surface. The Navy took no action until 1893, when fresh proposals were invited. Holland obtained a contract in 1895 and built a submarine, the *Plunger*. However, he was not happy with this boat and decided to build another at his own expense. His boat, the *Holland*, was of an advanced design and the first to use an internal combustion engine, in conjunction with a storage battery and an electric motor. This technical combination made Holland's submarine a viable weapon. Prior to this, some submarines had been steam driven on the surface and, once submerged with their boiler fires extinguished, had had to rely for propulsion on the latent power in the shut down boilers. Their interiors were consequently unbearably hot and extremely crowded, with spaces occupied by machinery and boilers. The *Holland* was cigar-shaped, relatively short, with a small superstructure and very little stability when surfaced. The desired depth was maintained by using the horizontal rudders as it was important to keep the centre of gravity constant and compensate for all variations in buoyancy. Twin tanks were also fitted in addition to the main ballast tanks. Motive power on the surface was provided by the newly-developed petrol engine; it was economical, which gave the *Holland* a great radius of action and also charged up the batteries. Another benefit was that, unlike steam machinery, it produced little heat. The armament comprised one torpedo tube in the bows firing a Whitehead torpedo, and one dynamite gun in the top of the casing using compressed air as a propellant.

Displacement: 63.3/74t
Dimensions: 53ft 10in x 10ft 3in (16.4m x 3.1m)
Machinery: single screw, petrol/battery. 45hp/75hp
Armament: one 18in (457mm) TT; one 10in (254mm)
Speed: 8/5 knots
Range: not known
Complement: 9

The *Holland* led to a whole series of submarines built by John P. Holland's company. He was later ousted from his own company.

HOUSATONIC

USA: 1861

Bark-rigged sloops with wooden hulls which followed established designs, the *Housatonic* and her three sisterships were the second tranche of a large increase in the US Navy authorized in 1861. The 100pdr Parrott rifle and 11in (280mm) Dahlgren smoothbore were on pivots on the centreline, with three 30pdrs and two 32pdrs on the broadside. Isherwood designed the engines, the first time he had designed the machinery for an entire class. *Housatonic* had one encounter with two Confederate ironclads off Charleston and was sunk while on blockade duty on 17 February 1864. Her executioner was the Confederate submarine, *Hunley* – the first time a warship had been sunk by a submarine.

Displacement: 1934t
Dimensions: 205ft x 38ft x 16ft 6in (62.5m x 11.6m x 5m)
Machinery: single screw, horizontal return connecting rod, two boilers; 700hp
Armament: one 100pdr; one 11in (280mm); three 30pdr; two 32pdr; two 24pdzr
Speed: 11.6 knots
Range: not known
Complement: 214

The wooden-hulled *Housatonic* fell victim to the first ever successful submarine attack.

HUASCAR

PERU: 1865

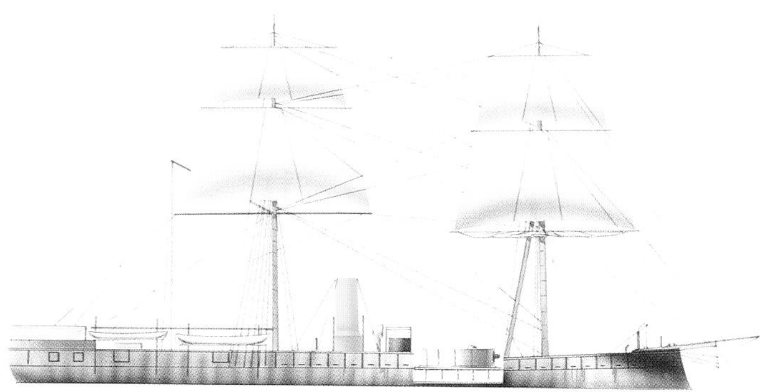

During Peru's war with Chile in 1879–81, the diminutive iron-hulled turret ship, *Huascar*, was to become the Peruvian Navy's main fighting force. She assumed this role after the ironclad *Independencia* was lost in action. *Huascar*'s iron belt was complete and ran from 5ft (1.5m) above

***Huascar* featured Coles turrets and unique tripod masts which cut down on the amount of rigging.**

Displacement: 2030t
Dimensions: 190ft x 35ft x 18ft (58m x 10.7m x 5.6m)
Machinery: single screw, single expansion, four boilers; 1650hp
Armament: two 10in (254mm); two 40pdr; one 20pdr
Armour: belt 4.5-2in (115-52mm); turret 8-5.5in (203-140mm); deck 2in; conning tower 3in (76mm)
Speed: 12.3 knots
Complement: 170

water (the maximum freeboard amidships) to 3ft (0.9m) below, backed by 13in (330mm) of wood. An armoured transverse bulkhead 4.5in (114mm) thick protected the turret mechanism, magazines, and boilers from raking fire. The single Coles turret housed two 10in (254mm) Armstrong muzzle loaders, each of which weighed 12.5t. On the quarter deck were two 40pdrs plus one 20pdr in the stern. The hull had a double bottom beneath the turret and machinery spaces. Amidships, hinged iron bulwarks were lowered when in action. *Huascar* was extremely handy, turning through 180 degrees in about two minutes. She was to have an active career. In May 1877, her crew mutinied and declared for Pierola, a claimant to the presidency of Peru. Later, she attempted the seizure of several British merchant ships, which brought her to the attention of Rear Admiral de Horsey in command of the Royal Navy's Pacific Squadron. He found *Huascar* and with his two ships, the large unarmoured frigate *Shah* and the smaller *Amethyst*, tried to capture her but, after a short engagement, failed to do so. This incident led the British Admiralty in the future to position an ironclad on overseas stations as, clearly, cruisers could not be expected to beat an ironclad in action. For many months, *Huascar* was the only serious opposition to the Chilean Navy but was eventually captured on 8 October 1879 by the ironclads *Blanco Encalada* and *Almirante Cochrane*. In 1891, *Huascar* saw more action during the Chilean Civil War. She is now preserved at Valparaiso, Chile.

IDAHO

USA: 1863

One of seven large, swift cruisers, *Idaho* was contracted out completely to Forbes and Dickerson. The hull was designed by Steers. The machinery, which had an 8ft (2.4m) stroke, was designed by Dickerson to compete with the Navy Departments' Engineer-in-Chief Isherwood. Designed for 15 knots, *Idaho* made only 8 knots and was rejected, but Forbes and Dickerson persuaded Congress to purchase the vessel despite its drawbacks. Accepted, minus machinery she was converted into a store-ship. *Idaho* became one of the fastest vessels afloat under sail making 18.5 knots.

***Idaho* was caught in a typhoon in 1869, dismasted and with 4ft (12m) of water on the upper deck, she limped to Yokohama and was sold for 4 per cent of the original cost.**

Displacement: 3241t
Dimensions: 298ft x 44ft 6in x 17ft (90.8m x 13.6m x 5.2m)
Machinery: twin screws, Dickerson engines, two boilers; 645hp
Armament: eight
Speed: 8.2 knots
Range: not known
Complement: 350

IDAHO

USA: 1905

Displacement: 14,465t
Dimensions: 382ft x 77ft x 24ft 8in (116.4m x 23.5m x 7.2m)
Machinery: twin screws, vertical triple expansion, eight boilers; 10,000hp
Armament: four 12in (305mm); eight 8in (203mm); eight 7in (178mm); two 21in (533mm) TT
Armour: belt 9-7in (229-178mm); turrets 12-8in (305-203mm); battery 7-3.5in (178-89mm); barbettes 10-6in (254-152mm)
Speed: 17 knots
Range: not known
Complement: 744

The last two pre-dreadnoughts of the US Navy, *Idaho* and her sistership, *Mississippi*, were an attempt to reproduce the successful *Vermont* class on 3000t less displacement. Their main belt armour was 244ft (74.4m) long, 9ft 3in (2.7m) deep, and weighed 3377t. The 12in (305mm) guns were in twin turrets fore and aft, with twin 8in (203mm) weapons on the upper deck, in the corners of the superstructure; the 7in (178mm) guns were in a battery on the main deck.

***Idaho* with cage masts. In 1914, both *Idaho* and *Mississippi* were sold to Greece. Both vessels were sunk by German aircraft in April 1941.**

IMPERIEUSE

GB: 1883

Displacement: 8500t
Dimensions: 315ft x 62ft x 26ft 9in (96m x 19m x 8.1m)
Machinery: twin screws, inverted compound, 12 boilers; 8000hp
Armament: four 9.2in (234mm); 10 6in (152mm)
Armour: belt 10in (254mm); bulkheads 9in (229mm); deck 4-2in (102-52mm); barbettes 8in (203mm)
Speed: 16.7 knots
Range: 5500nm (10,186km) at 10 knots
Complement: 555

In the first years of the 1880s, France built two large 6100t cruisers which were reduced copies of the *Amiral Duperré*, an 11,030t battleship armed with four 13.4in (340mm) guns. In reply, Britain laid down the *Imperieuse* and *Warspite* protected on the same principle as the contemporary British *Admiral*-class battleships, with the side armour concentrated in a short 140ft (43m), narrow 10in (254mm) belt. Above this ran a 2in thick

***Imperieuse* and *Warspite* served on foreign stations. The massive rig was soon removed and a single military mast substituted.**

armoured deck; at its ends, the thickness increased to 4in (102mm), the thickest in an armoured ship for 12 years. Between this deck and the main deck above, an elaborate subdivision was provided instead of armour. The four 9.2in (234mm) guns were mounted in single positions on the French lozenge system, with a pronounced tumblehome to the sides, so allowing the beam guns axial fire – though this layout was not repeated in a British ship. The 9.2in (234mm) guns were an improved type, and *Imperieuse* was the first to have them. Design changes, plus an increased coal supply and lack of control in the weight of material used, increased the displacement by 900t. The speed was an advance on previous armoured cruisers, but was still the same as contemporary battleships.

INCONSTANT

GB: 1868

The powerful cruiser *Inconstant* was able to make over 15 knots under sail alone. Her hull was not broken up until 1956.

The US Navy's *Wampanoag* class of fast cruisers were intended for commerce raiding. The British Admiralty immediately sought an answer to this threat, and ordered the construction of still more powerful cruisers, of which *Inconstant* was the first. In order to combine good sailing qualities with good steaming qualities, and at the same time carry a heavy armament, the design required very large dimensions and a displacement of 5780t, which was far greater than any other ship in her class. *Inconstant*'s designer, Sir Edward Reed, realized that a vessel of such size, length, and power would not be strong enough if built of wood, so iron was chosen instead. (For the first time, wood sheathing and coppering were used to reduce the fouling of the hull; later, it was used generally in cruising ships.) The armament was extremely powerful, with the 9in guns on the main deck and the 7in on the upper deck. No armour was fitted, protection being provided by coal bunkers. In order to obtain a steady gun platform, *Inconstant* initially had a small stability range, but this was altered when 300t of ballast was shipped.

Displacement: 5780t
Dimensions: 337ft 4in x 50ft x 25ft 6in (102.8m x 15.3m x 7.8m)
Machinery: single screw, horizontal single expansion; 7360hp
Armament: 10 9in (229mm); six 7in (178mm)
Speed: 16.2 knots
Range: not known
Complement: 600

INDEPENDENCIA

PERU: 1864

Displacement: 3500t
Dimensions: 215ft x 44ft 9in x 21ft 6in (65.6m x 13.6m x 6.5m)
Machinery: single screw; 2200hp
Armament: two 7in (178mm); 12 70pdr
Armour: belt 4.5in (115mm); battery 4.5in (115mm)
Speed: 12 knots
Range: not known
Complement:

The broadside ironclad *Independencia* was the largest armoured vessel built for Peru, and a typical capital ship much favoured by minor navies. In 1879, during the war with Chile, *Independencia* was lost in the early stages of the war. Built at Samunda's yard on the Thames, *Independencia* was an iron-hulled vessel with three watertight compartments. The complete iron belt extended to 4ft (1.2m) below the waterline with 10in (254mm) teak backing. The main battery housed 70pdr guns, and there were two 7in (178mm) pivot mounted guns on the spar deck.

While attempting to ram the Chilean 400t *Covadonga Independencia* ran aground and was lost.

INFANTA MARIA TERESA

SPAIN: 1890

The maritime needs of Spain differed from other, more powerful, European countries. Compared to France or Britain, Spain was not a rich country and, although she still needed powerful warships, only one battleship was ordered in the 1880s. Spain would continue to rely mainly on her large armoured cruisers to protect her colonies. *Infanta Maria Teresa* and her two sisterships were enlarged versions of the British *Galatea* class, with armour protection on the same principle. A narrow armour belt covered two-thirds of the waterline amidships, with the protective deck flat over the belt but curving down at the extremities, with a raised armoured glacis over the engine room. Wide coal bunkers were positioned above the belt, with a narrower set of bunkers abreast of the engine room below the waterline. The 11in Hontoria guns were placed fore and aft with the 5.5in Hontoria quick-firing guns on the upper deck behind shields. All three vessels of the class were sunk at Santiago in July 1898.

Displacement: 6890t
Dimensions: 364ft x 65ft x 21ft 6in (110.9m x 19.9m x 6.6m)
Machinery: twin screws, vertical triple expansion; 13,700hp
Armament: two 11in (280mm); 10 5.5in (140mm); eight TT
Armour: belt 12-10in (305-254mm); deck 3-2in (76-52mm); barbettes 9in (229mm)
Speed: 20.25 knots
Complement: 484

***Infanta Maria Teresa* was the flagship of Ceveras at Santiago when the Spanish Squadron tried to reach Havana.**

INFLEXIBLE

GB: 1876

Built as an answer to *Duilio* and *Dandolo*, the two powerful turret ships recently constructed by the Italians, *Inflexible* was originally planned to carry 60t guns. However, 80t guns were substituted, whereupon the Italians planned 100t weapons in place of the 60t weapons at first intended for their ships. Although there could be no question of a foreign navy having guns more powerful than those of the Royal Navy, design limitations forced the Admiralty to remain with the 80t guns. They were mounted in twin turrets *en échelon* in a 110ft (33.5m) central citadel plated with two layers of 12in (305mm) wrought iron armour – the thickest armour ever carried. Extensive sub-divisions of compartments either side of the citadel protected the ends of the ship.

***Inflexible* was built to tight limitations. She was not to exceed the size and cost of previous British battleships, yet was required to carry the heaviest guns.**

Displacement: 11,880t
Dimensions: 344ft x 75ft x 25ft 6in (104.8m x 22.9m x 7.8m)
Machinery: twin screws, compound expansion, 12 boilers; 8407hp
Armament: four 16in (406mm)
Armour: belt/citadel 24-16in (609-406mm); bulkheads 22-14in (575-356mm); turrets 17in (432mm); deck 3in (76mm)
Speed: 14.75 knots
Range: 5200 miles at 10 knots
Complement: 440

INTELLIGENT WHALE

USA: 1862

Responding to the Confederate threat of submarine craft, the Union forces began to experiment with their own in the form of the *Southern Pioneer*, which was built as a privateer. Later, the *Intelligent Whale* was designed by Scovel Merriam and Halstead. Hand-cranked by six of the crew of 13, it was hoped to achieve a speed of 4 knots. The boat was designed to anchor at a given depth so that divers could climb out of hatches in the bottom. After a series of unsuccessful and fatal trials, *Intelligent Whale* was condemned in 1872 and put on display at the old Washington Navy Yard.

Displacement: 30t
Dimensions: 30ft x 7ft (9.1m x 2.2m)
Machinery: single screw, hand-cranked
Speed: 3 knots
Complement: 13

***Intelligent Whale* was not completed until 1866. After her failure, no American submarine was planned for 30 years.**

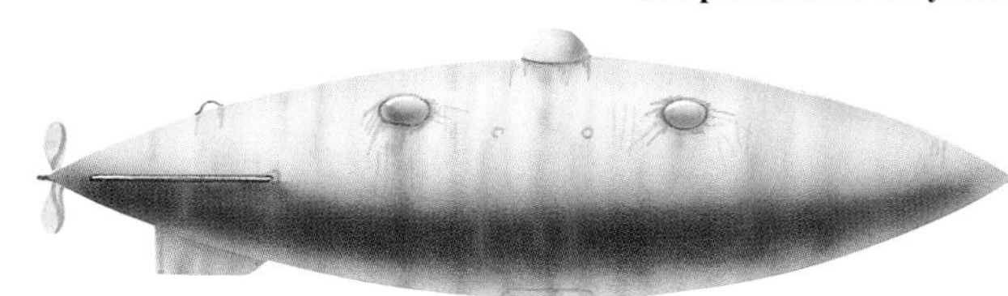

IOSCO

USA: 1863

Iosco was one of a class of 28 shallow-draught, double-ended side wheel steamers designed by Lenthall and Isherwood. All but three were laid down in 1862, and the rest begun in 1863. All had wooden hulls except one. The steamers were created especially to cope with operations against Confederate forces stationed along tortuous inland waterways, where trying to turn vessels round under fire proved hazardous and sometimes fatal. They had a rudder at each end, enabling them to steam backwards out of danger.

Great delays were experienced in the building of the *Iosco* class because of the shortage of skilled labour and machinery.

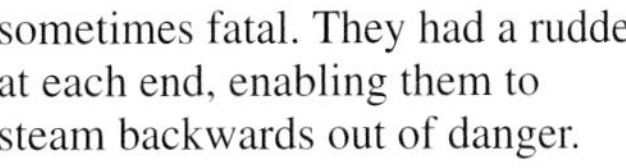

Displacement: 1173t
Dimensions: 240ft x 35ft (73m x 10.7m)
Machinery: side wheel, two boilers; 545hp
Armament: four 9in (229mm); two 6.4in (162mm)
Speed: 8.5 knots
Range: not known
Complement: 145

IOWA

USA: 1896

***Iowa* in 1911. Note the tumblehome of the hull to allow the 8in (203mm) guns axial fire.**

With a lighter armament on a larger displacement than the preceding *Oregon* class, *Iowa* was a more balanced design having a raised forecastle which gave her better sea-keeping qualities. The forward 12in (305mm) gun and the four twin-mounted 8in (203mm) guns were 25ft 6in (7.8m) above water. The 186ft (56.7m) main belt was 7ft 6in (2.3m) deep with 12in (305mm) transverse bulkheads. Above the main belt ran a short strake of 4in (102mm) armour up to the main deck. *Iowa* served in the Spanish-American War of 1898. She was sunk in 1923 as a radio-controlled target.

Displacement: 12,647t
Dimensions: 363ft 5in x 72ft x 24ft (110.5m x 22m x 7.3m)
Machinery: twin screws, vertical triple expansion, five boilers; 11,000hp
Armament: four 12in (305mm); eight 8in (203mm); six 4in (102mm); four 14in (356mm) TT
Armour: belt 14-4in (356-102mm); turrets 17-15in (432-381mm); secondary turrets 8-4in (203-102mm); barbettes 15-12.5in (381-317mm); deck 3in (76mm)
Speed: 16 knots
Range: 4500nm at 10 knots
Complement: 505

IRIS

GB: 1877

In the 1870s, the British Admiralty realized the importance of high speed and the advantages of less costly and more numerous vessels. It was decided to create a new type of cruiser by reducing displacement and increasing engine power. To achieve this, steel was to be used instead of iron in the hull, and more lightly-built engines coupled with the reduction in armament. Up until the 1870s, guns carried by cruisers and battleships were fairly matched, but now tests were conducted to determine the near ideal gun for these vessels. The conclusion was that a gun of between 3t and 5t seemed appropriate. *Iris* and her sistership, *Mercury*, were designed in accordance with these investigations. They were the first vessels in the Royal Navy to be built of steel, the guns were 3.2t 64pdrs and only a light rig was carried. It therefore became possible, on a relatively small displacement, to achieve a high speed. On completion, in 1879, *Iris* and *Mercury* were the fastest ships afloat, ideal for commerce protection in home waters. The complete absence of armour made it necessary to place the machinery as far below the waterline as possible; the engines were therefore arranged horizontally, and the coal bunkers positioned level with the machine spaces, continuing up to the main deck to provide some protection.

Steel for hulls had already been successfully used in the later Confederate blockade runners. *Iris* benefited from the experienced gained with these fragile but fast craft.

Displacement: 3730t
Dimensions: 330ft x 46ft x 22ft (91.5m x 14m x 6.7m)
Machinery: twin screws, horizontal direct acting compound, 12 boilers; 6000hp
Armament: 13 5in (127mm)
Speed: 18 knots
Range: 4400 miles at 10 knots
Complement: 275

ITALIA

ITALY: 1880

Displacement: 15407t
Dimensions: 409ft x 74ft x 28ft 9in (124.7m x 22.5m x 8.7m)
Machinery: four screws, vertical compound, 24 boilers; 11,986hp
Armament: four 17in (432mm); seven 5.9in (150mm); four 14in (356mm) TT
Armour: barbette 19in (483mm); funnel base 16in (406mm); deck 4in (102mm)
Speed: 17.8 knots
Range: 5000nm at 10 knots
Complement: 669

In the 1880s, Italy had a 3000 mile coastline and limited financial resources to defend it. She also had powerful neighbours, Austria and France; the latter especially had a powerful fleet that in number far exceeded that of the Italian Navy. The answer to Italy's limitations was to build a few large, very powerful vessels of high speed. The difficult balance of protection and armament was solved in a unique way, the result being the *Italia* and her sistership, *Lepanto*, battleships with unusual design features. Their designer, Benedetto Brin, discarded the side armour altogether and adopted the pure cellular raft principle type. The cellular layer was enclosed between a curved 4in (102mm) armoured deck which met the sides 6ft (1.8m) below the waterline and a deck 5ft (1.6m) above. Another deck was worked in between the two, with the top half used for coal stowage and the lower half minutely divided into spaces to be left empty. The four 110t guns were mounted on two turntables in a common barbette running diagonally across the ship, and armoured with 19in (483mm) compound plates set at 66 degrees.

Italia was faster than any capital ship afloat, had greater range, and heavier guns.

JAVARY

BRAZIL: 1875

For their time, the French-built *Javary* and her sistership, the *Solimoes*, were the most powerful vessels in the Brazilian Navy, which then comprised 18 ironclads. *Javary* was a double-turreted, iron-hulled shallow draught vessel with a 3ft 3in (1m) freeboard. The hull was completely armoured to 2ft 3in (0.7m) below the waterline with 10in (254mm) teak backing. The 10in (254mm) 22t Whitworth muzzle loaders fired a 400lb (182kg) shot. *Javary* had a 154ft (47m) flying bridge; ventilation was drawn down via the turrets and ventilators on the main superstructure.

Engaged in firing upon government shore positions during the Brazilian Revolution of 1893, _Javary_ sank due to leaks in her hull.

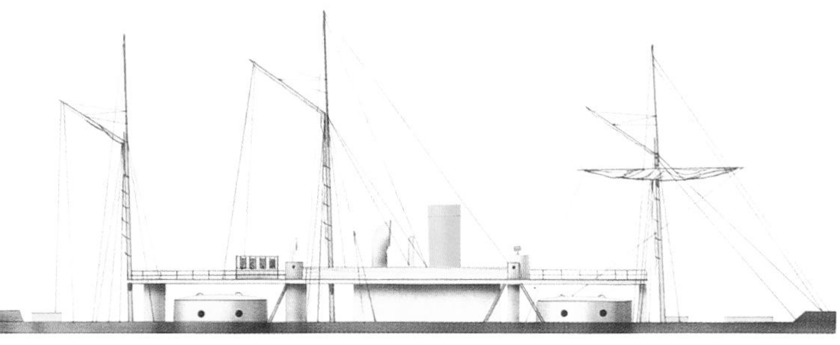

Displacement: 3543t
Dimensions: 240ft x 57ft x 11ft 5in (73m x 17.4m x 3.5m)
Machinery: twin screws, compound; 2200hp
Armament: four 10in (254mm)
Armour: belt 12–7in (305–178mm); turrets 12in (305mm)
Speed: 10 knots
Range: not known
Complement: 135

JEANNE D'ARC

FRANCE: 1899

The first of a series of large French armoured cruisers embodying Admiral Fournier's ideas on creating a fleet of commerce destroyers, *Jeanne D'Arc*'s designed speed was 23 knots. The waterline belt was complete and had an armoured deck 105in thick at its upper edge and another 2in at its lower edge, so forming a closed armoured box; inside the box was a cellular layer comprising cofferdams, passages, and 80 coal bunkers. The sides from the top of the second deck were protected from end-to-end by 3in (76mm) armour, and 1.5in armour was worked into the bow from the second deck to the upper deck. The 7.6in (194mm) guns were in single turrets fore and aft on the centreline, and the bow gun was 36ft (11m) above the waterline. In addition, there were 5.5in (140mm) guns on the broadside in armoured sponsons or protected by shields; nearly all of these guns could fire along the line of the keel. The engines were placed amidships between the two groups of boilers which gave this vessel its distinctive profile. On trials, only 22 knots was obtained from 33,000hp instead of the planned 28,500hp. Problems were experienced with ventilation and vibration, but these were successfully overcome and *Jeanne D'Arc* gave good service.

***Jeanne D'Arc* had a very large normal coal supply of 1400t which could be increased to 2000t.**

Displacement: 11,092t
Dimensions: 477ft x 63ft 8in x 27ft 6in (145.4m x 19.4m x 8.1m)
Machinery: triple screws, vertical triple expansion, 36 boilers; 33,000hp
Armament: two 7.6in (194mm); 14 5.5in (140mm)
Armour: belt 6-4in (152-102mm); upper belt 3in (76mm); deck 2in; turrets 6.3in (160mm)
Speed: 21.8 knots
Range: not known
Complement: 651

KAISER

GERMANY: 1874

Displacement: 8799t
Dimensions: 293ft x 62ft 8in x 26ft (89.3m x 19 x 7.9m)
Machinery: single screw, horizontal single expansion, eight boilers; 5779hp
Armament: eight 10.2in (260mm)
Armour: belt 10-5in (254-127mm); battery 8-7in (203-178mm); deck 2in
Speed: 14.6 knots
Range: 2470nm (4574km) at 10 knots
Complement: 656

Kaiser and her sistership, *Deutschland*, were the last foreign-built ironclads. Designed by Reed, these vessels demonstrated Germany's requirement for powerful cruising ironclads with which to maintain her newly-established colonies. The iron armour ran the full length of the vessel; bulkheads closed off the ends of the battery, with the forward bulkhead running down to the lower deck to provide added protection to the machinery and boilers. Four 10.2in (260mm) guns were mounted each side of the battery at main deck level, with the hull sides recessed to allow some axial fire aided by the battery protruding 3ft 6in (1m) beyond the sides.

***Kaiser* was a good sea-boat, and ship-rigged with 36,000sq ft (3344sq m) of canvas. She was rebuilt in 1895 as a heavy cruiser.**

KAISER FREDERICK III

GERMANY: 1896

With the five *Kaiser*-class battleships, Germany established a pattern that would last until the *Nassau* dreadnought class of 1908. These vessels were Germany's pre-dreadnoughts and, unlike those of other powers, had a lighter main armament and a greater number of secondary guns. The 9.4in (240mm) guns were in twin turrets fore and aft, with six 5.9in (150mm) in small single turrets on the upper deck and the rest in armoured casemates. The great weight of the armament meant that it was not possible on the limited displacement to adequately protect the hull: a narrow belt of armour ran for four-fifths of the length, and no protection was given to the high hull sides.

In 1907, four of the 5.9in (150mm) guns on *Kaiser Frederick III* were removed and the superstructure was cut down.

Displacement: 11,599t
Dimensions: 411ft x 67ft x 27ft (125.3m x 20.4m x 8.2m)
Machinery: triple screws, triple expansion, 12 boilers; 13,053hp
Armament: four 9.4in (240mm); 18 5.9in (150mm); six 17.7in (450mm) TT
Armour: belt 12-4in (305-102mm); main turrets 10in (254mm); secondary turrets 6in (152mm); deck 2.5in
Speed: 17.5 knots
Range: 3420 miles at 10 knots
Complement: 651

KATAHDIN

USA: 1893

Displacement: 2383t
Dimensions: 250ft 9in x 43ft 5in x 15ft (76.4m x 13.2m x 4.6m)
Machinery: twin screws, horizontal triple expansion, three boilers; 5068hp
Armament: four 6pdr
Armour: side 6in (152mm)
Speed: 16.1 knots
Range: not known
Complement: 97

The armoured coast-defence ram *Katahdin* was designed exclusively for ramming and carried no torpedoes. She was strongly built with a curved armoured deck, 6in (152mm) thick at the lower edge, 5.5in (140mm) on the slope, and 2in (52mm) on the flat. The knuckle was backed by 45in (1.1m) of timber, reminiscent of the Confederate ironclads. The hull top was 6ft (1.8m) above water, but was lowered 6in (152mm) when going into action by flooding the ballast tanks. There was a light bridge structure and one funnel.

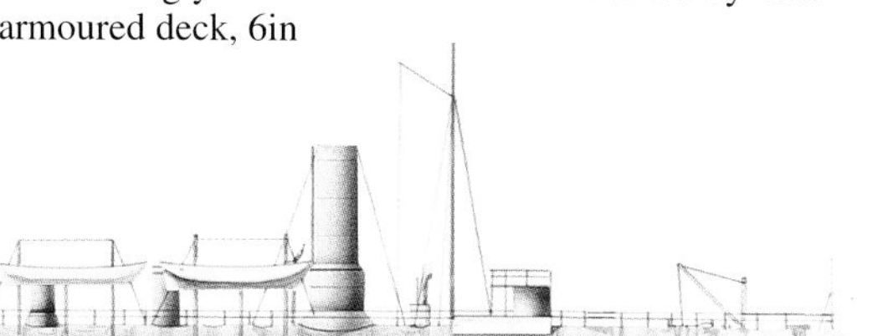

The ram *Katahdin* was designed by Admiral Ammen. Of the crew of 97, a total of 71 were engineers or stokers.

KEARSAGE

USA: 1861

A total of 18 screw sloops were built in the civil war; *Kearsage* was part of the huge US Navy expansion programme.

The wooden-hulled *Kearsage* was one of a group of cruisers laid down as part of the 1861 emergency programme designed to expand the US Navy as quickly as possible. Based upon the successful sloops of 1858, all the cruisers in the group were completed by 1862. *Kearsage* blockaded the Confederate raider *Sumter* at Gibraltar, forcing that vessel to be decommissioned. In June 1864, she fought and sank the raider *Alabama*. Sailing to Bluefields, Nicaragua, to safeguard American interests in the struggle between Nicaragua and Honduras, *Kearsage* ran aground on the Roncador Reef on 2 February 1894, and became a total wreck.

Displacement: 1457t
Dimensions: 198ft 6in x 33ft x 15ft 6in (60.5m x 10m x 4.7m)
Machinery: single screw, horizontal return connecting rod, two boilers; 840hp
Armament: two 11in (280mm); one 4.2in (107mm); four 32pdr
Speed: 12 knots
Range: not known
Complement: 163

KEARSAGE

USA: 1898

Displacement: 12,850t
Dimensions: 375ft 4in x 72ft x 23ft 6in (114.4m x 22m x 7.2m)
Machinery: twin screws, vertical triple expansion, five boilers; 10,000hp
Armament: four 13in (330mm); four 8in (203mm); 14 5in (127mm)
Armour: belt 16.5-4in (431-102mm); turrets 17in (432mm); secondary turrets 9in (229mm); battery 5.5in (140mm); deck 4in (102mm)
Speed: 16.8 knots
Range: not known
Complement: 553

Noted for the unusual arrangement of their armament, *Kearsage* and her sistership, *Kentucky*, mounted four 13in (330mm) guns in twin turrets fore and aft, with 8in (203mm) twin turrets superimposed on top and rigidly connected with the turrets below. The 5in (127mm) weapons were on the broadside in a long battery inside the superstructure, and protected all round with 5.5in (140mm) armour. Fitted between the guns were 2in splinter screens. The 5in (127mm) gun was chosen because it was the largest that could use shell and propellant. The combined main belt and the armour above it, which extended up to the main deck, formed a high armoured redoubt.

In the *Kearsage* a great deal was achieved on a limited displacement.

KNIAZ SOUVAROFF

RUSSIA: 1902

The ill-fated *Kniaz Souvaroff*. A sistership, *Orel*, was completed too late to join the Russian fleet on its way to Tshushima.

The five ships of the *Kniaz Souvaroff* class were the same type as the French-built *Tsessarevitch* of 1901, which gave such splendid service in the early stages of Russia's war with Japan. The principal armoured deck was 2in thick. Over the battery

Displacement: 13,516t
Dimensions: 397ft x 76ft x 27ft (121m x 23.2m x 8.1m)
Machinery: twin screws, vertical triple expansion, 20 boilers; 16,788hp
Armament: four 12in (305mm); 12 6in (152mm); four 15in (381mm) TT
Armour: belt 7.5-6in (190-152mm); turrets 10-4in (254-102mm); battery 3in (76mm)
Speed: 18.2 knots
Range: not known
Complement: 835

was another deck, 2.5–1.5in thick, plus another lower 1.5in deck. The main belt ran from 12in (305mm) turret to turret, and then thinned out towards the ends. In the Battle of Tsushima, four of the *Kniaz Souvaroff* class were engaged; heavily loaded down with coal and supplies, which brought the top of the armour belt almost level with the waterline, the ships were forced to rely for protection upon the thinner upper belt. The 6in (152mm) guns were in twin turrets, three per side, with most of the 11pdr anti-torpedo boat guns in a lightly armoured battery below. *Kniaz Souvaroff* was the flagship of Admiral Rozhdestvenski. During the action he was severely injured and transferred to another ship.

KÖNIG WILHELM (EX-FATIKH)

GERMANY: 1868

Originally intended to join the Turkish Navy as *Fatikh*, as part of a British policy of building up the Turkey Navy, this powerful central battery ship was purchased by Prussia and renamed *König Wilhelm*. The vessel was designed by Reed. The iron hull was built up on the bracket frame system and had a deep double bottom. The full-length belt covered the sides up to the main deck, but was reduced in depth in front of the battery. At each end of the battery, standing up clear of the upper deck, was a narrow structure. Each housed two guns – in the forward structure, the weapons fired ahead or on the beam; in the after structure, the guns fired on the beam or to the rear.

König Wilhelm was the largest unit in the Prussian Navy. Like all warships of the period, she had a ram bow.

Displacement: 11,591t
Dimensions: 368ft x 60ft x 28ft (112.2m x 18.3m x 8.5m)
Machinery: single screw, horizontal single expansion, eight boilers; 8345hp
Armament: 18 9.4in (240mm), five 8.2in (210mm)
Armour: belt 6-12in (152-305mm); battery 6-8in (152-203mm); deck 2in
Speed: 14.7 knots
Range: 1740 nm (3222km) at 10 knots
Complement: 730

KONIGSBERG

GERMANY: 1905

The evolution of the German light cruiser followed two lines, one for commerce destruction and one for fleet duties. As the types progressed, their speed and protection were greater than in many contemporary British cruisers, but they were more lightly armed, still retaining the 4.1in (105mm) weapon. It was maintained that it was a superior gun because it was semi-automatic, firing up to 20 rounds per minute, ideal against enemy cruisers and destroyers where volume of fire was essential. At the outbreak of World War I, *Konigsberg* was stationed in German East Africa. After a brief career as a raider, she was sunk in the Rufiji River after a lengthy campaign in 1915.

Displacement: 3814t
Dimensions: 376ft 8in x 43ft 4in x 17ft (114.8m x 13.2m x 5.2m)
Machinery: twin screws, vertical triple expansion, 11 boilers; 12,000hp
Armament: 10 4.1in (105mm)
Speed: 24 knots
Range: 5750nm (10,649km) at 12 knots
Complement: 322

Germany did not start to build large classes of cruisers until the 3033t *Gazelle* class of 1897 but they followed a distinct pattern which included the *Konigsberg* group.

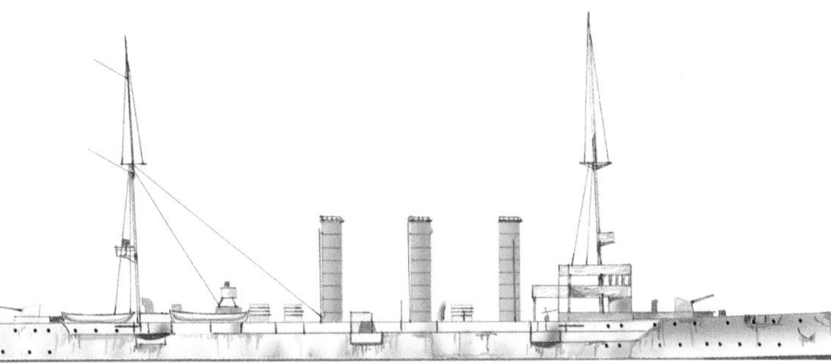

LEXINGTON

USA: 1861

Displacement: 448t
Dimensions: 177ft 7in x 36ft 10in x 6ft (54.2m x 11m x 1.8m)
Machinery: side wheel, high pressure, three boilers
Armament: four 8in (203mm); two 32pdr
Speed: 7 knots
Range: not known
Complement: 65

Lexington was built in 1860 as a wooden-hulled, side wheel passenger steamer but sold to the government at the outbreak of the American Civil War. She was converted into a gunboat under the direction of Commander Rogers. The boilers and steam pipes were lowered into the hold, the superstructure was removed and 5in (127mm) oak bulwarks were built all round the vessel to protect the crew from rifle fire. Decks were strengthened to take the extra weight of the guns. *Lexington* was one of the gunboats that saved the Union Army from defeat at Shilo.

Lexington was one of the first vessels to join the western flotilla that helped to break the Confederacy in two.

LIGHTNING

GB: 1877

The British steel-hulled *Lightning* was the world's first torpedo-boat to be armed with the Whitehead locomotive torpedo. Previous to this development, torpedo-boats had relied upon spar or towing torpedoes as their offensive weapons. Built by Thornycroft, the *Lightning* carried one bow tube with a reload carried on a trolley on either side amidships. The single screw was carried behind the divided rudder. Her type was soon copied by all navies, especially the minor ones who could not afford expensive ironclads.

The *Lightning* was the forerunner of a type of vessel that appeared to threaten the very existence of the battleship.

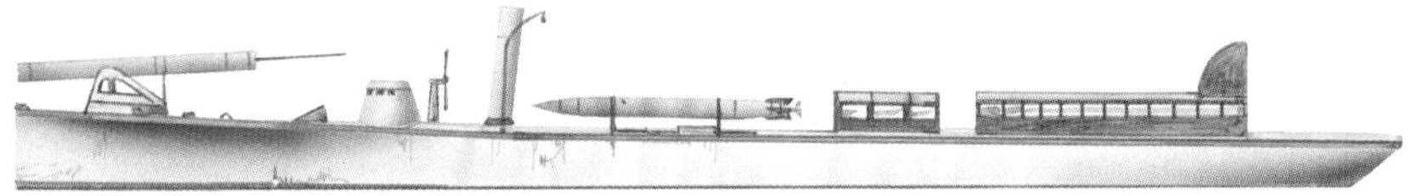

Displacement: 27t
Dimensions: 87ft x 10ft 9in x 5ft (26.5m x 3.3m x 1.6m)
Machinery: single screw, compound, one boiler; 460hp
Armament: one 14in (356mm) TT
Speed: 19 knots
Range: not known
Complement: 15

LOS ANDES

ARGENTINA: 1874

Displacement: 1500t
Dimensions: 186ft x 44ft x 10ft 6in (56.7m x 13.4m x 3.2m)
Machinery: twin screws, compound; 750hp
Armament: two 7.8in (198mm)
Armour: belt 6-4in (152-102mm); breastwork 8in (203mm); turret 9in (229mm)
Speed: 9.5 knots
Range: 2800 miles at 10 knots
Complement: 200

The low-freeboard turret ship *Los Andes* and her sistership, *La Plata*, were the first ironclads built for the Argentine Navy. The single turret, housing two Armstrong 12.5t guns, stood slightly forward of amidships. A light superstructure carried a bridge fore and aft, and was narrow enough to allow both turret guns to fire dead ahead as the gunports were widely spaced apart. Abreast the magazines and machinery, the iron belt extended from 2ft (0.6m) below the waterline to 5ft (1.5m) above. The hull had a 2ft (0.6m) deep double bottom ending 4ft (1.2m) from the sides in a continuous bulkhead running from end to end.

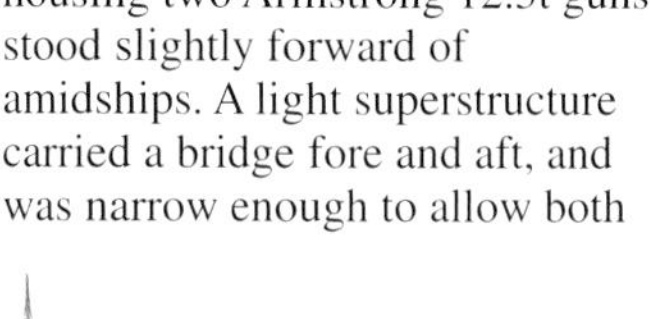

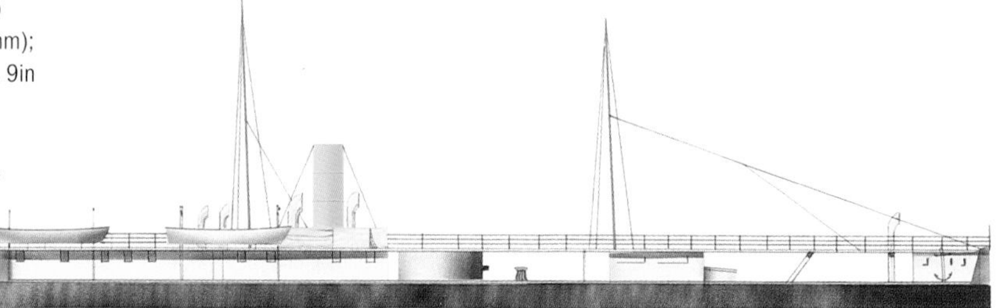

***Los Andes* as completed in September 1893, with an insurgent crew was in action with the 2300t coast-defence ship *Independencia*.**

LOUISIANA

CONFEDERATE STATES OF AMERICA: 1862

The large Confederate ironclad *Louisiana* was the main vessel defending New Orleans in 1862. Like all Confederate ironclads she suffered from unreliable engines and poor build quality. Nevertheless, by the end of 1861, several powerful armoured vessels were being built for the defence of the Mississippi – all of them planned before the Union Navy had even started their own ironclad programme, so highlighting Confederate Secretary Mallory's foresight. Delays were caused in the construction of *Louisiana* because of the lack of both skilled workers and seasoned timber; much green timber was used and further problems were experienced in obtaining armour plate. When *Louisiana* was launched, water poured into her gun deck and she was nearly swamped. The massive casemate sloped back at 45 degrees and was over 200ft (61m) long. This was covered by two layers of railroad iron. Propulsion was provided by four engines driving two huge paddle wheels set in tandem in a centre well. There were also two screws and twin rudders. When first afloat, the giant vessel could barely stem the tide. In action against a powerful Union force, and although unbeaten, *Louisiana* was set on fire and allowed to drift with the current until blowing up.

Great reliance was placed upon *Louisiana*. When the New Orleans forts fell she was set on fire not being able to get up river.

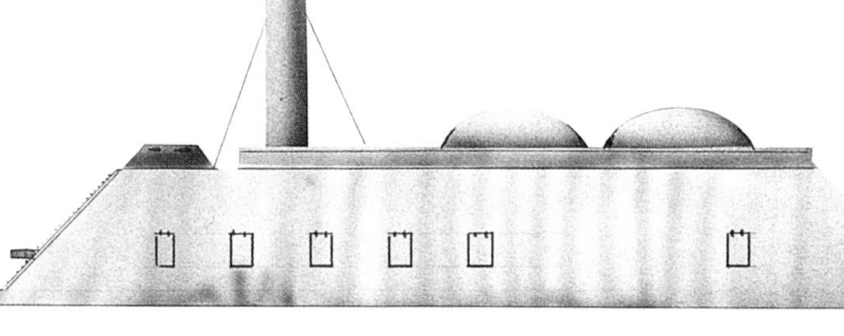

Displacement: 1400t
Dimensions: 264ft x 62ft (80.4m x 19m)
Machinery: twin screws, two paddle wheels
Armament: three 9in (229mm), four 8in (203mm), two 7in (178mm); seven 32pdr
Armour: belt/casemate 4in (102mm)
Speed: 4 knots
Range: not known
Complement: 300

LUFTI DJELIL

TURKEY: 1868

In 1877, when war with Russia broke out, Turkey had 15 ironclads, but because of neglect not much was achieved against a weaker Russian force during the 14-month-long conflict. She had originally been ordered by Egypt but was taken over by Turkey while still with the French builder. *Luftl Djelil* was an iron-hulled turret ship, the larger fore turret housed two 8in (203mm) guns with 7in (178mm) weapons in the aft turret; the turrets were hand worked. The waterline belt was 5ft (1.5m) deep, and evenly divided between above and below water. Hinged bulwarks could be lowered in action.

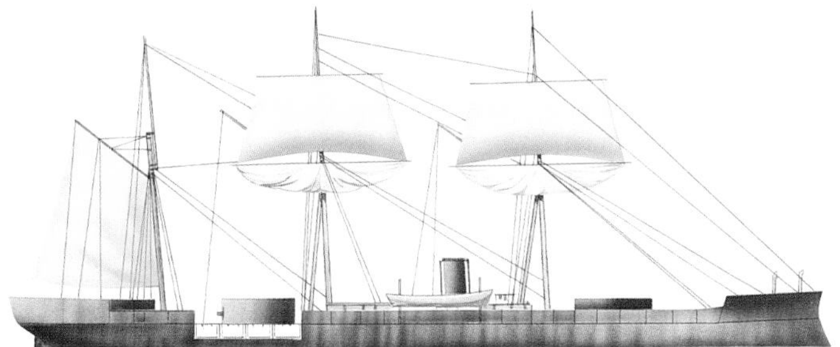

Lufti Djelil had an armoured forecastle, 24 men were needed to turn each of the turrets.

Displacement: 2540t
Dimensions: 204ft x 46ft x 14ft 6in (62.2m x 14m x 4.4m)
Machinery: twin screws, 2000HP
Armament: two 8in (203mm) two 7in (178mm)
Armour: belt 5.5in (140mm) - 4.6in (116mm) side 3in (76mm) turret 5.5in (140mm) deck 1.5in
Speed: 12 knots
Range: not known
Complement: 130

MAGENTA

FRANCE: 1861

Displacement: 6715t
Dimensions: 282ft x 56ft 8in x 27ft 8in (86m x 17.3m x 8.7m)
Machinery: single screw, horizontal return connecting rod, nine boilers; 3450hp
Armament: 16 55 PDR 34 6.4in (163mm)
Armour: belt 4.7in (119mm); battery 4.7-4.3in (119-110mm)
Speed: 13 knots
Range: not known
Complement: 674

The final element of France's ambitious naval building programme, which had begun in 1859, was the construction of *Magenta* and her sistership, *Solferino*. Several plans were prepared, and the one submitted by Dupuy De Lôme (after he had managed to see confidential plans of the British *Warrior*) was finally chosen. Determined that the French vessels would have more guns than those already building, Dupuy De Lôme planned for *Magenta* and *Solferino* to carry 52 rifled 30pdrs. Iron armour ran the length of the waterline in a shallow belt and on the two-tier battery (the only time this arrangement appeared in an ironclad). The wooden ends of the hull were left unprotected.

Magenta in 1864 was unique: her guns were housed on the main and upper decks.

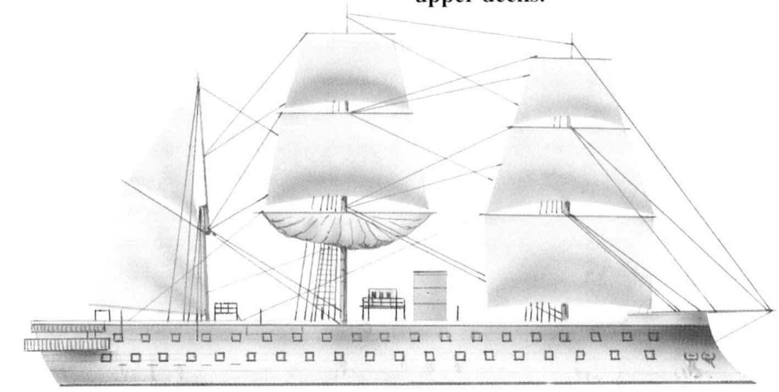

MAINE

USA: 1889

There is still controversy over the cause of the explosion that destroyed the _Maine_; she suffered either a magazine explosion or the effects of a mine planted by Spanish dissidents. She had been in commission for 30 months.

By the early-1880s, the US Navy had fallen to 20th in the ranking of the world's navies – below the navies of such South American countries as Chile and Brazil, which had two very fine powerful turret ships under construction that were to have a marked effect upon the USS *Maine*. At that time, there were no immediate plans to raise the level of the US Navy to the first rank, so only two capital ships were ordered. This decision resulted in the *Texas* and the *Maine*, the plans of the former being purchased in Britain. Initial plans for the *Maine* allowed for a full set of sails, but these were abandoned during construction and she emerged with two military masts. She was also described as an armoured cruiser, but this title was also dropped in favour of ranking her with battle-ships. The main armament of four 10in (254mm) guns were twin mounted in turrets set *en échelon* on the main deck with the fore turret to starboard and the aft turret to port. The barbettes protecting the turrets were sponsoned out over the ship's side to give axial fire. Each turret also had limited arcs of fire across the deck to the opposite side, and to aid this, the superstructure was angled back. Problems were experienced with blast damage and *Texas* and *Maine* were the only US battleships to have this armament layout. Six 6in (152mm) guns were carried, four on the main deck, two in the bows, and two aft with two on top of the centre superstructure. The 180ft (54.9m) armour belt extended 3ft (0.9m) above the waterline to 4ft (1.2m) below. The protective deck laid flat on the belt and curved down at the ends of the ship. The newly-formed US steel industry experienced problems supplying *Maine* with her armour and this caused delays in her completion. The *Maine* was sent to Havana, Cuba, in January 1898 to protect US interests, and while at anchor, she blew up on the evening of the 15 February with the loss of 260 lives.

Displacement: 7180t
Dimensions: 319ft x 57ft x 21ft 6in (97.3m x 17.4m x 6.5m)
Machinery: twin screws, vertical triple expansion, four boilers; 9000hp
Armament: four 10in (254mm); six 6in (152mm); four 14in (356mm) TT
Armour: belt 12-6in (305-152mm); turrets 8in (203mm); barbettes 12in (305mm); deck 3.5-2in (89-52mm)
Speed: 17 knots
Range: not known
Complement: 374

MAJESTIC

GB: 1895

By 1893, the British Admiralty had decided to construct nine powerful battleships, to be known as the *Majestic* class. This programme, which involved greater expense than the earlier Naval Defence Act of 1889, was authorized to enable the British Navy to keep pace with France and Russia, both nations having embarked on ambitious building programmes of their own. An important improvement in the design of the *Majestic* was made by sloping down the sides of the armoured deck so that it joined the bottom of the belt so greatly increasing the protection of the vitals as there were now two walls of armour that had to be penetrated before the ship received any serious damage at the waterline. This sloping deck became a standard feature in all British, and many foreign, battleships for many years. Major changes were also made to the side armour: instead of the shallow 18in (457mm) compound armour belt of the *Royal Sovereign*, the *Majestic* was given a uniform 9in (229mm) thickness of the newly-introduced harveyised armour. This was made possible because of the new armour's greater resistance inch-for-inch and partly because of the added protection given to the vitals by the 4in (102mm) thick sloping deck armour. Armoured bulkheads connected the ends of the belt, with the barbettes forming an enclosed citadel rising 9ft 6in (2.9m) above the water. It was thought that such an arrangement was adequate as armour-piercing projectiles would have to penetrate both the belt and deck before reaching the vitals. A new type of wire-bound 12in (305mm) gun was installed as the main armament, and was subsequently used in nearly all battleships for the next 15 years. All-round loading was also introduced as was better protection in the form of hoods. The secondary battery was increased to 12 6in (152mm) guns, all in single casemates, eight on the gun deck and four on the main deck between the main armament. The anti-torpedo battery was also greatly increased by installing 12pdrs instead of 6pdrs.

Displacement: 14890t
Dimensions: 421ft x 75ft x 27ft (128.3m x 22.9m x 8.2m)
Machinery: twin screws, triple expansion, eight boilers; 12000hp
Armament: four 12in (305mm); 12 6in (152mm); five 18in (457mm) TT
Armour: belt 9in (229mm); casemate 6in (152mm); bulkheads 14-12in (356-305mm); barbettes 14in (356mm); hoods 10in (254mm); deck 4-2.5in (102-64mm)
Speed: 17.9 knots
Range: not known
Complement: 672

Majestic was yet another major stride in battleship development, helping Britain to maintain her two-power standard.

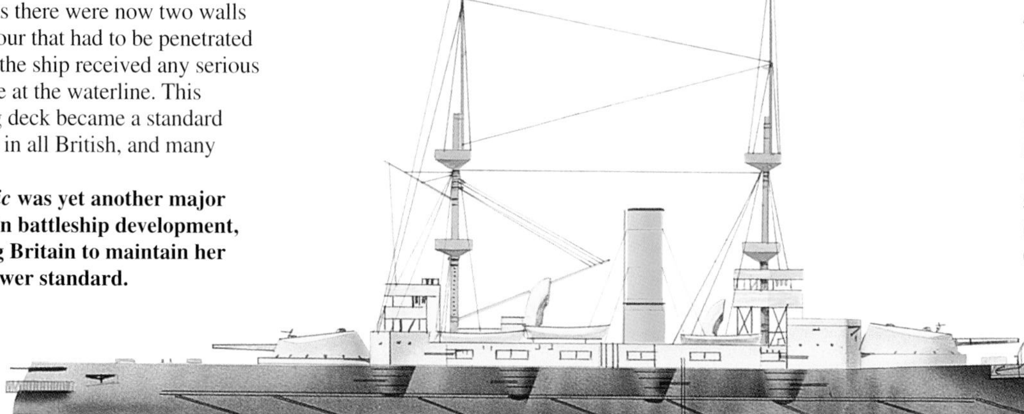

MATSUSHIMA

JAPAN: 1890

Displacement: 4217t
Dimensions: 301ft x 51ft 3in x 20ft (91.9m x 15.6m x 6m)
Machinery: twin screws, horizontal triple expansion, two boilers; 5400hp
Armament: one 12.6in (320mm); 12 4.7in (119mm)
Armour: barbette 12in (305mm); deck 2in
Speed: 16.5 knots
Range: not known
Complement: 360

In the 1880s, Japan ordered several warships from Europe, a decision taken in an atmosphere of growing tension with China, and the fact that the Chinese Navy by now possessed two powerful battleships with an assortment of modern cruisers. *Matsushima* and her two sisterships were ordered from France to the designs of Emile Bertin. They were armed with one large gun – a 12.6in (320mm) Canet breechloader which could fire one round every five minutes – on a 4000t displacement which seriously limited the amount of protection provided. The turret base was 12in (305mm) thick, with a 4in (102mm) shield over the gun and a 2in curved protective deck. The 4.7in (119mm) quick-firing guns were in an unprotected battery amidships.

Matsushima was the Japanese flagship at the Yalu in September 1894 where the massive 12.6in (320mm) gun scored some success.

MESSUDIEH

TURKEY: 1874

In the 1870s, the Turkish Navy and its fleet of ironclads ranked high among the navies of the world. At that time, they were some of the best warships afloat, but a lack of finance meant that this situation could not be maintained into the 1880s. The last major acquisition in the 1870s was that of the two iron-hulled, fully-rigged, central battery ships designed by Reed and built in Britain. These were *Messudieh* and *Memdouhied*; the latter was later sold to Britain and became HMS *Superb*. These vessels combined great firepower, good protection, and high speed with good sea-keeping qualities. They had a full-length iron belt extending 5ft (1.5m) below to 4ft (1.2m) above the waterline. The battery amidships was 153ft (46.6m) long, with a conning tower at the forward end of the battery. The 10in (254mm) 18t Armstrong muzzle loaders were in the battery, with two firing ahead and two astern, thanks to the

Displacement: 9710t
Dimensions: 331ft 5in x 59ft x 26ft (101m x 18m x 8m)
Machinery: single screw, horizontal compound, eight boilers; 7431hp
Armament: 12 10in (254mm); three 7in (178mm)
Armour: belt 12-6in (305-152mm); 3in (76mm) battery 10in (254mm) - 7in (178mm)
Speed: 13.7 knots
Range: not known
Complement: 700

recessed hull at each end of the battery. Two 7in (178mm) guns fired forward from the upper deck with another aft. *Messudieh* was totally reconstructed in Italy between 1898 and 1903. The ends were cut down and the midship section built up, 6in (152mm) quick-firing guns forming the main armament. In December 1914, *Messudieh* was torpedoed and she was sunk in the Dardanelles.

For many years *Messudieh* was the most powerful vessel in the Turkish Navy.

MIKASA

JAPAN: 1900

The last of a group of four battleships laid down under Japan's 1896 announcement of a 10-year naval expansion programme, the *Mikasa* benefited from the earlier improvements in armour and general layout. The main armament could be worked by electric, hydraulic, or manual power, and loaded at any elevation or bearing. The rate of fire was three rounds per gun every two minutes. The number of secondary guns was the same as in the earlier vessels but better protected, being placed in a main deck box battery with increased protection to the rear with 6in (152mm) armour – unlike casemate mounted guns which had only 2in of armour at the rear. Thanks to the use of Krupp cemented armour, a saving in weight was possible: the *Mikasa*'s total armour weighed 4097t, nearly 500t less than in the rest of the group. The *Mikasa* was the flagship of Vice Admiral Togo during the Russo-Japanese War of 1904–1905. She blew up in 1905 at Sasebo. Later, after being raised and maintained as a national monument, she was nearly destroyed in World War II. However, she was restored again and is now the last surviving battleship of her era.

Displacement: 15179t
Dimensions: 432ft x 76ft x 27ft (131.7m x 23.2m x 8.3m)
Machinery: twin screws, vertical triple expansion, 25 boilers; 15,000hp
Armament: four 12in (305mm); 14 6in (152mm); four 18in (457mm) TT
Armour: belt 9-4in (229-102mm); battery 6in (152mm); barbettes 14-8in (356-203mm); casemates 6-2in (152-52mm); deck 3-2in (76-52mm)
Speed: 18.6 knots
Range: 9000 miles at 10 knots
Complement: 830

One of the best examples of a pre-dreadnought battleship, the *Mikasa* combined all the best qualities of the type.

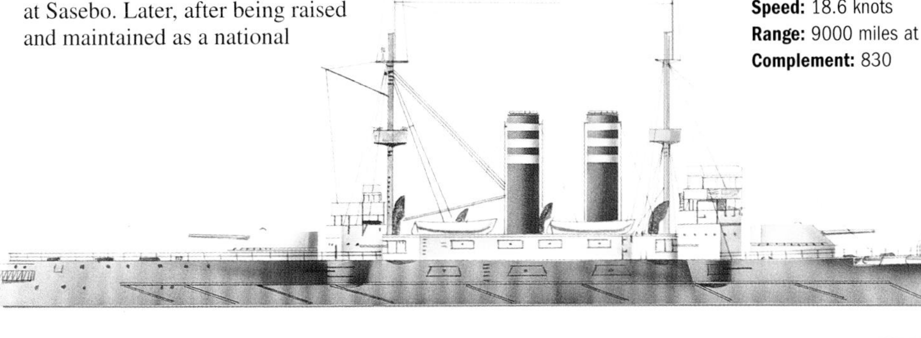

MININ

RUSSIA: 1869

Originally planned as a sistership to *Kniaz Pojarski*, a 5138t armoured corvette, *Minin* was altered to a turret ship. She was to have had an armament of four 11in (280mm) guns in twin turrets, plus four 6in (152mm) guns in armoured positions. However, following the loss of the British turret ship *Captain* in 1870, work on the *Minin* was halted after she was launched. She was not completed until 1878 – as an armoured cruiser with four 8in (203mm) guns in sponsons, with the secondary guns unprotected on the upper deck. The armour belt was 7ft (2.5m) deep and 5ft (1.5m) below water, with a protective steel deck flat on the belt.

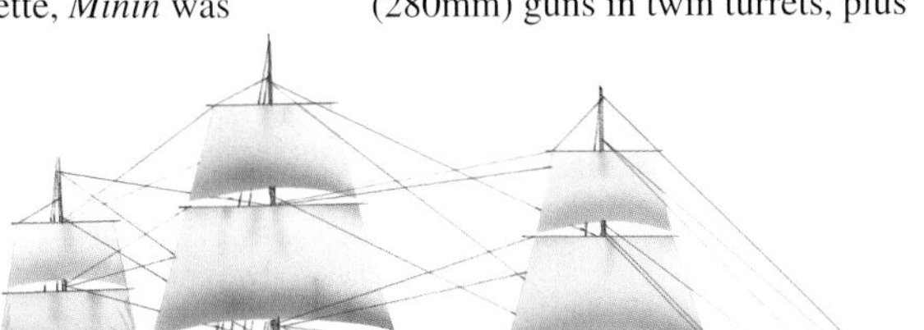

When first completed, the *Minin* carried a heavy ships' rig for extended ocean cruising.

Displacement: 6136t
Dimensions: 295ft x 49ft 6in x 25ft 5in (90m x 15m x 7.7m)
Machinery: single screw, vertical compound; 5290hp
Armament: four 8in (203mm); 12 6in (152mm)
Armour: belt 7-6in (178-152mm)
Speed: 14 knots
Range: 3000 miles at 10 knots
Complement: 545

MINNEAPOLIS

USA: 1893

The only large protected cruisers built for the US Navy up until 1900 were the *Minneapolis* and her sistership, *Columbia*. They were designed as commerce destroyers and were well-suited for this role, having a designed speed of 23 knots, higher than any cruiser or ocean liner then afloat. In addition, they had an enormous range thanks to a maximum coal supply of 1800t. During the

Spanish-American War of 1898, *Minneapolis* and *Columbia* did splendid service as scouts. The 8in (203mm) gun was aft, the two 6in (152mm) guns side-by-side on the forecastle, and the 4in (102mm) guns in sponsons on the gun deck.

The *Minneapolis* and her sistership, *Columbia*, were the first US warships with triple screws. The outer engines were separated by a centreline bulkhead.

Displacement: 3790t
Dimensions: 413ft x 58ft x 22ft 7in (126m x 17.7m x 6.9m)
Machinery: triple screws, vertical triple expansion, 10 boilers; 20,544hp
Armament: one 8in (203mm); two 6in (152mm); eight 4in (102mm); four 14in (356mm) TT
Armour: deck 4-2.5in (102-64mm)
Speed: 23 knots
Range: 6300nm (11,668km) at 10 knots
Complement: 477

MONADNOCK

USA: 1864

Displacement: 3400t
Dimensions: 258ft 6in x 52ft 9in x 12ft 8in (78.8m x 16m x 3.9m)
Machinery: twin screw, vibrating lever, four boilers; 1400hp
Armament: four 15in (381mm)
Armour: belt 5in (127mm); turrets 10in (254mm); deck 1.5in
Speed: 9 knots
Range: not known
Complement: 150

The four double-turreted monitors of the *Monadnock* class were thought to be the most successful group of monitors built for the US Navy in the Civil War. An earlier design of 1861 by Lenthall and Isherwood featuring Coles turrets was rejected after some behind-the-scenes activities by rivals. The revised design had a freeboard of 2ft 7in (0.8m). Laminated iron armour was used as the US could not roll solid plates at this time. On top of the turrets stood a pilothouse, and there was also a light bridge connecting the two turrets. The large ventilator stood behind the funnel.

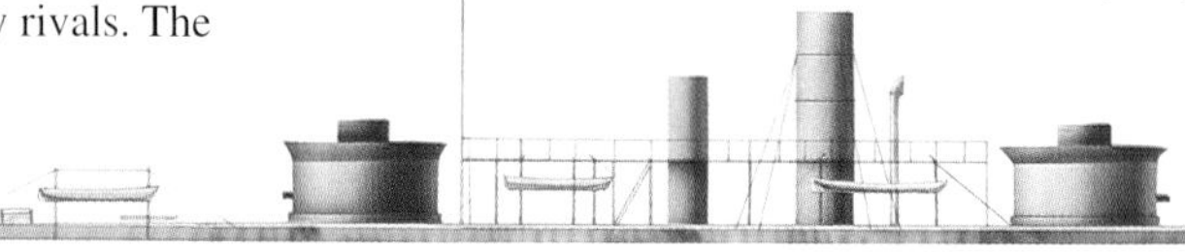

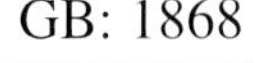

***Monadnock* in 1865. In heavy weather, water washed freely over the decks, but she was infact a steady ship.**

MONARCH

GB: 1868

The *Monarch* represented the British Admiralty's idea of a seagoing turret ship, unlike the low-freeboard type favoured by the Americans.

The first large seagoing turret ship was the British *Monarch* designed by Reed for service on foreign stations. With her high sides and full sail rig, *Monarch* departed widely from the monitor type. A complete armoured belt extended to the height of the second deck, and above this was a short armoured redoubt which protected the bases of the two turrets, each of which contained two 12in (305mm) 25t 600pdrs. The redoubt rose to the main deck and continued fore and aft in an unarmoured structure with a freeboard of 14ft (4.3m).

Displacement: 8322t
Dimensions: 330ft x 57ft 6in x 24ft (100.6m x 17.3m x 7.4m)
Machinery: single screw, horizontal return connecting rod, nine boilers; 7842hp
Armament: four 12in (305mm); three 7in (178mm)
Armour: belt 7-4in (178-102mm); redoubt 7in (178mm); turrets 10in (254mm)
Speed: 14.9 knots
Range: not known
Complement: 575

MONITOR

USA: 1862

Prior to the outbreak of the Civil War, the United States had shown little interest in the ironclad. In the spring of 1861, the US had 42 wooden vessels available, most of them on foreign service. Only the incomplete Stevens battery, begun in 1854, bore any resemblance, and then only passing, to the French oceangoing *Gloire* and the British *Warrior*. The situation in the South was different. Here work was started in 1861 on the rebuilding into an ironclad of the 4636t wooden frigate *Merrimack*. She had been launched in 1855 and had been set on fire and abandoned at the Norfolk Navy Yard when Union forces were compelled to evacuate this important naval establishment. In response to this threat, a bill was passed by the US Congress instructing the Navy Department to examine proposals for ironclads and to set aside $1.5 million for any vessels selected. Sixteen proposals were received, including one for a broadside frigate that eventually became the *New Ironsides*. Another design was for a small, poorly protected vessel, while the third proposal selected was submitted by John Ericcson and was to be named *Monitor*.

Ericcson's plans showed an unconventional vessel, with a low freeboard and a hull made up of two halves, one on top of the other. The lower section contained the machinery, furnaces, crew quarters and bunkers; the larger upper hull overlapped the lower, forming a large armoured raft with only 18in (457mm) of freeboard, so presenting a small target area. The sides were protected with laminated armour made up of five iron plates, each 1in thick, bolted to heavy wooden framing. To save time, the hull plates were not curved but flat for about 80ft (24.4m) of the length. The deck had 1in plating.

As an answer to the 7in (178mm) and 8in (203mm) guns likely to be carried by the *Merrimack*, two 11in (280mm) smooth-bores were considered adequate, and this heavy armament could be carried because the low freeboard allowed great savings in the weight of armour. The single turret, giving all-round fire, was covered with eight 1in plates and also acted as a giant ventilating shaft. *Monitor* arrived at Hampton Roads the day after the *Merrimack* (now renamed *Virginia*) had destroyed two large Union wooden warships hulled frigates.

Displacement: 987t
Dimensions: 172ft x 41ft 6in x 10ft 6in (52.4m x 12.6m x 3.2m)
Machinery: single screw, vibrating lever, two boilers; 320hp
Armament: two 11in (280mm)
Armour: turret 8-9in (203-229mm); side 2-4.5in (52-115mm); deck 1in
Speed: 6 knots
Range: not known
Complement: 49

During the action with the *Merrimack* on 9 March 1862, *Monitor* used diminishing charges in her guns, so reducing her chances of piercing *Merrimack*'s armour. *Monitor* sank in heavy weather on 31 December 1862.

NANIWA

JAPAN: 1885

Designed by Sir William White, *Naniwa* and her sistership, *Takachiho*, were improved versions of the successful Chilean cruiser *Esmeralda*. They were also the first protected cruisers built for the Japanese Navy. With increased freeboard, the sea-keeping qualities were better as was the armour protection, with an increase in the thickness of the deck. Above and below this protective deck were passages used as coal bunkers level with the machinery spaces. The 10.3in (264mm) guns were in barbettes at each end of the vessel.

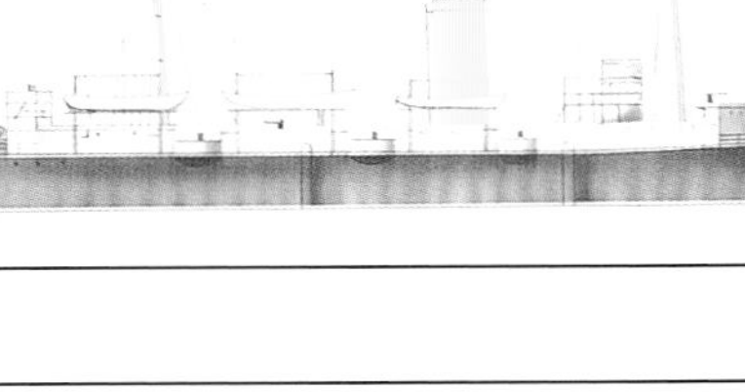

Naniwa was completed in 1885. It was eight years before another British-built protected cruiser was delivered to Japan.

Displacement: 3650t
Dimensions: 300ft x 46ft x 20ft 3in (91.4m x 14m x 6m)
Machinery: twin screws, horizontal compound, three boilers; 7600hp
Armament: two 10.3in (264mm); six 5.9in (150mm)
Armour: deck 3-2in (76-52mm)
Speed: 18.7 knots
Range: not known
Complement: 350

NASHVILLE

CONFEDERATE STATES OF AMERICA: 1864

Displacement: not known
Dimensions: 271ft x 95ft 6in x 10ft 9in (82.6m x 29m x 3.3m)
Machinery: side wheel, seven boilers
Armament: three 7in (178mm)
Armour: casemate 6in (152mm)
Speed: 5 knots
Range: not known
Complement: 120

The Confederate ironclad *Nashville* was one of the very few Confederate ironclad side wheel steamers (the rest were screw driven). She was built at Montgomery, Alabama and completed at Mobile after many delays caused by lack of materials and skilled labour. *Nashville* was not fully armoured, much of the side being left unprotected and any armour, made up of railroad iron, came mostly from the *Baltic* which by now was considered unsuitable for service. *Nashville* saw extensive action against Union forces, but was abandoned when Mobile eventually surrendered.

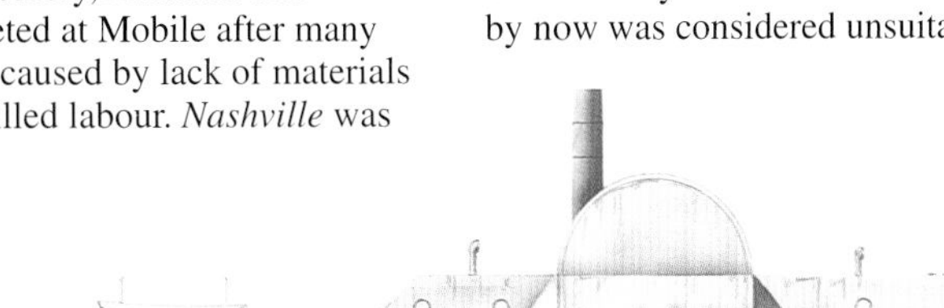

The imposing profile of the *Nashville*. The massive paddle boxes gave this vessel a beam of 95ft 6in (29m).

NEBRASKA

USA: 1904

Authorized in 1899, the *Nebraska* class of five vessels heralded the advent of US Navy battleships that now resembled in size and firepower contemporary European capital ships. These vessels had greater length, higher speed, and a higher freeboard, maintained throughout the entire length of the ship by fitting two complete decks above the armoured deck. The complete main belt extended from 3ft (0.9m) above to 5ft (1.5m) below the waterline. Above this rose a 6in (152mm) redoubt up to the main deck, closed at the ends with armoured bulkheads with a cofferdam packed with cellulose behind the main belt.

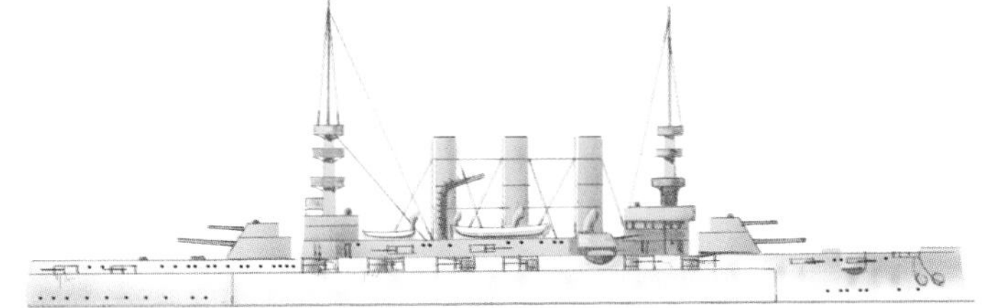

Nebraska with twin 8in (203mm) turrets superimposed on the 12in (305mm) turrets, and two more twin 8in (203mm) turrets on the main deck.

Displacement: 16,094t
Dimensions: 441ft 3in x 76ft 3in x 23ft 9in (134.5m x 23.2m x 7.2m)
Machinery: twin screws, triple expansion, 12 boilers; 19,000hp
Armament: four 12in (305mm); eight 8in (203mm); 12 6in (152mm)
Armour: belt 11-4in (280-102mm); redoubt 12-4in (305-102mm); turrets 12-6in (305-152mm); barbettes 10-6in (254-152mm; deck 3in (76mm)
Speed: 19 knots
Range: not known
Complement: 812

NEW IRONSIDES

USA: 1862

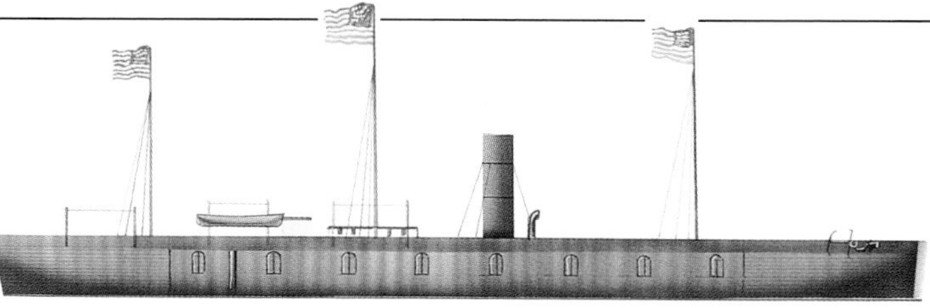

During the many actions before Charleston, sandbags were placed over the upper deck of the *New Ironsides* to reduce the effect of plunging fire.

In August 1861, the US Congress voted $1.5 million for the construction of ironclads to combat the growing number of Confederate ironclads then building. Three designs were selected, of which *New Ironsides* was the most conventional. Merrick and Sons supplied the engines and armour, with Cramp's shipyard building the wooden hull from designs by Charles Cramp and B. Bartol. Supplying heavy timber proved a serious problem, and soon the surrounding countryside for many miles around was denuded of trees. The battery was originally intended to carry 8in (203mm) guns but 11in (280mm) were substituted instead. The *New Ironsides* was considered a good sea-boat, but the weak engines could only drive her at 6.5 knots and then only by consuming 40t of coal per day, instead of the estimated 25t. Iron armour produced from scrap iron covered the midship battery for a length of 170ft (51.8m), with a continuous waterline belt extending from 3ft (0.9m) above to 4ft (1.2m) below the waterline. The *New Ironsides* was flagship at Charleston during the 7 April 1863 bombardment; she was struck 50 times in two hours and many hundreds of times during the following months. Severely damaged in a spar torpedo attack, *New Ironsides* was finally destroyed by fire in December 1865.

Displacement: 4120t
Dimensions: 232ft x 57ft 6in x 15ft (70.7m x 17.5m x 4.6m)
Machinery: single screw, horizontal direct acting, four boilers; 700hp
Armament: 14 11in (280mm); two 8in (203mm); two 5.1in (130mm)
Armour: belt 4.5-3in (115-76mm); battery 4.5in (115mm); deck 1in
Speed: 6.5 knots
Range: not known
Complement: 449

NEW YORK

USA: 1891

The construction of true armoured cruisers commenced in the United States with the *New York*. The system of protection consisted of a very heavy protective deck, with 6in (152mm) armour on the slopes and 3in (76mm) on the flat, while a partial 4in (102mm) belt was fitted along the waterline covering the machinery spaces only. A cellular layer was worked between the protective deck and the berth deck. Like all later American armoured cruisers, the *New York* carried a relatively heavy, well-protected main armament of six 8in (203mm) guns – this calibre becoming the standard main battery for American armoured cruisers for the next 10 years. These guns were mounted in twin turrets fore and aft, with one on each broadside amidships in a barbette protected by shields; the barbettes did not extend below the main deck but an armoured ammunition tube ran down to the protective deck. On the second deck, 4in (102mm) guns were mounted in sponsons. The engines were in tandem, so enabling the individual engine rooms to be made smaller and the height of the engines to be reduced.

The *New York* was Rear Admiral Sampson's flagship during the Spanish-American War. She was scuttled in December 1941 in the Philippines to avoid capture by the Japanese.

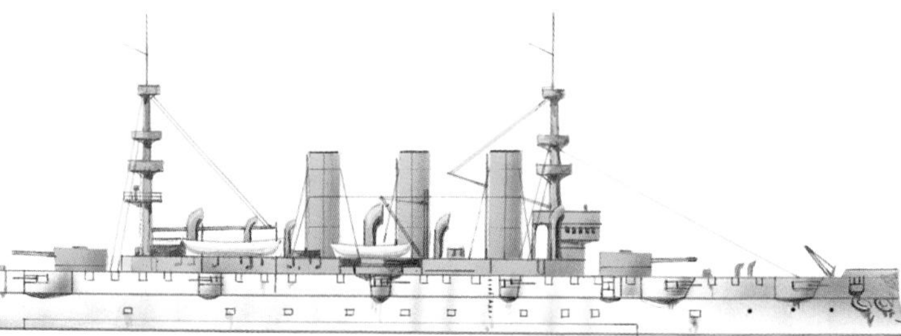

Displacement: 9021t
Dimensions: 384ft x 64ft 10in x 23ft 10in (117m x 19.8m x 7.2m)
Machinery: twin screws, vertical triple expansion, eight boilers; 17,401hp
Armament: six 8in (203mm); 12 4in (102mm)
Armour: belt 4in (102mm); turrets 5.5in (140mm); barbettes 10-5in (254-127mm); secondary weapons 4in (102mm); deck 6-3in (152-76mm)
Speed: 21 knots
Range: 5000nm (9260km) at 10 knots
Complement: 566

NILE

GB: 1888

The design of the *Nile* and her sistership, *Trafalgar*, owed much to the influence of the First Sea Lord, Admiral Sir Arthur Hood. It combined a heavy main armament with maximum protection. Subsequently, these two ships were the heaviest British battleships then built, having an extremely high percentage of armour to displacement of 33.5 per cent. The armour was concentrated amidships in a belt 230ft (70m) long, extending 5ft 6in (1.7m) below water to 3ft (0.9m) above, and terminating in 18in (457mm) bulkheads. Protection at each end of the ships was provided by an armoured deck 3in (76mm) thick; it extended over the 193ft (58.8m)-long armoured octagonal citadel above the main belt. The secondary battery consisted of six 4.7in (119mm) quick-firing guns, they were replaced in 1896 with 6in (152mm) weapons. With a freeboard of 11ft 9in (3.6m), both *Nile* and *Trafalgar*, were wet ships; this forbade high speed in heavy weather.

When completed it was thought that *Nile* would be the last battleship built because of the growing menace of the torpedo boat.

Displacement: 12590t
Dimensions: 345ft x 73ft x 28ft 6in (105.1m x 22.2m x 8.7m)
Machinery: twin screws, triple expansion, six boilers; 7500hp
Armament: four 13.5in (343mm); six 4.7in (119mm); four 14in (356mm) TT
Armour: belt 20-14in (508-356mm); citadel 18-16in (457-406mm); bulkheads 16-14in (406-356mm); turrets 18in (457mm); deck 3in (76mm)
Speed: 16.7 knots
Range: 6500 miles at 10 knots
Complement: 577

NORDENFELT I

GREECE: 1885

One of the greatest difficulties that faced the early designers of submarines was the lack of a suitable propulsion system. By the 1880s, Nordenfelt took up ideas already experimented with by Garret, who had built two submarines. Built in Sweden for the Greek government, *Nordenfelt I* had a long elliptical hull with the torpedo tube mounted externally on the hull at the bows. The hull was circular with frames spaced 2ft (0.6m) apart with a hull thickness of 0.7in (16mm) to 0.4in (10mm) at the ends. Most of the interior was taken up by a large marine boiler, a steam accumulator for storing steam to drive the craft below water, and a compound engine driving a propeller.

Laid down in 1882, she was one of the world's first steam-powered submarines.

Displacement: 60/75t
Dimensions: 64ft x 9ft (19.7m x 2.7m)
Machinery: single screw, compound, one boiler
Armament: one 14in (356mm) TT; one 1in
Speed: 10/5 knots
Complement: 3

NOVGOROD

RUSSIA: 1873

Displacement: 2491t
Dimensions: 101ft x 101t x 13ft 6in (30.8m x 30.8m x 4.1m)
Machinery: six screws, horizontal compound, eight boilers; 3000hp
Armament: two 11in (279mm); two 3.4in (86mm)
Armour: belt 9-7in (229-178mm); barbette 9in (229mm); deck 2.5in; funnel bases 4.5in (115mm)
Speed: 6.7 knots
Range: not known
Complement: 149

In the 1860s there was a tendency to build ironclads with a short length and wide beam, so reducing the side area to be armoured. This reached a climax with the circular Russian coast-defence ship *Novgorod*, designed by Vice-Admiral Popoff for service in the Black Sea. She was built in sections at St Petersburg and assembled at Nicolaiev. The protective armour extended from the deck edge 18in (457mm) above the waterline to 4ft 6in (1.4m) below. The deck stood 5ft 3in (1.6m) above water in the centre were the 7ft (2.2m) high barbettes stood which housed the two 11in (280mm) guns.

With her curved deck, *Novgorod* resembled an upturned saucer.

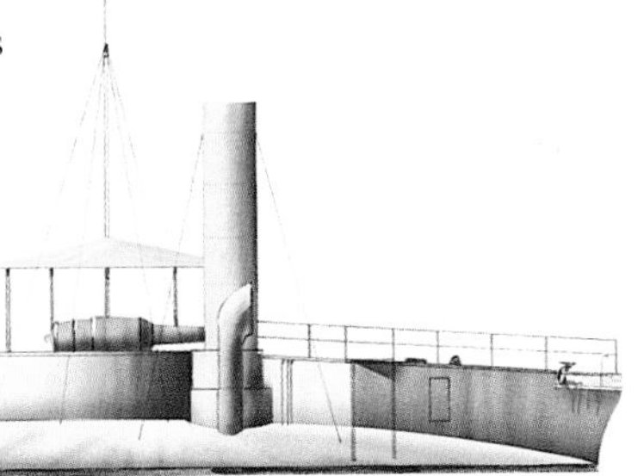

NUMANCIA

SPAIN: 1863

***Numancia* was the backbone of the Spanish fleet during the war in the Pacific against Peru and Chile in the 1860s.**

The iron-hulled broadside ironclad *Numancia* was the second unit in the ambitious Spanish building programme of the early 1860s, which gave Spain seven powerful capital ships by the end of the decade, ranking her amongst the top naval powers. The battery of 68pdr smooth-bore guns were all on one deck behind 4.7in (119mm) iron armour. By the 1880s, this armament had been replaced by four 10in (254mm), three 8in (203mm), and 16 6.5in (165mm) guns. *Numancia* was the flagship of Admiral Nuñez during the Spanish-Peruvian war; she bombarded Valparaiso in March 1866, and suffered damage in the abortive attack on Callao in May. She was also in action during the Carlist conflict in 1873. Refitted in 1897-98 at La Seyne, where she had been built, *Numancia* sank in December 1916 off the Portuguese coast while under tow to the breakers.

Displacement: 7189t
Dimensions: 315ft x 57ft x 27ft (96m x 17.4m x 8.2m)
Machinery: single screw, compound; 3700hp
Armament: 40 68pdr guns
Armour: belt 5.5in (140mm); battery 4.7in (119mm)
Speed: 13 knots
Range: 2450 m (4537km) at 10 knots
Complement: 500

OLYMPIA

USA: 1892

***Olympia* compared very favourably with contemporary foreign cruisers. She is still preserved at Philadelphia.**

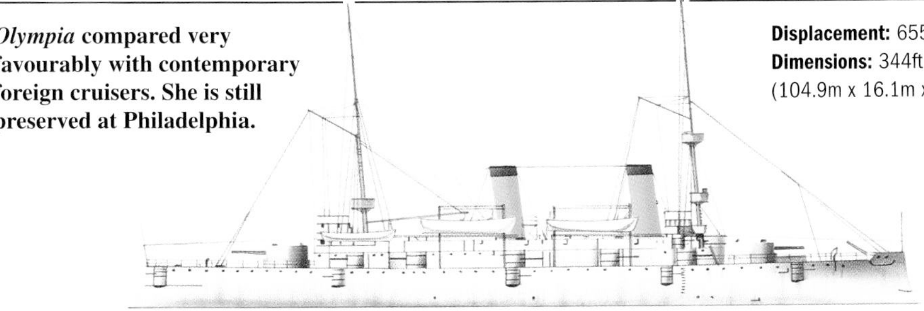

Displacement: 6558t
Dimensions: 344ft x 53ft x 21ft 6in (104.9m x 16.1m x 6.6m)
Machinery: twin screw, vertical triple expansion, six boilers; 17,313hp
Armament: four 8in (203mm), 10 5in (127mm); six 18in (457mm) TT
Armour: turrets 3.5in (89mm); barbettes 4.5in (115mm); shields 4in (102mm); deck 2-4.7in (54-119mm)
Speed: 21.7 knots
Range: 6000 miles at 10 knots
Complement: 411

Authorized in 1888, the second-class protected cruiser *Olympia* was probably the best cruiser of her type built for the US Navy in the 1890s, combining a powerful armament and good protection for a ship of this size. The armoured deck was 4.7in (119mm) thick on the slopes, 2in on the flat, and 3in (76mm) thick at the ends. A cellular layer 6ft (1.8m) high was worked over the machinery spaces. Better protection was provided for the main armament by mounting them in barbette turrets. The 5in (127mm) weapons were placed inside the long superstructure, and were provided with 4in (102mm) shields. *Olympia* was the flagship of Commodore Dewey at Manila on 1 May 1898 when the Spanish squadron was destroyed.

OREGON

USA: 1893

Oregon as completed in 1896. The original plans, the first for a major US capital ship for nearly 30 years, show a distinct monitor type armed with 12in (305mm) and 10in (254mm) guns.

In the 1880s, the idea promised in the United States was that the prime role of the navy was to defend the coast. To this end, three 'seagoing coastline battleships' were authorized in 1890. It had been hoped to build up a substantial navy over a period of 15 years, but a hostile Congress refused to vote for more funds. The *Oregon*, and her two sisters *Indiana* and *Massachusetts*, were characterized by a very heavy armament and protection, low freeboard, moderate speed, and small coal endurance in normal circumstances. The secondary battery of 8in (203mm) guns was heavy for this period, but here the US Navy took a lead which lasted for nearly 10 years until the British built the *Formidable* class of 15,800t. The *Oregon* class were the first US 'New Navy' battleships to approach foreign contemporaries in fighting capabilities. Nickel steel armour was specified for the *Oregon*, but Harvey armour became available during construction. The belt was 150ft (45.7m) long and 7ft 6in (2.3m) deep, with a maximum thickness of 18in (457mm), tapering to 8.5in (216mm) at its lower edge; 4ft 6in (1.4m) of it was below water. Above the main belt was a strake 4in (102mm) thick running up to the main deck. The belt terminated in 14in (356mm) bulkheads which connected up to the fore and aft barbettes. A flat armoured deck lay on the belt; the deck thickened to 3in (76mm) at each end of the vessel beyond the belt, sloping down to protect the ends. The twin 13in (330mm) gun turrets were mounted fore and aft on the centre line, but were only 17ft 9in (5.4m) above the water and were difficult to work in a seaway. Twin turrets equipped with 8in (203mm) guns were mounted two on each beam near the ends of the superstructure at upper deck level, 25ft (7.6m) above the water. Four 6in (152mm) guns were positioned in sponsoned casemates amidships at main deck level, where they too were hard to work in a seaway. Blast from the 8in (203mm) guns affected the crews of the 13in (330mm) turrets. *Oregon*'s normal coal supply was 400t and her maximum 1800t; at full power the vessel burnt about 10t an hour.

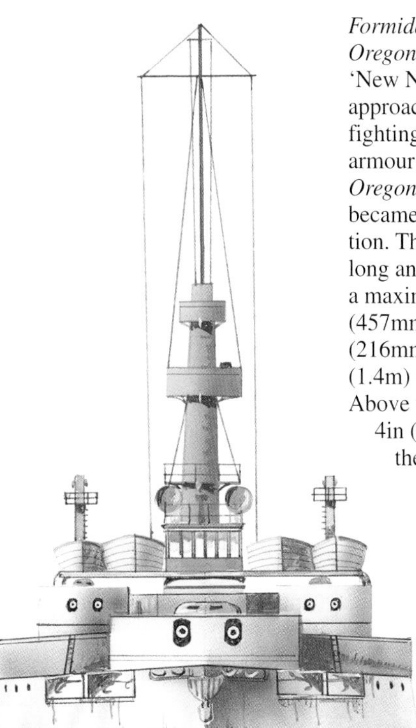

Oregon served finally as an ammunition ship at Guam in 1942 after being preserved at Portland, Maine. She was sold at Guam in 1956.

Displacement: 11,688t
Dimensions: 351ft x 69ft x 24ft (107m x 21m x 7.3m)
Machinery: twin screw, triple expansion, six boilers; 9700hp
Armament: four 13in (330mm), eight 8in (203mm), four 6in (152mm); six 18in (457mm) TT
Armour: belt 4-18in (102-457mm); turrets 15in (381mm); barbettes 17in (432mm); secondary guns 5-8in (127-203mm); deck 3in (76mm)
Speed: 16.7 knots
Range: 5000 miles at 10 knots
Complement: 473

In a later refit, the 6in (152mm) weapons and many of the 6pdrs were replaced with 12 3in (76mm) guns. At the same time, in 1905–08, the 13in (330mm) turrets were balanced, since the original unbalanced mountings made the vessel heel when trained on the beam. During this refit, the vessel was reboilered and received a cage mast aft; the torpedo tubes were also removed. On the eve of the outbreak of the war with Spain in 1898, *Oregon* was stationed on the Pacific coast at San Francisco. On 19 March, *Oregon* left on a 14,000-mile (26,000km) journey made in great haste to join the main US fleet under Sampson, as it was felt that the Spanish squadron of four armoured cruisers was the equal to the US force then near Cuba.

PANTHER

AUSTRIA: 1885

Austria ordered *Panther* and her sistership, *Leopard*, to be built in Britain in order to gain experience in modern shipbuilding techniques. Both were built by Armstrong's yard at Elswick, being good examples of torpedo cruisers intended to act with a battlefleet. Well armed, with four 14in (356mm) torpedo tubes (one in the bow, one in the stern, and one on either beam), and with two 4.7in (119mm) plus 10 smaller guns, these vessels were the first major Austrian warships with twin screws. When completed, there were only four torpedo boats available for torpedo warfare in the Austrian Navy.

A successful but short-lived type, as the torpedo boat grew in size so vessels such as *Panther* were no longer viable.

Displacement: 1557t
Dimensions: 234ft x 34ft x 14ft (71.4m x 10.4m x 4.3m)
Machinery: twin screws, vertical compound; 5940hp
Armament: two 4.7in (119mm); four 14in (356mm) TT
Armour: deck 0.5in (12mm)
Speed: 18.4 knots
Range: not known
Complement: 186

PASSAIC

USA: 1862

Displacement: 1875t
Dimensions: 200ft x 46ft x 10ft 6in (61m x 14m x 3.2m)
Machinery: single screw, vibrating lever, two boilers; 320hp
Armament: one 15in (381mm), one 11in (280mm)
Armour: side 5-3in (127-76mm); turret 11in (280mm); deck 1in
Speed: 7 knots
Complement: 75

In the early-1860s, the Union Navy sought to build some 20 ironclad monitors. Plans were already prepared by the Navy's own designers which featured a low freeboard ironclad, carrying two of the advanced Coles turrets, able to withstand most of the Confederate harbour defences. The rapidly-growing threat from Confederate ironclads then under construction made attractive an offer by a rival design team to build a group of 10 monitors of better quality, most to be ready by mid-1862. The *Passaic* class were designed as enlarged monitors with the hull made up in two sections, one above the other, with a single turret and good all-round firing positions made possible by mounting the pilot house on top of the turret. Increase in displacement enabled improvements to be made to the armament, including the substitution of two 15in (381mm) Dahlgren smoothbores for the 11in (280mm) guns. To save time, and because of delays in supplying these powerful weapons, only one smoothbore was eventually carried. Further problems arose over the production of protective armour as it was not yet possible to roll plates of sufficient thickness; single 1in plates were therefore bolted together. In action against the Confederate defences guarding Charleston, the seven *Passaic*-class vessels present were hit many times sustaining severe damage.

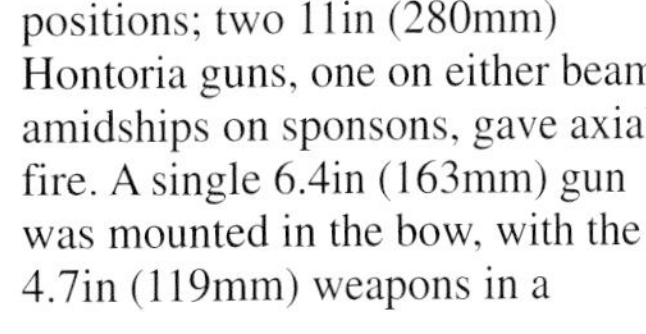

The *Passaic* class were the workhorses of the Union Navy during the Civil War, and served as coast defence ships during the Spanish-American War over 30 years later.

PELAYO

SPAIN: 1887

Pelayo was built at Le Seyne to a design by Lagane which resembled the French *Marceau* with slightly greater length, but with less draught to allow her to pass through the Suez Canal. *Pelayo* was originally rigged to carry 4000sq ft (372sq m) of canvas. There were two military masts. A complete belt of Creusot steel extended from 5ft (1.5m) below the waterline to 2ft (0.6m) above. There was extensive compartmentation below the armoured deck with 13 complete transverse bulkheads. Two 12.5in (318mm) Hontoria guns were carried fore and aft with all-round loading positions; two 11in (280mm) Hontoria guns, one on either beam amidships on sponsons, gave axial fire. A single 6.4in (163mm) gun was mounted in the bow, with the 4.7in (119mm) weapons in a battery amidships. *Pelayo* was Spain's most powerful warship for many years.

Displacement: 9745t
Dimensions: 334ft 8in x 66ft x 24ft 9in (102m x 20m x 7.6m)
Machinery: twin screw, vertical compound, 12 boilers; 9600hp
Armament: two 12.5in (318mm), two 11in (280mm), one 6.4in (163mm), 12 4.7in (119mm)
Armour: belt 11.7-17.7in (298-450mm); barbettes 11.7-15.7in (298-399mm); shields 6in (152mm); deck 2.7in (70mm)
Speed: 16.7 knots
Range: not known
Complement: 520

***Pelayo* headed the Spanish squadron sent to the Philippines in 1898, but was ordered back to protect the Spanish coastline against attack by US forces.**

PETR VELIKI

RUSSIA: 1872

Laid down in June 1869, she was, up until then, the most powerful vessel built for the Russian Navy. Completed in 1875, it was to be another eight years before a Russian battleship approaching her in power would be laid down. *Petr Veliki* had a freeboard of 8ft (2.4m), and the hull was recessed aft of the second turret to form a narrow platform of half the beam. The belt, made up of two 7in (178mm) strips with 22in (559mm) of wood between, ran the length of the vessel. Amidships was a citadel 160ft (48.8m) long supporting a small superstructure plus the two turrets.

***Petr Veliki* was the only major Russian battleship completed in 16 years.**

Displacement: 10406t
Dimensions: 339ft 8in x 62ft x 27ft (103.5m x 19m x 8.3m)
Machinery: twin screws, horizontal return connecting rod, 12 boilers; 8250hp
Armament: four 12in (305mm)
Armour: belt 15-11.5in (356-292mm); citadel 14-8in (356-203mm); turrets 14in (356mm); deck 3-1.5in (76-38mm)
Speed: 14 knots
Range: not known
Complement: 432

PETROPAVLOSK

RUSSIA: 1894

Displacement: 11,354t
Dimensions: 369ft x 70ft x 25ft 6in (112.5m x 21.3m x 7.8m)
Machinery: twin screw, vertical triple expansion, 12 boilers; 11,250hp
Armament: four 12in (305mm), 12 6in (152mm); six 18in (457mm) TT
Armour: belt 5-16in (127-406mm); turrets 14in (356mm); secondary turrets 5in (127mm); deck 3in (76mm)
Speed: 16.5 knots
Range: not known
Complement: 632

Petropavlosk was the lead ship in a class of three powerful battleships begun in 1892 at a time when Russia laid down seven capital ships in less than two years. The main belt ran for 240ft (74m); it was 7ft 6in (2.2m) deep and ended in 8-9in (203-229mm) bulkheads. Above the main belt was a shorter length of armour 7ft 6in (2.2m) high and 5in (127mm) thick. The 12in (305mm) guns were in twin turrets fore and aft; two 6in (152mm) twin turrets were positioned on each beam, with two more 6in (152mm) weapons between them on the main deck.

***Petropavlosk* was Admiral Makaroff's flagship at Port Arthur in 1904.**

PIEMONTE

ITALY: 1888

Designed by Philip Watts, *Piemonte* was another notable step in the development of the cruiser. Her protective armour was of an increased thickness, now raised to 3in on the slopes. All hatches that were to be left open during action were surrounded by cofferdams 4ft (1.3m) high above the waterline. There were also watertight flats under small compartments, but no double bottom. Extra protection was provided by patent fuel bunkers above the slopes amidships. The engines were four-cylinder triple expansion standing vertically, but with only a 27in (686mm) stroke. *Piemonte* was the first vessel armed exclusively with quick-firing guns, and these were provided with 4.5in (115mm) shields.

The forecastle and poop gave *Piemonte* good sea-keeping qualities, plus a raised platform for the newly introduced quick-firing gun.

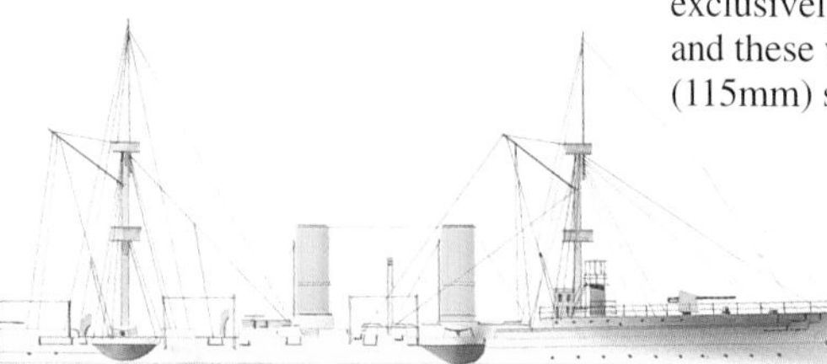

Displacement: 2597t
Dimensions: 321ft x 38ft x 16ft (97.8m x 11.6m x 4.9m)
Machinery: twin screws, vertical triple expansion, four boilers; 7100hp
Armament: six 6in (152mm), six 4.7in (119mm); two 14in (356mm) TT
Armour: deck 3in (76mm); shields 4.5in (115mm)
Speed: 22.3 knots
Range: 13,500nm (25,000km) at 10 knots
Complement: 298

PIONEER

CONFEDERATE STATES OF AMERICA: 1862

Displacement: 4t
Dimensions: 34ft x 4ft x 4ft (10m x 1.3m x 1.3m)
Machinery: single screw, hand-cranked
Armament: one spar torpedo
Speed: 3 knots
Complement: 3

The submarine was unique at the time of the US Civil War. *Pioneer* was amongst the first of these vessels to be built. Oval in shape, with conical ends, she was constructed at New Orleans by James McClintock and Baxter Watson. They co-owned the vessel with John Scott, who was to command her, and Robbin Barron. All four men had provided capital, and a letter of marque was issued by the Confederate Government, making *Pioneer* the only privateer submarine. Limited to inshore work because of the basic construction, and hand-cranked by a crew of two, *Pioneer*'s only possible source of prize money lay in sinking an enemy warship. The Confederate Government had undertaken to pay 20 per cent of the value of the destroyed vessel.

The unique iron-hulled submarine *Pioneer* was buried in a bayou until 1878, and then abandoned on a river bank until 1909.

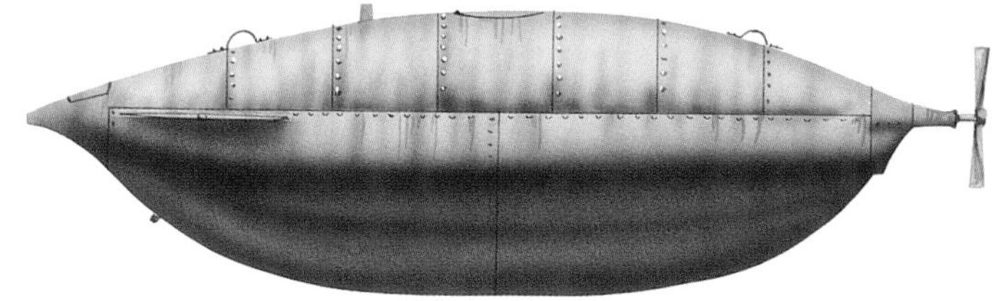

POLYPHEMUS

GB: 1881

Displacement: 2640t
Dimensions: 240ft x 40ft x 20ft 6in (73.2m x 12.2m x 6.2m)
Machinery: twin screw, compound; 7000hp
Armament: six 1in; five 14in (356mm) TT
Armour: deck 3-6in (76-152mm)
Speed: 17.8 knots
Range: 3400 miles at 10 knots
Complement: 146

***Polyphemus* had a light flying bridge with six 1in Nordenfelt machine guns in armoured towers to drive off attackers.**

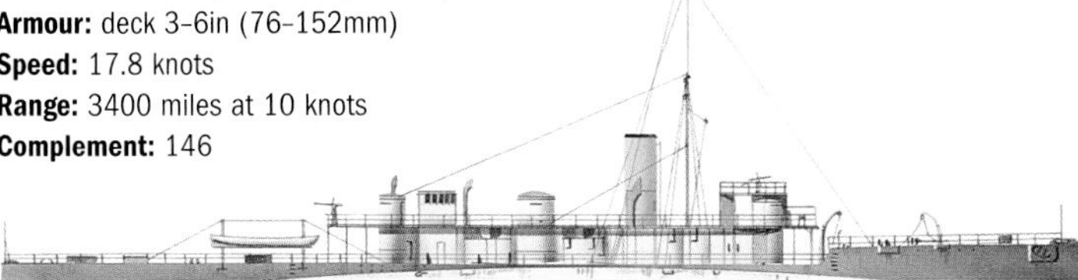

The English 'torpedo ram' was an experimental ship and grew out of an idea put forward by Admiral George Sartorius. The basic theme of this unusual craft was to obtain offensive power by combining the ram with a strong torpedo armament, while the defensive strength was secured by low armoured freeboard, high speed, and good manoeuvring capabilities. The upper hull was vaulted and projected 4ft 6in (1.4m) above the water; it was protected by 3in (76mm) of armour on the top and 6in (152mm) on the slope. The lower part of the hull was V-shaped amidships and housed 300t of iron ballast that could be dropped in an emergency. There were five torpedo tubes, one in the bow and two on each beam. The crew were housed below the armoured deck, this area being amongst the first such to be lit by electricity.

POWERFUL

GB: 1895

Powerful and her sister *Terrible* were built as an answer to the Russian armoured cruisers *Rurik* and *Rossia*. Britain needed to make great efforts to protect its commerce, so every type of cruiser built abroad, especially in France and Russia, was answered with another, more powerful type. Britain in the 1890s relied upon the thick armoured deck for protection, and in *Powerful* this deck was 6in (152mm) thick on the slopes, and reinforced along the sides by the upper coal bunkers, which were kept full for as long as possible; this could be done because the vessels had good inherent stability. The two-storey casemate was introduced in *Powerful* and *Terrible*, as was the use of large watertube boilers. The maximum coal supply was 3000t.

Displacement: 14,200t
Dimensions: 538ft x 71ft x 27ft (164m x 21.6m x 7.3m)
Machinery: twin screw, triple expansion, 48 boilers; 25,000hp
Armament: two 9.2in (234mm), 12 6in (152mm)
Armour: deck 2-6in (54-152mm); turrets 6in (152mm); casemates 6in (152mm)
Speed: 22.1 knots
Range: 7000 miles at 14 knots
Complement: 894

PRINCE ALBERT

GB: 1864

Displacement: 3687t
Dimensions: 240ft x 48ft x 19ft 8in (73m x 14.6m x 6m)
Machinery: single screw, horizontal direct acting, four boilers; 2128hp
Armament: four 9in (229mm)
Armour: belt 4.5in (115mm); turrets 10.5in (267mm); deck 1.1in (30mm)
Speed: 11.26 knots
Range: not known
Complement: 201

Captain Cowper Coles put forward several ideas for turret ships to the British Admiralty in the early 1860s. They were not approved: to carry adequate armour and maintain a good speed, a greater displacement was needed, and the cost would be greater per gun carried than that of any existing ironclad. In 1862, it was decided to build a six-turreted ironclad to test Coles' turrets, with each of the turrets to house one 300pdr gun. He maintained that such a large gun could not be worked on the broadside but only in his turrets. However, it was not until early 1865 that the go-ahead was given to construct this ship, to be named *Prince Albert*, and then only with four turrets, each containing one 300pdr gun. The vessel's sides were armoured in their entirety. The 5ft (1.5m) high hinged bulwarks were lowered in action.

***Prince Albert*, completed in 1866, was the first British iron turret ship and one of the longest lasting: 33 years on the Navy List.**

PROTECTOR

USA/RUSSIA: 1902

Displacement: 136t surfaced; 174.3t submerged
Dimensions: 54ft x 10ft 3in (16.5m x 3m)
Machinery: single screw; 60hp petrol/40hp electric
Armament: three 18in (457mm) TT
Speed: 7/5.5 knots
Complement: 6
Range: not known

Simon Lake of New York developed two submarines for purely commercial purposes. His object was to explore the ocean floor, but in his quest for official sponsorship, he proposed a design to the US Navy for a minelaying and minesweeping submarine, but it was turned down. Undaunted, he went ahead with *Protector*, which he sold to Russia in 1902, supplying four more vessels the following year.

Russia was an early entrant in the race to acquire submarines, with Lake's *Protector* amongst the first to be acquired.

Protector retained the wheels of the earlier Lake submarines for running along the seabed; these retracted into the hull. The circular pressure hull was surmounted by ballast tanks. Propulsion was by petrol engine on the surface and electric motor submerged. The torpedo tubes were in both the bow and stern.

PURITAN

USA: 1882

Displacement: 6060t
Dimensions: 296ft x 60ft x 18ft (90.3m x 18.3m x 5.5m)
Machinery: twin screw, horizontal compound, eight boilers; 3700hp
Armament: four 12in (305mm), six 4in (102mm)
Armour: belt 6-14in (152-356mm); turrets 8in (203mm); barbettes 14in (356mm); deck 2in (54mm)
Speed: 12.4 knots
Range: 6000 miles at 10 knots
Complement: 200

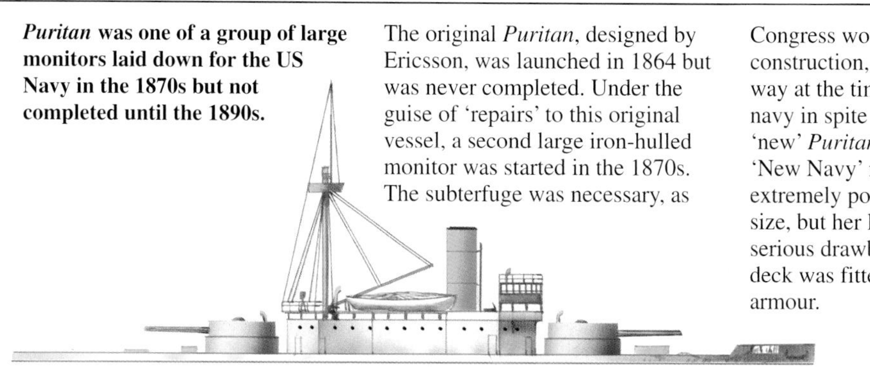

***Puritan* was one of a group of large monitors laid down for the US Navy in the 1870s but not completed until the 1890s.**

The original *Puritan*, designed by Ericsson, was launched in 1864 but was never completed. Under the guise of 'repairs' to this original vessel, a second large iron-hulled monitor was started in the 1870s. The subterfuge was necessary, as Congress would not vote funds for construction, and it was the only way at the time of building up a navy in spite of the politicians. The 'new' *Puritan* was the largest of the 'New Navy' monitors, and was an extremely powerful ship for her size, but her low freeboard was a serious drawback. The 2in steel deck was fitted over the iron armour.

RATTLESNAKE

GB: 1886

Displacement: 550t
Dimensions: 200ft x 23ft x 10ft 4in (61m x 7m x 3.1m)
Machinery: twin screw, triple expansion, four boilers; 3100hp
Armament: one 4in (102mm); four 14in (356mm) TT
Armour: deck 0.75in (19mm)
Speed: 19.5 knots
Range: 3050 at 10 knots
Complement: 66

During the 1880s, the rapidly growing number of torpedo boats created a need for vessels which could accompany the battleships and act as a defence against this new enemy. High speed, an armament of light guns, plus good seakeeping qualities were essential. The French took the initiative in 1885 with the 400t *Bombe* class, but these were too lightly built. The British responded with the 550t *Rattlesnake*, armed with one 4in (102mm) breech-loader forward and four torpedo tubes. The machinery spaces were protected by a steel deck 0.75in thick. The locomotive boilers used in vessels such as *Rattlesnake* gave much trouble, often obliging the large ships to slow down so that these vessels, generally referred to as torpedo gunboats, could keep up. Within only 10 years they were replaced by destroyers.

***Rattlesnake* was the first British torpedo gunboat. Vibration from the fast-running engines made life for the crew difficult.**

RE D'ITALIA

ITALY: 1863

***Re'D'Italia* with a barque rig. During the 1860s, Italy built up a powerful fleet.**

Italy ordered her second pair of ironclads from the United States early in the American Civil War, at a time when the Union Navy was still debating what type of warship was needed to counter the growing threat from Confederate ironclads. *Re D'Italia* and her sister *Re Di Portogallo* were the heaviest warships completed for the Italian Navy for five years. They were wooden-hulled with completely armoured sides, but had the steering gear left unprotected. This arrangement caused the loss of *Re D'Italia* at the Battle of Lissa in July 1866, when her steering gear was disabled and she was rammed and sunk. The vessel's powerful battery was all on one deck, and as she was built of wood there was no internal subdivision.

Displacement: 5869t
Dimensions: 326ft 9in x 55ft x 23ft 6in (99.6m x 16.8m x 6.2m)
Machinery: single screw, single expansion, four boilers; 1845hp
Armament: six 8in (203mm), 32 6.5in (165mm)
Armour: belt 4.7in (119mm); battery 4.7in (119mm)
Speed: 10.8 knots
Range: 1800 miles at 18.5 knots
Complement: 565

REGINA MARGHERITA

ITALY: 1901

Displacement: 14,093t
Dimensions: 455ft x 78ft 3in x 29ft (138.7m x 23.8m x 9m)
Machinery: twin screw, triple expansion, 28 boilers; 21,790hp
Armament: four 12in (305mm), four 8in (203mm), 12 6in (152mm)
Armour: belt 6in (152mm); battery 6in (152mm); turrets 8in (203mm); deck 3in (76mm)
Speed: 20.3 knots
Range: 8000 miles at 10 knots
Complement: 812

Designed by Benedetto Brin, *Regina Margherita* was a compromise. Protection was deliberately reduced in Brin's quest to produce an Italian battleship with the speed and firepower necessary for it to stand up to contemporary European capital ships. Originally she was to have carried two 12in (305mm) and 12 8in (203mm) guns, which would have given this vessel the most powerful secondary battery afloat. However, after Brin's death, the battleship was redesigned along the lines of her contemporaries, with three calibres of main and secondary guns, but retaining 6in (152mm) Terni armour for the 10ft (3m) deep belt that extended for most of the length of the ship.

***Regina Margherita* and *Benedetto Brin* were excellent sea boats; both were sunk in World War I.**

RETVISAN

RUSSIA: 1900

As part of the Russian naval expansion scheme of the late 1890s, warships were ordered from shipbuilders in France and America, in order to gain experience with foreign practice. *Retvisan* followed typical US practice, with high sides running the full length of the vessel. The main belt ran the entire length in two strakes, the lower strake stretching from 4ft (1.2m) below the water to 3ft 6in (1m) above, and maintaining a constant thickness of 9in (229mm) over 256ft (78m). The 12in (305mm) guns were in twin turrets fore and aft; eight of the 6in (152mm) guns were sited in the main deck battery, while four more were in casemates on the upper deck at each end of the superstructure.

A successful ship, *Retvisan* saw extensive service in 1904 in the war with Japan.

Displacement: 12,900t
Dimensions: 386ft 8in x 72ft x 26ft (117.8m x 22m x 7.9m)
Machinery: twin screw, vertical triple expansion, 24 boilers; 17,000hp
Armament: four 12in (305mm), 12 6in (152mm); six 15in (381mm) TT
Armour: belt 5-9in (127-229mm); battery 5in (127mm); turrets 9in (229mm); casemates 5in (127mm); deck 2-3in (54-76mm)
Speed: 18.8 knots
Range: not known
Complement: 738

RE UMBERTO

ITALY: 1888

Displacement: 15,454t
Dimensions: 418ft 7in x 76ft 10in x 30ft 6in (125.5m x 23.4m x 9.3m)
Machinery: twin screw, vertical compound, 18 boilers; 19,500hp
Armament: four 13.5in (343mm), eight 6in (152mm), 16 4.7in (119mm); five 17.7in (450mm) TT
Armour: belt 4in (102mm); battery 4in (102mm); barbettes 13.7in (347mm); deck 3in (76mm)
Speed: 18.5 knots
Range: 6000 miles at 10 knots
Complement: 733

The *Italia*-type capital ship lost favour in many quarters of the Italian Navy, and the next three battleships of the *Ruggiero di Lauria* class were slightly smaller versions of the *Duilio* class. When, however, Brin became Minister of Marine, the *Re Umberto* class were given hull protection similar to that of the *Italia*, but with the addition of 4in (102mm) of side armour amidships. This extended between the protective and main deck to combat the devastating effect of the newly introduced quick-firing gun. The inner bottom, which ran for almost the length of the ship, was carried up to the armoured deck, and was placed 5ft (1.5m) from the side. The main guns were central pilot mounting, the first guns to be so mounted shipboard.

When first completed, *Re Umberto*, and especially her sisters, were two or three knots faster than contemporary battleships.

RIACHUELO

BRAZIL: 1883

***Riachuelo* was a replacement for the large, masted turret ship *Independencia*, taken over by the Royal Navy during the Russian war scare.**

Riachuelo was for many years the most powerful vessel in the Brazilian Navy. Together with the similar *Aquidaban*, she made a distinct impression on US thinking in the 1880s. This led to the construction of the USS *Maine*. *Riachuelo* was a twin-turreted fully-rigged battleship with excellent armour and armament. A belt 250ft (76m) long covered the magazines and machinery. The twin gun turrets were arranged *en échelon* to provide fore-and-aft fire, plus the ability to fire across the deck to the opposite beam through gaps in the superstructure.

Displacement: 6100t
Dimensions: 305ft x 52ft x 19ft 8in (93m x 15.8m x 6m)
Machinery: twin screw, vertical compound, 10 boilers; 7300hp
Armament: four 9.2in (234mm), six 5.5in (140mm); five 14in (356mm) TT
Armour: belt 7-11in (178-280mm); turrets 10in (254mm)
Speed: 16.7 knots
Range: 4500 miles at 15 knots
Complement: 367

ROANOKE

USA: 1862

Displacement: 4395t
Dimensions: 265ft x 53ft x 22ft (80.8m x 16.2m x 6.7m)
Machinery: single screw, trunk, four boilers; 997hp
Armament: two 15in (381mm), two 11in (280mm), two 8in (203mm)
Armour: belt/side 3.5-4.5in (89-115mm); turrets 11in (280mm); deck 1in
Speed: 6 knots
Range: not known
Complement: 350

Roanoke was originally a wooden-hulled 40-gun frigate, launched in 1855, that was nearly lost at Hampton Roads in March 1862 when the Confederate *Merrimack* attacked the Union blockading force. *Roanoke* had the hull cut down to the battery deck and plated with armour; this protection was now rolled in one thickness instead of consisting of several thinner plates bolted together as before. Three Ericcson turrets were fitted on the centre line, making her the first ship with more than two turrets, but the weight of the iron armour and turrets caused the hull to hog. As converted, she rolled excessively, causing her to be employed during the Civil War as guardship at Hampton Roads.

***Roanoke* was a hasty conversion to help fill the gaps in the Union ironclad fleet.**

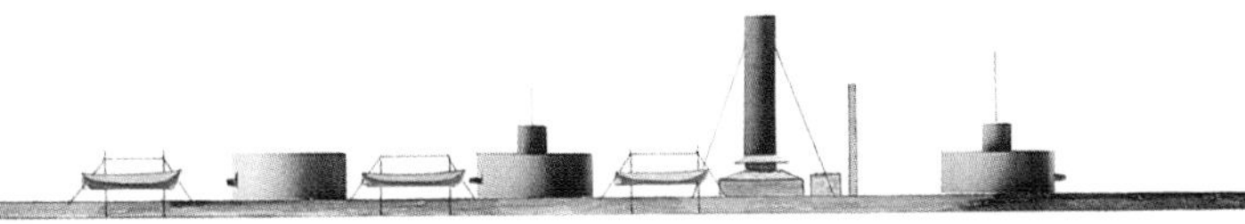

Rolf Krake

DENMARK: 1863

***Rolf Krake* was the first ship to carry Coles turrets, and this successful method of mounting heavy guns vindicated Coles' early work.**

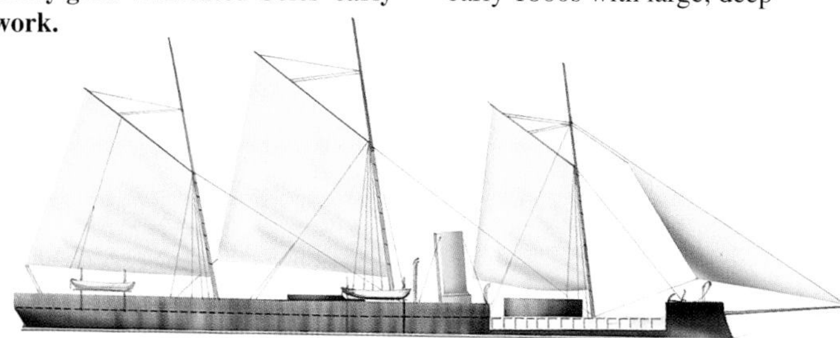

Denmark was the first Scandinavian country to build an ironclad fleet of any size, beginning in the early 1860s with large, deep-draught broadside ships. Due to the worsening relations with Prussia over Schleswig-Holstein, the Danes in 1862 decided to acquire a turret ship with reasonable freeboard for coastal operations in rough seas. *Rolf Krake* was built by Napier to fill this gap in Denmark's fleet. She had two Coles turrets and a light schooner rig. Hinged bulwarks were lowered when the ship was in action. The complete iron armour extended the length of the ship, and ran from the main deck, which was 1.5in thick, to 3ft (0.9m) below the waterline.

Displacement: 1320t
Dimensions: 183ft 9in x 38ft x 10ft 6in (56m x 11.6m x 3.2m)
Machinery: single screw, engine type not known; 750hp
Armament: four 68pdr
Armour: hull 4.5in (115mm); turret 4.5in (115mm); deck 1.5in
Speed: 9.5 knots
Range: 1500 miles at 10 knots
Complement: 150

Rossia

RUSSIA: 1896

With the laying down of the large armoured cruiser *Rossia* in 1894 as a follow up to the *Rurik*, Britain realized that in a possible conflict with Russia these two vessels could decimate British trade, and as a direct answer built the *Terrible* and *Powerful*. *Rossia*'s armour belt ran for almost the full length, with 4ft 6in (1.4m) above water and 4ft (1.2m) below; to protect the engine room, there was a short strip of 5in (127mm) armour plus a 5in (127mm) bulkhead forward. The 8in (203mm) were sited two forward in 9in (229mm) armoured sponsons, and two aft behind shields. Twelve 6in (152mm) guns were positioned on the main deck, with three more forward and one right aft. The vessel's coal supply was 2500t, and she burnt 18t per hour at full power.

For cruising, only *Rossia*'s centre screw was used. The twin outer screws were employed when top speed was required.

Displacement: 13,675t
Dimensions: 480ft 6in x 68ft 6in x 26ft (146.5m x 20.9m x 7.9m)
Machinery: triple screw, vertical triple expansion, 32 boilers; 18,466hp
Armament: four 8in (203mm), 16 6in (152mm); five 15in (381mm) TT
Armour: belt 4-8in (102-203mm); deck 2-3.7in (51-95mm)
Speed: 20.2 knots
Range: not known
Complement: 842

Royal Sovereign

GB: 1891

Displacement: 15,580t
Dimensions: 410ft 6in x 75ft x 27ft 6in (125m x 22.9m x 8.4m)
Machinery: twin screw, triple expansion, eight boilers; 13,360hp
Armament: four 13.5in (343mm), 10 6in (152mm); seven 18in (457mm) TT
Armour: belt 14-18in (356-457mm); upper belt 4in (102mm); barbettes 11-17in (280-432mm); casemates 6in (152mm); bulkheads 14-16in (356-406mm); deck 2-3in (51-76mm)
Speed: 18 knots
Range: not known
Complement: 712

The massive five-year building programme of the 1889 Act, which included the *Royal Sovereign* class, was eclipsed within a few years by an even bigger British naval programme.

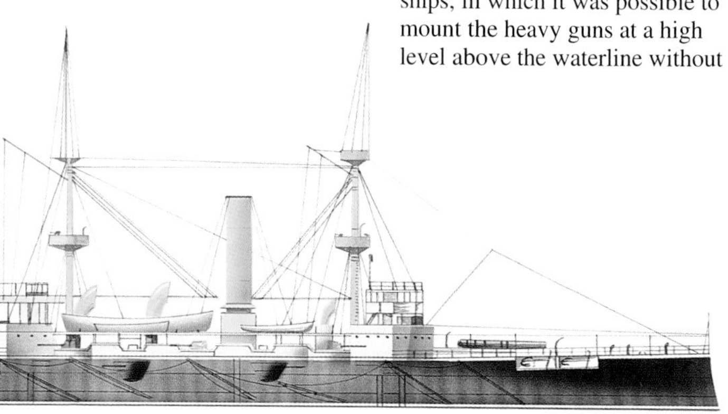

Between 1886 and 1889, no new battleships were laid down for the British Navy, but with the Naval Defence Act of 1889, a large and hitherto unequalled increase in naval strength was authorized to enable the Royal Navy to be equal in strength to any other two naval powers combined. A series of plans for battleships was considered, with the barbette system being selected. This basic design, created by Sir William White, formed the foundation for battleship design in the UK and many countries for the next 15 years. The basic idea behind the *Royal Sovereign* class of seven units was to increase fighting efficiency at sea, and the ability to maintain superior speed in a seaway. This had not been entirely possible with previous capital ships, such as the *Nile*, with its comparatively low freeboard, and was only attainable in barbette ships, in which it was possible to mount the heavy guns at a high level above the waterline without sacrificing too much weight in protection. An 18in (457mm) belt of compound armour 8ft 6in (2.6m) deep, with two thirds of it below the waterline, extended over two thirds of the length; there were transverse bulkheads at the ends, and a 3in (76mm) steel deck on top, forming a shallow armoured box. A second belt of steel armour 4in (102mm) thick was placed above the lower belt. At the ends, this armour was angled across to join the barbette walls. The 13.5in (343mm) guns were mounted two per barbette, with one barbette at each end of the ship. The 6in (152mm) guns were placed on the second and main decks, and were distributed as widely as possible to reduce the effect of the newly developed high explosive. Four of the 6in (152mm) weapons were placed in armoured casemates; the remaining six were positioned behind shields on the deck above. *Royal Sovereign* was the first capital ship to reach 18 knots.

RURIK

RUSSIA: 1892

Displacement: 11,690t
Dimensions: 435ft x 67ft x 27ft (132.6m x 20.4m x 8.3m)
Machinery: twin screw, vertical triple expansion, eight boilers; 13,250hp
Armament: four 8in (203mm), 16 6in (152mm), six 4.7in (119mm)
Armour: belt 5-10in (127-254mm); bulkheads 10in (254mm); deck 2.5-3.5in (64-89mm)
Speed: 18.7 knots
Range: not known
Complement: 683

When launched, *Rurik* caused major concern in British circles, as here was a ship with great offensive power and the ability to steam halfway round the world without refuelling, thanks to its 2000t coal capacity. *Rurik* had a displacement 5000t above that of the previous armoured cruiser, *Pamiat Azova*, launched four years earlier, clearly indicating Russia's plans to create a number of long-range cruisers. The belt was 320ft (98m) long and nearly 7ft (2.1m) deep, ending with 10in (254mm) bulkheads; these were taken to the upper deck, so providing protection against raking fire. The 8in (203mm) guns were in sponsons, the 6in (152mm) weapons were on the main deck, and the 4.7in (119mm) guns were sited on the upper deck.

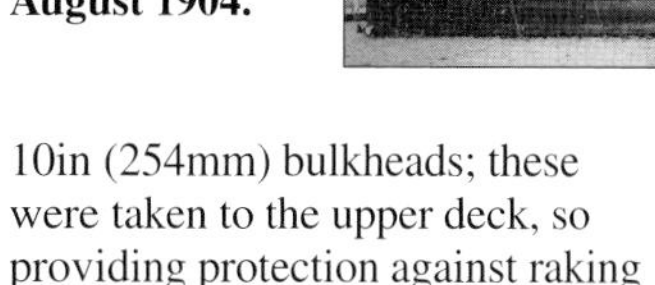

Rurik was originally barque-rigged. She was badly damaged at the Battle of Ulsan in August 1904.

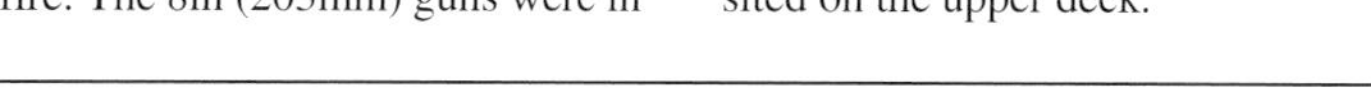

SALAMANDER

AUSTRIA: 1861

Displacement: 2750t
Dimensions: 206ft x 45ft 8in x 20ft 7in (62.8m x 14m x 6.3m)
Machinery: single screw, horizontal low pressure; 1842hp
Armament: 10 48pdr, 18 24pdr
Armour: belt 4.5in (115mm); battery 4.5in (115mm)
Speed: 11 knots
Range: not known
Complement: 346

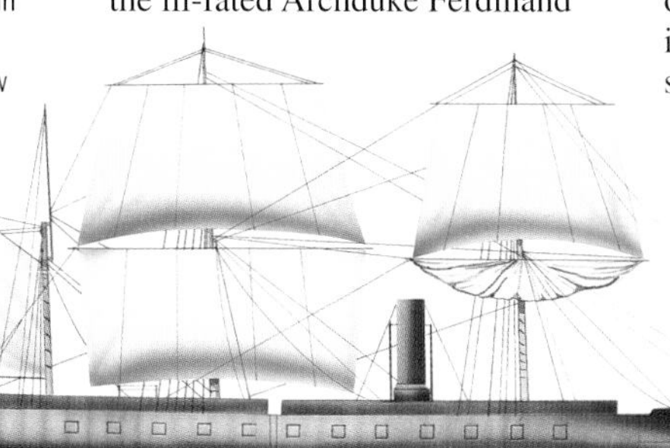

Under the far-sighted leadership of the ill-fated Archduke Ferdinand Maximilian, the Austria Navy was one of the first to construct ironclads. *Salamander* and her sister *Drache* were small wooden-hulled broadside armoured frigates designed by Joseph von Romako. The Styrian iron armour belt ran the full length of the vessel, and rose in height forward of the foremast to protect the battery. This armour was of a high quality, and although it was struck 35 times at the Battle of Lissa in 1866, no serious damage was inflicted. The Austrian guns, however, were of an old pattern and were inferior to the Italian rifled weapons.

***Salamander* and *Drache* were the first ironclads in Austria's fast-growing fleet.**

SAN FRANCISCO

USA: 1889

Displacement: 4583t
Dimensions: 324ft 6in x 49ft x 18ft 10in (98.9m x 14.9m x 5.7m)
Machinery: twin screw, horizontal triple expansion, four boilers; 10,500hp
Armament: 12 6in (152mm)
Armour: deck 2-3in (51-76mm)
Speed: 19.5 knots
Range: 6000 miles at 10 knots, 3000 miles at 17 knots
Complement: 384

San Francisco was one of the second-generation cruisers authorized in 1887. An attempt was now made to standardize the type of cruiser the US Navy needed. Initially sails were to be retained, but after the disastrous hurricane at Samoa, when three wooden-hulled fully rigged cruisers were wrecked, the value of sails was discredited and the plans of *San Francisco* were revised and the sails removed. The 6in (152mm) guns were positioned two side by side on the forecastle and poop, with four more on each beam amidships; two of these on each side were sponsoned out, giving axial fire.

***San Francisco* showed improvements in the design of US cruisers, but no attempt was made to build several of one type.**

SCIOTA

USA: 1861

The *Sciotas* were a successful but short-lived class of gunboats. They captured over 100 prizes.

A wooden-hulled gun-boat, *Sciota* was one of a class of 23 ordered as an emergency by the Navy Department in July 1861 without waiting for Congressional approval. Their rapid construction led to them being called the '90-day gunboats'. Such was the speed of building, all were launched by the end of the year. Although they were hastily built using poorly-seasoned wood, the *Sciotas* were well constructed and good sailors, though liable to roll badly. They were intended for use in close blockade work, and nearly all were sold at the end of the Civil War with the last, *Unadilla*, being sold in 1869.

Displacement: 691t
Dimensions: 158ft 4in x 28ft x 9ft 6in (48.3m x 8.5m x 3.1m)
Machinery: single screw, horizontal back acting, two boilers;
Armament: one 11in (280mm); two 24pdr, one 20pdr
Speed: 10 knots
Range: not known
Complement: 82

SEVASTOPOL

RUSSIA: 1864

Displacement: 6130t
Dimensions: 295ft x 52ft x 26ft (90m x 15.8m x 7.9m)
Machinery: single screw, horizontal return connecting rod, four boilers; 3090hp
Armament: 16 8in (203mm), one 6in (152mm), eight 3.4in (87mm)
Armour: belt 4.5in (115mm); battery 4.5in (115mm)
Speed: 12 knots
Range: 1300 miles at 14 knots
Complement: 607

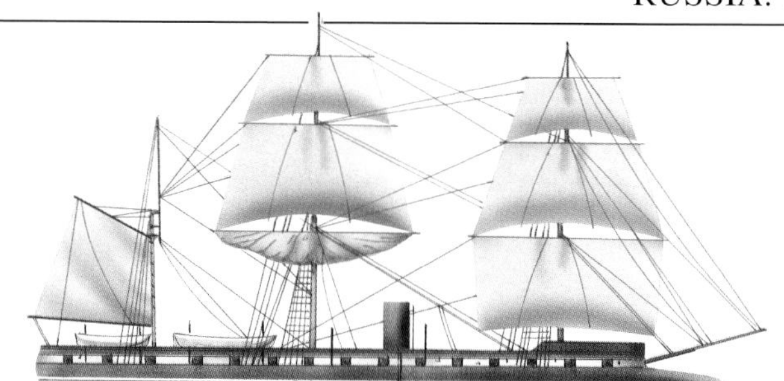

***Sevastopol* upon completion in 1865. Note the massive ram bow.**

Sevastopol, and her near-sister *Petropavlovsk,* were the first of six large, ocean-going Russian broadside ironclads; they were constructed before Russia built up a large fleet of turret ships, mostly for coast defence. *Sevastopol* was converted from a 5212t wooden unarmoured frigate that was to be armed with 28 60pdr smoothbore guns. The rebuilding gave her a complete waterline belt of wrought iron extending from 5ft 2in below water to the main deck. An armoured battery 195ft long, with armoured bulkheads at each end, was situated amidships.

SFAX

FRANCE: 1884

***Sfax* as she was first completed, with a barque rig of 21,400sq ft (1988sq m) of canvas. She represented a major advance in French cruiser development.**

While the first true protected cruiser, the Chilean *Esmeralda*, was under construction at Armstrong's yard in England, the French built the *Sfax*, which also had a complete protective deck entirely below the waterline. A minutely subdivided cellular layer was worked between the protective and gun decks, and comprised a cellulose-filled cofferdam along the sides. This additional method of protection had been adopted after trials made in 1872 by naval constructor Bertin, and formed the model for the cellular layer in warships of the French Navy and some other navies; it was later used by Bertin in the Japanese cruisers of the *Matsushima* class that fought at the Battle of the Yalu in 1894. Cellulose and other obturating materials used for filling cofferdams were abandoned in the 1890s because it was found that, in time, they deteriorated and lost their absorption properties.

Displacement: 4561t
Dimensions: 300ft 5in x 49ft 4in x 25ft (92m x 15m x 7.6m)
Machinery: twin screw, horizontal compound, 12 boilers; 6500hp
Armament: six 6.4in (162mm), 10 5.5in (140mm); five 15in (381mm) TT
Armour: deck 2.4in (62mm)
Speed: 16.8 knots
Range: not known
Complement: 486

The protective deck was 2.4in (62mm) thick and made up of four layers of steel; the hull was wrought iron on steel framing. The 6.4in (162mm) guns were sited on the upper deck, two in embrasured ports forward, with the rest in sponsons amidships and aft. The 5.5in (140mm) weapons were on the main deck.

SHAH

GB: 1873

Displacement: 6250t
Dimensions: 334ft x 52ft x 25ft 5in (101.8m x 15.8m x 8m)
Machinery: single screw, horizontal single expansion; 7480hp
Armament: two 9in (229mm), 16 7in (178mm), eight 64pdr
Armour: not applicable
Speed: 16.2 knots
Range: 6840 nm (12,668km) at 10 knots
Complement: 600

Designed by Sir Edward Reed, the *Shah* was one of three iron-hulled fully-rigged broadside frigates built as an answer to the large wooden-hulled US frigates of the *Wampanoag* class. *Shah* had three complete decks and a watertight lateral bulkhead which extended up to the main deck. She was an improved *Inconstant*, with an increased beam which improved stiffness. In addition to the broadside battery of 64pdr and 7in (178mm) guns, she had one 9in (229mm) gun mounted at each end of the main deck, allowing longitudinal fire through recessed ports. There was no armour protection. *Shah* was in an inconclusive action with the renegade Peruvian turret ship *Huascar* in May 1877.

As the powerful frigate *Shah* was unable to defeat *Huascar*, it became British policy to have an ironclad on most foreign stations after 1877.

SHENANDOAH

CONFEDERATE STATES OF AMERICA: 1863

By the summer of 1864, Confederate raiders had almost driven Union merchant shipping from the seas. The Confederacy decided, however, to fit out a suitable cruiser for operations in the Pacific where the Union whaling fleet would be. Bullock, the Confederate purchasing agent in Europe, acquired the *Sea King*, a newly completed army transport. Renamed *Shenandoah*, she was a

Shenandoah's captain did not know that the Civil War had ended and mistakenly carried on destroying Union whaling ships.

fully rigged wooden-hulled vessel with the funnel and machinery spaces aft. The guns were positioned on the upper deck, and comprised four 8in (203mm) smooth-bores plus smaller weapons. *Shenandoah* was a success as a raider. She covered 58,000 miles (107,400 km) and captured 30 vessels, many of great value.

Displacement: 1160t
Dimensions: 230ft x 32ft x 20ft (70m x 9.8m x 6.1m)
Machinery: single screw, engine type not known
Armament: four 8in (203mm), two 32pdr, two 12pdr guns
Armour: not applicable
Speed: 9 knots
Range: not known
Complement: 109

SOKOL — RUSSIA: 1895

Displacement: 220t
Dimensions: 190ft x 18ft 6in x 7ft 6in (57.9m x 5.6m x 2.3m)
Machinery: twin screw, vertical triple expansion, eight boilers; 3800hp
Armament: one 11pdr, two 3pdr; two 15in (381mm) TT
Speed: 30.2 knots
Range: not known
Complement: 54

Sokol, also known as *Pruitki*, was Russia's first destroyer. Built by Yarrow, she was an extremely successful vessel, achieving over 30 knots on trials; this speed was not possible under service conditions, as builders trials were usually run with the ship in a moderately light condition and with a picked crew, all experts in their own field. The hull was built of nickel steel with some aluminium used in the fittings. Aft of the turtle back was a low bridge upon which stood one 11pdr gun; the other, when later fitted, was situated aft. The 3pdrs were in the waist. One torpedo tube was sited in the bow, with the second aft on a turntable. When completed, *Sokol* was one of the fastest vessels afloat.

***Sokol* was the prototype to a class of 27 destroyers completed between 1898 and 1903, many of which served in the Russo-Japanese War of 1904-05.**

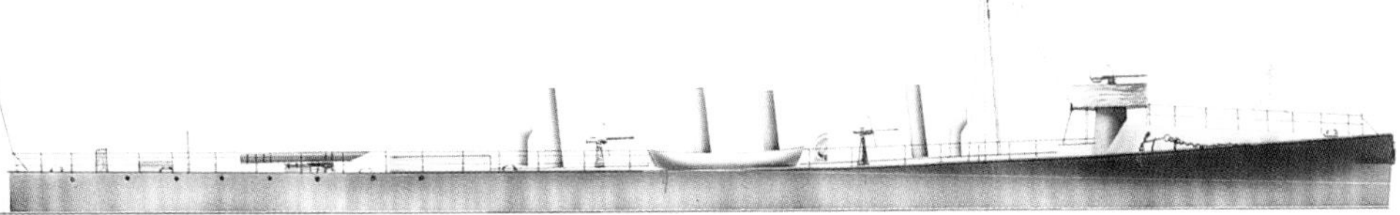

STILETTO — USA: 1886

Displacement: 31t
Dimensions: 94ft x 11ft 6in x 3ft (28.6m x 3.5m x 0.9m)
Machinery: single screw, vertical compound, one boiler; 359hp
Armament: none originally; two TT in 1898
Armour: not applicable
Speed: 18.2 knots
Range: not known
Complement: 6

***Stiletto* was built by Herreshoff as a private speculation, and was used in oil fuel trials in 1897.**

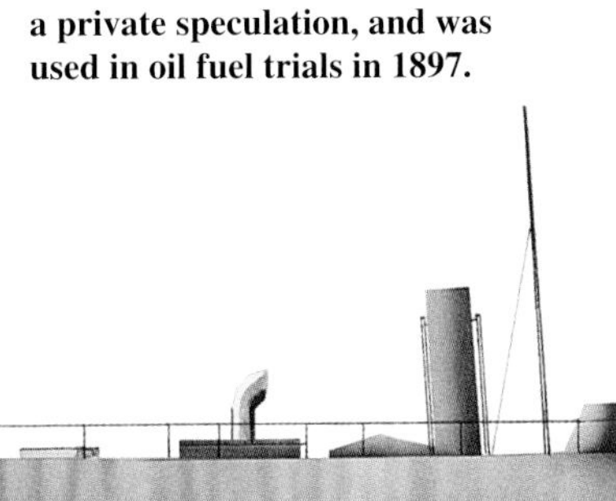

In 1876, the United States ordered a large wooden launch, the *Lightning*, from the Herreshoff Company. She was fitted with spar torpedoes and managed a commendable 17.5 knots on trial. In Europe, great interest was shown in torpedo boats at about this time, and the type continued to develop into the 1880s when the United States decided to order another torpedo boat which was built by the same company. This vessel was the wooden-hulled *Stiletto*, laid down in 1885. In 1898, she was armed with two Howell towing torpedoes, and was used extensively on experimental work. The Almy boiler was one long continuous copper pipe in the shape of a cone, with the fire in the centre.

STONEWALL — CONFEDERATE STATES OF AMERICA: 1864

Displacement: 1535t
Dimensions: 187ft x 32ft 8in x 14ft (57m x 10m x 4.3m)
Machinery: twin screw, return connecting rod, two boilers; 1200hp
Armament: one 9in (229mm), two 70pdr
Armour: hull 3.5-4.7in (89-119mm); turret 4in (102mm)
Speed: 10.8 knots
Range: not known
Complement: 135

In 1863, the Confederate Navy accepted an offer from the French shipbuilder Arman of Bordeaux to construct four sloops (one later became the Peruvian *Union*) and two armoured rams suitable for operations in the shallow waters of the Confederacy. *Stonewall*, one of the latter, had a composite hull – a wooden hull with iron frames – and a complete iron armour belt. The 9in (229mm) gun was housed forward, firing directly ahead over the lengthy ram. The two 70pdr weapons were carried aft in a fixed turret with four gunports, the guns being worked round to fire through the appropriate port. Twin rudders and screws made *Stonewall* and her sister very manoeuvrable. Delivery was planned for the summer of 1864, when they could safely weather an Atlantic crossing.

The Confederate ram *Stonewall* had an additional five names, three of which were to disguise her true identity. As *Azuma* she was sold to a fishing company in 1891.

Before completion, however, the French government stopped the sale. The vessels were then sold to Prussia and Denmark, then at war with each other and desperate to increase their weak naval forces. *Stonewall* was sold to the latter country, but once the war had ended, Denmark no longer needed her. Arman, through careful concealment, managed to sell *Stonewall* on to the South. Although shadowed by two large wooden Union frigates in Spanish waters, the formidable ironclad remained unchallenged and made her way to Cuba, where she surrendered, the Civil War having ended. She was then sold to Japan and renamed *Azuma*.

SULTAN

GB: 1870

Laid down before the early turret ships *Monarch* and *Captain* had been evaluated, *Sultan* was a ship-rigged central battery ship designed by Reed. She followed on from the *Hercules* of 1868 but had an improved armament layout, an additional armoured battery housing two 9in (229mm) guns having been sited on the upper deck with good all-round fire. There was a full-length waterline belt 9in (229mm) thick amidships, where it supported the 83ft (25.3m) battery which housed eight 10in (254mm) muzzle-loading rifled guns. Two 9in (229mm) guns were carried right forward beneath the topgallant forecastle. *Sultan* was a slow sail, mostly because of the drag of the screw. Although steady, she had 600t of ballast added to counter the topweight from the upper battery.

Displacement: 9540t
Dimensions: 325ft x 59ft x 26ft 5in (99m x 18m x 8m)
Machinery: single screw, horizontal trunk; 7720hp
Armament: eight 10in (254mm), four 9in (229mm)
Armour: belt 6-9in (152-229mm); battery 9in (229mm); upper battery 8in (203mm)
Speed: 14.1 knots
Range: 2140 miles at 10 knots
Complement: 633

***Sultan* with a full rig. This was reduced in 1876 because of fears about her stability. The central battery ship as a type continued to be built for another 10 years.**

TAGE

FRANCE: 1886

For nearly 10 years, *Tage* was the largest and one of the most powerful cruisers in the French Navy.

During the 1880s, France launched a number of powerful battleships but only four modern cruisers, *Tage* being one of them; 12 more cruisers were launched during this period but all had wooden hulls. *Tage* was the second modern French protected cruiser. She had a barque rig, three funnels, and a pronounced ram bow. The 6.4in (163mm) guns were on the upper deck, with two forward in embrasured ports and the remainder in sponsons; the 5.5in (140mm) weapons were on the main deck broadside. The protective deck was complete and curved down at the sides to 4ft 3in (1.3m) below the waterline. Above this deck was a cofferdam 3ft 3in (1m) wide.

Displacement: 7469t
Dimensions: 390ft x 53ft 6in x 25ft (118.9m x 16.3m x 7.6m)
Machinery: twin screw, horizontal triple expansion, 12 boilers; 12,500hp
Armament: eight 6.4in (163mm), 10 5.5in (140mm); seven 15in (381mm) TT
Armour: deck 2-2.2in (52-57mm)
Speed: 19.2 knots
Range: 4000 miles at 12 knots
Complement: 538

TEGETTHOFF

AUSTRIA-HUNGARY: 1878

Displacement: 7431t
Dimensions: 303ft x 71ft 5in x 24ft 10in (92.5m x 21.8m x 7.6m)
Machinery: single screw, horizontal low pressure, four boilers; 6706hp
Armament: six 11in (280mm)
Armour: belt 14in (356mm); battery 14in (356mm); bulkheads 10-12in (254-305mm)
Speed: 14 knots
Range: 3300 miles at 10 knots
Complement: 525

Tegetthoff was a central battery ship which had its main battery laid out in such a way as to allow it to fire forward during a chase and when ramming, a tactic that had proved so successful at Lissa in 1866. The six 11in (280mm) guns were in a well-protected central battery which overhung the sides, allowing the end guns on each side axial fire. There were three armoured bulkheads, one at each end, and one separating the forward pair of guns from those aft. The hull shape at the waterline meant that the armour plates were curved one way only. The armour and wood backing weighed 2160t.

***Tegetthoff* was designed by Von Romako. In a major refit she was given new engines, twin screws, and made 15.3 knots.**

TENNESSEE

CONFEDERATE STATES OF AMERICA: 1864

Tennessee was the largest ironclad built in the Confederacy. She was constructed at Selma, Alabama, and towed down to Mobile to become the major defensive unit afloat there. Mobile was about to come under attack by Union forces in an effort to close up the port, and to prevent it from being used by blockade runners. *Tennessee* had a long, wooden casemate covered in armour made up of railroad iron laid in 2in thicknesses. The sides were angled to deflect shots and continued to 6ft (1.8m) below the water. The casemate roof was made up of wrought iron grating bars 2in by 6in (152mm); the hull at each end was covered in 2in of armour. The engines were taken from a stranded transport, *Alonzo Child*. *Tennessee* surrendered to Union forces after a three-hour battle in Mobile Bay on 5 August 1864.

The *Tennessee* had two 7in (178mm) guns, one at each end of the casemate; her 6.4in (162mm) guns were sited on the broadside.

Displacement: 1273t
Dimensions: 209ft x 48ft x 14ft (64m x 14.6m x 4.3m)
Armament: two 7in (178mm), four 6.4in (163mm)
Armour: casemate 4-6in (102-152mm); deck 2in
Speed: 5 knots
Range: not known
Complement: 133

TEXAS

USA: 1892

Displacement: 6665t
Dimensions: 309ft x 64ft x 22ft 6in (94.1m x 19.5m x 6.9m)
Machinery: twin screw, vertical triple expansion, four boilers; 8600hp
Armament: two 12in (305mm), six 6in (152mm); four 14in (356mm) TT
Armour: belt 6-12in (152-305mm); turrets 12in (305mm); redoubt 12in (305mm); deck 2-3in (51-76mm)
Speed: 17.8 knots
Range: not known
Complement: not known

The delay in completing the armour manufacturing plant enabled improvements to be made to the *Texas'* armour.

Authorized in August 1886 and laid down three years later but not completed until August 1895, *Texas* was the first modern US capital ship. The design was prepared by Mr John of the Barrow Shipbuilding Company, England, and was one of 13 proposals submitted. The short waterline belt, 118ft (36m) long, was of Harvey nickel steel; two complete decks were fitted above the belt to give good seakeeping qualities. Two 12in (305mm) guns in single turrets were mounted on the upper, or main deck, *en échelon* and protected by a redoubt which did not extend right down to the waterline belt. Four 6in (152mm) guns were positioned on the second deck, and two more on the main deck. The main delay in completing *Texas* was that the armour plant was not ready to manufacture until 1891, two years later than planned.

TORDENSKJOLD

DENMARK: 1880

Displacement: 2462t
Dimensions: 222ft x 43ft 5in x 15ft 9in (68m x 13.2m x 4.8m)
Machinery: single screw, engine type not known; 2600hp
Armament: one 14in (356mm), four 4.7in (119mm); one 15in (381mm), three 14in (356mm) TT
Armour: barbette 8in (203mm); deck 1.5-3.7in (38-95mm)
Speed: 12.7 knots
Range: not known
Complement: 206

The 14in (356mm) gun carried by *Tordenskjold* was the most powerful afloat in the Baltic at the time.

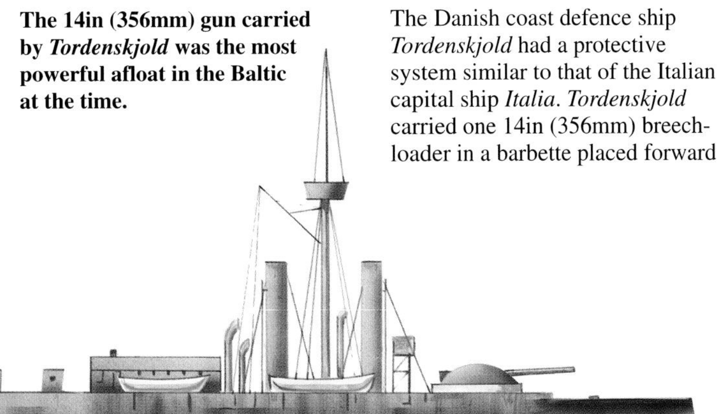

The Danish coast defence ship *Tordenskjold* had a protective system similar to that of the Italian capital ship *Italia*. *Tordenskjold* carried one 14in (356mm) breech-loader in a barbette placed forward on a turtle back, the top of which was slightly above the waterline. On the slopes, this deck was protected by Creusot steel plates, the lower slope being 3.7in (95mm) thick. Tests were carried out in 1883 near Copenhagen to determine the resistance of this deck armour under oblique impact; these tests proved the value of curved protected decks in cruisers. *Tordenskjold*'s 4.7in (119mm) battery was concentrated aft, as were three of the torpedo tubes; one 15in (381mm) tube was sited in the bow.

TRENTON

USA: 1876

The wooden-hulled broadside frigate *Trenton* was the largest cruiser in the US Navy for many years. Built of live oak (newly cut timber which is not allowed to season), she had a heavy cast-iron ram 8ft (2.4m) long, the point of which was 9ft (2.7m) below water. She was designed by chief constructor Isaiah Hanscom. *Trenton* had a fuller hull form than the previous class, with a beam to a length-ratio of 1:5.27. The 8in (203mm) muzzle-loading rifled guns were converted from 11in (280mm) smooth-bores; there were eight on the gundeck and three on the spar deck above, one aft and two forward able to fire ahead. *Trenton* was wrecked at Samoa on 16 March 1889 during a hurricane that destroyed the US and German squadrons in the harbour.

Displacement: 3900t
Dimensions: 253ft x 48ft x 20ft 6in (77m x 14.6m x 6.2m)
Machinery: single screw, compound return connecting rod, eight boilers; 3100hp
Armament: 11 8in (203mm)
Speed: 12.8 knots
Range: not known
Complement: 416

***Trenton* was the last major US warship built of wood. The United States did not possess a modern steel-hulled cruiser for another 10 years.**

TSESSAREVITCH

RUSSIA: 1901

Displacement: 12,915t
Dimensions: 388ft 9in x 76ft x 26ft (118.5m x 23.2m x 7.9m)
Machinery: twin screw, vertical triple expansion, 20 boilers; 16,500hp
Armament: four 12in (305mm), 12 6in (152mm); four 15in (381mm) TT
Armour: belt 4.7-7-10in (119-178-254mm); turrets 10in (254mm); secondary turrets 6in (152mm); deck 1.5-2.7in (38-69mm)
Speed: 18.5 knots
Range: not known
Complement: 782

The Russian battleship *Tsessarevitch* was built at La Seyne from Lagane's plans and was of a distinct French appearance with very pronounced tumblehome to the sides. The 12in (305mm) guns were in twin closed turrets at each end, the fore turret being 31ft (9.4m) above the waterline. The 12 6in (152mm) guns were mounted in twin turrets, four on the upper deck at corners of the superstructure, and two amidships on the main deck; all of the secondary battery had axial fire. Some of the 11pdrs were carried amidships on the second deck but without armour protection. The complete belt stretched from 5ft (1.5m) below to 7ft (2.1m) above the waterline. Above this was a strake of armour 7in (178mm) thick covered by a 2.7in (69mm) armoured deck, which at its maximum height was 7ft (2.1m) above the waterline. Six feet (1.8m) below this was a splinter deck 1.5in thick. This was slightly above the waterline, and curved down at the sides to form a lateral armoured bulkhead 6ft (1.8m) from the sides; this was intended as protection against underwater attack but ran only between the 12in (305mm) turrets.

***Tsessarevitch* in 1903. She was flagship at Port Arthur in 1904. When on full rudder at speed, her angle of heel was considerable.**

TSUKUBA

JAPAN: 1905

Displacement: 15,400t
Dimensions: 450ft x 75ft 5in x 26ft (137m x 23m x 7.9m)
Machinery: twin screw, vertical triple expansion, 20 boilers; 20,500hp
Armament: four 12in (305mm), 12 6in (152mm), 12 4.7in (119mm); three 18in (457mm) TT
Armour: belt 4-7in (102-178mm); upper belt 5in (127mm); turrets 7in (178mm); redoubt 5in (127mm); deck 3in (76mm)
Speed: 20.5 knots
Range: not known
Complement: 879

Tsukuba and her sister *Ikoma* were laid down in early 1905 as replacements for the battleships *Hatsuse* and *Yashima*, both of which were sunk off Port Arthur in 1904. *Tsukuba* was the first capital ship to be laid down in a Japanese yard, all previous battleships and armoured cruisers having been built abroad. As a result of battle experience, both vessels had 12in (305mm) guns as a main armament plus a secondary battery of 6in (152mm) weapons, but by the time of completion, the newly-introduced battlecruiser had superseded them in power and speed. There was a complete waterline belt with an armoured redoubt above, which housed eight of the 6in (152mm) weapons; four more were sited in casemates one deck higher.

***Tsukuba* was reclassified as a battlecruiser in 1912. She blew up in 1917 as a result of a magazine explosion.**

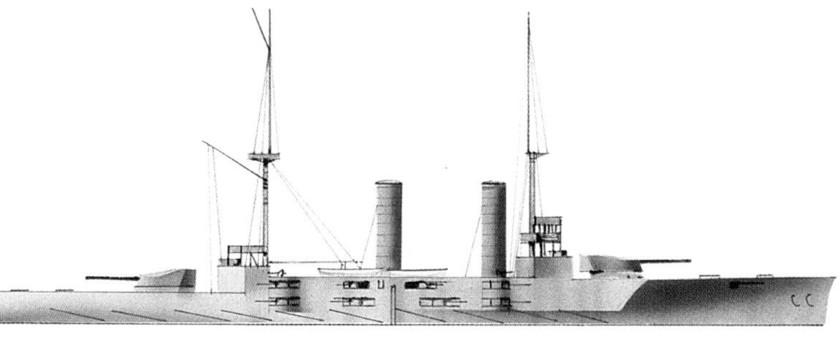

TSUKUSHI

JAPAN: 1880

Tsukushi was originally ordered by the Chilean government as the *Arturo Prat*. Laid down in October 1879 and completed in 1883, she was designed by Sir Edward Reed, and was a forerunner of the Chilean *Esmeralda*, which was launched in 1883. The 10in (254mm) 25t guns, which had a rate of fire of one round every 2.5 minutes, were positioned at each end of the superstructure and fired through ports on three sides. These were amongst the most powerful guns afloat at the time, and were only bettered by the massive guns on the British *Inflexible* and the Italian *Duilio* and *Dandolo*. As the war between Chile and Peru ended soon after she was completed, the vessel was sold to Japan and renamed *Tsukushi*.

Displacement: 1350t
Dimensions: 210ft x 31ft 9in x 14ft (64m x 9.7m x 4.3m)
Machinery: twin screw, reciprocating horizontal compound, five boilers; 2887hp
Armament: two 10in (254mm), four 4.7in (119mm)
Speed: 16.5 knots
Range: not known
Complement: 186

Like similar cruisers constructed by Armstrong, her builder, *Tsukushi* was an extremely powerful vessel for her size.

UNEBI

JAPAN: 1886

Displacement: 3615t
Dimensions: 321ft 6in x 43ft x 18ft 9in (98m x 13.1m x 5.7m)
Machinery: twin screw, reciprocating horizontal triple expansion, six boilers; 6000hp
Armament: four 9.4in (240mm), seven 5.9in (150mm); four 17in (432mm) TT
Armour: deck 2.5in 0
Speed: 18.5 knots
Range: not known
Complement: 280

At the same time as Japan ordered two protected cruisers from Armstrong in Britain, so she ordered from France a more conventional cruiser, the *Unebi*, which had a barque rig. The vessels ordered from Britain were without sails, an unusual feature in the early 1880s when these ships were first planned. *Unebi* was also more heavily armed than the British vessels building for Japan. Her 18t 9.4in (240mm) guns were mounted in sponsons, two on each beam; three 5.9in (150mm) weapons were also sited on each beam with one more in the bows. On the delivery journey, *Unebi* disappeared without trace between Singapore and Japan in October 1886.

In the 1870s and 1880s, France helped Japan establish a home shipbuilding industry.

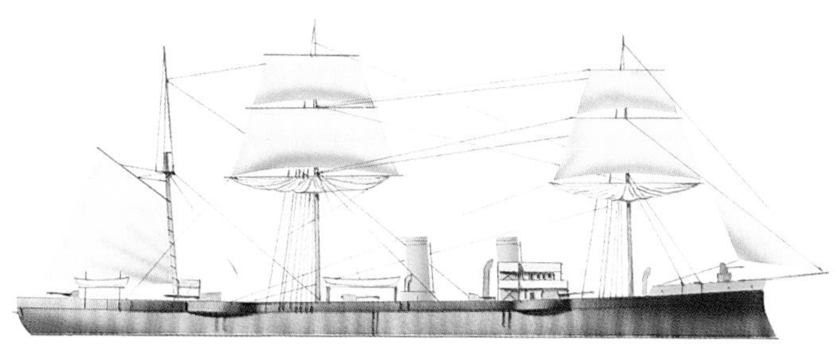

UNION (EX-GEORGIA)

PERU: 1865

All of the four vessels in *Union*'s class gave valuable service to their new owners; Prussia and Peru had two each.

Union was the former *Georgia*, one of a quartet of fast corvettes ordered in France for use as commerce raiders. All four were large examples of the type, with ample accommodation for long cruises, iron spars to avoid breakages, and a large spread of canvas. At the end of the American Civil War, *Georgia* was sold to Peru and renamed *Union*. She served in the war with Chile, fighting alongside the turret ship *Huascar;* when that ship was lost, *Union* became the only major warship in the Peruvian Navy. She was sunk at Callao in January 1881.

Displacement: 1827t
Dimensions: 267ft x 35ft 6in x 18ft (81.5m x 10.8m x 5.5m)
Machinery: single screw, single expansion, four boilers; 1300hp
Armament: 14 30pdr
Speed: 13.5 knots
Complement: 230

VANDALIA

USA: 1874

Displacement: 2033t
Dimensions: 216ft x 39ft x 17ft (65.8m x 11.9m x 5.2m)
Machinery: single screw, horizontal compound, return connecting rod, 10 boilers; 1150hp
Armament: six 9in (229mm), one 8in (203mm)
Armour: not applicable
Speed: 12 knots
Range: not known
Complement: 230

***Vandalia* in 1876. Such vessels as this were ideal cruising ships, but being built of wood, they had a short active career.**

Vandalia was one in a class of six wooden-hulled screw sloops laid down for the US Navy in 1872. She was barque-rigged and armed with rifled muzzle-loading guns. In the 1870s, the US Navy laid down 15 vessels of this type, ranging from the 1020t *Alert* class to the solitary 3900t *Trenton*. *Vandalia* was lost at Samoa in March 1889 during a violent hurricane; she ran aground, and *Trenton*, now no longer under control in spite of the valiant efforts of her crew, drifted down on her.

VASCO DA GAMA

PORTUGAL: 1875

Displacement: 2384t
Dimensions: 200ft x 46ft 6in x 19ft (60.1m x 14.2m x 5.8m)
Machinery: twin screw, vertical compound; 3625hp
Armament: two 10in (254mm), one 5.9in (150mm)
Armour: belt 4-9in (102-229mm); battery 6-10in (152-254mm)
Speed: 10.3 knots
Range: not known
Complement: 232

The Portuguese central battery ship *Vasco da Gama* was primarily intended for the defence of Lisbon and the River Tagus. The octagonal-shaped battery, which overhung the sides by 3ft (91cm), housed two 10.2in (259mm) 21t Krupp breech-loading rifled guns that could be moved around the battery on a complex set of rails. The sides of the hull were recessed, so providing fire ahead plus limited fire aft. The 5.9in (150mm) gun was placed aft below the poop. A full-length belt extended to the upper deck and down to the ram; the wood backing was 10in (254mm) thick. In 1901–03, *Vasco da Gama* was extensively modernized, being lengthened by 32ft (9.8m) and receiving 8in (203mm) guns, steel armour, and new machinery.

***Vasco da Gama* was a powerful, well-protected vessel on a small displacement. She was the only major vessel in the Portuguese Navy for 20 years.**

VAUBAN

FRANCE: 1882

Displacement: 5900t
Dimensions: 265ft 9in x 57ft x 25ft (81m x 17.4m x 7.6m)
Machinery: twin screw, vertical compound, eight boilers; 4060hp
Armament: four 9.4in (240mm), one 7.6in (194mm), six 5.5in (140mm); two 14in (356mm) TT
Armour: belt 6-10in (152-254mm); barbettes 8in (203mm)
Speed: 14.3 knots
Range: not known
Complement: 440

In the late 1860s and 1870s, the French built 14 cruising ironclads mainly for service on foreign stations, so allowing the major units of the French fleet to be concentrated in European waters. The *Vauban* was one of the last of this group. The wrought-iron belt extended from 5ft (1.5m) above the water to 5ft (1.5m) below. The barbettes had compound armour and housed two of the 9.4in (240mm) guns; there were two more guns aft of the single funnel on the upper deck. The 7.6in (194mm) gun was right forward in the bows, with the 5.5in (140mm) weapons concentrated amidships but without armour protection.

***Vauban* was built of steel and had a level of compartmentation not possible in the preceding wooden-hulled *Bayard* class.**

VESUVIUS

USA: 1888

Displacement: 929t
Dimensions: 252ft 4in x 26ft 5in x 9ft (76.9m x 8m x 2.7m)
Machinery: twin screw, vertical triple expansion, four boilers; 3200hp
Armament: three 15in (381mm) pneumatic guns
Armour: hull 1in
Speed: 21.6 knots
Range: not known
Complement: 70

The dynamite-gun cruiser *Vesuvius* was built by the US Navy to test the dynamite gun invented by Lieutenant Zalinsky of the US Army. Three 15in (381mm) barrels, each 55ft (16.8m) long, were fitted side by side in the bows at an angle of 18 degrees, parallel with the centre line of the ship; using compressed air as a propellant, the guns fired a 980lb (445kg) shell with a 500lb (225kg) warhead. The guns were aimed by pointing the ship at the target. The US were anxious to get ahead in one field of technical naval development, and preferred the dynamite gun to the torpedo, hence the torpedo boat found little favour in the US in the 1880s. However, money voted for a second dynamite cruiser was eventually allocated to torpedo-boat construction.

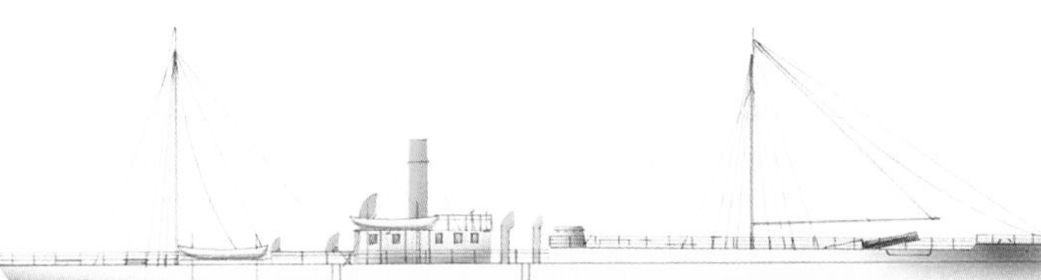

After completion, *Vesuvius* had 1in steel plating added abreast the machinery spaces. She took part in night attacks on Santiago in 1898.

VIBORG

RUSSIA: 1886

The first large Russian torpedo boat was the 160t *Vzruiv*, which was launched in 1877 and resembled a steam yacht. Six smaller torpedo boats followed over the next six years, but in 1886 Russia launched the *Viborg*, the first truly ocean-going torpedo boat to join the Russian Navy. The *Viborg* having proved successful, Russia embarked upon a major building programme that delivered 70 boats of 73 to 175t between 1886 and 1899. *Viborg* had two fixed bow torpedo tubes beneath the turtle-back foredeck, with another trainable tube behind the side-by-side twin funnels. She was converted to oil fuel in 1893, and stricken in 1910.

The total pumping power of *Viborg* was 2000t per hour, enough to move her own displacement in four minutes from the effective internal subdivision of small compartments.

Displacement: 166t
Dimensions: 142ft 6in x 17ft x 7ft (43.4m x 5.2m x 2.1m)
Machinery: twin screw, vertical compound, two boilers; 1300hp
Armament: three 15in (381mm) TT
Armour: not applicable
Speed: 20 knots
Range: not known
Complement: 24

VICTORIA

AUSTRALIA: 1884

Displacement: 530t
Dimensions: 145ft x 27ft x 11ft (44.2m x 8.2m x 3.3m)
Machinery: twin screw, compound; 800hp
Armament: one 10in (254mm), two 12pdr
Armour: not applicable
Speed: 12 knots
Range: not known
Complement: 60

In 1883, a number of gunboats were built for the British Colonial Forces in Australia, which was then divided into distinct individual authorities prior to the foundation of the Commonwealth of Australia in 1901. One of the original colonies was Victoria, which had a naval force comprising the old 4000t wooden line-of-battle ship *Nelson*, two first-class torpedo boats, and six gunboats, including *Victoria*. The steel-hulled *Victoria* was built by Armstrong, sent out from England in sections and reassembled on site. She mounted the 10in (254mm) 25t breech-loading gun forward in a covered structure. Two 12pdrs were carried right aft, firing through ports in the stern.

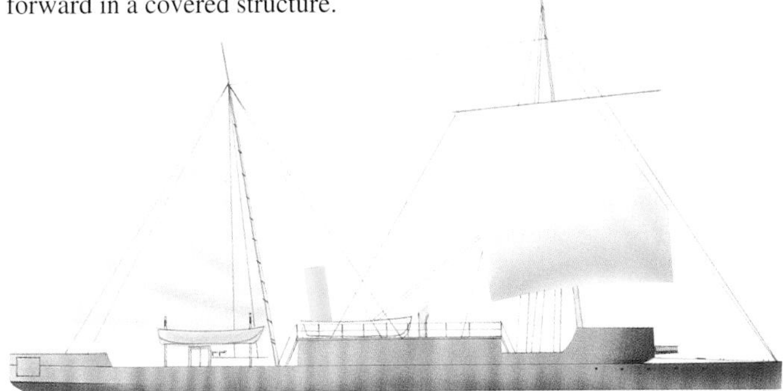

Designed strictly for coast defence, *Victoria*, with her powerful 10in (254mm) gun, could inflict serious damage on an enemy operating a long way from a friendly base.

VICTORIA

GB: 1887

The *Victoria* and her sister *Sans Pareil* were a logical follow-on to the *Admiral* class, and were protected in the same manner. They had a thick belt 162ft (49m) long covering the centre section of the waterline; this citadel was protected from above by a 3in (76mm) main deck, and the lower deck had similar protection either side of the citadel out to the bow and stern. The turret base was protected by a pear-shaped redoubt which extended down to the forward end of the citadel. The 6in (152mm) battery was amidships without protection, except for 6in (152mm) screens at each end to cover it from raking fire. A 3in (76mm) athwartship screen divided the battery in two. A single 10in (254mm) gun was positioned aft. As insufficient numbers of 13.5in (343mm) guns were available, two 16.25in (412mm) 110t Armstrong breech-loading guns were mounted in a single turret forward. To save weight, because of the limitations placed upon displacement, it was decided to adopt the one turret system. The turret also provided protection against the rapidly developing quick-firing gun, which up until a few years previously was represented only by the 6pdr. When the heavy guns on *Sans Pareil* were fired dead ahead, the deck caved in, and a man who had not been evacuated from the bow end of the ship was killed. On the 22 June 1893, *Victoria*, as flagship of Vice-Admiral Sir George Tryon, was sunk in collision with *Camperdown* off Tripoli.

***Victoria* was the first battleship to have triple-expansion engines.**

Displacement: 10,470t
Dimensions: 363ft x 70ft x 26ft 9in (110.6m x 21.3m x 8.1m)
Machinery: twin screw, triple expansion, eight boilers; 14,244hp
Armament: two 16.25in (412mm), one 10in (254mm), 12 6in (152mm); four 14in (356mm) TT
Armour: belt 18in (457mm); battery screens 3-6in (76-152mm); redoubt 18in (457mm); turret 17in (432mm); bulkheads 16in (406mm); deck 3in (76mm)
Speed: 17.3 knots
Range: 7000 miles at 10 knots
Complement: 550

VIPER

GB: 1899

Displacement: 344t
Dimensions: 210ft x 21ft (64m x 6.4m)
Machinery: quadruple screws, turbines
Armament: one 12pdr, three 6pdr; two 14in (356mm) TT
Armour: not applicable
Speed: 33.8 knots
Range: 920 miles at 17 knots
Complement: 70

Following on from the success of the first destroyers – such as the 27-knot 275t *Havock*, launched in 1893 – several groups of slightly larger destroyers with a speed of 30 knots were built. Attempts were made in the 490t *Albatross* of 1898 to reach a speed of 32 knots with reciprocating engines, but without success; it was not possible to achieve such speeds until the introduction of the turbine. It so happened that at this time the first destroyers fitted with Parsons turbines were under construction, but the loss of the first vessels so fitted, *Viper* and *Cobra*, caused a delay in the installation of turbines in major warships. *Viper* had three funnels, and the shafts each had two propellers, so cutting down on vibration and providing the ability to sustain high speed.

***Viper* was the first warship to be fitted with turbines.**

VITORIA

SPAIN: 1865

***Vitoria*, built at the Thames Ironworks, London, was part of the large building programme put in hand by Spain on the introduction of the ironclad.**

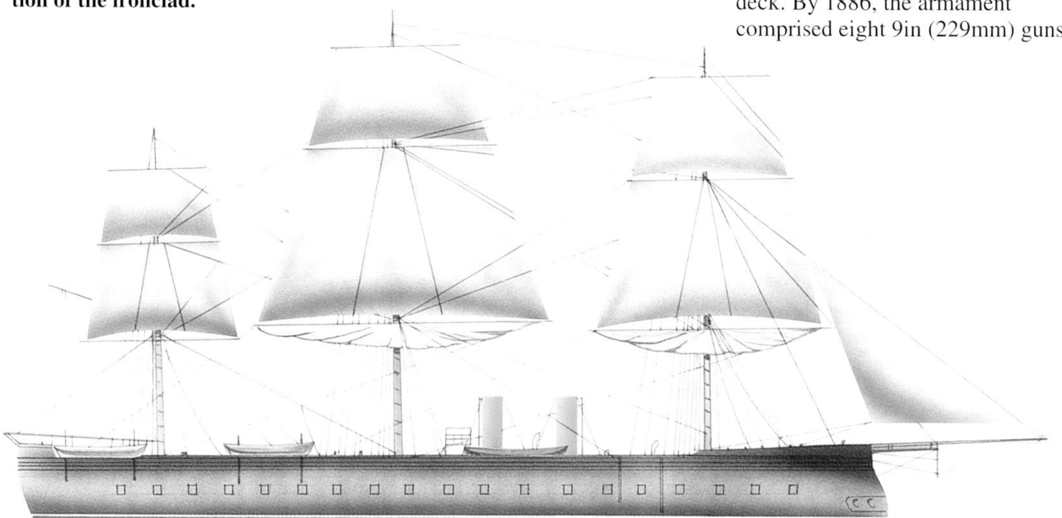

Vitoria was an ironclad broadside frigate; she was iron-hulled and ship-rigged, and had a ram bow. The full-length belt extended from 13ft (4m) above the waterline, covering the main battery, to 7ft (2.1m) below. The impressive battery was housed on the main deck. By 1886, the armament comprised eight 9in (229mm) guns mounted on the broadside, with two 8in (203mm) weapons in an armoured redoubt amidships on the deck above. In 1873, she was seized by insurgents at Cartagena, but was recovered by government forces, and was in action against three rebel ironclads within a few weeks. When completed in 1867, *Vitoria* helped put Spain fifth amongst the world's navies in relation to the amount of ironclads.

Displacement: 7135t
Dimensions: 316ft x 57ft x 26ft 5in (96.4m x 17.4m x 8m)
Machinery: single screw, engine type not known; 4500hp
Armament: 30 68pdr
Armour: belt 5.5in (140mm); battery 5.2in (133mm)
Speed: 12.5 knots
Range: not known
Complement: 500

VITTORIO EMMANUELE

ITALY: 1904

Displacement: 13,771t
Dimensions: 474ft 5in x 73ft 6in x 26ft (144.6m x 22.4m x 8m)
Machinery: twin screw, vertical triple expansion, 28 boilers; 19,424hp
Armament: two 12in (305mm), 12 8in (203mm)
Armour: belt 4-9.8in (102-252mm); redoubt 3in (76mm); turrets 8in (203mm); secondary turrets 6in (152mm); deck 1.5in
Speed: 21.3 knots
Range: 7000 miles at 10 knots, 1700 miles at 19 knots
Complement: 742

During the early 1890s, there was a pause in battleship construction in Italy, and only two capital ships were launched. Italy required fast and powerful ships to defend its extended coastline, and Cuniberti accordingly designed the *Vittorio Emmanuele* class of four ships. By abandoning the heavy quick-firing secondary battery and substituting 8in (203mm) guns in twin turrets, a far greater offensive power was obtained. This, coupled with exceptional speed and good protection, produced vessels closely resembling the later battle-cruisers of World War I. One of the two 12in (305mm) guns was mounted high up on the upper deck, which continued for two-thirds of the length of the ship; the second 12in (305mm) weapon was positioned aft. The 8in (203mm) turrets were on the broadside with axial fire.

***Vittorio Emmanuele* had a complete waterline belt with an armoured redoubt above.**

VOLAGE

GB: 1869

***Volage* was followed into the Royal Navy by 14 more unprotected cruisers before the *Comus* class of 1878, with limited deck protection, was introduced.**

In the late 1860s, the British Admiralty decided to accept the true concept of a cruising ship that broke away from the large and costly iron or wood frigates, and build cruisers which were of half the tonnage but had greater speed. Designed by Sir Edward Reed, *Volage* and her two near-sisters had a beam-to-length ratio of about 1:7. This, coupled with fine underwater lines, enabled *Volage* to exceed 15 knots, the first time such a speed had been reached in a cruiser of her type. Lateral watertight bulkheads reached up to the upper deck on which stood the six 7in (178mm) guns. They were sited in the waist on the broadside, together with two 64pdrs; there were two other 64pdr, one in the bows and one aft.

Displacement: 3080t
Dimensions: 270ft x 42ft x 22ft (82.3m x 12.8m x 6.7m)
Machinery: single screw, horizontal single expansion, five boilers; 4530hp
Armament: six 7in (178mm), four 64pdr
Speed: 15.3 knots
Range: 1850 miles at 10 knots
Complement: 340

VULCAN

GB: 1889

Displacement: 6600t
Dimensions: 373ft x 58ft x 22ft (113.7m x 17.7m x 6.7m)
Machinery: twin screw, triple expansion, four boilers; 12,550hp
Armament: eight 4.7in (119mm); six 14in (356mm) TT; six second-class torpedo boats
Armour: deck 2.5-5in (63-127mm)
Speed: 20.2 knots
Range: not known
Complement: 432

***Vulcan* experienced difficulties with the new type of boiler then also being tried in other warships. Only the French had a similar ship to *Vulcan*.**

Vulcan was a torpedo-boat depot ship able to carry its own group of six second-class vessels into action, as well as carry out repairs on other torpedo boats acting with the fleet. She could also act as a cruiser if required. Amidships, forming part of the superstructure, was a long gantry with cradles to hold the torpedo boats, which were handled by two large goose-necked cranes. The torpedo boats were 16t vessels, 60ft (18.3m) long, with a speed of 17 knots and armed with two 14in (356mm) torpedoes in dropping gear. Two of the 4.7in (119mm) guns were positioned side by side on the forecastle, two likewise aft, and two on each broadside at the ends of the gantry on the upper deck.

WARRIOR

GB: 1860

In the mid-1850s, Britain and France had been allies against Russia in the Crimean War, but the relationship began to deteriorate, especially when Britain saw the enormous increases in the number and quality of French steam-powered line-of-battle ships entering service. Britain responded with an increase in the rate of construction of these large wooden two- and three-deckers, which were armed with between 74 and 121 guns. The number of vessels completed rose from 29 in early 1859 to 40 by the summer of 1860. Meanwhile, France laid down three wooden-hulled ironclad broadside frigates that would change naval warfare forever. In May 1859, Britain answered with the *Warrior*, an iron-hulled ironclad broadside frigate intended to overtake and destroy any warship then afloat.

Although the French had led the way in the introduction of the ironclad, launching *Gloire* in 1859, Britain quickly took the lead by adopting iron for the hulls of

***Warrior* on completion in 1861. Designed by Isaac Watts, she was the forerunner of a long line of British capital ships, many of which were unmatched. *Warrior* was fully restored in the 1980s and is now a museum ship at Portsmouth Naval Dockyard.**

Displacement: 9137t
Dimensions: 420ft x 58ft 4in x 267ft (128m x 17.8m x 7.9m)
Machinery: single screw, horizontal single expansion trunk, 10 boilers; 5267hp
Armament: six 110pdr, 26 68pdr
Armour: belt 4.5in (115mm); battery 4.5in (115mm); bulkheads 4.5in (115mm)
Speed: 14 knots
Range: 1210 miles at 10 knots
Complement: 707

Warrior and her sister *Black Prince*; *Gloire* had been built of wood. *Warrior's* iron construction made it possible to build the British ship much larger – 9137t against 5630t – and also longer without any loss of structural strength; there was also less risk from the danger of fire. *Warrior* was also more than 1.5 knots faster than the fastest contemporary wooden line-of-battle ships and frigates. It had not been the fault of Dupuy de Lôme, *Gloire's* designer, that wood was used in his vessel; it was employed on the wishes of senior naval officers. There was also strong opposition in the Royal Navy to the use of iron for warship construction, and while the *Warrior* was being built, the Admiralty ordered the laying-down of several two- and three-deck wooden-hulled warships, as well as spending huge sums of money stocking up on wood for future shipbuilding. *Warrior* was protected by an iron waterline belt 213ft (65m) long and 4.5in (115mm) thick which extended up to cover the battery. This thickness, coupled with the 18in (457mm) of teak backing, was found to be sufficient to resist not only all the explosive shell of the day, but also 8in (203mm) solid spherical cast-iron shot at close range. Transverse armour bulkheads protected the battery from raking fire. The distribution of the armour in *Warrior* was different from that of the French *Gloire*, which was armoured from stem to stern. In *Warrior* the ends beyond the belt were left unprotected except for an unarmoured underwater watertight flat, although provision was made to reduce battle damage at the ends of the vessel by the construction of 92 watertight compartments. However, the steering gear remained exposed.

The graceful lines of *Warrior* are evident in this view. Under sail alone she made 13 knots and once made over 17 knots under sail and steam.

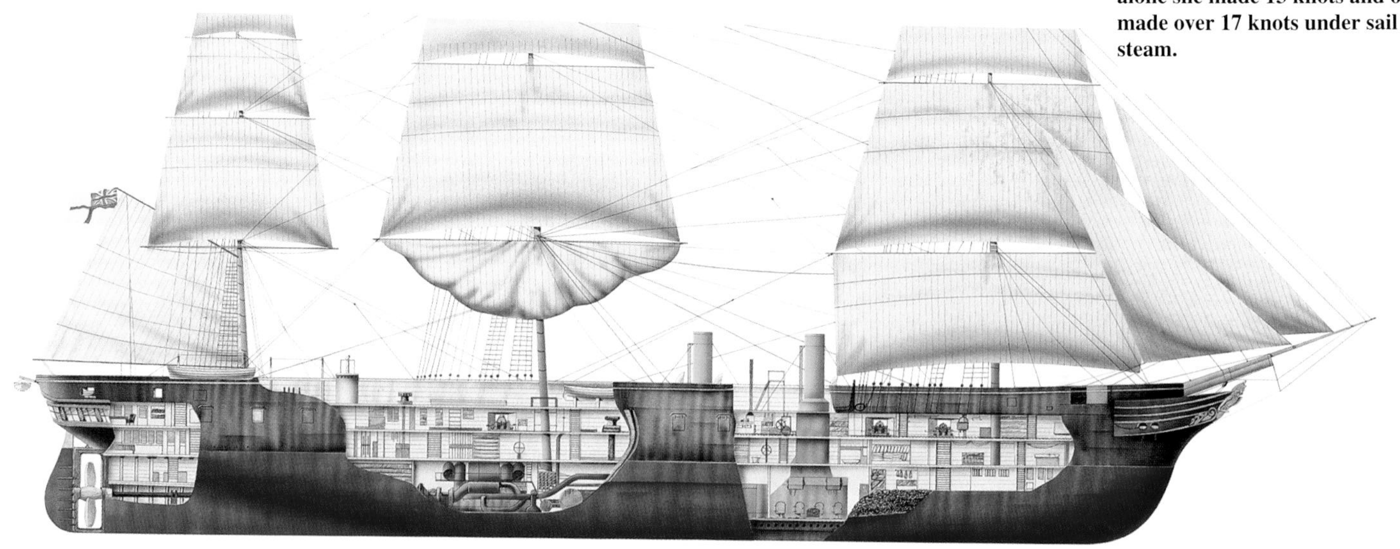

WILMINGTON

USA: 1895

Most of the gunboats built for the US Navy in the 1880s and 1890s had considerable seagoing qualities, being often required to navigate on the open sea. *Wilmington* and her sister *Helena* were designed, however, for service on Chinese rivers, their draught being only 9ft (2.7m). Large berthing capacity was provided by fitting a long superstructure that extended aft for nearly three quarters of the length of the vessel. This secured roomy accommodation for the crew and the capacity to carry large landing parties from other ships to the shallow ports on the Asiatic station. The hull aft was cut away to allow for the easy flow of water round the propellers in fast-flowing, shallow rivers. Twin rudders were also fitted to provide good handling.

Displacement: 1689t
Dimensions: 250ft 9in x 41ft x 9ft (76.4m x 12.5m x 2.7m)
Machinery: twin screw, vertical triple expansion, six boilers; 1900hp
Armament: eight 4in (102mm)
Armour: side 1in; deck 1.5in
Speed: 15 knots
Range: not known
Complement: 183

***Wilmington* had two 4in (102mm) guns forward and two more aft. A further four 4in (102mm) guns were on the broadside. There was a one-inch (25mm) armour strip amidships on the waterline.**

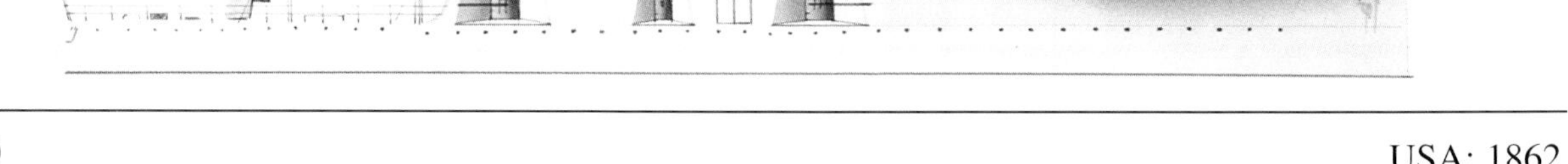

WINNEBAGO

USA: 1862

Displacement: 1300t
Dimensions: 229ft x 56ft x 6ft (69.8m x 17.1m x 1.8m)
Machinery: quadruple screw, horizontal non-condensing, seven boilers
Armament: four 11in (279mm)
Armour: turrets 8in (203mm); side 3in (76mm); deck 0.5-3in (12-76mm)
Speed: 9 knots
Range: not known
Complement: 120

In May 1862, the US Navy Department awarded a contract to James Eades for four double-turreted shallow-draught monitors for river use. *Winnebago* and her three sisters were screw-driven and not paddle-driven as were the earlier ironclad river gunboats. *Winnebago* had one Ericcson turret aft and one Eades turret forward, which made extensive use of steam power to elevate the guns, check the recoil, and lower the guns for reloading. The Eades turret also extended down into the hold and revolved on 6in (152mm) iron spheres in a circular groove. The turrets, funnel, and pilot house protruded up through the armoured turtle-back deck, which had solid 3in (76mm) iron plates.

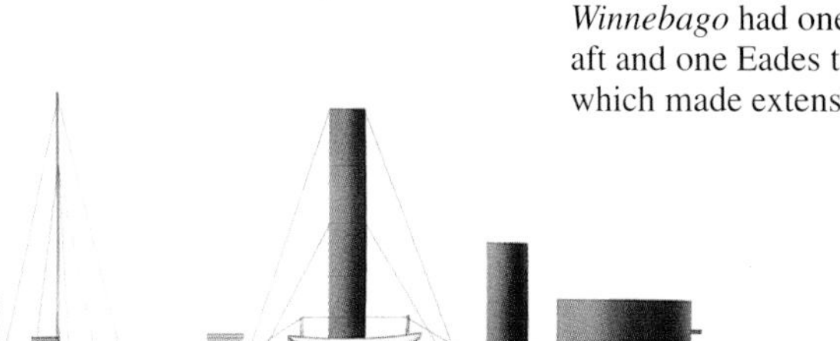

***Winnebago* and her sisters were amongst the most successful vessels of the monitor type.**

WIVERN

GB: 1863

***Wivern* showing the tripod masts designed by Coles to reduce the amount of rigging.**

Displacement: 2751t
Dimensions: 224ft 6in x 42ft x 16ft (68.4m x 12.8m x 4.9m)
Machinery: single screw, horizontal direct acting, four boilers; 1450hp
Armament: four 9in (229mm)
Armour: belt 2-4.5in (52-114mm); turrets 5-10in (127-254mm)
Speed: 10.5 knots
Range: 1150 miles at 10 knots
Complement: 153

In the early part of the American Civil War, poor shipbuilding facilities in the South led the Confederate Navy to put in hand a large purchasing programme in Europe for cruisers and ironclads. Two shallow-draught turret ships, suitable for service on the Mississippi and at its mouth, were ordered from Lairds of Birkenhead. The 6ft (1.8m) freeboard was increased by hinged bulwarks 5ft (1.5m) high which ran between the raised forecastle and poop. The hull was fully armoured from the upper deck down to 3ft 3in (1m) below the waterline, the armour backed by 22in (559mm) of wood. The two vessels were seized by the British government, named *Wivern* and *Scorpion*, and added to the Royal Navy. They were armed with a pair of 9in (229mm) guns (then the heaviest guns afloat in the Royal Navy) in each of the two polygonal turrets.

YOSHINO

JAPAN: 1892

Displacement: 4150t
Dimensions: 360ft x 46ft 6in x 17ft (109.7m x 14.2m x 5.2m)
Machinery: twin screw, reciprocating compound, 12 boilers; 17,750hp
Armament: four 6in (152mm), eight 4.7in (119mm); five 14in (356mm) TT
Armour: shields 4.5in (115mm); deck 1.7-4.5in (44-115mm)
Speed: 23.1 knots
Range: 9000 miles at 10 knots
Complement: 360

When completed in 1893, *Yoshino* was the fastest cruiser afloat.

The Japanese protected cruiser *Yoshino* was an improved version of the already successful 25 *de Mayo*, which was designed by Watts and built for Argentina. The 6in (152mm) quick-firing guns were positioned one forward, one aft and two in sponsons on either side of the bridge with ahead fire; the 4.7in (119mm) quick-firers were spread along each side, with one sponsoned out to give stern fire. This powerful armament was unmatched in a vessel of *Yoshino's* size. The protective deck was 1.7in (44mm) thick on the flat and 4.5in (115mm) thick on the slope with 4.5in (115mm) gunshields. *Yoshino* played a major role in the Battle of the Yalu in 1894. She was rammed and sunk in poor weather by the Japanese armoured cruiser *Kasuga* in May 1904.

ZIETEN

GERMANY: 1876

***Zieten* was the world's first torpedo cruiser, a type that gathered a following in several navies until replaced by the torpedo gunboat.**

The German scout or torpedo cruiser *Zieten* was built by the Thames Ironworks, and was the last major warship built abroad for the German Navy. She was the first vessel designed as a fast scout; two further enlarged versions were laid down in German yards in 1881. *Zieten* was armed with two submerged torpedo tubes, one in the bow and one astern. There were 10 torpedo reloads, and this armament, coupled with high speed and good seakeeping qualities, made this vessel a valuable addition to the fleet, especially as she entered service before the introduction of the quick-firing gun.

Displacement: 1152t
Dimensions: 260ft 8in x 28ft x 15ft (79.4m x 8.5m x 4.6m)
Machinery: twin screw, horizontal compound, six boilers; 2376hp
Armament: two 15in (381mm) TT
Armour: not applicable
Speed: 16.3 knots
Range: 1770 miles at 9 knots
Complement: 94

CHAPTER SIX

NAVAL VESSELS 1906–35

It was an era that would change the shape of naval warfare forever. It began in 1906, with the launch of the great battleship HMS *Dreadnought*; a vessel that made all other warships obsolete overnight. It was a time of innovation, a period that saw the debut of the battlecruiser, a hybrid warship that was to make its mark on the sea battles of the 20th century. The years that led up to World War I witnessed Great Britain's naval supremacy challenged first by Germany and then Japan, but at the end of that conflict the German High Seas Fleet had ceased to exist and the principal maritime powers were Britain, Japan and the United States, with France and Italy also in the running. Russia's naval strength, shattered by the Japanese fleet at Tsushima in 1905, had never recovered from that humiliation, and its post-war reconstruction was delayed by the economic effects of the Russian Revolution and its aftermath.

Left: ***New York*** **was launched on 30 October 1912 and completed on 15 April 1914. She immediately deployed to Vera Cruz, Mexico, in support of American military action there.**

The years between 1906 and 1935 were marked by undreamed-of techological innovation. Destroyers, once little more than coastal craft, were turned into hardy, seaworthy vessels with a role to play on the world's oceans, and World War I proved the destructive capability of the submarine beyond all doubt. During that war, Britain took the first tentative steps in the development of the aircraft carrier, the vessel that was to become the capital ship of the future. The carrier, perhaps, was the most significant naval design to emerge from the 1906–35 period; not only did it enable fleets to engage one another at distances far beyond visual range, but it also became a primary tool in hunting down the two greatest naval threats of World War II, the commerce raider and the submarine.

Yet the biggest single lesson to emerge from the 30 years or so on which this chapter concentrates has nothing to do with the design and application of warships. It is that treaties, naval or otherwise, mean nothing in the face of ruthless aggression and totalitarian ambition. The lesson was learned; but for yet another generation of seafarers, it was learned too late.

ACHILLES

GB: 1932

A cruiser of the *Leander* class, the only single-funnelled cruisers to be built for the Royal Navy since the 1880s, HMS *Achilles* was launched on 1 September 1932, and was loaned to the Royal New Zealand Navy 1937–1943. She became famous for her part in the Battle of the River Plate in December 1939. *Achilles* served in New Zealand waters 1940–43, home waters 1943–44, and joined the Pacific Fleet in 1945. She was sold to India and became INS *Delhi* in 1948.

Displacement: 6985t
Dimensions: 554ft 6in x 55ft 8in x 19ft 8in (169.01m x 16.97m x 5.99m)
Machinery: four screws, geared turbines; 72,000hp
Armament: eight 6in (152mm); eight 21in (533mm) TT
Armour: belt 3in (76mm); bulkheads 1.5in (38mm)
Speed: 32.5 knots
Range: 4500nm (8338km) at 15 knots
Complement: 570

Three of the eight cruisers in the *Leander* class, *Neptune*, *Sydney* (RAN) and *Perth*, were lost in action during World War II.

ADMIRAL GRAF SPEE

GERMANY: 1934

Popularly known as 'pocket battleships' due to their combination of light and heavy armament, the *Admiral Graf Spee* and her two sister ships, *Deutschland* and *Admiral Scheer*, were properly designated *Panzerschiffe* or armoured ships. Designed from the outset as commerce raiders with a large radius of action, their hulls were electrically welded and their armour plating reduced to the minimum considered necessary, achieving a substantial saving in weight, and permitting a higher maximum speed. When commissioned, they were faster and more powerful than most other warships then afloat. Laid down as the *Ersatz Braunschweig* (a replacement for the *Braunschweig*, a pre-dreadnought which was stricken in 1931) at the Wilhelmshaven Naval Dockyard, the *Graf Spee* was the last of the three constructed. She was launched on 30 June 1934, and completed in January 1936. Her operational career began almost immediately and she sailed for Spanish waters, where she carried out blockade duty off Republican ports during the Spanish Civil War. She sailed for the South Atlantic on 21 August 1939, 12 days before the outbreak of World War II. In a raiding spree that lasted until November (during which she was replenished by the fleet tanker *Altmark*, which had left Germany on 5 August), she sank or captured nine British merchant vessels before being brought to battle by a British naval force comprising the cruisers *Exeter*, *Ajax* and *Achilles* off the estuary of the River Plate. On 17 December, 1939 *Graf Spee* was scuttled off Montevideo; her captain, Hans Langsdorff, committed suicide.

The appearance of the *Graf Spee* and her sister ships aroused worldwide attention as it seemed that the so-called 'pocket battleships' outclassed the capital ships of other maritime nations.

Displacement: 12,100t standard; 16,200t full load
Dimensions: 610ft 3in x 71ft 2in x 23ft 9in (186m x 21.7m x 7.2m)
Machinery: two screws, diesel; 55,400hp
Armament: six 11in (280mm); eight 5.9in (150mm); eight 21in (533mm) TT
Armour: belt 3-2in (80mm-50mm); turrets 5.5in (140mm); deck 1.5in-0.71in (40mm-18mm)
Speed: 26 knots
Range: 10,000nm (18,530km) at 20 knots
Complement: 926

ADMIRAL NAKHIMOV

IMPERIAL RUSSIA: 1915

Launched on 6 November 1915, *Admiral Nakhimov* was one of a class of four light cruisers laid down in 1913–14. Only two were completed, *Admiral Nakhimov* in 1927 and *Admiral Lazarev* in 1932. Both were renamed before joining the Red Fleet, *Admiral Nakhimov* becoming *Chervona Ukraina*. Although these cruisers were virtually identical with the contemporary *Svetlana* class, their design was modified with the assistance of the British John Brown shipyard, giving an increased displacement and a higher speed.

While supporting German land forces in action at Sevastopol, *Chervona Ukrainia* was hit by three bombs, and sank in shallow water on 13 November 1941.

Displacement: 6833t standard; 8000t full load
Dimensions: 506ft 11in x 50ft 5in x 18ft 6in (154.5m x 15.36m x 5.65m)
Machinery: two screws, geared turbines, 46,300hp
Armament: 15 5.1in (130mm); six 21in (533mm) TT
Armour: belt 3in (76mm); deck 1.5in (38mm)
Speed: 29.5 knots
Range: 1200nm (2223km) at 14 knots
Complement: 630

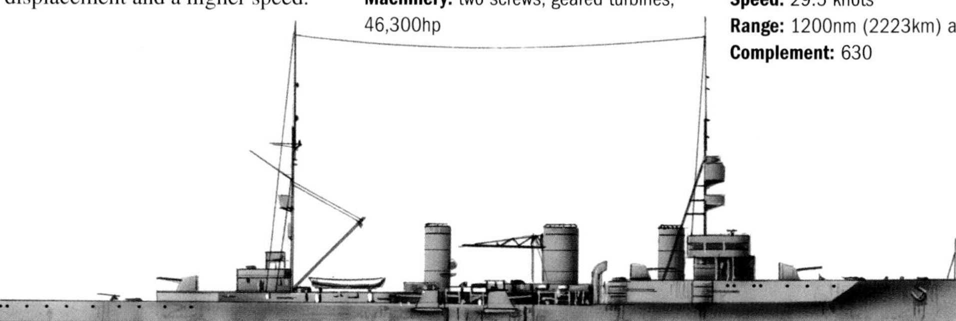

AIGLE

FRANCE: 1931

Aigle (Eagle) was one of a class of six large French destroyers which introduced a fast-firing (12–15 rounds per minute) semi-automatic 5.5in (140mm) gun into service. However, it could not be elevated at an angle greater than 28 degrees, so its range was less than that of previous models. Together with her sister ships *Gerfaut* (Falcon) and *Vautour* (Vulture), the *Aigle* was scuttled at Toulon on 27 November 1942 as German forces entered the port. She was refloated, but sunk later by Allied air attack in 1943.

As well as introducing the new quick-firing gun, the *Aigle* class destroyers were fitted with effective stereoscopic rangefinders.

Displacement: 2441t standard; 3140t full load
Dimensions: 421ft 7in x 38ft 10in x 16ft 4in (128.5m x 11.84m x 4.79m)
Machinery: two screws, geared turbines; 64,000hp
Armament: five 5.5in (140mm); four 37mm AA; six 21.7in (550mm) TT
Armour: belt 3in (76mm)
Speed: 36 knots
Range: 2700nm (5003km) at 14 knots
Complement: 230

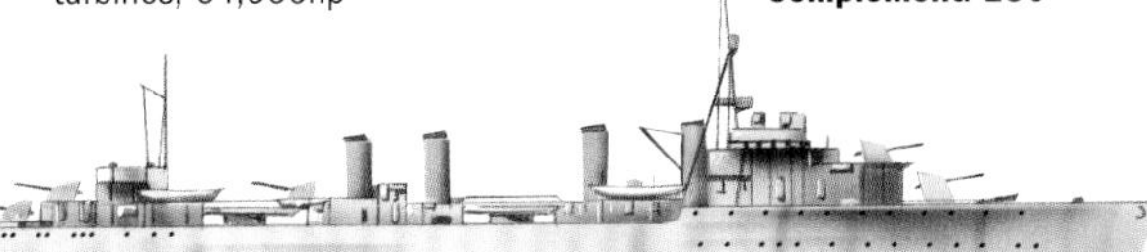

ALGERIE

FRANCE: 1932

As flagship of the 1st Cruiser Squadron, *Algerie* carried a crew of 729; her more usual complement was 616.

Displacement: 10,000t standard; 13,900t full load
Dimensions: 610ft 11in x 65ft 7in x 20ft 2in (186.2m x 20m x 6.15m)
Machinery: four screws, geared turbines, 84,000hp
Armament: eight 8in (203mm), 12 3.9in (100mm), eight 37mm AA; six 21.7in (550mm) TT
Armour: main belt 4.3in (110mm); deck 3in (76mm); turret faces 3.75in (95mm)
Speed: 31 knots
Range: 5500nm (10,192km) at 15 knots
Complement: 729

Launched on 21 May 1932, the French heavy cruiser *Algerie* was in a class of her own. In October 1939, she took part in the hunt for the German commerce raider *Admiral Graf Spee*, and in June 1940, following Italy's declaration of war on France, she bombarded shore installations at Genoa. She remained in the Mediterranean after the Armistice, and was fitted with radar early in 1942. On 27 November that year, she was scuttled at Toulon as German forces occupied the area.

ANDREA DORIA

ITALY: 1913

The *Andrea Doria* was one of two Italian dreadnoughts laid down in 1911, the other being the *Caio Duilio*. They were modified *Cavour*-class vessels with a 6in (152mm) secondary armament. Completed in 1916, *Andrea Doria* operated in the southern Adriatic during World War I. Both she and *Caio Duilio* underwent a major reconstruction programme in 1937; subsequently the *Andrea Doria* was not recommissioned until October 1940. A month later at Taranto, British naval aircraft damaged her with an aerial torpedo, but she was repaired by May 1941. She took part in a number of naval engagements against Allied forces in the Mediterranean in 1941–2, including the First Battle of Sirte on 17 December 1941. In March 1942, she was placed in the reserve, and on 9 September 1943, following the conclusion of an Armistice between Italy and the Allies, she sailed to Malta to be interned. She was reactivated for a time in 1947–49, as the flagship of the Italian Navy, but was stricken in 1956 and broken up in 1961.

Displacement: 22,964t standard; 25,200t full load
Dimensions: 577ft 9in x 91ft 10in x 31ft 2in (176.1m x 28m x 9.5m)
Machinery: four screws, geared turbines; 31,000hp
Armament: 13 12in (305mm); 16 6in (152mm); 13 3in (76mm); two 17.7in (450mm) TT
Armour: belt 9.2in-5in (235mm-127mm); turrets 11in (280mm); deck 6.6in (170mm)
Speed: 21.5 knots
Range: 4800nm (8894km) at 10 knots
Complement: 1233

In 1925 the *Andrea Doria* and the *Caio Duilio* were both provided with an M18 reconnaissance seaplane, with a catapult added a year later.

AOBA

JAPAN: 1926

The two *Aoba*-class cruisers, *Aoba* and *Kinugasa*, were laid down in 1924 as improved versions of the *Furutaka* class. Improvements included the mounting of 8in (203mm) guns in twin turrets, and replacement of the 3in (76mm) AA armament carried by the *Furutakas* with 4.7in (119mm). During World War II both *Aoba* and *Kinugasa* operated as a task force with the cruisers *Furutaka* and *Kako*, both of which were lost in late 1942, as was *Kinugasa*. *Aoba* survived until 28 July 1945, when she was sunk by air attack at Kure.

Sunk in shallow water by US carrier-borne aircraft, *Aoba* was later broken up in 1948. Her sister ship, *Kinugasa*, was sunk at Guadalcanal in November 1942.

Displacement: 9000t standard; 9300t full load
Dimensions: 602ft 6in x 75ft 9in x 18ft 6in (183.76m x 23.10m x 5.6m)
Machinery: four screws, geared turbines; 108,456hp
Armament: six 8in (203mm); four 4.7in (119mm); eight 24in (609mm) TT
Armour: turrets 5in (127mm); deck 2in (50mm)
Speed: 33.5 knots
Range: not known
Complement: 625

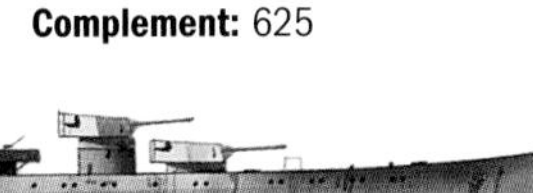

AQUILA

ITALY: 1926

Displacement: 23,350t standard: 27,600t full load
Dimensions: 759ft 2in x 96ft 7in x 24ft (211.6m x 29.4m x 7.31m)
Machinery: four screws, geared turbines; 151,000hp
Armament: eight 5.3in (135mm); 132 20mm AA; provision for 51 aircraft
Armour: 23.5in (600mm) bulge of reinforced concrete; 3in (76mm) plate on aviation fuel tanks and ammunition compartments
Speed: 30 knots
Range: 4150nm (7690km) at 18 knots
Complement: 1165 plus 243 aviation personnel

The only virtually complete aircraft carrier to be produced by Italy in World War II, *Aquila* was originally the passenger liner *Roma*, launched in 1926. Major conversion work began in November 1941, the liner's superstructure being removed and her internal structure rebuilt to accommodate new machinery and hangar space. Her engines were originally intended for the light cruisers *Cornelio Silla* and *Paolo Emilio*, construction of which had been stopped in 1941. The hangar was large enough to accommodate 26 Reggiane Re 2001 fighter-bombers, and there was provision to suspend another 15 from the hangar roof and park 10 more on the flightdeck. (A folding-wing version of the Re 2001 was under development at that time, which would have increased the air group to 66 aircraft.) In September 1943, the carrier was almost ready for sea trials, but her aircraft had not arrived. Seized by the Germans, she was damaged by Allied air attack and 'human torpedo' raids. She was scuttled, refloated in 1946, and broken up in 1951–2.

In addition to *Aquila*, the Italian Navy planned a second carrier, the *Sparviero*. This was to be a conversion from the passenger liner *Augustus*.

ARDENT

GB: 1929

HMS *Ardent* was one of a class of eight units with which the Royal Navy began a new era of destroyer construction, after a gap of eight years from the end of World War I. Laid down in 1929 and completed in 1930–31, the class introduced quadruple torpedo tubes, and had full shields for their 4.7in (120mm) guns. *Ardent* and her sister ship *Acasta* were sunk in June 1940 by the German battlecruisers *Scharnhorst* and *Gneisenau* while escorting the aircraft carrier *Glorious*, which also fell victim to the German guns.

The *A*-class destroyers were the first to introduce quadruple torpedo tubes. Four of the eight ships constructed were lost in action.

Displacement: 1360t standard; 1747t full load
Dimensions: 312ft x 32ft 3in x 12ft 3in (95.1m x 9.8m x 3.7m)
Machinery: two screws, geared turbines; 34,000hp
Armament: four 4.7in (120mm); eight 21in (533mm) TT
Armour: belt 3in (76mm)
Speed: 35 knots
Range: 2500nm (4632km) at 18 knots
Complement: 138

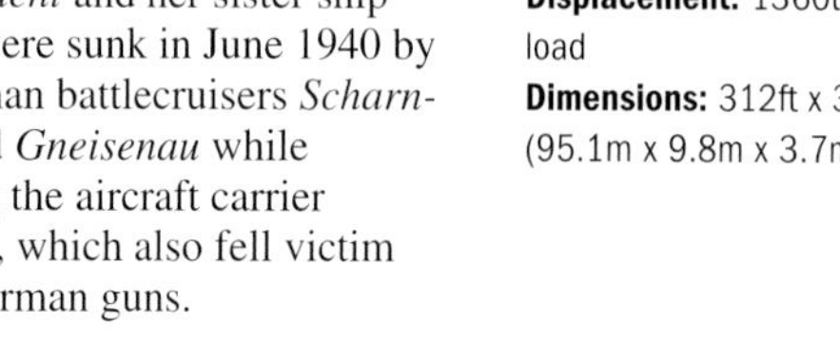

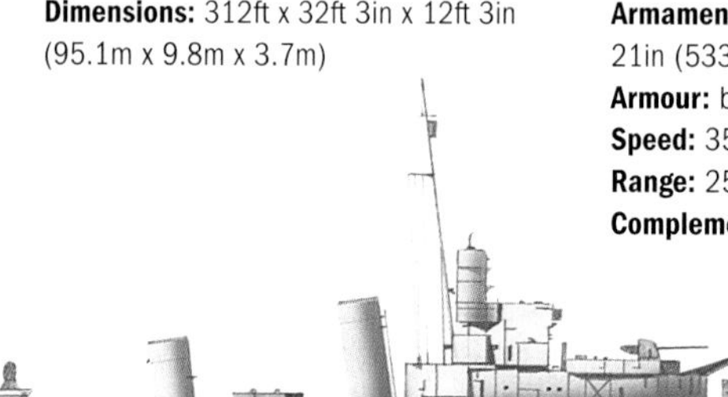

ARETHUSA

GB: 1930

Displacement: 5220t standard; 6665t full load
Dimensions: 506ft x 51ft x 16ft 6in (154.22m x 15.54m x 5.03m)
Machinery: four screws, geared turbines; 64,000hp
Armament: six 6in (152mm); four 4in (102mm); six 21in (533mm) TT
Armour: belt 2.75in (57mm); bulkheads 1in (25.4mm); turrets 1in (25.4mm)
Speed: 32 knots
Range: 3000nm (5559km)
Complement: 500

The *Arethusa*-class cruisers – of which there were four – represented an attempt to build the smallest possible useful cruiser. Though they proved to have a number of design shortcomings, they performed well in European waters during World War II. *Arethusa* survived an attack by torpedo-bombers in November 1942 that caused serious flooding and set her on fire, putting her out of action for over a year. Two of the class, *Galatea* and *Penelope*, were sunk by U-boats. *Arethusa* was broken up in 1950.

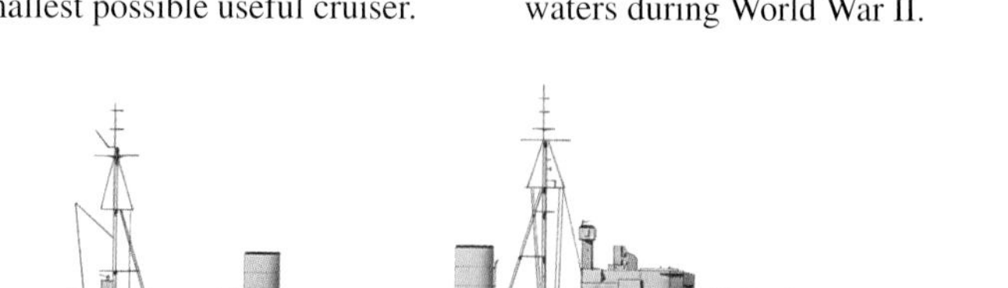

The other ship of the *Arethusa* class to survive the war was *Aurora*. She was sold to China in 1948 and re-named *Chung King*.

ARGONAUT

USA: 1927

Launched on 10 November 1927 and originally numbered V4 (later SM.1), *Argonaut* was the only purpose-built minelaying submarine to serve in the US Navy. She was the product of feasibility studies carried out in 1919 when the US Naval Staff, already perceiving a threat from Japan, realised that such a craft would be a vital asset in disrupting enemy commerce if war came to the Pacific. The specification for a long-range cruiser submarine called for a boat with an operating depth of 300ft (91.5m), an endurance of 90 days, and a combat radius of at least 600nm (1112km) with a normal fuel load, extending to 33,854nm (18,000nm) with maximum fuel. The submarine also required to maintain a continuous speed of 15 knots when surfaced. The specification also included an on-board reconnaissance aircraft and a large-calibre gun armament, a reflection on German submarine philosophy of World War I, which considerably influenced the American project. The Germans saw the submarine as a submersible torpedo-boat: it should be used in surface actions whenever possible, its ability to submerge being employed only as a means of concealment when approaching a

Displacement: 2710t surfaced; 4000t submerged
Dimensions: 381ft x 34ft x 15ft 6in (116m x 10.4m x 4.6m)
Machinery: two screws, diesels, plus electric motors; 3175hp/2200hp
Armament: four 21in (533mm) TT; two 6in (152mm); 60 mines
Speed: 15 knots surfaced; 8 knots submerged
Range: 5800nm (10,747km) at 10 knots, surfaced
Complement: 86

target, or as a means of escape. *Argonaut* was only one of the submarines envisaged by the US Navy planners; some schemes involved vessels with a displacement of as much as 20,000t. Her pre-war pendant number was A1 and she was later designated SS166. On 10 January 1943, *Argonaut* failed to return from a special operation off Lae.

The US Navy's only minelaying submarine (SM.1), *Argonaut* was converted to a transport submarine immediately after the attack on Pearl Harbor. Her long range made her ideal for special operations.

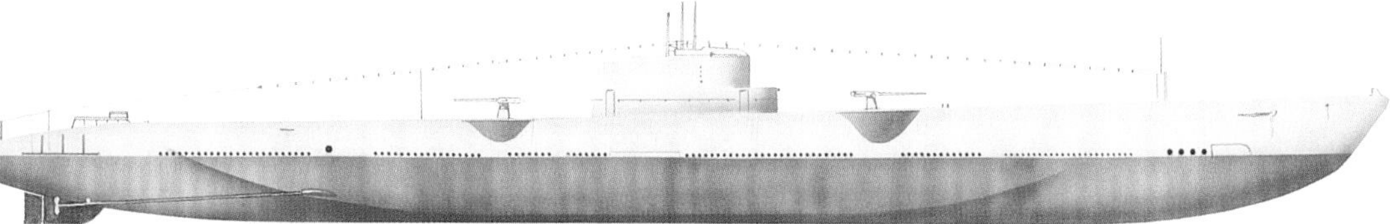

ARKANSAS

USA: 1911

During her reconstruction in the 1920s, *Arkansas* had her cage mainmast replaced by a small tripod mast. A catapult was also fitted.

The dreadnoughts *Arkansas* and *Wyoming* were enlarged versions of the *Florida* class with new 12in (305mm) guns. The *Arkansas* (BB-33) had served with the Atlantic Fleet during World War I, and in 1918 was attached to the British Grand Fleet. In 1925–6 she underwent substantial reconstruction. A further refit in 1942 saw her equipped with new AA guns. After service in the Atlantic and Pacific during World War II, she was expended in an atomic bomb test at Bikini on 25 July 1946.

Displacement: 26,000t standard; 27,243t full load
Dimensions: 562ft x 93ft 3in x 28ft 6in (171.3m x 28.4m x 8.7m)
Machinery: four screws, geared turbines; 26,000hp
Armament: 12 12in (305mm); 21 5in (127mm); two 21in (533mm) TT
Armour: belt 11in-5in (279mm-127mm); turrets 12in-9in (305mm-229mm); bulkheads 11in-9in (279mm-229mm)
Speed: 20.5 knots
Range: 8000nm (14,824km) at 10 knots
Complement: 1063

ASTORIA

USA: 1933

The USS *Astoria* was one of a class of seven heavy cruisers launched in 1933–36. These vessels were based on the *Northampton* class of 1927 which set the pattern for all succeeding American heavy cruisers – their silhouette was altered but they retained the same armament and machinery. *Astoria* (CA.34) was launched on 16 December 1933. Following the Japanese attack on Pearl Harbor, she formed part of the US naval force escorting aircraft carriers flying off reinforcements to Wake Island. In May 1942, she took part in the Battle of the Coral Sea and the Battle of Midway. In August that year, serving in the Solomon Islands, *Astoria* was part of the Northern Covering Force which supported the landings by US Marines on the island of Guadalcanal; during a night action with Japanese cruisers, she was badly damaged, abandoned, and sank. Two of her sister ships, *Quincy* (CA.39) and *Vincennes* (CA.44) were also sunk during this action, but the rest of the class survived the war, having taken part in almost every major engagement.

Displacement: 10,136t standard; 12,463t full load
Dimensions: 588ft x 61ft 9in x 22ft 9in (179.22m x 18.82m x 6.93m)
Machinery: four screws, geared turbines; 107,000hp
Armament: nine 8in (203mm); eight 5in (127mm); four aircraft
Armour: belt 5in (127mm); deck 2.25in (57mm)
Speed: 32.7 knots
Range: 10,000nm (18,530km) at 15 knots
Complement: 868

AUDACIOUS

GB: 1912

Once the concept of the dreadnought had been proven, construction of this revolutionary type of battleship for the Royal Navy proceeded rapidly, at the rate of three or four units per year. *Audacious* was one of four *King George V*-class battleships. Laid down at the Laird shipyard in March 1911, she was launched on 14 September 1912, and completed on 21 October 1913. Her operational career was destined to be short. On 27 October 1914, she was sunk by a mine north-east of Tory Island, Donegal. No lives were lost.

Displacement: 23,000t standard; 25,700t full load
Dimensions: 597ft 6in x 89ft x 28ft 8in (182.1m x 27.1m x 8.7m)
Machinery: four screws, geared turbines; 31,000hp
Armament: 10 13.5in (343mm); 16 4in (102mm); three 21in (533mm) TT
Armour: belt 12in-8in (305mm-203mm); turrets 11in (279mm); bulkheads 10in-4in (254mm-102mm); decks 4in-1in (102mm-26mm)
Speed: 21.7 knots
Range: 4060nm (7523km) at 18 knots
Complement: 782 (later 1132)

***Audacious* was the only ship of her class to become a war casualty. One of the others, *Centurion*, served as an AA battery in the Suez Canal in World War II.**

AUSTRALIA

AUSTRALIA: 1911

Of *Australia*'s sister ships, *Indefatigable* was destroyed at Jutland, and *New Zealand* was broken up in 1922 after touring the Dominions.

One of three battlecruisers of the *Indefatigable* class, *Australia* was paid for by the Australian government, and later became flagship of the embryonic Royal Australian Navy. Launched on 25 October 1911, she served with the Grand Fleet from 1915 to 1918. She was damaged in a collision in fog with her sister ship, *New Zealand*, on 22 April 1916, so missing the Battle of Jutland. In 1917 she was damaged in collision with the battlecruiser *Repulse*. She was sunk as a target off Sydney in April 1924.

Displacement: 18,800t standard; 22,080t full load
Dimensions: 590ft x 80ft x 27ft (179.8m x 24.4m x 8.2m)
Machinery: four screws, geared turbines; 44,000hp
Armament: eight 12in (305mm); 16 4in (102mm); two 18in (457mm) TT
Armour: belt 6in-4in (152mm-102mm); turrets 7in (178mm); bulkheads 4in (102mm); decks 2.5in-1in (63mm-25.4mm)
Speed: 25 knots
Range: 6330nm (11,729km) at 10 knots
Complement: 800

BADEN

GERMANY: 1915

Displacement: 28,600t standard; 32,200t full load
Dimensions: 590ft 6in x 98ft 6in x 30ft 6in (180m x 30m x 9.3m)
Machinery: triple screws, geared turbines; 35,000hp
Armament: eight 15in (381mm); 16 5.9in (150mm); five 24in (609mm TT)
Armour: belt 13.9in-6.7in (350mm-170mm); turrets 13.9in-10in (350mm-254mm); deck 3.9in (100mm)
Speed: 22 knots
Range: 5000nm (9265nkm) at 12 knots
Complement: 1171

The building of capital ships in Germany continued unabated in the years leading up to the outbreak of war in 1914. After the *Kaiser*-class dreadnoughts came the *Konig* class of 1911, *Grosser Kurfurst*, *Konig*, *Kronprinz* and *Markgraf*, the first German battleships to have all turrets mounted on the centreline. These vessels were followed by the *Baden* class of 1913, *Baden*, *Bayern*, *Sachsen* and *Warttemberg* – though the last two were never completed. The *Baden*s were modified *Konigs*, carrying a main armament of eight 15in (381mm) guns. They were built in response to the Royal Navy's *Queen Elizabeth* class, but were slower. Laid down in September 1913 as the *Ersatz Wirth* (the latter a pre-dreadnought of 1892 vintage, then still in commission), *Baden* was launched on 18 February 1915 and completed in the following March. She became the flagship of the High Seas Fleet in April 1916, replacing *Friedrich der Grosse*. Later, under the terms of the Armistice, *Baden* was not one of the ships originally scheduled to be surrendered, but the battlecruiser *Mackensen* was not seaworthy (in fact, she was never completed) so *Baden* was substituted. Interned at Scapa Flow on 14 December 1918, she was scuttled there on 21 June 1919, but instead of sinking she was towed ashore and beached. In July 1919, she was refloated for use as a naval gunnery target, and on 16 August 1921 she was sunk by British warships off Portsmouth. Her sister ship, *Bayern*, was also scuttled at Scapa Flow; she was raised and broken up at Rosyth in September 1934.

Baden and Bayern were Germany's last operational dreadnoughts. In many respects they were very advanced, and some of their more noteworthy features were incorporated in the later *Bismarck*.

BAHIA

BRAZIL: 1909

The two cruisers which constituted the Brazilian Navy's *Bahia* class were the *Bahia* and the *Rio Grande do Sul*. Their design was based on the British cruiser *Adventure*. They formed part of a Brazilian naval squadron which operated off the north-west coast of Africa during 1917–18. After being re-engined and re-boilered, both ships went on to see extensive service in World War II, operating with US naval forces in the Atlantic. On 4 July 1945, *Bahia* exploded without warning in mid-Atlantic and sank with the loss of 294 lives.

Brazil's entry into the war enabled her small cruisers, then the fastest of their type in the world, to make a valuable contribution to the Allied naval effort.

Displacement: 3100t standard
Dimensions: 380ft x 39ft x 14ft 6in (115.8m x 11.8m x 4.4m)
Machinery: triple screws, geared turbines; 18,000hp
Armament: 10 4.7mm (120mm); six 3pdr; two 18in (457mm) TT
Armour: deck 0.75in (19mm); conning tower 3in (76mm)
Speed: 26.5 knots
Range: not known
Complement: 350

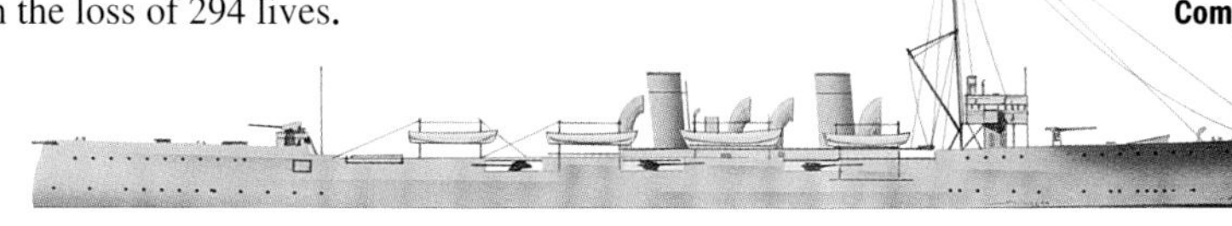

BALEARES

SPAIN: 1928

Ordered for the Spanish Navy in 1928, *Baleares* and her sister ship *Canarias* were modifed versions of the British *Kent* class. Both ships were completed just in time to take part in the Spanish Civil War on the Nationalist side. *Canarias* survived the conflict, but *Baleares* was sunk on 6 March 1938 in an engagement with three Republican destroyers, the *Barcaiztegui*, *Lepanto* and *Artequera*, off Cabo Palos. She was hit by a single torpedo which detonated her forward magazine.

***Canarias*, the sister ship of *Baleares*, was to remain in service with the Spanish Navy for many years. She was eventually scrapped in 1978.**

Displacement: 10,113t standard; 13,070t full load
Dimensions: 635ft 9in x 64ft x 17ft 4in (193.55m x 129.5m x 5.27m)
Machinery: four screws, geared turbines; 90,000hp
Armament: eight 8in (203mm); eight 4.7in (120mm) AA; 12 21in (533mm) TT
Armour: belt 2in (50mm); turrets 1in (25mm)
Speed: 33 knots
Range: 5600nm (10,377km) at 11 knots
Complement: 780

BEARN

FRANCE: 1920

In 1922, the French government authorised the provision of an aircraft carrier for the French Navy.

Displacement: 22,146t standard; 28,400t full load
Dimensions: 599ft x 89ft x 30ft 6in (182.6m x 27.13m x 9.3m)
Machinery: four screws, two geared turbines, plus two sets of reciprocating engines (outer shafts); 22,500/15,000hp
Armament: eight 6in (152mm); six 3in (76mm) AA; four 21.7in (550mm) TT
Armour: belt 3in (76mm); flightdeck 1in (25mm)
Speed: 21.5 knots
Range: 7000nm (12,971km) at 10 knots
Complement: 865

To save time and money, it was decided to convert the vessel from the incomplete hull of a *Normandie*-class battleship. This vessel had been laid down in 1914 as the *Vendee*, and was renamed *Bearn* at a later date. Construction was suspended when she was 25 per cent complete, and in April 1920 she was launched to clear the slip. Her conversion to an aircraft carrier began in 1923, and she was completed in 1926. Commissioned in May 1927, *Bearn* was inactive in 1939–40 and, following the fall of France, was demilitarized at Martinique. Later, she was rearmed and refitted at New Orleans in 1943–44 and reclassified as an aircraft transport, her slow speed precluding her from operating in any other role. In 1945–46 she served in the Far East, ferrying reinforcements to Indo-China. She was placed on the reserve in 1952, and broken up at La Spezia in 1967.

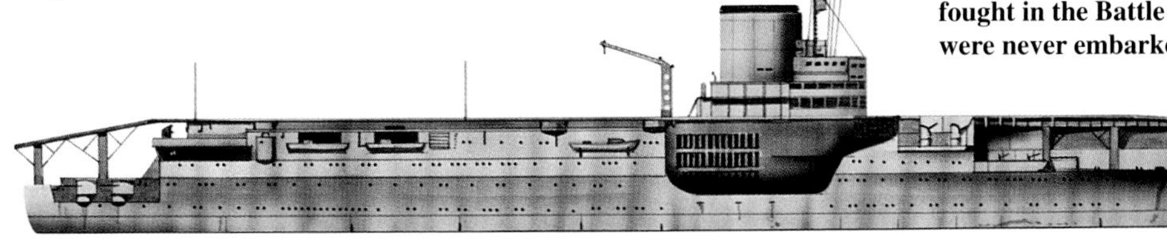

***Bearn* was to have had an air group of three dive-bomber squadrons, but although they fought in the Battle of France, they were never embarked.**

BIRKENHEAD

GB: 1915

The light cruisers *Birkenhead* and *Chester* began life as an order for the Greek Navy (which had a British Chief of Staff). In 1915, however, the British government directed that both vessels should be requisitioned by the Royal Navy. *Birkenhead*, fitted with an aircraft platform forward of the bridge, served with the 3rd Light Cruiser Squadron. In 1919, she was placed in reserve at Portsmouth, and paid off and sold for scrap in 1921.

Like *Birkenhead*, HMS *Chester* also served with the 3rd Light Cruiser Squadron and fought at Jutland, where her inadequately shielded gun crews suffered terribly.

Displacement: 5185t standard; 5795 full load
Dimensions: 446ft x 50ft x 16ft (136m x 15.2m x 4.9m)
Machinery: four screws, geared turbines; 25,000hp
Armament: 10 5.5in (140mm); two 21in (533mm) TT
Armour: belt 2in (50mm); conning tower 4in (102mm)
Speed: 26.5 knots
Range: 4500nm (8338km) at 15 knots
Complement: 500

BIRMINGHAM

GB: 1913

Displacement: 5440t standard; 6040t full load
Dimensions: 457ft x 50ft x 16ft (139.3m x 15.2m x 4.9m)
Machinery: four screws, geared turbines; 25,000hp
Armament: nine 6in (152mm); four 3pdr (47mm); two 21in (533mm) TT
Armour: belt 2in (50mm); conning tower 4in (102mm)
Speed: 26.5 knots
Range: 4140nm (7671km) at 16 knots
Complement: 480

HMS *Birmingham* joined the 1st Light Cruiser Squadron in 1914, and served until 1930. She was broken up the following year.

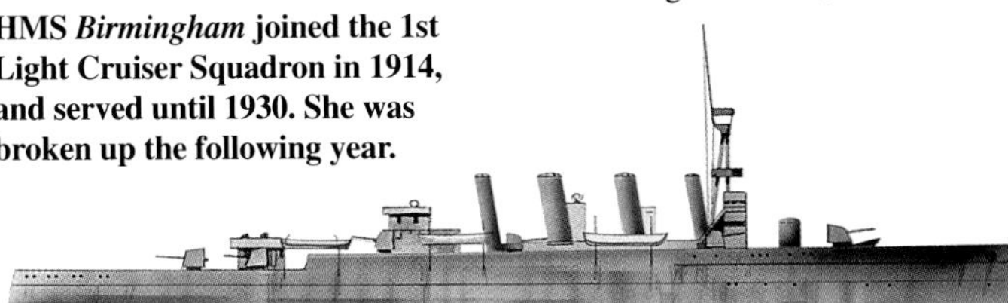

Launched on 7 May 1913, HMS *Birmingham* was leadship of a class of four light cruisers, the others being *Lowestoft*, *Nottingham* and *Adelaide*. They were near-repeats of the *Chatham* class and, like their forebears, proved very successful in service; the survivors were retained for use in the postwar fleet. *Nottingham* was sunk by the German submarine *U52* on 19 August 1916. *Adelaide* was not commissioned until 1922, and saw service in World War II.

BLÜCHER

GERMANY: 1908

Launched in April 1908, *Blücher* was a development of the *Scharnhorst* class. She was fitted with 8.2in (210mm), guns disposed in the same pattern as those of the *Westfalen* class, in the belief that British battlecruisers of the *Invincible* class, which the Germans knew were being built in 1906, would also have a main armament of this calibre. In fact, the *Invincibles* mounted 12in (305mm) guns. Classed as an armoured cruiser, *Blücher* had the general appearance of a battleship, except for the fact that her turrets were smaller. From 1911 to 1914 she served as a gunnery training ship, but became fully operational with the German High Seas Fleet in 1915. On 24 January that year, she was engaged by Royal Navy battlecruisers at Dogger Bank, and a 13.5in (343mm) shell from the *Princess Royal* pierced her armoured deck and ignited ammunition charges, causing a disastrous fire. She keeled over and sank after being hit by a further 50 heavy shells and two torpedoes.

***Blücher's* two forward beam turrets were supplied by ammunition rails from magazines below those for the after turrets – a disastrous arrangement.**

Displacement: 15,590t standard; 17,520t full load
Dimensions: 530ft 6in x 80ft 3in x 26ft 3in (161.7m x 24.5m x 8m)
Machinery: triple screws, vertical triple expansion; 34,000hp
Armament: 12 8.2in (210mm); eight 5.9in (150mm); 16 3.45in (88mm); four 17.7in (450mm) TT
Armour: belt 7in-2.4in (180mm-60mm); turrets 7in-2.4in (180mm-60mm); bulkheads 6in-3.2in (150-80mm)
Speed: 24.25 knots
Range: 6600nm (12,230km) at 12 knots
Complement: 847 (1026 at Dogger Bank)

BOLZANO

ITALY: 1932

Ordered for the Italian Navy under the 1929–30 re-equipment programme, the cruiser *Bolzano* attained over 36 knots during her trials, with her high speed achieved at the expense of armour protection. Later, in action off Calabria, she was hit by three shells; was subsequently torpedoed twice by the submarines HMS *Triumph* in 1941, and HMS *Unbroken* in 1942. She was still under repair at La Spezia when Italy surrendered. Captured by the Germans, she was sunk on 21 June 1944 by 'Chariots' (human torpedoes).

The cruiser *Bolzano* marked a return to the high speed and light armour of the earlier *Trento* class, with which she had many features in common.

Displacement: 10,890t standard; 13,665t full load
Dimensions: 646ft x 67ft 7in x 17ft 4in (196.9m x 20.6m x 6.8m)
Machinery: four screws, geared turbines; 150,000hp
Armament: eight 8in (203mm) and 16 3.9in (100mm); eight 21in (533mm) TT
Armour: belt 2.75in (70mm); decks 2in-1in (50-25.4mm); turrets 3.9in (100mm)
Speed: 36 knots
Range: 5500nm (10,191km) at 12 knots
Complement: 725

BRESLAU

GERMANY: 1911

Launched on 16 May 1911, *Breslau* was the second light cruiser in the *Magdeburg* class. These vessels were the first light cruisers to feature an armoured waterline belt, which consisted of 2.5in (60mm) nickel steel armour extending to about 80 per cent of the hull length. *Breslau*, together with the battlecruiser *Goeben*, formed the German Mediterranean Squadron. In 1914 she was assigned to the Turkish Navy, serving as the *Midilli*, but still manned by her German crew. The *Goeben* was renamed *Yavus Sultan Selim*, and the two warships continued to operate as a unit until the *Breslau* sank on 1 January 1918, after striking several mines during an operation against Imbros Island. There were three other vessels in the class: the leadship, *Magdeburg*, was destroyed by Russian cruisers after running aground in the Baltic on 26 August 1914; *Stralsund* was handed over to France, being broken up in 1935; and *Strassburg* was handed over to Italy as war booty. In World War II, *Strassburg* was sunk by aerial bombs in September 1944.

Displacement: 4570t standard; 5587t full load
Dimensions: 455ft x 43ft 11in x 16ft 10in (138.7m x 13.3m x 5.1m)
Machinery: four screws, geared turbines; 35,000hp
Armament: 12 4.1in (105mm); two 19.7in (500mm) TT
Armour: belt 2.75in (70mm); deck 2.25in-1.5in (57mm-38mm)
Speed: 25 knots
Range: 5820nm (10,784km) at 12 knots
Complement: 354

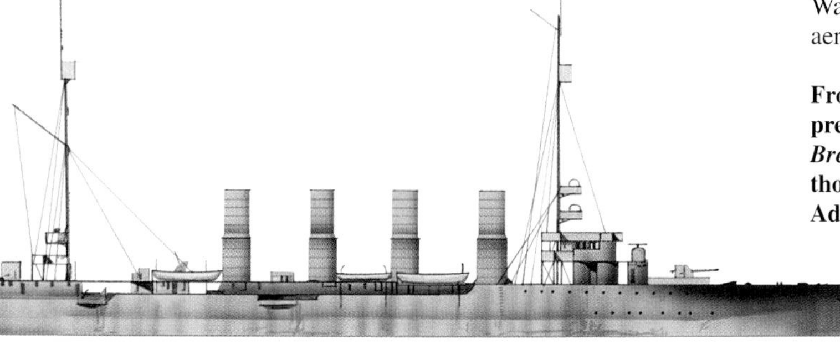

From the outset of WW1, the presence of the *Goeben* and *Breslau* in Turkish waters was a thorn in the side of the British Admiralty.

BRETAGNE

FRANCE: 1913

Ordered by Winston Churchill, the attack on Mers-el-Kebir, in which *Bretagne* was destroyed, was one of the tragedies of World War II.

The three dreadnoughts of the *Bretagne* class, *Bretagne*, *Lorraine*, and *Provence*, were similar to the earlier *Courbet* class, but with a heavier armament and a single turret amidships which replaced previous deck-edge turrets. In 1932–35, *Bretagne* and *Provence* were given a new main battery from guns originally intended for the *Normandie* class. In the early months of World War II, *Bretagne* served on Atlantic convoy duty. After the fall of France, *Bretagne* blew up and capsized after being hit by British gunfire in the attack on Mers-el-Kebir, 3 July 1940.

Displacement: 23,320t standard; 28,500t full load
Dimensions: 544ft 8in x 88ft 6in x 32ft 2in (166m x 27m x 9.8m)
Machinery: four screws, geared turbines; 29,000hp
Armament: 10 13.3in (340mm); 22 5.4 (138mm); four 17.7in (450mm) TT
Armour: belt 10.6in-7in (270mm-180mm); turrets 16.8in-9.8in (430mm-250mm); deck 2in (50mm)
Speed: 20 knots
Range: 4700nm (8709km) at 10 knots
Complement: 1113

C3

GB: 1906

C-class boats gave good service to the Royal Navy during World War I, and were well liked by their crews. The submarine C3, her operational days at an end, had a dramatic exit: on 23 April 1918 she was filled with high explosive and, commanded by Lieutenant Richard D. Sandford, crept into Zeebrugge harbour and was exploded under a steel viaduct as part of the British blocking operation there. Although wounded the two officers and four men aboard were picked up; Sandford was awarded the Victoria Cross.Approved in 1906, C-class boats were the first British submarines with an overseas (as distinct from coastal) patrolling ability.

Displacement: 290t surfaced; 320t submerged
Dimensions: 141ft x 13ft 1in x 11ft 4in (43m x 4m x 3.5m)
Machinery: single screw, petrol, plus one electric motor; 600/300hp
Armament: two 18in (457mm) TT
Speed: 12 knots surfaced; 7.5 knots submerged
Range: 1431nm (2414km) at 8 knots, surfaced
Complement: 16

CANADA

GB/CHILE: 1913

Displacement: 28,000t standard; 32,120t full load
Dimensions: 661ft x 92ft 6in x 32ft (201.5m x 28.2m x 9.8m)
Machinery: four screws, geared turbines; 37,000hp
Armament: 10 14in (355mm); 16 6in (152mm); four 21in (533mm) TT
Armour: belt 9in-4in (229-102mm); turrets 10in (254mm); decks 4in-1in (102mm-26mm)
Speed: 22.75 knots
Range: 4400nm (8153km) at 10 knots
Complement: 1167

The dreadnought *Canada* was originally laid down for the Chilean Navy as the *Almirante Latorre*, but was taken over by the British Admiralty in August 1914 on the outbreak of World War I. A sister ship, the *Almirante Cochrane*, was purchased by the British government in 1917, and converted into the aircraft carrier *Eagle*. A lengthened, *Iron Duke* type, *Canada* had 14in (356mm) guns. She was launched on 27 November 1913, served with the Grand Fleet, and took part in the Battle of Jutland. She was returned to Chile in 1920.

The *Canada* served in the Chilean Navy until October 1958 when she was stricken. She was broken up a year later.

CANARIAS

SPAIN: 1930

Canarias, together with her sister ship, *Baleares*, was ordered for the Spanish Navy in 1928, being a modified version of the British *Kent* class. A higher speed was achieved by reducing the beam, increasing the length slightly, and increasing the engine power, which added 1.5 knots to the design speed at full power. *Canarias* ran preliminary trials in 1934 and achieved 37.7 knots on full power over a four-hour period. *Baleares* was sunk during the Civil War. *Canarias* underwent a refit in 1953, emerging with two separate funnels in place of her earlier trunked ones. This was a reversion to the original design, which had never been carried out.

In her later years of service *Canarias* was completely overhauled and became the flagship of the Spanish Navy, being stricken in 1975.

Displacement: 10,113t standard; 13,070t full load.
Dimensions: 635ft 9in x 64ft x 17ft 4in (193.55m x 129.5m x 5.27m)
Machinery: four screws, geared turbines; 90,000hp
Armament: eight 8in (203mm); eight 4.7in (120mm) AA; 12 21in (533mm) TT
Armour: belt 2in (50mm); turrets 1in (25mm)
Speed: 33 knots
Range: 5600nm (10,377km) at 11 knots
Complement: 780

CAROLINE

GB: 1914

Displacement: 4219t standard; 4733t full load
Dimensions: 446ft x 41ft 6in x 16ft (135.9m x 12.6m x 4.9m)
Machinery: four screws, independent reduction turbines; 40,000hp
Armament: eight 4in (102mm); two 6in (152mm); four 21in (533mm) TT
Armour: belt 3in-1in (75mm-25mm); deck 1in (25mm)
Speed: 28.5 knots
Range: 4500nm (8338km) at 12 knots
Complement: 301

HMS *Caroline* was the leadship of a class of six light cruisers approved in the 1913 construction programme. In December 1914, she was leader of the Grand Fleet's 4th Destroyer Flotilla; she then served with the 1st Light Cruiser Squadron from February to November 1915. Early in 1916 she joined the 4th LCS and remained with it, including fighting at Jutland, until after the Armistice. In 1924 she became the Harbour Training Ship for the Ulster Division RNVR, Belfast. In World War II she served as an administrative centre for escort vessels based on Londonderry.

HMS *Caroline* had a lengthy career, serving as a reserve vessel for many years after her World War II service.

CASSIN

USA: 1913

The US Navy's eight *Cassin* class destroyers were the first with a design dominated by the US Navy's General Board philosophy – that the battle fleet operate as an integrated formation. The design emphasis was on sea-keeping and range at the expense of the small silhouette, which had been regarded as vital to the success of torpedo attacks. After World War I, *Cassin*, *Cummings* and *Downes*, served with the US Coast Guard.

Two of the *Cassin* class, *Cassin* and *Cummins*, had a reciprocating engine which could be clutched to one shaft for cruising below 15 knots.

Displacement: 1010t standard; 1235t full load
Dimensions: 305ft 5in x 30 ft 2in x 9ft 10in (91.5m x 9.2m x 3m)
Machinery: two screws, geared turbines, reciprocating gear for cruising; 16,000hhp
Armament: four 4in (102mm); eight 18in (457mm) TT
Armour: belt 2in (50mm)
Speed: 29 knots
Range: 1800nm (3335km)
Complement: 98

CERES

GB: 1917

Displacement: 4190t standard; 5020t full load
Dimensions: 450ft 3in x 43ft 5in x 14ft 8in (137.2m x 13.3m x 4.5m)
Machinery: two screws, geared turbines; 40,000hp
Armament: five 6in (152mm); two 3in (76mm); eight 21in (533mm) TT
Armour: belt 3in-1.5in (76mm-38mm); deck 1in (25mm)
Speed: 29 knots
Range: 3500nm (6485km) at 12 knots
Complement: 460

Launched on 11 July 1917, the light cruiser HMS *Ceres* was leadship in a class of five warships, the others being *Cardiff*, *Coventry*, *Curacao*, and *Curlew*. Their design incorporated a number of improvements over the earlier *Centaur* and *Caledon* classes, the most important being the rearrangement of the gun positions to allow more firepower to be brought to bear across wider arcs. *Ceres* served with the 5th Light Cruiser Squadron as part of the Harwich Force, 1917–19, and saw service in the Baltic.

HMS *Ceres* saw service in both world wars. During World War II she served in the Mediterranean and with the Eastern Fleet.

CHESTER

USA: 1906

Authorised under the US Navy Act of April 1904, USS *Chester* and her two sister ships, *Birmingham* and *Salem*, were classed as 'scout cruisers'. Their main distinguishing feature was a high freeboard forward. *Chester* and *Salem* were the first turbine-engined ships in the US Navy, the former being fitted with four-shaft Parsons turbines, and the latter with two-shaft Curtis turbines. However, the turbines gave constant trouble and were uneconomical, giving *Salem* a very high coal consumption. In April 1917, she was withdrawn from service to be re-engined with General Electric geared turbines of 20,000hp. *Birmingham* retained two-shaft vertical triple expansion engines. The ships carried very little armour protection, their maximum deck armour being 1in (25mm), with plate protecting the machinery of 2in (50mm). Armament was also very light, the main guns being on the forecastle deck forward and upper deck aft, with secondary armament positioned to port and starboard on the upper deck. In 1910, a wooden platform was positioned on the bow of *Birmingham* and from this, on 14 November, a civilian pilot named Eugene B. Ely took off in a Curtiss Golden Flyer, becoming the first aviator ever to fly from a ship. His aircraft struck the water, slightly damaging the propeller, but Ely retained control; he made a flight of 2.5 miles (4km), landing safely at Willoughby Spit. *Chester* was re-named *York* in July 1928 to allow her original name to be transferred to a *Northampton*-class cruiser. She was sold for scrap in 1930, as were *Birmingham* and *Salem*.

Displacement: 3750t standard; 4687t full load
Dimensions: 423ft 2in x 47ft 1in x 16ft 9in (128.98m x 14.34m x 5.1m)
Machinery: four screws; turbines; 16,000hp
Armament: two 5in (127mm); two 3in (76mm); two 21in (533m) TT
Armour: belt 2in (50mm); deck 1in (25mm)
Speed: 24 knots
Range: not known
Complement: 359

***Chester* and *Salem* were decommissioned in 1921. *Birmingham* continued in service for another two years, and was decommissioned in December 1923. The name *Chester* was then allocated to a *Northampton*-class cruiser.**

COLOSSUS

GB: 1910

Displacement: 20,000t standard; 23,050t full load
Dimensions: 546ft x 85ft x 28ft 6in (166.4m x 25.9m x 8.7m)
Machinery: four screws, turbines; 25,000hp
Armament: 10 12in (305mm); 16 4in (102mm); two 21in (533mm) TT
Armour: belt 11in-7in (279mm-178mm); bulkheads 10in-4in (254mm-102mm); decks 3in-1.5in (76mm-38mm); turrets 11in (279mm)
Speed: 21 knots
Range: 6680nm (12,378km) at 10 knots
Complement: 755

HMS *Colossus* was one of three dreadnoughts in the *Neptune* class laid down in 1908–9. They featured a new turret arrangement to provide greater broadside fire, with midships turrets in echelon, and 'X' turret superfiring over 'Y' turret. *Colossus* and *Neptune* differed from the third ship, *Hercules*, in having stronger armour and only one tripod mast, fitted abaft the forward funnel. *Colossus* fought at Jutland, and received two hits. In 1919 she became a training ship, and was scrapped in 1922.

Laid down at Scotts shipyard in July 1909, *Colossus* was launched on 9 April 1910 and completed in July 1911.

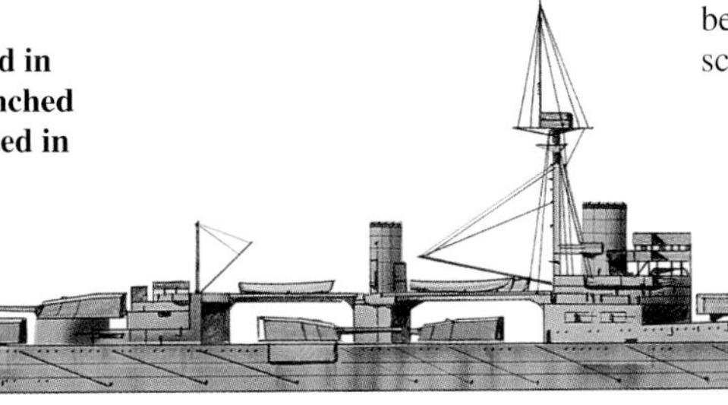

COMMANDANT TESTE

FRANCE: 1929

The *Commandant Teste* was designed to act both as an aircraft transport vessel and as a support ship for cruisers which carried reconnaissance aircraft. Aircraft were launched by means of four catapults and recovered by five cranes; a stern ramp was also fitted for winching aircraft aboard. The *Commandant Teste* escaped damage during the British attack on Mers-el-Kebir in July 1940, but was scuttled in November 1942 when German forces occupied Toulon. She was raised in 1946 and used as a store ship, and sold in 1950.

Displacement: 10,000t standard; 11,500t full load
Dimensions: 547ft 11in x 88ft 7in x 22ft 9in (167m x 27m x 6.9mm)
Machinery: two screws, geared turbines; 21,000hp
Armament: 12 3.9in (100mm); 26 aircraft
Armour: belt 2in (50mm); deck over machinery 1.5in (38mm)
Speed: 20.5 knots
Range: 5500nm (10,191km) at 10 knots
Complement: 686

After the *Commandant Teste* was raised in 1946, plans were made to convert her into a troop transport or training carrier, but were later abandoned.

CONQUEROR

GB: 1911

The battleship HMS *Conqueror*, and her sister ships *Monarch*, *Orion* and *Thunderer*, were the first British dreadnoughts to mount 13.5in (343mm) guns all on the centreline in superfiring turrets. The return to the 13.5in (343mm) main armament was the result of the Admiralty's dissatisfaction with the 12in (305mm) gun, which had poor accuracy at extreme range – its shells tended to 'wobble' in flight. The 'new' gun had no difficulty in ranging out to 24,000yds (21,936m). Its shell was also heavier, at 1400lb (634kg) against 1250lb (566kg), which in itself greatly improved the ballistics. *Conqueror* was launched on 1 May 1911 and commissioned in November 1912, joining the Home Fleet's 2nd Battle Squadron at Scapa Flow. In December 1914, her bow was seriously damaged in a collision with *Monarch*, but she was repaired in time to take part in the Battle of Jutland, in which she sustained no damage or casualties.

***Conqueror* was retained in the postwar fleet, but was discarded to comply with the Washington Treaty. She was broken up in 1922.**

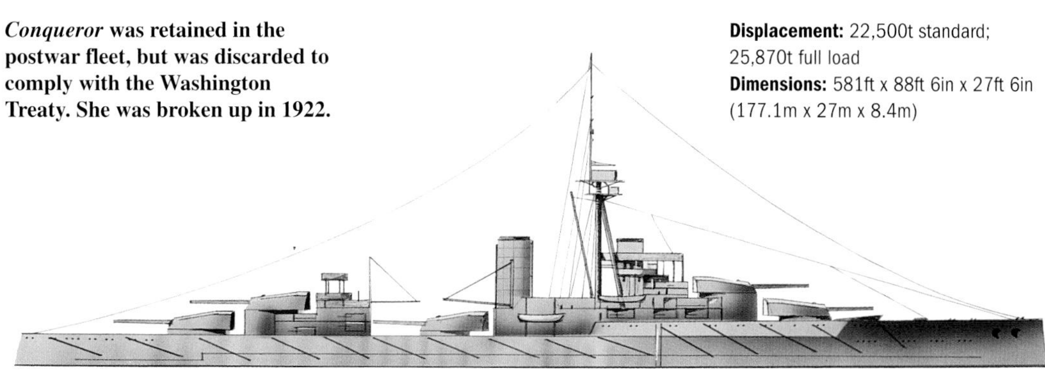

Displacement: 22,500t standard; 25,870t full load
Dimensions: 581ft x 88ft 6in x 27ft 6in (177.1m x 27m x 8.4m)
Machinery: four screws, turbines; 27,000hp
Armament: 10 13.5in (343mm); 16 4in (102mm); three 21in (533mm) TT
Armour: belt 12in-8in (305mm-203mm); deck 4in-1in (102mm-25mm); turrets 11in (279mm); bulkheads 10in-3in (254mm-76mm)
Speed: 21 knots
Range: 6730nm (12,470km) at 10 knots
Complement: 752

CONTE DI CAVOUR

ITALY: 1911

Named in honour of Count Camillo Benso di Cavour (1810–61), statesman and architect of the unification of Italy, the *Conte di Cavour* was laid down at La Spezia on 10 August 1910 and launched exactly a year later. After serving in the Adriatic in World War I, she undertook a cruise to the USA in 1919. Between October 1933 and October 1937, she underwent a complete reconstruction, emerging as virtually a new ship. On 12 November 1940, after taking part in preliminary naval skirmishes in the Mediterranean, she was sunk by aerial torpedoes during the attack on Taranto by British carrier-borne aircraft. Refloated in 1941, she was seized by the Germans in September 1943 while under repair at Trieste, and was sunk a second time by Allied bombs on 17 February 1945. The wreck was broken up after the end of the war. The *Conte di Cavour* had two sister ships, the *Giulio Cesare* and *Leonardo da Vinci*. The latter was sunk in Taranto on 2 August 1944.

***The Conte di Cavour* and her sisters were formidable battleships, having their main armament in three triple turrets and two twin superfiring turrets.**

Displacement: 23,088t standard; 25,086t full load
Dimensions: 577ft 9in x 91ft 10in x 30ft 9in (176.1m x 28m x 9.4m)
Machinery: four screws, turbines; 31,000hp
Armament: 13 12in (305mm); 18 4.7in (120mm); three 17.7in (450mm) TT
Armour: belt 10in-5in (250mm-127mm); turrets 11in (280mm); deck 6.6in (170mm)
Speed: 21.5 knots
Range: 4800nm (8894km) at 10 knots
Complement: 1000 (later 1236)

CORNWALL

GB: 1926

One of the seven *Kent*-class cruisers, HMS *Cornwall* was launched on 3 November 1926 and completed in May 1928. Two of the class, *Australia* and *Canberra*, were built for the Royal Australian Navy. The Kent class had 8in (203mm) guns in mountings of a novel design; this enabled elevation of the guns to an angle of 70 degrees, and shell and charge were rammed in one operation, thus increasing the firing rate. On 5 April 1942, while serving with the Eastern Fleet and operating in the vicinity of Ceylon, *Cornwall* and another cruiser, *Dorsetshire*, were attacked by Japanese carrier-borne aircraft and both were sunk. *Cornwall* sustained nine direct hits and six near misses in the space of 12 minutes, and all her engine and boiler rooms were put out of action. Out of a total of 1546 crew on both ships, 1112 were later rescued by the cruiser HMS *Enterprise* and two destroyers. *Canberra* was also sunk in World War II.

Displacement: 9750t standard; 13,400t full load
Dimensions: 630ft x 68ft 4in x 20ft 6in (192.02m x 20.83m x 6.25m)
Machinery: four screws, geared turbines; 80,000hp
Armament: eight 8in (203mm); four 4in (102mm); eight 21in (533mm) TT
Armour: ammunition lockers 4in-1in (100mm-25mm); deck and sides 1in (25mm)
Speed: 31.5 knots
Range: 4500nm (8338nm)
Complement: 685-710

The *Kent* class cruisers had good armoured protection around vital parts such as ammunition lockers, but elsewhere it was poor.

CORONEL BOLOGNESI

PERU: 1906

For half a century, the *Coronel Bolognesi* and her sister ship *Almirante Grau* were the largest and most powerful ships in the Peruvian Navy, both being classed 'scout cruisers'. They underwent a refit between 1923 and 1925: their boilers were retubed, they were modified to burn oil, and were fitted with Italian fire-control systems. In 1934–35, they were sent to Britain where they received new boilers at the Yarrow shipyard on the Clyde. Both ships were stricken in 1958.

In 1936, both *Coronel Bolognesi* and her sister ship, *Almirante Grau*, had an equipment update; this included the fitting of Japanese 3in (76mm) AA guns.

Displacement: 3100t standard
Dimensions: 380ft x 40ft 6in x 14ft 3in (115.8m x 12.3m x 4.3m)
Machinery: two screws, vertical triple expansion; 14,000hp
Armament: two 6in (152mm); eight 3in (76mm); two 18in (457mm) TT
Armour: deck 1.5in (38mm); gun shields 3in (76mm)
Speed: 24 knots
Range: 3276nm (6070km) at 10 knots
Complement: 320

COURAGEOUS

GB: 1916

Though they were defined as large light cruisers, *Courageous* and her sister ship, *Glorious*, were actually light battlecruisers. Ordered early in 1915, at a time when the British War Cabinet was reluctant to fund the building of more capital ships, they were the brainchild of Admiral Fisher who was drawing up plans to invade the German-occupied Baltic states, and who needed the ships to provide fire support. The operation never took place, and *Courageous* was decommissioned for conversion as an aircraft carrier in 1924.

Displacement: 19,230t standard; 22,690t full load
Dimensions: 786ft 3in x 81ft x 23ft 4in (239.7m x 24.7m x 7.1m)
Machinery: four screws, geared turbines; 90,000hp
Armament: four 15in (381mm); 18 4in (102mm); two 21in (533mm) TT
Armour: belt 3in-2in (76mm-50mm); bulkheads 3in-2in (76mm-50mm); turret faces 13in-11in (330mm-280mm); decks 1.5in-0.75in (38mm-20mm)
Speed: 32 knots
Range: 3200nm (5929km) at 19 knots
Complement: 828-842

***Courageous* was the first major British warship loss of World War II, being sunk by the U29 in September 1939 with the loss of 514 crew.**

COURBET

FRANCE: 1911

Displacement: 23,189t standard; 28,850t full load
Dimensions: 551ft 2in x 91ft 6in x 29ft 6in (168m x 27.9m x 9m)
Machinery: four screws, turbines; 28,000hp
Armament: 12 12in (305mm); 22 5.4in (137mm); four 17.7in (450mm) TT
Armour: belt 11.8in-7in (300mm-180mm); turrets 12.5in (320mm); deck 2.75in (70mm)
Speed: 21 knots
Range: 4200nm (7782nm) at 10 knots
Complement: 1108

The *Courbet*-class battleships of 1910–11, *Courbet*, *France*, *Jean Bart*, and *Paris*, were the first French dreadnoughts, and designed by Lyasse. Their armament was mounted in six turrets, including one on each beam amidships. In an action off Albania on 16 August 1914, *Courbet* sank the Austrian cruiser *Zenta*. Both *Courbet* and *Jean Bart* underwent substantial reconstruction in 1926–29, their two forward funnels being trunked into one, and a tripod replacing the pole mast. *Courbet* was seized by the British at Portsmouth in June 1940, where she was based after lending fire support to Allied forces evacuating Cherbourg. She was later returned to the Free French, but was considered obsolete and decommissioned in April 1941. In June 1944 she was sunk as part of an artificial harbour in Normandy to assist the invasion forces.

Courbet was named in honour of Amadée Anatole Prosper Courbet (1827–85), the French admiral who played a prominent part in the occupation of Indo-China.

CYCLOP

GERMANY: 1916

Displacement: 4010t full load
Dimensions: 308ft 5in x 64ft 4in x 20ft 8in (94m x 19.6m x 6.3m)
Machinery: two screws, vertical triple expansion; 1800hp
Armament: none
Armour: none
Speed: 9 knots
Range: not established
Complement: 124

***Cyclop* actually began building in the Imperial Yard at Danzig, but because of overcrowding she was finished at Vegesack.**

Completed in 1917 at Danzig, the submarine salvage vessel *Cyclop* was developed from the earlier *Vulcan*, which was designed to be an integrated part of the German submarine force. *Vulcan* had two hulls, rather resembling a large catamaran, but because of the hull shape and large topside, she suffered from very bad seaworthiness. Her successor, *Cyclop*, underwent extensive trials to remedy some of these faults, and was not commissioned until July 1918. At the war's end, *Cyclop* was ceded to Britain. She was scrapped in 1923.

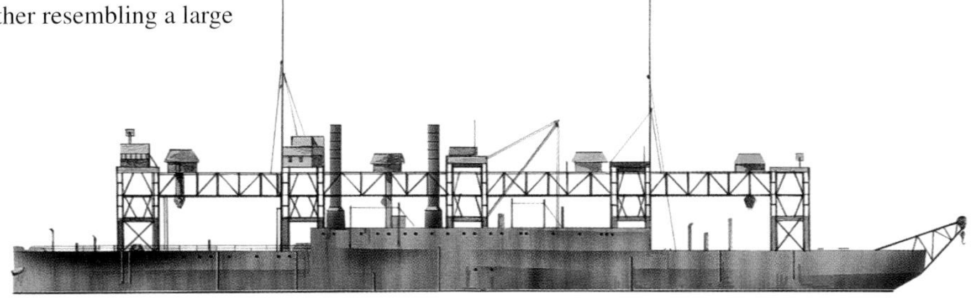

D1

GB: 1908

Displacement: 483t surfaced; 595t submerged
Dimensions: 163ft x 20ft 6in x 10ft 5in (50m x 6m x 3m)
Machinery: two screws, diesels, plus electric motors; 1200/550hp
Armament: three 18in (457mm); one 12pdr
Speed: 14 knots surfaced; 9 knots submerged
Range: 2500nm (4632km) at 10 knots, surfaced
Complement: 25

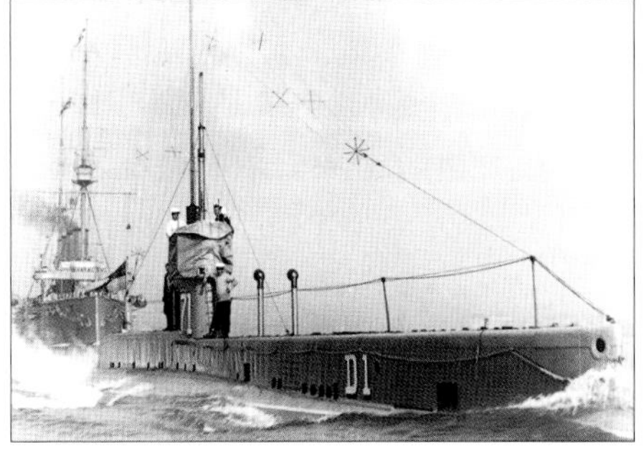

Built in 1908–11, the eight British *D*-class submarines had an increased displacement, diesel engines, and greater internal space.

The *D*-class boats were an improvement on previous submarine designs, introducing diesel engines.

They were intended for deployment on extended patrols away from coastal areas. Unlike earlier classes, the *D*-class boats could send wireless messages as well as receive them. On the outbreak of World War I in August 1914, they were assigned to convoy protection in the English Channel, and to offensive patrol duties in the Heligoland Bight. *D1* was sunk as a floating target in 1918.

Dante Alighieri

ITALY: 1910

Designed by Masdea, *Dante Alighieri* was Italy's first dreadnought. She was also the first battleship to have the main armament mounted in triple turrets, all arranged on the centreline to permit maximum broadside fire.

Following a romantic Italian practice, and a rather unusual one whan applied to a battleship, *Dante Alighieri* was named after a poet.

Laid down at Castellammare in June 1909 and launched on 20 August 1910, *Dante Alighieri* was flagship of the Italian fleet in the southern Adriatic during World War I, but she did not play an active part in hostilities. She was stricken in 1928.

Displacement: 19,500t standard; 21,800t full load
Dimensions: 551ft 6in x 87ft 3in x 30ft 2in (168.1m x 26.6m x 9.2m)
Machinery: four screws, turbines; 32,200hp
Armament: 12 12in (305mm); 20 4.7in (120mm); three 17.7in (450mm) TT
Armour: belt 9.8in-4.7in (250mm-120mm); turrets 11in (280mm)
Speed: 23 knots
Range: 5000nm (9265nm) at 10 knots
Complement: 987

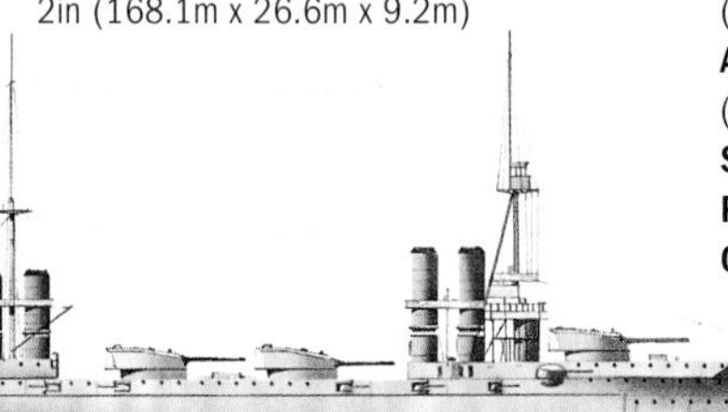

Danton

FRANCE: 1909

Most of the surviving *Danton*-class battleships had been discarded by the late 1920s, some being used as target vessels.

The *Danton* class pre-dreadnought battleships, *Condorcet*, *Danton*, *Diderot*, *Mirabeau*, *Vergniaud* and *Voltaire*, were laid down in 1906. They were the first large French warships to be fitted with turbines. Despite this, they were obsolete when they were laid down, and were not particularly successful. *Danton*, named after the famous leader of the French Revolution, was laid down at Brest in 1908 and launched in July the following year. During the early months of World War I, this battleship served on convoy escort duty in the Mediterranean; she then deployed to the Adriatic in 1915 and the Aegean in 1916. On 19 March 1917, torpedoed twice off Sardinia by the German submarine *U64*, *Danton* sank with the loss of 296 lives. *Voltaire* was also torpedoed twice (in the Aegean, by *UB48*) but survived. Later, in 1923–24, a refit was carried out, but the vessel was discarded, she was used as a target in 1935, and broken up in 1938.

Displacement: 18,318t standard; 19,450t full load
Dimensions: 480ft 11in x 84ft 8in x 30ft 2in (146.6m x 25.8m x 9.2m)
Machinery: four screws, turbines; 22,500hp
Armament: four 12in (305mm); 12 9.4in (240mm); 16 3in (76mm); two 17.7in (250mm) TT
Armour: belt 10in-7.86in (255mm-200mm); main turrets 12.5in (320mm)
Speed: 19 knots
Range: 5100nm (9450km) at 10 knots
Complement: 921

Defence

GB: 1907

The three *Minotaur*-class warships, to which *Defence* belonged, were the last and largest conventional British armoured cruisers. They were actually completed after the first battlecruisers entered service and were of the enlarged *Warrior* type, with displacement increased by 1000t to permit the carriage of heavier armament. *Defence* was sunk by the gunfire of the German battleship *Friedrich der Grosse* at Jutland, with the loss of 893 lives.

Serving in the Mediterranean in the early weeks of World War I, *Defence* took part in the pursuit of the German battlecruiser *Goeben*.

Displacement: 14,600t standard; 16,100t full load
Dimensions: 519ft x 74ft 6in x 26ft (158m x 22.7m x 7.9m)
Machinery: two screws, vertical triple expansion; 27,000hp
Armament: four 9.2in (234mm); ten 7.5in (190mm); 16 12pdr; five 18in (457mm) TT
Armour: belt 6in-3in (152mm-76mm); main turrets 8in-4.5in (203mm-114mm); decks 2in-1in (50-25mm)
Speed: 23 knots
Range: 8150nm (15,102km) at 10 knots
Complement: 755

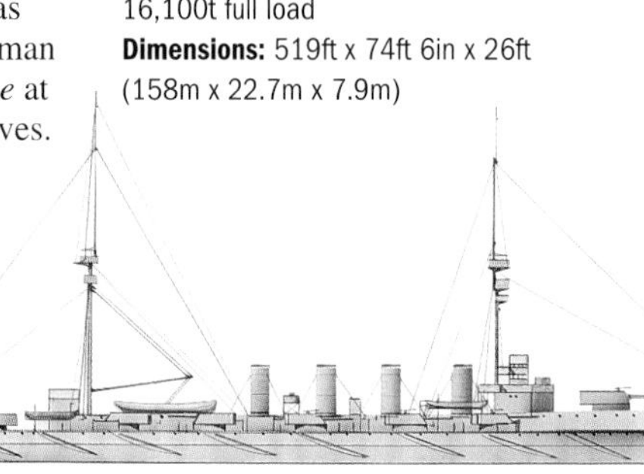

DELAWARE

USA: 1909

The first dreadnoughts built in the United States were the *Michigan* and *South Carolina*. Though laid down after HMS *Dreadnought*, they were in fact the first battleships designed with an 'all big-gun' armament comprising eight 12in (305mm) guns and superfiring turrets, features that were copied by all other nations. Their propulsion system of twin screw, vertical triple expansion engines left much to be desired. The *Delaware* and *North Dakota* suffered similarly, although they were generally a much more successful class with a larger-calibre secondary armament. *Delaware* (BB-28) was launched on 6 February 1909 and assigned to the Atlantic Fleet. During World War I, she was assigned to the British Grand Fleet. She was decommissioned in 1923, sold and broken up at Philadelphia in 1924.

Displacement: 20,380t standard; 22,060t full load
Dimensions: 518ft 9in x 85ft 3in x 28ft 10in (158.1m x 26m x 808m)
Machinery: two screws, vertical triple expansion; 25,000hp
Armament: 10 12in (305mm); 14 5in (127mm); two 21in (533mm) TT
Armour: belt 11in-3in (279mm-76mm); turrets 12in-8in (305mm-203mm); deck/conning tower 12in (305mm)
Speed: 21 knots
Range: 9000nm (16,677km) at 12 knots
Complement: 945

One of the main features of the *Delaware* class was its large-calibre secondary armament, which brought it into line with British battleships of the period.

DELHI

GB: 1918

Delhi was part of the second group of *Danae*-class light cruisers. There were to have been 12 in all, but the last four were cancelled.

One of eight *Danae*-class light cruisers, HMS *Delhi* was launched on 23 August 1918 and completed in May 1919. In the early years of World War II, she served in northern waters, the Mediterranean, and the South Atlantic. After a refit in the United States she joined the Home Fleet, then deployed to the Mediterranean in 1943, where she spent the remainder of the war. She was placed in the reserve in 1945, and was scrapped in May 1948. Only one of this class, HMS *Dunedin*, became a war loss.

Displacement: 4970t standard; 5870t full load
Dimensions: 471ft x 45ft 6in x 16ft 6in (143.6m x 13.9m x 5m)
Machinery: two screws, geared turbines; 40,000hp
Armament: six 6in (152mm); two 3in (76mm); 12 21in (533mm) TT
Armour: belt 3in-1.5in (75mm-40mm); deck 1in (25mm)
Speed: 29 knots
Range: 4500nm (8338km) at 14 knots
Complement: 450

DERFFLINGER

GERMANY: 1913

Derfflinger and her sister ships, *Hindenburg* and *Lutzow*, were without doubt the best capital ships of their day. Launched on 12 July 1913 (after an earlier unsuccessful attempt in June), *Derfflinger* served with the German High Seas Fleet throughout World War I, taking part in the bombardment of the English north-east coast (1914), the Dogger Bank battle (1915), and the Battle of Jutland (1916). Interned at Scapa Flow after the Armistice, she was scuttled there with the rest of the High Seas Fleet.

***Derfflinger* was severely damaged at the Battle of Jutland, suffering 21 heavy shell hits; 157 of her crew were killed.**

Displacement: 26,180t standard; 30,700t full load
Dimensions: 690ft 3in x 95ft 2in x 27ft 3in (210.4m x 29m x 8.3m)
Machinery: four screws, turbines; 63,000hp
Armament: eight 12in (305mm); 12 5.9in (150mmm); four 3.45in (88mm); four 19.7in (450mm) TT
Armour: belt 12in-4in (300mm-100mm); bulkheads 10in-4in (250mm-100mm); turrets 10.7in-3.2in (270mm-80mm)
Speed: 26.5 knots
Range: 5600nm (10,376km) at 14 knots
Complement: 1112 (1391 at Jutland)

DEUTSCHLAND

GERMANY: 1916

Before the United States entered into the war in 1917, the Germans were quick to recognise the potential of large, cargo-carrying submarines as a means of beating the blockade imposed on Germany's ports by the Royal Navy. Two *U151*-class submarines, the *U151* and *U155*, were converted for mercantile use and named *Oldenburg* and *Deutschland* respectively. Both were unarmed. *Deutschland* made one commercial run to the United States before America's involvement in the war brought an end to the venture; she was then converted back to naval use as a submarine cruiser, as was *Oldenburg*. A third merchant conversion, *Bremen*, was lost on her first voyage in 1917, possibly mined off the Orkneys. *Oldenburg* was never commissioned into service as a submarine freighter; by the time she was ready for commercial operations, the United States had entered the war. After the war, *Deutschland* was scrapped in England, at Morecambe in 1922, and *Oldenburg* was sunk as a target off Cherbourg in 1921.

Although the double crossing of the Atlantic by the submarine *Deutschland* was undoubtedly a considerable achievement, it was more of a propaganda success than a commercial one.

Displacement: 1512t surfaced; 1875t submerged
Dimensions: 213ft 3in x 29ft 2in x 17ft 5in (65m x 8.9m x 5.3m)
Machinery: two screws, diesels, plus electric motors, 800bhp/800hp
Armament: none
Speed: 12.4 knots surfaced; 5.2 knots submerged
Range: 11,284nm (20,909km) at 10 knots, surfaced
Complement: 56

DOLPHIN

USA: 1932

Displacement: 1560t surfaced; 2240t submerged
Dimensions: 19ft 3in x 27ft 9in x 13ft 3in (97m x 8.5m x 4m)
Machinery: two screws, diesels, plus electric motors; 3500/1750hp
Armament: six 21in (533mm) TT; one 4in (102mm)
Speed: 17 knots surfaced; 8 knots submerged
Range: 6000nm (1,118km) at 10 knots, surfaced; 50nm (93km) at 10 knots, submerged
Complement: 63

Dolphin was an experimental boat, originally designated V7 and then given the serial number SS169. She was a distinct move away from the large ocean-going submarines that were then popular. However, she was not considered a success due to the attempt to incorporate most of the features of the preceding class into a hull half the size. During World War II, the US Navy relegated *Dolphin* to training duties. She was broken up in 1946. As a matter of interest, the previous class – the *Narwhal* boats – were successful.

The unsuccessful *Dolphin* marked the beginning of a trend away from the large cruiser submarine concept, and a preference for a more modest long-range type.

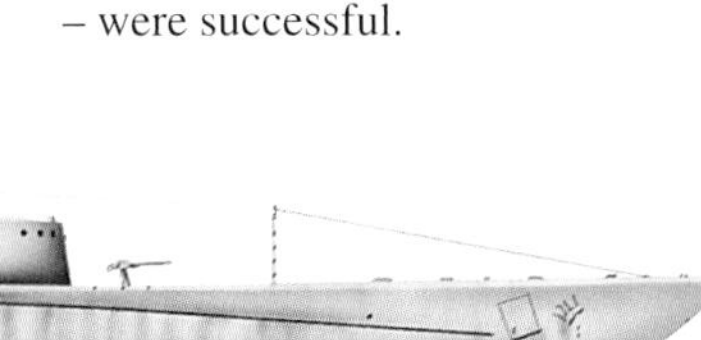

DREADNOUGHT

GB: 1906

Admiral Lord Fisher, who became First Sea Lord in October 1904, was a rarity in Queen Victoria's navy: an excellent sailor with a scientific mind. An exponent of gunnery, he harboured a long-standing ambition to improve the Royal Navy's standard of shooting. During his time in command of the Mediterranean Fleet, he demonstrated that engagements were feasible at ranges of 6000yds (5484m), and that modern guns could achieve an acceptable hit rate at up to 8000yds (7312m), provided they were deliberately aimed and that full salvoes were fired. It followed that the chances of success in a long-range naval duel would rise in direct proportion to the number of large-calibre guns that could be brought into action. By the time he took over as First Sea Lord at the age of 58, Fisher had already put much thought into the concept of a battleship armed with a maximum number of 10in (254mm) guns at the expense of secondary armament. Within weeks of his appointment, he appointed a committee to define a battleship armed with the maximum number of 12in (305mm) guns, the calibre preferred by the Admiralty. The committee was also set up to study the concept of a second type of warship, which would carry a battery of 12in (305mm) guns, and which would have a speed of around 25 knots. This vessel would be in the nature of a hybrid, a cross between a heavy cruiser and a battleship – in other words, a 'battlecruiser'. The 'super-

Displacement: 17,900t standard; 21,845t full load
Dimensions: 527ft x 82ft x 26ft 6in (160.6m x 25m x 8.1m)
Machinery: four screws, turbines; 23,000hp
Armament: 10 12in (305mm); 27 12pdr; five 18in (457mm) TT
Armour: belt and barbettes 11in-4in (279mm-102mm); bulkheads 8in (203mm); turrets 11in (279mm); decks 4in-1in (102mm-25mm)
Speed: 21 knots
Range: 6620nm (12,266km) at 10 knots
Complement: 697

***Dreadnought* had a brief moment of glory in World War I; she rammed and sank the German submarine, *U29*, in the North Sea on 18 March 1915. She was broken up in 1923.**

battleship' concept took shape rapidly, its development spurred on by the acceleration of the international naval arms race. A prototype was laid down by Portsmouth Dockyard in October 1905. Constructed in great secrecy and in record time, the vessel was ready for initial sea trials a year and a day later. The name given to this formidable new ship was *Dreadnought*. She was revolutionary in that she was armed with 10 12in (305mm) guns, two in each of five turrets centrally placed on the ship. (In fact, only eight guns in the first of these ships could be fully brought to bear, but this was remedied in its successors.) From 1906 onwards, a first-class battleship was to be a ship capable of firing 10 heavy guns on either side. Thus, a dreadnought could engage one of the older vessels with a superiority of 10-to-4, or two of them with a superiority of 10-to-8. As well as being the first battleship with main armament of a single calibre, *Dreadnought* was also the first with steam turbines and quadruple screws, which machinery that gave her a top speed of 21 knots. She carried a crew of 697 and displaced 17,900t. Once the concept of the dreadnought had been proven, construction of this revolutionary type of battleship proceeded rapidly, at the rate of three or four per year.

***Dreadnought* was a brilliant concept, and revolutionised naval warfare. Her appearance, however, sparked off a naval arms race between Britain and Germany that quickly became unstoppable.**

DROTTNING VICTORIA

SWEDEN: 1917

Launched on 15 September 1917, *Drottning Victoria* was one of a planned class of four so-called 'coastal battleships' laid down for the Royal Swedish Navy between 1912 and 1915. Economic constraints and other factors meant that only three were completed, the other two being the *Sverige* and *Gustav V*. All three vessels underwent substantial modification over the years, to the point where they became a drain on Sweden's financial resources. However, they were not stricken until the 1950s.

***Drottning Victoria* and *Gustaf V* were both built as icebreakers, the first and only Swedish warships ever assigned this role.**

Displacement: 7125t standard; 7633t full load
Dimensions: 399ft x 61ft x 20ft 4in (121.6m x 18.6m x 6.2m)
Machinery: two screws, geared turbines; 23,910hp
Armament: four 11.1in (283mm); eight 6in (152mm); two 21in (533mm) TT
Armour: belt 7.8in-5.8in (200mm-150mm); turrets 7.8mm-3.9mm (200mm-100mm)
Speed: 22.5 knots
Range: not known
Complement: 427

DUGUAY-TROUIN

FRANCE: 1923

During her war service with the Allies, *Duguay-Trouin* took part in the invasion of Provence, August 1944, as part of the Flank Force.

Authorised in 1922, the *Duguay-Trouin*-class cruisers were the first major French warship design after World War I. The three vessels, *Duguay-Trouin*, *Lamotte-Picquet*, and *Primaguet*, were generally considered to be successful and seaworthy vessels, and were well armed: their armament included eight 6.1in (155mm) guns. This gun was also in use with the French Army, and could fire four rounds per minute to a distance of 21,000yds (19,200m). *Duguay-Trouin* was disarmed at Alexandria in 1940, but later joined the Free French; she was broken up in 1952.

Displacement: 7249t standard; 9350t full load
Dimensions: 595ft 9in x 56ft 5in x 17ft (181.6m x 17.2m x 5.2m)
Machinery: four screws, geared turbines; 100,000hp
Armament: eight 6.1in (155mm); four 3in (76mm); 12 21.7in (550mm) TT
Armour: turrets 1in (25mm); main deck 0.75in (19mm)
Speed: 33 knots
Range: 4500 (8338km) at 15 knots
Complement: 578

DUNKERQUE

FRANCE: 1935

Modelled on the Royal Navy's *Nelson* class, *Dunkerque* and her sister ship *Strasbourg* were the French Navy's fastest battleships at the outbreak of World War II, in September 1939. They formed the nucleus of a fast raiding force, based on the Atlantic port of Brest, that also included seven heavy cruisers, three light cruisers, and some 50 destroyers. These French warships were capable of a sustained speed of 30 knots which, at that time, could not be matched by any other naval force in the world. *Dunkerque* was launched on 2 October 1935. After the fall of France, she joined other French warships at Mers-el-Kebir in North Africa where, on 3 July 1940, she was attacked and heavily damaged by British warships. Three days later, she was damaged again and partly sunk by Swordfish torpedo-bombers. She was refloated and sailed to Toulon, where she was blown up in dry dock on 27 November 1942 when German forces occupied the port.

Displacement: 25,500t standard; 33,000t full load
Dimensions: 703ft 9in x 102ft x 31ft 6in (214.5m x 31.1m x 9.6m)
Machinery: four screws, geared turbines; 100,000hp
Armament: eight 12.9in (330mm); 16 5in (130mm) DP; eight 37mm AA
Armour: belt 8.8in-4.9in (225mm-125mm); turrets 13.5in-13in (345mm-330mm); deck 5.5in-5in (140mm-130mm)
Speed: 30 knots
Range: 7500nm (13,897nm) at 15 knots
Complement: 1431

***Dunkerque's* hulk was undocked in August 1945, and was designated Q56. Classed as damaged beyond repair, it was broken up in 1958.**

E11

GB: 1913

The victorious *E11* returning to Malta after a successful Mediterranean patrol. The *E*-class boats performed well in this theatre.

Completed from 1913 through to 1916, the *E*-class submarines ran to 55 hulls. Once war was declared, construction work was shared between 13 private yards. Five major groups were built, differences, being primarily in torpedo layout and the adaptation of six boats to carry 20 mines in place of ther midships tubes. *E11*, under the commander of the talented Lieutenant-Commander Martin Nasmith, was arguably the most famous of them all. She scored many successes, including the sinking of the Turkish battleship *Hairredin Barbarossa*. For these operations in the Dardanelles, the British submarines adopted a blue camouflage to conceal themselves in the shallow, clear waters. The class was also active in the North Sea and the Baltic; in 1916–17, some of the boats operating in these areas were fitted with high-angle 3in (76mm) or 12pdr guns for anti-aircraft defence. In all, 22 *E*-class boats were lost.

Displacement: 667t surfaced; 807t submerged
Dimensions: 181ft x 22ft 8in x 12ft 6in (55.17m x 6.91m x 3.81m)
Machinery: two screws, diesels, plus two electric motors; 1600/840hp
Armament: five 18in (457mm) TT; one 12pdr
Speed: 14 knots surfaced; 9 knots submerged
Range: 300nm (560km) at 10 knots, surfaced
Complement: 30

EAGLE

GB: 1918

Displacement: 22,600t standard; 26,400t full load
Dimensions: 667ft x 92ft 9in x 27ft (203.3m x 28.3m x 8.2m)
Machinery: four screws, geared turbines; 50,000hp
Armament: nine 6in (152mm); five 4in (102mm) AA
Armour: belt 4.5in (114mm); deck 1.5in (38mm)
Speed: 24 knots
Range: 4400nm (8153nm) at 10 knots
Complement: 748

Originally laid down as a battleship for Chile, and acquired in 1917 for conversion to an aircraft carrier, *Eagle* was extensively modified after trials and rebuilt in 1922–23, when she was fitted with a full-length flightdeck and heavy armament. She was the first aircraft carrier with an island superstructure. In the early months of World War II, *Eagle* was in the West Indies, subsequently deploying to the Mediterranean. On 11 August 1942, she was torpedoed and sunk by the German submarine *U73* during a Malta convoy support operation.

***Eagle* met her end while providing support for Operation Pedestal, the attempt to run a supply convoy to Malta during August 1942.**

EAGLE BOAT

USA: 1919

Displacement: 500t standard; 615t full load
Dimensions: 200ft 10in x 33ft 2in x 8ft 6in (61.2m x 10.1m x 2.6m)
Machinery: single screw, geared turbine; 2500hp
Armament: two 4in (102mm); one 3in (76mm)
Armour: steel hull; no special protection
Speed: 18.3 knots
Range: 3500nm (6485km) at 10 knots
Complement: 61

Most of the *Eagle*-class boats were relegated to reserve training in the 1920s, and some were used for underwater sound experiments.

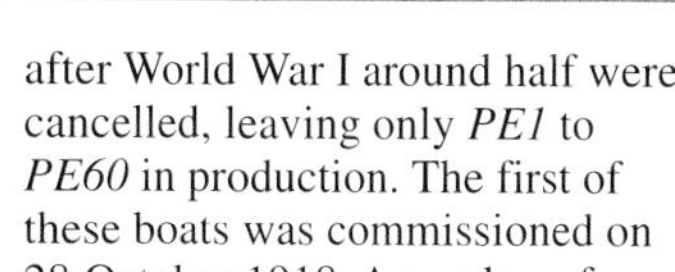

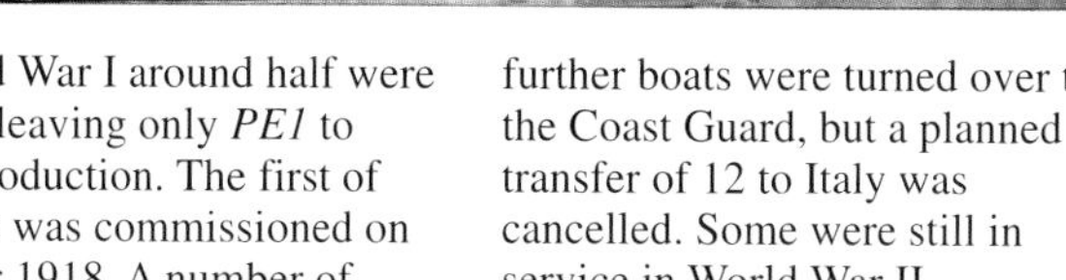

The US Navy's *Eagle*-class patrol vessels were designed as an inexpensive yet efficient substitute for destroyers, intended for anti-submarine warfare operations in open water. The original plan was to build 112 units, but immediately after World War I around half were cancelled, leaving only *PE1* to *PE60* in production. The first of these boats was commissioned on 28 October 1918. A number of further boats were turned over to the Coast Guard, but a planned transfer of 12 to Italy was cancelled. Some were still in service in World War II.

EDGAR QUINET

FRANCE: 1907

Displacement: 13,847t standard
Dimensions: 521ft 4in x 70ft 7in x 27ft 7in (158.9m x 21.51m x 8.41m)
Machinery: triple screws, vertical triple expansion; 36,000hp
Armament: 14 7.6in (194mm); 20 9pdrs; two 18in (457mm) TT
Armour: belt 6in-1.5in (152mm-38mm); turrets 8in (203mm)
Speed: 23 knots
Range: 5300nm (9820nm) at 10 knots
Complement: 859

The *Edgar Quinet* and her sister ship, the *Waldeck-Rousseau*, were the most powerful French armoured cruisers. As was the case with other French warships of this period, both vessels were virtually obsolete by the time they were completed. In World War I, the *Edgar Quinet*, together with the cruisers *Jules Michelet* and *Ernest Renan*, formed the 1st Light Division, which hunted for the German warships *Goeben* and *Breslau*. Later, on 4 January 1930, the *Edgar Quinet* foundered off Algeria after striking an uncharted rock.

Converted as a training ship, the *Edgar Quinet* saw much service in the Mediterranean in the 1920s. She was modified to carry two floatplanes.

EMANUELE FILIBERTO DUCA D'AOSTA

ITALY: 1935

There were 12 *Condottieri*-class light cruisers in all, named after famous Italian conductors. The *Emanuele Filiberto Duca D'Aosta*, together with her sister ship, *Eugenio di Savoia*, formed the fourth group. In general, the armoured protection of the *Condottieri*s was inadequate against gunfire from British cruisers. Of the class, five were sunk in World War II: three by submarines, one in a naval gunnery action, and one by aerial bombing. Both *Duca D'Aosta* and *Eugenio di Savoia* saw a great deal of war service, much of their activity involving convoy escort and running essential supplies to the Axis forces in North Africa. However, both vessels survived. *Duca D'Aosta* was ceded to the Soviet Union early in 1949 under the designation Z.15. Fully commissioned in the Soviet Navy, she was re-named *Stalingrad* and later became the *Kerch*. She was discarded in around 1957. Her sister ship, *Eugenio di Savoia*, was transferred to Greece in July 1951 and re-named *Helle*. She was removed from the active list in 1964.

The *Duca D'Aosta* and *Eugenio di Savoia* were very fast ships, making over 37 knots during their trials. Maximum sea speed was 34 knots.

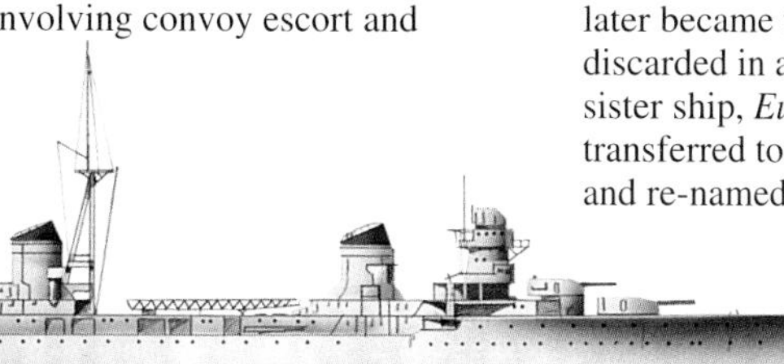

Displacement: 8317t standard; 10,374t full load
Dimensions: 613ft 2in x 57ft 5in x 21ft 4in (186.9m x 17.5m x 6.5m)
Machinery: two screws, geared turbines; 110,000hp
Armament: eight 6in (152mm); six 3.9in (100mm) AA; six 21in (533mm) TT
Armour: belt 2.75in (70mm); bulkheads 2in-1.2in (50mm-30mm); turrets 3.5in (90mm)
Speed: 36.5 knots
Range: 4300nm (7968km)
Complement: 578 (694 during war service)

EMANUELE PESSAGNO

ITALY: 1929

Displacement: 1943t standard; 2580t full load
Dimensions: 352ft x 33ft 6in x 11ft 2in (107.3m x 10m x 3.4m)
Machinery: two screws, geared turbines; 50,000hp
Armament: six 4.7in (120mm); two 40mm AA; six 21in (533mm) TT
Armour: belt 3in (76mm)
Speed: 32 knots
Range: 1850nm (3428km) at 10 knots
Complement: 225

The *Emanuele Pessagno* was ordered in 1926 and launched in August 1929. She saw extensive service in World War II, as did the other 11 vessels which comprised the *Navigation* class. When first completed, the vessels were classified as scouts, but by 1938 they were listed as destroyers. Only one vessel survived the war; eight were sunk in combat, two were scuttled and one was mined. In May 1942, the *Emanuele Pessagno*, while escorting Italian supply convoys to Benghazi, was torpedoed and sunk by the British submarine HMS *Turbulent* (Commander Linton).

The *Navigatori*-class destroyers, to which the *Emanuele Pessagno* belonged, were ordered to counter the large French destroyers of the *Jaguar* and *Guepard* classes.

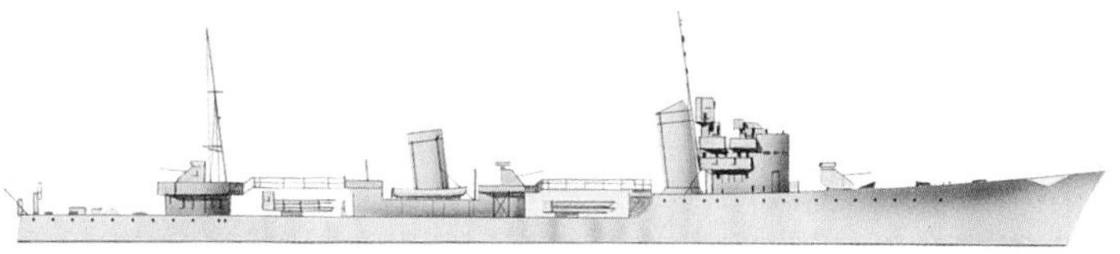

EMDEN

GERMANY: 1908

One of the most famous warships of the 20th century, the German light cruiser *Emden* served in Far Eastern waters from 1909, providing support for the various German colonies in the region. At the outbreak of World War I, she was at Tsingtao in China and, on the orders of Admiral von Spee, she sailed immediately to begin independent commerce raiding. In September 1914 she appeared in the Bay of Bengal, where she began her spree of merchant sinkings interspersed with shore bombardments. Her sudden appearance off Madras on 22 September, where she bombarded the Burma Company's oil storage tanks, caused widespread alarm, and the mere fact of her presence caused delays in the sailing of troopships from Calcutta to the Middle East. On 9 November, after further merchant sinkings, she destroyed the wireless station at the Cocos Islands, but on that same day she was intercepted by the Australian cruiser HMAS *Sydney*, which had been detached from convoy escort duties. Following the first sea battle in the history of the Royal Australian Navy, *Emden* was left ablaze and beached on the reefs off North Keeling Island. The survivors of her crew managed to capture a schooner and a steamer and reached Mecca, from where they embarked on an adventurous journey across Saudi Arabia, Syria and Turkey to Constantinople, arriving back in Germany to be hailed as heroes. *Emden*'s sister ship, *Dresden*, fought in the Falklands battle and embarked on commerce raiding in the Pacific. On 14 March 1915, she was caught by British warships and scuttled after being shelled into submission.

The wreck of the *Emden* remained stranded on its reef for 40 years. In the 1950s, it was was partially dismantled by a Japanese company.

Displacement: 3664t standard; 4268t full load
Dimensions: 386ft 10in x 44ft 4in x 18ft (117.9m x 13.5m x 5.5m)
Machinery: two screws, vertical triple-expansion engines; 13,500hp
Armament: ten 4.1in (105mm); two 17.7in (450mm) TT
Armour: deck 1.75in-0.75in (30mm-20mm); gunshields 2in (50mm)
Speed: 23.5 knots
Range: 3760nm (6967km) at 12 knots
Complement: 361

EMDEN

GERMANY: 1925

Launched on 7 January 1925, *Emden* was the first medium-sized German warship built after World War I. Originally coal-fired, she converted to oil in 1934. Intended primarily for overseas service, she made nine foreign cruises as a training ship from 1926. In World War II, after service as a minelayer and as an escort during the Norwegian campaign, she deployed to the Baltic for operations in support of the German Army during the invasion of Russia. Damaged by a bombing attack, she was scuttled at Kiel in April 1945.

One of the last tasks of *Emden* during World War II was to evacuate the coffin of Field Marshal von Hindenburg from Konigsberg before the Russians arrived.

Displacement: 5600t standard; 6990t full load
Dimensions: 508ft 10in x 46ft 11in x 19ft (155.1m x 14.3m x 5.8m)
Machinery: twin screws, geared turbines; 45,900hp
Armament: eight 5.9in (150mm); three 3.5in (88mm); four 21in (533mm (TT)
Armour: belt 1.5in (38mm); deck 0.75in (20mm); gunshields 2in (50mm)
Speed: 29.4 knots
Range: 4600nm (8524km) at 18 knots
Complement: 650

EMERALD

GB: 1920

Ordered in March 1918, the three *Emerald*-class light cruisers, *Emerald*, *Enterprise*, and *Euphrates* had their origin in a British Naval Staff requirement for warships capable of intercepting the fast German minelayers *Brummer* and *Bremse*. The essential requirement was speed, rather than armament and endurance. *Emerald* was completed in 1926, and served on convoy escort duty in the Atlantic and with the Eastern Fleet in World War II. She was scrapped in 1948.

Of the three *Emerald*-class vessels, *Euphrates* was cancelled in November 1918, soon after the Armistice. She was never launched.

Displacement: 7300t standard; 9450t full load
Dimensions: 570ft x 54ft 6in x 18ft 6in (173.7m x 16.6m x 5.6m)
Machinery: four-screws, geared turbines; 80,000hp
Armament: seven 6in (152mm); five 4in (102mm); 12 21in (533mm) TT
Armour: belt 3in-1.75in (76mm-38mm); deck 1in-0.5in (25mm-15mm)
Speed: 33 knots
Range: 4800nm (8894km) at 15 knots
Complement: 450

EMILE BERTIN

FRANCE: 1933

Displacement: 5886t standard; 8480t full load
Dimensions: 580ft 8in x 52ft 6in x 21ft 8in (177m x 16m x 6.6m)
Machinery: four screws, geared turbines; 102,000hp
Armament: nine 6in (152mm); four 3.5in (89mm) AA; six 21.7in (550mm) TT
Armour: deck and magazine protection 1in (25mm)
Speed: 34 knots
Range: 6000nm (11,118km) at 15 knots
Complement: 567 (711 during war service)

Launched on 5 May 1933, the light cruiser *Emile Bertin* saw pre-war service as the flagship of a squadron of 12 super-destroyers of the *Malin* and *Maille Breze* classes, tasked with anti-submarine and anti-commerce raider operations in the Atlantic. The French collapse in June 1940 found her at Martinique, where she was immobilised and disarmed along with the aircraft carrier *Bearn*. She was broken up in 1959.

***Emile Bertin* underwent an extensive refit in the USA in 1944–45, during which her armament was modernised and her aircraft catapult removed.**

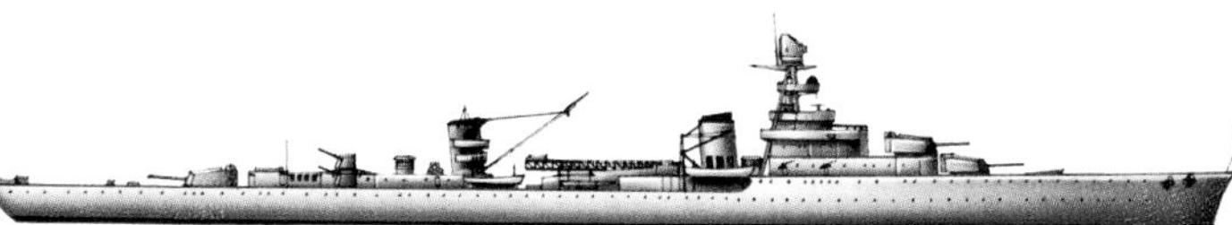

ENGADINE

GB: 1911

The last of three cross-Channel steamers impressed into Royal Navy service on the outbreak of World War I, *Engadine* was fitted out as a seaplane carrier with hangar space for three aircraft. On 24 December, from a position in the German Bight, she launched her seaplanes in an unsuccessful attack on the Zeppelin sheds at Nordholz. At Jutland in 1916, one of her Short seaplanes shadowed the German High Seas Fleet and made abortive attempts to radio its position to *Engadine*.

During the Battle of Jutland, *Engadine* took the damaged cruiser *Warrior* under tow, and rescued 600 of her crew when she sank.

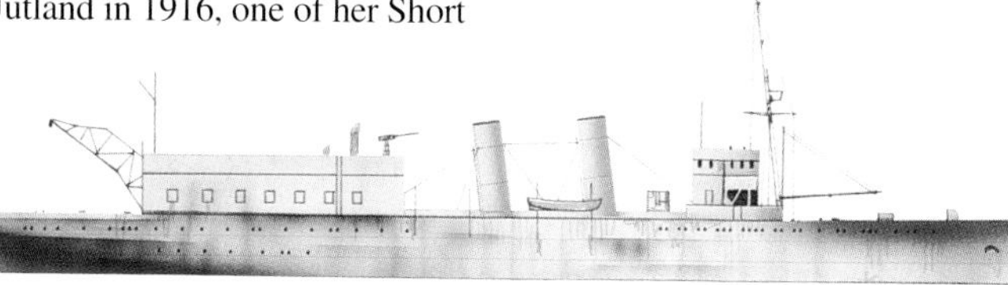

Displacement: 1881t standard; 1676t full load
Dimensions: 316ft x 41ft x 16ft (96.3m x 12.5m x 4.9m)
Machinery: triple screws, turbines; 6000hp
Armament: two 4in (102mm); one 6pdr
Armour: none
Speed: 21.5 knots
Range: not known
Complement: 250

ERIN

GB: 1913

Displacement: 22,780t standard; 25,250t full load
Dimensions: 559ft 6in x 91ft 7in x 28ft 5in (170.5m x 27.9m x 8.7m)
Machinery: four screws, turbines; 26,500hp
Armament: 10 13.5in (345mm); 16 6in (152mm); four 21in (533mm) TT
Armour: belt 12in-4in (300mm-100mm); bulkheads 8in-4in (200mm-100mm); deck 3in-1.5in (76mm-38mm); turret faces 11in (280mm)
Speed: 21 knots
Range: 5300nm (9821km) at 10 knots
Complement: 1070

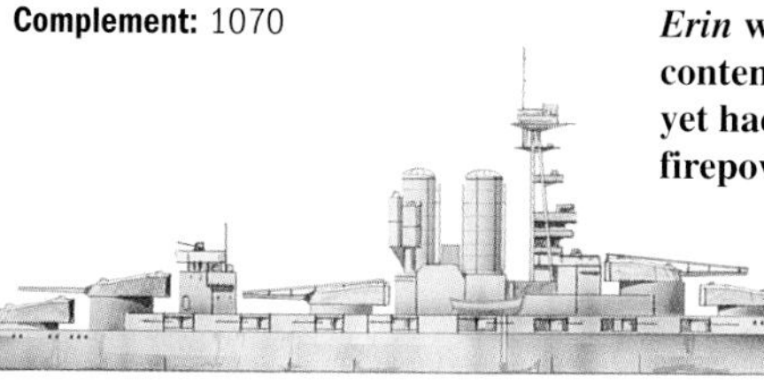

The dreadnought *Sultan Mehmed Reshad V* was originally laid down at Vickers Shipbuilders in 1911 for the Turkish Navy. She was renamed *Reshadieh* before being launched on 3 September 1913, and was virtually complete when she was seized by the British government on the outbreak of World War I in August 1914. Renamed HMS *Erin*, she served with the Grand Fleet throughout the war, and fought in the Battle of Jutland. She was broken up in December 1922.

***Erin* was shorter and wider than contemporary British battleships, yet had the formidable offensive firepower of an *Iron Duke* type.**

ESPANA

SPAIN: 1912

The three vessels of the *Espana* class, *Espana*, *Alfonso XIII* and *Jaime I*, were the smallest battleships of the dreadnought type ever constructed. Built in Spain with British technical assistance, their relatively small size was explained by the reluctance of the Spanish government to incur the additional expense of building new docks, or rebuilding existing ones. *Espana* was lost on 26 August 1923 when she hit an uncharted reef in dense fog off Cape Tres Forces, near Mililla, Morocco.

***Espana* and her sister ships paid the price for the Spanish government's cost-cutting exercise.**

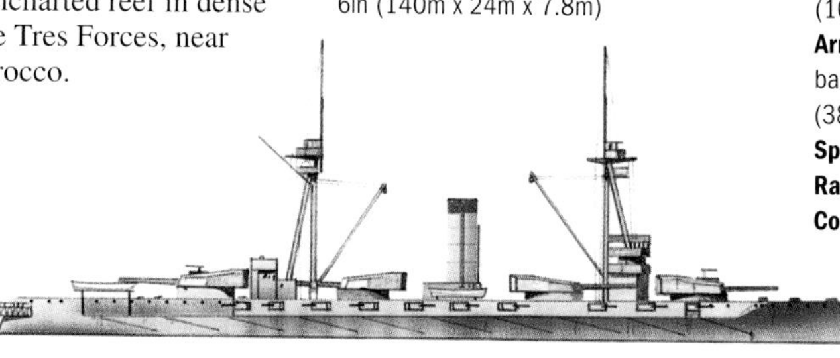

Displacement: 15,452t standard; 15,700t full load
Dimensions: 459ft 2in x 78ft 9in x 25ft 6in (140m x 24m x 7.8m)
Machinery: four screws, turbines; 15,500hp
Armament: eight 12in (305mm); 20 4in (102mm)
Armour: belt 8in-4in (203mm-102mm); barbettes 10in (254mm); deck 1.5in (38mm)
Speed: 19.5 knots
Range: 5000nm (9265km) at 10 knots
Complement: 854

EXETER

GB: 1929

Launched on 18 July 1929, the cruiser HMS *Exeter* became famous for her part in the action against the German armoured ship – the 'pocket battleship' – *Admiral Graf Spee* off Montevideo in December 1939. During this engagement she received direct hits from seven 11in (280mm) shells, and took splinter damage from several more which dropped short. She was out of action for 14 months, returning to service just in time to take part in the hunt for the German battleship *Bismarck* in May 1941. She later deployed to the Far East, and took part in combined naval operations against the Japanese in the Dutch East Indies, forming part of the Allied Eastern Force under Admiral Doorman. During the Battle of the Java Sea, she was hit in the aft boiler room by an 8in (203mm) shell, reducing her speed to 16 knots; two days later on 1 March 1942, she became trapped between two Japanese naval forces. Together with the destroyer *Encounter*, the *Exeter* was sunk by gunfire and torpedoes from the destroyer *Inazuma*.

Exeter was similar to the cruiser HMS *York*, launched a year earlier, but had vertical funnels.

Displacement: 8390t standard; 10,490t full load
Dimensions: 575ft x 58ft x 20ft 3in (175.25m x 17.68m x 6.17m)
Machinery: four screws, geared turbines; 80,000hp
Armament: six 8in (203mm); four 4in (102mm); six 21in (533mm) TT
Armour: box protection to ammunition spaces 4in-1in (100mm-25mm); side 3in (76mm); turrets 1in (25mm)
Speed: 32 knots
Range: 5200nm (9635km) at 12 knots
Complement: 630

FAULKNOR GB/CHILE: 1914

Displacement: 1610t standard; 2000t full load
Dimensions: 330ft 10in x 32ft 6in x 21ft 1in (100m x 10m x 6.4m)
Machinery: twin screws, turbines; 30,000hp
Armament: six 4in (102mm); four 21in (533mm) TT
Armour: belt 3in (76mm)
Speed: 31 knots
Range: 2000nm (3706km) at 10 knots
Complement: 197

In 1912, the ship builder J. S. White designed four large, powerful destroyers ordered by the Chilean Navy. One of these, the *Almirante Simpson*, was taken over by the Royal Navy in August 1914 and renamed *Faulknor*. In 1915, she joined other light forces in hunting U-boats in the Irish Sea, and in November 1916 she operated intensively against submarine traffic off the Norwegian coast. After World War I, Faulknor was refitted and returned to Chile, where she served until she was removed from the effective list in 1933.

Chile's decision to acquire a powerful, modern fleet had its origins in a border dispute with Argentina dating from the 1890s.

FLORIDA USA: 1910

Displacement: 21,825t standard; 23,033t full load
Dimensions: 521ft 6in x 88ft 3in x 30ft 4in (159m x 26.9m x 9.1m)
Machinery: four screws, turbines; 28,000hp
Armament: 10 12in (305mm); 16 5in (127mm); two 21in (533mm) TT
Armour: belt 11in-3in (279mm-76mm); turrets 12in-8in (305mm-203mm)
Speed: 20.75 knots
Range: 6720nm (12,452km) at 10 knots
Complement: 1000

The two *Florida*-class dreadnoughts, *Florida* and *Utah*, were improved *Delawares*, completed with five twin turrets. They were the first US battleships with four shafts. *Florida* (BB-30) was launched on 12 May 1910, and completed in September the following year. She was assigned to the Atlantic fleet, and served with the British Grand Fleet from 1917 to 1919, escorting convoys and assisting in the repatriation of American froces from France. She was broken up in 1931.

The completion of the *Florida*-class ships was delayed by changes in design, and by failure to deliver turbine casings.

FROBISHER GB: 1920

The *Frobisher* was a *Cavendish*-class cruiser. These ships were designed specifically for long-range operations against armed commerce raiders, the British Admiralty being conscious of the fact that, in 1914, efforts to hunt down these elusive vessels had seriously overstretched the Royal Navy's light cruiser squadrons. *Frobisher* was launched on 20 March 1920, but was not completed until 1924. She was rearmed for service in World War II and broken up in 1949.

Of the other *Cavendish*-class cruisers, *Effingham* and *Raleigh* were wrecked, *Hawkins* was scrapped, and *Cavendish* became the carrier *Vindictive*.

Displacement: 9750t standard; 12,190t full load
Dimensions: 605ft x 65ft x 19ft 3in (184.4m x 19.8m x 5.9m)
Machinery: four screws, geared turbines; 65,000hp
Armament: seven 7.5in (190mm); six 12pdr; six 21in (533mm) TT
Armour: belt 3in-1.5in (76mm-40mm); deck 1.5in-1in (38mm-25mm)
Speed: 30.5 knots
Range: 4500nm (8338nm) at 12 knots
Complement: 712

FURIOUS

GB: 1916

Displacement: 19,513t standard; 22,890t full load
Dimensions: 786ft 6in x 88ft x 21ft (239.7m x 26.8m x 6.4m)
Machinery: four screws, geared turbines; 90,000hp
Armament: two 18in (457mm); 11 5.5in (140mm); two 21in (533mm) TT
Armour: belt and bulkheads 3in-2in (75mm-50mm); turret faces 9in (230mm); decks 3in-0.75in (76mm-20mm)
Speed: 31.5 knots
Range: 6000nm (11,118km) at 12 knots
Complement: 880

Launched on 15 August 1916, the light battlecruiser *Furious* was a modified *Courageous* type, designed with two 18in (457mm) guns in two single turrets. In 1917, in the course of a refit, one of her 18in guns was removed, together with her mainmast, and a hangar and flightdeck installed aft. Recommissioned in March 1918, her aircraft successfully attacked the Zeppelin sheds at Tondern on 19 July. In 1921–25, *Furious* was fully converted to aircraft carrier status with the fitting of a complete flightdeck. During World War II, after two refits in the 1930s, she served in northern waters, including the Norwegian campaign. Later, she ferried vital aircraft reinforcements to the besieged island of Malta, and formed part of the covering force during the Allied invasion of North Africa in November 1942. After further operations in northern waters against the battleship *Tirpitz*, she was placed in reserve in 1944 and broken up in 1948.

***Furious* was virtually complete when, on 17 March 1917, the Admiralty decided to convert her to a carrier, the Grand Fleet then being short of aircraft.**

FURUTAKA

JAPAN: 1925

Furutaka and her sister ship *Kako* were authorised in 1922; the first Japanese heavy cruisers built to the restrictions by the Washington Treaty. They were part of the crash building programme designed to compensate, at least in part, for the capital ships that had had to be cancelled under the terms of the Treaty. During World War II both ships formed part of the 6th Cruiser Squadron; both were sunk during the heavy fighting at Guadalcanal, *Furutaka* being destroyed by the American cruiser *Boise* on 11 October 1942.

The *Furutaka* class were designed by Vice-Admiral Y. Higara. They incorporated new techniques pioneered in the building of the cruiser *Yubari*.

Displacement: 7100t standard; 8450t full load
Dimensions: 607ft 6in x 51ft 9in x 18ft 3in (185.17m x 15.77m x 5.56m)
Machinery: four screws, geared turbines; 102,000hp
Armament: six 8in (203mm); four 3in (76mm) AA; 12 24in (609mm) TT
Armour: belt 3in (76mm); deck 1.5in (38mm)
Speed: 34.5 knots
Range: 3800nm (7041km)
Complement: 625

FUSO

JAPAN: 1914

At the time of her completion, in November 1915, *Fuso* was the most powerfully armed and fastest battleship in the world. Her main turrets were all mounted on the centreline and she featured two tripod masts of uneven height. Fire-control platforms were added to these during a refit in 1927–28; new AA armament and searchlights were also fitted. *Fuso* and her sister ship *Yamashiro* were both reconstructed in 1930–35, new engines and boilers being fitted, the forward funnel removed, anti-torpedo bulges added, the elevation of the main battery increased, and the tripod masts replaced by towers fore and aft. Catapults were installed on the 'P' turret of *Fuso* and on the stern of *Yamashiro*. Until the Battle of Leyte Gulf, *Fuso* had seen little action in World War II. However, on 24 October, 1944 the Japanese Fleet approached Leyte sailing in two forces, the Centre and Southern. The Centre Force was attacked by four waves of American carrier-borne aircraft; during these attacks the battleship *Musashi* was hit by 10 bombs and six torpedoes and sank in about eight hours, with the loss of 1039 of her crew. Her sister ship, *Yamato*, was also hit by two bombs, but they had little effect on her. The Southern Force was then engaged by the battleships *West Virginia*, *California*, *Tennessee*, *Maryland*, and *Mississippi*, as well as American and Australian cruisers. *Fuso* was sunk by gunfire and torpedoes in Surigao Strait. *Yamashiro* sank, hit by numerous shells and three torpedoes, Vice-Admiral Nishimura going down with her.

A plan to convert *Fuso* and *Yamashiro* to 'carrier battleships', with a flightdeck installed in place of the after turrets, was abandoned.

Displacement: 30,600t standard; 35,900t full load
Dimensions: 673ft x 94ft x 28ft 3in (205.1m x 28.7m x 8.6m)
Machinery: four screws, turbines; 40,000hp
Armament: 12 14in (355mm); 16 6in (152mm); five 21in (533mm) TT
Armour: belt 12in-4in (305mm-102mm); turrets 12in-4.5in (305mm-114mm); deck 2in (50mm)
Speed: 22.5 knots
Range: 8000nm (14,824km) at 14 knots
Complement: 1193

G101

GERMANY: 1914

Displacement: 1116t standard; 1843t full load
Dimensions: 321ft 6in x 30ft 9in x 12ft 9in (98m x 9.4m x 3.9m)
Machinery: two screws, turbines; 28,000hp
Armament: four 3.3in (85mm); six 20in (508mm) TT
Armour: belt 3in (76mm)
Speed: 33.5 knots
Range: 2000nm (3706km) at 12 knots
Complement: 104

One of a quartet of *G*-class destroyers laid down in 1914 for Argentina at the yard of Germaniawerft, Kiel, *G101* was originally named *Santiago*. She and her sister ships were completed in 1915 but taken over by the German Navy. Had these vessels entered service with the Argentine Navy, they would have been among the most powerful destroyers in South American waters. All four were interned after World War I, and scuttled by their crews at Scapa Flow on 21 June 1919. *G101* was raised and later taken to the USA where she was scrapped at Charleston in 1926.

After the war, raised from Scapa Flow, *G102* was sunk as a target in 1920, *G103* sank in a heavy gale in 1925, and *G104* was scrapped.

Galatea

GB: 1914

Displacement: 3750t standard, 4400t full load
Dimensions: 436ft x 39ft x 13ft 5in (132.9m x 11.9m x 4.1m)
Machinery: four screws, turbines; 40,000hp
Armament: two 6in (152mm); six 4in (102mm; four 21in (533mm) TT
Armour: belt 3in-1in (76mm-25mm); deck 1in (25mm)
Speed: 28.5 knots
Range: 2500nm (4632km) at 15 knots
Complement: 276

The *Arethusa* class of eight light cruisers, of which *Galatea* was one, was built in response to an urgent Admiralty requirement. These vessels were to have enough speed to match that of the latest destroyers, and subsequently would not carry as much armour as traditional 'scout' cruisers, but they would have better protection than destroyers. Winston Churchill, then First Lord of the Admiralty, invented a name for them: 'Light Armoured Cruisers.' *Galatea* was broken up in 1921.

On 4 May 1916, *Galatea* together with her sister ship *Phaeton* shot down Zeppelin L7 off the island of Sylt.

Gangut

IMPERIAL RUSSIA/USSR: 1911

Gangut and her three sister ships, *Petropavlovsk*, *Poltava* and *Sevastopol*, were the first Imperial Russian Navy dreadnoughts. Their original design was modified to include ice-breaking bows. *Gangut* was launched on 7 October 1911, and served with the Baltic Fleet during World War I. After the Russian Revolution, she was re-named *Oktyabrskaya Revolutsia* and became part of the Red Fleet. During World War II she took part in the defence of Leningrad, where she was severely damaged by German bombs. She was broken up in 1956–59.

***Gangut* was named in honour of the great Russian naval battle fought on 27 July 1714, resulting in victory over Sweden.**

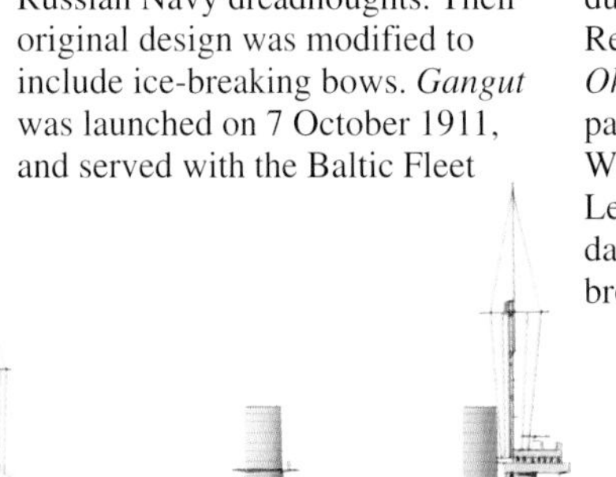

Displacement: 23,400t standard; 25,850t full load
Dimensions: 600ft x 87ft x 27ft 3in (182.9m x 26.5m x 8.3m)
Machinery: two screws, vertical quadruple expansion engines; 50,000hp
Armament: 12 12in (305mm); 16 4.7in (120mm); four 17.7in (450mm) TT
Armour: belt 10in-3.9in (279mm-100mm); turrets 12in-4.9in (305mm-125mm); deck 3in (76mm)
Speed: 24.6 knots
Range: 4000nm (7412km) at 16 knots
Complement: 1125

Garland

GB: 1913

HMS *Garland* was one of the *Acasta* class of 20 destroyers, built as part of Britain's 1911–12 naval construction programme. Designed to counter the, not inconsiderable, threat posed by the latest German destroyers, the *Acasta*s were to be armed with two 4in (102mm) guns, plus four 12pdrs. However, three 4in (102mm) guns were chosen instead, making them the most powerful destroyers of the period. Ships of this class were normally deployed in support of the Royal Navy's light cruiser forces.

Displacement: 1072t standard; 1300t full load
Dimensions: 267ft 6in x 27ft x 9ft 6in (81.5m x 8.2m x 2.9m)
Machinery: two screws, semi-geared turbines; 24,500shp
Armament: three 4in (102mm); two 21in (533mm) TT
Armour: belt 3in (76mm)
Speed: 29 knots
Range: not known
Complement: 73

HMS *Garland* was one of the *Acasta* class destroyers. Built by Cammell Laird, she was originally to have been named *Kenwulf*.

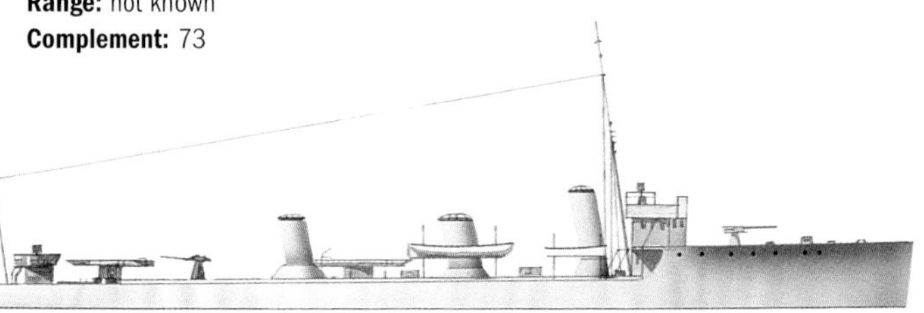

GEORGIA

USA: 1904

The pre-dreadnought battleship USS *Georgia* (BB-15) was one of five *Virginia*-class warships, laid down under the authority of the Navy Act of 1902. This class reintroduced superimposed 8in (203mm) turrets, with the result that the ships rolled excessively. The torpedo tubes were installed after completion. *Georgia* served with the Atlantic Fleet during World War I, and made five transatlantic voyages as a troop transport. She served with the Pacific Fleet in 1919–20, and was broken up in 1923.

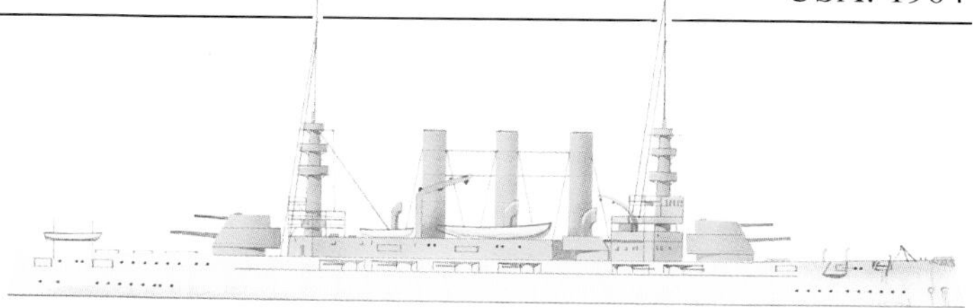

Displacement: 14,948t standard; 16,094t full load
Dimensions: 441ft 3in x 76ft 3in x 23ft 9in (134.5m x 23.2m x 7.2m)
Machinery: two screws, vertical triple expansion engines; 19,000hp
Armament: four 12in (305mm); eight 8in (203mm); 12 6in (152mm); four 21in (533mm) TT
Armour: belt 11in-4in (279mm-102mm); turrets 12in-8in (305mm-203mm); deck 3in (76mm)
Speed: 19 knots
Range: 4920nm (9117km) at 10 knots
Complement: 905

The *Virginia*-class vessels had cagemasts installed in 1910–11. After some had suffered storm damage, they were strengthened in 1918.

GEORGIOS AVEROF

GREECE: 1910

Laid down in 1907 at the Livorno yard of the Italian shipbuilding company Orlando & Co, *Georgios Averof* was a sistership of the *Pisa*-type armoured cruiser. She was built as a speculative venture, Orlando being certain that a buyer would be found. In the event, the purchaser was the Greek Admiralty; the ship was named in honour of a Greek millionaire who had donated a large sum of money for the expansion of the Greek Navy. In 1912–13 *Georgios Averof*, as the Greek flagship, played a prominent part in the Balkan wars, being slightly damaged in actions against the Turkish fleet in the Dardanelles on 16–22 December 1916. In 1919 she was partially refitted at HM Dockyard, Malta. When the Germans invaded Greece in 1941, *Georgios Averof* escaped to Alexandria. Later, she served as a station ship at Piraeus. Stricken in 1946, she is now on display at the Poros Island Naval Museum, south of Athens.

***Georgios Averof* differed from her Italian-built sister ships in that they were armed with 10in (254mm) guns, whereas she carried 9.2in (234mm).**

Displacement: 9960t standard
Dimensions: 462ft 6in x 69ft x 24ft 8in (141m x 21m x 7.5m)
Machinery: two screws, vertical triple expansion engines; 19,000hp
Armament: four 9.2in (234mm); eight 7.5in (190mm); three 18in (457mm) TT
Armour: belt 8in-3in (203mm-76mm); turrets 6.48in (165mm)
Speed: 23 knots
Range: 7125nm (13,203km) at 10 knots
Complement: 550

GLASGOW

GB: 1909

A much-travelled ship, HMS *Glasgow* was one of the five *Bristol*-class light cruisers. Launched on 30 September 1909, she spent much of her early career in South Atlantic waters. On 16 August 1914, she captured the German merchantman *Catherina* off South America. *Glasgow* escaped destruction at Coronel and in the later Falklands battle she assisted in the destruction of the German light cruiser *Leipzig*. In 1917–18 she served with the 8th Light Cruiser Squadron in the Adriatic. She was scrapped in 1927.

In 1915 *Glasgow* deployed to the Mediterranean. She took part in the hunt for the German raider *Möwe* there in 1916.

Displacement: 4800t standard; 5300 full load
Dimensions: 453ft x 47ft x 15ft 6in (138.1m x 14.3m x 4.7m)
Machinery: four screws, turbines; 22,000hp
Armament: two 6in (152mm); 10 4in (102mm); two 18in (457mm) TT
Armour: deck 2in-0.75in (50-20mm)
Speed: 25 knots
Range: 5070nm (9395km) at 16 knots
Complement: 480

GLATTON

GB: 1914

HMS *Glatton* and her sister ship, *Gorgon*, were originally ordered as small coastal defence battleships for service with the Royal Norwegian Navy. In 1915, they were acquired by the British government prior to completion, both being converted as monitors. *Glatton* commissioned at Newcastle in 1918, and joined the Dover Patrol in September. She had been there barely a week when, on 16 September 1918, her midships 6in (152mm) magazine exploded; she caught fire and 77 lives were lost. Later, she was sunk by British destroyers.

Displacement: 5700t standard; 5746t full load
Dimensions: 310ft x 73ft 7in x 16ft 4in (94.5m x 22.5m x 5m)
Machinery: two screws, vertical triple expansion engines; 4000hp
Armament: two 9.2in (234mm); four 6in (152mm); two 3in (76mm)
Armour: belt 7in-3in (180-100mm); bulkheads 4in-3in (100mm-76mm); turret faces 8in (200mm); decks 2.5in-1in (65mm-25mm)
Speed: 12 knots
Range: 2700nm (5003km) at 11 knots
Complement: 305

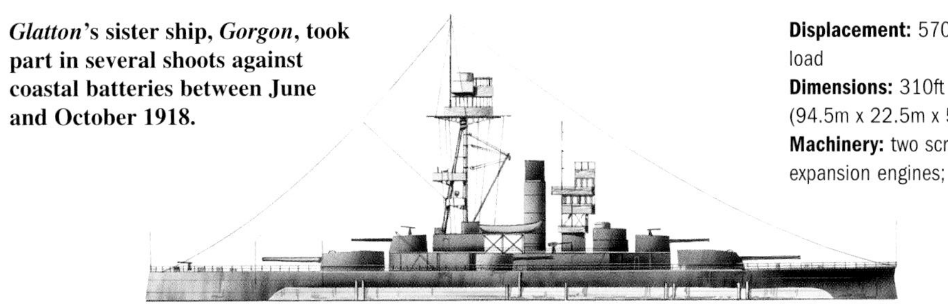

***Glatton*'s sister ship, *Gorgon*, took part in several shoots against coastal batteries between June and October 1918.**

GLOIRE

FRANCE: 1935

Displacement: 7600t standard; 9120t full load
Dimensions: 588ft 11in x 57ft 4in x 17ft 7in (179.5m x 17.48m x 5.35m)
Machinery: two screws, geared turbines; 84,000hp
Armament: nine 6in (152mm); eight 3.5in (89mm); four 21.7in (550mm) TT
Armour: belt 4.7in-3in (120mm-76mm); turret faces 4in (102mm); deck 1.5in (38mm)
Speed: 31 knots
Range: 5440nm (10,080km) at 15 knots
Complement: 540

French naval designers had every reason to be proud of the six *La Galissonniere*-class light cruisers of the mid-1930s, of which *Gloire* was one. They were an outstanding success, with excellent sea-going characteristics and splendid armament. Three of the class (*La Galissonniere*, *Jean de Vienne* and *Marseillaise*) were scuttled at Toulon in November 1942 to prevent their capture by the Germans. The *Georges Leygues*, *Montcalm*, and *Gloire* fought on the Allied side, supporting the landings in France in 1944.

All three surviving light cruisers served in the post-war French fleet. *Gloire* was sold for scrap in 1958.

GLORIOUS

GB: 1916

As early as 1907, the British Admiralty had plans that, in the event of hostilities with Germany, it would result in the sending of a strong naval force into the Baltic. The intention was to capture the island of Borkum opposite the Ems estuary, for use as a stepping stone, and to blockade the north German ports. This operation would support an expeditionary force sent to occupy the Baltic States, as a prelude to an attack on Germany from the north. The First Sea Lord, Admiral Fisher, was a staunch advocate of this plan; in the event, it was never worked out in detail and, had it taken place, would probably have been more disastrous than the Gallipoli landings later in the war. Nevertheless, the plan gave Fisher a pretext for ordering warships to support the northern invasion, at a time when the British Cabinet was reluctant to release funds for the building of more capital ships. Two ships were built, the *Courageous* and her sister ship, *Glorious*. Though defined as large light cruisers, they were in fact light battlecruisers with a 15in (381mm) armament. In practical terms, they proved of little use; they were used as cruisers and converted for minelaying in 1917. Both saw action in the Heligoland Bight on 17 November 1917 against German light forces, their gunfire damaging the German cruiser *Pillau*. Both ships were converted to aircraft carriers in the 1920s, and both became early World War II losses: *Courageous* was torpedoed by *U29* on 17 September 1939, and *Glorious* was sunk by the gunfire of *Scharnhorst* and *Gneisenau* while ferrying aircraft from Norway to Scotland on 8 June 1940.

Displacement: 19,230t standard; 22,690t full load
Dimensions: 786ft 3in x 81ft x 23ft 4in (239.7m x 24.7m x 7.1m)
Machinery: four screws, geared turbines; 90,000hp
Armament: four 15in (381mm); 18 4in (102mm); two 21in (533mm) TT
Armour: belt 3in-2in (76mm-50mm); bulkheads 3in-2in (76mm-50mm); turret faces 13in-11in (330mm-280mm); decks 1.5in-0.75in (38mm-20mm)
Speed: 32 knots
Range: 3200nm (5929km) at 19 knots
Complement: 828 to 842

The 15in (381mm) guns removed from *Glorious* and *Courageous* on their conversion to aircraft carriers were mounted in Britain's last battleship, HMS *Vanguard*.

GNEISENAU

GERMANY: 1906

The *Gneisenau* and her sister armoured cruiser, *Scharnhorst*, were enlarged and improved versions of the earlier *Roon* class, and were completed respectively by the A. G. Weser Shipyard, Bremen and Blohm & Voss, Hamburg, in 1907–8. Both vessels were considered to be too weak to form part of the main battle force, the High Seas Fleet, but adequate for overseas duty in support of

German colonies. From 1911, they were deployed to Tsingtao in China to form the spearhead of the German Asiatic Squadron under Admiral von Spee. The outbreak of World War I found them still there, together with the three light cruisers *Leipzig*, *Dresden*, and *Nurnberg*. The Asiatic squadron immediately sailed east for home waters, avoiding pursuing Japanese warships. In October, off the Pacific coast of Chile, it destroyed Admiral Sir Christopher Cradock's South Atlantic Squadron at Coronel, and then rounded Cape Horn. Sighting the Falklands Islands on 8 December, Von Spee decided to raid but, shortly afterwards, was engaged by a strong British naval force that included the battlecruisers *Inflexible* and *Invincible*. Realising that he could not outrun the British, Von Spee turned his flagship *Scharnhorst* broadside on and engaged the *Invincible*, while the *Gneisenau* took on the *Inflexible*. After a running fight of some three hours, the *Scharnhorst* went down by the stern, and the two British battlecruisers turned their joint fire on the *Gneisenau*. She very gallantly continued the fight until, battered into a blazing wreck, she also sank. Some 200 survivors were rescued from *Gneisenau*'s 800 crew; all 860 men aboard the *Scharnhorst* perished.

The armoured cruiser *Gneisenau* bore the name of Count August Neithardt von Gneisenau, a Prussian field marshal who fought against Napoleon.

Displacement: 11,600t standard, 12,900t full load
Dimensions: 474ft 4in x 70ft 10in x 26ft (144.6m x 21.6m x 7.9m)
Machinery: three screws, vertical triple expansion engines; 26,000hp
Armament: eight 8.25in (210mm); six 5.9in (150mm); four 17.7in (450mm) TT
Armour: belt 5.9in-3.2in (150mm-80mm); turrets 6.6in (170mm); deck 2.3in (60mm)
Speed: 22.5 knots
Range: 5120nm (9487km) at 12 knots
Complement: 764

GOEBEN

GERMANY: 1911

The *Goeben* and her sister ship, *Moltke*, were enlarged *Von der Tann* battlecruiser types. They had stronger protection, an extra turret mounted aft, and the same turret arrangement as in the *Kaiser*-class battleships. *Goeben* was in the Mediterranean from the outset of World War I, and on the day hostilities started, 4 August, she bombarded the French Algerian ports of Bone and Philippeville. Determined efforts were made to intercept her, but she outran all her pursuers, including the battle-cruisers *Indomitable* and *Indefatigable*, entering Turkish waters through the Dardanelles on 10 August 1914. Although she retained her German crew, *Goeben* was nominally transferred to the Turkish Navy on 16 August and renamed the *Yavuz Sultan Selim*. In September, she was operating in the Black Sea, together with her consort, the light cruiser *Breslau*. On 18 November, she bombarded Batum but was damaged the next day in action with Russian warships off Samsoun. She sustained further damage on 26 December when she struck two mines in the approaches to the Bosphorus. In May 1915, in action against Russian battleships, she was damaged again, and on January 20 she ran aground after striking two mines off Mudros – but not before she had sunk the British monitors *Raglan* and *M28*. *Goeben* was formally handed over to Turkey in November 1918, and at a later date her name was shortened to *Yavuz*. *Moltke* served with the High Seas Fleet, engaging in the Dogger Bank and Jutland battles. She survived two torpedo attacks by British submarines, only to be scuttled by her crew at Scapa Flow in 1918.

Displacement: 22,979t standard; 25,400t full load
Dimensions: 611ft 10in x 69ft 9in x 30ft 2in (186.5m x 29.5m x 9.2m)
Machinery: four screws, turbines; 52,000hp
Armament: 10 11in (280mm); 12 5.9in (150mm); four 19.6in (500mm) TT
Armour: belt 10.5in-3.7in (266mm-95mm); turrets 8in (203mm); deck 2in (50mm)
Speed: 20.3 knots
Range: 3600nm (6670km) at 14 knots
Complement: 1107

Goeben, alias *Yavuz*, underwent a refit in the late 1920s, and was recommissioned in 1930. She was decommissioned and broken up in 1954.

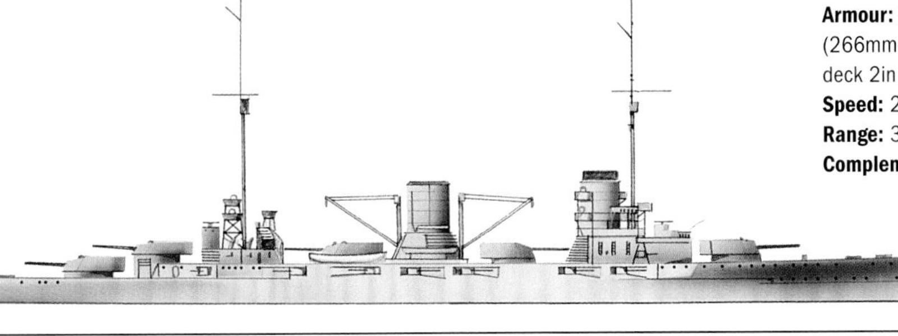

GOTLAND

SWEDEN: 1933

The cruiser *Gotland* was originally projected as a small aircraft carrier, with an air group of 12 floatplanes and twin catapults, the aircraft recovering to a coastal base after launch. However, financial constraints dictated a reappraisal of this concept; the air group was reduced to six aircraft (Hawker Ospreys), and one catapult was deleted. *Gotland* consequently emerged as a cross between an aircraft carrier and a cruiser and, in 1943–44, she was converted to an AA cruiser.

Displacement: 4700t standard; 5550t full load
Dimensions: 442ft 3in x 50ft 7in x 18ft (134.8m x 15.4m x 5.5m)
Machinery: two screws, geared turbines; 33,000hp
Armament: six 6in (152mm); four 3in (76mm); six 21in (533mm) TT; 80-100 mines
Armour: bulkheads 2in-1in (50mm-25mm); deck 2in (50mm)
Speed: 28 knots
Range: 4000nm (7412km) at 14 knots
Complement: 467

As an AA cruiser, *Gotland* was armed with four 3in (76mm) and eight 40mm guns; she also eventually carried 16 25mm guns.

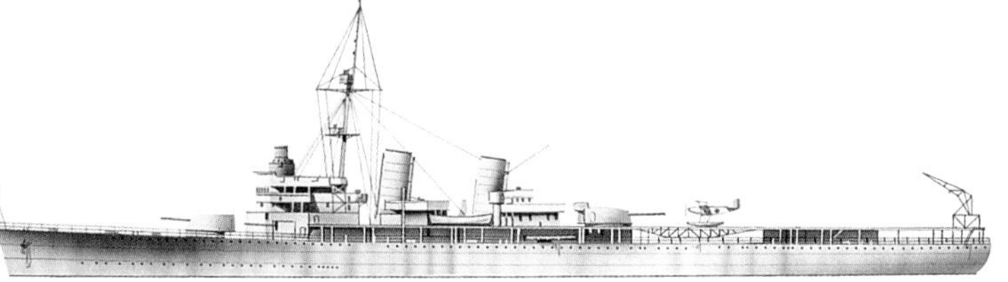

GRAF SPEE

GERMANY: 1917

Of the four *Mackensen*-class battlecruisers laid down in 1915, only the *Mackensen* and *Graf Spee* were actually launched, in April and September 1917 respectively. As a consequence, the other two never had their names formally allocated: *Fürst Bismarck* was broken up on the slip after construction was suspended in 1917, and the hull of the *Prinz Eitel Friedrich* was launched to clear the slip in 1920, and broken up at Hamburg in 1922.

The *Mackensens* were truly formidable warships. Much of their design went into the *Scharnhorst* and *Gneisenau* of World War II.

Displacement: 31,000t standard; 35,300t full load
Dimensions: 734ft 10in x 99ft 7in x 30ft 6in (224m x 30.4m x 9.3m)
Machinery: four screws, geared turbines; 90,000hp
Armament: eight 14in (356mm); 14 5.9in (150mm); five 24in (600mm) TT
Armour: belt and turrets 12in-4.7in (305mm-120mm); deck 1.17in (30mm)
Speed: 27 knots
Range: 5500nm (10,191km) at 14 knots
Complement: 1186

GRAUDENZ

GERMANY: 1913

Displacement: 4912t standard; 6382t full load
Dimensions: 468ft 3in x 45ft 3in x 18ft 10in (142.7m x 13.8m x 5.75m)
Machinery: two screws, turbines; 29,000hp
Armament: 12 4.1in (105mm); two 19.7in (250mm) TT
Armour: belt 2.25in-0.75in (60mm-18mm); deck 2.25in-1.5in (60mm-40mm)
Speed: 27.5 knots
Range: 4300nm (7967km) at 12 knots
Complement: 442

Authorised under the 1911 naval construction programme, *Graudenz* and her sister light cruiser, *Regensburg*, underwent armament changes during building. Both vessels served with the High Seas Fleet Scouting Force during World War I. After the Armistice, she was ceded to Italy as war booty, and re-named to serve as the *Ancona*; she was broken up in 1938. Similarly, *Regensburg* went to France and became the *Strasbourg*. She was broken up in 1944.

Completed in 1914–15, *Regensburg* and *Graudenz* were similar to the *Karlsruhe* class, but with three funnels instead of four.

GRAYLING

USA: 1909

Built at the Fore River Company and launched on 16 June 1919, *Grayling* was numbered D2 but later redesignated SS18. She was one of the last submarines in the US Navy to have petrol engines, a source of constant anxiety to her 15 crew. Her engines developed 600hp, giving a surface range of 1270nm (2356km) at cruising speed. These three *D*-class boats – *Narwhal* (D1) and *Salmon* (D3) were the other two – had a designed diving depth of 200ft (61m), and began their operational service off the US east coast, D3 being deployed to the Caribbean in 1912. All three were stricken in 1922. When the USA entered World War II, over half of their commissioned submarines were of World War I vintage. US Navy submarines were named after fish; during World War II, so many new boats were built that the Navy ran out of existing fish names, so they invented names that in the future could be given to fish of newly-discovered species.

The *D*-class submarines had a designed diving depth of 200ft (61m). All three began their service off the US east coast.

Displacement: 288t surfaced; 337t submerged
Dimensions: 135ft x 13ft 9in x 12ft (41m x 4.2m x 3.6m)
Machinery: two screws, petrol engine, plus electric motor; 600hp/260sp
Armament: four 18in (457mm) TT
Speed: 12 knots surfaced; 9.5 knots submerged
Range: 1270nm (23,56km) at 10 knots
Complement: 15

GRILLO

ITALY: 1918

Displacement: 8t
Dimensions: 52ft 6in x 10ft 2in x 2ft 4in (16m x 3.1m x 0.7m)
Machinery: single screw, two electric motors; 10hp
Armament: two 17.7in (450mm)TT
Armour: not known
Speed: 4 knots
Range: not known
Complement: 1 + 3

Towards the end of World War I, Italian naval engineers produced a quite remarkable range of fast motor-boats and assault craft for use in the confined waters of the Adriatic. Among them were the four *Grillo*-class 'climbing boats', which were equipped with two lateral climbing chains for surmounting harbour barrages. The main objective of these unusual craft was the Austrian naval base at Pola, but attempts to breach the powerful defences there ended in failure, and three of the craft were lost.

The main Austrian fleet base at Pola was a constant thorn in the Italian Navy's side, and many attempts were made to penetrate it.

GROMKI

IMPERIAL RUSSIA: 1913

Displacement: 1320t standard; 1460t full load
Dimensions: 321ft 6in x 30ft 6in (98m x 9.3m x 3.2m)
Machinery: two screws, turbines; 25,500hp
Armament: three 4in (102mm); two 47mm AA; 10 18in (457mm) TT, 80 mines
Armour: belt 3in (76mm)
Speed: 34 knots
Range: 1800nm (3335km) at 10 knots
Complement: 125

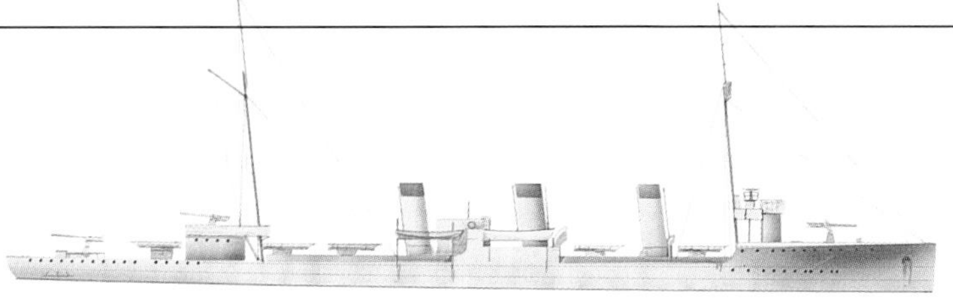

Launched on 18 December 1913, *Gromki* was one of the *Bespokoiny* class of nine destroyers that were reduced versions of the 1280t *Novik*. The class were part of a new naval construction programme, the primary aim of which was to increase the size of the Black Sea Fleet. Design studies had begun in 1907; revised designs showed a 50t increase in displacement to enable the vessels to carry more armament. *Gromki* was scuttled at Novorossisk on 18 June 1918.

The *Bespokoiny*-class destroyers proved something of a disappointment in service, none of the vessels achieving design speed.

GROSSER KÜRFURST

GERMANY: 1913

One of the *Konig* class of dreadnoughts, *Grosser Kürfurst* was launched on 5 May 1913 and completed in July 1914, just before the outbreak of World War I. She took part in the Battle of Jutland and sustained eight shell hits; on 5 November 1916, she was damaged in a torpedo attack by the British submarine *J1* off Utsira. On 5 March 1917, she was damaged yet again, this time in a collision with the battleship *Kronprinz* in the Heligoland Bight. Scuttled at Scapa Flow, *Grosser Kürfurst* was raised and broken up in 1936.

Grosser Kürfurst was named in honour of the Great Elector (Friedrich Wilhelm, Elector of Brandenburg), a distinguished 17th-century military commander.

Displacement: 25,796t standard; 28,600t full load
Dimensions: 575ft 6in x 96ft 9in x 30ft 2in (175.4m x 29.5m x 9.2m)
Machinery: three screws, turbines; 31,000hp
Armament: 10 12in (305mm); 14 5.9in (150mm; five 19.7in (500mm) TT
Armour: belt 13.8in–4.7in (350mm–120mm); turrets 11.79in (300mm); deck 3.9in (100mm)
Speed: 21 knots
Range: 8000nm (14,824km) at 12 knots
Complement: 1150

GUSTAVE ZÉDÉ

FRANCE: 1913

One of the last steam-driven submarines built for the French Navy, *Gustave Zédé* was, at the time of her completion in October 1914, one of the fastest submarines in the world. In 1921–22 she was fitted with diesel engines taken from a former German submarine, *U165*. At the same time, the boat was fitted with a new bridge, and two of the aft buoyancy tanks were converted to carry diesel fuel. *Gustave Zédé* was stricken from the Navy List in 1937.

Gustave Zédé was employed in the Adriatic during World War I while her sister submarine, Nereide, served in the Atlantic.

Displacement: 849t surfaced; 1098t submerged
Dimensions: 242ft 9in x 19ft 8in x 12ft 2in (74m x 6m x 3.7m)
Machinery: two screws, reciprocating steam engines, plus electric motors; 3500hp/1640hp
Armament: eight 17.7in (450mm) TT; one 3in (75mm)
Speed: 9.2 knots surfaced; 6.5 knots submerged
Range: 1433nm (2660km) at 10 knots, surfaced; 90nm (167km) at 4 knots, submerged
Complement: 47

GWIN

USA: 1916

At the time of the Japanese attack on Pearl Harbor in December 1941, of the 171 US destroyers in commission, over one-third were of World War I vintage. The USS *Gwin*, launched in December 1917, was an early 'flushdecker', many of which served alongside their modern counterparts in World War II. She had three funnels and a raised superstructure amidships which carried two of the 4in (102mm) guns. She was sold in 1939. The name *Gwin* was later allocated to a light minelayer in 1944.

The *Caldwell*-class destroyers, to which *Gwin* belonged, were intermediate between the 'thousand-tonners' and the mass-production destroyers of World War I.

Displacement: 1120t standard; 1187t full load
Dimensions: 315ft 7in x 30ft x 9ft (96.2m x 9.3m x 2.7m)
Machinery: two screws, turbines; 18,500hp
Armament: four 4in (102mm); 12 21in (533mm) TT
Armour: belt 3in (76mm)
Speed: 30 knots
Range: 2500nm (4632km) at 20 knots
Complement: 100

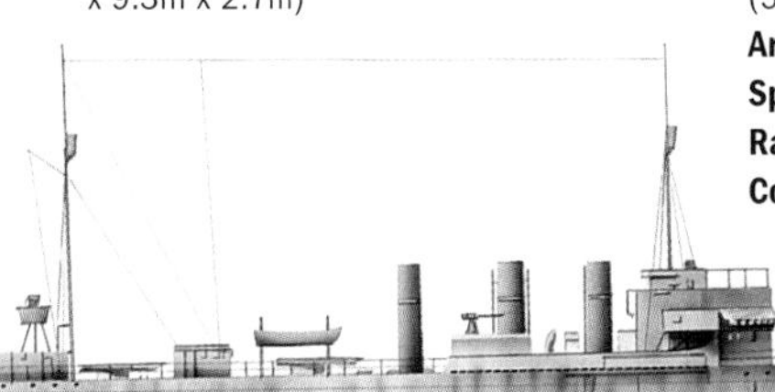

HARUNA

JAPAN: 1913

The battlecruiser *Haruna* and her three sisters, *Hiei, Kirishima,* and *Kongo,* were designed by an Englishman, Sir George Thurston. He included some improvements as a result of experience in the building of the British *Lion* class. *Kongo* was the last Japanese capital ship to be built outside the country while, due to a lack of slipways in Japanese government-owned yards, *Haruna* and *Kirishima* became the first Japanese capital ships to be constructed in private yards (Kawasaki and Mitsubishi respectively). *Haruna* was launched on 14 December 1913 and completed in April 1915. The class had a new arrangement of main armament turrets, heavy secondary armament, and good protection; they outclassed contemporary ships. All four ships, with the exception of *Hiei*, underwent two periods of extensive reconstruction between the wars (*Hiei* was rebuilt only once), and were then re-classified as battleships. They were named after mountains, and all went on to serve in the Pacific in World War II.

Displacement: 27,500t standard; 32,200t full load
Dimensions: 659ft 4in x 92ft x 27ft 6in (201m x 28m x 8.4m)
Machinery: three screws, geared turbines; 64,000hp
Armament: eight 15in (380mm); 16 6in (152mm); eight 3in (76mm); four 21in (533mm) TT, later removed
Armour: belt 8in-3in (203mm-76mm); turrets 9in (230mm); barbettes 10in (255mm); bulkheads 9in-5.5in (230mm-140mm), conning tower 10in (255mm)
Speed: 27.5 knots
Range: 8000nm (14,824km) at 14 knots
Complement: 1221

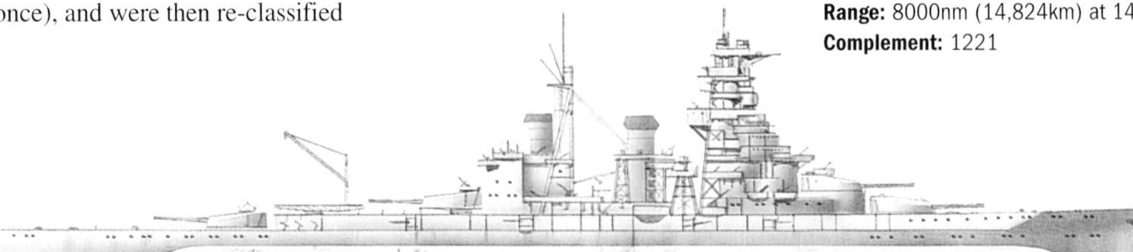

***Haruna* was sunk by US carrier aircraft at Kure on 28 July 1945. She was refloated and broken up in 1946.**

HELGOLAND

GERMANY: 1909

Displacement: 22,800t standard; 24,700t full load
Dimensions: 548ft 6in x 93ft 6in x 29ft 3in (167.2m x 28.5m x 8.9m)
Machinery: three screws, vertical triple expansion engines; 28,000hp
Armament: 12 12in (305mm); 14 5.9in (150mm); six 19.7in (500mm) TT
Armour: belt 11.79in-6.6in (300mm-170mm); turrets 11.79in-4in (300mm-100mm); deck 2.35in (60mm)
Speed: 20.3 knots
Range: 3600nm (6670km) at 18 knots
Complement: 1100

The *Helgoland*-class dreadnoughts, *Helgoland, Oldenburg, Ostfriesland,* and *Thüringen* were enlargements of the *Nassau* class of 1906, with 12in (305mm) guns. They were the only German dreadnoughts with three funnels, and were characterised by a very small superstructure. Launched on 25 September 1909, *Helgoland* was commissioned for trials on 23 August 1911, a few weeks after her sister ships *Thüringen* and *Ostfriesland*. Present at the Battle of Jutland, *Helgoland* sustained one hit. *Ostfriesland* was more badly damaged, striking a mine. In October 1918, *Helgoland* was at the centre of the mutiny that broke out among the sailors of the Imperial German Navy. Stricken in November 1919, she was allocated to Great Britain in 1920, and broken up at Morecambe in 1924. *Ostfriesland* became famous as the first battleship sunk by air attack during the US bombing trials of 1921. She and *Thuringen* were broken up in 1921 and 1924 respectively.

The greater beam of the *Helgoland* class allowed the wing turrets to be positioned further inboard, permitting the magazines to be better protected.

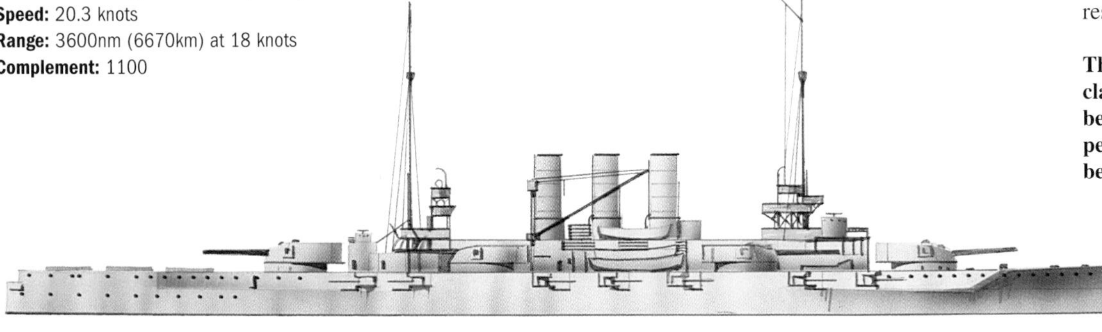

HELLE

GREECE: 1912

Built by the New York Shipbuilding Co and originally ordered by the Chinese Navy under the name *Fei Hung*, this cruiser was never delivered. As a result of revolution in China, she was put up for sale and bought by the Greek Navy. Re-named *Helle*, she served under the French flag in 1916–17 and, in 1928, was rebuilt as a cruiser-minelayer, her superstructure being substantially modernised, her engine renewed, and her boilers replaced. Her armament was also modified.

Displacement: 2600t standard
Dimensions: 322ft x 39ft x 14ft (98.1m x 97.5m x 4.3m)
Machinery: three screws, turbines; 6000hp
Armament: two 6in (152mm); four 4in (102mm); two 18in (457mm) TT
Armour: deck 2in-1in (50mm-25mm)
Speed: 18 knots
Range: 3500nm (6485km) at 12 knots
Complement: 232

At anchor off Tinos Island, just before Italy invaded Greece, *Helle* was torpedoed and sunk on 15 August 1940 by the Italian submarine *Delfino*.

HERMES

GB: 1919

At the end of World War I, Great Britain was a significantly ahead of the rest of the world in the development of vessels which could be truly defined as aircraft carriers – in other words, fitted with flight decks, from which land-based aircraft could operate. The first such vessel was HMS *Furious*, laid down shortly after the war as a light battlecruiser and converted at a later date; a similar ship, HMS *Cavendish*, was commissioned as an aircraft carrier in October 1918 and renamed HMS *Vindictive*. However, the first vessel to be designed from the outset as an aircraft carrier, with a small cruiser-type hull and engines, a full flight deck, and a large island, was HMS *Hermes*. Laid down on 15 January 1918, she was launched on 11 September 1919 and was fully fitted out by February 1925. She served mainly in the Far East. At the outbreak of World War II, she was in the South Atlantic, and her aircraft were involved in the attack on the French base at Dakar in July 1940. In February 1941, while on station in the Indian Ocean, she supported the British offensive against the Italians in Somaliland, and in the following months was involved in convoy protection in the Indian Ocean and South Atlantic. Early in 1942, *Hermes* was part of the Royal Navy's Eastern Fleet, based on Trincomalee, Ceylon. On 8 April that year, air reconnaissance reported a Japanese carrier task force approaching Ceylon; *Hermes* was ordered to put to sea, along with the Australian destroyer *Vampire*, the corvette *Hollyhock*, and two tankers. The ships were attacked by some 80 Japanese aircraft and all five were sunk. *Hermes* had no aircraft on board, and was therefore defenceless. Over 300 of her crew perished.

***Hermes* proved to be an excellent sea-boat. Her main disadvantage was her small air group of only 20 aircraft.**

Displacement: 10,850t standard; 12,900t full load
Dimensions: 598ft x 70ft x 21ft 6in (182.3m x 21.3m x 6.6m)
Machinery: two screws, geared turbines; 40,000shp
Armament: six 5.5in (140mm); four 3pdr AA
Armour: belt 3in (76mm); deck 1in (25mm)
Speed: 25 knots
Range: 4200nm (7783km) at 14 knots
Complement: 664

HOOD

GB: 1918

HMS *Hood*, destined to become one of the most famous warships of all time, was a prime example of how the ongoing quest for naval supremacy in World War I influenced warship design in just a few short years. She was designed as an enlarged version of the *Queen Elizabeth*-class battlecruisers, and owed her existence to the threat posed by the German *Mackensen*-class battlecruisers. (These were never completed, although their design formed the basis of the later *Scharnhorst* and *Gneisenau*.) At the time of her launch on 22 August 1918, *Hood* was the largest warship in the world. In 1923–24 she undertook a much-publicised world cruise. She remained the largest warship afloat throughout the inter-war years – and, with a speed of 32 knots, she was also one of the fastest, deck armour having been sacrificed to produce a higher speed. Her armour was increased after an analysis of British battlecruiser losses during the Battle of Jutland, but she still remained poorly protected, and a proposed reconstruction, scheduled for 1939, was cancelled due to the advent of World War II. Her first wartime operational sortie was to form part of a blocking screen across the Iceland-Faeroes-UK gap, searching for enemy blockade runners. Later, she took part in the British naval bombardment of French naval bases in North Africa in July 1940, and at the end of that year underwent a refit. In May 1941, together with the battleship *Prince of Wales*, the *Hood* sailed to intercept the German battleship *Bismarck* and the heavy cruiser *Prinz Eugen* in the Denmark Strait, between Greenland and Iceland. A salvo from Bismarck penetrated her deck and exploded in her magazine. *Hood* blew up and sank with the loss of 1338 lives.

Displacement: 41,200t standard; 45,200t full load
Dimensions: 860ft 7in x 105ft x 31ft 6in (262.3m x 32m x 9.6m)
Machinery: four screws, geared turbines; 144,000hp
Armament: eight 15in (381mm); 12 5.5in (140mm); four 4in (102mm); six 21in (533mm) TT
Armour: belt and barbettes 12in-5in (305mm-127mm); turrets 15-11in (381mm-279mm); conning tower 11in-9in (279mm-229mm); bulkheads 5in-4in (127mm-102mm); decks 3in-1in (76mm-26mm)
Speed: 32 knots
Range: 6300nm (11,674km) at 12 knots
Complement: 1477

***Hood* was to have been followed by three more powerful battlecruisers, *Anson, Howe,* and *Rodney*, but they were cancelled, and their names were later allocated to battleships of the *King George V* class.**

HOSHO

JAPAN: 1921

Initially to have been named *Hiryu*, and projected in 1919 as an auxiliary tanker and specialist transport capable of carrying aircraft, *Hosho* was in fact completed as Japan's first dedicated aircraft carrier. She was launched on 13 November 1921, and completed in December 1922. It has been suggested that much of the design work was attributed to a British Aviation Mission which was present in Japan at the time. *Hosho* had a small bridge and three funnels, which could be swung down during flying operations. The bridge was removed in 1923, the flight deck made flush to improve aircraft operation, and a system of mirrors and lights fitted to assist pilots in landing. *Hosho* served during the Sino-Japanese war and was recalled to active duty in December 1941, but was later relegated to a training role. Damaged by air attack at the end of World War II, she was broken up at Osaka in 1947.

***Hosho*'s flight deck originally sloped down at the bow, but this was raised and made horizontal in 1936.**

Displacement: 7470t standard; 9630t full load
Dimensions: 552ft 6in x 59ft 1in x 20ft 3in (168.4m x 18m x 6.2m)
Machinery: two screws, geared turbines; 30,000hp
Armament: four 5.5in (140mm); 26 aircraft
Armour: Not applicable
Speed: 25 knots
Range: 8680nm (16,084km) at 12 knots)
Complement: 550

HUMBER

GB: 1913

The small river monitor *Humber* and her two sister ships, *Severn* and *Mersey*, were originally completed for Brazil early in 1914. However, the Brazilian government could not afford to pay for them, and they were laid up until August 1914 when they were taken over by the Royal Navy. *Humber* saw active service on bombardment duty off the Belgian coast and the Mediterranean, and in 1919 was deployed to Murmansk, North Russia, in support of the Allied intervention force. She was sold to a Dutch salvage firm in 1920.

***Humber* was converted to a crane barge and was still carrying out salvage work in 1938, but her eventual fate is unknown.**

Displacement: 1260 standard; 1520t full load
Dimensions: 266ft 9in x 49ft x 5ft 7in (81.3m x 14.9m x 1.7m)
Machinery: two screws, triple expansion engines; 1450hp
Armament: two 6in (152mm); two 4.7mm (120mm) howitzers
Armour: belt 3in–1.5in (76mm–38mm); turret face 4in (100mm)
Speed: 9.5 knots
Range: not known
Complement: 140

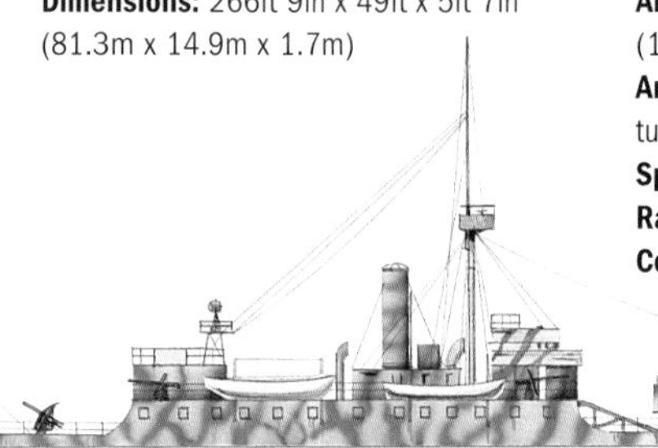

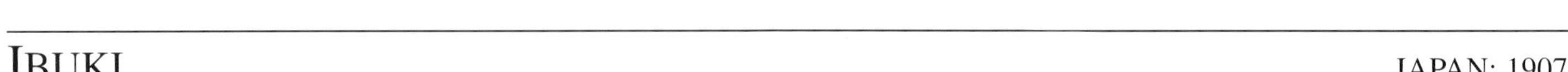

IBUKI

JAPAN: 1907

Although construction was begun later than intended, *Ibuki* was built in record time, being launched less than six months after she was laid down.

Launched on 21 November 1907 as an armoured cruiser, *Ibuki* was the first major ship of the Imperial Japanese Navy to be completed with turbines. The decision to fit them was taken when her construction was unavoidably delayed by overcrowding of the Yokosuka shipyard. *Ibuki* and her sister ship, *Kurama*, were both redesignated battlecruisers in 1912. In World War I, *Ibuki* took part in the hunt for the German commerce raider *Emden*, and carried out convoy escort duty in the Indian Ocean. She was scrapped in 1924.

Displacement: 14,636t standard; 17,200t full load
Dimensions: 485ft x 75ft 4in x 26ft 1in (147.8m x 23m x 8m)
Machinery: two screws, turbines; 24,000hp
Armament: four 12in (305mm); eight 8in (203mm); 14 4.7in (120mm); three 14.7in (375mm) TT
Armour: belt 7in–4.7in (178mm–102mm); turrets 7.7in–6in (178mm–152mm); deck 2in (50mm)
Speed: 21.5 knots
Range: 4500nm (8338km) at 12 knots
Complement: 820

IDAHO

USA: 1917

One of three *New Mexico*-class dreadnoughts, USS *Idaho* (BB-42) was launched on 30 June 1917. She was assigned to the US Pacific Fleet in 1919, and underwent a major reconstruction programme in 1931–34. Among other refinements, her cagemasts were removed, a tower superstructure was added, her AA armament was increased, anti-torpedo bulges were fitted, and she was re-engined and re-boilered. After a brief assignment to the Atlantic Fleet in 1941, *Idaho* returned to the Pacific, her service in World War II taking her to Attu, the Gilbert Islands, Kwajalein, Saipan, Guam, Palau, Iwo Jima, and Okinawa. On 13 June 1945,

she ran aground off Okinawa, effectively bringing her operational career in the Pacific to a close. In September that year, together with other US battleships, she sailed for the USA with high priority personnel on board. She was decommissioned in July 1946, to be sold and broken up in the following year.

All three vessels in the *New Mexico* class were to have been armed with 16 5in (130mm) dual-purpose guns, but only the *Idaho* received them, in 1944.

Displacement: 32,000t standard; 33,000t full load
Dimensions: 624ft x 97ft 5in x 30ft (190.2m x 29.7m x 9.1m)
Machinery: four screws, geared turbines; 32,000hp
Armament: 12 14in (356mm); 14 5in (127mm); two 21in (533mm) TT
Armour: belt 13.5in-8in (343mm-203mm); turrets 18in-9in (457mm-229mm); deck 6in (152mm)
Speed: 22 knots
Range: 10,000nm (18,530km) at 10 knots
Complement: 1080

IMPERATOR PAVEL

IMPERIAL RUSSIA/USSR: 1907

Displacement: 17,400t standard; 18,580t full load
Dimensions: 460ft x 80ft x 28ft (140.2m x 24.4m x 8.5m)
Machinery: two screws, vertical triple expansion engines; 17,600hp
Armament: four 12in (305mm); 14 8in (203mm); 12 4.7in (120mm); three 18in (457mm) TT
Armour: belt 8.48in-3.1in (216mm-79mm); turrets 8in-5in (203mm-127mm); deck 2.3in-1.4in (60mm-35mm)
Speed: 18.6 knots
Range: 6000nm (11,118km) at 12 knots
Complement: 933

The *Imperator Pavel* and her sister pre-dreadnought, *Andrei Pervozannyi*, were laid down as part of a plan to modernise Russia's Baltic Fleet, shortly before the outbreak of the Russo-Japanese war. As a result of lessons learned from that conflict, some re-design took place but, nonetheless, both dreadnoughts were obsolete even before they entered service. They took little part in the Baltic fighting during World War I. In April 1917, the *Imperator Pavel* was re-named *Respublika* and saw service briefly with the Red Fleet. She was broken up in 1923.

The two ships in this class had no scuttles, requiring air to be forced below through deck-mounted ventilators. The health of their crews suffered as a result.

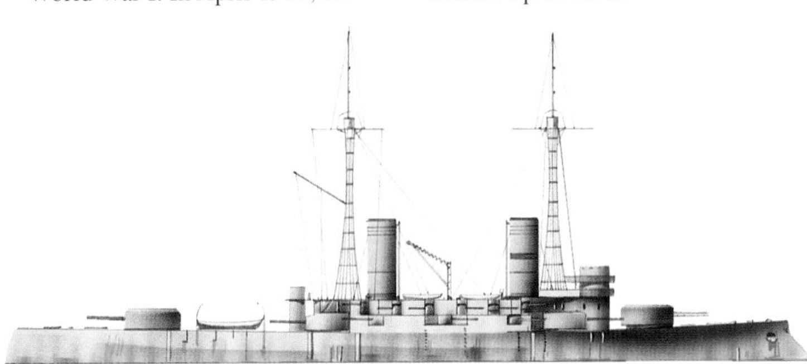

INDIANAPOLIS

USA: 1931

Indianapolis and her sister ship, *Portland*, were improved *Northampton*-class cruisers with extra protection, notably around the magazines and on top of the machinery. Both were fast ships: during her trials, *Indianapolis* achieved 32.86 knots at a displacement of 11,144t and an output of 108,317shp. Both ships were designated as flagships. *Indianapolis* was launched on 7 November 1931, some six months before *Portland*. During the early months of the Pacific War, she took part in attacks on Japanese-held objectives and undertook convoy escort duty. Operating mostly with Task Force 8, she carried out a number of bombardment missions in 1943, including attacks on Attu in January and February and, in November that year, formed part of the naval force supporting the American landings in the Gilbert Islands. Early in 1944, *Indianapolis* undertook similar operations at Kwajalein and Eniwetok, and in June and July lent her firepower to the assault on Saipan by the US V Amphibious Force. In August she operated off Guam. The next year, 1945, saw her as part of the huge escort assembled in February to protect American carriers engaged in launching the first major seaborne raid on Tokyo. In March she supported the landings on Iwo Jima. Operating as flagship of the Fifth Fleet on 30 March, *Indianapolis* was damaged by a *kamikaze* off Okinawa. After repair she was detailed for a special mission, which involved transporting components of the first atomic bomb from San Francisco to Tinian. She had completed this task, and was proceeding to Leyte, when she was hit by a salvo of six torpedoes from the Japanese submarine *I-58*, and sank with heavy loss of life. Only 316 of her 1199 crew were later picked up by US flying-boats.

***Indianapolis* served as flagship of the United States 5th Fleet. She had the unfortunate distinction of being the last major American warship loss of World War II.**

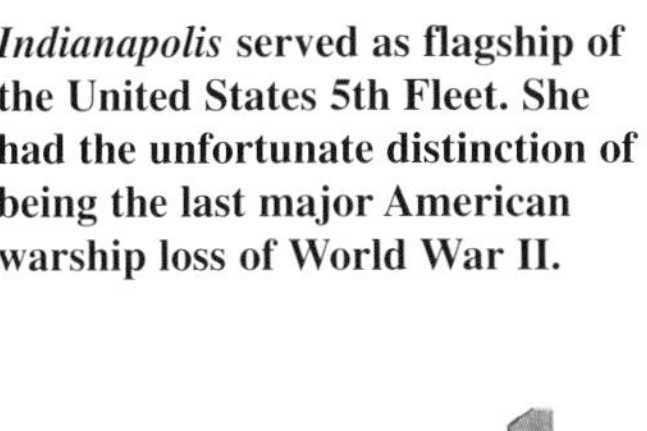

Displacement: 10,258t standard; 12,755t full load
Dimensions: 610ft x 66ft x 21ft (185.93m x 20.12m x 6.4m)
Machinery: four screws, turbines; 107,000hp
Armament: nine 8in (203mm); eight 5in (127mm)
Armour: belt 2.25in (57mm); deck 5.75in-2.5in (146mm-63mm)
Speed: 32.5 knots
Range: 10,00nm (18,530km) at 15 knots
Complement: 917

INFLEXIBLE

GB: 1907

In parallel with Admiral Fisher's dreadnought development, there ran another revolutionary warship concept – the battlecruiser. This vessel was to be nearly equal in armament to the new battleships but very much swifter, a ship that could cruise ahead and scout for the main battle fleet, and be capable of overwhelming any conventional cruiser. The concept arose simply because existing armoured cruisers had evolved into ships so large and expensive that they had reached the end of their potential. The first ship of the new class was the *Inflexible*, completed in 1908. She carried eight 12in (305mm) guns, and had a speed of 26 knots. Her firepower was four-fifths that of a dreadnought, but much had to be sacrificed in the cause of speed. While the machinery power of the dreadnought was 18,000hp, that of the *Inflexible* was 41,000hp, so a large hull was required to accommodate the necessary 31 boilers. With a reduced armament, and protection sacrificed for speed, the battlecruisers were inevitably more vulnerable, as events at Jutland in 1916 were to show in a tragic manner: *Invincible*, the sister ship of *Inflexible*, blew up and sank with the loss of 1026 lives after a shell penetrated her deck and exploded in a magazine. All three original battlecruisers, *Inflexible*, *Invincible*, and *Indomitable*, were built under conditions of extreme secrecy. After the war, *Inflexible* was sold and, rather ironically, broken up in Germany in 1921.

Displacement: 17,250t standard; 20,125t full load
Dimensions: 567ft x 78ft 5in x 26ft 8in (172.8m x 23.9m x 8.1m)
Machinery: four screws, turbines; 41,000ihp
Armament: eight 12in (305mm); 16 4in (102mm); five 18in (457mm) TT
Armour: belt 6in-4in (152mm-102mm); turrets 7in (178mm); decks 2.5in-1.5in (63mm-37mm)
Speed: 25 knots
Range: 3000nm (5559km) at 10 knots
Complement: 784

The *Invincible* class suffered from relatively poor protection, which was to lead directly to the loss of *Invincible* and her crew at the Battle of Jutland. *Inflexible* also suffered shell damage from Turkish guns in the Dardanelles.

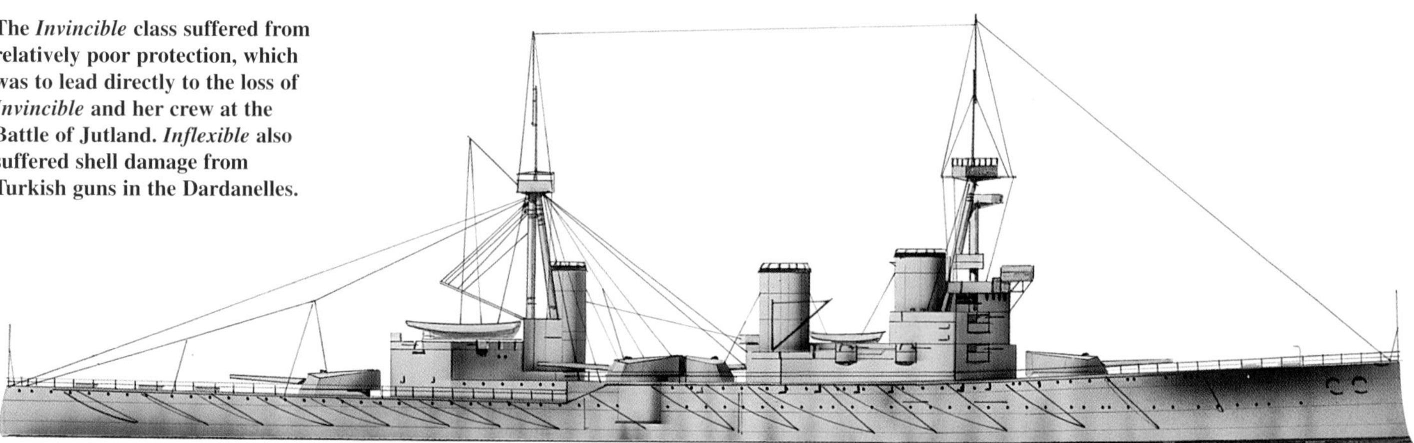

IRON DUKE

GB: 1912

***Iron Duke* was the last battleship completed with anti-torpedo nets, which were removed after trials. She became a training ship from 1931, with much of her armour and two turrets removed.**

The *Iron Duke*-class dreadnoughts were similar to the earlier *King George V* class, but with better underwater protection and a secondary 6in (152mm) battery. The four ships of the class were *Iron Duke*, *Benbow*, *Emperor of India*, and *Marlborough*. *Iron Duke*, completed in 1914, was the flagship of Admiral Jellicoe at Jutland as part of the 2nd Battleship Squadron, with which she continued to serve until she was deployed to the Mediterranean in 1919 as part of the naval component of the Allied intervention force. Here, she supported the loyalist Russian forces during the revolution. During 1919–20, she operated in the Black Sea, giving fire support to White Russian and Allied forces, and also assisting in the evacuation of refugees. After these operations she rejoined the Mediterranean Fleet and, following a period with the Atlantic Fleet during 1926–29, was paid off to be disarmed and converted to the training role. Her main and secondary armament was removed for installation in shore defences, and she was assigned to the Home Fleet in Scapa Flow as a depot ship. On 17 October 1939 she was badly damaged by near misses during a German air attack on Scapa and had to be beached. She was repaired and continued to serve as a depot ship throughout World War II, before being sold for scrap and broken up at Faslane in 1946. Of the other ships in the class, *Marlborough* survived a torpedo attack at Jutland and remained active until 1929, *Benbow* was also paid off in that year, and *Emperor of India* was sunk as a gunnery target in 1931, and raised and broken up in the following year.

Displacement: 26,100t standard; 30,380t full load
Dimensions: 622ft 9in x 90ft x 29ft 6in (189.8m x 27.4m x 9m)
Machinery: four screws, turbines; 29,000hp
Armament: 10 13.5in (343mm); 12 6in (152mm); four 21mm (533mm) TT
Armour: belt 12in-4in (305mm-102mm); barbettes 10in-3in (254mm-76mm); decks 2.5in-1in (64mm-26mm)
Speed: 21 knots
Range: 7780nm (14,416km) at 10 knots
Complement: 925 (later 1193)

ISAAC PERAL

SPAIN: 1916

Isaac Peral was Spain's first major submarine. She was built by the Fore River Company in the USA. The boat was modelled on the Holland design, and she attained a surface speed of 15.36 knots during trials. She was renumbered O1 in 1930, later being reduced to a hulk and numbered AO. Her single 3in (76mm) gun was fixed to a collapsible mount and was not a permanent feature. *Isaac Peral* closely resembled the US submarine *M1*; her Nelseco diesels were German MAN engines, built in the US under licence.

The *Isaac Peral* had a 3in (76mm) deck gun which was on a collapsible mounting, an arrangement that greatly reduced underwater drag.

Displacement: 491t surfaced; 750t submerged
Dimensions: 196ft 10in x 19ft x 11ft 2in (60m x 5.8m x 3.4m)
Machinery: two screws, two diesels, plus electric motors; 1000bhp/480shp
Armament: four 18in (457mm) TT; one 3in (76mm) AA
Speed: 15 knots surfaced; 10 knots submerged
Range: 240nm (445km) at 11 knots surfaced; 70nm (130km) at 4.5 knots submerged
Complement: 24

ISE

JAPAN: 1916

The dreadnought *Ise* and her sister ship, *Hyuga*, were of an improved *Fuso* type, with 'P' and 'Q' turrets repositioned aft of both funnels. Laid down by Kawasaki in May 1915, *Ise* was launched on 12 November 1916, and completed in December the following year. From 1935–37 she was completely reconstructed at Kure, having new engines and boilers fitted, her forward funnel removed, and anti-torpedo bulges and an aircraft catapult added. All this increased her displacement to over 40,000t full load; her overall length was also increased to 708ft (215.8m). The original Brown-Curtis engines were replaced by Kanpon geared turbines, increasing power to 80,825shp and the maximum speed to 25.3 knots. Armament changes included the removal of six 5.5in (140mm) guns and the addition of eight 5in (127mm) and 20 25mm AA guns. *Ise* saw action at the Battle of Midway in June 1942; as a result of the staggering carrier losses sustained by the Japanese in this battle, both *Ise* and *Hyuga* were converted into 'battleship-carriers' by replacing the two aft turrets with a flight deck, and installing a hangar which could house 22 seaplanes. The plan was that all the aircraft could be launched within 20 minutes, being hoisted aboard by crane on returning to the vessel at the end of their mission. However, it was thwarted by the fact that the special floatplanes never became available. Both battleships took part in the Battle of Leyte Gulf, where they formed part of Admiral Ozawa's decoy force. Both ships were sunk by US carrier aircraft near Kure in July 1945; they were later refloated and broken up.

Even if *Ise* and *Hyuga* had received their complement of combat aircraft, it is likely that the desperate shortage of naval pilots would have prevented their use in action.

Displacement: 31,260t standard; 36,500t full load
Dimensions: 683ft x 94ft x 29ft 1in (208.2m x 28.7m x 8.9m)
Machinery: four screws, turbines; 45,000hp
Armament: 12 14in (355mm); 20 5.5in (140mm); six 21in (533mm) TT
Armour: belt 12in-4in (305mm-102mm); turrets and barbettes 12in (305mm); deck 2.16in-1in (55mm-25mm)
Speed: 23.5 knots
Range: 9680nm (17,937km) at 14 knots
Complement: 1360

JAVA

THE NETHERLANDS: 1921

***Java*'s sister ship, *Sumatra*, was laid up at Portsmouth and used as a breakwater at Normandy; *Celebes* was cancelled while incomplete.**

Java and her sister cruisers, *Sumatra* and *Celebes*, were built to a Dutch design but with materials, technical supervision, and some labour supplied by Krupp. They were planned for completion by 1918, but their construction was delayed by World War I; by 1925–6, when they were finished, they were already obsolete. The class was to be equipped with two seaplanes (Fairey IIIDs). *Java* was torpedoed and sunk by the Japanese heavy cruiser *Nachi* in the Battle of the Java Sea.

Displacement: 6670t standard; 7050t full load
Dimensions: 509ft 6in x 52ft 6in x 18ft (155.3m x 16.0m x 5.5m)
Machinery: three screws, turbines; 72,000hp
Armament: 10 5.9in (150mm)
Armour: belt 3in-2in (76mm-50mm); deck 2in-1.5in (50mm-38mm)
Speed: 31 knots
Range: 3400nm (6300km) at 14 knots
Complement: 480

JEANNE D'ARC

FRANCE: 1930

Displacement: 6496t standard; 8950t full load
Dimensions: 557ft 7in x 57ft 5in x 20ft 7in (170m x 17.5m x 6.3m)
Machinery: two screws, geared turbines; 32,500hp
Armament: eight 6.09in (155mm); four 3in (76mm); two 21.7in (550mm) TT
Armour: belt 4.75in (120mm); turrets 3.75in (95mm); deck 3in (76mm)
Speed: 25 knots
Range: 5000nm (9265km) at 14.5 knots
Complement: 505 (plus 156 midshipmen and 20 officers when a training ship)

After the Allied invasion of the French Riviera in August 1944, *Jeanne d'Arc* ferried troops and material from North Africa.

Launched in February 1930, the light cruiser *Jeanne d'Arc* was disarmed by Allied intervention at Martinique in May 1942; she was subsequently refitted for service with the Free French Forces in June 1943. She took part in operations off Corsica, and later formed part of the naval task force which shelled enemy positions along the Italian Riviera. After World War II, *Jeanne d'Arc* became a training ship for midshipmen. She remained on the French Navy's inventory until 1964, when she was stricken.

K4

GB: 1916

In 1915, the British Admiralty decided on a class of exceptionally fast ocean-going submarines, known as K-boats. Their design called for them to keep up with the battlefleet; as diesel engines of the period could not develop adequate power to sustain a surface speed of 24 knots, steam turbines were used instead, with electric motors for underwater operation. The turbine machinery took up nearly 40 per cent of a K-boat's length and had to be shut down when she was submerged, with large lids covering the funnel uptakes. The boats were a disaster, no fewer than five of the 17 built prior to 1919 being lost in accidents. It was hardly surprising that morale in the Submarine Flotillas to which the K-boats were assigned was not at its highest level. Although a failure operationally, the K-boats represented a bold technical concept that was unmatched by either the Germans or Britain's allies. In January 1918, *K4* was accidentally rammed and sunk.

Displacement: 2140t surfaced; 2770t submerged
Dimensions: 351ft 6in x 28ft (107m x 8.5m)
Machinery: two screws, steam turbines, plus electric motors; 10,500hp/1440hp
Armament: 10 21in (533mm) TT; three 4in (102mm)
Speed: 23 knots surfaced; 9 knots submerged
Range: 3000nm (5559km) at 13.5 knots, surfaced
Complement: 50-60

On 31 January 1918, *K4* was sunk after a collision with the battlecruiser *Inflexible* off May Island, Fife, Scotland during night exercises.

KAGA

JAPAN: 1921

Launched on 17 November 1920, *Kaga* was originally laid down as an improved *Nagato*-type dreadnought, with increased armour protection and an enlarged main battery. She was cancelled in February 1922 to comply with the terms of the Washington Naval Treaty but, instead of scrapping her, the Japanese Naval Staff decided to complete her as an aircraft carrier to replace another carrier, the *Amagi*, which had been destroyed in an earthquake while under construction. (A sister ship, *Tosa*, was stricken and her incomplete hull sunk as a target in 1925.) *Kaga* was completed in March 1928 and joined the Combined Fleet in 1930. Reconstructed in 1934–35, she gained a full-length flight deck and island. Recommissioned in June 1935, *Kaga* was assigned to the 1st Carrier Division with the *Akagi*, her air group seeing action during the Sino-Japanese war. Her career during World War II was short but spectacular. In December 1941, her aircraft attacked Pearl Harbor, and subsequently operated over Rabaul, Darwin and Java. She then formed part of the Japanese carrier task force assembled for the assault on Midway Island. Concentrating on the destruction of Midway's air defences, the Japanese carriers were caught unprepared when American dive-bombers and torpedo-bombers launched their counter-attack; *Akagi*, *Kaga*, and *Soryu* were all sunk. *Kaga* sustained 800 fatalities. The Battle of Midway was a blow from which the Japanese Navy never recovered.

Displacement: 26,000t standard; 33,693t full load
Dimensions: 789ft x 108ft x 31ft (240.48m x 32.91m x 9.44m)
Machinery: four screws, geared turbines; 91,000hp
Armament: 25 20mm; 30 13.2mm AA
Armour: belt 11in (279mm); deck 2.3in (58.42mm)
Speed: 27.5 knots
Range: 5500nm (10,191km) at 16 knots
Complement: 1340

***Kaga* was not the only ship reprieved for conversion to an aircraft carrier. Two battlecruisers, *Akagi* and *Amagi*, were also retained for similar conversion.**

KAISER

GERMANY: 1911

Launched on 22 March 1911, *Kaiser* was leader of a class of five dreadnoughts, the others being *Friedrich der Grosse*, *Kaiserin*, *Konig Albert*, and *Prinzregent Luitpold*. She served with the High Seas Fleet throughout World War I, being damaged by two hits at Jutland and, in 1918, giving fire support to German forces operating in the eastern Baltic. She was interned at Scapa Flow after the Armistice, and was scuttled there on 21 June 1919. She was refloated and broken up in 1929.

The *Kaiser* class vessels were the first German battleships with turbines. *Friedrich der Grosse* was the fleet flagship.

Displacement: 24,724t standard; 27,000t full load
Dimensions: 565ft 8in x 95ft 2in x 29ft 9in (172.4m x 29m x 9.1m)
Machinery: three screws, turbines; 31,000hp
Armament: 10 12in (305mm); 14 5.9in (150mm); five 19.7in (500mm) TT
Armour: belt 13.8in-5.9in (350mm-150mm); turrets 12in-3.2in (305mm-80mm); deck 4in (100mm)
Speed: 21 knots
Range: 7900nm (14,638km) at 12 knots
Complement: 1088

KAMIKAZE

JAPAN: 1922

Ordered in 1921–22, the nine *Kamikaze* class destroyers actually formed Group II of the preceding *Minekaze* class. They were the first destroyers in the Imperial Japanese Navy to be built with a bridge strengthened by steel plating. The ships of this class had a distinguished record in World War II. In 1944, four were sunk by American submarines, and a fifth in an air attack on Truk. *Kamikaze* survived the war but, in June 1946, she became stranded on a reef and was scrapped where she lay.

Displacement: 1030t standard; 1150t full load
Dimensions: 336ft 3in x 29ft 6in x 9ft 6in (102.6m x 9m x 2.89m)
Machinery: two screws, geared steam turbines; 38,000hp
Armament: four 4.7in (120mm); six 21in (533mm) TT
Armour: belt 3in (76mm)
Speed: 37.5 knots
Range: 2700nm (5003km) at 15 knots
Complement: 148

The Japanese *kamikaze* is about the storm that destroyed the invasion fleet of the Mongol Emperor Kublai Khan in 1281.

KARLSRUHE

GERMANY: 1912

Displacement: 4900t standard; 6191t full load
Dimensions: 466ft 6in x 44ft 11in x 18ft (142.2m x 13.7m x 5.5m)
Machinery: two screws, turbines; 26,000hp
Armament: 10 4.1in (105mm); two 19.7in (500mm) TT; 120 mines
Armour: belt 2.25in-0.75in (60mm-18mm); deck 2.25in-1.5in (60mm-38mm-); gunshields 2in (50mm)
Speed: 27 knots
Range: 5500nm (10,191km) at 12 knots
Complement: 373

The two light cruisers *Karlsruhe* and *Rostock* were laid down in 1911, and launched exactly a month apart, on 11 November and 11 December 1912 respectively. At the outbreak of World War I, *Karlsruhe* was en route to relieve the light cruiser *Dresden* on the West Indies station, and to take part in the opening ceremony of the Panama Canal. She at once began commerce raiding, sinking 17 merchant ships before she herself sank as the result of an internal explosion on 4 November 1914.

***Rostock*, the sister ship of *Karlsruhe*, served with the High Seas Fleet. She sank after being badly damaged by a torpedo hit at Jutland.**

KÖLN

GERMANY: 1916

In 1915, the German Navy, aware that losses of its light cruisers were reaching serious levels, embarked on an ambitious programme to build 10 new vessels. The ships were, in effect, to be improved versions of the second generation of the *Königsbergs*. Seven units were launched but due to manpower and material shortages only two, *Köln* and *Dresden*, were commissioned. Both were scuttled at Scapa Flow on 21 June 1919; the other five were sold for scrap and broken up in the 1920s.

The five *Köln*-class light cruisers launched but not completed were the *Wiesbaden*, *Magdeburg*, *Leipzig*, *Rostock*, and *Frauenlob*.

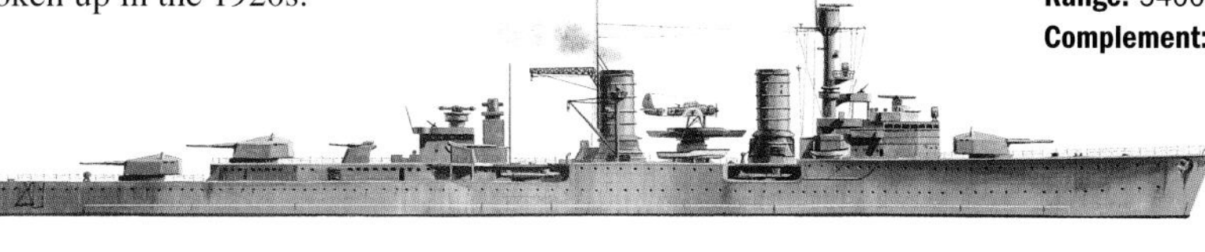

Displacement: 5620t standard; 7486t full load
Dimensions: 510ft 2in x 46ft 11in x 19ft 8in (155.5m x 14.3m x 19m)
Machinery: two screws, turbines; 31,000hp
Armament: eight 5.9in (150mm); three 3.45in (88mm); four 23.6in (600mm) TT; 120 mines
Armour: belt 2.25in-0.75in (60mm-18mm); deck 2.25in-1.5in (60mm-38mm); gunshields 2in (50mm)
Speed: 27.5 knots
Range: 5400nm (10,006km) at 12 knots
Complement: 511-522

KÖLN

GERMANY: 1928

Completed in 1928, the light cruiser *Köln* was in action from the very first day of World War II. She served in northern waters until 1943, when she was transferred to the Baltic Fleet. During the closing months of the war, she provided fire support for German forces on the Eastern Front. On 30 March 1945, while refitting at Wilhelmshaven, she was badly damaged in an Allied air attack. She was decommissioned on 6 April and her guns used for local defence. She was scrapped in 1946.

One of *Köln*'s last tasks before she was bombed was to evacuate German troops and civilian refugees from East Prussia.

Displacement: 6650t standard; 8130t full load
Dimensions: 570ft 10in x 50ft 2in x 18ft 3in (174m x 15.3m x 5.56m)
Machinery: two screws, geared turbines; 65,000hp
Armament: nine 5.9in (150mm); 12 19.7in (500mm) TT
Armour: belt 2.7in (68.58mm); deck 1.5in (38mm); turrets 1in (25mm)
Speed: 32 knots
Range: 4500nm (8338km) at 14 knots
Complement: 850

L1

USA: 1915

Displacement: 450t surfaced; 548t submerged
Dimensions: 167ft 4in x 17ft 4in x 13ft 5in (51m x 5.3m x 4m)
Machinery: two screws, diesel/electric motors; 1200/800hp
Armament: four 18in (457mm) TT: one 3in (76mm)
Speed: 14 knots surfaced; 8 knots submerged
Range: 3380nm (6270km) at 112 knots, surfaced
Complement: 35

The L1 class were the first American submarines to be fitted with a deck gun. It retracted vertically into a deckhouse until only a small portion of the barrel was left exposed, so reducing underwater drag. The USA ended World War I with around 120 submarines, although by this time she had lost her submarine design lead to the European naval powers. At this stage, America's best submarines were roughly comparable with Britain's H and L classes. In 1917–18 the submarines L1-L4 and L9-L11 were based at Bantry Bay, Ireland.

L10

GB: 1918

After the Battle of Jutland in May 1916, German surface forces rarely put to sea, and targets for Allied submarines were few and far between. However, in April 1918, the German High Seas Fleet once more ventured out in strength to attack convoys plying between Britain and Scandinavia. During one of these sorties, on 3 October 1918, the British submarine *L10* intercepted the German destroyer *S33* and sank her – only to be sunk herself by other enemy warships.

Originally intended to be modified *E*-class boats, these submarines embodied so many improvements that they were allocated the new *L* designation.

Displacement: 890t surfaced; 1080t submerged
Dimensions: 238ft 6in x 23ft 8in x 11ft 2in (72.7m x 7.2m x 3.4m)
Machinery: two screws, diesel/electric motors; 2400/1600hp
Armament: four 21in (533mm) TT; one 4in (102mm) gun
Speed: 17.5 knots surfaced, 10.5 knots submerged
Range: 4500nm (8338km), surfaced
Complement: 38

LANGLEY

USA: 1912

The USS *Langley* (CV-1) was the US Navy's first aircraft carrier. She was converted from the fleet collier *Jupiter*, which was launched in 1912 and subsequently used as a testbed for turbo-electric propulsion. The collier's superstructure was removed and a flight deck erected the full length of the hull; the cranes were also removed, and the coal bunkers converted to accommodate disassembled aircraft. The carrier had no island, and smoke was vented by means of a hinged funnel on the port side. A second funnel was fitted later. Conversion was completed in March 1922, and the *Langley* joined the Pacific Fleet in 1924. In 1937 she was converted to a seaplane tender and re-classified AV-3. When Pearl Harbor was attacked in December 1941, *Langley* was in the Far East. In February 1942, she was assigned the task of ferrying aircraft reinforcements to Java; on 27 February, off Tjilatjap, Java, she was attacked and sunk by bombers of the Japanese 21st and 23rd Naval Air Flotillas.

During her conversion to the role of seaplane tender in 1937, *Langley*'s forward section underwent a number of changes, including removal of part of the flight deck.

Displacement: 12,700t standard; 13,900t full load
Dimensions: 542ft x 65ft 5in x 24ft (165.2m x 19.9m x 7.3m)
Machinery: two screws, turbo-electric drive; 7200hp
Armament: four 5in (127mm); 36 aircraft
Armour: none
Speed: 15 knots
Range: 3500nm (6485km) at 10 knots
Complement: 468

LEOPARD

FRANCE: 1923

Displacement: 2126t standard; 2950t full load
Dimensions: 415ft 11in x 37ft 2in x 13ft 5in (126.78m x 11.32m x 4.1m)
Machinery: two screws, geared turbines; 50,000hp
Armament: five 5.1in (130mm); six 21.7in (550mm) TT
Armour: belt 3in (76mm); deck 2in (50mm)
Speed: 35 knots
Range: 3000nm (5559km) at 13 knots
Complement: 195

One of six French destroyers of the *Chacal* class, *Leopard* was launched on 29 September 1924. On 3 July 1940 she was in Portsmouth, and was taken over by the Royal Navy. She was assigned to the Free French Naval Forces on 31 August 1940, and subsequently served on convoy escort duty in the Atlantic. On 21 July 1942, together with RN escorts, she sank the German submarine *U136*. She was badly damaged near Tobruk on 27 May 1943 and was beached, being considered a total loss.

To compensate for *Leopard*'s lack of radius, her first boiler was removed and a fuel tank installed in its place.

LEXINGTON

USA: 1925

***Lexington* and *Saratoga* were the first US Fleet carriers. They provided the US Navy with invaluable experience which resulted in the design of the *Yorktown* class of the early 1930s.**

Displacement: 37,681t standard; 43,055t full load
Dimensions: 888ft x 105ft 5in x 33ft 4in (270.66m x 32.12m x 10.15m)
Machinery: four screws, turbines; 180,000hp
Armament: eight 8in (203mm); 12 5in (127mm); 63 aircraft
Armour: belt 7in-5in (178mm-127mm); deck 2in (50mm)
Speed: 33.25 knots
Range: 10,500nm (19,456km) at 15 knots
Complement: 2327

In 1916–17, as a counter to the powerful Japanese *Kongo* class,the US Naval Staff ordered a class of six new battlecruisers, *Constellation* (CC-2), *Constitution* (CC-5), *Lexington* (CC-1), *Ranger* (CC-4), *Saratoga* (CC-3), and *United States* (CC-6). To comply with the terms of the 1922 Washington Naval Treaty, construction of these warships was suspended when they were partially complete and the contract was cancelled. However, it was decided to complete two vessels as aircraft carriers, the *Constitution* (rather confusingly re-named *Lexington*) and the *Saratoga*. The *Lexington* was re-ordered as a carrier in July 1922 and given the designation CV-2; *Sarotoga* was designated CV-3, although in fact she was the first to be launched, on 7 April 1925. Launched on 3 October that year, *Lexington* took part in Pacific Fleet exercises for the first time in January 1929, together with her sister ship. As finally completed, both ships were armed with 8in (203mm) rather than 6in (152mm) guns, these weapons being designed to match the new generation of cruisers which were similarly armed. As a defensive measure, there were also plans, never implemented, to incorporate torpedo tubes. As the two biggest aircraft carriers in the world at the time of their completion, *Lexington* and *Saratoga* received much publicity. In December 1929, for example, *Lexington* made headlines when she served as a floating power plant for the city of Tacoma, Washington, following a massive power failure. After the Japanese attack on Pearl Harbor, *Lexington*'s air group was involved in the battle for Wake Island, followed by limited raids on Japanese-held objectives in the Pacific and convoy escort duty. In May 1942, Allied naval intelligence learnt that the Japanese were about to mount an amphibious assault on Port Moresby, New Guinea, as a preliminary to an invasion of Australia. *Lexington* was assigned to Task Force 11, a joint Allied naval force formed to counter this move. In the Battle of the Coral Sea, which began on the morning of 8 May 1942 after the opposing carrier task forces sighted one another and launched their respective strike forces, *Lexington* was hit by two torpedoes and three bombs and had to be abandoned, being sunk later by the destroyer USS *Phelps*. Casualties included 216 fatalities. *Saratoga* survived the war, despite being twice torpedoed in 1942 and hit by four *kamikazes* in 1945, only to be expended in the atomic bomb tests at Bikini in 1946.

When Japanese aircraft attacked the carrier *Lexington* in the Coral Sea battle, she was without her 8in (203mm) main armament and also without the 5in (127mm) dual purpose guns that were to have replaced them.

L'INDOMPTABLE

FRANCE: 1933

The *Fantasque* class of six destroyers, one of which was *L'Indomptable*, was the penultimate class in a French series that set new destroyer standards. However, the design had little real influence on construction abroad because it stemmed largely from naval rivalry with the Italians. At the height of the Norwegian campaign, *Le Triomphant*, *L'Indomptable*, and *Le Malin* carried out an audacious raid into the Skagerrak, engaging a force of German patrol boats. *L'Indomptable* was scuttled at Toulon in 1942.

Displacement: 2569t standard; 3300t full load
Dimensions: 434ft 4in x 40ft 6in x 16ft 4in (132.4m x 12.35m x 5m)
Machinery: two screws, geared turbines; 81,000hp
Armament: five 5.46in (138.6mm); three triple 21in (533mm) TT
Armour: belt 3in (76mm); turret faces and decks 1in (25mm)
Speed: 37 knots
Range: 3000nm (5559km) at 14 knots
Complement: 210

Although the design speed of the *Fantasque* class was 37 knots, all six vessels in fact exceeded 40 knots during trials.

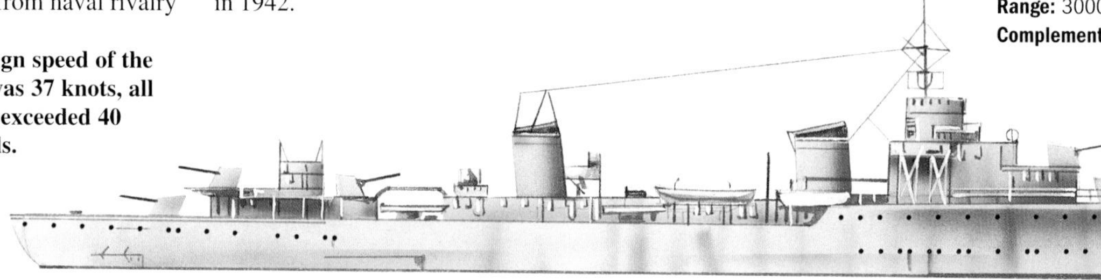

LION

GB: 1910

Displacement: 26,350t standard; 29,680t full load
Dimensions: 700ft x 88ft 6in x 28ft 10in (213.4m x 27m x 8.8m)
Machinery: four screws, turbines; 70,000hp
Armament: eight 13.5in (343mm); 16 4in (102mm); two 21in (533mm) TT
Armour: belt 9in-4in (229mm-102mm); turrets 9in (229mm), deck 1in (25mm)
Speed: 26 knots
Range: 5610nm (10,395km) at 10 knots
Complement: 997

The two vessels which constituted the *Lion* class warships of 1909–10, *Lion* and *Princess Royal*, were the first battlecruisers to surpass battleships in size. They had a number of deficiencies, the most glaring of which was that they were provided with adequate protection only to resist 11in (280mm) shellfire, and then only in limited areas. They were extremely vulnerable to 12in (305mm) shells, the calibre employed by most German capital ships, and in some areas their armour could be penetrated by shells of lesser calibre; they were also several knots slower than their design speed. Launched on 6 August 1910, *Lion* commissioned in June 1912 and was assigned to the 1st Cruiser Squadron in January 1913 as the flagship of Rear-Admiral Beatty. She was in action against German light forces in the Heligoland Bight. At the Dogger Bank battle on 24 January 1915, she expended 243 shells but scored only four hits. On the other hand, she was hit by 18 shells, suffering such serious damage that she had to be towed home by *Indomitable*.

During the Battle of Jutland, *Lion* suffered even worse damage, coming under withering fire from

Both *Lion* and *Princess Royal* underwent frequent changes to their secondary and AA armament during their service. In 1919, *Lion*'s AA armament comprised two 3in (76mm) and two 2pdr guns.

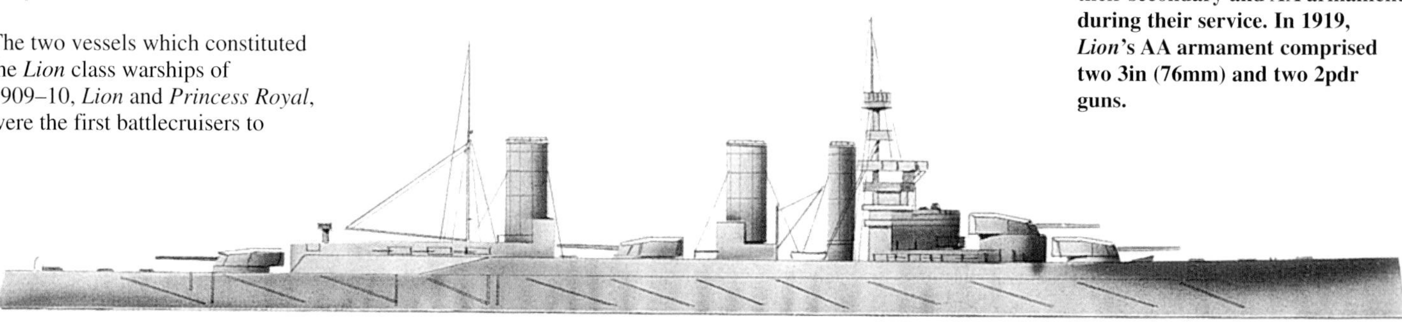

the battlecruiser *Lutzow* and taking 12 hits, one of which started a fire in 'Q' turret. Only an order to flood the magazine, issued by a dying Royal Marines officer, Major Harvey, prevented a disaster. *Lion* suffered 99 dead in this action. In November 1916, she became flagship of Rear-Admiral Pakenham, and undertook numerous further sorties as leader of the 1st CS before the war's end. She continued on active service until 1923, being sold and broken up at Blyth, Northumberland, in 1924.

LORD NELSON

GB: 1906

Displacement: 16,500t standard; 17,820t full load
Dimensions: 443ft 6in x 79ft 6in x 27ft (135.2m x 24.2m x 8.2m)
Machinery: two screws, vertical triple expansion engines; 16,750hp
Armament: four 12in (305mm); 10 9.2in (234mm); five 18in (457mm) TT
Armour: belt 12in-4in (305mm-102mm); turrets 12in (305mm)
Speed: 18 knots
Range: 9180nm (17,010km) at 10 knots
Complement: 697

The pre-dreadnought battleships *Lord Nelson* and *Agamemnon* were designed with a battery of mixed large-calibre guns, all mounted in turrets, no barbettes being used. They were the first British battleships to feature tripod masts, and the last to be fitted with reciprocating engines. *Lord Nelson* was launched on 4 September 1906. At the outbreak of World War I, she was flagship of the Channel Fleet, and subsequently served in the Dardanelles, Aegean and Black Sea. She was broken up in 1920.

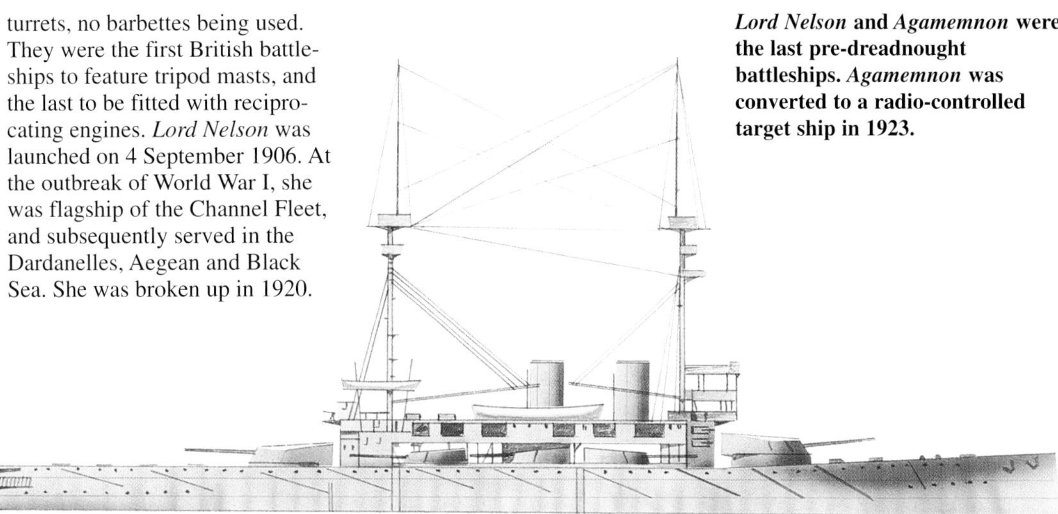

Lord Nelson and Agamemnon were the last pre-dreadnought battleships. Agamemnon was converted to a radio-controlled target ship in 1923.

LUIGI CADORNA

ITALY: 1930

Luigi Cadorna and her sister ship *Armando Diaz* formed the second group of the *Condottieri* class of light cruisers. The *Luigi Cadorna* was launched on 30 September 1931 and completed in August 1933. Both ships were fitted out for use as fast minelayers, being operated in that capacity in the Mediterranean and Aegean during World War II. Half the class became war casualties, but the *Luigi Cadorna* survived and remained active until 1951, when she was stricken.

Although *Cadorna* survived the war, her sister ship, *Armando Diaz*, was sunk by HM submarine *Upright* on 25 February 1941.

Displacement: 5232t standard; 7001t full load
Dimensions: 555ft 5in x 50ft 10in x 18ft (169.3m x 15.5m x 5.5m)
Machinery: two screws, geared turbines; 95,000hp
Armament: eight 6in (152mm); six 4.7in (100mm); four 21in (533mm) TT
Armour: belt 1in-0.70in (25mm-18mm); turrets 1in (25mm); deck 0.78in (20mm)
Speed: 36.5 knots
Range: 4200nm (7782km) at 14 knots
Complement: 544

M1

GB: 1917

In 1917, the British Admiralty suspended construction work on four K-boats, and revised plans to turn them into 'submarine monitors'. They became known as M-boats and featured a single 12in (305mm) gun mounted in the front part of an extended conning tower. The gun could be fired from periscope depth within 30 seconds of a target being sighted, or in 20 seconds if the submarine was surfaced. The *M1* was the only M-boat to see war service.

Displacement: 1594t surfaced; 1946t submerged
Dimensions: 295ft 7in x 24ft 7in x 16ft (90.1m x 7.5m x 4.9m)
Machinery: two screws, diesel/electric motors; 2400/1600hp
Armament: four 21in (533mm) TT; one 12in (305mm)
Speed: 15 knots surfaced; 9 knots submerged
Range: 10,000nm (18,530km) at 10 knots, surfaced; 100nm (185km) at 5 knots, submerged
Complement: 65

Of the three *M*-class boats completed, two were lost in accidents, *M1* in a collision with the freighter *Vidar* in November 1925.

M2

GB: 1917

Displacement: 1594t surfaced; 1946t submerged
Dimensions: 295ft 7in x 24ft 7in x 16ft (90.1m x 7.5m x 4.9m)
Machinery: two screws, diesel/electric motors; 2400/1600hp
Armament: four 21in (533mm) TT; one 12in (305mm)
Speed: 15 knots surfaced; 9 knots submerged
Range: 10,000nm (18,530km) at 10 knots, surfaced; 100nm (185km) at 5 knots, submerged
Complement: 65

Although often referred to as 'ex-*K* class', the four M-boats were a new design, bearing no resemblance to the steam-driven Ks.

The second of the M-boats, *M2* was converted to the role of seaplane carrier in April 1928 and foundered off Portland in 1933. A principal drawback with the *M*-class submarines was that the gun could not be reloaded under water, so the submarine had to surface after each round was fired – earning the M-boats the nickname 'Dip Chicks'.

MARSHAL SOULT

GB: 1915

Displacement: 6670t standard; 6900t full load
Dimensions: 355ft 8in x 90ft 3in x10ft 6in (108.4m x 27.5m x 3.2m)
Machinery: two screws, diesel engines; 1500hp
Armament: two 15in (381mm); eight 4in (102mm), added in 1916
Armour: deck 4in (102mm); turrets 13in (330mm)
Speed: 6.5 knots
Endurance: 1000nm (1853km) at 5 knots
Complement: 228

Presumably named in order to cement the *entente cordiale*, the monitor *Marshal Soult* (M14) and her sister ship, *Marshal Ney* (M13), were fitted with 15in (381mm) turrets from the battleship *Ramillies*, then under construction. Both *Marshal Soult* and *Marshal Ney* were launched in 1915, in May and June respectively, and assigned to the Dover patrol. In April 1918, *Marshal Soult* carried out bombardment duty in support of the raid on Zeebrugge. After postwar service as a gunnery training ship, she was hulked in 1940 and broken up in 1946.

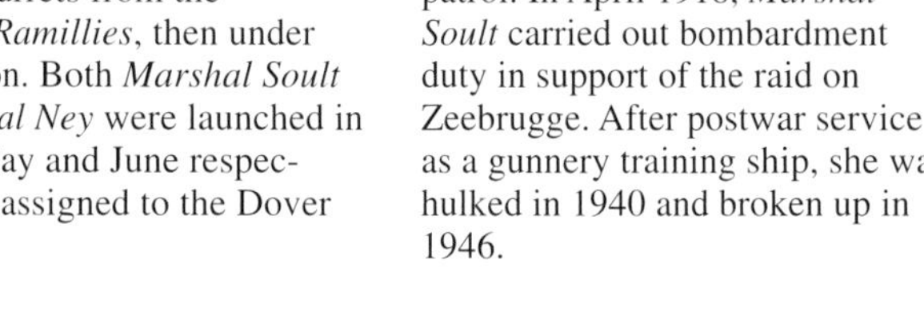

The engines of these two monitors were taken from oilers under construction. Both ships were too slow, never achieving their design speed.

MAS 9

ITALY: 1916

Launched in 1916, *MAS 9* was one of a group of unusual vessels designed for rapid attack by Engineer Bisio. The small size of the boats made them very difficult targets for the enemy, especially when manoeuvring at high speed. Torpedoes were carried one each side amidships, on the whaleback foredeck. On the night of 9 December 1917, *MAS 9*, commanded by Luigi Rizzo, successfully penetrated Trieste harbour and sank the Austrian battleship *Wien*. In 1922, *MAS 9* was discarded.

Displacement: 16t standard
Dimensions: 52ft 6in x 8ft 8in x 4ft (16m x 2.6m x 1.2m)
Machinery: two screws, petrol engines; 450hp
Armament: one 1.85in (47mm); two 17.7in (450mm) TT
Armour: none
Speed: 25.2 knots
Range: not known
Complement: eight

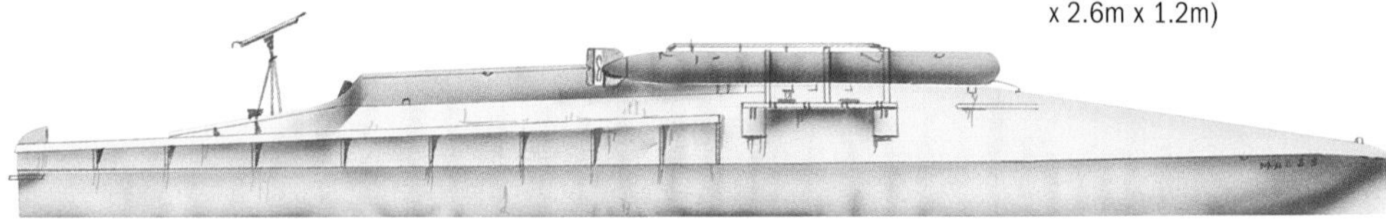

In addition to its petrol engines, *MAS 9* was also fitted with two Rognini electric motors, developing 10hp, for silent running.

MAYA

JAPAN: 1930

The cruiser *Maya* was one of four laid down in 1927–28, the others being *Takao*, *Atago*, and *Chokai*. They were a slightly improved version of the previous *Nachi* class, the main alterations being a larger bridge structure, torpedo tubes in a rotating mount on the upper deck, and an upright second funnel. Following bomb damage in November 1943, 'C' turret on *Maya* was removed and replaced by two twin 5in (127mm) AA turrets. *Maya* was sunk by four torpedoes from the US submarine *Dace* on 23 October 1944.

All cruisers of the *Takao* class carried three aircraft for general reconnaissance. One of *Maya*'s was removed in 1943.

Displacement: 9850t standard; 12,781t full load
Dimensions: 668ft 6in x 59ft 2in x 20ft 1in (203.76m x 18.03m x 6.11m)
Machinery: four screws, geared turbines; 130,000hp
Armament: 10 8in (203mm); four 4.7in (120mm); eight 24in (609mm) TT
Armour: belt 3.9in (100mm); magazines 4.9in (125mm); deck 1.5in (38mm)
Speed: 35.5 knots
Range: 5000nm (9265km) at 14 knots
Complement: 773

MEMPHIS

USA: 1924

Displacement: 7050t normal; 9508t full load
Dimensions: 555ft 6in x 55ft 5in x 13ft 6in (169.4m x 16.9m x 4.1m)
Machinery: four screws, turbines; 90,000hp
Armament: 12 6in (152mm); 10 21in (533mm) TT
Armour: belt 3in (76mm); deck 1.5in (38mm)
Speed: 34 knots
Range: 10,000nm (18,530km) at 10 knots
Complement: 458

Launched on 17 April 1924, the cruiser USS *Memphis* was one of the first such vessels to be authorised since 1904, and one of the last of the *Omaha*-class cruisers. Ten units were built, the design being based on pre-World War I concepts, and emphasising end-on firing at the expense of broadside. Later, makeshift steps had to be taken to strengthen these weak points, two twin 6in (152mm) gun mounts being added to increase the broadside, and additional torpedo tubes also being fitted. The overall result was an increase in personnel required to operate the extra equipment, so that the *Omaha*s were criticised for being badly overcrowded. They were, however, good sea-boats and fast and manoeuvrable. *Memphis* served on the South Atlantic patrol during World War II, and was one of the US warships that implemented the Neutrality Patrol in the summer of 1941. In 1944, she formed part of a task group operating against German blockade runners coming from East Asia. *Memphis* was stricken in 1946.

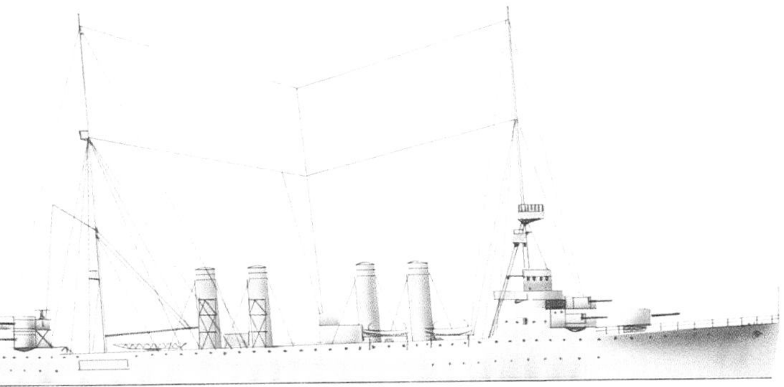

By the end of World War II, the armament of the *Omaha* class varied considerably. *Memphis* was reduced to seven 3in (76mm) guns.

MENDEZ NUÑEZ

SPAIN: 1923

Displacement: 4650t standard
Dimensions: 462ft x 46ft x 14ft 4in (140.8m x 14m x 4.7m)
Machinery: four screws, geared turbines; 45,000hp
Armament: six 6in (152mm); 12 21in (533mm) TT
Armour: belt 3in-1.25in (76mm-1.75mm); deck 1in (25mm)
Speed: 29 knots
Range: 4200nm (7782km) at 12 knots
Complement: 343

The Spanish cruisers *Mendez Nuñez* and her sister ship, *Blaz de Lezo*, were authorised in 1915. The *Mendez Nuñez* was launched on 3 March 1923 and completed in 1924, *Blaz de Lezo* having been launched some months earlier. Construction was hampered and subjected to lengthy delays due to a shortage of shipbuilding material during and after World War I. The vessels were similar in design to the British *C*-class light cruisers. *Blaz de Leno* was wrecked off Cape Finisterre in 1932, but *Mendez Nunez* was not stricken until 1963.

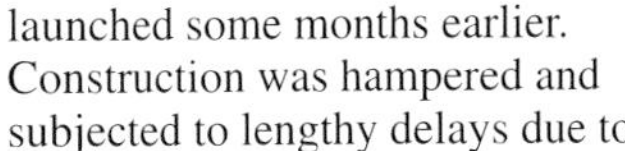

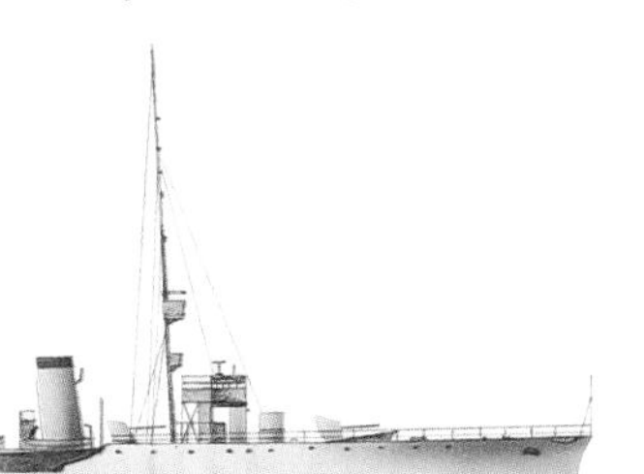

The Spanish Navy planned two more cruisers in the *Mendez Nuñez* class, but they were cancelled in 1919.

MICHIGAN

USA: 1906

The USS *Michigan* and her sister ship USS *South Carolina* were the first dreadnought battleships built in the USA. Although laid down after HMS *Dreadnought*, they were in fact the first battleships designed with an all-big-gun armament of eight 12in (305mm) guns and superfiring turrets, features that were copied by all other nations. This turret arrangement was arrived at through default of an earlier design, which involved twin 12in (305mm) turrets mounted fore and aft on the centreline, and four single turrets replacing the twin 8in (203mm) mounts of earlier pre-dreadnoughts. However, this concept gave rise to serious structural problems, presumably because a Congress mandate restricted displacement to 16,000t (they were the last American battleships to be subject to this restriction). The superfiring concept, where the main turrets were mounted one above the other, was first tested in the monitor *Florida* in March 1907. *Michigan* was launched on 26 May, and *South Carolina* on 11 July 1908. Their propulsion system of two screw, vertical triple expansion engines left much to be desired, producing a maximum speed of barely 17 knots. As a result, they could not operate tactically with later dreadnoughts; for example,

Building of the *Michigan* and *North Carolina* revolutionised battleship construction techniques in the USA, forming the basis for successive classes.

Displacement: 16,000t standard; 17,617t full load
Dimensions: 452ft 9in x 80ft 3in x 24ft 6in (138m x 24.5m x 7.5m)
Machinery: two screws, vertical triple expansion engines; 16,500hp
Armament: eight 12in (305mm); 22 3in (76mm); two 21in (533mm) TT
Armour: belt 11in-9in (279mm-229mm); turrets 12in-8in (305mm-203mm); bulkhead 10in (254mm); deck 3in (76mm); conning tower 12in (305mm)
Speed: 18.5 knots
Range: 5000nm (9265km) at 10 knots
Complement: 869

they did not serve in battle groups with the later vessels in European waters during World War I. On 15 January 1915, *Michigan* lost her cage foremast in a violent storm off Cape Hatteras, North Carolina, which led to all cage masts being redesigned and strengthened. She made two voyages as a troop transport in 1919, bringing American personnel home from France. She was decommissioned on 11 February 1922 and stricken on 17 October 1917, being sold and broken up at Philadelphia in the following year.

MINAS GERAIS

BRAZIL: 1908

Minas Gerais was one of two battleships built in Britain for the Brazilian Navy, the other being the *Sao Paolo*. Both were of the enlarged dreadnought type with superfiring turrets. Launched on 10 September 1908, *Minas Gerais* was completed in January 1910. In November that year she was involved in an anti-government rebellion, shelling Rio de Janeiro. In 1917, Brazil offered to attach both warships to the British Grand Fleet, but this was rejected. *Minas Gerais* was broken up in 1954.

Reconstructed in 1934–37, *Minas Gerais* served as a floating battery at Salvador, Bahia, during World War II.

Displacement: 19,280t standard; 21,200t full load
Dimensions: 543ft x 83ft x 25ft (165.5m x 25.3m x 7.6m)
Machinery: two screws, vertical triple expansion engines; 23,500hp
Armament: 12 12in (305mm); 22 4.7in (120mm)
Armour: belt 9in–4in (230mm–102mm); turrets 9in–8in (230mm–203mm)
Speed: 21 knots
Range: 8000nm (14,824nm) at 10 knots
Complement: 850

MOGAMI

JAPAN: 1934

Displacement: 8500t standard; 10,993t full load
Dimensions: 661ft 1in x 59ft 1in x 18ft 1in (201.5m x 18m x 5.5m)
Machinery: four screws, geared turbines; 152,000hp
Armament: 15 6in (152mm); eight 5in (127mm) DP; 12 24in (609mm) TT
Armour: belt 3.9in (100mm); magazines 4.9in (124mm); deck 2.4in–1.4in (61mm–31.36mm)
Speed: 37 knots
Range: 4400nm (8153km) at 14 knots
Complement: 850

The four Japanese light cruisers of the *Mogami* class were in effect 'mini battleships', designed to mount the heaviest possible armament on the restricted tonnage set by the London Naval Treaty of 1930. They featured triple gun turrets and, like Germany's 'pocket battleships', their hulls were electrically welded to save weight. At an early stage in the trials of the first two ships, *Mogami* and *Mikuma*, they were found to be top-heavy and had to be withdrawn for modification. Launched on 14 March 1934, *Mogami* took part in the Battle of Midway in June 1942, where she was severely damaged by carrier aircraft from the USS *Yorktown*. After a lengthy period of reconstruction she was returned to service in 1943, having been fitted with a flight deck on which it was intended to carry 11 seaplanes. *Mogami* was sunk by air attack in the Battle of the Surigao Strait on 25 October 1944. None of the ships of the *Mogami* class survived the war.

***Mogami* saw most of her war service with the 7th Light Cruiser Squadron, and was in the forefront of the action throughout.**

MONTANA

USA: 1906

The USS *Montana* (ACR-13) was one of four *Tennessee*-class armoured cruisers, the others being *North Carolina* (ACR-12), *Tennessee* (ACR-10), and *Washington* (ACR-11). They were improvements of the *Pennsylvania* class of 1899–1900, with heavier armour and armament. The first aircraft catapult launch from a ship was made from one of this class, *North Carolina*, on 5 November 1915. *Montana* was laid down at Newport News in April 1905, and launched on December 15 1906. Completed in July 1908, she was assigned to the Atlantic Fleet until 1917, with occasional deployments to the Mediterranean. During World War I she escorted convoys across the Atlantic, and in 1919 she made one voyage as a troop transport, bringing home American personnel from Europe. In June 1920 she was renamed *Missoula*, and was decommissioned in the following year. She was sold and broken up in 1930.

All the *Tennessee*-class armoured cruisers were re-named. *Tennessee* and *Washington* became *Memphis* and *Seattle* in 1916, while *North Carolina* became *Charlotte* in 1920.

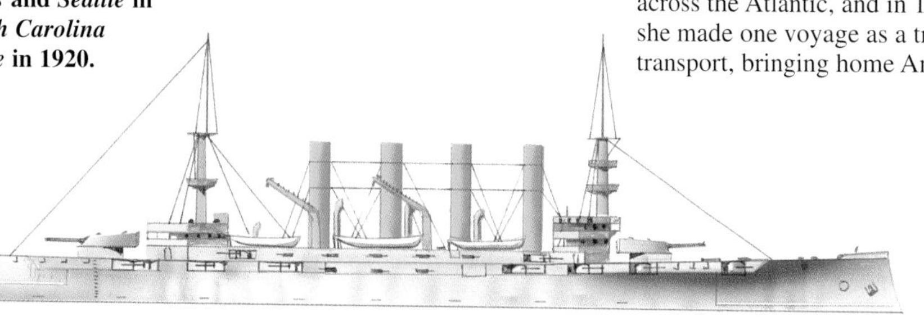

Displacement: 14,500t standard; 15, 715t full load
Dimensions: 504ft 6in x 72ft 11in x 25ft (153.76m x 22.23m x 7.62m)
Machinery: two screws, vertical triple expansion engines; 23,000hp
Armament: four 10in (254mm); 16 6in (152mm); four 21in (533mm) TT
Armour: belt 5in (127mm); turrets 9in–5in (229mm–127mm)
Speed: 22 knots
Range: 5500nm (10,191km) at 10 knots
Complement: 858

MORENO

ARGENTINA: 1911

Displacement: 28,000t standard; 30,600t full load
Dimensions: 604ft x 95ft 6in x 27ft 9in (181.4m x 29.1m x 8.5m)
Machinery: three screws, turbines; 39,500hp
Armament: 12 12in (305mm); 12 6in (152mm); 12 4in (102mm); two 21in (533mm) TT
Armour: belt 11in-8in (279mm-203mm); turrets 12in-9in (305mm-229mm); deck 3in (76mm)
Speed: 22.5 knots
Range: 11,000nm (20,383nm) at 11 knots
Complement: 1080

***Moreno* and *Rivadavia* were very heavily armed, their main guns disposed in six turrets, two diagonally placed on the wings.**

The Argentine Navy's *Rivadavia*, class dreadnoughts, *Rivadavia* and *Moreno*, were built in the USA, the former by Fore River and the latter by the New York Shipbuilding. Ordered in 1908, *Moreno* was launched on 23 September 1911, and completed in March 1915. In 1937, together with *Rivadavia*, she undertook a cruise to Europe, the first Argentine warships to do so. In the 1950s, she served successively as a depot ship and a prison ship before being scrapped in Japan in 1957. *Rivadavia* was also scrapped that year.

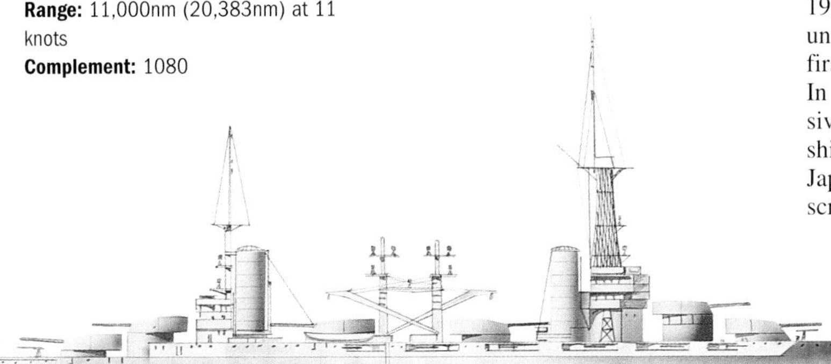

NACHI

JAPAN: 1927

The *Myoko*-class cruisers, to which *Nachi* belonged, were Japan's first generation 10,000t vessels built under the restrictions of the Washington Treaty. Their advanced design, and the construction techniques used, combined to produce warships that were able to attain the highest possible speeds while mounting the maximum armament. The ships had inclined side armour, its thickness being increased from 3in (76mm) to 3.9in (99mm), while there was extra protection against torpedoes in the form of an arched protective bulkhead inside the main armour belt. The four ships in the class were *Ashigara*, *Haguro*, *Myoko*, and *Nachi*, all of which became casualties in World War II. *Nachi* was sunk in an attack by US carrier aircraft in Manila Bay, *Haguro* by British destroyers off Penang, and *Ashigari* by HM submarine *Trenchent* near the Banka Strait. *Myoko* was scuttled in the Malacca Straits after the war.

During World War II, *Nachi* and her sister ships formed the 5th Cruiser Division, operating mainly in the Indian Ocean.

Displacement: 10,000t standard; 13,380t full load
Dimensions: 668ft 6in x 56ft 11in x 19ft 4in (203.76m x 17.34m x 5.9m)
Machinery: four screws, geared turbines; 130,000hp
Armament: 10 8in (203mm); six 4.7in (120mm); 12 24in (609mm) TT
Armour: belt 3.9in (100mm); deck 1.4in (35.56mm)
Speed: 35.5 knots
Range: 4500nm (8338km) at 15 knots
Complement: 773

NAGARA

JAPAN: 1921

The *Nagaras* were the second class of Japanese 5000t cruisers to be completed. There were six ships in the class: *Abukuma*, *Isuzu*, *Kinu*, *Nagara*, *Natori*, and *Yura*. A new feature of the design was the bridge built above main deck level, such that a seaplane could be housed underneath it. A flying-off platform was fitted in front of the aircraft shelter. At a later date, the platform was equipped with a catapult. Both aircraft and catapult were moved aft in 1934. *Nagara* was sunk by the US submarine *Bowfin* on 7 August 1944.

During World War II, the *Nagara*-class light cruisers were used as the flagships of cruiser, destroyer and submarine squadrons.

Displacement: 5170t standard; 5570t full load
Dimensions: 532ft x 46ft 6in x 15ft 9in (162.1m x 14.2m x 4.8m)
Machinery: four screws, geared turbines; 90,000hp
Armament: seven 5.5in (140mm); eight 24in (609mm) TT
Armour: belt 2.5in (63mm); deck 1.25in (32mm)
Speed: 36 knots
Range: 5000nm (9265km) at 14 knots
Complement: 450

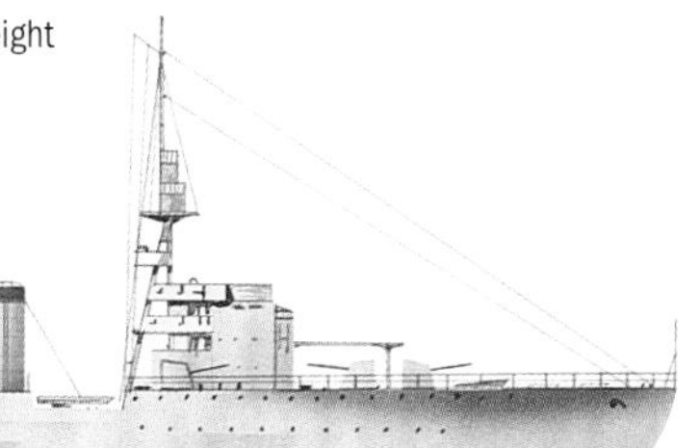

NASSAU

GERMANY: 1908

In 1908, Germany passed yet another Navy Act, making provision for an increase in the number of heavy warships. The 'large cruisers' that were the outcome of the earlier 1908 Navy Act were now re-classified as 'battlecruisers', so that the planned combined battleship and battle-cruiser strength envisaged for the Imperial German Navy over the coming years rose to 58 ships. Germany's first dreadnoughts were the four vessels of the *Nassau* class, initiated in 1906. Shorter and wider than the British dreadnoughts, and less heavily armed, they were nevertheless well protected and well armed: their main armament comprised 12 11in (280mm) guns with a secondary armament of 12 5.9in (150mm). The disposition of the main armament, however, was poor, broadside fire being restricted by the positioning of two turrets on each side amidships, and one each fore and aft. The ships of this class were the *Nassau*, *Posen*, *Rheinland*, and *Westfalen*.

Displacement: 18,873t standard; 20,535t full load
Dimensions: 479ft 4in x 88ft 4in x 28ft 9in (146.1m x 26.9m x 8.7m)
Machinery: three screws, vertical triple expansion engines; 22,000hp
Armament: 12 11in (280mm); 12 5.9in (150mm); six 17.7in (450mm) TT
Armour: belt 3.9in-3.2in (100mm-80mm); turrets 11in-8.6in (280mm-220mm); deck 3.2in (80mm)
Speed: 19.5 knots
Range: 9400nm (17,418km) at 10 knots
Complement: 1008

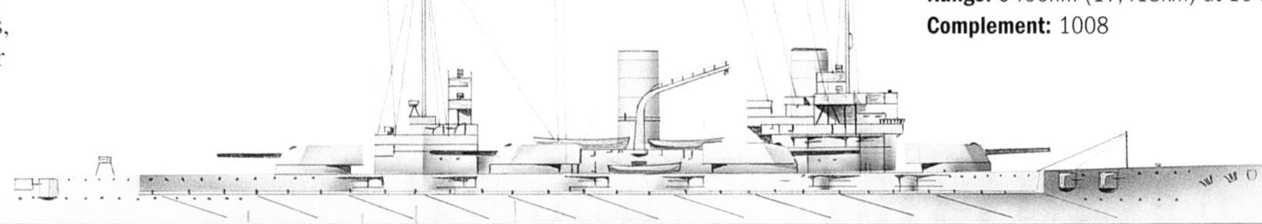

In the Battle of Jutland, *Nassau* rammed and sank the British destroyer *Spitfire*. *Nassau* was scrapped in 1920.

NAUTILUS

USA: 1930

Displacement: 2730t surfaced; 3900t submerged
Dimensions: 370ft x 33ft 3in x 15ft 9in (113m x 1m x 4.8m)
Machinery: two screws, diesel/electric motors; 5450/2540hp
Armament: six 21in (533mm) TT, two 6in (152mm)
Speed: 17 knots surfaced, 8 knots submerged
Range: 10,000nm (18,350km) at 10 knots, surfaced
Complement: 90

Launched on 15 March 1930, the USS *Nautilus* (SS168, formerly V6) was one of three *V*-class boats designed as long-endurance, ocean-going submarines with a heavy armament, the others being *Argonaut* and *Narwhal*. In 1940, *Nautilus* was refitted to carry 19,320gal (5104l) of aviation fuel for long-range seaplanes, the idea being that she should make an ocean rendezvous with the latter. She was one of a force of submarines patrolling north-west of Midway Island in June 1942. Their role was to counter an anticipated Japanese invasion force, and in August, together with *Argonaut*, she landed US raiders on Makin, in the Gilbert Islands. In October 1942 she sank two freighters off the east coast of Japan, and in May 1943, together with *Narwhal*, she acted as a marker submarine in Operation 'Landcrab', the reconquest of Attu in the North Pacific. In March 1944, *Nautilus* sank another large freighter off the Mandate Islands. She was scrapped in 1945.

***Nautilus* and *Narwhal*, designed from the outset as long-range cruiser submarines, were the largest American submersibles until the advent of the nuclear submarine.**

NELSON

GB: 1925

The principal aim of the 1922 Washington Treaty, which was engineered by the USA and which, in effect, was the first disarmament treaty in history, was to limit the size of the navies of the five principal maritime powers. At that time, the five were Great Britain, the USA, France, Italy, and Japan. For Britain, this meant a reduction in capital ship assets to 20 by scrapping existing warships and dropping new projects. However, because her capital ships were older and less heavily armed than those of the USA, she would be permitted to build two new vessels as replacements for those existing. The new vessels were the battleships *Nelson* and *Rodney*, both of which were laid down in December 1922. In effect, they were scaled-down versions, but adopted the same design as the *G3* class of four un-named battle-cruisers, cancelled due to the Washington Treaty. All main armament was positioned forward in three triple turrets, while all machinery was concentrated aft so as to save on weight of armour.

Displacement: 33,950t standard; 38,000t full load
Dimensions: 710ft x 106ft x 30ft (216.4m x 32.3m x 9.1m)
Machinery: two screws, geared turbines; 45,000hp
Armament: nine 16in (406mm); 12 6in (152mm); six 4.7mm (120mm); two 24.5in (622mm) TT
Armour: belt 14in-11in (355mm-279mm); turrets 16in-9in (406mm-229mm); deck 6.5in (165mm)
Speed: 23 knots
Range: 16,500nm (30,574km) at 12 knots
Complement: 1314

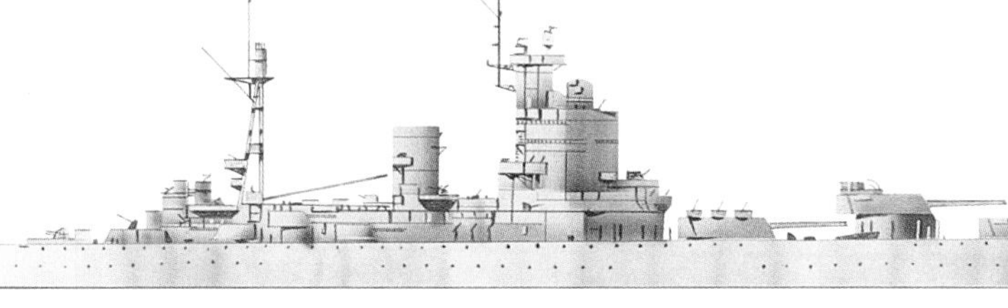

On 28 September 1943, the Armistice with Italy was signed aboard the battleship HMS *Nelson*. She was broken up in 1948.

NEVADA

USA: 1914

Displacement: 27,500t standard; 28,400t full load
Dimensions: 583ft x 95ft 3in x 28ft 6in (177.7m x 29m x 8.7m)
Machinery: two screws, turbines; 26,500hp
Armament: 10 14in (356mm); 21 5in (127mm); four 21in (533mm) TT
Armour: belt 13.5in-8in (343mm-203mm); turrets 18in-9in (457mm-229mm); deck 3in (76mm)
Speed: 20.5 knots
Range: 10,000nm (18,530km) at 10 knots
Complement: 1049

In 1946, *Nevada* was used as a target vessel in the Bikini atom bomb tests. Decommissioned in August 1946, she was sunk as a target by aircraft and naval gunfire off Hawaii on 31 July 1948.

Nevada (BB-36) and her sister ship *Oklahoma* (BB-37) were second generation American dreadnoughts. Of revolutionary design, they featured so-called 'all or nothing' protection. The designers decided that, since armour-piercing shells did not burst when penetrating thin plating, there was nothing to be gained from using thin armour, which would serve only to detonate the missiles; the choice, therefore, was between using only the thickest possible armour, which would not be penetrated, or none at all. In the *Nevada* design, the main armoured deck was moved to the top of the upper belt, with a splinter deck placed below it to protect machinery and magazines from shells bursting after they had penetrated the main armoured deck. The upper and lower armoured belts were merged into a single belt, while the upper casemate armour was abandoned in favour of heavy casemate armour. The *Nevadas* were the first US battleships to burn only fuel oil, and to feature triple turrets. Reconstructed in 1927–30, they were fitted with new engines and boilers, their cagemasts were replaced by tripods, the secondary battery was raised one deck, aircraft catapults were installed on 'X' turret, and stern and anti-torpedo bulges were added. When the Japanese bombed Pearl Harbor, the *Oklahoma* was sunk and the *Nevada* was severely damaged and beached. However, she was refloated and reconstructed in time to take part in the Normandy landings. Later, in the final stages of the Pacific war, *Nevada* was damaged by a *kamikaze* and also hit by shore batteries off Okinawa.

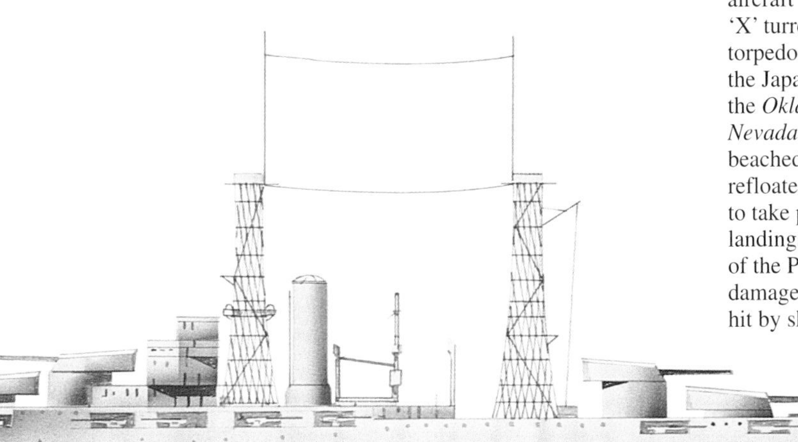

NEW YORK

USA: 1912

The USS *New York* (BB-34) and her sister ship *Texas* (BB-35) were the first American 'super-dreadnoughts'. It was originally planned to install turbines in them, but trials with these engines mounted in USS *North Dakota* produced disappointing results, and seemed to indicate that the new ships would be able to achieve a range of only about 5600nm (10,377km) at 12 knots with turbines, compared to 7060nm (13,082km) with reciprocating engines. Since turbine power would clearly be insufficient to propel the warships from the West Coast of the USA to the Philippines, the US Navy selected reciprocating engines, even though they were aware that these were at the end of their development. *New York* and *Texas* served with the 6th Battle Squadron of the British Grand Fleet in the closing stages of World War I and, while in British waters, *Texas* had flying-off platforms fitted – the first American battleship to be so equipped. Both ships underwent reconstruction in the mid-1920s; in 1939, *New York* became the first American vessel to be fitted with experimental shipborne radar. Her World War II service included Atlantic convoy escort duty and shore bombardment off North Africa, Iwo Jima and Okinawa – where she was slightly damaged by a *kamikaze*. She was used as a target vessel in the 1946 Bikini atomic tests and, on 8 July 1948, was sunk as a target by aircraft off Hawaii. *Texas* was stricken in April 1948, and preserved as a memorial at Galveston in her name state.

New York was launched on 30 October 1912 and completed on 15 April 1914. She immediately deployed to Vera Cruz, Mexico, in support of American military action there.

Displacement: 27,000t standard; 28,367 full load
Dimensions: 572ft 8in x 95ft 3in x 28ft 6in (174.6m x 29m x 8.7m)
Machinery: two screws, vertical triple expansion engines; 28,100hp
Armament: 10 14in (355mm); 21 5in (127mm); four 21in (533mm) TT
Armour: belt 12in-6in (305mm-152mm); turrets 14in-8in (355mm-203mm); deck 2in (50mm)
Speed: 21 knots
Range: 10,000nm (18,530km) at 10 knots
Complement: 1040

NORFOLK

GB: 1929

The cruiser HMS *Norfolk* was launched on 29 January 1929, and had a long and distinguished career. In World War II, together with her sister ship, *Dorsetshire*, she took part in the final action against the battleship *Bismarck*, expending 527 8in (203mm) shells and eight torpedoes (*Dorsetshire* 254 shells and two torpedoes) before the German warship sank. Just under a year later, *Dorsetshire* was herself sunk by Japanese air attack. *Norfolk* also took part in the action against the battlecruiser *Scharnhorst*.

***Norfolk* remained on the active list for some time after World War II, being broken up in 1950.**

Displacement: 9925t standard; 13,425t full load
Dimensions: 635ft 5in x 66ft x 20ft 11in (193.67m x 20.12m x 6.37m)
Machinery: four screws, geared turbines; 80,000hp
Armament: eight 8in (203mm); four 4in (102mm)s; eight 21in (533mm) TT
Armour: 4in-1in (100mm-25mm) box protection to ammunition spaces; turrets 1in (25mm)
Speed: 32.3 knots
Range: 4500nm (8338km) at 12 knots
Complement: 710

NORTHAMPTON

USA: 1929

Displacement: 9006t standard; 11,420t full load
Dimensions: 600ft 3in x 66ft 1in x 19ft 5in (182.96m x 20.14m x 5.92m)
Machinery: four screws, turbines; 107,000hp
Armament: nine 8in (203mm); four 5in (152mm); six 21in (533mm) TT
Armour: belt 3in-2in (76mm-50mm); turret faces 2.5in (63mm)
Speed: 32.5 knots
Range: 10,000nm (18,530km) at 15 knots
Complement: 697

The USS *Northampton* (CA26) was leader of a class of six heavy cruisers. She set the pattern for all succeeding US Navy heavy cruisers, with the main armament reduced to nine 8in (203mm) guns in three triple turrets. Three of the class, including *Northampton* herself, were lost in World War II. She was sunk by Japanese torpedoes on 1 December 1942 in a fierce night action, during which three other American heavy cruisers were badly damaged. Three vessels of this class, *Augusta*, *Chicago*, and *Houston*, were built as flagships.

Pre-war modifications to the *Northampton* class included the removal of the torpedo tubes and the strengthening of the AA armament.

OBERON

GB: 1926

Launched on 24 September 1926, *Oberon* was a prototype overseas patrol submarine of the saddle-tank type. Her pressure hull plating was 0.75in (19.4mm) thick, she had a maximum diving depth of 500ft (152m), and her design speeds (though never attained) were 15 knots surfaced and 9 knots submerged. *Oberon* was followed by eight more *O*-boats, five of which were lost in World War II. One of these, *Oxley*, was rammed and sunk in error by HM submarine *Triton* off Norway on 19 September 1939.

Displacement: 1598t surfaced; 1831t submerged
Dimensions: 269ft 8in x 28ft x 15ft 6in
Machinery: two screws, diesels, electric motors; 2950/1350hp
Armament: eight 21in (533mm) TT; one 4in (102mm)
Speed: 13.75 knots surfaced; 7.5 knots submerged
Range: 5650nm (10,469km) at 10 knots surfaced; 105nm (195km) at 5 knots submerged
Complement: 54

***Oberon* (centre) was laid up in 1944 and scrapped at Rosyth in 1945.**

OPYTNYI

USSR: 1935

Displacement: 1670t standard; 1870t full load
Dimensions: 387ft 2in x 38ft x 13ft 9in (118m x 11.6m x 4.2m)
Machinery: two screws, geared turbines; 70,000hp
Armament: three 5.1in (130mm); eight 21in (533mm) TT, 60 mines
Armour: belt 3in (76mm)
Speed: 42 knots
Range: not known
Complement: 197

During trials *Opytnyi* reached a speed of 41.6 knots. She survived World War II and was scrapped in 1950.

Opytnyi, formerly the *Sergei Ordzhonikidze*, was an experimental destroyer. She was the first to be built in the Soviet Union without assistance from abroad. Every attempt was made to make her as light and as fast as possible. Only one gun was mounted on the forecastle, and only one of the three boiler rooms was fitted forward, so as not to restrict the lifting of the bow at high speed. *Opytnyi* was launched in December 1935, but she was not commissioned until late 1941 due to ongoing experimental work.

PAULDING

USA: 1910

Displacement: 742t standard; 887t full load
Dimensions: 293ft x 26ft 3in x 8ft (89.6m x 8m x 2.4m)
Machinery: three screws, turbines; 12,000hp
Armament: five 3in (76mm); six 18in (457mm) TT
Armour: belt 3in (76mm)
Speed: 29.5 knots
Range: 3000nm (5559km) at 16 knots
Complement: 86

The US Navy's *Paulding* class were the first American destroyers to use oil fuel. Most had three shafts, but four ships in the class were fitted with two turbines. The vessels had four funnels, but some had the two midships funnels trunked together. *Paulding* was launched on 12 April 1910; together with her sister ships, *Roe*, *McCall*, and *Burrows*, she served in the US Coast Guard from 1924 to 1930. She was broken up in 1934; and scrapped in 1934–35.

Two of the *Paulding* class, *Mayrant* and *Henley*, were fitted with 13,000hp Westinghouse-geared turbines in 1915.

PENNSYLVANIA

USA: 1915

The dreadnoughts *Pennsylvania* and her sister ship *Arizona* were improved developments of the *Nevada* class, their main armament mounted in four triple turrets. Neither saw overseas service in World War I due to a shortage of tankers for re-supply; *Pennsylvania*, launched on 15 March 1915 and completed in June 1916, was assigned as flagship of the Atlantic Fleet. In 1922 she was assigned to the Pacific Fleet as flagship, undergoing a second period of reconstruction in 1929–31. On 7 December 1941, at Pearl Harbor, she was badly damaged by Japanese bombs while in dry dock (*Arizona* exploded and sank during the attack) and was reconstructed again in 1942. She rejoined the Pacific Fleet in 1943, and took part in all the major naval campaigns. She was badly damaged by a Japanese aerial torpedo in Buckner Bay, Okinawa, on 12 August 1945. Only temporary repairs were made following the end of the war.

Displacement: 31,400t standard; 32,567t full load
Dimensions: 608ft x 97ft x 28ft 10in (185.3m x 29.6m x 8.8m)
Machinery: four screws, geared turbines; 31,500hp
Armament: 12 14in (355mm); 22 5in (127mm); two 21in (533mm) TT
Armour: belt 13.5in–8in (343mm–203mm); turrets 18in–9in (457mm–229mm); deck 4in (102mm)
Speed: 21 knots
Range: 10,000nm (18,530km) at 10 knots
Complement: 1040 (later 1314)

***Pennsylvania* was decommissioned on 24 August 1946, and was expended as a target vessel off Kwajalein on 10 February 1948, sunk by US aircraft.**

PENSACOLA

USA: 1929

Displacement: 9097t standard; 11,512t full load
Dimensions: 585ft 8in x 65ft 3in x 19ft 6in (178.51m x 19.89m x 5.94m)
Machinery: four screws, turbines; 107,000hp
Armament: 10 8in (203mm); four 5in (127mm); six 21in (533mm) TT
Armour: belt 4in–2.5in (100mm–63mm); deck 1.75in (45mm); turret faces 2.5in (63mm)
Speed: 32.5 knots
Range: 10,000nm (18,530km) at 15 knots
Complement: 631

The first American cruisers built under the restrictions of the Washington Treaty were the *Pensacola* and her sister ship *Salt Lake City*. In World War II, USS *Pensacola* fought in every Pacific naval campaign from Midway, taking in Santa Cruz and Guadalcanal. During the latter battle, while engaging Japanese naval forces with three other heavy cruisers, *Pensacola* was badly damaged, as was *Minneapolis*, *Northampton* was sunk and *New Orleans* lost her bow. *Pensacola* returned to action in November 1943, in time to lend her fire support to the American landings in the Gilbert Islands, and she was in action at Kwajalein in January 1944. As part of the US Task Force 94, she took part in many bombardment operations before the last drive against Japan took her to Iwo Jima and Okinawa. Both *Pensacola* and *Salt Lake City* were sunk as target ships in 1948.

The *Pensacolas* were the oldest heavy cruisers in US Navy service in 1941. Their tendency to roll was eliminated by modifications to the hull and superstructure.

PILLAU

GERMANY: 1914

Displacement: 4390t standard; 5252t full load
Dimensions: 443ft 11in x 44ft 7in x 19ft 8in (135.3m x 13.6m x 6m)
Machinery: two screws, turbines; 30,000hp
Armament: eight 5.9in (150mm); two 19.7in (500mm) TT
Armour: deck 3in-0.75in (76mm-20mm)
Speed: 27.5 knots
Range: 4300nm (7968km) at 12 knots
Complement: 442

In Italian service, *Pillau* had her funnels reduced from three to two. She was modified and rebuilt for colonial duties.

Originally laid down in 1913 for the Imperial Russian Navy, and nearing completion at the outbreak of World War I, the *Muaviev Amurski* and the *Admiral Nevelski* were taken over by the Imperial German Navy. Renamed *Pillau* and *Elbing*, they became light cruisers. *Elbing* had to be scuttled during the Battle of Jutland, but *Pillau* saw action with the German Navy Scouting Forces, and was ceded to Italy after the war, and given the name *Bari*. In World War II, she was sunk by Allied aircraft off Livorno in September 1943.

PLUTON

FRANCE: 1929

Launched on 10 April 1929, *Pluton* was an unarmoured minelaying cruiser. Later in her career, she was used as a gunnery training ship at Toulon but, in 1939, was re-named *La Tour d'Auvergne* and pressed into service as a training vessel for midshipmen. She was destroyed as the result of an internal explosion, caused by the accidental detonation of mines, while at Casablanca on 18 September 1939. She was declared a constructive total loss on 24 February 1940.

Displacement: 4773t standard; 6500t full load
Dimensions: 500ft 4in x 51ft 2in x 17ft (152.5m x 15.6m x 5.18m)
Machinery: two screws, geared turbines; 57,000hp
Armament: four 5.5in (140mm); four 3in (76mm); 290 mines
Armour: None
Speed: 30 knots
Range: Not known
Complement: 424

Early in 1940, the French Admiralty proposed building a new light cruiser to replace *La Tour d'Auvergne*, but this was prevented by the defeat of France.

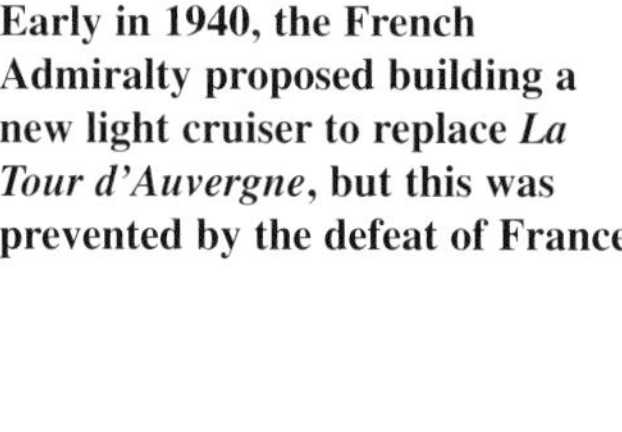

PORTER

USA: 1935

Displacement: 1834t standard; 2597t full load
Dimensions: 381ft 1in x 37ft x 13ft (116.15m x 11.28m x 3.96m)
Machinery: two screws, turbines; 50,000hp
Armament: eight 5in (127mm); eight 21in (533mm) TT
Armour: belt 3in (76mm)
Speed: 37 knots
Range: 6500nm (12,044km) at 12 knots
Complement: 194

The eight destroyers of the *Porter* class were designed as destroyer leader, attempts by the US Navy having failed to persuade Congress to authorise a new class of light cruiser to fulfil this role. The *Porters* introduced the twin 5in (127mm) gun mount and, in practice, resembled light cruisers. The heavy tripod masts, with which they were originally fitted, were replaced by pole masts early in World War II; the 'X' turret was also removed, and 12 40mm anti-aircraft guns added. Of the eight ships, only *Porter* herself became a war casualty (although *Selfridge* lost her bow at Vella Lavella on 6 October 1943), being sunk by the Japanese submarine *I-21* on 26 October 1942. Two ships, *Winslow* and *McDougal*, became training vessels and were discarded in 1957 and 1949 respectively; the rest were all discarded in 1946–47. Neither of the ships that were converted saw much service in their new roles.

Two of the *Porter* class ships saw brief service as radar pickets right at the very end of World War II.

QUARTO

ITALY: 1911

Displacement: 3271t standard; 3442t full load
Dimensions: 439ft 9in x 42ft x 13ft 5in (134mm x 12.8mm x 4.1mm)
Machinery: four screws, turbines; 25,000hp
Armament: six 4.7in (120mm); six 3in (76mm); two 17.7in (450mm) TT
Armour: deck 1.5in (38mm)
Speed: 28.6 knots
Range: 2300nm (4262km) at 15 knots
Complement: 247

Launched on 19 August 1911, the scout cruiser *Quarto* was the brainchild of the talented Italian naval engineer Giulio Trucconi, who was later responsible for the splendid *Maestrale*-class destroyers of 1931. *Quarto* had a very shallow keel and, on several occasions during World War I, torpedoes fired at her passed harmlessly under her keel. Between the wars, she suffered a serious accident when one of her boilers exploded in August 1938. She was stricken in January 1939.

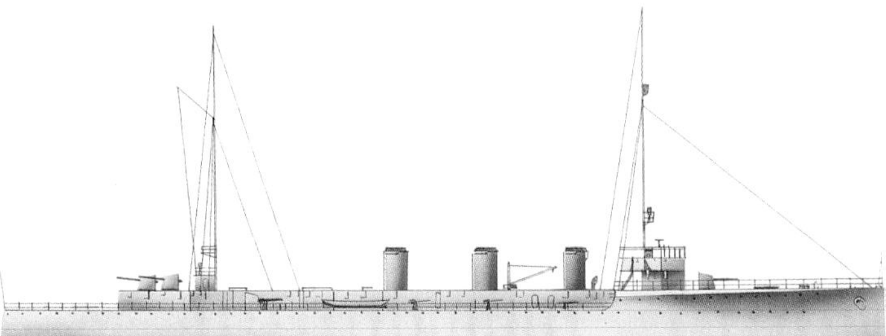

***Quarto* was modernised in the 1920s, being equipped with a reconnaissance seaplane.**

QUEEN ELIZABETH

GB: 1913

Laid down in 1912, the *Queen Elizabeth* class of dreadnoughts, included the *Barham*, *Malaya*, *Valiant*, and *Warspite*. A sixth vessel, *Agincourt*, was never built. *Queen Elizabeth* was launched on 16 October 1913 and completed in January 1915. She was almost immediately deployed to the Mediterranean, where she formed part of the naval force (mostly composed of pre-dreadnoughts) tasked with providing fire support to Allied troops during the Dardanelles campaign. From 1916 to 1918 she was flagship of the Grand Fleet, replacing the *Iron Duke* in that capacity. She served in the Mediterranean between the two world wars, undergoing substantial reconstruction in 1926–27 and again in 1937–40. By the time she emerged from her second period of reconstruction she was virtually a new ship, having been re-engined, re-boilered, and rearmed. She was recommissioned in January 1941 and again deployed to the Mediterranean, where she took part in fleet engagements against the Italian Navy. On 19 December 1941, together with her sister ship *Valiant*, she was heavily damaged at Alexandria in a daring attack by Italian frogmen, who entered the harbour and laid explosive charges under the two warships. She was made seaworthy and sent to Norfolk, Virginia, for repair, being recommissioned in June 1943. After service with the Home Fleet, *Queen Elizabeth* was sent to join the Eastern Fleet in the Indian Ocean, where she took part in several bombardment operations against enemy positions in Burma and Sumatra. She was broken up in 1948.

Displacement: 27,500t standard; 33,000t full load
Dimensions: 640ft x 90ft 6in x 34ft 1in (195m x 27.6m x 10.4m)
Machinery: four screws, turbines; 75,000hp
Armament: eight 15in (381mm); 14 6in (152mm); four 21in (533mm) TT
Armour: belt 13in-6in (330mm-152mm); turrets 13-113in (330mm-279mm); decks 3in-1in (76mm-25mm)
Speed: 24 knots
Range: 6450nm (11,952km) at 10 knots
Complement: 951 (later 1297)

During her first period of reconstruction, at Portsmouth in 1926–27, *Valiant* had her bridge remodelled, her two funnels trunked into one, and anti-torpedo bulges fitted.

RANGER

USA: 1933

Displacement: 14,500t standard; 15,575t full load
Dimensions: 769ft x 80ft 1in x 24ft 6in (234.4m x 24.4m x 7.5m)
Machinery: two screws, geared turbines; 53,500hp
Armament: eight 5in (127mm); 86 aircraft
Armour: belt 2in (50mm); deck 1in (25mm)
Speed: 29.5 knots
Range: 11,500nm (21,309km) at 15 knots
Complement: 1788

The USS *Ranger* (CV-4) was the US Navy's first purpose-built aircraft carrier, rather than a conversion. She was originally designed with a flush deck, but in the course of construction it was decided to incorporate an island which, together with other structural changes, added greatly to her tonnage. Her original air group comprised 36 bombers, 36 fighters, and four general purpose aircraft. Under the restrictions of the Washington Treaty, speed was sacrificed in order to incorporate other essentials, reducing her effectiveness as a front-line unit. Too slow for use with the Pacific carrier task forces, *Ranger* served in the Atlantic during World War II, operating off North Africa in November 1942, escorting convoys, and participating in Allied carrier raids on German targets in Norway. She was relegated to training duties in 1944, decommissioned in 1946, and broken up the following year.

In 1945, *Ranger* participated in early trials with airborne early warning (AEW) aircraft. She also specialised in night training operations.

REPULSE

GB: 1916

Launched in 1916 and completed in record time in the same year, the battlecruiser HMS *Repulse* served with the British Grand Fleet for the rest of World War I. She underwent two refits, in 1921–22 and 1932–36, in which her armour protection was increased, torpedo tubes added, superstructure modified, and her anti-aircraft armament increased. *Repulse* was sunk off the coast of Malaya by Japanese air attack on 10 December 1941, along with the battleship *Prince of Wales*.

Repulse saw considerable active service, and was involved in the hunt for the *Bismarck* before her fateful deployment to the Far East.

Displacement: 26,500t standard; 32,727t full load
Dimensions: 794ft x 90ft x 30ft 3in (242m x 27.4m x 9.2m)
Machinery: four screws, turbines; 112,000hp
Armament: six 15in (381mm); 17 4in (102mm); two 21in (533mm) TT
Armour: belt 6in-3in (152mm-76mm); turrets 11in-7in (279mm-178mm); decks 3.5in-1in (89mm-26mm)
Speed: 29.9 knots
Range: 4200nm (7782km) at 10 knots
Complement: 967

REVENGE

GB: 1915

Displacement: 27,500t standard; 31,200t full load
Dimensions: 624ft 3in x 88ft 6in x 28ft 7in (190.3m x 27m x 8.7m)
Machinery: four screws, turbines; 40,000hp
Armament: eight 15in (381mm); 14 6in (152mm); four 21in (533mm) TT
Armour: belt 13in-4in (330mm-102mm); turrets 13in-5in (330mm-127mm); decks 4in-1in (102mm-25mm)
Speed: 23 knots
Range: 6,800nm (12,600km) at 10 knots
Complement: 936

Launched on 29 May 1915, HMS *Revenge* was leader of a class of dreadnoughts which, in effect, were improved *Iron Dukes* with 15in (381mm) guns. Rather confusingly, the ships later became widely known as the *Royal Sovereign* class, although contemporary Admiralty records refer to them as the *Revenge* class. They were a much cheaper design than the *Queen Elizabeth* class that preceded them, and were also smaller, although the armour protection was more effectively dispersed. *Revenge* served with the 1st Battle Squadron of the Grand Fleet for the remainder of the war, being present at Jutland. On 5 November 1918, days before the Armistice brought an end to World War I, *Revenge* was in collision in the Firth of Forth with the aircraft carrier *Campania*, which foundered; the carrier had dragged her cables during a gale and drifted across the battleship's bows. *Revenge* served with the Mediterranean Fleet for much of the 1920s and underwent three separate refits between 1928 and 1937. In World War II she served on Atlantic convoy escort duty and, in September 1941, was involved in a collision with the cruiser *Orion*, which fortunately survived the experience. In 1942, *Revenge* and four other battleships, *Ramillies*, *Resolution*, *Royal Sovereign*, and *Warspite*, all of World War I vintage, formed the nucleus of the Far Eastern Fleet. *Revenge* was retired from front-line service in 1944 to become a stokers' training ship at Gairloch, Scotland. She was sold and broken up in 1948.

Unlike earlier dreadnoughts which had twin balanced rudders, the *Revenge* class had a single large rudder with a small auxiliary rudder ahead of it.

ROYAL OAK

GB: 1914

One of the *Revenge*-class dreadnoughts, HMS *Royal Oak* was launched on 17 November 1914 and completed in May 1916, just in time to take part in the Battle of Jutland. She served with the Grand Fleet throughout the rest of World War I and, after a refit in 1922–24, was deployed to the Mediterranean, where she served for the best part of a decade. She underwent a second refit in 1934–45, having a tripod mainmast fitted, and was then assigned to the Home Fleet. At the outbreak of World War II, *Royal Oak* was on patrol duty in northern waters. In October 1939, the German Admiralty ordered units of the German Fleet to make a sortie towards the southern coast of Norway; the force comprised the battlecruiser *Scharnhorst*, the light cruiser *Koln* and nine destroyers, the intention being to draw the British Home Fleet across a concentration of four U-boats and within range of the Luftwaffe. The German force turned back on being sighted, and British warships sent out to intercept them returned to their base at Loch Ewe. There was an exception: the *Royal Oak* had been detached from the main force to guard the Fair Isle Channel, between the Shetland and Orkney Islands; when the German threat receded she made her way to the anchorage at Scapa Flow. On the night of 13/14 October, the German submarine *U47*, commanded by Kapitanleutnant Günther Prien, penetrated the defences of Scapa Flow and sank the *Royal Oak* with three torpedo hits. The attack, in which 833 lives were lost, was carried out with great coolness, skill and daring, and came as a severe shock to the Royal Navy, and indeed Britain.

Displacement: 27,500t standard; 31,200t full load
Dimensions: 624ft 3in x 88ft 6in x 28ft 7in (190.3m x 27m x 8.7m)
Machinery: four screws, turbines; 40,000hp
Armament: eight 15in (381mm); 14 6in (152mm); four 21in (533mm) TT
Armour: belt 13in-4in (330mm-102mm); turrets 13in-5in (330mm-127mm); decks 4in-1in (102mm-25mm)
Speed: 23 knots
Range: 6,800nm (12,600km) at 10 knots
Complement: 936

The loss of the *Royal Oak* was felt particularly keenly in the north-east of England, from where many of her crew were recruited.

RURIK

IMPERIAL RUSSIA/USSR: 1906

Displacement: 15,190t standard; 16,930t full load
Dimensions: 529ft x 75ft 2in x 26ft (161.2m x 22.9m x 7.9m)
Machinery: two screws, vertical quadruple expansion engines; 19,700hp
Armament: four 10in (254mm); eight 8in (203mm); 20 4.7in (120mm); two 18in (457mm) TT
Armour: belt 6.1in-3in (155mm-76mm); turrets 8in-7in (203mm-178mm); deck 1.5in (38mm)
Speed: 21 knots
Range: 8000nm (14,824km) at 10 knots
Complement: 899

Built in England by Vickers, the armoured cruiser *Rurik* was a very successful design, characterised by a long low profile with three funnels and a pole mainmast. Her guns were mounted in two twin turrets fore and aft, and four twin turrets at the corners of her superstructure; the turrets were of a new design, which allowed an elevation of 35 degrees. The magazines were fitted with flooding and spraying equipment to counteract fire in the event of flashback from the turret. *Rurik* was the largest and finest armoured cruiser laid down for the Imperial Russian Navy, and is generally considered to have been one of the finest armoured cruisers ever built. In World War I, during minelaying operations in the Baltic (she sometimes carried as many as 400 mines) she was severely damaged when she herself struck a mine on 7 November 1916. She was repaired and served with the Red Fleet before being scrapped in 1923.

Named after the semi-legendary founder of Russia, *Rurik* was well endowed with protection, and fitted with two armoured decks.

RYUJO

JAPAN: 1931

The Japanese light carrier *Ryujo* ('Fighting Dragon') was designed to conform to Washington Treaty limitations. Laid down in November 1929 and launched on 2 April 1931, she incorporated improvements in her design from experience gained in the building of the carriers *Akagi* and *Kaga*. Her design was modified in the course of construction to add a second hangar deck; this resulted in her being top-heavy at sea, so a ballast keel had to be fitted and part of her armament removed. Further improvements were made in 1935, the front of the bridge being rebuilt to a new design, and a new deck one level higher built on the forecastle to improve seaworthiness. In World War II, *Ryujo* formed the nucleus of the 4th Carrier Division; she took part in actions around the Philippines and in the Battle of Midway, before being sunk by US carrier aircraft in the Eastern Solomons on 24 August 1942.

Displacement: 8000t standard; 10,150t full load
Dimensions: 575ft x 66ft 8in x 18ft 3in (175.3m x 20.3m x 5.6m)
Machinery: two screws, geared turbines; 65,000hp
Armament: 12 5in (127mm); 48 aircraft
Armour: not applicable
Speed: 29 knots
Range: 10,000nm (18,530km) at 14 knots
Complement: 600

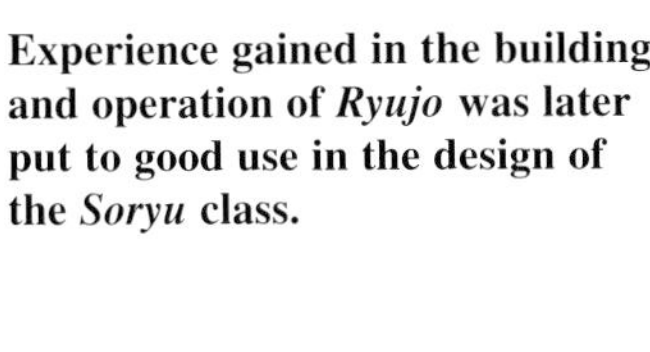

Experience gained in the building and operation of *Ryujo* was later put to good use in the design of the *Soryu* class.

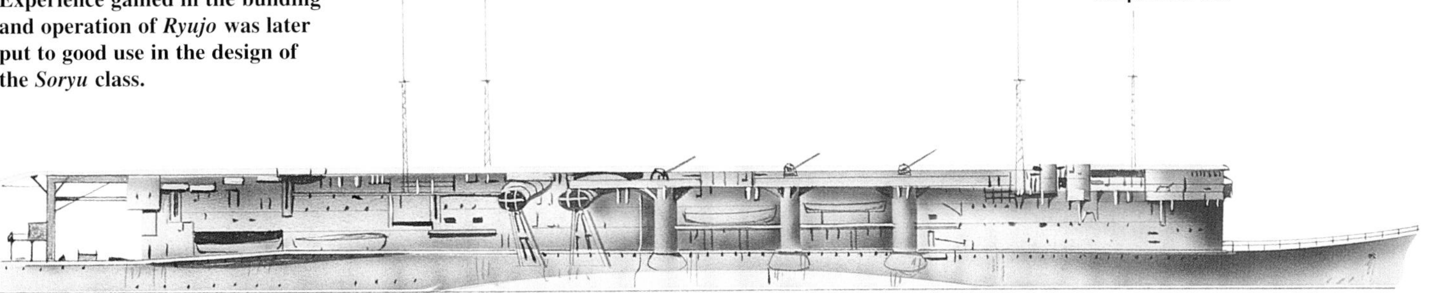

SAMPSON

USA: 1916

Displacement: 1100t standard; 1225t full load
Dimensions: 315ft 3in x 29ft 10in x 9ft 6in (96.1m x 9.1m x 2.9m)
Machinery: two screws, turbines; 17,500hp
Armament: four 4in (102mm); 12 21in (533mm) TT
Armour: belt 2in (50mm); turret faces 1in (25mm)
Speed: 29.5 knots
Range: 3500nm (6485km) at 14 knots
Complement: 99

Authorised in June 1914, the *Sampson*-class destroyers, *Sampson, Rowan, Dvis, Allen, Wilkes,* and *Shaw*, were the last of the US Navy's 'thousand-tonners'. They incorporated a new 21in (533mm) triple torpedo tube mount, and also a pair of 1pdr anti-aircraft guns, the first American destroyers to do so. Two vessels of this class, *Shaw* and *Allen*, served in European waters during 1917–18, following America's entry into World War I. These two ships had a single cruising turbine that could be geared to one shaft.

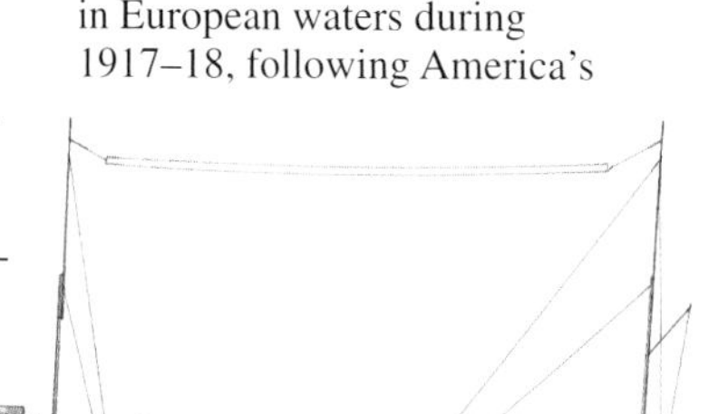

The USS *Sampson* was launched on 4 March 1916 and broken up in 1936; most of the other vessels in the class were scrapped around this time.

SAN GIORGIO

ITALY: 1908

Launched on 27 July 1908, the armoured cruiser *San Giorgio* was reconstructed as a training ship at La Spezia in 1937–38, and armed mostly with anti-aircraft weaponry. In the early months of World War II, she was used as a floating AA battery at Tobruk, where she was scuttled on 2 January 1941 as Australian troops broke into the town. She was refloated in 1952, but as she was being towed to Italy her tow-rope parted and she sank in heavy seas some 100 miles from Tobruk.

***San Georgio*'s sister ship, *San Marco*, was converted to a radio-controlled target ship in the early 1930s. She was sunk at La Spezia in September 1943.**

Displacement: 10,167t standard; 11,300t full load
Dimensions: 462ft 2in x 68ft 11in x 24ft (140.8m x 21m x 7.3m)
Machinery: two screws, vertical triple expansion engines; 19,500hp
Armament: four 10in (254mm); eight 7.5in (190mm); three 17.7in (450mm) TT
Armour: belt and main turrets 8in (200mm); deck 2in (50mm)
Speed: 23.2 knots
Range: 6270nm (11,618km) at 10 knots
Complement: 700

SCHLESIEN

GERMANY: 1906

Displacement: 13,191t standard; 14,218t full load
Dimensions: 418ft 4in x 72ft 10in x 27ft (127.6m x 22.2m x 8.2m)
Machinery: three screws, vertical triple expansion engines; 20,000hp
Armament: four 11in (280mm); 14 6.6in (170mm); six 17.7in (450mm) TT
Armour: belt 9.4in-4in (240mm-100mm); turrets 11in (280mm); deck 1.57in (40mm)
Speed: 18 knots
Range: 4800nm (8894nm) at 12 knots
Complement: 743

The *Deutschland*-class battleships, of which *Schlesien* was one, were Germany's last pre-dreadnoughts. *Schlesien* served with the High Seas Fleet during World War I and, together with her sister ships *Hannover* and *Schleswig-Holstein*, formed the nucleus of Germany's post-war fleet. She was reconstructed in 1935, and used as a cadet training ship during World War II. On 4 May 1945, she was scuttled at Swinemünde after being damaged by an aircraft mine.

***Schlesien* saw active service in World War II, bombarding Polish targets in September 1939 and Russian troops near Danzig in 1945.**

SKATE (F4)

USA: 1912

The submarine *Skate* and her three sisters were *F*-boats, similar to and contemporaries of the *E* class, where a tendency towards a smaller type of submarine had originated. All boats of both classes were withdrawn from service in 1915 for re-engineering. *Skate* left Honolulu harbour on 25 March 1915 for a short trial run, but she never returned. She was located at a depth of 300ft (91m) just off Pearl Harbor, well beyond the depth from which such a vessel had hitherto been successfully raised.

Five months later, American salvage crews achieved the seemingly impossible and brought

The *F*-class submarines had a design depth of 200ft (61m). Their early American diesel engines gave constant trouble.

Displacement: 330t surfaced; 400t submerged
Dimensions: 142ft 9in x 15ft 5in x 12ft 2in (43.5m x 4.7m x 3.7m)
Machinery: two screws, diesels, plus electric motors; 800/620hp
Armament: four 18in (457mm) TT
Speed: 13.5 knots surfaced; 11.5 knots submerged
Range: 2300nm (4262km) at 11 knots, surfaced
Complement: 22

Skate to the surface, setting up a new world deep-sea diving record in the process. Another boat in the class, *Carp*, was lost in a collision with her sister boat *Pickerel* on 17 December 1917. *Pickerel* survived and was stricken in 1922.

In the years to come America was always to be at the forefront of such salvage operations, with specially-designed deep submergence craft.

SMITH

USA: 1909

The Smith-class destroyers, Smith, Lamson, Preston, Flusser, and Reid, were designed from the outset as fully sea-going vessels, unlike their predecessors which were essentially coastal craft. At the time, the Smiths were regarded as the ultimate in destroyer technology, but within just a few years they would be entirely overshadowed by the first of the 'thousand-tonners'. Designed to use either reciprocating engines or turbines, and with an armament of five 3in (76mm) guns, the Smiths represented a considerable improvement over earlier models. The USS Smith served in European waters in 1917–18, being based at the French Atlantic port of Brest.

Displacement: 700t standard; 900t full load
Dimensions: 293ft 8in x 26ft x 8ft (89.6m x 7.9m x 2.4m)
Machinery: three screws, turbines; 10,000hp
Armament: five 3in (76mm); three 18in (457mm) TT
Armour: belt 2in (50mm)
Speed: 28 knots
Range: 2800nm (5188km) at 10 knots
Complement: 87

SURCOUF

FRANCE: 1929

Displacement: 3250t surfaced; 4304t submerged
Dimensions: 360ft 10in x 29ft 9in x 29ft 9in (110m x 9.1m x 9.07m)
Machinery: two screws, diesel/electric motors; 7600/3400hp
Armament: four 15.75in (400mm) TT ; two 8in (203mm); eight 21.7in (550mm)
Speed: 8.5 knots submerged; 18 knots surfaced
Range: 10,000nm (18,530km) surfaced; 70nm (130km) at 4.5 knots submerged
Complement: 118

It had been intended to deploy *Surcouf* to the Pacific, where her long range and powerful armament would have been very effective.

The *Surcouf* was, in effect, an experimental, one-off boat, described by the French Navy as a 'Corsair submarine'. She was fitted with the largest calibre guns permitted to be mounted on submarines under the terms of the Washington Treaty. At the outbreak of World War II, *Surcouf* was the largest and heaviest submarine in the world, and would remain so until the Japanese 400 series entered service. In June 1940, *Surcouf* escaped from Brest, where she was refitting, and sailed for Plymouth, where she was seized by the Royal Navy (her crew resisting, with casualties on both sides) at the time of the British attacks on French warships at Mers-el-Kebir on 3 July. She was later turned over to the Free French Navy and carried out patrols in the Atlantic, and also took part in the seizure of the islands of St Pierre and Miquelon off Newfoundland, which were loyal to Vichy France. *Surcouf* was lost on 18 February 1942, in collision with an American freighter in the Gulf of Mexico.

SUSSEX

GB: 1928

Displacement: 9830t standard; 13,315t full load
Dimensions: 630ft x 66ft x 20ft 9in (192.02m x 20.12m x 6.32m)
Machinery: four screws, geared turbines; 80,000hp
Armament: eight 8in (203mm); four 4in (102mm); eight 21in (533mm) TT
Armour: ammunition spaces 4in-1in (100mm-25mm); sides and turrets 1in (25mm)
Speed: 32.3 knots
Range: 5000nm (9265km) at 14 knots
Complement: 700

One of four *London*-class cruisers, HMS *Sussex* was launched on 22 February 1928. In September 1940, while on the Clyde after a refit, she was hit by a single 550lb (250kg) bomb which started a disastrous fire, enveloping the whole after part of the ship. Returning to service after 21 months, she sank the German tanker *Hohenfriedburg* off Cape Finisterre on 20 February 1943. In 1944, the *Sussex* was deployed to the Eastern Fleet, and operated in the Indian Ocean until the end of World War II. She was scrapped in 1950.

In September 1945, HMS *Sussex* was one of the Allied warships covering the landing of British and Indian troops at Soerabaya, Indonesia.

SWIFT

GB: 1907

Originally known as the *Flying Scud* (a name mercifully abandoned in April 1916), the destroyer HMS *Swift* was based on the successful *River* class of 1901–4. She was designed as a flotilla leader at the instigation of the First Sea Lord, Admiral Fisher. The requirement called for a vessel capable of a top speed of 36 knots, which in the event was never attained. *Swift* was built by Cammell Laird and launched on 17 December 1907, after many alterations had been made to the original design. Her trials lasted nearly two years and she was accepted for service in February 1910. At the outbreak of World War I, *Swift* was leader of the 4th TBD Flotilla and, in 1915 after a short refit, she joined the Dover Patrol (6th Destroyer Flotilla). She was badly damaged in action with German destroyers in the Channel, on 20 April 1917, but after repair rejoined the Dover Patrol. *Swift* was paid off after the Armistice and scrapped in 1921.

Although *Swift* was initially assigned to the Grand Fleet at Scapa Flow, she was not structurally strong enough for service in northern waters.

Displacement: 2170t standard; 2390t full load
Dimensions: 353ft 9in x 34ft 2in x 10ft 6in (107.8m x 10.4m x 3.2m)
Machinery: four screws, turbines; 30,000hp
Armament: four 4in (102mm); two 18in (457mm) TT
Armour: belt 2.5in (63mm)
Speed: 35 knots
Range: 3200nm (5929km) at 14 knots
Complement: 126

SWORDFISH

GB: 1916

Displacement: 932t surfaced; 1105t submerged
Dimensions: 231ft 4in x 23ft x 14ft 9in (70.5m x 7m x 4.5m)
Machinery: two screws, geared impulse-reaction steam turbines, plus two electric motors; 4000/1400hp
Armament: two 21in (533mm) and four 18in (457mm) TT
Speed: 18 knots surfaced; 10 knots submerged
Range: 3000nm (5559km) at 8.5 knots, surfaced
Complement: 25

The original *Swordfish* design was based on a proposal by the engineer Laurenti, developed further by Scott.

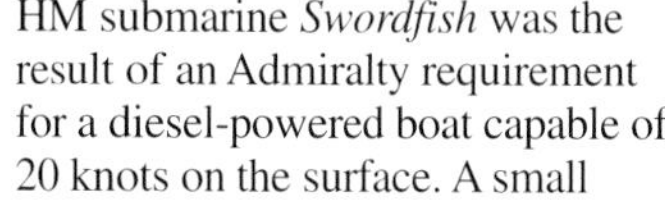

HM submarine *Swordfish* was the result of an Admiralty requirement for a diesel-powered boat capable of 20 knots on the surface. A small funnel was lowered electrically, and then well-covered by a plate. Closing down the funnel took a minute and a half, the heat inside the submarine proving bearable. *Swordfish* was the first submarine to have an experimental emergency telephone buoy fitted. In 1917, after a few months of trials work, she was converted into a surface patrol craft. *Swordfish* was broken up in 1922.

SYDNEY

GB/AUSTRALIA: 1934

Originally named *Phaeton*, the cruiser *Sydney* was launched on 22 September 1934 and completed a year later for the Royal Australian Navy. She was equipped with a catapult launcher and a Fairey Seafox reconnaissance aircraft. *Sydney* was sunk on 19 November 1941 in a gun and torpedo battle with the German commerce raider *Kormoran*, which was also sunk in the engagement. The Australian cruiser was last seen limping over the horizon, blazing fiercely. Most of *Kormoran*'s crew reached the Australian coast.

Although *Sydney* outgunned *Kormoran*, her fate was sealed by a torpedo, which put her 'A' and 'B' turrets out of action.

Displacement: 6830t standard; 8850t full load
Dimensions: 562ft 3in x 56ft 8in x 18ft 6in (171.37m x 17.27m x 5.64m)
Machinery: four screws, geared turbines; 72,000hp
Armament: eight 6in (152mm); four 4in (102mm); eight 21in (533mm) TT
Armour: belt 3in (76mm); turrets 1in (25mm)
Speed: 32.5 knots
Range: 4500nm (8338nm) at 14 knots
Complement: 570

TENNESSEE

USA: 1920

Begun in 1915, the dreadnoughts *Tennessee* (BB-43) and her sister ship *California* (BB-44) were repeats of the *New Mexico* class, with the hull line clear of gunports and two slender funnels. *Tennessee* was launched on 30 April 1920 and *California* in the following November, both vessels joining the Pacific Fleet. *California* was sunk in the Japanese attack on Pearl Harbor on 7 December 1941, but was later refloated, repaired and recommissioned. *Tennessee* was damaged by two bombs in the same attack but reconstructed in 1942 and recommissioned in May 1943. Joined by the reconstructed *California*, *Tennessee* was in action off Saipan in June 1944, both ships

Displacement: 32,300t standard; 33,190t full load
Dimensions: 624ft 6in x 97ft 4in x 30ft 3in (190.3m x 29.7m x 9.2m)
Machinery: four screws, turbo-electric drive; 26,800hp
Armament: 12 14in (355mm); 14 5in (127mm); two 21in (533mm) TT
Armour: belt 13.5in-8in (343mm-203mm); turrets 18in-9in (457mm-229mm); deck 3.5in (89mm)
Speed: 21 knots
Range: 10,000nm (18,530km) at 10 knots
Complement: 1083 (later 1480)

being damaged by shore batteries; August, the two dreadnoughts were involved in a collision. In 1945, they sustained further damage when both were hit by *kamikazes*. Decommissioned in 1947, *Tennessee* and *California* were both sold and broken up in 1959.

Both *Tennessee* and *California* were completely reconstructed in 1942–43. A massive single funnel was fitted, AA armament increased and anti-torpedo bulges added.

THAMES

GB: 1932

The *Thames* class submarines were combined fleet and patrol type boats, completed in 1932–35. It was planned to build 20, but only three, *Thames*, *Severn*, and *Clyde*, were produced. They featured welded external fuel tanks, which solved the problem of leakage affecting earlier designs. *Thames* differed from her two sisters in various respects, and was fitted with buoyancy tanks in the superstructure to improve stability. She was lost on 23 July 1940, believed to have hit a mine off Norway.

All three submarines of the *Thames* class could carry up to 12 M2 mines as an alternative to torpedoes.

Displacement: 2165t surfaced; 2680t submerged
Dimensions: 345ft x 28ft 3in x 15ft 7in (105.15m x 8.61m x 4.76m)
Machinery: two screws, diesels, plus electric motors; 10,000/2500hp
Armament: six 21in (533mm) TT; one 4in (102mm)
Speed: 22.5 knots surfaced; 10 knots submerged
Complement: 61

TIGER

GB: 1913

Displacement: 28,500t standard; 35,160t full load
Dimensions: 704ft x 90ft 6in x 32ft 4in (214.6m x 27.6m x 10.4m)
Machinery: four screws, turbines; 108,000hp
Armament: eight 13.5in (343mm); 12 6in (152mm); four 21in (533mm) TT
Armour: belt 9in-3in (229mm-76mm); turrets 9in (229mm); decks 3in-1in (76mm-25mm)
Speed: 29 knots
Range: 5700nm (10,562km) at 12 knots
Complement: 1121

The battlecruiser HMS *Tiger* was originally planned as a fourth unit of the *Lion* class, but was redesigned, with secondary armament added and increased horsepower, when the powerful Japanese *Kongo* class made its appearance. *Tiger* was launched on 15 December 1913, and served with the British Grand Fleet throughout World War I, being damaged at Dogger Bank on 24 January 1915 and at Jutland on 31 May 1916. Anti-aircraft guns were added to her armament in 1924. She was sold for scrap in 1932.

Tiger was one of the first battlecruisers to feature a flying-off platform, installed on 'Q' turret in 1917. It was removed in 1924.

TONE

JAPAN: 1907

The second-class light cruiser *Tone* was to have been one of two ships laid down in 1905, but funds were not made available for the second vessel. *Tone* was the first Japanese warship to feature a clipper-type bow. She underwent some armament changes soon after completion, including the installation of 3.1in (78mm) anti-aircraft guns. The cruiser was stricken on 1 April 1933 and was used as a floating target, sunk by aerial bombs off Amami-O Smima.

During her trials, *Tone* reached a speed of over 23 knots at a displacement of 4103t and 15,215hp.

Displacement: 4113t standard; 4900t full load
Dimensions: 373ft 4in x 47ft 3in x 16ft 9in (113.8m x 14.4m x 5.1m)
Machinery: two screws, vertical triple expansion engines; 15,000hp
Armament: two 6in (152mm); 10 4.7in (120mm); three 18in (457mm) TT
Armour: deck 3in-1.5in (76mm-38mm)
Speed: 23 knots
Range: 7340nm (13,601km) at 10 knots
Complement: 370

TRIESTE

ITALY: 1927

The first Italian cruisers to be armed with 8in (203mm) guns under the terms of the Washington Treaty, *Trieste* and her sister ship, *Trento*, were originally classed as light cruisers. They were among the fastest of the first-generation 10,000t vessels, speed being achieved at the expense of protection. Both vessels took part in the battle of Cape Matapan in March 1941. *Trento* saw action at Calabria in July 1941 and at Sirte in March 1942. *Trieste* was sunk by Allied air attack off Sardinia on 10 April 1943.

Both *Trieste* and *Trento* had an aircraft catapult and an aircraft hangar; three aircraft could be carried.

Displacement: 10,339t standard; 13,326t full load
Dimensions: 646ft 2in x 67ft 7in x 22ft 4in (196.96m x 20.6m x 6.8m)
Machinery: four screws, geared turbines; 150,000hp
Armament: eight 8in (203mm); 16 3.9in (100mm); eight 21in (533mm) TT
Armour: belt 2.75in (70mm); bulkheads 2.3in-1.57in (60mm-40mm); turrets 3.9in (100mm); decks 2in-0.78in (50mm-20mm)
Speed: 36 knots
Range: 5500nm (10,191km) at 12 knots
Complement: 723 (781 on war footing)

U1

GERMANY: 1906

Displacement: 238t surfaced; 283t submerged
Dimensions: 139ft x 12ft 6in x 10ft 6in (42.4m x 3.8m x 3.2m)
Machinery: two screws, heavy oil (kerosene), plus electric motors; 400hp/400hp
Armament: one 17.7in (450mm) TT
Speed: 10.8 knots surfaced; 8.7 knots submerged
Range: 1536nm (2850km) at 10 knots, surfaced
Complement: 22

Strangely enough, the German Naval Staff at the turn of the century failed to appreciate the potential of the submarine. Indeed, the first submarines built in Germany were three *Karp*-class vessels ordered by the Imperial Russian Navy in 1904. Germany's first practical submarine, *U1*, was not completed until 1906. She was, however, one of the most successful and reliable of the period. Her two kerosene engines developed 400hp, as did her electric motors. She had an underwater range of 43nm (80km). Commissioned in December 1906, *U1* was used for experimental and training purposes. In February 1919 she was stricken, sold, and refitted as a museum exhibit by her builders, Germaniawerft of Kiel. She was damaged by bombing in World War II, but subsequently restored. She was donated to the Deutsches Museum in Munich, where she is still exhibited today.

The early years of submarine development in Germany were adversely affected by rivalry between civilian designers and the Germany Navy's 'experts'.

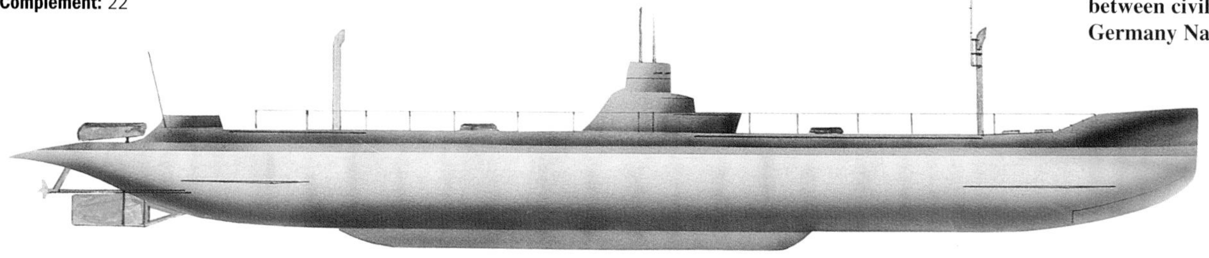

U2

GERMANY: 1935

Under the terms of the Versailles Treaty, Germany was forbidden to build submarines, but during the 1920s she set up clandestine design teams in Spain, Holland, and the Soviet Union. The first boat, built for Finland in 1927, was used as the prototype for *U2*, one of the first Type II submarines intended for coastal service. The diesel engines developed 350hp and the electric motors 180hp. All the early Type IIs were used for training. *U2* was lost in a collision in the Baltic on 8 April 1944.

Displacement: 250t surfaced; 298t submerged
Dimensions: 133ft 2in x 13ft 5in x 12ft 6in (40.9m x 4.1m x 3.8m)
Machinery: two screws, heavy oil, plus electric motors; 600/630hp
Armament: three 21in (533mm) TT; one 20mm AA
Speed: 13 knots surfaced; 7 knots submerged
Range: 912nm (168km), surfaced
Complement: 22

Despite strenuous efforts by the C-in-C U-boats, Karl Dönitz, the German Navy only had 46 submarines ready for action in September 1939.

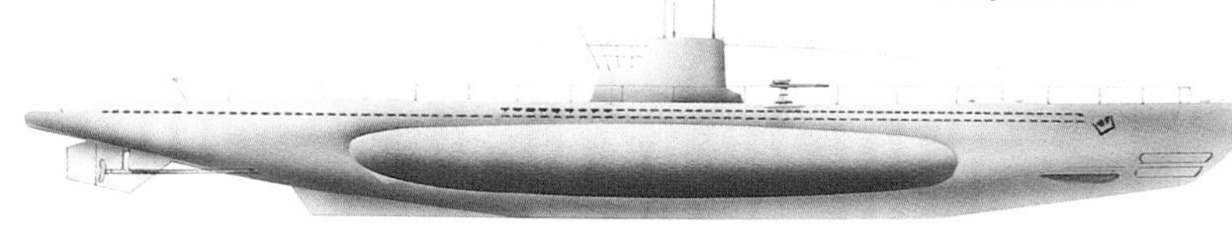

U21

GERMANY: 1914

Although the Germans got away to a slow start in their submarine construction programme before World War I, the vessels were well engineered, and used double hulls and twin screws from the start. German engineers refused to employ petrol engines in the early boats, preferring to use smellier but safer kerosene fuel. In 1908, suitable diesel engines were designed and these were installed in the *U19* class and used exclusively thereafter. One of the four boats of the *U19* class, *U21* was constructed at Danzig and completed in 1913.

As the war progressed, various modifications were introduced to German U-boat designs, including the familiar shark-like bows.

Displacement: 650t surfaced; 837t submerged
Dimensions: 210ft 6in x 20ft x 11ft 9in (64.2m x 6.1m x 3.5m)
Machinery: two screws, two diesels, plus two electric motors; 1700/1200hp
Armament: four 20in (508mm TT); one 3.4in (86mm)
Speed: 15.5 knots surfaced; 9 knots submerged
Range: 7600nm (14,082km) at 8 knots surfaced; 80nm (145km) at 5 knots submerged
Complement: 35

U151

GERMANY: 1917

Before the USA entered the war in 1917, the Germans were quick to recognise the potential of large, cargo-carrying submarines as a means of beating the blockade imposed on Germany's ports by the Royal Navy. Two *U151*-class boats, the *U151* and *U155*, were converted for mercantile use and named *Oldenburg* and *Deutschland* respectively. *Deutschland*, unarmed, made two mercantile trips to the USA. After 1917, the two boats were converted back to naval use as heavily-armed submarine cruisers, forming two of a class of seven (*U151–U157*). The class suffered casualties: a third merchant conversion, *Bremen*, was lost on her first voyage in 1917, possibly mined off the Orkneys; on 24 November 1918, *U151* was surrendered to France and was sunk as a target vessel off Cherbourg on 7 June 1921; and *U155*, formerly *Deutschland*, was scrapped at Morecambe, England, in 1922.

The cruiser submarine concept developed by Germany in World War I was sound, and other nations attempted to adopt it.

Displacement: 1512t surfaced; 1875t submerged
Dimensions: 213ft 3in x 29ft 2in x 17ft 5in (65m x 8.9m x 5.3m)
Machinery: two screws, diesel engines, plus electric motors; 800/800hp
Armament: two 5.9in (150mm); two 3.4in (86mm); two 20in (509mm) TT
Speed: 12.4 knots surfaced; 5.2 knots submerged
Range: 11,284nm (20,909km) at 10 knots, surfaced
Complement: 56

Von der Tann

GERMANY: 1909

Launched on 20 March 1909 and completed in September 1910, the *Von Der Tann* was the first German battlecruiser and also the first large German ship to have turbines and quadruple screws. In 1916, her 3.4in (88mm) guns were removed and four anti-aircraft guns of similar calibre substituted. Such was the urgency of the construction schedule applied to *Von Der Tann* that she was completed in less than two years, the shortest construction time for any German capital ship.

Much thought had gone into the arrangement of *Von Der Tann*'s armament. Her four twin turrets were all able to fire on broadside.

She was considerably better protected than any contemporary British battlecruiser, following the German design philosophy that it was cheaper to repair an existing

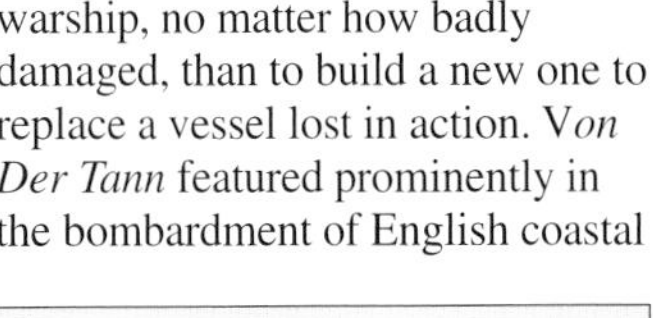

warship, no matter how badly damaged, than to build a new one to replace a vessel lost in action. *Von Der Tann* featured prominently in the bombardment of English coastal

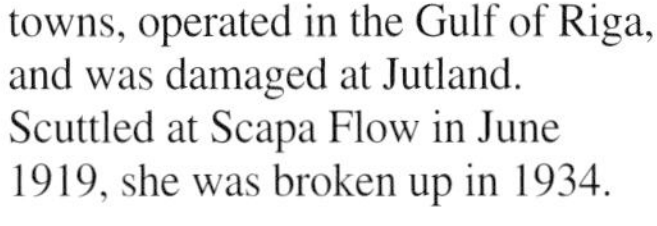

towns, operated in the Gulf of Riga, and was damaged at Jutland. Scuttled at Scapa Flow in June 1919, she was broken up in 1934.

Displacement: 19,370t standard; 21,300t full load
Dimensions: 563ft 4in x 87ft 3in x 29ft 10in (171.7m x 26.6m x 9.1m)
Machinery: four screws, turbines; 42,000hp
Armament: eight 11in (280mm); 10 5.9in (150mm); four 17.7in TT450mm
Armour: belt 9.8in–3.9in (250mm–100mm); turrets 9in (230mm); deck 3in–2in (76mm–50mm)
Speed: 24.7 knots
Range: 4400nm (8153km) at 14 knots
Complement: 910

Wadsworth

USA: 1915

The USS Wadsworth (DD60) was one of six Tucker-class destroyers, which in effect formed the second group of the O'Brien class. Several of these boats served in European waters following America's entry into World War I in 1917, and one of them, the Jacob Jones, was torpedoed and sunk by the German submarine U53 off the Scillies on 6 December that year. Wadsworth was designated flagship of the US Navy destroyer forces in British waters from April 1917. The Tucker-class destroyers continued to serve for some years after World War I. All were scrapped between 1934 and 1937.

Displacement: 1060t standard; 1205t full load
Dimensions: 315ft 3in x 29ft 9in x 9ft 2in (96.1m x 9.1m x 2.8m)
Machinery: two screws, turbines; 17,500hp
Armament: four 4in (102mm); eight 21in (533mm) TT
Armour: belt 3in (76mm)
Speed: 29.5 knots
Range: 3400nm (6300km) at 12 knots
Complement: 99

WALRUS

USA: 1914

Walrus, one of an eight-unit class and the last US submarine to be given a name for many years to come, was later renumbered *K4*. She served in the Azores during World War I and was broken up in 1931. Many of the American submarine classes of World War I vintage were designed for purely defensive use, not being suitable for oceanic operations. Nevertheless, many were still on the active list when America entered World War II. Other named *K* class boats were *Haddock*, *Cachalot* and *Orca*.

***Walrus* experienced early problems with her diesel engines, a situation that arose in three of the other *K*-class boats but was never completely cured.**

Displacement: 392t; 521t submerged
Dimensions: 153ft 10in x 16ft 9in x 13ft 2in (47m x 5m x 4m)
Machinery: two screws, diesel, plus electric motors; 950/680hp
Armament: four 18in (457mm) TT
Speed: 14 knots surfaced; 10.5 knots submerged
Range: 4500nm (8338km) at 10 knots, surfaced
Complement: 28

WEST VIRGINIA

USA: 1921

The *West Virginia* was the second vessel in the *Colorado* class of dreadnoughts. They were repeats of the *Tennessee* class, but with a 16in (406mm) main armament in four twin turrets. The third ship of the class was the *Maryland*; the fourth, *Washington*, was destroyed when 75 per cent complete, in order to comply with the terms of the Washington Naval Treaty of 1922. None of the *Colorados* were modernised before the USA entered World War I, except for an increase in anti-aircraft protection between 1935 and 1941. *West Virginia* (BB-48) was launched on 19 November 1921, completed in 1923, and assigned to the Pacific Fleet after her trials (during which she ran aground in Hampton Roads). She underwent two refits in the 1930s. On 7 December 1941, she was torpedoed during the Japanese attack on Pearl Harbor. *Maryland* was also damaged by bombs in the same attack. Both vessels were subsequently repaired and returned to active service. Despite having sunk at her moorings, *West Virginia* was refloated in 1942, totally reconstructed in similar fashion to *Tennessee*, and recommissioned in September 1944, rejoining the Pacific Fleet. Later, she was damaged by a *kamikaze* off Okinawa on 1 April 1945. *West Virginia* was decommissioned on 9 January 1947 and broken up at Seattle in 1959. The lead ship of the class, *Colorado*, fought through the whole of the Pacific War. She was damaged during a *kamikaze* attack at the Battle of Leyte Gulf, and by friendly gunfire at Lingayen. Along with the *Maryland*, the *Colorado* was broken up in 1959.

The decision to arm the *Colorado*-class battleships with 16in (406mm) guns was made in response to the new classes of Japanese dreadnoughts then under construction.

Displacement: 32,600t standard; 33,590t full load
Dimensions: 624ft x 97ft 6in x 30ft 6in (190.2m x 29.7m x 9.3m)
Machinery: four screws, turbo-electric drive; 28,900hp
Armament: eight 16in (406mm); 12 5in (127mm); two 21in (533mm) TT
Armour: belt 13.5in-8in (343mm-203mm); turrets 18in-9in (457mm-229mm); deck 3.5in (89mm)
Speed: 21 knots
Range: 10,000nm (18,530km) at 10 knots
Complement: 1407

WICKES

USA: 1918

Displacement: 1090t standard; 1247t full load
Dimensions: 314ft 4in x 30ft 10in x 9ft 2in (95.8m x 9.4m x 2.8m)
Machinery: two screws, turbines; 24,200hp
Armament: four 4in (102mm); 12 21in (533mm) TT
Armour: belt 2.5in (63mm)
Speed: 35 knots
Range: 2500nm (4632km) at 20 knots
Complement: 114

The USS *Wickes* was class leader of the famous American 'flush deck' destroyers, over 100 of which formed the bulk of the US Navy's light forces between the two world wars. The first 50 were authorized as part of the massive 1916 building programme. Although standard in layout and type (but not make) of equipment, the destroyers' performance varied radically, depending on the designer and manufacturer. For example, it was found that the Yarrow boilers installed in many of the vessels deteriorated badly in service and, in 1929, the US Navy decided to scrap 60 of the vessels fitted with this equipment. In 1940, *Wickes* herself and 23 of the class, were turned over to the Royal Navy where they were used to good effect on the Atlantic convoy routes at a time when the RN desperately needed such ships. *Wickes* was renamed HMS *Montgomery* and, in 1942, allocated to the Royal Canadian Navy. She was scrapped on the River Tyne in 1945.

The USS *Wickes* was one of 50 elderly destroyers of various classes transferred to the Royal Navy in September 1940.

X1

GB: 1923

Designed to evaluate the performance of a very large submarine underwater, *X1* would probably never have existed at all had it not been for the legacy of the large German 'submarine cruisers' of World War I. Though few of the latter ever became operational, they left behind an inflated reputation, appearing to validate the concept of a big submersible which, carrying a heavy armament, could fight it out on the surface with destroyers and armed merchant cruisers. *X1* was laid up in 1933.

X1 stored most of her fuel in external tanks, and had a designed depth unit of 350ft (106.6m).

Displacement: 3050t surfaced; 3600t submerged
Dimensions: 363ft 6in x 29ft 10in x 15ft 9in (110.8m x 9m x 4.8m)
Machinery: two screws, diesels, plus electric motors; 7000/2400hp
Armament: six 21in (533mm) TT; four 5.2in (132mm)
Speed: 20 knots surfaced; 9 knots submerged
Range: not established
Complement: 75

YORK

GB: 1928

The cruiser HMS *York* was a smaller version of the earlier *Kent*, *London* and *Norfolk* classes. A catapult and aircraft became part of her equipment in 1931. She was fitted out in much the same way as that of the *Norfolk* class, except for better protection around the machinery spaces, with the main armament reduced from eight to six guns. On 26 March 1941, *York* was damaged by an Italian explosive boat and had to be beached. She was wrecked by bombing.

The bombed-out wreck of HMS *York* remained beached at Suda Bay until 1952, when it was broken up.

Displacement: 8250t standard; 10,350t full load
Dimensions: 575ft x 57ft x 20ft 3in (175.25m x 17.37m x 6.17m)
Machinery: four screws, geared turbines; 80,000hp
Armament: six 8in (203mm); six 21in (533mm) TT
Armour: belt 3in (76mm); box protection to ammunition spaces 4in-1in (100mm-25mm)
Speed: 32.3 knots
Range: 4400nm (8153km) at 14 knots
Complement: 623

ZARA

ITALY: 1930

Displacement: 11,680t standard; 14,300t full load
Dimensions: 557ft 2in x 62ft 10in x 21ft 11in (182.8m x 20.62m x 7.2m)
Machinery: two screws, geared turbines; 95,000hp
Armament: eight 8in (203mm); 16 3.9in (100mm)
Armour: belt 9in-4-5in (150-100mm); decks 2.75-0.75in (70-20mm)
Speed: 32 knots
Range: 4000nm (7412km) at 15 knots
Complement: 841

The Italian *Zara*-class ships were originally classed as light cruisers, then armoured cruisers, and finally heavy cruisers. They were intended to be an improvement on the earlier *Trento* class, completed in the 1920s, but it was soon realized that the intended increase in armour protection, speed and gunnery could not be provided under the 10,000t limit imposed by the various naval treaties between the wars. When all improvements were incorporated, in fact, the displacement of the vessels exceeded the treaty limit by 1500t. There were four ships in the class, *Zara*, *Fiume*, *Gorizia*, and *Pola*, equipped with a launch catapult and a hangar capable of accommodating two spotter aircraft which fitted beneath the forecastle. Although the ships were capable of over 33 knots, higher speed was sacrificed for greater armour protection; in fact, the weight of armour installed was three times that of the *Trento* class. *Zara* was launched on 27 April 1930, and completed on 20 October 1931. Her operational career almost exactly matched that of her sister ships, *Fiume* and *Pola*, all three vessels being sunk at the Battle of Cape Matapan in March 1941.The British battleships *Warspite* and *Barham*, and the cruiser *Ajax*, annihilated the Italian warships in a close-range night engagement thanks to the use of radar, which the Italian vessels did not have. In 1944, *Gorizia*, was sunk by British 'human torpedoes' at La Spezia.

The designers of the *Zara* class used the two-screw, lightweight machinery developed for the successful *Condottieri* class light cruisers, one of the more effective Italian designs of the inter-war years.

CHAPTER SEVEN

WORLD WAR II 1936–45

The last day of 1936 saw the end of the warship 'building holiday' imposed by the Washington Treaty of 1922, which had constrained the five most powerful navies for a period of 15 years. They were now allowed to resume construction unrestricted save by their ability to fund it, and with the depression of the early 1930s – a significant factor in itself – over, economic restraints, too, disappeared. Germany was not subject to the Washington Treaty (and neither was the Soviet Union; it was to be many years before she became a major naval power), but had had to face a different set of problems, for her fleet had been dismantled by the Versailles Treaty of 1919. This had placed an entirely different set of restrictions on her, and already she had repudiated them. The stage was thus set for naval re-armament on a grand scale, and seamen agreed that unlike World War I, when the opposing battle fleets had barely brushed sleeves, the global conflict which was looming would test them as severely as it would their brothers-in-arms ashore.

Left: The battleships USS *West Virginia* (BB.48) and USS *Tennessee* (BB.43) ablaze after the Japanese attack on Pearl Harbor.

When war came – and war was approaching fast – it would be a new sort of war, and would quickly demonstrate the vulnerability of the old capital ships to the new weapons, and the ascendency of the aircraft carrier and the submarine as means of force projection. There were factors other than re-armament at work, too: the new technologies of radio- and sound-direction and ranging ('radar' and 'sonar') would soon begin to go some way towards redressing the balance, and allow men to seek out and track ships and aircraft at hitherto unimaginable distances, at night, in bad weather and below the surface of the sea, stripping the submarine of its cloak of invisibility and leaving it vulnerable. However, it would be some years before they became commonplace.

Two things remained certain within this framework: the skill and courage of the seaman had lost none of its importance, and there would always be an extra adversary present in any naval battle – the sea herself.

ACANTHUS

GB: 1940

Before World War II, the Royal Navy had only a minimal requirement for small warships, but in 1939 it was forced to cast around for a small escort vessel which could be constructed rapidly by non-specialist yards. The requirement was met by modifying the design of a commercial whale-catcher, Smith's Dock's *Southern Pride*, lengthening it by 30ft (9.2m) to improve crew space, and giving it more sheer and flare forward, deeper bilge keels, and splinter protection. The *Flower* class, as the resulting corvettes became known, was one of the biggest in British service and ran to almost 150 ships, while Empire and other Allied navies, principally that of Canada, operated about 130 more. They were to be employed much more widely than first envisaged, escorting convoys as far afield as the USA and Russia. HMS *Acanthus* was one of the first of them, built by Ailsa Shipbuilding. She was transferred to Norway as the Andenes in 1941 and remained in service until 1957.

HMS *Acanthus* was one the *Flower*-class corvettes, employed to escort merchant convoys across the Atlantic and around the North Cape to Russian ports.

Displacement: 980t standard; 1245t full load
Dimensions: 205ft x 33ft 2in x 15ft 9in (62.5m x 10.1m x 4.8m)
Machinery: one-shaft, vertical triple-expansion engine; 2750hp
Armament: one 4in (102mm); two 6pdr; four 20mm
Speed: 16.5 knots
Range: 4000nm (7400km) at 12 knots
Complement: 85–109

ACCIAIO

ITALY: 1941

Displacement: 697t surfaced; 850t submerged
Dimensions: 197ft 6in x 21ft 2in x 15ft 8in (60.2m x 6.45m x 4.8m)
Machinery: two-shaft, FIAT diesels, plus two CRDA electric motors; 1400bhp/800hp
Armament: six 21in (533mm) TT (four bow, two stern: 12 torpedoes); one 3.9in (100mm); one 20mm
Speed: 14 knots surfaced; 7.5 knots submerged
Range: 5000nm (9250km) at 8 knots surfaced
Complement: 45

Between 1932 and 1942, the Italian Navy commissioned five classes of 600t submarines, all of them designed by Bernardis, with single hulls and saddle tanks. They were smaller and less sophisticated than previous Italian coastal boats, and were thus significantly cheaper to build (though they were hardly inferior to the bigger boats in operation). *Acciaio* was the lead boat of the last group of 13. Built by Odero Terni Orlando (OTO) at Muggiano, she was sunk by HM Submarine *Unruly* in July 1943.

The 600t-class Italian submarines were optimized for operation in the shallow waters of the Mediterranean, where manoeuvrability was at a premium.

ACTIVITY

GB: 1942

Displacement: 11,800t standard; 14,300t full load
Dimensions: 512ft 9in x 66ft 6in x 26ft 1in (156.3m x 20.3m x 7.95m)
Machinery: two-shaft, two Burmeister & Wain diesels; 12,000bhp
Armament: two 4in (102mm); 24 20mm; 10 aircraft
Speed: 18 knots
Range: 12,000nm (22,200km) at 15 knots
Complement: 700

Constructed as a fast refrigerated ship, the *Telemachus*, but converted before completion by her builders, Caledon, HMS *Activity* was commissioned in September 1942. One of the few British-built escort carriers, she was used for deck-landing training initially, but spent much of her wartime career escorting Atlantic and Russian convoys. In 1945 she carried aircraft to the Far East. After the war she was reconverted to mercantile use as the *Breconshire*. Despite her considerable size – she was 475ft (145m) between perpendiculars – *Activity* had only a very small hangar, under 100ft (31m) long; this severely limited her aircraft capacity, to either six torpedo bombers and four fighters, or vice-versa. In this respect, she was distinctly inferior to American-built escort carriers such as the *Bogues*, which could operate twice as many aircraft on a smaller displacement. *Activity* was equipped with a single lift aft, 42ft x 20ft (13m x 6m), with a capacity of under 2t, and was not fitted with a catapult.

The escort carrier HMS *Activity* began life as a 'reefer', and was chosen for conversion by reason of the type's performance.

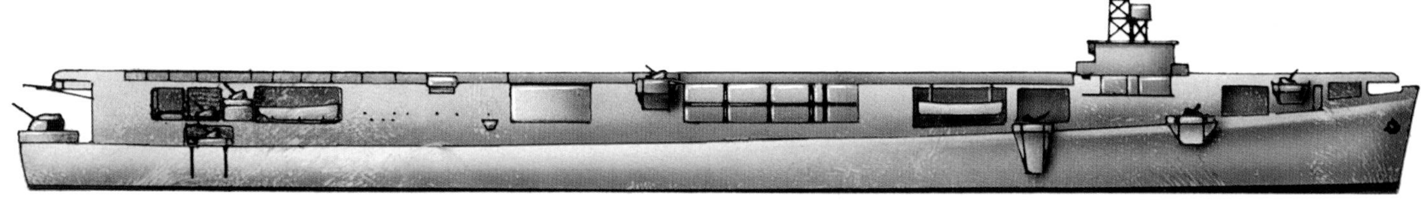

ADAMANT

GB: 1940

Most of the depot- and repair ships operated by the Royal Navy during World War II were converted merchantmen, but eight were specially constructed. HMS *Adamant*, built to replenish up to 20 submarines, was the biggest of them, with powerful AA armament and substantial protection in the form of armoured decks and internal anti-torpedo bulges and bulkheads. She was constructed in Belfast by Harland & Wolff and had a long career, remaining in commission for almost 30 years.

Depot ships like the *Adamant* were floating factories-cum-warehouses, able to carry out major repair work.

Displacement: 12,700t standard, 16,500t full load
Dimensions: 658ft x 70ft 6 in x 21ft 3in (200.55m x 21.5m x 6.5m)
Machinery: two-shaft, Parsons geared turbines; 8000hp
Armament: eight 4.5in (114mm) HA; 16 2pdr pom-poms; six 20mm
Armour: 1.25in (31.7mm) torpedo bulkheads; 2in (50mm) NC deck
Speed: 17 knots
Range: 6000nm (11,100km) at 12 knots
Complement: 1273

AGANO

JAPAN: 1941

The *Aganos* were almost the last cruisers constructed for the Imperial Japanese Navy. They were intended to operate as leaders for destroyer squadrons. Their armament included the oxygen-powered 'Long Lance' 24in (610mm) torpedo, which had a range three times that of any Allied torpedo and a 50 per cent bigger warhead. *Agano* was built at Sasebo Navy Yard, and entered service in October 1942. She was torpedoed by an American submarine USS *Skate*, off the island of Truk in February 1944.

The four *Aganos* were the last conventional cruisers built for the Imperial Japanese Navy; by mid-1944 they were carrying over 60 anti-aircraft guns.

Displacement: 6650t standard; 8535t full load
Dimensions: 571ft 2in x 49ft 10in x 18ft 6in (174.1m x 15.2m x 5.63m)
Machinery: four-shaft, geared turbines; 100,000hp
Armament: six 6in (152mm); four 3in (76mm) AA; 32 (later 46) 25mm; eight 24in (610mm) TT; 16 DC; two aircraft
Armour: belt 2.2in (56mm); deck 0.7in (18mm); turrets 1in (25mm)
Speed: 35 knots
Range: 8000nm (14,800km) at 20 knots
Complement: 730

AKITSUKI

JAPAN: 1941

Displacement: 2700t standard; 3700t full load
Dimensions: 440ft 3in x 38ft 1in x 13ft 7in (134.2m x 11.6m x 4.15m)
Machinery: two-shaft, geared turbines; 52,000hp
Armament: eight 3.9in (100mm); four (later, up to 5) 25mm; four 24in (610mm) TT; DC racks; DC throwers
Speed: 33 knots
Range: 8000nm (14,800km) at 20 knots
Complement: 300

The Imperial Japanese Navy's last class of destroyers, the *Akitsukis*, was authorized in 1939. Innovative ships, and somewhat ahead of the general run of destroyer development, they were intended originally to act as fast escorts for carrier task forces. They were armed with a newly-developed dual-purpose 3.9in (100mm) gun; before the design was finalized it was amended to include anti-submarine weaponry and four 24in (619mm) tubes for long-range torpedoes. The *Akitsukis* proved to be very successful and were certainly superior to the American destroyers of the period even if, on paper at least, they seemed to have inferior principal armament. Six of the 12 units completed actually survived the war (a rare occurrence in a Navy which was almost entirely destroyed) but *Akitsuki* was not one of them. Constructed at Maizuru Navy Yard, and launched on 2 July 1941, she was sunk on 25 October 1944 by American carrier-borne aircraft, during the epic Battle of Leyte Gulf.

The *Akitsuki*-class destroyers were the biggest ships of the type constructed for the Imperial Japanese Navy, armed with a new high-velocity dual-purpose gun.

ALLEN M SUMNER

USA: 1943

USS *Allen M Sumner* was the lead ship of a large class of destroyers, an improvement on the *Fletchers* with whose construction theirs was interleaved, with three, rather than five, single 5in (127mm) guns. The arrangement of the *Fletchers'* guns caused crowding on the centreline, and the introduction of the new twin mounting, the 5in/38 Mark 32, solved this problem. The extra space thus released was unfortunately, and almost ironically, filled by extra AA guns. This was the undoing of the *Sumners*: the addition of 12 40mm Bofors and 11 20mm Oerlikon cannon made them overweight and both slowed them down and cut their range.

USS *Allen M Sumner* was commissioned at the New York Navy Yard on 26 January 1944 after construction by Federal Shipbuilding at Kearny, New Jersey. Having seen service during World War II in the Pacific, she also took part in both the Korean and Vietnam Wars, winning a total of five battle stars before she was finally stricken in August 1973.

The *Sumners* introduced twin gun mountings into US destroyers – earlier classes had singles, and were very overcrowded as a result – but were soon overburdened with light AA guns.

Displacement: 2610t standard; 3220t full load
Dimensions: 376ft 6in x 40ft 10in x 14ft 2in (114.75m x 12.45m x 4.3m)
Machinery: two-shaft, General Electric geared turbines; 60,000hp
Armament: six 5in (127mm); 12 1.6in (40mm); 11 0.8in (20mm); 10 21in (533mm) TT; six DC throwers; two DC racks
Speed: 36.5 knots
Range: 3300nm (6100km) at 20 knots
Complement: 336

AMMIRAGLIO CAGNI

ITALY: 1940

Displacement: 1672t surfaced; 2125t submerged
Dimensions: 288ft 5in x 25ft 5in x 18ft 9in (87.9m x 7.75m x 5.7m)
Machinery: two-shaft, CRDA diesels, plus two CRDA electric motors; 4370bhp/1800hp
Armament: 14 17.7in (450mm) TT (eight bow, six stern: 36 torpedoes); two 3.9in (100mm); four 0.5in MG
Speed: 17 knots surfaced; 8.5 knots submerged
Range: 13,500nm (25,000km) at 9 knots surfaced
Complement: 85

In 1939, the Italian Navy ordered a group of four large submarines, intended for long-duration ocean patrols. They were first employed, however, as supply carriers to Italian garrisons in North Africa, and three were lost in this service. *Ammiraglio Cagni* was luckier and made two sorties into the South Atlantic in 1942–43; she surrendered at the end of the second sortie, in Durban on 9 September 1943. She was employed as a training boat for the rest of the war, and discarded in 1948.

The *Cagni*'s first operational patrol took her to the South Atlantic and lasted for four and a half months before she returned to her base at Bordeaux.

ARIETE

ITALY: 1943

The *Arietes* were the last of four classes of destroyer escorts constructed for the Italian Navy prior to and during World War II. Only the named ship was actually commissioned into the *Regia Marina*; the rest were taken over before completion by the German Navy, in September 1943. *Ariete* was constructed by Cantieri Riuniti dell'Adriatico at Trieste. Along with two others, she survived the war and was transferred to Yugoslavia as a reparation in 1949; as the *Durmitor*, she remained in service until 1963.

A total of 16 *Ariete*-class destroyer escorts were constructed; 15 were seized by the Germans, and 13 of them were destroyed or scuttled.

Displacement: 745t standard; 1110t full load
Dimensions: 274ft x 28ft 3in x 10ft 4in (83.5m x 8.6m x 3.15m)
Machinery: two-shaft, Parsons geared turbines; 22,000hp
Armament: two 3.9in (100mm); 10 0.8in (20mm); six 17.7in (450mm) TT; two DC throwers
Speed: 31.5 knots
Range: 1500nm (2800km) at 16 knots
Complement: 150

ARK ROYAL

GB: 1937

HMS *Ark Royal* was the first large aircraft carrier to be purpose-built for the Royal Navy. The flight deck had a useable area of 720ft x 95ft (219.5m x 29m); at the bow were two catapults which could each launch a 12,000lb (5455kg) load at a velocity of 66 knots. Constructed by Cammell Laird at Birkenhead, 'The Ark' was commissioned on 16 November 1938, and had a short but eventful career: one of her Blackburn Skua aircraft scored the first aerial victory of the war, and another, a Fairey Swordfish, crippled the *Bismarck* with a torpedo, forcing her into a fatal gunnery duel. *Ark Royal* did sterling service as part of Force 'H' in the Mediterranean. She was sunk there on 14 November 1941, by a single torpedo fired from a German Type VIIC U-boat, *U81*. The torpedo opened a 130ft x 30ft (40m x 9m) hole in her starboard side and bottom, abreast of the starboard boiler room; she capsized and went down after 14 hours, near to Gibraltar. It was something of a lucky shot which

The fleet carrier HMS *Ark Royal* played a major role in the sinking of the *Bismarck*, but was sunk herself, six months later, by a single torpedo from a German submarine.

sank 'The Ark': whether accidentally or on purpose, the German torpedo was set to run very deep and thus evaded both her armoured belt and the cellular system within the hull itself. The juxtapositioning of the three boiler rooms and the location of the unbaffled smoke ducts which joined them – allowing them all to be flooded at an angle of list of just 10 degrees – was perhaps the only serious mistake *Ark Royal*'s designers made, but it was to prove fatal.

Displacement: 22,000t standard; 27,700t full load
Dimensions: 800ft x 96ft x 27ft 9in (243.8m x 29.3m x 8.5m)
Machinery: three-shaft, Parsons geared turbines; 102,000hp
Armament: 16 4.5in (114mm); 32 2pdr pom-poms; four 3pdr; 72 aircraft
Armour: belt 4.5in (114mm); bulkheads 3in (76mm); decks 3.5in (89mm)
Speed: 31 knots
Range: 7600nm (14,100km) at 20 knots
Complement: 1580

ARMADA — GB: 1943

HMS *Armada* was the lead ship of the *Battle* class of destroyers, the biggest of their type constructed for the Royal Navy during World War II. Intended to serve in the Pacific theatre, these destroyers were multi-role ships; their 4.5in (114mm) guns, mounted forward in twin turrets, were capable of elevation to 80 degrees, and they had a heavy secondary AA armament. Constructed by Hawthorne Leslie, HMS *Armada* entered service in September 1944. She was placed in reserve in 1960, and sold for breaking up in 1965.

The multi-role *Battle*-class destroyers were the biggest constructed for the Royal Navy during World War II.

The *Battles* were criticized as being somewhat under-gunned, and a follow-on group of eight more ships, which were otherwise identical, received an extra 4.5in (114mm) gun mounted amidships in the 'P' position. Post-war, *Armada* lost her 4in (102mm) gun, gaining two single 40mm in its place, and also lost the single 40mm on the quarter deck to make room for a Squid anti-submarine mortar.

Displacement: 2315t standard; 3300t full load
Dimensions: 379ft x 40ft 3in x 15ft 2in (115.5m x 12.3m x 4.6m)
Machinery: two-shaft, Parsons geared turbines; 50,000hp
Armament: four 4.5in (114mm) DP; one 4in (102mm); eight 40mm; two 2pdr; two 0.8in(20mm); eight 21in (533mm) TT; two DC racks
Speed: 35.75 knots
Range: 4800nm (8900km) at 20 knots
Complement: 308

ARTEMIS — USA: 1942

Displacement: 6740t full load
Dimensions: 426ft x 58ft x 15ft 6in (129.85m x 17.7m x 4.7m)
Machinery: two-shaft, Westinghouse geared turbines; 6000hp
Armament: 12 20mm
Speed: 18 knots
Range: 8000nm (14,800km) at 16 knots
Complement: 303

The original attack cargo ships were converted merchantmen. They performed an essential function, but were not optimized for the task, and it became clear that purpose-built ships were needed. *Artemis* was the first, and leader, of a class which ran to 32 vessels. She carried a mix of specialist landing-craft on deck, disembarked them empty using her own derricks, and then loaded them alongside from the 900t of cargo and the 850 or so troops she carried.

The *Artemis*-class attack cargo ships were based on the standard S4 merchantman, which served in many guises during World War II.

ASASHIO — JAPAN: 1936

The Imperial Japanese Navy constructed a class of 10 2000t fleet destroyers under its 1934 Programme. They were larger than earlier ships, marking the end of the restrictions imposed by the Washington Treaty, and setting a pattern for future construction. The *Asashios*' powerplant was of a new design which gave considerable trouble at first, and the steering gear was deficient, but both problems were solved before war broke out in December 1941. Like all Japanese destroyers of the period, the *Asashio* class's principal armament of 5in (127mm) dual-purpose guns was mounted in twin turrets, one forward and two aft. From 1943, the 'X' turret was removed and replaced by additional light AA guns; by that time, however, the *Asashio*, first of the class to be constructed at Sasebo Navy Yard, had already been lost, sunk by American carrier-based aircraft. Of the 10 constructed, not one was to survive the war.

Despite some initial problems with their powerplant, the Japanese *Asashio*-class destroyers were to become effective warships, though all were lost during World War II.

Displacement: 1960t standard; 2610t full load
Dimensions: 388ft x 33ft 11in x 12ft 1in (118.25m x 10.35m x 3.7m)
Machinery: two-shaft, geared turbines; 50,000hp
Armament: six 5in (127mm) DP; four 25mm; eight 24in (610mm) TT; 16 DC
Speed: 35 knots
Range: 6000nm (11,100km) at 20 knots
Complement: 200

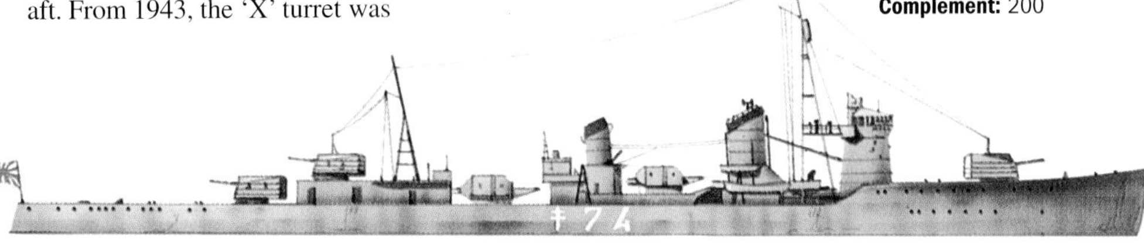

ASHLAND

USA: 1942

The landing-ship, dock (LSD) was essentially a self-propelled drydock. It could be flooded down at the stern by pumping seawater into ballast tanks so that the landing-craft it carried in the well deck – for example, three US-pattern LCTs, each with five medium tanks aboard – could be floated out through stern gates. USS *Ashland* was the first of the type. She had a comparatively long career, and was broken up in 1970.

USS *Ashland* was the first landing-ship, dock. She was designed and built in the United States to fulfil a British requirement.

Displacement: 4030t standard; 7930t full load
Dimensions: 457ft 9in x 72ft 2in x 15ft 10in (139.5m x 22m x 4.8m)
Machinery: two-shaft, Skinner Uniflow vertical triple-expansion reciprocating engines; 7400hp
Armament: one 5in (127mm) gun; 12 40mm; 16 20mm
Speed: 15.5 knots
Range: 8000nm (15,000km) at 15 knots
Complement: 254

ATHERSTONE

GB: 1939

Britain constructed just one class of escort destroyers during World War II, but it ran to four groups (though the last group numbered only two ships, and they were markedly different in appearance). All 86 ships in the class were named after hunts; the first of them, HMS *Atherstone* was constructed by Cammell Laird at Birkenhead. Once at sea it was clear that she was dangerously unstable; the problem was corrected by the hurried removal of one of the three twin 4in (102mm) gun turrets and adding ballast. These *Hunt*-class escort destroyers were amongst the first ships of the Royal Navy to be fitted with Denny fin stabilisers. Later groups had their beam increased by 2ft 6in (609mm x 152mm); this both cured the stability problem definitively, and enabled them to revert to their designed armament. Somewhat surprisingly, for their role was a dangerous one, all but 17 of the *Hunts* survived the war. HMS *Atherstone* was broken up in 1957.

The three major groups of *Hunt*-class escort destroyers were all basically similar, differing only in their weapons mix. They were a mainstay of the Battle of the Atlantic.

Displacement: 1000t standard; 1450t full load
Dimensions: 280ft x 29ft x 12ft 6in (85.35m x 8.85m x 3.8m)
Machinery: two-shaft, Parsons geared turbines; 19,000hp
Armament: four 4in (102mm) HA; four 2pdr pom-poms; two 20mm; 50 DC
Speed: 28 knots
Range: 6000nm (11,100km) at 18 knots
Complement: 147

ATLANTA

USA: 1941

USS *Atlanta* was the leader of a class of 11 anti-aircraft cruisers constructed in three groups during World War II. The basic design was forced upon the US Navy by the last of the between-the-wars Naval Treaties, concluded in London in 1936. The treaty terms effectively prevented the Navy from building more 10,000t ships. Instead, the Navy evolved a 6000t design to replace the ageing *Omahas*, and to work alongside destroyers engaged in screening carrier battle groups. There was a question mark against the *Atlantas* initially; much of the responsibility for their shortcomings as warships rests with the unavailability of a new twin 6in (152mm) dual-purpose gun mounting with which they were supposed to be equipped. Later groups, particularly the third, were a great improvement over the original design; the weapons mix was altered and their topsides weight reduced, which made them much more stable. USS *Atlanta* was built by Federal Ship Building at Kearny, New Jersey, and joined the fleet on Christmas Eve 1941. She was lost at Guadalcanal, eleven months later, on 13 November 1942, along with her sister ship, the original *Juneau*. One of the major disappointments associated with the *Atlantas* concerned their performance: the designers had concluded that in ships of this size and displacement, 75,000hp would allow them to make almost 40 knots, but they were wrong – *Atlanta* herself could not make 34 knots on trial, and this was a serious shortcoming, for the ships they were intended to escort could all equal that and did so in service.

The *Atlantas* were the smallest of the American cruisers engaged in World War II. They are generally rated as the least successful, though only two were lost during the course of the war.

Displacement: 6720t standard; 8340t full load
Dimensions: 541ft 6in x 53ft 2in x 20ft 6in (165.05m x 16.2m x 6.25m)
Machinery: two-shaft, Westinghouse geared turbines; 75,000hp
Armament: 16 5in (127mm) DP; 16 40mm; 16 1.1in; eight 20mm; eight 21in (533mm) TT; DC racks
Armour: belt and bulkheads 3.75in (95mm); deck 1.25in (32mm); gunhouses 1.25in (32mm)
Speed: 32.5 knots
Range: 8500nm (15,750km) at 15 knots
Complement: 623

ATLANTIS

GERMANY: 1938

Displacement: 17,600t full load
Dimensions: 508ft 6in x 61ft 4in x 28ft 6in (155m x 18.7m x 8.7m)
Machinery: one-shaft, two MAN double-acting 6-cyl. diesels; 7600bhp
Armament: six 5.9in (150mm); one 75mm; two 37mm; four 20mm; four 21in (533mm) TT; two aircraft
Speed: 16 knots
Range: 12,000nm (22,200km) at 12 knots
Complement: 351

In 1937, AG Vulcan, Bremen laid down a motor ship, the *Goldenfels*, of 7862grt. She was to have a very different career than that envisaged for her; on 30 November 1939 she was impressed into the *Kriegsmarine* as *Schiff 16*, armed as a commerce raider. The captains of such vessels were allowed to name them themselves, and she became the *Atlantis*. She went on to wreak havoc with Allied shipping for two years, sinking 22 vessels before running foul of the British heavy cruiser HMS *Devonshire*.

The *Atlantis*, known to the British as 'Raider C', accounted for over 145,000t of Allied shipping before she was sunk by the cruiser HMS *Devonshire*.

ATTILIO REGOLO

ITALY: 1940

Attilio Regolo was the first of 12 ships of the *Capitani Romani* class laid down for the Italian Navy in 1939, only four of which were completed (one of them not until the mid-1950s, after she had been raised from the sea bed where she had lain since being scuttled in 1943). These ships reverted to the role originally intended for the bigger *Condottieri* type, built in five groups from 1928. The *Attilio Regolo* class were actually very large, fast destroyers – they regularly achieved 36 knots without undue effort, even when fully loaded, and one was reported to have exceeded 41 knots. Built by Odero Terni Orlando (OTO) at Leghorn (Livorno), *Attilio Regolo* was completed on 14 May 1942. She saw action with the Italian Navy on both sides, and was eventually ceded to France under the terms of the Armistice at Toulon on 15 August 1948. She served with the French Navy as the *Chateau-renault* until she was stricken in 1962.

Displacement: 3690t standard; 5335t full load
Dimensions: 468ft 10in x 47ft 3in x 16ft (142.9m x 14.4m x 4.9m)
Machinery: two-shaft, Belluzzo geared turbines; 110,000bhp
Armament: eight 5.3in (135mm); eight 37mm; eight 20mm; eight 21in (533mm) TT
Armour: 0.6in (15mm) splinter protection to bridge and 0.8in (20mm) turrets
Speed: 40 knots
Range: 4250nm (7870km) at 18 knots
Complement: 418

***Attilio Regolo* was the first of the *Capitani Romani* class, only three of which saw action during World War II; she was later transferred to France as the *Chateaurenault*.**

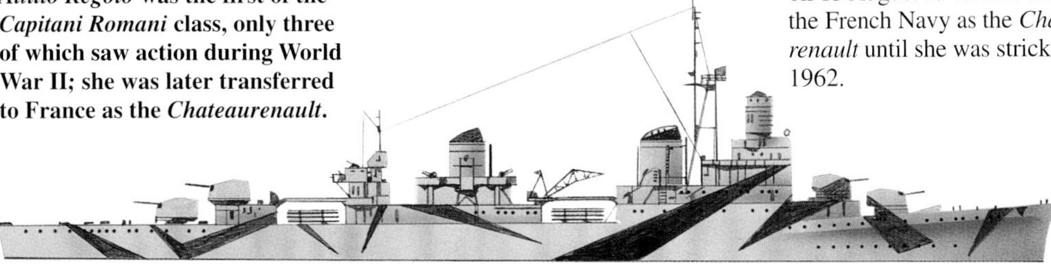

ATTU

USA: 1944

Displacement: 8190t standard; 10,900t full load
Dimensions: 512ft 4in x 108ft 1in x 20ft 9in (156.15m x 32.95m x 6.3m)
Machinery: two-shaft, two Skinner Uniflow vertical triple-expansion reciprocating engines; 9000hp
Armament: one 5in (127mm); eight 40mm; 12 20mm; 27 aircraft
Speed: 19 knots
Range: 10,200nm (18,850km) at 15 knots
Complement: 860

In mid-1942, Henry J. Kaiser, the American industrial hero of World War II, proposed mass-producing escort carriers by the same production-line methods he was already using to turn out merchant ships at an almost incredible rate. The result was the *Casablanca* class, 50 escort carriers constructed for the US Navy at a specially-built yard in Vancouver, on the Columbia River in Washington State, between 1942 and 1944. USS *Attu* (she was originally to have been named *Elbour Bay*, but the name was changed before building commenced) was the last but two of the *Casablanca* class. By that stage of the war, Kaiser's men had refined the construction process to something resembling an art form: USS *Attu* took just 75 days to build, from the laying of the first plates for her keel to her commissioning on 30 June 1944. She got under way for her first mission on active service – ferrying replacement aircraft and fresh aircrew to Guadalcanal via Pearl Harbor – on 7 August. She continued in that role until the war's end, when she began to carry out the process in reverse as part of Operation 'Magic Carpet'. Like all her sister ships, she was laid up at the war's end, and was broken up in 1949. The *Casablanca*s were austere ships, based on the same general-purpose S4 hull which Kaiser was already using for his merchant ships. They were relatively lightly armed and without armour, but with a very useful air wing comprising nine fighter aircraft, nine bombers, and nine torpedo bombers.

Built by Henry Kaiser's production-line methods, it was just 75 days from USS *Attu's* keel being laid to her joining the fleet.

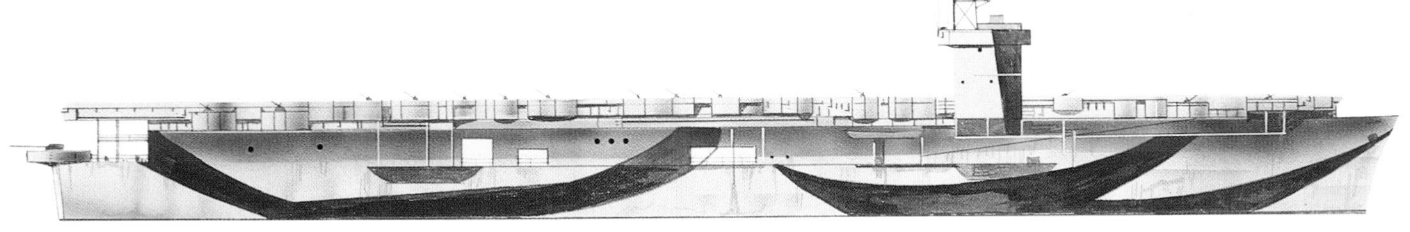

AUDACITY

GB: 1939

Following the fall of France, Allied shipping in the Atlantic faced a new threat in the shape of ultra-long range Focke Wulf FW.200 *Kondor* bombers. In an attempt to provide much-needed air cover, merchant ships were converted to become expedient aircraft carriers; the first of them was HMS *Audacity*. Constructed by AG Vulcan at Vegesack, Bremen as the 5500grt *Hannover*, she was launched on 29 March 1939 only to be captured by the Allies in February 1940. Work on converting her was put in hand by Blythe Shipbuilding in January 1941; she was commissioned as HMS *Audacity* in June that year. Only very rudimentary equipment was installed. There was no hangar and consequently no need for a lift – her six aircraft were kept on deck. Tanks to hold 10,000 gallons of aviation fuel were installed. Navigation and control of air operations were carried out from a simple platform to starboard. *Audacity* escorted Gibraltar convoys for six months until torpedoed by *U751* off Portugal on 20 December 1941.

HMS *Audacity* started life as a motor-cargo ship under German ownership. She was captured in the Caribbean in 1940 and converted into an escort carrier the following year.

Displacement: 12,000t full load
Dimensions: 467ft 3in x 60ft x 21ft 7in (142.4m x 18.3m x 6.6m)
Machinery: one-shaft, one 7-cyl. MAN diesel; 5200bhp
Armament: one 4in (102mm) HA; one 6pdr; four 2pdr pom-poms; four 20mm; six aircraft
Speed: 15 knots
Range: 12,000nm (22,200km) at 13 knots
Complement: 480

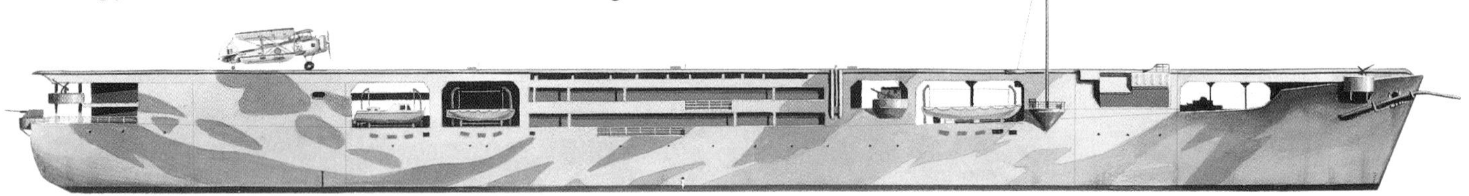

AURORE

FRANCE: 1939

The *Aurores* were the final form of a type of submarine which had its origins in the mid-1920s, the 630-tonners. In all, five quite distinct and different classes were constructed, of which the *Aurores* were very much the largest, having grown to almost 900t standard displacement. They were considerably more robust than earlier classes, with an operational depth limit increased from 250ft to 330ft (77m to 100m). *Aurore* was built at the Arsenal de Toulon. She was launched on 26 July 1939, and completed the following year. She was the only one of the class actually completed in time to see war service, serving with the Vichy French Navy in the Mediterranean and, like virtually all its vessels, scuttled at Toulon on 27 November 1942, to prevent her falling into German hands. One more unit was completed by the Germans and others were completed postwar, to two very different designs, incorporating many new elements developed during the course of the war.

The *Aurore*, one of only two boats of the class to see wartime service, was the best of the French second-class 630t submarine types.

Displacement: 893t surfaced; 1170t submerged
Dimensions: 241ft 2in x 21ft 4in x 13ft 9in (73.5m x 6.5m x 4.2m)
Machinery: two-shaft, two Sulzer diesels, plus electric motors; 3000bhp/1400hp
Armament: nine 21.7in (550mm) TT (four bow, two stern, three external amidships); one 3.9in (100mm); two 13.2mm MG
Speed: 14.5 knots surfaced; 9 knots submerged
Range: 5600nm (10,300km) at 10 knots, surfaced
Complement: 44

AVON

GB: 1943

Displacement: 1460t standard; 2180t full load
Dimensions: 301ft 4in x 36ft 8in x 12ft 9in (91.8m x 11.2m x 3.9m)
Machinery: two-shaft, two vertical triple-expansion reciprocating engines; 5500hp
Armament: two 4in (102mm); Hedgehog; 126 DC
Speed: 19 knots
Range: 7000nm (13,000km) at 12 knots
Complement: 140

The *Rivers* were ocean-going convoy escorts. Built to first-class mercantile standards, most were produced in yards in Britain and Canada that had little or no experience of building warships. All but a very few of the class had simple two-shaft reciprocating machinery and could not make 20 knots. HMS *Avon* was built by Charles Hill and entered service late in 1943. She was transferred to Portugal in 1948 as the *Nuño Tristao*, and was discarded in 1972.

The *River*-class ocean-going escorts were built to replace the *Flower*-class corvettes, and had largely taken over from them by 1944.

BALTIMORE

USA: 1942

The *Baltimores* were heavy cruiser equivalents of the *Clevelands*, armed with three triple 8in (203mm) guns in place of the *Clevelands*' four triple 6in (152mm) mountings. Direct descendants of the solitary *Wichita* of 1937, and freed from the restrictions imposed by the inter-war Naval Treaties, the *Baltimores*' extra displacement went into strengthening the hull and mounting extra weapons.

Unlike the *Clevelands* (the most prolific of all the World War II cruiser classes), the *Baltimores* did not suffer from excessive top weight and were altogether superior ships, a fact confirmed when most units stayed in service into the 1970s. In all, the class contained 14 identical ships and four which were somewhat modified. A further six were planned but cancelled before they were begun. USS *Baltimore* herself was constructed by Bethlehem Steel at Quincy, Massachusetts, where all save six of the class were built; she was completed on 15 April 1943. She remained in service until February 1971 but, unlike some of her sister ships, was not extensively modernized. Four of the class were modified to fire Regulus, the US Navy's first-generation cruise missile. Two more lost their aft 8in (203mm) turret and one 5in (127mm) turret, and at the same time gained two launchers for Terrier surface-to-air missiles, being recommissioned as the US Navy's first guided-missile cruisers. Three more of the *Baltimores* had even more extensive modifications made to them, losing all their 8in (203mm) turrets and their 5in (127mm) turrets (though they subsequently regained a pair of the latter), and gaining both Talos and Tartar SAMs, the ASROC anti-submarine guided-missile system, and six 12.75in (324mm) torpedo tubes. Their superstructure was also extensively modified.

The *Baltimores* were the US Navy's most extensive class of heavy cruisers of World War II. All units survived, most remaining in service until the 1970s.

Displacement: 14,470t standard; 17,030t full load
Dimensions: 673ft 5in x 70ft 10in x 24ft (205.25m x 21.6m x 7.3m)
Machinery: four-shaft, General Electric geared turbines; 120,000hp
Armament: nine 8in (203mm); 12 5in (127mm); 48 40mm; 24 20mm; four aircraft
Armour: belt 6in-4in (152mm-102mm); deck 2.5in (63mm); turret face 8in (203mm)
Speed: 33 knots
Range: 10,000nm (18,500km) at 15 knots
Complement: 2039

BELFAST

GB: 1938

Displacement: 10,550t standard; 13,175t full load
Dimensions: 613ft 6in x 63ft 4in x 21ft 3in (187m x 19.3m x 6.5m). Later, after repair: 613ft 6in x 66ft 4in x 23ft 2in (187m x 22.2m x 7.1m)
Machinery: four-shaft, Parsons geared turbines; 80,000hp
Armament: 12 6in (152mm); 12 4in (102mm); four 3pdr; 16 2pdr pom-poms; six 21in (533mm) TT; three aircraft
Armour: belt 4.5in (114mm); bulkheads 2.5in (64mm); deck 3in-2in (76mm-51mm); turrets 4in-2in (102mm-51mm)
Speed: 32.5 knots
Range: 12,000nm (22,200km) at 20 knots
Complement: 850

HMS *Belfast* was the second of the two *Edinburghs*, the biggest cruisers (if only by a narrow margin) ever constructed for the Royal Navy. They were the last of the 10 large light cruisers designed within the limits set by the Naval Treaties, but were some 5 per cent overweight when completed. While the *Belfast* and the *Edinburgh* were based on the *Southamptons*, they differed from them in minor but important ways: the 'X' and 'Y' turrets were each raised by one deck, the anti-aircraft battery was enlarged, and its armour extended, reinforced, and rearranged (repeating the much better turret protection introduced with the interim *Gloucester* class). Their machinery was also marginally uprated over that of the *Southamptons*, giving them half a knot more on their top speed. It had been the Admiralty's intention that these cruisers should mount 15 guns, but to accommodate them would have required an increase in their overall length, and finding drydocks would then have become problematic. An alternative – quadruple 6in (152mm) mountings – proved unworkable. HMS *Belfast* was built, fittingly enough, in that city by Harland & Wolff and was launched on St Patrick's Day, 17 March 1938. She was completed on 3 August 1939, just a month before Britain and France declared war on Germany. She had her back broken by a magnetic mine in November 1939, and repairs (and the bulging of her hull) dragged on until October 1942, although she later played a major role in the sinking of the *Scharnhorst*. She finally paid off in 1962, and is preserved as a museum in the Pool of London.

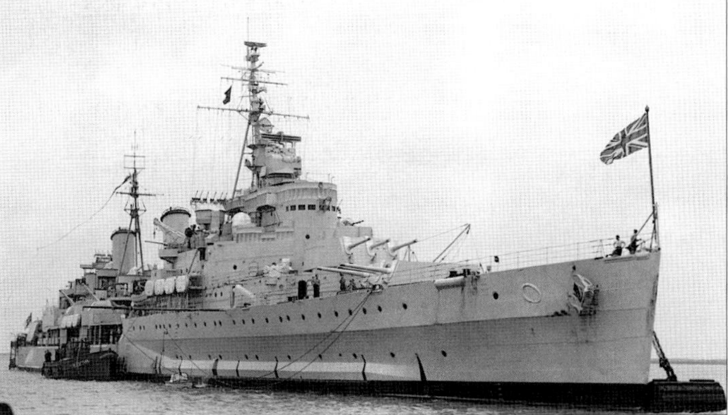

Though she was out of action for much of World War II, HMS *Belfast* was probably the most effective light cruiser the Royal Navy had during that period.

BELLONA

GB: 1942

HMS *Bellona* was the leader of a class of five anti-aircraft cruisers, a follow-on from the earlier *Didos* with only very minor modifications (the absence of rake to masts and funnels distinguished them). By the time the *Bellonas* were constructed, problems with the production of the semi-automatic, 5.25in (133mm) Mk I HA gun had been resolved. Now, all the *Bellonas* mounted the weapon for which they had been designed, though in four, rather than five, twin turrets that in the 'Q' position having been deleted in favour of adding more light AA guns. HMS *Bellona* was built at Fairfield's yard on the Clyde, and entered service late in 1943. Four of the five units survived the war, the exception being the ill-fated *Spartan*, sunk by a single 'Fritz-X' guided glider bomb on 29 January 1944. *Bellona* was loaned to New Zealand from 1948 to 1956, and was then returned to the Royal Navy. She was broken up in 1959.

The *Bellonas* were purpose-built anti-aircraft ships. They were armed with four pairs of semi-automatic 5.25in (133mm) guns of a new design, as well as many light AA guns.

Displacement: 5950t standard; 7350t full load
Dimensions: 512ft x 50ft 6in x 17ft 11in (156.05m x 15.4m x (5.45m)
Machinery: four-shaft, Parsons geared turbines; 62,000hp
Armament: eight 5.25in (133mm) HA; 12 2pdr pom-poms (later eight 40mm and 20 20mm); six 21in (533mm) TT
Armour: sides 3in (76mm); bulkheads 1in (25mm); deck 2in-1in (51mm-25mm)
Speed: 32 knots
Range: 6000nm (11,100km) at 18 knots
Complement: 530

BENHAM

USA: 1938

The US Navy did not build an entirely effective fleet destroyer until the *Bensons* of 1939; earlier, it had persisted in constructing ships which were over-armed and too lightly built. The 10 *Benhams* were repeats of the earlier *Bagleys*, but with somewhat more efficient machinery, retaining their unbalanced four gun/16 torpedo tube armament. USS *Benham* was built by Federal Ship Builders at Kearny, New Jersey. She was sunk in November 1942, torpedoed at the Battle of Guadalcanal.

The *Benhams* were very vulnerable to air attack. At the start of the war, they had only four machine guns, though surviving units later had both 40mm and 20mm cannon.

Displacement: 1657t standard; 2250t full load
Dimensions: 340ft 9in x 35ft 6in x 12ft 10in (103.85m x 10.8m x 3.9m)
Machinery: two-shaft, Westinghouse geared turbines; 50,000hp
Armament: four 5in (127mm); four 0.5in MG; 16 21in (533mm) TT
Speed: 38 knots
Range: 6500nm (12,000km) at 12 knots
Complement: 184

BENSON

USA: 1939

Displacement: 1830t standard; 2385t full load
Dimensions: 348ft 4in x 36ft 1in x 13ft 2in (106.2m x 11m x 4m)
Machinery: two-shaft, Westinghouse geared turbines; 50,000hp
Armament: five 5in (127mm); six 0.5in MG; 10 21in (533mm) TT (later four 5in; four 40mm; six 20mm; five TT)
Speed: 35 knots
Range: 6500nm (12,000km) at 12 knots
Complement: 208 (later 250)

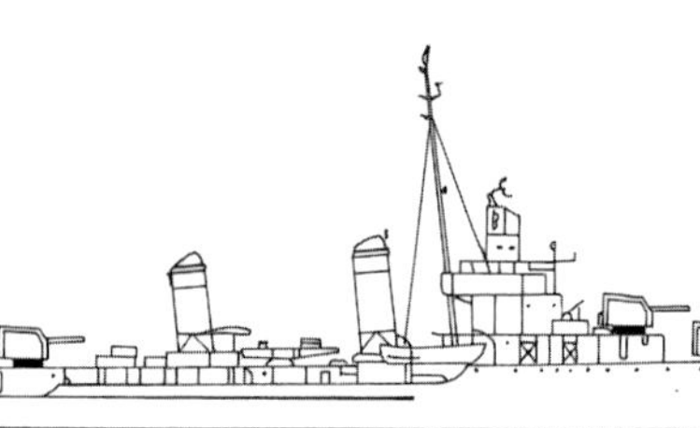

The *Bensons*, and the almost identical *Gleaveses*, were the first effective US fleet destroyers of the World War II era. They were based on the *Sims*, with two additional torpedo tubes, and established the pattern for future destroyer classes throughout the war. A total of 97 were built, of which USS *Benson* was one of the first, launched by Bethlehem Steel at Quincy, Massachusetts in November 1939. She was transferred to Taiwan in 1954, and served as the *Lo Yang* until 1975.

The *Bensons* were a distinct improvement over earlier US destroyers, but as originally designed they still had almost no defence against air attack.

BILOXI

USA: 1943

Displacement: 11,745t standard; 14,130t full load
Dimensions: 610ft 1in x 66ft 4in x 24ft 6in (185.95m x 20.2m x 7.5m
Machinery: four-shaft, General Electric geared turbines; 100,000hp
Armament: 12 6in (152mm); 12 5in (127mm); 24 40mm; 21 20mm; four aircraft
Armour: belt 5in-3.5in (127mm-89mm); deck 2in (51mm); bulkheads 5in (127mm); turret faces 6.5in (165mm); conning tower 5in (127mm)
Speed: 32.5 knots
Range: 11,000nm (20,350km) at 15 knots
Complement: 1285

Even though the original order for 52 ships of the *Cleveland* class was reduced to 27 (nine were converted on the stocks into light aircraft carriers), this was still the biggest class of light cruisers ever constructed. The *Clevelands* were modified *Brooklyns*, and suffered from the exigencies of wartime production. Their design called for a largely aluminium superstructure, but shortages saw steel employed instead and the *Clevelands* were very top-heavy as a result. They were dual-purpose ships, mounting 12 6in (152mm) guns for use against surface targets, and 12 5in (127mm) and large numbers of 40mm and 20mm as anti-aircraft guns. A 1942 re-design saw the superstructure and deckhouses lowered and watertight integrity improved by heightening the bulkheads. The result was a much more seaworthy ship. USS *Biloxi* was built by Newport News Shipbuilding, and launched some 15 months after the class leader. She was laid up in reserve for many years after the war, until finally discarded in 1962.

The *Cleveland*-class cruisers were built in large numbers, not so much because they were the best available but because they could be constructed quickly.

BISMARCK

GERMANY: 1939

Displacement: 41,700t standard; 50,900t full load
Dimensions: 813ft 8in x 118ft 1in x 34ft 9in (248m x 36m x 10.6m)
Machinery: three-shaft, Blohm & Voss geared turbines; 138,000hp
Armament: eight 15in (38cm); 12 5.9in (15cm); 16 4.1in (10.5cm); 16 37mm; 12 20mm; four aircraft
Armour: belt 12.5in-10.5in (318mm-267mm); deck 4.75in (121mm); 2in (51mm); main turrets 14.25in-7in (362mm-178mm); secondary turrets 4in-1.5in (102mm-37mm); conning tower 14in (356mm)
Speed: 29 knots
Range: 8500nm (15,750km) at 19 knots
Complement: 2092

***Bismarck* and her sister ship *Tirpitz* were actually designed and built to be a match for the French *Richlieus*, but fate was to see *Bismarck* pitted against the heavier guns of the British battleship *Rodney*.**

The Treaty of Versailles, which ended World War I, prevented Germany from constructing new warships. Later, in 1935, the Anglo-German Naval Treaty permitted her to build up to 35 per cent of British naval tonnage. This was when work on reconstructing the German fleet began (though design work actually started as early as 1932). *Bismarck* and her sister ship *Tirpitz* were the second pair of battleships built (after the *Scharnhorst* and the *Gneisenau*). Designed under the direction of MinRat Burkhardt, *Bismarck* was built (originally as battleship 'F', *Ersatz Hannover*) by Blohm & Voss at Hamburg and commissioned, under the command of *Kapitän zur See* Ernst Lindemann, on 24 August 1940. Officially, *Bismarck* was to have been a ship of 35,000t, but that was a fiction; the true figure was considerably higher – her hull armour alone weighed 17,500t. She was an outstanding sea-boat, with a shallow pitching movement and very slight roll, and required no weather helm to maintain her heading. She was very responsive, too, and would answer to a rudder movement as small as 5 degrees, but was difficult to control at low speed and when going astern; tugs were always on standby in narrow waters. *Bismarck* put to sea for her first – and last – combat mission, Operation '*Rheinübung*' (Rhine Crossing), in company with the cruiser *Prinz Eugen* (in place of the *Tirpitz*, which had not yet worked up) on 19 May 1941, refuelled in Norway, and attempted to break out into the Atlantic via the Denmark Strait. Located in the early hours of 24 May by the battlecruiser HMS *Hood* and the new battleship *Prince of Wales* at a range of 17nm (at which distance *Hood* was very vulnerable), Lindemann gave battle, sinking the *Hood* (almost instantaneously) with his fifth salvo, a single 15in (381mm) shell penetrating a magazine and setting off 150t of cordite. *Bismarck* did not escape unscathed, however, and Lindemann decided to break off '*Rheinübung*' and head for St Nazaire for repairs at reduced speed, shadowed by elements of the British fleet. He managed temporarily to shake off his pursuers, but was located again on 26 May. At the very end of the day, *Bismarck* was hit by an aerial torpedo launched from a Swordfish aircraft from the carrier HMS *Ark Royal*, the projectile hitting aft and jamming her rudders at an angle of 12 degrees to port. The next day the battleships *Rodney* and *King George V*, battered her and she was later sunk by torpedoes from HMS *Dorsetshire*, 300 miles west of Ushant. Only 115 men were saved. The wreck was located in 1989 and extensively filmed.

Despite her very short combat career, the *Bismarck* was an excellent example of a modern battleship, her extremely wide beam making her a superb gun platform, even in heavy weather.

BLOCK ISLAND

USA: 1944

The *Commencement Bay* class, the last of the escort carriers of World War II, was developed from the *Sangamons*, and retained the capacity to carry oil as cargo – 12,000 tons of it. They were the only escort carriers capable of operating the Grumman F6F Hellcat, the most effective maritime fighter-bomber of World War II. The *Commencement Bays* were heavily armed for self-defence, and their 16,000hp turbine powerplant gave them a top speed of 19 knots on a displacement of almost 21,500t. Even without oil from their cargo tanks, they had a very long endurance, and could stay at sea for around 60 days. All were built by a single yard: Todd-Pacific at Tacoma, Washington. USS *Block Island* was the second of the *Commencement Bay* class. She served in the Pacific in 1945, and later, during the 1950s (after a period as a school ship), with the Atlantic Fleet.

The US Navy commissioned a total of 19 *Commencement Bay*-class escort carriers. The largest of their type, they could accommodate up to 33 aircraft.

Displacement: 18,910t standard; 21,400t full load
Dimensions: 557ft 1in x 80ft x 28ft (169.8m x 24.4m x 8.5m)
Machinery: two-shaft; Allis-Chalmers geared turbines producing 16,000hp
Armament: two 5in (127mm); 36 40mm; 20 20mm; 33 aircraft
Speed: 19 knots
Range: 21,500nm (39,800km) at 15 knots
Complement: 1066

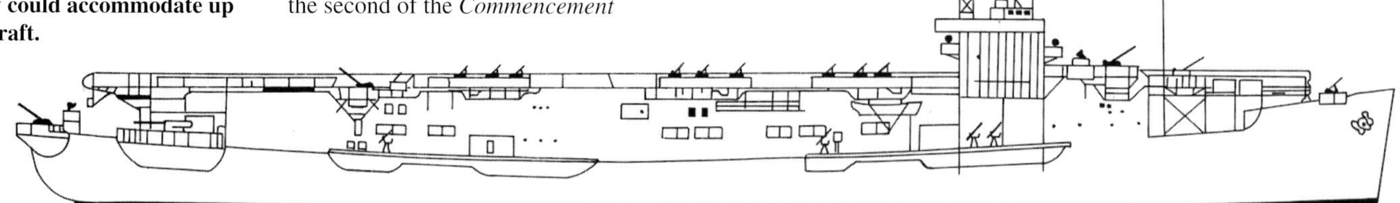

BOGUE

USA: 1942

In 1941, the US Navy began taking over C3-type merchant ships and completing them as escort carriers, as successors to the prototype *Long Islands*. A total of 21 ships were converted in this way, and one more was built from the keel up. The *Long Islands*, with low-powered diesel machinery, proved too slow in service (they were used later for transportation and training duties), and surprisingly, this shortcoming was not remedied in the *Bogues*, which had the same installed power. It is perhaps evidence of the general dissatisfaction with the new class that when the better *Casablancas* became available, the remaining *Bogues* were transferred to the Royal Navy on Lend-Lease, and entered service as the *Attacker* class, the US Navy retaining 11. Poor performance was not their only shortcoming: the hangar decks were built upon the main deck of the original hulls, and the considerable sheer and camber sometimes caused difficulty in handling aircraft below. The *Bogues*/ *Attackers* were fitted with two 6.5t lifts close to the extremities of the wooden flight deck, and a single catapult capable of launching a 3t aircraft. USS *Bogue* started life as the *Steel Advocate*. She was built by Seattle-Tacoma Shipbuilders and converted there for the US Navy before commissioning on 26 September. Her war service was principally in the Atlantic, on transportation and anti-submarine duties. She was placed in reserve in 1946. In 1955, she was re-designated as a helicopter carrier and scrapped in 1960.

Displacement: 10,200t standard; 14,400t full load
Dimensions: 496ft x 82ft x 26ft (151.2m x 25m x 7.9m)
Machinery: one-shaft, one Allis-Chalmers geared turbine; 8500hp
Armament: two 5in (127mm); four 40mm; one 20mm; 28 aircraft
Speed: 16.5 knots
Range: 26,000nm (48,150km) at 15 knots
Complement: 890

The *Bogue*-class escort carriers were never entirely satisfactory, but they filled a desperate need and gave sound service. Just one was lost; the survivors all stayed in service post-war as aircraft transports.

BOMBARDA

ITALY: 1942

Displacement: 660t standard; 730t full load
Dimensions: 211ft x 28ft 7in x 8ft 4in (64.35m x 8.7m x 2.5m)
Machinery: two-shaft, four FIAT diesels; 3500bhp
Armament: one 3.9in (100mm); seven 20mm; two 17.7in (450mm) TT; 10 DC throwers
Speed: 18 knots
Range: 3000nm (5500km) at 15 knots
Complement: 110

Italy began building the *Gabbiano* class of small, cheap escorts in 1941. They were constructed by virtually all yards which had the required capacity, to little more than mercantile standards. Though smaller and less hardy, they were comparable to the British *Flower* class, but rather more heavily armed. The majority, including the Breda-built *Bombarda*, were seized by the Germans after the Italian Armistice. She was scuttled in 1945, but was later salvaged and put back into service until 1975.

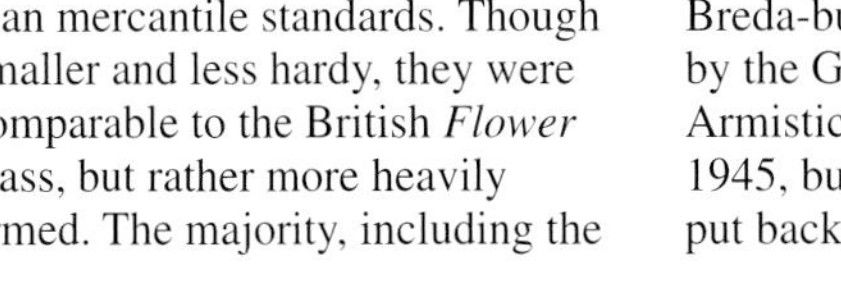

Some of the *Gabbianos* – though not the *Bombarda* – were fitted with two small electric motors, which allowed them to 'creep' in almost complete silence, and made them effective anti-submarine ships.

BOMBARDIERE

ITALY: 1942

It was not until the Italian Navy introduced the 1600t *Maestrales* of 1934 that it had destroyers with the required levels of performance. Ships thereafter were built to the same basic hull form, with its 10.5:1 length-to-beam ratio. The *Soldatis* were the last and best of them, ordered in two groups in 1936 and 1940, with the same powerplant and performance as the preceding *Orianis*. Originally they mounted four 50-calibre 4.7in (120mm) guns and one only 15 calibres in length, to fire starshell; the latter was deleted in the second group and a fifth 50-calibre gun substituted. All gained large numbers of light AA guns, and some depth charge throwers, during the course of their wartime careers. *Bombardiere* was the penultimate ship of the class, constructed by Cantieri Navale Riuniti at Ancona. She had but a short career, being sunk off Marettimo on 17 January 1943 by the British submarine HMS *United*.

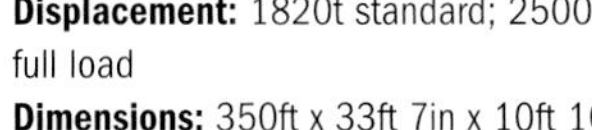

Displacement: 1820t standard; 2500t full load
Dimensions: 350ft x 33ft 7in x 10ft 10in (106.7m x 10.15m x 3.3m)
Machinery: two-shaft, Belluzzo geared turbines; 48,000hp
Armament: five 4.7in (120mm); 12 20mm; six 21in (533mm) TT; four DC throwers
Speed: 38 knots
Range: 2500nm (4650km) at 14 knots
Complement: 206

The *Soldatis* were the best Italian destroyers of World War II, even though nine were sunk by enemy action and one more foundered.

BRIN

ITALY: 1938

Displacement: 1000t surface; 1245t submerged
Dimensions: 237ft 8in x 21ft 11in x 14ft 11in (72.5m x 6.7m x 4.55m)
Machinery: two-shaft, Tosi diesels, plus two Ansaldo electric motors; 3400bhp/1300hp
Armament: eight 21in (533mm) TT (four bow, four stern: 14 torpedoes); one 4.7in (120mm); four 13.2mm MG
Speed: 17 knots surfaced; 8 knots submerged
Range: 11,000nm (20,400km) at 8 knots, surfaced
Complement: 58

From early in the type's history, the Italian Navy was firmly committed to the use of submarines. During the 1920s and 1930s, many small classes – no less than 23 – were produced, to a variety of specifications. Only a very few ran to more than a handful of boats, and the *Brin* class of 1938 was no exception; initially, just three were to be constructed, but two more were added later (in conditions of some secrecy) to replace two earlier *Archimede*-class boats transferred surreptitiously to Franco's rebels in Spain. The *Brins* were designed by their constructor, Tosi. They were ocean-going boats of a partial double-hull design, with an operational depth limit of 360ft (110m). *Brin* managed to survive until the Italian Armistice, surrendering to the Allies in 1943. She was employed as an anti-submarine training target thereafter, and discarded in 1948.

The *Brins* were ocean-going submarines. They operated largely in the Indian Ocean and in the South Atlantic. Four more were later built to an improved, enlarged design.

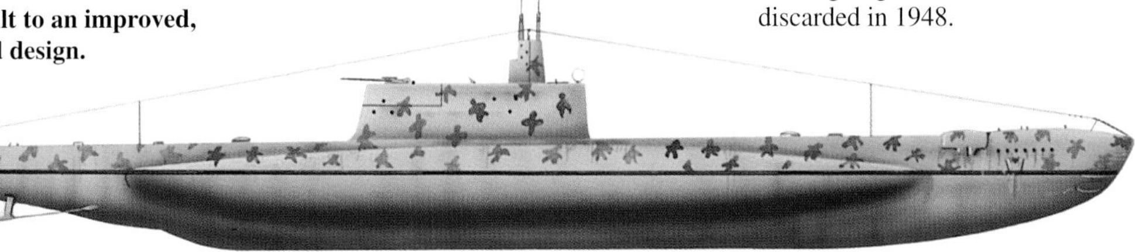

BROOKLYN

USA: 1936

The *Brooklyns* were of roughly the same size as the heavy cruisers which had preceded them into service, but were very much more modern in appearance, with an all-new hull form, flush-decked with a high transom stern which housed a hangar capable of accommodating four aircraft, accessible via a sliding hatch. They were the first of the American 'large light cruisers', and were to provide a model for the later *Clevelands*. By 1933, when design work on *Clevelands* was begun, the US Navy's Bureau of Ships had become convinced that a cruiser armed with 12 6in (152mm) guns of a newer, quicker-firing pattern, with some of the weight saved going to improve protection, could actually overwhelm an 8in-gun heavy cruiser. Before the design was finalized, however, Japan launched the first of the *Mogamis*, which mounted 15 6.1in (155mm) guns on a standard displacement of 8500t, and this caused a hasty revision of the *Brooklyns*' weapons plan, the weight of an extra 6in triple being 'stolen' from the hull. In fact, the *Mogamis* were hopelessly underspecified, and the first pair had to be rebuilt, emerging at 11,200t, but by the time that happened, the *Brooklyn* was in construction, fittingly at New York Navy Yard. There was some speculation that these ships, too, were too lightly constructed, but all but one of the nine-strong class survived the war, and most continued for many decades more in foreign service. *Brooklyn* was sold to Chile in 1951 to serve as the *O'Higgins*. She was finally decommissioned in 1992, and foundered on the way to the breakers.

The designers of the *Brooklyns* tried to achieve too much on the 10,000t displacement laid down by the Washington Treaty, especially when they were required to add a fifth triple 6in (152mm) gun turret. Nonetheless, the *Brooklyns* were successful ships for all that.

Displacement: 9770t standard; 12,210t full load
Dimensions: 608ft 4in x 61ft 9in x 22ft 9in (185.4m x 18.8 x 6.95m
Machinery: four-shaft, Parson geared turbines; 100,000hp
Armament: 15 6in (152m); eight 5in (127mm); eight 0.5in MG (later 28 40mm and 20 20mm); four aircraft
Armour: belt 5in (127mm); deck 2in (51mm); turret faces 6.5in (166mm); conning tower 5in (127mm)
Speed: 32.5 knots
Range: 10,000nm (18,500km) at 15 knots
Complement: 868

C1 CLASS

JAPAN: 1938–39

Displacement: 2185t surfaced; 3561t submerged
Dimensions: 358ft 7in x 29ft 10in x 17ft 7in (109.3m x 9.1m x 5.35m)
Machinery: two-shaft, diesels, plus electric motors; 12,400bhp/2000hp
Armament: eight 21in (533mm) TT; one 5.5in (140mm); two 25mm
Speed: 23.5 knots surfaced; 8 knots submerged
Range: 14,000nm at 16 knots surface
Complement: 101

The Imperial Japanese Navy ordered a class of five large submarines under the 1937 Programme. The *C1*s were developed from the *KD6*s of six years before, but considerably larger, essentially similar to the *A*s and *B*s, but without the ability to operate aircraft; instead, they were equipped to carry a midget submarine on the deck casing aft, and did so for the attack on Pearl Harbor. The leadboat of the class, *I16*, was later modified to carry a 46ft (14m) landing-craft.

With the entire Pacific Ocean to cover, Japan built many large submarines. Many of these boats were equipped to carry aircraft or, as in the case of the *C1*s, midget submarines or landing-craft.

CA1

ITALY: 1937

Though better known for its aircraft, the Caproni company also built midget submarines; perhaps the most interesting were the 'CA Type 1s' designed to attack shipping in harbours. The first two boats of this class were modified (and two more were completed to the new specification) to be transported across the Atlantic aboard an ocean-going submarine, to attack shipping off the eastern seaboard of the United States. For this purpose the diesel engine was removed and they were to operate on battery power alone, the extra space thus liberated allowing them to carry and lay a total of eight 100kg explosive charges. While the planned operation was feasible, the invasion of Italy forced its cancellation, and *CA1* was scuttled at La Spezia in 1943.

Displacement: 13.3t surfaced; 16.1t submerged
Dimensions: 32ft 10in x 6ft 5in x 5ft 3in (10m x 1.96m x 1.6m)
Machinery: one-shaft, MAN diesel, plus Marelli electric motor; 60bhp/25hp
Armament: two 17.7in (450mm) TT
Speed: 6.25 knots surfaced; 5 knots submerged
Range: 700nm (1300km) at 4 knots surfaced
Complement: 2

CHAPAYEV

USSR: 1940

The Soviet Union constructed only six cruisers before World War II (and completed three more which had been begun before the Revolution). The *Kirovs* and the very similar *Gorkiys* were fairly uninspired, with 7.1in (180mm) rather than the more usual 8in (203mm) guns of a heavy cruiser. Later, under the third Five Year Plan (1938–42), the design was enlarged to accommodate a fourth triple turret, and this time the ships were to mount 6in (152mm) guns to qualify as a light cruisers. The *Chapayev* was to have been the first of 17 ships, and was intended for service in the Baltic (others in the class were destined for the Black Sea); the programme was curtailed after seven ships had been laid down, however, and two of those were broken up before launch. Constructed at the Ordzhonikidze Yard in Leningrad (St Petersburg), *Chapayev* was a very long time in the building. She was launched in 1940, but not completed – albeit to an improved design – until May 1950. She was hulked 10 years later, and broken up in 1964.

The *Chapayev*-class ships were entirely conventional light cruisers, on a par in most respects with vessels of the type constructed in Britain and the USA.

Displacement: 11,300t standard; 15,000t full load
Dimensions: 659ft 5in x 64ft 8in x 21ft (201m x 19.7m x 6.4m)
Machinery: two-shaft, geared turbines, plus cruising diesels; 130,000hp
Armament: 12 6in (152mm); eight 3.9in (100mm); 24 37mm; six 21in (533mm) TT
Speed: 34 knots
Range: 10,000nm (18,500km) at 18 knots
Complement: 840

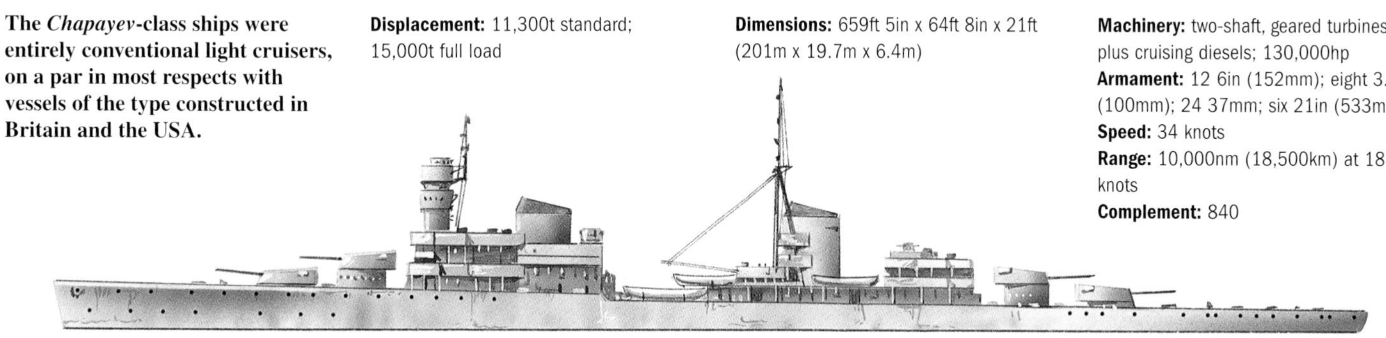

CHITOSE

JAPAN: 1936

Japan relied on converted oilers to operate as seaplane carriers until 1934, when the first of two purpose-built ships, the *Chitose* and the *Chiyoda*, was laid down. They were quite unconventional in appearance, clearly warships as far back as the funnel, but with no superstructure whatsoever, from there aft, save for a large open-sided platform (the after legs of which contained the uptakes for their secondary diesel engines), which served to protect the seaplane handling area from the elements. *Chitose* and her sister ship were built at Kure Navy Yard, *Chitose* being launched in November 1936. In 1943–44, both were reconstructed as conventional aircraft carriers, their superstructures razed and a full-length flight deck installed, with a hangar beneath; this conversion had been envisaged from the outset. *Chitose* was taken in hand last, by Sasebo Navy Yard. In this form, they carried 30 aircraft. Both were sunk on 25 October 1944, during the Battle of Leyte Gulf.

The *Chitose* was ostensibly constructed as a seaplane carrier, but it was always intended that she should be converted to become a conventional aircraft carrier.

Displacement: 11,000 (later 11,200t) standard; c15,300t full load
Dimensions: 631ft 7in x 61ft 8in (later 68ft 3in) x 23ft 8in (192.5m x 18.8m (later 20.8m) x 7.2m)
Machinery: two-shaft COSAD, geared turbines, plus diesel engines; 44,000hp/12,800bhp
Armament: four (later eight) 127mm (5in) DP; 12 (later 30) 25mm; 24 (later 30) aircraft
Speed: 29 knots
Range: 8000nm (14,800km) at 18 knots
Complement: (later) c800

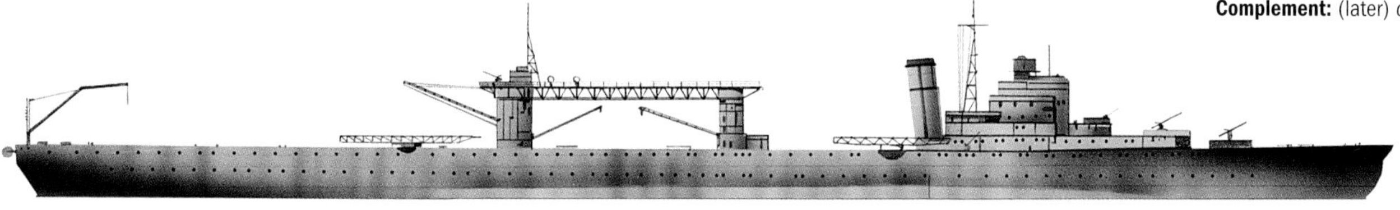

CICLONE

ITALY: 1942

Displacement: 910t standard; 1625t full load
Dimensions: 287ft 10in x 32ft 6in x 12ft 4in (87.75m x 9.9m x 3.75m)
Machinery: two-shaft, Parsons geared turbines; 16,000hp
Armament: two 3.9in (100mm); eight (later 12) 20mm; four 17.7in (450mm) TT; four DC throwers
Speed: 26 knots
Range: 4000nm (7400km) at 14 knots
Complement: 177

During the late 1930s, Italy built a class of 32 600t torpedo boats, the *Spica*s, which resembled miniature destroyers, and later added four more, of 30 percent greater displacement. The design of these boats, enlarged again, was repeated during the war as the 16-strong *Ciclone* class, the name-ship of which was constructed by Cantieri Riuniti dell'Adriatico at Trieste. She sank on 8 March 1943 after hitting a mine. The *Ciclone*s were the equivalent of the British *Hunt* class, and proved to be very effective small warships.

The *Ciclone*s were optimized for service in the Mediterranean. Some units received a third 3.9in (100mm) gun, and all had an enlarged light AA battery by 1943.

COMET

GB: 1944

Displacement: 1730t standard; 2510t full load
Dimensions: 362ft 9in x 35ft 8in x 14ft 5in (110.55m x 10.85m x 4.4m)
Machinery: two-shaft, Parsons geared turbines; 40,000hp
Armament: four 4.5in (114mm); two (later 4) 40mm; four 21in (533mm) TT
Speed: 36.5 knots
Range: 6000nm (11,100km) at 16 knots
Complement: 186-222

HMS *Comet* was one of a large group of general-purpose fleet destroyers, constructed in three classes towards the end of World War II. They were to incorporate many improvements introduced in earlier classes, such as the transom stern of the *Q*s and the flared bow of the *Tribal*s. These classes, known as the *Ch*, *Co*, and *Cr*, also had improved guns, and lost one bank of torpedo tubes to compensate for the additional weight of their mountings. *Comet* was built by Yarrow on the Clyde; she survived the war, to be broken up in 1962.

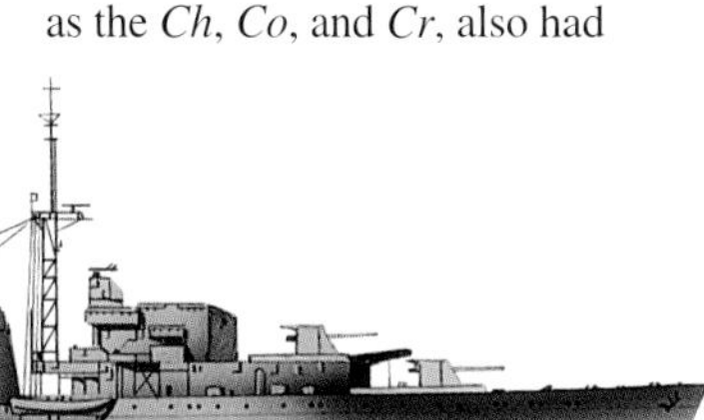

The ships of the three classes, *Ch*, *Co*, and *Cr*, were the last fleet destroyers constructed for the Royal Navy during World War II. All stayed in service until the 1960s.

Corallo

ITALY: 1936

The *Corallo* was one of the Italian *Perla*-class coastal or second-class submarines, the third of five groups which originated with the *Argonautas* of 1931. She was constructed by Cantieri Riuniti dell'Adriatico at Monfalcone. All five classes were essentially similar and all had problems of stability. Many had their conning towers much reduced in size, a modification made to the *Corallo* in 1942, only months before she was sunk on 13 December, in the western Mediterranean by the British sloop HMS *Enchantress*.

Displacement: 680t surfaced; 845t submerged
Dimensions: 197ft 6in x 21ft 2in x 15ft 5in (60.2m x 6.45m x 4.7m)
Machinery: two-shaft, CRDA diesels, plus CRDA electric motors; 1200bhp/800hp
Armament: six 533mm (21in) TT (four bow, two stern: 12 torpedoes); one 3.9in (100mm); two 13.2mm MG;
Speed: 14 knots surfaced; 7.5 knots submerged
Range: 5000nm (9250km) at 8 knots surfaced
Complement: 45

The *Perlas* were reasonably successful coastal submarines. Two of them were modified to carry *maiale* ('pigs'), the name the Italians gave to their successful human torpedoes.

Curtiss

USA: 1940

Displacement: 12,050t on trial
Dimensions: 527ft 4in x 69ft 3in x 21ft 4in (160.75m x 21.1m x 6.5m)
Machinery: two-shaft, Parsons geared turbine; 12,000hp
Armament: four 5in (127mm); 10 0.5in MG
Speed: 18 knots
Range: 12,000nm (22,200km) at 12 knots
Complement: 1195

Despite their shortcomings, before and during World War II, the US Navy operated considerable numbers of seaplanes (small aircraft which rested on floats, not on their fuselage, like the larger so-called 'flying boats'), mostly in the reconnaissance role, but also as strike aircraft. Pre-war, the seaplane-tender force had comprised a converted 'Hog Island' cargo ship, a converted collier, and USS *Langley*, the first American aircraft carrier, de-rated and cut down. In 1937, the USN ordered a pair of large tenders, each capable of looking after 24 such aircraft; not just providing maintenance and repair facilities, including refuelling and re-supplying, but also housing their crews. This pair formed the *Curtiss* class, and they were joined towards the end of the war by the four rather more capable *Curritucks*, which incorporated a larger hangar and a flush-decked catapult, and which were to have operated as seaplane carriers. USS *Curtiss* was constructed by New York Ship Builders, and launched in 1940; she was discarded in 1963.

USS *Curtiss* was the US Navy's first purpose-built seaplane tender; she had extensive workshop facilities, and carried a full range of spare parts.

D3 Type

USSR: 1939–45

Imperial Russia's flirtation with motor torpedo-boats (MTB) – it was the first nation to use the Whitehead torpedo successfully, in 1878 – continued after the Revolution, although, the Soviet Union was never as committed to MTBs as the USA or Germany. The *D3* type was probably the most effective of Soviet designs. A total of about 130 were completed in a variety of forms, mostly for service in the Baltic. Their torpedoes were launched from cradles.

The Soviet *D3* type MTBs were small in comparison to German types. They were good sea-boats, and could operate in fairly heavy weather.

Displacement: 32t standard; 35t full load
Dimensions: 71ft x 13ft x 4ft 6in (21.6m x 3.95m x 1.35m)
Machinery: three-shaft, three GAM-34FN petrol engines; 3600bhp
Armament: two 21in (533mm) TC; one, or two, 20mm or between one and four 12.7mm MG
Speed: 39 knots
Range: 600nm (1100km) at 20 knots
Complement: 9–14

Dagabur

ITALY: 1936

Displacement: 680t surfaced; 845t submerged
Dimensions: 197ft 6in x 21ft 2in x 15ft 5in (60.2m x 6.45m x 4.7m)
Machinery: two-shaft, Tosi diesels, plus Marelli electric motors; 1200bhp/800hp
Armament: six 21in (533mm) TT (four bow, two stern: 12 torpedoes); one 3.9in (100mm); two 13.2mm MG
Speed: 14 knots surfaced; 7.5 knots submerged
Range: 5000nm at 8 knots surfaced
Complement: 45

The Italian Navy commissioned five groups of coastal submarines in the 600t class from 1931. The fourth, the last to be constructed before the outbreak of war, was the *Adua* class. They were repeats of the earlier *Perlas*, and were indistinguishable from them. A total of 20 boats were built, of which three were sold to Brazil. *Dagabur* was constructed by Tosi; she was run down and sunk by the British destroyer *Wolverine* off Algiers on 12 August 1942.

Just one of the Italian *Adua*-class coastal submarines survived World War II: three were scuttled to avoid capture, one was wrecked, and the rest were sunk.

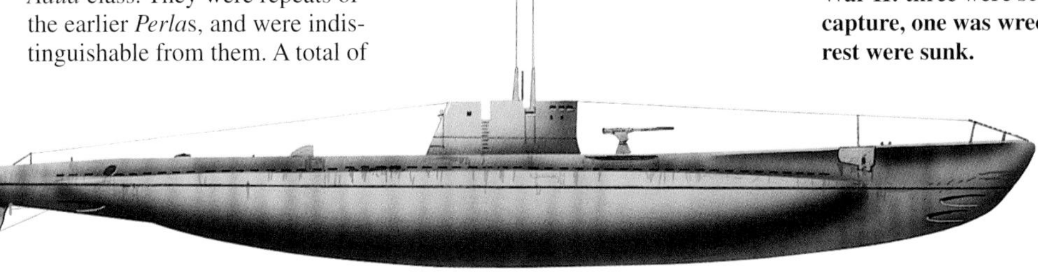

DANDOLO

ITALY: 1937

Prior to 1925, when Italy acquired interests in East Africa, her navy had no need of ocean-going submarines; construction of the first important class of such boats, the *Marcellos*, was not started until the late 1930s. *Dandolo* was one of the first of the class, constructed by Cantieri Riuniti dell'Adriatico at Monfalcone. The *Marcellos* had partial double hulls and internal ballast tanks, and were able to operate to 330ft (100m). When submerged, they proved to be very manoeuvrable, but their transverse stability was poor, due to their large, long conning towers, and they tended to roll heavily on the surface. Their endurance was limited, but their respectable turn of speed, and comparatively heavy armament, should have made them formidable opponents; like many units of the Italian fleet, the *Marcellos* were not generally well employed. *Dandolo* alone of the class survived the war. She was discarded in 1948.

The *Marcello*-class submarines were the first effective ocean-going boats in service with the *Regia Marina*. They were designed to operate in the Indian Ocean.

Displacement: 1045t surface; 1290t submerged
Dimensions: 239ft 6in x 23ft 7in x 16ft 8in (73m x 7.2m x 5.1m)
Machinery: two-shaft, CRDA diesels, plus two CRDA electric motors; 3600bhp/ 1100hp
Armament: eight 21in (533mm) TT (four bow, four stern: 16 torpedoes); two 3.9in (100mm); four 13.2mm GM
Speed: 17.5 knots surfaced; 8 knots submerged
Range: 7500nm (13,900km) at 9.5 knots surfaced
Complement: 57

DE/GMT TYPE

USA: 1942–44

Displacement: 1190t standard; 1415t full load
Dimensions: 289ft 5in x 35ft 2in x 10ft 1in (88.2m x 10.7m x 3.05m)
Machinery: two-shaft, four General Motors diesels; 6000bhp
Armament: three 3in (76mm); four 1.1in MG; nine 20mm; Hedgehog AS mortar; DC throwers; DC racks
Speed: 19.5 knots
Range: 6000nm (11,100km) at 12 knots
Complement: 156

Of all the destroyer escorts the US Navy operated during World War II, the short-hulled, diesel-powered *GMT*s were probably the least satisfactory. *GMT*s (General Motors Tandem; their diesel engines were coupled in pairs) were a compromise. Originally designed with turbine engines, problems with gear cutting slowed down delivery, so they were re-drawn to take eight submarine-type diesels. Orders for landing-craft now took priority, and their powerplant was halved, to four engines, nevertheless some 75 *GMT*s were constructed. The last *GMT* to be launched was USS *Finnegan* was on 2 February 1944.

The US Navy built destroyer escort in six sub-classes. The *GMT*s were the least satisfactory.

DE RUYTER

THE NETHERLANDS: 1944

The design for a pair of light cruisers was drawn up in the Netherlands in 1936, and work commenced on them in 1939. The class leader was to have been *De Zeven Provincien*, but became *De Ruyter* on the loss of an earlier ship of that name, in 1942. During the German occupation of the Netherlands in World War II, she was barely touched and was left in good condition at the Wilton-Fijenoord Yard, where she was launched in December 1944 to clear the slip. New plans to complete her to contemporary standards were drawn up with the aid of the British, and the work was carried out by Rotterdamsche Droogdok. She entered service with the Royal Dutch Navy on 18 November 1953. Plans to convert her to a guided-missile cruiser in the mid-1960s came to nothing, and she was sold to Peru in March 1973, and served initially as the *Almirante Grau* and later, substantially modernized and additionally armed with OTOMAT surface-to-surface missiles after a refit from 1985–88, as the *General Garzoni*.

Displacement: 8350t standard; 10,800t full load
Dimensions: 613ft 6in x 56ft 7in x 18ft 6in (187m x 17.25m x 5.6m)
Machinery: three-shaft, Parsons geared turbines; 78,000hp
Armament: 10 5.9in (150mm); 14 40mm; eight 12.7mm MG; six 533mm (21in) TT
Armour: belt 4in-3in (100mm-75mm); decks 1in-0.8in (25mm-20mm); turrets 4in-2in (100mm-50mm)
Speed: 32 knots
Range: 10,000nm (18,500km) at 18 knots
Complement: 700

The designers of HNLMS *De Ruyter* can never have suspected that she would still be in service six full decades after her keel was laid in 1939.

DIDO

GB: 1939

The Royal Navy ordered HMS *Dido* from Cammell Lairds in 1936. She was to be the lead ship in a new class of light cruisers, armed not with the almost obligatory 6in (152mm) gun, but with a new 50-calibre 5.25in (134mm). This high-velocity gun in a powered mount could elevate to 70 degrees, allowing the ships to function as anti-aircraft cruisers. *Dido* should have had five pairs, but was completed with four, plus a 4in (105mm) short-barrelled starshell gun in the 'Q' position, a situation which was not rectified until September 1941. The *Dido*s were relatively small ships, scarcely bigger than the *Arethusas*, which were a frank attempt to build the smallest-possible effective cruiser. Nonetheless, they still managed 3in (76mm) side armour and 2in (51mm) decks over the ammunition spaces, though the turrets were really nothing more than gunhouses, with protection only against splinters. Their four-shaft, 62,000-horsepower machinery gave them the same sort of performance as the *Town*-class large light cruisers. In all, 11 *Dido*s were commissioned between HMS *Bonaventure* – the first of them to be completed, on 24 May 1940 – and HMS *Argonaut*, which entered service only in August 1942. The *Dido*s were succeeded by the five *Bellona*s, which differed in detail and are considered by some to be members of the same class. Six remained in service until the 1950s, and HMS *Dido* herself was one of the last to go, not being scrapped until 1958. Four wartime losses were all to submarines, while a fifth ship, HMS *Scylla*, was almost broken in two by a ground mine off the Normandy beaches, and was salvaged but never repaired.

Displacement: 5600t standard; 6850t full load
Dimensions: 512ft x 50ft 6in x 16ft 9in (156.05m x 15.4m x 5.1m)
Machinery: four-shaft, Parsons geared turbines; 62,000hp
Armament: eight (later 10) 5in (127mm); one (later 0) 4in (102mm); eight 2pdr pom-poms (later 14 20mm); six 21in (533mm) TT
Armour: sides 3in (76mm); decks 2in (51mm) over magazines, 1in (25mm) over machinery; bulkheads 1in (25mm)
Speed: 32.5 knots
Range: 6000nm (11,100km) at 18 knots
Complement: 480-530

The *Dido*s were the first British ships to break the light cruiser mould, being equipped as anti-aircraft ships instead of with single-purpose 6in (152mm) guns.

DUNCAN

USA: 1944

The *Gearing*s were the best destroyers the US Navy had during World War II. They were equipped with the same weapons suite as the *Sumner*s they succeeded but with enhanced performance. This was achieved by lengthening their hulls by 14ft (4.25m) to increase maximum speed in the seaway. This also increased their range considerably, their fuel capacity being upped from 500t to 740t. One of the prime responsibilities of the US Navy's destroyers was to protect the fleet aircraft carriers and, to a lesser extent, the battleships which, by the end of the war, were being used exclusively for shore bombardment. This requirement meant the destroyers had to be fast, achieved by installing very powerful machinery; the last three classes of the period all developed 60,000 horsepower to give them top speeds in excess of 33 knots, even at a full load displacement of around 3500t. In all, some 93 *Gearing*s were launched between October 1944 and July 1946. USS *Duncan* was one of the very earliest of them, built by Consolidated Shipbuilders at Orange, Texas. She was one of 12 ships converted to become a radar picket in January 1945, before she had seen action. Her forward bank of torpedo tubes was replaced by a tripod mainmast to hold the radar antennae. She later lost her after bank of tubes, too, to be replaced by additional anti-aircraft guns. *Duncan* was finally stricken only in September 1973.

Displacement: 2615t standard; 3460t full load
Dimensions: 390ft 6in x 40ft 10in x 14ft 4in (119m x 12.45m x 4.35m)
Machinery: two-shaft, General Electric geared turbines; 60,000hp
Armament: six 5in (127mm); 12 40mm; 11 20mm; 10 21in (533mm) TT
Speed: 36.5 knots
Range: 4500nm (8350km) at 20 knots
Complement: 336

The *Gearing*s were the last and best destroyers the US Navy put into service during World War II. Many remained active until the 1970s, with modifications to their weapons and sensor suites.

EDSALL

USA: 1942

Even before the United States entered World War II, the US Navy had begun ordering destroyer escorts, largely to pass on to Britain under Lend-Lease. Eventually, more than 1000 were to be ordered (many were later cancelled) in six very similar classes. The chief difference between the types was in their machinery: those fitted with diesel engines driving through a reduction gearbox (other diesel-powered ships were actually diesel-electric) were known as the 'FMRs'. USS *Edsall* was the first of them, and entered service early in 1943.

Displacement: 1255t standard; 1600t full load
Dimensions: 306ft x 36ft 7in x 10ft 5in (93.3m x 11.15m x 3.2m)
Machinery: two-shaft, four Fairbanks-Morse diesels; 6000bhp
Armament: three 3in (76mm); two 40mm; eight 20mm; three 21in (533mm) TT; one Hedgehog; eight DC throwers; two DC racks
Speed: 21 knots
Range: 11,000nm (20,350km) at 12 knots
Complement: 186

USS *Edsall* was actually the first of the American destroyer escorts to be launched; she was designed in conjunction with the Royal Navy.

ENTERPRISE

USA: 1936

Displacement: 19,875t standard; 25,485t full load
Dimensions: 824ft 9in x 109ft 6in x 26ft (251.4m x 25.35m x 7.9m)
Machinery: four-shaft, Parsons geared turbines; 120,000hp
Armament: eight 5in (127mm); 16 1.1in; 24 0.5in (later 60 40mm); 32 20mm); up to 96 aircraft
Speed: 32.5 knots
Range: 12,000nm (22,200km) at 15 knots
Complement: 1890 (1938) 2175 (1942)

After 1922, the USA was limited by the Washington Treaty to a total of 135,000t for all its aircraft carriers. The converted battle-cruisers *Lexington* and *Saratoga*, completed late in 1927, consumed 66,000t, and the unsatisfactory *Ranger* took another 14,000t. Even before the latter was completed, the Bureau of Ships was having second thoughts about minimum-displacement carriers and, rather than taking the option of constructing four more, decided to build two at 20,000t each. The first of these was the *Yorktown*, and the *Enterprise* followed six months later. Both ships were built by Newport News Shipbuilding,

Little more than half the displacement of the *Lexington*s but able to operate 20 per cent more aircraft, the *Enterprise* set the style for the fleet carriers, the bigger *Essex* class, which followed her into service and won victory in the Pacific.

entering service in September 1937 and May 1938 respectively (the commissioning of *Enterprise* was delayed by problems with her powerplant). Though both ships were to define the form of the modern aircraft carrier and become legends in their own lifetime, they were fault-free. For example, the hangars were built up as light superstructures, rather than as an integral part of the hull, with large side apertures closed by roller shutters, to allow aircraft engines to be run up before they were elevated to the flight

There was a strong popular movement to preserve the 'Big E', as *Enterprise* was universally known. She was a symbol of everything the US Navy's carriers had achieved in the Pacific but, sadly, was demolished nevertheless.

deck and to allow easy access for loading stores and supplies – a configuration leaving essential areas unprotected and, worse, meaning that the flight deck itself could not be armoured (it was constructed of 6in (152mm) thick wooden planking). This was probably the most unsatisfactory element of the ships' design and one that contrasted with British (and later Japanese) practice; given the total displacement available to the designers, however, it was unavoidable. Save for the Battle of the Coral Sea, USS *Enterprise* was involved in almost every carrier battle of World War II. At Midway, her aircraft and those of her two sister ships, sank four Japanese carriers and inflicted a blow from which Japan never recovered. *Enterprise* herself was damaged at Guadalcanal and again at Santa Cruz, but was repaired in time for her aircraft to sink the battleship *Hiei* in November 1942. She had a major refit in the latter half of 1943, which included bulging her hull to restore buoyancy and stability. From then until the end of the war in the Pacific, she was employed to strike at Japanese-held islands in support of the American invasion forces, and took part in the 'Great Marianas Turkey Shoot' and the Battle of Leyte Gulf. In May 1945, she was the victim of a serious kamikaze attack, which destroyed her forward elevator, and she took no further part in hostilities. Placed in reserve in February 1947, she was sold for breaking on 1 July 1958. Her wartime service won *Enterprise* a Presidential Unit Citation, a Navy Unit Commendation, and 20 battle stars.

ERIE

USA: 1936

The London Naval Treaty of 1930 was aimed at restricting the number of major warships. However, 'sloops' – defined as ships of under 2000t, armed with guns of under 6.1in (154mm) calibre, and capable of no more than 20 knots – were exempt from its limits. The US Navy concluded that ships to that specification might prove very useful indeed. By way of an experiment, two were constructed to operate in the Caribbean and around the coast of Central America. They were somewhat anachronistic in appearance, with long clipper bows and counter sterns in an attempt to maximize deck space, especially aft, where mine rails and depth charge racks would be fitted in time of war, while minimizing waterline length. Unusual features for a ship of this size included storage space for a floatplane amidships, along with a crane to launch and recover it. USS *Erie*, the leadship of the class, was constructed at New York Navy Yard. She was torpedoed in 1942.

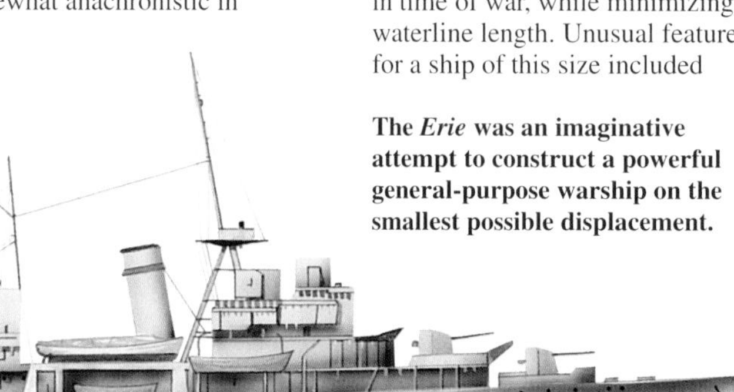

The *Erie* was an imaginative attempt to construct a powerful general-purpose warship on the smallest possible displacement.

Displacement: 2000t standard; 2340t full load
Dimensions: 328ft 6in x 41ft 3in x 11ft 4in (100.1m x 12.55m x 3.45m)
Machinery: two-shaft, geared turbines; 6200hp
Armament: four 6in (152mm); 16 1.1in; one aircraft
Speed: 20 knots
Range: 8000nm (14,800km) at 12 knots
Complement: 236

ERITREA

ITALY: 1936

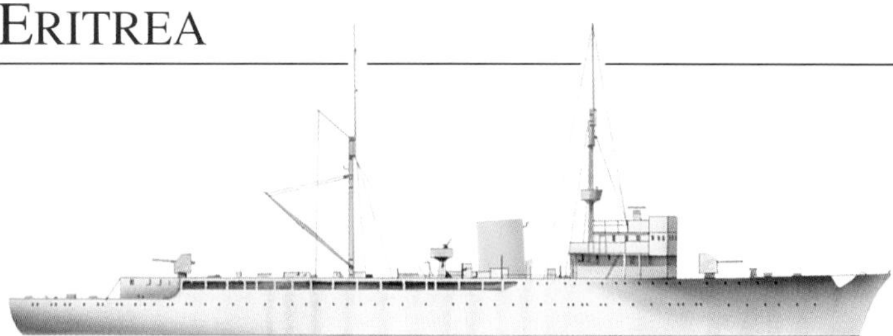

The *Eritrea* was Italy's one and only colonial sloop, built during the Fascist era to show the flag around the Mediterranean and in the Indian Ocean.

The *Eritrea* was built to serve two purposes: in time of peace she was intended to 'show the flag', and in wartime to act as a coastal escort and to lay mines. Perhaps her most unusual feature was her machinery. The *Eritrea* was constructed by Cantieri di Castellammare di Stabia, and entered service in 1937. She surrendered to the Allies at Colombo in September 1943, and in 1948 was formally ceded to France, serving as the *Francis Garnier* until 1966.

Displacement: 2165t standard; 3070t full load
Dimensions: 317ft 11in x 43ft 7in x 15ft 5in (96.9m x 13.3m x 4.7m)
Machinery: two-shaft, FIAT diesels, plus FIAT/Marelli diesel-electric drive; 7800bhp/1300hp
Armament: four 120mm (4.7in); two 40mm (later four 37mm); four 13.2mm MG
Armour: deck 1.25in–1in (32mm–25mm); conning tower 4in (100mm)
Speed: 20 knots
Range: 6950nm (12,900km) at 11.5 knots (diesel-electric drive)
Complement: 234

ESPEIGLE

GB: 1942

The *Bangors* were the first large class of minesweepers built for the Royal Navy during World War II. They proved satisfactory, but cramped, and a new, enlarged design was soon evolved as the *Algerines*, built in two groups with either turbine or VTE engines. The former were in short supply and just 29 ships, including *Espiegle*, had them. All but two of the *Bangors* were built by Harland & Wolff in Belfast. HMS *Espeigle* survived the war, and remained in service, but was soon made obsolete by a new generation of magnetic mines.

The *Algerines* were the best Allied minesweepers of World War II. They continued to give excellent service afterwards.

Displacement: 980t standard; 1265t full load
Dimensions: 225ft x 35ft 6in x 10ft 6in (65.6m x 10.8m x 3.2m)
Machinery: two-shaft, geared turbines; 2000hp
Armament: one 4in (102mm); eight 20mm
Speed: 16.5 knots
Range: 12,000nm (22,200km) at 12 knots
Complement: 85

EVANGELISTA TORRICELLI

ITALY: 1934

The *Archimede* class was an attempt by constructor Tosi to stretch his earlier second-class *Settembrini* to produce an ocean-going submarine which would be more economical to build and operate than the true first-class boats completed in Italy in the 1920s. The four boats constructed were robust partial double-hull types, with an operating depth in excess of 360ft (110m). *Torricelli* was transferred in conditions of secrecy to Franco's Nationalist forces in April 1937. She served as the *General Mola*, and was stricken only in 1959.

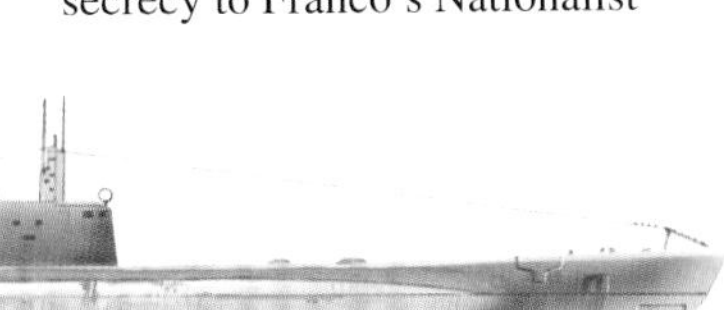

With a comparatively small increase in dimensions over those of the preceding submarine design, the constructors of the *Torricelli* managed to up her range by 15 per cent and stow four more torpedoes.

Displacement: 970t surfaced; 1240t submerged
Dimensions: 231ft 4in x 22ft 6in x 13ft 6in (70.5m x 6.87m x 4.12m)
Machinery: two-shaft, Tosi diesels, plus Marelli electric motors; 3000bhp/1100hp
Armament: eight 533mm (21in) TT (four bow, four stern: 16 torpedoes); two 100mm (3.9in); two 13.2mm MG
Speed: 17 knots surfaced; 8 knots submerged
Range: 10,500nm (19,450km) at 8 knots surfaced
Complement: 55

FAIRMILE TYPE C

GB: 1941

Displacement: 69t standard; 75t full load
Dimensions: 110ft x 17ft 5in x 5ft 8in (33.55m x 6.5m x 1.75m)
Machinery: three-shaft, Hall-Scott petrol engine; 2700bhp
Armament: two 2pdr pom-poms; four 0.5in MG (later four 20mm); four 0.303in MG; four DCs
Speed: 27 knots
Range: 800nm (1500km) at 25 knots
Complement: 16

The Royal Navy operated 24 Fairmile Type C motor gun-boats from 1941. Wooden-hulled hard-chine craft, they were a modified version of the Type A motor launch. Though fitted with more powerful triple Hall-Scott petrol engines, they were to exhibit the same basic faults, being very noisy, with poor overall performance, a large turning circle, and short range. The more numerous Type Ds, slightly larger, with a sharper entry and with four Packard-built Rolls-Royce Merlin aero-engines, were more successful, but were more often armed as motor torpedo-boats.

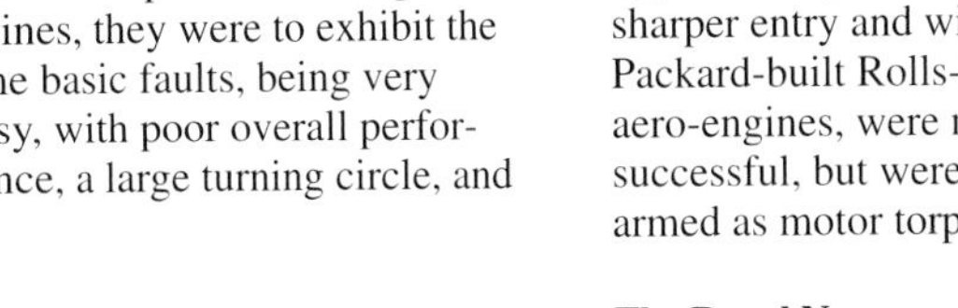

The Royal Navy operated a plethora of MGB types during World War II. The Fairmile Type C was one of the most numerous.

FANNING

USA: 1936

The US Congress barred all the Navy's attempts to obtain new destroyers from the end of World War I until 1932. That year's programme saw the authorization of the *Farraguts*, the basic hull form of which was to be employed in four successive classes. The first follow-on class was the *Mahans*, which introduced new high-pressure boilers developed by Babcock & Wilcox; these boilers became standard for medium and large American warships for many years to come, and provided almost 20 percent extra power. There were also changes made to the way the guns were distributed, allowing an extra quadruple bank of torpedo tubes to be mounted. USS *Fanning* was the last of the *Mahans*, constructed by Bethlehem Steel at Staten Island, New York. She was extensively refitted in 1944, when her weapons suite was modified to improve her anti-aircraft defences. The *Fanning* survived World War II but was decommissioned into reserve immediately afterwards. She was sold for breaking up in 1948.

The *Mahans*, of which USS *Fanning* was the last, introduced the high-pressure boilers which were employed by most US warships for the next two decades.

Displacement: 1490t standard; 2100t full load
Dimensions: 341ft 4in x 35ft 5in x 12ft 4in (104.05m x 10.7m x 3.75m)
Machinery: two-shaft, General Electric geared turbines; 49,000hp
Armament: five (later 4) 5in (127mm); four 0.5in MG (later four 40mm and five 20mm); 12 21in (533mm) TT
Speed: 36.5 knots
Range: 6500nm (12,000km) at 12 knots
Complement: 158

FLETCHER

USA: 1942

USS *Fletcher* was the lead ship of the largest class of destroyers – 179 in all – constructed for the US Navy during World War II, and the first to break entirely with the designs which had evolved during the 1930s. The standard displacement of the *Fletchers* was 25 per cent up on that of the previous class. This allowed them to be much more heavily armed and easier to modify subsequently (though in fact lack of deck space would become a restricting factor). Flush-decked, they were considerably more robust than earlier ships.

Displacement: 2325t standard; 2925t full load
Dimensions: 376ft 5in x 39ft 7in x 13ft 9in (114.75m x 12.05m x 4.2m)
Machinery: two-shaft, General Electric geared turbines; 60,000hp
Armament: five 5in (127mm) (later 10 40mm); four 1.1in (later deleted); four (later seven) 20mm; 10 21in (533mm) TT
Speed: 38 knots
Range: 6500nm (12,000km) at 15 knots
Complement: 273

USS *Fletcher* was constructed by Federal Shipbuilding at Kearny, New Jersey, and entered service in mid-1942. She saw very extensive service during World War II, and was awarded 15 battle stars. Placed in reserve from August 1946 until October 1949, she was reactivated for the Korean War (winning five more battle stars). She remained in service until 1962 when she returned to the reserve. *Fletcher* was stricken in 1967.

Though more cramped and less well-armed than the succeeding *Sumners*, the *Fletchers* were more popular with their crews, perhaps because of their speed advantage.

FLEURET

FRANCE: 1938

Fleuret was the second of the *Le Hardi* class, built to serve as escorts for the *Dunkerque*-class battleships. The primary requirement of the *Le Hardis* was that they should be able to maintain 35 knots at full load, and this they did without undue effort. If they had a shortcoming, it was in their main armament which was complex and unreliable, and could not elevate to more than 30 degrees. It was planned to equip the last four units (which were abandoned while building) with a new dual-purpose gun, which would have turned them into some of the most capable ships of their type in the world. *Fleuret* was constructed by Forges et Chantiers de la Méditerranée at La Seyne near Toulon, and entered service officially in July 1940. Renamed *Foudroyant* in April 1941 to commemorate the *L'Adroit*-class ship of that name sunk off Dunkirk, she was scuttled at Toulon in November 1942, raised and later sunk as a blockship in August 1944.

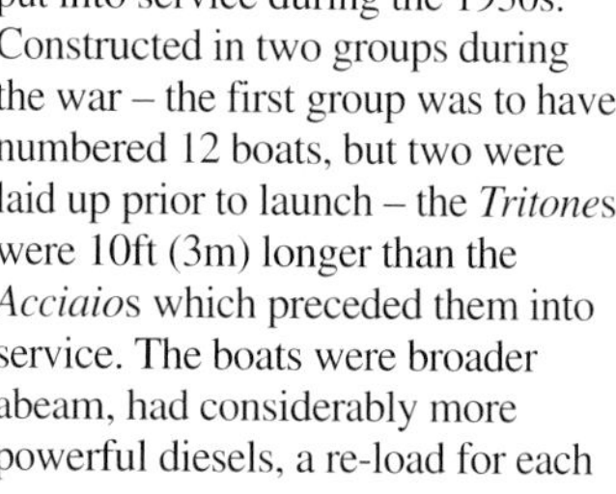

The *Le Hardis*, of which *Fleuret* was the second, should have been one of the best destroyer classes in the world, but were let down by their main guns.

Displacement: 1770t standard; 2575t full load
Dimensions: 384ft 6in x 36ft 5in x 13ft 9in (117.2m x 11.1m x 4.2m)
Machinery: two-shaft, Rateau-Bretagne geared turbines; 58,000hp
Armament: six 5.1in (130mm); two 37mm (later two 25mm); four (later eight) 13.2mm MG; later, five 8mm MG; seven 21.7in (550mm) TT; one towed AS torpedo; one DC rack
Speed: 37 knots
Range: 1900nm (3520km) at 25 knots
Complement: 187

FLUTTO

ITALY: 1942

Displacement: 888t surfaced; 1050t submerged
Dimensions: 207ft 4in x 22ft 11in x 16ft (63.15m x 6.98m x 4.85m)
Machinery: two-shaft, FIAT diesels, plus CRDA electric motors; 2400bhp/800hp
Armament: six 21in (533mm) TT (four bow, two stern: 12 torpedoes); one 3.9in (100mm); two 20mm
Speed: 16 knots surfaced; 8 knots submerged
Range: 5400nm (10,150km) at 8 knots surface
Complement: 50

The enlarged *Tritones* were successors to the numerous 600t coastal submarines the Italian Navy put into service during the 1930s. Constructed in two groups during the war – the first group was to have numbered 12 boats, but two were laid up prior to launch – the *Tritones* were 10ft (3m) longer than the *Acciaios* which preceded them into service. The boats were broader abeam, had considerably more powerful diesels, a re-load for each torpedo tube, dived more quickly and deeper, and were more manoeuvrable underwater. Sometimes described as the class leader, *Flutto* was the first built, by Cantieri Riuniti dell'Adriatico at Monfalcone. She entered service on 20 March 1943, but had a very short career: encountering a trio of British Fairmile Type D motor torpedo-boats in the Straits of Messina on 11 July 1943, she was sunk. A second group of 16 boats was planned, marginally longer but otherwise unchanged; only three were launched, and they were scuttled before completion.

***Flutto* was one of the last class of Italian coastal submarines put into service during World War II; only two survived.**

FOCA

ITALY: 1937

The Italian Navy operated a few small coastal minelaying submarines during World War I, but did not construct a first-class submarine minelayer, the *Micca*, until the mid-1930s. She was designed by Cavallini, and some years later he improved on his work with the three *Foca*-class boats which Tosi constructed at Taranto. These were partial double-hulled designs, based on the *Archimede*, dispensing with stern torpedo tubes in favour of mine chutes. (Submarine minelaying is made complicated by the need to adjust the boat's trim as the mines are ejected; vertical chutes, either within the pressure hull, as in the *Focas*, or in the saddle tanks, facilitate the process.) *Foca* was the only one of the three boats lost during the war, disappearing without trace off Haifa on 15 October 1940. There was speculation in Italian circles that she had touched off one of her own mines – by no means an impossibility.

Displacement: 1305t surface; 1625t submerged
Dimensions: 271ft 10in x 23ft 6in x 17ft 1in (82.85m x 7.2m x 5.2m)
Machinery: two-shaft, FIAT diesels, plus Ansaldo electric motors; 2880bhp/1250hp
Armament: six 533mm (21in) TT (bow: eight torpedoes); one 100mm (3.9in); four 13.2mm MG; two MC (36 mines)
Speed: 16 knots surfaced; 8 knots submerged
Range: 8500nm (15,750km) at 8 knots surface
Complement: 60

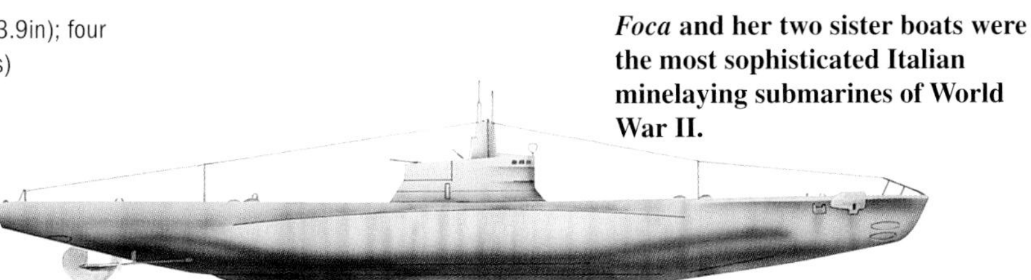

***Foca* and her two sister boats were the most sophisticated Italian minelaying submarines of World War II.**

FORMIDABLE

GB: 1939

The three *Illustrious*-class fleet aircraft carriers constructed for the Royal Navy at the end of the 1930s were the first in the world to have fully armoured hangars, with sides 4.5in (115mm) thick, topped by a 3in (76mm) armoured flight deck and with a similar deck of its own, which rested on the main armour belt. This configuration meant that the class had but one hangar deck, against the two of the *Ark Royal*, and could only operate half the number of aircraft, despite being of similar size and displacement. Whether the reduction in capacity was acceptable, or whether they would have been more effective fighting ships if they had been more like the prototype British fleet carrier, is a matter of some contention. By 1944, aircraft capacity had been increased to over 50 by the expedient of adding a 'parking' area extension to the flight deck, on outriggers. HMS *Indomitable*, laid down as the fourth member of the class, was completed with 3in (76mm) less armour on the hangar sides and the flight deck raised to allow an additional (shortened) hangar, to accommodate 50 per cent more aircraft on the same displacement. Despite her protection, *Formidable* was out of action for six months after she was hit by two 2205lb (1000kg) bombs, neither of them on the armour, but she survived two kamikaze attacks in May 1945. HMS *Indomitable* was built in Belfast by Harland & Wolff, and entered service in November 1940. She was the first of the *Illustrious* class to go, being sold for breaking up in 1953. Her sister ship, HMS *Victorious*, was later modified to operate jet aircraft and stayed in service for a further 15 years.

Displacement: 23,000t standard; 29,100t full load
Dimensions: 743ft 9in x 95ft 9in x 28ft (226.7m x 29.2m x 8.5m)
Machinery: three-shaft, Parsons geared turbines; 111,000hp
Armament: 16 4.5in (114mm) HA; 48 2pdr pom-poms (later 12 40mm and 34 20mm); 33 (later 50-54) aircraft
Speed: 30.5 knots
Range: 11,000nm (20,400km) at 14 knots
Complement: 1229 (later 1997)

The *Illustrious*-class carriers were designed to meet the threat of attack from land-based aircraft, particularly in the Mediterranean.

FULTON

USA: 1940

Displacement: 9250t full load
Dimensions: 529ft 6in x 73ft 4in x 23ft 6in (161.4m x 22.35m x 7.15m)
Machinery: two-shaft, General Motors diesels; 12,000bhp
Armament: four 5in (127mm)
Speed: 20 knots
Range: 12,000nm (22,200km) at 16 knots
Complement: 1303

USS *Fulton* was the leader of a class of seven submarine support ships, offering services which ranged from routine re-supply and refurbishment to a dockyard-standard refit. She was constructed at Mare Island Navy Yard and commissioned less than three months before the start of World War II, during which she acted as a submarine tender and as a general repair ship in the Pacific theatre. Placed in reserve 1947–51, she was subsequently recommissioned and remained in service, latterly tending to nuclear-powered submarines, until the 1960s.

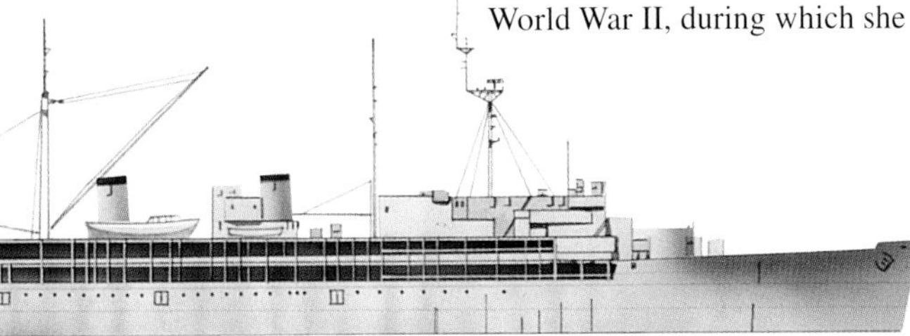

The *Fulton* and her six sister ships were the largest submarine tenders in service with the US Navy during World War II.

GATO

USA: 1941

The *Gatos*, together with the *Balao* and *Tench* classes – the three were almost indistinguishable, one from the other, save for various small improvements made in the light of experience – were the American fleet submarines of World War II. They were a successful design, with 10 torpedo tubes and a total of 24 torpedoes or 40 mines, and a fairly powerful gun armament – eventually one 5in (127mm), one 40mm and one 20mm – and a range sufficient to allow them to span the Pacific Ocean.

The most significant difference between them and earlier fleet submarines was a lengthening of the hull, to allow an increase in the size of ballast tanks and to improve habitability and stability. It was planned to increase the power of the four diesel engines from 1600bhp to 2000bhp, but this never took place. Originally, operating depth was 300ft (91.5m) but later boats could dive to 400ft (122m) or more. Many remained in service after the war's end, and most went throught the GUPPY (Greater Underwater Propulsive Power) programme, which saw them streamlined and fitted with effective snorkels and more powerful batteries. Stripped of their guns, with faired-in hulls and a new streamlined fin replacing the conning tower, the converted boats could make 16 knots underwater for short periods. USS *Gato*, the leadboat of the class and also the first to be constructed, by the Electric Boat Co. at Groton, Connecticut, entered service in 1942, and survived the war; she was decommissioned and placed in reserve in 1946, and was not refurbished or modernized; she was stricken from the Navy List in 1960.

Displacement: 1525t surfaced; 2410t submerged
Dimensions: 311ft 9in x 27ft 3in x 15ft 3in (95m x 8.3m x 4.65m)
Machinery: two-shaft, diesel engines, plus electric motors; 6400bhp/2740hp
Armament: 10 21in (533mm) TT (six bow, four stern; 24 torpedoes); one 3in (76mm), later 5in (127mm); two 0.5in MG; two 0.3in MG (later one 40mm and one 20mm)
Speed: 20.25 knots surfaced; 8.75 knots submerged
Range: 11,000nm (20,350km) at 10 knots surfaced
Complement: 60–80

The early *Gatos* were subject to a programme of modernization aimed at keeping them up to the same specification as later boats; including reworking their conning towers and re-arming them.

GIULIO CESARE

ITALY: 1911–37

Displacement: 29,032t full load
Dimensions: 611ft 6in x 91ft 10in x 34ft 5in (186.4m x 28m x 10.5m)
Machinery: two-shaft, Belluzzo geared turbines; 75,000hp/93,000hp forced draught
Armament: 10 12.6in (320mm); 12 4.7in (120mm); eight 3.9in (100mm) AA; 12 37mm; 12 13.2mm MG (later 12, and later again 16, 20mm)
Armour: belt 10in (254mm); deck 4.4in–3.15in (112mm–80mm); barbettes 11in (280mm); turrets 10in (254mm); conning tower 10.2in (260mm); torpedo bulkheads 1in (25mm)
Speed: 28 knots
Range: 6500nm (12,000km) at 13 knots
Complement: 1235

The rebuilding of the Italian dreadnoughts in the mid-1930s was a major feat of naval engineering. The results were at least comparable to those the US Navy achieved when it rebuilt the *Nevadas* and the *Pennsylvanias*.

Giulio Cesare was one of the *Cavour*-class battleships, launched in 1911. As constructed, she mounted 13 12in (305mm) guns arranged as a triple and a superfiring double fore and aft, and a triple amidships. Her four-shaft 30,700 horsepower machinery gave her a top speed of 21.5 knots at a displacement of around 24,000t. In October 1933, she was taken in hand at Cantieri del Tirreno's Genoa yard. She was rebuilt from a stripped-out hull and re-engined with two-shaft machinery, giving 75,000 horsepower for 27 knots under normal conditions, and 93,000 horsepower for 28 knots under forced draught, a speed she exceeded marginally on trial. She received a cellular underwater protection system, and more extensive sub-division, and was extended fore and aft, increasing her length by just over 33ft (10m). The embrasures for the secondary battery were plated over to forecastle deck level, and she received additional horizontal armour and all new superstructure. Her main armament was reduced to 10 guns in the original superfiring double/triple arrangement fore and aft. The guns themselves were bored out and re-linered, and the mountings were modified to allow them to elevate to 27 degrees. New secondary and anti-aircraft batteries were added. One of the most extensive rebuilds ever attempted (three other battleships were also reconstructed), it was very successful. Recommissioned on 1 October 1937, she survived World War II. In 1948 she was transferred to the Soviet Union in reparation where, renamed *Novorossiisk*, she was either sunk after hitting a mine, or badly damaged and then broken up, in 1955.

GIUSEPPE GARIBALDI

ITALY: 1936

The Italian light cruisers known as the *Condottieri* type were divided into five groups, each group being sufficiently different as to qualify as a class of its own, though there was a definite progression, rather than any abrupt major change, between one group and the next. *Giuseppe Garibaldi* was one of the two *Abruzzis*, the fifth and most effective group, put into service by the Italian Navy during the 1930s. The *Abruzzis* were almost twice the displacement of the first group, with increased protection and heavier armament and more powerful geared turbines, but did not achieve the high speeds of the earlier ships as a result. *Giuseppe Garibaldi* was built by Cantieri Riuniti dell'Adriatico at Trieste, and entered service on 20 January 1937. On Italy's surrender, she came under Allied control and was employed as a convoy escort, but never again saw action. She was returned to Italy in 1946 and, in 1957–61, was reconstructed as a guided-missile cruiser. *Giuseppe Garibaldi* was stricken in January 1972.

***Giuseppe Garibaldi* was a very successful light cruiser, a type at which Italy excelled. She was later reconstructed as a guided-missile cruiser.**

Displacement: 9050t standard; 11,120t full load
Dimensions: 187m x 18.9m x 6.8m (613ft 6in x 62ft x 22ft 4in)
Machinery: two-shaft, Parsons geared turbines; 100,000hp
Armament: 10 6in (152mm); eight 3.9in (100mm) AA; eight 37mm; eight 13.2mm MG (later 10 20mm); six 21in (533mm) TT
Armour: belt 3.9in (100mm); bulkheads 3.9in (100mm); decks 40mm–30mm (1.6in–1.2in); barbettes 3.9in (100mm); turrets 5.3in (135mm); conning tower 3.9in (100mm)
Speed: 34 knots
Range: 5000nm (9250km) at 20 knots
Complement: 640–692

GLASGOW

GB: 1936

In 1933, the Royal Navy began work on a new class of light cruiser. The *Southamptons* were to be substantially bigger than those cruisers then in service (which were of World War I design) or already under construction. The ships were to provide a basic pattern for future classes, specifically the *Gloucesters* and *Edinburghs*, but also influenced the design of the *Fijis*. Though they were protected for the length of their machinery space by an armoured belt, brought up to the upper deck level to cover the boiler rooms, only box protection of similar thickness was provided for the magazines. Their four-shaft machinery was enough to give them a maximum speed, on trial, of 32 knots, which was comparable with most of their contemporaries. HMS *Glasgow* was built by Scotts at Greenock, and entered service in September 1937. She was hit by two aerial torpedoes in December 1940; repairs took nine months, but she survived the war and was stricken in 1958.

Displacement: 9100t standard; 11,350t (later 12,190t) full load
Dimensions: 591ft 6in x 61ft 8in x 20ft 4in - later 21ft 6in (180.3m x 18.8m x 6.20m - later 6.55m)
Machinery: four-shaft, Parsons geared turbines; 75,000hp
Armament: 12 6in (152mm); eight 4in (102mm) AA; four 3pdr; eight (later 28) 2pdr pom-poms; six 21in (533mm) TT; three aircraft
Armour: belt 4.5in (114mm); ammunition spaces 4.5in (114mm); bulkheads 2.5in (64mm); turrets 1in (25mm)
Speed: 32 knots
Range: 6000nm (11,100km) at 14 knots
Complement: 748

The *Southampton* class set the style for the Royal Navy's large light cruisers. A total of 21 were constructed between the mid-1930s and the end of World War II.

GLOUCESTER

GB: 1937

The three *Gloucester*-class large light cruisers, which entered service with the Royal Navy just before the outbreak of World War II, were slightly enlarged versions of the *Southamptons*. They were provided with somewhat better protection and more powerful machinery. HMS *Gloucester* was the last of them, entering service in January 1939. She had but a short career, being sunk by at least four direct hits and three near misses by 1000lb (2200kg) bombs off Crete on 21 May 1941, in the run-up to the German invasion.

HMS *Gloucester* was the leader of the second class of large light cruisers, armed with 12 6in (152mm) guns, constructed for the Royal Navy in the late 1930s.

Displacement: 9400t standard; 11,650t full load
Dimensions: 591ft 6in x 62ft 4in x 20ft 7in (180.3m x 19m x 6.3m)
Machinery: four-shaft, Parsons geared turbines; 82,500hp
Armament: 12 6in (152mm); eight 4in (102mm) AA; four 3pdr; eight 2pdr pom-poms; six 21in (533mm) TT
Armour: belt 4.5in (114mm); ammunition spaces 4.5in (114mm); bulkheads 2.5in (64mm); turrets 4in-2in (102mm-51mm))
Speed: 32.5 knots
Range: 6000nm (11,100km) at 14 knots
Complement: 800

GNEISENAU

GERMANY: 1936

Hitler took a personal interest in the design of the *Scharnhorst*-class battleships. He originally wished them to be similar to the *Deutschland*-class 'pocket battleships', but with much-improved protection. The German Navy resisted the idea of building ships on a displacement of 19,000t armed with only six 11in (280mm) guns, and eventually persuaded Hitler that a bigger ship, mounting nine guns, would be more satisfactory. *Gneisenau* was constructed at Kiel, by Deutsche Werke, initially as Ship E (*Ersatz Hessen*). She entered service on 21 May 1938, six months before her sister ship, the *Scharnhorst*. The following year both received the so-called 'Atlantic' bow, which increased overall length by 16ft 9in (5.1m) and made them more satisfactory sea-boats. *Gneisenau*'s most important mission was Operation 'Berlin'; in late January 1941, in company with the *Scharnhorst*, she broke out into the North Atlantic and spent two months attacking merchant convoys before running into Brest. Having come

Displacement: 32,100t standard; 38,100t full load
Dimensions: 753ft 11in x 98ft 5in x 27ft 3in (229.8m x 30m x 8.3m)
Machinery: three-shaft, Germania geared turbines; 165,000hp
Armament: nine 11in (280mm); 12 5.9in (150mm); 14 4.1in (105mm); 16 37mm; eight 20mm; three or four aircraft
Armour: belt 13.75in-6.75in (350mm-170mm); deck 2in (50mm); armoured deck 4in-3in (100mm-75mm); main turret faces 14in (355mm); secondary turret faces 5.5in (135mm); conning tower 350mm (13.75in)
Speed: 32 knots
Range: 6200nm (11,450km) at 19 knots
Complement: 1670-1840

under air attack for almost a year, the two battleships, plus the cruiser *Prinz Eugen*, made the celebrated 'Channel dash' of Operation 'Cerberus' – evading the efforts of both the Royal Air Force and the Royal Navy to stop them – arriving in Wilhelmshaven on 13 February 1942. The RAF proved more effective a fortnight later, when a mixed force of medium and heavy bombers attacked the floating dock at Kiel, to which *Gneisenau* had been moved. A direct hit near the bow demolished her as far back as 'A' turret. This was the end of the ship as a combat unit. Her guns were later removed for employment ashore, and she was towed to Gotenhafen (Gdynia), where she was scuttled on 27 March 1945.

***Scharnhorst* and *Gneisenau* were constructed to operate as a pair, and were inseparable until the latter was crippled in February 1942.**

GÖTA LEJON

SWEDEN: 1945

A pair of light cruisers were ordered for the Swedish Navy in mid-1943 to a state-of-the-art specification, including dual-purpose fully-automatic 6in (152mm) guns in mountings which could elevate to 70 degrees. The cruisers were both fast and well protected, their armour accounting for a quarter of their entire standard displacement. *Göta Lejon* was the second of them, built by Eriksberg. She was modernized in 1950–52 and partially rebuilt in 1957–58, and sold to Chile as the *Latorre* in 1971. She was discarded in 1984.

Displacement: 8200t standard; 9200t full load
Dimensions: 597ft 1in x 54ft 9in x 21ft 4in (182m x 16.7m x 6.5m)
Machinery: two-shaft, De Laval geared turbines; 90,000hp
Armament: seven 6in (152mm), later four 57mm; 27 (later 10) 40mm; six 21in (533mm) TT; 160 mines
Armour: belt 1in-0.8in (25mm-20mm) plus 3.15in-2.75in (80mm-70mm); decks 1.2in (30mm); turret fronts 5in (125mm); conning tower 1in-0.8in (25mm-20mm)
Speed: 33 knots
Range: 6000nm (11,100km) at 20 knots
Complement: 610

The layout of the *Göta Lejon* was somewhat unconventional, with a single triple turret forward and two superfiring twins aft.

GRAF ZEPPELIN

GERMANY: 1938

Displacement: 26,930t standard
Dimensions: 861ft 3in x 103ft 4in x 23ft 7in (262.5m x 31.5m x 7.2m)
Machinery: four-shaft, Brown-Boveri geared turbines; 200,000hp
Armament: 16 5.9in (150mm); 12 4.1in (105mm) AA; 22 37mm; 28 20mm; 41-43 aircraft
Armour: belt 3.5in (88mm); hangar deck 1.5in (37mm); flight deck 0.8in (20mm)
Speed: 35 knots
Range: 8000nm (14,800km) at 19 knots
Complement: 1760 (est.)

In 1936 the German Navy, now released from treaty restrictions, began building a fleet aircraft carrier, the *Graf Zeppelin*. She had a planned standard displacement of 22,000t, with side armour similar to that of a heavy cruiser, but both her hangar deck and flight decks were comparatively thin. Some elements of her design, including automated fire-fighting equipment and the provision of retractable Voith-Schneider propulsors at the bow, were quite advanced, but others fell far behind contemporary practice. Deutsche Werke began her construction at Kiel and she was launched in December 1938; work was halted in May 1940 when she was 85–90 per cent complete. Work restarted two years later (during which time she was used as a timber store at Gotenhafen (Gdynia)), but stopped again in early 1943. She was later towed to Stettin (Szczecin) and was scuttled there in January 1945. Raised by Soviet engineers in 1946, with the intention of completing her, *Graf Zeppelin* sank under tow to Leningrad in September 1947.

The *Graf Zeppelin* was to have operated a mixture of marinized Bf.109F or -G fighters and Ju.87G dive bombers.

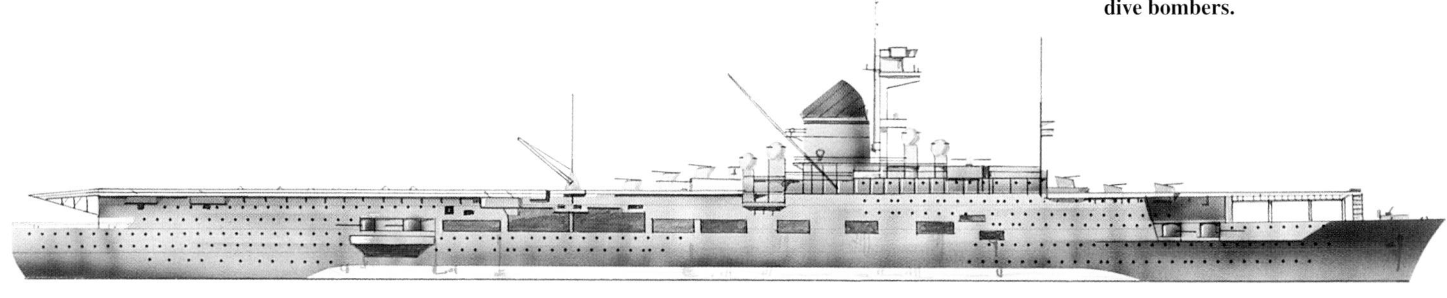

GROM

POLAND: 1936

Displacement: 2010t standard; 3385t full load
Dimensions: 374ft x 36ft 1in x 10ft 10in (114m x 11m x 3.3m)
Machinery: two-shaft, Parsons geared turbines; 54,500hp
Armament: seven 4.7in (120mm), later one 4in (102mm) AA; four 40mm; eight 13.2mm MG; six (later three) 21in (533mm) TT; 44 mines
Speed: 39 knots
Range: 4500nm (8350km) at 15 knots
Complement: 180

The pair of *Grom*-class destroyers were constructed for Poland in the United Kingdom, by White at Cowes. Somewhat surprisingly, for the Polish Navy was barely even third-rate at the time, these destroyers were held to be the best in the world, and were certainly amongst the fastest, when they commissioned in 1937. Designed for service in the Baltic, they proved to be equally at home in the harsher conditions of the North Atlantic. They both escaped from Poland even as war was breaking out, the Warsaw government deciding that these precious assets would be safer in British ports. After short refits, which included exchanging a bank of torpedo tubes for a 4in (102mm) AA gun, both ships were immediately committed to active service. *Grom* was sunk by German aircraft in Rombaksfjord during the invasion of Norway. Her sister ship, *Blyskawica*, survived the war and returned to Poland in 1947. There she served as the flagship of the Polish Navy until the early 1960s, and was later preserved.

The Polish *Grom* was amongst the fastest destroyers in the world when she was put into service in 1937.

GRYF

POLAND: 1936

The *Gryf* was an unsuccessful attempt to combine three quite different functions – those of minelayer, training ship, and state yacht – in one ship. To make matters worse she was under-funded, and undersize as a result, though she retained her full battery as designed. Built in France by Augustin-Normand, *Gryf* was delivered to the Polish Navy in 1938. On 1 September 1939 she was sunk, in a floating drydock, to act as a defensive battery at Hela. She was destroyed in a German air attack two days later.

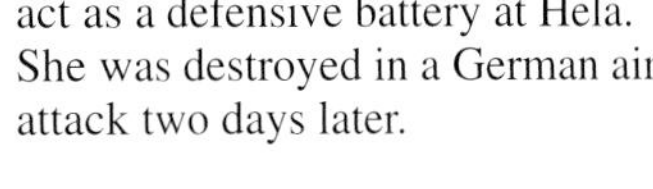

Too much was expected of the *Gryf*, and on too low a displacement. She ended her brief career as a static gun battery.

Displacement: 2250t standard
Dimensions: 338ft 7in x 43ft x 11ft 10in (103.2m x 13.1m x 3.6m)
Machinery: two-shaft, Sulzer diesel engines; 6000bhp
Armament: six 4.7in (120mm); four 40mm; four 13.2mm MG; 600 mines
Speed: 20 knots
Range: 6000nm (11,100km) at 18 knots
Complement: 205

GUAM

USA: 1943

In 1941, the US Navy's cruiser development programme reached its peak with a class of ships sometimes called 'super-cruisers'. Though they had 12in (305mm) guns, a significant amount of armour, and enough power to give them 33 knots, their design appeared very much a return to the discredited battlecruiser formula of earlier years. Six ships were ordered, as the *Alaska* class; three were laid down and two were actually completed in 1944, even though the tactical requirement which had spurred their development had long since disappeared. The *Alaska*s had very little in common with other US ships of the period – though there was a thread of consistency running through into other classes of smaller cruisers which never got past the design stage – and had been expensive to build. They soon proved to be very costly to maintain and, since they had no useful function, they were decommissioned into reserve as soon as the war was over. The *Alaska*s never returned to service, though there was a plan to complete the *Hawaii* (which had been launched and then mothballed incomplete) as a guided-missile cruiser and, another, rather better thought-out, to convert her as a command ship. USS *Guam* was constructed by New York Shipbuilding, and was commissioned on 17 September 1944. She arrived at Pearl Harbor for combat duty in February 1945, and took part in operations off Japan, both supporting the carrier task forces and engaging shore targets with her main guns. Later, she became the flagship of the North China Force, before returning to the USA in December 1945 for decommissioning at Bayonne in February 1947. Stricken in 1960, she was sold for scrap the following year.

Displacement: 29,800t standard; 34,250t full load
Dimensions: 808ft 6in x 91ft 1in x 31ft 10in (246.4m x 27.8m x 9.7m)
Machinery: four-shaft, General Electric geared turbines; 150,000hp
Armament: nine 12in (305mm); 12 5in (127mm); 56 40mm; 34 20mm
Armour: belt 9in-5in (229mm-127mm); deck 4in (102mm); barbettes 13in (330mm); turret faces 13in (330mm); conning tower 10.5in (267mm)
Speed: 33 knots
Range: 12,000nm (22,200km) at 15 knots
Complement: 1517

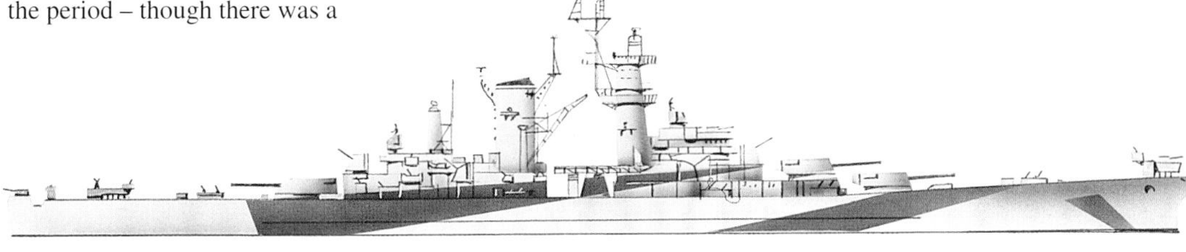

The *Guam* and her sister ship *Alaska* were white elephants which served no useful purpose. The tactical role they were built to play had long since disappeared, though they added their considerable weight to the US fleet off the home islands of Japan in the last months of the war.

Guglielmo Marconi

ITALY: 1939

The *Guglielmo Marconi* was the lead boat of a class of six ocean-going submarines, improved versions of the *Marcello*s, which entered service with the Italian Navy in 1940. She was built by Cantieri Riuniti dell'Adriatico and newly-delivered when Italy declared war in June 1940. Unsuitable for operations in the Mediterranean, *Guglielmo Marconi* was soon transferred to Bordeaux, to operate in the Atlantic, along with most other Italian first-class submarines. She was sunk, torpedoed in error by the German submarine *U67*, in October 1941.

Displacement: 1175t surfaced; 1465t submerged
Dimensions: 251ft x 22ft 4in x 15ft 6in (76.5m x 6.8m x 4.7m)
Machinery: two-shaft, CRDA diesel engines, plus Marelli electric motors; 3600bhp/1500hp
Armament: eight 533mm (21in) TT (four bow, four stern: 12 torpedoes); one 3.9in (100mm); four 13.2mm MG
Speed: 17.8 knots surfaced; 8.2 knots submerged
Range: 10,500nm (19,500km) at 8 knots surfaced
Complement: 57

All six *Marconi*-class submarines operated in the Atlantic out of Bordeaux; one, converted to carry cargo, was seized by the Japanese in Singapore.

Gustaf V

SWEDEN: 1918/1930/1938

Laid down during World War I but not completed until the 1920s, the *Gustaf V* was the last of Sweden's three *Sverige*-class battleships. Though no bigger than small cruisers, these small coastal battleships were armed with four heavy guns and protected by a substantial belt of armour. All three were to remain in service for over three decades, having passed through successive stages of modification. *Gustaf V* was first taken in hand in 1927: she received a heavy tripod mast with control tops, 75mm AA guns, and a director, and had her two funnels trunked into one – this latter modification was not made to her two sister ships, and she was readily distinguishable thereafter as a result. In 1936 she was partially re-boilered to allow her to burn oil as well as coal; those bunkers not replaced by oil tanks were left in place for protection. Her forward 152mm guns were also replaced, by 40mm Bofors. *Gustaf V* was stricken in April 1957, but not broken up until 1970.

The three *Sverige*-class battleships, of which *Gustaf V* was the last, were never intended to venture far from Swedish home waters.

Displacement: 7125t standard; 7635t full load
Dimensions: 399ft x 61ft x 22ft (121.6m x 18.6m x 6.7m)
Machinery: two-shaft, Motala geared turbines; 23,900hp
Armament: four 11.1in (283mm); eight (later six) 6in (152mm); six 3in (75mm), later four 3in (75mm) AA); two 57mm, later four 40mm; two MG; two 21in (533mm) TT
Armour: belt 7.8in-2.4in (200mm-60mm); turrets 7.8in-3.9in (200mm-100mm); conning tower 6.8in (175mm)
Speed: 22.5 knots
Range: 3000nm (5500km) at 15 knots
Complement: 427-443

HA201

JAPAN: 1945

Displacement: 320t surfaced; 440t submerged
Dimensions: 173ft 11in x 13ft 1in x 11ft 3in (53m x 4m x 3.45m)
Machinery: one-shaft, diesel engine, plus two electric motors; 400bhp/1250hp
Armament: two 21in (533mm) TT (bow: two torpedoes); one 0.303in (7.7mm) MG
Speed: 10.5 knots surfaced; 13 knots submerged
Range: 3000nm (5500km) at 10 knots surfaced
Complement: 22

The Japanese *STS*-class coastal submarines were constructed hurriedly for the last-ditch defence of the home islands, but were never used.

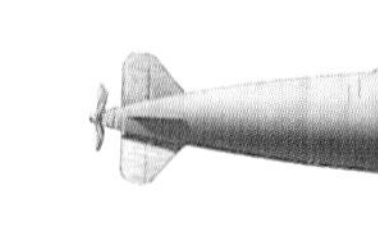

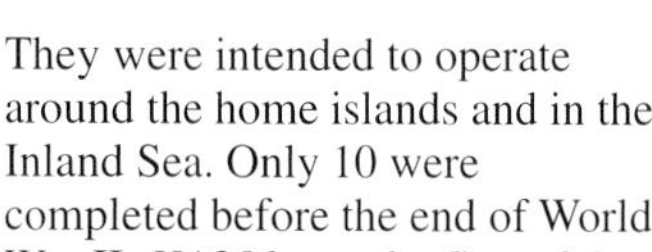

The Imperial Japanese Navy began constructing small third-class submarines, lightly armed but with exceptionally good underwater performance, from March 1945. They were intended to operate around the home islands and in the Inland Sea. Only 10 were completed before the end of World War II. *HA201* was the first of the class. Built at Sasebo Navy Yard, she was commissioned in May 1945, but crew training was never completed and she never saw active service.

Hamakaze

JAPAN: 1940

The *Kagero*-class destroyers were authorized within the 1937 and 1939 construction programmes. In November 1939 – when the leadship entered service, problems with the powerplant and steering gear experienced in the preceding *Asashio*s having been eliminated – the Imperial Japanese Navy believed the *Kagero*s were the best fleet destroyers in the world. Like all Japanese destroyers of the period, their principal armament of 5in (127mm) dual-purpose guns was mounted in twin turrets, one forward and two aft; the 'X' turret was removed from survivors from 1943, and replaced with additional light AA guns. *Hamakaze* was the first Japanese destroyer to be equipped with radar. She was constructed by Uraga in Tokyo and entered service in 1941. She was sunk by US aircraft on 7 April 1945. All but one of the *Kagero* class of 18 were lost; the sole survivor, the *Yukikaze*, was transferred to China and then to Taiwan. Here she remained in service, extensively modified, until May 1970.

The destroyer *Hamakaze* was the first Japanese ship of this type to be equipped with radar, in 1943.

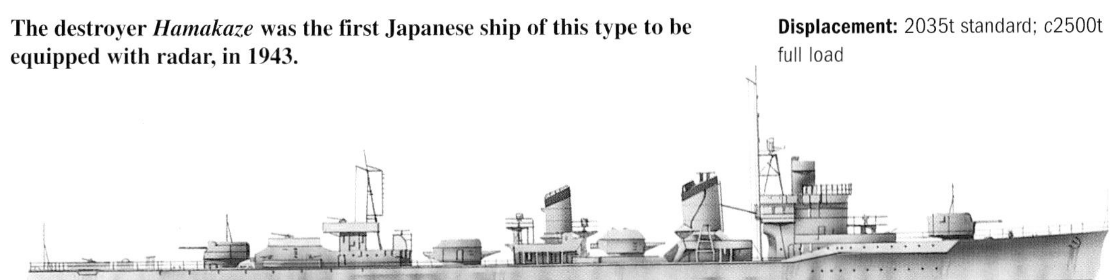

Displacement: 2035t standard; c2500t full load
Dimensions: 388ft 9in x 35ft 5in x 12ft 4in (118.5m x 10.8m x 3.75m)
Machinery: two-shaft, geared turbines; 52,000hp
Armament: six (later four) 5in (127mm); four (later 14) 25mm; eight 24in (610mm) TT; DCs
Speed: 35 knots
Range: 6000nm (11,100km) at 20 knots
Complement: 240

HASHIDATE

JAPAN: 1936

Displacement: 1000t standard; 1150t full load
Dimensions: 257ft 7in x 31ft 10in x 8ft (78.5m x 9.7m x 2.45m)
Machinery: two-shaft, geared turbines; 4600hp
Armament: three 4.7in (120mm); four (later nine) 25mm; later, DCs
Speed: 19.5knots
Range: not available
Complement: 170

***Hashidate* and her sister ship *Uji* were built to operate in coastal and estuarine waters in support of the Japanese forces invading China.**

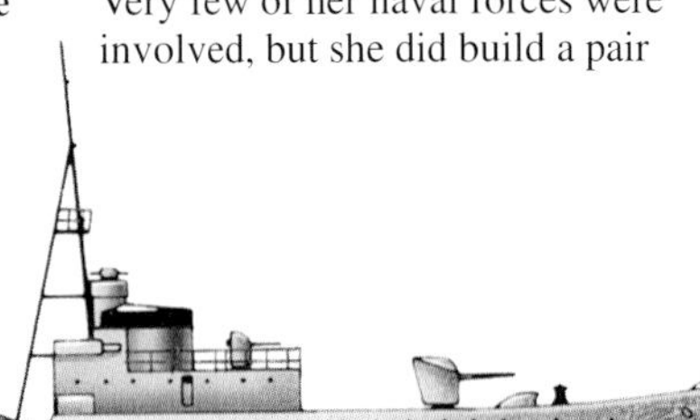

Japan was at war in China long before she entered World War II. Very few of her naval forces were involved, but she did build a pair of gunboats to operate in coastal waters and in the estuaries of the major rivers, primarily as mobile firebases to bombard shore targets. *Hashidate* was the first of them, built by Sakurajima in Osaka; she was later modified to operate as a coastal escort. She was sunk, torpedoed by an American submarine, on 22 May 1944.

HATSUTAKA

JAPAN: 1939

Prior to and during World War II, the Imperial Japanese Navy constructed or converted a considerable number of ships to operate as minelayers and also to deploy anti-submarine net defences. Many of them, including the three purpose-built vessels of the *Hatsutaka* class, were later converted to act as coastal escorts, with depth charge racks substituted for their minelaying and net handling gear. *Hatsutaka*, like her sister ships, was constructed by Harima at Aioi. She entered service in 1939 and was sunk in May 1945.

***Hatsutaka* was the leader of a small class of minelayers and netlayers, constructed to operate in the shallow waters around Japan's coast.**

Displacement: 1610t standard; 1900t full load
Dimensions: 298ft 3in x 37ft 1in x 14ft 5in (90.9m x 11.3m x 4.4m)
Machinery: two-shaft, geared turbines; 6000hp
Armament: four 40mm; four 25mm; 360 mines, later 36 DCs
Speed: 20 knots
Range: not available
Complement: not available

HIEI

JAPAN: 1912/1940

Displacement: 32,350t standard; 36,400t full load
Dimensions: 738ft 7in x 92ft x 31ft 11in (222.05m x 28m x 9.7m)
Machinery: four-shaft, Parsons geared turbines; 136,000hp
Armament: eight 14in (356mm); 14 6in (152mm); eight 5in (127mm) DP; four 40mm; 20 25mm; three aircraft
Armour: belt 7.9in-3in (200mm-75mm); decks 4.7in-3.2in (120mm-80mm); barbettes 9.9in (250mm); turrets 8.9in (225mm); conning tower 9.9in (250mm)
Speed: 30.5 knots
Range: 12,000nm (22,200km) at 15 knots
Complement: 1437

Hiei was constructed as a *Kongo*-class battlecruiser, launched in 1912. These were the first ships to be armed with 14in (356mm) guns. She was kept up to date after World War I, but was de-militarized under the 1930 London Treaty to serve as a school ship, her armour and half her 14in (356mm) battery removed and with less than half her powerplant in operation. *Hiei* was later substantially reconstructed – with an extension to the hull aft, entirely new machinery which produced more than twice the power of the original engines for a 3 knot increase in top speed, an effective AA battery, aircraft, and extra armour – to recommission as a fast battleship in 1940. Her rebuilt bridge structure and fire control system were later duplicated for the *Yamato*s. She was the first Japanese capital ship lost during World War II, sunk at Guadalcanal on 13 November 1942 by torpedo bombers from USS *Enterprise*, having already been substantially crippled by shellfire.

As reconstructed, the *Hiei* was reclassified as a fast battleship. Her protection proved insufficient to justify the classification as she was crippled by shellfire of no more than 8in (203mm) calibre.

HIRYU

JAPAN: 1937

The *Hiryu* was constructed at Yokosuka Navy Yard and completed in July 1939. She was a slightly enlarged version of the *Soryu*, the ship which set the style for the Japanese large light carriers of World War II, with her 3.3ft (1m) greater beam increasing her bunkerage by 20 per cent. Though protection was minimal, consisting of an armoured waterline belt and flight deck, the *Hiryu* had a two-level hangar, the upper some 20 per cent longer than the lower, which connected to the flight deck by three lifts, and could operate up to 64 aircraft. Her island was, unusually, but like the earlier *Akagi*, positioned to port, and served to balance the horizontal funnels to starboard, just below the level of the flight deck. *Hiryu* was one of the four Japanese carriers sunk at the Battle of Midway in early June 1942: she was hit four times by dive bombers, sustained insupportable damage to flight deck and hangars, and was abandoned and then torpedoed by the destroyer *Mikagumo*.

The *Hiryu* was one of the four Japanese carriers sunk at Midway, the battle which changed the course of the war in the Pacific.

Displacement: 17,300t standard; 21,900t full load
Dimensions: 745ft 11in x 73ft 3in x 25ft 9in (227.4m x 22.3m x 7.85m)
Machinery: four-shaft, geared turbines; 153,000hp
Armament: 12 5in (127mm) DP; 31 25mm; 64 aircraft
Armour: belt 5.9in-3.6in (150mm-90mm); deck 1in (25mm)
Speed: 34.5 knots
Range: 9500nm (17,600km) at 18 knots
Complement: 1100

HOWE

GB: 1940

Displacement: 36,725t standard; 42,075t full load
Dimensions: 745ft x 103ft x 32ft 7in (227.05m x 31.4m x 9.95m)
Machinery: four-shaft, Parsons geared turbines; 110,000hp
Armament: 10 14in (356mm); 16 5.25in (135mm) AA; eight (later 22) 40mm; 32 (later 88) 2pdr pom-poms; up to 64 20mm; two aircraft
Armour: belt 15in-13in (380mm-356mm); bulkheads 12in-4in (305mm-102mm); barbettes 13in (356mm); turret faces 13in (356mm); conning tower 4.5in (114mm)
Speed: 28 knots
Range: 15,000nm (27,800km) at 10 knots
Complement: 1422

HMS *Howe* was the flagship of the Royal Navy's Pacific Fleet in 1945, having taken part in the invasions of Sicily and Italy.

HMS *Howe* was the third of the *King George V*-class battleships. They were built to the Treaty limit of 35,000t even though the treaty itself had expired before any of them was laid down. Improvements in propulsion technology made it possible to generate 110,000hp, carry 10 14in (356mm) guns, and still have first-class protection within that limit, so the designer was hardly hampered by artificial restrictions. *Howe* was built by Fairfield, and commissioned in August 1942, by which time one of her sister ships, the *Prince of Wales*, had already been sunk by Japanese aircraft. The upper strake of her protective belt ran for over half the total length of the ship, between the forward and the after 14in (356mm) magazines, covering the machinery located between them. It terminated in 10in (254mm) and 12in (305mm) bulkheads, while the somewhat lighter lower strake continued for 40ft (12m) more on each end. She had a system of torpedo protection which consisted of three vertical bands of compartments below the belt: the outer and the inner were voids, the middle band being filled with fuel which was replaced with seawater as it was consumed. This system was expected to be proof against a 1000lb (454kg) TNT charge; the four aerial torpedoes which sank the *Prince of Wales* had warheads much smaller than this, but the two most important strikes were on the propeller shafts. The 14in (356mm) guns were in mountings, which allowed elevation to 40 degrees, and were arranged with quadruples forward and aft, and a superfiring pair forward. HMS *Howe* survived the war, was placed in reserve in 1951 and scrapped in 1957.

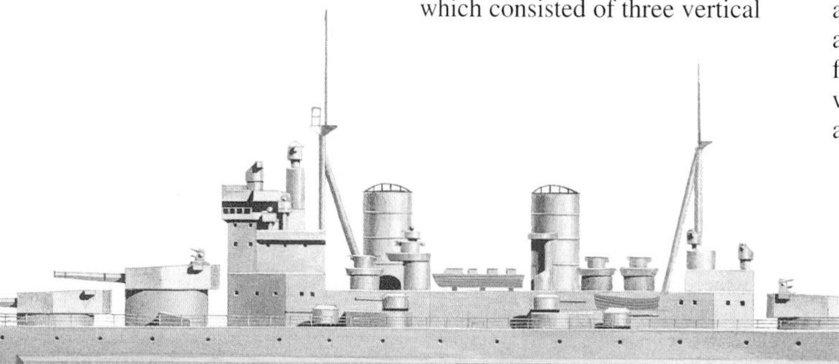

I13

JAPAN: 1944

The *AM*-class submarines Japan constructed under the 1941 War Programme were the biggest built up until that time. Planned to operate as flotilla leaders, these boats were modified to act as scouts for the *STO*-class submarine aircraft carriers. The conning tower was to starboard of the centreline, with the aircraft hangar alongside, giving straight on to the inclined catapult. Only two units were completed; the first of them, *I13*, was sunk off the Japanese coast in July 1945.

Many Japanese headquarters and scout submarines carried one or two aircraft, which were launched by catapult and recovered alongside.

Displacement: 2620t surfaced; 4762t submerged
Dimensions: 373ft x 38 5in x 19ft 4in (113.7m x 11.7m x 5.9m)
Machinery: two-shaft, diesel engines, plus electric motors; 4400bhp/600hp
Armament: six 21in (533mm) TT; one 5.5in (147mm); seven 25mm; two aircraft
Speed: 16.5 knots surfaced; 5.5 knots submerged
Range: 21,000nm (38,900km) at 16 knots surfaced
Complement: 114

I201

JAPAN: 1944

The *ST* class, of which *I201* was the first, represented Japan's first attempt to construct a true submarine. The class was designed to be comparable with the German Type XXI, including streamlined hulls and conning towers, snorkels, and increased battery capacity. Like the Type XXIs, they were largely prefabricated, the sections being electro-welded together. Only three of the class were completed; both *I201* and *I203* were captured by the US Navy, and elements of their design were incorporated into the GUPPY programme.

Displacement: 1070t surfaced; 1450t submerged
Dimensions: 259ft 2in x 19ft x 18ft (79m x 5.8m x 5.5m)
Machinery: two-shaft, diesel engines, plus electric motors; 2750bhp/5000hp
Armament: four 21in (533mm) TT; two 25mm
Speed: 15.5 knots surfaced; 19 knots submerged
Range: 5800nm (12,600km) at 14 knots surfaced
Complement: 31

The *ST*-class boats were some of the first true submarines. They had considerably better performance submerged than on the surface.

I351

JAPAN: 1944

Displacement: 2650t surfaced; 4290t submerged
Dimensions: 364ft 3in x 33ft 4in x 20ft 2in (111m x 10.15m x 6.15m)
Machinery: two-shaft, diesel engines, plus electric motors; 3700bhp/1200hp
Armament: four 21in (533mm) TT; two 3in (76mm) mortars; seven 25mm
Speed: 15.5 knots surfaced; 6 knots submerged
Range: 13,000nm (24,000km) at 14 knots surfaced
Complement: 90

The large submarines of the *SH* class were built as replenishers for seaplanes and flying-boats. They carried up to 300t of aviation fuel, as well as fresh water, food, and ordnance. Their armament was largely defensive, though they did have four torpedo tubes. The first of just two units built, at Kure Navy Yard, *I351* was the only one completed. She entered service early in 1945, and was sunk on 14 July by a US submarine in the East Indies.

The *SH*-class submarines were designed as mobile forward supply bases for reconnaissance aircraft, a practice which began with modified boats in 1940.

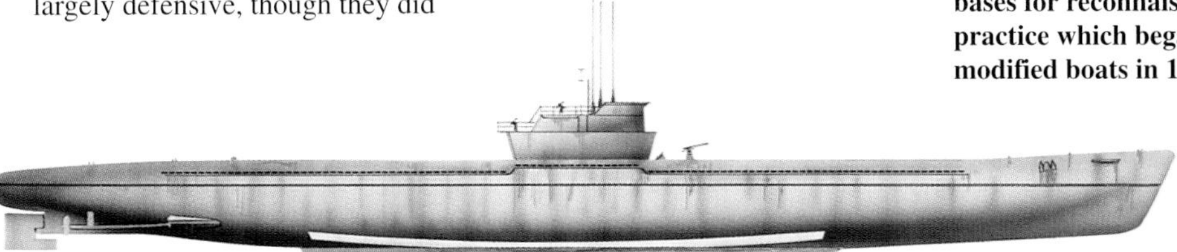

INDEPENDENCE

USA: 1942

As an emergency measure, when the building programme for the *Essex*-class fleet carriers seemed to be slipping behind in 1942, the US President, Franklin D. Roosevelt, ordered that nine *Cleveland*-class large light cruisers then building at New York Shipbuilders in Camden, New Jersey be completed as light aircraft carriers. The resulting ships were cramped, but proved a useful addition to the wartime fleet. The conversion process was simple, and based on the method evolved for adapting merchant ships as escort carriers: the hulls were bulged, which necessitated modifications to the armour belt (*Independence* and *Princeton*, the first and second units delivered, actually had no belt) and the hangar was built up from the (armoured) upper deck level and topped with a wooden flight deck. There was a small island to starboard, ahead of four offset funnels supported by outriggers. USS *Independence* originally mounted 5in (127mm) guns, which were removed after her trials. She survived the war, and was sunk as a target in 1951.

Displacement: 10,660t standard; 14,750t full load
Dimensions: 622ft 6in x 109ft 2in x 24ft 3in (189.75m x 33.25m x 7.4m)
Machinery: four-shaft, General Electric geared turbines; 100,000hp
Armament: 24 (later 28) 40mm; 22 (later 4) 20mm; 30 aircraft
Armour: belt 5.5in (140mm); bulkheads 5in (127mm); deck 2in (51mm)
Speed: 31 knots
Range: 13,000nm (24,000km) at 15 knots
Complement: 1569

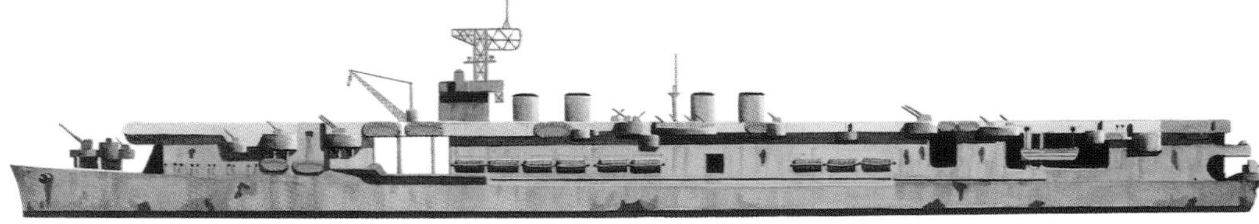

The *Independence*-class light carriers operated 12 fighters, nine dive bombers, and nine torpedo bombers.

INDIANA

USA: 1941

USS *Indiana* was the second of the *South Dakota* class. These were the penultimate class of battleships constructed for the US Navy and the last to be constrained by the between-the-wars naval treaties (though they were overweight as constructed). They were smaller than the preceding *North Carolinas* but roughly the same displacement, having somewhat heavier armour, with the objective of protecting them against 16in (406mm) shells; the real improvement was brought about through design changes rather than enhancement. The internal belt sloped steeply, was taken down to the armoured bulkhead of the torpedo protection system, and experimentation suggested later that it would not be entirely effective; it was never tested in practice. As a result of the reduction in overall length, the upperworks were cramped, and there was considerable potential for blast damage. The powerplant was enlarged slightly to maintain the required top speed of 28 knots. Design work began in 1936. Initially, only *South Dakota* and *Indiana* were to authorized for construction in 1938. *Indiana* was built by Newport News Shipbuilding. Begun in late November

1939, she was completed less than 30 months later, a considerable feat even by American standards. By the time she joined the fleet, the nature of warfare at sea had already changed. Her wartime career was typical of the US Navy's capital ships, consisting largely of protecting carriers and bombarding shore installations; the worst damage she sustained was caused when she collided with USS *Washington* in February 1944, while manoeuvring to refuel destroyers at night. *Indiana* was placed in reserve in 1946, decommissioned in 1947, and stricken in 1962.

Displacement: 37,970t standard; 44,520t full load
Dimensions: 680ft x 108ft 2in x 35ft (207.25m x 32.95m x 10.7m)
Machinery: four-shaft, General Electric geared turbines; 130,000hp
Armament: nine 16in (406mm); 20 5in (127mm), later 48 40mm; 12 1.1in (later deleted), later 56 20mm; 12 0.5in MG (later deleted); three aircraft
Armour: belt 12.2in (310mm); deck 6in (152mm); bulkheads 11in (280mm); barbettes 17.3in–11.3in (440mm–287mm); turret faces 18in (457mm); conning tower 16in (406mm)
Speed: 27.5 knots
Range: 15,000nm (27,800km) at 15 knots
Complement: 1793

The *South Dakota* class was smaller than the preceding *North Carolinas*, with the result that the ships were better protected on the same displacement.

INDOMITABLE

GB: 1940

Displacement: 23,000t standard; 29,730t full load
Dimensions: 753ft 11in x 95ft 9in x 29ft (229.8m x 29.2m x 8.85m)
Machinery: three-shaft, Parsons geared turbines; 111,000hp
Armament: 16 4.5in (114mm); later 12 and later again 25 40mm; 24 (later 48) 2pdr pom-poms (later 36 20mm); 45 (later 56) aircraft
Armour: belt 4.5in (114mm); hangar sides 1.5in (37mm); bulkheads 3in (76mm); flight deck 3in (76mm)
Speed: 30.5 knots
Range: 11,000nm (20,400km) at 14 knots
Complement: 1392 (later 2100)

The carrier *Indomitable* was to have been the fourth ship of the *Illustrious* class, but was extensively modified before completion. Her hangar side armour was reduced from 4.5in (115mm) to 1.5 in, and she was built up to take a second hangar deck; though it did not run the full length of the ship, and had only 14ft (of headroom, it allowed her to operate 50 per cent more aircraft. Like her half-sisters, she had a 3in-thick armoured flight deck as an integral part of her structure. HMS *Indomitable* was constructed by Vickers-Armstrong at Barrow-in-Furness, and was completed and entered service in October 1941. She had a very eventful wartime career, being very severly damaged twice, by bombs in August 1942, which kept her out of action for six months, and by an aerial torpedo in August 1943. She returned to service in April 1944, and survived the rest of the war, to be sold for breaking-up in 1955.

HMS *Indomitable* was something of a compromise, with lighter armour but more hangar space than her half-sisters, but that allowed her to operate 50 per cent more aircraft.

IOWA

USA: 1942

The *Iowa*-class battleships were the largest and fastest battleships ever constructed for the US Navy – and also the last. Freed of treaty-imposed restrictions, their designers were allowed to attempt to create the best ship possible: that all those ships actually completed were in service almost half a century after they were first commissioned perhaps speaks for itself. The designers' only 'artificial' constraint was that the ships be able to make the passage through the Panama Canal; this required that their beam be no more than 110ft (33.55m). The *Iowas* displaced close to 60,000t at extra-deep load. The extra charge hardly affected their performance; they were still capable of well over 30 knots at will (one is said to have made 35 knots, but at reduced displacement). Such impressive performance was obtained by giving them 60 per cent more power than the preceding class of *South Dakotas*, and by increasing their length by almost 30 per cent. The long, narrow bow in particular, with its considerable sheer, was an unmissable feature of the *Iowas*. They had the same protection as the earlier class (though it was never tested in practice), and the same basic 16in (406mm) armament, too, but with the barrels lengthened by 5 calibres. This development increased their offensive range

On average, during deployment during World War II, the *Iowas* consumed fuel at the rate of about 200 gallons per mile (565 litres per km) at a mean speed of just under 18 knots.

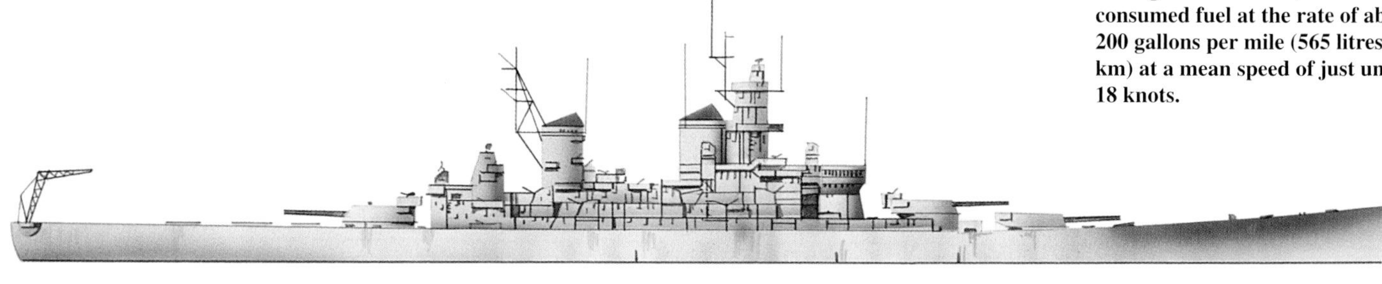

Displacement: 48,110t standard; 57,540t full load
Dimensions: 887ft 3in x 108ft 2in x 36ft 2in (270.45m x 32.95m x 11m)
Machinery: four-shaft, General Electric geared turbines; 212,000hp
Armament: nine 16in (406mm); 20 5in (127mm) HA; 76 40mm; 52 20mm; three aircraft
Armour: belt 12.2in (310mm); deck 6in (152mm); bulkheads 11in (280mm); barbettes 17.3in-11.3in (440mm-287mm); turret faces 19.7in (500mm); conning tower 17.3in (440mm)
Speed: 33 knots
Range: 15,000nm (27,800km) at 15 knots
Complement: 1921

With all 16in (406mm) guns in action, the *Iowa* could deliver 200t of ordnance onto a target over 20 miles (32km) away in less than 10 minutes, at a cost which was calculated at US$1511 per ton.

by around 5,500yd (5030m), to a maximum of over 21nm (39km) – this for a shell which weighed as much as a small car, 2700lb (1225kg). These battleships also carried enormous numbers of light AA guns, though most of them were removed at the end of World War II. *Iowa* was reactivated twice, in 1951–58 and 1983-90. In her later incarnation, she carried two types of surface-to-surface guided weapons: the Tomahawk cruise missile and the Harpoon anti-ship missile. Everything about the ships was massive. They carried 9,320t of fuel and almost 1500t of provisions; the super-firing No 2 ('B') turret, with its barbette, weighed 1240t, and each of its three Mk 7 guns weighed 107t (rated as a 'lightweight' design). The guns could fire just 300 rounds before their barrels had to be re-lined. USS *Iowa* was constructed at New York Navy Yard and entered service on 22 February 1943. She operated out of Atlantic ports for almost a year, before deployment to the Pacific where she was engaged for the rest of the war. She was decommissioned into reserve in 1949 and recommissioned two years later. Laid up in 1958, she returned to active service in April 1984. In 1990, she was again laid up. *Iowa* was stricken from the Navy List, along with her three sister ships, on 13 January 1995, but reinstated in January 1999.

JASON

USA: 1943

The US Navy's repair ships were a vital part of the fleet during World War II. This was especially true of the Pacific Theatre where any reasonably sheltered anchorage was soon turned into a fully-equipped dockyard. The *Vulcan* class, of which USS *Jason* was the last, were the most sophisticated of repair ships, with foundries, forges, and machine shops able to fabricate virtually any component part of a warship. *Jason* had a long career: commissioned in June 1944, she was launched on 3 April 1943; she was decommissioned only in 1995, and sold for scrap.

The *Jason* was rated as a heavy hull-repair ship. Most of her World War II service saw her stationed at Ulithi, and later at Leyte.

Displacement: 9350t standard; 16,900t full load
Dimensions: 529ft 6in x 73ft 4in x 23ft 6in (161.4m x 22.35m x 7.2m)
Machinery: two-shaft, geared turbines; 11,000hp
Armament: four 5in (127mm); eight 40mm
Speed: 19 knots
Complement: 1158

JUNYO

JAPAN: 1941

Junyo was laid down as a 27,500grt passenger liner, *Kashiwara Maru*. While still on the stocks at Mitsubishi's Nagasaki yard, she was taken over by the Imperial Japanese Navy for completion as an aircraft carrier (there is some doubt as to whether it had ever been intended to complete her otherwise). Her spacious hull allowed two hangar decks to be included, though headroom was limited. Two lifts served the 690ft x 89.5ft (210m x 27m) wooden flight deck. No catapult was fitted. She was the first Japanese carrier with the funnel trunked into the island (which was sponsoned out to starboard) as was common American and British practice.

Junyo was commissioned in May 1942, and took part in the Aleutian Islands operation the following month and was also present at Santa Cruz. She was damaged in the Battle of the Philippine Sea and, again, by torpedoes in December 1944. *Junyo* was never repaired and was broken up in 1947.

Displacement: 24,140t standard; 28,300t full load
Dimensions: 719ft 7in x 87ft 8in x 26ft 10in (219.3m x 26.7m x 8.15m)
Machinery: two-shaft, geared turbines; 56,250hp
Armament: 12 5in (127mm) DP; 24 (later 40, later again 76) 25mm; (later six 28-barrelled R/L); 53 aircraft
Armour: deck 1in (25mm) over machinery
Speed: 25 knots
Range: 8000nm (14,800km) at 18 knots
Complement: 1200

The *Junyo* and her sister ship *Hiyo* were laid down as passenger liners. The limited hangar headroom restricted the types of aircraft they could operate.

KAIYO

JAPAN: 1938

Displacement: 13,600t standard; c16,900t full load
Dimensions: 546ft 6in x 71ft 10in x 26ft 6in (166.55m x 21.9m x 8.05m)
Machinery: two-shaft, geared turbines; 52,000hp
Armament: eight 5in (127mm); 24 (later 44) 25mm; (later two 28-barrelled R/L); (later DCs); 24 aircraft
Speed: 24 knots
Complement: 829

The *Kaiyo* began life as the 12,750grt diesel-powered passenger ship, the *Argentina Maru*. The Imperial Japanese Navy took her for use as a troop ship in December 1941. A year later she was taken in hand for conversion to an escort carrier: destroyer-type turbines were fitted, a hangar built over the upper deck, and a wooden flight deck installed. She was employed as an aircraft transport and for aircrew training. She was disabled in 1945 by British aircraft, and later broken up *in situ*.

By the end of 1942, the Japanese had no more use for troop transports. The ex-passenger liner *Argentina Maru* was converted into the escort carrier *Kaiyo*.

KATORI

JAPAN: 1939

The four ships which made up the *Katori* class were ordered in two pairs, in 1938 and 1940. They were designated training ships, the size of small cruisers but only comparatively lightly armed, but only three were completed and they subsequently saw service in World War II as headquarters ships to escort vessels and submarine flotillas. They were actually of rather limited value as warships: even though their anti-aircraft armament was considerably enhanced by 1944, they were badly underpowered, and only barely capable of achieving as their maximum the cruising speed of the main body of the Japanese fleet. *Katori* was constructed, like all the ships of the class, by Mitsubishi at Yokohama. She entered service in April 1940. Crippled off the island of Truk in mid-February 1944, the *Katori* was subsequently sunk by gunfire from US cruisers and destroyers.

The size of a small cruiser, the *Katoris* were nonetheless of only limited value as warships. They served as headquarters ships to escort vessels and submarine flotillas.

Displacement: 5890t standard; c6400t full load
Dimensions: 425ft 9in x 52ft 4in x 18ft 10in (129.8m x 15.95m x 5.75m)
Machinery: two-shaft COSAD, geared turbines plus diesel engines; 8000hp
Armament: four 140mm (5.5in); two (later six) 127mm (5in) DP; four (later 20, later 30) 25mm; (later eight 13.2mm MG); DC racks; one aircraft (later deleted)
Speed: 18 knots
Range: not available
Complement: not available

KD7 Class

JAPAN: 1941–43

Displacement: 1630t surfaced; 2600t submerged
Dimensions: 346ft 2in x 27ft 1in x 15ft 1in (105.5m x 8.25m x 4.6m)
Machinery: two-shaft, diesel engines, plus electric motors; 8000bhp/1800hp
Armament: six 533mm (21in) TT; one 4.7in (120mm); two 25mm
Speed: 23 knots surfaced; 8 knots submerged
Range: 8000nm (14,800km) at 16 knots surfaced
Complement: 88

The *KD*-type submarines were first-class ocean-going boats, though comparatively small by later Japanese standards. They were constructed in nine quite separate groups (some of only one unit, clearly as experiments). The *KD7*s were the last group, 10 of which were completed between August 1942 and September 1943. All but one – *I 179* – were sunk by Allied action, the exception having foundered during an accident in training in July 1943. Many were converted to transports, some to carry a landing-craft.

When the *KD7*s were running on the surface, with their powerful machinery on a relatively light displacement, they were among the fastest submarine classes.

Kelly

GB: 1938

Displacement: 1760t standard; 2330t full load
Dimensions: 356ft 6in x 35ft 8in x 13ft 8in (108.65m x 10.85m x 4.2m)
Machinery: two-shaft, Parsons geared turbines; 40,000hp
Armament: six 4.7in (119mm); four 2pdr pom-poms; 10 21in (533mm) TT; DC racks
Speed: 36 knots
Range: 6000nm (11,100km) at 15 knots
Complement: 218

HMS *Kelly* was the designated leader of the eight-ship 'K' flotilla of fleet destroyers constructed, along with the 'Js' and 'Ns', from 1937 onwards. Their construction introduced the more robust longitudinal framing into British destroyers. They mounted the improved 4.7in (119mm) Mk XII gun in twin gunhouses, instead of single Mk IXs, which made their centrelines much less crowded. HMS *Kelly* was constructed by Hawthorne Leslie and was commissioned in 1939. She was sunk off Crete in May 1941.

The *Kelly* was to become one of the most famous ships of the Royal Navy during World War II. Her career was dramatised by Noel Coward in his film *In Which We Serve*.

Kirov

USSR: 1936

The *Kirov* was the first cruiser ever constructed from the keel up by the Soviet Union, under the second Five Year Plan (1933–37). She was built at the Ordzhonikidze Yard in Leningrad (St Petersburg) from designs prepared by Ansaldo in Italy. It is not surprising, therefore, that she bore a close resemblance to Italian cruisers of the period. The design was modified by Russian naval architects, who rated the original as too weak, and planned displacement went up by 10 per cent as a result. *Kirov* was ready for trials in August 1937, but did not commission until over a year later, it being necessary to make many modifications, probably as a result of the yard's inexperience. She never moved further than Tallin during World War II, mainly operating in the defence of Leningrad, and she was twice damaged in air raids. She had a nondescript career post-war, and spent much of her time laid up, but was not stricken until 1975.

Kirov is probably best regarded as an over-gunned light cruiser, with inadequate protection and high speed; in the latter respects she betrayed her Italian origins.

Displacement: 7880t standard; 9436t full load
Dimensions: 626ft 8in x 57ft 11in x 23ft 9in (191m x 17.65m x 7.25m)
Machinery: two-shaft COSAD, geared turbines plus cruising diesels; 113,000hp
Armament: nine 7.1in (180mm); six (later eight) 3.9in (100mm); six 45mm (later deleted); later five, later 10, later 18 37mm; four 12.7mm MG; six 21in (533mm) TT; four DC throwers; 100 mines; two aircraft
Armour: belt 2in (50mm); deck 2in (50mm); barbettes 2in (50mm); turrets 3in (75mm); conning tower 5.9in (150mm)
Speed: 36 knots
Range: not available
Complement: 734

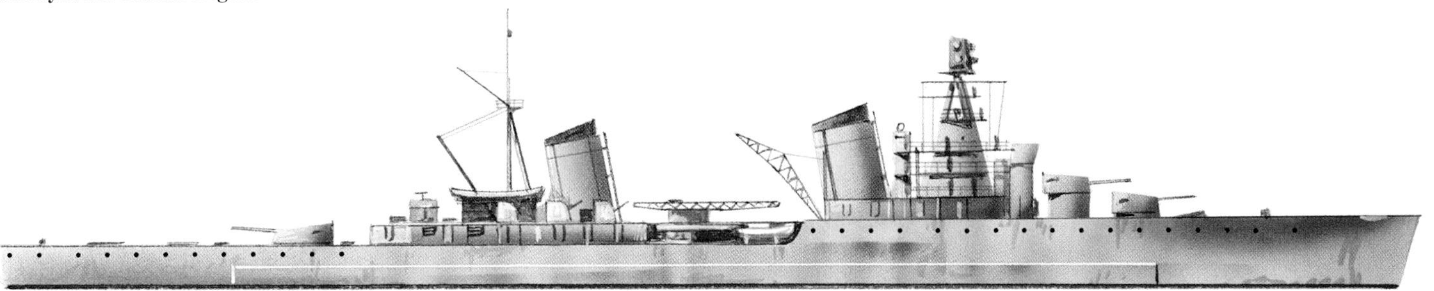

KOMET

GERMANY: 1938

Komet was the smallest of the German armed raiders of World War II. She was built by Deutschewerft as the MS *Ems* and commissioned as *Schiff 45* in June 1940. *Komet* had a reinforced stem, and her first voyage took her along the Arctic coast of the Soviet Union and, via the Bering Straits, into the Pacific. There she sank 10 ships, and eventually returned to Hamburg after a voyage of 516 days. She was less lucky on her second sortie, being sunk in the English Channel by a British MTB.

Many armed raiders carried a midget MTB. The one carried by the *Komet* was actually a midget minelayer, 17.7in (450mm) torpedoes not then being available, and magnetic mines having been substituted.

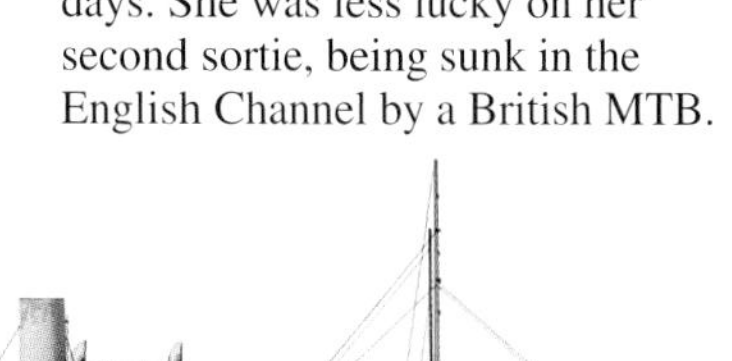

Displacement: 7500t normal
Dimensions: 377ft 3in x 50ft 2in x 21ft 4in (115m x 15.3m x 6.5m)
Machinery: one-shaft, two MAN two-stroke diesels; 3900bhp
Armament: six 5.9in (150mm); one 60mm; two 37mm; four 20mm; six 21in (533mm) TT; two aircraft; one MTB
Speed: 14.5 knots
Range: 12,000nm (22,200km) at 12 knots
Complement: 269

KORMORAN

GERMANY: 1939

Displacement: 19,900t normal
Dimensions: 538ft x 66ft 3in x 27ft 10in (164m x 20.2m x 8.5m)
Machinery: two-shaft diesel electric, four Krupp four-stroke diesels plus two Siemens electric motors; 16,000hp
Armament: six 5.9in (150mm); one 75mm (later deleted); four 37mm; five 20mm; six 21in (533mm) TT; 360 mines; two aircraft; one MTB
Speed: 18 knots
Range: 12,000nm (22,200km) at 12 knots
Complement: 400

Kormoran, the former MS *Steiermark*, was the only German armed raider to sink a major warship (though the destruction was mutual). Built by Germaniawerft, she was commissioned as *Schiff 41* in October 1940. She sank or captured 11 Allied ships in the course of a 350-day cruise into the Indian Ocean. She met – and surprised – the cruiser HMAS *Sydney* off Shark Bay, Western Australia, on 11 November 1941, and sank her with gunfire with great loss of life, but was herself crippled and later scuttled.

Armed raiders were chosen for their resemblance to well-known merchantmen. *Kormoran* played the ruse out to the last, taking the *Sydney* completely by surprise.

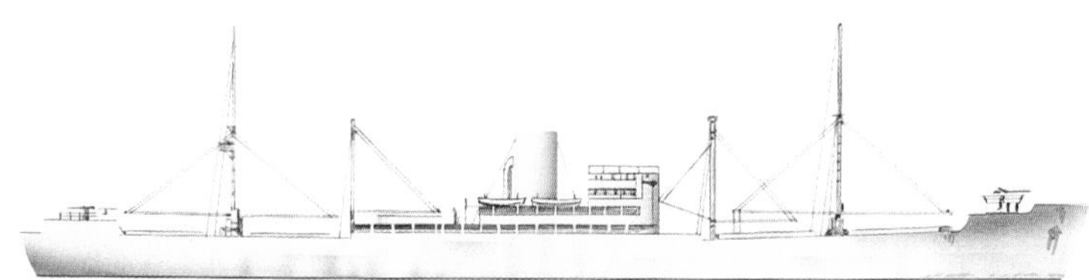

LA ARGENTINA

ARGENTINA: 1937

Vickers-Armstrong at Barrow-in-Furness constructed a somewhat modified *Arethusa*-class light cruiser for the Argentine Navy in the latter part of the 1930s. Its purpose was to serve primarily as a training ship with space for 60 cadets on top of her normal complement. *La Argentina* was longer and heavier than the British ships and, in terms of both habitability and sea-kindliness, was all the better for it, the *Arethusas* being very cramped. She had similar levels of protection but carried 50 per cent more 6in (152mm) guns, having exchanged twin turrets for triples. (One of the most frequently-voiced criticisms of the *Arethusas* was that they were under-gunned; mounting triple turrets was a very sensible solution.) Less powerful machinery, plus an increase in displacement. meant that she was at least 3 knots slower than her half-sisters. She was delivered a year late, in January 1939, thanks to the sheer volume of work in British yards at the time. *La Argentina* was to remain in service for 35 years.

***La Argentina* was an enlarged and improved version of the British *Arethusas*, held to be the smallest viable cruisers of the period.**

Displacement: 6500t standard; 7500t full load
Dimensions: 541ft 2in x 56ft 6in x 16ft 6in (164.95m x 17.2m x 5.05m)
Machinery: four-shaft, Parsons geared turbines; 54,000hp
Armament: nine 6in (152mm); four 4in (102mm); eight 2pdr; six 21in (533mm) TT; one aircraft
Armour: belt 3in (76mm); deck 2in (51mm); turrets 2in (51mm); conning tower 3in (76mm)
Speed: 30 knots
Range: 8000nm (14,800km) at 20 knots
Complement: 556

LA BAYONNAISE

FRANCE: 1936

In 1934, France elected to exploit, as too did Italy, the provision of the 1930 London Treaty which permitted the unlimited construction of warships of under 600t. She laid down *La Melpomène* as the leader of a class of 12, designated as *torpilleurs* (torpedo-boats), and intended for service in the Mediterranean. They proved to be fast – all made 36.5 knots at standard displacement on trial, and were capable of 32 knots at full load. Speed was widely held to be their only virtue, for they were generally unstable and were poor sea-keepers. *La Bayonnaise* was to be the fifth of them, constructed by Chantiers Maritime du Sud Ouest at Bordeaux; she entered service in 1937. She was scuttled at Toulon on 27 November 1942, but raised by the Italians, and enlisted as *FR 45*. With repairs incomplete she was transferred to the *Kriegsmarine* as *TA 13* in April 1943. Still not completed, she was scuttled again as a block-ship, in August 1944.

The *La Melpomène* class were undistinguished and unsatisfactory small warships, overweight, wet and unstable. One actually capsized.

Displacement: 680t standard; 895t full load
Dimensions: 264ft 9in x 26ft 1in x 10ft 1in (80.7m x 7.95m x 3.05m)
Machinery: two-shaft, Parsons geared turbines; 22,000hp
Armament: two 100mm (3.9in); four 13.2mm MG; two 550mm (21.7in) TT; one towed AS torpedo; one DC rack
Speed: 35 knots
Range: 1000nm (1850km) at 20 knots
Complement: 105

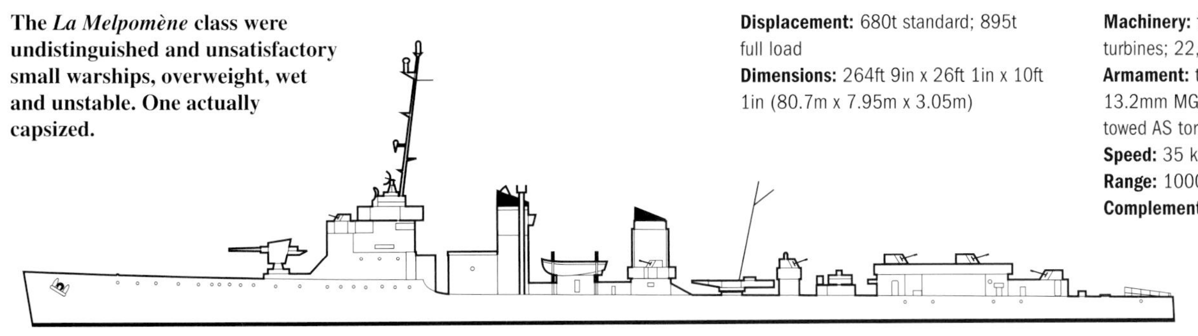

LCI(L)

GB/USA: 1942–1944

Displacement: 194t standard; 387t full load
Dimensions: 158ft 6in x 23ft 8in x 2ft 8in (forward), 5ft (aft) (48.3m x 7.2m x 0.8m, 1.5m)
Machinery: two-shaft, diesel; 2320bhp
Armament: four 20mm; 188 troops or 75t
Speed: 15.5 knots
Range: 8500nm (15,750km) at 12 knots (fuel as cargo)
Complement: 24

Well over a thousand LCI(L)s were built for the invasion of Europe; they crossed the Atlantic under their own power.

The 200-ton Landing Craft, Infantry (Large) was designed, in the United Kingdom, as a vehicle for raiding parties. They were relatively seaworthy – most had conventional stems and troops disembarked via gangways, but others had ramps – and crossed the Atlantic from the USA under their own power. Some were converted as fire support ships in many different forms, and others as flotilla flagships. Construction began in the USA in October 1942 and ended two years later, by which time well over a thousand had been built.

Lexington

USA: 1942

Displacement: 27,200t standard; 34,880t full load
Dimensions: 872ft x 96ft x 27ft 6in (265.8m x 29.25m x 8.4m)
Machinery: four-shaft, Westinghouse geared turbines; 150,000hp
Armament: 12 5in (127mm); 32 (later 68) 40mm; 46 (later 60) 20mm; (later 20 0.5in MG); 91 aircraft
Armour: belt 4in-2.5in (102mm-62mm); hangar deck 2.5in (62mm); deck 1.5in (37mm)
Speed: 32.5 knots
Range: 15,000nm (27,800km) at 15 knots
Complement: 2682

By 1937, the Washington Treaty had lapsed, and the only restrictions on the ships the US Navy could build were imposed by Congress. In May, it voted funds to construct carriers up to 40,000t; the *Hornet*, a third *Yorktown*, took up less than half that, and designers began drawing up plans for a slightly improved version based on a requirement to carry 10 per cent more aircraft and offer improved protection. The result was a design for a ship some 30 per cent bigger than the *Yorktowns*, which when realised would set a standard for fleet aircraft carriers of the period, the *Essex* class. The designers had one thing working in their favour – advances in steam machinery since the *Yorktown* was built meant they could make considerable weight savings in that area, while actually increasing the installed power by 25 per cent. The new ships were to be 50ft (15.2m) longer on the waterline than the *Yorktowns*, and 10ft (3m) broader abeam, still allowing them to pass the Panama Canal easily; they were almost 50 per cent heavier at standard displacement, and much of the disproportionate increase came about as a result of their protection being increased by the addition of a second, thicker, armoured deck. USS *Lexington* was the second or third *Essex* to be laid down – her sister ship *Bunker Hill* was laid down alongside her the same day – by Bethlehem Steel at Quincy, Massachusetts (as USS *Cabot*; her name was changed after the original 'Lady Lex' was scuttled after the Battle of the Coral Sea in

As completed, *Lexington* had two hydraulic catapults (of the class, only *Oriskany* had the more powerful steam catapults), one forward on the flight deck, the other athwartships on the hangar deck. This latter proved to be less than useful.

The *Essex*-class carriers were the first to have deck-edge lifts. This development simplified flight deck organization and would later become standard. The single unit fitted amidships, opposite the island, folded up when not in use.

May 1942). She entered service, the second of the class, just 73 weeks later on 17 February 1943. She was to have the longest career of any of them, not finally decommissioning, to be preserved as a museum at Corpus Christi, Texas, until December 1991. She served as the flagship of Task Force 58 during the war in the Pacific, and was present at every major engagement from Tarawa to Tokyo. During the Battle of Leyte Gulf, in October 1944, her aircraft were solely responsible for sinking the carrier *Zuikako* and the cruiser *Nachi*, and were instrumental in sinking the battleship *Musashi* and the carriers *Chitose* and *Zuiho*. In reserve from April 1947, she was transferred to Puget Sound Navy Yard in September 1953, where she underwent the SCB-125 conversion. This re-configured her flightdeck to incorporate an angled landing area, enclosed her foredeck, modified her island, strengthened her arrester gear, and enlarged her forward lift, and she recommissioned in August 1955. She succeeded *Antietam* as the US Navy's training carrier in 1963.

LONG ISLAND

USA: 1940

USS *Long Island* was the first American escort carrier, converted from the merchantman *Mormacmail*, a diesel-power C-3 type. In the event, the powerplant proved unsatisfactory and her captain recommended that future conversions employ steam-powered ships of the same type. As a result, the USS *Bogues* had turbine machinery, though it proved to be no more powerful. Four other diesel-powered ships were built: of these, three were passed on to Britain and served as the *Avengers* and one, USS *Charger*, was retained as a training ship. The *Long Island* conversion was simple: a light structure, 70 per cent the length of the ship, enclosed for its after third, built on the upper deck to serve as a hangar and topped with a wooden flight deck, the two communicating by a single lift. The flight deck was subsequently lengthened by 60ft (18m), her aircraft capacity quadrupling. *Long Island* later served as an aircraft transport, survived the war, and was sold back into the merchant service in 1949. She was hulked at Rotterdam in 1966.

Since she was diesel powered, *Long Island* had no need of a funnel. She had no island, the navigating bridge being below the leading edge of the flight deck.

Displacement: 11,800t standard; 15,130t full load
Dimensions: 492ft x 102ft x 25ft 2in (149.95m x 31.1m x 7.65m)
Machinery: one-shaft, diesel; 8500bhp
Armament: one 4in (102mm) (later one 5in (127mm)); two 3in (76mm); (later 40 20mm); four 0.5in MG (later deleted); 16 aircraft
Speed: 16.5 knots
Range: 10,000nm (18,500km) at 14 knots
Complement: 856

LOOKOUT

GB: 1940

The Royal Navy's *L*- and *M*-class destroyers were enlarged versions of the *J* class. They were fitted with higher-power machinery and new, much more powerful, 4.7in (120mm) guns. These guns, on twin mounts in weatherproof gunhouses, were delivered late so four ships had four pairs of 4in (102mm) in high-angle mounts instead. HMS *Lookout* had the 4.7in (120mm). She was built by Scotts, and entered service in 1941. She survived the war but was immediately decommissioned. *Lookout* was broken up in 1948.

Save for the *Tribal* class, the *L* and *M* classes were the best-armed destroyers in service with the Royal Navy during World War II.

Displacement: 1920t standard; 2660t (later 2810t) full load
Dimensions: 362ft 6in x 36ft 9in x 14ft 6in (110.50m x 11.2m x 4.4m)
Machinery: two-shaft, Parsons geared turbines; 48,000hp
Armament: six 4.7in (120mm); (later one 4in (102mm) HA); four 2pdr pom-poms; (later 10 20mm); eight (later four) 21in (533mm) TT; DC racks
Speed: 36 knots
Range: 6000nm (11,100km) at 20 knots
Complement: 190

LSM(R)

USA: 1944–1945

The design for the Landing Ship, Medium was evolved during 1943 and construction began the following year. It was supposed to fill the gap between the Landing Ship (Tank) and the Landing Craft (Tank) and be seaworthy enough to make ocean passages under its own power. In fact, many of these vessels were converted to act as fire support ships and designated as LSM(R)s; they mounted both guns and mortars, and had large numbers of rocket launchers installed in the open well deck.

The LSM(R)s were designed to give massive close-range fire support to opposed amphibious landings.

Displacement: 783t (later 826t; 924t) standard
Dimensions: 203ft 6in x 34ft 6in x 5ft 6in (later 5ft 9in; 6ft 9in) (62m x 10.5m x 1.68m (later 1.75m; 2.05m))
Machinery: two-shaft, diesel; 2800bhp
Armament: one 5in (127mm); (later four 4.2in (108mm) mortars); two (later four) 40mm; three (later eight) 20mm; 105 (later 85; 20) R/L
Speed: 13 knots
Range: 4900nm (9100km) - later 3000nm (5600km) - at 12 knots
Complement: 81 (later 143)

LST

USA: 1944–1945

Displacement: 1625t standard; 4080t full load
Dimensions: 328ft x 50ft x 3ft 11in (forward), 9ft 10in (aft) (100m x 15.25m x 1.2m (3m))
Machinery: two-shaft, diesel; 1800hp
Armament: seven (later eight) 40mm; 12 (later 20) 20mm; 20 tanks; 163 troops
Speed: 12 knots
Range: 24,000nm (44,450km) at 9 knots (fuel as cargo)
Complement: 111

The Landing Ship, Tank (they were popularly known as Large Slow Targets) were constructed in the USA in response to a British requirement for a class of ships which could transport tanks from the American factories where they were built directly to the invasion beaches of Europe. They proved very adaptable, and many were converted to carry tank and personnel landing craft, or to act as tenders or repair ships; a total of over 1150 were built.

The LSTs were the biggest ships of World War II, and capable of both crossing an ocean and delivering their cargo straight to the beach.

M261

GERMANY: 1941

The German minesweepers of World War II were very versatile small warships. They were equally at home as escorts or employed as small AA ships.

The coal-burning 1940-type minesweepers built for the German Navy were simpler than the previous class, the 1935 type. They owed much to ships constructed during World War I. The design itself was prepared by Deutsche-werft, but the ships were built at a large number of yards, *M261*, the first of the class, being constructed by Atlas. She was commissioned in September 1942 and taken as a British prize in 1945. She was broken up in 1948.

Displacement: 545t standard; 775t full load
Dimensions: 204ft 5in x 27ft 10in x 9ft 2in (62.3m x 8.5m x 2.8m)
Machinery: two-shaft, vertical triple-expansion, plus exhaust-driven turbines; 2400hp
Armament: one (later two) 4.1in (105mm); later three 40mm; one 37mm (later deleted); seven (later eight) 20mm
Speed: 16.5 knots
Range: 4000nm (7400km) at 10 knots
Complement: 68-80

M601

GERMANY: 1944

For successors to the 1940-type minesweepers, the *Kriegsmarine* commissioned a design which would allow similar-sized ships to be prefabricated in seven sections right across Europe from Rostock to Toulon, and assembled at the rate of one per week per yard. They were to be built in four standard versions for employment in the original role; as submarine chasers; as torpedo boats and as training ships. A total of just 21 were completed and commissioned between November 1944 and the war's end. *M601* was the first of the type, constructed at the Neptun yard. She was taken as a British prize in 1945, and broken up three years later.

Displacement: 580t standard; 820t full load
Dimensions: 222ft 5in x 29ft 6in x 8ft 10in (67.8m x 9m x 2.7m)
Machinery: two-shaft, vertical triple-expansion, plus exhaust-driven turbines; 2400hp
Armament: two 4.2in (105mm) DP; two 37mm; 8 20mm; one 73mm R/L
Speed: 16.5 knots
Range: 4000nm (7400km) at 10 knots
Complement: 107

MAGPIE

GB: 1943

Displacement: 1350t (later 1490t) standard; 1880t (later 1950t) full load
Dimensions: 299ft 6in x 38ft 6in x 11ft 6in (91.3m x 11.75m x 3.5m)
Machinery: two-shaft, Parsons geared turbines; 4300hp
Armament: six 4in (102mm) DP; (later four 40mm); five 20mm; (later Hedgehog); DC throwers; DC racks
Speed: 20 knots
Range: 6000nm (11,100km) at 12 knots
Complement: 192

The last class of sloops built for the Royal Navy were a modified version of the *Black Swans* of 1938. They were more heavily armed than frigates of similar displacement and, as they were designed for colonial duties in peacetime, they were rather more habitable. The extra space available was soon taken over for additional weapons, and the weight of depth charges carried aft soon caused problems with hull deformation and sprung welds. These were complex ships and therefore expensive to construct. Only 29 were built, two of them for the Royal Indian Navy, and five more were cancelled. Many were to remain in service until the 1960s or even later. In World War II five were lost, all in actions involving German submarines. HMS *Magpie* was built by Thornycroft at Portsmouth and was completed on 30 August 1943. Her wartime service was in the North Atlantic. She survived and was later scrapped, in 1959.

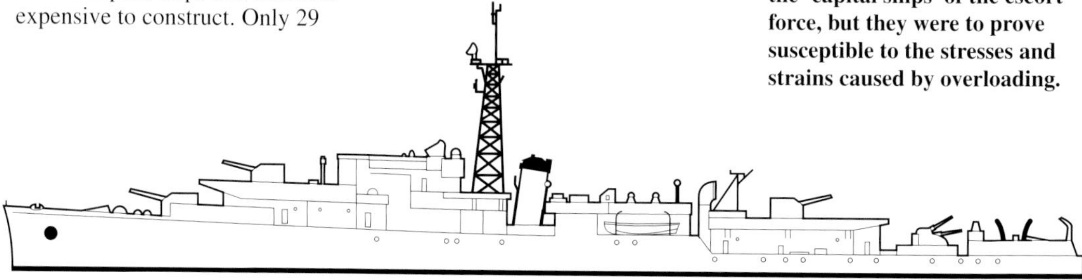

The *Black Swans* were regarded as the 'capital ships' of the escort force, but they were to prove susceptible to the stresses and strains caused by overloading.

MATSU

JAPAN: 1944

Japan began constructing escort destroyers only in 1943, and it was April of the following year before *Matsu*, the leader of the first class, entered service. The equivalent of the American destroyer escorts or the British *Hunts*, and designed to be built quickly by non-specialist yards, the *Matsus* carried considerably heavier armament, including the 'Long Lance' torpedo. A follow-up class, the *Tachibanas*, had similar dimensions and weapons but a simpler hull form, to reduce construction costs even further.

The *Matsus* were the Japanese equivalent of the American *Des* or the British *Hunts*, but were more heavily armed than either.

Displacement: 1260t standard; 1660t full load
Dimensions: 328ft x 30ft 8in x 10ft 10in (100m x 9.35m x 3.3m)
Machinery: two-shaft, geared turbines; 19,000hp
Armament: three 5in (127mm); 24 25mm; four 24in (610mm) TT; DC racks
Speed: 27.5 knots
Range: 6000nm (11,100km) at 18 knots
Complement: not available

MIKURA

JAPAN: 1943

In addition to its escort destroyers, Japan also constructed smaller, even less sophisticated escorts, in four groups, latterly making use of prefabrication and electro-welding. These techniques combined to reduce construction times (of what were rather smaller ships) to less than four months. *Mikura* was the lead ship of the second group. She was optimized for anti-submarine operations, with reduced AA armament and a total of 120 depth charges. This configuration enabled her to carry four times the load carried by the escort destroyers, though in 1945 many light AA guns were added.

The Japanese 1000t-class escorts were similar in character to the British *Castles*, but were more heavily armed, in accordance with Japanese practice.

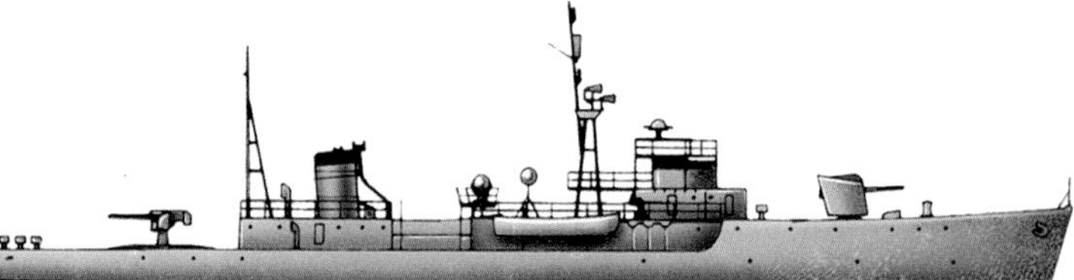

Displacement: 940t standard; 1060t full load
Dimensions: 258ft 6in x 29ft 10in x 10ft (78.8m x 9.1m x 3.05m)
Machinery: two-shaft, diesel; 4200bhp
Armament: three 4.7in (120mm); four 25mm; DC racks
Speed: 19.5 knots
Range: 6000nm (11,100km) at 16 knots
Complement: 150

MINAS GERAIS

BRAZIL: 1908–36

Brazil ordered two dreadnought battleships from Britain in 1906, while engaged in a building 'war' with its neighbours, Argentina and Chile. The first ship, built at Armstrong's famed Elswick yard, was the *Minas Gerais*; for a brief period after she was first commissioned, in 1910, she was the most powerful ship in the world. In 1934, she was taken in hand for a reconstruction which – despite being nowhere near as extensive as those carried out in American and Italian battleships – was to last five years. The first essential was to re-boiler the ship, to allow her to burn oil instead of coal; in the process her two wide-set funnels were trunked into one, and she was given a tripod mast and new bridge works. Most of the 4.7in (119mm) guns mounted in main deck casemates were removed and a pair of similar-calibre AA guns were added. *Minais Gerais* was sold in 1953. *São Paulo* was lost at sea in bad weather.

The *Minas Gerais* and her sister ship *São Paulo* were unique amongst post-1906 battleships in having reciprocating, rather than turbine, engines; the *Minas Gerais* powerplant was not renewed during her 1934 reconstruction.

Displacement: 19,200t standard; 21,200t full load
Dimensions: 543ft x 83ft x 28ft (165.5m x 25.3m x 8.5m)
Machinery: two-shaft, vertical triple expansion engines; 23,500hp
Armament: 12 12in (305mm); 12 4.7in (120mm); two 4.7in (120mm) AA; eight 3pdrs
Armour: belt 9in-4in (228mm-102mm); turret faces 9in (228mm); conning tower 12in (305mm)
Speed: 21 knots
Range: 10,000nm (18,500km) at 10 knots
Complement: 900

MIZUHO

JAPAN: 1938

The *Mizuho* was virtually a repeat of the *Chitose*, but with several important differences: her powerplant was diesel-only, which cut 7 knots from her top speed, she lacked the protective deck over the seaplane handling area, and was more heavily armed. In 1941 she was modified: her after seaplane recovery gear was landed, and she was equipped to carry and operate 12 midget submarines instead. *Mizuho* was sunk by the US submarine *Drum*, on 2 May 1942.

It is likely that, had *Mizuho* not been sunk in 1942, she would have followed her half-sisters *Chitose* and *Chiyoda* and been converted to a light aircraft carrier.

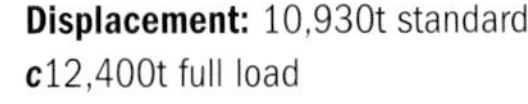

Displacement: 10,930t standard; **c**12,400t full load
Dimensions: 631ft 6in x 61ft 8in x 23ft 3in (192.5m x 18.8m x 7.1m)
Machinery: two-shaft, diesel; 15,200bhp
Armament: six 5in (127mm); 12 25mm; 24 (later 12) aircraft, later 12 midget submarines
Speed: 22 knots
Range: 8000nm (14,800km) at 16 knots
Complement: not available

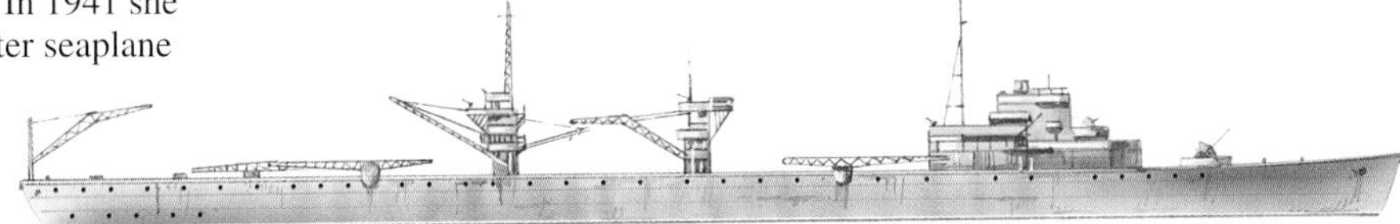

MOHAWK

GB: 1937

The *Tribal*-class destroyers were a new departure for the Royal Navy, inspired by France, Germany, Japan and the United States – all nations with heavily-armed destroyers already at sea (or, as with the US Navy's *Somers* class, in construction). The displacement of any new class of destroyers was limited by treaty to 1850t (though the *Tribal*s were to exceed that), with guns of less than 5.1in (130mm) calibre. The Admiralty's decision was to mount new models of 4.7in (119mm) guns in five twin mountings in the belief that their faster rate of fire would make up for their lighter weight. A design review later concluded that one pair, in the 'Q' position replacing a bank of torpedo tubes, could be replaced by a pair of quad 2pdr pom-poms. As completed, the *Tribal*s were thus the first British destroyers to have an effective light AA armament; later, many ships would lose the 4.7in (120-mm) in the 'X' position, too, replaced by a pair of 4in (102mm) HA guns. Some of the extra length gained went into the foreship: the class had a sharply-raked stem which was to find its way into the largest group of British destroyers, the *S* to *W* classes. All the British *Tribal*s were laid down during 1936/37 and took about two years to complete. HMS *Mohawk* was built by Thornycroft at Portsmouth and entered service in October 1938. She was sunk in the course of a fierce battle on 16 April 1941 with the very similar Italian *Navigatori*-class destroyer *Luca Tarigo*, which managed to torpedo *Mohawk* while under fire from her and her sister ship *Nubian*, as well as the two *J*-class destroyers *Jervis* and *Janus*, before succumbing herself.

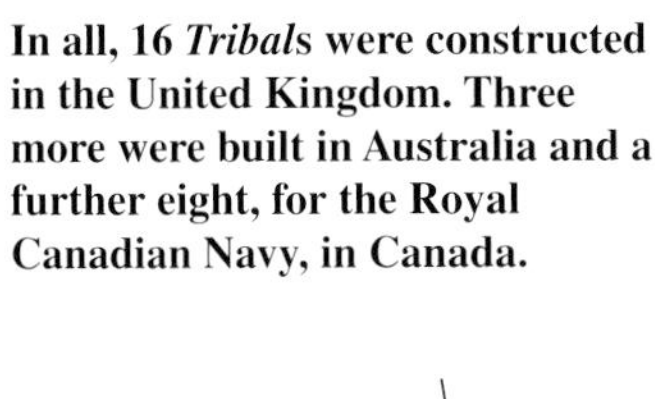

In all, 16 *Tribal*s were constructed in the United Kingdom. Three more were built in Australia and a further eight, for the Royal Canadian Navy, in Canada.

Displacement: 1960t standard; 2520t full load
Dimensions: 377ft x 36ft 6in x 13ft (114.9m x 11.15m x 3.95m)
Machinery: two-shaft, Parsons geared turbines; 44,000hp
Armament: eight 4.7in (120mm); eight 2pdr pom-poms; four 21in (533mm) TT; DC racks
Speed: 36 knots
Range: 6000nm (11,100km) at 20 knots
Complement: 190

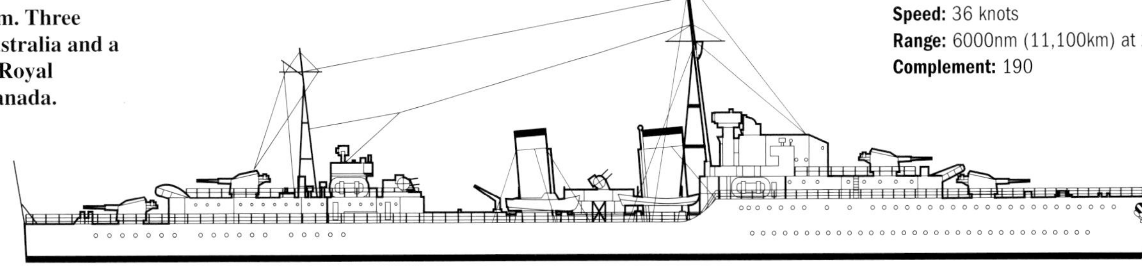

No 71

JAPAN: 1938

Displacement: 195t surfaced; 240t submerged
Dimensions: 140ft 5in x 10ft 11in x 10ft 2in (42.8m x 3.3m x 3.1m)
Machinery: one-shaft, diesel engines, plus electric motors; 300bhp/1800hp
Armament: three 18in (457mm) TT
Speed: 13 knots surfaced; 21 knots submerged
Range: 2200nm (4100km) at 12 knots surfaced
Complement: 11

In August 1938, the Imperial Japanese Navy began experimenting with a small submarine. The boat was a testbed for new battery and powerplant technology designed to optimize underwater performance. The results fell short of aspirations and expected surface performance proved poor, thanks to substituting Japanese diesels for the 1200bhp German units specified. However, the boat was to provide important data which would be incorporated into the design of the wartime *ST* and *STS* classes.

***No 71* was a purely experimental submersible, her three torpedo tubes included only for trials purposes. She was broken up in 1940.**

North Carolina

USA: 1940

The USS *North Carolina* and her sister ship the *Washington* were the first new battleships constructed for the US Navy since the *West Virginia* was completed in December 1923. The new class broke with the American tradition of emphasising protection and firepower at the expense of speed. This was in line with capital ship development in Britain, France, and Germany; these countries were building ships of over 35,000t permitting inclusion of all three elements. Initially, the new ships were to have mounted nine 14in guns, with enough installed power to drive the ships at 30 knots, but, at the last minute, the Chief of Naval Operations added two (later three) guns at the expense of two knots off the top speed. All along, it had been a stipulation that the triple/quadruple 14in (356mm) turrets should be replaceable by 16in (406mm) triples. This forethought was rewarded when the Japanese refused to accept the clause in the 1936 London agreement which limited this class to 14in (356mm) guns; subsequently, the *North Carolinas* were completed with nine 16in (406mm) guns. USS *North Carolina* was constructed at the New York Navy Yard and completed in April 1941. She was not fully worked up until early 1942, but after that took part in most of the major actions until the war's end. She was only once seriously damaged, by a submarine torpedo, just after Guadalcanal. The *North Carolina* was decommissioned in June 1960 and, the following year, presented to the people of the State whose name she bears, to be preserved as a memorial at Willmington.

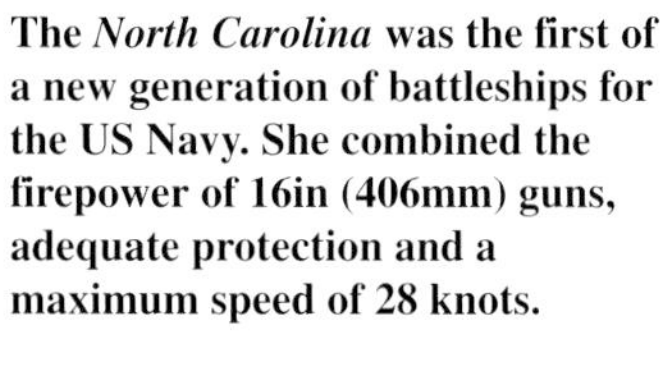

The *North Carolina* was the first of a new generation of battleships for the US Navy. She combined the firepower of 16in (406mm) guns, adequate protection and a maximum speed of 28 knots.

Displacement: 37,485t standard; 44,380t full load
Dimensions: 728ft 9in x 108ft 4in x 33ft (222.1m x 33m x 10m)
Machinery: four-shaft, General Electric geared turbines; 121,000hp
Armament: nine 16in (406mm); 20 5in (127mm), (later 60 40mm); 16 1.1in (later deleted), (later 83 20mm; 12 0.5in MG (later deleted); three aircraft
Armour: belt 12in (305mm); deck 5.5in (140mm); bulkheads 11in (280mm); barbettes 16in-14.7in (406mm-373mm); turret faces 16in (406mm); conning tower 16in (406mm)
Speed: 28 knots
Range: 15,000nm (27,800km) at 15 knots
Complement: 1793

Norton Sound

USA: 1943

Displacement: 12,800t standard; 15,100t full load
Dimensions: 540ft 5in x 69ft 3in x 22ft 3in (164.7m x 21.1m x 6.8m)

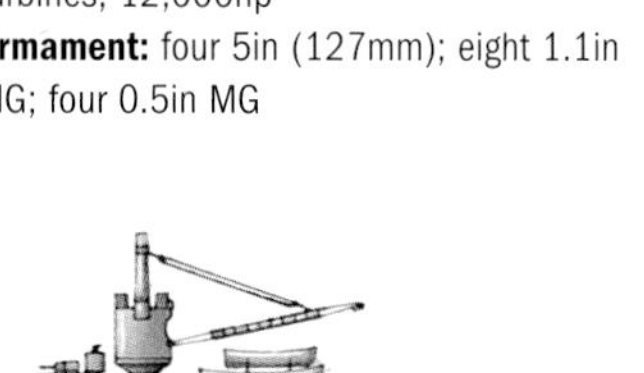

Machinery: two-shaft, Parsons geared turbines; 12,000hp
Armament: four 5in (127mm); eight 1.1in MG; four 0.5in MG
Speed: 19 knots
Range: 12,000nm (22,200km) at 12 knots
Complement: 1247

The *Curtiss*- and the *Currituck*-class tenders were built to warship standards. This proved too expensive, and the majority of US seaplane tenders were built on C-3-type merchant hulls.

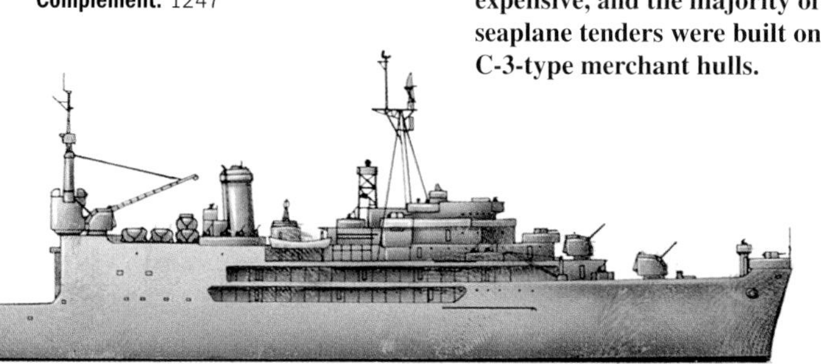

The four *Currituck* class seaplane tenders the US Navy put into service in 1944 were a significant improvement over the earlier *Curtiss* class. The much enlarged afterdeck housed a flush-mounted H-5 hydraulic catapult, sufficiently powerful (though never implemented) to launch US Marine Corps dive bombers. USS *Norton Sound*, the second of the class, was to have a very long career. She remained in service, latterly as a guided-missile trials ship, until the 1980s.

OGNEVOI

USSR: 1940

The design for what was known to the Red Navy as Project 30 was finalized in 1937. At least 24 of these destroyers were ordered but construction was much delayed, and only two, *Ognevoi* and *Vnushitelnyi*, were completed before the end of World War II. Post-war, 12 more were completed. The *Ognevoi* was constructed at the 61 Kommunar Yard at Nikolayev on the Black Sea. Little is known about her service history, but she is believed to have remained in commission until the 1960s.

The *Ognevois* were the best destroyers the Soviet Union constructed during World War II. They formed the basis for the post-war *Skoryi* class.

Displacement: 2240t standard; 2950t full load
Dimensions: 383ft 10in x 36ft 1in x 13ft 9in (117m x 11m x 4.2m)
Machinery: two-shaft, geared turbines; 54,000hp
Armament: four 5.1in (130mm); two 3in (76mm); three 37mm; four 12.7mm MG; six 21in (533mm) TT; 96 mines
Speed: 37 knots
Range: 4000nm (7400km) at 20 knots
Complement: 250

ONSLAUGHT

GB: 1941

The Royal Navy's *O* and *P* class destroyers were a utility version of the earlier *J*s, with the same machinery on a new, smaller, hull and with single 4.7 on manual high-angle mounts and two quad pom-poms. *Onslaught* got older guns in 40° mounts, and exchanged a bank of torpedo tubes for a single 4in HA. She was built by Fairfield and was originally to have been HMS *Pathfinder*. She was transferred to Pakistan, in 1951 remaining in service as the *Tughril* until 1971.

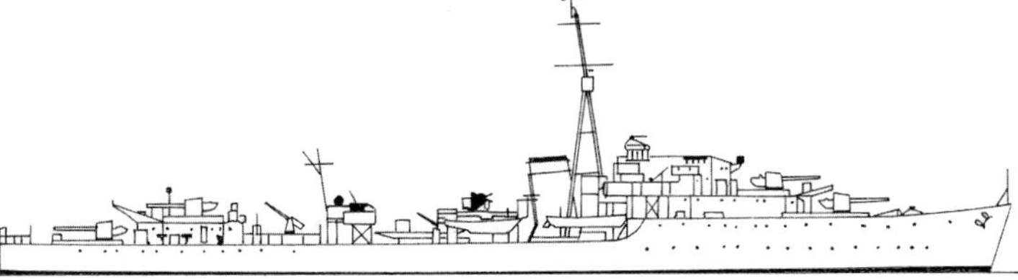

In the early years of World War II, British destroyers were being completed with all possible speed. However, not all of them, *Onslaught* included, received the weapons suite they were designed to carry.

Displacement: 1550t standard; 2270t full load
Dimensions: 345ft x 35ft x 13ft 6in (105.15m x 10.65m x 4.1m)
Machinery: two-shaft, Parsons geared turbines; 40,000hp
Armament: four 4.7in (120mm); one 4in (102mm) HA; eight 2pdr pom-poms, (later eight 20mm); four 21in (533mm) TT; DC throwers
Speed: 37 knots
Range: 3850nm (7130km) at 20 knots
Complement: 176

ORZEL

POLAND: 1938

Displacement: 1100t surfaced; 1650t submerged
Dimensions: 275ft 7in x 22ft x 13ft 8in (84m x 6.7m x 4.15m)
Machinery: two-shaft, Sulzer diesel engines, plus Brown-Boveri electric motors; 4740bhp/1100hp
Armament: 12 21in (533mm) TT (four bow, four stern, four midships trainable: 20 torpedoes); one 4.1in (105mm); two 40mm; two 13.2mm MG;
Speed: 20 knots surfaced; 9 knots submerged
Range: 7000nm (13,000km) at 10 knots surfaced
Complement: 60

Two *Orzel*s were constructed in Holland for the Polish Navy. They were a double-hull design, divided into five watertight compartments, tested to a depth of 260ft (80m). At a time when little attention was paid to stream-lining, these boats were notable for their fine lines, particularly the conning tower and the gunhousing forward of it. They had superior performance on the surface, and rather greater endurance than other submarines designed to operate in the Baltic. Only the lead boat was completed and commissioned on 2 February 1939. The *Orzel* was at sea when war broke out and, forced by mechanical problems to put in to Tallin in Estonia on 15 September 1939, briefly interned. Three days later, she broke out and made Rosythe in Scotland on 14 October. She later served as part of the Free Polish Navy and was lost, probably after hitting a mine, in the North Sea on 8 June 1940.

The Polish *Orzel* was built at Flushing (Vlissingen) to a Dutch design. Although her career was all too brief, she proved to be an excellent warship.

OYODO

JAPAN: 1942

The cruiser *Oyodo* was a singular ship, with a split personality. She was designed as a flagship for the scouting submarine flotillas, and from her mainmast forward was a perfectly conventional cruiser, with six 6.1in guns, as fitted to the *Mogami* class; from there aft, however, she was a seaplane carrier in the mould of the American *Curritucks*. She was designed with a large, 45m-long high-capacity catapult, capable of launching one of the six reconnaissance float-planes she was to carry, but the scheduled aircraft was not ready when she was launched in 1942, and she was completed with a normal 18m-long catapult, offset to port, She carried just two smaller aircraft and proved to be of limited value, the role she was designed for having long since disappeared. *Oyodo* was sunk by American carrier-based aircraft in shallow water close to Kure in July 1945. She was broken up *in situ* three years later.

The *Oyodo* was an attempt to produce an early carrier/cruiser. She resembled the Italian *Vittorio Veneto* of the 1960s in her general form.

Displacement: 8165t standard; 11,430t full load
Dimensions: 630ft 3in x 54ft 6in x 19ft 6in (192.1m x 16.6m x 5.95m)
Machinery: four-shaft, geared turbines; 110,000hp
Armament: six 6.1in (155mm); eight 3.9in (100mm) AA; 12 25mm; two aircraft
Armour: belt 2in (50mm); deck 1.4in (35mm); turrets 1in (25mm)
Speed: 35 knots
Range: not available
Complement: not available

PC CLASS

USA: 1940–44

Displacement: 414t standard; 463t full load
Dimensions: 173ft 8in x 23ft 2in x 7ft 9in (52.95m x 7.05m x 2.35m)
Machinery: two-shaft, diesel; 2880bhp
Armament: two (later one) 3in (76mm), later one (or two) 40mm; two Mousetrap AS mortars; DC throwers; DC racks
Speed: 19 knots
Range: 4800nm (8900km) at 12 knots
Complement: 59

The *PC* class was the US Navy's maid-of-all-work small warship, simple and cheap to build and to operate.

The 'PCs' were conceived as multi-purpose ships, to serve as submarine chasers, anti-submarine pickets, and coastal convoy escorts, and some were later completed as minesweepers, though they were not entirely successful in the role. They were built in huge numbers between 1940 and 1944 by small yards all over the United States. The choice of low-powered diesel engines gave them good endurance, and they were frequently operated with much greater payloads than they were designed to carry.

PINGUIN

GERMANY: 1936

Schiff 33 began life as the 7766 merchantman, *Kandelfels*, built by AG Weser. She was renamed the *Pinguin* by the *Kriegsmarine* in February 1940, armed largely with guns taken from the secondary batteries of *Deutschland*-class pre-dreadnought battleships, and put under the command of *Kpt. z. S.* Ernst-Felix Krüder. She left Gotenhafen (Gdynia) on 15 June for a raiding voyage which took her to the Antarctic icepack, sailing 59,188nm (109,616km) and sinking or seizing 32 Allied ships totalling 154,619. Her first prize was a Norwegian tanker, which was converted into an auxiliary minelayer in three days, then used to mine the entrances to Adelaide, Melbourne, and Sydney harbours. The most useful of *Pinguin*'s catches were whaling ships, which she sent back to Europe as prizes. Her luck ran out on 8 May 1941 when she ran foul of HMS *Cornwall*, near the Seychelles; a shell fired by the heavy cruiser exploded *Pinguin*'s remaining stock of mines.

Displacement: 17,600t normal
Dimensions: 508ft 6in x 61ft 4in x 28ft 6in (155m x 18.7m x 8.7m)
Machinery: two-shaft, MAN double-acting diesels; 7600bhp
Armament: six 4.9in (150mm); one 3in (75mm); one 37mm; four 30mm; four 21in (533mm) TT; 420 mines; two (later one) aircraft
Speed: 16 knots
Range: 12,000nm (22,200km) at 12 knots
Complement: 401

In terms of the number of ships she captured or sank, the *Pinguin* was the most successful of the 10 armed raiders deployed by the German Navy in World War II.

PRETORIA CASTLE

GB: 1938

Displacement: 19,650t standard; 23,450t full load
Dimensions: 594ft 7in x 76ft 6in x 28ft (181.25m x 23.3m x 8.55m)
Machinery: two-shaft, Burmeister & Wain diesels; c16,000bhp
Armament: four 4in (102mm) HA; 16 2pdr pom-poms; 20 (later 28) 20mm
Speed: 18 knots
Range: 12,000nm (22,200km) at 14 knots
Complement: not available

Constructed by Harland & Wolff in Belfast as a Union Castle Line steamer, *Pretoria Castle* was by far the largest of escort carriers, equipped to operate 15 bomber and six fighter aircraft. She was initially armed as a light cruiser, and employed as a convoy escort. Purchased in July 1942, she was converted to the carrier configuration by Swan Hunter, and commissioned as HMS *Pretoria Castle* on 9 April 1943. She never saw combat, and was used solely as a trials and training carrier.

Constructed as a passenger liner, the *Pretoria Castle* served first as an armed merchant cruiser and then as a training carrier. She reverted to the merchant service in 1947.

PRINZ EUGEN

GERMANY: 1938

The *Kriegsmarine* constructed just three heavy cruisers – there would have been five, but one was converted to an aircraft carrier (but never completed), and the other was sold to the Soviet Union (and likewise was never finished, though she did see a considerable amount of combat). These cruisers handsomely contravened the displacement limit of the 1935 Anglo-German Agreement. The *Hipper*s were built in two groups, the sole survivor of the second, *Prinz Eugen*, being marginally longer and broader and proportionally heavier than the first pair. She was constructed by Germaniawerft at Kiel and commissioned in August 1940. She had an active career early on, accompanying *Bismarck* when she broke out into the North Atlantic to mount Operation 'Rheinübung', and *Scharnhorst* and *Gneisenau* on their return to Germany from Brest during Operation 'Cerberus'. *Prinz Eugen* was awarded to the USA as reparation and later used as a target during the 1946 Bikini Atoll atom bomb tests, sinking in Kwajalein lagoon on 22 December that year.

There was considerable opposition to the building of the *Hipper* class cruisers in German naval circles; their range was thought to be nowhere near sufficient for a commerce raider.

Displacement: 14,680t standard; 18,750t full load
Dimensions: 679ft 1in x 70ft 6in x 23ft 7in (207.7m x 21.5m x 7.2m)
Machinery: three-shaft, Brown-Boveri geared turbines; 132,000hp
Armament: eight 8in (203mm); 12 4.1in (105mm), later 17 40mm; 12 37mm (later deleted); eight (later 26) 20mm; 12 21in (533mm) TT; three aircraft
Armour: belt 3.3in (80mm); deck 2in-1.2in (50mm-30mm); turret faces 4.1in (105mm) conning tower 5.9in (150mm)
Speed: 32.5 knots
Range: 6800nm (12,600km) at 20 knots
Complement: 1600

RAVEN

USA: 1940

Displacement: 810t standard; 1040t full load
Dimensions: 220ft x 32ft 2in x 9ft 4in (67.05m x 9.8m x 2.85m)
Machinery: two-shaft, diesel; 2880bhp
Armament: two 3in (76mm); four (later eight) 20mm; one Hedgehog; four DC throwers; two DC racks; 80 mines
Speed: 18 knots
Range: 6500nm (12,000km) at 16.5 knots
Complement: 105

USS *Raven* was the leader of a class of minesweeper/minelayers which were also expected to serve as anti-submarine escorts; the demands were probably too much to make on a small warship, particularly when the requirement to deal with magnetic mines, which needed considerable electrical power, was also imposed. There was no room in the original design to house the necessary generator, and instead, diesel-electric drive was specified for the follow-on *Auk* class, its generators being used to power the magnetic sweeps.

USS *Raven* was built at Norfolk Navy Yard as a prototype; other vessels in the class were built in hundreds at commercial yards throughout the USA.

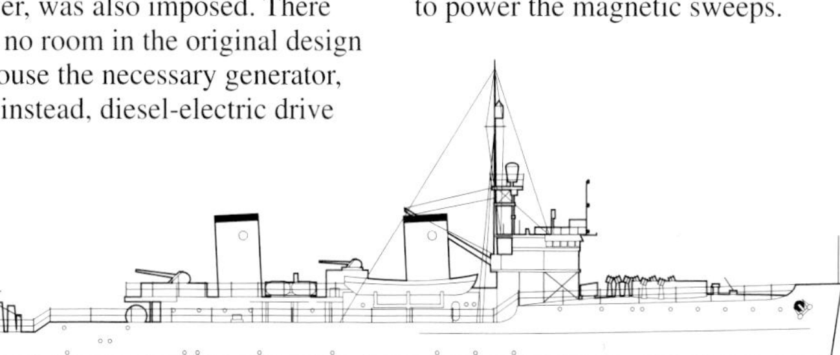

REDOUBT

GB: 1942

Reducing the size of the hulls of the Royal Navy's *O*- and *P*-class destroyers did not improve them. The next group, the *Q*s and *R*s reverted to the form of the *J* class, modified by the addition of a transom stern, introduced in the *Colony*-class cruisers at the same time. *Q* and *R* classes were carbon copies of the 4.7in (119mm)-armed *O*s and underwent the same sort of modification, which consisted of little more than the addition of extra light AA weapons, though they never swapped torpedo tubes for the 4in (102mm) AA gun. Constructed in 1941/42, they were only roughly finished, but the general build quality was good, so much so that four *R*-class ships were retained in British service after the war and extensively rebuilt to serve as anti-submarine frigates. *Redoubt* was not amongst them; she was transferred to India in 1949 and served there as the *Ranjit*. She was stricken in 1979 after a career which spanned 37 years.

Displacement: 1720t standard; 2480t full load
Dimensions: 358ft 3in x 35ft 8in x 14ft in (109.2m x 10.9m x 4.25m)
Machinery: two-shaft, Parsons geared turbines; 40,000hp
Armament: four 4.7in (120mm); four 2pdr pom-poms; (later eight 20mm); eight 21in (533mm) TT; DC throwers
Speed: 37 knots
Range: 4500nm (8330km) at 20 knots
Complement: 175

With the *Q* and *R* class, the Royal Navy had almost achieved the optimum utility destroyer; very little modification followed in later classes.

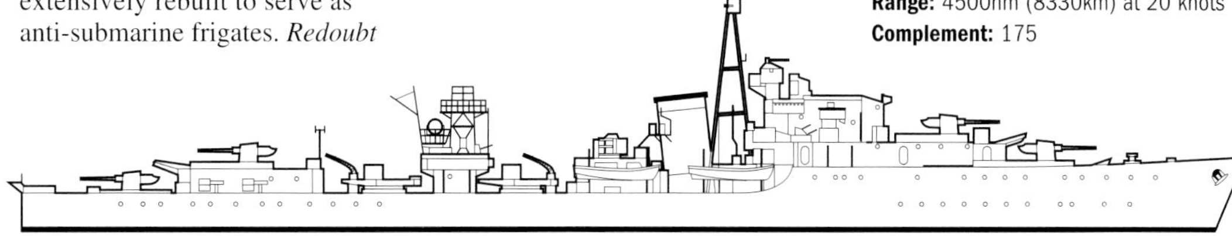

REMO

ITALY: 1943

In 1942, the Italian Navy ordered 12 large ocean-going *R*-class submarines, intending to use them as freighters, transporting essential cargoes to and from Japan. Designed by Cavallini, their cargo capacity was to be 600cu m (21,170cu ft), and their powerplants small, and their armament very light (the first two units had lightweight torpedo tubes; deleted from subsequent boats). *Remo* was the second and last to be commissioned; both were destroyed during their trials, in the third week of July 1943 – *Remo* torpedoed by the

British submarine *United*, and *Romolo* bombed by Allied aircraft. Two boats were delivered incomplete, the construction of two was suspended, and the remaining six were seized by the Germans and either sunk while fitting out or scuttled. Like all Cavallini designs, they were partial double-hulled, and were divided into 13 watertight compartments, six of which were cargo holds. Their maximum operating depth was 330ft (100m).

Displacement: 1300t surfaced; 2560t submerged
Dimensions: 283ft 10in x 25ft 9in x 17ft 6in (86.5m x 7.85m x 5.35m)
Machinery: two-shaft, Tosi diesel engines, plus Marelli electric motors; 2600bhp/900hp
Armament: two 17.7in (450mm) TT (bow); three 20mm
Speed: 14 knots surfaced; 6.5 knots submerged
Range: 12,000nm (22,200km) at 9 knots surfaced
Complement: 63

Only two of Italy's *R*-class submarine freighters were actually commissioned; both were sunk within two days of each other, while still running trials.

RENOWN

GB: 1916/1926/1939

Displacement: 30,750t standard; 36,100t full load
Dimensions: 794ft x 102ft 4in x 32ft 3in (242m x 31.2m x 9.8m)
Machinery: four-shaft, Parsons geared turbines; 120,000hp
Armament: six 15in (381mm); 20 4.5in (114mm); 24 (later 28) 2pdr pom-poms, (later 64 20mm); eight 21in (533mm) TT (later deleted); two aircraft (later deleted)
Armour: belt 9in (229mm); decks 4in-2in (102mm-51mm); bulkheads 4in-3in (102mm-76mm); secondary battery 2.5in (64mm); turret faces 11in (280mm); barbettes 6in (152mm); conning tower 10in (254mm)
Speed: 31 knots
Range: 3650nm (6760km) at 29 knots
Complement: 1200

The 28,000t battlecruisers *Renown* and *Repulse* were commissioned in 1916. That they were built at all, further battlecruiser construction having been barred, was a tribute to the personal power of the the newly-returned First Sea Lord, Fisher. They mounted six 15in (381mm) guns and were lightly protected, but their 112,000hp machinery gave them a top speed of over 30 knots. *Renown* was rebuilt in 1923–26: she was bulged, a 9in (229mm) armour belt replaced the earlier 6in (152mm), thicker deck armour was fitted, and her secondary battery was renewed. Her standard displacement increased to *c*31,000t. She was reconstructed again in 1936–39: her machinery was renewed with more powerful turbines and improved boilers, and her secondary battery was replaced again. A catapult and aircraft hangars were added, though both were later removed. During World War II, modifications consisted chiefly of additions to her light AA weaponry. *Renown* alone survived the war, her sister ship being sunk in December 1941, to be broken up in 1948.

The high-speed of the battlecruiser *Renown* made her an obvious candidate to escort fast aircraft carriers. She was employed in that role for much of World War II.

RICHELIEU

FRANCE: 1939

The *Richelieu* was the most important naval asset France possessed during World War II. Though incomplete until 1943, she saw action as part of the British fleet in the Far East.

Discounting the two *Dunkerque*s, which were really battecruisers, the *Richelieu* was the only modern battleship France possessed during World War II, her sister ships, *Jean Bart* and *Clemenceau* having been begun but not completed. She was characteristic of the new breed of fast battleships, mounting 15in guns in quadruple turrets, with almost 40 per cent of her entire standard displacement given over to protection and with 150,000-horsepower machinery to give her a top speed of 30 knots. *Richelieu*, launched in January 1939,was only 95 per cent complete when France surrendered to the Germans in June 1940. Like most of the French fleet, she made her way to an African port, in her case Dakar in Senegal. There she was damaged following Churchill's decision to disable the fleet lest it be employed by the *Kriegsmarine*. She joined the Allies in 1942 and was sent to the United States, where she was refitted. She emerged in October 1943 with radar added, her aircraft removed, and her 37mm and 13.2mm light AA guns replaced by greater numbers of 40mm and 20mm. Her fuel capacity was increased by 500 tons and her total displacement by 3000 tons. She served with the British Far Eastern Fleet for the rest of the war. Later, with some of her light AA weapons removed, she became the French flagship in Indo-China. She was paid off at Brest and hulked as an accommodation ship in 1959, and sold for demolition in 1964.

Displacement: 35,000t (later 37,500t) standard; 43,300t (later 46,000t) full load
Dimensions: 813ft 2in x 108ft 3in x 31ft 3in (247.85m x 33m x 9.6m)
Machinery: four-shaft, Parsons geared turbines; 150,000hp
Armament: eight 15in (381mm); nine 6in (152mm) DP; 12 3.9in (100mm) AA; eight 37mm, later 56 40mm; 48 20mm; 16 13.2mm MG; three aircraft (later deleted)
Armour: belt 13.5in-9.5in (345mm-240mm); bulkheads 15in-9.5in (380mm-240mm); decks 6in-2in (150mm-50mm); turret faces 17.5in (445mm); secondary armament 5in (125mm)
Speed: 30 knots
Range: 15,000nm (27,800km) at 15 knots
Complement: 1670

RO100

JAPAN: 1941

The Japanese *KS*-class coastal submarines were built in two groups of nine boats each, between 1941 and 1943 (a further group was cancelled). They were small, second-class boats, suited to operating in relatively shallow waters, and had only limited endurance. All 18 were lost in combat – many of them around the Philippines – including five to a single US destroyer escort, the *England*, in an eight-day period in the last week of May 1944. *RO100* was the class leader, constructed at Kure Navy Yard.

Displacement: 525t surfaced; 780t submerged
Dimensions: 199ft 10in x 19ft 8in x 11ft 6in (60.9m x 6m x 3.5m)
Machinery: two-shaft, diesel engines, plus electric motors; 1100bhp/760hp
Armament: four 21in (533mm) TT; one 3in (76mm) AA
Speed: 14 knots surfaced; 8 knots submerged
Range: 3500nm (6500km) at 12 knots surfaced
Complement: 38

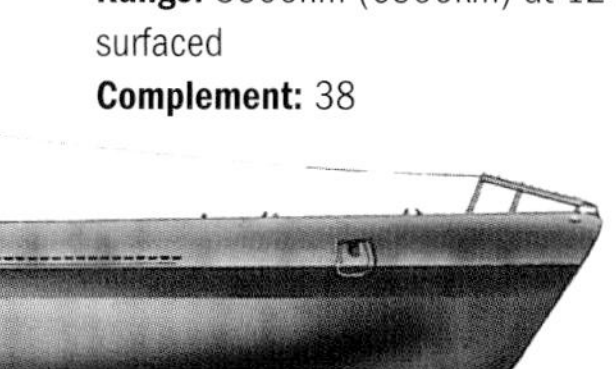

The Japanese *KS* class were similar in character to the British-*U*-class submarines, but had inferior underwater performance.

ROBERTS

GB: 1941

Displacement: 7975t standard; 9150t (later c9500t) full load
Dimensions: 373ft 4in x 89ft 9in x 13ft 6in (113.8m x 27.35m x 4.1m)
Machinery: two-shaft, Parsons geared turbines; 4800hp
Armament: two 15in (381mm); eight 4in (102mm) AA, (later eight 40mm); 16 2pdr pom-poms, (later 20 20mm)
Armour: belt 5in-4in (127mm-102mm); deck 6in-4in (152mm-102mm); barbette 8in (203mm); turret face 13in (330mm); conning tower 3in (76mm)
Speed: 12.5 knots
Range: 2000nm (3700km) at 10 knots
Complement: 442

HMS *Roberts* saw action in the Mediterranean and off the Normandy beaches.

Three World War I-vintage coastal monitors were still in RN service in 1939, but the following year *Marshall Soult*, was disarmed and her 15in twin turret mounted aboard a new construction, HMS *Roberts*. She had much more in the way of superstructure than the earlier types, and looked rather like a miniature *Nelson*-class battleship. As a prime target for shore-based aircraft, *Roberts* was given a significant AA battery.

S4

USSR: 1936

The Soviet *S*-class submarines were designed in the Netherlands in 1933–34 by the (German-run) Ingenieurskantoor voor Scheepsbouw. They also produced the German *Type IA*, and the two submarine classes were very similar. The Series *IXbis* was the largest sub-group, numbering 44 boats. They were the best Soviet submarines produced before World War II, they were saddle-tank types, able to operate to a depth of 260ft (80m).Constructed at the Ordzhonikidze Yard in Leningrad (St Petersburg), *S4* was the first of the series. She entered service in 1937 and sank on 6 January 1945 having been rammed by the German torpedo-boat *T33*, off Danzig (Gdansk).

Displacement: 856t surfaced; 1090t submerged
Dimensions: 255ft 1in x 21ft x 13ft 4in (77.75m x 6.4m x 4.05m)
Machinery: two-shaft, diesel engines, plus electric motors; 4000bhp/1100hp
Armament: six 21in (533mm) TT (four bow, two stern: 12 torpedoes); one 3.9in (100mm); one 45mm; one 7.6mm MG
Speed: 18.9 knots surfaced; 8.9 knots submerged
Range: 9500nm (17,600km) at 10 knots surfaced
Complement: 45

S38

GERMANY: 1939

The *S38* group had their forecastles built up to enclose the torpedo tubes. Later boats of the class had armoured bridgeworks.

It was only in 1939 that the *Kriegsmarine* began operating *S*-boats (*schnellboote*) in significant numbers. A number of classes were designed, and the majority constructed, by Lürssen Werft at Vegesack, an acknowledged master of the type. The *S38* group was the most numerous; their round-bilged hull form made them much more sea-kindly than equivalent British boats (such as the Fairmile *C*s and *D*s) and they were more effective, their highly-evolved Daimler-Benz diesel powerplant providing very superior performance. From mid-1940 to 1944 (when they were known to the British as E-boats), *S*-boats operated in the North Sea, the Channel, and even the Thames Estuary from hardened bases in the Low Countries. In addition they saw service in both the Baltic and the Mediterranean (via the Rhine and Rhône rivers). A total of 249 German *S*-boats of all types were constructed though less than 100 survived the war. This constituted a very high fatality rate for what was always an extremely hazardous operation.

Displacement: 92t standard; 115t full load
Dimensions: 115ft x 17ft x 5ft (34.95m x 5.1m x 1.5m)
Machinery: three-shaft, Daimler-Benz diesels; 6000bhp
Armament: two 21in (533mm) TT; two 20mm
Armour: (later conning tower)
Speed: 40 knots
Range: 850nm (1600km) at 35 knots
Complement: 21

SALMON

USA: 1937

The *Salmon* and similar *Sargo/Seadragon* classes were an interim design on the way to the ideal fleet boats as represented by the *Gatos*, and were themselves effective in the role, though their development had some way to go. In particular, the diesel-electric propulsion system was still in the process of development, and the *Salmons* and *Sargos* actually reverted to direct drive via hydraulic couplings (though they were the last American boats to be so equipped). This arose because of concern over the integrity of electric drive if compartments were flooded. Improved power-plants allowed the boats to exceed their specified performance. They had a fuller hull form aft than earlier classes, enabling them to mount two more torpedo tubes, and they carried two reloads for the bow tubes and one for the stern, plus four extra torpedoes externally. USS *Salmon* was constructed by the Electric Boat Co. at Groton, Connecticut. She survived the war, but was immediately decommissioned and broken up in 1946.

The *Salmons* had a much-increased battery capacity. They could operate submerged for up to 48 hours at 2 knots, with air conditioning and auxiliary systems running.

Displacement: 1450t surfaced; 2210t submerged
Dimensions: 308ft x 26ft 2in x 15ft 7in (93.9m x 8m x 4.75m)
Machinery: two-shaft, diesel engines, plus electric motors; 5500bhp/2660hp
Armament: eight 21in (533mm) TT (four bow, four stern: 24 torpedoes); one 3in (76mm); two 12.7mm MG; two 7.62mm MG
Speed: 21 knots surfaced; 9 knots submerged
Range: 11,000nm (20,400km) at 10 knots surfaced
Complement: 59

SAN GIORGIO

ITALY: 1908/1938

Displacement: 9470t standard; 11,500t full load
Dimensions: 462ft 2in x 68ft 11in x 24ft (140.8m x 21m x 7.3m)
Machinery: two-shaft, vertical triple-expansion; 19,500hp
Armament: four 254mm (10in); eight 190mm (7.5in); eight (later 10) 100mm (3.9in); (later 12 0.8in (20mm); 14 13.2mm MG; three 450mm (17.7in) TT
Armour: side 8in (200mm); deck 2in (50mm); turret faces 8in (200mm); conning tower 10in (255mm)
Speed: 18 knots
Range: 4250nm (7900km) at 12 knots
Complement: 699

San Giorgio began life as an armoured cruiser, entering service before World War I. In 1937 she was taken in hand at La Spezia for conversion to a training ship: her boilers were reduced from 14 to eight and converted to burn oil only, the first and third funnels were removed and the others modified along with the superstructure, and her tertiary armament was modernised. In 1940 she was deployed as a coastal battery at Tobruk, where she was later scuttled.

The *San Giorgio* was scuttled amidst considerable controversy on 22 January 1941 by her captain; he had the option of saving her, since she was not disabled.

SANGAMON

USA: 1939

The *Sangamons* (and the later *Commencement Bays*, which were very similar) were amongst the most successful escort carrier conversions. The four ships started life as commercial T-3 tankers, and were purchased by the US Navy in 1940–41 for use as fleet oilers. Considerably bigger than the *Bogues*, when converted they had greater hangar space and their more powerful twin-shaft machinery (which was conveniently situated right aft) provided much-improved performance. Converted in much the same manner as the *Bogues*, with a hangar deck built up on the upper deck, lightly plated-in at the sides and supporting a wooden flight deck, the *Sangamons* had twin lifts, a single catapult and a small island forward on the starboard side. They retained the capacity to carry 12,000 tons of oil meaning that they were frequently called upon to carry out their original role but also giving them a theoretical range far beyond that of any other carriers.

Completed in time for the North African landings, *Sangamon* later served in the Pacific. Three times damaged in air raids, she was stricken in 1946.

Displacement: 10,495t standard; 23,875t full load
Dimensions: 553ft x 105ft 2in x 30ft 7in (168.55m x 32.05m x 9.3m)
Machinery: two-shaft, Allis-Chalmers geared turbines; 13.500hp
Armament: two 5in (127mm); eight (later 28) 40mm; 12 (later 27) 20mm; 30 (later 36) aircraft
Speed: 18 knots
Range: 24,000nm (44,450km) at 15 knots
Complement: 1080

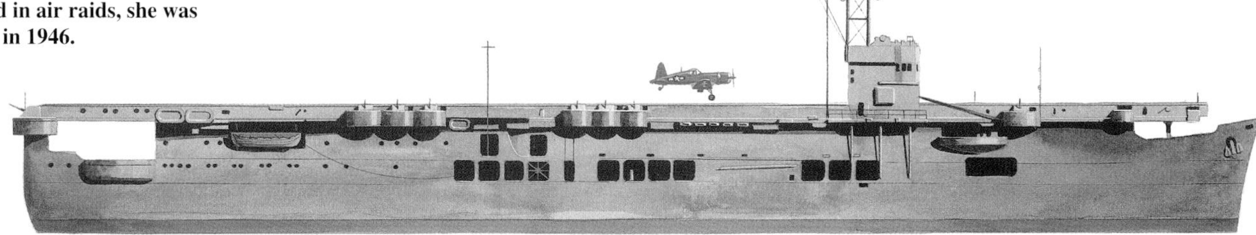

SAUMAREZ

GB: 1942

The British *S*- to *W*-class fleet destroyers were some of the best the Royal Navy had during World War II. They were, essentially, repeats of the *Q*s and *R*s, but with the extended bow first seen on the *Tribal*s which made them considerably drier. The 4.7in (119mm) guns were in an improved mounting, allowing an elevation to 55 degrees, and the quadruple 2pdr pom-poms of the earlier class were replaced in most ships by twin 40mm Bofors in the three-dimensional stabilized mount developed in pre-war Holland by Hazemeyer. The leader of the *S* flotilla, HMS *Saumarez* was constructed by Hawthorn Leslie and had extra accommodation for a Captain (D) and his small staff. She survived the war only to be mined (along with a sister ship, HMS *Volage*) by Albanian pirates in the Corfu Channel in October 1946. *Saumarez* was laid up thereafter, and scrapped four years later. Many of the *S* and *W* class were retained, converted to frigates.

After *Saumurez* and *Volage* were mined, one suggestion put forward was that they should be re-constructed as a single ship, to be called HMS *Sausage* . . .

Displacement: 1810t standard; 2545t full load
Dimensions: 362ft 9in x 35ft 8in x 14ft in (110.55m x 10.9m x 4.25m)
Machinery: two-shaft, Parsons geared turbines; 40,000hp
Armament: four 4.7in (119mm); two (later 10) 40mm; (later eight 20mm, later deleted); eight (later four) 21in (533mm) TT; DC throwers
Speed: 37 knots
Range: 4500nm (8330km) at 20 knots
Complement: 180 (later 225)

SERAPH

GB: 1942

The Royal Navy's *S*-class submarines were constructed in two (large) groups between 1941 and the end of World War II, after which many of them remained in service. They were intended for coastal operations around the British Isles, but also proved to be very satisfactory in the Mediterranean. They were developed from the *Shark* class of the mid-1930s, with improvements such as welded framing. The boats of the first group could operate to 300ft (91.5m), but the second group had welded pressure hulls and could dive 50ft (15m) deeper. HMS *Seraph* was one of the first group, built in Barrow-in-Furness by Vickers-Armstrong. She was taken in hand in 1944 and extensively modified: with higher-capacity batteries, up-rated powerplant and bigger propellers (from the *T*-class boats) and her hull and casing cleaned up, *Seraph* reached 12.5 knots at periscope depth and 16.75 knots on the surface. She was the longest-serving member of the group, not being broken up until 1965.

The British *S*-class submarines were reckoned to be some of the handiest of all. In particular, they could crash-dive in half the time it took a German Type VII.

Displacement: 715t surfaced; 990t submerged
Dimensions: 217ft x 23ft 9in x 14ft (66.15m x 7.25m x 4.3m)
Machinery: two-shaft, Vickers diesel engines, plus electric motors; 1900bhp/1300hp
Armament: seven 21in (533mm) TT (six bow, one external: 13 torpedoes); one 3in (76mm)
Speed: 14.75 knots surfaced; 9 knots submerged
Range: 6000nm (11,100km) at 10 knots surfaced
Complement: 48

SHCH 135

USSR: 1940

Displacement: 585t surfaced; 705t submerged
Dimensions: 192ft 9in x 20ft 4in x 14ft (58.75m x 6.2m x 4.2m)
Machinery: two-shaft, diesel engines, plus electric motors; 1600bhp/800hp
Armament: six 21in (533mm) TT (four bow, two stern: 10 torpedoes); two 45mm
Speed: 13.5 knots surfaced; 8 knots submerged
Range: 6500nm (12,000km) at 8.5 knots surfaced
Complement: 39

The Soviet union constructed large numbers of coastal submarines. The Series *X bis*, such as *Shch 135*, were the best of them.

The Soviet Union began building what became known as *Shch*-type medium submarines in 1930. The designation came from the Series III prototype, *Shchuka* – 'Pike'. Six groups were constructed, of which the Series *X* and *X bis* were the most numerous and evolved, in the 600 ton class, intended to operate in coastal waters. *Shch 135* was the first boat of the latter group. She was constructed at the Dalzavod Yard in Vladivostock – though material was assembled in Leningra – and launched in 1940. She survived the war and was discarded in the early 1960s.

SHIMAKAZE

JAPAN: 1942

Shimakaze was the prototype of a new, very fast heavy destroyer type, initially planned as a class of 16 ships. The project was cancelled, perhaps due to problems associated with maintaining the advanced powerplant, leaving *Shimakaze* as a unique example. Her design speed was 39 knots, and on trial she bettered that by almost two knots. Typical of the Japanese destroyers of the period, she had six 5in (127mm) dual-purpose guns in three twin gunhouses, one forward and two aft, closely-grouped and super-

The *Shimakaze* had very advanced machinery, almost 50 per cent more powerful than the standard destroyer installation.

firing, but she also mounted no less than 15 24in (609mm) torpedo tubes. Early in 1944, her 'X' turret was replaced with 10 additional 25mm AA guns and, by the summer of that year, when American carrier-based aircraft came to represent the most significant threat to Japanese warships, the total had climbed to 28. It was to no avail; *Shimakaze* was sunk in an air attack on 11 November 1944.

Displacement: 2570t standard; 3300t full load
Dimensions: 413ft 5in x 36ft 9in x 13ft 7in (125m x 11.2m x 4.15m)
Machinery: two-shaft, geared turbines; 75,000hp
Armament: six (later four) 5in (127mm); six (later 16, later 28) 25mm; 15 24in (610mm) TT; DC racks
Speed: 39 knots
Range: not available
Complement: c250

SHIMUSHU JAPAN: 1939

The Imperial Japanese Navy began building utility escorts in the sub-1000t class in 1938. The *Shimushu*, constructed by Matsui at Tamano, was the first of them. Only four of this class were completed, and it was two years more before construction of an improved version began. They were the Japanese equivalent of the British *Flower* class, though following normal Japanese practice, they were more heavily armed and somewhat faster. *Shimushu* survived the war and was transferred to the Soviet Union in 1947.

Displacement: 860t standard; 1150t full load
Dimensions: 250ft x 29ft 19in x 10ft (77.7m x 9.1m x 3.05m)
Machinery: two-shaft, diesels; 4200bhp
Armament: three 4.7in (120mm); four (later 15) 25mm; DC racks
Speed: 19.5 knots
Range: not available
Complement: 150

The *Shimushu* was the first modern general-purpose escort built by the Imperial Japanese Navy, just prior to World War II.

SHINANO JAPAN: 1944

Displacement: 64,800t standard; 71,900t full load
Dimensions: 872ft 8in x 119ft 1in x 33ft 10in (266m x 36.3m x 10.3m)
Machinery: four-shaft, Kampon geared turbines; 150,000hp
Armament: 16 5in (127mm) DP; 145 25mm; 12 28-barrelled R/L; 70 aircraft
Armour: belt 8.1in (205mm); hangar deck 7.5in (190mm); flight deck 3.1in (80mm)
Speed: 27 knots
Range: not available
Complement: 2400

The Imperial Japanese Navy's *Shinano* was by far the biggest aircraft carrier of her day, a record she was to hold until the nucelar-powered USS *Enterprise* was launched in 1960.

The aircraft carrier *Shinano* was originally laid down as the third *Yamato*-class battleship. The only substantial difference between her and the class leader was to have been marginally lighter armour and modified AA batteries. In December 1941, by which time she was about 50 per cent complete, construction was suspended, and after the Battle of Midway, six months later, it was decided that she should be completed as a carrier. She retained a considerable degree of protection, though nothing like that of her erstwhile sisters, and was intended as a reserve/support ship for carrier task forces. At 65,000t, *Shinano* was the biggest aircraft carrier in the world by some considerable margin, yet capable of 27 knots due to her 150,000hp powerplant. In appearance, she was rather more like the British and American carriers, with her uptake trunked into her starboard island like that of the *Taiho*. As in the British *Illustrious* class, the weight of armour she carried precluded her from having more than one hangar deck (though, unlike them, she had no vertical protection to the hangar itself, which was open save for roller shutters). Nonetheless, she could still accommodate at least 70 aircraft in comfort, plus vast quantities of aviation spirit and ordnance. On 29 November 1944 – despite her prodigious protection – as she was being moved from Yokosuka Navy Yard, where she was built, to Kure Navy Yard for final fitting out, *Shinano* proved to be easy prey for the submarine USS *Archerfish*, which torpedoed her four times. Pumps and watertight doors had not yet been mounted and she slowly filled and sank.

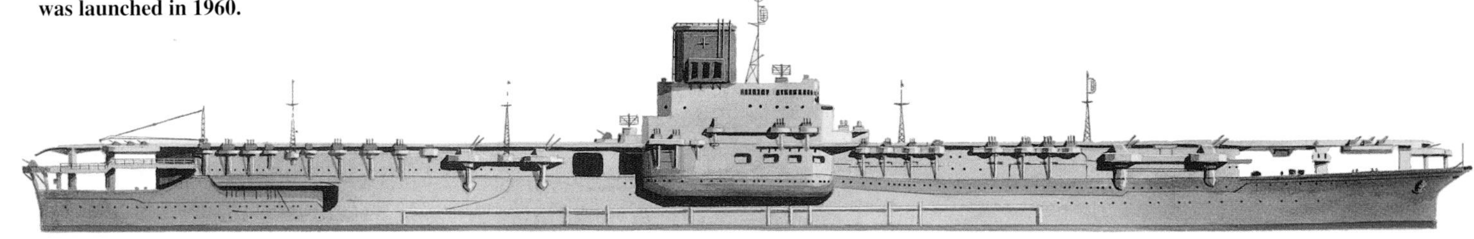

SILNYI

USSR: 1938

Displacement: 2192t standard; 2405t full load
Dimensions: 370ft 7in x 22ft 6in x 13ft 5in (112.8m x 10.2m x 4.1m)
Machinery: two-shaft, geared turbines; 54,000hp
Armament: four 5.1in (130mm); two 3in (76mm); three (later six) 37mm; four 0.5in MG; six 21in (533mm) TT; 60 mines
Speed: 36 knots
Range: 3200nm (5920km) at 20 knots
Complement: 207

The first destroyers constructed by the Soviet Union were the Type 7 *Gnevnyi* class, authorized under the second Five Year Plan (1933–1937). It appears that the design was stolen from Italy. They had many faults, some of which were corrected in the *Storozhevoi* class, of which *Silnyi* was the first, having been modified during construction. The class were built at the Zhdanov Yard in Leningrad (St Petersburg) and designed to operate in the Baltic. *Silnyi* remained in service until the 1960s.

***Silnyi* was laid down as a Type 7 destroyer, but work on her was halted, and she was altered to the upgraded standard of the Type 7U, with a strengthened hull and more powerful machinery.**

SIMS

USA: 1938

With the *Sims* class, the US Navy struck a satisfactory balance in its fleet destroyers, and established a pattern which was to result in the *Benson/Gleaves* class. This was the first very large class to be constructed since World War I. The three principal preceding classes had four 5in (127mm) guns and 16 torpedo tubes (the exception was the *Somers* class, which was more like a small cruiser), but the *Sims* class reverted to the five gun/eight tube arrangement of the *Farraguts*. Their 50,000hp machinery gave them a top speed of 35 knots, and their fuel reserves allowed them to transit the Atlantic Ocean, or reach Pearl Harbor from California, at flank speed. Unfortunately, they came out considerably overweight, most of the excess being in the powerplant where little could be done to rectify the situation. USS *Sims* was constructed by Bath Iron Works and entered service in 1939. She was sunk by Japanese aircraft in the Coral Sea on 7 May 1942.

The *Sims* class marked the last stage in the transition which began with the *Farraguts*, and resulted in the effective fleet destroyers of World War II.

Displacement: 1765t standard; 2315t full load
Dimensions: 348ft 4in x 36ft x 12ft 10in (106.15m x 10.95m x 3.9m)
Machinery: two-shaft, Westinghouse geared turbines; 50,000hp
Armament: five 5in (127mm) DP; eight 21in (533mm) TT; 2 DC racks
Speed: 35 knots
Range: 6500nm (12,000km) at 12 knots
Complement: 192

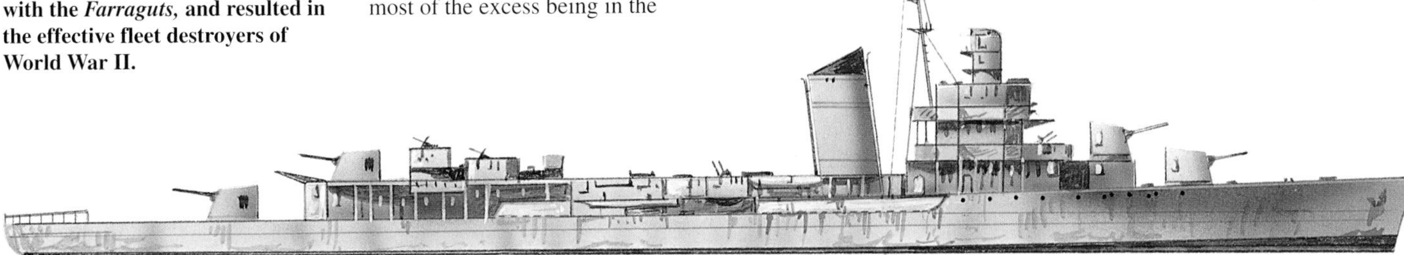

SOMERS

USA: 1939

Despite being somewhat overweight, *Somers* exceeded her design speed by 2.5 knots on trial, at less than design power.

The *Somers* class was a departure from the line of development which stretched through American destroyers from the *Farraguts* to the *Bensons*; rather, they evolved from the *Porters*, and like them were designed to operate as flotilla leaders, armed like scout cruisers. They were distinctly top-heavy as completed; the solution was to remove one of the three banks of torpedo tubes and one of the twin gunhouses, but that modification was only carried out to two of the five ships of the class.

Displacement: 2045t standard; 2765t full load
Dimensions: 381ft x 36ft 11in x 12ft 5in (116.15m x 11.25m x 3.8m)
Machinery: two-shaft, General Electric geared turbines; 52,000hp
Armament: eight 5in (127mm) DP; eight 1.1in MG; two 0.5in MG; 12 21in (533mm) TT
Speed: 37 knots
Range: 7500nm (13,900km) at 15 knots
Complement: 294

SRI AYUTHIA

THAILAND: 1937

The Siamese (Thai) coastal defence ships *Sri Ayuthia* and *Dhonburi* were designed and built by Kawasaki in Japan. They resembled miniature heavy cruisers in appearance, armament, and protection, though not in their machinery, and were the biggest and most powerful ships in the Siamese Navy by some considerable margin. (They were to have been followed by a pair of 5000t light cruisers being built by Cantieri Riuniti dell'Adriatico in Italy; however, in 1941, these were taken over for the *Regina Marina* and completed as the *Etna* and *Vesuvio*.) Both the *Sri Ayuthia* and the *Dhonburi* attempted to engage the French light cruiser *Lamotte-Picquet* in a night action at Koh-Chang in the Gulf of Siam on 17 January 1941, after Siam had ill-advisedly invaded French Indo-China. Both ships were badly battered and eventually driven ashore. *Sri Ayuthia* was later repaired in Japan, but *Dhonburi* capsized and sank while under tow there. *Sri Ayuthia* was sunk in July 1951 by artillery fire from dissident elements of the Siamese Army.

Displacement: 2265t normal
Dimensions: 252ft 8in x 47ft 4in x 13ft 8in (76.5m x 14.45m x 4.15m)
Machinery: two-shaft, MAN diesels; 5200bhp
Armament: four 8in (203mm); four 3in (76mm); four 40mm
Armour: belt 2.5in (65mm); deck 1.5in–1in (37mm–25mm); barbettes 3.9in (100mm); turrets 3.9in (100mm)
Speed: 15.5 knots
Range: 4000nm (7400km) at 14 knots
Complement: 155

The Siamese coastal defence ship *Sri Ayuthia* resembled a miniature heavy cruiser, with paired 8in (203mm) guns mounted fore and aft, and significant protection.

SWIFTSURE

GB: 1943

Displacement: 8800t standard; 11,130t full load
Dimensions: 555ft 6in x 63ft x 20ft 8in (169.3m x 19.2m x 6.3m)
Machinery: four-shaft, Parsons geared turbines; 72,500hp
Armament: nine 6in (152mm); 10 4in (102mm) HA; 16 2pdr pom-poms; (later 13 40mm); (later 22 20mm, later deleted); six 21in (533mm) TT
Armour: belt 3.5in (140mm); bulkheads 2in (51mm); turrets 2in (51mm)
Speed: 31.5 knots
Range: 8,000nm (14,800km) at 16 knots
Complement: 855–960

In 1941, the Royal Navy ordered a pair of light cruisers, essentially follow-on *Colonys*, on the same basic hull with a 1ft (305mm) greater beam and with nine, rather than 12, 6in (152mm) guns and a heavier AA battery. Only one, HMS *Swiftsure*, the class leader, constructed by Vickers-Armstrong at Elswick on the Tyne, was destined for British service. The second unit, originally named *Minotaur* but now the *Ontario*, was transferred to the Royal Canadian Navy on completion, just after the end of the war in Europe. *Swiftsure*, in contrast, had a year of war service, but suffered little harm. She remained in service after the war and there was a plan to modernize her by replacing both her principal and secondary batteries with new fully-automatic guns. Work actually started in February 1957 at Chatham, but two and a half years later it was halted. By then, it was clear that the result would still be an obsolete ship. *Swiftsure* was broken up in 1962.

HMSs *Swiftsure* and *Superb*, virtually identical except in detail, were the last cruisers ever built for the Royal Navy. They were obsolete within a few years of completion.

T1

GERMANY: 1938

The designation 'torpedo-boat' as used in this era was somewhat misleading, for these were actually miniature destroyers. The Type 35s, of which *T1* was the first, were built by Schichau at Elbing and Deschimag of Bremen, who were to construct 36 similar vessels for the *Kriegsmarine*, some of them considerably bigger. Though more capable than French and Italian ships with the same designation, and very much faster and thus more effective, the Type 35s were very expensive to construct and operate.

By 1935, torpedo-boats were largely obsolete, but the relatively high speeds of the German ships made them useful as coastal raiders.

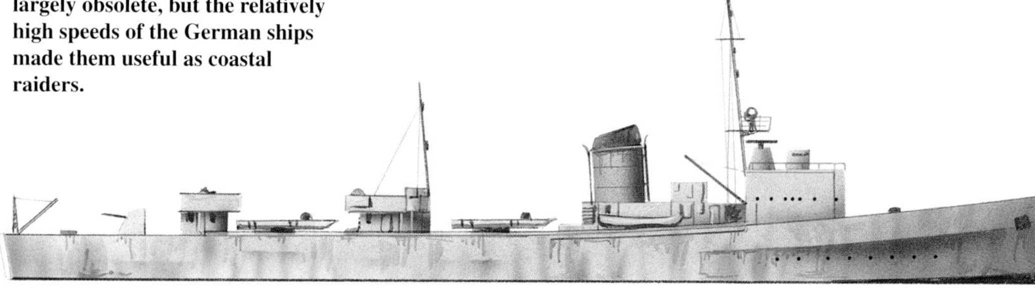

Displacement: 845t standard; 1090t full load
Dimensions: 276ft 7in x 28ft 3in x 7ft 8in (84.3m x 8.6m x 2.35m)
Machinery: two-shaft, Wagner geared turbines; 31,000hp
Armament: three 21in (533mm) TT; one 4.1in (105mm); one (later three) 37mm; eight (later 12) 20mm
Speed: 35 knots
Range: 600nm (1100km) at 35 knots
Complement: 119

T1

JAPAN: 1944

The Japanese *T1*-class landing-ships were actually an intelligent attempt to solve the very serious problem of how to support and re-supply isolated island garrisons. They were fast and well armed for ships of this type, each carrying five landing-craft which were launched, fully loaded, from rails at the stern. By 1945, surviving units were being modified to carry and deploy cradle-mounted midget submarines in the same way. A total of 22 landing-ships were constructed, but most were lost.

The Japanese T1-class landing-ships were an innovation, designed to offload laden landing-craft at high speed.

Displacement: 1500t standard; 2200t full load
Dimensions: 315ft x 33ft 5in x 11ft 10in (96m x 10.2m x 3.6m)
Machinery: one-shaft, geared turbine; 9500hp
Armament: two 5in (127mm); 15 25mm; five landing-craft
Speed: 22 knots
Range: not available
Complement: not available

T22

GERMANY: 1941

Considerably larger than the earlier Type 35s and Type 37s, the German Type 39 torpedo-boats, of which *T22* was the first, were actually more akin to destroyer escorts. They were effective in the role and were also employed as minelayers – fatally for *T22* and two sister ships. They were sunk when navigational errors drove them into a minefield they had laid, in the Gulf of Finland in August 1944. Wartime modifications included mounting additional light AA weaponry.

Displacement: 1295t standard; 1755t full load
Dimensions: 334ft 8in x 32ft 10in x 10ft 6in (102m x 10m x 3.2m)
Machinery: two-shaft, Wagner geared turbines; 29,000hp
Armament: six 21in (533mm) TT; four 4.1in (105mm); four 37mm; seven (later 12) 20mm; DC racks; 50 mines
Speed: 32.5 knots
Range: 5000nm (9250km) at 19 knots
Complement: 206

The Type 39 torpedo-boats were the *Kriegsmarine*'s most effective World War II coastal escorts.

T371

USSR: 1943

Displacement: 150t standard; 180t full load
Dimensions: 127ft 11in x 18ft x 4ft 11in (39m x 5m x 1.5m)
Machinery: two-shaft, diesels; 1440bhp
Armament: two 45mm; four 12.7mm MG; 18 mines
Speed: 14 knots
Range: not available
Complement: 32

The Soviet *T371*-class coastal minesweepers were very crude vessels, roughly welded together from steel sections and powered by tank engines.

The Soviet *T301*, and slightly larger *T371*-class coastal minesweepers were among the crudest of small warships. Designed to be built from the simplest of materials (their hulls employed flat steel sheet sections only; there was not a curve in sight) and using modified tank engines, they were mass-produced in small yards in Leningrad (St Petersburg) at the rate of five per month from 1943 onwards. By the end of the war, 145 had been completed – and perhaps another 100 units were constructed afterwards, many of them for use by the smaller Soviet-bloc satellite navies. They carried only minimal gun armament and, though they could also function as minelayers, had little in common with the pre-war *Tral*-class coastal minesweepers. That the *T371* class were effective at all was thanks only to their sheer weight of numbers.

TAIHO

JAPAN: 1943

The *Taiho* was the largest purpose-built Japanese carrier. She was similar in overall size to the *Essex* class, but with two-storey hangar decks topped by an armoured flight deck, the first Japanese carrier to be so constructed. She was developed from the *Shokaku*, but incorporated a number of features not found in that ship, notably the sponsonned-out island of the *Hiyos*, with its trunked-in, angled-out funnel. She had a 'hurricane' bow, plated up to the level of the flight deck, something the *Essex* class would not have until well after the war was over. For all her sophistication and extensive protection, the *Taiho* had a very brief career; she completed on 7 March 1944, and after her shakedown cruise she was committed to the Battle of the Philippine Sea. On 19 June she was hit by just one torpedo from the US submarine *Albacore*; some hours later, she suffered a devastating explosion when petrol vapour ignited, probably as a result of negligence or poor damage-control procedures.

Displacement: 29,300t standard; 37,720t full load
Dimensions: 855ft x 98ft 6in x 31ft 6in (260m x 30m x 9.6m)
Machinery: four-shaft, Kampon geared turbines; 160,000hp
Armament: 12 3.9in (100mm) AA; 51 25mm; 53 aircraft
Armour: belt 5.9in–2.2in (150mm–55mm); hangar deck 4.9in (125mm); flight deck 3.1in (80mm)
Speed: 33.3 knots
Range: 8000nm (14,800km) at 18 knots
Complement: 1751

On paper, the *Taiho* was the best of all the Japanese carriers, but she was destroyed in her first combat action by a single torpedo.

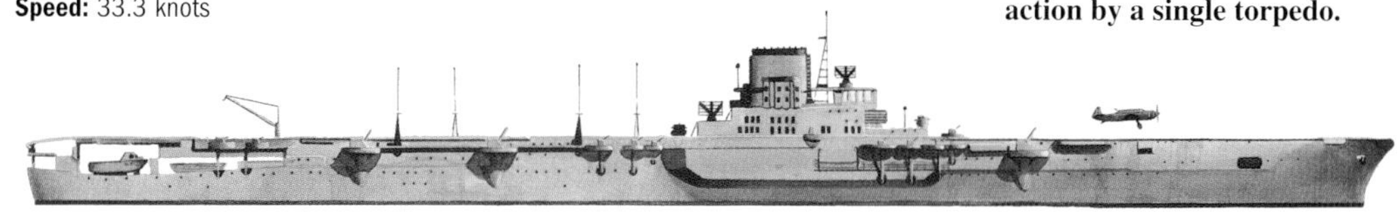

TAIYO

JAPAN: 1940

The *Taiyo* was converted from the passenger liner *Kasuga Maru*, taken over by the Imperial Japanese Navy while fitting out in May 1941, and moved from Mitsubushi's yard at Nagasaki to Sasebo Navy Yard for the purpose. Two other similar ships were also taken over before completion. The design of these vessels was not unlike Allied escort carriers, but they were destined to be used for aircrew training and as aircraft transports. All three were sunk by American submarines, *Taiyo* by USS *Rasher* off Luzon in August 1944.

***Taiyo* alone of her class was actually sent into the combat zone, sailing in a supporting role with the *Yamato* to the East Solomons in August 1942.**

Displacement: 17,830t standard; 21,200t full load
Dimensions: 591ft 4in x 75ft 6in x 26ft 3in (180.25m x 23m x 8m)
Machinery: two-shaft, Kampon geared turbines; 25,200hp
Armament: six 4.7in (120mm) AA (later four 5in (127mm) DP); eight (later 24, later 64) 25mm, (later 10 13.2mm MG); 27 aircraft
Speed: 21 knots
Range: 6500nm (12,000km) at 18 knots
Complement: 747

TAMBOR

USA: 1939

Displacement: 1475t surfaced; 2240t submerged
Dimensions: 307ft 2in x 27ft 3in x 15ft (93.65m x 8.3m x 4.55m)
Machinery: two-shaft, diesel-electric, plus electric motors; 5400hp/2740hp
Armament: 10 21in (533mm) TT (six bow, four stern: 24 torpedoes or four torpedoes and 40 mines); one 3in (76mm); two 0.5in MG
Speed: 20 knots surfaced; 8.75 knots submerged
Range: 11,000nm (20,350km) at 10 knots surfaced
Complement: 60

The US submarine *Tambor* was the leader of the last of the transitional classes produced pre-World War II, in which almost all the elements found in the later definitive fleet boats, the *Gatos*, *Balaos*, and *Tenches*, were present. Finally, after years of debate, US submariners accepted that it would be possible to add two more torpedo tubes forward without increasing displacement by 15 per cent (in fact, the weight penalty was just 15t). Thus, the *Tambors* were the first American boats to be equipped with 10 tubes. Otherwise, they were almost identical to the diesel-electric *Seadragons*, apart from the deletion of the externally carried re-load torpedoes, which produced considerable drag; all subsequent re-loads were held internally (with mines as an alternative). Standard operating depth was 250ft (76m), but that was often exceeded by 20 per cent. Seven of the 12 boats in the class were war losses. USS *Tambor* herself survived, to be broken up in March 1960.

The *Tambor*-class submarines were hardly inferior to the later *Gatos*, the definitive American fleet boats of World War II.

TASHKENT

USSR: 1937

The destroyer leader *Tashkent* was constructed for the Soviet Union in Italy by Odero Terni Orlando at Leghorn (Livorno). She was a singular ship and there is no evidence that more of the same design were ever contemplated. Entirely different in character from the *Leningrad*-class flotilla leaders which preceded her, *Tashkent* was armed in the Soviet Union after delivery from Leghorn; thus, she ran her acceptance trials at much less than standard displacement and at 20 per cent over specified power, making over 44 knots as a result. A more realistic service maximum would have been 39 knots. She was not completed until 1941 and had a short career, being badly damaged twice in air attacks: first, whilst berthed in Odessa and later, after having been repaired, on her way from Sebastopol to Novorossisk. She was taken in tow by the destroyer *Bditelnyi* but, with 1900t of water in her hull, foundered before she could be berthed.

Thanks to running her trials underweight and overpowered, the *Tashkent* made an almost incredible 44.2 knots for an hour.

Displacement: 2895t standard; 3200t full load
Dimensions: 458ft 6in x 44ft 11in x 12ft 2in (139.75m x 13.7m x 3.7m)
Machinery: two-shaft, Parsons geared turbines; 110,000hp
Armament: four (later six) 5.1in (130mm); two 3in (76mm); six 45mm (later six 37mm); six 12.7mm MG; nine 21in (533mm) TT; DC throwers; 80–110 mines
Speed: 39 knots
Range: 5000nm (9250km) at 20 knots
Complement: 250

Terror

USA: 1941

Though she was built as a minelayer, *Terror* was of more use as a flagship and support ship during mine clearing operations.

The only purpose-built minelayer in service with the US Navy in World War II, USS *Terror* was used to lay defensive minefields to protect US installations, served as a minesweeping support ship, and even performed casualty evacuation under fire. Her mine deck was totally enclosed, with splinter protection which extended to the mine holds; she was double-bottomed, and the void chambers were filled with water to the load waterline. She deployed her mines from six tracks which ran the length of the ship and held 648 mines, with another 478 stowed on tracks in the hold, accessible by means of lifts. *Terror* was constructed at the Philadelphia Navy Yard and commissioned in July 1942. Most of her service was in the Pacific – and regularly in the combat zone. She fell victim to a kamikaze attack on 1 May 1945 which put her out of action for the rest of the war. She remained in service until 1966.

Displacement: 5875t standard; 8640t full load
Dimensions: 454ft 10in x 60ft 2in x 19ft 7in (138.65m x 18.35m x 6m)
Machinery: two-shaft, General Electric geared turbines; 11000hp
Armament: four 5in (127mm); eight 0.5in MG; c 1150 mines
Speed: 18 knots
Range: 10,000nm (18,500km) at 15 knots
Complement: 481

Thistle

GB: 1938

The original British *T*-class submarines were the pre-war *Tritons*, which superseded the *Thames* class as the Royal Navy's long-range patrol submarines. They were saddle-tank types, with 0.5in (12mm) pressure plating and an operating depth of 300ft (91m). Modified types were built in two groups during the war. Improvements included greater operatonal depth and much-increased fuel capacity, as well as alterations to the distribution of the torpedo tubes. Though she was one of the original group, constructed by Vickers-Armstrong at Barrow-in-Furness, *Thistle* was an early loss, being torpedoed by the German submarine *U4* off Utsira, on 10 April 1940, and thus was not later modified as were other boats of the group. Modifications included the two external tubes forward removed from some boats, to improve their sea-keeping and depth capability; and most boats had their external midships tubes altered to fire astern instead of ahead, and an additional external stern tube mounted. All survivors received a 20mm cannon in 1943. Some had their fuel capacity increased by the simple expedient of adapting their main tanks.

The *T*-class submarines, with their distinctive bulbous bows, were the British long-range patrol boats of World War II.

Displacement: 1090t surfaced; 1575t submerged
Dimensions: 275ft x 26ft 7in x 15ft (83.8m x 8.1m x 4.55m)
Machinery: two-shaft, Vickers diesel engines, plus electric motors; 2500bhp/1450hp
Armament: 10 21in (533mm) TT (six bow, four external: 16 torpedoes); one 4in (102mm)
Speed: 15.25 knots surfaced; 9 knots submerged
Range: 8000nm (14,800km) at 10 knots surfaced
Complement: 59

Thor

GERMANY: 1939

The armed raider *Thor* was second only to the *Pinguin* in the amount of Allied shipping she took or destroyed. During her first sortie, she sank the British armed merchant cruiser *Voltaire* and 11 other ships in the course of 329 days; her second voyage lasted 321 days and resulted in the loss of 10 more ships. She was destroyed by an explosion aboard the supply ship *Uckermark* while she was lying alongside her at Yokohama on 30 November 1942.

In the course of two sorties totalling almost 22 months, the *Thor* sank or captured over 150,000t of Allied shipping.

Displacement: 9200t normal
Dimensions: 400ft 3in x 54ft 9in x 26ft 7in (122m x 16.7m x 8.1m)
Machinery: one-shaft, AEG geared turbines; 6500hp
Armament: six 5.9in (150mm); one 37mm; four 20mm; four 21in (533mm) TT; one aircraft
Speed: 18 knots
Range: not available
Complement: 345

TIGER

GB: 1945

Displacement: 8885t (later 9550t) standard; 11,560t (later 11,700t) full load
Dimensions: 555ft 6in x 64ft x 21ft (later 23ft) (169.3m x 19.5m x 6.45m (later 7m))
Machinery: four-shaft, Parsons geared turbines; 72,500 (later 80,000)hp
Armament: four (later two) 6in (152mm) HA guns; six (later two) 3in (76mm) HA; (later two GWS22 Seacat SAM launchers; four helicopters)
Armour: belt 3in (76mm); engine room and magazine crowns 2in (51mm); bulkheads 2in (51mm); turrets 2in (51mm)
Speed: 31.5 knots
Range: 6500nm (12,000km) at 13 knots
Complement: 880

HMS *Tiger* began life as the third ship of the *Swiftsure* class of light cruisers, and was to have been named *Bellerophon*. Laid down at John Brown's yard on the Clyde in October 1941, she was soon modified to increase her beam by 1ft (305mm). Four other ships were begun to the same design of which only one, *Superb*, was ever completed as planned. *Tiger* was launched in October 1945 with no clear idea of how – or even if – she would ever be finished; work on demolishing her existing upper works began in 1954 and she was finally completed, as an AA cruiser, in March 1959. Two other ships of the class followed, but it was obvious that they were an anachronism. In the late 1960s, the two survivors each lost everything aft of the mainmast and gained a hangar and platform for four large helicopters, as well as Seacat surface-to-air missiles, and proved effective but hopelessly uneconomic in a hybrid AA/ASW role. After much discussion, *Tiger* was laid up in in 1979 and finally sold for demolition in 1986.

The *Tigers* were a brave – some would say forlorn – attempt to take a World War II cruiser and bring it into the modern age simply by updating its weapons systems.

TINTAGEL CASTLE

GB/CANADA: 1943

Displacement: 1060t standard; 1590t full load
Dimensions: 252ft x 36ft 8in x 13ft 6in (76.8m x 11.2m x 4.1m)
Machinery: one-shaft, vertical triple-expansion reciprocating engine; 2750hp
Armament: one 4in (102mm); two to six 20mm; Squid AS mortar; DC racks
Speed: 16.5 knots
Range: 9500nm (17,600km) at 10 knots
Complement: 120

The *Castle*-class corvettes were less effective than the *Loch*-class frigates of the same period, and were only built in limited numbers.

The British *Castle*-class corvettes were similar to the earlier *Flowers*, with the same powerplant in a hull stretched by almost 25 per cent, which improved sea-keeping and habitability but also provided space for the Squid anti-submarine mortar. Squid was a three-barrel 12in (305mm) mortar; it fired a pattern of 440lb (200kg) hydrostatically-fused bombs out to a range of 440yd (400m) using position data derived directly from the ship's sonar. *Tintagel Castle* was built by Ailsa, and remained in service until 1957.

TIRPITZ

GERMANY: 1939

Because her career consisted largely of hiding in Norwegian fjords, the *Tirpitz* is often regarded as being somehow of less value than her sister ship *Bismarck*. However, as a 'ship-in-being' she probably troubled the British more than her short-lived sister ship ever did and certainly for much longer. The RAF alone mounted no less than 12 bombing missions against her, both in German ports and later in Norway, finally destroying her on 12 November 1944 with 'Tallboy' 12,000lb (5443kg) penetration bombs. Earlier, she had been a priority target of the Royal Navy: carrier-borne Fairey Barracuda aircraft from HMS *Victorious* and HMS *Furious*

Displacement: 42,900t standard; 52,600t full load
Dimensions: 813ft 8in x 118ft 1in x 34ft 9in (248m x 36m x 10.6m)
Machinery: three-shaft, Brown-Boveri geared turbines; 138,000hp
Armament: 8 15in (380mm); 12 5.9in (150m); 16 4.1in (105mm); 16 37mm; 12 (later 58) 20mm, later eight 21in (533mm) TT; four aircraft
Armour: belt 12.5in-10.5in (318mm-267mm); deck 4.75in-2in (121mm-51mm); main turrets 14.25in-7in (362mm-178mm); secondary turrets 4in-1.5in (102mm-37mm); conning tower 14in (356mm)
Speed: 29 knots
Range: 8500nm (15,750km) at 19 knots
Complement: 2092

attacked her on 3 April 1943 and, in an extremely hazardous operation mounted in September 1943, the famous *X*-class midget submarines effectively crippled her. *Tirpitz* was virtually identical to *Bismarck* in most respects, save that she had machinery from Brown-Boveri and additional AA guns, though she displaced 1200t more.

Tirpitz was a supreme example of the power of a 'ship-in-being'; though she never made an effective sortie, she occupied the attention of the British for five years, at enormous cost.

TOGO

GERMANY: 1940

The motor-ship *Togo* was constructed as a merchantman by AG Vulcan, Bremen. Taken up by the *Kriegsmarine* for conversion to an armed commerce raider, the *Coronel*, she attempted to break out through the Channel in February 1943, but was bombed off Dunkirk. She returned to Germany, and was refitted as a fighter direction ship under her original name, operating 'Freya' and 'Würzburg' radar systems. She served in the Baltic, and at the end of the war was used as a troop transport and, later, refugee ship.

Having failed as an armed commerce raider, the _Togo_ was reequipped as a fighter direction ship.

Displacement: 12,700t normal
Dimensions: 439ft 7in x 58ft 9in x 25ft 11in (134m x 17.9m x 7.9m)
Machinery: one-shaft, double-acting, two-stroke diesel; 5100bhp
Armament: three 4.1in (105mm); two 40mm; four 37mm; 20 20mm; four 73mm R/L
Speed: 16 knots
Range: not available
Complement: not available

TONE

JAPAN: 1937

Displacement: 11,215t standard; 15,200t full load
Dimensions: 661ft 1in x 60ft 8in x 21ft 3in (201.5m x 18.5m x 6.5m)
Machinery: four-shaft, Kampon geared turbines; 152,000hp
Armament: eight 8in (203mm); eight 5in (127mm) DP; 12 25mm; 12 13.2mm MG; 12 24in (610mm) TT; six aircraft
Armour: belt 4.9in-3.9in (125mm-100mm); deck 2.5in-1.2in (65mm-30mm); turrets 1in (25mm)
Speed: 35 knots
Range: 12,000nm (22,200km) at 14 knots
Complement: 850

The *Tone* and her sister ship the *Chikuma* were laid down as light cruisers, but were modified during construction (the Washington and London Treaties having expired) and completed as heavy cruisers. They were unusual – all their armament was forward of the superstructure, leaving the quarter-deck largely clear for aircraft operations, save for light AA emplacements – but not unique; *Mogami* was converted to a similar configuration. Their light float-planes were launched by catapult and recovered by cranes. These were the biggest cruisers the Imperial Japanese Navy ever constructed (though the more heavily-armed *Takaos* were marginally longer), fast and well protected, with a double bottom and inclined side decks in addition to an armoured belt covering the magazines and machinery. Both ships were constructed by Mitsubishi at Nagasaki, and entered service in 1938 and 1939. *Tone* was sunk in shallow water near Kure by American aircraft in July 1945, and was broken up *in situ* in 1948.

The two _Tones_ were built and equipped as large scout cruisers and proved to be very successful in the role.

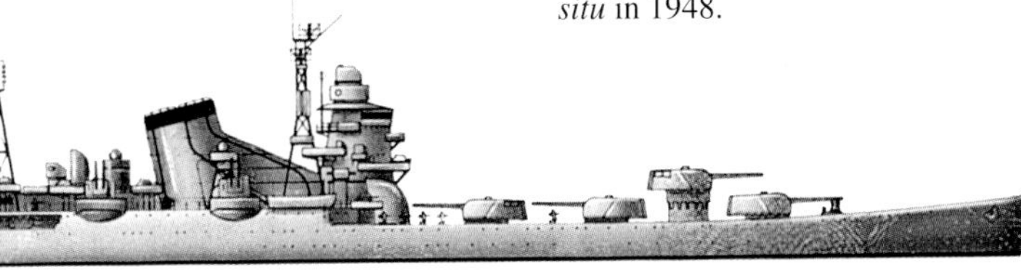

TROMP

THE NETHERLANDS: 1937

HNLMS *Tromp* and her sister ship *Jacob van Heemskerck* were originally conceived in 1931 as 2500t flotilla leaders, but when they were authorized in 1936, they had gained over 50 per cent displacement and evolved into conventional scout cruisers. They had comparatively heavy armament, concentrated forward, at the cost of reduced protection consisting of a splinter-proof box enclosing the machinery and magazines, something like the citadel found in ships of an earlier generation but much lighter. It had always been intended that these cruisers would operate in the Dutch East Indies, but when war broke out in Europe, only *Tromp* had been completed. She and her sister ship escaped to Britain in 1940, where *van Heemskerck* was completed as an AA cruiser, with 10 4in (102mm) HA guns of British design and British gunnery directors, and extra light weapons. Both ships survived the war and were to be the mainstay of the Royal Netherlands Navy immediately postwar. On being stricken in 1958, they became accommodation ships.

Displacement: 4150t standard; 4860t full load
Dimensions: 433ft x 40ft 8in x 13ft 9in (132m x 12.4m x 4.2m)
Machinery: two-shaft, Parsons geared turbines; 56,000hp
Armament: six 4.9in (150mm); (later four 3in (76mm) AA); eight (later 12) 40mm; (later two 20mm); four 12.7mm MG; six 21in (533mm) TT; one aircraft
Armour: belt 0.7in (15mm); sides and bulkheads 1.2in (30mm); decks 1in (25mm); gunshields 0.7in (15mm)
Speed: 33.5 knots
Range: 10,000nm (18.500km) at 15 knots
Complement: 309

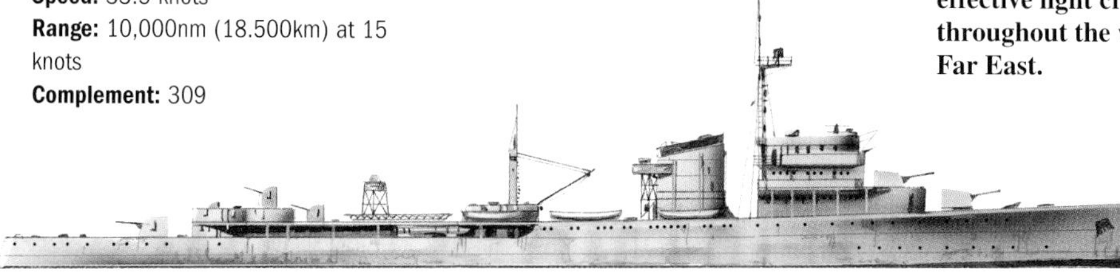

Despite being only lightly protected, the *Tromps* proved to be effective light cruisers and served throughout the war, chiefly in the Far East.

TSUGARU

JAPAN: 1940

Displacement: 4000t standard; 6600t full load
Dimensions: 408ft 6in x 51ft 3in x 16ft 2in (124.5m x 15.6m x 4.9m)
Machinery: two-shaft, Kampon geared turbines; 9000hp
Armament: four 5in (127mm) DP; four 25mm; 600 mines; one aircraft
Speed: 20 knots
Range: 10,000nm (18,500km) at 14 knots
Complement: not available

The Imperial Japanese Navy began building modern minelayers (most of which were also equipped to lay anti-submarine nets, though the two operations actually had very little in common) as early as 1929. Many were relatively small ships, intended for harbour and coastal operations, others were in the range 1000–2000t. In 1931, a cruiser-minelayer, the *Okonishima*, much closer in character to those in service with some European navies, was authorized and followed six years later by an almost identical ship with some basic improvements, the *Tsugaru*. She was constructed at Yokosuka Navy Yard and entered service in 1941. Like all ships of this type, she had considerable freeboard and very little sheer, her mine deck running the full length of the ship, fitted with parallel sets of rails upon which the mines were transported and then laid. She also operated as a general transport, with temporary wooden decks covering the rails.

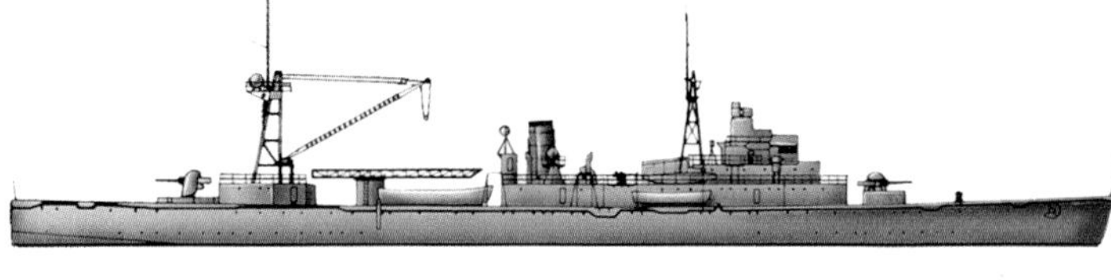

The *Tsugaru* was one of only two important minelayers in service with the Imperial Japanese Navy during World War II. She could also function as a fast transport and long-range escort.

Tsugaru was torpedoed by an American submarine in June 1944.

TYNE

GB: 1940

The two *Tyne*-class destroyer depot ships were essentially combat-prepared freighters with a considerable number of AA guns and protection against torpedoes. The latter featured internal sandwich bulges and a bulkhead 10ft (3m) inboard – its efficacy demonstrated when no less than five torpedoes from *U505* were required to sink HMS *Hecla*. The class carried 2000t of fuel as cargo, 80 torpedoes and depth charges and ammunition, and also had extensive repair facilities and a hospital. *Tyne* survived the war and remained in service until the 1960s.

The *Tyne* was a floating warehouse; her bakery could turn out 25,000 loaves a day.

Displacement: 11,000t standard; 14,000t full load
Dimensions: 621ft 2in x 66ft x 20ft 6in (189.35m x 20.1m x 6.25m)
Machinery: two-shaft, Parsons geared turbines; 7500hp
Armament: eight 4.5in (114mm) HA; eight 2pdr pom-poms; (later 15 20mm)
Armour: deck 2in (51mm)
Speed: 17 knots
Range: 8000nm (14,800km) at 12 knots
Complement: 818

TYNWALD

GB: 1936

Displacement: not available
Dimensions: not available
Machinery: two-shaft, geared turbines
Armament: six 4in (102mm) HA; eight 2pdr pom-poms
Speed: 21 knots
Range: 5000nm (9250km) at 16 knots
Complement: not available

Tynwald was one of the smaller British anti-aircraft ships, but with a turn of speed which made her a useful escort for fast convoys.

Tynwald was one of eight auxiliary anti-aircraft ships in service with the Royal Navy during World War II.

Constructed as a merchant ship in 1936, she was taken up from trade in 1940 and converted. Her superstructure was demolished, magazines were constructed in her cargo space, and a warship-type bridge was built, together with reinforced supports for her gunhouses. She spent most of her brief service career in the Mediterranean, where she was sunk by a mine (or an Italian submarine) in November 1942.

U3

GERMANY: 1936

The German Type II U-boats were small coastal submarines, the first constructed in any number for the *Kriegsmarine*, from 1934. They were based on the Finnish *Vesikko*, built with German assistance in 1932 and purchased by Germany in 1936. They were single-hull types, divided into three watertight compartments, with an operating depth of 260ft (80m) and crush depth of (490ft (150m). Only six of the first group, the Type IIAs, were produced, and the three units which survived up until that time (including *U*3) were all stricken before the war's end, in August 1944. Later groups were progressively increased in size, but retained the same powerplant and armament. Six Type IIBs were laboriously transported to the Black Sea via the Elbe and the Danube. This involved cutting them into three sections, removing all the heavy components, and loading them aboard 50t pontoons, before transporting them overland on specially-built vehicles between Dresden and Linz in Austria. Here they were reassembled, to continue their journey between two barges.

Displacement: 250t surfaced; 374t submerged
Dimensions: 134ft x 13ft 5in x 12ft 5in (40.9m x 4.1m x 3.8m)
Machinery: two-shaft, MWM diesel engines, plus Siemens-Schuckert electric motors; 700bhp/360hp
Armament: three 21in (533mm) TT (bow: six torpedoes); one 20mm
Speed: 13 knots surfaced; 7 knots submerged
Range: 1600nm (2950km) at 8 knots surfaced
Complement: 25

A total of 49 coastal Type II U-boats were constructed from 1934 to 1940; they were obsolete by the war's end.

U31

GERMANY: 1936

The 10 Type VIIA submarines were all completed within a 10-month period; all but two were sunk during the war, those were scuttled at its end.

The first of the German Type VII submarines was commissioned in June 1936. The last of the 10 units which made up the group (*U*27 to *U*36) was in service by April of the following year. These boats were the prototypes for the most successful class of – German World War II submarines. Built by Deschimag, *U31* had a brief but eventful career, being sunk twice, first by the RAF off the mouth of the Jade in 1940, and the second time, some eight months later, by HMS *Antelope*, off Ireland.

Displacement: 616t surfaced; 899t submerged
Dimensions: 211ft 7in x 19ft x 14ft 5in (64.5m x 5.8m x 4.4m)
Machinery: two-shaft, Germaniawerft diesel engines, plus Brown-Boveri electric motors; 2100bhp/750hp
Armament: five 21in (533mm) TT (four bow, one stern: 11 torpedoes); one 3.5in (88mm); one 20mm
Speed: 16 knots surfaced; 8 knots submerged
Range: 6200nm (11,450km) at 10 knots surfaced
Complement: 44

U47

GERMANY: 1938

The Type VII ocean-going submarines, known as the 'Atlantic' boats, were the most common by far in German service during World War II, a total of 715 being produced in five variants, of which the most numerous, were the Type VIICs, bult until 1944. They were saddle-tank types, divided into six watertight compartments, with an operating depth of 330ft (100m), and they proved to be highly seaworthy and very manoeuvrable. The 23 Type VIIBs were enlarged versions of the original, their standard displacement upped to a nominal 740t, with the single stern torpedo tube incorporated within the hull (in the Type VIIAs it had been external). They also had an increased torpedo or mine storage capacity (though three boats had only two forward tubes, one had no stern tube and five were not equipped to deploy mines). Their conning towers were enlarged, to allow the single 20mm AA gun to be mounted on a platform abaft the bridge. Of the few which survived beyond the end of 1943, some lost their 3.5in (88mm), and had extra light AA guns added. The 'Atlantic' U-boats were actually not well suited to oceanic operations at all, having been designed for service in the North Sea and the Western Approaches. Their design was the minimum acceptable for open-ocean work by reason of their limited torpedo capacity in particular. Nonetheless, their one

The Type VII U-boats were the backbone of the German submarine service during World War II. German success during the Battle of the Atlantic came largely as a result of their very successful deployment in 'wolf packs'.

Displacement: 741t surfaced; 1021t submerged
Dimensions: 218ft 2in x 20ft 4in x 15ft 5in (66.5m x 6.2m x 4.7m)
Machinery: two-shaft, Germaniawerft diesel engines, plus AEG electric motors; 2800bhp/750hp
Armament: five 21in (533mm) TT (four bow, one stern: 14 torpedoes); one 3.5in (88mm); one 20mm
Speed: 18 knots surfaced; 8 knots submerged
Range: 8700nm (16,100km) at 10 knots surfaced
Complement: 44

_U47_, while she was not the most successful German submarine of the war, was certainly the most celebrated; she successfully penetrated the Home Fleet's anchorage at Scapa Flow and sunk the battleship _Royal Oak_.

vital attribute was that they were available and they worked – reason enough to ensure the boat's employment (and even continuing construction), even after it was functionally obsolete. *U47* was constructed by Germaniawerft, Krupp's yard in Kiel. She was begun in 1936 and commissioned on 17 December 1938. In the hands of the celebrated *Korvettenkapitän* Günther Prien, Germany's ninth-ranking U-boat ace (despite his short career), she sank almost 165,000 tons of Allied mercantile shipping. On 14 October 1939, in one of the most daring attacks of the entire war, Prien also sank the battleship HMS *Royal Oak*, whilst she was at anchor in Scapa Flow (scene of the scuttling of the German High Seas Fleet in 1919), and would probably have sunk another, the *Warspite*, had the torpedoes used in the attack not malfunctioned. Prien got another shot at the *Warspite* off the Norwegian coast during the invasion in April 1940. He fired two torpedoes at her, at a range of about 1000yd (914m), but missed. On 8 March 1941, *U47* was sunk by the depth charges of a British World War I-vintage destroyer, HMS *Wolverine*, off Rockall. Despite her age, *Wolverine* was no mean submarine killer: as well as *U47*, she also sank *U76* and the Italian submarine *Dagabur*.

U106

GERMANY: 1940

The German Type IX submarines were true ocean-going boats of over 1000t. They were developed from the Type IA, itself an improved version of the Spanish *E1* (designed in Holland by the German-run IvS bureau) and which in turn owed much to the UEII Type of 1915. The Type IX was constructed as a combat boat and later, in small numbers, as cargo-carriers. They were double-hulled and divided into five watertight compartments; maximum operating depth was 100m (330ft), and crush depth was double that. *U106* was a Type IXB, constructed by Deschimag in Bremen. She was commissioned on 24 September 1940 and, during a combat career which spanned 35 months, she was credited with having sunk a total of 20 ships. She was herself sunk by depth charges dropped from Sunderland flying-boats of the RAF and RAAF, northwest of Cape Ortegal, on 2 August 1943. Only one boat of the class, *U123*, survived the war; she was taken into the French service as *Blaison*.

Displacement: 1034t surfaced; 1405t submerged
Dimensions: 251ft x 22ft 4in x 15ft 5in (76.5m x 6.8m x 4.7m)
Machinery: two-shaft, MAN 9-cyl. diesel engines, plus Siemens-Schuckert electric motors; 4400bhp/1000hp
Armament: six 21in (533mm) TT (four bow, two stern: 22 torpedoes, or 44 Type TMA or 66 Type TMB mines); one 4.1in (105mm); one 37mm; one 20mm
Speed: 18.2 knots surfaced; 7.3 knots submerged
Range: 12,000nm (22,200km) at 10 knots surfaced
Complement: 48

_U106_ operated first out of Wilhelmshaven and later, after the massive complex of armoured pens was constructed there, out of Lorient, as part of the 2nd Flotilla _(Flotilla Salzwedel)_.

U219

GERMANY: 1942

Germany constructed just eight purpose-built minelaying submarines during World War II; these were the Type XB, double-hulled ocean-going boats with an outer hull which was almost square in section, with two groups of six mine chutes each side of the outer hull and six more in the forward outer hull. They were adapted to carry cargo in the mine chutes. *U219* was taken over by Japan in May 1945. She served briefly as *I505*, and was surrendered at Djakarta.

Displacement: 1735t surfaced; 2660t submerged
Dimensions: ft in x ft in x ft in (89.8m x 9.2m x 4.7m)
Machinery: two-shaft, Germaniawerft 9-cyl. supercharged diesel engines, plus AEG electric motors; 4800bhp/1100hp
Armament: two 21in (533mm) TT (stern: 15 torpedoes); 66 Type SMA mines; one 4.1in (105mm); one 37mm; one 20mm
Speed: 17 knots surfaced; 7 knots submerged
Range: 18,450nm (34,250km) at 10 knots surfaced
Complement: 52

_U219_ was one of only eight purpose-built minelaying submarines constructed for the _Kriegsmarine_; like her, most also served as freighters.

U459

GERMANY: 1941

In 1940 work began on the Type XIV submarine tanker, which would meet the fleet boats out in the Atlantic and refuel them from the 425 tons of fuel they carried in tanks in the outer hull, allowing them to prolong their operational patrols. The tankers also carried four reload torpedoes in pressurized external canisters. *U459* was the first of the so-called 'milch cows' to enter service, in November 1941; she was sunk in July 1943 by RAF Coastal Command.

Alone amongst operational German submarines of World War II, the Type XIV 'milch cows' had no torpedo armament, only three light AA guns.

Displacement: 1660t surfaced; 2260t submerged
Dimensions: 220ft 2in x 30ft 10in x 21ft 4in (67.11m x 9.4m x 6.5m)
Machinery: two-shaft, Germaniawerft diesel engines, plus Siemens-Schuckert electric motors; 3200bhp/750hp
Armament: two 37mm; one 20mm
Speed: 14.5 knots surfaced; 6 knots submerged
Range: 12,500nm (23,150km) at 10 knots surfaced
Complement: 53

U2326

GERMANY: 1944

The Type XXIII U-boats, like the larger Type XXI, represented the culmination of submarine development in Germany up to and during World War II. Like the ocean-going 'electro-boats' they were designed largely by the 'Glückauf' Design Office at Blankenburg, in the Harz Mountains, where many of Hitler's secret weapons were to have been produced. The XXIII was a small coastal boat of under 230t standard displacement, divided into three watertight compartments. The pressure hull was in a 'figure-eight' configuration amidships and cylindrical towards the bow and stern, with tanks for ballast and fuel below, an outer fairing casing covering all to reduce drag to a minimum. The conning tower was small and streamlined. Like the Type XXI boats, the XXIII had very large-capacity batteries, creeping motors and snorkels incorporated into the conning tower casing; underwater performance (and handling) were better than when they were running on the surface. Maximum operating depth was 260ft (80m) and crush depth was twice that. The boats were constructed in four sections; it was the intention that they be assembled in Hamburg, Kiel, Linz, and at the captured facilities in Genoa, Monfalcone, Toulon, and Nikolayev. In the event, boats were only completed at the first two named locations. Of the boats commissioned, few made operational sorties. *U2326* was one of the first batch assembled in Hamburg and commissioned in August 1944. She was surrendered to the British at Loch Foyle on 14 May 1945, and was taken into the Royal Navy as HMS *Meteorite*. Transferred to France the following year, she was lost in an accident off Toulon, with all hands, on 6 December 1946.

Displacement: 230t surfaced; 270t submerged
Dimensions: 113ft 10in x 9ft 10in x 12ft 2in (34.7m x 3m x 3.7m)
Machinery: one-shaft, MWM diesel engine, plus AEG electric motor, plus creeping motor; 630bhp/580hp/35hp
Armament: two 21in (533mm) TT (bow: two torpedoes)
Speed: 10 knots surfaced; 12.5 knots submerged
Range: 2600nm (4800km) at 8 knots surfaced
Complement: 14

The Type XXIII U-boats could dive faster than any other submarine: when running on the surface, the boat took just 14 seconds to submerge.

U2501

GERMANY: 1944

By a very clear margin, the German Type XXI submarines were the best ocean-going boats produced anywhere during World War II. With their streamlined form, integral snorkel, and high-capacity batteries, they were the first true submarines. Their design derived from that of the experimental anaerobic-engined Type XVIII, two of which were laid down in 1942 but never finished. The work of Professor Hellmuth Walter – who was also active in the field of rocketry, and had built the motor which powered the first thrust-driven aircraft – the Type XVIII boat had the distinctive streamlined double pressure-hull form and the low faired-in conning tower which were to become familiar in the Type XXI. The powerplant was entirely conventional, save for its secondary single-commutator electric motors, designed for silent running. The battery compartment, on the other hand, was much more sophisticated than in other classes, with three 124-cell AFA batteries for 33,900ampère/hours, some three times the capacity of the batteries of the Type IX. Construction of the

Type XXI was modular; they were produced in eight sections in 11 different yards and assembled in four. A total of 740 were ordered, only 121 were completed and just two made operational sorties. *U2501* was the first constructed, by Blohm & Voss in Hamburg; she commissioned on 28 June 1944 but never saw service. She was scuttled by her crew on 3 May 1945 in Hamburg; the wreck was later broken up. A total of six boats survived the war intact, one was salvaged (and is now preserved at Bremerhaven), and perhaps 30 more were later completed by the Russians.

Displacement: 1595t surfaced; 2060t submerged
Dimensions: 251ft 8in x 21ft 8in x 20ft 8in (76.7m x 6.6m x 6.3m)
Machinery: two-shaft, MAN supercharged diesel engines, plus electric motors, plus creeping motors; 4000bhp/4200hp/226hp
Armament: six 21in (533mm) TT (bow: 23 torpedoes or 14 torpedoes plus 12 Type TMC mines); four 20mm
Speed: 15.5 knots surfaced; 17.2 knots submerged
Range: 15,000nm (27,800km) at 10 knots surfaced
Complement: 57

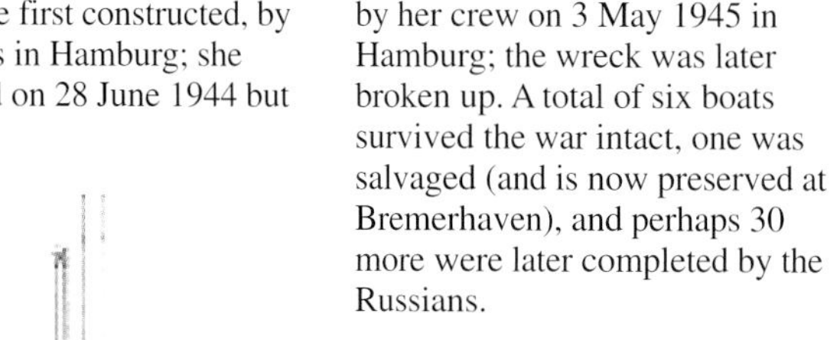

The German Type XXI U-boats were the world's first true submarines, faster submerged than they were on the surface.

UNICORN

GB: 1941

HMS *Unicorn* was ordered and constructed as an aircraft maintenance ship, but served as a light fleet carrier. Considerably smaller than the *Implacables* of the same period, she still had two-storey hangars with 16ft 6in (5m) of clear headroom, two lifts and a catapult able to launch a 14,000lb (6350kg) aircraft at 66 knots. She was constructed by Harland and Wolff in Belfast, and commissioned in March 1943. She supported the landings at Salerno, and again at Okinawa, and was finally sold for demolition in 1959.

Displacement: 14,750t standard; 20,300t full load
Dimensions: 646ft x 90ft x 24ft (196.9m x 27.45m x 7.3m)
Machinery: two-shaft, Parsons geared turbines; 40,000hp
Armament: eight 4in (102mm) HA; 16 (later 24) 2pdr pom-poms; 16 20 mm; 35 aircraft
Armour: flight deck 2in (51mm); box protection to magazines 3in-2in (76mm-51mm)
Speed: 24 knots
Range: 11,000nm (20,400km) at 13.5 knots
Complement: 1200

HMS *Unicorn* was built to support the *Illustrious*-class carriers, and repair their aircraft, but did not function in that role until the Korean War.

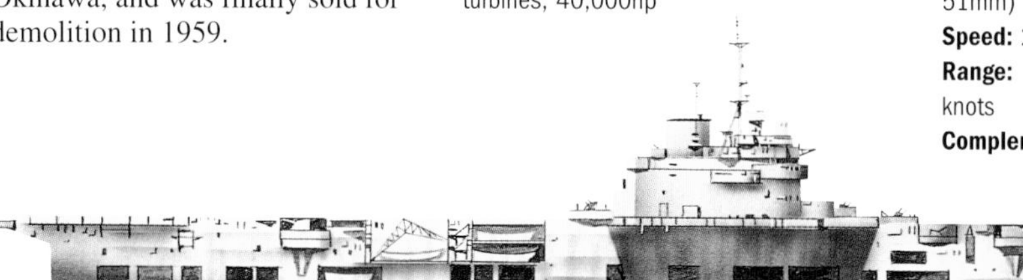

UNRYU

JAPAN: 1943

Displacement: 17,150t standard; 22,500t full load
Dimensions: 746ft 1in x 88ft 6in x 25ft 9in (227.4m x 27m x 7.85m)
Machinery: four-shaft, Kampon geared turbines; 152,000hp
Armament: 12 5in (127mm) DP; 51 (later 89) 25mm; (later 48 R/L); 65 aircraft
Armour: belt 5.9in-1.8in (150mm-45mm); deck 2in-1in
Speed: 34 knots
Range: 8000nm (14,800km) at 18 knots
Complement: 1595

The *Unryu*-class vessels were the last, and theoretically the most advanced, Japanese carriers of World War II. Six were launched (and 11 more were proposed) but only three were completed. They were essentially copies of the *Hiryu*, but with a larger island and two lifts. Some, including the class leader, were fitted with cruiser-type powerplants, the others had double destroyer machinery. *Unryu* was constructed at Yokosuka Navy Yard. She never saw combat, and was sunk by the submarine *Redfish* in December 1944.

Unryu was designed as a strike carrier, to attack convoys, rather than to fight fleet actions.

URSULA

GB: 1938

Displacement: 540t surfaced; 730t submerged
Dimensions: 191ft x 16ft 1in x 15ft 2in (58.2m x 4.9m x4.6 m)
Machinery: two-shaft, Paxman-Ricardo diesel engines, plus electric motors; 615bhp/825hp
Armament: six 21in (533mm) TT (four bow, two external: eight torpedoes); one 3in (76mm)
Speed: 11.25 knots surfaced; 9 knots submerged
Range: c5000nm (9250km) at 8 knots surfaced
Complement: 27

HMS Submarine *Undine* and her two sisterboats were built in the mid-1930s to replace the few remaining World War I-vintage *H*-class coastal submarines. They were single-hull types, with an operational depth of 200ft (60m) and were unusual in having diesel-electric drive when surfaced. They served as the prototypes for the wartime *U* class. Two external torpedo tubes in the bows gave them a rather ungainly aspect. Of the three, *Ursula* alone mounted a 3in (76mm) gun. She was loaned to the USSR from 1944–49.

The *Undine* class were intended to serve as training boats. They proved to be very successful, and large numbers of modified craft were built during World War II.

VANGUARD

GB: 1944

HMS *Vanguard* was the last battleship constructed for the Royal Navy (and save for the *Jean Bart*, 10 years in construction, the last in the world). Strictly speaking *Vanguard* was obsolete even before she was commissioned in August 1946. Plans for her were first drawn up in 1939, to make use of the four 15in twin turrets which had been removed from the *Courageous*-class battlecruisers when they were converted to aircraft carriers in the 1920s, by installing them, suitably modified, in a ship capable of 30 knots, and she was authorized in 1941. She was markedly different from earlier British battleships, with a transom stern and considerable sheer forward, which made her a much better sea-boat than her predecessors. (And better all-round than the US Navy's *Iowas*; during heavy weather in a combined exercise in 1953, *Vanguard* was observed to roll through 30 degrees while *Iowa* rolled through 52 degrees.) *Vanguard* was built by John Brown on the Clyde. She was decommissioned after only 10 years service, and scrapped from 1960.

HMS *Vanguard* was the biggest, heaviest, fastest, and most expensive battleship the Royal Navy ever constructed – she cost £9 million at 1944 values.

Displacement: 44,500t standard; 51,420t full load
Dimensions: 814ft 4in x 108ft x 34ft 10in (248.2m x 32.9m x 10.6m)
Machinery: four-shaft, Parsons geared turbines; 130,000hp
Armament: eight 15in (381mm); 16 5.25in (135mm) DP; 73 40mm; four 3pdr
Armour: belt 14in-4.5in (355mm-115mm); bulkheads 12in-4in (305mm-102mm); barbettes 13in-11in (332mm-280mm); turret faces 13in (332mm); conning tower 3in (76mm)
Speed: 30 knots
Range: 14,000nm (26,000km) at 15 knots
Complement: 1893

VENERABLE

GB: 1943

Displacement: 13,200t standard; 18.050t full load
Dimensions: 694ft x 80ft x 23ft 3in (211.5m x 24.4m x 7.1m)
Machinery: two-shaft, Parsons geared turbines; 40,000hp
Armament: 24 2pdr pom-poms; 32 20mm; 48 aircraft
Speed: 25 knots
Range: 12,000nm (22,200km) at 14 knots
Complement: 1300

HMS *Venerable* was the third ship launched of the 10-strong *Colossus* class of light fleet aircraft carriers. These ships were of much lighter construction than the earlier fleet carriers, lighter even than *Unicorn*, with no protection save for an armoured mantlet round the torpedo magazine, and no watertight longitudinal bulkheads save in the machinery spaces. The *Colossus* class were designed early in 1942, in response to the realization that the war had become global, that the large fleet carriers then in design, the *Eagles*, would not be ready until 1945 at the very earliest, and that escort carriers – the first of which, *Audacity* and *Archer*, had just completed – would clearly be incapable of providing air cover during fleet actions. There were no obviously suitable fast-but-obsolete warships to convert. The solution was to specify ships which could be built quickly (and relatively cheaply) by non-specialist divisions of the leading yards. Hence, a design emerged with a single-storey hangar, on a large cruiser's displacement, and with a destroyer's machinery for a maximum of 25 knots. The basic principle was sound, and later proven when 10 more such ships, in two classes and to somewhat modified designs so that they could operate bigger, heavier aircraft, were constructed. *Venerable* was built by Cammell Laird and entered service in January 1945, in time to see service in the Pacific. She was sold to Holland as the *Karel Doorman* in 1948, there receiving an angled flight deck; she was sold again to Argentina, as the *Vienticinco de Mayo* and, after being laid up for 10 years, was eventually sold for scrap in 1996 for about $60 per ton.

HMS *Venerable* was to have two more identities during the course of a long life. She served as HNLMS *Karel Doorman* from 1948–1969, and then as the Argentinian *Vienticinco de Mayo*.

VINDEX

GB: 1943

During the latter part of her career, HMS *Vindex* operated Fairey Fulmars as night fighters, on the Arctic run to Murmansk.

Vindex was one of a pair of fast 'reefers', converted while still on the stocks to become escort carriers in a similar fashion to HMS *Activity*. They had a single-storey hangar and a flight deck 495ft (151m) long, and a single lift to connect them. Somewhat longer than *Activity*, *Vindex* and her sister ship *Nairana* could operate more aircraft. Both were commissioned in December 1943 and spent the war in the North Atlantic. *Vindex* was reconverted to a merchant ship, post-war, and stayed in service until 1970.

Displacement: 13,445t standard; 16,830t full load
Dimensions: 528ft 6in x 68ft x 25ft 2in (161.1m x 20.75m x 7.65m)
Machinery: two-shaft, Doxford diesels; 10,700bhp
Armament: two 4in (102mm) HA; 16 2pdr pom-poms; 16 20mm; 18-21 aircraft
Speed: 16 knots
Range: 12,000nm (22,200km) at 15 knots
Complement: 700

VITTORIO VENETO

ITALY: 1937

In addition to the four entirely reconstructed World War I battleships, the *Regina Marina Italiana* also operated three brand-new fast battleships during World War II. The first to enter service was the *Vittorio Veneto*, constructed by Cantieri Riuniti dell'Adriatico (CRDA) at Monfalcone; the second, *Littorio*, was built by Ansaldo in Genoa (Genova); and the third, the *Roma*, was also built by CRDA, but at Trieste. A fourth unit, the *Impero*, was laid down and launched at Trieste but never completed. The *Littorio*s were of a thoroughly modern design, the work of Umberto Pugliese, and were the first battleships laid down since the British *Nelson*s of 1922. Perhaps they were never intended to come in under the 35,000t limit set by the Naval Treaties: by the time they were authorized in 1934, the legend weight would seem to have been around 40,000t. Had Italian ordnance factories been able to turn out guns and mountings up to the Treaty limit of 16in (406mm), it is probably safe to say that the battleships would have mounted them – and been even heavier as a result. *Vittorio Veneto* entered service in April 1940; she was hit by an aerial torpedo at the Battle of Matapan in March 1941, and repairs took five months. She was torpedoed again in December 1941, this time by the British submarine *Urge*, and was out of action until March, 1942. She was interned in the Bitter Lakes from late 1943, and returned in 1946. *Vittorio Veneto* was awarded to Britain as a reparation in 1947 and later broken up.

In the spring of 1940, the *Vittorio Veneto* was the most modern battleship in the world. All English and Italian commercial sources claim she was built at Trieste, but the Italian Navy's historical list states Monfalcone.

Displacement: 40,520t standard; 45,030t full load
Dimensions: 780ft x 107ft 7in x 34ft 6in (237.75m x 32.8m x 10.5m)
Machinery: four-shaft, Belluzzo geared turbines; 128,200hp
Armament: nine 15in (381mm); 12 6in (152mm); four 4.7in (120mm); 12 3.6in (90mm) AA; 20 37mm; 16 20mm
Armour: belt 11in (280mm); bulkheads 8.25in (210mm); decks 6.4in–1.8in (162mm–45mm); barbettes 13.8in–11in (350mm–280mm); turret faces 13.8in (350mm); conning tower 10.2in (260mm)
Speed: 30 knots
Range: 4600nm (8500km) at 16 knots
Complement: 1830

VLADIMIR POLUKHIN

USSR: 1940

The *Vladimir Polukhin* class, built in the Soviet Union both during and after World War I, were the best large minesweepers the Red Navy had. They only entered service in small numbers, the locations where they were built – Leningrad (St Petersburg) and Sevastopol – being either beseiged or overrun by the German Army in 1941. *Polukhin* was constructed in Leningrad, and completed, under difficult conditions, in November 1942. It is believed that she remained in service until sometime in the 1960s.

The Soviet *Vladimir Polukhin*-class minesweepers were fast, handy small warships which could also function as minelayers.

Displacement: 700t standard; 900t full load
Dimensions: 249ft 4in x 26ft 3in x 7ft 5in (76m x 8m x 2.25m)
Machinery: two-shaft, geared turbines; 8000hp
Armament: two 3.9in (100mm); three 37mm; two 20mm; 15 mines
Speed: 24 knots
Range: not available
Complement: 120

VOLTA

FRANCE: 1936

Displacement: 2885t standard; 4020t full load
Dimensions: 451ft 1in x 41ft 7in x 15ft (137.5m x 12.65m x 4.55m)
Machinery: two-shaft, Rateau-Bretagne geared turbines; 92,000hp
Armament: eight 5.5in (140mm); four (later two) 37mm, later two 25mm; four (later eight) 13.2mm MG, later eight 8mm MG; 10 21in (550mm) TT; 40 mines
Armour:
Speed: 39 knots
Range: 4000nm (7400km) at 18 knots
Complement: 264

The two *Mogador*-class destroyer leaders were the biggest and most heavily-armed ships of the type constructed for the French Navy prior to World War II, with heavier armament on 10 per cent greater displacement than that of earlier classes. *Volta* was built by Ateliers et Chantiers de Bretagne at Nantes and entered service in 1937. In order to ensure no deterioration of performance, it was necessary to install a still larger powerplant than that fitted to the *Le Fantasques*, with over 100,000hp available in an emergency (on trial, *Volta* produced almost 105,000hp, for a top speed of almost 43 knots). Sadly, these magnificent ships were spoiled by their twin 5.5in (140mm) gun mounts, which were both complex and delicate, and unreliable as a result. Having served with the French High Seas Fleet, *Volta* was scuttled at Toulon on 27 November 1942, together with her sister ship, and was later raised and broken up.

Had it not been for their unreliable main guns, *Volta* and *Mogador* would have been two of the best destroyers of their day.

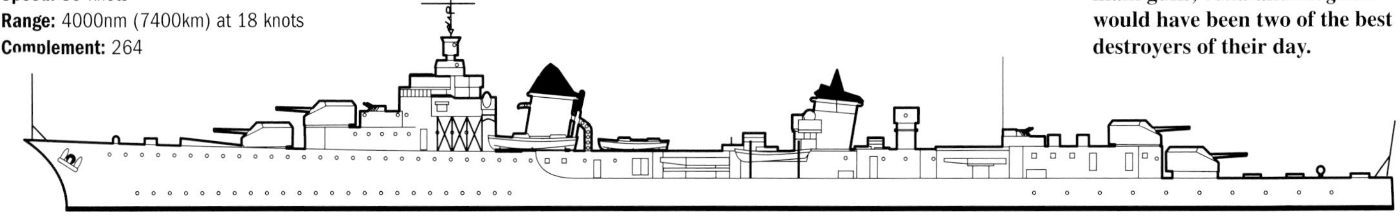

WALKER

GB: 1917/42

During World War II, the Royal Navy made very good use of the late-World War I destroyers it still had in service. These were *V*- and *W*-class ships, constructed in 1917–19, and many were converted to one of three new configurations: as AA ships, with appropriate armament; as short-range escorts, with a reduced weapons suite and fuel load, to boost performance; and as long-range escorts, with the forward boiler room converted to a fuel bunker to increase their range and the now-redundant fore funnel removed. HMS *Walker* was one of the latter. Built by Denny, she was completed originally as a minelayer and commissioned on 12 February 1918. Her weapons suite was only slightly modified – she lost a triple bank of torpedo tubes and the aftermost 4in (102mm) gun in order to ship a Hedgehog AS mortar, depth charge throwers and depth charge racks – and she gained some 20mm guns. *Walker* survived the war but was sold for breaking up immediately afterwards.

Displacement: 1100t (later 1200t) standard; 1490t (later 1690t) full load
Dimensions: 312ft x 29ft 6in x 10ft 6in (95.1m x 9m x 3.2m)
Machinery: two-shaft, Brown-Curtis geared turbines; 27,000hp (later 15,000hp)
Armament: four (later three) 4in (102mm); one 3in (76mm) AA, later five 20mm; six (later three) 21in (533mm) TT, later Hedgehog; DC throwers; DC racks
Speed: 34 (later (25) knots
Range: 3500nm (6500km) - later 4500 nm (8350km) - at 15 knots
Complement: 127

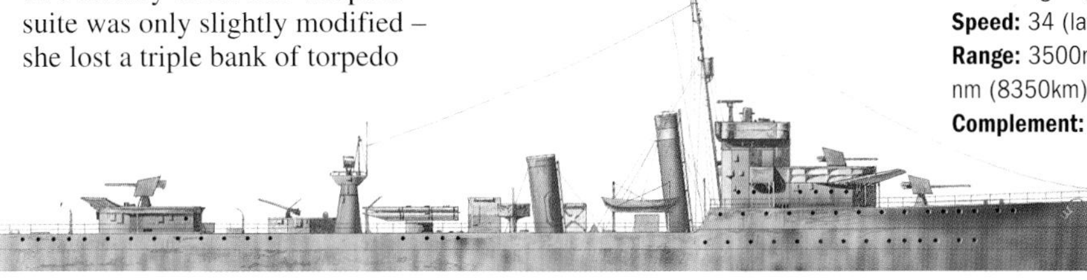

HMS *Walker* was one of the World War I-vintage destroyers converted to the convoy escort and protection role in World War II.

WASP

USA: 1939

Displacement: 14,700t standard; 18,450t full load
Dimensions: 741ft 3in x 93ft x 24ft 6in (225.9m x 28.35m x 7.45m)
Machinery: two-shaft, Parsons geared turbines; 70,000hp
Armament: eight 5in (127mm) DP, later four 40mm; 16 1.1in MG; 16 0.5in MG, later deleted; 20 20mm
Armour: deck 1.5in (37mm)
Speed: 29.5 knots
Range: 12,500nm (23,150km) at 15 knots
Complement: 1889 (later 2167)

Though she was not laid down until after the Washington Treaty had lapsed, USS *Wasp* was built in accordance with its provisions, to use up the 15,000t displacement left over after the completion of the *Yorktown* and *Enterprise*. Unfortunately, her designers were forced to try to incorporate as many of the features of those ships as possible into one which was only 75 per cent of their displacement. The compromise was most obvious in the powerplant and in the lack of protection – there was provision made to add an armour belt in time of war, but it was never fitted. *Wasp* was commissioned in April 1940 and joined the Atlantic Fleet, contributing significantly to Malta's survival by delivering a total of about 100 Spitfire fighters to the island. In June 1942, she transferred to the Pacific and on 15 September was torpedoed by *I19* off Guadalcanal and set ablaze. She was subsequently abandoned and sunk.

The *Wasp* was a compromise, forced on the US Navy by the Washington Treaty, but she proved invaluable in the relief of Malta.

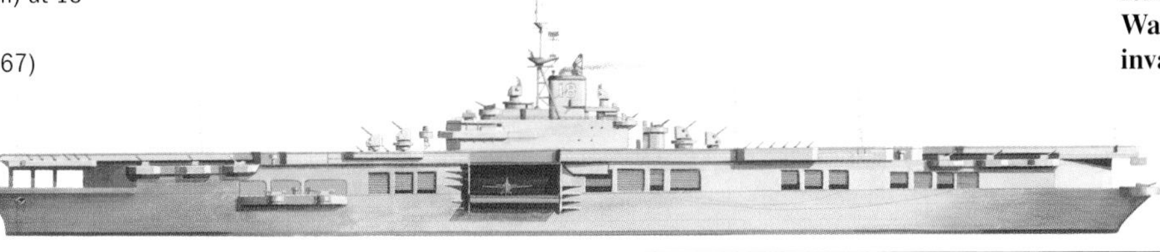

WELSHMAN

GB: 1940

Displacement: 2650t standard; 4000t full load
Dimensions: 418ft x 40ft x 14ft 9in (127.4m x 12.2m x 4.5m)
Machinery: two-shaft, Parsons geared turbines; 72,000hp
Armament: six 4in (102mm) HA; four 2pdr pom-poms; 156 mines
Speed: 40 knots
Range: 1000nm (1850km) at 38 knots
Complement: 242

Designed from the outset as fast minelayers, the Royal Navy's *Abdiel*-class vessels were smaller than the smallest light cruisers (the *Arethusas*) but had the machinery of the bigger *Perths*. They were, thus, very fast ships indeed, capable of over 41 knots at light displacement and good for 1,000 miles (1850km) at 38 knots, heavily laden. Capable of out-running even motor torpedo-boats, they were much in demand as transports for urgent cargo, and were often employed to run ammunition to the besieged garrisons at Malta and Tobruk. They were lightly armed for ships of their size – more lightly, in fact, than the destroyers of the period – and had protection only against splinters. HMS *Welshman* was constructed by Hawthorn Leslie on the Tyne, a yard better known for its destroyers (though a second *Abdiel*, HMS *Apollo*, was also built there, as well as four cruisers and the light fleet carrier *Triumph*). She entered service on 25 August 1941. Her initial employment was in home waters; in early February 1942, together with *Manxman* she sowed over 1000 mines along the probable line of Operation 'Cerberus' (the 'Channel Dash' of the German battleships *Scharnhorst* and *Gneisenau*). In May 1942, she began what were to be regular full-speed runs between Gibraltar and Malta, carrying ammunition. This she was still doing when, with her route often extended to Tobruk, she was torpedoed off that port by *U617*, a Type VIIC U-boat, on 1 February 1943. Together with USS *Wasp*, *Welshman* received much of the credit for enabling the island fortress of Malta to hold out.

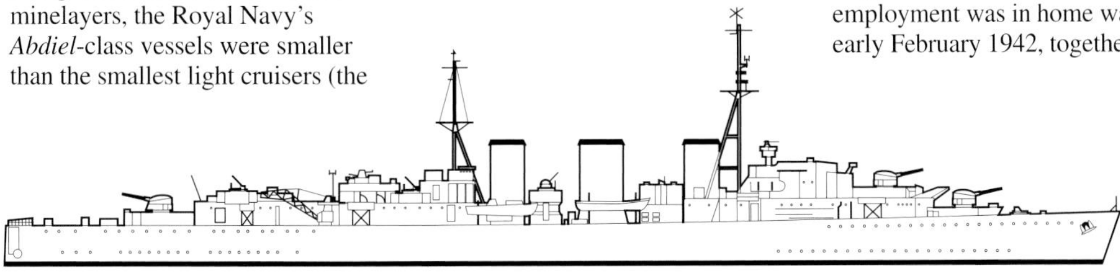

HMS *Welshman* was built as a fast minelayer. She and her sister ships were the fastest ocean-going ships in the British fleet.

WICHITA

USA: 1937

A singular and unique ship, USS *Wichita* was a heavy cruiser version of the *Brooklyns*, on the same hull and with the same machinery, but with heavier armour and 8in (203mm) in place of 6in (152mm) guns. She was a significant improvement over the earlier *New Orleans* class, since she was able to incorporate many of the light cruisers' features and also had a new design of triple turret, which cured some of the problems experienced with the earlier vessels. To some extent, *Wichita* was a prototype for the later *Baltimores*, though it would perhaps be more accurate to say that she provided a model to be modified. Her most important shortcoming was her excessive top-weight, but it was not a major problem. *Wichita* was commissioned in February 1939; she survived World War II both unscathed and largely unchanged, save that in August 1945 her light AA armamant was modernized. There were plans, which came to nothing, to convert her to a guided-missile cruiser after the war. She was sold for breaking up in 1959.

USS *Wichita* was a transitional design. Many of her features are discernable in the later *Baltimores*.

Displacement: 10,590t standard; 13,015t full load
Dimensions: 608ft 4in x 61ft 9in x 23ft 9in (185.4m x 18.8m x 7.25m)
Machinery: four-shaft, Parsons geared turbines; 100,000hp
Armament: nine 8in (203mm); eight 5in (127mm) DP, later 24 40mm; 18 20mm; eight 0.5in MG (later deleted); four aircraft
Armour: belt 6in-4in (152mm-102mm); deck 2.25in (58mm); barbettes 7in (178mm); turret faces 8in (203mm); conning tower 6in (152mm)
Speed: 33 knots
Range: 10,000nm (18,500km) at 15 knots
Complement: 929

WRIGHT

USA: 1945

Displacement: 14,500t standard; 18,750t full load
Dimensions: 683ft 7in x 108ft x 27ft (208.35m x 32.9m x 8.2m)
Machinery: four-shaft, General Electric geared turbines; 120,000hp
Armament: 40 (later eight) 40mm; 32 20mm (later deleted); 48 (later four) aircraft
Armour: belt 4in (102mm); bulkheads 4in (102mm); deck 2.5in (64mm)
Speed: 33 knots
Range: 13,000nm (24,000km) at 15 knots
Complement: 1821 (later 1317)

USS *Wright* began her life as a light fleet carrier, but ended up as a floating command centre.

In 1943, the US Navy ordered two additional light carriers, improved versions of the *Independence*, based on the hull of the *Brooklyn*-class cruisers, rather than that of the *Clevelands*. In fact, a completely new (but generally similar) hull was designed for them, both longer and broader abeam; they were also given the machinery of the *Baltimores*, protected like the *Essex* class, with a flight deck strengthened to allow them to operate heavier aircraft. The single hangar deck communicated with the flight deck via two centreline lifts, and there were two hydraulic catapults fitted. They had a small starboard island, similar to that fitted to the *Commencement Bays*. USS *Wright* was the second of the pair; she commissioned in 1947 and operated as a training carrier. She was deactivated in 1956. Later, she recommissioned, converted to a command ship (actually, a National Emergency Command Post Afloat, with presidential accommodation) in 1963. She was decommissioned again in 1970 and stricken seven years later.

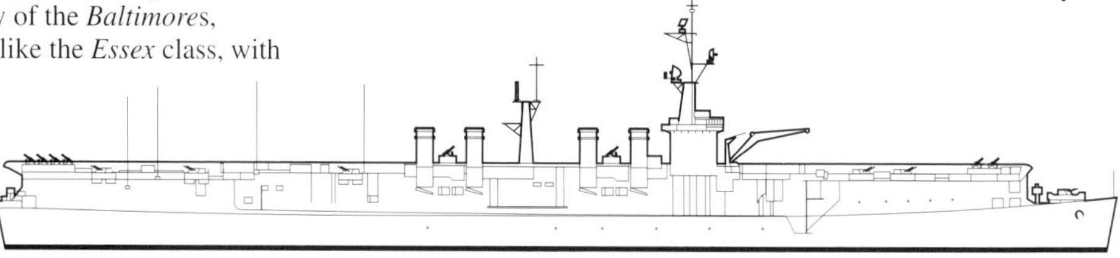

X5

GB: 1942

The British *X*-class midget submarines were developed from an experimental boat designed for riverine use by the British Army. They were intended to attack stationary shipping in harbours and sheltered anchorages, being towed, submerged, to within range of their targets behind *S* and *T*-class submarines. Two prototypes, *X3*

Despite their diminutive size, the *X* craft could dive to 300ft (92m); they had a wet-and-dry lock and carried a diver, whose task was to clear obstacles.

and *X4* were built, and from these the *X5* was the first operational unit developed. She was constructed by Vickers-Armstrong, and entered service in 1942. The most notable event involving the class was the unsuccessful attempt to sink the German battleship *Tirpitz* on September 22 1943, *X5* disappeared without trace during the mission. *X*-craft were also used successfully against Japanese shipping in Singapore in 1945.

Displacement: 26.9t surfaced; 31.7t submerged
Dimensions: 51ft 7in x 5ft 9in x 7ft 4in (15.7m x 1.75m x 2.25m)
Machinery: one-shaft, Gardner diesel engine, plus electric motor; 42bhp/30hp
Armament: two 10,500lb (4770kg) explosive charges
Speed: 6.5 knots surfaced; 5.5 knots submerged
Range: 1320nm (2445km) at 4 knots surfaced
Complement: 4

XIIBIS CLASS

USSR: 1937–41

Displacement: 210t surfaced; 261t submerged
Dimensions: 146ft x 10ft 10in x 10ft 1in (44.5m x 3.3m x 3.1m)
Machinery: one-shaft, diesel engine, plus electric motor; 800bhp/400hp
Armament: two 21in (533mm) TT (bow); one 45mm; one 7.62 mm MG
Speed: 13.5 knots surfaced; 7.7 knots submerged
Range: 3000nm (5600km) at 8 knots surfaced
Complement: 20

The Soviet Union constructed Series XII submarines – small coastal boats in the 200t class – in two groups. The first, consisting of only four units, can be considered as prototypes for the second, the XIIbis. These latter boats had streamlined conning towers and increased bunkerage. They were built in six sections, small enough to be transported by rail or canal, in many of the Baltic and Black Sea yards and at Gorki, and assembled where they were needed. Of the 50 constructed, 19 survived the war.

The 200-ton *M*-type (Malyutka – 'small') submarines of the Red Navy were the smallest practicable design of World War II.

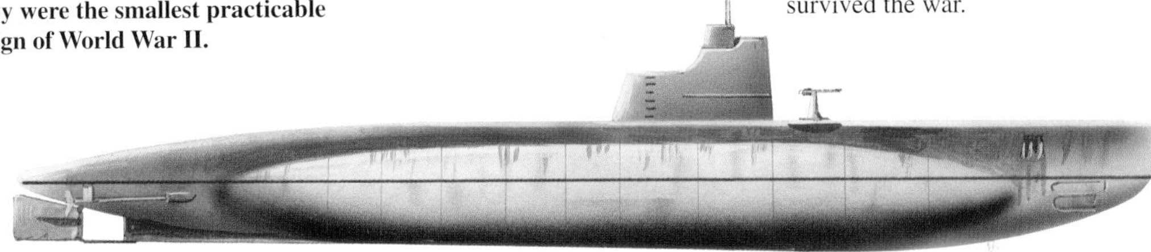

XIIIBIS CLASS

USSR: 1939–1941

Displacement: 1123t surfaced; 1416t submerged
Dimensions: 273ft 3in x 23ft x 13ft 5in (83.3m x 7m x 4.1m)
Machinery: two-shaft, diesel engines, plus electric motors; 4200bhp/2400hp
Armament: one 3.9in (100mm); one 45mm; two 7.62mm MG; eight torpedo tubes (six bow, two stern); 20 mines
Speed: 18 knots surfaced; 10 knots submerged
Range: not available
Complement: 55

The Soviet Union constructed just 24 purpose-built minelaying submarines between 1930 and the outbreak of war against Germany in 1941. The Series XIIIbis proved to be the most sophisticated. Six only were constructed: three in Leningrad and three in Nikolayev (though earlier types were also built in Vladivostock). They were a saddle-tank design, with mines carried in a pair of horizontal stern tubes, a system developed by the Imperial Russian Navy during World War I.

The three Soviet Series XIIIbis minelaying submarines which survived World War II remained in service until the 1950s.

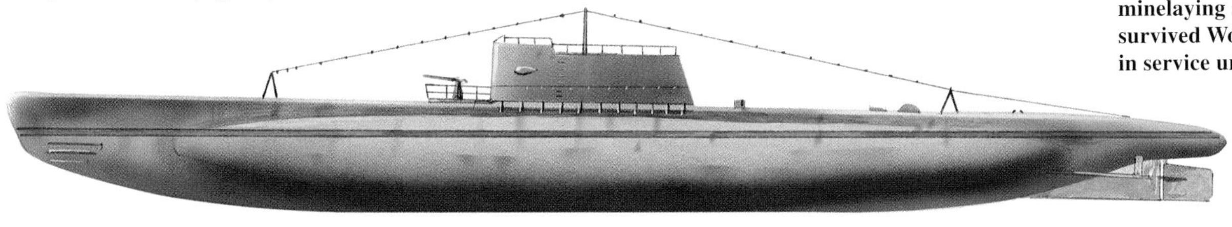

XV CLASS

USSR: 1940

The final series of *M*-type submarines constructed for the Soviet Union during World War II were quite different from the preceding groups and an entirely new design, somewhat bigger and with two-shaft machinery for rather better performance on the surface. Like earlier groups, these boats were constructed in seven sections (but only in Leningrad), and then transported by rail and canal to wherever they were needed. Maximum operating depth was 260ft (79m). Three were operational during the war, and more were constructed later.

The Soviet *M*-type submarines proved to be effective despite (or perhaps because of) their size. Some Series XV boats were still active in the 1960s.

Displacement: 281t surfaced; 351t submerged
Dimensions: 162ft 5in x 14ft 5in x 9ft (49.5m x 4.4m x 2.75m)
Machinery: two-shaft, diesel engines, plus electric motors; 1600bhp/875hp
Armament: four 21in (533mm) TT (bow); one 45mm; two 7.62mm MG
Speed: 15.7 knots surfaced; 7.8 knots submerged
Range: 3000nm (5600km) at 8 knots surfaced
Complement: 24

YAMATO

JAPAN: 1940

Displacement: 63,000t (later 65,000t) standard; 71,660t (later 72,810t) full load
Dimensions: 862ft 9in x 121ft 1in x 34ft 1in (263m x 36.9m x 10.4m)
Machinery: four-shaft, Kampon geared turbines; 150,000hp
Armament: nine 18.1in (460mm); 12 (later six) 6.1in (155mm); 12 (later 24) 5in (127mm) DP; 24 (later 150) 25mm; six or seven aircraft
Armour: belt 16.1in (410mm); deck 9.1in–7.9in (230mm–200mm); turret faces 25.6in (650mm); conning tower 19.7in (500mm)
Speed: 27 knots
Range: 7200nm (13,320km) at 16 knots
Complement: 2500

Many design elements of the Japanese super-battleships still remain shrouded in secrecy. In August 1945, all the drawings – and even the official photographs – of the ships were destroyed.

The battleships *Yamato* and *Musashi* were the ultimate of the type: the biggest, best-protected, and best-armed warships of all time. Indeed, *Musashi* set a minor record of her own: the biggest warship ever launched from a slipway, at 35,737t. Their design was initiated in 1934, and the first presentation submitted on 10 March 1935, in the knowledge that the Washington and London Treaties, which controlled the construction of new capital ships, were to expire on 31 December 1936. There were to be no less than 22 more design submissions prepared before authorization to proceed was finally given, and construction of the *Yamato* began, at Kure Navy Yard, on 4 November 1937. She was followed, in March 1938, by *Musashi* at Mitsubishi's Nagasaki yard – later the target for the second atomic bomb. Two more units were authorized: *Shinano* was completed as an aircraft carrier but the unnamed 'No 111' was broken up incomplete. Much of the design work concentrated on the possibility of giving the ships a combined steam and diesel powerplant (and diesel-only was also considered), but the necessary 30,000hp engines were unavailable. *Yamato* was floated out of the specially-enlarged dry-dock at Kure on 8 August 1940; her main guns, transported by a specially-

The *Yamato* and her sister ship *Musashi* were the ultimate gun-armed warships, supposedly impregnable to (2200lb)1000kg AP bombs, and with guns which could fire 1.46t shells to a range of almost 23nm, at a rate of up to two rounds per barrel per minute.

built heavy-lift ship, the *Kashino*, were mounted between May and July 1941. On 16 December, nine days after the attack on Pearl Harbor, *Yamato* was commissioned. She became Admiral Yamamoto's flagship on 12 February 1942, and served in that capacity at Midway, with the intention of using her 18.1in (460mm) rifles to bombard the island itself. Ironically, it was the overwhelming effectiveness of carrier-based aircraft during that battle which finally brought home the fact that the days of the battleship were numbered. *Yamato* was hit by a single torpedo from the US submarine *Skate* off Truk on Christmas Day 1943, and took on 3000t of water. However, she made Kure on 16 January and was repaired, during which her heavy AA battery was modified and she rejoined the fleet on 1 May 1944. She was in combat in the Marianas in June. Later, on 25 October (the day after the *Musashi* was sunk, by 17 bombs and perhaps as many torpedoes), *Yamato* finally fired her guns, 104 rounds in all, at US warships in the Battle of the Samur Sea, sinking an escort carrier and a destroyer. She was herself sunk off Okinawa, on what was effectively the most involved Kamikaze mission of the war, on 7 April 1945. Hit by six bombs and perhaps 10 torpedoes, she went down at 1423hrs, with the loss of all but about 280 officers and men aboard.

YASTREB

USSR: 1941

During the 1930s and 1940s the Soviet Union constructed a number of fast, lightly-armed, lightly-built shallow-draught ships for coastal guard duties. Manned by NKVD as well as Red Navy personnel, they replaced torpedo boats left over from the Imperial Navy, which had never been entirely suitable. The production of such ships in wartime was severely curtailed; some under construction in Leningrad (St Petersburg) were sent to Gorki via the canal and river system, and completed there.

A total of eight Yastreb-class guard-ships were laid down; the lead ship was completed in Leningrad 1943.

Displacement: 905t standard; 1060t full load
Dimensions: 275ft 7in x 27ft 3in x 9ft 10in (84m x 8.3m x 3m)
Machinery: two-shaft, geared turbines; 23,000hp
Armament: three 3.9in (100mm); four 37mm; six 0.5in MG; three 17.7in (450mm) TT; 20 mines
Speed: 30 knots
Range: not available
Complement: 148

YMS 100 CLASS

USA: 1942

Displacement: 270t standard; 360t full load
Dimensions: 136ft x 24ft 6in x 7ft 9in (41.45m x 7.45m x 2.35m)
Machinery: two-shaft, diesels; 800bhp
Armament: one 3in (76mm); one 20mm
Speed: 15 knots
Range: not available
Complement: 60

The 'Yard Mine Sweepers' were constructed for the US Navy from 1942 for purely inshore duties. They were built out of wood for simplicity (though that would render them immune to magnetic mines in a later era) and had low-powered diesel machinery. In fact, ships of this class often made trans-oceanic voyages, and were employed to sweep ahead of invasion forces. A submarine-chaser version was a failure due to the inadequate maximum speed. Many of the class were used for general duties.

The wooden YMS-class minesweepers were to prove useful not only at the task for which they were designed, but for general duties.

Z20

GERMANY: 1938

The Third Reich built its first destroyers in 1934. Subsequent classes were modelled on them, and all shared their shortcomings to some extent. Though they were amongst the fastest in the world at the time, these destroyers were unstable, steered and manoeuvred poorly and were very wet indeed. Halfway through the production of the Type 36, improvements were introduced, beginning with a new 'clipper' bow profile for the *Karl Galster*, otherwise known as *Z20*. The type were heavily built, with innovative high-performance high-pressure steam machinery which often proved unreliable. They were well-armed ships, even from the outset, but *Karl Galster*, the only survivor of the invasion of Norway (during which all five of her sister ships were sunk) received many more AA guns. She was constructed, like all the class, by Deschimag in Bremen, and entered service in March 1939. She survived the war and was taken as a Russian prize. Re-named *Procniy*, she served in the Baltic until about 1960.

The *Karl Galster* (*Z20*) was the only ship of her class not to be sunk in the vicinity of Narvik during 10–13 June 1940.

Displacement: 1810t standard; 3415t full load
Dimensions: 410ft 1in x 38ft 8in x 13ft 1in (125m x 11.8m x 4m)
Machinery: two-shaft, Wagner geared turbines; 70,000hp
Armament: five 5in (127mm); four (later six) 37mm; six (later 15) 20mm; eight 21in (533mm) TT; 60 mines
Speed: 36 knots
Range: 2050nm (3800km) at 19 knots
Complement: 330
Country: Germany

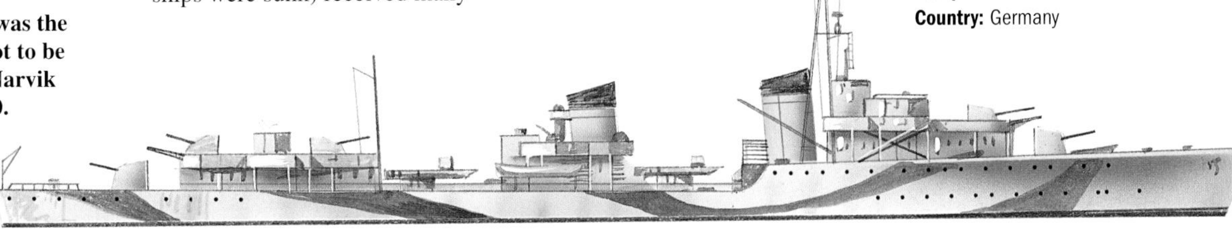

Z30

GERMANY: 1940

A total of just eight Type 1936A destroyers were constructed for the *Kriegsmarine* from November 1938, numbered *Z23 – Z30*. They were more heavily armed than the Type 1936 and earlier classes with a new 5.9in (150mm) gun – the biggest mounted aboard any destroyer – which proved to be unsatisfactory, since its ammunition consisted of separate charge and projectile, and difficult to manage. Designed with a twin mounting forward, they were completed with a single; the four ships which later received the twin were hampered by the extra weight forward, which badly affected their already poor sea-keeping. Two of the class were later modified to the 'Barbara' AA configuration with 12 37mm and 18 20mm light AA guns in place of the (5.9in) 150mm guns in the 'Q', 'X', and 'Y' positions. *Z30* was built by Deschimag at Bremen and commissioned in November 1941. She was unmodified in service, taken as a British prize at the war's end, and expended in underwater explosives experiments.

Displacement: 2657t standard; 3691t full load
Dimensions: 416ft 8in x 39ft 4in x 15ft 2in (127m x 12m x 4.6m)
Machinery: two-shaft, Wagner geared turbines; 70,000hp
Armament: four 5.9in (150mm); four 37mm; five 20mm; eight 21in (533mm) TT
Speed: 38.5 knots
Range: 2950nm (5460km) at 19 knots
Complement: 321

The *Narvik* class, as these destroyers are sometimes known, were poor sea-keepers and never entirely effective.

Z51

GERMANY: 1944

In 1943, Deschimag began construction of a single 'fleet torpedo boat' to serve as a trials ship for an all-diesel powerplant. She was to be considerably larger than previous types, with her machinery arranged to allow a great degree of flexibility – she had three shafts, the wing shafts driven directly by a single 5620bhp engine each, the central shaft driven through a Vulcan gearbox by four 11,650bhp engines. All the units were manufactured by MAN and were normally-aspirated two-stroke double-acting V-12s and V-24s. There is no indication whether the propellers on the wing shafts were a different size and/or pitch from that on the central shaft, though that may have been the case. She was to have had lighter main armament than any preceding class, but many more light AA guns. *Z51* was launched, but never completed; she was sunk by RAF Mosquito bombers in the fitting-out dock, on 21 March 1945, and was later broken up *in situ*.

Despite her destroyer pennant number, *Z51* was to have served as the prototype for the Type 1942 'fleet torpedo boats', none of which were ever constructed.

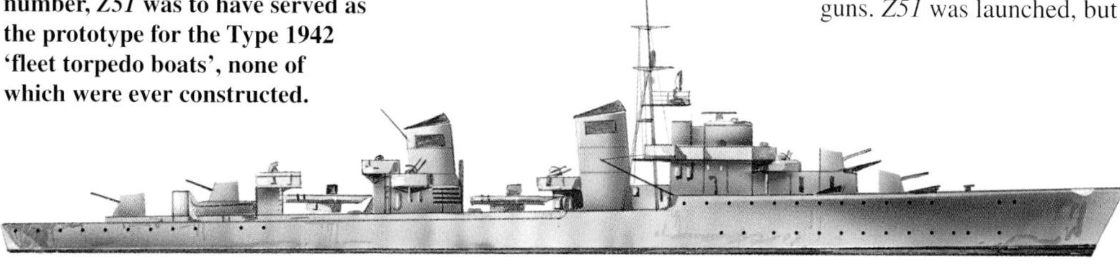

Displacement: 2330t standard; 2632t full load
Dimensions: 375ft x ft in x ft in (114.3m x 11m x 4m)
Machinery: three-shaft, MAN diesels; 57,8400bhp
Armament: four 5in (127mm); eight 37mm; 12 20mm; six 21in (533mm) TT
Speed: 36 knots
Range: 5500nm (10,190km) at 19 knots
Complement: 235

Zealous

GB/ISRAEL: 1944

Displacement: 1730t standard; 2575t full load
Dimensions: 362ft 9in x 35ft 8in x 14ft 6in (110.55m x 10.85m x 4.4m)
Machinery: two-shaft, Parsons geared turbines; 40,000hp
Armament: four 4.5in (114mm); two 40mm; four 2pdr pom-poms; eight 21in (533mm) TT
Speed: 36.5 knots
Range: 6000nm (11,100km) at 15 knots
Complement: 186

The Z-class destroyers were repeats of the *S* to *Ws*. They were armed with the much more powerful Mk IV 4.5in (115mm) gun which, despite its marginally smaller calibre, fired a heavier shell further than the Mk IX 4.7in (119mm) gun of the earlier class. The Zs were laid up immediately after the war, but in 1955 HMS *Zealous* was sold to Israel and became the *Elath* (*Eilat*), the flagship of the Israeli Navy. She was the first warship sunk by a surface-to-surface missile (Styx), off Port Said on 21 October 1967.

The Z-class destroyers were the first in British service to mount the 4.5in (115mm) gun, which was the standard calibre until the end of the century.

ZG3

GREECE/GERMANY: 1938

The destroyer *Vasilefs Georgios* was constructed by Yarrow at Scotstoun for the Greek Navy from 1937. One of two British *G*-class ships with modified armament, her 5in (127mm) guns were substituted for the 4.7in (119mm) guns of the British ships, her 37mm light AA guns replaced the 2pdr pom-poms, she received 20mm guns in addition, and her quadruple banks of torpedo tubes replaced the quintuple of her class. She was damaged in a German bombing raid on 13 April 1941 at Salamis, and the floating dock in which she was being repaired was subsequently sunk a week later by Ju.87 dive bombers. When Greece fell to the Axis invasion, she was salvaged, repaired at the Skaramanga Navy Yard, which had been taken over by Germaniawerft, and put back into service with the *Kriegsmarine* on 21 March 1942 as *ZG3*. The following August, she was named *Hermes*. Disabled off Trapani on 30 April 1943 by RAF bomber aircraft, with the loss of 23 crew, she was towed to Tunis and scuttled in the harbour mouth on 7 May.

Displacement: 1415t standard; 2090t full load
Dimensions: 332ft x 34ft 1in x 9ft 10in (101.2m x 10.4m x 3m)
Machinery: two-shaft, Parsons geared turbines; 34,000hp
Armament: four 5in (127mm); four 37mm; four (later eight) 20mm; eight 21in (533mm) TT
Speed: 32 knots
Range: 5500nm (10,200km) at 15 knots
Complement: 215

***ZG3*, later named *Hermes*, was the only major German surface warship to operate in the Mediterranean during World War II.**

ZUIHO

JAPAN: 1936

The carrier *Zuiho* and her sister ship *Shoho* were laid down as submarine support ships in the mid-1930s, being converted to light carriers (*Zuiho*, originally the *Takasaki*, while fitting out, *Shoho* after she had been in commission, as the *Tsurugisaki*, for two years). These ships were part of the large 'shadow fleet' programme and were constructed in such a way as to facilitate the conversion. They were built up to provide a hangar deck topped by a flight deck which allowed them to operate 30 aircraft, the flight deck extending to 80 per cent of their overall length (*Zuiho*'s was subsequently extended to almost the full length of the ship). The original diesel machinery was replaced by destroyer-type boilers and geared turbines. *Zuiho* suffered serious damage at Santa Cruz, inflicted by aircraft from USS *Enterprise*. She was repaired and later took part in the fighting at Guadalcanal and the Marianas, but was sunk at Cape Engano during the Battle of Leyte Gulf.

Displacement: 11,260t standard; 14,200t full load
Dimensions: 671ft 11in x 59ft 9in x 21ft 9in (204.8m x 18.2m x 6.65m)
Machinery: two-shaft, Kampon geared turbines; 52,000hp
Armament: eight 5in (127mm) DP; eight (later 46) 25mm; (later 48 R/L); 30 aircraft
Speed: 28 knots
Range: 7800nm (14,450km) at 18 knots
Complement: 785

With no protection at all, *Zuiho* was very vulnerable; her sister ship *Shoho* was sunk in just minutes at the Battle of the Coral Sea.

ZUIKAKU

JAPAN: 1939

Displacement: 25,675t standard; 32,105t full load
Dimensions: 844ft 10in x 95ft x 29ft 1in (257m x 29m x 8.85m)
Machinery: four-shaft, Kampon geared turbines; 160,000hp
Armament: 16 5in (127mm) DP; 42 (later 82, later 108) 25mm; 72 aircraft
Armour: belt 6.5in-1.8in (175mm-45mm); deck 5.9in-3.9in (155mm-100mm
Speed: 34 knots
Range: 10,000nm (18,500km) at 18 knots
Complement: 1660

The *Zuikaku* and her sister ship, the class leader *Shokaku*, were enlarged and improved versions of the *Soryu* and *Hiryu*. Much of the additional displacement went to thicken their protective decks, though the flight deck and intermediate hangar deck remained unarmoured, as did the hangar sides – the main shortcoming in these vessels. Nonetheless, they are considered by many to have been the most succesful of all the Japanese carriers, and were certainly to have the longest careers. Wartime modification consisted of adding light AA weapons, as usual, but in May 1944 *Zuikaku* had the air spaces around her aviation spirit bunkers filled with concrete in an effort to exclude the air and make explosion less likely. *Zuikaku* was built by Kawasaki at Kobe and entered service in late September 1941. With those of her sister ship, her aircraft sank the USS *Lexington*. She herself was badly damaged in the Philippine Sea, and was sunk at Cape Engano during the Battle of Leyte Gulf.

The timing of the Japanese attack on Pearl Harbor was determined by the availability of the *Zuikaku* and the *Shokaku*, which were two of its mainstays.

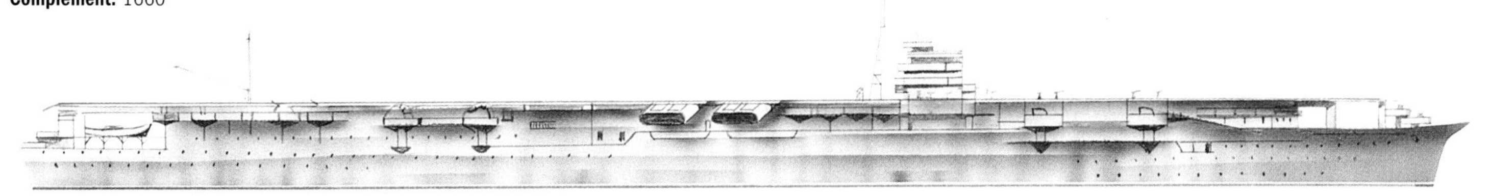

375

CHAPTER EIGHT

THE NUCLEAR ERA 1946–2000

The six years of World War II put an end to centuries of conventional thinking on naval forces. The capital ship was no longer an all-powerful force. In the North Atlantic, and more so in the Pacific, the supremacy of the battleship ended when air power defeated sea power. The aircraft carrier has brought a whole new dimension to naval warfare and it has been the dominant element of every major application of sea power since 1945.

Today, the anti-ship missile has long since replaced the gun as the primary offensive weapon of most naval vessels, and small missile-armed attack craft are one of the most dangerous and unpredictable threats facing any naval commander. Increasingly also, modern warships have to fight and win an electronic war – both to find their targets and to protect themselves from attack.

Left: The Type 22 frigates have proved to be a great success for the RN. HMS *Beaver* (F93) seen here, was one of the Batch Two ships, lengthened to accommodate the towed-array sonar.

'Stealth' is becoming an increasing factor in warship design and many of the most modern surface combatants have incorporated low-observable construction techniques in an attempt to reduce their radar signatures and their vulnerability to detection and attack. This has led to a generation of ships that look very different to their predecessors – these changes are most noticeable on vessels like Israel's *Sa'ar* 5-class corvettes and France's *Lafayette-class.*

Underwater, submarines continue to play their cat-and-mouse games with surface fleets and the advances in undersea warfare technology have been immense. The Soviet Union made impressive gains in submarine development during the Cold War and this pace has been maintained, to a lesser degree, by Russia today.

ABUKUMA

JAPAN: 1988

The six ships of Japan's *Abukuma* class are large and capable escort frigates, comparable to some of the fleet's smaller destroyers. They were laid down between 1988 and 1991; *Abukuma* (DE 229) was launched on 21 December 1988 and completed on 12 December 1989. The class incorporate some 'stealthy' design features to reduce their radar signature, by using non-vertical and rounded surfaces throughout the hull and superstructure. The effect of these refinements is undermined by the decidedly 'non-stealthy' lattice mainmast and air-search radar antenna.

***Abukuma*'s main armament is a 3in (76mm) main gun and Harpoon anti-ship missiles – the latter carried in two quad launchers at the rear of the ship.**

Displacement: 2050t standard; 2550t full load
Dimensions: 357ft 7in x 44ft x 12ft 6in (109m x 13.4m x 3.8m)
Machinery: two-shaft CODOG, two gas turbines; 26,650hp
Armament: eight Harpoon SSM; one 3in (76mm); one Mk 15 Phalanx 20mm CIWS; one ASROC; six 12.7in (324mm) ASW TT
Sensors: air-search radar; sea-search radar; fire-control radar; hull-mounted sonar
Speed: 27 knots
Range: not available
Complement: 115

ACTIVE

GB: 1972

The Royal Navy acquired eight Type 21 *Amazon*-class frigates between 1974 and 1978, of which HMS *Active* (F 171) was the third. She was laid down at the Vosper Thornycroft yard on 23 July 1971, launched on 23 November 1972 and completed on 17 June 1977. From *Active* onwards, the Type 21s were fitted with a quad launcher for MM38 Exocet anti-ship missiles, in the 'B' position (behind the main gun). The *Amazon*-class vessels were well liked by those who served on them because they were comfortable and handled well. However, they had very limited growth potential and were not big enough to accommodate the new weapons and sensors that were required during their service lifetime. At war during the Falkland Islands campaign of 1982, the lightweight aluminium construction of the Type 21s proved unable to withstand the rigours of heavy seas and combat. However, HMS *Active* survived the Falklands conflict, unlike two of her sisterships, and was sold to the Pakistan Navy.

The six surviving *Amazons* were sold to Pakistan in 1993–94 and renamed the *Tariq* class. HMS *Active* is now the *Shahjahan* and has been comprehensively upgraded with new weapons and systems.

Displacement: standard 3100t; full load 3600t
Dimensions: 384ft x 41ft 7in x 19ft 5in (117m x 12.7m x 5.9m)
Machinery: two-shaft CODOG, two gas turbines; 56,000hp
Armament: four MM38 Exocet SSM; one Seacat SAM system; one 4.5in (114mm); two 20mm cannon; six 12.75in (324mm) TT
Sensors: search radar; fire-control radar; hull-mounted sonar
Speed: 30 knots
Range: 4000nm (7408km) at 17 knots
Complement: 175-192

ADELAIDE

AUSTRALIA: 1978

Displacement: 4100t full load
Dimensions: 453ft x 45ft x 14ft 8in (138.1m x 13.7m x 4.5m)
Machinery: one-shaft, two gas turbines; 40,000hp
Armament: eight Harpoon SSM and Standard SAMs using a common launcher; one 3in (76mm); one Mk 15 Phalanx 20mm CIWS; up to six 12.7mm MG; six 12.7in (324mm) TT; two Seahawk helicopters
Sensors: air-search radar; surface-search/navigation radar; fire-control radar; hull-mounted sonar
Speed: 29 knots
Range: 4,500nm (8334km) at 20 knots
Complement: 176

The *Adelaide*-class guided missile frigates of the Royal Australian Navy are essentially identical to the US Navy's FFG-7 *Oliver Hazard Perry*-class ships. Australia decided to acquire the American warships having cancelled plans to develop its own *DDL* class in 1974. There are six vessels in the *Adelaide* class – four built in Seattle and the remainder built in Williamstown, Australia. At one time it had been hoped to acquire four additional, larger, *Adelaide*s but these plans were shelved. *Adelaide* (01) was laid down on 29 July 1977, launched on 21 June 1978 and completed on 15 November 1980. These vessels have a multi-role air defence, anti-submarine and anti-surface vessel capability and, like their equivalent FFGs, can deploy two Seahawk helicopters. However, the most important role of the *Adelaide*s in RAN service is fleet air defence, for which they rely on the Standard SM-1 SAM system.

Only her flags and pennant number distinguish *Adelaide* from her US counterparts – the *Oliver Hazard Perry*-class FFGs. Australia's six *Adelaide*-class frigates are among the most potent warships of their kind.

ADMIRAL PETRE BARBUNEANU

ROMANIA: 1981

Romania's four *Tetal*-class frigates are small anti-submarine escort vessels based largely on the Soviet *Koni*-class, though with some changes. *Admiral Petre Barbuneanu* (260) is the lead ship in the class, launched from the Manglia yard in 1981 and completed in February 1983. Romania also has two additional modified *Tetal*-class ships, each with a redesigned superstructure and a helicopter deck. The *Admiral Petre Barbuneanu*'s primary offensive weapons are its 16-tube RBU-2500 anti-submarine mortars.

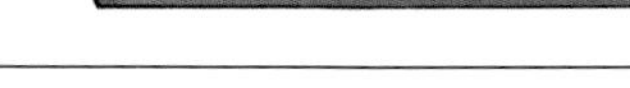

The *Admiral Petre Barbuneanu*'s chief distinguishing feature is the very long forecastle, with its 3in (76mm) gun turret.

Displacement: 1440t full load
Dimensions: 303 ft 1in x 38ft 4in x 9ft 8in (95.4m x 11.7m x 3m)
Machinery: two-shaft, two diesel engines; 20,000hp
Armament: two twin 3in (76mm); four 30mm; two 14.5in (368mm) MG; two RL; four 21in (533mm) TT
Sensors: air/surface-search radar; fire-control radar; hull-mounted sonar
Speed: 24 knots
Range: not available
Complement: 95

ADMIRAL SENYAVIN

USSR: 1952

Displacement: 13,600t standard; 16,640t full load
Dimensions: 672ft 4in x 22ft 7in x 72ft (210m x 22m x 6.9m)
Machinery: unknown, estimated rating of 110,000hp
Armament: 12 6in (152mm); 12 3.9in (100mm); 32 37mm AA; 10 21in (533mm) TT
Sensors: hull-mounted sonar
Speed: 32.5 knots
Range: 9000nm (16,668km) at 18 knots
Complement: 1250

As part of her 1970–72 refit, the *Admiral Senyavin* was equipped with four twin 30mm gun turrets and a pop-up SA-N-4 SAM launcher above the helicopter hangar.

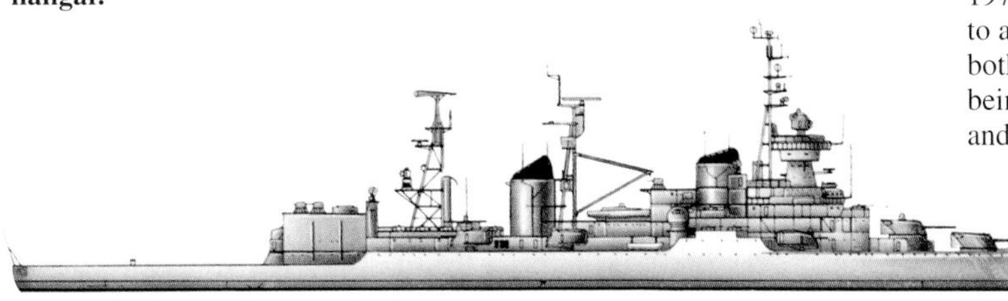

The Soviet Union was unique among the world's navies in continuing to build large capital ships after World War II. One such vessel was the *Admiral Senyavin*, the fifth example of the *Sverdlov*-class of heavy cruisers all of which had long operational careers; the *Admiral Senyavin* was not stricken from the fleet until 1991. Between 1970 and 1972 she was modified to act as a command ship, with both rear 6in (152mm) gun turrets being replaced by a helicopter deck and hangar.

ADMIRAL ZOZULA

USSR: 1965

Until its political priorities changed during the mid-1960s, the Soviet Union built four *Kresta I*-class ships, as 'large anti-ship rocket cruisers'. The *Admiral Zozula* was the leadship, launched in October 1965 and completed in October 1967. The vessels in this class were armed with SS-N-3 anti-ship missiles, which they retained throughout their operational careers despite many plans to modernise them. In 1991 the *Admiral Zozula* was refitted with four 30mm 'Gatling' gun turrets, abaft the SS-N-3 launchers.

Two twin SS-N-3 anti-ship missile launchers were mounted in stand-alone fairings, fore and aft, on all the *Kresta I*-class cruisers.

Displacement: 6000t standard; 6500t full load
Dimensions: 508ft 6in x 55ft 9in x 18ft 1in (155m x 17m x 5.5m)
Machinery: two-shaft steam turbines; four pressure-fired boilers; 100,000hp
Armament: two twin SS-N-3 SSM; two twin SA-N-1 SAM; four 57mm; four RL; 10 21in (533mm) TT; one helicopter
Speed: 34 knots
Range: 10,500nm (19,446km) at 14 knots
Complement: 380

AGOSTA

FRANCE: 1974

The French Navy's four *Agosta*-class ocean-going attack submarines were a modern design for the 1970s, with a double-hulled construction and conventional motors. These boats spent their early operational life in the Mediterranean, before being deployed in the Atlantic. The *Agosta* was launched on 19 October 1974 and completed in July 1977; she can dive to a maximum of 984ft (300m) and is capable of a maximum underwater speed of 17.5 knots for 60 minutes. An emergency boost allows 20.5 knots to be reached for five minutes of evasive action, and a small 'creep' motor provides a capability for silent operations at just 3.5 knots. Four torpedo tubes are fitted in the bow and a maximum of 20 highly-accurate wire-guided torpedoes can be carried. *Agosta* is also armed with submarine-launched SM39 Exocet anti-ship missiles. Similar submarines have been exported to Pakistan.

Displacement: 1490t surfaced; 1740t submerged
Dimensions: 222ft x 22ft x 18ft 1in (67.6m x 6.8m x 5.5)
Machinery: one-shaft, two diesels and one electric motor; 3600hp/4600hp
Armament: four 21.6in (550mm) TT; MM38 Exocet missiles
Speed: 17.5 knots surfaced; 12 knots submerged
Range: 8500nm (15,742km) at 9 knots
Complement: 54

The blunt, bull-nosed bow of the *Agostas* is fitted with a sonar housed in a cylindrical fairing above the nose, just forward of the diving planes. Since their introduction into service these boats have been refitted with a DSUV 62A towed sonar array, to increase target detection capability.

AGUIRRE

PERU: TRANSFERRED 1976

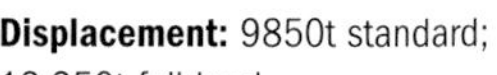

Originally the Dutch-built cruiser *De Zeven Provincien*, which was transferred to Peru in August 1976, the *Aguirre* (CH 84) is one of two such cruisers currently in service and effectively the Peruvian Navy's flagship. A *De Ruyter*-class ship, she was refitted between 1962 and 1964 with the stern-mounted Tartar SAM system launcher, becoming a guided missile cruiser. On transfer to her Peruvian ownership, the Tartar system was removed and replaced by a capacious helicopter flight deck and hangar, typically embarking up to three Agusta-built ASH-3D Sea Kings. *Aguirre* now serves as a 'helicopter cruiser'. Her sistership, the *Admirante Grau*, is unmodified and retains the *De Ruyter* standard pair of twin 6in (152mm) gun turrets at the rear of the ship. In fact, the two cruisers differ on many levels, *Aguirre* lacking *Grau*'s MM38 Exocet launchers and several other weapons and radar systems.

The *Aguirre* is a vessel of the 1940s and, as such, she has distinctly 'old style' lines and design features.

Displacement: 9850t standard; 12,250t full load
Dimensions: 614ft 7in x 56ft 8in x 22ft (182.4m x 22m x 6.7m
Machinery: two-shaft, geared turbines, four boilers; 85,000hp
Armament: four 6in (152mm); six 40mm; four 30mm; depth charges (two racks), helicopters
Sensors: air-search radar; surface-search/targeting radar; navigation radar; fire-control radar; hull-mounted sonar
Speed: 32 knots
Range: 7000nm (12,964km) at 12 knots
Complement: 953

AKULA CLASS

USSR: 1984

Displacement: 7500t surfaced; 9100t submerged
Dimensions: 360ft 1in x 45ft 9in x 34ft 1in (110m x 14m x 10.4m)
Machinery: one-shaft, one nuclear reactor; 43,000hp
Armament: four 21in (533mm) and four 25.5in (650mm) TT; plus SS-N-21 SLCMs and SS-N-15/16 anti-ship missiles
Speed: 32 knots surfaced; 18 knots submerged
Range: not available
Complement: approximately 70

The Russian for 'Shark' is 'Akula' and on the appearance of a new generation of nuclear-powered fast attack submarines (SSNs) that entered Soviet service in the mid-1980s, NATO applied the code-name accordingly. However, the constructors knew the boats as 'Project 971' and the Soviet Navy named the lead boat *Bars*. The SSNs incorporated a new powerplant, weapons, and sensor technology that made them challenging opponents. Indeed, these deep-diving boats were rated 'as good as', if not better than, many Western counterparts and they have proved to be very difficult to detect.

These big SSNs are effective fighting submarines, but their steel-hulled design and new reactor type have proved to have a short operational life.

AL MADINA

SAUDI ARABIA: 1983

Saudi Arabia's four French-built *Al Madina*-class frigates are based on the Type F 2000S design. Their acquisition, in the mid-1980s, marked a major step forward in Saudi naval capability. *Al Madina* was launched on 23 April 1983 and completed on 5 January 1985. The frigates are all well armed and helicopter capable, embarking a single SA 365F Dauphin helicopter as required. Their primary role is surface attack, though they are equally well suited to anti-submarine and air defence missions.

Despite their compact size, the *Al Madina*-class frigates are well armed and very capable warships.

Displacement: 1990t standard; 2610t full load
Dimensions: 377 ft 3 in x 41 ft x 16 ft (115m x 12.5m x 4.9m)
Machinery: two-shaft, eight diesels; 32,000hp
Armament: eight Otomat Mk 2 SSM; one Crotale SAM launcher (24 missiles; one 3.9in)100mm); four 40mm cannon; four 17.33in (440mm) TT; one AS-15-armed SA 365F Dauphin helicopter
Sensors: air/surface-search radar; navigation radar; fire-control radar; hull-mounted sonar
Speed: 30 knots
Range: 8000nm (14,816km) at 16 knots
Complement: 179

ALBACORE

USA: 1953

Displacement: 1500t surfaced; 1850t submerged
Dimensions: 210ft 6in x 27ft 4in x 18ft 6in (64.2m x 8.3m x 5.6m)
Machinery: one-shaft, two diesels and one electric motor; 1500hp/15,000hp
Armament: none
Speed: maximum 33 knots submerged
Range: varied, depending on powerplant configuration
Complement: 52

Though she could be described as 'just' an experimental vessel, the USS *Albacore* (AGSS 569) holds a key place in the history of submarine development. She was the first US submarine designed to operate entirely underwater and so she pioneered the bullet-shaped streamlined design of modern submarines. From the earliest days of submarine warfare, the 'boats' conducted all of their transits on the surface because their underwater drag reduced their speed, and range dramatically. Submarines would only submerge when initiating an attack, or being attacked themselves. To all intents and purposes, they were 'submersible torpedo boats'. The smooth new lines of *Albacore* allowed her to maintain an operationally useful underwater speed without using excessive power – for the very first time in a submarine. *Albacore* was laid down on 15 March 1952 and launched on 1 August 1953. Thanks to her large onboard battery pack, she was capable of astonishing 'dash' speeds of 27 knots. By the end of her operational career new developments in high-capacity silver-zinc batteries had boosted that speed to 33 knots. Coupled with the advent of the first onboard nuclear powerplants, the *Albacore*-type hull-form introduced greatly increased endurance, speed and manoeuvrability for all the submarines that followed her. Throughout her life, *Albacore* was modified many times, as new control surfaces and new (conventional) power packs were fitted. In 1961, her hull length was stretched from 203ft 9in (62.1m) to 210ft 6in (64.2m) and her conventional stern control surfaces were replaced by new X-form planes, a dorsal rudder, a new bow-mounted sonar dome and diving brakes.

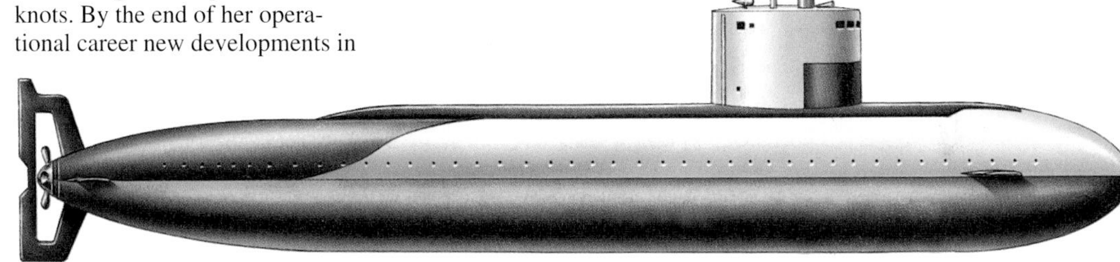

USS *Albacore* made a major contribution to the design and development of modern submarines. Her revolutionary new streamlined shape set her apart from the other submarines of the 1950s.

ALBANY

USA: 1962

For the United States, the cruiser USS *Albany* was one of the great symbols of that bold new 'nuclear navy' that was born in the heady days of the late 1950s. She was a World War II veteran, one of the 16 large *Baltimore*-class cruisers launched between 1942 and 1945. In November 1962 she was recommissioned as the lead ship (of three) in a new class of converted nuclear-powered guided-missile cruisers. In this much-modified form, the *Albany* (CG10) was a radical vessel, armed primarily with the Talos and Tartar SAMs. Only a pair of 5in (127mm) guns were retained on this warship of the 'missile age'. Plans to fit the Regulus II cruise missile – and later even Polaris ICBMs – to *Albany*-class ships did not proceed, but *Albany* herself had a long service career as the flagship of the Second Fleet. She was decommissioned in 1980. Even then, *Albany* was held in reserve, despite the withdrawal from service of her primary Talos missile system.

Albany carried 52 missiles for her long-range Talos SAM system (twin launchers mounted on the bow and stern) and a further 42 for the smaller Tartar system.

Displacement: 14,394t standard; 18,777t full load
Dimensions: 674ft 11in x 69ft 9in x 25ft 9 in (205.8m x 21.3m x 7.9m)
Machinery: four-shaft, geared turbines, four boilers; 120,000hp
Armament: two twin Talos and Tartar SAM launchers; two 5in (127mm); one ASROC; six 12.75in (324mm) TT
Sensors: air-search radar; surface-search/targeting radar; navigation radar; fire-control radar; hull-mounted sonar
Speed: 32 knots
Range: 7000nm (12,964km) at 15 knots
Complement: 1266

ALFA CLASS

USSR: 1967

Displacement: 2800t surfaced; 3680t submerged
Dimensions: 267ft 1in x 31ft 2in x 23ft (81.4m x 9.5m x 7m)
Machinery: one-shaft (nuclear), one nuclear reactor; approximately 45,000hp
Armament: six 21in (533mm) TT (18 torpedoes, 36 mines or SS-N-15 ASM)
Speed: 43–45 knots submerged
Range: not available
Complement: approximately 31

The Soviet Union's Project 705 *Lira* attack submarines appeared in the 1970s and were acknowledged as the first Soviet submarine design to rival that of its Western equivalents. Code-named *Alfa* by NATO, this class introduced several unusual technologies, such as liquid metal-cooled nuclear reactors and very strong titanium hulls. These hulls allowed the *Alfa*s to dive as deep as 2330ft (710m), outside the range of most Western torpedoes of that time. However, the class relied on a high degree of automation which was prone to failure and the nuclear powerplants also suffered several failures.

The prototype *Alfa* (K-377) was launched in 1967. This boat was followed by a further five production-standard units which entered service between 1979 and 1983. The *Alfa*s proved to be unsuccessful pioneers. K-377 was broken up after a reactor failure in 1974. The others were mostly retired by the late 1980s.

ALLIGATOR CLASS

USSR: 1964

The Project 1171 Nosorog large landing ships (BDK) were better known to NATO as the *Alligator* class. The first vessel, *Voronezhskiy Komsomolets* (BDK-10), was completed in 1966. All the *Alligators* had large bow and stern ramps and could carry between 25 and 30 APCs or 1500t of cargo. Early production ships had three deck cranes, while later examples had just one. These later ships also had an enclosed bridge, plus gun and rocket armament.

The Soviet Navy built 16 *Alligator* class BDKs at Kaliningrad, in four slightly differing classes, between 1964 and 1967.

Displacement: 3400t standard; 4700t full load
Dimensions: 370ft 6in x 50ft 2in x 14ft 5in (112.8m x 15.3m x 4.4m)
Machinery: two diesels; 8000hp
Armament: two or three SA-N-5 SAM launchers (some examples); two 37mm; four 25mm; one 4.8in (122mm) RL (fit varies from ship to ship)
Speed: 18 knots
Range: 14,000nm (25,910km) at 10 knots
Complement: 75, plus 300 troops

ALMIRANTE BROWN

ARGENTINA: 1981

Argentina's *Almirante Brown* (D 10) was the first of four German-designed MEKO 360 *H2*-class frigates acquired during the early 1980s. These vessels are Argentina's most modern warships. Along with her sisterships, *Almirante Brown* has a primary anti-surface and air defence tasking, armed with Exocet and Aspide missile systems. She also boasts credible gun and torpedo armament and can embark two Alouette III helicopters for limited ASW capability.

In 1990 the *Almirante Brown* sailed to the Persian Gulf and joined the coalition naval forces deployed for Operation Desert Shield/Desert Storm.

Displacement: 2900t standard; 3660t full load
Dimensions: 413ft x 49ft 3in x 19ft (125.9m x 15m x 5.8m)
Machinery: two-shaft, COGOG four gas turbines; 51,800hp/10,200hp
Armament: eight MM40 Exocet SSM; one octuple SAM launcher; one 5in (127mm); four 40mm; six 12.75in (324mm) TT; two helicopters
Sensors: air/surface-search radar; surface-search radar; navigation radar; fire-control radar; hull-mounted sonar
Speed: 30.5 knots
Range: 4500nm (8334km) at 18 knots
Complement: 200

ALMIRANTE RIVEROS

CHILE: 1958

Displacement: 2730t standard; 3300t full load
Dimensions: 402ft x 43ft x 13ft 4in (122.5m x 13.1m x 4m)
Machinery: two-shaft, geared turbines, two boilers; 54,000hp
Armament: four MM38 Exocet SSM; one Seacat SAM system; four 4in (102mm), four 40mm; six 12.75in (324mm) TT; two Squid ASW mortars
Sensors: air-search radar; air/surface-search radar; navigation radar; fire-control radar; hull-mounted sonar
Speed: 34.5 knots
Range: 6000nm (11,112km) at 16 knots
Complement: 266

Built in England, at Vickers' Barrow yard, during the late 1950s, Chile's two *Almirante*-class large destroyers are among the oldest warships still in front-line service. *Almirante Riveros* (18) was laid down in 1957 and launched in December 1958. She is armed with an 'old and new' mix of four 4in (102mm) main guns, Seacat SAMs and Exocet anti-ship missiles. The Vickers-designed main guns, on a unique mounting that can be elevated up to 75°, have a maximum range of 12,400yds (11,340m).

Chile's *Almirante Riveros* entered service in 1961, a few months after her equally venerable sistership, the *Almirante Williams*.

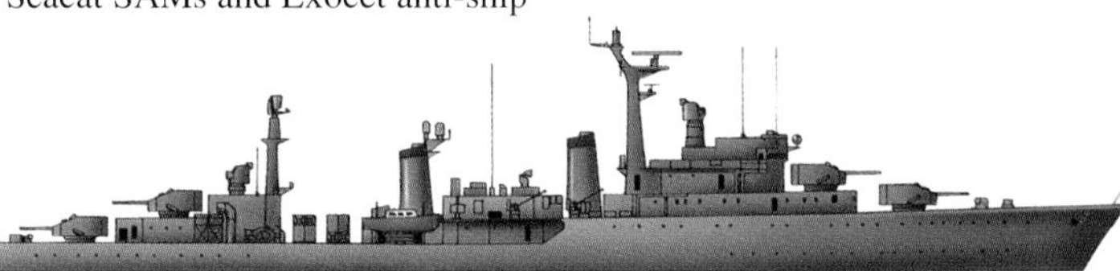

ALVAND

IRAN: 1968

Iran's four *Alvand*-class frigates were based on the British Vosper Thornycroft Mk 5 design and, as such, resemble scaled-down Type 21 frigates. They were built as the *Saam* class, but were renamed in 1985 – when the *Saam* (DE 12) became the *Alvand* (71). The Mk 5 used the new generation of compact but powerful gas turbines, lightweight weapons and computerised systems to provide a good compromise between cost and capability. One vessel was sunk by US aircraft in 1988.

***Alvand* has mounted on her stern a distinctive combination of Sea Killer SSM launchers, A/S mortar and 35mm gun turret.**

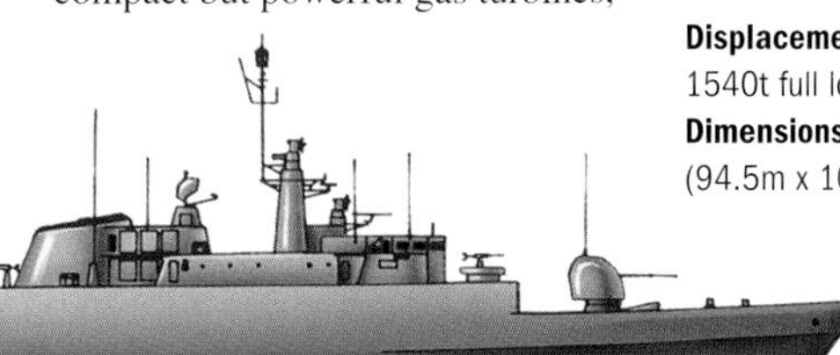

Displacement: 1250t standard; 1540t full load
Dimensions: 310ft x 34ft 5in x 11ft 6in (94.5m x 10.5m x 3.5m)
Machinery: two-shaft, CODOG, two gas turbines, plus two diesels; 46,000hp/3800hp
Armament: one SSM launcher; one Seacat SAM system (now deleted); one 4.5in (114mm), two 35mm, two 20mm; two 12.7mm MG; one Limbo Mk 10 ASW mortar
Sensors: air/surface-search radar; surface-search radar; navigation radar; two fire-control radar; hull-mounted sonar
Speed: 40 knots
Range: 5000nm (9260km) at 15 knots
Complement: 125–135

ALVSBORG

SWEDEN: 1969

Displacement: 2500t standard; 2660t full load
Dimensions: 303ft 1in x 48ft x 13ft 2in (92.4m x 14.7m x 4m)
Machinery: one-shaft (CP propeller), two 12-cyl. diesels, plus 16-cy. diesels; 42,000hp/3800hp
Armament: three 40mm; 300 mines; one helicopter
Sensors: radar-scanner and other national systems
Speed: 17 knots
Range: not available
Complement: 95

The *Alvsborg* and the *Visborg* were the two vessels built for the Swedish Navy's *Alvsborg* class of large minelayers. The lead ship, *Alvsborg*, was launched from Karlskrona in November 1969 and commissioned in 1971. Later, she was modified to act as a submarine tender with accommodation for up to five crews (205 personnel). The *Visborg* was launched in 1974 and was also converted from its original task: this time to serve as a command ship for the Commander-in-Chief of Sweden's Baltic fleet.

For a minelayer, Sweden's *Alvsborg* was a comparatively large ship and her capacious size served her well when she later took on the role of submarine tender.

AMERICA

USA: 1964

Between 1956 and 1964 the US Navy laid down four new aircraft carriers, known as the *Kitty Hawk* class. They were the last US carriers to be built with conventional (non-nuclear) propulsion, and were based on the earlier *Forrestal* class. The USS *America* (CVA 66), the third of the *Kitty Hawks*, was laid down in January 1961, launched in February 1964 and completed in January 1965. Compared to the *Forrestals*, the *Kitty Hawks* had their islands moved further aft, with two aircraft elevators located forward of the bridge (compared to one on the *Forrestals*). Though built to a common design, the four *Kitty Hawks* had such a degree of detail differences that they almost belonged to separate classes. *America* was launched four years after her sisterships and so incorporated many important improvements, chiefly in weapons fit. Between May 1969 and March 1973 *America* made three combat deployments to Vietnam. Attached to the East Coast fleet she spent most of her later years in the Atlantic and also in the Mediterranean, where she supported operations over Lebanon and against Libya. In January 1991 aircraft from *America*'s air wing took part in Operation Desert Storm. At that time *America*'s standard air wing comprised 20 F-14A Tomcats, 20 F/A-18C Hornets, 16 A-6E/KA-6D Intruders, four EA-6B Prowlers, six S-3B Vikings and four E-2C Hawkeyes. Anti-submarine operations were flown by eight SH-3G/H Sea King helicopters, later replaced by SH-60F Ocean Hawks. *America* did not receive the service life extension programme applied to other US carriers in the 1990s and she was decommissioned in September 1996.

The USS *America* was the first (and so far the only) *Kitty Hawk* carrier to be withdrawn from service, as a result of the severe budget cuts imposed on the US Navy during the 1990s.

Displacement: 60,005t standard; 80,945t full load
Dimensions: 1047ft 6in x 251ft 8in x 36 ft (319.4m x 76.7m x 11.4m)
Machinery: four-shaft, geared turbines, eight boilers; 280,000hp
Armament: three Sea Sparrow SAM; three Mk 15 Phalanx 20mm CIWS
Sensors: air-search radar; surface-search radar; navigation radar; fire-control radar, hull-mounted sonar
Speed: 33.6 knots
Range: 12,000nm (22,224km) at 20 knots
Complement: 3306, plus 1379 air wing

ANNAPOLIS

CANADA: 1962

Canada built two *Annapolis*-class destroyers in the early 1960s, and both are still in service. Completed in 1964, *Annapolis* (DDH 265) was designed with a primary anti-submarine mission in mind and built around a large flight deck and hangar for an ASW helicopter – a CH-124 Sea King. This extra top-weight saw *Annapolis* adopt a US-pattern Mk 33 3in (76mm) gun instead of the heavier British Mk 6s that had been fitted to earlier Canadian ships.

The high-rounded, contoured breakwater, which stretches from the bow of the *Annapolis* to her breakwater, is a common feature on other Canadian warships of her vintage.

Displacement: 2400t standard; 2600t full load
Dimensions: 366ft x 42ft x 13ft 2in (111.6m x 12.8m x 4.2m)
Machinery: two-shaft, geared steam turbines, two boilers; 30,000hp
Armament: two 3in (76mm); six 12.75in (324mm) TT; one helicopter
Sensors: air/surface-search radar; surface-radar; fire-control radar; hull-mounted sonar
Speed: 28 knots
Range: 4570nm (8464km) at 14 knots
Complement: 228

ANQING

PEOPLE'S REPUBLIC OF CHINA: 1991

The *Jiangwei*-class frigates are the most modern of their type in Chinese service. Four vessels are currently active, with a fifth under construction and a sixth planned. *Anqing* (539) is the lead ship and entered service in late 1991/early 1992. Armed with the latest Chinese-developed weapons, *Anqing* is also equipped to operate a Harbin Z-9A helicopter from its rear deck. China has made strenuous efforts to sell the *Jiangwei* class abroad, offering non-Chinese weapons and systems to make them more attractive.

The six-tube launcher for *Anqing*'s HQ-61 surface-to-air missiles is mounted on the bow, behind the 3.9in (100mm) main gun turret.

Displacement: 2180t full load
Dimensions: 367ft 5in x 40ft 7in x 14ft 1in (112m x 12.4m x 4.3m)
Machinery: two-shaft (CP propellers), four diesels; 21,460hp
Armament: six SSM; one SAM launcher; two 3.9in (100mm), eight 37mm; two ASW mortars
Sensors: air/surface-search radar; navigation radar; fire-control radar; hull-mounted sonar
Speed: 28 knots
Range: 2500nm (4630km) at 18 knots
Complement: 180

ANZAC

AUSTRALIA: 1994

Australia's ANZAC frigates are the most modern vessels in its surface fleet. These new warships are being acquired in conjunction with New Zealand.

In 1989 Australia and New Zealand launched the joint ANZAC frigate project. The two countries signed a contract to acquire 10 vessels based on the German MEKO 200. The project has struggled with funding limitations and some of the capabilities envisaged for the ANZACs – most notably advanced air-defence systems – have been left out of the basic configuration. Budget cuts also forced the Royal New Zealand Navy to relinquish two options, ordering just two ANZACs. The first ship in the class, HMAS *Anzac* (150) was laid down in March 1992, launched in March 1994 and completed in March 1996. The Royal Australian Navy had planned to equip its ANZACs with a 3in (76mm) main gun, but pressure from the Army (which had concerns about future fire-support requirements) saw this replaced by a larger, longer-range 5in (127mm) gun. All the ANZACs are fitted with an eight-cell Mk 41 vertical launching system for the Sea Sparrow SAM. Under a proposed warfighting improvement programme, it was planned to increase the number of launchers and to upgrade them for Standard SM-2 Block III SAMs and the Harpoon anti-ship missile. However, the proposal has been scaled back to improve only the ship's anti-missile defences and countermeasures. Both Australia and New Zealand have acquired new helicopters for their ANZACs in the shape of the Kaman SH-2G Seasprite. Australia's SH-2G(A)s and New Zealand's SH-2G(NZ)s have been heavily upgraded with a new digital cockpit, advanced radar and mission systems and new weapons (such as the Penguin anti-ship missile). The 10th and final ANZAC for Australia, HMAS *Perth*, is due for delivery in 2004. The first ANZAC frigate for New Zealand, HMNZS *Te Kaha*, was launched in 1997 and followed by HMNZS *Te Mana* in 1999.

Displacement: 3600t full load
Dimensions: 387ft 1in x 47ft 1in x 14ft 5in (118m x 14.4m x 4.4m)
Machinery: one-shaft CODOG, one gas turbine, plus two diesels; 30,000hp/8840hp
Armament: one eight-cell Mk 41 VLS for Sea Sparrow SAM; one 5in (127mm); two 12.7mm MG; six 12.75in (324mm) TT; one helicopter
Sensors: air-search radar; air/surface-search radar; navigation radar; fire-control radar; hull-mounted sonar
Speed: 31.75 knots
Range: 4100nm (7593km) at 18 knots
Complement: 163

ARAGUA

VENEZUELA: 1955

Displacement: 2600t standard; 3300t full load
Dimensions: 402ft x 43ft x 12ft 9in (122.5m x 13.1m x 3.9m)
Machinery: two-shaft, geared turbines, two boilers; 50,000hp
Armament: six 4.5in (114mm); 16 40mm; three 21in (533mm) TT; two Squid ASW mortars; two DC racks
Sensors: not available
Speed: 34.5 knots
Range: 5000nm (9260km) at 11 knots
Complement: 254

***Aragua* was typical of the destroyers and other smaller warships built in British shipyards for various South American navies in the years following the end of World War II.**

Venezuela's *Nueva Esparta*-class destroyers were spacious vessels, designed from the outset to be completely air-conditioned so as to facilitate operations in tropical waters. A total of three were constructed, all in British yards. The *Aragua* (D31) was the first to be launched; she was laid down in (what was then) the Vickers-Armstrong yard at Barrow during June 1953, launched in January

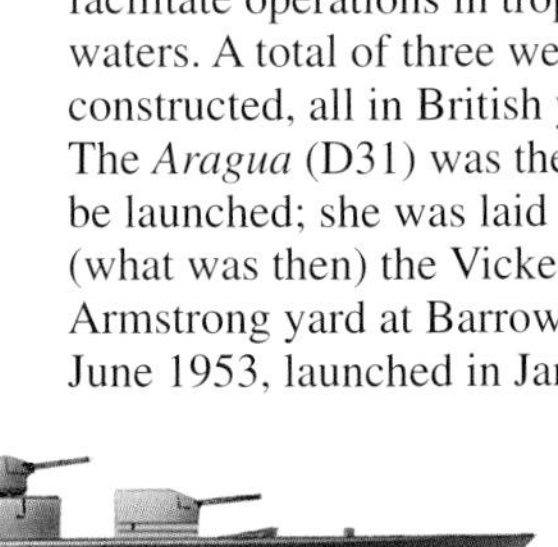

1955 and completed in February 1956. Though the ship had only a single smoke stack and uptake she had two independent engine and boiler rooms. The main guns, in twin turrets, were all British Mk IVs. *Aragua* never received any of the improvements applied to her sisterships, *Nueva Esparta* and *Zulia*; these included Seacat SAM, to replace the outdated 40mm AA guns, and more modern radars. In contrast, *Aragua* retained the pair of Squid ASW mortars she had been built with. She remained in service until 1975.

ARGUS

UK: 1988

Built as a roll-on/roll-off container ship, the *Contender Bezant*, but acquired by the Royal Navy in 1984, HMS *Argus* (A 135) became an aviation training ship. She was converted to that role by Harland & Wolff, acquiring an armoured flight deck and new bulkheads, an operations centre and military communications equipment. During peacetime, *Argus* carries ASW helicopters to their operations area for deep-water training, but in wartime she would act as a 'ferry' carrier for Sea Harrier aircraft.

HMS *Argus* carries the name of a World War II auxiliary carrier. She saw service during Operation Desert Storm as a Commando HC Mk 4 helicopter carrier.

Displacement: not available
Dimensions: 402ft x 43ft x 12ft 9in (122.5m x 13.1m x 3.9m)
Machinery: two-shaft, geared turbines, two boilers; 50,000hp
Armament: none, but can embark up to 12 Sea King helicopters and Sea Harrier aircraft
Sensors: not available
Speed: 34.5 knots
Range: 5000nm (9260km) at 11 knots
Complement: 254

ARK ROYAL

GB: 1950

Displacement: 43,340t standard; 53,060t full load
Dimensions: 744ft 4in x 164ft 6in x 29ft (226.9m x 50.1m x 8.8m)
Machinery: two-shaft, geared steam turbines, four boilers; 76,000hp
Armament: (1969) all original gun armament deleted, fitted for (but not with) four Seacat SAM launchers; 36 aircraft
Sensors: fire-control and other radar systems
Speed: 28 knots
Range: 5000nm (9260km) at 24 knots
Complement: 2637, including air group

The name 'Ark Royal' is one of the most illustrious in Royal Navy history. The aircraft carrier HMS *Ark Royal* (R 09) carried the name until the late 1970s and was perhaps one of the best known of all Royal Navy warships. This was due largely to her starring role in the celebrated TV series *Sailor*, which gave 'the Ark' a public profile out of all keeping with her troublesome service career. Just 18 months after the previous HMS *Ark Royal* was sunk in 1941 by a German U-boat, a new carrier was laid down and given the same name. The new 'Ark' had a protracted development as many changes were made to her design and construction. She was not launched until May 1950 and finally completed only in February 1955. Her lines changed several times throughout her career, with the most important modifications coming between 1967 and 1970 when she was converted to operate Phantom and Buccaneer aircraft. *Ark Royal* had been scheduled for withdrawal by 1972, but when her planned successor, the CVA-02 carrier, was abandoned she struggled on for another decade. HMS *Ark Royal* was paid off in 1978.

Throughout her long career, HMS *Ark Royal* saw action only during the Indonesian confrontation of the late 1960s. After her retirement, in 1978, she gave her name to the third of the new *Invincible*-class carriers.

ARLEIGH BURKE

USA: 1989

Displacement: 6624t standard; 8315t full load
Dimensions: 504ft 7in x 66ft 11in x 20ft (153.8m x 20.4m x 6.1m)
Machinery: four gas turbines; 100,000hp
Armament: two Mk 41 VLS (over 90 cells) for eight Harpoon SSM, Tomahawk TLAM and Standard SAM; one 5in (127mm); two Mk 15 Phalanx 20mm CIWS; six Mk 32 12.75in (324mm) TT
Sensors: air-search/fire-control radar; surface-search radar; navigation radar; fire-control radar; hull-mounted and passive towed array sonar
Speed: 30 knots
Range: 4500nm (8334km) at 20 knots
Complement: 341

The *Arleigh Burke* class of fleet escorts (destroyers) augment the US Navy's larger *Ticonderoga* class of escort cruisers in the protection of US carrier battle groups. Like the *Ticonderogas*, the *Arleigh Burkes* are fitted with the Aegis automated air-defence system, which is built around the SPY-1 radar. The first vessel in the class, the USS *Arleigh Burke* (DDG-51), was laid down in December 1988, launched in September 1989 and completed in 1991. The US Navy has plans to acquire over 30 vessels of this class. They have phenomenal striking power for their size, being armed with two Mk 41 vertical launcher systems for Tomahawk land-attack cruise missiles, Harpoon anti-ship missiles and Standard SM-2MR Block IV SAMs. The class is also very well armoured, with steel upperworks and 130t of Kevlar armour alone. Three different 'Flights' emerged within the class, with detail differences between them.

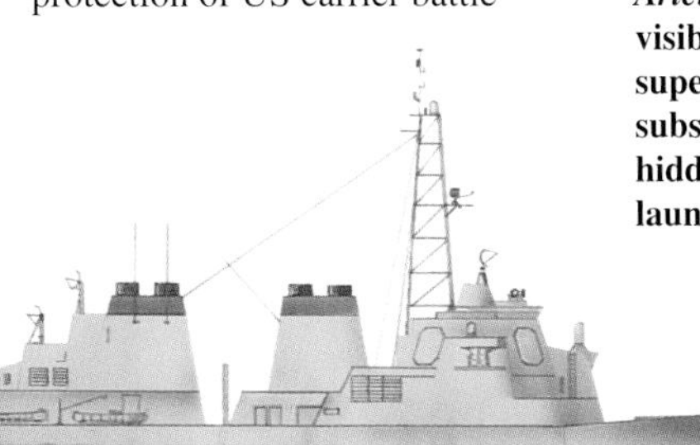

The electronic arrays for the *Arleigh Burke*'s SPY-1 radars are visible as flat panels on its forward superstructure. The warship's substantial load of missiles is hidden below decks in two vertical launcher systems boxes.

ARROMANCHES

FRANCE: 1946

Displacement: 14,000t standard; 17,900t full load
Dimensions: 693ft x 80ft x 23ft (211.2m x 24.5m x 7.2m)
Machinery: two-shaft, geared steam turbines, four boilers; 40,000hp
Armament: 24 2pdr; 19 40mm; up to 24 aircraft
Sensors: not available
Speed: 25 knots
Range: 12,000nm (22,224km) at 14.6 knots
Complement: 1224, including air group

The French carrier *Arromanches* was the former HMS *Colossus*, leased from the Royal Navy in 1946 and bought outright in 1951. *Arromanches* saw action throughout the French campaigns in Indo-China until 1954, and in the Suez conflict of 1956. In 1957–58 she was refitted with an angled deck and became a training carrier for jet aircraft. In 1962 *Arromanches* took on the role of an assault helicopter carrier.

***Arromanches* had a long and varied career which began with launching Dauntless and Seafire air strikes against Communist insurgents in Indo-China.**

ARTEMIZ

IRAN: 1965

Iran's *Damavand*, formerly the *Artemiz*, was believed to be still operational in the early 1990s but her present status is uncertain.

Iran acquired the former British *Battle*-class destroyer HMS *Sluys* in 1965. After an extensive refit, she was renamed the *Artemiz* (D 60). A further refit, in South Africa in the mid-1970s, saw her fitted with Standard SAM launchers and her associated radars and systems were also modernised. In post-Revolution Iran, the *Artemiz* was renamed the *Damavand*. At least two of her unserviceable Seacat launchers were replaced with Soviet 23mm AA guns in 1985.

Displacement: 2780t standard; 3430t full load
Dimensions: 379ft x 40ft 6in x 15ft 4in (115.5m x 12.3m x 4.7m)
Machinery: two-shaft, geared turbines, two boilers; 50,000hp
Armament: one Seacat SAM launcher (deleted); four 4.5in (114mm), four (later two) 40mm, two 23mm AA; one Squid ASW mortar
Sensors: air-search radar; fire-control radar; sonar
Speed: 23 knots
Range: 4500nm (8334km) at 15 knots
Complement: 270

ASTER

BELGIUM: 1985

During the 1980s and early 1990s, Belgium acquired 10 minesweepers under the French-led 'Tripartite' programme, which also involved the Netherlands. *Aster* (M 915) was the lead ship in her class and was launched in June 1985. She can carry a varying crew, depending on her mission, and has provision for up to six divers including a portable decompression chamber carried above deck. Three of the class served during Operation Desert Storm as part of the Coalition naval effort.

Displacement: 511t standard; 595t full load
Dimensions: 168ft 9in x 29ft 2in x 8ft 2in (51.5m x 8.9m x 2.5m)
Machinery: one-shaft, twin active rudders and bow thruster, one diesel; 1900hp
Armament: one 20mm cannon; one 12.7mm MG (optional); two PAP 104 remote-controlled mine-locating vehicles
Sensors: navigation radar; sonar
Speed: 15 knots
Range: 2500nm (4630km) at 12 knots
Complement: 34–46

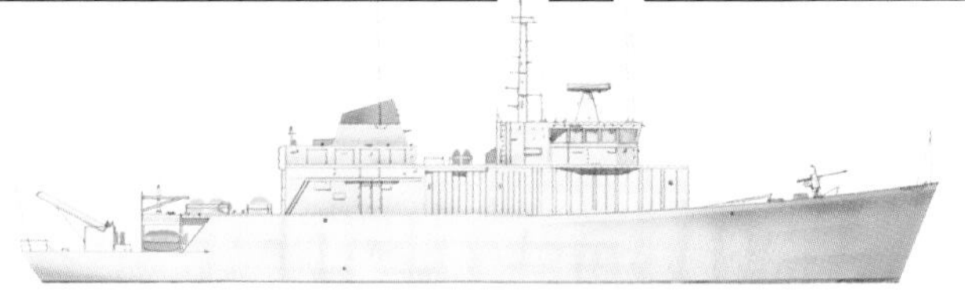

The *Aster* is fitted with a pair of PAP 104 remote-controlled mine locators, carried on her rear deck. She uses mechanical sweep gear to clear the mines it finds.

ATHABASKAN

CANADA: 1970

Displacement: 3551t standard; 5100t full load
Dimensions: 423ft x 50ft x 14ft 6in (128.9m x 15.2m x 4.4m)
Machinery: two-shaft COGOG, two gas turbines, plus two 'cruising' gas turbines; 50,000hp/7400hp
Armament: one SAM launcher; one 3in (76mm); one Mk 15 Phalanx 20mm CIWS; six 12.75in (324mm) TT; two helicopters
Sensors: air-search radar; surface-search/navigation radar; fire-control radar; sonar
Speed: 29 knots
Range: 4500nm (8334km) at 20 knots
Complement: 285 (including 30 aircrew)

***Athabaskan* was built with a 5in (127mm) main gun armament, but this was replaced in the TRUMP modernisation programme with a Mk 41 vertical launching system 'missile box'.**

In the late 1960s, Canada ordered four *Iroquois*-class general-purpose frigates, to replace an earlier class of similar ships that had been cancelled. *Athabaskan* (282) was the third vessel to enter service – launched in November 1970 and completed in July 1972. Like her sisterships, *Athabaskan* is well equipped and has been progressively modified to take on an air-defence role, using Standard missiles in a Mk 41 vertical launcher. She can also embark two CH-124A Sea King ASW helicopters.

AUDACE

ITALY: 1971

Displacement: 3600t standard; 4400t full load
Dimensions: 448ft 3in x 47ft 3in x 15ft 1in (136.6m x 14.4m x 4.6m)
Machinery: two-shaft, geared steam turbines, four boilers; 73,000hp
Armament: eight SSM; one launcher for Standard SAMs; one octuple SAM launcher; one 5in (127mm); four 3in (76mm); six 12.75in (324mm) TT; two helicopters
Sensors: long-range air-search radar; air-search radar; air/surface-search radar; surface-search radar; navigation radar; fire-control radar; hull-mounted sonar
Speed: 33 knots
Range: 3000nm (5556km) at 20 knots
Complement: 380

***Audace*, and her sistership *Ardito*, both have a large helicopter hangar and flight deck capable of housing two AB 212ASWs or one ASH-3D Sea King.**

The two *Audace*-class destroyers of the Italian Navy, *Audace* and her sistership *Ardito*, are optimised for the air-defence role. *Audace* (D 551) was launched in October 1971 and completed in November 1972. Originally fitted with two forward 5in (127mm) gun turrets and a Tartar SAM system, she was refitted for close-in defence in 1991, an Aspide SAM launcher replacing the rear 'B' turret and Super Rapido 3in (76mm) guns being added. Now, modern Standard missiles have replaced the Tartars and the original 21in (533mm) torpedo tubes have been removed.

BABUR

PAKISTAN: 1956

The Pakistan Navy's cruiser *Babur* is named in honour of the famous Moghul emperor. She was originally one of Britain's five *Bellona*-class cruisers, HMS *Diadem*. A World War II veteran, *Diadem* was launched in 1942 and, along with three of her sisterships, she survived into the 1950s (one of the *Bellonas*, HMS *Spartan*, was sunk by the Luftwaffe in 1944). In 1956, ownership of *Diadem* was transferred to Pakistan; she underwent an extensive refit and modernisation in the Portsmouth dockyards between 1956 and 1957, receiving a new bridge, radar and lattice masts, to re-emerge as the cruiser *Babur* (C 84) in July 1957. In 1961, she was taken out of the front-line and became a training ship and, in the years that followed, was reduced to harbour service only. In 1982 one of Pakistan's former Royal Navy Type 21 frigates was named *Babur*, and the cruiser *Babur* was re-named *Jahanqir*. She was broken up in 1985.

The cruiser *Babur* was the flagship of, and the largest ever warship in, the Pakistan Navy.

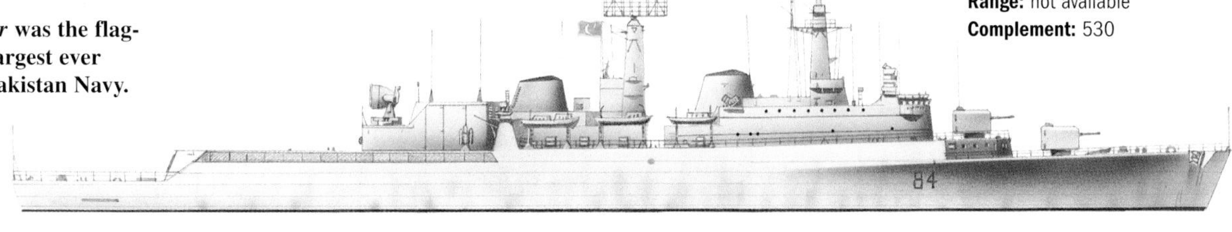

Displacement: 5950t standard; 7410t full load
Dimensions: 512ft x 50ft 6in x 17ft 11in (156.05m x 15.39m x 5.46m)
Machinery: four-shaft, geared turbines, four boilers; 62,000hp
Armament: eight 5.2in (133mm); 12 2pdr pom-poms; six 21in (533mm) TT
Sensors: not available
Speed: 34.5 knots
Range: not available
Complement: 530

BADR

EGYPT: 1980

The *Ramadan*-class fast patrol-boats of the Egyptian Navy are small but effective craft based on the Royal Navy's *Tenacity* class. *Badr* (566, formerly 678) was the last of the six FPBs to be built (different vessels with the same name are also in Pakistani and Saudi service). She was launched in November 1980 with a primary armament of four OTO Melara/Matra Otomat Mk 1 anti-ship missiles, housed in box launchers amidships. *Badr* is also equipped with a sophisticated fire-control and target-tracking system.

***Badr* has a distinctive arrangement of spherical radomes, with the primary air/surface-search radar mounted above the pyramidal mainmast.**

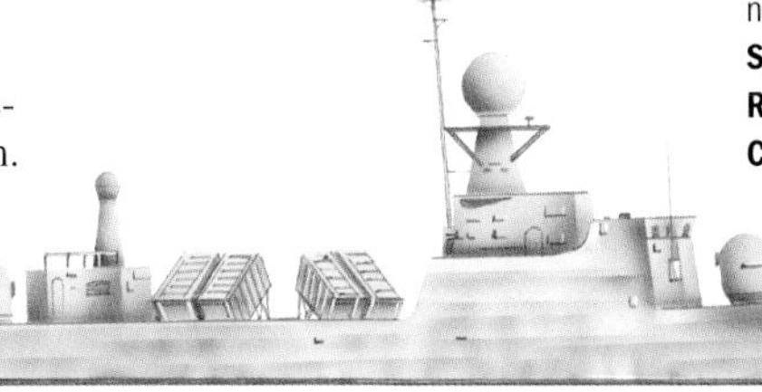

Displacement: 307t standard; 350t full load
Dimensions: 170ft 7in x 25ft x 6ft 7in (52m x 7.6m x 2m)
Machinery: four-shaft, four 20-cyl. diesels; 18,000hp
Armament: four SSM; one 3in (76mm); two 40mm
Sensors: air/surface-search radar; navigation radar; fire-control radar
Speed: 37 knots
Range: 2000nm (3704km) at 15 knots
Complement: 40

BAINBRIDGE

USA: 1961

The cruiser USS *Bainbridge* was the development ship for a whole class of US nuclear-powered vessels that followed her.

Displacement: 7250t standard; 7982t full load
Dimensions: 565ft x 56ft x 19ft 5in (172.3m x 17m x 5.9m)
Machinery: two-shaft, nuclear, two reactors, two geared turbines; 60,000hp
Armament: two twin Terrier SAM launchers; one ASROC launcher; four 20mm; one Mk 15 Phalanx 20mm CIWS; six 12.75in (324mm) TT
Sensors: navigation radar; air/surface-search radar; fire-control radar; hull-mounted sonar
Speed: 30 knots
Range: limited only by reactor fuel state
Complement: 459

The cruiser USS *Bainbridge* (CGN 25, formerly DLGN 25) served as the prototype nuclear-powered fleet escort vessel for the US Navy and, as such, was a 'one-off' vessel. *Bainbridge* was launched in April 1961 and completed in October 1962. She was essentially similar to the *Leahy*-class cruisers, but was fitted with an early-model two-reactor nuclear powerplant. To accomplish her air defence role the *Bainbridge* was fitted with a prominent twin launcher for Terrier SAMs on both bow and stern. Each launcher was armed with a magazine of 40 missiles. *Bainbridge* was built with minimal gun armament and had an ASROC launcher (firing rocket-boosted ASW torpedoes) behind the forward Terrier launcher. During the mid-1970s, she was modernised with an improved anti-air warfare package including 20mm cannon replacing the earlier 3in (76mm) guns. Harpoon missile launchers were also added and, in the mid-1980s, she acquired two Phalanx CIWS. *Bainbridge* was decommissioned in 1995.

BALEARES

SPAIN: 1970

Though similar to the US Navy's *Knox* class, the five Spanish *Baleares*-class frigates replaced the helicopter deck of the American ships with a Standard missile launcher. *Baleares* (F 71) was launched in August 1970 and completed in September 1973. She features unusual internal Mk 32 torpedo tubes (angled out at 45°) along with larger Mk 25 tubes at the stern. A mid-life update between 1985 and 1991 saw *Baleares* fitted with Harpoon missile launchers and the Spanish-developed Meroka CIWS.

An unusual feature of the *Baleares* is the large cylindrical main mast and combined funnel, which also carries most of the vessel's radar antennae.

Displacement: 3015t standard; 4177t full load
Dimensions: 438ft x 46ft 9in x 24ft 7in (133.5m x 14.25m x 7.5m)
Machinery: one-shaft, geared turbines, two boilers; 35,000hp
Armament: eight Harpoon SSM; 16 Standard SAM; one ASROC launcher; one 5in (127mm); two Mk 15 Phalanx 20mm CIWS; two 19in (483mm) TT, four internal 12.75in (324mm) TT
Sensors: air-search radar; surface-search radar; navigation radar; two fire-control radar; hull-mounted sonar
Speed: 28 knots
Range: 4500nm (8334km) at 20 knots
Complement: 256

BAPTISTA DE ANDRADA

PORTUGAL: 1973

The four *De Andrada*-class frigates of the Portuguese Navy were based on the earlier *Countinho*-class vessels, but had an improved weapons and systems fit, along with provision for a Lynx-size helicopter. The lead ship, *Baptista De Andrada* (F 486), was launched in March 1973 and completed in November 1974. Portugal planned to sell the entire class to Colombia in 1977, but the deal fell through. Afterwards, the *De Andradas* were never modernised and remained useful only as coastal patrol vessels.

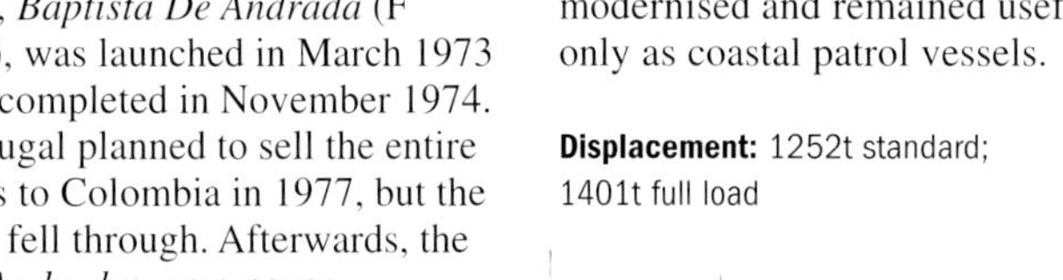

With its simple gun and torpedo armament the *Baptista De Andrada* was not an effective warship for a NATO navy.

Displacement: 1252t standard; 1401t full load
Dimensions: 277ft 8in x 33ft 10in x 10ft 10in (84.6m x 10.3m x 3.3m)
Machinery: two-shaft, two diesels; 10,560hp
Armament: one 3.9in (100mm); two 40mm; six 12.75in (324mm) TT; one helicopter
Sensors: air/surface-search radar; navigation radar; fire-control radar; hull-mounted sonar
Speed: 24.4 knots
Range: 5000nm (9260km) at 18 knots
Complement: 113

BARRY

USA: 1955

Displacement: 2734t standard, 4916t full load
Dimensions: 418ft 6in x 44ft 11in x 15ft (127.6m x 13.7m x4.6m)
Machinery: two-shaft, geared turbines, four boilers; 70,000hp
Armament: three 5in (127mm), four 3in (76mm); four 21in (533mm) TT, six 12.75in (324mm) TT; two Hedgehog ASW mortars
Sensors: air-search radar; hull-mounted sonar
Speed: 33 knots
Range: 4500nm (8334km) at 20 knots
Complement: 324

By the early 1980s, the ageing engines and boilers of the USS *Barry* were becoming increasingly difficult to maintain. She was quickly retired.

The *Forrest Sherman*-class destroyers were the only general-purpose, gun-armed destroyers built for the post-war US Navy. As completed, they had an unusual gun arrangement, with two Mk 42 5in (127mm) gun turrets aft and only one forward. She was launched in October 1955 and completed in August 1956.

From the next vessel (USS *Decatur*, DD 936) onwards some changes were made to the basic *Forrest Sherman* lines, with the bow raised by about 3ft (1m). By the mid-1950s, the old-style general-purpose destroyer classification had fallen into disuse and the Navy wanted more fast escorts for dedicated air defence or anti-submarine warfare. It was planned to equip all the class with the Tartar SAM, but the missile's high cost and low effectiveness limited this to four ships. The USS *Barry* was one of those chosen for ASW tasks and she became a trials ship for the new bow-mounted SQS-23 sonar. She was decommissioned in 1982 and is now a museum ship.

BASS

USA: 1950

The *Barracuda*-class submarine USS *Bass* was one of a group of three such vessels which were to serve as prototypes for a mass-produced class of 'ambush' submarines. This new concept for US Navy small attack submarines required that they lie in wait on the approaches to Soviet naval bases and attack enemy submarines as they emerged. *Bass* had to prove that it could be both quiet and cheap to build. The key to the new submarine's success was a large passive sonar, housed in a stream-lined bow fairing and designed to detect its hapless underwater targets.

However, the three *Barracudas* were felt to be too small, both for the crews and for maintaining an adequate ocean-going capability. Furthermore, resources at that time were limited for the development of dedicated attack submarines, or SSKs, and it was ultimately felt that money would be better spent on the conversion of existing submarines rather than building a whole new class. The USS *Bass* was launched as the K2 in May 1950, and completed in November 1951. She did not receive her 'B' name until 1955 and, just four years later, was finally withdrawn from the SSK development task. The same fate befell her two sisters, the distinctive bow sonar dome being removed from all three boats. Of the three former K-class submarines the USS *Barracuda* became a training submarine and remained in service until 1973, while the USS *Bonita* was used as a target during nuclear bomb tests in 1958. USS *Bass* was finally broken up in 1967.

The USS *Bass* was a small stepping stone on the road that led to modern hunter/killer submarines, such as today's *Los Angeles* class.

Just a few short years after her launch, the blunt lines of the USS *Bass* – so typical of World War II submarines – would give way to a whole new era of far more efficient streamlined designs.

Displacement: 765t surfaced; 1160t submerged
Dimensions: 196ft 1in x 24ft 7in x 14ft 5in (59.8m x 7.5m x 4.4m)
Machinery: two-shaft, two diesels plus electric motors; 1050hp
Armament: four 21in (533mm) TT
Sensors: sonar
Speed: 13 knots surfaced; 8.5 knots submerged
Range: not available
Complement: 37

BELKNAP

USA: 1963

The *Belknap*-class escort cruisers had a convoluted design history and failed in their aim to be less expensive than equivalent ships. *Belknap* (DG 26, formerly DLG 26) was launched in July 1963 and completed in November 1964. She had several innovative features, such as a combined ASROC and Terrier launcher. A modernisation programme during the 1980s saw the addition of Harpoon missiles and the Phalanx CIWS. *Belknap* served as the flagship of the US Sixth Fleet and had the longest service career of any of her class; she was decommissioned only in 1995.

The cruiser USS *Belknap* underwent many changes throughout her service life as new weapons and radars were added. She was also converted to act as a senior command vessel.

Displacement: 5409t standard; 7890t full load
Dimensions: 547ft x 54ft 9in x 18ft 2in (166.8m x 16.7m x 5.5m)
Machinery: two-shaft, geared turbines, four boilers; 85,000hp
Armament: one Terrier/ASROC SAM/ASW system; one 5in (127mm); two 3in (76mm); six 12.75in (324mm) TT; two 21in (533mm) TT
Sensors: navigation radar; air/surface-search radar; hull-mounted sonar
Speed: 32 knots
Range: 7100nm (13,149km) at 20 knots

BERK

TURKEY: 1971

Displacement: 1450t standard; 1950t full load
Dimensions: 312ft 4in x 39ft 10in x 18ft 1in (95.2m x 12.1m x 5.7m)
Machinery: one-shaft, four diesels; 24,000hp
Armament: four 3in (76mm); two ASW mortars; six 12.75in (324mm) TT; depth charges; one helicopter
Sensors: air-search radar; surface-search radar; navigation radar; fire-control radar; hull-mounted sonar
Speed: 25 knots
Range: 10,000nm (18,520km) at 9 knots
Complement: 175

Laid down in the late 1960s, the *Berk*-class frigates were the first major warships to be built in Turkey since before the outbreak of World War I. The two ships were based on the US *Claud Jones* class, but modified with a different hull and machinery, a single funnel and upgunned armament. The lead ship in the class, *Berk* (D 358), was launched in June 1971 and completed in July 1972. Her main deck is dominated by a

A high central mast rises above the *Berk*, using a distinctive tripod construction. The large curved mesh antenna for the SPS-40 radar is particularly prominent.

single 3in (76mm) gun mounting, with a pair of Hedgehog anti-submarine mortars located behind the 'A' turret position, below the bridge. A helicopter platform for a single AB 212ASW helicopter is situated above the break in the main deck, but *Berk* has no hangar to permit sustained helicopter operations. Behind the helicopter deck is a second pair of 3in (76mm) guns, but this time in an open mount. *Berk* and her sistership, *Peyk*, are still active in Turkey as coastal patrol and ASW vessels.

BESKYTTEREN

DENMARK: 1975

Displacement: 1540t standard; 1970t full load
Dimensions: 244ft x 41ft x 14ft 9in (74.4m x 12.5m x 4.5m)
Machinery: one-shaft, three diesels; 7440hp
Armament: one 3in (76mm); one helicopter
Sensors: air/surface-search radar; navigation radar; hull-mounted sonar
Speed: 18 knots
Range: 6000nm (11,112km) at 13 knots
Complement: 60

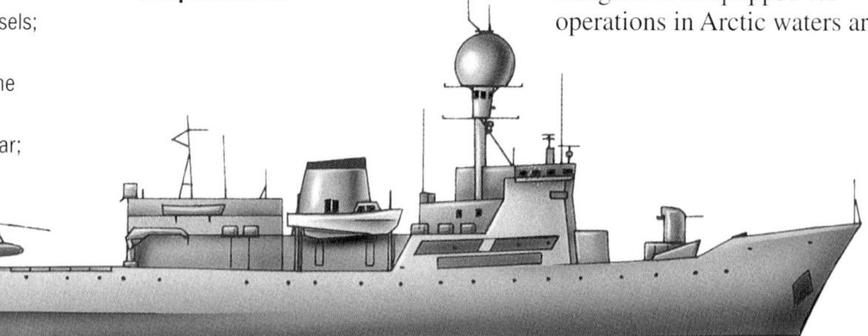

The Danish patrol vessel *Beskytteren* (F 340) is a modified *Hvidbjørnen*-class frigate. It is designed and equipped for operations in Arctic waters around Greenland (a Danish protectorate). *Beskytteren* was built some years after the other *Hvidbjørnens* and has a different machinery fit, additional and more modern radars, and can also embark a Lynx helicopter. She is classed as a fishery protection 'inspection vessel' and has limited armament only, a single 3in (76mm) gun.

***Beskytteren* has a large radome above her main mast. It houses an AWS 6 air/surface-search radar, fitted in the late 1980s.**

BLANCO ENCALADA

CHILE: 1987

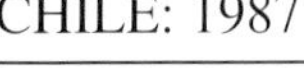

***Blanco Encalada* and the other *Prat*-class destroyers are the flagships of the Chilean Navy and, despite their age, they remain formidable combatants.**

One of four *County*-class destroyers acquired by Chile from the Royal Navy during the 1980s (largely in gratitude for Chilean assistance during the Falklands conflict), this vessel began her career as HMS *Fife*. Originally launched in July 1964, she was handed over in July 1987, as the last of the four to enter service with the Chilean Navy. Renamed the *Blanco Encalada* (15) she was substantially modified, along with her sistership the *Cochrane*, to serve as a helicopter carrier. An entirely new and enlarged helicopter deck, with a hangar capable of accommodating two Super Pumas, was added – replacing the stern-mounted Sea Slug SAM system and original small helicopter deck. These changes give *Blanco Encalada* the appearance of a flush-decked design, very different from that of the two unmodified *Prat* (the former *County*)-class ships. *Blanco Encalada*, along with her three sisters, has been progressively updated with new radars, sonar and defensive systems. She is expected to be fitted with Israeli-supplied Barak SAMs for close-in defence.

Displacement: 6200t standard; 6800t full load
Dimensions: 521ft 6in x 54ft 000in x 20ft 6in (158.9m x 16.4m x 6.2m)
Machinery: two-shaft, COSAG-geared steam turbines, two boilers, plus four gas turbines; 30,000hp plus/30,000hp
Armament: four MM38 Exocet SSM; two 4.5in (114mm); four/two 40mm; 12.7mm MG; six 12.75in (324mm) TT; two helicopters
Sensors: air-search radar; navigation radar; fire-control radar; hull-mounted sonar
Speed: 30 knots
Range: 3500nm (6482km) at 28 knots
Complement: 440-471

BOLD PATHFINDER

GB: 1951

Displacement: 130t standard; 150t full load
Dimensions: 122ft 8in x 20ft 5in x 6ft 7in (37.4m x 6.2m x 2m)
Machinery: experimental Gatric gas turbine
Armament: two 4.5in (114mm); one 40mm cannon (as a gunboat); one 40mm cannon and four 21in (533mm) TT (as a torpedo-boat)
Complement: 20

Between 1950 and 1953 the Vosper and White shipyards built two *Bold*-class experimental fast attack craft. They were testbeds for the new Gatric gas turbine engine, though they initially went to sea with Mercedes diesels scavenged from wartime German E-boats. *Bold Pathfinder* (P 5701, formerly MTB 5720) was the first to be built and, along with her primary engine development task, she also served as a trials ship for the new 3.3in (84mm) gun developed for the *Brave*-class attack craft. *Bold Pathfinder* was withdrawn in 1962.

HMS *Bold Pathfinder* had an aluminium hull with a wooden frame. This was a different hull-form from that of her sistership, HMS *Bold Pioneer*.

BONAVENTURE

CANADA: 1957

In 1957 the former British aircraft carrier, HMS *Powerful*, was transferred to the Royal Canadian Navy as HMCS *Bonaventure* (RML 22). Launched in 1945, *Powerful* was refitted before entering Canadian service with an angled deck and American radar and armament. Her original air wing comprised F2H Banshees and S-2F Trackers, but the F2Hs gave way to HO4S-3 Whirlwinds (later CHSS-2 Sea Kings) when *Bonaventure* adopted an ASW role in the 1960s. Re-designated RRSM 22 in 1957, and later CVL 22, *Bonaventure* was paid off in 1970.

Between 1966 and 1967 *Bonaventure* was modernised with new radars, improved crew accommodation and better deck aircraft handling. Her two forward 3in (76mm) gun mounts were also removed.

Displacement: 16,000t standard; 20,000t full load
Dimensions: 704ft x 128ft x 25ft (214.6m x 39m x 7.69m)
Machinery: two-shaft, geared steam turbines, four boilers; 40,000hp
Armament: eight 3in (76mm) (originally); four 3pdr saluting cannon; 21–24 aircraft
Sensors: radar
Speed: 24.5 knots
Range: not available
Complement: 1370

BOYKIY

USSR: 1960

As a *Krupny*-class missile destroyer, *Boykiy* was one of the very first missile-armed Soviet warships. She was launched in December 1960 and completed in June 1961 – the seventh of eight ships constructed. The *Krupny*-class was charged with surface attack and shore bombardment, using the SS-N-1 missile but, lacking sufficient self-defence armament, these vessels were transferred to ASW tasks. This conversion proved to be both difficult and expensive and was never again attempted with any other similar class of Soviet ship.

As part of her conversion to the ASW role, *Boykiy* received a new bow sonar, torpedo tubes, an anti-submarine mortar, an aft helicopter pad to accommodate a Ka-25, sonobouys, the SA-N-1 SAM system and new 23mm guns. Her machinery had to be uprated to cope with the increased weight.

Displacement: 3850t standard; 4192t full load
Dimensions: 455ft 9in x 48ft 8in x 13ft 9in (138.9m x 14.84m x 4.2m)
Machinery: two-shaft, geared turbines, four boilers; 72,000hp
Armament: two SSM launchers with 12 missiles; 16 57mm; two ASW RL; six 21in (533mm) TT; one helicopter
Sensors: air-search; missile-control and naviagation radar; hull-mounted sonar
Speed: 34.5 knots
Range: 3000nm (5556km) at 18 knots
Complement: 310

BRANDENBURG

GERMANY: 1992

Displacement: 3660t standard; 4275t full load
Dimensions: 455ft 8in x 57ft 1in x 20ft 8in (138.9m x 16.7m x 6.3m)
Machinery: two-shaft (CP propellers), two gas turbines, plus two diesels; 25,480hp/5630hp
Armament: four MM38 Exocet SSM; one VLS for Sea Sparrow SAM; two 21-cell RAM launchers; one 3in (76mm); six 12.75in (324mm) TT; two helicopters
Sensors: air-search radar; air/surface-search radar; navigation radar; two trackers (fire-control); hull-mounted sonar
Speed: 29 knots
Range: 4000nm (7408km) at 18 knots
Complement: 219

The *Brandenburg*-class destroyers (also known as Type 123s) were built by a consortium of three German shipyards. They were introduced to replace the earlier *Hamburg*-class ships which dated back to the early 1960s. Four ships were ordered in all, *Brandenburg* (F 215) being the lead ship. She was launched in August 1992 and completed in October 1994. The primary role for the Type 123s is air defence; the destroyers are armed with medium-range Sea Sparrow SAMs and the close-in Rolling Airframe Missile (RAM) system. The Sea Sparrows are housed in a vertical launching system forward of the bridge, while two boxy Mk 49 RAM launchers are located forward and aft. *Brandenburg* is also equipped with Exocet anti-ship missiles and can embark a pair of Lynx Mk 88 helicopters (with a flight deck and hangar aft). Similar ships are in service with the navies of Portugal and Turkey.

Notable design features of the *Brandenburg* include her large, solid main mast and the bridge layout set well back from the bow.

BRAVYY

USSR: 1955

The *Kotlin*-class destroyers were a hard-working and well-liked family of ships that entered Soviet Navy service in substantial numbers during the 1950s. The *Bravyy* – launched in February 1955 and completed in January 1956 – was the 14th unit to be built. Between 1959 and 1963 she served as a testbed for the new 'Volga' (SA-N-1) SAM system. The launcher, along with its magazine, replaced all other aft-mounted weapons. Along with her sisterships, *Bravyy* served into the late 1980s.

The Project 56 (Soviet designation) destroyer *Bravyy* acted as the prototype for eight successive missile-armed Project 56A conversions.

Displacement: 2662t standard; 3230t full load
Dimensions: 413ft 9in x 41ft 8in x 13ft 9in (126.1m x 12.7m x 4.2m)
Machinery: two-shaft, geared turbines, four boilers; 72,000hp
Armament: (as modified) one SAM launcher with 16 missiles; two 5.1in (130mm); two (later four) 45mm; two ASW RL; four 21in (533mm) TT; one helicopter
Speed: 38 knots
Range: not available
Complement: 284

BRECON

GB: 1978

Displacement: 750t full load
Dimensions: 197ft x 32ft 3in x 7ft 3in (60m x 9.8m x 2.2m)
Machinery: two-shaft, two diesels, plus hydraulic drive and bow thruster; 3540hp
Armament: one 30mm (replaced 40mm)
Sensors: navigation radar; variable-depth minehuntingsonar
Speed: 17 knots
Range: not available
Complement: 45

The Royal Navy's *Hunt*-class minesweepers are among the most advanced vessels of their type ever built – and in terms of cost per ton are also among the most expensive. When they were drawn up the *Hunts* were the largest ships ever to be built from glass-reinforced plastic (GRP). HMS *Brecon* (M 29) was the lead ship in the class. After the Falklands War, *Hunt*-class ships swept Port Stanley harbour and later, in 1991, saw action in the Persian Gulf.

Among the innovations found on HMS *Brecon* are sophisticated thrusters and position-fixing gear for precise low-speed handling.

BRISTOL

GB: 1969

The guided-missile destroyer HMS *Bristol* was intended to be the first of four ships dedicated to the air defence of the Royal Navy's future CVA-01 carrier battle groups. However, when the CVA-01 carriers were cancelled the requirement for the *Bristols* disappeared too. Nonetheless, construction of HMS *Bristol* (D 23) proceeded on the grounds that she would act as a trials ship for new weapons and systems. Launched in June 1969 and completed in March 1973, *Bristol* undertook several important development tasks and was the first Royal Navy ship to be fitted with the Australian Ikara anti-submarine missile system. She conducted early Sea Dart SAM trials and made a major contribution to the development of modern, supportable powerplants. She was hampered by her lack of a helicopter deck, but her unique Action Data Automatic Weapons System (which integrates radar and sonar plots) made her invaluable for R&D.

HMS *Bristol* survived a serious engine fire in 1973, enabling her to continue her vital role as a weapons trials ship. Later, she ended her days as a training vessel.

Displacement: 6700t standard; 7700t full load
Dimensions: 507ft x 55ft x 22ft 6in (154.3m x 16.8m x 6.8m)
Machinery: two-shaft, COSAG geared steam turbines, two boilers, plus two gas turbines; 30,000hp plus/40,000hp
Armament: one twin launcher for SAM system (40 missiles); one launcher for ASW system (32 missiles); one 4.5in (114mm); one ASW mortar
Sensors: navigation radar; air-search radar; fire-control radar
Speed: 30 knots
Range: 5000nm (9260km) at 18 knots
Complement: 407

BROADSWORD

GB: 1976

The *Broadsword*-class frigates were the first iteration of the Royal Navy's Type 22 vessels and proved to be excellent ships. They were developed to counter the Soviet Union's new fast, deep-diving attack submarines which began to appear during the 1970s. The *Broadswords* had to be capable of finding and destroying these submarines, while coping with the latest submarine-launched anti-ship missiles that were also being introduced. For this, they fielded the Sea Wolf SAM, which was designed to defeat high-speed, close-in targets. HMS *Broadsword* (F 88) and her three sisterships were all big, could maintain high speed in high seas and had plenty of room for future modernisation – the latter a primary design consideration. She was launched in May 1976 and completed in May 1979. *Broadsword* went to war during the Falklands conflict in 1982 and was damaged by Argentine air attack, but survived. In 1998–89 she was refitted, gaining new funnels and expanded crew quarters to handle training details.

All four Batch 1 frigates of the *Broadsword* class were sold to Brazil in the mid-1990s, beginning with HMS *Broadsword* herself in June 1995. In Brazilian service she is now the *Greenhalgh* (F 46).

Displacement: 4000t standard; 4400t full load
Dimensions: 430ft x 48ft 6in x 19ft 10in (131.2m x 14.8m x 6.1m)
Machinery: two-shaft, COGOG, four gas turbines; 54,600hp plus/9700hp
Armament: four MM38 Exocet SSM; two six-round launchers for SAM system; two 40mm (or two 30mm); six 12.75in (324mm) TT; two helicopters
Sensors: air/surface-search radar; navigation radar; fire-control radar; hull-mounted sonar
Speed: 30 knots
Range: 4500nm (8334km) at 18 knots
Complement: 407

CAIO DUILIO

ITALY: 1962

Displacement: 5000t standard; 6500t full load
Dimensions: 489ft 9in x 56ft 5in x 16ft 5in (149.3m x 17.3 x 5m)
Machinery: two-shaft, geared steam turbines, four Foster-Wheeler boilers; 60,000hp
Armament: one Terrier SAM launcher, eight (later six) 3in (76mm); six 40mm cannon; six Mk 32 12.75in (324mm) TT (Mk 46 ASW torpedoes); three helicopters
Sensors: long-range air-search radar; fire-control radar; naviagation radar; hull-mounted sonar
Speed: 30 knots
Range: 5000nm (9260km) at 7 knots
Complement: 485

The Italian helicopter cruiser *Caio Duilio* (C 554) was one of two *Doria*-class ships developed to provide ASW cover and air defence for large naval forces and convoys. Her primary armament was the Terrier SAM system but, to back up the SAMs, eight newly-developed OTO Melara 3in (76mm) guns were fitted, adding another layer of anti-aircraft and anti-missile defence. An aft flight deck and helicopter hangar were also provided, to accommodate up to three ASH-3D Sea Kings. In fact, the *Doria*s proved to be too small to comfortably operate the Sea Kings and AB 212ASWs were used instead. *Caio Duilio* was the lead ship in the class and so became the first Italian warship to be fitted with a fully-automated combat data system. She was launched in December 1962 and completed in February 1964. Her sistership, the *Andrea Doria*, was modernised in 1976–78. The *Caio Duilio* was held back for conversion into a training ship, during 1979 and 1980.

In her final role as a training ship, *Caio Duilio* received a partial systems modernisation, but had some weapons deleted to make way for classroom facilities. She remained in the fleet until 1991.

CALIFORNIA

USA: 1971

Displacement: 10,150t full load
Dimensions: length 596ft x 61ft x 20ft 6in (181.7m x 18.6m x 6.3m)
Machinery: two-shaft nuclear, two D2G reactors, two geared turbines; 60,000hp
Armament: two twin Standard SAM launchers (40 missiles each); two 5in (127mm); four 20mm cannon; one ASROC rocket-boosted ASW torpedo launcher (deleted); four 12.75in (324mm) TT (Mk 32 ASW torpedoes)
Sensors: navigation radar; air/surface-search radar; fire-control radar
Speed: 30+ knots
Range: limited only by reactor fuel state
Complement: 533

Two nuclear-powered *California*-class cruisers were built for the US Navy after plans for a pair of earlier guided missile destroyers fell through. They proved to be very different from the ships they notionally succeeded, as they incorporated a host of new systems – most importantly their nuclear powerplants. As a result, their cost escalated sharply and funding was only released by the Pentagon after Congress stepped in to rewrite the budget (as often happens in the US procurement system). The *Californias* were redesignated as nuclear-powered cruisers (CGNs) in 1975. The original design had called for heavyweight 5in (127mm) main guns and tubes for Mk 48 torpedoes but the guns were replaced with lighter weapons and the torpedo tubes deleted. Standard SAMs replaced the earlier Tartars and *California* had a much-improved reactor design (compared to ships like the *Bainbridge* or *Truxton*), with three times the reactor fuel life. A helicopter deck was fitted, but no hangar. The USS *California* (CGN 36, formerly DLGN 36) was launched in September 1971 and completed in February 1974. She was built with an ASROC system located behind the forward 5in (127mm) gun, under the bridge (it was removed in 1993). Over the years the *California* underwent progressive stages of modernisation. For example, she received Kevlar armour protection over vital superstructure areas and her initial SPS-40 radar was replaced by an improved SPS-49. In 1992–93 the nuclear refuelling process was carried out in both the *California* and her sistership, the USS *South Carolina*, thereby extending their service lives to the end of the 1990s, when they were finally decommissioned.

***California's* primary weapons system, her two twin Standard missile launchers, were located fore and aft, in front of the 5in (127mm) main gun turrets.**

CARL VINSON

USA: 1980

Known to her crews as the 'Starship Vinson', the nuclear-powered aircraft carrier USS *Carl Vinson* (CVN-70) was the third of the giant *Nimitz*-class carriers to enter service. Their design drew heavily on the experience gained from the USS *Enterprise*, the first nuclear carrier. However, the oldest ship in the class, the USS *Nimitz* is 12 years younger than the 'Big E' and so is considerably more modern. One big advance found in the class is a new form of compact two-reactor powerplant which frees up more internal space. All vessels in the class were built at the Newport News yard, where the *Carl Vinson* was laid down in October 1975, launched in March 1980 and completed in April 1982. Along with her two predecessors, the *Carl Vinson* is different from the rest of the *Nimitz* class – they can be distinguished by the single bridle-catching 'broom' at the end of the starboard bow catapult. The US Navy claims that the *Carl Vinson* can carry 90 per cent more aviation fuel and 50 per cent more aviation ordnance for its air wing than a *Forrestal*-class carrier; thanks to the modern design, and careful attention to self-protection measures, the Navy also claims that she could absorb three times the (typically) severe damage suffered by the *Essex*-class carriers in Japanese air attacks during World War II. After her shakedown cruise in the Atlantic, and a spell in the Mediterranean, the *Carl Vinson* made a round-the-world cruise to join the Pacific Fleet. She has remained in the Pacific since the mid-1980s and currently has Carrier Air Wing 11 (CVW-11) embarked. The *Carl Vinson* is the next carrier in line for the complex three-year nuclear refuelling process that will extend her service life by up to 50 years.

The USS *Carl Vinson* is armed with three Sea Sparrow launchers and four Phalanx CIWS systems for last-ditch self-defence against air or missile attack.

Displacement: 73,973t standard; 91,440t full load
Dimensions: 1,088ft x 257ft 6in x 36ft 8in (331.7m x 78.5m x 11.2m)
Machinery: four-shaft nuclear, two A4W reactors, four geared turbines; 260,000hp
Armament: three Mk 29 Sea Sparrow octuple launchers; four Mk 15 Phalanx 20mm CIWS; 90 aircraft
Sensors: air-search radar; surface-search radar; navigation radar; fire-control radar
Speed: 30+ knots
Range: limited only by reactor fuel state
Complement: 5621 ship, plus air wing

CASMA

PERU: 1978

Displacement: 1180t surfaced; 1300t submerged
Dimensions: 183ft 5in x 20ft 4in x 17ft 11in (55.9m x 6.2m x 5.4m)
Machinery: one-shaft, four diesels, plus one electric motor; 2,250hp/ 3,600hp
Armament: eight 21in (533mm) TT
Sensors: surface-search radar; sonar fit
Speed: 21.5 knots surfaced; 11 knots submerged
Range: 400nm (741km) at 4 knots submerged
Complement: 31

The Peruvian Type 209 submarine *Casma* is fitted with eight 21in (533mm) torpedo tubes and typically carries 14 warshot torpedoes.

The *Casma* (S 31) is one of six German-built Type 209 submarines in service with the Peruvian Navy. The single-hulled, conventionally-powered Type 209 was a very successful export design, and variations of the basic vessel are in service with 12 countries around the world. The *Casma* is a Type 209/1200 – a larger and heavier variant, almost identical to the Greek *Glavkos* class of Type 209s. *Casma* was launched in August 1978 and completed in December 1980.

CASSARD

FRANCE: 1985

The French destroyer *Cassard* (D 614) is one of two dedicated air-defence ships, built as the *C 70 AA* class. In France they are known as FAA (Frégates Anti-Aériennes) vessels and are built around the US-supplied Standard SAM, with a sophisticated fit of French radars and tactical data systems. *Cassard* was launched in February 1985 and competed in July 1988. Particular attention was paid to anti-missile defences and the *Cassard* is fitted with SANDRAL point-defence missiles and a comprehensive suite of decoys and countermeasures.

The French destroyer *Cassard* has a hangar and a small flight deck located aft, to support Lynx helicopter operations.

Displacement: 3900t standard; 4500t full load
Dimensions: 456ft x 46ft x 18ft (139.1m x 14m x 5.6m)
Machinery: two-shaft, four SEMT-Pielstick 18 PA 6 V280 BTC diesels; 42,300hp
Armament: eight MM40 Exocet SSM; one Mk 13 launcher for Standard SM-1MR SAM (40 missiles); two sextuple launchers for SANDRAL point-defence SAM; one 3.9in (100mm), two 20mm; four 12.7mm MG; two launchers for L5 torpedoes (10 carried); one helicopter
Sensors: air-search radar; air/surface-search radar; navigation radar; fire-control radar; hull-mounted sonar
Speed: 29.6 knots
Range: 8000nm (14,816km) at 17 knots
Complement: 225

CENTAURO

ITALY: 1954

Italy's *Canopo* class were conventional European-style frigates of the 1950s, but their unusual main gun arrangement set their apart from their contemporaries.

Italy built four *Canopo*-class frigates during the mid-1950s, with support from the United States' MDAP military aid fund. The *Centauro* (F 554) was the third of the class. She was launched in April 1954 and completed in May 1957 and, like her sisterships, had an unusual 'over and under' arrangement in the gun turrets. However, this arrangement proved to be unreliable and conventional mounts were later adopted. *Centauro* remained in Italian naval service until the early 1980s, but was stricken in 1984.

Displacement: 1807t standard; 2250t full load
Dimensions: 338ft 4in x 39ft 4in x 12ft 6in (103.1m x 12m x 3.8m)
Machinery: two-shaft, geared steam turbines, two boilers; 22,000hp
Armament: eight Teseto Mk 2 SSM; one Mk 13 Mod 4 launcher for Standard SM-1MR SAM; four (later three) 3in (76mm); four (later two) 40mm cannon; one Menon ASW mortar; two 21in (533mm) TT, later Mk 32 12.75in (324mm) TT
Sensors: air-search radar; radar; hull-mounted sonar
Speed: 26 knots
Range: 3000nm (5556km) at 20 knots
Complement: 207

CHAKRI NARUEBET

THAILAND: 1996

Displacement: 11,300t full load
Dimensions: 599ft 1in x 110ft 1in x 20ft 4in (182.5m x 30.5m x 6.15m)
Machinery: two-shaft (CP propellers) CODOG, two gas turbines, plus two diesels; 44,250hp/11,780hp
Armament: two launchers for Mistral SAM; two 12.7mm MG; six AV-8S Harriers, four S-70B Seahawks
Sensors: surface-search radar; fire-control radar; navigation radar; aircraft-control radar; hull-mounted sonar
Speed: 26 knots
Range: 10,000nm (18,520km) at 12 knots
Complement: 455, plus 162 air crew

A new chapter in the history of the Royal Thai Navy, and in the story of Pacific Rim sea-power, opened with the introduction of Thailand's aircraft carrier *Chakri Naruebet* (911*)*. This ship is the first such vessel to enter Thai service and the only aircraft carrier – apart from those Japan-based US Navy vessels – to be based in the region. *Chakri Naruebet* was built in Spain and is a smaller version of the *Principe de Asturias*. She was launched in January 1996, completed in March 1997 and features a 12° ski jump designed to operate Harrier VSTOL jets as well as helicopters. Thailand bought up the former-Spanish Navy fleet of AV-8A(S) Harriers and built an entirely new maritime air group around them. Seven AV-8A(S)s and two, two-seat, TAV-8A(S)s were delivered in September 1997. Six S-70B Seahawks were also acquired to operate alongside them. However, the Harriers have proved to be maintenance intensive and very expensive to operate, while funding troubles have also hit the *Chakri Naruebet* itself. As a result the Thai carrier has seen little sea time since commissioning in August 1997.

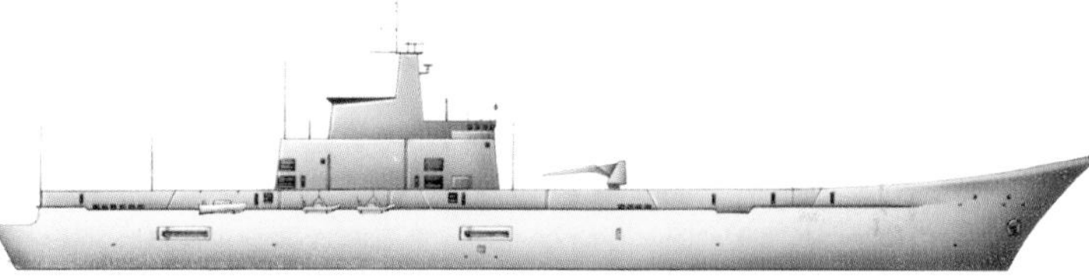

The *Chakri Naruebet* can carry six Harriers and four Seahawks, and represents a major step forward in capability for the Thai Navy.

CHARLES DE GAULLE

FRANCE: 1994

The *Charles De Gaulle* (F 91) is the first nuclear-powered carrier to enter French service and is the single vessel that, under current plans, will replace France's two existing carriers *Clemenceau* and *Foch*. Her construction order was placed in 1986 but the rising cost of the carrier – and her nuclear powerplant in particular – ensured the process would be slow. Though a far more modern ship, the *Charles De Gaulle* has hull dimensions which are essentially the same as the 1950s-era *Clemenceau* – the dimensions ruled by what can be accommodated in the Brest shipyard. The flight deck has considerable overhang, with two aircraft lifts mounted on the starboard side behind the island. The *Charles De Gaulle* has a striking slab-sided appearance that incorporates 'stealthy' design features to reduce her radar signature. Though the angled deck is conventional, the forward catapult intrudes into the area occupied by the offset catapult, so the carrier cannot conduct simultaneous take-off and landing operations. This arrangement frees up additional aircraft parking space at the stern. *Charles De Gaulle* was laid down in April 1989, launched in May 1994 and was scheduled to be commissioned in mid-1999. This was delayed until October 2000 after problems cropped up during sea trials. She is intended to operate an Air Wing of Rafale M multirole fighters and E-3C Hawkeye AEW aircraft. In 1999 it was discovered that the flight deck, in certain conditions, is too short to conduct safe Hawkeye operations.

Despite rising costs, long delays and early technical troubles, France has stuck with its nuclear-powered carrier programme, and so will have a strategic maritime capability that is unique outside the United States.

Displacement: 34,500t standard; 36,600t full load
Dimensions: 858ft x 211ft x 28ft (261.5m x 64.4m x 8.5m)
Machinery: two-shaft nuclear, two 150 MW pressurised water reactors, double reduction-geared steam turbines; 82,000hp
Armament: four 16-cell vertical launch SAM systems (ASTER); two SANDRAL point-defence missile launchers; eight 20mm AA; 40 aircraft
Sensors: air-search radar; air/surface-search radar; fire-control radar
Speed: 27 knots
Range: limited only by reactor fuel state
Complement: 1750 (including air group)

CHARLIE II CLASS

USSR: 1973

The Soviet Union's Project 670M 'Skat-M' cruise missile submarines were given the NATO code-name *Charlie-II* when they first appeared in 1973. Six *Charlie-II*s are believed to have followed on from 12 *Charlie-I*s, which were smaller, shorter submarines with a different missile armament. The *Charlie-II*s were armed with the SS-N-9 'Siren' anti-ship missile, which could be fitted with a nuclear warhead for use against US carrier battle groups. The *Charlie-II* class was, in effect, the finished version of what the *Charlie-I* design had tried to be – after the latter was rushed into production to cover problems with the *Papa*-class attack submarines. The fleet remained in Russian service until the late-1990s.

Throughout their service lives the *Charlie* class was hampered by its single reactor powerplant, which did not provide enough speed to keep up with US carrier battle groups.

Displacement: 4300t surfaced; 5100t submerged
Dimensions: 340ft x 32ft 10in x 26ft 3in (103.6m x 10m x 8m)
Machinery: one-shaft, nuclear, one reactor; 15,000hp
Armament: eight SS-N-9 SLCM; four 21in (533mm) TT, four 16in (406mm) TT
Speed: 24 knots surfaced
Range: limited only by reactor fuel state
Complement: 98

CLEMENCEAU

FRANCE: 1957

Clemenceau (R 98) holds the distinction of being the first aircraft carrier to be built in France. Together with her sistership, *Foch*, she has sustained French naval aviation operations for nearly 30 years, but is now on the verge of retirement pending the introduction of the nuclear-powered carrier *Charles De Gaulle*. For her day, the *Clemenceau* was a modern ship, with a fully-angled deck, a mirror landing-aid system and a comprehensive radar fit. *Clemenceau* is also remarkably powerful, her two-shaft machinery having a combined output of 126,000hp – a figure surpassed only by the US Navy's own 'super carriers' which were built years later. *Clemenceau* was laid down in November 1955, launched in December 1957 and completed in November 1961. She has two steam catapults and two aircraft deck elevators. Unusually, at least for a modern carrier, both her flight deck and machinery compartments are armoured. *Clemenceau* was intended to carry up to 60 aircraft, but her standard air wing usually numbered around 40. At the start of her service life, *Clemenceau* embarked Aquilon (Sea Venom) interceptor, Etendard IVM attack and Alizé ASW aircraft. Super Etendards replaced the Etendard IVs and F-8F Crusaders took over from the Aquilons – the Crusaders were only retired in late-1999. In 1977–78 *Clemenceau* underwent a major modernisation and received stronger catapults, new boilers, improved tactical systems and new landing aids; she was also modified to safely accommodate nuclear stores in her aircraft ordnance lockers. In a second major refit, during 1985–86, she had four of her 3.9in (100mm) guns replaced by two Crotale SAM batteries. *Clemenceau* is scheduled to be withdrawn and held in reserve in 2000/01.

There had been hopes that *Clemenceau* would carry on in service alongside the new *Charles De Gaulle*, but she will be withdrawn – as was her sistership, the *Foch*.

Displacement: 22,000t standard; 32,780t full load
Dimensions: 870 ft x 168 ft x 28 ft (265m x 51.2m x 8.6m)
Machinery: four-shaft, Parsons geared steam turbines, six boilers; 126,000hp
Armament: four 3.9in (100mm); two Crotale SAM launchers
Sensors: long-range air-surveillance radar; low-altitude targeting radar; height-finding radar; air-surveillance/tracking radar; sonar
Speed: 32 knots
Range: 7500nm (13,890km) at 18 knots
Complement: 1338

COLBERT

FRANCE: 1956

Displacement: 9085t standard; 11,100t full load
Dimensions: 593ft x 66ft x 21ft (180.5m x 20.3m x 6.5m)
Machinery: two-shaft, CEM Parsons geared steam turbines, four boilers; 87,000hp
Armament: one Mascura twin SAM launcher (later); 16 5in (127mm) (original fit), 20 57mm (original fit)
Sensors: long-range air-surveillance radar; height-finding radar; fire-control radar; sonar
Speed: 33 knots
Range: 4500nm (8334km) at 25 knots
Complement: 977

The French cruiser *Colbert* (C 611) spent most of her active life as a fleet command ship. Her service career lasted from the late 1950s until 1991, but it was not until 1970 that any changes were made to her basic armament fit of 16 5in (127mm) main guns. At this point, a battery of Masurca anti-aircraft missiles replaced some of the original gun positions, giving the *Colbert* a much-improved fleet defence capability. In 1980 Exocet anti-ship missiles were also added.

The cruiser *Colbert* was a fast and elegant ship that spent most of her career as the flagship of France's Mediterranean fleet.

COLLINS

AUSTRALIA: 1993

In 1987 a lengthy Australian evaluation of a new attack submarine (SSK) to replace its *Oxley* (Oberon)-class boats resulted in an order for six Swedish-designed (Kockums) Type 471s. Dubbed the *Collins* class, and built by the Australian Submarine Corporation, the new SSKs are loosely based on the *Vastergötland*-class. However, they do not have the advanced air-independent diesels of the Swedish submarines, relying instead on conventional diesel-electric power. It had been hoped to acquire eight SSKs, but two options were not taken up. The lead ship, HMAS *Collins* (S 71), was launched in August 1990 and completed in 1995. Her introduction into service was far from trouble-free and the *Collins* submarines attracted major criticism for failing to be operationally effective. Though based on a proven design, they suffered from unreliable diesel engines, excessive noise from the propellers and from water flow around the hull, vibration and optical flaws in the periscope and problems with the all-important on-board tactical combat data management system. Since 1998, major efforts have been made to rectify these problems by a joint Royal Australian Navy/industry team with assistance from both the US Navy and Sweden. Changes have been made to the hull shape and propeller design and HMAS *Collins* has trialled an interim fit for a new combat management system. These changes, and the complete replacement of the original tactical mission system with entirely new equipment, should see the *Collins* class regain full operational effectiveness by 2002. In June 2000, HMAS *Collins* made the first ever Sub-Harpoon missile launch by an Australian submarine, during exercises with the US Navy.

Australia's *Collins*-class SSKs have suffered from several teething troubles, but the replacement of their combat data management system and some design refinements should allow the new submarines to reach optimum combat effectiveness. Prior to the introduction of the *Collins* class, the old diesel-powered *Oxley*-class boats were the only submarines to ever serve in the Royal Australian Navy.

Displacement: 3051t surfaced; 3353t submerged
Dimensions: 254ft x 25ft 7in x 23ft (77.5m x 7.8m x 7m)
Machinery: one-shaft, diesel electric, two 18-cyl. diesels, plus one electric motor; 3.5MW
Armament: six 21in (533mm) TT (23 Mk 48 Mod 4 torpedoes and Sub-Harpoon anti-ship missiles or mines)
Sensors: bow and flank sonar arrays; plus passive towed array
Speed: 10 knots surfaced; 20 knots submerged
Range: 9000nm (16,668km) at 10 knots
Complement: 42

CONQUEROR

GB: 1969

Displacement: 4000t surfaced; 4900t submerged
Dimensions: 285ft x 33ft 3in x 27ft (64.2m x 8.3m x 8.2m)
Machinery: one-shaft, nuclear, one pressurised water-cooled reactor with geared steam turbine, plus diesel-electric auxiliary; 15,000hp
Armament: six 21in (533mm) TT (Mk 23 Tigerfish torpedoes and Sub-Harpoon anti-ship missiles)
Sensors: search-and-navigation radar; sonar
Speed: 32 knots (maximum) submerged
Range: limited only by reactor fuel state
Complement: 52

The *Valian*- class nuclear attack submarines were the first mass-produced SSNs to enter Royal Navy service. They were based on HMS *Dreadnought*, the first British nuclear submarine, but were equipped with six tubes for Mk 24 Tigerfish torpedoes, though they could also use the older Mk 8s and wire-guided Mk 23s. In the early 1980s the *Valiant*s were modified to carry the Sub-Harpoon. HMS *Conqueror* (S 48) was the fourth of five in the class, being launched in August 1969 and completed in November 1971. During the Falklands conflict, *Conqueror* sank the Argentinean cruiser *General Belgrano*, an action much discussed both at the time and to this day. During the attack, on 2 May 1982, *Conqueror* fired two Mk 8 torpedoes to defeat the armour of a ship built in 1938. The Mk 8 design dates back to 1927, but it has a larger warhead than the more modern Tigerfish. By 1988, *Conqueror*'s reactor was beginning to cause concern and the *Valiant*s were withdrawn in the early-1990s.

HMS *Conqueror* was withdrawn from service in 1990 having become the first Royal Navy submarine to score a kill in action since the end of World War II. Her place in the RN submarine fleet was taken by the more modern *Swiftsure*-class SSNs.

CORAL SEA

USA: 1946

The USS *Coral Sea* (CV-43, formerly CVB-43) was a *Midway*-class aircraft carrier – the mainstay of the US Navy's post-war carrier fleet. The *Midways* featured heavy anti-aircraft armament and deck armour, after the lessons learned during the Pacific campaign. In the early 1950s they were also the only US carriers capable of carrying nuclear weapons. The USS *Coral Sea* was the third of the class to be built. She was laid down in July 1944, launched in April 1946 and commissioned in October 1947 and spent most of her operational life with the US Sixth Fleet, making many North Atlantic and Mediterranean cruises. From the 1970s onwards, the question of her retirement was repeatedly raised but the demand for carrier hulls kept the *Coral Sea* in service. By the end of her service life, she could carry an air wing of 65 aircraft. The USS *Coral Sea* was finally withdrawn for scrapping in October 1989, and was formally decommissioned in April 1991.

Displacement: 65,200t full load
Dimensions: 1,003ft x 236ft x 35ft (307.5m x 72m x 10.7m)
Machinery: four-shaft, steam turbines, 12 boilers; 212,000hp
Armament: three Mk 15 Phalanx 20mm CIWS (final configuration); 65 aircraft
Sensors: not available
Speed: 33 knots
Range: not available
Complement: approximately 4,104

The USS *Coral Sea* was one the last World War II-era carriers to remain in US Navy service, outlasted only by the USS *Midway* herself. The *Midways* were small, uncomfortable ships with relatively poor sea-keeping qualities that were kept in service only by the Cold War need for sea-power.

CORNWALL

GB: 1985

Britain ordered four Batch 3 Type frigates, otherwise known as the *Cornwall* class, to make up for losses suffered during the Falklands conflict. These warships used the proven Batch 2 hull-form, albeit with a steeper-angled stern profile and introduced a substantially improved weapons and systems fit. Chief among these changes was the addition of a new CACS-5 tactical battle management system (replacing the earlier CACS-1), Harpoon anti-ship missiles and the large-calibre Goalkeeper close-in weapons system. Other notable modifications were made to the forward deck area to allow the addition of a single Mk 8 4.5in (114mm) main gun – the first time that a gun turret had been incorporated into a Type 22 vessel. The gun is controlled by a pair of GSA 8A Sea Archer electro-optical fire directors, mounted above the wheelhouse, to port and starboard. The Mk 8 replaced the earlier Exocet missile launcher, which had been made redundant by the addition of Harpoons to the Batch 3s. In yet another armament change, Oerlikon 30mm cannon replaced the previous Bofors 40mm. Such were the differences between the Batch 3 Type 22s and their predecessors, that they were awarded all-new 'C' type names. The Type 22s have been recognised as superb – not to mention elegant – warships, but they come at a high cost.HMS *Cornwall* (F 99) was the lead ship in the class and was laid down in the Yarrow shipyard in December 1983. She was launched in October 1985 and completed in April 1988. *Cornwall* has a flight deck and hangar that can accommodate two Lynx or a single Sea King helicopter (soon to be replaced by the Merlin HAS.Mk 3).

The Batch 3s are primarily designed for ASW operations, and have facilities for a flag officer and his staff.

Displacement: 4200t standard; 4900t full load
Dimensions: 485ft 9in x 48ft 6in x 21ft (148.1m x 14.8m x 6.4m)
Machinery: two-shaft, COGOG, four gas turbines; 52,300hp/9700hp
Armament: eight Harpoon SSM; two sextuple launchers for GWS25 Mod 3 Sea Wolf SAM; one 4.5in (114mm); two 30mm cannon; one Goalkeeper 30mm CIWS; six 12.75in (324mm) TT (Stingray ASW torpedoes); one/two helicopters
Sensors: air/surface-search radar; navigation radar; fire-control radar; hull-mounted sonar ; towed array
Speed: 28.5 knots
Range: 8000nm (14,805km) at 18 knots
Complement: 250

CORONEL BOLOGNESI

PERU: 1955

Displacement: 8530t standard; 11450t full load
Dimensions: 555ft 6in x 62ft x 20ft 9in (169.4m x 18.9m x 6.4m)
Machinery: four-shaft, Parsons geared turbines, eight three-drum boilers; 72,500hp
Armament: (as delivered) nine 6in (152mm); eight 4in (102mm); 18 40mm AA;
Sensors: long-range air-search radar; height-finding radar; air/surface-search radar; surface radar; fire-control radar
Speed: 31.5 knots
Range: not available
Complement: 920

When she arrived in Peru, the cruiser *Coronel Bolognesi* was already an ageing ship, but she remained in service for another 20 years.

In the early years of World War II, the *Fiji*-class cruisers were considered to be the best available to the Royal Navy. All 11 ships were named after British possessions or overseas territories. Of those that survived the war, one was sold to India and two went to Peru. *Coronel Bolognesi* (82) was formerly HMS *Ceylon* and was acquired in February 1960. She was refitted with a new mast, a covered bridge and improved AA armament before delivery and remained in service with the Peruvian Navy until May 1982.

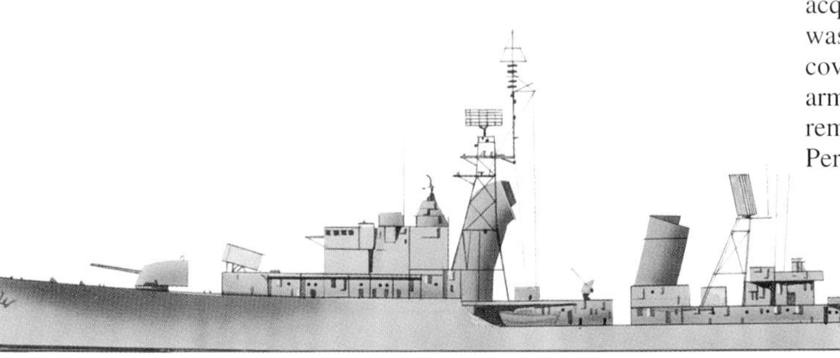

D'ESTIENNE D'ORVES

FRANCE: 1973

The French *D'Estienne d'Orves* (A 69)-class corvettes are a numerically important type, designed for coastal anti-submarine work and colonial patrol tasks and with accommodation for a detachment of 18 troops. The first of 17 vessels (plus two for Argentina), *D'Estienne d'Orves* (F 781) was launched in June 1973 and completed in September 1976. She is built around a DUBA 25 sonar and an ASW rocket launcher. Like her sisterships she was modified to carry Exocet anti-ship missiles and (later) a new type of 3.9in (100mm) gun.

Displacement: 1100t standard; 1250t full load

The *D'Estienne d'Orves* class is a simple and austere design, optimised for long-endurance patrols. All 17 of the class are still in service.

Dimensions: 262ft x 34ft x 1 ft (80m x 10.3m x 5.3m)
Machinery: two-shaft, two diesels; 11,000hp
Armament: four MM40 or two MM38 Exocet SSM; one 3.9in (100mm); two 20mm cannon (later); one Mk 54 14.75in (375mm) six-tube ASW RL; four launchers for L5 torpedoes
Sensors: air/surface-search radar; navigation radar; fire-control radar; hull-mounted sonar
Speed: 23.5 knots
Range: 4500nm (8334km) at 25 knots
Complement: 105

DALE

USA: 1962

Displacement: 5146t standard; 7590t full load
Dimensions: 533ft x 53ft 4in x 19ft (162.5m x 16.3m x 5.8m)
Machinery: two-shaft, geared turbines, four boilers; 85,000hp
Armament: one quadruple launcher for Harpoon SSM; two twin launchers for Terrier SAM (later SM-2ER Standard); four 3in (76mm) (deleted); two Mk 15 Phalanx 20mm CIWS; four .50-cal MG; one ASROC rocket-boosted ASW torpedo launcher; six 12.75in (324mm) TT (Mk 32 ASW torpedoes)
Sensors: air-search radar; fire-control radar; hull-mounted sonar
Speed: 32 knots
Range: 8000nm (14,816km) at 20 knots
Complement: 377

Once they had matured in service, the *Leahy*-class cruisers were effective combat ships-but the heavy budget cutbacks in the US Navy of the 1990s inevitably saw them taken out of action.

The US Navy's *Leahy*-class escort cruisers became the first American 'all-missile' ships, with guns playing a very minor role in their armament fit. They were developed to meet the growing need for fleet air defence against long-range Soviet bombers and were built around the Terrier missile system and its associated air-search radars. Once in service, Terrier proved not to be as capable as had been hoped and all the *Leahys* underwent substantial modernisation in later years. The USS *Dale* (DLG 19, later CG 19) was the fourth of nine ships in her class. She was launched in July 1962 and completed in November 1963. In time, the Terrier missiles were replaced by Standards and Harpoon anti-ship missiles took the place of the 3in (76mm) guns. By the 1980s, the *Dale* had been further upgraded to fire the Standard SM-2ER and had also been fitted with the Phalanx CIWS. The *Dale* was finally stricken from service in 1994.

DANIEL BOONE

USA: 1963

Displacement: 7325t surfaced; 8251t submerged
Dimensions: 425ft x 33ft x 27ft 10in (129.6m x 10.1m x 8.5m)
Machinery: two-shaft nuclear, one S5W reactor; 15,000hp
Armament: 16 UGM-73A Poseidon SLBM (later UGM-96A Trident I/C-4); four 21in (533mm) TT
Sensors: active/passive sonar and towed array
Speed: 20 knots submerged
Range: limited only by reactor fuel state
Complement: 140

Until the mid-1980s, the backbone of the US Navy's nuclear-powered strategic missile submarine (SSBN) fleet was its *Lafayette* class boats. They were an enlarged version of the *Ethan Allen*-class, which was armed with 16 Polaris A-1/A-3 SLBMs; the first *Lafayettes* were also armed with Polaris, until soon replaced by the UGM-73A Poseidon – for which the *Lafayettes* had been designed. The Poseidon was the first SLBM with a MIRV warhead, carrying 10 50kT devices. Within the *Lafayette* class were three sub-classes, which featured several important design refinements. The USS *Daniel Boone* (SSBN 629) was the first boat of the second sub-class (known as the *James Madison* class) to be built. She was launched in June 1963 and completed in April 1964. The Poseidon missile had a troubled service history and proved to be unreliable. It was replaced by the Trident. In all, 12 *Lafayettes* were modified to carry the Trident I missile; the USS *Daniel Boone* was the first to be converted (though not to sail), in September 1980.

The USS *Daniel Boone* helped introduce the Trident SLBM into US Navy service, but with the coming of the dedicated *Ohio*-class SSBNs she was finally retired in 1993. The *Daniel Boone* holds the distinction of being the first fleet ballistic missile submarine to ever visit Hawaii.

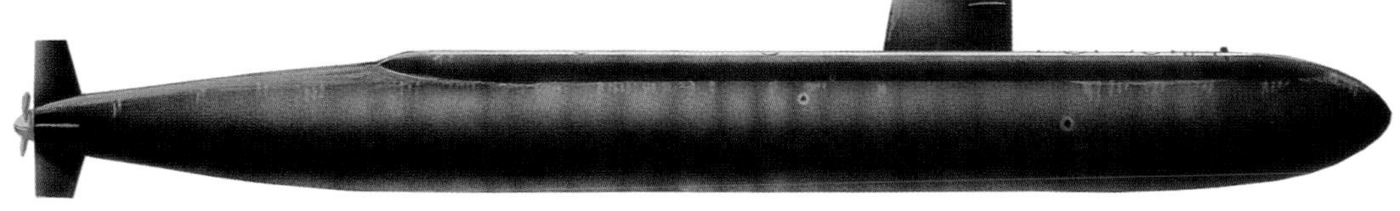

DAPHNÉ

FRANCE: 1959

The 11 *Daphné*-class submarines which entered French service between 1964 and 1970, were designed as affordable but effective craft. Though they lacked the range of the larger *Narval*-class ocean-going submarines, they were quiet, manoeuvrable boats and featured strong double-hulled construction. *Daphné* (S 641) was launched in June 1959 and completed in June 1964. She is no longer active, though three of the class remain in French service.

The *Daphné* design has proved to be popular. Similar submarines have been adopted by the navies of Portugal, Pakistan, South Africa and Spain.

Displacement: 869t surfaced; 1043t submerged
Dimensions: 190 ft x 22 ft x 17 ft (57.8m x 6.8m x 5.25m)
Machinery: two-shaft, two diesels, plus one electric motor; 1300hp/1600hp
Armament: 12 21.6in (549mm) TT (ECAN E15 torpedoes)
Sensors: search and attack sonar
Speed: 16 knots surfaced; 13.5 knots submerged
Range: 10,000nm (18,520km) at 7 knots, surfaced
Complement: 45

DARING

GB: 1949

Displacement: 2830t standard; 3580t full load
Dimensions: 390ft x 43ft x 13ft (118.8m x 13.1m x 4.1m)
Machinery: two-shaft, double reduction-geared turbines, two boilers; 54,000hp
Armament: six Mk 6 4.5in (114mm); two/six 40mm; one Squid ASW mortar
Sensors: tracking radar; air-search radar; hull-mounted sonar
Speed: 34.75 knots
Range: 6000nm (11,112km) at 16 knots
Complement: 297–330

Eight *Daring*-class ships were built, starting with HMS *Daring* (D 05); she was laid down in September 1945, launched in August 1949 and completed in March 1952. *Daring* was armed with three twin 4.5in (114mm) gun turrets but, in 1963, trials were conducted on one of the other ships to replace the aft turret with a Seacat SAM launcher. This did not prove a success and though some changes were made to the configuration of her 40mm guns, *Daring* remained essentially unchanged. At the wish of Lord Mountbattan, HMS *Daring* was fitted with a streamlined aft funnel, but this was returned to its original form when it was found to restrict the arc of fire of the twin Bofors. While several of her sisterships were sold abroad, HMS *Daring* was retired and broken up in 1971. The first ship in the Royal Navy's forthcoming class of new Type 45 frigates has now been named HMS *Daring*.

Though built as destroyers, and unremarkable in their size, the Admiralty decreed that HMS Daring and her sisterships should be classed as '*Daring*-type ships' and treated as light cruisers.

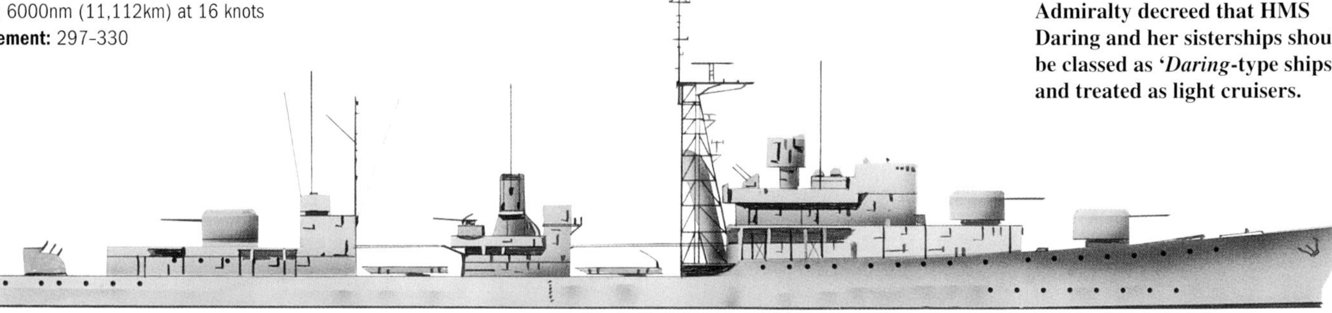

DAT ASSAWARI

LIBYA: 1969

By far the largest vessel in the Libyan Navy is the British-built frigate *Dat Assawari* (211, formerly F 01). Based on the Vosper Thornycroft Mk 7 design, she was launched in October 1969 and completed in February 1973. She was refitted in Italy during 1991, having sustained bomb damage in the US air action against Libya. Some of her older British-built weapons and radar were replaced by Italian equipment; for example, Otomat SSM were added and Albatros SAMs replaced one Seacat system.

Displacement: 1325t standard; 1625t full load
Dimensions: 330ft x 35ft x 11ft 2in (100.6m x 11m x 3.4m)
Machinery: two-shaft, CODOG, two gas turbines, two diesels; 46,400hp/3500hp
Armament: four Otomat Mk 1 SSM; one four-round launcher for Albatros SAM, one three-round launcher for Seacat SAM; one 4.5in (114mm); two 35mm cannon; six 12.75in (324mm) TT (ASW torpedoes)
Sensors: search radar; radar; hull-mounted sonar
Speed: 30 knots
Range: 5700nm (10,556km) at 17 knots
Complement: 132

Libya's *Dat Assawari* is similar to the Mk 5 frigates developed and built for Iran, but is larger and was outfitted with different weapons.

DE GRASSE

FRANCE: 1946

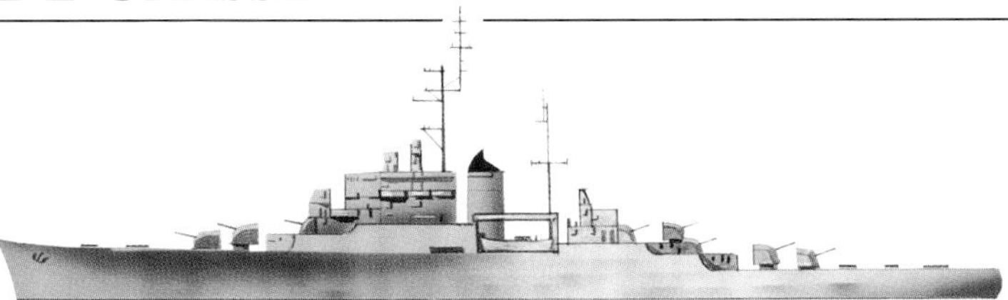

In the final years of her service, *De Grasse* was fitted with a tall communications mast on her aft decking, added for her new role as a test and trials support vessel.

The French cruiser *De Grasse* (C 610) was laid down in 1938 but the outbreak of World War II halted progress. The unfinished ship remained at the Lorient yard until Germany's defeat in 1945, when work resumed. *De Grasse* was launched in August 1946 and completed in September 1956. She was heavily armed with standard French pattern 5in (127mm) and 57mm guns. This fit was revised in 1966 when the cruiser was modified to support French nuclear tests in the Pacific, and several turrets were deleted.

Displacement: 9380t standard (later 9000t); 11,545t full load
Dimensions: 618ft x 61ft x 18ft (188.3m x 18.6m x 5.6m)
Machinery: two-shaft, geared steam turbines, four boilers; 110,000hp
Armament: 16 (later 12) 5in (127mm); 20 57mm (later deleted)
Sensors: medium-range air-surveillance radar; air/surface-search radar; height-finding radar; fire-control radar
Speed: 33 knots
Range: not available
Complement: 950 (983 as flagship, 560 as trials vessel, plus 120 support technicians)

DE RUYTER

THE NETHERLANDS: 1950

The two *De Ruyter* class cruisers were the flag-ships of the Dutch Navy throughout the 1950s and 1960s. Both were sold to Peru; *De Ruyter* was the first to go, in 1973.

The Dutch cruiser *De Ruyter* (C 801) was laid down in 1939 as *De Zeven Provincien*. In World War II, the Germans launched her in their 1944 attempt to prevent the Allies using Rotterdam docks. *De Ruyter* was finally completed for Dutch service in November 1953, her entire propulsion system and armament being revised and updated. She never did receive the Terrier SAMs that were fitted to her sistership (confusingly named *De Zeven Provincien*), and retained her all-gun armament.

Displacement: 9529t standard; 11,850t full load
Dimensions: 615ft x 57ft x 22ft (187.3m x 17.3m x 6.7m)
Machinery: two-shaft, De Schelde Parsons geared steam turbines, four boilers; 85,000hp
Armament: eight 6in (152mm); eight 57mm; eight 40mm cannon
Sensors: long-range air-surveillance radar; medium-range air/surface-surveillance radar; height-finding radar; fire-control radar
Speed: 32 knots
Range: not available
Complement: 926

DÉDALO

SPAIN: 1967

Displacement: 13,000t standard; 16,416t full load
Dimensions: 623ft x 109ft 2in x 26ft (189.9m x 33.7m x 7.9m)
Machinery: four-shaft, geared turbines, four boilers; 100,000hp
Armament: 26 40mm AA; seven Matadors and up to 20 helicopters
Sensors: air-surveillance radar; surface-search radar; height-finding radar; radar; fire-control radar; TACAN
Speed: 31 knots
Range: 7500nm (13,890km) at 15 knots
Complement: 1112 (ship's company)

The *Dedalo* could carry about 20 aircraft, chiefly AV-8 Matadors and SH-3 Sea Kings. It had been hoped to retain her in service alongside the more modern *Principe de Asturias*, but she proved to be too expensive to sustain.

In 1967 the former US Navy *Independence*-class escort carrier, the USS *Cabot*, was transferred to Spain under the MDAP military aid programme – and purchased outright in 1973. The ship was rechristened the *Dédalo* (R 01) and pioneered Spanish shipboard naval aviation operations. *Dédalo* was extensively refitted and modernised and two of her original four funnels were removed. To serve aboard the *Dédalo*, Spanish Naval Aviation acquired a total of 11 AV-8A and two TAV-8A Harriers – known as AV-8A(S) Matadors. *Dédalo* never received a ski jump to fully exploit the Matador's VSTOL capabilities, but the rear deck was given a metal re-skinning to allow vertical take-offs and landings. *Dédalo* was acquired to operate as a helicopter carrier, and so she routinely carried SH-3G/H Sea Kings. By the 1980s the *Dédalo* was becoming too old to carry on and was replaced by the purpose-built carrier *Principe de Asturias*. *Dedalo* was returned to the USA in 1989 and will be preserved as a museum ship.

DELTA-III CLASS

USSR/RUSSIA: 1976

The Soviet-era Project 667B ballistic missile submarines (NATO code-name *Delta* class) are still a vital element of the Russian Navy's strategic fleet. The type's origins lie in the *Yankee*-class submarines of the mid-1960s, which were steadily improved into the today's *Deltas*. Four sub-types of the *Delta*-class have been identified, each with new systems and improved main missile armament. The *Delta-I* carried 12 SS-N-8 'Sawfly' SLBMs while the larger *Delta-II* carried 16 missiles. The SS-N-8 was fitted with a single warhead in the megaton-class, and

The humpbacked appearance of the *Delta*-class missile submarines is unmistakable. They are roughly equivalent to the US Navy's *Lafayette*-class missile boats. When it entered service with the *Delta-IIIs*, the SS-N-18 'Stingray' SLBM was the largest missile of its kind.

had a range of less than 5000nm (9260km). With the introduction of the *Delta-III* class (Project 677 BDR Kalmar), Soviet SLBM capability took a major step forward. The first *Delta-III* (K-441) was launched and completed in 1976 and a total of 13 followed by 1982 – when the further improved *Delta-IV* came on stream. A *Delta-III* is armed with 16 SS-N-18 'Stingray' SLBMs, the first Soviet naval multiple-warhead missile. The latest versions of the missile can carry up to seven kiloton-class warheads over an estimated range of 4350nm (8056km). All the *Delta* missile submarines have a distinctive hump behind the main sail, housing their bulky SLBM payload. On the *Delta-III* this hump is much larger, to accommodate the new missiles – approximately 147ft 6in (44.96m) long. The *Delta-III boats* operate at a depth of about 1200ft (366m) and are understood to have test dived to 1900ft (579m). The improved *Delta-IV* boats are fitted with a housing for a towed-sonar array/towed decoy, and the same system has been retrofitted to some *Delta-IIIs*.

Displacement: 10,500t surfaced; 13,250t submerged
Dimensions: 459ft 4in x 39ft 4in x 28ft 7in (140m x 12m x 8.7m)
Machinery: two-shaft, nuclear, one reactor, rated at approximately 500,000hp
Armament: 16 SS-N-18 SLBMs, four 21in (533mm) TT; two 16in (406mm) TT
Sensors: sonar suite
Speed: 25 knots submerged
Range: limited only by reactor fuel state
Complement: approximately 120

DENVER

USA: 1983

Displacement: 10,000t standard; 16,900t full load
Dimensions: 570ft x 84ft x 23ft (173.8m x 25.6m x 7m)
Machinery: two-shaft, geared turbines, two boilers; 24,000hp
Armament: two/four Mk 33 3in (76mm); two Mk 15 Phalanx 20mm CIWS; up to six CH-46A Sea Knight helicopters
Sensors: air-search radar; surface-search radar; navigation radar
Speed: 20 knots
Range: 7700nm (14,260km) at 20 knots
Complement: 410–447, plus 840 Marines

In common with all the *Austin*-class LPDs, the USS *Denver* is no longer the most modern type in the US Navy's amphibious assault force.

The *Austin*-class dock landing ships (LPDs) were built in the mid-1960s as assault ships and, as part of the Marine Corps' dedicated 'Gator Navy', the 11 vessels in the class sustained the US amphibious assault force for three decades. All are still in use, largely as general-purpose 'swing' ships, but some have been diverted to other tasks. The capacious hulls of the *Austins* made them well-suited to the flagship/command-ship mission and some were converted to serve in this dedicated role. The USS *Denver* (LPD 9) was launched in January 1965. From the beginning, she was fitted out as an amphibious squadron flagship, with an extra bridge level to house additional command staff. The same changes were made to the last five *Austin*-class ships (*Denver* was the sixth to be built). *Denver* retains all the amphibious assault capabilities of her sisterships and can embark three LCM-6, four LCM-8 or 20 LVT landing craft. She can also accommodate CH-46A helicopters on her rear deck.

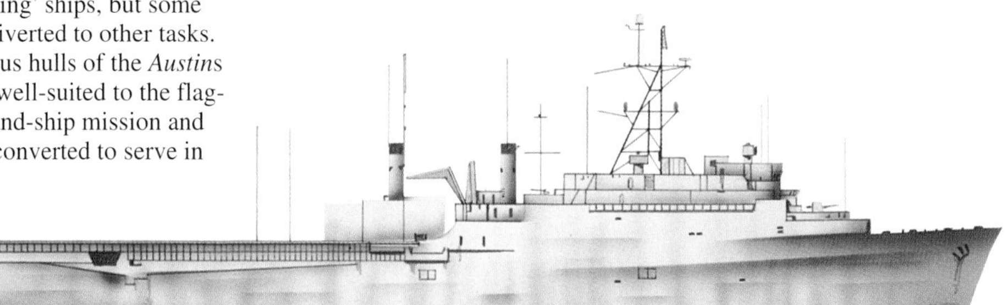

DES MOINES

USA: 1946

The three vessels of the US Navy's *Des Moines* class were the peak of World War II cruiser design. They were armed with the automated 8in (203mm) /55 dual-purpose gun that tripled the range of existing 8in (203mm) guns – and matched the rapid firing rate of the smaller 6in (152mm) guns while outranging them. It was felt that only an all-new cruiser design could take advantage of this new armament and such ships would also provide a credible capability in the post-war years. The plan to build eight *Des Moines*-class ships was curtailed by the war coming to an end; just three were completed (with a fourth ship laid down but then cancelled). The USS *Des Moines* (CA 134) was launched in September 1946 and completed in November 1948. Along with her sisterships, she proved to be a capable and effective vessel. *Des Moines* remained in the active fleet until 1961, when she was transferred to the reserve. She was finally stricken in 1991.

The USS *Des Moines* was an elegant, all-gun cruiser that survived the great cutbacks at the end of World War II to serve the US Navy for another 20 years.

Displacement: 17,255t standard; 20,934t full load
Dimensions: 716ft 6in x 75ft 4in x 26ft (218.4m x 22.96m x 7.92m)
Machinery: two-shaft, General Electric turbines, four boilers; 120,000hp
Armament: nine 8in (203mm); 12 5in (130mm); 24 3in (76mm); 24 20mm AA
Sensors: not available
Speed: 33 knots
Range: 1500nm (19,432km) at 15 knots
Complement: 1799

DEUTSCHLAND

GERMANY: 1960

The *Deutschland* (A 59) was built as a Type 440 multi-purpose vessel, though she was never intended to have a combat role. However, she did have a full armament fit and could have been pressed into emergency wartime tasks. Launched in November 1960, she served as a naval training ship and was also used to test new gear and equipment – such as her unusual mixed propulsion system. After 30 years of service *Deutschland* was decommissioned in 1990 and broken up in 1993.

The training ship *Deutschland* was fitted with every type of weapon in German naval service, apart from guided missile systems.

Displacement: 4880t standard; 5684t full load
Dimensions: 453ft 6in x 52ft 9in x 16ft 8in (138.2m x 16.1m x 5.1m)
Machinery: three-shaft (CP propellers), steam turbines with two boilers, plus four diesels; 16,000hp (combined)
Armament: four 3.9in (100mm); six 40mm cannon; two 21in (533mm) TT (ASW torpedoes); two 14.75in (375mm) ASW mortars
Sensors: air-search radar; hull-mounted sonar
Speed: 22 knots
Range: 3800nm (7038km) at 18 knots
Complement: 172, plus 250 cadets

DEVONSHIRE

GB: 1960

Displacement: 6200t standard; 6800t full load
Dimensions: 521ft 6in x 54ft x 20ft 6in (158.3m x 16.4m x 6.2m)
Machinery: two-shaft COSAG, geared steam turbines, two Babcock & Wilcox boilers, plus four gas turbines; 30,000hp/30,000hp
Armament: one launcher for Seaslug SAM; four 4.5in (114mm); two 20mm cannon; one helicopter
Sensors: air-surveillance radar; air/surface-search radar; height-finding radar; fire-control radar; hull-mounted sonar
Speed: 30 knots
Range: 3500nm (6482km) at 28 knots
Complement: 440–471

The *County*-class guided-missile destroyers recorded some notable firsts for the Royal Navy. They were the first vessels capable of embarking a medium helicopter (Wessex), the first to be armed with operational anti-ship missiles (Exocet) and, together with the *Tribal* class, the first to be fitted with COSAG (COmbined Steam And Gas) machinery. HMS *Devonshire* (D 02) was the lead ship in the class. She was launched in June 1960 and completed in November 1962, mounting Mk 6 gun turrets and the (then) new Seaslug SAM system. On later ships, Seaslug was replaced by the more advanced Seacat. *Devonshire* was never fitted with the Exocets that replaced the 'B' turret on some of her sisterships. The *County*-class fleet was due to be eliminated after the 1981 defence cuts, but the Falklands conflict prolonged their service lives. Four ships were later sold to Chile and one to Pakistan, but HMS *Devonshire* was expended as a target in July 1984.

The beam-riding Seaslug was a first-generation surface-to-air missile. It was carried in a complicated lattice-frame launcher mounted aft.

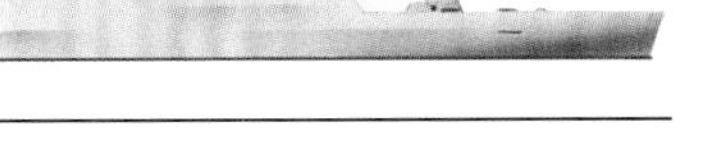

DIDO

GB: 1961

The Royal Navy's *Leander*-class frigates proved to be an innovative design that allowed smaller ships to once more take on the role of multi-purpose escorts, instead of being dedicated single-role vessels. The *Leander*s are generally considered to have been among the best of their type ever built and they proved to be immensely popular in service. HMS *Dido* (F 104), was the third vessel of the 16 frigates in the class; she was launched in December 1961 and completed in September 1963. *Dido* was one of the eight ships to receive the Batch 1 conversion – replacing its 4.5in (114mm) main gun turret with a GWS40 Ikara ASW missile system. The other *Leander*s were modified, through the Batch 2 conversion, to carry the Exocet anti-ship missile. HMS *Dido* was recommissioned in her new form in October 1978, as the last of the Batch 1 conversions. She remained in Royal Navy service until 1983 when she was sold to New Zealand, becoming HMNZS *Southland*.

The *Leander*-class frigates boasted a new kind of automatically-controlled machinery which conferred remarkable manoeuvrability and handling.

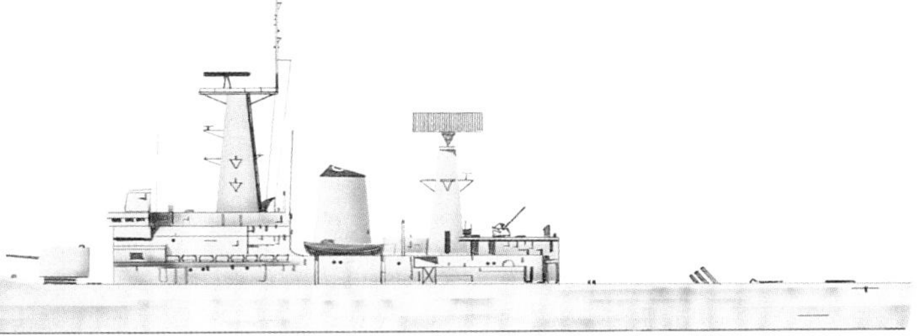

Displacement: 2350t standard; 2860t full load
Dimensions: 372ft x 41ft x 18ft (113.4m x 12.5m x 5.5m)
Machinery: two-shaft, geared steam turbines, two boilers; 30,000hp
Armament: one launcher for Seaslug SAM; one GWS22 Seacat SAM system; two 4.5in (114mm), two 40mm AA guns (deleted); one GWS40 Ikara ASW missile system (added); one helicopter
Sensors: air-surveillance radar; air/surface-search radar; navigation radar; fire-control radar; hull-mountedsonar
Speed: 28 knots
Range: 4000nm (7408km) at 15 knots
Complement: 251–263

DMITRY POZHARSKI

USSR: 1953

Displacement: 13,600t standard; 16,640t full load
Dimensions: 672 ft 4in x 72ft x 22ft 7in (210m x 22m x 6.9m)
Machinery: unknown, estimated rating of 110,000hp
Armament: 12 6in (152mm); 12 3.9in (100mm); 32 37mm AA; 10 21in (533mm) TT (ASW torpedoes)
Sensors: air-surveillance radar; air-warning rader; air/surface-search radar; fire-control radar; hull-mounted HF sonar
Speed: 32.5 knots
Range: 9000nm (16,668km) at 18 knots
Complement: 1250

The Soviet Union continued to build large gun-armed cruisers well into the 1950s, long after most Western navies had started the transition to missile-armed warships. At one time, the Soviet Navy had plans to build 30 *Sverdlov*-class cruisers (known to their designers as Project 68B ships). Stalin gave his support for these large warships, which were far more imposing than the flagships of most other navies. However, on his death the planned total of 30 was cut back to 21 and only 16 were actually completed. The *Dmitry Pozharski* was the sixth to be built. She was launched in June 1953 and completed in December 1954. Over the years, new radar and weapons fits were added to different vessels, but the *Dmitry Pozharski* retained her original armament. Some *Sverdlovs* were retired as early as 1961, but others soldiered on into the late 1980s. *Dmitry Pozharski* was not finally stricken until 1987.

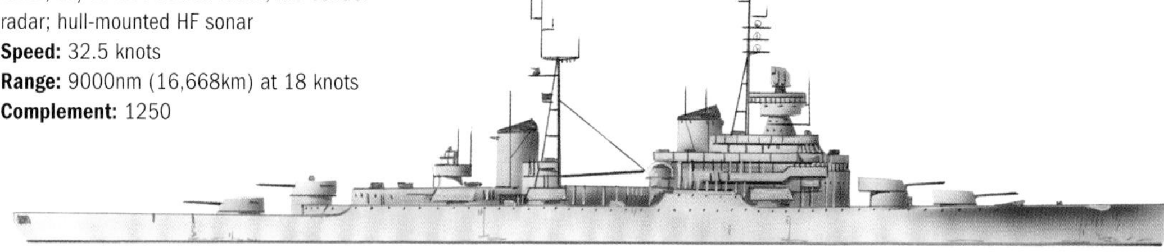

The *Dmitry Pozharski* was a large light cruiser, one of the Soviet Union's substantial fleet of unique (at least in the pos-war world) *Sverdlov*-class cruisers.

DOLFIJN

THE NETHERLANDS: 1959

Displacement: 1494t surfaced; 1826t submerged
Dimensions: 261ft x 26ft x 16ft (79.5m x 7.9m x 5m)
Machinery: two-shaft, two diesels, plus two electric motors; 2800hp/4000hp
Armament: four 21in (533mm) TT
Sensors: navigation radar; sonar
Speed: 14.5 knots surfaced; 17 knots submerged
Range: 12,000nm (22,208km) at 10 knots
Complement: 64

The first post-World War II submarine class laid down for the Dutch Navy used a unique triple-hulled design and, for a while, consideration was given to making them nuclear-powered. Four *Dolfijn* -class boats were built; the lead boat, *Dolfijn* (S 808), was launched in May 1959 and completed in December 1960. The final two submarines to be built were later re-engined, but *Dolfijn*, and her sister-submarine *Zeehond*, remained in their original configuration. *Dolfijn* was finally broken up in 1985.

The Dutch submarine *Dolfijn* had a long service career, but was finally replaced by the current *Walrus* class in the mid-1980s.

DOUDART DE LAGRÉE

FRANCE: 1961

***Doudart De Lagrée* and her sister-ships were designed to combine good range and operating economics, and so were designed around a two-shaft diesel engine.**

The French *Commandant Riviere*-class frigates were designed for the dual roles of colonial patrol and wartime NATO convoy escort. The *Doudart De Lagrée* (F 728) was the fourth of nine such vessels to be built; she was launched in April 1961 and completed in May 1963. Her main armament was a trio of 3.9in (100mm) guns and an anti-submarine mortar; in the late 1970s the rear 'X' gun mount was replaced by an Exocet launcher. *Doudart De Lagrée* was finally stricken in 1991.

Displacement: 1750t standard; 2230t full load
Dimensions: 338ft x 38ft x 14ft (103m x 11.5m x 4.3m)
Machinery: two-shaft, four SEMT-Pielstick 12-cyl. diesels; 16,000hp
Armament: four launchers for MM38 Exocet SSM (later); three 3.9in (100mm) (original fit); two 30mm (later 40mm) cannon; six 21.6in (549mm) TT; one 12in (305mm) ASW mortar
Sensors: search radar; fire-control radar; hull-mounted sonar
Speed: 25 knots
Range: 7500nm (13,890km) at 16 knots
Complement: 166

DREADNOUGHT

GB: 1960

The submarine HMS *Dreadnought* holds an important place in British naval history. As befits her illustrious name (the original *Dreadnought* of 1906 was the first big gun, steam turbine-powered battleship), the *Dreadnought* of 1960 opened up another new era for the Royal Navy – that of nuclear power. Britain was a world leader in nuclear research from the late 1930s onwards, but developing that technology was hugely expensive. (The first British plans for a nuclear-powered submarine were drawn up as early as 1943, but the vessel could not then be built.) Construction of a naval nuclear powerplant was, in any case, dependent on Britain's nuclear power stations which would secretly provide the necessary fuel. The establishment of Britain's own post-war nuclear industry (and with it the fundamentals of reactor design) went so slowly that the US government was asked to supply one of its S5W reactors (as fitted to the US Navy's *Skipjack* class). So, the first British nuclear submarine went to sea with a US powerplant – albeit one built in the UK by Rolls-Royce. In fact, the whole rear section of the *Dreadnought* was essentially the same as the US boats, but grafted on to the British-built vessel. HMS *Dreadnought* (S 101) was laid down in the Vickers-Armstrong yard at Barrow in June 1959. She was launched in October 1960 and completed in April 1963. In 1982 she was declared to have reached the end of her structural life and was laid up in preparation for the removal of her reactor. *Dreadnought* was paid off in the Chatham yard and towed to Rosyth in 1983, to await disposal.

HMS *Dreadnought* had an operational life of nearly 20 years and the experience she provided the Royal Navy was irreplaceable.

Displacement: 3000t surfaced; 4000t submerged
Dimensions: 265ft 9in x 32ft x 26ft (81m x 9.8m x 7.9m)
Machinery: one-shaft, nuclear, one S5W reactor with geared steam turbines, plus diesel-electric auxiliary; 15,000hp
Armament: six 21in (533mm) TT
Sensors: search-and-navigation radar; sonar
Speed: 28 knots submerged (maximum)
Range: limited only by reactor fuel state
Complement: 88

DUGUAY-TROUIN

FRANCE: 1973

Displacement: 4850t standard; 5800t full load
Dimensions: 501ft x 50ft x 21ft (152.5m x 15.3m x 6.5m)
Machinery: two-shaft, geared steam turbines with four boilers; 54,400hp
Armament: four launchers for MM38 Exocet SSM; one octuple launcher for Crotale Navale SAM (26 missiles); one 3.9in (100mm); two 20mm cannon; four 12.7mm MG; two launchers for L5/Mk 46 torpedoes; two helicopters
Sensors: air-search radar; air/surface-search radar; navigation radar; fire-control radar; hull-mounted and towed-array sonar
Speed: 31 knots
Range: 5,000nm (9260km) at 18 knots
Complement: 282

The *Tourville*-class (F 67) guided-missile destroyers were the first French naval vessels designed from the outset to carry a helicopter. They were well-armed, powerful ships which introduced a new generation of air-surveillance radar – the DRBV 26. This radar removed the need for the large bulbous radome fitted to earlier generations of French missile destroyers. *Duguay-Trouin* (D 611) was the second of the three F 67s. She was launched in June 1973 and completed in September 1975. For a short period, *Duguay-Trouin* was fitted with a third 3.9in (100mm) gun turret above the helicopter hangar, but an early decision was made to replace this with a Crotale SAM system. The third *Tourville* destroyer, *De Grasse*, was built with Crotale in place and *Duguay-Trouin* was retrofitted in 1979. *Duguay-Trouin* has a large double flight deck and hangar for Lynx helicopters, fitted with a Harpoon deck-landing system and SPHEX handling equipment. She has received successive upgrades to keep her at the cutting-edge of current French naval forces.

The *Tourville*-class destroyers were based on the earlier *Aconit* class, but were larger ships that boasted twice as much available horsepower.

DUPLEIX

FRANCE: 1978

It had been planned to equip the *Leygues*-class destroyers with more than one main gun turret but a reduction in their planned length forced the current configuration.

The French C 70 destroyer programme was launched with the aim of providing a single hull design that could support a dedicated anti-submarine or anti-air warfare vessel. The destroyer *Dupleix* (D 641) was the second of seven ships to be laid down, in what became formally known as the *Georges Leygues* class. *Dupleix* was launched in December 1978 and completed in June 1981. The *Leygues*-class ships were fitted with a gas turbine powerplant – the first time such an engine was used in a French ship.

Displacement: 3550t standard; 4350t full load
Dimensions: 456ft x 46ft x 19ft (139.1m x 14m x 5.7m)
Machinery: two-shaft, CODOG, two gas turbines plus two diesels; 52,000hp/10,400hp
Armament: four launchers for MM38 Exocet SSM; one octuple launcher for Crotale Navale SAM (26 missiles); one 3.9in (100mm); two 20mm cannon; four 12.7mm MG; two launchers for L5/Mk 46 torpedoes; two helicopters
Sensors: air-search radar; air/surface-search radar; navigation radar; fire-control radar; hull-mounted sonar
Speed: 31 knots
Range: 9500nm (17,594km) at 17 knots
Complement: 216

EAGLE

GB: 1946

The aircraft carrier HMS *Eagle* was laid down in 1942, as HMS *Audacious*. She was conceived as one of four carriers that would improve on the *Implacable* class, but when World War II ended in 1945 only she was far enough advanced to avoid cancellation. In January 1946, *Audacious* was renamed HMS *Eagle* (R 05) (taking the place of an intended HMS *Eagle* which had been cancelled). Two months later she was launched and, upon her completion in October 1951, *Eagle* became the most modern aircraft carrier in the Royal Navy. Though notionally a sistership to HMS *Ark Royal*, *Eagle* and the 'Ark' were quite different ships. *Eagle* would prove to be the sounder of the two, her design following traditional British lines, trading internal space for thorough armour protection. She also incorporated very heavy AA gun armament, backed up by an array of modern radar-controlled fire-directors. During 1954–55, *Eagle* was refitted with a 5° angled deck (increased to 8° by 1964) and the latest mirror landing-aid system. Unlike *Ark Royal*, HMS *Eagle* had a very active operational career and was involved in most of the Royal Navy's major actions during the 1950s and 1960s. The most important of these was the Suez crisis of 1956. Later, she was involved in the confrontation with Indonesia, the unrest in Aden and the 'Beira Patrol' blockade of Rhodesia. In her final years, *Eagle* embarked an air wing of approximately 60 aircraft, typically Sea Vixens, Scimitars and Gannets. Although she was the Navy's most modern carrier, *Eagle* was hastily withdrawn from service following the 1966 defence cuts, leaving *Ark Royal* to soldier on in failing health.

The career of HMS *Eagle* was overshadowed by that of her contemporary HMS *Ark Royal*, but *Eagle* was a much better ship with a far more impressive operational record.

Displacement: 45,000t standard; 53,390t full load
Dimensions: 811ft 9in x 171ft x 36ft (247.4m x 52.1m x 11m)
Machinery: four-shaft, geared steam turbines, eight three-drum boilers; 152,000hp
Armament: : six GWS22 Seacat SAM (replaced all AA from 1962); 16 (later eight) 4.5in (114mm), 48 (later 42) 40mm AA, nine (later six) 40mm AA, four 40mm guns; 60 aircraft (1952, 45 aircraft (1964)
Sensors: not available
Speed: 31 knots
Range: 5000nm (9260km) at 24 knots
Complement: 2750, including air group

ECHO CLASS

USSR: 1960

Displacement: 4500t surfaced; 5500t submerged
Dimensions: 360ft 11in x 29ft 10in x 24ft 7in (110m x 9.1m x 7.5m)
Machinery: two-shaft, nuclear, one HEN nuclear reactor; approximately 25,000hp
Armament: eight SS-N-8 SSM; six 21in (533mm) TT; four (aft) 16in (406mm) TT
Sensors: search radar and sonar
Speed: 20 knots surfaced; 25 knots submerged
Range: limited only by reactor fuel state
Complement: 75

The Soviet nuclear-powered '*Echo I*'-class cruise-missile submarines were designed to carry the SS-N-3 'Shaddock' over-the-horizon anti-ship missile. The SS-N-3 was designed to attack US carriers, but needed mid-course guidance from an aircraft to find its target. Five *Echo I* submarines entered service between 1960 and 1962. They proved to be incapable of carrying out their intended role and were converted to standard torpedo-armed vessels instead. Over the years three of these boats were either lost or badly damaged through various accidents.

The *Echo I* (Project 659) class was a first-generation Soviet nuclear-powered design, using the HEN powerplant. After unsuccessful careers the survivors were retired by the early 1990s.

EILAT

ISRAEL: 1994

The futuristic, angular lines of Israel's flagship *Eilat* (501) mark her as a *Saar V*-class corvette. She combines 'stealthy' design techniques in a compact hull, with a heavy weapons load resulting in an extremely effective medium-sized warship. *Eilat* and her two sisterships are primarily intended to act as lead ships for Israel's fleet of smaller attack boats, but they are also the most capable vessels in the Israeli Navy. The *Saar Vs* are the latest member of the *Saar* ship family, and are built in the United States. *Eilat* was launched in 1994 and carries a mix of US and Israeli-supplied weapons and systems. There is an interchangeable gun position on the forward deck that is capable of mounting either an OTO Melara 3in (76mm) gun, a Bofors 57mm gun or a Phalanx CIWS system. The rest of *Eilat*'s armament is dedicated to missile systems, including both the Harpoon and Gabriel II anti-ship missiles. She can also embark a Dauphin helicopter on her aft flight deck.

Displacement: 1275t full load
Dimensions: 283ft 6in x 39ft x 10ft 6in (86.4m x 11.9m x 3.2m)
Machinery: two-shaft (CP propellers), CODAG, one LM2500 gas turbine, plus two turbocharged diesels; 23,000hp/6600hp
Armament: eight Harpoon SSM, eight Gabriel II SSM; VLS for Barak SAM (64 missiles); one 3in (76mm) or one 57mm or one Mk 15 Phalanx 20mm CIWS; two 25mm Sea Vulcan cannon; six Mk 32 12.75in (324mm) TT (Mk 46 torpedoes); one helicopter
Sensors: air-search radar; surface-search radar; navigation radar; fire-control radar; hull-mounted sonar with VDS or towed-array
Speed: 33 knots
Range: 3500nm (6482km) at 17 knots
Complement: 74

***Eilat*'s flat angular design is intended to reduce her radar reflectivity, making her a more difficult to detect, 'stealthy' vessel. Though classed as a corvette, *Eilat* has a combat power out of all proportion to her size.**

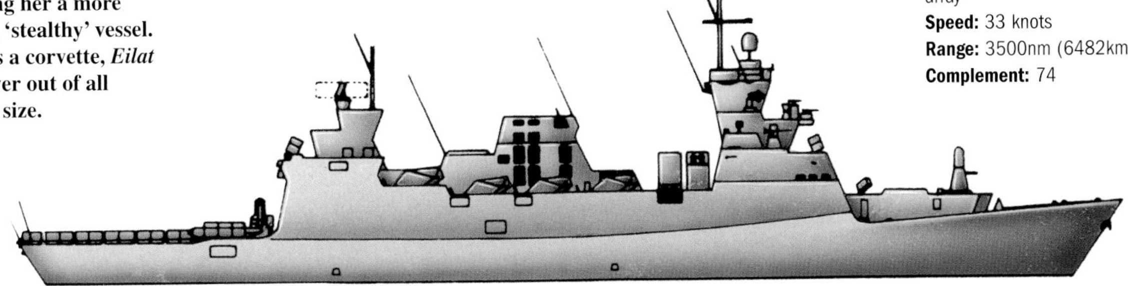

ENGADINE

GB: 1966

Ordered under the 1964–65 Naval Estimates, the helicopter support ship HMS *Engadine* was the first of its type dedicated to the training of helicopter crews in deep-water operations. As a result, *Engadine* was fitted with Denny Brown stabilisers to provide a greater degree of control and steadiness when conducting flying operations in rough seas. HMS *Engadine* was laid down in August 1965 and launched the following year. She was fitted with a small single funnel forward of amidships. Behind this funnel, on the rear of the long superstructure, was a helicopter pad, with a second, larger, landing pad aft on the poop deck. This stretched out in a clean line from the end of the superstructure, which enclosed the helicopter hangars, to right aft.

Displacement: 9000t standard
Dimensions: 424ft x 58ft 4in x 22ft (129.2m x 17.8m x 6.7m)
Machinery: one-shaft, one diesel engine; 5500hp; six helicopters (four Wessex and two Wasps/Sea Kings)
Sensors: not available
Speed: 16 knots
Range: 5000nm (9260km) at 14 knots
Complement: 75–188

HMS *Engadine* was devoted to training Fleet Air Arm ASW helicopter crews for North Atlantic operations against the Soviet submarine fleet.

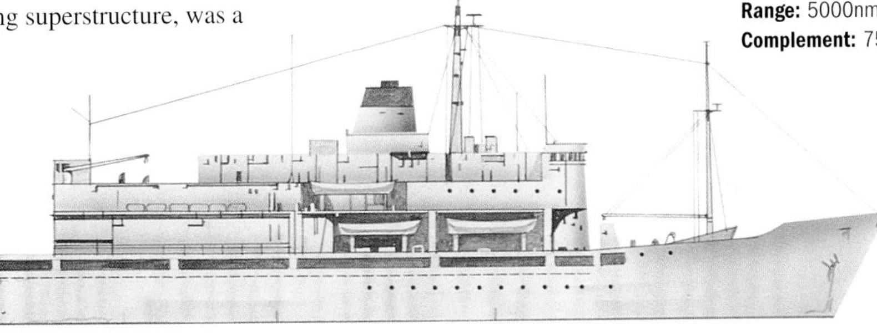

ENRICO TOTI

ITALY: 1967

Displacement: 535t surfaced; 591t submerged
Dimensions: 151ft 8in x 15ft 5in x 13ft 1in (46.2m x 4.7m x 4m)
Machinery: one-shaft, two diesels, plus one electric motor; 2200hp
Armament: four 21in (533mm) TT (four wire-guided Canguro ASW torpedoes, four ASW torpedoes; later six A-184 torpedoes
Sensors: surface-search radar; sonar fit
Speed: 13 knots surfaced; 9 knots submerged
Range: 3000nm (5556km) at 5 knots surfaced
Complement: 26

The first Italian submarines to appear after World War II were the *Toti*-class boats. They were unusually small craft, their original design probably inspired by the US Navy's 'ambush' submarine concept, which was being explored during this period. Designs for the *Toti*s were drawn up in the mid-1950s but in the 10 years that elapsed between then and construction of the first boat, they changed considerably. In fact, so great were the changes that the class was re-ordered in 1964 – having become smaller, lighter, slower and less well-armed. It was decided that the *Toti*s would fill the lower tier in a two-tier Italian submarine force. Plans to build nuclear-powered attack submarines were abandoned, however, and conventional submarines were substituted instead. *Enrico Toti* (S 506) was the first of four boats built. She was launched in March 1967 and completed in January 1968. Like her sisterships, the *Enrico Toti* survived into the 1990s and was stricken from the fleet in 1992.

The basic design of the *Enrico Toti* changed many times and, during her service career, she was modified again through the addition of new sonar systems.

ENTERPRISE

USA: 1960

As the world's first nuclear-powered aircraft carrier, the USS *Enterprise* (CVN 65, formerly CVAN 65) was an epoch-making ship. The first 'super carrier', she owed much of her great size to a bulky first-generation nuclear powerplant, but this allowed her to use space once reserved for ship's fuel for aviation fuel instead. This gave *Enterprise* not only substantial below-the-waterline protection, but also allowed her to sustain air operations at an unprecedented level. *Enterprise*, or 'Big E' as she became known to her crews, was built with SPS-32/SPS-33 electronically-scanned phased-array radar mounted in flat panels around her main island. Only the guided-missile cruiser USS *Long Beach* (which formed part of *Enterprise*'s original task group) was fitted with a similar system. However, the radar were not as successful as had been hoped, proved difficult to maintain and were replaced with more conventional antennae in 1980. The USS *Enterprise* was laid down in February 1958, launched in September 1960 and completed in

After a complex overhaul in 1991, *Enterprise* today serves with the Atlantic Fleet and currently has Carrier Air Wing 3 embarked.

November 1961. She was fitted with no air-defence armament – cost overruns in her construction left her with provision only for the Terrier SAM system. Eventually, Sea Sparrow was fitted in 1967. *Enterprise* joined the Atlantic fleet in 1961 and participated in the blockade of Cuba in 1962. In May 1963 she made a round the world cruise to join the Pacific Fleet and, in 1964, began the first of her eight combat deployments during the Vietnam War. *Enterprise* was badly damaged in a fire during 1973, but she bounced back to become the first carrier to operate F-14 Tomcats, in 1974.

The USS *Enterprise* is scheduled to be withdrawn in 2013, when the first of the US Navy's next-generation aircraft carriers (CVX-1) is due to enter service.

Displacement: 71,277t standard; 89,084t full load
Dimensions: 1123ft 2in x 255ft x 37ft 1in (342.4 x 77.7m x 11.3m)
Machinery: four-shaft, nuclear, eight A2W reactors, four geared turbines; 280,000hp
Armament: three Mk 29 Sea Sparrow octuple launchers; 90 aircraft
Sensors: air-search radar; surface-search radar; navigation radar; fire-control radar
Speed: 32 knots
Range: limited only by reactor fuel state
Complement: 3325, plus 1891 air wing

ERIDAN

BELGIUM: 1979

Displacement: 562t standard; 595t full load
Dimensions: 168ft 9in x 29ft 2in x 8ft 2in (51.5m x 8.9m x 2.5m)
Machinery: one-shaft, one diesel, twin active rudders and bow thruster; 1900hp
Armament: one 20mm cannon; two 12.7mm MG (optional); two PAP 104 remote-controlled mine-locating vehicles
Sensors: navigation radar; search sonar
Speed: 15 knots
Range: 2500nm (4630km) at 12 knots
Complement: 34–46

The French Navy's *Eridan*-class minehunters were part of the Belgian/Dutch/French 'Tripartite' programme, and drew on the earlier *Circé*-class vessels. All the Tripartite ships had a common GRP hull, to which was added French minehunting systems and electronics, Belgian electrical generators and minehunting propulsion systems, and Dutch main machinery. *Eridan* (M 641) was launched in February 1979, as the first of 10 such vessels for the French Navy. The chief role of the *Eridans* is to patrol harbour approaches and protect French ballistic missile submarines.

While *Eridan* is a minehunter, and not a minesweeper, she does have some limited sweeping capabilities, being fitted with an advanced DUBM 21B search sonar, light mechanical sweep gear and explosive charges.

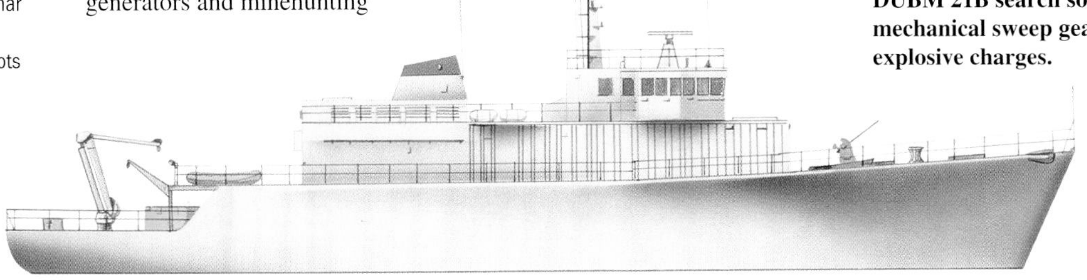

ESMERELDAS

ECUADOR: 1980

Ecuador's *Esmeraldas*-class corvettes are very similar to the *Wadi M'ragh*-class corvettes.

The most modern vessels currently in service with Ecuador's very modest naval forces are its Italian-built corvettes. These (modified) *Esmeraldas*-class vessels, though not large, are fast and well-armed warships, capable of dealing with air and surface threats. Ecuador acquired six of these corvettes from CNR Tirreno in the early 1980s. The lead ship, *Esmeraldas* (CM 11), was launched in October 1980 and completed in August 1982; she is fitted with a helicopter flight deck, but no hangar.

Displacement: 605t standard; 685t full load
Dimensions: 204ft 5in x 30ft 6in x 9ft 3in (62.3m x 9.3m x 2.8m)
Machinery: four-shaft, four diesels; 24,400hp
Armament: six MM40 Exocet SSM; one Albatros octuple SAM launcher; one 3in (76mm); two 40mm cannon; six ILAS 3 12.75in (324mm) TT (A 244/S torpedoes); one helicopter
Sensors: air/surface-search radar; navigation radar; fire-control radar; hull-mounted sonar
Speed: 37 knots
Range: 4000nm (7408km) at 18 knots
Complement: 51

ESPORA

ARGENTINA: 1982

Displacement: 1560t standard; 1790t full load
Dimensions: 283ft 6in x 40ft x 10ft 11in (86.4m x 11.1m x 3.33m)
Machinery: two-shaft, two diesels; 22,600hp
Armament: four MM40 (replacing MM38) Exocet SSM; one 3in (76mm); four 40mm cannon; two 12.7mm MG; six ILAS 3 12.75in (324mm) TT (A244/S torpedoes); one Lynx helicopter
Sensors: air-search radar; navigation radar; fire-control radar; hull-mounted sonar
Speed: 27 knots
Range: 4000nm (7408km) at 18 knots
Complement: 93

Argentina's *Espora*-class corvettes are sometimes referred to as the *Espora 140* class. Their design is based on the German MEKO 140 modular approach which allows the addition and deletion of different weapons and features between individual ships during development or construction. For example, the first three *Esporas* do not have a helicopter hangar while the fourth vessel does (and all are being refitted with one). The MEKO philosophy has proved popular in Argentinean naval service, with the larger *Almirante Brown*-class (MEKO 360) frigates also currently active. The *Espora* corvettes were built in Argentina, the lead ship of the class, *Espora* (F 4), being launched in January 1982 and completed in July 1985. Two of her sisterships were deployed to the Persian Gulf in 1990–91 to support the Allied naval effort in Operation Desert Shield/Desert Storm. A fifth and sixth unit were added to the *Espora* class in 1985–86, but they were not completed and instead put up for sale.

The *Espora 140*-class corvettes were originally fitted with MM38 Exocet missiles, but these have been replaced by the improved MM40 version.

EXPLORER

GB: 1954

In the early 1950s, the Royal Navy built two *Explorer*-class experimental submarines to serve as fast underwater targets. These boats were needed to help develop new ASW tactics to counter the expanding and improving Soviet submarine fleet. HMS *Explorer* and her sister-submarine, HMS *Excalibur*, replaced former German U-boats in this important trials task. *Explorer* (S 30) was launched in March 1954 and completed in November 1956. Both the British submarines were built around a new hydrogen peroxide-powered turbine, which promised very high-speed performance. However, the HTP fuel for the engines was dangerous and unstable. It had to be held in conditions of extreme isolation and purity – conditions which proved impossible to maintain in a submarine. Despite being purpose-built for her job, HMS *Explorer* soon gained the unfortunate nickname 'HMS Exploder' on account of the many (small) HTP-fired incidents she suffered (likewise, HMS *Excalibur* became 'HMS Excruciator'). The Royal Navy made much better progress in taming HTP propulsion than was ever achieved by the Russians or the Americans, but the system was never perfected and the constant risk forced its abandonment – and the withdrawal of the two submarines.

Displacement: 776t surfaced; 1076t submerged
Dimensions: 225ft x 15ft 8in x 18 ft 2in (68.7m x 4.8m x 5.5m)
Machinery: two-shaft, hydrogen-peroxide turbine, plus electric motor; 15,000hp/400hp
Armament: none
Sensors: trials fit only
Speed: 27 knots surfaced; 18 knots submerged
Range: not available
Complement: 41–49

Due to the continuous complications with her HTP turbine, HMS *Explorer* left the fleet in the early 1960s and was broken up in 1965.

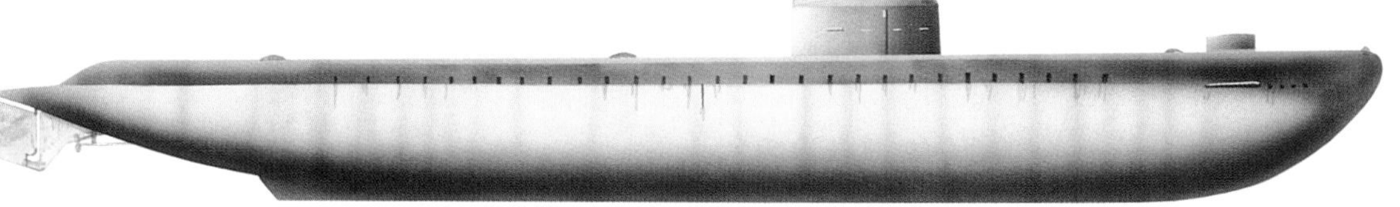

FARRAGUT

USA: 1958

Displacement: 4167t standard; 5648t full load
Dimensions: 512ft 6in x 52ft 4in x 17ft 9in (156.3m x 15.9m x 5.3m)
Machinery: two-shaft, geared turbines, four boilers; 85,000hp
Armament: one Terrier (later Standard) SAM system (40 missiles); one 5in (127mm); one ASROC rocket-boosted ASW torpedo launcher; six 12.75in (324mm) TT (Mk 32 torpedoes)
Sensors: air-search radar; fire-control radar; hull-mounted sonar
Speed: 32 knots
Range: 5000nm (9260km) at 20 knots
Complement: 360

Though they were the first missile-armed ships of their type to enter service with the US Navy, the *Farragut*-class fleet escorts (destroyers) had not been designed as such. Their armament of quick-firing 5in (127mm) guns and a limited ASW weapons fit was intended for their role of fast screening tasks undertaken for US carrier battle groups. However, as the US Navy accelerated plans for the transition to an 'all-missile' fleet and, at the same time, as the Soviet submarine threat was becoming increasingly serious, more emphasis was placed on the *Farraguts'* ASW capabilities. The USS *Farragut* (CLG 6, later DDG 6) was launched in July 1959 and completed in December 1960 and, being in the right place at the right time, benefitted from the transition to the new weapons fit. Thus, *Farragut* and her sisterships were among the first to be armed with the ASROC system, which used rocket-boosted anti-submarine torpedoes and could be fitted with a nuclear warhead.

The *Farragut* was upgraded to carry the Naval Tactical Data System for air-defence command and control. Later, Harpoon missiles and the Phalanx CIWS were added. She was decommissioned in October 1989.

FATAHILLAH

INDONESIA: 1977

The first modern new-build ships to be acquired by the Indonesian Navy in recent times, the compact *Fatahillah*-class frigates were ordered from The Netherlands in 1975. *Fatahillah* (361) was the lead ship of the three vessels in the class. She was launched in December 1977 and completed in July 1979. *Fatahillah* has many sophisticated features, such as an NBC-protected combat centre, all-digital tactical systems and full air-conditioning. The third ship in the class, *Nala*, has a small helicopter deck aft.

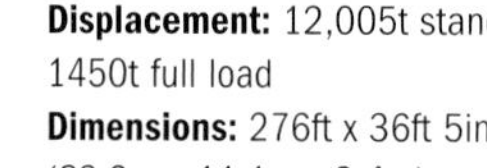

Displacement: 12,005t standard; 1450t full load
Dimensions: 276ft x 36ft 5in x 10ft 9in (83.9m x 11.1m x 3.4m)
Machinery: two-shaft, CODOG (two CP propellers), two gas turbines, plus two diesels; 28,000hp/6000hp
Armament: four MM38 Exocet SSM; one 4.7in (119mm); one 40mm cannon, two 20mm cannon; six 12.75in (324mm) TT (Mk 46/A224S torpedoes); one 14.75in (375mm) ASW mortar
Sensors: air/surface-search radar; surface-search radar; fire-control radar; hull-mounted sonar
Speed: 30 knots
Range: 4250nm (7871km) at 16 knots
Complement: 89

Indonesia's *Fatahillah*-class ships are officially classed as corvettes but their weapons and systems fit make them far more capable than this description would suggest.

FERRE

PERU: 1969

***Ferre* was modified several times during her time in Peruvian service. Twin 40mm guns replaced her original single guns, while all her ASW weapons and sonar were eventually removed.**

Displacement: 2830t standard; 3580t full load
Dimensions: 390ft x 43ft x 13ft 7in (118.8m x 13.1m x 4.1m)
Machinery: two-shaft, double reduction-geared turbines, two boilers; 54,000hp
Armament: six (four for a period) 4.5in (114mm); two twin 40mm cannon; one Squid ASW mortar (deleted)
Sensors: air/surface-search radar; hull-mounted sonar, later deleted
Speed: 34.75 knots
Range: 6000nm (11,112km) at 16 knots
Complement: 297-330

In 1969, the Peruvian Navy acquired two *Daring*-class destroyers from the UK. The former HMS *Decoy* became the *Ferre* (DM 74) and her sistership, HMS *Diana*, the *Palacios*. Before delivery, both ships were refitted by Cammell Laird. To prepare them for their new role, each destroyer was armed with eight Exocet anti-ship missile launchers and a new Plessey AWS-1 radar was mounted on the newly-enclosed foremasts. *Ferre* was commissioned in April 1973 and, two years later, she received a helicopter deck. A more extensive refit in 1977–78 added a helicopter hangar in place of the aft gun turret (this hangar was later removed and the turret was reinstated once more), and a second funnel was streamlined and raised. Twin Breda 40mm cannon were mounted on either side of the bridge, replacing the original single gun mounts. *Ferre* survived intact into the late-1990s, but not as an active service vessel and she has now been formally withdrawn.

FLAGSTAFF

USA: 1968

During the late-1960s and early-1970s, the US Navy flirted with armed hydrofoil designs. One such development vessel to explore the concept was the USS *Flagstaff* (PGH 1). She was built by Grumman and used for comparative evaluation against her Boeing-built rival, USS *Tucumcari*. Both vessels were deployed to Vietnam and tested with a variety of weapons fit. *Flagstaff* was later loaned to the Coast Guard. However, she was badly damaged in a collision with a whale and was sold off in 1978.

The US once had grand plans for combat hydrofoils, large and small, but they proved too difficult to integrate into the US Navy as a whole and few were ever built.

Displacement: 56.8t standard
Dimensions: 74ft 5in x 21ft 5in x 13ft 6in (22.7m x 6.5m x 4.1m)
Machinery: one-shaft, gas turbine, plus two diesels for hull-borne water-jet propulsion; 3620hp/300hp
Armament: one 40mm cannon; two .50.cal-MG; one 3.2in (81mm) mortar
Sensors: trials fit only
Speed: 48 knots
Range: not available
Complement: 13

FLORÉAL

FRANCE: 1990

Displacement: 2600t standard; 2950t full load
Dimensions: 307ft x 46ft x 14ft (93.5m x 14m x 4.3m)
Machinery: two-shaft, four diesels; 8800hp
Armament: two MM38 Exocet SSM; one 3.9in (100mm); two 20mm cannon
Sensors: air/surface-search radar; navigation radar
Speed: 20 knots
Range: 9000nm (16,668km) at 15 knots
Complement: 80, plus 24 embarked troops

The *Floréal* class of frigates/corvettes are lightly armed ships and, to further keep costs down, they have few of the expected battleworthy design features of regular warships.

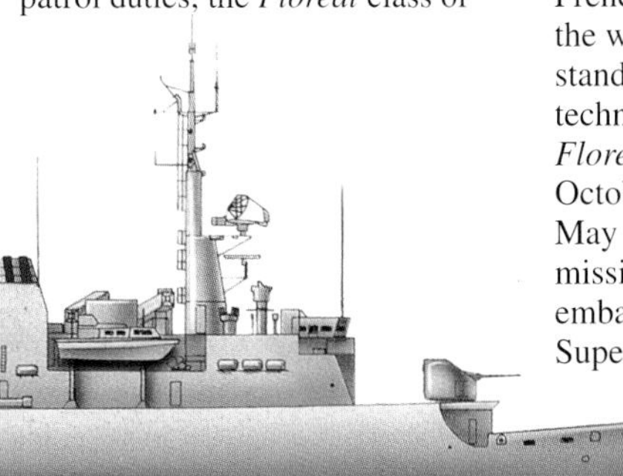

Responding to the French Navy requirement for a new, and affordable, vessel for general patrol duties, the *Floréal* class of frigates/corvettes was authorised in the late-1980s. The first warships to be built by a private yard for the French military in over 30 years, the work involved the use of standard mercantile construction techniques and modular assembly. *Floréal* (F 730) was launched in October 1990 and completed in May 1992. She has a modern mission systems fit and can embark a helicopter as large as a Super Puma.

FORRESTAL

USA: 1954

The development of the US Navy's post-war carriers was, in the main, driven by the advent of jet combat aircraft which required longer flight decks and also larger accommodation to meet the huge appetite for aviation fuel. In 1950, the Korean War breathed new life into the Navy's carrier plans and led directly to the birth of the *Forrestal* class. The first US carriers to have an angled deck, and the first to have the flight deck as an integral part of the ship's structure, the *Forrestals* were made larger so they could operate the Navy's new A3D Skywarrior – the first carrier-borne jet-powered nuclear bomber. There were to have been six ships in the class, but the last two were so different as to deserve a separate *Improved Forrestal* class, all their own. Even within the four *Forrestals*, there were notable differences as design changes were incorporated in successive vessels. The USS *Forrestal* (CVA 59, later CV 59) was laid down in July 1952, launched in December 1954 and commissioned in October 1955. Joining the fleet in 1956, *Forrestal* deployed to the Mediterranean in response to the Suez crisis. In August 1967 her only combat deployment to Vietnam was cut short when she suffered a disastrous accidental explosion and fire on board. However, *Forrestal* was repaired and later joined the Atlantic Fleet. She underwent an 18-month service life extension programme in 1983–85 and, in 1992, replaced the USS *Lexington* as the Navy's designated training carrier (AVT 59). As a result of wider cutbacks across the Navy's carrier fleet, the *Forrestal* was decommissioned in September 1993.

When she left the front-line fleet in 1992, *Forrestal* had Carrier Air Wing 6 (CVW-6) embarked. It comprised F-14As (two squadrons), F/A-18As (two squadrons), A-6E/KA-6Ds (one squadron), EA-6Bs (one squadron), E-2Cs (one squadron), S-3Bs (one squadron) and SH-3Hs (one squadron).

Displacement: 61,163t standard; 78,509t full load
Dimensions: 1039ft x 250ft x 33ft 10in (316.7m x 76.2m x 10.3m)
Machinery: four-shaft, geared turbines, eight boilers; 260,000hp
Armament: three Mk 29 Sea Sparrow octuple launchers; three Mk 15 Phalanx 20mm CIWS
Sensors: air-search radar; surface-search radar; navigation radar; fire-control radar
Speed: 33 knots
Range: 12,000nm (22,224km) at 20 knots
Complement: 2764 crew, plus 1912 air wing

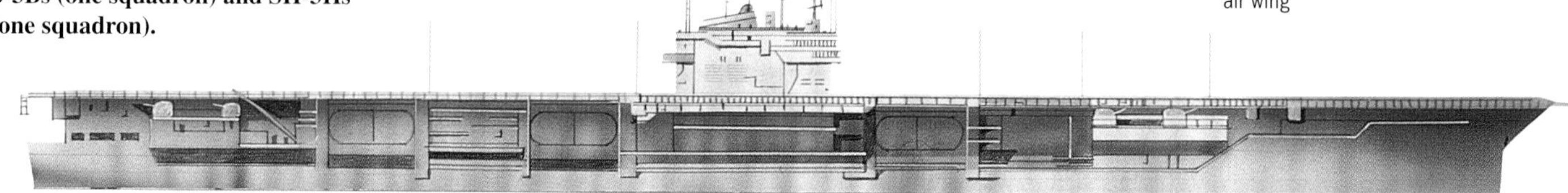

FORT GRANGE

GB: 1976

In the early-1970s, the Royal Navy ordered a pair of helicopter-capable fleet replenishment ships. The first of these was HMS *Fort Grange* (A 385), which was launched in December 1976 and completed in April 1978. A sistership, *Fort Austin*, followed in 1979. The *Fort Grange* was designed to refuel and rearm other ships at sea and, using her helicopter capability, to perform 'vertrep' (vertical replenishment) missions. However, she also provided a useful additional combat helicopter platform and carried offensive stores for her own aircraft accordingly.

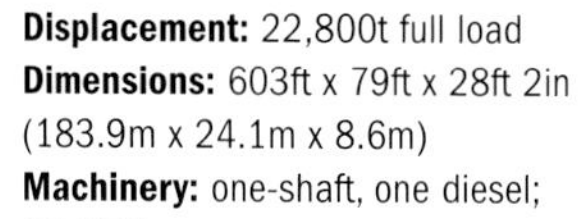

Displacement: 22,800t full load
Dimensions: 603ft x 79ft x 28ft 2in (183.9m x 24.1m x 8.6m)
Machinery: one-shaft, one diesel; 23,200hp
Armament: two 20mm cannon; up to four Sea King helicopters
Sensors: navigation radar
Speed: 22 knots
Range: not available
Complement: 140, plus 36 aircrew detachment

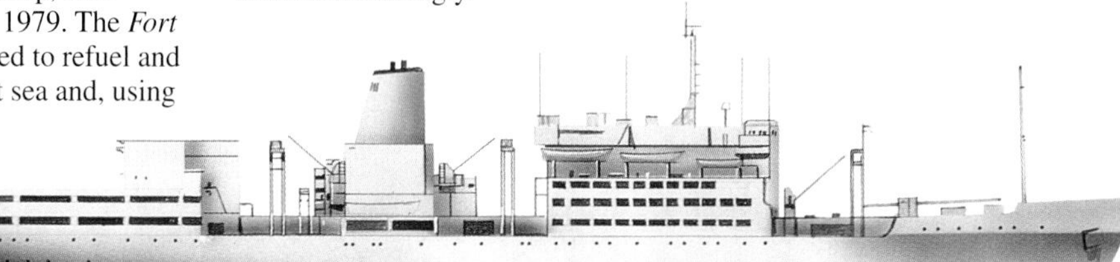

HMS *Fort Grange* could carry up to 3500t of naval stores in her hold, and was fitted with six deck cranes for loading and unloading.

FOUDRE

FRANCE: 1988

Displacement: 9300t standard; 11,880t full load
Dimensions: 551ft x 77ft x 17ft (168m x 23.5m x 5.2m)
Machinery: two-shaft, two diesels; 21,600hp
Armament: two Simbad SAM systems; one 40mm cannon; two 20mm cannon; two 12.7mm MG; four Super Pumas/Cougar helicopters
Sensors: air/surface-search radar; surface-search radar; navigation radar
Speed: 21 knots
Range: 11,000nm (20,358km) at 15 knots
Complement: 210, plus 350-1200 troops

The *Foudre*-class (TCD 90) dock-landing ships are designed to accommodate a 350-man mechanised regiment of the French Force d'Action Rapide, along with their combat vehicles and supplies. *Foudre* (L 9011) is the lead ship of four planned vessels and was launched in November 1988. She has hangar space for four Super Puma helicopters and docking space for 20 standard CTM landing craft, or two CDIC tank landing craft. The docking well is also large enough to handle any of the standard French overseas patrol craft.

***Foudre* has a secondary role as a mobile logistic and support ship, as distinct from her primary amphibious assault role.**

FOXTROT CLASS

USSR: 1959

Displacement: 1957t surfaced; 2484t submerged
Dimensions: 299ft 6in x 24ft 7in x 19ft 8in (91.3m x 7.5m x 6m)
Machinery: three-shaft, three diesels, rated at 6000hp, plus four 112-cell batteries and three electric motors; rated between 2700hp and 1350hp
Armament: 10 21in (533mm)TT (six bow, four stern)
Sensors: search radar; active sonar, passive array
Speed: 15.9 knots submerged
Range: not available
Complement: 75

The Soviet Union's *Foxtrot*-class attack submarines (Project 641) were an enlarged version of the *Romeo*-class and designed to operate with a snorkel. The prototype *Foxtrot* was launched in 1957 and from then on 62 examples were built. The majority went to the Soviet Fleet but many more to export customers including Cuba, India, Libya and Poland. The *Foxtrot*s could dive deeper and had greater range than the *Zulu*-class that preceded them. They were an important part of the Brezhnev-era planned expansion of the Soviet Navy. There were over 70 members of the class, and planned service life was 27 years. Some boats class were still in service during the late-1980s, but most had been retired by then and none are currently active.

Both a passive and an active sonar array were concealed within the bow fairings of *Foxtrot*-class submarines.

FRANK CABLE

USA: 1978

The USS *Frank Cable* is fitted with a helicopter deck, but no hangar. Like her four sisterships, she is dedicated to the US Navy's attack submarine fleet.

The US Navy's support fleet of the late-1960s era took some time to catch up with the technology of the front-line fleet. It was not until the 1970s that the Navy commissioned the first tenders specifically designed to support nuclear attack submarines. The USS *Frank Cable* (AS 40) joined the fleet in 1980 and was a member of the *Emery S. Land* class, which itself was an improved version of the earlier *Spear*-class tenders. The USS *Frank Cable* is dedicated to supporting *Los Angeles*-class attack submarines and can handle four simultaneously.

Displacement: 13,840t standard; 23,000t full load
Dimensions: 645ft 7in x 85ft x 28ft (196.7m x 25.9m x 8.7m)
Machinery: one-shaft, steam turbines, two boilers; 20,000hp
Armament: two Mk 19 40mm cannon; two Mk 67 20mm cannon
Sensors: not available
Speed: 20 knots
Range: 10,000nm (18,520km) at 12 knots
Complement: 1158

FREMANTLE

AUSTRALIA: 1979

Displacement: 240t standard; 275t full load
Dimensions: 137ft 10in x 23ft 5in x 6ft 11in (42m x 7.1m x 1.9m)
Machinery: three-shaft, two diesels, plus cruising diesel; 6000hp
Armament: one 40mm cannon; two 12.7mm MG; one 3.2in (81mm) mortar
Sensors: navigation radar
Speed: 30 knots
Range: 4800nm (8890km)
Complement: 22

The 20 fast-attack patrol craft of Australia's *Fremantle* class were based on a British design, though all but one were built in Australia. The one exception was the lead ship, HMAS *Fremantle* (P 203); she was laid down in Lowestoft, Suffolk in 1977 and commissioned in March 1979. All ships of the class were in service by 1984, replacing the RAN's earlier *Attack*-class coastal patrol boats. The *Fremantle*s were bigger, faster and better-armed ships and some 15 of them remain in current RAN service.

The *Fremantle*-class patrol craft are the mainstay of Australia's coastal patrol force and, despite their compact size, are fast and long-legged ships.

FRET

THE NETHERLANDS: 1953

The *Fret* was a slow, lightly-armed ship from a class that quickly became outdated. However, she did find a useful peacetime role as a patrol vessel.

The *Roofdier*-class frigates of the Royal Netherlands Navy were built with US-supplied MDAP funding. They were a conservative 1950s design, intended to provide slow convoy escorts for NATO in the English Channel and North Sea. The *Fret* (F 818) was the second of six units to be built. Launched in July 1953 and completed in May 1954. The *Roofdiers* were soon outclassed in their intended role, but proved to be excellent second-line ships and served into the 1980s as fisheries patrol vessels. The *Fret* was finally broken up in 1998.

Displacement: 808t standard; 975t full load
Dimensions: 185ft x 33ft x 10ft (56.2m x 10m x 2.9m)
Machinery: two-shafts, two diesels; 1600hp
Armament: one 3in (76mm); six/four 40mm cannon; eight 20mm AA cannon (later removed); one Hedgehog ASW mortar
Sensors: sonar
Speed: 15 knots
Range: 4300nm (7964km) at 10 knots
Complement: 96

FROSCH

GERMAN DEMOCRATIC REPUBLIC: 1976

Displacement: 1774t standard; 1950t full load
Dimensions: 297ft 7in x 36ft 5in x 11ft 2in (90.7m x 11.1m x 3.4 m)
Machinery: two-shaft, two diesels; 9500hp
Armament: four 57mm cannon, four 30mm cannon; 40 mines; seven tanks embarked
Sensors: search radar; navigation radar; IFF interrogators; fire-control radar
Range: 2000nm (3704km)
Complement: 42

The East German *Frosch*-class (Project 108) landing ships were the largest vessels to serve with the Volksmarine (People's Navy). The *Hoyerswerda* (611) was launched in November 1976, the first of the class. In all, a total of 14 units were eventually constructed, either as *Frosch I* or – modified as armed support ships – *Frosch II* vessels. Designed to carry 12 armoured vehicles, the *Frosch*-class vessels were fitted with a bow ramp but no bow doors. They were all withdrawn from use in 1990 and sold to Indonesia in 1993.

East Germany's *Frosch*-class landing ships were designed to support Warsaw Pact operations in the Baltic region, and to form part of any future invasion fleet.

GALATEA

GB: 1963

The Royal Navy's *Leander*-class frigates were well designed and well liked warships that followed on from the progress made with the contemporary *Tribal*-class ships. The *Leanders* themselves were inspired by development work done for the Royal New Zealand Navy and its Type 12 design. The final *Leander* design managed to combine an effective heavy armament with long-range air-search radar and a shipboard helicopter capability – all in a vessel that was very stable and seaworthy. The *Leanders* featured self-compensating fuel tanks, which replaced separate fuel and ballast tanks. As fuel was consumed, water was drawn into the tanks to keep the ship stable. This arrangement increased stability and saved internal space but also led to fuel contamination problems. Twin tanks were later reinstated on some ships. HMS *Galatea* (F 18) was the seventh *Leander*-class frigate. She was launched in May 1963 and completed in April 1964. She received the Batch 1 Ikara conversion in 1974 and remained in service until the 1980s. She was expended as a target in 1988.

During the 1970s, the Royal Navy converted its *Leander*-class frigates to carry either the Ikara ASW system (Batch 1) or the Exocet anti-ship missile (Batch 2). HMS *Galatea* was one of the eight Batch 1 conversions.

Displacement: 2450t standard; 2960t full load (post-conversion)
Dimensions: 372ft x 41ft x 18ft (113.4m x 12.5m x 5.5m)
Machinery: two-shaft, geared steam turbines, two boilers; 30,000hp
Armament: one Seaslug SAM system, one Seacat SAM system; two 4.5in (114mm), two 40mm (deleted); one Ikara ASW system (added); one helicopter
Sensors: air/surface-search radar; navigation radar; fire-control radar; hull-mounted sonar (all post-conversion)
Speed: 28 knots
Range: 4000nm (7408km) at 15 knots
Complement: 257 (post-conversion)

GALVESTON

USA: 1958

Displacement: 11,066t standard; 15,152t full load
Dimensions: 610ft x 65ft 8in x 25ft 8in (186m x 20m x 7.8m)
Machinery: four-shaft, geared turbines, four boilers; 100,000hp
Armament: one Talos SAM system; six 6in (152mm), six 5in (127mm)
Sensors: air-search radar; height-finding radar; fire-control radar; hull-mounted sonar
Speed: 32 knots
Range: 8000nm (14,816km) at 15 knots
Complement: 1382

The USS *Galveston* retained her original gun armament alongside her new missile and radar systems. She was fitted with the Talos long-range SAM system, while some of her sisterships carried Terrier SAMs.

At the end of the 1950s, the US Navy took six of its World War II-era *Cleveland*-class cruisers and recommissioned them as 'austere' air defence missile ships. Mating the newly developed Talos and Terrier SAM systems with these large, existing hulls provided an affordable answer to the big demand for missile ships at that time. The USS *Galveston* (CLG 3) was recommissioned in May 1958 as the first of six modified *Clevelands*. She remained in service until 1970 and was stricken in 1973.

GATINEAU

CANADA: 1957

Canada's *Restigouche*-class destroyers were developed from the earlier *St Laurent*-class ships, and the two are very similar in terms of size and shape. *Gatineau* (DDE 236) was the third of seven to be built; she was launched in June 1957 and completed in February 1959. Between 1966 and 1973, *Gatineau* was one of four ships in the class to be modernised with a variable-depth sonar mounted on the stern and an ASROC launcher fitted aft. This replaced the original ASW mortar and a twin 3in (76mm) gun mounting. The *Restigouches* have had a long service career and three are still active, including *Gatineau*. These vessels are now known as the *Improved Restigouche* class, following a further upgrade driven by their service in the Gulf War and subsequent deployments to the Gulf. Beginning with *Terra Nova*, the three ships have been fitted with Harpoon anti-ship missiles (replacing the ASROC), a Phalanx CIWS, additional cannon and machine guns, modernised systems and radar.

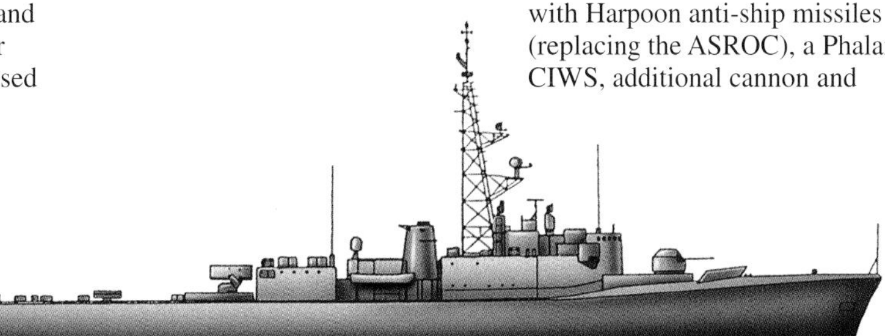

The Canadian frigate *Gatineau* is over 40 years old but has been progressively modernised and remains a capable warship today.

Displacement: 2000t standard; 2600t full load
Dimensions: 366ft x 42ft x 13ft 2in (111.6m x 12.8m x 4.2m)
Machinery: two-shaft, geared steam turbines, two boilers; 30,000hp
Armament: one Harpoon octuple SSM; two 3in (76mm); two 40mm; one Mk 15 Phalanx 20mm CIWS; two 12.7mm MG; six 12.7in (324mm) TT
Sensors: air/surface-search radar; surface radar; navigation radar; fire-control radar; VDS and hull-mounted sonar
Speed: 28 knots
Range: 4570nm (8464km) at 14 knots
Complement: 290

GENERAL BELGRANO

ARGENTINA: 1951

In 1951, the former *Brooklyn*-class cruiser USS *Phoenix*, originally launched in 1938, was acquired by Argentina. Rechristened *General Belgrano* (C 4), she was commissioned on 5 December 1951 and was joined by a sistership, the *Nueve De Julio*. The *De Julio* was decommissioned in 1978, but the *Belgrano* continued to serve as the largest capital ship in the Argentine Navy. During the Falklands conflict in 1982, the *Belgrano* sailed with two Exocet-armed destroyer escorts and took up station to the southwest of the islands. The British Task Force feared a pincer attack by *Belgrano*'s group from the south and another group led by the carrier *Veinticinco De Mayo* from the north. The decision was taken to sink the *Belgrano*. On 2 May 1982, the submarine HMS *Conqueror* fired two Mk 8 torpedoes at the cruiser and within 45 minutes the ship had sunk. Of her crew of 1201, 321 men were killed and 880 rescued.

Displacement: 10,000t standard
Dimensions: 608ft 4in x 61ft 9in x 19ft 5in (185.4m x 18.86m x 5.94m)
Machinery: unknown
Armament: two Seacat SAM; 15 6in (152mm), eight 5in (127mm)
Sensors: not available
Speed: 33 knots
Range: not available
Complement: 868

The sinking of the *General Belgrano* was a key point in the Falklands conflict and effectively eliminated the Argentine surface fleet as a factor in the war.

GEORGE WASHINGTON

USA: 1959

Displacement: 5989t surfaced; 6709t submerged
Dimensions: 381ft 8in x 33ft x 26ft 8in (116.33m x 10.06m x 8.13m)
Machinery: one-shaft, nuclear, one S5W reactor; 15,000hp
Armament: 16 UGM-27 Polaris A-1 (later A-3) SLBM; six 21in (533mm) TT
Sensors: sonar
Speed: 20 knots submerged
Range: limited only by reactor fuel state
Complement: 140

The sleek lines of the *Skipjack* class, from which the USS *George Washington* was derived, were distorted by the addition of a bulky centre section that housed the launch tubes for 16 Polaris missiles.

The first US fleet ballistic missile submarines, the *George Washington* class, were based on the much smaller *Skipjack*-class attack submarines. These new vessels were developed as part of a rush programme by the United States to field a submarine-launched nuclear force with a striking range of 1300 miles (2092 km), by 1960. Armed with the Polaris A-1 missile, the *George Washington* class would provide an important interim capability before the purpose-built *Ethan Allen*-class SSBNs entered service, just a short period later. Five *Skipjack* submarines, already under construction, were modified by the insertion of a large 130ft (39.62m) centre-section 'plug' containing 16 launch tubes for the UGM-27 Polaris A-1 SLBM. The A-1 was the first submarine-launched ballistic missile (SLBM) to be developed and fielded, and was one of the most important weapons systems ever developed by the USA. It was armed with a single 500kT W-47 thermonuclear warhead and a total of 163 were built, by the Lockheed Missile & Space Co. Once in service, about 80 Polaris A-1 missiles were on active patrol at any one time. The USS *George Washington* (SSBN 598) was laid down as the USS *Scorpion* in 1957, but was launched in its modified form in June 1959. She was formally commissioned on 30 December that year. The *George Washington* launched its first test Polaris missile in July 1960 and undertook its first 64-day operational cruise just four months later. In 1964 the *Washington* was refitted to carry the longer-range (2,800miles, 4506km) Polaris A-3 missile, equipped with three W-58 300kT MIRV warheads. Refurbished and rearmed, the *Washington* went back out on patrol in June 1966 – becoming the first US submarine to sail with the Polaris A-3. By 1967 all five of the *Washington* class had been thus modified and were attached to the US Navy's Atlantic Fleet. In the early 1970s they were modified once again, this time to carry the improved Polaris A-3T missile, and were then transferred to the Pacific Fleet Ballistic Missile Force. Based at Guam, the *Washingtons* spent the rest of their operational careers in the Pacific Fleet. The *George Washington* class was only ever intended as a stop-gap solution, and none of the SSBNs ever carried the more modern Poseidon missile. The decommissioning of the class began in 1981, when the *Theodore Roosevelt* and *Abraham Lincoln* were retired. Along with her two remaining sisterships, the *George Washington* had its missile tubes deactivated and was redesignated as an attack submarine (SSN). She also adopted a special forces role and was used as a clandestine transport for US Navy SEALS. The *George Washington* was finally decommissioned in 1985.

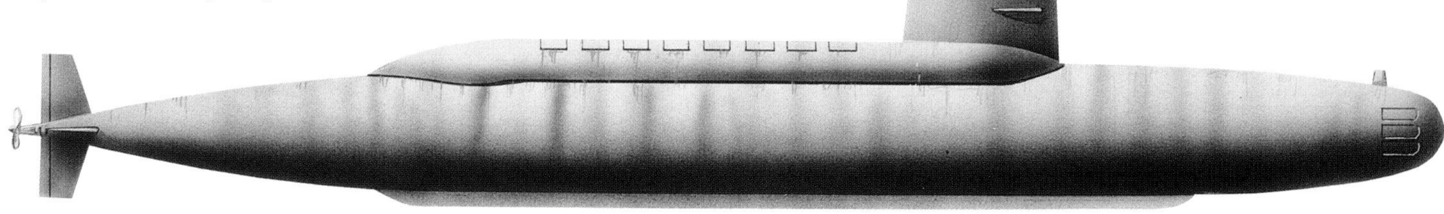

The USS *George Washington* and her sisterships were the result of a crash programme to provide the US fleet with missile submarines. They were not a refined design but served without incident for over 20 years.

GIULIANO PRINI

ITALY: 1987

In 1983, Italy commissioned two *Salvatore Pelosi*-class attack submarines to fill a gap in its fleet caused by delays in the S90 submarine programme. These vessels were based on the earlier *Sauro* class but were lengthened and incorporated many improvements. *Giuliano Prini* (S 523) was the second of the two, launched in December 1987 and completed in November 1989. The *Pelosi* class are capable, deep-diving submarines that could be armed with the Sub-Harpoon anti-ship missile in addition to their regular torpedo load.

The *Giuliano Prini* and her sistership are further developments of Italy's successful *Sauro* class of attack submarines.

Displacement: 1476t surfaced; 1662t submerged
Dimensions: 211ft 2in x 22ft 5in x 18ft 7in (64.36m x 6.8m x 5.66m)
Machinery: one-shaft, three diesels and one electric motor; 3210hp/3650hp
Armament: six 21in (533mm) TT
Sensors: navigation/surface-search radar; sonar
Speed: 11 knots surfaced; 19 knots submerged
Range: 7000nm (12,964km)
Complement: 50

GIUSEPPE GARIBALDI

ITALY: 1983

When the *Giuseppe Garibaldi* (C 551) was laid down in 1981, the Italian Navy was still restricted by a 1923 law that forbade the operation of combat aircraft from its ships. As a result, Italy's first aircraft carrier spent the early years of her life as a helicopter carrier. The *Garibaldi* was launched in June 1983 and completed in September 1985. Her original design foresaw the *Giuseppe Garibaldi* operating VSTOL aircraft in the Harrier class, but initially the ship embarked Agusta-built ASH-3D Sea Kings. *Garibaldi*'s below-deck hangar can accommodate up to 12 Sea Kings. Typically, the *Giuseppe Garibaldi* serves as a flagship, but it also has a secondary amphibious assault capability with space for 600 troops on board. In 1992, the anachronistic restrictions on shipborne aircraft were finally lifted and Italy ordered 16 McDonnell Douglas (now Boeing) AV-8B Harrier II+ jets and a pair of TAV-8B trainers. The Harrier II+s are very capable all-weather day/night air defence and attack aircraft. The Harriers made their first deployment aboard in December 1994. *Garibaldi* does not have a ski jump in the style of the British carriers, but she does have an inclined forward flight deck to aid Harrier operations. The Marina Militare Italiana has an option to acquire further Harriers and is now preparing to introduce the EH101 and NH90 helicopters to replace its ageing ASH-3Ds and AB 212ASWs. Italy is examining its options for its future carrier fleet and is considering building both a sistership for the *Garibaldi* (which has long been proposed) and a much larger ship which would be a true 'all-up' aircraft carrier.

The *Giuseppe Garibaldi* is typical of the small carriers that have been adopted by some European navies as a cost-effective, if limited, means of providing shipborne airpower.

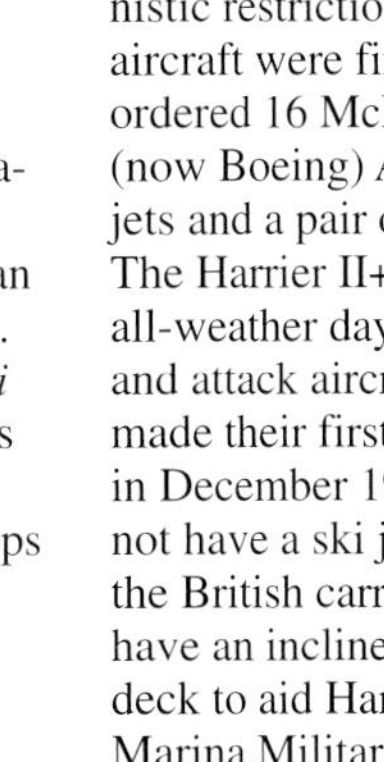

Displacement: 10,000t standard; 13,850t full load
Dimensions: 591ft 2in x 99ft 9in x 26ft 9in (180.2m x 30.4m x 8.2m)
Machinery: two-shaft, two gas turbines; 80,000hp
Armament: four Teseo Mk 2 SSM; two Albatros SAM; six 40mm; six 12.7in (324mm) TT; 16 aircraft or 18 helicopter
Sensors: air-search radar; air/surface-search radar; surface-search/target indication radar; navigation radar, fire-control radar; hull-mounted sonar
Speed: 29.5 knots
Range: 7000nm (12,964km) at 20 knots
Complement: 550, plus 230 air group

GODAVARI

INDIA: 1980

Displacement: 3500t standard; 4100t full load
Dimensions: 414ft 9in x 47ft 11in x 29ft 6in (126.4m x 14.6m x 9m)
Machinery: two-shaft, geared steam turbines, two boilers; 30,000hp
Armament: four SS-N-2C SSM; one SA-N-4 SAM; one 57mm, eight 30mm; six 12.75in (324mm) TT; two helicopters
Sensors: air-search radar; air/surface-search radar; navigation/air traffic control radar; fire-control radar, hull-mounted sonar
Speed: 27 knots
Range: 4500nm (8334km) at 12 knots
Complement: 313

India's unmistakable *Godavari*-class frigates feature a unique combination of a Western hull design (British *Leander* class) with a suite of Soviet-supplied weapons and systems. The design was further modified to incorporate an extended helicopter flight deck aft, with either two Sea King or Chetak helicopters embarked. *Godavari* (F 20) was the first of three ships to be built before the *Improved Godavari* class appeared (these ships look quite different again). She was launched in May 1980 and completed in December 1982.

Godavari's lines are dominated by the cluster of major weapons systems on its bow, including the SS-N-2C 'Styx' SSM, SA-N-4 'Gecko' SAMs and the 57mm gun mounting.

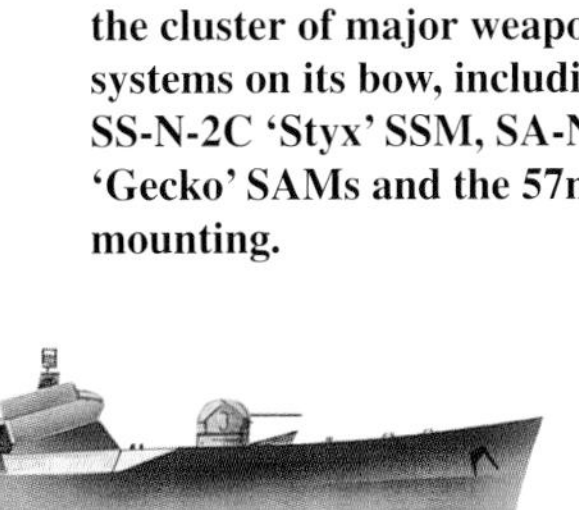

GOLF CLASS

USSR: 1959

Displacement: 2500t surfaced; 2900t submerged
Dimensions: 328ft 1in x 27ft 11in x 21ft 8in (100m x 8m x 6.6m)
Machinery: three-shaft, three diesels; 5300hp
Armament: three SS-N-4 SLBM; 10 21in (533mm) TT
Sensors: radar; sonar suite
Speed: surfaced speed unknown; 12 knots submerged
Range: 9000nm (16,668km) at 5 knots
Complement: 59

The lines of the basic Project 628 submarine changed several times over the years as a range of major sub-types from *Golf I* to *Golf IV* appeared.

The Project 628 (NATO code-name *Golf*) ballistic missile submarines were designed to carry the SS-N-4 SLBM. These submarines made some of the very first launches of an operational SLBM, and over the years a range of modifications and sub-types were introduced. The first *Golf* (B-92, later K-96) was launched from the Severodvinsk yard in 1959. A total of 23 were built, along with one produced in China from Soviet-supplied components. A handful of *Golfs* survived into the early 1990s, but none are now in service.

GRAFTON

GB: 1954

The Royal Navy's Type 14 frigates, the *Blackwood* class, were single-purpose ASW ships that followed on from the *Whitby* class. Driving their design was the need to keep costs to a minimum and so the *Blackwoods* had none of the multi-purpose utility of standard frigates. This made them excellent anti-submarine platforms but limited their day-to-day usefulness. HMS *Grafton* (F 51) was the fifth of 12 to be built. She was launched in September 1954 and completed in January 1957. She was withdrawn from use in the early 1970s.

Displacement: 1180t standard; 1535t full load
Dimensions: 310ft x 35ft x 15ft 6in (94.5m x 10.7m x 4.7m)
Machinery: one-shaft, geared steam turbine, two boilers; 15,000hp
Armament: three (later two) 40mm; four 21in (533mm) TT (later removed); one Limbo ASW mortar
Sensors: air-warning radar; navigation radar; hull-mounted sonar
Speed: 27 knots
Range: 4500nm (8334km) at 12 knots
Complement: 140

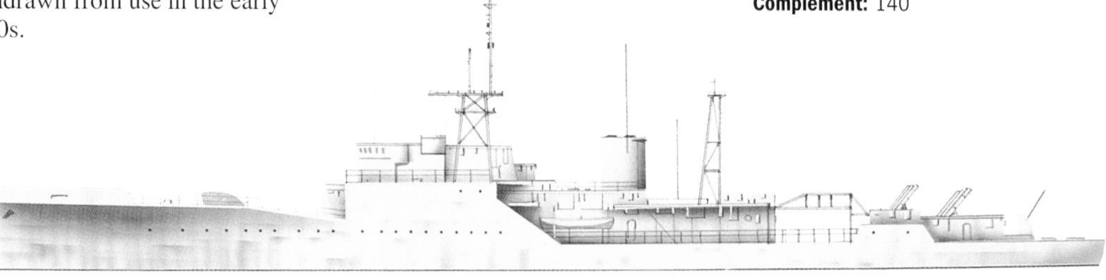

The *Blackwood*-class frigates were an uneasy compromise between cost and capability. Although they would have been valuable assets in time of war, their inflexibility hampered regular peacetime operations.

GRAYBACK

USA: 1954

Displacement: 2287t surfaced; 3638t submerged
Dimensions: 322ft 4in x 30ft x 17ft 4in (98.3m x 9.1m x 5.3m)
Machinery: two-shaft, three diesels and two electric motors; 4500hp/5600hp
Armament: four SSM-N-9 Regulus II (intended); eight 21in (533mm) TT
Sensors: sonar
Speed: 15 knots surfaced; 12 knots submerged
Range: not available
Complement: 84

Before modern intercontinental ballistic missiles were developed, the United States relied on a short-lived series of large cruise missiles, with nuclear warheads, to back up its strategic bomber force. These cruise missiles were short-ranged, bulky, slow and inaccurate weapons. The US Navy adopted the Vought Regulus I to arm several of its surface ships and submarines. For the latter, it was hugely impractical. A submarine had to surface to launch its missiles – which was a lengthy process – and the huge plume of rocket booster exhaust immediately betrayed the submarine's position. The USS *Grayback* (SSG 574) was one of the very first submarines designed to carry nuclear missiles. Earlier vessels had been converted to carry the Regulus I, but *Grayback* was purpose-designed around the larger, more sophisticated supersonic Regulus II. However, the US Navy opted to fund only the Polaris SLBM programme, and Regulus II was cancelled. *Grayback* was converted to special missions transport, with her missile 'hangar' modified to carry swimmers and small submarines.

The USS *Grayback* never took on her intended role as a cruise missile carrier. Instead, the large forward 'hangar' built for Regulus missiles was used to carry special forces divers.

GRAYLING

USA: 1967

Displacement: 4246t surfaced; 4777t submerged
Dimensions: 292ft 3in x 31ft 8in x 25ft 6in (89.1m x 9.7m x 7.8m)
Machinery: one-shaft, one nuclear reactor; 15,000hp
Armament: four 21in (533mm) TT firing ASW torpedoes, SUBROC, Sub-Harpoon or Tomahawk cruise missiles
Sensors: long-range sonar
Speed: surfaced speed unknown; 26 knots submerged
Range: limited only by reactor fuel state
Complement: 99

Until the introduction of the *Los Angeles* class, the *Sturgeon* class was the backbone of the US Navy's attack submarine fleet.

The *Permit/Sturgeon* class was a combined family of attack submarines that shared a common design with some important differences – such as their relative size and sophistication. The USS *Grayling* was a 'full-spec' *Sturgeon*-class vessel, although some of her early sisterships were hybrid 'overlaps' between the two classes.

Officially there were two classes – the *Permit* and *Sturgeon*. Although similar, the later *Sturgeons* are larger than the *Permits* and were fitted with a more advanced sonar and Sub-Harpoon anti-ship missiles (ultimately these changes were retrofitted to all vessels). The

Sturgeons were dedicated hunter-killer submarines, designed to seek out and destroy the Soviet submarine fleet. They could carry a wide range of ASW weapons – even the Mk 45 ASTOR nuclear torpedo, before that weapon was retired from the US inventory in the late 1970s – but the total onboard weapons capacity was relatively low. This made the *Sturgeon* class less effective than it might otherwise have been and hastened the introduction of the multi-purpose Mk 48 torpedo. The USS *Grayling* (SSN 646) was the seventh *Sturgeon*-class submarine to be built. She was launched in June 1967 and completed in October 1969. She is still active.

GREMYASHCHIY

USSR: 1959

When they appeared in the late 1950s, the *Krupny*-class guided missile destroyers became the first missile-armed warships in the Soviet fleet. Drawn up as Project 57Bis, the *Krupnys* were designed to carry the SS-N-1 'Scrubber' anti-ship missile. This was an outdated and cumbersome system. The missiles had to be extracted from their launch tubes and then fitted with their control surfaces (wings) before being fired from a launch rail. This whole process took about 40 minutes and so lacked a certain amount of military effectiveness. It did give the *Krupnys* a useful anti-ship and land-attack capability, but the great failing of the design was the lack of adequate self-defence armament, which severely limited the destroyers' usefulness. The *Gremyashchiy* was the first of nine in her class. She was launched in April 1959 and completed in June 1960. Like all her sisterships she was eventually converted for ASW tasks – a process which proved hugely expensive and time-consuming. *Gremyashchiy* was finally stricken in 1991.

Displacement: 3850t standard; 4192t full load
Dimensions: 455ft 9in x 48ft 8in x 13ft 9in (138.9m x 14.84m x 4.2m)
Machinery: two-shaft, geared turbines, four boilers; 72,000hp
Armament: two SS-N-1 SSM (later deleted); 16 57mm; two ASW RL (later three); six 21in (533mm) TT; one helicopter
Speed: 34.5 knots
Range: 3000nm (5556km) at 18 knots
Complement: 310

The guided missile destroyer *Gremyashchiy* holds an important place in Soviet naval history but ultimately proved to be a flawed design that was almost too vulnerable to use.

GRISHA CLASS

USSR: 1968

The Soviet Union's Project 1124 Albatros, or *Grisha* class, frigates were small coastal patrol ships that were widely built in a range of versions. The first example of a *Grisha I* was launched in 1968. The SA-N-4 missile launcher of this version was replaced by a 57mm main gun in the *Grisha II* – many of which served with the KGB Border Guards. The *Grisha III* was similar, while the *Grisha IV* was a one-off ASW trials ships (with SA-N-9 SAMs). The *Grisha V* was fitted with a 3in (76mm) main gun, a single RBU-6000 launcher and hand-held SAMs.

The *Grisha* class, in all its incarnations, was chiefly intended for coastal patrol and ASW tasks, using a dipping sonar and 'sprint-and-dash' tactics to hunt submarines.

Displacement: 950t standard; 1200t full load
Dimensions: 234ft 11in x 32ft 2in x 13ft 9in (71.6m x 9.8m x 4.2m)
Machinery: CODAG, two cruise diesels and one boost gas turbine; 40,000hp/18,000hp
Armament: one SA-N-4 SAM (not *Grisha II*); one twin 57mm gun (two on *Grisha II*), one 30mm Gatling (not *Grisha II*); two ASW RL; four 21in (533mm) TT; two depth charge racks
Sensors: air/surface-search radar; fire-control radar; sonar
Speed: 34.5 knots
Range: 4500nm (8334km) at 18 knots
Complement: 60

GRONINGEN

THE NETHERLANDS: 1954

Displacement: 2497t standard; 3070t full load
Dimensions: 381ft x 38ft x 17ft (116m x 11.7m x 5.2m)
Machinery: two-shaft, geared steam turbines, four boilers; 60,000hp
Armament: four 4.73in (120mm); six 40mm (later four); two ASW RL; two depth charge racks
Sensors: air/surface-search radar; fire-control radar; hull-mounted sonar
Speed: 36 knots
Range: 4000nm (7408km) at 18 knots
Complement: 284

The *Friesland*-class destroyers, introduced by the Dutch Navy in the mid-1950s, were effective ASW vessels that gave decades of good service. They used the machinery of the US *Gearing*-class destroyers, which allowed them to be bigger and faster than their Dutch-built predecessors.

Groningen (D 813) was the second of eight to be built. She was launched in January 1954 and completed in March 1956.

Groningen remained in Dutch service until the early 1980s, when she and her six surviving sister-ships were sold to Peru.

Over the years, the *Friesland* class introduced several changes in its armament fit but never really progressed beyond 1950s-era gun and ASW mortar systems.

GUADIARO

SPAIN: 1950

Spain's *Guadiaro*-class minesweepers were based on the German Type 1940 design of World War II. Seven were launched between 1950 and 1953, beginning with *Guadiaro* (M 11) and *Tinto* (M 12) in June 1950. In a neat design touch the ships' auxiliary turbine was driven by steam extracted from the main reciprocating engines. As built, the *Guadiaros* had a 3.5in (89mm) and 37mm gun armament, but this was removed during an early-1960s overhaul. *Guadiaro* was finally stricken from the fleet in 1977.

The *Guadiaro*-class minesweepers were withdrawn from use in the late 1970s, by which time all had been re-roled to serve as coastal patrol ships.

Displacement: 671t standard; 770t full load
Dimensions: 243ft 10in x 33ft 6in x 12ft 3in (74.3m x 10.2m x 3.7m)
Machinery: two-shaft, triple expansion plus auxiliary turbine, two boilers; 2400hp
Armament: one 3.5in (89mm) gn, one 37mm, two 20mm
Sensors: radar; sonar
Speed: 16 knots
Range: 1000nm (1852km) at 16 knots
Complement: 79

GURKHA

GB: 1960

Displacement: 2300t standard; 2700t full load
Dimensions: 360ft x 42ft 3in x 13ft 3in (109.7m x 12.9m x 4m)
Machinery: one-shaft, COSAG, geared steam turbine (one boiler) and one gas turbine; 12,500hp/7500hp
Armament: two 4.5in (114mm); two 40mm or two 20mm (deleted) cannon; one Seaslug SAM (added later); one Limbo ASW mortar; one helicopter
Sensors: air-search radar; surface/air-search radar; fire-control radar; navigation radar; sonar
Speed: 27 knots
Range: 4500nm (8334km) at 12 knots
Complement: 253

With the *Tribal*-class frigates, the Royal Navy returned once more to the concept of general-purpose frigates – single-purpose ships having risen to post-war prominence. The *Tribal*s were fitted with surface and anti-submarine weapons, along with air-search radar (though not, initially, any missiles). HMS *Gurkha* (F 122) – launched in July 1960 and completed in February 1963 – was the third of seven *Tribal*s to be built. She was later re-equipped with the Seacat SAM system, which replaced her original 40mm cannon. By 1979, the Royal Navy was suffering from such a shortage of manpower that it was forced to withdraw ships from the fleet. The entire *Tribal* class was put up for disposal. HMS *Gurkha* was decommissioned, only to be returned to service, for a period, after the Falklands conflict. In October 1985, she became the second of three Tribal-class ships to be sold to Indonesia, where she is still active as the *Wilhelmus Zakarias Yohannes*.

The *Tribal*-class frigates were developed largely to replace the Royal Navy's ageing *Loch*-class frigates, on station in the Persian Gulf.

GUS CLASS

USSR: 1969

The Soviet Union developed several types of air cushion (hovercraft) landing craft and pushed that technology much further than other nations. The Project 1205 Skat, or *Gus* class, troop transport hovercraft were the smallest to be built. They were not outfitted to carry or deliver cargo, and several were later modified to serve as hovercraft trainers. About 30 were built between 1969 and 1974 and, while the status of the current fleet is uncertain, it is likely that some are still active.

Displacement: 27t standard
Dimensions: 70ft 3in x 23ft 11in x 1ft 8in (21.4m x 7.3m x 0.5m)
Machinery: two propellers, two gas turbines; 1800hp
Armament: none
Sensors: not available
Speed: 60 knots
Range: 230nm (426km) at 43 knots
Complement: 4, plus 25 troops

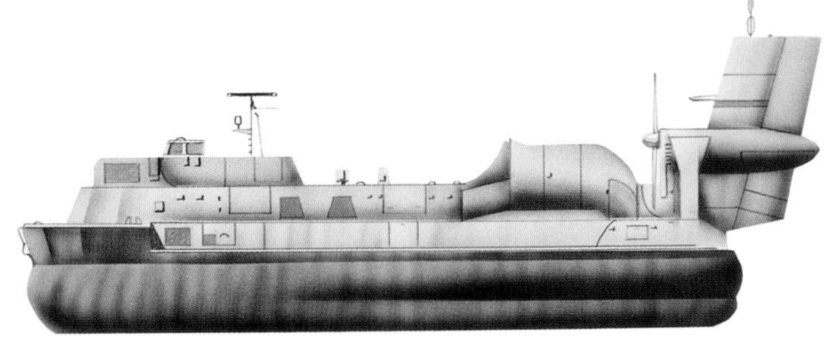

The *Gus*-class hovercraft were developed from the civilian 'Skate' transports and were far removed from the Soviet Union's giant assault hovercraft, such as the *Pomornik* class.

HAI LUNG

TAIWAN: 1986

The decision by Taiwan to acquire new submarines in the 1980s was met with fierce opposition from the People's Republic of China. The Taiwanese ordered two modified Dutch-designed *Zwaardvis*-class submarines as the *Hai Lung* class – the first warships to be purpose-built for the Republic of China since 1949. Both *Hai Lung* (793) and her sistership *Hai Hu* (795) were launched in late 1986. *Hai Lung* was delivered, by ship, in 1987. Attempts to buy more submarines were turned down by the Dutch, following increased pressure from mainland China.

Before the introduction of the *Hai Lung*-class attack submarines, the Republic of China Navy had to rely on two World War II-vintage *Tench*/*Guppy II*-class boats.

Displacement: 2376t surfaced; 2660t submerged
Dimensions: 219ft 7in x 27ft 7in x 22ft (66.92m x 8.4m x 6.7m)
Machinery: one-shaft, three diesels and one electric motor; 4050hp (diesels)
Armament: four 21in (533mm) TT
Sensors: search radar; integrated sonar system
Speed: 11 knots surfaced; 22 knots submerged
Range: 10,000nm (18,520km) at 9 knots (surfaced)
Complement: 67

HALIBUT

USA: 1959

Displacement: 3846t surfaced; 4895t submerged
Dimensions: 350ft x 29ft 6in x 20ft 9in (106.7m x 9m x 6.3m)
Machinery: two-shaft, one nuclear reactor; 6600hp
Armament: five SSM-N-8 Regulus I or two SSM-N-9 Regulus II (intended); six 21in (533mm) TT
Sensors: sonar
Speed: 15 knots surfaced; 15.5 knots submerged
Range: limited only by reactor fuel state
Complement: 111

Until her decommissioning in 1976, the USS *Halibut* had a highly classified career as a 'spy sub', which included recovering Soviet weapons and exploring wrecked submarines on the seabed.

Almost a sistership to the USS *Grayback*, the USS *Halibut* (SSGN 587) was among the handful of cruise missile carrying submarines built in the 1950s by the US Navy.

Like *Grayback*, the *Halibut* was designed to fire the Regulus missile, but unlike any of the other cruise missile submarines she was nuclear-powered. When the Regulus II programme was cancelled, the bulky 'hangars' were removed from *Halibut* and she served as a research vessel and then as an intelligence ship carrying deep-diving mini-submarines.

HALIFAX

CANADA: 1988

Displacement: 4750t full load
Dimensions: 440ft x 53ft 9in x 16ft 2in (134.1m x 16.4m x 4.9m)
Machinery: two-shaft, COGOG, gas turbines and one diesel; 46,000hp/8800hp
Armament: eight Harpoon SSM; two VLS for Sea Sparrow SAM; one 57mm; one Mk 15 Phalanx 20mm CIWS; eight 12.7mm MG; four 12.75in (324mm) TT; one helicopter
Sensors: air-search radar; air/surface-search radar; navigation radar; fire-control radar; sonar
Speed: 28 knots
Range: 7100nm (13,149km) at 15 knots
Complement: 225

Canada's *City*-class (or *Halifax*-class) frigates are large and somewhat boxy ships, with a distinctive oversized and squared-off funnel, which is offset to port.

When the plans for Canada's *City*-class frigates (also known as the *Halifax* class) were drawn up in 1977, it was intended to be a major programme, totalling 20 ships. The Canadians have described these vessels as 'helicopter frigates', although their (single) helicopter capability is a standard feature of most frigates in most navies. The plans to acquire such a large fleet of ships were progressively scaled back as lengthy delays arose, and the initial order, for six frigates, was not signed until 1983. A total of 12 *City*-class ships have been ordered to date – the second batch was signed for in December 1987.

The first ship in the class, *Halifax* (FFH 330), was launched in May 1988 and completed in June 1992. For a frigate, *Halifax* is a comparatively large vessel, but she is equipped with a modern suite of anti-surface and air defence weapons, plus an embarked ASW helicopter.

HALLAND

SWEDEN: 1952

Displacement: 2630t standard; 3400t full load
Dimensions: 397ft 2in x 41ft 4in x 18ft (121m x 12.6m x 5.5m)
Machinery: two-shaft, geared turbines (two boilers) and two diesels; 58,000hp/3800hp
Armament: one SSM launcher; four 4.73in (120mm), two 57mm; six 40mm cannon; two ASW RL; eight 21in (533mm) TT; six rocket flare launchers; mines
Sensors: navigation and fire-control radar
Speed: 35 knots
Range: 3000nm (5556km) at 20 knots
Complement: 290

The *Halland*-class destroyers were the largest new-build ships to serve with the post-war Swedish Navy.

Sweden's two *Halland*-class destroyers were the first vessels, outside the USSR, armed with anti-ship missiles – a mark of Sweden's consistent post-war prowess in weapons technology. *Halland* (J 18) was launched in July 1952 and completed in June 1955. She had a single sistership, *Smaland*, but two additional vessels were cancelled. *Halland* was armed first with Saab Rb 315 missiles, followed by the Rb 08 and the Rb 20. Her Bofors main guns were fully automatic and could fire 40 rounds per minute. *Halland* was decommissioned in 1982.

HAMAYUKI

JAPAN: 1983

The *Hatsuyuki*-class destroyers are yet another example of the well-balanced, medium-sized warships that have been consistently developed and fielded by the Japanese Maritime Self Defence Force. Although relatively small ships, they combine effective anti-air, anti-surface and anti-submarine capability – and also have a helicopter flight deck and hangar. A Mitsubishi-built HSS-2B Sea King is typically embarked. *Hamayuki* (DD 126) was the fifth of 12 such ships to be built. She was launched in May 1982 and completed in November 1983.

The *Hatsuyuki*-class destroyers were an important element of the modernisation plan implemented across the Japanese Maritime Self Defence Force during the 1980s.

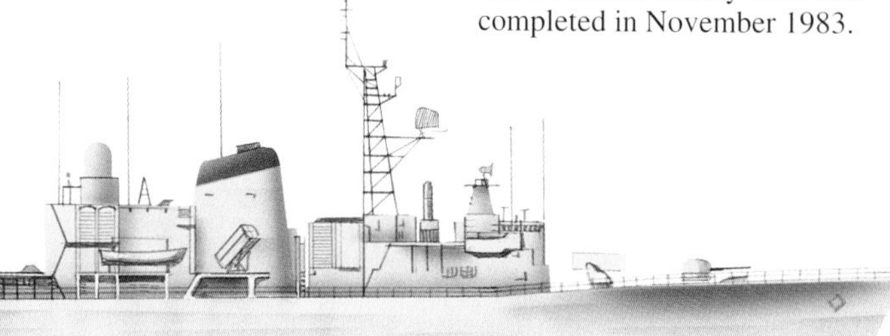

Displacement: 2850t standard; 3700t full load
Dimensions: 432ft 4in x 44ft 11in x 14ft 3in (131.7m x 13.7m x 4.3m)
Machinery: two-shaft, CODOG (CP propellers), two gas turbines plus two gas turbines; 56,780hp/10,860hp
Armament: eight Harpoon SSM; one Sea Sparrow SAM; one 3in (76mm); two Mk 15 Phalanx 20mm CIWS; one ASROC; six 12.7in (324mm) ASW TT; one helicopter
Sensors: air-search radar; sea-search radar; fire-control radar; hull-mounted sonar
Speed: 30 knots
Range: not available
Complement: 190

HAMBURG

GERMANY: 1960

Displacement: 3340t standard; 4330t full load
Dimensions: 438ft 9in x 44ft x 17ft (133.7m x 13.4m x 5.2m)
Machinery: two-shaft, turbines (four boilers) and two diesels; 72,000hp/5630hp
Armament: one SSM launcher; four 4.73in (120mm), two 57mm; six 40mm cannon; two ASW RL; eight 21in (533mm) TT; six rocket flare launchers; mines
Sensors: radar; hull-mounted sonar
Speed: 36 knots
Range: 6000nm (11,112km) at 13 knots
Complement: 284

By the end of their careers the *Hamburg*-class destroyers carried a mix of gun and missile armament, with one Exocet launcher replacing the original 3.9in (100mm) 'X' turret position.

In the late 1950s, the German Navy had hoped to acquire as many as 12 Type 101 or *Hamburg*-class destroyers. In the event, only four were ordered, but they became the largest warships to be built in Germany post-1945. *Hamburg* (D 181) was launched in March 1960 and completed in March 1964. She and her sisterships were modernised several times, and notable changes included the addition of Exocet missiles and an enclosed bridge. *Hamburg* was decommissioned in 1994.

HAN

PEOPLE'S REPUBLIC OF CHINA: 1970

Displacement: 5000t submerged
Dimensions: (401) 328ft x 36ft x 28ft (100m x 11m x 8.5m)
Machinery: one-shaft, one nuclear reactor, turbo-electric drive; 15,000hp
Armament: six 21in (533mm) TT; Ying Ji (Eagle Strike) SSM
Sensors: naviagtion radar; sonar
Speed: 30 knots surfaced; 25 knots submerged
Range: limited only by reactor fuel state
Complement: 75

These attack submarines were the first nuclear-powered vessels (and the first submarines) to be built in Communist China – albeit with considerable (West) German help. The People's Liberation Army Navy has acquired four *Han*-class submarines, the first of which (401) was launched in 1970. These submarines use a teardrop hull shape, as pioneered by the US Navy submarine *Albacore* in the early 1950s. Much of the design expertise for the nuclear propulsion system came from Germany, but the only other Chinese vessel to have adopted a reactor powerplant is the single *Xia*-class ballistic missile submarine. A total of five *Han*-class boats were built over the next 20 years, so overall progress can best be described as leisurely. Once in service, the *Han*-class has suffered from build-quality and reliability problems, but the three late-build vessels are understood to have been armed with the Chinese-developed YJ-1 anti-ship missile. All are currently in service.

The last three of five *Han*-class submarines are some 26ft (7.92m) longer than their predecessors, to accommodate the Ying Ji (Eagle Strike) missile tubes behind the sail.

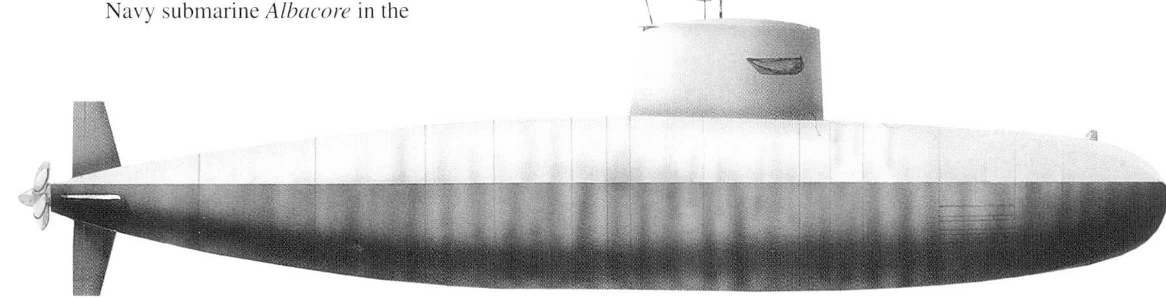

HARUSHIO

JAPAN: 1967

The *Oshio*-class submarines are notable as the first fleet submarines to be built in Japan after 1945. The lead ship, *Oshio*, differed from the rest of the class in having a unique bow shape and a preliminary sonar fit. *Harushio* (SS 563) was the second of the remaining four 'standard' *Oshios* to be built. She was launched in February 1967 and completed in December that year. The primary role of the *Oshios* was to act as ASW targets for exercises.

Displacement: 1650t surfaced; 2150t submerged
Dimensions: 288ft 8in x 26ft 11in x 16ft (88m x 8.2m x 4.9m)
Machinery: two-shaft, two diesels and two electric motors; 2300hp/6300hp
Armament: eight 21in (533mm) TT
Sensors: sonar fit
Speed: 18 knots surfaced; 14 knots submerged
Range: not available
Complement: 80

Before the *Oshio*-class, Japan had built just a handful of small, coastal submarines in the post-war years.

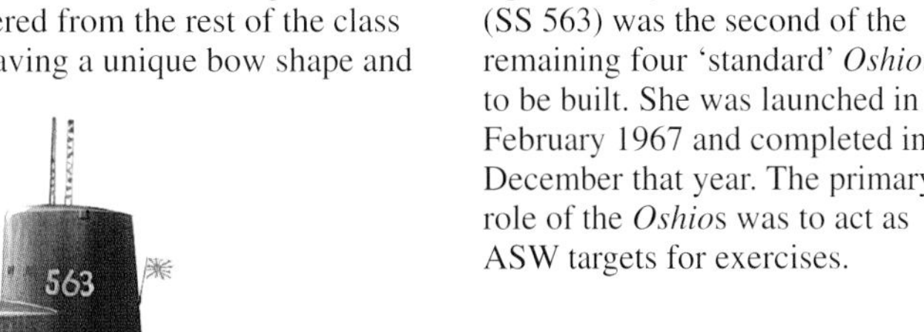

HATAKAZE

JAPAN: 1984

Displacement: 4600t standard; 6800t full load
Dimensions: 521ft x 57ft 5in x 17ft 5in (151.8m x 17.5m x 5.3m)
Machinery: two-shaft, geared turbines, two boilers; 70,000hp
Armament: eight Harpoon SSM; one Standard SM-1MR SAM; two 5in (127mm); two Mk 15 Phalanx 20-mm CIWS; one ASROC; six 12.7in (324mm) ASW TT
Sensors: air-search radar; sea-search radar; fire-control radar; hull-mounted sonar
Speed: 32 knots
Range: not available
Complement: 370

Japan's two *Hatakaze*-class destroyers were built with a primary air defence mission but are well equipped to operate as multi-purpose warships. It had been planned to acquire four ships, but only two were ever funded. *Hatakaze* (DD 171) was the lead vessel – launched in November 1984 and completed in March 1986. While she is fitted with a helicopter deck, she has no hangar – unlike most of her modern counterparts in the Japanese Maritime Self Defence Force.

***Hatakaze*'s forward deck is packed with weapons, including a Mk 112 ASROC launcher, Mk 42 5in (127mm) main gun and a Mk 13 Standard missile launcher.**

HENGAM — IRAN: 1973

Hengam and her sisterships are scaled-down versions of the British _Sir Lancelot_-class LSTs and, during the 1990s, Iran has tried to replicate the design in its own shipyards.

Iran ordered six tank landing ships (LSTs) from the British

Displacement: 2540t full load
Dimensions: 305ft 1in x 49ft x 7ft 3in (93m x 14.9m x 2.2m)
Machinery: two-shaft, two CP propellers, four diesels; 5600hp
Armament: four 40mm; two rocket flare launchers (some Soviet-supplied weapons later added)
Sensors: navigation radar
Speed: 14.5 knots
Range: 4000nm (7408km) at 12 knots
Complement: 80, plus 227 troops

Yarrow yard in the early 1970s, but only four were built. The first of these was *Hengam* (511), launched in September 1973. *Hengam* can carry up to nine tanks, depending on their size. Overall cargo capacity is 700t and the vessel is equipped to handle standard cargo containers using its upper-deck crane. *Hengam* has an aft helicopter deck and whereas she has limited armament, two of her sisterships are operated as unarmed 'hospital ships'.

HERMES (LATER VIRAAT) — GB: 1953

Displacement: 23,900t standard; 28,700t full load
Dimensions: 744ft 4in x 160ft x 29ft (226.9m x 48.8m x 8.8m)
Machinery: two-shaft, geared steam turbines, four boilers; 76,000hp
Armament: 10 40mm (replaced by two Seacat SAM); 28 aircraft (as completed)
Sensors: long-range air-search radar; height-finding radar; tracking radar; navigation radar
Speed: 28 knots
Range: 6000nm (11,112km) at 13 knots
Complement: 1830, plus 270 air group

HMS _Hermes_ is best known for her vital role, alongside HMS _Invincible_, in the Falklands conflict of 1982. During that time she carried 20 Sea Harriers and 10 Sea Kings.

The Royal Navy originally intended to acquire six *Centaur*-class aircraft carriers, but the final vessel was cancelled. The intended name for that ship, HMS *Hermes*, was applied to the fifth and last *Centaur*, which had been laid down (in 1944) as HMS *Elephant*. She was redesigned with post-war innovations such as an angled flight deck, steam catapults and long-range radar.

HMS *Hermes* (R 12) was launched in February 1953 and completed in November 1959. Because of her *Centaur* origins, *Hermes* was always too small. In 1959, her air group consisted of just 20 Sea Vixens, Scimitars and Buccaneers, plus eight Gannets. With the advent of the Phantom, *Hermes* was re-roled as an ASW helicopter carrier because she could not accommodate the larger jets. When the Sea Harrier was introduced, *Hermes* returned to jet status, with a new ski jump, and went to war during the Falklands crisis as the Task Force flagship. She was finally paid off in 1984 and transferred to India in 1987, as the *Viraat*.

HOLLAND (LATER GARCIA Y GARCIA) — THE NETHERLANDS: 1953

Displacement: 2215t standard; 2765t full load
Dimensions: 371ft x 37ft x 17ft (113.1m x 11.4m x 5.1m)
Machinery: two-shaft, geared steam turbines, four boilers; 45,000hp
Armament: four 4.73in (120mm); one 40mm; two RL; two depth charge racks
Sensors: air-search radar; air/surface-search radar; surface-search radar; fire-control radar; hull-mounted sonar
Speed: 32 knots
Range: 4000nm (7408km) at 18 knots
Complement: 247

The *Holland*-class were the first European destroyers to be built without anti-ship torpedoes. They had a primary escort role and were fitted with heavy 4.73in (120mm) guns that were fully automatic and radar-guided. Plans were drawn up

The _Holland_ class were compromised by their undersized powerplants, which were salvaged from the pre-war _Isaac Sweeters_-class ships. This problem was remedied in the _Friesland_-class destroyers that followed the _Hollands_.

to acquire 12 vessels, but this proved to be impossible as Dutch industry had not fully recovered from World War II. The lead ship, *Holland* (D 808), was launched in April 1953 and completed in December 1954. She was sold to Peru in 1978, becoming the *Garcia Y Garcia*.

HOTEL CLASS

USSR: 1958

The nuclear-powered Project 658 (NATO code-name 'Hotel') missile submarines were contemporaries of the *Golf* class. They were intended to carry the SS-N-4 (later SS-N-5) and were essentially a missile-carrying development of the *November* class. The first *Hotel* (K-19) was launched in August 1959, and by 1964 eight had been completed. The *Hotels* had a poor safety record and their dismantling began in the early 1980s. By 1989, none still had their missile firing systems and all have now been withdrawn.

The lead submarine in the class, K-19, had an appalling safety record and was involved in three separate nuclear incidents that led to the deaths of nearly 40 crew members. This earned her the macabre nickname 'Hiroshima'.

Displacement: 5000t surfaced; 6000t submerged
Dimensions: 377ft 4in x 29ft 6in x 23ft (115m x 9m x 7m)
Machinery: two-shaft, one nuclear reactor; 30,000hp
Armament: three SS-N-4 (later SS-N-5) SLBM; six 21in (533mm) TT, four 16in (406mm) TT
Sensors: search radar; sonar active
Speed: 25 knots surfaced; 20 knots submerged
Range: limited only by reactor fuel state
Complement: 80

HUNLEY

USA: 1961

Displacement: 10,500t standard; 19,000t full load
Dimensions: 599ft x 83ft x 23ft 4in (182.6m x 25.3m x 7.1m)
Machinery: one-shaft, six diesels, diesel-electric; 15,000hp
Armament: two 5in (127mm) (later four 20mm)
Sensors: not available
Speed: 15 knots
Range: 10,000nm (18,520km) at 12 knots
Complement: 2568

The USS *Hunley* was a specialist support ship, designed to operate with the Polaris SSBN fleet. In 1974, she was modified to handle the more modern Poseidon C3 missiles.

The tender USS *Hunley* (AS 31) was the first ship designed and built to support US nuclear-powered ballistic missile submarines – specifically the early Polaris submarines. The *Hunley* was launched in September 1961 and was commissioned in June 1962. She was capable of undertaking any maintenance or repair task at sea, short of a full major overhaul. During the early 1960s, she operated from the Holy Loch base in Scotland. In 1964, she was modernised to handle the Polaris A3 missile, and in 1966 she returned to the United States.

IBN KHALDOUN

IRAQ: 1978

Displacement: 1850t full load
Dimensions: 317ft 4in x 36ft 8in x 14ft 10in (96.7m x 11.2m x 4.5m)
Machinery: two-shaft, CODOG (CP propellers), one gas turbine and two diesels; 22,000hp/7500hp
Armament: one 57mm; one 40mm; eight 20mm cannon; one ASW mortar; depth charges
Sensors: search radar; surface-search radar; navigation radar; hull-mounted sonar
Speed: 26 knots
Range: 4000nm (7408km) at 18 knots
Complement: 93, plus 100 trainees

This sleek vessel resembles the export frigates built by Britain's Vosper Thorneycroft, but was, in fact, designed and built in Yugoslavia. Iraq's *Ibn Khaldoun* (507) was launched in 1978 and entered service in 1980. She was intended as a training ship, while having some of the combat capabilities of a small frigate. *Ibn Khaldoun* was used as a transport during the first Gulf War against Iran but was badly damaged during Operation Desert Storm. Her current status is unknown.

Alongside her basic gun armament, *Ibn Khaldoun* had provision to carry anti-ship missiles, but none were ever fitted.

ILLUSTRIOUS

GB: 1978

HMS *Illustrious*, one of Britain's trio of *Invincible*-class carriers, was born in the aftermath of the CVA-01 debacle. With the death of the Royal Navy's big carrier plans in 1966, a new programme of large helicopter-carrying ships was drawn up. Redesigned to have a proper (if short) flight deck, they became known as 'through-deck cruisers'. With the advent of the Sea Harrier they became fully fledged VSTOL aircraft carriers. HMS *Illustrious* was laid down in October 1976, launched in December 1978 and completed in June 1982. Immediately afterwards, she replaced *Invincible* on station in the Falklands – although she was rushed to completion, *Illustrious* was not available in time to participate in the recapture of the islands. She was fully completed in May 1983. *Illustrious* was built with a 6.5° ski jump for her Sea Harriers, but this has now been refitted and increased to 12 degrees.

Today the *Invincibles* are rated as support carriers (CVS). In 1998, *Illustrious* completed a major overhaul that remodelled her bow, adding a new ski jump and a Goalkeeper anti-missile gun system.

Displacement: 16,000t standard; 20,600t full load
Dimensions: 677ft x 90ft x 24ft (206.3m x 27.5m x 7.3m)
Machinery: two-shaft, COGOG, four gas turbines; 112,000hp
Armament: one twin Sea Dart SAM; one 30mm Goalkeeper CIWS; two 20mm; nine aircraft; 12 helicopters (maximum)
Sensors: air-search radar; surface-search radar; navigation radar; fire-control radar; hull-mounted sonar
Speed: 20 knots
Range: 5000nm (9260km) at 18 knots
Complement: 557, plus 318 air group

IMPAVIDO

ITALY: 1962

Just as the US Navy developed its *Charles F. Adams*-class missile destroyers from the earlier *Sherman* class, so did *Impavido* and *Intrepido* follow on from the *Impetuoso* and the *Indomito*.

Displacement: 3201t standard; 3990t full load
Dimensions: 430ft 11in x 44ft 9in x 14ft 6in (131.3m x 13.7m x 4.4m)
Machinery: two-shaft, geared steam turbines, four boilers; 70,000hp
Armament: one Tartar SAM (later Standard SM-1MR); two 5in (127mm); four 3in (76mm); six 12.7in (324mm) ASW TT
Sensors: air-search radar; navigation radar; fire-control radar; hull-mounted sonar
Speed: 33 knots
Range: 3300nm (6112km) at 20 knots
Complement: 340

With the *Impavido*-class destroyers, Italy followed the US practice of re-equipping an existing ship design (in this case the *Impetuoso* class) with the newly developed missile systems of the 1950s. This resulted in two new missile destroyers, both laid down in the late 1950s. The lead ship, *Impavido* (D 570), was launched in May 1962 and completed in November 1963. The *Impavidos* were very similar in size, shape and machinery to the earlier *Impetuoso* class but were fitted with the Tartar long-range SAM system in place of a rear 5in (127mm) gun turret. The Tartar was eventually replaced by the more modern Standard SM-1 missile. *Impavido* was equipped with a highly developed long-range sonar system and relied on 3in (76mm) guns (instead of the 40mm guns fitted to the *Impetuosos*) for additional anti-aircraft protection. In later years, *Impavido*'s SPS-39 radar was modernised with a flat planar array, and a new EW system was fitted. *Impavido* was finally stricken from the fleet in June 1992.

INDIA CLASS

USSR: 1979

Displacement: 3900t surfaced; 4800-6840t submerged
Dimensions: 347ft 8in x 31ft 8in x 32ft 8in (106m x 9.7m x 10m)
Machinery: two-shaft, two diesel-electric engines and two propulsion motors; 4000hp/3500hp
Armament: none
Sensors: general purpose radar; active/passive sonar
Speed: 15 knots surfaced; 11.5-15 knots submerged
Range: 45 days endurance
Complement: 94

Carrying two deep-submergence rescue vehicles (DSRVs), the Soviet Union's Project 940 Lenok (*India* class) vessels were built to locate other submarines in distress and rescue their crews. Launched in 1979 and 1980, the *India*s had medical facilities and decompression chambers to treat several dozen individuals. The DSRVs could dive from 1640 to 3281ft (500–1000m), rescuing crews by docking with a submarine's escape hatch. The *India*s could also be used in salvage operations. Both submarines were placed in reserve around 1990 and scrapped in 1995.

The Poseidon-class DSRVs operated in pairs and were generally carried on board an *India*-class submarine. They could each carry 24 passengers and a crew of three.

INHAÚMA

BRAZIL: 1986

Displacement: 1670t standard; 1970t full load
Dimensions: 314ft 3in x 37ft 5in x 18ft (95.8m x 11.4m x 5.5m)
Machinery: two-shaft, CODOG (CP propellers), one gas turbine and four diesels; 23,000hp/7,800hp
Armament: four MM40 Exocet SSM; one 4.5in (114mm); two 40mm; six 12.7in (324mm) ASW TT
Sensors: surface-search radar; navigation radar; fire-control radar; hull-mounted sonar
Speed: 27 knots
Range: 4000nm (7408km) at 15 knots
Complement: 162

The compact *Inhaúma*-class frigates were designed for Brazil in Germany. They were ordered in the mid-1980s, but plans to acquire up to 16 ships have so far resulted in just four. The lead vessel, *Inhaúma* (V 30), was launched in December 1986 and completed in December 1989. *Inhaúma* is fitted with a wide range of weapons and systems, including a Swedish fire control system, a British combat data system, US engines and French missiles. She also has a flight deck for a Lynx helicopter.

The *Inhaúma* class proved to be more expensive than planned, and while Brazil will acquire at least one more (improved) example, the fleet will not expand to the levels once hoped for.

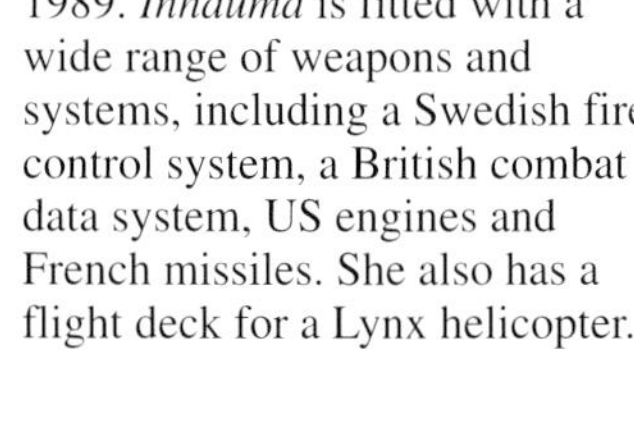

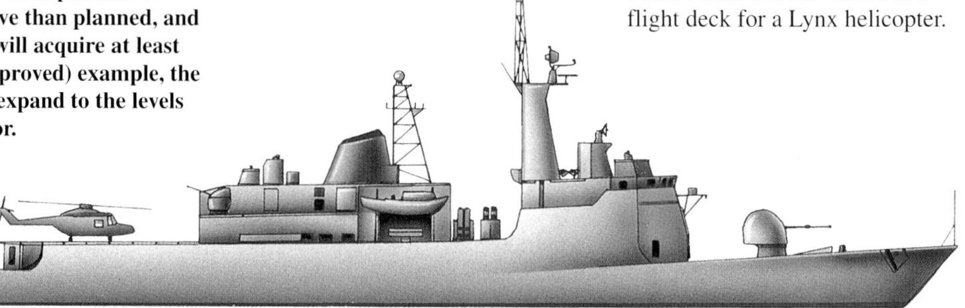

INTREPID

GB: 1964

Displacement: 11,060t standard; 12,120t full load
Dimensions: 520ft x 80ft x 20ft 6in (158.5m x 24.4m x 6.3m)
Machinery: two-shaft, geared steam turbines, two boilers; 2000hp
Armament: four Seacat SAM; four 30mm, two 20mm; up to four helicopters
Sensors: surface-search radar; navigation radar
Speed: 21 knots
Range: 5000nm (9260km) at 20 knots
Complement: 580, plus 400–700 troops

HMS *Intrepid* was refitted in 1984-85 but was not given any of the modern systems applied to HMS *Fearless*. She is now overdue for replacement.

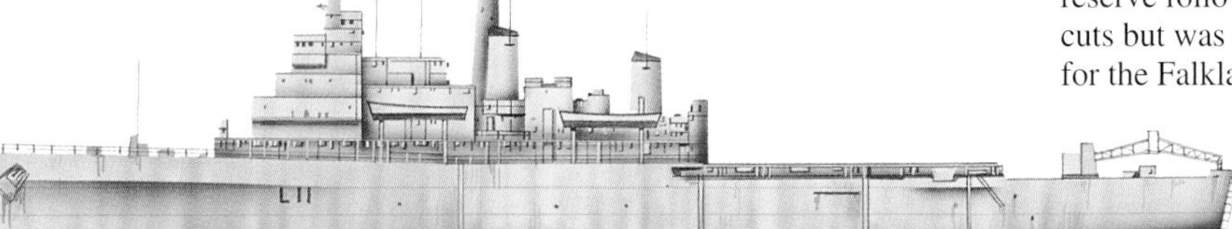

HMS *Intrepid* (L 11) was one of two *Fearless*-class assault ships ordered for the Royal Marines in 1962. Described as LSTs, they could accommodate up to 700 troops (400 was a more normal load) plus 15 tanks and 27 vehicles. *Intrepid* was launched in June 1964 and completed in March 1967. She was rotated in and out of the reserve following the 1976 defence cuts but was pressed into service for the Falklands conflict in 1982.

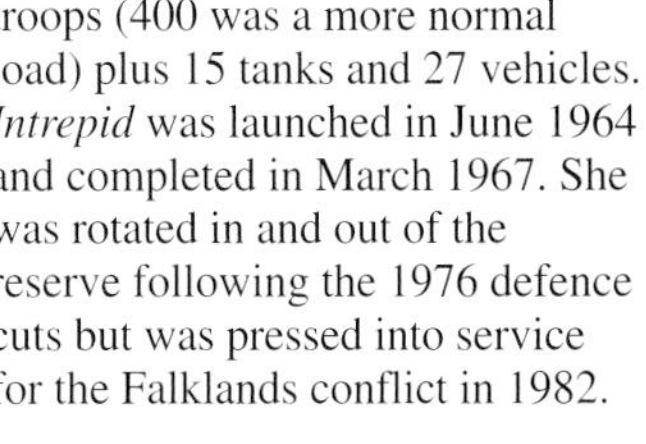

IOWA

USA: RECOMMISSIONED 1951

The *Iowa*-class battleships were the largest and fastest to serve with the US Navy during World War II, and remain among the most imposing and effective combat vessels afloat. They were intended to operate with US carriers, protecting them while they attacked Japanese surface units. Six were planned but only four were built – the USS *Iowa*, USS *New Jersey*, USS *Missouri* and USS *Wisconsin*. The USS *Iowa* was laid down on 27 June 1940, launched on 27 August 1942 and commissioned on 22 February 1943. The *Iowa*s operated with great distinction as part of the US Navy's Fast Carrier Task Forces, often as command ships. They were popular with their crews but were also expensive to operate and were mothballed soon after the war. *Iowa* was reactivated for the Korean War and again during Vietnam. Mothballed a third time in the early 1970s, the *Iowa*s were reactivated in the free-spending Reagan years to become imposing symbols of America's military power and prestige. The battleships were re-armed with Tomahawk cruise missiles and Harpoon anti-ship missiles, while still retaining their highly accurate 16in (406mm) main guns. The *Iowa* made a show-of-force sailing off Nicaragua in 1984 and undertook tanker escorts in the Persian Gulf in 1988. The other battleships undertook fire support duties off the Lebanon during the 1980s and saw action against Iraqi targets in Kuwait during Operation Desert Storm. In 1989, *Iowa* suffered an explosion in one of her main turrets which kept her out of Desert Storm and led to her decommissioning in October 1990. The *Iowa*-class ships are now held in reserve awaiting a decision on their fate, but the *Iowa* herself has been slated for preservation.

The US Navy spent about $1.7 billion to modernise and reactivate the four *Iowa*-class battleships. The USS *Wisconsin* is shown here.

Displacement: 48,110t standard; 57,540t deep load
Dimensions: 887ft 3in x 108ft 2in x 36ft 2in (270m x 33m x 11m)
Machinery: four-shaft, turbines, eight boilers; 212,000hp
Armament: six Harpoon SSM; 32 TLAM-N Tomahawk; nine 16in (406mm); 12 5in (127mm); four Mk 15 20mm Phalanx CIWS,
Sensors: air-search radar; surface-search radar; fire-control radar; gun directors
Speed: 33 knots
Range: not available
Complement: 1515, plus 58 Marines

IVAN ROGOV

USSR: 1977

Displacement: 8260t standard; 14,080t full load
Dimensions: 518ft 4in x 78ft 9in x 26ft 11in (158m x 24m x 8.2m)
Machinery: two-shaft, geared gas turbines with thrusters; 20,000hp
Armament: two SS-N-3 SSM; two SA-N-4 SAM; one Grad-M rocket launcher; one twin 3in (76mm); four 30mm
Sensors: navigation radar; air-search radar; fire-control radar; helicopter-landing control radar
Speed: 23 knots
Range: 12,000nm (22,224km) at 14 knots
Complement: 239, plus 520 troops

The appearance of the *Ivan Rogov* amphibious assault ship, launched in 1976, seemed to signal the beginning of a major elevation in the Soviet Union's international power-projection and intervention capabilities. The *Ivan Rogov* was three times the size of the preceding Alligator-class large landing ships and was compared by some to a US Navy LPH. *Ivan Rogov* was completed in 1978. She could carry an entire naval infantry battalion plus 10 tanks and 30 APCs – and introduced a new class of 'Lebed' assault hovercraft to take them ashore. If no landing craft were carried, the *Ivan Rogov* could carry up to 55 tanks. A flight deck, situated aft, was large enough to accommodate four helicopters. *Ivan Rogov* also had bow doors to allow a beaching landing, if necessary. However, production of the subsequent ships progressed very slowly and, by 1989, only three had been built. *Ivan Rogov* was stricken in 1996, while the status of the two remaining vessels is unclear.

The *Ivan Rogov*-class amphibious dock landing ships were a symbol of the great rise in Soviet naval capability during the 1970s.

IWO JIMA

USA: 1960

The development of the large helicopter assault ship by the US Marine Corps was driven by the Cold War concept of conducting landings opposed by nuclear weapons. Concentrations of conventional landing craft were felt to be very vulnerable to nuclear attack. Helicopters provided greater stand-off range and concentrated delivery, offered higher speeds and allowed the assault fleet to remain dispersed. The *Iwo Jima*-class LPHs were developed with an all-new hull design and a large flight deck. *Iwo Jima* could carry 2000 troops and had space on deck for seven CH-46s or four CH-53s, with hangar space below for another 19 and 11 respectively. *Iwo Jima* (LPH 2) was the lead ship in a class of seven and was launched in September 1960. In 1963, she made the first of several deployments to Vietnam and later joined the Atlantic Fleet. *Iwo Jima*'s original 3in (76mm) guns were replaced by Sea Sparrow SAMs and Phalanx (later Bushmaster) CIWS'. Having proved the LPH concept admirably, *Iwo Jima* was decommissioned in 1993.

Displacement: 10,717t standard; 18,004t full load
Dimensions: 602ft 4in x 84ft 2in x 26ft 1in (103.6m x 25.7m x 8m)
Machinery: one-shaft, geared turbine, two boilers; 22,000hp
Armament: two Sea Sparrow SAM; two Mk 15 Phalanx 20mm CIWS (later 25mm Bushmaster); up to 30 helicopters
Sensors: air-search radar; surface-search radar
Speed: 23.5 knots
Range: 6000nm (11,112km) at 18 knots
Complement: 667, plus 2057 marines

The *Iwo Jimas* were a major step forward for the US Marine Corps because they were designed carry up to 2000 troops in a single accommodation block – in earlier assault ships troops had to be spread far and wide.

IZUMRUD

USSR: 1970

Displacement: 950t standard; 1200t full load
Dimensions: 234ft 11in x 33ft 3in x 11ft 3in (71.6m x 10.15m x 3.45m)
Machinery: two shaft, CODAG, two cruise diesels and one boost gas turbine; 40,000hp/18,000hp
Armament: two 57mm; two ASW RL; four 21in (533mm) ASW TT; two depth charge/mine racks
Sensors: air/surface-search radar; sonar
Speed: 34 knots
Range: 4500nm (8334km) at 18 knots
Complement: 310

The Soviet anti-submarine frigate *Izumrud* was a Project 1124P *Grisha II*-class ship, one of 14 ships known to have been completed in this *Grisha* sub-type. Like all the *Grisha IIs*, *Izumrud* was built at the Zelenodol'sk Zavod yard in Kazan. The *Grisha II* was not fitted with the SA-N-4 SAM system of the *Grisha I* and had a dual 57mm gun as its primary armament. *Izumrud* was operated by the KGB Border Guards, but its current status is unknown.

The *Grisha II* craft are unique among the Project 1124 family (*Grisha*-class) in having no missile armament.

JACOB VAN HEEMSKERCK

THE NETHERLANDS: 1983

Also known as the *L* class, the Dutch Navy's pair of *Jacob Van Heemskerck*-class missile frigates are dedicated air defence ships.

Displacement: 3000t standard; 3750t full load
Dimensions: 427ft x 47ft x 20ft (130.2m x 14.4m x 6m)
Machinery: two-shaft, COGOG, two gas turbines plus two gas turbines; 51,600hp/9800hp
Armament: eight Harpoon SSM; Standard SM-1MR SAM; Sea Sparrow octuple launcher; Goalkeeper 30mm CIWS; two 20mm; four 12.7in (324mm) TT
Sensors: surface-search radar; air/surface-search radar; fire-control radars; hull-mounted sonar
Speed: 30 knots
Range: 4000nm (7408km) at 20 knots
Complement: 197

When the Dutch decided to develop an air defence version of their *Kortenaer* multi-purpose frigates, the result was the *Jacob Van Heemskerck* class. These did away with the ASW system of the previous class, removed the forward 3in (76mm) gun and carried a more advanced fit of Standard missiles (compared with the *Kortenaer*'s Sea Sparrows). *Jacob Van Heemskerck* (F 812) was launched in November 1983 and completed in January 1986. She is an important element of the modern Dutch fleet.

JEANNE D'ARC

FRANCE: 1961

The helicopter carrier *Jeanne D'Arc* (R 97) was built to undertake a range of wartime roles, including ASW warfare, amphibious assault and troop transport. She also has an important training role. *Jeanne D'Arc* was launched in September 1961 and completed in June 1964. Designed to accommodate up to four Super Frelon helicopters, *Jeanne D'Arc* has tended to operate smaller types such as the Lynx and Dauphin. While the ship's gun armament has never been replaced, she now carries Exocet missiles.

Displacement: 10,000t standard; 12,365t full load
Dimensions: 597ft x 79ft x 24ft (182m x 24m x 7.3m)
Machinery: two-shaft, geared steam turbines, four boilers; 40,000hp
Armament: six MM38 Exocet SSM; four 3.9in (100mm) guns; eight helicopters
Sensors: air-search radar; air/surface-search radar;, navigation radars; fire-control radar; hull-mounted sonar
Speed: 26.5 knots
Range: 6000nm (11,112km) at 15 knots
Complement: 627, including 183 cadets

***Jeanne D'Arc* is still a very active vessel and is a regular platform for joint French Army and Navy deployments and exercises.**

JIANGHU III

PEOPLE'S REPUBLIC OF CHINA: 1986

Displacement: 1865t full load
Dimensions: 338ft 7in x 35ft 6in x 10ft 2in (103.2m x 10.83m x 3.10m)
Machinery: two-shaft, two diesels; 16,000hp
Armament: eight YJ-1 Eagle Strike SSM; two twin 3.9in (100mm); four twin 37mm; two ASW mortars; two depth charge racks
Sensors: air/surface-search radar; surface search/fire-control radar; navigation radar; fire-control radars
Speed: 25.5 knots
Range: 3000nm (5556km) at 18 knots
Complement: 180

In an attempt to improve the obsolete *Jianghu I/II*-class frigates, China's People's Liberation Army Navy developed the *Jianghu III* during the late 1980s. The real differences between the classes are limited, although the *Jianghu III* does have a revised superstructure and carries more modern anti-ship missiles. The first ship in the class, *Huangshi* (535), was launched in 1986, followed by *Wuhu* (536) in 1987 and *Zhoushan* (537) in 1992. Four more examples were built for Thailand, two with a helicopter deck.

Described as frigates, China's *Jianghu III*-class ships are little more than well-armed coastal patrol boats.

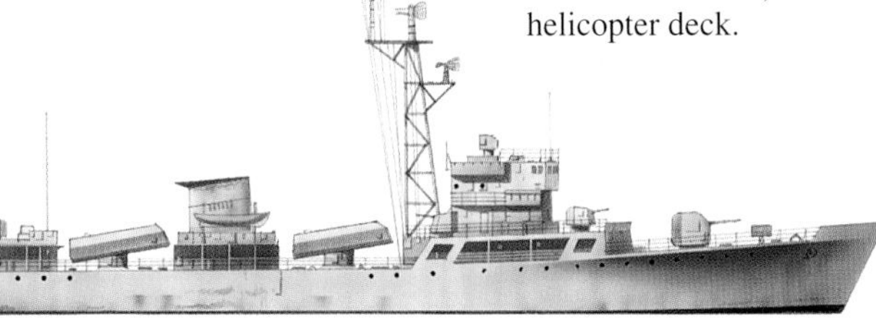

JOHN F. KENNEDY

USA: 1967

Although nominally one of the four *Kitty Hawk*-class carriers, the USS *John F. Kennedy* (CV 67) has substantial design differences that almost set her in a class apart. The *Kennedy* incorporates an all-new underwater protection system, designed for the nuclear-powered carriers, but entered service with no defensive weapons (Sea Sparrows were added later). The *Kennedy* was launched in May 1967 and completed in September 1968. *Kennedy* spent most of her operational life in the North Atlantic and Mediterranean. She was the first carrier to deploy the S-3 Viking, and during the 1980s she saw action off Lebanon and Libya. During Operation Desert Storm the *Kennedy* was the only carrier to deploy with A-7 Corsairs, and her air wing flew a total of 11,000 combat sorties. Today, the *Kennedy* is one of only two non-nuclear carriers remaining in US Navy service. She is officially classed as a Naval Reserve vessel but spends almost her entire time in the regular fleet.

At one time it was planned to build the *John F. Kennedy* as a nuclear-powered carrier, but her conventional powerplant was eventually retained for cost reasons.

Displacement: 60,005t standard; 80,945t full load
Dimensions: 1052ft x 251ft 8in x 36ft (320m x 76.7m x 11.4m)
Machinery: four-shaft, geared turbines, eight boilers; 280,000hp
Armament: three Sea Sparrow octuple launchers; three Mk 15 Phalanx 20mm CIWS
Sensors: air-search radars; surface-search radar; navigation radars; fire-control radars; fitted for hull-mounted sonar
Speed: 33.6 knots
Range: 12,000nm (22,224km) at 20 knots
Complement: 3306, plus 1379 air wing

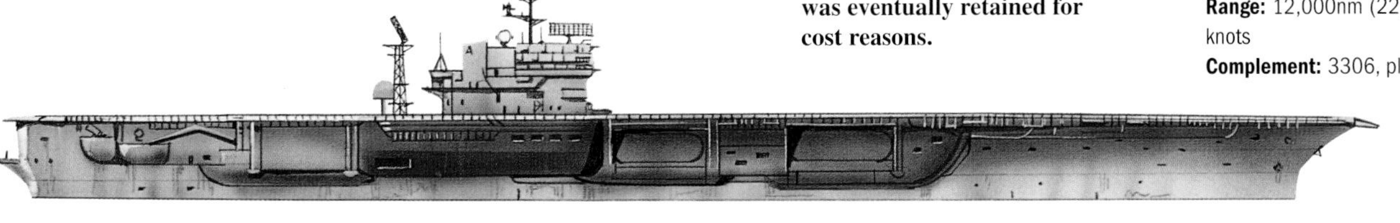

JOSEPH STRAUSS

USA: 1961

The sleek lines of the *Charles F. Adams*-class destroyer escorts (DDGs), with their upswept bows, were particularly distinctive. These ships followed the *Sherman* class but incorporated the Tartar missile instead of a 5in (127mm) gun mounting. A total of 23 served with the US Navy, along with others for Germany and Australia. The USS *Joseph Strauss* (DDG 16) was the 15th built – launched in December 1961 and completed in 1963. The *Strauss* served until 1990 and was transferred to Greece in 1992.

The *Strauss* was the second ship in the class to be built with the more reliable single-arm Tartar SAM launcher.

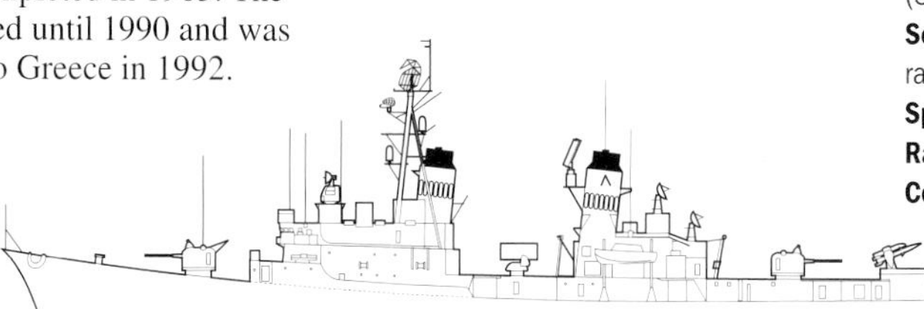

Displacement: 3277t standard; 4526t full load
Dimensions: 437ft x 47ft x 15ft (133.2m x 14.3m x 4.6m)
Machinery: two-shaft, geared turbines, four boilers; 70,000hp
Armament: one Tartar SAM; two 5in (127mm); one ASROC; six 12.75in (324mm) TT
Sensors: air-search radar; fire-control radar; hull-mounted sonar
Speed: 33 knots
Range: 4500nm (8334km) at 20 knots
Complement: 333-350

JULIETT CLASS

USSR: 1966

The Project 651 ('Juliett' class) cruise missile submarines were conventionally powered equivalents of the *Echo*-class nuclear submarines. Armed with the same SS-N-3 missiles, they carried half as many as the *Echoes*. The four missiles were carried in flat tubes that had to be raised above deck level to be fired. The first Project 651 (K-137) was launched in August 1966, and a total of 34 were built by 1972. The withdrawal of the 'Juliett's began in the 1980s and by 1994 none remained in service.

The Project 651 submarines were a sophisticated design and incorporated an innovative powerplant that used a combined drive/battery-charging generator.

Displacement: 3000t surfaced; 3750t submerged
Dimensions: 295ft 3in x 32ft 10in x 23ft (90m x 10m x 7m)
Machinery: two-shaft, diesel-electric; 5000hp
Armament: four SS-N-3 cruise missiles; six 21in (533mm) TT; four 16in (406mm) TT
Sensors: search radar; missile tracking radar; actove/passive sonar array
Speed: 16 knots submerged
Range: 9000nm (16,668km) at 7 knots (submerged)
Complement: 78

KASHIN CLASS

USSR (RUSSIA): 1960

The Soviet Union's *Kashin*-class (Project 61) destroyers hold the distinction of being the first major warships in the world to use a gas turbine powerplant. The *Kashin*'s were one of several types of Soviet warships developed during the great modernisation drive of the early 1960s. They were intended to provide area defence for surface fleets, primarily against aircraft, but with an important ASW function also. The lead ship in the class, *Komsomolets Ukrainy*, was launched in December 1960 and completed in December 1962. From then until 1973, a total of 20 *Kashins* were built at. The *Kashins* were the first Soviet warships designed to survive a nuclear blast. The primary ship control centre was housed deep inside the hull, well away from the regular bridge. The Project 61M modernisation was introduced on late-production ships and added an improved array of air defence weapons.

About half the *Kashin* fleet remained in service into the mid-1990s, but many have now been stricken by funding crisis.

Displacement: 3400t standard; 4390t full load
Dimensions: 472ft 5in x 51ft 10in x 15ft 1in (144m x 15.8m x 4.6m)
Machinery: two-shaft, CODAG, four gas turbines; 72,000hp
Armament: two SA-N-1 SSM launchers; four 3in (76mm); two RBU-6000 and two RBU-1000 ASW RL; five 21in (533mm) TT (original fit)
Sensors: air-search radar; navigation radar; fire-control radar; hull-mounted sonar
Speed: 18 knots
Range: 3500nm (6482km) at 18 knots
Complement: 266

KASZUB

POLAND: 1986

Given the NATO code-name 'Balcom 6', the Type 620 corvette *Kaszub* (240) was the first ocean-going warship ever to be built in Poland. Based on the Soviet *Grisha* class, *Kaszub* was powered by diesel engines instead of the *Grisha*'s gas turbines. *Kaszub* was launched in October 1986 and completed in March 1987. Several of the intended elements of *Kaszub*'s armament fit were never installed – such as its SA-N-4 missiles – and before 1990 the vessel rarely went to sea, due to technical troubles.

Prior to the collapse of the Warsaw Pact, it was planned to build seven Type 620s. Poland still hopes to build more ships, but *Kaszub* remains the sole example.

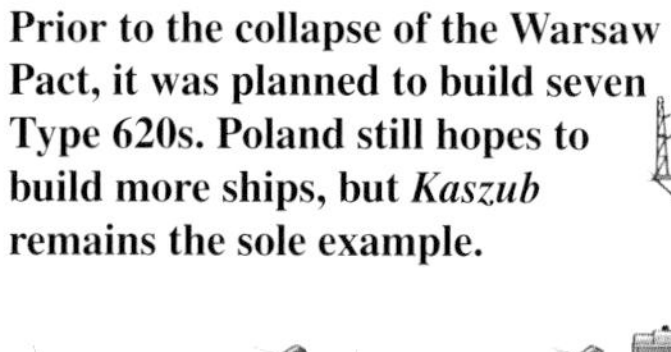

Displacement: 1051t standard; 1183t full load
Dimensions: 270ft 2in x 32ft 9in x 9ft 2in (82.3m x 10m x 2.8m)
Machinery: four-shaft, CODAD, four diesels; 17,500hp
Armament: two SA-N-5 SAM launchers (eight missiles); one 3in (76mm); six 23mm cannon; two RBU-6000 ASW RL; two 21in (533mm) TT; two DC rails
Sensors: air/surface-search radar; surface-search radar; hull-mounted sonar
Speed: 28 knots
Range: 2800nm (5186km) at 14 knots
Complement: 67

KATORI

JAPAN: 1968

Displacement: 3372t standard; 4100t full load
Dimensions: 418ft 2in x 49ft 1in x 14ft 4in (127.5m x 15m x 4.4m)
Machinery: two-shaft, gas turbines; 20,000hp
Armament: four 3in (76mm); one ASW RL; six 12.5in (317mm) TT; one helicopter
Sensors: air/surface-search radar; hull-mounted sonar
Speed: 25 knots
Range: 3500nm (6482km) at 18 knots
Complement: 460 (including trainees)

The Japanese Maritime Self Defence Force training ship *Katori* is a comparatively large vessel, weighing in at over 4000t with a full load. *Katori* was launched in November 1986 and completed in September 1969. In time of war, *Katori* is equipped to operate as an escort command ship, but since she was commissioned crew training has remained her operational role. Plans to build a more modern replacement were delayed throughout the 1990s.

For many years *Katori* was the 'flagship' of Japan's small but very active naval training fleet. A more modern vessel has now taken on her role.

KERCH

USSR (RUSSIA): 1972

The *Kara*-class guided missile destroyers were a further development of the mid-1960s *Kresta II* design, with gas turbines replacing the steam turbine plants of the previous classes. This resulted in major modifications to the layout of the section amidships, but the extra space was used to house new command and control facilities. It has been suggested that the main motivation behind the introduction of the gas turbine powerplants was simply that the Soviet Union's sole gas turbine factory was located near the Black Sea shipyards where the *Karas* were laid down. However, it is also true that gas turbine engines are much quieter and more efficient than the older steam turbine units. Although larger than the *Kresta II* cruisers, and with significant anti-air and anti-submarine capabilities, these ships are classified as destroyers rather than cruisers by the Russian Navy. The fourth unit was modified during construction as a test ship for the SA-N-6 SAM system, which replaced the aft SA-N-3 SAM system. Only one ship, the *Kerch*, which was the Russian Black Fleet flagship until 1997, remains in service, but it may not be deployable. There is considerable disagreement among sources as to the build chronology of the units of this class. The first *Kara*-class destroyer, *Nikolayev*, was launched in December 1969. Launched in February 1972 and commissioned in December 1974, the *Kerch* was the third *Kara* to appear. The *Kerch* spent the majority of her operational life in the Mediterranean.

Displacement: 8200–8565t standard; 8825–9700t full load
Dimensions: 568ft 9in x 55ft 1in x 17ft 5in (173.3m x 16.8m x 5.3m)
Machinery: two-shaft, COGAG, four gas turbines; 96,000–120,000hp
Armament: six quadruple SA-N-6, four twin SA-N-3 and two twin SA-N-4 SAM launchers; two twin 3in (76mm); four 30mm AK-630 CIWS; two RBU-6000 and two RBU-1000 ASW RL; one Ka-25 'Hormone' helicopter
Sensors: air/surface-search radar; navigation radar; fire-control radar; hull-mounted sonar
Speed: 34 knots
Range: 6500nm (12,038km) at 18 knots
Complement: 350–525

The *Kara*-class destroyers were a very distinct sub-type of the original Project 1134 design, which gave birth to the *Kresta I* and *Kresta II* ships of the mid- to late-1960s.

KIDD

USA: 1979

Displacement: 5826t standard; 9200t full load
Dimensions: 563ft 4in x 55ft x 20ft 6in (171.7m x 16.8m x 6.25m)
Machinery: two-shaft, four gas turbines; 80,000hp
Armament: two quad Harpoon SSM; twin Mk 46 VLS for Standard SM-2R SAM and ASROC; two 5in (127mm); two 20mm Phalanx CIWS; four 12.7mm MG; six 12.75in (324mm) TT
Sensors: air-search radar; surface-search radar; navigation radar; fire-control radar; hull-mounted sonar and towed array
Speed: 30 knots
Range: 6000nm (11,112km) at 18 knots
Complement: 296

The US Navy's *Kidd*-class destroyer escorts are something of an anomaly. They are a derivative of the *Spruance*-class, originally ordered by the Imperial Iranian Navy in 1973–74. Iran took the existing *Spruance* design but considerably improved its air defence capabilities by adding the Standard missile system, Phalanx CIWS and other weapons. The first of four vessels for Iran, *Kouroush*, was laid down in June 1978, but the order was cancelled following the Islamic Revolution in 1979. *Kouroush* became the USS *Kidd*, which was launched in August 1979 and completed in June 1981. All four *Kidd*-class destroyers are still in service.

Though the USS *Kidd* and her sisterships closely resembled the *Spruance*-class destroyers, they were much better armed and equipped – thanks to the Iranian petrodollars that paid for their design.

KIEV

USSR (RUSSIA): 1972

The Soviet Union's large and heavily armed Project 1143 Krechyet (*Kiev* class) 'aircraft carriers' marked a dramatic step forward in Soviet naval capabilities in the 1970s, and were vessels with no real equivalent in the Western navies. In Soviet service they were classified as heavy aircraft-carrying cruisers and were capable of engaging in surface, anti-submarine and anti-air warfare with ease. The *Kiev* class featured a large flight deck (with two deck lifts to the hangar below) and was fitted with arrestor wires and a bow ski jump. The *Kievs* could carry over 20 fixed-wing Yak-38 'Forger' VTOL aircraft and a further 15 helicopters. The ships' Bazalt anti-ship missile system had eight (or 12) missile launchers, while the Krechyet air defence system consisted of 24 reinforced vertical launchers and 192 SAMs. Each of the Project 1143 warships had significant differences from the others, and some of the later vessels were almost one-off designs. Following on from the much smaller *Moskva* class, *Kiev* was the lead ship in the second generation of Soviet aircraft carriers. She was laid down in July 1970, launched in December 1972 and completed in December 1975. *Kiev* passed through the Dardanelles on 18 July 1976, to loud international protests about possible infractions of the Montreaux Convention. Three more ships were built in the class: *Minsk*, *Baku* (later renamed *Admiral Gorshkov*) and *Novorossiysk*. A fifth Project 1143 was approved in 1979, but not built. *Kiev* remained in service with the Northern Fleet until 1993, when she was retired from the fleet and held pending her scrapping. In August 2000 it was reported that a shipyard in China had bought *Kiev* from Russia.

It had been intended to replace Kiev's Yak-38 'Forgers' with the newly developed Yak-141 'Freehand', but that programme ended with the collapse of the Soviet Union – which finished the Kiev also.

Displacement: 36,000t standard; 43,500t full load
Dimensions: 902ft x 154ft 10in x 26ft 11in (275m x 47.2m x 8.2m)
Machinery: four-shaft, four steam turbines, eight turbo-pressurised boilers; 200,000hp
Armament: eight SS-N-12 SSM tubes; two twin SA-N-3 and SA-N-4 SAM launchers; two twin 3in (76mm); eight 30mm AK-630 CIWS; 10 21in (533mm) TT; 12-13 Yak-38 'Forger' attack fighters, 14-17 Ka-25 'Hormone' or Ka-27/-29 'Helix' helicopters
Sensors: air/surface-search radar; navigation radar; fire-control radar; hull-mounted sonar
Speed: 32 knots
Range: 13,500nm (25,002km) at 18 knots
Complement: 1200–1600, including air group

KILO CLASS

RUSSIA: 1980

The *Kilo* class (Project 877) attack submarines are modern and effective fighting vessels designed for anti-submarine and anti-ship warfare. They are considered to be among the quietest diesel submarines in the world. Russia operates three variants of the *Kilo* 877. These include the basic 877, the 877K with an improved fire-control system, and the 877M armed with wire-guided torpedoes. Export models, designated with an 'E' suffix, are generally similar though less capable. The first *Kilo* (B-248) was launched in September 1980 and commissioned in December 1982. At least 26, and perhaps as many as 30, were built for the Soviet/Russian Navy, one of which was subsequently exported to Iran. All *Kilos* built for home service were designated Project 877, although late-production examples were built to the improved 636 standard. By early 2000, 14 Kilos were believed to be active with the Russian Navy, with seven in reserve. The latest Project 636 *Kilo* design is an improved version of the Project 877EKM *Kilo* class that was an interim development of the basic *Kilo*. The Project 636 is being actively promoted on the world market. This version has improved range, firepower, acoustic characteristics and reliability. Distinguished by a step on the aft casing, the length of the hull is extended by two frame spacings. The additional length permitted an increase in the power of the diesel generators, now mounted on improved shock-absorbing supports, with a slower main propulsion shaft speed. With these improvements both speed and endurance were increased, while the noise level was significantly reduced. Russia has exported 21 Project 877 and 636 submarines to India (10), China (four), Iran (three), Algeria (two), Poland (one) and Romania (one).

Kilos are renowned for their low-noise characteristics, achieved through the selection of quiet machinery, vibration and noise isolation, and a special anti-acoustic rubber coating applied on the outer hull.

Displacement: 2300t (877), 2350t (636) surfaced; 3950t (877), 4000t (636) submerged
Dimensions: 238ft 2in x 242ft 2in x 32ft 5in x 21ft 4in (72.59m (636) (877) 73.8m (636) x 9.9m x 6.5m) (877),
Machinery: one-shaft, two diesel generators, one electric propulsion motor; 3650hp/5790hp
Armament: six 21in (533mm) TT with 18 torpedoes, eight SA-N-8 or SA-N-10 SAM
Sensors: general-purpose radar; active/passive sonar
Speed: 12 knots (877), 11 knots (636) surfaced; 25 knots (877), 20 knots (636) submerged
Range: 5214nm (9656km) at 7 knots with snorkel; 45 days endurance
Complement: 350–525

KIROV

USSR (RUSSIA): 1977

Displacement: 24,300-25,860t standard; 25,396-26,396t full load
Dimensions: 813ft 8in x 93ft 6in x 24ft 7in (248m x 28.5m x 7.5m)
Machinery: two-shaft, two nuclear reactors, four steam turbines; 280,000hp
Armament: 20 SS-N-19 SSM; S-300F (SA-N-6) ADGM (12 launchers, 96 SAM); two twin SA OSA-MA (SA-N-4, 40 missiles); 10 21in (533mm) TT with SS-N-14; two 3.9in (100mm); eight 30mm AK-630 CIWS; two RBU-1000 and one RBU-6000 ASW RL; three Ka-25/-27 helicopters
Sensors: air/surface-search radar; navigation radar; fire-control radar; hull-mounted sonar
Speed: 32 knots
Range: 13,500nm (25,002km) at 18 knots
Complement: 1200-1600, including air group

Russia's Project 1144.2 Orlan (*Kirov* class) are the world's largest cruisers and might best be termed 'battle cruisers'. Originally designed as large anti-submarine warships to seek and destroy ballistic missile submarines, their role was expanded to engage large surface targets; and to provide air and anti-submarine defence for naval forces, after the introduction of the Granit system. *Kirov* was launched in December 1977 and completed in December 1980. *Kirov* was armed with the Granit (SS-N-19 'Shipwreck') long-range anti-ship missile. Twenty missiles were installed under the upper deck, mounted at a 60° elevation. The S-300F Kashtan air defence missile system was also installed, with 12 launchers and 96 vertical launch SAMs. The S-300F is capable of engaging both air and surface targets. In addition, *Kirov* had two Osa-Ma (SA-N-4) double launchers with 40 air defence missiles. The ship's propulsion system is based on a combination of nuclear power and steam turbine, with two nuclear reactors and two auxiliary boilers.

In 1990, *Kirov* (newly renamed as the *Admiral Ushakov*) suffered a major nuclear accident that put her out of service. She was stricken in 1998 to provide spares for the only other active ship of the class, *Admiral Nakhimov*. However, in January 1999 the Russian Duma (lower parliament) voted the *Admiral Ushakov* should be repaired and restored to service.

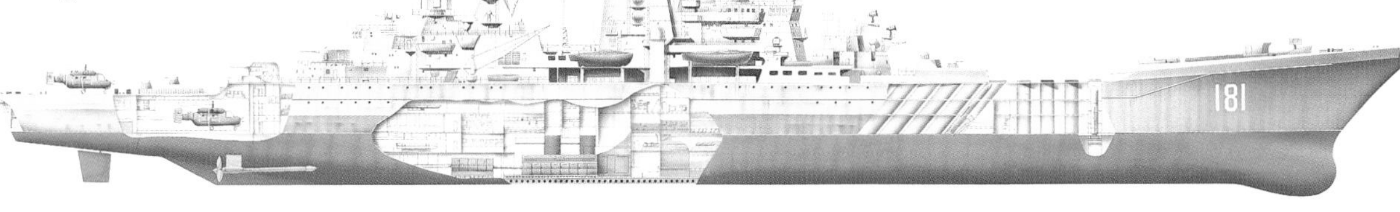

The four ships in the *Kirov* class – *Admiral Ushakov* (ex-*Kirov*), *Admiral Lazarev* (ex-*Frunze*), *Admiral Nakimov* (ex-*Kalinin*) and *Peter Velikiy* (ex-*Yuri Andropov*) – are easily among the most powerful warships afloat, but only one or two are currently operational.

KNOX

USA: 1966

As designed, the *Knox* class proved to be 'wet' ships and from 1980 onwards they were modified with raised bulwarks and spray strakes to improve their sea-keeping.

With the *Knox* class, the US Navy sought to develop an ocean-going escort destroyer that could be manned by a crew fewer in number than had previously been the case. The ships were designed around a new type of pressure-fired boiler, which promised better cruise performance (in terms of range). The *Knox* class had a primary anti-submarine role, but the ships were surprisingly lightly armed, with just one 5in (127mm) gun and an ASROC launcher as their primary offensive weapons. USS *Knox* (DE 1052) was launched in November 1966 and completed in April 1969. Over the next seven years a total of 45 other *Knox* class vessels were launched. With the end of the Cold War, they were among the first US Navy vessels to be retired under the new financial climate – a reflection of their small size and lack of overall capability. Most were sold abroad. USS *Knox* herself was decommissioned in 1992 and transferred to Taiwan a few years later.

Displacement: 3020t standard; 4066t full load
Dimensions: 438ft x 47ft x 25ft (133.5m x 14.3m x 7.6m)
Machinery: one-shaft, geared turbines, two boilers; 35,000hp
Armament: one Sea Sparrow SAM launcher; one ASROC launcher; one 5in (127mm); two 21in (533mm) and four 12.75in (324mm) TT; one SH-2 Seasprite (LAMPS I) helicopter
Sensors: air/surface-search radar; navigation radar; fire-control radar; hull-mounted sonar
Speed: 27 knots
Range: 4500nm (8334km) at 20 knots
Complement: 224

KONGO

JAPAN: 1991

Sharing a name with the mainstay class of the Japanese destroyer force during World War II, the *Kongo* class destroyers of today's Japanese Maritime Self Defence Force are equally important vessels. Japan's status as a valued ally of the United States is reflected in the technological sophistication of these warships. They are based on the US Navy's *Arleigh Burke* (DDG 51) class missile destroyers and are fitted with the Aegis air defence radar and missile system found only on the *Burke*s and the *Ticonderoga* class cruisers. Until the arrival of the *Kongo* class, Japan did not possess a truly modern air defence ship – and, to date, Japan is the only foreign navy to be allowed access to this technology. The Aegis system combines the Standard SM-2 missile with the SPY-1 phased-array radar and a highly sophisticated computerised battle management and fire control system. Aegis ships are easily identifiable by the flat-panel electronic radar arrays for the SPY-1 system that are fitted to their forward superstructure. Using Aegis, the *Kongo*-class destroyers can defend an entire battle group against simultaneous multiple attacks from airborne and missile threats. So sensitive is the Aegis system that the USA was reluctant to export it to Japan, but eventually relented. Ships such as the *Kongo* are hugely expensive and Japan has so far built just four, when once it planned to acquire eight. *Kongo* (DD 173) was launched in September 1991 and completed in March 1993. The ship has a flight deck aft for an SH-60J Seahawk, but no hangar. *Kongo* is armed with two Mk 41 vertical launch systems, fore and aft, that carry up to 29 and 61 SM-2MR missiles respectively.

Thanks to their Aegis air defence system, Japan's *Kongo*-class destroyers are arguably the most capable air defence ships in service outside the USA.

Displacement: 7250t standard; 9485t full load
Dimensions: 528ft 2in x 68ft 7in x 20ft 4in (160.9m x 20.9m x 6.2m)
Machinery: two-shaft, COGAG, four gas turbines; 102,160hp
Armament: eight Harpoon SSM; two Mk 41 VLS with 90 Standard missiles and ASROC torpedoes; one 5in (127mm); two 20mm Phalanx CIWS; six 12.75in (324mm) TT; one SH-60J Seahawk helicopter
Sensors: Aegis air defence system; air/surface-search radar; navigation radar; fire-control radar; hull-mounted sonar and towed array
Speed: 30 knots
Range: 4500nm (8334km) at 20 knots
Complement: 300

KONI CLASS

USSR: 1978

Displacement: 1440t standard; 1900t full load
Dimensions: 311ft 8in x 42ft x 13ft 9in (95m x 12.8m x 4.2m)
Machinery: three-shaft, CODAG, two diesels and gas turbine; 35,000hp
Armament: four SS-N-2C SSM (some ships); one twin SA-N-4 SAM launcher; two twin 3in (76mm); four twin 30mm cannon
Sensors: air/surface-search radar; surface-search radar; hull-mounted sonar
Speed: 27 knots
Range: 1800nm (3334km) at 14 knots
Complement: 110

Based on the *Grisha* class of small frigates, the *Koni* class (Project 1159) coastal anti-submarine warfare ships were built in the Soviet Union entirely for foreign customers. The first example, *Delfin*, was launched in 1978. *Delfin* proved to be the only example of the class to be retained by the Soviet Union, for demonstration and training purposes, but was eventually transferred to Bulgaria in 1990. A total of 14 *Koni*s were built for export to Algeria (three), Bulgaria (one), Cuba (three), East Germany (three), Libya (two) and Yugoslavia (two). All of the ships were designed to carry the SS-N-2 anti-ship missile, but these were never fitted to those supplied to Algeria, Cuba or East Germany. The Yugoslavian ships had the improved SS-N-2C missiles, while the Libyan vessels were also fitted with 15.75in (400mm) torpedo tubes. All the *Koni*s except for the East German ships are believed to still be extant.

For the small navies that acquired and operated them, the *Koni*-class frigates were important warships and small Soviet-era status symbols.

KOTOR

YUGOSLAVIA: 1984

Having taken delivery of two Soviet-built Koni-class frigates in 1980 and 1982, Yugoslavia next built two similar ships of its own, under licence. These two ships of the *Kotor* class are similar to the *Koni* design, but are larger and incorporate distinct structural changes. The upper lines of the *Kotor*s are very different to the Soviet-built ships and they also lack the rear gun turret of the Konis. *Kotor* (33), the lead ship in her class, was launched in 1984 and completed in 1988. Her sistership, *Pula*, was launched in 1986. *Kotor* was armed and equipped with a mixture of Soviet and Western systems – a typical arrangement in 'neutral' Yugoslavia during the Tito years. Both *Kotor* and *Pula* were operational at the beginning of the Balkan wars of the 1990s, but their current status is unclear.

One unusual feature of the *Kotor* was its powerplant, which combined a Soviet-supplied gas turbine with a French-built diesel engine.

Displacement: 1700t standard; 1900t full load
Dimensions: 317ft 3in x 42ft x 13ft 9in (96.7m x 12.8m x 4.2m)
Machinery: three-shaft, CODAG, two diesels and one gas turbine; 9600hp/18,000hp
Armament: four SS-N-2C SSM; one twin SA-N-4 SAM launcher; one twin 3in (76mm); two twin 30mm cannon; six 12.75in (324mm) TT; two RBU-6000 ASW RL
Sensors: air/surface-search radar; surface-search radar; hull-mounted sonar
Speed: 27 knots
Range: 1800nm (3334km) at 14 knots
Complement: 110

KRIVAK II CLASS

USSR (RUSSIA): 1975

Displacement: 3300t standard; 3800t full load
Dimensions: 405ft 3in x 46ft 3in x 15ft 1in (123.5m x 14.1m x 4.6m)
Machinery: two-shaft, COGAG, two cruise gas turbines, two boost gas turbines; 24,000hp/48,600hp
Armament: four SS-N-14 ASW missiles; two SA-N-4 SAM launchers; one 3.9in (100mm); eight 21in (533mm) TT; two RBU-6000 ASW RL; mines
Sensors: air/surface-search radar; navigation radar; fire-control radar; hull-mounted sonar
Speed: 32 knots
Range: 4600nm (8519km) at 20 knots
Complement: 181-200

The Project 1135 Burevestnik (*Krivak I* class) was an entirely new design, intended as a defensive ASW ship. When they first appeared, Western agencies were convinced that the *Krivaks* had a primary surface warfare role, but this was not the case. The *Krivak* design was intended to be a less expensive and less capable counterpart to the *Kresta II* and *Kara* ships. The Project 1135M *Krivak II* that followed differed chiefly from its predecessor in having a revised-calibre main gun, but they were otherwise almost impossible to tell apart. The most distinctive feature of the *Krivak Is* and *Krivak IIs* is the flat, rounded four-tube launcher for the SS-N-14 boosted torpedoes. This was misidentified as an SS-N-10 anti-ship missile launcher, thus giving rise to the confusion over the ships' role. There is still some confusion over the numbers of *Krivak*'s built, but there is general agreement that the *Krivak II* series consisted of 11 ships, all completed between 1975 and 1982. The lead ship was the *Rezvy*, but like all the *Krivaks* she has now been retired.

The *Krivak I* and *Krivak II* destroyers were followed by the *Krivak III* class, which deleted the SS-N-14 launcher in favour of the SS-N-15 and had the main gun mounted forward instead.

KRONSTADT

USSR (RUSSIA): 1968

The *Kresta* class (Project 1134) ships were designed for ASW and surface warfare tasks, and to provide additional air defence for Soviet task forces. There were two variants in the class. The Project 1134 Berkut (*Kresta I*) ships were surface warfare cruisers. Responding to an urgent ASW requirement, the SS-N-14 anti-submarine system was fitted to the much more capable Project 1134A Berkut-A (*Kresta II*) ships. This replaced the SS-N-3 anti-ship missiles of the *Kresta I*. The *Kresta II* could carry a Ka-25 'Hormone A' helicopter, which could deliver nuclear depth bombs. The *Kresta II* was also equipped with 3in (76mm) guns, replacing the 57mm mounts on *Kresta Is*. Four *Kresta I* class cruisers became operational during 1967–69 and 10 *Kresta II* cruisers entered service during 1969–78. Launched in October 1968 and commissioned in December 1969, *Kronstadt* was the lead *Kresta II*. All *Kresta* class ships had been stricken by 1994 and, as of early 2000, most are believed to have been sold to foreign ship-breakers.

Displacement: 5600t standard; 7535t full load
Dimensions: 521ft 6in x 54ft 10in x 17ft 5in (158.9m x 16.7m x 5.3m)
Machinery: two-shaft, two steam turbines, four boilers; 100,000hp
Armament: two quad SS-N-14 launchers; two twin SA-N-3 SAM launchers; two twin 57mm; four 30mm AK-630 CIWS; two 21in (533mm) TT; two RBU-1000 ASW RL; one Ka-25 helicopter
Sensors: air/surface-search radar; navigation radar; fire-control radar; hull-mounted sonar
Speed: 34 knots
Range: 10,500nm (19,446km) at 14 knots
Complement: 380

The *Kresta II* class uses a gas turbine propulsion system that is lighter and more compact than the boilers used on the *Kresta I*.

KYNDA CLASS

USSR (RUSSIA): 1961

Bulky launchers for SS-N-3 anti-ship missiles, fore and aft, dominated the lines of the *Kynda* class.

Displacement: 4400t standard; 5500t full load
Dimensions: 464ft 9in x 51ft 10in x 17ft 5in (141.6m x 15.8m x 5.3m)
Machinery: two-shaft, two steam turbines, four boilers; 100,000hp
Armament: two SS-N-3b SSM launchers (eight missiles, eight reloads); one twin SA-N-1 SAM launcher (24 missiles); two twin 3in (76mm); four 30mm AK-630 CIWS; six 21in (533mm) TT
Sensors: air-search radar; navigation radar; fire-control radar; hull-mounted sonar
Speed: 34 knots
Range: 7000nm (12,964km) at 14.5 knots
Complement: 304-375

Deployed between 1962 and 1965, the Project 58 Groznyy (*Kynda* class) guided missile cruisers were among the first modern Soviet warships. Laid down as destroyers, they were redesignated as 'rocket cruisers' in 1962. The lead ship, *Groznyy*, was launched in March 1961 and completed in December 1962. Only slightly longer than the *Krupnyy* and *Kildin* destroyers, the *Kyndas* had significantly more firepower. However, their excessive top-weight prompted the decision to build the larger *Kresta* class, and only four *Kyndas* were built. All have now been retired.

LA GALISSONNIERE

FRANCE: 1960

The French Type T 56 destroyer *La Galissonniere* (D 638) was a one-off trials and development ship, used to provide the necessary experience for a whole new generation of ASW ships. *La Galissonniere* was launched in March 1960 and completed in July 1962. She conducted early trials of the Malafon boosted ASW torpedo system and also holds the distinction of being the first French naval vessel to operate a helicopter. *La Galissonniere* later dropped her trials role and joined the active fleet, but was retired in 1990.

***La Galissonniere* was fitted with a most unusual helicopter deck arrangement, located above the Malafon torpedo magazine with a fold-down hangar.**

Displacement: 2750t standard; 3470t full load
Dimensions: 436ft x 42ft x 18ft (132.8m x 12.8m x 5.5m)
Machinery: two-shaft, geared steam turbines, four boilers; 63,000hp
Armament: two 3.9in (100mm); one Malafon ASW system; six 21.66in (550mm) TT; one 12in (305mm) ASW mortar; one Alouette II/I helicopter
Sensors: air-search radar; navigation radar; fire-control radar; hull-mounted sonar
Speed: 34 knots
Range: 5000nm (9260km) at 18 knots
Complement: 347

LE TRIOMPHANT

FRANCE: 1993

The SNLE-NG (Sous-Marins Nucleaires Lanceurs Engins-Nouvelle Generation), or *Le Triomphant* class SSBNs, will replace the *Redoutable* class SSBNs in French Navy service. Plans for six boats were initially cut back to three for budgetary reasons, but President Chirac himself decided that the SNLE-NG programme should include four submarines. With four SNLE-NGs, three could be operational at any one time. The first of the class, *Le Triomphant* (S-616), was laid down in 1989, launched in July 1993 and commissioned in March 1997. *Le Téméraire*, the second SNLE-NG, was commissioned in December 1999. The third boat, *Le Vigilant*, will enter service in 2004, followed by the final vessel in 2008. The upgraded M-45 SLBM will equip the first three SNLE-NGs once fully operational. The fourth will receive a new model missile, the M-51. *Le Vigilant* was intended to be the first to commission with the M-51, with the others being retrofitted, but delays in the M-51 programme have forced the use of the interim M-45. As a major design objective, the *Le Triomphant* class aimed to be 1000 times quieter than the *Le Redoubtable* submarines they were replacing. Strenuous efforts have been made to reduce all emitted noise, and the hydrodynamic effect of water flow around the submarine. To ensure that machinery noise is not propagated outside the hull, the rigid connec-tions that secure hardware to the hull have been replaced by a kind of cradle which avoids any direct connections. To avoid the cavitation problems caused by standard propellers, *Le Triomphant* uses a new form of ducted propeller, called a 'propeller pump' or propulsor.

The *Le Triomphant* class SSBNs represent a huge investment for France, which has funded and developed the submarines, their nuclear powerplants and new M-51 missiles completely independently.

Displacement: 12,640t surfaced; 14,335t submerged
Dimensions: 453ft x 55ft 8in x 41ft (138m x 17m x 12.5m)
Machinery: one-shaft, nuclear with pump jet propulsor; one pressurised-water reactor, two turbo-alternators, one motor, two auxiliary diesels and one emergency motor; 41,500hp.
Armament: 16 Aerospatiale M45/TN 71 SLBM with six 150kT MRV each (to be replaced by M5/TN 75 with 10–12 MRV each); four 21in (533mm) TT for L5 torpedoes or SM 39 Exocet SSM (18 torpedoes and SSM carried in mixed load)
Sensors: general-purpose radar; active/passive multi-function sonar
Speed: 20 knots surfaced; 25 knots submerged
Range: limited only by reactor fuel state
Complement: 111

LONDON

GB: 1984

Displacement: 4100t standard; 4800t full load
Dimensions: 490ft 6in x 48ft 6in x 21ft (149.5m x 14.8m x 6.4m)
Machinery: two-shaft, COGOG, four gas turbines; 54,600hp/9700hp
Armament: four MM38 Exocet SSM; two GWS25 Sea Wolf SAM launchers; two 40mm or two 30mm cannon; six 12.75in (324mm) TT; two Lynx or one Sea King/Merlin helicopter
Sensors: air-search radar; navigation radar; fire-control radar; hull-mounted sonar
Speed: 28.5 knots
Range: 8000nm (14,816km) at 18 knots
Complement: 273

The *Boxer*-class frigates, otherwise known as Improved *Broadsword* or *Broadsword* Batch 2, were based on the initial Type 22 (*Broadsword* class) frigates, but were lengthened to accommodate the Type 2031Z towed sonar array. Beginning in 1979, they were ordered to supersede the original *Broadsword* design. After the Falklands conflict, their design was re-examined and revised and as a consequence only six were built. HMS *London* (F 95) was the fourth of the *Boxer* class and, as such, featured an enlarged flight deck to accommodate a Merlin helicopter.

HMS *London* was built as HMS *Bloodhound*, but was renamed at the request of the Lord Mayor of London.

LONG BEACH

USA: 1959

The nuclear-powered fleet escort missile cruiser USS *Long Beach* (CGN 9) holds the distinction of being the largest warship built by the US Navy in the post-war years – with the exception of its aircraft carriers. The three *Albany* class cruisers that were her contemporaries could rival the *Long Beach* in terms of size, but they were World War II-vintage vessels that had been recommissioned in the early 1960s. The USS *Long Beach* was the only American warship to be built post-1945 that ever reached traditional cruiser size and, as such, she remained alone in her class. She also had another notable distinction. Along with the carrier USS *Enterprise*, she was the only US naval vessel to be fitted with the flat-panel fixed-arrays for the SPS-32/33 long-range air-search radar. The USS *Long Beach* was launched in July 1959 and completed in September 1961. She was one of the early nuclear-powered vessels, using two reactors, and carried a very heavy air defence weapons load. She boasted two Terrier SAM launchers with 120 missiles, alongside a single longer-range Talos system with 52 SAMs. While operating in the Gulf of Tonkin during May–June 1968, *Long Beach* shot down two North Vietnamese MiG fighters in what was the first successful recorded naval SAM engagement. In the early 1980s, the USS *Long Beach* underwent a modernisation programme that saw the removal of the troublesome SPS-32/33 radar antennas, though her distinctively slab-sided superstructure remained. At the same time, the Phalanx CIWS were added and Harpoon anti-ship missiles replaced the obsolete Talos launcher. USS *Long Beach* was due for a further upgrade in the 1990s, but instead force reductions resulted in her retirement in 1994.

Displacement: 15,111t standard; 16,602t full load
Dimensions: 721ft 3in x 73ft 4in x 23ft 9in (219.8m x 22.3m x 7.2m)
Machinery: two-shaft, nuclear, two reactors, two geared turbines; 80,000hp
Armament: one Talos SAM system (replaced by eight Harpoon SSM); two Terrier SAM systems; two 5in (127mm); two 20mm Phalanx CIWS (later); one ASROC launcher; six 12.75in (324mm) TT
Sensors: long-range air-search radar; air/surface-search radar; navigation radar; fire-control radar; hull-mounted sonar
Speed: 30+ knots
Range: limited only by reactor fuel state
Complement: 1107

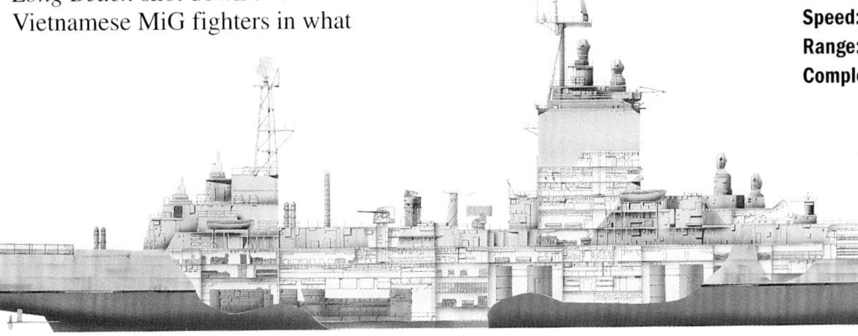

The original design for the USS *Long Beach* included provision for Regulus II or Polaris nuclear missiles, but such plans were quickly dropped.

LOS ANGELES

USA: 1974

The *Los Angeles* class submarines are very large, weighing in at about 2000t more than their predecessors, the *Sturgeon* class.

Displacement: 6000t surfaced; 6900t submerged
Dimensions: 360ft x 33ft x 32ft 4in (109.7m x 10m x 9.8m)
Machinery: one-shaft, nuclear, one reactor; 30,000hp
Armament: four 21in (533mm) TT (maximum of 26 Mk 48 torpedoes, up to eight Tomahawk cruise missiles); 20 vertical launch Tomahawks (SSN 719 onwards)
Sensors: general-purpose radar; active/passive multi-function sonar
Speed: 31 knots submerged
Range: limited only by reactor fuel state
Complement: 127

The *Los Angeles*-class is the mainstay of the US Navy's attack submarine fleet and one of the largest vessels of their kind in Western service. The '688s' are they are known (after the pennant number of the lead boat, *Los Angeles*) were intended to replace the *Sturgeon* class. The lead ship in the class, USS *Los Angeles* (SSN 688) was launched in April 1974 and completed in November 1976. A total of 62 examples have been built, making this class by far the most important type in the US submarine fleet. Over the life of the design many important changes have been made to the 688s. From 1984 onwards, with the launch of the USS *Providence* (SSN 619), all the *Los Angeles* class have been fitted with vertical launch tubes for the Tomahawk land-attack cruise missile. Earlier vessels can fire Tomahawks from their torpedo tubes – but carry far fewer missiles (eight). From the USS *San Juan* (SSN-751) onwards, the 'Improved 688' class appeared. These were fitted with the new BSY-1 submarine combat system. A more obvious change was the replacement of the sail-mounted diving planes, with bow planes – for better under-ice operations. Though they were designed as classic hunter/killer submarines, the role of the *Los Angeles* class has been greatly expanded in the modern US Navy by their stand-off land attack capability. In fact, the *Los Angeles* class actually provides the United States with a second-tier attack force, quite apart from the fleet ballistic missile submarines. US Navy attack submarines have been capable of launching nuclear weapons since the 1950s, when the Regulus cruise missile was introduced (albeit unsuccessfully). However, it is the matching of *Los Angeles* class with the Tomahawk cruise missile that makes them so deadly effective. Until 1990 *Los Angeles*-class vessels would have gone to sea with a small, but significant, quantity of BMG-109 Tomahawks, armed with 200-kt thermonuclear warheads. The nuclear-tipped version of the Tomahawk is no longer deployed, and the missiles now carry 1,000lb of high-explosive instead. This switch to the conventional land attack role has made the *Los Angeles* class a far more militarily useful asset. Submarines, by their very nature, have a covert striking power and can be deployed to a crisis or potential trouble spot without ever betraying their presence. The long-range and phenomenal striking power of the submarine-launched Tomahawk, as first demonstrated during operation Desert Storm and more recently during Operation Allied Force in the Balkans, is well-proven.

The first *Los Angeles*-class boats could carry 12 Tomahawk cruise missiles, but from SSN-719 (USS *Providence*) onwards that number rose significantly.

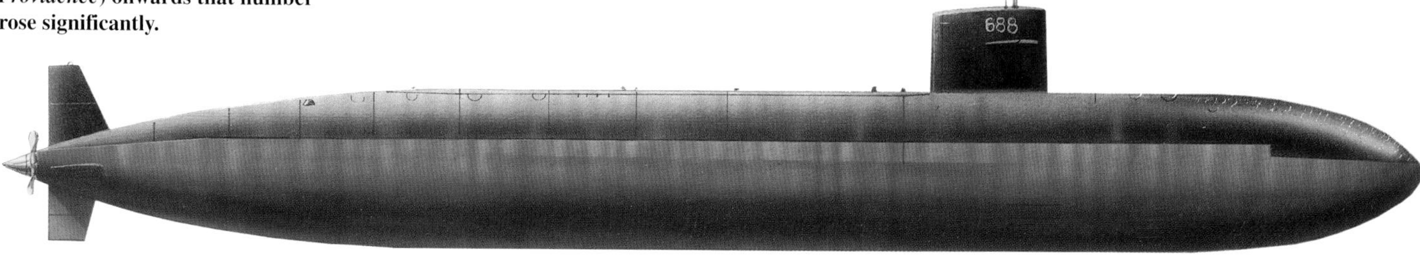

LÜBECK

GERMANY: 1960

The Type 122 Frigate *Lübeck* (F 214) is a *Bremen*-class warship that replaced a 1960s-vintage Type 120 frigate of the same name. Launched in October 1987 and completed in March 1990, *Lübeck* was the eighth and last of the Type 122s to be built. The *Bremen* class are capable multi-purpose ships that replaced the remaining Type 119 (Fletcher class) and Type 120 ships in German Navy service, though not on a one-for-one basis. Their design is modelled on the Dutch *Kortenaer* class.

The *Bremen*-class frigates are among the most modern in Germany's Navy. They have an effective mix of offensive and defensive capabilities thanks to their Harpoon, Sea Sparrow and RAM missile armament.

Displacement: 3700t standard; 3800t full load
Dimensions: 440ft x 47ft 9in x 19ft 9in (134.1m x 14.5m x 6m)
Machinery: two-shaft, CODOG, two gas turbines and two diesels; 50,000hp/10,400hp
Armament: eight Harpoon SSM; one Sea Sparrow VLS (21 missiles); one RAM launcher; one 3in (76mm); four TT
Sensors: air/surface-search radar; navigation radar; fire-control radar; hull-mounted sonar
Speed: 30 knots
Range: 4000nm (7408km) at 18 knots
Complement: 189

LUIGI DURAND DE LA PENNE

ITALY: 1989

Named in honour of Italian heroes of World War II, the *Luigi Durand De La Penne* class destroyers replaced the *Impavido* class air defence ships. The lead ship, *Luigi Durand De La Penne* (D 56), was launched in October 1989 and completed in December 1993. She is armed with an integrated Aspide SAM, 3in (76mm) gun and quad fire-control radar system for her primary role. It had originally been planned to build a total of four ships, but funding was diverted to other projects and just two were completed. The funding earmarked was instead used to acquire four *Lupo*-class frigates built for Iraq but later embargoed.

Displacement: 4500t standard; 5600t full load
Dimensions: 484ft 7in x 52ft 10in x 16ft 5in (147.7m x 16.1m x 5m)
Machinery: two-shaft, CODOG, two gas turbines and two diesels; 55,000hp/12,600hp
Armament: eight Otomat SSM; one Albatros SAM launcher (eight Aspide missiles); one 5in (127mm), three 3in (76mm); six 12.75in (324mm) TT; two helicopters
Sensors: air/surface-search radar; navigation radar; fire-control radar; hull-mounted sonar
Speed: 21 knots
Range: 3450nm (6389km) at 18 knots
Complement: 400

LUPO

ITALY: 1976

Displacement: 2208t standard; 2500t full load
Dimensions: 370ft 2in x 39ft 4in x 12ft (112.8m x 12m x 3.6m)
Machinery: two-shaft, CODOG, two gas turbines and two diesel engines; 50,000hp/8490hp
Armament: eight Otomat SSM; one Sea Sparrow SAM launcher (eight missiles); one 5in (127mm); four 40mm cannon, two 20mm cannon (optional); six 12.75in (324mm) TT; two helicopters
Sensors: air/surface-search radar; navigation radar; fire-control radar; hull-mounted sonar
Speed: 35 knots
Range: 4350nm (8056km) at 16 knots
Complement: 185

The *Lupo* has deck space to operate a pair of helicopters, but standard Italian practice is to carry just one.

The Italian *Lupo* class frigates are a modern and efficient design that have proved popular with export customers. The Italian Navy has acquired a fleet of eight *Lupo*s, including four examples built for Iraq but which were never delivered. The lead ship in the class, *Lupo* (F 564), was launched in June 1976 and completed in September 1977. Together with the *Sparviero*-class attack boats, the *Lupo* was the first Italian ship to introduce the Otomat SSM into service. The *Lupo* is noteworthy for adopting the US Sea Sparrow SAM. She is built around a SADOC automated combat control system, allowing her to work as part of an integrated, data-linked surface battle group.

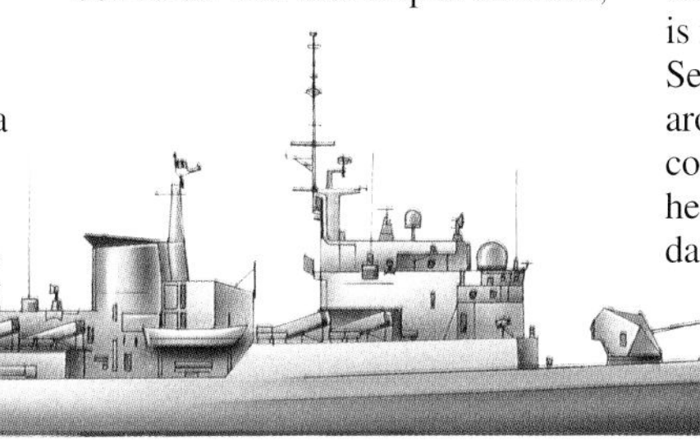

LÜTJENS

GERMANY: 1967

To improve its naval air defences during the mid-1960s, Germany looked to build six *Charles F. Adams*-class guided missile destroyers in its own shipyards. This plan proved to be too expensive and, in the end, just three ships were ordered from ongoing production in the US. These vessels were modified *Charles F. Adams* class, with side-exhausting funnels and a different mast arrangement. The lead ship was the *Lütjens*, which was launched in August 1967 and completed in March 1969. The *Lütjens* was comprehensively upgraded in the mid-1980s.

During her upgrade, *Lütjens* was re-armed with new systems including Harpoon and Standard missiles, and had her electronics updated.

Displacement: 3370t standard; 4717t full load
Dimensions: 441ft 3in x 47ft 3in x 14ft 9in (134.5m x 14.4m x 4.5m)
Machinery: two-shaft, geared turbines, four boilers; 70,000hp
Armament: combined Mk 13 launcher for Harpoon SSM and Standard SAM; one RAM launcher; one ASROC launcher; two 5in (127mm); six 12.75in (324mm) TT
Sensors: air/surface-search radar; fire-control radar; hull-mounted sonar
Speed: 36 knots
Range: 4500nm (8334km) at 20 knots
Complement: 333

LYNX

GB: 1955

HMS *Lynx* served with the Royal Navy until 1982, when she was sold to Bangladesh to become the *Abu Bakr*.

Displacement: 2300t standard; 2520t full load
Dimensions: 340ft x 40ft x 11ft 10in (103.6m x 12.2m x 3.6m)
Machinery: two-shaft, diesel, eight diesel engines; 14,400hp
Armament: two twin 4.5in (114mm); two 40mm cannon; one Squid ASW mortar
Sensors: long-range air/surface-search radar; fire-control radar; hull-mounted sonar
Speed: 25 knots
Range: 7500nm (13,890km) at 16 knots
Complement: 205

The Royal Navy decided to split its '1945' frigates along two distinct lines, with different powerplants. One result was the *Leopard* class (Type 41), which did away with steam plants in favour of diesel engines. One unusual aspect of their design was the lack of any funnels, with the engines exhausting through trunking inside the masts. This was not a happy arrangement and the masts had to be plated to prevent corrosion. HMS *Lynx* (F 27) was the second Type 41 to be laid down. She was launched in January 1955 and completed in March 1957. By the standards of the day HMS *Lynx* had a very capable air defence fit, with a long-range search radar and radar-directed fire control for its 4.5in (114mm) main guns. The great weakness of the Type 41 class was its Admiralty Standard Range 1 diesel engines, which were not a successful design. The Leopards were finally withdrawn from use in the mid- to late 1970s.

MAESTRALE

ITALY: 1981

Displacement: 2990t standard; 3250t full load
Dimensions: 402ft 9in x 42ft 9in x 27ft 5in (122.7m x 13m x 8.3m)
Machinery: two-shaft, CODOG, two gas turbines and two diesel engines; 50,000hp/11,000hp
Armament: four Otomat SSM; one Albatros SAM launcher (eight missiles); one 5in (127mm); four 40mm cannon; two 21in (533mm) and six 12.75in (324mm) TT; two helicopters
Sensors: air/surface-search radar; navigation radar; fire-control radar; hull-mounted sonar
Speed: 33 knots
Range: 6000nm (11,112km) at 16 knots
Complement: 232

Italy's *Maestrale*-class frigates are based on the Lupo design but are about 10 per cent bigger. This increase in size means that they are slightly slower than the *Lupo*s, but also more seaworthy. Several Lupo systems were changed on the Maestrales. The Sea Sparrow SAM was replaced by the Albatros/Aspide system, which, unlike the Mk 29 Sea Sparrow launcher, has a powered reloader. Additional hangar space was 'bought' by cutting the load of Otomat missiles by half. Another interesting feature of the *Maestrale* class is the pair of large-calibre torpedo tubes mounted in the stern, for the heavyweight A-184 torpedoes. The *Maestrale*s also have a towed VDS sonar to back up the hull-mounted system. The *Maestrale* (F 570), the first of eight ships in its class, was launched in February 1981 and completed in March 1982. In 1977 the class was cut back to just six ships, but the final two were reinstated in 1980. All eight ships had entered service with the Italian Navy by 1985.

The *Maestrale* is typical of modern Italian frigate designs: a well armed but lightweight ship optimised for Mediterranean conditions.

MANCHESTER

GB: 1980

The original Type 42 (*Sheffield* class) design was a larger and heavier ship than those that were actually built. The Falklands conflict of 1982 underlined the shortcomings of those Batch 1 and Batch 2 destroyers, but even before then, the Royal Navy had moved to change the design with a revised Batch 3 Type 42. In terms of systems fit and machinery, the Batch 3 (or *Manchester* class) destroyers are almost identical to the *Sheffield* class. The only major change is the replacement of their Type 965 air-warning radar by the more advanced Type 1022. The *Manchester*s are, however, nearly 140ft (42.67m) longer at the waterline than their Batch 1/2 sisterships, and about 1000t heavier. This dramatic stretch of the Type 42 class has resulted in a vessel with sleek and sweeping lines – in the eyes of many they are the most handsome warships afloat. A side-effect of the stretch is the prominent stiffening beam that runs the length of the upper hull. This actually adds 2ft (61cm) to the width of each ship. HMS *Manchester* (D 95) was the lead ship of the Type 42 Batch 3s. She was laid down in November 1980 and completed in December 1982. A total of four *Manchester* class frigates were built and all had entered service by 1985. For close-in defence the *Manchester*s can be fitted with both individual 20mm cannon and the Phalanx CIWS. During the 1991 Gulf War, HMS *Gloucester* (the second of the Batch 3s) engaged and destroyed an Iraqi 'Silkworm' anti-ship missile with her Sea Dart system, but this is now being replaced by the more modern Sea Dart missile on all the *Manchester*s, starting with HMS *Edinburgh*.

Displacement: 4750t standard; 5350t full load
Dimensions: 463ft x 49ft x 19ft (141.1m x 14.9m x 5.8m)
Machinery: two-shaft, CODOG, four gas turbines; 50,000hp/8000hp
Armament: one Sea Dart GWS30 SAM launcher (22 missiles); one 4.5in (114mm); four 20mm cannon; one or two 20mm Phalanx CIWS; six 12.75in (324mm) TT; one Lynx helicopter
Sensors: air/surface-search radar; navigation radar; fire-control radar; hull-mounted sonar
Speed: 30 knots
Range: 6000nm (11,112km) at 16 knots
Complement: 312

The lengthened hull of the *Manchester*-class frigates makes them slightly faster than their *Sheffield*-class relatives.

MARANON

PERU: 1951

Two quite distinctive *Ucayali* class river gunboats were built in Great Britain (by Thornycroft) for the Peruvian Navy in 1951. The second of these, *Maranon* (13), was launched in April 1951, a month after her sistership *Ucayali* – and both are still in service today. Their very unusual lines were dictated by the shallow draught required for riverine operations along the Amazon River. Both vessels were specifically designed for tropical conditions. Peru has a tradition of acquiring ex-British ships dating back to the post-war era.

The *Ucayali* class craft were the largest in a small fleet of patrol gunboats specially built for operations along the Amazon River.

Displacement: 365t full load
Dimensions: 154ft 9in x 32ft x 4ft (47.2m x 9.7m x 1.2m)
Machinery: two-shaft, two diesel engines; 800hp
Armament: two 3in (76mm); seven 20mm cannon
Sensors: none
Speed: 12 knots
Range: 5000nm (9260km) at 12 knots
Complement: 40

MARLBOROUGH

GB: 1985

Displacement: 3500t standard; 4200t full load
Dimensions: 436ft 4in x 52ft 10in x 24ft (133m x 16.1m x 7.3m)
Machinery: two-shaft, CODLAG, two gas turbines, two electric motors and four generators; 37,540hp/7000hp
Armament: eight Harpoon SSM; one Sea Wolf VLS (32 missiles); one 4.5in (114mm); two 30mm cannon; six 12.75in (324mm) TT; one Sea King/Merlin helicopter
Sensors: air/surface-search radar; navigation radar; fire-control radar; hull-mounted sonar
Speed: 28 knots
Range: 8500nm (15,742km) at 15 knots
Complement: 169

The Type 23 *Duke*-class frigate is a scaled-down version of the Royal Navy's very capable – but also very expensive – Type 22 ships. The Type 23 has much of the ASW capability of the Type 22 but also proved to be an effective multi-purpose warship. The *Dukes* were designed around the Sea Wolf SAM, the much-improved successor to the Sea Dart. This was to have used a standard two-headed launcher, but by the time the *Dukes* were laid down a vertical launcher for the Sea Wolf had been developed. Because the Type 23 uses a towed sonar for ASW tasks, it was important to keep its own radiated noise down to a minimum. For this reason a unique combined diesel-electric and gas turbine (CODLAG) propulsion system was chosen, using Spey gas turbines for cruising and diesel-electric motors for 'silent running' while sub-hunting. HMS *Marlborough* (F 233) was launched in January 1989 and completed in June 1991.

The conventional appearance of the Type 23s hides a number of 'stealthy' design features. The class is claimed to have one of the lowest radar signatures of any major warship, whilst also being among the quietest.

MARLIN

USA: 1953

The US Navy submarine *Marlin* was a small and simple vessel used largely as a training target for other naval forces, alongside her sistership *Mackerel*.

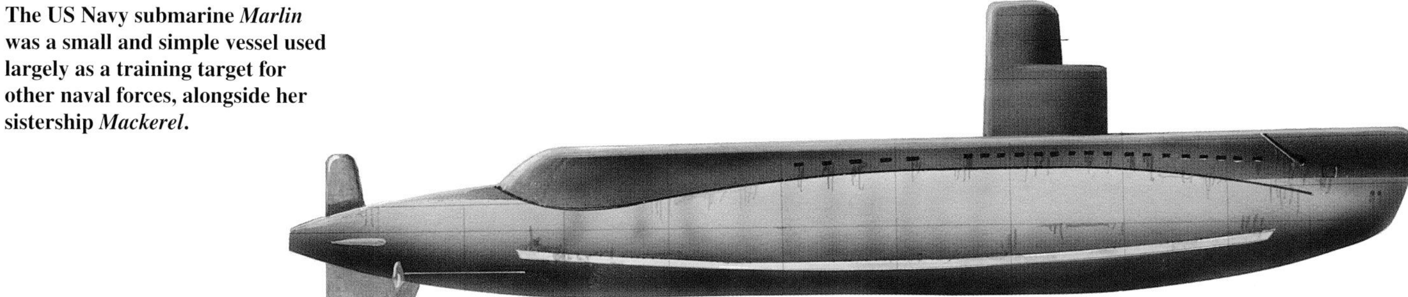

The training submarine USS *Marlin* (SST 2) was among the smallest operational submarines ever built for the US Navy. One of just two *Mackerel* class (T1) vessels built, *Marlin* was launched in July 1953 and completed in October 1953. She undertook valuable service as a target and training submarine, helping to evaluate submarine and anti-submarine equipment and tactics. In addition to duty with the Fleet Sonar School at Key West, *Marlin* participated in various fleet operations. She was finally stricken in 1973.

Displacement: 303t surfaced; 347t submerged
Dimensions: 131ft 2in x 13ft 6in x 12ft 2in (40m x 4.1m x 3.7m)
Machinery: one-shaft, two diesels and electric motors; 380hp/1050hp
Armament: one 21in (533mm) TT
Sensors: limited sonar fit
Speed: 8 knots surfaced; 9.5 knots submerged
Range: 2000nm (3704km) at 8 knots
Complement: 18

MELBOURNE

AUSTRALIA: 1949

Displacement: 16,000t standard; 19,966t full load
Dimensions: 701ft 6in x 80ft 3in x 25ft 6in (213.8m x 24.5m x 7.8m)
Machinery: two-shaft, geared steam turbines, four three-drum boilers; 42,000hp
Armament: 12 40mm cannon; 24 aircraft (eight A-4G Skyhawks, six S-2E Trackers, 10 Sea King Mk 50s)
Sensors: long-range air/surface-search radar; fire-control radar; hull-mounted sonar
Speed: 23 knots
Range: 12,000nm (22,224km) at 14 knots
Complement: 1070, plus 347 (air group)

HMAS *Melbourne* was the last Australian post-war aircraft carrier.

The aircraft carrier *Melbourne* (R 21), the former HMS *Majestic*, was transferred to the Royal Australian Navy in 1949. She was modernised with steam catapults and an angled deck before delivery. Initially her air wing consisted of Sea Venoms, Gannets and Wessex helicopters. In the late 1960s, *Melbourne* was modified to accommodate A-4G Skyhawks and S-2E Trackers, and given a new radar and electronics suite. HMAS *Melbourne* was paid off in 1982 and broken up in 1985.

MERMAID

GB: 1966

The frigate *Mermaid* was based on the *Leopard*-class design, and was ordered as the presidential yacht for Ghana's President Nkrumah. However, he was toppled by a *coup d'état* before the ship was named, and so she was acquired by the Royal Navy to serve as a training ship. HMS *Mermaid* was launched in December 1966 and completed in May 1973. Though HMS *Mermaid* gave good service to the Royal Navy, she was always 'odd ship out' and was sold to the Royal Malaysian Navy in 1977.

HMS *Mermaid* was styled after the Type 41 (*Leopard* class) frigates but without the raised forecastle deck, and with the addition of a conventional funnel.

Displacement: 2300t standard; 2520t full load
Dimensions: 340ft x 40ft x 11ft 10in (103.6m x 12.2m x 3.6m)
Machinery: two-shaft, diesel, eight diesel engines; 14,400hp
Armament: two twin 4.5in (114mm); four 40mm cannon; one Limbo Mk 10 ASW mortar
Sensors: search radar; hull-mounted sonar
Speed: 24 knots
Range: 7500nm (13,890km) at 16 knots
Complement: 235

MIKE CLASS

USSR: 1983

Project 685 (NATO code-name 'Mike') was a nuclear-powered test-bed for advanced submarine technologies. The design was initially developed in the 1960s, but the first unit was not laid down until 1978. Submarine K-278 *Komsomolets* ('member of the Young Communist League') was launched in May 1983 and commissioned in late 1984. The inner pressure hull was titanium, making her the world's deepest-diving submarine. While underwater on 7 April 1989, fire broke out in the aft compartment. *Komsomolets* sank off the coast of Norway with the loss of 42 of her 69 crew.

In addition to her own reactor, *Komsomolets* was carrying two nuclear torpedoes when she sank.

Displacement: 5750t surfaced; 8000t submerged
Dimensions: 393ft 8in x 36ft 1in x 29ft 6in (120m x 11m x 9m)
Machinery: one-shaft, nuclear, one pressurised-water reactor, two steam turbines; 43,000–47,000hp
Armament: six 21in (533mm) TT (two SS-N-15 and SS-N-16 SSM)
Sensors: surface-search radar; low-frequency active sonar
Speed: 14 knots surfaced; 30 knots submerged
Range: endurance 4500 power hours
Complement: 68

MINAS GERAIS

BRAZIL: 1956

Brazil's aircraft carrier, *Minas Gerais* (A 11), is the former HMS *Vengeance* and was transferred from Great Britain in 1956. She was then rebuilt in the Netherlands with steam catapults, an angled deck and a mirror deck landing system. Because of a dispute between the Brazilian Air Force and Navy regarding roles and missions, *Minas Gerais* spent most of her life as an ASW ship and helicopter carrier. However, the Brazilian Navy is now launching fully-fledged naval aviation operations with A-4MB Skyhawks acquired from Kuwait.

Displacement: 15,890t standard; 16,144t full load
Dimensions: 695ft x 105ft x 24 ft (211.8m x 32m x 7.3m)
Machinery: two-shaft, geared steam turbines, four three-drum boilers; 40,000hp
Armament: three Sandral/Mistral SAM launchers; two 12.7mm MG; approximately 15 aircraft (seven S-2E Trackers, eight SH-3D Sea Kings; now A-4MB Skyhawks also)
Sensors: long-range air/surface-search radar; fire-control radar; hull-mounted sonar
Speed: 24 knots
Range: 12,000nm (22,224km) at 14 knots
Complement: 1300

After decades of sterling service, *Minas Gerais* will be replaced in 2002–03 by the ex-French carrier *Foch*, which will become the *Sao Paulo*.

MIRKA CLASS

USSR:1964

Displacement: 950t standard; 1150t full load
Dimensions: 270ft 4in x 30ft 2in x 9ft 6in (82.4m x 9.2m x 2.9m)
Machinery: two-shaft, CODAG, two diesels and two gas turbines; 12,000hp/30,000hp
Armament: two twin 3in (76mm); five (*Mirka I*) or 10 (*Mirka II*) 15.75in (400mm) TT; four (*Mirka I*) or two (*Mirka II*) RBU-6000 ASW RL
Sensors: air/surface-search radar; surface-search radar; hull-mounted sonar
Speed: 32 knots
Range: 4800nm (8890km) at 14 knots
Complement: 98

This class of small Soviet frigates was designed for inshore ASW tasks. All were built rapidly between 1964 and 1966, with production split between two variants. The *Mirka I* ships had five torpedo tubes and four RBU-6000 launchers. In the later *Mirka II* ships, the aft ASW launchers were replaced by another set of torpedo tubes. Some *Mirka II* frigates were later fitted with a dipping sonar in place of the internal depth charge racks.

A total of 18 of these light frigates were built at the Kaliningrad yard, at the same time as the more successful 'Petya' programme. All *Mirka Is* and *Mirka IIs* had been discarded by 1990–91.

MITSCHER

USA: 1952

The USS *Mitscher* holds the distinction of being the first US destroyer to operate a helicopter.

The four fleet escorts laid down as the *Mitscher* class in the late 1940s were planned during World War II. They were large, all-gun destroyers that had to be adapted to meet the changing needs of the escort role, such as long-range air defence. For this task, the *Mitschers* acquired an advanced CIC and radar fit, used for directing aircraft from their own carrier battle group. ASW capability was secondary, with the *Mitschers* relying on high speed to evade enemy submarines in the first place. A new type of small turbine plant that promised high speed from a compact size powered the four ships; but it proved to be consistently troublesome and both the *Mitscher* and her sistership *John S. McCain* were reboilered. The USS *Mitscher* (DL 2) was launched in January 1952 and completed in May 1953. She was later converted to a Tartar-armed DDG, but was decommissioned in the 1970s.

Displacement: 3642t standard; 4855t full load
Dimensions: 490ft x 47ft 6in x 14ft 8in (149.3m x 14.5m x 4.5m)
Machinery: two-shaft, geared turbines, four boilers; 80,000hp
Armament: one Tarter SAM launcher (later); two 5in (127mm), four 3in (76mm) (later two, then none); eight 20mm cannon; four 21in (533mm) TT; two Weapon Alfa ASW RL (later one, then none); one DC rack
Sensors: air/surface-search radar; navigation radar; fire-control radar; hull-mounted sonar
Speed: 36.5 knots
Range: 4500nm (8334km) at 20 knots
Complement: approximately 300

MOSKVA

USSR (RUSSIA): 1964

At the time of her construction, *Moskva* was the largest ship ever built by the Soviet Union.

Displacement: 14,590t standard; 17,500t full load
Dimensions: 620ft 1in x 85ft 4in x 42ft 8in (189m x 26m x 13m)
Machinery: two-shaft, two steam turbines and four oil-fired steam boilers; 90,000-100,000hp
Armament: two twin SA-N-3 SAM launchers (44 missiles); one twin SUW-N-1 missile launcher; two twin 57mm AA; 10 21in (533mm) TT (later removed); 14 Ka-25 'Hormone' helicopters
Sensors: air/surface-search radar; fire-control radar; hull-mounted sonar
Speed: 31 knots
Range: 13,500nm (25,002km) at 12 knots
Complement: 850 (including air group)

The two Project 1123 Kondor ships were developed to counter Western strategic missile submarines. Their task was to hunt down Polaris submarines in the open ocean and then call the accompanying battle group to destroy them. As such, the *Moskvas* carried a relatively small number of helicopters (about 14 Ka-25 'Hormone As') and tried to keep the overall ship size down, while still retaining a measure of flexibility. These were the first Soviet aviation ships, and their design was something of a hybrid, with features of a missile cruiser forward and a flight deck aft of the superstructure. The design was heavily influenced by the French helicopter carrier *Jeanne D'Arc* and the Italian helicopter carrier *Vittorio Veneto*. *Moskva* was laid down in December 1962, launched in January 1964 and commissioned in December 1967. The two ships deployed to the Mediterranean, the Atlantic and the Indian Ocean. They were designated as 'aviation cruisers' at least in part to avoid problems with the 1936 Montreaux Convention, which prohibited the passage of 'aircraft carriers' through the Dardanelles. Despite their graceful appearance, the *Moskvas* had a tendency to ride down in the bow, and ultimately they proved ineffective and unreliable. Western predictions that up to 12 Project 1123 carriers would eventually be built proved to be very wide of the mark. *Moskva* was retired to the reserve in 1983 and scrapped in 1997. *Leningrad* was scrapped even earlier, in 1991.

MOUNT WHITNEY

USA: 1970

The US Navy command ship USS *Mount Whitney* (AGC 20, later LCC 20) is a sistership of the USS *Blue Ridge* and, despite their origins in the late 1960s, they are the successors of the merchant-hull conversions of World War II. They follow the same design lines as the earlier LPH helicopter carriers, but with a completely rearranged interior to allow for command space and communications facilities. It had been planned to build six such ships, but the advent of the new LHAs largely did away with the need for dedicated command ships. However, *Mount Whitney* and *Blue Ridge* have been deployed as command flagships in nearly every major US naval operation staged since their commissioning. The USS *Mount Whitney* was launched in January 1970, and soon replaced the command cruiser USS *Oklahoma City*. She has been improved and upgraded, and is still an important part of the active fleet.

USS *Mount Whitney's* flight deck is no longer used for regular helicopter operations, though she can accommodate one utility helicopter of her own.

Displacement: 19,290t full load
Dimensions: 620ft x 108ft x 27ft (189m x 32.9m x 8.2m)
Machinery: one-shaft, geared turbines, two boilers; 22,000hp
Armament: two Sea Sparrow SAM launchers (later removed); four 3in (76mm) (later removed); two 20mm Phalanx CIWS; one helicopter
Sensors: air/surface-search radar; navigation radar; fire-control radar; hull-mounted sonar
Speed: 20 knots
Range: 13,000nm (24,076km) at 20 knots
Complement: 720, plus 700 (flag staff)

MOURAD RAIS

ALGERIA: 1978

Displacement: 1440t standard; 1900t full load
Dimensions: 311ft 8in x 42ft x 13ft 9in (95m x 12.8m x 4.2m)
Machinery: three-shaft, CODAG, two diesels and gas turbine; 35,000hp
Armament: one twin SA-N-4 SAM launcher; two twin 3in (76mm); two twin 30mm cannon; two RBU-6000 ASW RL; two DC racks
Sensors: air/surface-search radar; navigation radar; hull-mounted sonar
Speed: 27 knots
Range: 1800nm (3334km) at 14 knots
Complement: 110

Beginning in 1980, the Algerian Navy took delivery of three Soviet-built *Koni*-class frigates. The *Koni* class was built entirely for export to 'friendly' nations. These vessels (more accurately described as corvettes) are still the largest naval vessels in Algerian service and provide a small degree of ocean-going capability. Launched in 1979, the *Mourad Rais* was the first of the *Konis* to be delivered, arriving in Algeria in December 1980. The last of the three ships arrived in 1984.

The Algerian Navy's *Koni* class ASW frigates were never fitted with the SS-N-2 anti-ship missiles delivered to other customers.

MURASAME

JAPAN: 1994

The *Murasame* class ships are the latest destroyers to enter Japanese service. Designed to operate alongside the *Kongo* class Aegis destroyers, the *Murasames* are essentially air defence missile carriers, armed with two large vertical launch Sea Sparrow SAM systems. The launcher boxes can also fire ASROC missiles and may yet be upgraded to carry Standard SAMs. Japan hopes to acquire nine of these ships. The first, *Murasame* (DD 101), was launched in September 1994 and commissioned in 1996.

***Murasame*'s advanced fire control system is capable of guiding up to 16 Sea Sparrow missiles simultaneously.**

Displacement: 4400t standard; 5100t full load
Dimensions: 495ft 5in x 55ft 7in x 17ft 1in (151m x 16.9m x 5.2m)
Machinery: COGAG, four gas turbines; 84,630hp
Armament: eight Harpoon SSM; two Mk 41 VLS with 100 Standard missiles and ASROC torpedoes; one 3in (76mm); two 20mm Phalanx CIWS; six 12.75in (324mm) TT; one SH-60J helicopter
Sensors: air/surface-search radar; navigation radar; fire-control radar; hull-mounted sonar and towed array
Speed: 33 knots
Range: 4500nm (8334km) at 20 knots
Complement: 170

MUTENIA

ROMANIA: 1982

The Romanian missile destroyer *Mutenia* was an ambitious attempt at indigenous shipbuilding, using Soviet weapons, systems and engines. *Mutenia* is a large vessel, but was under-armed and lacked the kind of modern ASW fit essential to a vessel of her intended class. *Mutenia* (111) was launched in 1982 and commissioned in June 1985. She has spent long periods out of service due to lack of funds and has been offered for sale.

Displacement: 4500t standard; 5790t full load
Dimensions: 474ft 4in x 48ft 6in x 23ft (144.6m x 14.8m x 7m)
Machinery: two-shaft, four diesel engines; 31,000hp
Armament: eight SS-N-2C SSM; two twin 3in (76mm); eight 30mm cannon; six 21in (533mm) TT; two RBU-120 ASW RL (later RBU-6000); two Alouette III helicopters
Sensors: air/surface-search radar; navigation radar; fire-control radar; hull-mounted sonar
Speed: 31 knots
Range: not available
Complement: 270

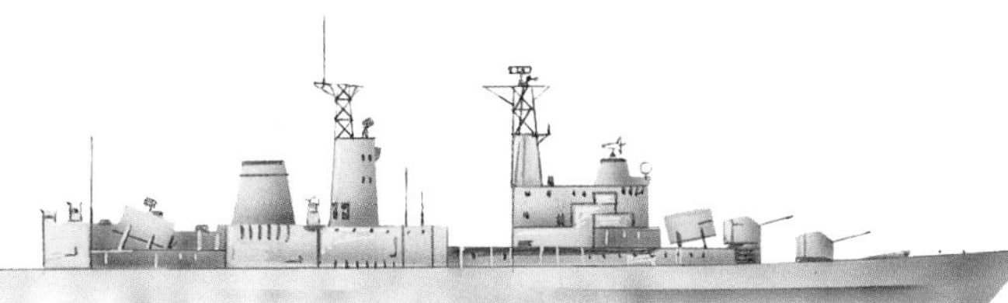

Between 1990 and 1992, *Mutenia* was refitted with smaller masts and re-equipped with different ASW systems.

NÄCKEN

SWEDEN: 1978

Displacement: 980t surfaced; 1150t submerged
Dimensions: 162ft 5in x 18ft 8in x 18ft (49.5m x 5.7m x 5.5m)
Machinery: one-shaft, diesel engine, electric motor; 2100hp/1150kW (later with AIP)
Armament: six 21in (533mm) and two 15.75in (400mm) TT (12 torpedoes)
Sensors: surface-search radar; active sonar
Speed: 20 knots surfaced; 25 knots submerged
Range: not available
Complement: 19

Sweden has long maintained a sophisticated submarine design and manufacturing capability of its own. During the early 1980s, the most advanced vessels in its submarine fleet were the three *Näcken* class (A14) boats, which were all laid down in 1976. The lead ship in the class, *Näcken*, was launched in April 1978 and completed in April 1980. Each of the submarines carried large three-letter pennant letters on their conning towers – in *Näcken*'s case they read 'Näk'. During 1987–88, the three *Näckens* were taken back into dry dock and fitted with a new closed-cycle air independent propulsion (AIP) system. These new powerplants required the submarines' hulls to be extended by 26 ft 3in (8m) – a not insubstantial amount. Experience with these AIP engines paved the way for the latest generation of AIP-powered Swedish submarines, the *Vastergötland* class, which are now entering service. As a result of substantial cuts to the Swedish defence budget, only the three *Vastergötlands* will ultimately remain in service, so the *Näcken* class has now been retired.

Thanks to its new AIP engines, *Näcken* no longer needed to surface to feed air to its diesel engines and could stay completely submerged for 14 days.

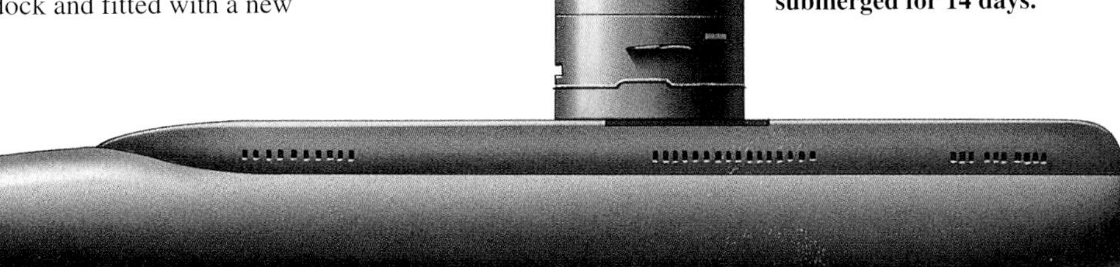

NAJIN

NORTH KOREA: 1972

The two *Najin*-class frigates built in North Korea in the early 1970s were obsolete before they were ever launched. They were armed with World War II-vintage Soviet-supplied main guns and a radar fit from the 1950s. Even the SS-N-2A SSMs they carried were removed from *Osa*-class attack craft and bolted on. The lead ship (3025) was launched in 1972 and completed the following year. The name and pennant numbers of both ships have been changed and are no longer clear.

The *Najin* class is reminiscent of the Soviet *Kola*-class frigates, but featured alternative diesel engines.

Displacement: 1200t standard; 1500t full load
Dimensions: 328ft x 32ft 6in x 8ft 10in (100m x 9.9m x 2.7m)
Machinery: two-shaft, two diesels; 15,000hp
Armament: two 3.9in (100mm), four 57mm; four 25mm cannon (later 12); eight 14.5mm MG (later removed); three 21in (533mm) TT; two RBU-1200 ASW RL
Sensors: air/surface-search radar; navigation radar; fire-control radar; hull-mounted sonar
Speed: 33 knots
Range: 4000nm (7408km) at 14 knots
Complement: 155–180

NANUCHKA I CLASS

USSR: 1969

The heavily armed Project 1234 *Nanuchka I*-class guided missile corvettes bristled with more gun and air defence systems than previous Soviet missile ships. The remarkable amount of firepower and combat electronics mounted on such a small platform was apparently purchased at the price of poor sea-keeping characteristics. All *Nanuchka Is* are being scrapped, though it is difficult to establish how many remain operational and in particular, which ships remain in service.

Known as small missile ships (Malyy Raketnyy Korabl, MRK), all 'Nanuchka Is' served with Soviet forces. The 'Nanuchka II' was built for India and the 'Nanuchka III' for Algeria and Libya.

Displacement: 560t standard; 660t full load
Dimensions: 194ft 7in x 41ft 4in x 7ft 11in (59.3m x 12.6m x 2.4m)
Machinery: three paired diesel engines; 30,000hp
Armament: six SS-N-9 SSM; one SA-N-4 SAM launcher (20 missiles); one 3in (76mm) or two 57mm
Sensors: search radar; navigation radar; fire-control radar; hull-mounted sonar
Speed: 32 knots
Range: 2500nm (4630km) at 12 knots
Complement: 60

NAREUSAN — THAILAND: 1993

In 1989, Thailand ordered two Type 25T frigates from China. These vessels are based on the *Jianghu* class but are far more combat-capable. They incorporate Western machinery, armament and electronic systems, much of which was fitted in Thailand after the ships had been delivered from China. The lead vessel in the class, *Nareusan* (621), was launched in April 1993 and the second ship followed in 1994. *Nareusan* is capable of embarking a helicopter in the *Lynx* or SH-2 *Seasprite* class.

Thailand is so far the only foreign nation to order large combat vessels from the Chinese State shipyards.

Displacement: 2500t standard; 2980t full load
Dimensions: 393ft 8in x 42ft 8in x 12ft 6in (119.99m x 13m x 3.81m)
Machinery: two-shaft, CODOG, two gas turbines and two diesel engines; 44,000hp/14,720hp
Armament: eight Harpoon SSM; one Mk 41 VLS (eight Sea Sparrow SAM); one 5in (127mm), two twin 37mm; six 12.75in (324mm) TT
Sensors: air/surface-search radar; navigation radar; fire-control radar; hull-mounted sonar
Speed: 32 knots
Range: 4000nm (7408km) at 18 knots
Complement: 150

NARWHAL — USA: 1967

Displacement: 4246t surfaced; 4777t submerged
Dimensions: 292ft 3in x 31ft 8in x 25ft 6in (89.1m x 9.6m x 7.8m)
Machinery: one-shaft, nuclear, one reactor; 15,000hp
Armament: four 21in (533mm) TT
Sensors: general-purpose radar; active/passive multi-function sonar
Speed: 26 knots submerged
Range: limited only by reactor fuel state
Complement: 99

The third US Navy submarine to carry the name 'Narwhal' was laid down in January 1966 as a member of the *Sturgeon* class of nuclear-powered attack submarines. The USS *Narwhal* (SSN 671) was launched in September 1967 and commissioned in July 1969. Like her sisterships, *Narwhal* assumed the status of one the largest 'straight' nuclear-powered attack submarines then built by the US Navy. The *Sturgeon* class followed on from the *Thresher/Permit* class attack submarines but were much larger ships, partly because of their different nuclear reactor. As a one-off trials fit, *Narwhal* incorporated a new type of S5G natural convection powerplant that promised greater endurance than had hitherto been possible. This new reactor also reduced the submarine's noise level and, at the time of her commissioning, *Narwhal* was reputed to be the quietest submarine in US naval service. *Narwhal* was de-activated, while still in commission, in January 1999. Along with all the other retiring nuclear-powered vessels, she will be disposed of through the US Navy's Nuclear Powered Ship and Submarine Recycling Program in Bremerton, Washington.

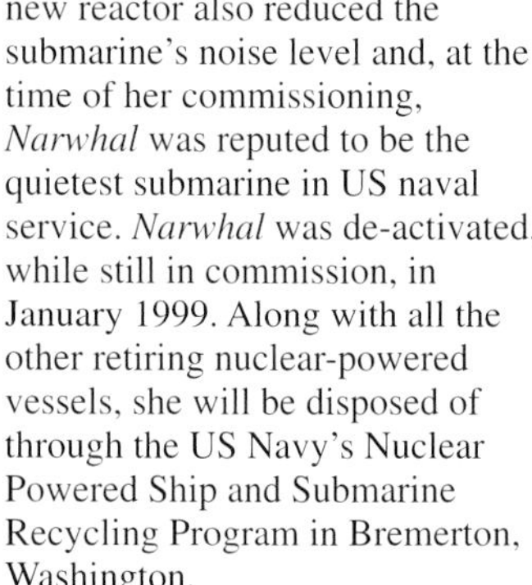

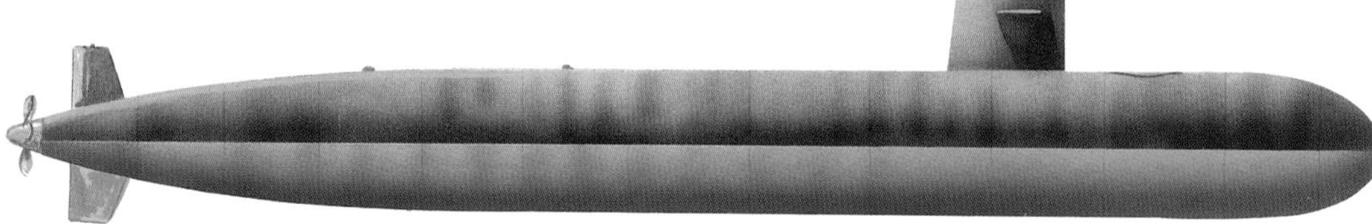

Like the other remaining *Sturgeon*-class boats, *Narwhal* was retired to make way for an all-*Los Angeles*-class attack submarine fleet.

NASR AL BAHR — OMAN: 1984

Displacement: 2500t full load
Dimensions: 305ft 1in x 50ft 10in x 7ft 6in (93m x 15.5m x 2.3m)
Machinery: two-shaft, two diesel engines; 7800hp
Armament: four 40mm and two 20mm cannon
Sensors: navigation radar
Speed: 16 knots
Range: 4000nm (7408km) at 13 knots
Complement: 81 plus 240 troops

The Omani Navy ordered this Algerian-built *Kalaat* class landing ship in 1982. Christened *Nasr Al Bahr* (L 2), she was launched in May 1984 and completed in February 1985, by Brooke Marine in Great Britain. *Nasr Al Bahr* has a vehicle deck that can accommodate seven main battle tanks, and is fitted with a beaching ramp and two Sea Truck LCVP landing craft. There is also a stern-mounted flight deck, capable of handling a Sea King helicopter.

By far the largest ship in the Omani Navy, *Nasr Al Bahr* can carry a maximum load of 650t.

NAUTILUS

USA: 1954

Displacement: 3533t surfaced; 4092t submerged
Dimensions: 323ft 9in x 27ft 8in x 21ft 9in (98.7m x 8.4m x 6.6m)
Machinery: two-shaft, nuclear, one reactor; 15,000hp
Armament: six 21in (533mm) TT
Sensors: sonar
Speed: 23 knots submerged
Range: limited only by reactor fuel state
Complement: 105

***Nautilus* holds the great distinction of being the world's first nuclear-powered warship and the first vessel to reach the North Pole.**

The fourth *Nautilus* was the world's first nuclear-powered warship. Her name not only commemmorated two previous US submarines, but also Fulton's early submersible. Her keel was laid down on 14 June 1952, by President Truman. The USS *Nautilus* (SSN 571) was launched in January 1954 and commissioned in September 1954. She was a great success, not least because the hull design was conventional to avoid unnecessary risk. Captain Hyman G Rickover, USN, the head of a group of scientists and engineers at the Naval Reactors Branch of the Atomic Energy Commission, had stressed reactor safety as an absolute priority. The penalty for failure of this revolutionary submarine would be immense; not only was a large amount of money at stake, but the prestige of the United States was involved. On 17 January 1955, at 1100 hours, she cast off and reported 'underway on nuclear power' for the very first time. During her shakedown trials, she remained submerged *en route* to Puerto Rico, covering 1200nm (2222km) in 89.8 hours – the longest submerged cruise to date by any submarine and at the highest sustained submerged speed ever recorded. On 4 February 1957, *Nautilus* logged her 60,000th nautical mile (111,120km), bringing to reality the fictional achievements of her famed literary namesake in Jules Verne's novel *20,000 Leagues Under the Sea*. In August 1957, she departed for her first voyage, of 1202nm (2226km), under polar pack ice. A year later, on 3 August 1958, she became the first ship to reach the geographic North Pole. From there she continued on course and, after 96 hours and 1590nm (2945km) under the ice, she surfaced north-east of Greenland, having completed the first successful voyage across the North Pole. *Nautilus* participated in several NATO exercises and, during 1962, she was deployed as part of the naval blockade of Cuba. Afterwards, she headed east again for a two-month Mediterranean tour in August 1963. Most of her subsequent operational career was spent in the Atlantic, but from 1969 onwards, she took up a permanent trials role. *Nautilus* was finally retired to a museum in 1982.

***Nautilus* went on to operate with the Atlantic fleet, conducting evaluation tests for ASW improvements.**

NAZARIO SAURO

ITALY: 1976

Ordered in 1967 but later delayed, Italy's *Nazario Sauro* (S 518) was the first of four *Sauro*-class attack submarines. The class was cancelled and then reordered in 1972, with the *Nazario Sauro* launched in October 1976 and completed in March 1980. Equipped with MD100S passive ranging and a French Velox sonar receiver, the *Nazario Sauro* is armed with 12 A184 wire-guided torpedoes. The first Italian submarine constructed from HY-80 steel, the *Nazario Sauro* has an operating depth of 820ft (250m).

Displacement: 1456t surfaced; 1641t submerged
Dimensions: 209ft 7in x 22ft 5in x 18ft 9in (63.9m x 6.8m x 5.7m)
Machinery: one-shaft, three diesels plus one electric motor; 3210hp/3650hp
Armament: six 21in (533mm) TT (12 torpedoes)
Sensors: navigation/surface-search radar; sonar
Speed: 11 knots surfaced; 19 knots submerged
Range: 7000nm (12,964km) at 12 knots
Complement: 45

The *Nazario Sauro* underwent an upgrade during the 1990s, with new batteries, improved accommodation and a BSN-716 integrated combat system being fitted.

NEUSTRASHIMYY

USSR: 1951

The *Neustrashimyy* was planned as the first of 110 Project 41 destroyers. This new class was to have been the first Soviet destroyer of post-war design, and introduced a range of innovations including dual-purpose guns, pressure-fired steam plant, AC electrical power, new weapons and minimal superstructure. The ship's primary armament was similar to the secondary battery of the *Sverdlov*-class cruiser, with a pair of twin 5.1in (130mm) stabilised gun turrets. Designed to survive in a nuclear environment, the ship also introduced radiator heating and air-conditioning, and lacked conventional air-ports. In the event, only the lead ship was built, and the class was cancelled before trials were complete. Some Soviet sources even suggest that the class was cancelled while the *Neustrashimyy* was still under construction, purely on the grounds of its size and cost. Built by Zhdanov and launched on 29 January 1951, the *Neustrashimyy* was completed on 31 January 1955, but proved slower than expected, while also suffering from excessive vibration aft and excessive spray forward. Judged to be too large, unwieldy and impractical, the *Neustrashimyy* was replaced by the smaller but similarly equipped *Kotlin* class (Project 56). The plans were then sold to China, forming the basis of the 'Luda' class. The ship's innovative pressure-fired KV-41 boilers also formed the basis of the steam plant used in subsequent Soviet surface combatants. The *Neustrashimyy* was modernised in 1959, with four four-gun SM-20 ZiF turrets replacing the original four SM-16s, and with new propellers, radar, and communications antennae. Thereafter, the vessel (known to NATO as the *Tallinn* class) was used as a Baltic Fleet staff ship and as a training ship for construction workers, before being broken up in 1975.

Displacement: 3100t standard; 3830t full load
Dimensions: 439ft 1in x 44ft 6in x 14ft 6in (133.8m x 13.6m x 4.4m)
Machinery: two-shaft, geared turbines, four boilers; 66,000hp
Armament: four 5.1in (130mm), eight 45mm; two unidentified ASW rocket launchers; 10 21in (533mm) ASW TT; depth charges; mines
Sensors: air-search radar; surface-search radar; sonar
Speed: 36 knots
Range: not available
Complement: 305

The rakish-looking *Neustrashimyy* was exceptionally sleek, with very little superstructure above the weather deck.

NEUSTRASHIMYY

USSR: 1988

Displacement: 3500t full load
Dimensions: 426ft 6in x 50ft 11in x 18ft 5in (130m x 15.5m x 5.6m)
Machinery: two-shaft, four gas turbines; 110,000hp
Armament: one SS-N-25 SSM launcher; one SA-N-9 SAM launcher; two CADS-N-1 gun/missile CIWS; one RBU-12000 ASW RL; six torpedo launchers (can be used with SS-N-15); one helicopter
Sensors: air/surface-search radar; navigation radar; fire-control radar; hull-mounted sonar and VDS/towed array
Speed: 32 knots
Range: 4500nm (8334km) at 25 knots
Complement: 210

The new Project 1154 *Neustrashimyy*-class frigate was designed to meet a 1972 specification for a small ASW frigate to replace the Project 1124 *Grisha* class, and also the Project 1135 *Krivak* class. Designed for low signature, the *Neustrashimyy* had a flat-flared hull, with superstructure levels broken up and the stacks shaped to reduce and disperse radar returns. The *Neustrashimyy* was designed to fire a version of the standard submarine ASW missile (the SS-N-15) from catapults, leaving the rear deck free for a helicopter.

Although four ships were built, the class was not a success, and the vessels were replaced by *Parchim*-class corvettes bought from East Germany, and by modernised the *Grisha*-class frigates.

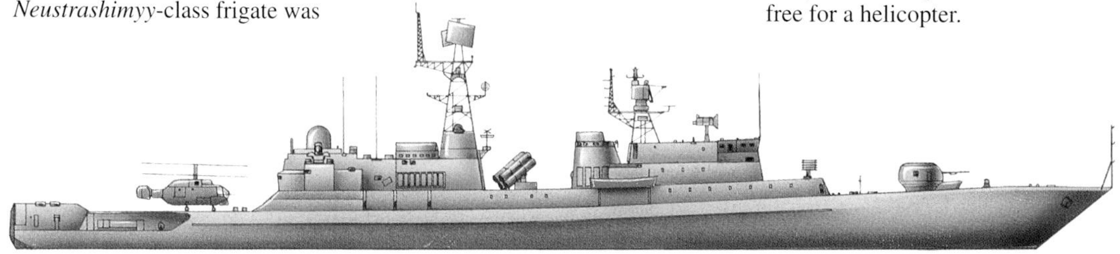

NIELS JUEL

DENMARK: 1978

The Aalborg-built *Niels Juel* (F 354) was the lead ship in a class of three indigenous Danish corvettes. Ordered in 1975, the *Niels Juel* was launched on 17 February 1978 and completed in January 1979. Equipped with Harpoon and Sea Sparrow missiles, the ship never received the ASW torpedo system that had been planned for it. sistership the *Olfert Fischer* served with UN Forces in the Gulf during 1991. The class was refitted from 1995, with various improvements.

Although indigenously designed and built, the *Niels Juel* incorporated armament and equipment produced by a variety of Denmark's NATO partners, from US gas turbines to Dutch electronics.

Displacement: 1190t standard; 1320t full load
Dimensions: 275ft 6in x 33ft 9in x 13ft (84m x 10.3m x 4m)
Machinery: two-shaft, CODOG: one diesel and one gas turbine; 4800hp/18,400hp
Armament: two quad Harpoon SSM launchers; one Mk 29 Sea Sparrow SAM launcher; one OTO Melara 3in (76mm); four Oerlikon 20mm cannon; depth charges
Sensors: air-search radar; surface-search radar; navigation radar; fire-control radar; hull-mounted sonar
Speed: 28 knots
Range: 2500nm (4630km) at 18 knots
Complement: 90

NIGERIA

NIGERIA: 1965

Displacement: 1724t standard; 2000t full load
Dimensions: 360ft 3in x 37ft x 11ft 6in (109.8m x 11.2m x 3.5m)
Machinery: two-shaft, four diesels; 16,000hp
Armament: two Mk 19 4in (101mm); four Oerlikon Mk 7 40mm cannon; one Admiralty Squid ASW mortar system
Sensors: search radar; fire-control radar; hull-mounted sonar
Speed: 26 knots
Range: 3500nm (6482km) at 15 knots
Complement: 216

The frigate *Nigeria* (F 87) was ordered from the Netherlands Shipbuilding Bureau for a price of £3.5m, and was completed in September 1965. She participated in a surprisingly effective blockade during the Biafran crisis, and was refitted at Birkenhead in 1973. The ship was refitted again at Schiedam in 1977, and was renamed as the *Obuma* in 1981. She was increasingly relegated to training duties following the Nigerian Navy's acquisition of the newer *Aradu*. In recent years, patchy funding has often left the *Obuma* unable to put to sea.

***Nigeria* was designed to serve as a combined escort, training ship and flagship for the Nigerian Navy.**

NITEROI

BRAZIL: 1974

The *Niteroi* (F 40) was the lead ship in a class of six frigates designed by Vosper Thorneycroft for the Brazilian Navy as the Mk 10, under a 1970 contract. Similar in size and complexity to the British *Sheffield* class (Type 42), the Brazilian Navy ships required 100 fewer men to operate them, and were extremely modern. They bore a passing resemblance to the Royal Navy's Type 21 Amazon class frigates. The *Niteroi* was laid down on 8 June 1972, launched on 8 February 1974 and completed on 20 November 1976. While *Niteroi*, *Defensora*, *Constituicao* and *Liberal* were built in Great Britain, *Independencia* and *Uniao* were built in Brazil by Arsenal de Marinho, the latter two vessels being completed in 1979 and 1980, having been laid down on 11 June 1972. This was an impressive achievement by the new shipyard. Arsenal de Marinho had the two largest dry-docks in Latin America and this allowed the nation to participate in the construction of its vital Mk 10 frigates. A seventh ship based on the *Niteroi* was ordered from Arsenal de Marinho as the training ship *Brazil*. Two of the Vosper Thorneycroft-built ships were built as general-purpose frigates, and had an extra 4.5in (114mm) gun and four MM38 Exocet SSM in place of the other (ASW-dedicated) ships' Lynx helicopter, hangar and Ikara (Branik) ASW missile system. All seven remain in service and are a source of enormous pride within the Brazilian Navy.

Brazil's *Niteroi*-class frigates have been divided for specific tasks, with some as dedicated ASW vessels and the others serving as general-purpose frigates.

Displacement: 3200t standard; 3800t full load
Dimensions: 424ft x 44ft 2in x 18ft 2in (129.2m x 13.5m x 5.5m)
Machinery: two-shaft, CODAG, two gas turbines, four diesels; 56,000hp/18,000hp
Armament: four MM40 Exocet SSM; two GWS34 Seacat SAM launchers; one Ikara ASW missile system; one Vickers Mk 8 4.5in (114mm); two Bofors 40mm cannon;, six Mk 32 12.75in (324mm) ASW TT; one depth charge rack; one helicopter
Sensors: air/surface-search radar; surface-search radar; fire-control radar; hull-mounted sonar
Speed: 30 knots
Range: 5,300nm at 17 knots
Complement: 200

NORFOLK

USA: 1961

Based on the older *Atlanta*-class cruisers, the USS *Norfolk* (DL 1) was laid down as an ASW cruiser, but was actually completed as a 'Destroyer Leader' or Ocean Escort. This was a new category of ship aimed at countering the latest generation of Soviet submarines. Unfortunately, the ship was so large and so expensive that a planned sistership was never laid down. The ship incorporated some lessons from the Bikini Atoll nuclear bomb tests, with decks designed to allow fallout to 'wash away', and an enclosed bridge. The ship was fitted with slow-turning propellers for minimum noise, and relied on homing torpedoes as its primary weapon, with an automatic rocket launcher as back-up and with guns for anti-aircraft use. Completed in March 1953, the USS *Norfolk* was very much a one-off, and was used primarily for trials of new equipment, sensors and weapons, including ASROC and electronically-scanned radar. The ship was stricken in 1973.

The *Norfolk* closely resembled the earlier *Atlanta*-class cruisers, except in its armament and enclosed bridge.

Displacement: 2950t full load
Dimensions: 375ft 6in x 39ft 8in x 18ft (114.4m x 12.1m x 5.5m)
Machinery: two-shaft, geared turbines; 60,000hp
Armament: two 5in (127mm), four 3in (76mm) secondary guns; eight 20mm cannon; one Weapon System Alfa ASW system (automatic rocket launcher); one Hedgehog anti-submarine mortar; four 21in (533mm) TT
Sensors: air-search radar; hull-mounted sonar
Speed: 33 knots
Range: 6000nm (11,112km) at 16 knots
Complement: 546

NORTHAMPTON

USA: 1951

Displacement: 17,049t full load
Dimensions: 677ft 2in x 69ft 9in x 24ft (206.4m x 21.3m x 7.3m)
Machinery: four-shaft, four geared turbines, four boilers; 120,000hp
Armament: four 5in (127mm), eight 3in (76mm)
Sensors: long-range air-search radar; air/surface-search radar
Speed: 32.8 knots
Range: 7000nm (12,964km) at 20 knots
Complement: 1635

The *Northampton* (CLC 1) was laid down as a cruiser, but was redesigned as a specialised Amphibious Command Ship. Before completion, she was redesigned again as a fast carrier force flagship, equipped with the long-range air defence radar and combat information centre that could not easily be accommodated in the new aircraft carriers themselves. The advent of the angled flight deck removed the limitations on carrier island size and, as new carriers were built with their own radar and CIC facilities, *Northampton* remained unique. She was decommissioned in 1970.

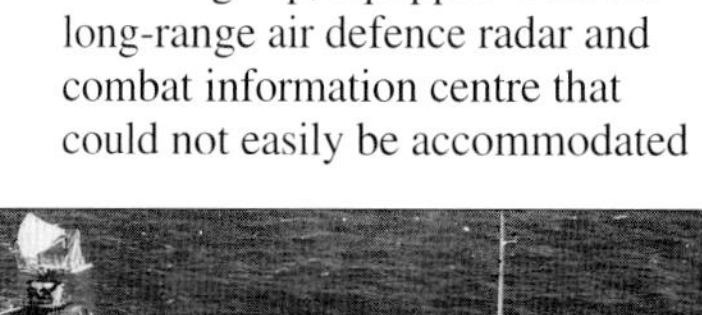

The *Northampton* remained a one-off, plans to convert the battle cruiser *Hawaii* to a similar standard being cancelled on cost grounds in 1954.

NOVEMBER CLASS

RUSSIA:1957

The *November* class (Project 627 Kit) submarines were Russia's first nuclear-powered submarines. The first example of 14 built, *K-3*, was delivered in March 1959. Originally conceived as a strategic anti-ship submarine firing a single 25-mile (40km) range nuclear torpedo, the design was refined into an attack submarine with eight torpedo tubes in the bow, capable of firing 24 conventional torpedoes. Early problems with reactor cooling often limited the performance of the *November* class submarines, but when working properly, the vessels were extremely fast, as one demonstrated in February 1968 when chasing the US aircraft carrier *Enterprise*. Her good performance became a factor in the US Navy's acquisition of its new *Los Angeles*-class attack submarines. Attempts to produce versions of the *November* armed with Ilyushin P-20 cruise missiles did not progress beyond a single prototype stage. The operational career of the *November*s was overshadowed by a series of accidents and incidents, two being lost to fires following steam-generator faults and two more suffering severe reactor accidents.

Perhaps the most obvious distinguishing feature of the *November*-class submarine was its exceptionally small and rounded sail.

Displacement: 4500t surfaced; 5300t submerged
Dimensions: 363ft 11in x 29ft 6in x 23ft 5in (110.9m x 9m x 7.1m)
Machinery: two-shaft, nuclear, one nuclear reactor; 30,000hp
Armament: eight 21in (533mm) TT (24 torpedoes)
Sensors: surface-search radar; attack sonar
Speed: 30 knots submerged
Range: limited only by reactor fuel state
Complement: 80

OBERON

GB: 1959

The Royal Navy's HMS *Oberon* (S 09) was the first in a class of 14 diesel-electric patrol submarines derived from the successful eight-boat *Porpoise* class, but with detailed improvements, including a maximum dive depth in excess of 1000ft (305m). *Oberon*, *Onslaught*, *Ocelot* and *Onyx* were built at Chatham (*Onyx* going straight to the Royal Canadian Navy); *Odin*, *Oracle*, *Opossum* and a replacement *Onyx* by Cammell-Laird; *Orpheus*, *Olympus* and *Osiris* by Vickers-Armstrong and *Otter*, *Otus* and *Opportune* by Scotts. Exceptionally quiet, the *Oberons* were renowned as being deadly hunter-killers, and one was bought 'on the stocks' by the Royal Canadian Navy, along with two more which were 'built-to-order'. Extensively modified and modernised in the 1980s, most Oberons received a new sonar, EW and combat systems and a clip-on towed array. Intended to remain in service until fully replaced by new *Upholder* class submarines, the *Oberons* were retired early as part of the 1991 defence cuts.

The *Oberon* class were among the quietest submarines ever built, and were extremely hard to detect. They proved to be well suited to special missions tasks.

Displacement: 2030t surfaced; 2410t submerged
Dimensions: 290ft 3in x 26ft 6in x 18ft 3in (88.5m x 8.1m x 5.6m)
Machinery: two-shaft, diesel-electric, two diesels plus two electric motors; 3680hp/6000hp
Armament: eight 21in (533mm) TT (30 Mk 24 torpedoes)
Sensors: search radar; navigation radar; sonar
Speed: 12 knots surfaced; 17 knots submerged
Range: 9000nm (16,668km) at 12 knots
Complement: 64

OBSERVATION ISLAND

USA: 1956

Displacement: 17,015t standard
Dimensions: 564ft x 76ft x 28ft 7in (171.9m x 23.2m x 8.7m)
Machinery: one-shaft, geared turbines, two boilers; 19,250hp
Armament: none
Sensors: phased-array radar; dish antenna
Speed: 20 knots
Range: not available
Complement: varies

Officially described as a missile range instrumentation ship, the US Naval Ship *Observation Island* (T-AGM-23) is designed to detect, track and collect intelligence data on US, Russian and other ballistic missile tests over the Pacific Ocean. *Observation Island* carries the huge AN/SPQ-11 'Cobra Judy' phased-array radar, designed to detect and track ICBMs launched by Russia in their west-to-east missile range. She is a converted merchant ship, modified first as a fleet ballistic missile test launch platform, then as a missile-tracking platform.

***Observation Island* was laid down as the SS *Empire State Mariner* in 1952.**

OCEAN

GB: 1998

Displacement: 20,000t standard
Dimensions: 668ft x 107ft x 21ft 4in (203.6m x 32.6m x 6.5m)
Machinery: two-shaft, two diesels; 23,904hp + bow thruster
Armament: four BAE/Oerlikon twin 30mm cannon; three Mk 15 Phalanx 20mm CIWS; up to 12 Merlin and six Lynx helicopters; landing and refuelling facilities for Harrier GR.7/Sea Harrier FA.2 aircraft and Chinook HC.2/.3 helicopters
Sensors: combat data system
Speed: 18 knots
Range: 8000nm (14,816km) at 18 knots
Complement: 255, crew plus 686 (206 aircrew, 480 marines); up to 800 troops can be embarked

HMS *Ocean* (L 12) was ordered in 1992 to fulfil a 1987 requirement for a lightly armed Aviation Support ship whose primary role would be as a helicopter carrier for training and deployments. The vessel was designed to be capable of embarking, supporting and operating a full squadron of helicopters, while simultaneously carrying the bulk of a full Royal Marine Commando with its vehicles, weapons and equipment. Kvaerner Govan built the hull on the Clyde, sailing under its own power to VSEL at Barrow in November 1996 for fitting out. HMS *Ocean* was commissioned in September 1998, and has made operational deployments to the Adriatic and Sierra Leone.

HMS *Ocean* is a Commando Helicopter Support Ship and not an aircraft carrier, but could carry up to 20 Harrier GR.7s/Sea Harrier FA.2s.

OGNEVOY

USSR (RUSSIA): 1963

The Soviet Project 61 design was an air defence/ASW patrol ship to replace the *Kotlin* and *Riga* classes. *Ognevoy* was the third of 20 Project 61 guided missile destroyers (known to NATO as the *Kashin* class), and one of six ships in the class modernised in the mid-1970s with improved air defence armament, sonar and cruise missiles. She was one of the last in the class to be retired, and was broken up in 1990. Five additional *Kashins* were built for India, entering service from 1980.

Although designed as an air defence and ASW destroyer, the air defence role soon came to dominate the operations of *Ognevoy* and her sisterships.

Displacement: 3400t standard; 4390t full load
Dimensions: 472ft 5in x 51ft 10in x 15ft 1in (144m x 15.8m x 4.6m)
Machinery: two-shaft, CODAG, four gas turbines; 72,000hp
Armament: two SA-N-1 SSM launchers; four 3in (76mm); two RBU-6000 and two RBU-1000 ASW RL (replaced by 30mm AK-630 CIWS); five 21in (533mm) TT (original fit)
Sensors: air-search radar; navigation radar; fire-control radar; hull-mounted sonar
Speed: 18 knots
Range: 3500nm (6482km) at 18 knots
Complement: 266

OHIO

USA: 1979

A replacement for the *Ohio* class, still known simply as the New Attack Submarine, is already under development.

Displacement: 16,000t surfaced; 18,700t submerged
Dimensions: 560ft x 42ft x 35ft 6in (170.7m x 12.8m x 10.8m)
Machinery: one-shaft, nuclear, one reactor; 35,000hp
Armament: 24 Trident D-5 SLBM; four 21in (533mm) TT
Sensors: general-purpose radar; active/passive multi-function sonar and towed array
Speed: 25 knots submerged
Range: limited only by reactor fuel state
Complement: 133

USS *Ohio* (SSBN 726) was the first in a class of 18 nuclear-powered SSBNs for the US Navy. The *Ohio* class carries 24 Trident SLBMs and also has four torpedo tubes (for 21-in Mk 48 torpedoes) for self defence. The vessels carry a passive BQQ-6 or modified BQQ-5 sonar, and a passive towed array. The first eight boats in the class were delivered with Trident C-4 missiles, with 14 later vessels carrying the longer-range Trident D-5 missile. Trident is as accurate as ground-based ICBMs, with the same response time and greater destructive effect. Under the START II (Strategic Arms Reduction) Treaty, which comes into effect in 2002, the US Navy will be limited to 14 *Ohio*-class submarines, while the number of re-entry vehicles per missile deployed will reduce from the theoretical maximum of 12 or the START I limit of eight to a START II limit of four or five. The *Ohio*-class programme was subject to considerable delays, such that the *Ohio*, scheduled for delivery in 1977, wasn't launched until April 1979, and did not complete trials until 1981. The USS *Ohio* was commissioned on 11 November 1981 and immediately sailed on a shake-down cruise. On 13 March 1982 the submarine launched its first Trident 1 missile. The following August the vessel was loaded with operational missiles for the first time and on 1 October the *Ohio* sailed on its first deterrent patrol. The *Ohio* class is a major improvement over the previous *Lafayette*-class SSBNs – they are faster, quieter, easier to maintain, cheaper to operate and have far superior crew facilities (including two onboard libraries). Because each *Ohio* carries 24 missiles, compared to the 16 of a *Lafayette*, the US Navy has replaced all of its 31 *Lafayette*-class boats with 20 *Ohios* – which still provide a far superior striking force. The last of the class, USS *Louisiana*, was commissioned in June 1997. The *Ohio*-class submarines remain highly-classified, though it is known that they are among the quietest nuclear-powered submarines in service, with an advanced turbo-electric drive for 'silent running'. Despite their sophistication, the submarines are remarkably maintainable, and are able to average 66 per cent of their time at sea, usually following a 70-day at sea/25 day maintenance schedule. Shipyard overhauls are due every nine years. The previous Poseidon submarines averaged 55 per cent of their time at sea.

Only the Soviet *Typhoon* is bigger than the *Ohio* class, which is the world's most destructive weapons system. It bears a passing resemblance to the smaller *Sturgeon* class SSN.

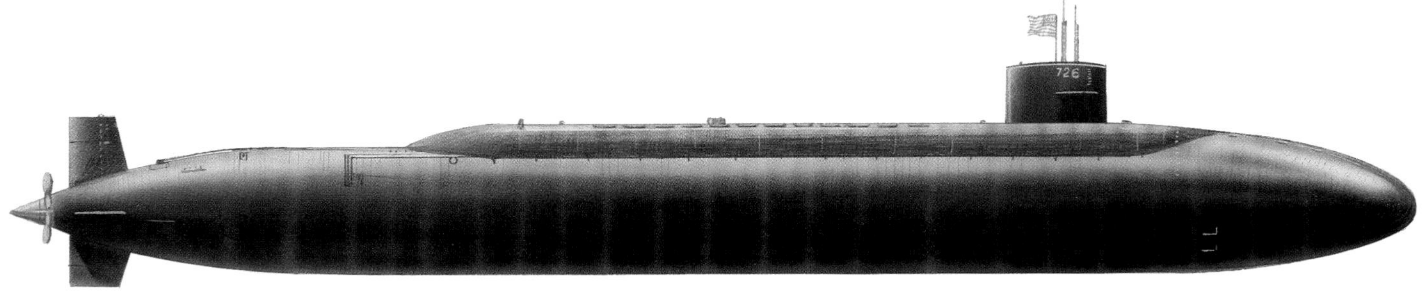

OLIVER HAZARD PERRY

USA: 1976

The US Navy has acquired 51 *Oliver Hazard Perry*-class frigates (FFGs). USS *Oliver Hazard Perry* (FFG 7) led the class, being launched on 25 September 1976. The class was conceived as a direct successor to the *Knox* class ASW destroyers, and to replace the remaining FRAM destroyers that had not been replaced by the *Spruance* class. These new ships were deliberately austere, with more emphasis placed on anti-ship and anti-aircraft capability than on ASW. There was no shortage of sonar-equipped ASW vessels, and a multi-role ship was felt to be prohibitively expensive. The *Perry* class was optimised as AAW vessels, though the combination of towed sonar and helicopter-delivered ordnance soon provided a formidable stand-off ASW capability. This was limited on earlier vessels in the class by having only one helicopter. From USS *Underwood* (FFG 36) onwards, an enlarged flight deck and hangarage for two LAMPS helicopters were fitted, these features being retrofitted to many of the earlier vessels. Despite their lightweight construction, the *Oliver Hazard Perry* vessels have proved to be remarkably robust. The USS *Stark* survived two Exocet hits, while the USS *Samuel B. Roberts* withstood a contact mine explosion. Both vessels were repaired and returned to service. Many of the class were once expected to be transferred to allied nations after the end of the Cold War, but most were retained in an effort to cope with over-stretch, and to provide a relatively cheap method of ensuring a US Navy presence wherever it might be required. A handful were transferred (to Egypt, Bahrain and Turkey, for example) and others were built specifically for Australia and Taiwan.

The *Oliver Hazard Perry* class enjoys a considerable degree of redundancy, with well-separated radar, auxiliary engines and twin-channel fire control systems.

Displacement: 2648t standard; 3486t full load
Dimensions: 445ft x 47ft 6in x 14ft 5in (135.6m x 14.5m x 4.4m)
Machinery: one-shaft, two LM-2500 gas turbines; 40,000hp
Armament: one Mk 13 launcher for Harpoon SSM (four) and Standard SAM (36); one 3in (76mm); six 12.75in (324mm) TT; one SH-60B Seahawk (LAMPS III) helicopter
Sensors: air/surface-search radar; navigation radar; fire-control radar; hull-mounted sonar
Speed: 28.5 knots
Range: 4500nm (8334km) at 20 knots
Complement: 176

OSA CLASS

USSR (RUSSIA): 1959

Displacement: 172t standard; 209t full load
Dimensions: 123ft x 24ft 11in x 12ft 6in (37.5m x 7.6m x 3.8m)
Machinery: three-shaft, diesels; 12,500hp
Armament: four SS-N-2 SSM; SA-N-5 SAM (some *Osa IIs*); four 30mm cannon
Sensors: surface-search radar; fire-control radar
Speed: 35 knots (*Osa I*); 37 knots (*Osa II*)
Range: 400nm (741km) at 34 knots (*Osa I*); 500nm (926km) at 35 knots (*Osa II*)
Complement: 26

The USSR built 193 Project 205 Tsunami 'rocket cutters' (NATO code-name *Osa I*) and 28 Project 205Us (*Osa II*), together with eight 205Es with P-25 missiles and bow-mounted hydrofoils. A further 125 or so *Osa Is* were built in China. There were also 146 similar Project 205M and 205P Tarantul patrol/coastal ASW boats for the Border Guards, built on Project 205 hulls and known to NATO as the *Stenka* class. These had a helicopter-style 'dipping sonar' from a Ka-25 'Hormone', and were armed with torpedoes, depth charges and four 30mm cannon. The same hull was also used on the rival Project 206 *Bogomol*, *Matka*, *Mol*, *Shershen* and *Turya* torpedo and gun boats and hydrofoils, approximately 65 of which were built. The first Project 205 boat was launched in 1959 and commissioned in 1960. It was armed with four P-15 Termit missiles in box-like 'hangars', though four were completed with eight Strela AAMs instead. The basic SS-N-2A/B-armed *Osa I* was exported widely, about 100 going to Algeria, Benin, Bulgaria, China, Cuba, Egypt, East Germany, India, Iraq, North Korea, Poland, Romania, Syria and Yugoslavia. The Project 205U was armed with four increased-range SS-N-2B/C Rubezh missiles in smaller, circular-section tubes. Some 98 vessels (presumably converted from *Osa Is* or newly-built) were exported to Algeria, Angola, Bulgaria, Cuba, India, Iraq, Libya, Somalia, Syria, Vietnam, North Yemen and Yugoslavia. Small numbers of *Osa Is* remain in service in Russia, though many have been retired, some going to civilian owners for sporting purposes.

The *Osa I* and *Osa II* were among the first Soviet small attack craft to be armed with missiles, following on from the Project 183R *Komar* fast attack craft.

OSCAR CLASS

RUSSIA: 1980

The Project 949 submarines were designed as cruise missile launchers, and combined the Artika reactor designed for the Project 941 *Typhoon* class with the sonar systems of the *Victor III* class. Two Project 949 submarines with 24 SS-N-19 Granit cruise missiles, four 21in (533mm) and two 25.6in (650mm) torpedo tubes were built from 1978, followed by about seven or eight Project 949A Anteiy (*Oscar II*) submarines, launched between 1990 and 1996. These vessels were successors to the *Echo* class and were designed to be able to launch their cruise missiles from underwater, obtaining targeting data from a mast-mounted 'Punch Bowl' radar antenna or from a towed VLF buoy. The Project 949A production programme was abandoned in early 1992, when the Russian Defence Ministry announced that six incomplete submarines were being broken up. One *Oscar II* class submarine hit the headlines during August 2000, when the *Kursk* (K-141) sank with all hands during a major exercise.

Unusually, the *Oscar*'s missile tubes are located between the inner and outer pressure hulls, canted at 40° from the vertical, with pairs of launch tubes covered by single doors.

Displacement: 12,500t (*Oscar I*), 13,900t (*Oscar I*) surfaced; 14,600t (*Oscar I*), 16,000t (*Oscar II*) submerged
Dimensions: 469ft 2in (*Oscar I*), 505ft 2in (*Oscar I*) x 59ft 9in x 29ft 6in (143m (*Oscar I*), 153.97m (*Oscar II*) x 18.21m x 8.99m)
Machinery: two-shaft, nuclear, two pressurised-water nuclear reactors, two steam turbines; 90,000hp
Armament: four 21in (533mm) and four 25.6in (650mm) TT (for 24 torpedoes/tube-launched weapons including SS-N-19, SS-N-15, SS-N-16 Stallion)
Sensors: general-purpose radar; active/passive sonar
Speed: 32 knots submerged
Range: 50 days endurance
Complement: 94

OSLO

NORWAY: 1964

The *Oslo* (F 300) was the first of five Norwegian frigates built between 1963 and 1967, based on the US *Dealey* class but with modifications to better suit them to local conditions. These modifications included increased forward freeboard. The ships also featured electronic and mission systems from a number of sources, with French search radar, Dutch fire control systems and British navigation equipment. Built in the Norwegian Naval Yard (Marinens Hoverdvert, Horten) the five ships were half-funded by the US Government. Between 1987 and 1990, the five ships underwent a major modernisation programme with improved sonar, weapons and systems. The lead ship of the class sank after running aground on 25 January 1994, forcing the reinstatement of the *Bergen*, placed in reserve in 1993. During 1995–96, the surviving ships had their hulls strengthened, these having become stressed by towing VDS equipment in heavy seas.

The *Oslo* class gave the Royal Norwegian Navy a modern, indigenous warship, and the four survivors have already given more than 30 years of service.

Displacement: 1450t standard; 1760t full load
Dimensions: 318ft x 36ft 7in x 17ft 4in (97m x 11.1m x 5.3m)
Machinery: one-shaft, double reduction geared turbines, two boilers; 20,000hp
Armament: six Penguin SSM; one Sea Sparrow SAM launcher (24 missiles); four 3in (76mm); one Terne III ASW RL; six 12.75in (324mm) TT
Sensors: air/surface-search radar; navigation radar; fire-control radar; hull-mounted sonar
Speed: 25 knots
Range: 4500nm (8334km) at 15 knots
Complement: 150

OYASHIO

JAPAN: 1997

The *Oyashio* (SS 590) is the lead ship in a new class of diesel-electric attack submarines built at Kobe by Kawasaki and Mitsubishi, beginning in 1994. Named after Japan's first indigenous post-war submarine, the second *Oyashio* is an improved *Harushio* class submarine, with large sonar arrays on its flanks. The *Oyashio* class is the latest in a line of Japanese attack submarines and there are plans to acquire 10 such vessels through to 2007.

The *Oyashio* class is conventional in appearance, with a teardrop-shaped hull and diving planes mounted on the well-proportioned sail.

Displacement: 3600t submerged
Dimensions: 268ft x 29ft 2in x 25ft 9in (81.7m x 8.9m x 7.8m)
Machinery: one-shaft, diesel and electric motor; 7750hp
Armament: six 21in (533mm) TT (torpedoes and Harpoon SSM)
Sensors: hull/flank sonar arrays and towed array
Speed: 20 knots submerged
Range: not available
Complement: 75

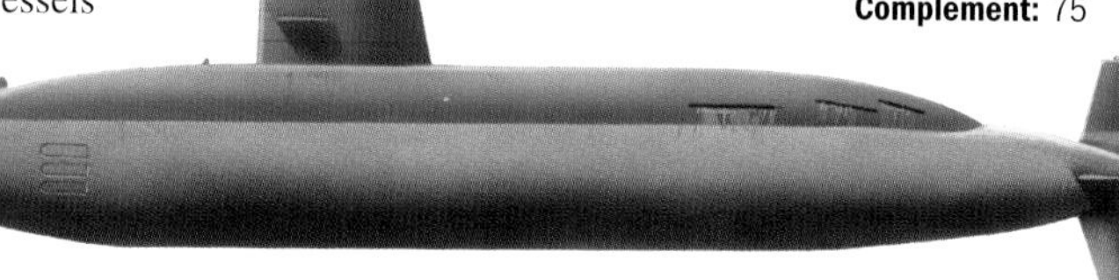

PAPA CLASS

USSR: 1968

Completed in 1969, K-222 (later K-162) was the sole Project 661 Anchar fast cruise missile submarine (NATO code-name 'Papa'). This submarine proved even faster than required (clocking up 42 knots in service, against the 38 knots requirement) but was slow and uneconomic to build, and produced excessive noise levels at high speed. Despite its unique high-speed capability, K-162 was withdrawn from use in 1988, and probably remains in storage at Severodvinsk.

K-162 was the world's fastest submarine, reportedly reaching a speed of 44.7 knots during trials, causing significant damage to topside equipment in the process. Such high speed came at a price of high noise and high construction costs.

Displacement: 5200ft surfaced; 7000t submerged
Dimensions: 350ft 9in x 37ft 9in x 26ft 3in (106.9m x 11.5m x 8m)
Machinery: two-shaft, nuclear, two pressurised-water nuclear reactors and two steam turbines; 80,000hp
Armament: 10 SS-N-9 cruise missiles; four 21in (533mm) TT
Sensors: sonar fit
Speed: 20 knots submerged
Range: limited only by reactor fuel state
Complement: 82

PEDER SKRAM

DENMARK: 1965

Displacement: 2200t standard; 2720t full load
Dimensions: 395ft 5in x 39ft 5in x 14ft 1in (120.5m x 12m x 4.3m)
Machinery: two-shaft, COGOG, one gas turbine and one diesel; 18,400hp/4800hp
Armament: four Harpoon SSM (later); one Sea Sparrow SAM launcher (later); four 5in (127mm) (later two); four 40mm cannon; three 21in (533mm) TT (deleted); depth charges
Sensors: air-search radar; navigation radar; fire-control radar; hull-mounted sonar
Speed: 28 knots
Range: 2500nm (4630km) at 18 knots
Complement: 200

Peder Skram (F352) was the first of a pair of indigenously designed Danish frigates built by Helsingör in the mid-1960s, using US offshore funding. *Peder Skram* was completed in June 1966, and modernised in 1977–78, gaining Harpoon and Sea Sparrow missiles. Never as useful as the helicopter-equipped *Hvindbjørnen* class, both ships were placed in reserve in 1987, and were subsequently stricken and broken up. Four helicopter-equipped Thetis class frigates subsequently replaced the *Hvindbjørnen* frigates and the Peder Skrams.

The two *Peder Skram*-class frigates enjoyed a 20-year service life before being placed in reserve in 1987. Both have since been scrapped.

PERTH

AUSTRALIA: 1963

HMAS *Perth* (38) was the first of three *Charles F. Adams*-class destroyers ordered by Australia in 1962–63. Virtually identical to the US Navy ships, the Australian destroyers used Ikara instead of ASROC, requiring a new magazine between the funnels. The ships were modernised in the mid-1970s with Standard AAMs and new radar and systems, and again in the late 1980s when the upgrade included provision for Harpoon anti-shipping missiles, Phalanx CIWS, and the removal of Ikara.

The Royal Australian Navy's three *Perth* class destroyers are Australia's most powerful surface warships, and have already given 35 years of service.

Displacement: 3277t standard; 4526t full load
Dimensions: 437ft x 47ft 3in x 14ft 9in (133.2m x 14.4m x 4.5m)
Machinery: two-shaft, geared turbines, four boilers; 70,000hp
Armament: combined Mk 13 launcher for Harpoon SSM and Standard SAM; two 5in (127mm); two 20mm Phalanx CIWS (later); six 12.75in (324mm) TT; two Ikara boosted ASW torpedo systems (deleted)
Sensors: air/surface-search radar; fire-control radar; hull-mounted sonar
Speed: 33 knots
Range: 4500nm (8334km) at 20 knots
Complement: 333

PETYA CLASS

USSR:1961

The *Petya* class was a light frigate that was produced in larger numbers than the similar *Mirka* class, indicating a more successful design. A total of 45 *Petyas* (18 *Petya Is* and 27 *Petya IIs*) were built for the Soviet Navy between 1961 and 1969. All *Petya I* class corvettes had been discarded by 1989, followed by all *Mod Petya Is* by 1990–91 and all *Petya IIs* by 1994. The *Petya III* was the export version.

The *Petya* class light frigate (or Project 159) was the first purpose-built Soviet ASW ship. The later examples (*Petya II*) had improved armament and a different sonar fit.

Displacement: 950t standard; 1150t (*Petya I*), 1160t (*Petya II*) full load
Dimensions: 268ft 4in x 30ft 2in x 9ft 6in (81.8m x 9.2m x 2.9m)
Machinery: two-shaft, CODAG, one diesel and two gas turbines; 6000hp/30,000hp
Armament: four 3in (76mm) AA; five (*Petya I*) or 10 (*Petya II*) 15.75in (400mm) TT; four RBU-2500 (*Petya I*) or two RBU-6000 (*Petya II*) ASW RL
Sensors: surface-search radar; navigation radar; hull-mounted and dipping sonar (some)
Speed: 32 knots
Range: 4870nm (9019km) at 10 knots
Complement: 90

PIGEON

USA: 1973

Displacement: 3,411t full load
Dimensions: 251ft x 86ft x 21ft 8in (76.5m x 26.2m x 6.6m)
Machinery: two-shaft, four Alco diesels; 6,000hp
Armament: two 20mm cannon
Sensors: surface-search radar; navigation radar; search sonar
Speed: 15 knots
Range: 8500nm (15,742km) at 13 knots
Complement: 24, plus submarine operatios team of 24

The two *Pigeon*-class ships (USS *Pigeon* and USS *Ortolan*) were the first in the world to be built specifically for the submarine rescue mission. They were capable of transporting, servicing, lowering, and raising two Deep Submergence Rescue Vehicles and supporting saturation or conventional diving operations to depths of 850ft (259m). USS *Pigeon* (ASR 21) was launched in April 1973 and decomissioned in 1991. Saved from scrapping, she was sold on to a commercial operator in 1998.

Except for one Military Sealift Command ship, the USS *Pigeon* was the first catamaran to be built for the US Navy since Robert Fulton's *Demologos* in 1812.

PRAT

CHILE:1937/1951

The *Brooklyn*-class cruiser USS *Nashville* (launched in 1937) gained a new lease of life in 1951, transferring to the Chilean Navy as the *Prat*. At the same time, USS *Brooklyn* transferred to Chile as the *O'Higgins*, while Brazil and Argentina each also received a pair of surplus *Brooklyn*-class cruisers. The two Chilean *Brooklyns* were refitted in the USA during 1957–58. *Prat* was decommissioned in 1984, with *O'Higgins* following in 1992.

The *Prat* and her sistership were retired after the Falklands conflict, being replaced by four ex-Royal Navy *County*-class guided missile destroyers.

Displacement: 10,000t standard
Dimensions: 608ft 4in x 61ft 9in x 19ft 5in (185.4m x 18.8m x 5.9m)
Machinery: four-shaft, eight boilers; 100,000hp
Armament: 15 6in (152mm), eight 5in (127mm); 28 40mm cannon, 12 20mm cannon; one JetRanger helicopter
Sensors: air/surface-search radar
Speed: 33 knots
Range: not available
Complement: 868

PRINCIPE DE ASTURIAS

SPAIN:1982

Following on from a US design intended to meet an unfunded 1975 requirement for a Sea Control Ship, the Spanish Navy adopted the same basic concept and produced the VSTOL carrier *Principe de Asturias* (R11). Built by Bazan, at Ferrol, the *Principe de Asturias* was launched in May 1982 and completed in May 1988. The commissioning of the *Principe de Asturias* finally allowed the retirement of the elderly wooden-decked *Dedalo*. The *Principe de Asturias* is optimised for the operation of Spain's EAV-8B Harrier IIs and features a 12° ski jump. A total of 37 aircraft and helicopters can be embarked, but only 24 can be operated simultaneously. Limited aircrew accommodation usually restricts the air wing to eight Harrier IIs and 10 helicopters, usually including two AEW-configured SH-3 Sea Kings. The *Principe de Asturias* is fully equipped for a fleet flagship role, with a lower 'flag' bridge and additional command and control facilities.

The *Principe de Asturias* is rather smaller than the otherwise broadly similar British *Invincible* class, and typically embarks a slightly smaller air wing.

Displacement: 16,700t standard
Dimensions: 642ft 8in x 79ft 8in x 30ft 10in (195.9m x 24.3m x 9.4m)
Machinery: one-shaft, two gas turbines; 46,400hp
Armament: two 20mm Baroka CIWS; two 37mm saluting guns; 6-12 AV-8B Harrier II+ fighters, 2-4 AB212ASW/EW, two SH-60B, two SH-3 AEW helicopters
Sensors: air-search radar; navigation radar; fire-control radar; hull-mounted sonar
Speed: 26 knots
Range: 6500nm (12,038km) at 10 knots
Complement: 763

QUEBEC CLASS

USSR: 1950

A single Project 615 submarine was launched on 31 August 1950 and completed in May 1953. Thirty Project A615s, delivered between 1955 and 1958 followed it. These remarkable submarines were powered by three closed-cycle diesels, based on pre-war research, and produced by a design team freed from an NKVD prison after the war. The *Quebecs* proved extremely prone to fires and minor explosions, leading to the type becoming known as the 'cigarette lighters'. A planned rectification programme was cancelled in 1968, and most had been withdrawn by the mid-1970s. Four remained in use in 1982.

The *Quebec*-class submarine was based on pre-war closed-cycle powerplant technology, but also borrowed heavily from wartime German U-boats.

Displacement: 460ft surfaced; 540t submerged
Dimensions: 183ft 9in x 16ft 5in x 12ft 6in (56.m x 5m x 3.8m)
Machinery: three-shaft, liquid oxygen AIP powerplant with auxiliary diesel engines; 2300hp/2200hp
Armament: four 21in (533mm) TT; two 25mm cannon (deleted)
Sensors: surface-search radar; active/passive sonar
Speed: 18 knots surfaced; 16 knots submerged
Range: 7000nm (12,964km) cruising
Complement: 51

RALEIGH

USA: 1962

Displacement: 805t standard; 13,745t full load
Dimensions: 513ft 1in x 84ft x 20ft 6in (156.4m x 25.6m x 6.25m)
Machinery: two-shaft, geared turbines, two boilers; 24,000hp
Armament: three dual 3in (76mm)
Sensors: surface-search radar
Speed: 21 knots
Range: 13,000nm (24,076km) at 20 knots
Complement: 501, plus 932 troops

USS *Raleigh* (LPD 1) was the first of three amphibious transport dock ships which preceded the larger *Austin* class. The *Raleigh* class featured a built-in dock to allow the carriage of landing craft, a sizeable helicopter deck (but no hangar), and accommodation for up to 932 troops. A heavy-lift crane was provided to allow landing craft to be carried on and launched from the helicopter flight deck. Launched in 1962, USS *Raleigh* was decommissioned in July 1992.

The *Raleigh*-class LPDs looked similar to the later, slightly larger *Austin* class, but lacked a hangar and were marginally smaller.

LE REDOUBTABLE

FRANCE: 1967

Displacement: 8045t surfaced; 8940t submerged
Dimensions: 422ft x 35ft x 33ft (128.6m x 10.7m x 10m)
Machinery: one-shaft, nuclear, one PWR, two turbines with two turbo-alternators, one electric motor plus one auxiliary diesel engine; 15,000hp/2670hp
Armament: 16 Aerospatiale M-1/-2/-4 SLBM; four 21.66in (550mm) TT (18 torpedoes)
Sensors: general-purpose radar; active/passive multi-function sonar
Speed: 20 knots surfaced; 25 knots submerged
Range: limited only by reactor fuel state
Complement: 111

When France left NATO's command structure, the country had to develop its nuclear submarines from scratch, without US assistance. The French were unable to buy American reactors, and the supply of enriched uranium (then beyond France's capability to produce) was limited to experimental use for power stations on land. To build the *Redoubtable* class SSBNs therefore, France had to design all-new reactors, new missiles and their associated guidance systems, and the submarines themselves. *Le Redoubtable* (S 611) was the first of six submarines in its class. She was launched in March 1967 and completed in December 1971. The first two submarines were armed with the M-1 SLBM, broadly equivalent to the US *Poseidon*, but with a range of only 1554 miles (2500km) and armed with a single 500kT warhead. The next three had the 1864-mile (3000km) range M-2 missile. The M-20, with a 1MT thermonuclear warhead and improved re-entry vehicle replaced these early weapons. From the fourth submarine in the class, a new reactor with a metallic core was fitted, while the sixth vessel (*L'Inflexible*) had M-4 missiles with six 150kT MIRVs and a range of 2486 miles (4000km), together with new sonar and improved systems. *Le Redoubtable* decommissioned in 1991, but the remaining vessels in the class were brought up to the same standards as *L'Inflexible*. The two oldest vessels were withdrawn in 1996, and another in 1999, as the second *Le Triomphant*-class submarine commissioned. The remaining two will retire as they are replaced, leaving France with a four-boat deterrent.

Development of the *Redoubtable* class SSBNs, built to form the backbone of the national nuclear deterrent, was a symbol of General Charles de Gaulle's push for French independence in defence.

REQUIN

FRANCE: 1955

The *Requin* (S 634) was the fourth in the *Narwal* class of six diesel-electric patrol submarines completed between 1957 and 1960. These were closely based on the German Type XXI U-boat, but with improved performance and some advanced features from more contemporary US designs. The *Narwal* class originally had a quite distinctive appearance, with a raised section at the rear part of the fin; this was later rebuilt, resulting in a more conventional profile. The submarines were built with six torpedo tubes in the bows and two in the stern, and carried 14 torpedoes in all. The stern tubes would later be removed, but the number of torpedoes carried was raised to 20. *Requin* was launched in December 1955 and completed in April 1960. Despite early propulsion problems, the class were refitted during the late 1960s and then remained active into the 1980s. *Requin* became a trials vessel for the SM-39 Exocet before being stricken in 1985.

The *Narwal*-class submarines were optimised for long-range patrols, not least of the waters around French colonial territories. For this reason, the specification called for a range of 15,000nm (27,780km).

Displacement: 1635t surfaced; 1910t submerged
Dimensions: 257ft x 26ft x 17ft (78.3m x 7.9m x 5.2m)
Machinery: two-shaft, two diesels with two electric motors; 4400hp/5000hp
Armament: eight 21.66in (550mm) TT
Sensors: sonar fit
Speed: 18 knots surfaced; 16 knots submerged
Range: 15,000nm (27,780km) at 8 knots
Complement: 63

RESOLUTION

GB: 1966

HMS *Resolution* (S 22) was the first of a class of four ballistic missile submarines built for the Royal Navy and based on the US Navy's *Lafayette* class. These submarines allowed the Royal Navy to take over responsibility for Great Britain's strategic nuclear deterrent from the RAF's Blue Steel-armed Vulcan and Victor bombers, as agreed at the 1962 Nassau Conference. The four submarines (a fifth was cancelled) used US Polaris missiles, missile tubes, and fire control systems plus British engines and other equipment. The British Polaris boats lacked the fin-mounted diving planes of the original *Lafayettes*, and instead borrowed certain features from the British *Valiant* class of attack submarines. The planned fifth submarine had been judged to be necessary to guarantee that one submarine would always be on patrol, and was cancelled by the incoming Labour Government in 1964 as an economy measure and as a sop to those calling for nuclear disarmament. Officially, there was never a gap in submarine patrols; unofficially, it is believed that the RAF's Vulcans took back the strategic deterrent commitment on at least one occasion in the late 1960s. Launched in September 1966, HMS *Resolution* was completed in October 1967, and went on her first patrol in 1968 as planned. To improve the ability of the Polaris missile to penetrate Moscow's fabled ABM defences, Great Britain embarked on an expensive and ambitious upgrade programme code-named Chevaline, adding decoys to the Polaris warhead. The *Resolution* class submarines were replaced from 1995 by the new Trident-armed *Vanguard* class. HMS *Revenge* was withdrawn in 1992, and *Resolution* followed in 1994. The remaining two submarines in the class were withdrawn during 1995–96.

Design, construction and deployment of the *Resolution* class was claimed to have been the only British defence procurement programme to be completed under-budget.

Displacement: 7500t surfaced; 8500t submerged
Dimensions: 425ft x 33ft x 30ft (129.5m x 10m x 9.1m)
Machinery: one-shaft, nuclear, PWR1 reactor with two geared steam turbines plus auxiliary diesel engine; 15,000hp/4000hp
Armament: 16 UGM-27C Polaris A-3 SLBM; six 21in (533mm) TT
Sensors: general-purpose radar; active/passive multi-function sonar
Speed: 20 knots surfaced; 25 knots submerged
Range: limited only by reactor fuel state
Complement: 143

RICHARD L. PAGE

USA: 1966

The *Garcia* class and *Brooke* class escort destroyers were conceived as fast escorts to replace remaining wartime destroyers, and the Dealey class destroyers and unsuccessful *Claud Jones*-class and *Bronstein*-class destroyers. The decision was taken to aim for a performance of 30 knots, using pressure-fired powerplants. Ten *Garcias* were configured for ASW duties, while six *Brookes* were armed with Tartar SAMs. Launched in April 1966, USS *Richard L. Page* (DEG 5) was the fifth of the *Brooke*-class ships.

Displacement: 2710t standard; 3246t full load
Dimensions: 414ft x 44ft x 24ft (126.2m x 13.4m x 7.3m)
Machinery: one-shaft, geared turbine, two pressure-fired boilers; 35,000hp
Armament: one Tarter SAM launcher (16 missiles); one 5in (127mm); one ASROC launcher; six 12.75in (324mm) TT; one helicopter
Sensors: search radar; hull-mounted sonar
Speed: 27 knots
Range: 4000nm (7408km) at 20 knots
Complement: 228

The *Garcia* class and *Brooke* class were withdrawn during the late 1980s, eight going to Pakistan and others to Brazil.

RIGA CLASS

USSR (RUSSIA): 1954

Development of what NATO called the *Riga* class (Project 50) frigate was launched at the personal order of Josef Stalin as a simple replacement for the Project 42 *Kola* class. Designed around a pressure-fired powerplant, the new frigate was deliberately small, light and cheap, but performance proved disappointing. Despite this, Kaliningrad built 41 of the class, with Nikolaev building 20 more and Komsomolsk producing another seven. Nine Project 50s were built in China, five of them improved as the *Kiangnan* class.

Many of the Soviet *Rigas* were modernised, and some became dedicated ASW frigates. All survivors were withdrawn from use between 1986 and 1992.

Displacement: 1260t standard; 1480t full load
Dimensions: 295ft 3in x 33ft 6in x 10ft (90m x 10.2m x 3m)
Machinery: two-shaft, geared steam turbines, two boilers; 21000hp
Armament: three 3.9in (100mm), four 37mm and four 25mm AA; two or three 21in (533mm) TT; two RBU-2500 ASW RL
Sensors: surface-search radar; navigation radar; hull-mounted sonar (some)
Speed: 28 knots
Range: 3609nm (6684km) at 10 knots
Complement: 170

ROGER DE LAURIA

SPAIN: 1957

During 1947, the Spanish Navy ordered nine destroyers based on the pre-war French *Le Hardi* class. Six were cancelled in 1953, and only the first, *Oquendo*, was completed to the original design, being completed in 1960. The ship suffered from excessive top-weight and proved unstable. It was modified, while the second and third ships (*Roger de Lauria* (D42) and *Marques de la Enseneda*) were dismantled and completed to a revised and enlarged design. The *Roger de Lauria* was relaunched after being lengthened and broadened in 1967, and was completed in 1969. The two *Roger de Lauria*-class destroyers were equipped to broadly the same standards as the US Navy's *Gearing* class FRAM IIs, but were handicapped by boiler problems. The *Marques de la Enseneda* was repaired after being damaged in a terrorist attack in 1981, using parts from the *Roger de Lauria*, which was withdrawn in 1982. Her rebuilt sistership followed in 1988.

Displacement: 3012t standard; 3785t full load
Dimensions: 391ft 6in x 42ft 8in x 18ft (119.3m x 1m x 5.5m)
Machinery: two-shaft, geared turbines and three three-drum boilers; 60,000hp
Armament: six 5in (127mm); six 12.75in (324mm) and two 21in (533mm) TT; one helicopter
Sensors: air/surface-search radar; navigation radar; fire-control radar; hull-mounted sonar
Speed: 31 knots
Range: 4000nm (7408km) at 15 knots
Complement: 318

The *Roger de Lauria* was unusual in being a 1960s derivative of what was originally a pre-war French design.

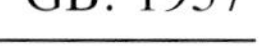

ROTHESAY

GB: 1957

The *Rothesay*-class frigates were developed from the outstanding Type 12 *Whitby* class using the same hull-form. The first of nine ships, HMS *Rothesay* (F 107), was launched in December 1957 and completed in April 1960. The success of the *Leander* class led to a major modernisation of the *Rothesays*, which gained provision for a Wasp helicopter and improved armament and systems. The class fell victim to the 1981 Defence Review, and *Rothesay* was broken up in 1988.

The *Rothesay* class was a stepping-stone between the seaworthy but sparsely equipped *Whitbys* and the much-improved *Leander* class, all using a common hull-form.

Displacement: 2150t standard; 2560t full load
Dimensions: 370ft x 41ft x 17ft (112.8m x 12.5m x 5.2m)
Machinery: two-shaft, geared steam turbines, two boilers; 30,000hp
Armament: GWS22 Seacat SAM launcher (added later); two 4.5in (114mm); two 20mm cannon; 12 21in (533mm) TT (deleted); one Limbo Mk 10 ASW mortar; one Wasp helicopter
Sensors: air/surface-search radar; navigation radar; fire-control radar; hull-mounted sonar
Speed: 31 knots
Range: 4500nm (8334km) at 12 knots
Complement: 220-235

ROTTERDAM

THE NETHERLANDS: 1997

The *Rotterdam* was the result of a joint venture between the Netherlands and Spain, and was launched by builders Royal Schelde in February 1997. An amphibious transport dock, the *Rotterdam* can transport a full Marine battalion, while also having facilities for landing craft and a two-spot flight deck with hangarage for six NHI NH-90s or four EHI EH 101s. The ship has full hospital facilities and can be used in the disaster relief/emergency SAR role.

The *Rotterdam* was built to commercial standards, but incorporates military command, control and NBC decontamination facilities.

Displacement: 1200t full load
Dimensions: 523ft x 82ft x 19ft 4in (159.4m x 25m x 5.9m)
Machinery: two-shaft, four diesel engines with auxiliary electric motors; 16,628hp
Armament: two 30mm Goalkeeper CIWS; four 20mm cannon
Sensors: search radar
Speed: 20 knots
Range: 6000nm (11,112km) at 12 knots
Complement: 127, plus 600 troops

SAGINAW

USA: 1970

***Saginaw* was one of 20 *Newport*-class tank landing ships, characterised by the massive bow 'prongs' for the retractable bow ramp.**

The tank landing ship USS *Saginaw* (LST 1188) was the tenth in the *Newport* class. The lead ship was ordered in 1965 and launched in February 1968; *Saginaw* following in 1970. The ships had conventional bows to allow them to reach 20 knots (impossible with bow doors), and a split upper section through which a 112ft (34.14m) ramp, supported by prominent derricks, could be extended. There was also a stern door to allow amphibious vehicles directly into the water, into a landing craft, or onto a pier. The *Saginaw* was transferred to *Australia* (along with another *Newport*-class vessel) to replace a planned class of indigenous helicopter support ships. The bow ramp was removed and a six-helicopter hangar (capable of accommodating four S-70s) was fitted before the ship recommissioned as HMAS *Kanimbla* (L-51) in August 1984, with the conversion being completed in 1997.

Displacement: 8342t full load
Dimensions: 442ft x 62ft x 13ft 6in (134.7m x 18.9m x 4.1m)
Machinery: two-shaft, six diesel engines; 15000hp
Armament: six 3in (76mm)
Sensors: navigation radar
Speed: 17.2 knots
Range: 14,000nm (25,928km) at 14 knots
Complement: 195, plus 634 (troops)

SALISBURY

GB: 1953

Displacement: 2170t standard; 2350t full load
Dimensions: 340ft x 40ft x 11ft 10in (103.6m x 12.2m x 3.6m)
Machinery: two-shaft, diesel, eight diesel engines; 14,400hp
Armament: GWS22 Seacat SAM launcher (later); two 4.5in (114mm); two 40mm cannon; one Squid ASW mortar
Sensors: long-range air/surface-search radar; fire-control radar; hull-mounted sonar
Speed: 25 knots
Range: 7500nm (13,890km) at 16 knots
Complement: 207

The much-praised hull-form of the Type 12 frigate actually originated in the Type 41 and Type 61 frigates – its diesel-powered equivalents – though these ships had a shorter forecastle and no funnel, and so looked less 'elegant'. While the Type 41 *Leopard* class were anti-aircraft frigates, the Type 61 *Salisbury*-class frigates were aircraft direction frigates, using their radar to guide carrierborne fleet air defence aircraft. Both types supported the primarily ASW-roled Type 12s. *Salisbury* (F 32) was the first of the four Type 61s, launched in June 1953 and completed in February 1957. The ship, the last of its class in Royal Navy service, ended its days as a target on 30 September 1985. One other had already gone to Bangladesh, where it remains in service.

The *Salisbury* class of aircraft direction frigates foreshadowed the more flexible *Leanders*, and marked the end of the single-role 'futility' frigate in Royal Navy service.

SAN GIORGIO

ITALY: 1987

Italy's *San Giorgio* was the first of three unusual dock landing ships ordered in 1984. Each is armed with weapons taken from scrapped frigates and each have slightly different roles. *San Giorgio* was a standard LPD, launched in February 1987 and commissioned in October 1987. *San Marco* was financed by the Ministry of Civil Protection and is earmarked for disaster relief.

Because she is better equipped than the others, she was used as a hospital ship during Operation Desert Storm. *San Giusto* is a peacetime training ship and lacks a bow ramp.

Displacement: 5000t standard; 7665t full load
Dimensions: 437ft 4in x 67ft 3in x 17ft 3in (133.30m x 20.50m x 5.26m)
Machinery: two-shaft, two diesel engines; 116,800hp
Armament: one 3in (76mm); two 20mm cannon; two 12.7mm MG
Sensors: surface-search radar; navigation radar; fire-control radar
Speed: 21 knots
Range: 7500nm (13,890km) at 16 knots
Complement: 163 plus 345 (troops)

The *San Giorgio* class are conventional LPDs with stern doors, carrier-type helicopter flight decks, and a large island offset to starboard.

SANTISIMA TRINIDAD

ARGENTINA: 1974

A largely standard Royal Navy Type 42 destroyer, the *Santisima Trinidad* (D2) was the second of two such ships ordered by Argentina in 1970. The first example, *Hercules*, was built at Barrow and launched in 1972, but *Santisima Trinidad* was constructed locally. The ship was launched in November 1974, but was sabotaged during fitting out, and was not commissioned until 1981. *Santisima Trinidad* functioned as flagship for the invasion force which took the Falkland Islands in 1982, and the first wave of commandos landed on 1 April 1982 were carried in from her by helicopter. As the British Task Force arrived in the area, the two Type 42s operated in support of the Argentine Navy's sole aircraft carrier. Post-war operations were somewhat restricted by a British embargo, and both ships spent long periods laid up following the war. The two vessels were offered to Turkey in 1986, but the spares situation then began to ease, and they returned to service.

Displacement: 3850t standard; 4350t full load
Dimensions: 410ft x 46ft x 19ft (124.99m x 14m x 5.8m)
Machinery: two-shaft, CODOG, four gas turbines; 50,000hp/8000hp
Armament: one GWS30 Sea Dart SAM launcher (22 missiles); one 4.5in (114mm); four 20mm cannon; six 12.75in (324mm) TT; one Lynx helicopter
Sensors: air/surface-search radar; navigation radar; fire-control radar; hull-mounted sonar
Speed: 30 knots
Range: 6000nm (11,112km) at 16 knots
Complement: 312

The *Santisima Trinidad* became a spares source for *Hercules* by 1996, and is now little more than a hulk.

SERVIOLA

SPAIN: 1990

Displacement: 836t standard; 1106t full load
Dimensions: 225ft 5in x 34ft x 11ft (68.7m x 10.4m x 3.3m)
Machinery: two-shaft, two diesel engines; 7500hp
Armament: one 3in (76mm); two MG; one AB212 helicopter
Sensors: surface-search and navigation radar
Speed: 19 knots
Range: 8000nm (14,816km) at 12 knots
Complement: 42

The four *Serviola*-class corvettes should perhaps be more accurately described as offshore patrol vessels. They can embark an Agusta-Bell AB212 helicopter.

The *Serviola* (P71) was the lead ship in a class of four corvettes ordered by Spain in 1988. These ships followed the design of 11 *Halcon* class frigates built by Bazan during the early 1980s for Argentina and Mexico. The *Serviola* class was adopted following the rejection of a larger, faster and more heavily armed *Milano* class. Launched in May 1990 (after all the other ships in the class), *Serviola* was completed in March 1991.

SHREVEPORT

USA: 1966

The USS *Shreveport* (LPD-12) was one of 12 *Austin*-class dock landing ships ordered to augment the three slightly smaller *Raleigh* class ships. They had increased accommodation for troops (930), cargo and landing vehicles, and most (after LPD-4) also had extending, telescopic hangarage for up to six CH-46 Sea Knights. Seven of the ships (including *Shreveport*) were fitted out as amphibious squadron flagships with slightly reduced troop accommodation.

Displacement: 10,000t standard; 16,900t full load
Dimensions: 570ft x 84ft x 23ft (173.74m x 25.60m x 7m)
Machinery: two-shaft, geared turbines, two boilers; 24,000hp
Armament: two or four 3in (76mm); two 20mm Phalanx CIWS
Sensors: air/surface-search radar; navigation radar
Speed: 20 knots
Range: 7700nm (14,260km) at 20 knots
Complement: 410-447, plus 932 troops

Although a planned SLEP for the *Austin* class was cancelled in 1987, the ships are expected to remain in service for some time.

SIERRA CLASS

USSR: 1983

Displacement: 5200–7200t surfaced; 6800–10,100t, 10,400t (*Sierra II*) submerged
Dimensions: 351ft, 369ft 2in (*Sierra II*) x 39ft 5in x 28ft 11in (107m, 112.5m (*Sierra II*) x 12m x 8.8m)
Machinery: one-shaft, nuclear, one pressurised-water nuclear reactor with steam turbines; 47,000–50,000hp
Armament: four 21in (533mm) and four 25.6in (650mm) TT with provision for SS-N-22, SS-N-16, Shkval underwater rockets, SET-72, TEST-71M, USET-80 torpedoes; 42 mines (in lieu of torpedoes); one SA-N-5/SA-N-8 position
Sensors: surface-search radar; active/passive sonar suite
Speed: 8 knots surfaced; 36 knots submerged
Range: endurance 4500 power hours
Complement: 61

Designed as a follow-on to the Project 671 *Victor III*, only four examples of the Project 945 *Sierra*-class attack submarine were built before production switched to the cheaper Project 971 *Akula* (not to be confused with the Project 941 *Akula* ballistic missile submarine, known to NATO as *Typhoon*). Designed by the Lazurit OKB, the Project 945 submarines used the *Victor III* acoustics suite and a very quiet powerplant based on the Arktika reactor. The titanium-hulled vessels combined a deep-diving capability (variously quoted as 700, 800 or 1000m) with excellent accommodation and safety systems for the crew, including an escape pod (or two pods on the third and fourth Project 945A *Sierra II* submarines) in the wide sail. The lead ship, *Barrakuda*, was launched in June 1983 and completed in June 1984, while K-534, the first Project 945A submarine, was launched in May 1988 and completed one year later. Three Project 945 submarines were scrapped before completion in 1992.

Though similar in appearance to the successful *Akula*, the Project 945 submarines marked a major shift in Soviet submarine design practice, placing much greater emphasis on crew accommodation and safety. Unfortunately, these priorities proved impossibly expensive.

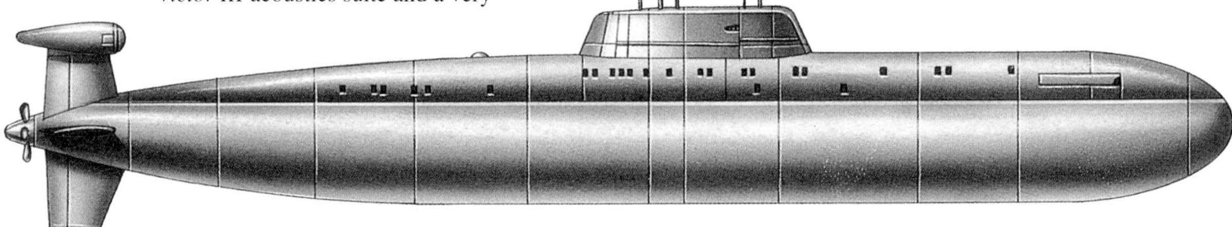

SIR GALAHAD

GB: 1966

The Royal Fleet Auxiliary *Sir Galahad* (L3005) was the third of six landing ships in the *Sir Lancelot* class, though she was actually the second to be launched (in April 1966). *Sir Galahad* and her sistership, *Sir Tristram*, were attacked and badly damaged by Argentine aircraft during the Falklands conflict. So severe was the damage to *Sir Galahad* that she was sunk at sea as a war grave. *Sir Tristram* was eventually brought home and repaired.

A new ship was ordered in 1984 to replace the original *Sir Galahad*. This new *Sir Galahad* (L3005) was launched in December 1986 and commissioned in November 1987.

Displacement: 3270t standard; 5674t full load
Dimensions: 412ft 1in x 59ft 8in x 13ft (125.6m x 18.1m x 3.9m)
Machinery: two-shaft, diesel, two diesel engines; 9400hp
Armament: two 40mm cannon
Sensors: navigation radar
Speed: 17 knots
Range: 8000nm (14,816km) at 15 knots
Complement: 68, plus 534 troops

SJÖORMEN

SWEDEN: 1967

Displacement: 1125t surfaced; 1400t full load
Dimensions: 165ft 7in x 20ft x 19ft (50.5m x 6.1m x 5.8m)
Machinery: one-shaft, diesel engines, two electric motors; 1600hp/1680kW
Armament: four 21in (533mm) and two 15.75in (400mm) TT (12 torpedoes)
Sensors: surface-search radar; active sonar
Speed: 17 knots surfaced; 22 knots submerged
Range: not available
Complement: 36

The Swedish attack submarine *Sjöormen* (pennant letter 'Sor') was the lead ship in a class of five diesel-electric attack boats. Funded in 1961, these two-deck submarines featured a teardrop hull, diving planes on the sail, X-configured stern planes and a single five-bladed propeller. *Sjöormen* was launched in January 1967 and completed in July 1968. The class received a new fire control and sonar suite in the mid-1980s, but most were then laid up in 1993 due to a lack of funding. Two submarines were extensively modified in 1992–93 with towed arrays and improved electronics for service until the end of 1997. One of the ships laid up in 1993 was sold to Singapore in 1997 for training. The five ships in the class were to have been replaced by five *Vastergötland*-class submarines, but two of the latter were cancelled.

These small Swedish submarines proved extremely effective and popular in service, and enjoyed a 25-year service life.

SKATE

USA: 1957

Displacement: 2550t surfaced; 2848t submerged
Dimensions: 267ft 8in x 25ft x 20ft 7in (81.6m x 7.6m x 6.3m)
Machinery: two-shaft, nuclear, one reactor; 6600hp
Armament: eight 21in (533mm) TT (12 torpedoes)
Sensors: surface-search radar; active/passive sonar
Speed: 20 knots submerged
Range: limited only by reactor fuel state
Complement: 84

The four attack submarines of the *Skate* class represented the first 'production' nuclear submarines for the US Navy, the larger single class Poseidons and Seawolfs being one-off prototypes used mainly for research and trials. The USS *Skate* (SSN 578) was launched in May 1957 and completed in December that year. Similar in size to the conventionally powered *Tangs*, the *Skates* served until the late 1980s, although production was abandoned in favour of the larger *Skipjack* class after only four submarines.

The *Skate* class were among the last US submarines with a conventional (non-teardrop) hull, and this prompted the end of production for the class.

SKIPJACK

USA: 1958

Displacement: 3070t surfaced; 3500t submerged
Dimensions: 251ft 9in x 31ft 8in x 25ft 3in (76.7m x 9.6m x 7.7m)
Machinery: one-shaft, nuclear, one reactor; 15,000hp
Armament: six 21in (533mm) TT (24 torpedoes)
Sensors: surface-search radar; active/passive sonar
Speed: 30 knots submerged
Range: limited only by reactor fuel state
Complement: 85

Until the advent of the one-off experimental boat USS *Albacore*, submarines were designed for making headway on the surface, as well as underwater. *Albacore* adopted a teardrop hull optimised for underwater operation, and led directly to the diesel-electric *Barbel* class and the nuclear-powered *Skipjacks*. USS *Skipjack* (SSN 585) herself was launched in May 1958 and completed in April 1959. Equipped with six torpedo tubes in the bow, the *Skipjack* class lacked sonar and SUBROC, but (apart from one accidental loss) the class nevertheless remained in use until the late 1980s. *Skipjack* was the last of the class to decommission, on 19 April 1990.

The teardrop-hulled *Skipjack* class proved efficient and popular attack submarines, and formed the basis of the *Los Angeles*-class missile boats.

SLAVA CLASS

USSR (RUSSIA): 1979

The Project 1164 Atlant (NATO code-name *Slava*) class were surface strike ships, with some anti-air and ASW capability. As a smaller contemporary of the *Kirovs*, the *Slavas* may have been intended as a less-expensive complement to the larger ships. Sixteen SS-N-12 anti-ship missiles are mounted in four pairs on either side of the superstructure, giving the ship a distinctive appearance. Initially designated 'Black Com1' by Western intelligence and subsequently the *Krasina* class, the first *Slava* class cruiser became operational in 1983, and by 1990 three were in the fleet, with the third beginning sea trials in August 1989. Some sources suggest that the Soviet Navy intended to build as many as 21 units of this class, which would have enabled them to replace the *Kynda* and *Kresta* classes as they retired in the 1990s. But such plans were not evident in actual Cold War-era building activity. The first of four ships in the class, *Slava*, was laid down in November 1976 and launched in July 1979. Completed one day before the end of 1982, *Slava* made her first deployment (with the Black Sea Fleet) in September 1983, while *Ustinov* went to the Northern Fleet. The end of the Cold War and the break-up of the Soviet Union led to the transfer of two ships to the Ukraine, with *Lobov* (originally *Komsomolets*) becoming *Poltava*, *Bohdan Khmenytsky* and finally *Vilna Ukraina*. The ship was then sold back to Russia in 1995. *Slava* was sent to the Ukraine and began a refit in December 1990, but this was stopped when only 40 per cent complete. Its future remains uncertain.

The *Slava* was the first of four *Slava*-class missile-armed cruisers built between 1976 and 1984. Two more ships in the class were cancelled in 1990.

Displacement: 10,000t standard; 12,500t full load
Dimensions: 613ft 6in x 68ft 3in x 24ft 7in (187m x 20.8m x 7.5m)
Machinery: four-shaft, COGOG, four gas turbines; 108,800–110,000hp
Armament: 16 SS-N-12 SSM; eight SA-N-6 SAM launchers (64 missiles), two SA-N-4 SAM launchers (40 missiles); two 5.1in (130mm); six 30mm AK-630 CIWS; 10 21in (533mm) TT; two RBU-6000 ASW RL; one Ka-25 'Hormone' helicopter
Sensors: air/surface-search radar; navigation radar; fire-control radar; hull-mounted sonar
Speed: 34 knots
Range: 9000nm (16,668km) at 15 knots
Complement: 529

SMYGE

SWEDEN: 1991

To develop stealth technology for its new *Visby* class (YS-2000) corvettes, now under construction, Sweden built the unique trials vessel *Smyge* (meaning 'stealth') – the only purpose built 'stealth ship' known to have been produced outside the USA. *Smyge* was a surface effect ship (air cushion) that used radar reflectant and absorbent material in its compact and low-profile design.

In addition to her technological features, *Smyge* also adopted a form of the Swedish 'Model 90' camouflage, which further reduced its visual signature, particularly in a littoral environment. Launched in March 1991, *Smyge* undertook a lengthy series of trials in the Baltic, including weapons firing and test and development work with new mine-hunting sonar. Once this research programme was completed, *Smyge* was retired and is held in floating storage at the Karlskronavarvet shipyard, where it was built.

Smyge made a substantial contribution to the development of Sweden's much larger *Visby* class corvettes – revolutionary 'stealth' warships unlike anything in service with any other navy.

Displacement: 140t full load
Dimensions: 99ft 9in x 37ft 5in x 6ft 3in (30.4m x 11.4m x 1.9m)
Machinery: two waterjets, two diesel engines, two lift fans with two diesels; 5550hp/1250hp
Armament: two RBS-15 SSM; one 40mm cannon; one, 15.75in (400mm) TT
Sensors: navigation radar
Speed: 50 knots
Range: not available
Complement: 14

SOVREMENNYY

USSR(RUSSIA): 1978

Displacement: 6200t standard; 7800t full load
Dimensions: 511ft 10in x 56ft 9in x 21ft 4in (155.5m x 17.3m x 5.8m)
Machinery: two-shaft, two steam turbines, four high-pressure boilers; 100,000–102,000hp
Armament: two SS-N-22 SSM launchers (eight missiles); two SA-N-7 SAM launchers (48 missiles), one SA-N-12 SAM launcher (24 missiles); two 5.1in (130mm); four 30mm AK-630 CIWS; four 21in (533mm) TT; two RBU-1000 ASW RL; 40 mines; one Ka-27 helicopter
Sensors: air/surface-search radar; navigation radar; fire-control radar; hull-mounted sonar
Speed: 35 knots
Range: 10,500nm (19,446km) at 14 knots
Complement: 380

The *Sovremennyy* was the first of a class of 20 missile cruisers (actually designated as destroyers in the Soviet Navy) which replaced the *Kresta* class in production at Zhdanov. The new vessels used basically the same hull, and the same pressure-fired steam plants, and had broadly similar armament, albeit with the addition of fore and aft turrets each containing a pair of 5.1in (130mm) guns. These were new weapons, liquid-cooled and capable of firing 70.5lb (32kg) shells over a range of just under 16.20nm (30km) at a rate of 86rpm. The primary SAM used by the new ships was the SA-N-7, with six guidance channels available for the two 24-round launchers. The primary offensive weapon was the Moskit (SS-N-22), a deadly anti-ship missile with a range of about 70nm (129km). The *Sovremennyy*-class ships were originally conceived as amphibious assault support ships, but they were revised to have a more general multi-purpose role, and entered service as the light RKR which would complement the heavy *Slava* class. The *Sovremennyy* was laid down in March 1976, launched in November 1978 and completed on Christmas Day, 1980. Zhdanov has completed some 19 ships in the class. At the end of the 1990s, the only large Russian Navy surface combatants active in significant numbers were the newer units of the dozen remaining *Sovremennyy*-class guided-missile destroyers and a few of the half-dozen remaining operational *Udaloy* class destroyers. At that time the two remaining unfinished Sovremennyys, *Vazhniy* and *Aleksandr Nevskiy* (ex-*Vdumchivyy*), were lying 65 per cent and 35 per cent complete, respectively, at St Petersburg, with only the first in the water. The first was delivered to China in early 2000, with a second to follow.

***Sovremennyy* and her sisterships formed the short-range elements within Soviet Navy's RKR divisions, operating alongside the heavyweight *Slavas* and *Kirovs*.**

SPARVIERO

ITALY: 1973

Displacement: 62.5t full load
Dimensions: (hull) 80ft 7in x 23ft x 6ft 2in (24.5m x 7m x 1.9m)
Machinery: one gas turbine with waterjet; (hull-borne) one-shaft, one diesel; 4500hp/180hp
Armament: two Otomat SSM; one 3in (76mm)
Sensors: surface-search radar
Speed: 50 knots
Range: 1200nm (2222km) at 18 knots
Complement: 10

The *Sparviero*-class hydrofoils were the product of a new collaboration between the Italian Government, the commercial hydrofoil manufacturer Carlo Rodriguez and Boeing, and marked the death of conventional Italian fast patrol boat development. The vessels use Boeing's jetfoil system, with a single forward foil, and two aft. The

The surviving *Sparviero*-class hydrofoils are now being retired, but the related Japanese-built PG 1 fast attack hydrofoils are likely to remain in service.

boats were powered by a Proteus gas turbine driving a waterjet when 'foilborne', while using a diesel when waterborne. This gave the boats a maximum speed of around 45 knots in the water, and about 50 knots when 'foilborne'. *Sparviero* (P420) was launched in May 1973, and after extensive trials, a production series of six more were completed during 1980–83. While the prototype used a single-cell missile launcher, the later boats used the Teseo system, with two Otomat Mk 2 sea-skimming missiles. All vessels in the class also had a compact turret forward housing a single 3in (76mm) gun. The boats have been modernised, gaining a new diesel powerplant, though plans to fit new, more powerful gas turbines were abandoned. Although enjoying excellent performance characteristics and a relatively heavy 'punch', the *Sparviero* class was always limited by the lack of onboard accommodation for the crew, restricting the type's radius of action and rendering it reliant on support ships or harbour facilities. *Sparviero* was the first of the class to be stricken, in September 1991, while another was paid off in 1996. The remainder will have been withdrawn from service by the end of 2002. The *Sparviero* class formed the basis of the Japanese PG 1 class of fast attack hydrofoils, three of which were built by Sumitomo, with assistance from Fincantieri, the Italian manufacturers.

SPICA

ITALY: 1989

Spica (P 403) was the third and penultimate vessel in what had been planned as a six-ship class of corvettes authorised in late 1982 and formally ordered in late 1986. Funded by the Ministry of the Merchant Navy, the four ships were built by Fincantieri at Muggiano. They are operated by the Italian Navy on behalf of the Coast Guard, and are tasked with EEZ (Exclusive Economic Zone) patrols. Broadly equivalent to some of the cutters used by the US Coast Guard, the Cassiopeia class ships were armed with 3in (76mm) guns and turrets stripped from redundant Bergamini class frigates, along with the associated SPG-70 fire-control radar. The ships have a telescopic hangar and a generously proportioned helicopter flight deck, and can carry a single AB212. The vessels are fitted out for search and rescue, resupply and fire-fighting. They are also capable of limited pollution control tasks, using a 17,657 cubic feet (500m³) tank to store polluted water. The lead ship in the class (*Cassiopeia*, P401) was launched in July 1988, with *Spica* following in May 1989. Plans for four extra ships did not materialise, but the fifth and sixth vessels were ordered and then cancelled. Their roles have partly been fulfilled by the larger, better-armed and more sophisticated *Minerva*-class corvettes, and also by four of the newer *Lupo* class frigates which were originally ordered by Iraq but whose delivery was delayed by the Iran-Iraq war, and which were subsequently purchased back following Operation Desert Storm. With their non-standard sonar and EW equipment removed, they are ideal (if a little large) for patrol duties.

The *Spica* was one of four patrol cutters (of a class once planned to consist of eight ships) delivered to the Italian Navy for operations on behalf of the Coast Guard.

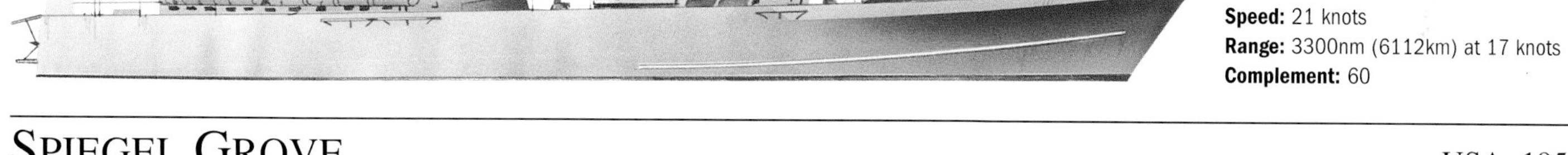

Displacement: 1110t standard; 1475t full load
Dimensions: 261ft 10in x 38ft 9in x 11ft 10in (79.8m x 11.8m x 3.6m)
Machinery: two-shaft, two diesel engines; 8800hp
Armament: one 3in (76mm); two 20mm cannon; one helicopter
Sensors: surface-search radar
Speed: 21 knots
Range: 3300nm (6112km) at 17 knots
Complement: 60

SPIEGEL GROVE

USA: 1955

Displacement: 6880t standard; 12,150t full load
Dimensions: 510ft x 84ft x 19ft (155.5m x 25.6m x 5.8m)
Machinery: two-shaft, steam turbines, two boilers; 24,000hp
Armament: 16 3in (76mm) (later 12, then six); 12 20mm cannon
Sensors: navigation radar
Speed: 22.5 knots
Range: 10,000nm (18,520km) at 20 knots
Complement: 404, plus 341 troops

Launched in November 1955, USS *Spiegel Grove* (LSD 32) was one of eight *Thomaston* class dock landing ships built for the US Navy during the mid-1950s. These ships had deeper well-decks than on previous LSDs, with portable mezzanine and super-decks for cargo or helicopter operation. The ships all had large cranes, and strengthened bows for ice navigation. The last two ships in the class were also air-conditioned. *Spiegel Grove* was finally stricken in February 1994, after a period in reserve.

The *Thomaston* class LSDs proved to be effective, if unglamorous, and gave the USA's amphibious forces a much needed boost following the Korean War.

SPOKOINYY

USSR (RUSSIA): 1953

The destroyer *Spokoinyy* was the first of 27 Project 56 *Kotlin* class ships – lighter, cheaper alternatives to the planned *Neustrashimyys*. They were the last gun- and torpedo-armed Soviet destroyers and production ran from 1954 to 1961. Four of the hulls initially laid down as *Kotlins* were completed as *Kildin* missile destroyers. An additional eight *Krupnyy*/*Kanin* missile destroyers were built to a similar design. Subsequently, 11 or 12 units were modernised under Project 56-PLO *Kotlin Mod*. *Bravy* was completed as the sole Project 56-K *Kotlin SAM* ship, to serve as an experimental prototype to test the SA-N-1 missile before seven or eight other ships were modernised under the Project 56-A *Kotlin SAM* programme. With an SA-N-1 mount aft, in place of their original guns, the ships became the first Soviet anti-air warfare oriented destroyers. One *Kotlin SAM* ship, *Spavedlivy*, was transferred to Poland and renamed the *Warszawa*. The last of the *Kotlin*, *Kotlin SAM* and *Kildin MOD* destroyers were retired in the late 1980s.

The high bows of *Spokoinyy* and the rest of her class made them extremely 'dry' when underway, even in heavy seas, and they were popular with their crews.

Displacement: 2662t standard; 3230t full load
Dimensions: 413ft 9in x 41ft 8in x 13ft 9in (126.1m x 12.7m x 4.2m)
Machinery: two-shaft, steam turbines; 72,000hp
Armament: one twin SA-N-1 SAM launcher (16–22 missiles); four 5.1in (130mm) and 16 45mm; 10 21in (533mm) TT; six depth charge projectors, two depth charge racks; two RBU-6000 ASW RL
Sensors: air/surface-search radar; navigation radar; fire-control radar; hull-mounted sonar
Speed: 36 knots
Range: 4000nm (7408km) at 14 knots
Complement: approximately 300

SPRUANCE

USA: 1973

USS *Spruance* (DD 963) was the lead ship in a class of 30 fleet escort destroyers ordered in June 1970 from Litton Industries' new Ingalls Shipbuilding Division. Launched in November 1973 and completed in September 1975, *Spruance* was a large destroyer, its size dictated by the requirement for a 30 knots speed and by a common hull for planned ASW and anti-aircraft versions. The 30 *Spruance* class destroyers entered service between 1975 and 1980, and the class has been subject to a succession of modifications and upgrades. Nine ships were fitted with pairs of armoured launcher boxes for Tomahawk cruise missiles from 1984, but since then, Mk 41 vertical launchers for 45 TLAMs and 16 ASROCs have been fitted in place of the original Mk 26 launchers which contained Standard SAMs and/or ASROC. The class is also receiving improved ASW and sonar equipment. Four further *Spruance*-based anti-aircraft destroyers were ordered by pre-Revolution Iran, and these were subsequently purchased for the US Navy as the Kidd class. These were followed by a 31st *Spruance* class destroyer, the only one of seven planned extra ships to be built.

***Spruance*-class destroyers have been among the US Navy's b usiest and most useful warships in the post-Cold War era. Eleven participated in Operation Desert Storm, and the type has been a regular delivery platform for Tomahawk TLAMs fired at Iraqi targets.**

Displacement: 5826t standard; 7800t full load
Dimensions: 563ft 4in x 55ft x 20ft 6in (171.70m x 16.76m x 6.25m)
Machinery: two-shaft, four gas turbines; 80,000hp
Armament: one Sea Sparrow SAM launcher (24 missiles); one ASROC launcher; two 5in (127mm); six 12.75in (324mm) TT; one SH-2 Seasprite (LAMPS I) helicopter
Sensors: air/surface-search radar; navigation radar; fire-control radar; hull-mounted sonar
Speed: 30 knots
Range: 6000nm (11,112km) at 20 knots
Complement: 296

SRI INDERA SAKTI

MALAYSIA: 1980

Displacement: 1800t standard; 4300t full load
Dimensions: 328ft x 49ft 2in x 15ft 8in (99.8m x 14.9m x 4.8m)
Machinery: two-shaft, two diesels; 5986hp
Armament: one 40mm cannon
Sensors: navigation radar; optronic fire control
Speed: 16.5 knots
Range: 60 days endurance
Complement: 215

The *Sri Indera Sakti* (1503) was the first in a two-ship class of logistic support ships for the Royal Malaysian Navy, and was launched in 1980. Each ship features a 15-tonnes capacity crane amidships, along with a massive vehicle hold, a divers' compression chamber, and a large operations room. Both ships had a helicopter landing spot aft, while the second vessel has an extended flight deck replacing the normal funnel. The latter ship, *Mahawangsa* (1504), is specially equipped to carry ammunition.

The *Sri Indera Sakti* class are used for cadet training as well as long-range transport and support. The first ship had a prominent funnel; the second lacked this feature.

ST LAURENT

CANADA: 1951

With a pressing need for additional ASW capability, the then Royal Canadian Navy opted to build an indigenous type. The resulting design was similar to the British Type 12, without being too close in appearance, and used the same machinery with US and Canadian electronics. The first of the new class, *St Laurent* (DDE 205), was launched in November 1951 and completed in October 1955. All seven ships were extensively modernised between 1961 and 1966, losing their 40mm guns and a Limbo Mk 10 mortar to make way for variable-depth sonar on the stern. A raised helicopter deck (for a single CH-124A Sea King) was added on the rear deck, with a new hangar forward of this. *St Laurent* was the first of the class to be retired; she was laid up in 1974 and sold for scrap in 1979. The remaining six ships were given a Destroyer Life Extension (DELEX) upgrade in 1980–81, and the last of the class were finally put up for disposal in 1994.

The *St Laurent* class destroyers were broadly equivalent to the Royal Navy's *Whitbys*, using much of the same equipment, but were designed to look different; their Canadian origin.

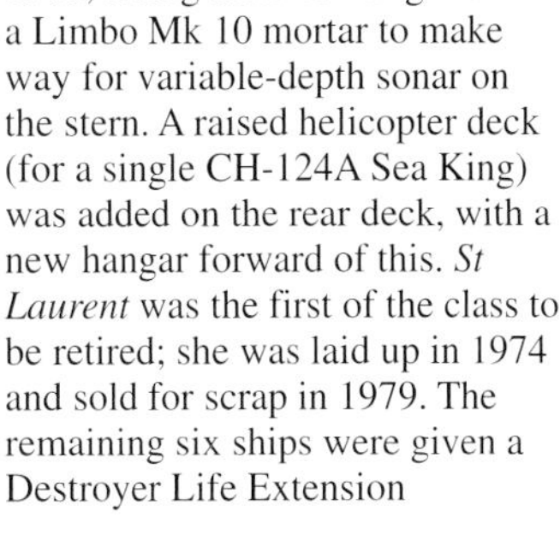

Displacement: 2000t standard; 2600t full load
Dimensions: 366ft x 42ft x 13ft 2in (111.6m x 12.8m x 4m)
Machinery: two-shaft, geared steam turbines, two boilers; 30,000hp
Armament four 3in (76mm); two 40mm cannon; two Limbo Mk 10 ASW mortars (as built)
Sensors: air/surface-search radar; fire-control radar; hull-mounted sonar
Speed: 28 knots
Range: 7500nm (13,890km) at 16 knots
Complement: 290

SUFFREN

FRANCE: 1965

Displacement: 5090t standard; 6090t full load
Dimensions: 517ft x 51ft x 24ft (157.6m x 15.5m x 7.3m)
Machinery: two-shaft, geared steam turbines, four boilers; 72,500hp
Armament: one Masurca SAM system (48 missiles); one Malafon ASW system (13 missiles); two 3.9in (100mm); four 20mm cannon; catapults for torpedoes
Sensors: air-search radar; navigation radar; fire-control radar; hull-mounted sonar
Speed: 34 knots
Range: 5000nm (9260km) at 18 knots
Complement: 355

France originally planned to acquire three *Suffren*-class guided missile destroyers, with more to follow, but only two were actually completed. *Suffren* (D 602) was launched in 1965 and completed in 1967. The two ships were designed to protect the carriers *Foch* and *Clemenceau*. Their primary air defence weapon was the Masurca SAM, with Malafon missiles or torpedoes for ASW. From 1977, the two ships gained Exocet ASMs, and they have since been extensively modernised.

The massive spherical radome of the *Suffren*-class destroyers housed a DRBI 23 3-D air search and tracking radar, vital for their carrier air defence role.

SURCOUF

FRANCE: 1953

The 12-ship *Surcouf* (T 47) class of destroyers were based on pre-war French designs, bore a strong resemblance to the *Hardi* class, and were larger than most of their contemporaries. *Surcouf* (D 521) was launched in October 1953 and completed in November 1955. During the 1960s, *Surcouf* had her forward 57mm gun position removed and was converted to command ship status. *Surcouf* was broken up in 1971 – one of the first two of the class to be withdrawn from use.

Four T 47s were fitted with the Tartar missile, while five were converted to ASW configuration, gaining Malafon ASW missile launchers and a new air-search radar.

Displacement: 2750t standard; 3740t full load
Dimensions: 422ft x 42ft x 18ft (128.6m x 12.8m x 5.5m)
Machinery: two-shaft, geared steam turbines, four boilers; 63,000hp
Armament: six 5in (127mm), six 57mm (later four); four 20mm cannon; 12 21.66in (550mm) TT
Sensors: air-search radar; navigation radar; fire-control radar; hull-mounted sonar
Speed: 34 knots
Range: 5000nm (9260km) at 18 knots
Complement: 347

SWIFTSURE

GB: 1971

HMS *Swiftsure* (S 126) was the first of a class of six nuclear attack submarines that were, in some respects, improved *Valiant* class submarines. With a shorter, fuller hull-form, the *Swiftsures* had only five torpedo tubes in the bow, though full height and full width are maintained for a greater length of the hull. *Swiftsure* was launched in September 1971 and completed in April 1973. The remainder of the class entered service between 1974 and 1981, and the final boat, HMS *Splendid*, then participated in the Falklands conflict. HMS *Swiftsure* was paid off in 1992, well in advance of her sisterships. The other five *Swiftsures* remain in front-line service, now armed with torpedoes, Sub-Harpoon SSM and Tomahawk TLAMs, following a major refit between 1987 and 1997. HMS *Splendid* became the first *Swiftsure* to receive a full load of Tomahawk TLAMs, and then became the first to fire Tomahawk in anger during Operation Allied Force.

Despite their age, the Royal Navy's *Swiftsure*-class submarines remain among the service's most important and most potent assets.

Displacement: 4000t surfaced; 4900t submerged
Dimensions: 272ft x 32ft 4in x 27ft (82.9m x 9.8m x 8.2m)
Machinery: one-shaft, nuclear, one PWR1 reactor with two geared steam turbines and one diesel-electric auxiliary motor; 15,000hp/4000hp
Armament: five 21in (533mm) TT (maximum of 21 Tigerfish torpedoes, four Sub-Harpoon missiles and Tomahawk cruise missiles)
Sensors: general-purpose radar; active/passive multi-function sonar
Speed: 20 knots surfaced; 30 knots submerged
Range: limited only by reactor fuel state
Complement: 116

SYDNEY

AUSTRALIA: 1944/1948

Displacement: 14,000t standard; 17,780t full load
Dimensions: 695ft x 80ft x 23ft (211.8m x 24.4m x 7m)
Machinery: two-shaft, geared steam turbines, four three-drum boilers; 40,000hp
Armament: 24 40mm cannon; 37 aircraft (12 Sea Furies, 24 Fireflies, one Sea Otter)
Sensors: air-search and height-finding radar
Speed: 25 knots
Range: 9320nm (17,261km) at 14 knots
Complement: 1300

The aircraft carrier HMS *Terrible* was launched in April 1944, but was transferred to Australia in 1948, before her completion in February 1949. As HMAS *Sydney* (R17), the carrier played a major part in the Korean War, but a planned modernisation due in 1954 was cancelled. From 1953 onwards, the carrier was used only for training and her place in the front-line was taken on by the borrowed HMS *Vengeance*, prior to the introduction of HMAS *Melbourne*. From 1962, *Sydney* was used as a fast transport, most notably taking trucks and military vehicles to Vietnam.

HMAS *Sydney* was the former Royal Navy *Colossus*-class carrier HMS *Terrible*.

TACHIKAZE

JAPAN: 1974

Tachikaze (DDG-168) was the first of three graceful destroyers built for the Japanese Maritime Self Defence Force between 1973 and 1979. They introduced a considerable improvement in air defence capability over their predecessors. Each ship in the class had a progressively more advanced combat data system, and all have been upgraded since being commissioned. *Tachikaze* gained Harpoon SSM and Phalanx CIWS in 1983, and the other ships in the class followed in 1987.

The three *Tachikaze*-class destroyers were designed as general-purpose combatants, with a useful mix of Standard SAMs, ASW ASROC and Harpoon SSM.

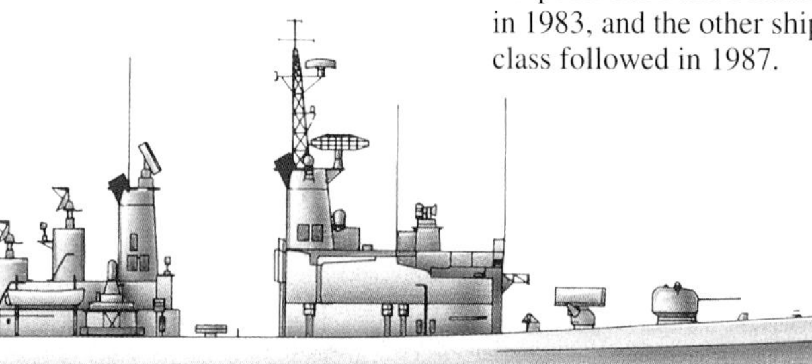

Displacement: 3850t standard; 4800t full load
Dimensions: 469ft 2in x 46ft 10in x 15ft 1in (143m x 14.3m x 4.6m)
Machinery: two-shaft, geared turbines, two boilers; 70,000hp
Armament: eight Harpoon SSM; one Mk 13 Standard SAM launcher; one ASROC launcher; two 5in (127mm); two 20mm Phalanx CIWS; six 12.75in (324mm) TT; one SH-60J helicopter
Sensors: air/surface-search radar; fire-control radar; hull-mounted sonar
Speed: 32 knots
Range: not available
Complement: 277

TAMANDARE

BRAZIL: TRANSFERRED 1951

Displacement: 10,000t standard
Dimensions: 608ft 4in x 61ft 9in x 19ft 5in (185.4m x 18.8m x 5.9m)
Machinery: four-shaft, eight boilers; 100,000hp
Armament: 15 6in (152mm), eight 5in (127mm); 28 40mm cannon, eight 20mm cannon; one helicopter
Sensors: air/surface-search radar
Speed: 33 knots
Range: not available
Complement: 868

The USS *St Louis* was built as the eighth of nine *Brooklyn* class cruisers, and was launched in December 1936. She differed from the seven earlier ships in the class (including *Philadelphia*, delivered to Brazil as the *Barroso*) in having revised armament and superstructure, giving her a considerably different outline. Six of the class were eventually transferred to Latin American navies: two (*Phoenix* and *Boise*) to Argentina, two (*Brooklyn* and *Nashville*) to Chile, and two (*Philadelphia* and *St Louis*) to Brazil. The best known of these was USS *Phoenix*, which became the *General Belgrano*, sunk by the Royal Navy in 1982. The *St Louis*, transferred to Brazil in 1951 as the *Tamandare* (C12), gave valuable service until 1973, when she was put up for disposal. Fitted with a sizeable hangar and catapults in US Navy service, the ship used helicopters while with the Brazilian Navy. Finally sold for scrap in 1980, the ship foundered and sank while under tow to Taiwan!

With its twin funnels and four stacked gun turrets, *Tamandare* looked every inch the pre-war battle wagon that she was. Limited upgrades in Brazilian Navy service did little to change her fundamental appearance.

TANG

USA: 1951

USS *Tang* (SS 563) was the first of six attack submarines designed using lessons learned from the influential German Type XXI U-boats. They were as much experimental/research vessels as they were front-line fleet submarines. The first four boats were powered by a novel (and exceptionally unreliable) compact radial ('pancake') diesel, and had to be lengthened by 9ft (2.74m) in 1957 to allow installation of a more conventional powerplant. Before this stretch, the boats were characterised by their extremely low drag, and were exceptionally fast underwater. Using a developed Schnorkel, the boats could remain submerged for extended periods, and one of the class circumnavigated the globe during September 1957–February 1958. *Tang* received a further stretch in 1967, of 15ft (4.57m). Plans to transfer *Tang* and two others to Iran were halted by the Islamic Revolution in 1979, and two of the boats were instead passed to Turkey, initially under a lease agreement. Tang became the *Piri Reis* in 1980, and was purchased outright in 1987.

Originally similar in appearance to the experimental *Seawolf*, the *Tang* later had its conning tower revised, and was lengthened and re-engined, significantly changing its appearance.

Displacement: 1560t surfaced; 2260t submerged
Dimensions: 269ft 2in x 27ft 2in x 17ft (82m x 8.3m x 5.2m)
Machinery: two-shaft, three diesel engines and two electric motors; 4500hp/5600hp
Armament: eight 21in (533mm) TT
Sensors: sonar fit
Speed: 15 knots surfaced; 18.8 knots submerged
Range: not available
Complement: 83

TANGO CLASS

USSR: 1972

Displacement: 3100t surfaced; 3900t submerged
Dimensions: 300ft 3in x 29ft 6in x 23ft (91.5m x 9m x 7m)
Machinery: three-shaft, diesel engines; 6000hp
Armament: six 21in (533mm) TT
Sensors: active/passive sonar fit
Speed: 20 knots surfaced; 16 knots submerged
Range: not available
Complement: 72

Project 641 BUKI (NATO codename *Tango*) submarines were a derivative of the earlier Project 641 (*Foxtrot*), with more automated systems, a sonar complex linked to a combat information control system, and an autopilot. The class carried 20 per cent more torpedoes, had improved silencing and crew accommodation. The first example was launched in 1972 and 18 BUKIs were used to provide a defensive screen for the Northern Fleet.

The BUKI designation was derived from the Russian phrases for armament change (B), enlarged (U), new command system (K) and emergency design (I).

TARAWA

USA: 1973

The USS *Tarawa* (LHA 1) was the first of a class of five assault ships. She was launched in December 1973 and commissioned in May 1976. The *Tarawa* class ships routinely embark up to six AV-8B Harrier II+ fighters in addition to a mix of helicopters, or they can operate nine CH-53 Sea Stallion or as many as 12 CH-46 Sea Knight helicopters. The ships incorporate comprehensive command and control facilities, allowing them to fulfil a flagship role. They also have an austere 3-D radar, enabling them to perform limited fighter control functions. There have been periodic attempts to produce a full carrier conversion of the *Tarawa* class LHA hull, for the US Navy or for export customers like Australia. Apart from its 'Air Wing', each *Tarawa* class ship has a floodable well-deck for landing craft, and can carry up to 1903 troops who have access to a 5000 square feet (464.5m²) acclimatisation/training room.

***Tarawa* is exceptionally large for an amphibious assault ship; larger (but lighter) than the last conventional British carrier, *Ark Royal*.**

Displacement: 25,588t standard; 38,761t full load
Dimensions: 820ft x 126ft x 25ft 9in (249.9m x 38.4m x 7.8m)
Machinery: two-shaft, geared turbines, two boilers; 70,000hp
Armament: two RAM launchers; two 5in (127mm); six Mk 24 25mm cannon; two 20mm Phalanx CIWS; one helicopter
Sensors: air/surface-search radar; navigation radar; fire-control radar
Speed: 24 knots
Range: 10,000nm (18,520km) at 20 knots
Complement: 892, plus 1903 troops

THETIS

DENMARK: 1989

Four Stanflex 2000 ships were ordered in 1987 to replace Denmark's *Hvindbjørnen* class 'inspection vessels', which were frigates in all but name. It was planned that the new *Thetis* class would receive Harpoon and Sea Sparrow to augment their 3in (76mm) gun and 20mm cannon, but this has not yet happened. *Thetis* (F357) was the lead ship in the class, launched in July 1989 and commissioned in 1991.

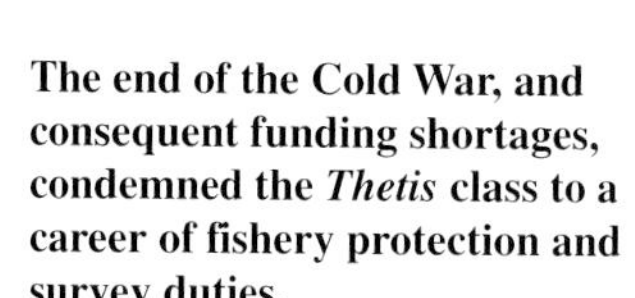

Displacement: 2600t standard; 3500t full load

The end of the Cold War, and consequent funding shortages, condemned the *Thetis* class to a career of fishery protection and survey duties.

Dimensions: 369ft 1in x 47ft 3in x 19ft 8in (112.5m x 14.4m x 6m)
Machinery: one-shaft, three diesel engines; 12,000hp
Armament: one 3in (76mm); one 20mm cannon; depth charge racks; one helicopter
Sensors: air/surface-search radar; navigation radar; hull-mounted and towed array sonar
Speed: 21.5 knots
Range: 8500nm (15,742km) at 15.5 knots
Complement: 61

THRESHER

USA: 1960

Displacement: 3705t surfaced; 4311t submerged
Dimensions: 278ft 6in x 31ft 8in x 25ft 2in (84.9m x 9.6m x 7.7m)
Machinery: one-shaft, nuclear, one reactor; 15,000hp
Armament four 21in (533mm) TT (torpedoes, SUBROC and Sub-Harpoon SSM)
Sensors: active/passive sonar fit
Speed: 27 knots submerged
Range: limited only by reactor fuel state
Complement: 94

The USS *Thresher* (SSN 593) was the lead ship in a class of 11 attack submarines that were officially distinct from the 42 *Sturgeon* class submarines which followed, although the two classes were extremely similar, the *Sturgeons* representing no more than an improved derivative of the earlier submarines. In fact, the 42-ship total includes three vessels originally laid down as *Permit*-class submarines. The *Permit* class itself included four submarines originally intended as SSGNs that would have been armed with Regulus II missiles. These submarines were completed as *Threshers* after the 1958 cancellation of the Regulus programme. The USS *Thresher* was launched in July 1960, but was lost off New England during diving trials in April 1963, with the 108 crewmen, four officers and 17 civilian trials specialists. The class was then renamed after the second submarine, USS *Permit* (SSN 594). The submarines used the same S5W reactor as the earlier, smaller *Skipjack* class, and a lengthened version of the same 'Albacore-type' teardrop hull. But because they were bigger and heavier, the new submarines were quite slow, reportedly able to make no more than 26 knots. This limited their effectiveness as attack submarines, and all had been withdrawn by 1992. One ship in the class, USS *Jack*, was fitted with a unique contra-rotating, coaxial dual propeller in an effort to improve performance. This produced a 10 per cent improvement in efficiency and reduced noise, but there was no increase in speed, and it was not fitted fleet-wide. The later *Sturgeons* remained in use, but several were converted for special forces insertion duties, and others for the use of Harpoon and Tomahawk cruise missiles.

The *Thresher/Permit*-class attack submarines were slightly shorter than the *Sturgeons* that followed. They had a shorter, lower-drag sail, and were fitted with more primitive electronics.

TICONDEROGA

USA: 1981

Based on the hull of the *Spruance* class destroyer, the *Ticonderoga* class was originally conceived as the conventional part of a conventional/nuclear mix of missile frigates, later re-designated as cruisers. The nuclear strike cruiser programme was subsequently cancelled. The Aegis air defence system (originally fitted to the California class nuclear cruisers *California* and *South Carolina*) was installed in what was viewed as a minimum platform for Aegis, affordable in relatively large numbers. USS *Ticonderoga* (CG 47) led a class of 27 ships, and was launched in April 1981. She was less powerfully armed than the planned nuclear strike cruiser, with no 8in (203mm) gun, and with only two quadruple canisters of Harpoon missiles. The ship also carried Standard SAMs, ASROC, torpedoes and two 5in (127mm) guns, and two SH-60B Seahawk (LAMPS III) helicopters. Later ships in the class (CG 52 onwards) had enlarged missile storage, increased to 122 rounds, and Tomahawk cruise missiles.

Displacement: 6560t standard; 8910t full load
Dimensions: 563ft x 65ft x 31ft (171.60m x 19.81m x 9.45m)
Machinery: two-shaft, four gas turbines; 80,000hp
Armament: eight Harpoon SSM; two Mk 26 launchers (68 Standard SAM and 20 ASROC torpedoes); two 5in (127mm); six 12.75in (324mm) TT; one SH-60J helicopter
Sensors: Aegis air defence system; air/surface-search radar; navigation radar; fire-control radar; hull-mounted sonar and towed array
Speed: 30 knots
Range: 6000nm (11,112km) at 16 knots
Complement: 343

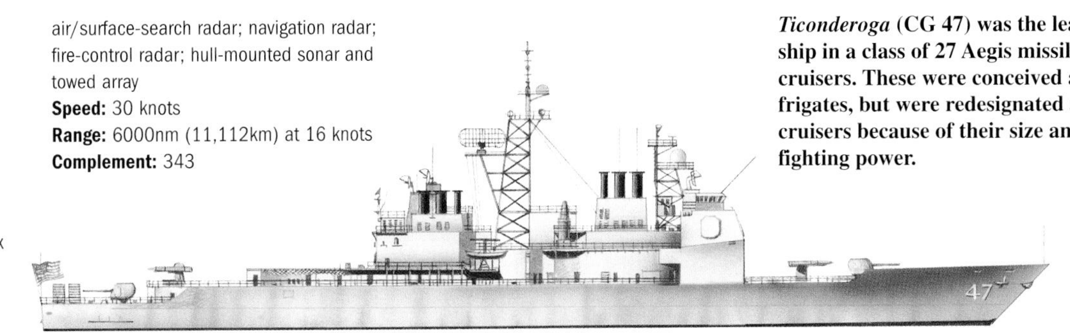

***Ticonderoga* (CG 47) was the lead ship in a class of 27 Aegis missile cruisers. These were conceived as frigates, but were redesignated as cruisers because of their size and fighting power.**

TORBAY

GB: 1985

The first submarine in the Trafalgar class was launched on 1 July 1981, having been ordered in 1977. The new class followed on directly from the *Swiftsure* attack boats, which it closely resembled. These deadly hunter-killers today form the backbone of the Royal Navy's ASW capability, detecting, identifying, and stalking enemy submarines while remaining undetected themselves. Exceptionally quiet (they are reckoned to be the world's quietest nuclear submarines), the *Trafalgars* are covered with conformal anechoic tiles and have retractable foreplanes and a strengthened fin for under-ice operations. They are also capable of operating at extreme depths (below 1640ft (500m) according to some sources). Armed with 20–21 Mk 24 Mod 2 Tigerfish wire-guided torpedoes (fired from five bow tubes) and four UGM-84A Sub-Harpoon anti-ship missiles, the *Trafalgar* class submarines also have a powerful anti-ship capability, and can also be used for surveillance duties. HMS *Torbay* was the fourth of the seven submarines in the *Trafalgar* class, and was ordered in June 1981. Laid down by VSEL at Barrow in December 1982, she was launched in March 1985 and commissioned in February 1987. While early boats in the class had a conventional seven-bladed propeller, *Torbay* and some of her sisterships have a shrouded propulsor instead. Colloquially known as 'T-boats' in service, the *Trafalgar* class boats serve with the 2nd Submarine Squadron at Devonport. The submarines were extensively modified during the 1990s, receiving sonar and countermeasures improvements. They also received Spearfish torpedoes, and will gain Tomahawk cruise missiles.

***Torbay* was the fourth of seven *Trafalgar*-class attack submarines, an advanced derivative of the previous *Swiftsure* class.**

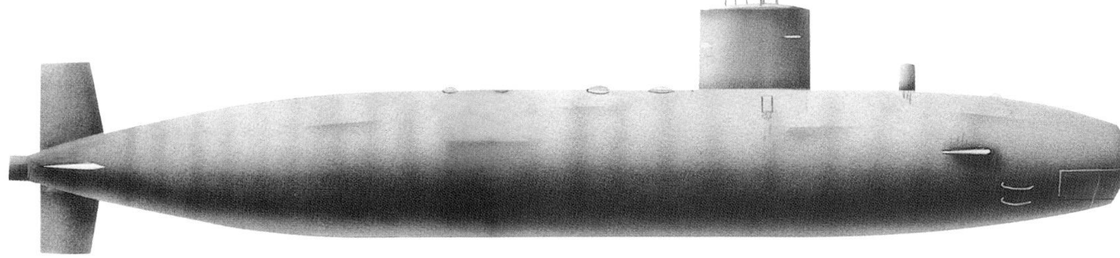

Displacement: 4700t surfaced; 5200t submerged
Dimensions: 280ft 2in x 32ft 2in x 31ft 3in (85.4m x 9.8m x 9.5m)
Machinery: one-shaft, nuclear, one PWR1 reactor with two geared steam turbines, one diesel-electric auxiliary motor and two batteries; 15,000hp/4000hp
Armament: five 21in (533mm) TT (maximum of 21 Tigerfish torpedoes, four Sub-Harpoon anti-ship missiles)
Sensors: general-purpose radar; active/passive multi-function sonar
Speed: 20 knots surfaced; 30 knots submerged
Range: limited only by reactor fuel state
Complement: 97

TORQUAY

GB: 1954

Displacement: 2150t standard; 2560t full load
Dimensions: 370ft x 41ft x 17ft (112.8m x 12.5m x 5.2m)
Machinery: two-shaft, geared steam turbines, two boilers; 30,000hp
Armament: two twin 4.5in (114mm); two 40mm cannon (later one); 12 21in (533mm) TT; one Limbo Mk 10 ASW mortar
Sensors: air/surface-search radar; fire-control radar; hull-mounted sonar
Speed: 29 knots
Range: 4500nm (8334km) at 12 knots
Complement: 231

Planned as the second of the Royal Navy's *Whitby* class frigates, HMS *Torquay* (F 43) was actually launched one day before Cammell Laird's HMS *Whitby*, on 1 July 1954. This hull had a sharp V-form forward, with a widened, deep square cross-section. These features allowed very high sustained speeds, even in rough seas, while the raised topgallant forecastle kept the bridge free of spray and 'green water', although it did mean that the bridge was located well aft. The large, 12ft (3.66m) diameter screws turned slowly, and quietly, making the class highly effective sub-hunters and sub-chasers. *Torquay* and her two initial sisterships were built with an unusually thin, 'stove-pipe' funnel, but this caused smoke corrosion to the radar array, and was replaced by the thicker, raked and capped funnel used on later ships in the class. Weight-saving on the ships also went 'too far' initially, and all six ships had to be replated soon after they entered service.

The Type 12 *Whitby* class frigate introduced the outstanding hull-form later used by the *Rothesay* class and the *Leander* class.

TRIBAL (PROJECT, NOT BUILT) CANADA: 1960

Canada's *Tribal* class ships evolved into the very similar *Iroquois* class DDHs.

This class of eight large frigates for the Royal Canadian Navy was announced in 1960 as the *Tribal* class. However, the entire programme was cancelled in 1963, before any orders had been placed. In 1986, rhw long-deferred plans to build AAW ships came to fruition, and a contract was awarded to Litton Systems Canada Ltd for the *Tribal*-class Update and Modernisation Programme (TRUMP). The basic hull was used to form the basis of the *Iroquois* class.

Displacement: 3551t standard; 4700t full load
Dimensions: 423ft x 50ft x 14ft 6in (128.9m x 15.2m x 4.4m)
Machinery: two-shaft, geared steam turbines; 30,000hp
Armament: one Tartar SAM system; one 5in (127mm); ASW TTs
Sensors: air/surface-search radar; fire-control radar; hull-mounted sonar (assumed)
Speed: 30 knots
Range: not defined
Complement: 232, plus air crew

TRITON USA: 1958

Displacement: 5963t surfaced; 7773t submerged
Dimensions: 447ft 6in x 36ft 11in x 23ft 6in (136.4m x 11.2m x 7.2m)
Machinery: two-shaft, nuclear, two reactors; 34,000hp
Armament: six 21in (533mm) TT
Sensors: long-range air-surveillance radar; sonar
Speed: 27 knots surfaced; 20 knots submerged
Range: limited only by reactor fuel state
Complement: 180

The radar picket submarine USS *Triton* (SSRN 586) was a massive vessel, with a huge sail into which radar antennae could retract, and a surprisingly high surface speed of 27 knots. The vessel was powered by two S4G reactors, producing 34,000hp – roughly the same power output as enjoyed by the mighty Ohio class missile submarines today. The ship served for only two years before being reclassified as an attack submarine in 1961. The two Sailfish class radar pickets were reclassified at the same time, having been rendered unnecessary by developments in land-based radar and AEW, and by the success of the DEW (Distant Early Warning) line. The ship proved too unwieldy and too expensive to operate in the attack role, and was decommissioned in May 1969. Plans to use the vessel as an alternative National Command Post Afloat (like the cruiser *Northampton*) came to nothing. USS *Triton* then gained the dubious distinction of being the world's first nuclear submarine to be laid up.

The massive *Triton* was the US Navy's largest nuclear submarine until the introduction of the *Ethan Allen* class and *Lafayette* class strategic submarines; larger even than the mighty *Los Angeles* class attack submarines.

TRITON GB: 2000

The research vessel *Triton* is the world's first large powered trimaran ship. It is a revolutionary vessel which has been described as 'the most significant development in warship design since the ironclads'. *Triton*'s size will allow an excellent range of 3000nm which will allow her to cross the Atlantic.

Launched on 6 May, 2000, once complete *Triton* will undertake two years of trials to fully evaluate the trimaran concept and determine its suitability for a new generation of warships. If successful, the first trimaran frigate for the Royal Navy could be in service by 2010.

Displacement: 1200t
Dimensions: 324ft x 74ft x 29ft 7in (98.7m x 22.5m x 9m)
Machinery: one-shaft, two thrusters; two diesel generators, three electric motors; 2085kW at 1800rpm
Speed: 20 knots
Range: 3000nm (5556km) at 12 knots
Complement: 24

***Triton* is the final stepping stone to the trimaran warship becoming a reality.**

TROMP THE NETHERLANDS: 1973

The guided missile frigate *Tromp* (F 801) was one of two ordered by the Royal Netherlands Navy as replacements for its ageing de Ruyter class 6in (152mm) gun cruisers. The *Tromp* was launched in June 1973 and completed in October 1975. Heavily influenced by the contemporary British Leander class, the two Tromps used the same powerplant. Both vessels have been extensively modernised and upgraded in service, and they remain useful flagships for the Dutch anti-submarine task groups.

Displacement: 3665t standard; 4308t full load
Dimensions: 453ft x 49ft x 22ft (138.1m x 14.9m x 6.7m)
Machinery: two-shaft, CODOG, four gas turbines; 44,000hp/8200hp
Armament: eight Harpoon SSM; one Mk 13 Standard SAM launcher (40 missiles), one octuple Sea Sparrow SAM launcher; two 4.7in (120mm); one 30mm Goalkeeper CIWS; two 20mm cannon; six 12.75in (324mm) TT
Sensors: air/surface-search radar; navigation radar; fire-control radar; hull-mounted sonar
Speed: 28 knots
Range: 5000nm (9260km) at 18 knots
Complement: 306

The missile frigate *Tromp* and her sistership were distinguished by a massive radome above and behind the bridge. The original aluminium dome was replaced by plastic in a 1980 upgrade.

TRUXTON

USA: 1964

The one-off USS *Truxton* (DLGN 35, later CGN 35) was a nuclear-powered version of the Belknap class cruiser, enlarged to accommodate a nuclear powerplant and ordered because Congress ordered that one of the seven frigates approved in FY62 must be nuclear-powered. The *Truxton* thereby became the fourth nuclear-powered ship in the US Navy, following the cruiser *Long Beach*, the carrier *Enterprise* and the missile frigate *Bainbridge*. It was the fifth US Navy ship to be named after Commodore Thomas Truxton, a notable naval commander of the late 18th century. The escort cruiser *Truxton* was laid down in June 1963, launched in December 1964 and completed in May 1967. Over the years she was subjected to modest improvements, such as the replacement of her 3in (76mm) gun mount with Harpoon missiles in 1980. A Phalanx CIWS was added later in the 1980s, along with an improved EW suite. *Truxton* was decommissioned in 1993.

Though derived from the *Belknap*-class cruisers, *Truxton* bore a passing resemblance to the nuclear-powered *Bainbridge*.

Displacement: 8149t standard; 8927t full load
Dimensions: 564ft x 57ft 10in x 19ft 10in (171.9m x 17.6m x 6m)
Machinery: two-shaft, nuclear, two reactors, two geared turbines; 60,000hp
Armament: one combined Terrier SAM/ASROC launcher; one 5in (127mm), two 3in (76mm) (later replaced by Harpoon SSM); two 20mm Phalanx CIWS (later); six 12.75in (324mm) TT
Sensors: air/surface-search radar; navigation radar; fire-control radar; hull-mounted sonar
Speed: 30+ knots
Range: limited only by reactor fuel state
Complement: 490

TYPE 82/42 DESTROYER

GB: 1969

Displacement: 6700t standard; 7700t full load
Dimensions: 507ft x 55ft x 22ft 6in (154.5m x 16.8m x 6.9m)
Machinery: two-shaft, COSAG, geared steam turbines, two boilers, two gas turbines; 30,000hp/40,000hp
Armament: one GWS30 Sea Dart SAM launcher (40 missiles); one 4.5in (114mm); one Ikara ASW torpedo launcher; one Limbo Mk 10 ASW mortar
Sensors: long-range air/surface-search radar; navigation radar; fire-control radar; hull-mounted sonar
Speed: 30 knots
Range: 5000nm (9260km) at 18 knots
Complement: 407

The Type 82 was drawn up as a Destroyer Leader Guided Missile (DLG) escort for Great Britain's proposed new CVA-01 carriers, and four were ordered. Three were cancelled in 1966, along with the new carrier, but HMS *Bristol* (D 23) was completed as a trials ship for a new Anglo-Dutch radar project, and subsequently evaluated various new weapons and systems. The Type 42 was originally seen as a cheaper, 'telescoped' version and eventually emerged as the 10-ship *Sheffield* class of guided-missile destroyers.

TYPHOON CLASS

USSR (RUSSIA): 1980

The massive *Typhoon* class SSBNs are characterised by their side-by-side pressure hulls, giving an unusual flattened cross-section.

The enormous Project 941 *Akula* submarines known to NATO as the *Typhoon* were the world's largest and arguably most sinister weapons of war. Optimised as a means of delivering a retaliatory strike, the vast *Akula* submarine was designed to be able to lie on the seabed under the ice for up to a year, surviving any nuclear exchange before emerging to unleash as many as 20 SLBMs, with 200 warheads, on the enemy's heartland. The D-19 launch system uses 20 solid-fuel propellant R-39 (SS-N-20) missiles which have a range of up to 10,000 km (6,219 miles). They are arranged in silos in two rows in front of the sail between the main hulls. The *Typhoon* has an automated torpedo and missile loading system including six torpedo tubes. The *Akula*/SS-N-20 combination is known in Russia as *Taifun*, and the programme was launched in direct response to the USA's Trident missile programme. The *Typhoons*'are multi-hulled with two separate pressure hulls, five inner habitable hulls and 19 compartments. The pressure hulls are arranged parallel to each other and symmetrical to a centerplane. The missile compartment is arranged in the upper part of the bow between the pressure hulls. Both hulls and all compartments are connected by transitions. The pressure hulls, the centerplane and the torpedo compartment are made of titanium and the outer light hull is made of steel. A protected

Displacement: 24,500t surfaced; 48,000t submerged
Dimensions: 562ft 9in x 75ft x 40ft (171.5m x 22.9m x 12.2m)
Machinery: two-shaft, nuclear, two pressurised-water reactors, two steam turbines; 100,000hp
Armament: D-19 launch system (20 SS-N-20 SLBM); two 25.6in (650mm) and four 21in (533mm) TT
Sensors: general-purpose radar; active/passive multi-function sonar
Speed: 16 knots surfaced; 27 knots submerged
Range: limited only by reactor fuel state
Complement: 150

module, comprising the main control room and electronic equipment compartment, is arranged behind the missile silos above the main hulls. The *Akula* submarine's huge size includes crew accommodation that is spacious enough to allow the provision of a sauna and even an aviary! TK-208, the first of six *Typhoons*, was laid down at Severodvinsk in March 1977 and launched in 1980, following Brezhnev's 1974 warning to then US President Gerald Ford that the *Taifun* would go ahead if the USA persisted with Trident. A seventh *Typhoon* was broken up on the slipway, and a further seven planned submarines in the class were cancelled. As of June 2000 the Russian Navy claimed that it operates 26 strategic nuclear submarines carrying 2,272 nuclear warheads on 440 ballistic missiles. This force was said to include five *Typhoons*, but according to one report as of 1999 only a single *Typhoon* remained operational (probably TK-20), and most estimates would suggest that no more than three boats were in service by early 2000. were cancelled. As of June 2000, the Russian Navy claimed that it operates 26 strategic nuclear submarines carrying 2272 nuclear warheads on 440 ballistic missiles. This force was said to include five *Typhoons*; but according to one report, as of 1999 only a single *Typhoon* remained operational (probably TK-20), and most estimates would suggest that no more than three boats were in service by early 2000.

The first Project 941 heavy ballistic missile submarine 'TK-208' was commissioned in September 1980 and introduced into the Northern fleet on 12 December 1981. Another six followed between 1981 and 1989.

U12

GERMANY: 1968

After just three examples, Germany's Type 201 coastal submarines had to be rebuilt as Type 205s, when it was discovered that their non-magnetic steel hulls corroded easily. *U4–U8* were modified with a tin covering, but *U9–U12* were built with a new corrosion-resistant steel. This was then used to rehull the original *U1* and *U2*. *U12* was launched in September 1968 and was one of the last Type 205s to remain operational.

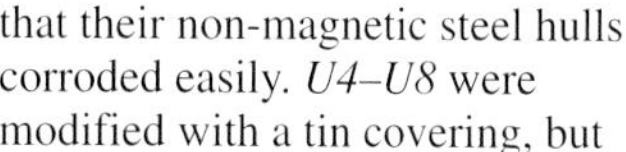

The Type 205s used four different conning tower arrangements, while *U11* and *U12* also had a new rudder arrangement.

Displacement: 419t surfaced; 455t submerged
Dimensions: 150ft x 15ft x 13ft 9in (45.7m x 4.6m x 4.2m)
Machinery: one-shaft, electric drive, two diesels with one electric motor; 1200hp/1500hp
Armament: eight 21in (533mm) TT
Sensors: surface-search radar; active/passive sonar
Speed: 10 knots surfaced; 17.5 knots submerged
Range: 3800nm (7038km) at 10 knots
Complement: 21

U28

GERMANY: 1974

Displacement: 456t surfaced; 500t submerged
Dimensions: 159ft 6in x 15ft x 14ft (48.6m x 4.6m x 4.3m)
Machinery: one-shaft, electric drive, two diesels with one electric motor; 1200hp/1500hp
Armament: eight 21in (533mm) TT
Sensors: surface-search radar; active/passive sonar
Speed: 10 knots surfaced; 17.5 knots submerged
Range: 3800nm (7038km) at 10 knots
Complement: 21

The Type 206 coastal submarine introduced sonar in a swollen, rounded bow, and also had wire-guided torpedoes, improved manoeuvrability and lower noise characteristics. The first of the class (*U13*) was launched in 1971, the last (*U30*) in 1974. *U28* was launched in January 1974 and commissioned that December. She was the penultimate submarine in the class to be built by Rheinstahl Norseewerke at Emden, which produced eight; Howardtswerke at Kiel built the rest. IKL developed external GRP mine containers that

Apart from its swollen, rounded bow, the sonar-equipped Type 206 closely resembled the earlier Type 205 and Type 201, and the wartime Type XXIII.

could be fitted as an option. Otherwise, the submarine could carry either 16 torpedoes for its eight bow tubes, or 24 mines. Twelve of the Type 206 submarines were extensively modernised in 1987–92, emerging as Type 206As with new sonar, periscopes, ESM and GPS navigation, together with engine and accommodation improvements. *U28* was one of the six boats modernised by HDW at Kiel, the remainder being upgraded at Emden by Thyssen Nordseewerke.

UDALOY

USSR (RUSSIA): 1980

The Project 1155 cruiser *Udaloy* was the first in a class of 14 ASW cruisers described by some as being broadly equivalent to the US Navy's *Spruance* class. Embarking a pair of helicopters and armed with SS-N-14 SSM, SA-N-9 SAMs and two 3.9in (100mm) cannon, the *Udaloy* and her sisterships succeeded the *Kara* class and acted as ASW flotilla leaders. *Udaloy* was laid down in July 1977, launched in February 1980 and completed on the last day of 1980. Integration of the SA-N-9 on the *Udaloy*s was delayed, and the first two ships were originally delivered without the weapon; the fourth ship was the first with both the missiles and their associated directors. Two late vessels were ordered as Project 1155.1s, with SS-N-15s or SS-N-22s as used by the *Krivak III* class, and these were ultimately taken over by the Border Guards. *Simferopol* and *Admiral Vinogradov* were designated as Project 1155 bis cruisers.

The *Udaloy* and her sisterships remain among the most modern and powerful ships in Russian Navy service.

Displacement: 6200t standard; 7900t full load
Dimensions: 531ft 6in x 63ft 4in x 20ft 4in (162m x 19.30m x 6.20m)
Machinery: two-shaft, COGAG, two cruise gas turbines and two boost gas turbines; 120,000hp
Armament: eight SS-N-14 SSM; eight SA-N-9 SAM launchers (64 missiles); two 3.9in (100mm); four 30mm AA cannon; four 30mm AK-630 CIWS; eight 21in (533mm) TT; two RBU-6000 ASW RL; two helicopters
Sensors: air/surface-search radar; navigation radar; fire-control radar; hull-mounted sonar
Speed: 34 knots
Range: 10,500nm (19,446km) at 14 knots
Complement: 300

ULSAN

SOUTH KOREA: 1980

Built by Hyundai and launched in April 1980, *Ulsan* (951, also known as *Ulsan Ham*) was the first of a class of nine lightweight, fast general-purpose frigates built for the Republic of Korea Navy. With steel hulls and alloy superstructures, the HDF-2000 ships had British and Dutch electronics, and European and American armament. The same hull was used as the basis for a class of patrol vessels for India.

The nine Korean-designed *Ulsan* class fast general-purpose frigates have proved successful and popular in service.

Displacement: 1600t standard; 2180t full load
Dimensions: 321ft 6in x 39ft 4in x 11ft 6in (98m x 12m x 3.5m)
Machinery: two-shaft, CODOG, two gas turbines and two diesel engines; 54,400hp/7200hp
Armament: eight Harpoon SSM; one 3in (76mm); eight 30mm or six 40mm cannon; six 12.75in (324mm) TT; depth charge racks
Sensors: air/surface-search radar; surface-search radar; hull-mounted sonar
Speed: 35 knots
Range: 4000nm (7408km) at 14 knots
Complement: 145

UPHOLDER

GB: 1986

Displacement: 2220t surfaced; 2455t submerged
Dimensions: 230ft 7in x 25ft x 17ft 8in (70.3m x 7.6m x 5.4m)
Machinery: one-shaft, diesel-electric, diesel engines and one electric motor with two 120-cell batteries; 5400hp
Armament: six 21in (324mm) TT (14 Tigerfish torpedoes, four Sub-Harpoon SSM)
Sensors: general-purpose radar; active/passive multi-function sonar
Speed: 12 knots surfaced; 20 knots submerged
Range: 8000nm (14,816km) at 8 knots
Complement: 47

Originally planned to be the first in a class of 12 submarines, HMS *Upholder* (S40) was launched on 2 December 1986, and was completed in June 1990. The *Upholder*s were planned as replacements for the elderly *Oberon*s, especially for coastal use, special forces insertion, and surveillance. The number on order was reduced first to 10, then to nine, and in 1990–91's defence cuts, to just four submarines. Plans to retrofit the updated Type 2075 sonar (intended for subsequent submarines) were cancelled at the same time. These four vessels were felt by many to be the most useful submarines ever taken on charge by the Royal Navy, and it was expected that they would remain in use for many years. However, the four *Upholder*s were put up for disposal in 1995, having been withdrawn from use during 1994–95. These extremely capable submarines were eventually sold to Canada.

The *Upholder*-class submarines had only the briefest career with the Royal Navy before being withdrawn and sold to Canada.

VALIANT

GB: 1963

The first British nuclear submarine was the one-off *Dreadnought*, which was in many respects a British copy of the US Skipjack class. The first British production nuclear submarines, the *Valiant* class, were essentially productionised copies of the Dreadnought, enlarged to accommodate the bulkier British reactors. *Valiant* (S 102), the first of the class, was launched in December 1963 and completed in July 1966. By the end of the 1980s, the age of the *Valiant* class reactors was causing concern and the five submarines were withdrawn from service from 1990.

Although there were only five submarines in the class, the *Valiant* submarines gave valuable service, not least in the Falklands conflict, when *Conqueror* torpedoed the cruiser *General Belgrano*.

Displacement: 4000t surfaced; 4900t submerged
Dimensions: 285ft x 33ft 3in x 27ft (86.7m x 10.1m x 8.2m)
Machinery: one-shaft, nuclear, one PWR1 reactor with geared steam turbine plus diesel-electric auxiliary; 15,000hp
Armament: six 21in (533mm) TT (Mk 23 Tigerfish torpedoes and Sub-Harpoon SSM)
Sensors: search and navigation radar; active/passive sonar and towed array
Speed: 32 knots submerged
Range: limited only by reactor fuel state
Complement: 52

VAN SPEIJK

THE NETHERLANDS: 1965

Displacement: 2200t standard; 2850t full load
Dimensions: 372ft x 41ft x 18ft (113.4m x 12.5m x 5.5m)
Machinery: two-shaft, geared steam turbines, two boilers; 30,000hp
Armament: Harpoon SSM (later); two Seacat launchers (eight missiles); two 4.5in (114mm) (later one 3in (76mm)); one Limbo Mk 10 ASW mortar (deleted); six Mk 32 TT; one helicopter
Sensors: air/surface-search radar; navigation radar; fire-control radar; hull-mounted sonar
Speed: 28.5 knots
Range: 5000nm (9260km) at 12 knots
Complement: 251

Although they incorporated as much local equipment as possible, the Dutch *Van Speijk*-class frigates were in other respects minimum-change copies of the British *Leander* class, with the same hull and armament. The *Van Speijk* class did use Dutch radar and since this used smaller antennas, an extra Seacat missile launcher was added. The *Van Speijk* (F 802) was launched in May 1965 and completed in February 1967, the first of six frigates in the class. All were upgraded in the late 1970s and early 1980s, with increased automation and revised armament and electronics. The ships were retired in the late 1980s.

The *Van Speijk*-class frigates were Dutch-built adaptations of Great Britain's *Leander* class. All six were sold to Indonesia between 1986 and 1989.

VANGUARD

GB: 1992

The *Vanguard* class are the largest submarines ever used by the Royal Navy – and the most devastatingly powerful, with their Trident D5 missiles.

In 1980, the British Ministry of Defence announced that it would replace the Royal Navy's Polaris missile submarines (the *Resolution* class) with four new submarines armed with Trident I (C4) missiles. By 1982, the choice of missile had changed to the Trident II (D5). The new submarines were to be much larger than those they replaced, but had similar features and a slightly smaller complement. Lead ship HMS *Vanguard* (S 28) was ordered in April 1986, and was laid down that September. Launched in March 1992, she was completed in August 1993 and conducted missile firings in May 1994. *Vanguard* made her first operational patrol in early 1995, and the first three new Trident submarines had fully replaced the Polaris boats by the end of 1996. The end of the Cold War has led to the Trident missiles being armed with fewer than their theoretical maximum number of warheads (16 missiles with 12 MIRVs each give a total of 192, and the Vanguard submarines deploy with a maximum of only 96). There is also the option of arming the missiles with low-yield, 'sub-strategic' warheads.

Displacement: 14,000t surfaced; 15,900t submerged
Dimensions: 491ft 8in x 42ft x 39ft 4in (149.8m x 12.8m x 12m)
Machinery: one-shaft, nuclear, one PWR2 reactor with geared steam turbine plus diesel-electric auxiliary; 27,500hp
Armament: 16 Trident D5 SLBM; four 21in (533mm) TT
Sensors: search and navigation radar; active/passive sonar and towed array
Speed: 25 knots submerged
Range: limited only by reactor fuel state
Complement: approximately 150

VASTERGÖTLAND

SWEDEN: 1986

Displacement: 1070t surfaced; 1143t submerged
Dimensions: 162ft 5in x 18ft 8in x 18ft (49.5m x 5.7m x 5.5m)
Machinery: one-shaft, diesel engine, electric motor; 2100hp/1150kW
Armament: six 21in (533mm) and two 15.75in (400mm) TT (12 torpedoes)
Sensors: surface-search radar; active sonar
Speed: 20 knots surfaced; 25 knots submerged
Range: not available
Complement: 19

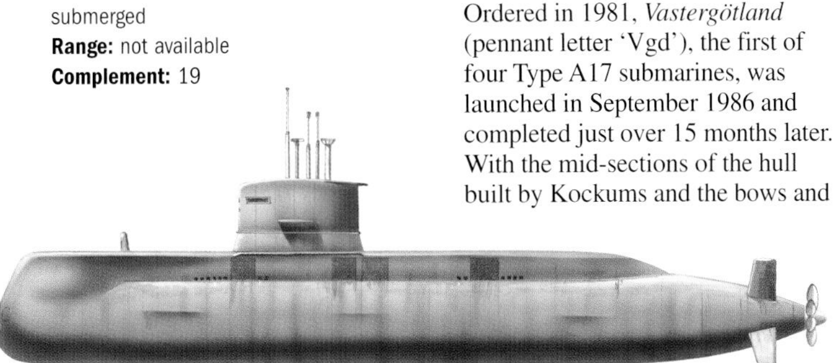

Ordered in 1981, *Vastergötland* (pennant letter 'Vgd'), the first of four Type A17 submarines, was launched in September 1986 and completed just over 15 months later. With the mid-sections of the hull built by Kockums and the bows and sterns coming from Karlskronavarvet, the submarines featured 10 bow-mounted torpedo tubes, external containers for mines, and an anechoic coating on the hull.

Plans to mount four vertical launch tubes for SSM in the sail of the *Vastergötland* class have been abandoned, and the submarines' armament remains torpedoes and mines.

VEINTICINCO DE MAYO

ARGENTINA: 1943/1968

The former Dutch Navy carrier *Karel Doorman* (formerly HMS *Venerable*) was acquired by Argentina as the *Veinticinco de Mayo* (V 2) in 1968, replacing the *Independencia* (the former HMS *Warrior*). The carrier had been damaged in a boiler room fire, but was repaired after its premature retirement. In Argentine Navy service, the carrier embarked its first aircraft in September 1969 and gained extra flight deck area in 1979. Following the Falklands conflict, the carrier was modified to operate Super Etendard fighters and British mission systems were replaced, but she was non-operational after 1985.

The *Veinticinco de Mayo* was placed in reserve in 1993 pending re-engining, and remains out of service.

Displacement: 15,892t standard; 19,896t full load
Dimensions: 693ft 2in x 121ft x 25ft (211.3m x 36.9m x 7.6m)
Machinery: two-shaft, geared steam turbines, four three-drum boilers; 42,000hp
Armament: 12 40mm cannon; 22 aircraft/helicopters (A-4Q Skyhawks, Super Etendards, S-2A Trackers, SH-3 Sea Kings)
Sensors: long-range air/surface-search radar; fire-control radar; hull-mounted sonar
Speed: 23 knots
Range: 12,000nm (22,224km) at 14 knots
Complement: 1250

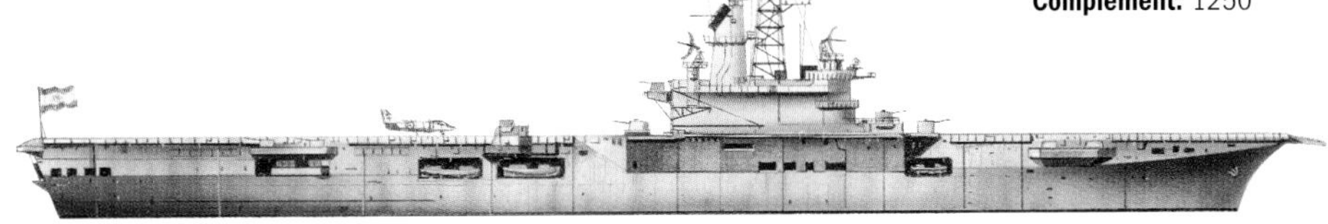

VENDETTA

AUSTRALIA: 1954

The Australian *Voyager* class destroyers differed from the Royal Navy's *Daring* class only in minor details. When one of the *Voyagers* was lost, it was replaced by a British-built *Daring*.

The Royal Australian Navy ordered four locally built destroyers based on the British *Daring* class, but the fourth vessel was cancelled before launch. HMAS *Vendetta* (D08) was the second in the class, and was launched in May 1954. The first ship in the class, *Voyager*, sank after a collision with HMAS *Melbourne* in 1964. She was replaced by HMS *Duchess* on loan from the Royal Navy, the latter ship being purchased outright in 1972. Both *Vendetta* and *Duchess* were put on the disposal list in 1979, but the remaining ship joined a training squadron until 1985.

Displacement: 2800t standard; 3600t full load
Dimensions: length 390ft x 43ft x 13ft 7in (118.87m x 13.11m x 4.14m)
Machinery: two-shaft, double reduction-geared turbines, two boilers; 54,000hp
Armament: six 4.5in (114mm); six 40mm cannon; five 21in (533mm) TT; one Limbo Mk 10 ASW mortar
Sensors: air/surface-search radar; navigation radar; fire-control radar; hull-mounted sonar
Speed: 34.75 knots
Range: 6000nm (11,112km) at 16 knots
Complement: 320

VICTOR III CLASS

USSR(RUSSIA): 1977

The original *Victor I* class was developed as follow-on to the Project 627 *November* class submarine, and was drawn up as a second-generation nuclear-powered attack submarine with a modern teardrop hull. The first boat was launched in October 1965, and delivered in November 1967. Some 15 were built (mainly for the Pacific Fleet), before production switched to the lengthened *Victor II*. These seven submarines carried a new ASW weapon (the SS-N-16) and were assigned to the Northern Fleet. Komsomolsk and Leningrad built 26 improved (and further lengthened) *Victor III*s, in two distinct sub-variants. Ten were sent to the Pacific Fleet and the remainder to the Northern Fleet. The 671RTMs had a new sonar suite, silenced engines and four (instead of six) torpedo tubes. They also had a towed VLF buoy, and most had an innovative new propeller system, with two four-bladed screws turning on a common shaft but inclined 22.5° apart to reduce cavitation. Some reports suggest that some *Victor IIIs* were configured as ASW platforms and others for anti-ship duties, though with no change in external appearance. Eight of the Northern Fleet 'Victor IIIs' were fitted with a new command system based on a captured/compromised Norwegian system and redesignated as Project 671RTMKs. During the 1980s, the surviving RTMs and RTMKs were modernised and re-equipped with new SS-N-21 subsonic cruise missiles. Like the earlier *Victors*, the *Victor IIIs* were retired from the mid-1990s as and when the time came for their reactors to be recored.

The Project 671RTM transformed the combat capability of the *Victor* class, and it remained in production after the introduction of the *Sierra* class.

Displacement: 4900t surfaced; 6000t submerged
Dimensions: 341ft 2in x 32ft 10in x 23ft (104m x 10m x 7m)
Machinery: one-shaft, nuclear, one pressurised-water reactor; 30,000hp
Armament: six 21in (533mm) TT (18 torpedoes and SS-N-15)
Sensors: surface-search radar; low-frequency active sonar
Speed: 30 knots submerged
Range: endurance 4500 power hours
Complement: 94

VIKRANT

INDIA: 1945/1961

Displacement: 16,000t standard; 19,500t full load
Dimensions: 700ft x 128ft x 24ft (213.4m x 39m x 7.3m)
Machinery: two-shaft, geared steam turbines, four three-drum boilers; 42,000hp
Armament: 15 40mm cannon; 16 aircraft
Sensors: long-range air/surface-search radar; fire-control radar; hull-mounted sonar
Speed: 23 knots
Range: 12,000nm (22,224km) at 14 knots
Complement: 1250

India ordered an aircraft carrier in 1957, buying the former RN Light Fleet Carrier *Hercules* and having her modernised and converted by Harland and Wolff. Completed in 1961, INS *Vikrant* (R11) emerged with a steam catapult, angled flight deck, and other new equipment and systems. The new carrier was broadly equivalent to the Australian carrier *Melbourne* and embarked an air wing of Sea Hawk fighter-bombers, Alizé ASW aircraft, and Alouette helicopters. The carrier participated in the 1971 Indo-Pakistan war, and spearheaded the Indian Navy fleet for 25 years, undergoing a succession of major overhauls and upgrades. India acquired a second carrier, *Viraat* (the former *Hermes*) in 1986, this having a ski jump that maximised the Sea Harrier's payload/range capabilities. In 1987–89, the original carrier was rebuilt with a ski jump to allow similarly unrestricted Sea Harrier operations, but was withdrawn from service in 1996, with the hope that it would be replaced by a second-hand former Soviet carrier.

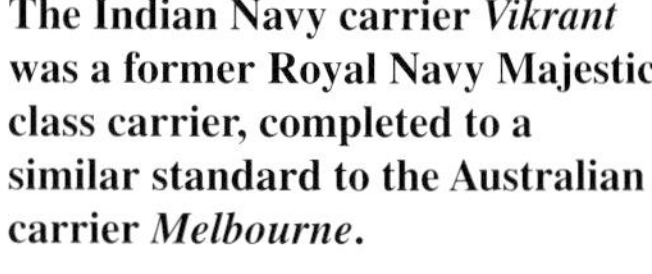

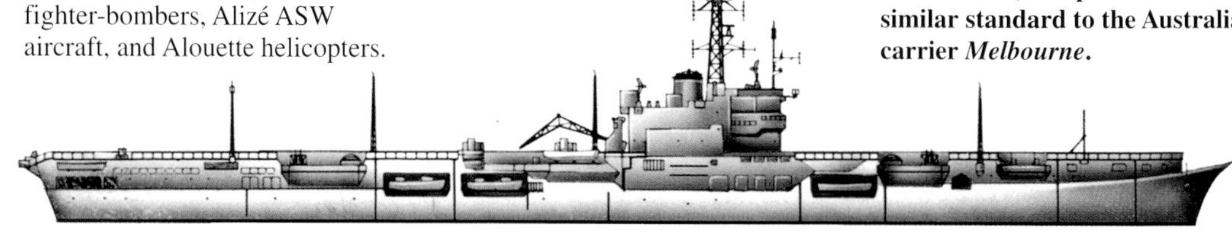

The Indian Navy carrier *Vikrant* was a former Royal Navy Majestic class carrier, completed to a similar standard to the Australian carrier *Melbourne*.

VIRGINIA

USA: 1974

Displacement: 11,000t full load
Dimensions: 585ft x 63ft x 21ft (178.3m x 19.2m x 6.4m)
Machinery: two-shaft, nuclear, two reactors, two geared turbines; 60,000hp
Armament: two Mk 26 combined Standard/ASROC launchers; two 5in (127mm); six 12.75in (324mm) TT; one helicopter
Sensors: long-range air/surface-search radar; fire-control radar; hull-mounted sonar
Speed: 30 knots
Range: limited only by reactor fuel state
Complement: 519

Built as guided missile destroyers, the four ships of the *Virginia* class were reclassified as cruisers in 1975. Intended as nuclear-powered equivalents of the *Spruance* class, the Virginia class actually emerged as a slightly improved version of the earlier California class. Lead ship USS *Virginia* (DLGN 38) was launched in mid-December 1974 and completed in September 1976. A planned fifth ship was cancelled in 1976, when it became clear that the class would not be receiving the Aegis system. Because of their long endurance and ability to operate independently, the *Virginia* class cruisers were provided with a

Ironically, the more modern *Virginia* class cruisers were retired before the two older *California* class ships, which had been refuelled in 1991–92.

pair of missile launchers, containing 24 missiles forward and 44 aft, and with two SPG-51D guidance radar. They later gained Harpoon anti-ship missiles and eight Tomahawk TLAMs in armoured boxes, the latter replacing the ships' helicopter facility. The four *Virginia* class cruisers proved relatively noisy because of their reactor's recirculation pumps, and so, despite being well equipped with ASW sensors and weapons, the ships were used primarily in the anti-aircraft role. This shift in emphasis was highlighted when the ships lost their helicopters (which had been accommodated in unusual 'below deck' hangars), and by the removal of ASROC. Helicopters were seldom deployed anyway, not least because the elevator to the hangar was prone to water leaks. Nuclear refuelling was required every 10 years, and the high cost of this led to the deactivation of *Texas* and *Virginia* in 1993 and 1994, and of *Mississippi* and *Arkansas* in 1996 and 1997. The latter two ships were initially classified as being 'in commission, in reserve'.

VITTORIO VENETO

ITALY: 1967

The helicopter carrier *Vittorio Veneto* (C 550), officially classed as a Guided Missile Helicopter Cruiser, was built instead of a planned third Andrea Doria, *Enrico Dandolo*, which was cancelled. The larger hull of the new ship allowed a larger flight deck, with the hangar located below instead of in front of it. This allowed the ship to embark six SH-3 Sea Kings or up to nine AB212s, compared to the four AB212s embarked aboard the Andrea Doria class ships. The ship was laid down in June 1965, and the design was recast several times before launch on 5 February 1967; sea trials began on 30 April 1969. The ship proved extremely efficient, with its two sets of stabilisers proving particularly effective. Originally armed with ASROC and Terrier ASW and anti-aircraft missiles, the *Vittorio Veneto* later received Standard SAMs. The ship also had six torpedo tubes and eight 3in (76mm) gun turrets. An upgrade in the early 1980s saw the addition of three new gun turrets, each containing a pair of Breda 40mm cannon, mounted on each forward corner of the flight deck and in front of the bridge on the centreline. These formed two (fore and aft) Dardo point defence systems, linked to new RTN-20X radar. The same upgrade also encompassed the provision of four Teseo Mk 2 SSM launchers. The *Vittorio Veneto* served as the Italian fleet flagship until replaced by the new carrier *Giuseppe Garibaldi* in the late 1980s, at which point she was relegated to training duties.

Displacement: 7500t standard; 8850t full load
Dimensions: 589ft 3in x 63ft 7in x 19ft 9in (179.6m x 19.4m x 6m)
Machinery: two-shaft, geared steam turbines, four boilers; 73,000hp
Armament: one Mk 26 combined Standard/ASROC launcher; eight 3in (76mm); six 12.75in (324mm) TT; nine helicopters
Sensors: long-range air/surface-search radar; fire-control radar; hull-mounted sonar
Speed: 30.5 knots
Range: 5000nm (9260km) at 17 knots
Complement: 550

The Guided Missile Helicopter Cruiser *Vittorio Veneto* served for many years as the Italian fleet flagship, but has now been relegated to training duties.

WALRUS

GB: 1959

The boats constructed for the two British submarine classes, *Porpoise* and *Oberon*, were externally identical, but the *Oberon*s incorporated detailed improvements to weapons and mission systems. The first new post-World War II Royal Navy production submarines, the *Porpoise* class, had two sets of batteries which could be connected together in series, enabling them to make short dashes at very high speed and yet remain notably quiet. The lead boat, HMS *Porpoise* (S 01), was launched in April 1956 and completed in April 1958. HMS *Walrus* (S 08) was the last in the class, launched on 22 September 1959 and completed in February 1961; both *Walrus* and another in the class, *Sealion*, were actually completed to *Oberon* standards, though they were never officially classed as such. The first of the *Porpoise*s to be withdrawn was broken up in 1977, the rest following during the 1980s. *Walrus* was sold in 1987.

Displacement: 1565t surfaced; 2303t submerged
Dimensions: 290ft 3in x 26ft 6in x 18ft 3in (88.5m x 7.9m x 5.5m)
Machinery: two-shaft, diesel-electric, two 16-cyl. diesels plus two electric motors; 3680hp/6000hp
Armament: eight 21in (533mm) TT (20 torpedoes)
Sensors: search and navigation radar; sonar
Speed: 12 knots surfaced; 17 knots submerged
Range: not available
Complement: 71

HMS *Walrus* was the final boat of Britain's first post-World War II class of production submarines.

WALRUS

THE NETHERLANDS: 1985

The Netherlands launched its own *Walrus*-class submarines in 1975. This followed the failure of attempts to develop a new submarine with Great Britain, which had a contemporary and parallel requirement; consideration was briefly given to using a nuclear powerplant, but this proposal was soon rejected on both financial and technical grounds. The new boat was closely based on the two *Zwaardvis*-class submarines built at Rotterdam during the late-1960s. The most obvious difference lay in the adoption of 'X' type surfaces, which provided excellent control characteristics in shallow water and in precise manoeuvring. A last-minute demand for a 50 per cent increase in maximum depth led to a switch to different steel and a need for intercooling, a pressurised fuel system and a 'wet' exhaust system. *Walrus* (S 801) was the first of four submarines in the class (two more being cancelled) and was launched in October 1985. These boats were extremely advanced submarines, commanded from a low-manpower single control room and equipped with the Sub-Harpoon missile and a British Type 2026 towed array.

The Dutch *Walrus*-class submarines carry their diving planes well forward, adjacent to the leading edge of the sail.

Displacement: 2450t surfaced; 2800t submerged
Dimensions: 222ft x 28ft x 23ft (67.7m x 8.4m x 7m)
Machinery: one-shaft, three diesels, plus one electric motor; 6300hp/6910hp
Armament: four 21in (533mm) TT (wire-guided torpedoes or anti-ship missiles)
Speed: 20 knots submerged; 13 knots surfaced
Range: 10,000nm (18,507km) at 9 knots
Complement: 52

WARSPITE

GB: 1965

Displacement: 4000t surfaced; 4900t submerged
Dimensions: 285ft x 33ft 3in x 27ft (64.2m x 8.3m x 8.2m)
Machinery: one-shaft nuclear, one pressurised water-cooled reactor, geared steam turbine, plus diesel-electric auxiliary; 15,000hp
Armament: six 21in (533mm) TT (torpedoes and anti-ship missiles)
Sensors: search and navigation radar; sonar
Speed: 32 knots submerged
Range: limited only by reactor fuel state
Complement: 52

Despite the priority given to the Polaris ballistic missile programme, and the associated *Resolution*-class missile submarines, Vickers was able to simultaneously produce the *Valiant*-class nuclear attack submarines. Based loosely on the experimental *Dreadnought*, the *Valiants* used a new type of bulkier, British-designed, reactor. HMS *Warspite* (S 102) was the second boat in the class, being launched in September 1965 and completed in April 1967. Starting with HMS *Courageous*, the class underwent a refit with Type 2020 long-range sonar, also gaining the Sub-Harpoon missile and Mk 48 torpedoes. During the Falklands War, *Warspite*'s sister-boat, HMS *Conqueror*, sank the Argentine cruiser *General Belgrano*. The five *Valiant*-class submarines formed a vital part of the Fleet throughout the 1970s and 1980s, before being put up for disposal between 1990 and 1992. Still giving valuable service, the submarines were retired because of concerns over the age of their early-generation reactors.

HMS *Warspite* was the second of five *Valiant*-class attack submarines. With HMS *Conqueror*, she was one of the first to be withdrawn from use in 1990.

USS WASP

USA: 1987

The six *Wasp*-class assault ships were especially designed to be able to handle military hovercraft landing vessels.

The first of seven assault ships, USS *Wasp* (LHD 1) was built in a hurry. The *Wasps* were ordered to fill a gap in the US Navy's fleet and designed to handle air cushion landing craft (LCACs). Production was actually brought forward by three years, such was the urgency accorded to the programme. USS *Wasp* was launched in August 1987; two further batches, each of three ships, followed her. At one time it seemed likely that 12 *Wasps* would be funded, but it now seems likely that the remaining, and earlier, *Iwo Jima*-class LHAs will be replaced by an all-new class. As LHDs rather than LHAs, the *Wasp*-class ships have a secondary sea-control role, and can embark up to 20 AV-8B Harrier IIs and six ASW helicopters. The flight deck is long enough and wide enough to allow the Harriers to make heavyweight rolling take-offs without a ski jump, and has projecting deck-edge elevators which may be folded down.

Displacement: 28,233t standard; 40,532t full load
Dimensions: 844ft x 140ft x 26ft 4in (257.3m x 42.7m x 8.1m)
Machinery: two sets of geared turbines, two boilers; 77,000hp
Armament: two missile launchers; three 20mm CIWS; eight 12.7mm MG; up to 42 assault helicopters; 6 to 8 (but up to 20) Harriers
Sensors: air-search radar; surface-search radar; navigation radar
Range: 9500nm (17,582 km) at 20 knots
Complement: 1080, plus 1873 marines

WHALE

USSR: 1952

The Soviet submarine S-99, unofficially named *Whale* by NATO, was the first Soviet submarine capable of exceeding 20 knots when submerged. Her designers based the new boat very closely on the stillborn German Type XVI U-boat – and built its hydrogen peroxide steam gas turbine from captured German parts. A plan, Project 616, to simply copy the Type XVI, was abandoned. Nonetheless, despite the inclusion of Soviet weapons and other equipment, Project 617 was, essentially, a U-boat copy. Covered in a rubber coating (again captured), the submarine even looked like a German U-boat when it was finally completed in December 1955. Though not built as the basis for a production submarine, because the unique powerplant could not be replicated, S-99 went to sea 98 times, proving herself both fast (by the standards of the day) and manoeuvrable. The Walter engine was extremely efficient at shallow depths, but performance reduced with depth, because exhaust gases needed to be dumped overboard; hydrogen peroxide was carried in plastic bag tanks below the main pressure hull. The success of S-99 did lead to development work, the long-range Project 643, though this was abandoned in 1960. In May 1959, S-99's service life came to an abrupt end. She suffered a hydrogen peroxide explosion while starting the Walter engine underwater; a hole in the pressure hull began to flood, but she surfaced and limped home under her own power. Repairing her German powerplant was impossible and S-99 was unceremoniously scrapped. By 1959, the writing was on the wall for submarines with closed-cycle powerplants and all effort would soon be switched to the new nuclear boats.

The *Whale* marked an interesting one-off blend of Soviet and German technologies, but its novel powerplant ultimately proved to be a technological dead-end.

Displacement: 950t surfaced
Dimensions: 204ft x 19ft 11in x 16ft 7in (62.2m x 6.1m x 5m)
Machinery: one-shaft, hydrogen peroxide air independent powerplant, one 26-cell battery, plus electric motor, plus electric creep motor, auxiliary 8-cyl. 4-stroke diesel engine; 7250hp/540hp/140hp/450hp
Armament: six 21in (533mm TT (12 torpedoes)
Sensors: search radar; sonar
Speed: 11 knots surfaced; 20 knots submerged
Range: 120nm (222km) submerged
Complement: 51

WHIDBEY ISLAND

USA: 1983

Displacement: 11,125t standard; 15,726t full load
Dimensions: 609ft 6in x 84ft x 19ft 8in (185.8m x 25.6m x 6m)
Machinery: two-shafts, two diesels; 41,600hp
Armament: two 20mm CIWS; two 20mm cannon; eight 12.7mm MG; platform for two assault helicopters
Sensors: air-search radar; surface-search radar; navigation radar
Speed: 22 knots
Range: 8000nm (14,805km) at 18 knots
Complement: 376, plus 440 marines

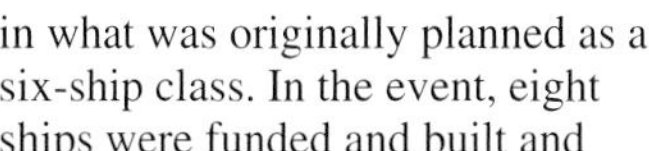

Loosely based on the earlier *Anchorage* class, the USS *Whidbey Island* (LSD 41) was the lead ship in what was originally planned as a six-ship class. In the event, eight ships were funded and built and these were designed to be able to handle air cushion landing craft as well as conventional landing craft. This necessitated a deeper well deck, with a raised helicopter deck above. *Whidbey Island* was launched in June 1983, while the eighth and last ship was launched in November 1989.

The US Navy has eight *Whidbey Island*-class dock landing ships, and four more of the modified *Harpers Ferry* class.

WHISKEY CLASS

USSR(RUSSIA): 1950

Displacement: 1050t surfaced; 1340t submerged
Dimensions: 249ft 4in x 20ft 8in x 14ft 11in (76m x 6.3m x 4.55m)
Machinery: two-shaft, diesel-electric, two Type 37D diesels; two electric motors, two creep motors; 4000hp/2700hp/100hp
Armament: 10 21in (533mm) TT (22 torpedoes or 44 mines); two 57mm; two 25mm cannon
Speed: 13.7 knots surfaced; 18.25 knots submerged
Range: 8580nm (15,879km) at 10 knots surfaced
Complement: 70

The *Whiskey*-class submarines were extremely versatile and efficient submarines, and had a long and productive career. It was a *Whiskey* (S-137) which ran aground near the Swedish naval base at Karlskrona in October 1981, causing an international incident.

In 1946, the Soviet Union began projects for construction of three post-World War II submarine classes. Project 611 resulted in the large *Zulu*-class; Project 612 was a small submarine design which remained unbuilt; and Project 613 became a medium-size attack submarine which would form the backbone of the Soviet submarine

force throughout the 1950s and 1960s – the submarine class named by NATO, *Whiskey*. The design was heavily influenced by wartime German submarines, particularly the Type XXI U-boat. Several of the latter were evaluated by the Soviet Navy; while widely respected the type was not universally admired and was seen to have weaknesses. These were addressed in the design of Project 613. The Soviet shipyards involved in the construction adopted mass-production techniques, using prefabricated components. The *Whiskeys* had better handling and seaworthiness than the Type XXI, were better insulated and had a simpler and more reliable drive shaft arrangement. The first of the class (S-80) was launched in 1951 and production continued until 1959: the *Whiskeys* built for the Soviet Navy totalled 215, with 113 built at Gorki, 72 at Nikolayev, 19 in the Baltic Yard, and 11 at Komsomolsk. A further 21 were assembled in China and more were exported to Albania, Bulgaria, Cuba, Egypt, Indonesia, North Korea, Poland and Syria. The *Whiskeys* were built in several versions, with various armament and equipment options; some boats were converted for use as radar pickets. About 18 of these versatile submarines remained in use at the beginning of the 1990s. All are now believed to have been withdrawn.

WIELINGEN

BELGIUM: 1976

The first of a class of four Belgian frigates, designs for the *Wielingen* (F 910) were begun in 1969. Procurement was dependent on a high degree of indigenous content, costs being minimised by tailoring the vessels for operations in the North Sea and English Channel. The ships incorporated French Exocet missiles, American Sea Sparrow SAMs and Dutch radar and tactical data systems. The *Wielingen* was launched in March 1976 and completed in January 1978. Two *Wielingens* remain in service, with a third in reserve or refit.

Despite being tightly designed-to-cost, the *Wielingen*-class frigates are highly automated and extremely seaworthy.

Displacement: 1880t standard; 2283t full load
Dimensions: 349ft x 40ft x 17ft (106.4m x 12.3m x 5.3m)
Machinery: two-shaft CODOG, one gas turbine, plus two diesels; 28,000hp/6000hp
Armament: four SSM; one octuple launcher; one 3.9in (100mm); one 14.75in (375mm) six-tube ASW rocket launcher; two launchers for torpedoes
Sensors: air/surface-search radar; navigation radar; surface-search/fire-control radar; sonar (hull-mounted)
Speed: 20 knots
Range: 4500nm (8328km) at 18 knots
Complement: 160

WORCESTER

USA: 1947

Displacement: 14,700t standard
Dimensions: 680ft x 71ft x 26ft (207m x 21.6m x 7.92m)
Machinery:
Armament: 12 6in (152mm); 22 3in (76mm); 24 20mm cannon
Sensors: not available
Speed: 33 knots
Range:
Complement: 1070

Combining destroyer manoeuvrability with cruiser size, and given a main battery that could deal not only with surface targets but with aircraft as well, the USS *Worcester* (CL-144) embodied many of the lessons learned during World War II. She and her sistership, *Roanoke*, epitomised the hard-hitting dual-purpose cruiser. *Worcester* was launched in February 1947 and commissioned in June 1948. She saw action during the Formosa crisis and the Korean War (supporting the Inchon landings). *Worcester* was finally struck-off on 1 December 1970.

Only two *Worcester*-class cruisers were completed, two more planned ships in the class being cancelled. Had World War II continued longer, the class might well have replaced the overloaded *Cleveland*-class cruisers.

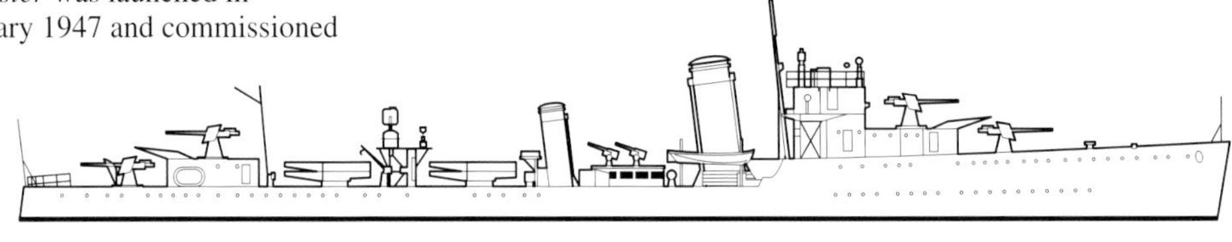

X1

USA: 1955

Built by Fairchild at Farmingdale, the four- to eight-man midget submarine *X1* was launched in September 1955, using a hydrogen-peroxide fuelled powerplant. An internal explosion in 1958 broke the submarine into three pieces, but these were recovered and the submarine was rebuilt. She joined the NSRDC in December 1960 and was finally stricken in February 1973.

The US Navy submarine *X1* was heavily influenced by the wartime British X-craft, and enjoyed a long test and development career.

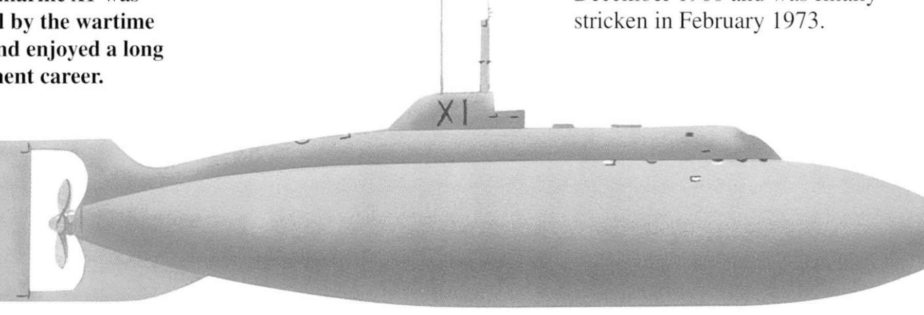

Displacement: 31t surfaced; 36t submerged
Dimensions: 49ft 2in x 7ft x 7ft (15m x 2.1m x 2.1m)
Machinery: one-shaft, diesels, plus electric motor; 30hp
Armament: none
Sensors: none
Speed: 12 knots surfaced; 15 knots submerged
Range: 500nm (925km)
Complement: four to eight

XIA

PEOPLE'S REPUBLIC OF CHINA: 1981

China's only ballistic missile submarine, *Xia* (Type 092 SSBN), resembles a scaled-down Soviet *Yankee*-class boat. Built by the same Huludao Shipyard which built China's five *Han* (Type 091)-class nuclear-powered attack submarines, this new boat is based on the *Hans*, with a similar *Albacore*-type teardrop hull, but lengthened and with a pannier extending aft from the sail which covers six side-by-side pairs of missile launch tubes. *Xia* has the same type of nuclear powerplant as used for the *Hans*, developed with extensive help from West Germany. Armed with six 21in (533mm) torpedo tubes in the bows, *Xia* also deploys up to 12 JL2 (CSS-N-3) ICBMs, an 4970 mile (8000km) range missile with a two-stage solid-fuel rocket motor carrying three or four 90kT MIRVs, or a single 250kT warhead. The *Xia* (406) was launched in 1981 and completed in 1987, though it was unable to make a successful missile firing until 1988. Since then, the submarine has spent a great deal of time in refit and has made only a few operational patrols. The *Xia* is probably a one-off, though some sources suggest that a sister-submarine was built but lost in service; further units, with four more missile launch tubes, might be under construction. A Soviet-built 'Golf' submarine was used as a trials vessel for the JL2 missile and more boats of this class are believed to be in service with the Chinese Navy. It is widely believed, also, that a longer-range Type 094 SSBN is under development to replace the *Xia*.

Displacement: 8000t submerged
Dimensions: 394ft x 33ft x 26ft (120m x 10m x 8m)
Machinery: one-shaft nuclear, one pressurised water reactor, turbo-electric drive
Armament: 12 SLBMs; six 21in (533mm) TT
Sensors: not available
Speed: 22 knots submerged
Range: not available
Complement: 100

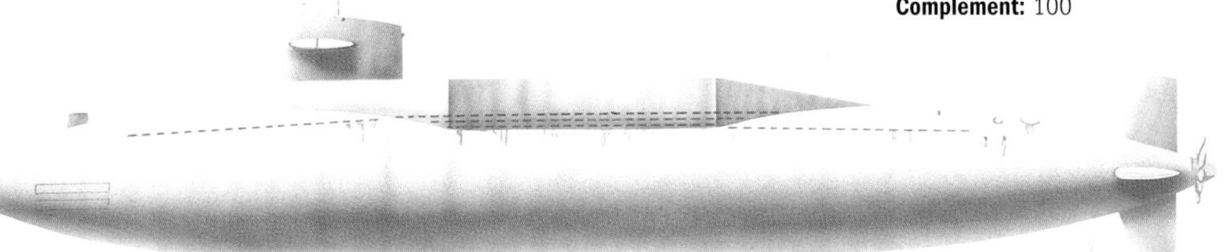

The *Xia* has a very similar outline to the much larger Soviet *Yankee*-class boats, although the hull ahead of the sail curves away more dramatically.

YANKEE CLASS

USSR/RUSSIA: 1966

The Project 667A SSBNs were the first Soviet submarines designed to fire their missiles from underwater and the first with SLBM launch tubes inside the pressure hull. The first boat of the 34 in this class was launched in August 1966. The *Yankees* were withdrawn from 1980 to comply with SALT treaty limitations. Those boats withdrawn had their missile sections cut away, though some were later converted for other roles. The last non-strategic *Yankee* was withdrawn in 1994.

The *Yankee*-class submarines ceased patrols of the US coast in 1987. The number of these submarines in strategic service dwindled: 12 in 1991, six in 1992, and none by the end of 1993.

Displacement: 4300t surfaced; 5100t submerged
Dimensions: 340ft x 32ft 10in x 26ft 3in (103.6m x 10m x 8m)
Machinery: one-shaft nuclear, one reactor; 15,000hp
Armament: eight SLCMs; four 21in (533mm) TT; four 16in (406mm) TT
Speed: 24 knots surfaced
Range: limited only by reactor fuel state
Complement: 98

YUBARI

JAPAN: 1982

Displacement: 1470t standard; 1690t full load
Dimensions: 298ft 6in x 35ft 5in x 11ft 6in (91m x 10.8m x 3.5m)
Machinery: two-shaft CODOG, one gas turbine, one diesel; 28,400hp/4650hp
Armament: eight SSM; one 3in (76mm); one 14.75in (375mm) mortar; six 12.75in (324mm) TT (ASW)
Sensors: sea-search radar; navigation radar; fire-control radar; sonar (hull-mounted)
Speed: 25 knots
Range: not available
Complement: 98

Japan's *Yubari*-class escorts were developed because the preceding *Ishikari* class was too small to accommodate the weapons, sensors and systems necessary for the escort role. The *Yubaris* therefore had about 250t greater displacement, being slightly larger and having a greater fuel capacity. *Yubari* (DE 227) was launched in February 1982 and commissioned in March the following year. She is armed with two quad Harpoon launchers, a 3in (76mm) gun, two triple torpedo tubes, plus an anti-submarine mortar. A Phalanx CIWS was intended but never fitted.

The *Yubari* and her sistership, *Yubetsu*, are improved and slightly enlarged derivatives of the *Ishikari*.

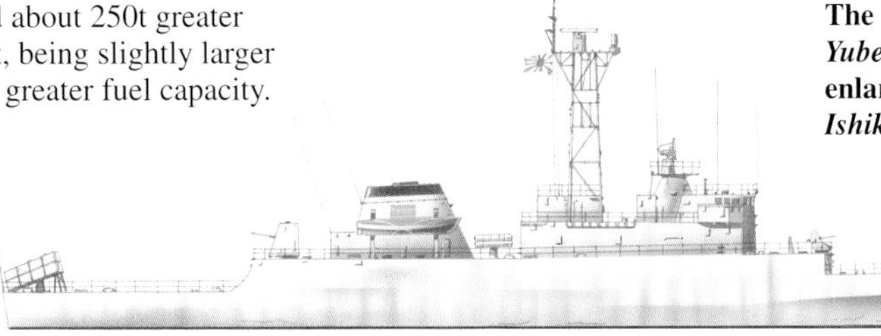

YUKIKAZE

JAPAN: 1955

Although she was the second of Japan's two A-Type, *Harukaze*-class destroyers, the Mitsubishi Kobe-built *Yukikaze* (DD 102) was actually launched one month before the lead ship, in August 1955. She was completed three months later, in July 1956 and named after a wartime destroyer, which was, by coincidence, still in service in Taiwan. Both the *Harukazes* were fitted with American electronics and mission systems and gained an ASW role in March 1959, when torpedo launchers were installed. *Yukikaze*

Displacement: 1700t standard; 2340t full load
Dimensions: 348ft 9in x 34ft 5in x 12ft 2in (106.3m x 10.5m x 3.
Machinery: two-shaft, geared-tu boilers; 30,000hp
Armament: three 5in (127mm) 40mm cannon; two ASW morta guns; one depth charge rack (a completed)
Sensors: search radar; sonar (h mounted)
Speed: 30 knots
Range: 6000nm (11,104km) a
Complement: 240

also gained a towed passive sonar array in the mid-1970s, simultaneously losing her aft mast, depth charge rack, 5in (127mm) gun and K-guns. Both ships in the class were reallocated to training and development duties with the Fleet Training and Development Command in 1981, before being withdrawn in 1985. During this last period, *Yukikaze* was classified as a Special Use Auxiliary, under a new pennant number (ASU 7003), and undertook trials of a more modern active towed sonar array.

The two *Harukaze*-class destroyers deliberately used different powerplants to allow in-service evaluation. *Yukikaze* had US Westinghouse geared turbines.

YUSHIO — JAPAN: 1979

The first teardrop-hulled submarines made in Japan were the seven *Uzushio*-class boats.

Displacement: 2200t surfaced
Dimensions: 249ft 4in x 32ft 6in x 24ft 7in (76m x 9.9m x 7.5m)
Machinery: one-shaft, two diesels, plus electric motors; 3400hp/7200hp
Armament: six 21in (533mm) TT
Sensors: bow sonar; towed array
Speed: 13 knots surfaced; 20 knots submerged
Range: not available
Complement: 80

Launched between 1970 and 1978, these submarines have now all been retired. The 10 *Yushio*-class submarines which followed were developed versions of the *Uzushio* design, with improved electronics and deeper diving capability. The lead ship *Yushio* (SS 573) was launched in March 1979 and commissioned in 1980. *Yushio* became a training submarine (ATSS 8008) in August 1996 and thus became the only submarine in the class not to receive the Sub-Harpoon missile.

The *Yushio*-class submarines closely resembled the *Uzushio* class from which they were derived, and the later *Harushio*-class submarines which replaced them in production.

ZINNIA — BELGIUM: 1967

Instead of procuring an exact copy of the *Godétia* for mine countermeasures support, Belgium chose to modify the design to produce a second logistics ship, the *Zinnia* (A 961). While *Godétia* doubled as a Royal Yacht and oceanographic laboratory, the *Zinnia* had a helicopter landing platform and a telescopic hangar. *Zinnia* also had stern-mounted winch reels for towed minesweeping gear from the start, whereas when the gear was deployed on *Godétia* a 40mm gun had to be removed to make room.

***Zinnia* deployed to the Gulf in 1987–88 in support of Belgian MCM vessels and again during Operation Desert Storm. Both vessels remain in use.**

Displacement: 1705t standard; 2685t full load
Dimensions: 326ft x 46ft x 12ft (99.5m x 14m x 3.6m)
Machinery: one-shaft, two diesels; 5000hp,
Armament: three 40mm cannon; one helicopter
Sensors: not available
Speed: 18 knots
Range: 14,000nm (25,910km) at 12.5 knots
Complement: 123

ZULU CLASS — USSR: 1951

The Soviet submarines constructed under Project 611 (NATO codename *Zulu*) were larger counterparts to the *Whiskey*-class. The first of the *Zulus* was launched in July 1951 and completed in December 1953. It was followed by 26 similar vessels, the last being completed in July 1958. The first examples were surprisingly anachronistic, with deck guns but no snorkel. All were eventually converted to 611M configuration, with snorkels but no guns. After retirement from the attack role, the surviving *Zulus* were converted to fulfil a range of duties, from minelaying to weapons trials.

Displacement: 1900t surfaced; 2350t submerged
Dimensions: 295ft 3in x 24ft 7in x 19ft 8in (90m x 7.5m x 6m)
Machinery: three-shaft, diesel; 5300hp
Armament: 10 21in (533mm) TT (22 torpedoes or 44 mines); two 57mm; two 25mm cannon
Speed: 18 knots surfaced; 16 knots submerged
Range: 20,000nm (37,014km) surfaced; 9500nm (17,582km) at 9 knots (snorkelling)
Complement: 70

The *Zulu*-class submarines were heavily influenced by the wartime German Type XXI U-boats, and early versions closely resembled that design.

GLOSSARY

AA Anti-aircraft, as in 'anti-aircraft artillery' (AAA); air-to-air, as in 'air-to-air missile' (AAM).
Ahead; Astern Forward; backward (in reverse).
Armour Plates of iron, later steel and alloys, later still more exotic metals such as titanium, added to the hull and essential components of a ship to protect its integrity, its vital parts and its crew from battle damage.
ASDIC Perhaps an acronym for the (British) Anti-Submarine Detection Investigation Committee established by the Admiralty during World War I, ASDIC was the name given to the technique of using sound waves to detect objects underwater, and by extension, to the hardware employed; see **Sonar**, by which name such equipment was later known.
ASM Anti-**submarine** missile; anti-**submarine** mortar (also air-to-surface missile, air-to-ship/anti-ship missile).
ASW Anti-**submarine** warfare.
Axial fire Gunfire ahead or astern, along the major axis of the vessel.

Ballast The weight added to a ship or boat to bring her to the desired level of floatation and to increase stability. Originally in the form of gravel, later metal and sometimes concrete, now more commonly water, which latter has the advantage of being easy to remove and replace. **To ballast** The act of adding ballast. **In ballast** Sailing without cargo; ie, with empty holds.
Barbette Originally an open-topped armoured enclosure, inside which a gun was mounted on a turntable. The addition of an armoured hood, which rotated with the gun mount, turned it into a **turret**. Latterly, the fixed (armoured) cylinder upon which a turret rotated.
Barge Most commonly, a flat-bottomed vessel of shallow draught used to carry cargo on inland waterways, both from port to port and to and from ocean-going ships. Most sailing barges, once common in northern Europe, have now been turned over to recreational uses; motor barges are still widespread; see **lighter**. Also a ceremonial boat of state, invariably rowed by many oarsmen; also a motorboat as used by senior naval officers.
Barque-rigged A ship with three or more masts, square-rigged on all but the aftermost.
Battlecruiser The made-up designation for a hybrid warship armed like a **battleship** but sacrificing passive protection in the form of **armour** plate for speed.
Battleship Originally the biggest and most powerful ships of the fleet, mounting guns of usually 10in (254mm) or larger **calibre** (the biggest were those of the Japanese *Yamato* class, which were 18.1in (460mm)), and heavily armoured. The word was derived from 'line-of-battle ships', the equivalent warships in the days of sailing navies.
Beam The width of a ship's hull.
Beam engine The original form of single-cylinder steam engine, the piston of which acted on a beam by way of a connecting-rod. The beam itself formed a simple Class I lever, its **reciprocating** action being translated into rotation by a link to a crank or eccentrically to a flywheel.
Bilge The 'floor' of the hull of a ship; ie that portion of the hull which has a horizontal, rather than a vertical aspect.
Bilge keels Long, narrow wing-like plates located at or about the turn of the **bilge** along the length of the hull, designed to dampen or reduce the ship's rolling motion and aid steering; they perform the secondary function, especially in modern yachts, of allowing the vessel to remain upright when beached.
Blue Riband/Hales Trophy The 'Blue Riband' (more formally, the Blue Riband of the Atlantic) was, since the 1840s, the non-existent prize awarded to the (passenger) ship making the fastest trans-Atlantic passage in either direction. In 1935, a minor British parliamentarian, Thomas K Hales, put up a silver trophy to be held by the shipping line which owned the then-fastest passage-maker in either direction.
Bofors A Swedish armaments manufacturer, best known for its 40mm anti-aircraft gun. First produced in the 1930s and adopted widely from 1942, the recoil-actuated 40mm L/60 Bofors was the most effective weapon of its type; improved versions were still in production at the end of the 20th century.
Boiler A device for heating water to boiling point, to turn it into steam so that it could be employed to power machinery. The development of boilers paralleled that of steam engines – flue boilers gave way to cylindrical, which in turn were superseded by tubular types, initially fire tube boilers, in which hot gases passed through the **feed water**, latterly water tube types, which inverted the arrangement.
Bonaventure An extra **mizzen** sail; it fell out of use towards the end of the 17th century.
Boom A **spar** used to extend the **foot** of a sail; also a floating barrier, usually across the entrance to a harbour.
Bore The diameter of a cylinder or gun barrel.
Bowsprit A **spar** protruding over the bows of a sailing vessel, to serve as an outboard anchorage for the **tack** of a flying **jib**.
Break A change in the level of a deck, eg 'the break of the **forecastle**'.
Breastwork A built-up armoured surround within which a battery of guns was located, especially in a ship with low **freeboard**.
Breech block The removeable part of a gun's breech, through which projectile and charge could be loaded.
Breech-loading (BL) Guns loading from the breech, via a removable segment.
Broadside The side of the ship; the simultaneous firing of the guns located there.
Bulges/Blisters Chambers added to the outside of a warship's hull to provide protection against torpedos; outer sections were generally water-filled, to absorbe splinters, inner, air-filled, to diffuse blast. They were also often retro-fitted to increase buoyancy when a ship's displacement had been increased during re-building.
Bulk Carrier A single-deck ship expressly designed to accommodate loose cargo such as grain or ore.
Bulkhead/Water-tight bulkhead A vertical partition employed to divide up a ship's internal space, both longitudinally and transversely. These partitions may be water-tight, in which case the openings in them to allow passage must be capable of being sealed, preferably by remote control.
Bunker/Bunkerage The part of a ship allocated to the storage of fuel; the fuel itself, and the quantity carried.
Bunt The centre part of a sail (especially a square sail), cut and stitched to form a shallow bag.
Burthen An antiquated expression of a vessel's carrying capacity, usually expressed in tons, originally 'tuns', or wine casks.

Calibre the diameter of the bore of a gun barrel; the number of times that diameter fits into the length of the barrel, expressed as 'L/(calibre)'; eg, a gun of 10in bore with a barrel 300in long would be described as '10in L/30', or just '10in/30'.
CAM ship Catapult-Armed Merchant ship A merchant ship equipped to fly off a fighter aircraft; a temporary expedient adopted during 1940.
Capesize A ship with too great a **draught** to allow her to pass through the Suez Canal, or too great a **beam** to allow her to pass through the Panama Canal; *see* **Panamax**; **Suezmax**.
Capital Ship A term coined around 1910 to describe the most important naval assets, and group together **battleships** and **battlecruisers** (chiefly to give extra credibility to the latter); it was later extended to include **monitors**.
Careening The process of tipping a ship onto her side to facilitate cleaning her bottom.
Carrier battle group A force designation coined during World War II; it was made up of one or more **fleet aircraft carriers** together with associated defensive elements – **destroyers** and **cruisers** – but often included **battleships**, which had by then largely been relegated to the shore bombardment role.
Carronade A short-barrelled, lightweight muzzle-loading gun, produced by the Carron Ironworks in Scotland from the 1770s.
Carvel a construction method in which hull planking is placed edge-to-edge; see **Clinker**
Casemate A fixed armoured box within which a gun was mounted. It allowed the weapon to be elevated and trained, and usually protruded from the hull or superstructure to increase its arc of fire.
Catamaran A boat (and later ship) with two hulls joined by a continuous deck or decks.
cb cabin class
Central battery
Citadel/Central citadel A heavily-armoured redoubt within which the ship's main battery was housed.
Clew The lower after corner of a **fore-and-aft** sail or either lower corner of a square sail.
Clinker A construction method in which hull planking is placed so that the lower edge of a plank overlaps the top edge of the plank below it; see **Carvel**.
Clipper An ultimately meaningless term used to describe any fast sailing ship, particularly one engaged in the grain, opium or tea trades, widely used in the mid-19th century.
Close-hauled The point of sailing as near as possible to the reciprocal of the direction of the wind, achieved by hauling the **sheets** taught. The best **square-rigged** ships could come within 70° of the wind, while modern yachts approach 45°.
Cofferdam A continuous series of watertight compartments, often filled with coal or cork, arranged longitudinally within a warship's hull, usually to increase the protection of the machinery space.
Combined Carrier A cargo ship of the latter part of the 20th century, adapted to carry both bulk and containerised cargoes.
Composite construction A construction method employing iron or steel **frames** and wooden hull planking.
Compound engine A multi-cylinder steam engine in which the steam is employed at least twice, at decreasing pressures; theoretically, all multi-cylinder engines are compound engines, but those which employ the steam three times are known as **triple-expansion**, and those which employ it four times as **quadruple-expansion** engines.
Conbulker see **Combined Carrier**.
Controllable-pitch (variable-pitch) propeller A propeller which incorporates a mechanism within its boss or hub for collectively changing the pitch of the blades.
Coppering The practice of cladding the wooden hull of a ship with copper, to inhibit the growth of marine flora and fauna; 19th century iron- and steel-hulled warships built for tropical service were often clad with wood and then coppered.
Corvette Originally a (French) sailing ship of war, too small to warrant a rate (and thus the equivalent of the British **sloop**); more recently, a warship smaller than a **frigate** or **destroyer-escort**.
Counter/Fantail While not quite identical, both refer to the overhanging portion of a ship's stern, above the waterline.

Course The sails set from the lower **yards** of a **square-rigged** ship, eg fore course, main course.
Crossjack yard The lower **yard** on the **mizzen mast** of a **square-rigged** ship.
Cruiser A warship, larger than a frigate or destroyer, much more heavily armed and often armoured to some degree, intended for independent action or to act as a scout for the battlefleet. Modern cruisers operate as defensive elements within **carrier battle groups**.
Cutter Originally a small, decked boat, lightly-armed, with a single **mast** and **bowsprit**, carrying a **fore-and-aft** (**gaff**) **mainsail** and a square **topsail**, with either two **jibs** or a jib and **staysail**, frequently used as an auxiliary to the fleet or on preventive duties. Latterly a single-masted sailing boat with two **fore-and-aft headsails**. Also a small to medium-sized service vessel, especially with pilotage organisations or the Coast Guard.
CVA Attack aircraft carrier.

Davitts A pair of small goose-neck cranes equipped with hoisting and lowering gear (falls), commonly used to carry, and facilitate the launching and recovery of, boats (especially lifeboats) from a larger vessel; there exist a variety of patent patterns.
DDG Guided-missile destroyer.
DDH Helicopter destroyer.
Deadrise The angle to the vertical of the planking in the floor of a vessel's hull, and thus a measure of the 'sharpness' of her lines.
Deadweight *see* **Tonnage**.
Deck The continuous horizontal platforms, the equivalent of floors in a building, which separate a ship. Each has its proper name (though there is often duplication and some confusion); the orlop is the lowest, then the lower, main, upper, shelter, bridge and boat, though many passenger **liners** have many more, with names like promenade deck and hurricane deck. In sailing navies, the upper deck was often known as the **spar deck**, and the main deck as the **gundeck**. Halfdecks such as the **forecastle** and **poop** do not, properly speaking, qualify as decks, but are usually thus described.
Derrick A form of lifting gear comprising a single spar attached at its heel low down to a **mast** or **kingpost** and pivoted there, equipped with stays, a topping lift and guy pendants, so that its attitude and position may be positively controlled, and with a block attached at its head, through which a runner may be rove and led, if necessary, to a winch. There exist a variety of patent patterns, of which the most important is the Stülcken, a heavy-lift version capable of handling loads of 50 tons and more.
Destroyer Originally torpedo-boat destroyer; a small warship of little more than 200 tons **displacement**, itself equipped to launch **torpedoes**, but also armed with light guns. By the end of Word War I, the first major conflict in which they played a serious role, they had grown to well over 1000 tons, and by the end of World War II, to over triple that. In more modern times, the type has largely disappeared, and been replaced by enlarged **frigates**.
Destroyer-escort A small warship, bigger than a **corvette** of the period, designed and constructed to guard convoys of merchant ships, especially on the Atlantic routes, during World War II.
Diesel A form of internal-combustion engine which ignites its fuel/air mixture by compression alone, invented by Rudolf Diesel in 1892. By the 1970s, by which time it had been much refined, it had taken over almost completely from steam engines as the propulsion unit for ships of all types, the only serious competition coming from **gas turbines**, fitted to many warships.
Diesel-electric A form of propulsion in which the compression-ignition internal-combustion engine drives a generator, which in turn drives an electric motor which turns the propeller shaft. This method offers advantages in terms of flexibility, but at the cost of considerable power loss; see **Turbo-electric**.
Displacement A measure of the actual total weight of a vessel and all she contains obtained by calculating the volume of water she displaces. Normally used only for warships, displacement is expressed in a variety of ways – standard- or normal displacement is the ship as ready for sea with a small allowance of fuel and stores; full-load displacement is exactly what it suggests, with the maximum possible weight of fuel, supplies and ordnance.
Down Easter Wooden sailing ships originating in New England, especially Maine, during the 19th century.
Draught (also **Draft**) The measure of the depth of water required to float a ship, or how much she 'draws'.
Dreadnought The generic name given to a **battleship** modelled after HMS *Dreadnought*, the first with all-big-gun armament; it fell into disuse once all **capital ships** were of this form.
Driver An additional sail hoisted on the **mizzen**; see **Spanker**.

ECM Electronic Countermeasures; measures taken to decoy or confuse an enemy force's sensors.
EEZ Economic Exclusion Zone; a coastal strip, 200nm wide measured from the mean low water mark, within which a nation is held to have the exclusive right to exploit natural resources; it supplements, but does not replace, the territorial limit (originally three miles, the effective range of coastal artillery, later extended to 12 miles).
En échelon Diagonally.

Fast attack craft Gun, torpedo and/or guided-missile-armed warships, characterised by their small size and high speed. Such craft only ever had limited success.
Feed water Water – as pure as possible – which is translated to steam in the **boilers**. Any contamination – from seawater, for example – quickly leads to serious, often irreparable, damage.
FEU Forty-foot Equivalent Unit. A double-length standard container; *see* **TEU**
Fire control A (centralised) system of directing the firing of a ship's guns, based on observation of the fall of shot relative to the target, taking into account movements of both the target and the firing platform.
Flag of Convenience see **Registry**.
Flare The outward (usually concave) curve of the hull of a ship towards the bow.
Floflo Float on/float off loading operations; *see* **Lolo**; **Roro**.
Flotilla In the Royal Navy up to World War II, an organised unit of (usually eight) smaller warships – **destroyers** and **submarines** in particular, but also **minesweepers** and **fast attack craft**; **cruisers** and **capital ships** were grouped into **squadrons**, and squadrons and flotillas made up fleets – derived from the diminutive of the Spanish *flota*, fleet.
Flush decked Commonly, a ship with no **forecastle** or **poop**.
Foot The bottom edge of a sail.
Forced draught A means of increasing the efficiency of a ship's boilers by forcing air at higher than normal pressure through the furnace element.
Fore-and-aft Sails which, when at rest, lie along the longitudinal axis of a vessel; a vessel rigged with such sails.
Forecastle Originally the superstructure erected at the bows of a ship to serve as a fighting platform, later the (raised) forward portion and the space beneath it, customarily used as crews' living quarters. Pronounced fo'c'sle.
Frames The ribs of a vessel, upon which the hull planking is secured, set at right-angles to the keel.
Freeboard The distance between the surface of the water and the upper deck of a ship or the **gunwale** of a boat.
Frigate Originally, fifth- or sixth rate ships carrying their guns on a single deck, employed as scouts, and the counterpart of the later **cruiser**. The term fell into disuse from the mid-1800s and was revived a century later to designate a small warship, between **corvette** and **destroyer** in size, used for convoy escort duties; later it became the generic term for smaller warships.

Gaff A spar used to extend the **head** of a four-sided **fore-and-aft** sail; the sail is attached to the gaff, and the two are hoisted together.
Gas turbine A rotary internal-combustion engine in which a fuel/air mixture is burned and the rapidly-expanding gas thus produced used to drive turbine blades arranged upon a shaft; a gas turbine bears the same relationship to a steam turbine that a **reciprocating** internal-combustion engine does to a reciprocating steam engine.
Gundeck The name given to the main deck in sailing warships of the Royal Navy.
Gunwale a timber set atop the hull planking as a finishing strip.

Halyard A rope or cable used to hoist a sail (or flag) and retain it in position.
Head The bows of a ship (and as in '(down) by the head'), and by extension in the plural, because they were traditionally located there, the latrines; also the top of a four-sided sail.
Headsail Those sails – **jibs** and **staysails** in the main, but also **spinnakers** – which are set before the (fore)mast.
Heel, to The act of temporarily tipping a vessel to one side, usually caused by the pressure of wind on sails.
Heeling tanks Ballast tanks set on a ship's sides to allow her to be deliberately heeled over.
Hogging The tendency for a vessel's bows and stern to fall in relation to her midships section, generally as a result of the buoyancy there being greater and her longitudinal stiffness insufficient to resist the pressure. Hogging was common in wooden ships, particularly those over about 150 feet overall.
Horsepower A measure of the power produced by an engine; one horsepower = 550 foot/pounds per second ('the power required to raise 550 pounds through one foot in one second') as defined by James Watt. Various forms were and are used – brake horsepower (bhp) is the useable power delivered by an engine or motor as measured by a brake on its output shaft (and is, to all intents and purposes, the same as shaft horsepower (shp), commonly employed in relation to **turbines**). Indicated horsepower (ihp) was derived from a calculation using the pressure and volume of the steam within a cylinder; typically, it produced a value some 25% greater than the power actually available, and was used exclusively to decribe the output of **reciprocating** steam engines. Nominal horsepower (nhp) was derived from a calculation based on the geometry of the engine, and was even less reliable an indication of its actual output.

Immune Zone The area within which shells fired by an adversary would not penetrate a vessel's **armour**.
Ironclad The contemporary name for wooden warships clad with iron, and by extension, to the first iron warships; it continued in use up until the arrival of the **dreadnought**.

Jib A triangular sail (usually loose-footed) set on a forestay. Modern yachts carry no more than two, as a rule (and the second is more commonly known as a **staysail**), but **clippers** often carried as many as six. The **clew** of larger jibs – genoas and yankees – extends well abaft the mast.
Jib-boom A continuation of the **bowsprit**.
Jumboising The act of enlarging a ship (usually a **bulk carrier**) by cutting her in two and inserting an extra section amidships.

Keel The main longitudinal timber of a ship or boat, effectively her spine and certainly her strongest member. In yachts, a downwards extension in the form of a wing (or wings) which balances the pressure of the wind upon the sails; also, the flat-bottom lighters used in ports in the northeast of England.

Ketch A two-masted sailing vessel; in modern terms, a yacht with a reduced **mizzen** stepped before the rudder post (see **yawl**).
Kingpost/Samson post A cut-down **mast**, used as the vertical, static, component of a **derrick**.
Knees Timbers in a form similar to that of an angle bracket – usually grown to shape, rather than formed by cutting – attached to the **frames** and used to support the **deck** beams.
Knot Internationally, the measure of a ship's speed – one **nautical mile** per hour.
Kort nozzle A duct or tube surrounding the **propeller**, designed to control the flow of water across it and thus increase the thrust it develops. The device dates from 1932, and was fixed originally, but later became part of the rudder, and turned with it.

LASH An acronym for Lighters Aboard Ship, a system of carrying loaded **lighters** aboard ocean-going ships to simplify on- and off-loading operations at terminal ports. They are lifted on and off by means of a gantry crane at the stern of the ship; see **Seabee**.
Lateen A loose-footed triangular **fore-and-aft** sail set on a **yard** which extended both forward and aft of the mast. An unhandy rig using sails of this type.
Lee/Leeward The side of the vessel away from the wind, but a coast onto which the wind is blowing.
Leeboard A primative form of drop-**keel**, hung over the side of a vessel from a forward pivot. Two were carried, one to **port** and one to **starboard**, though only the one on the **lee** side was employed.
Lifting screw A screw propeller designed to be lifted clear of the water, fitted to sailing ships with auxiliary machinery, the object of the exercise being to reduce drag when sailing.
Lighter A 'dumb' (ie, unpowered) **barge**, used as a transit vehicle to load and unload ships in port and also in places where proper port facilities are deficient.
Liner A ship carrying passengers to a fixed schedule, usually on trans-oceanic routes; the term became current from the mid-1800s. A cargo liner also operates on fixed schedules, with space for a limited number of passengers.
Lolo Lift on/lift off loading operations; *see* **Floflo**; **Roro**.

Magazine Secure storage for explosives.
Masts Spars, mounted vertically or close to it, normally stayed (guyed) at either side and fore and aft, employed to allow sails to be carried. Bigger ships had **topmasts** and even **topgallant masts** mounted above the lower mast. A secondary use was to provide a platform for lookouts and signal flags, and that continued, especially in warships, long after sails had been eliminated. Latterly masts acted solely as platforms for radio and radar antennae.
Maierform A hull (and especially bow) form which reduced resistance, developed in the 1930s.
MGB/MTB Motor gun boat/motor torpedo boat; *see* **Fast attack craft**.
Minesweeper A small ship, roughly the size of a trawler (many were, in fact, converted fishing boats originally) adapted and equipped to locate and neutralise submarine mines. Later supplemented by specialist minehunters.
Mizzen The third **mast**, counting from the bows; since most ships had three masts, it was also the aftermost, and invariably carried a **fore-and-aft** steadying sail.

NATO North Atlantic Treaty Organisation.
Nautical mile Internationally, the measure of distance at sea which has become standardised at 6080ft (1852m).

OBO Ore/Bulk/Oil carrier.
Oerlikon A Swiss arms manufacturer whose 20mm cannon, widely acknowledged to be the best of its type, was adopted by both sides during World War II. Improved versions were still in production at the end of the 20th century.
Ordinary An antiquated Royal Navy term used to describe a ship laid up, usually with a temporary roof erected over the upper deck, and with masts and spars, sails and rigging and guns removed ashore for storage.

Packet A ship employed on a regular, scheduled service, carrying passengers and/or cargo.
Panamax The largest a ship can be (by virtue of her beam dimension; the limit is fractionally under 106ft (32.3m)) and still be able to transit the Panama Canal; *see* **Capesize**.
Paravane A mechanical 'fish', used to support the outward end of a cable designed to snag the mooring cable of a tethered mine.
Periscope An optical device allowing an observer to change his plane of vision; it works by means of right prisms, or mirrors placed in parallel planes, which reflect incident rays at identical but opposed angles. At sea they were commonly used to allow submerged **submarines** a view of the surface, and also in gun turrets.
Plough A bow form similar in appearance to a **ram**, with a forward-protruding section at and just below the waterline; its purpose, however, was quite different, in that it served only to increase buoyancy right forward.
Pom-pom A heavy recoil-operated machine gun developed by Maxim and his successor, the Vickers Company. It got its name, which was purely onomatopoeic, during the Boer War. It was widely employed as a light **AA** gun aboard British warships especially, until replaced by the more effective **Bofors** cannon.
Poop The short raised deck at the stern of a vessel, originally known as the aftercastle. The word is derived from the Latin *puppis*, stern.
Propeller Properly speaking, the screw propeller; as essential to steam- and motor ships as their powerplant, the rotation of the screw propeller and the angle of its blades or vanes combine to generate thrust against the mass of water, which pushes the vessel through it.
Propulser Commonly, any propulsive device – a water jet, for example – which is not a propeller; the most effective is probably the **Voith-Schneider**.

Quadruple-expansion A type (the most advanced) of **reciprocating compound engine**, with a minimum of four cylinders of graduated sizes housing pistons connected to a common crankshaft; the steam, introduced at very high pressure into the smallest, is condensed, and passes to the second, slightly larger, cylinder, where it is condensed once more, and so on until it reaches the largest cylinder(s). Developed (from the **triple-expansion** engine, thanks to improvements in boiler technology, which allowed steam at higher temperatures and thus greater pressure to be generated) late in the 19th century, it was soon overtaken by the **steam turbine**, and indeed, was never taken up by the world's navies, though such engines did power the fastest passenger ships of the day.
Quarterdeck That part of the upper deck abaft the mainmast (or where the mainmast would logically be in a steam- or motor ship), traditionally the reserve of commissioned officers.
Quick-firing A designation applied to small- and medium-calibre guns to indicate that they used unitary ammunition (ie, with projectile and propellant cartridge combined). Developed in the latter part of the 19th century, such guns had a very much higher rate of fire than earlier types which used separate projectile and propellant.

Radar An acronym for Radio Direction and Range – a means of using electromagnetic radiation (in this case at the very top of the radio spectrum) to locate an object in space by bouncing signals off it and measuring the time elapsed before they return to the plane of the emitter, the orientation of the receiving antanna providing directional data.
Ram A strengthened, usually armoured, projection from the bow of a warship, designed to allow her to pierce the hull of an adversary with relative impunity. Widely used in the age of the galley, it fell into disuse with the coming of sail, but enjoyed a brief revival after the Battle of Lissa in 1866, and was found on most major warships from just after that date until the coming of the **dreadnoughts**, even though it actually figured in more peacetime disasters than ever it did in wartime successes.
Reciprocating engine By far the most common type of engine, in which a piston moves along the axis of a cylinder, being pushed out by the expansion of the gas filling the cylinder (internal combustion or compressed air engine) or pulled back within it by a partial vacuum forming there (in the case of a condenser steam engine), transferring its up-and-down (or to-and-fro) motion by means of a connecting rod to a crankshaft, where it is translated into rotation.
Reefer A refrigerated cargo-carrier.
Registry All merchant ships must be registered within a territory chosen by their owners. This does not necessarily have to be within the territory in which the vessel is owned (though some countries do require it), but can be in any country which permits open registry. Some countries have much stricter regulations regarding the manning and operation of ships than others, and since a ship and its crew are operated according to the laws and practices of the country of registry, not that of ownership, it has long been common practice to register ships in those which are less stringent; a ship thus registered is said to be sailing under a **flag of convenience**. The practice dates effectively from the 1920s, when laws prohibiting the sale of alcohol aboard US-registered ships caused their owners to transfer them to shell companies in Panama, and register them there.
Reserve Warships not in active commission are said to be in reserve; this may be a temporary measure, in which case maintenance work will be kept fully up to date, or a long-term measure, in which case the ship will be 'mothballed' – effectively sealed up, with precautions taken to ensure that any machinery liable to deteriorate is well protected.
Rifle/Rifling The practice of cutting a series of grooves in a spiral the length of a gun's barrel, in order to impart spin to a projectile and thus stabilise it in flight. The system was widely adopted for naval ordnance from the mid-1800s; see also **smooth-bore**.
Roro Roll on/roll off loading operations; *see* **Lolo**; **Floflo**.
Rudder A vertical board or fin hung on the centreline of the vessel at the **stern post**, originally (and still, in small boats) from simple hinges known as pintels, and connected either directly to the **tiller** or by ropes or chains to the steering wheel, which, when it is angled relative to the vessel's course, causes a change of direction.
Running Rigging That portion of a ship's rigging – **halyards** and **sheets**, for example – which is actively employed in raising, setting and striking her sails; see also **Standing rigging**.

Sagging Less common than **hogging**, of which it is the antithesis, sagging is a temporary phenomena, caused when a ship's midships section wallows in a trough while bows and stern are supported on wave crests. In the event of a ship being long enough for three or more wave crests to be come into play, the effect is known as shearing.
SAM Surface-to-air missile.
sc single class.
Schooner-rigged A boat or ship with two or more masts of equal height (or with the foremast lower than the main and others), **fore and aft rigged** on all of them, with or without topsails.
Schnorkel/Snorkel A tube with a ball-valve at its upper extremity, which allows a **submarine** to take in air, and thus continue to operate its internal-combustion engines, while remaining

below the surface. Invented in the Netherlands in the 1930s, it was not used extensively until the German Navy took it up during World War II, but since then it has been universal.
Seabee A system of carrying loaded cargo **barges** aboard ocean-going ships to simplify on- and off-loading operations at terminal ports. Barges (more properly, **lighters**) were lifted on and off by means of an elevator at the stern of the ship; *see* **LASH**.
Sheer The upward curve of a ship's upper deck towards bow and stern.
Sheet The rope or cable employed to secure the **clew** of a **fore-and-aft** sail, and thus determine how it is set.
Sloop In the 18th and 19th centuries, a small warship similar to a **corvette**, later a somewhat larger steam warship, often fitted out for service in distant waters, where it served as the flagship of the State's representative; more commonly a single-masted yacht with a single **headsail**, and by far the most common type of sailing pleasure craft.
Smooth-bore A gun with a smooth (ie, **unrifled**) barrel, used as naval ordnance until the second half of the 19th century.
Sonar An acronym for Sound Navigation and Ranging, a technique of using sound waves to detect objects underwater, and by extension, to the hardware employed; see also **ASDIC**.
Spanker Originally an additional sail hoisted on the **mizzen** mast to take advantage of a following wind, later taking the place of the mizzen **course**; see **Driver**.
Spar A free wooden or metal beam used in the rigging of a ship, generally as a **boom**, **gaff** or **yard**.
Spar deck Strictly speaking, a temporary **deck**, but later used to describe the upper deck of a **flush-decked** ship.
Spinnaker a loose-footed three-cornered sail, usually of light material, with a considerable **bunt**, set before a yacht's mast to take advantage of a following wind.
Sponson A platform built outside the hull, at main- or upper deck level, usually to allow guns on the **broadside** to be sited so as to allow them to fire axially.
Squadron In the Royal Navy, originally an organised unit of (usually eight) major warships – **cruisers** and **capital ships**, but in the US Navy (and the practice became widespread), an organised unit of ships of any type, from minesweepers upwards, the term having taken over from **flotilla**.
Square-rigged A sailing vessel whose sails are set on yards, which when at rest are at right-angles to the longitudinal axis of the hull.
SSM Surface-to-surface missile.
SSN Nuclear-powered submarine.
Standing Rigging That portion of a ship's rigging – stays and shrouds, for example – which is employed to steady her masts; see also **Running rigging**.
Steam Turbine A rotary engine in which steam is used to drive turbine blades arranged upon a shaft; invented by Parsons at the end of the 19th century, the turbine was to replace the **reciprocating compound engine** in most sophisticated marine applications. Parsons and others later devised a system of gearing (single-reduction; double-reduction) which made the powerplant considerably more efficient than the original direct-drive turbine by allowing it to operate at much higher speeds.
Steerage (st) A large space below decks, above the propellers and adjacent to the rudder post, where passengers who could not afford cabins were lodged. The space was lined with bunks, with additional tiers ranked centrally; normally, steerage passengers provided their own bedding and food.
Stem The foremost member of a ship's **frame**, fixed at its lower extremity to the **keel**.
Stern post The aftermost member of a ship's frame, fixed at its lower extremity to the **keel**.
Strake A structural timber running the length of a ship or boat's hull, along the major axis.
Stroke The distance the piston of a **reciprocating engine** travels in the cylinder; also, one rowing cycle.
Studding sails Additional square sails employed in fine weather outboard of the normal sails, set from **booms** which extended the **topmast** and **topgallant yards**. Pronounced 'stunsail'.
Submarine Properly speaking, a vessel capable of indefinite (or at least very prolonged) underwater operation; early submarines were in fact submersibles, and it was not until the advent of air-independent propulsion systems that true submarines were constructed.
Suezmax The largest (by virtue of her draught) a ship can be and still pass through the Suez Canal; the actual value changes according to the progress of dredging operations; see **Capesize**.

Tack The lower forward corner of a **fore-and-aft** sail; a reach sailed (in a sailing vessel) with the wind kept on one side.
TEU Twenty-foot Equivalent Unit. The standard size for a cargo container is 20ft x 8ft x 8ft 6in, and the carrying capacity of container ships is expressed in terms of the number of such units they can load; the size of containers therefore effectively governs the dimensions of container ships. See also **FEU**.
Tiller A wooden or metal bar attached rigidly to the rudder and used to control its movement.
Tonnage The load carrying capacity of a merchant ship or the **displacement** of a warship. In a merchant ship, tonnage (the term comes from 'tun' – a wine cask – the original standard cargo unit; 'ton' means not 2240lbs, but 100 cubic feet) may be calculated in a number of ways. Gross tonnage is the total internal volume of a ship's hull derived from a calculation based on her dimensions; net tonnage is the internal volume available for the loading of cargo (ie, the gross tonnage minus space allocated to crew accomodation, machinery, bunkerage etc). Deadweight tonnage is a measurement of the total weight of cargo, fuel and stores a vessel can carry when fully loaded. Increasingly, **bulk carriers**'s capacity is expressed in cubic metres. There are also archaic forms of measurement such as Old Measure and Builders Old Measure; yachts were measured according to different rules and their size described in tons, Thames Measure, but modern rating rules (eg, Quarter-ton, Half-ton) are derived from very complex calculations mased on a boat's dimensions. See also **Burthen**.
Topgallant mast The third and topmost section of the **mast**, stepped above the **topmast**, where the topgallant **yard** is located.
Topmast The second section of a mast, stepped above the lower mast, carrying the (upper and lower) topmast yard(s).
Topping Lift A rope or wire tackle by means of which a spar is lifted.
Topsail In a **square-rigged** vessel, the square sails set immediately above the **course**, from the **topmast yard(s)** (bigger ships carried paired topsails, upper and lower, for ease of working); in a **fore-and-aft** rigged vessel, the topsails may be either square or themselves fore-and-aft.
Torpedo Originally a moored mine, later an explosive charge on the end of a spar hung from the bows of a small boat. In modern terms, a torpedo is a self-propelled explosive device, with or without some form of guidance, running on or below the surface of the sea; in this form it was invented by Robert Whitehead in the 1860s. The name derives from that of a small fish capable of delivering an electric shock.
tr tourist class.
Trainable tubes Tubes intended for launching **torpedoes**, mounted on a turntable, to allow them to be aligned with the target.
Tramp A merchant ship operating on an irregular basis, not to a fixed schedule (*cf* **Packet**, **Liner**), picking up cargoes as and when it can, its next port-of-call often determined by the consignee's requirements.
Transom A squared-off stern form, adopted both because it saved weight and resulted in better hydrodynamic perfromance.
Trawler A fishing boat (in fact, the largest are substantial ships) which drags behind it on two **warps** a roughly cone-shaped net. Modern trawlers have substantial refrigeration plant and freezers, and stay at sea for weeks at a time.
Trenails Hardwood pins or dowels used to fix a ship's planks to her **frames**.
Triple-expansion A type of **reciprocating compound engine**, with a minimum of three cylinders of graduated sizes housing pistons connected to a common crankshaft; the steam, introduced at very high pressure into the smallest, is condensed, and passes to the second, slightly larger, cylinder, where it is condensed once more, and then passed to the largest cylinder(s). Developed late in the 19th century, it was soon overtaken by the **steam turbine**, but was still employed in smaller ships, particularly those employed as **tramp** steamers, which had no requirement to make high speeds. It was finally superseded by the marine diesel, post-World War II.
Tumblehome The convex line of a ship's hull; the degree to which the sides of a ship are brought together towards the centreline after reaching the maximum beam, and thus the opposite of **flare**.
Turbo-electric A form of propulsion in which the **steam turbine** drives a generator, which in turn drives an electric motor which turns the propeller shaft. This method offers advantages in terms of flexibility, but at the cost of considerable power loss; see **Diesel-electric**.
Turret Originally an armoured shell or covering for a gun, which rotated with the platform upon which the gun is mounted; later the armoured cover became an integral part of the rotating mounting, and itself supported the gun or guns.
Turret ship A design of cargo carrier developed in the 1890s, its upper deck being about half the full beam of the ship; slightly below this was the so-called 'harbour deck', which joined the main vertical plating in a wide-radius curve. It was basically a subterfuge, which came about as a result of the Suez Canal Company's policy of charging dues based on the ship's beam at the upper deck.

VLCC/ULCC Very/Ultra-Large Crude Carrier; the biggest oil tankers, with a deadweight capacity of over 200,000 tons (VLCC) and over 300,000 tons (ULCC).
Voith-Schneider propulsor An alternative propulsion system to the screw **propeller**, which also replaces the **rudder**. The drive shaft of a Voith-Schneider propulsor arrives vertically, and terminates in a carousel, from which orientable paddles are suspended. Since the orientation of these paddles can be controlled, and they are feathered as the carousel revolves, thrust generated by the revolution of the device can be vectored, dispensing with the need for a moveable rudder (instead a large fixed fin or skeg is mounted) and also permitting very precise station-keeping.

Walking beam see **Beam engine**.
Warp Usually the heaviest rope or cable a vessel carries, used for mooring or towing.
Weather helm The degree of compensation a helmsman needs to apply to the wheel or **tiller** to counteract a vessel's tendency to deviate from the desired course; originally the predominant factor was the pressure of wind on the sails, but in steam- and motor ships the hull form aft and the positioning of the **rudder**(s) *vis-à-vis* the **propeller**(s) became more significant.
Whaleback/Turtleback A convex deck form, especially of the forecastle deck; in extreme cases, the deck may actually be faired into the side planking or plating.
Windward The side of the ship towards the direction from which the wind is blowing.

Yard (also **yard-arm**) A large wooden or metal spar crossing the mast of a ship from which a sail is set; also an abbreviation for 'dockyard'.
Yawl A two-masted sailing yacht with a reduced **mizzen** stepped abaft the rudder post (see **ketch**).

INDEX

Headings in italics refer to classes or types of ship. Soviet ships are referred to their NATO designation where this is used in the text.

PICTURE CREDITS

Aerospace Publishing: 328c, 330cb, 356t, 357b, 358cb, 360c, 364ct, 371c, 388c, 389c, 393b, 394c, 404t and b, 406c, 407t, 409b, 416b, 417b, 419t, 432t, 437ct, 479c, 496t.

BP: 119t, 123t, 137t, 141c, 157b, 181b, 229b, 260c, 359b, 364cb and b, 366t, 391t, 430b, 447t, 460c, 463t, 473c, 487t, 488b, 491t, 493cb, 496cb, 502b, 504b, 508t, 521t, 522c, 527t and c, 529b.

Chrysalis Picture Library: 18b, 23c, 32t, 37b, 40b, 60t, 126, 130c, 170c, 179c, 198t, 216b, 217t, 227t, 266b, 279cb, 323cb and b, 388b, 390b, 402t and c, 409t, 413c, 429b, 436t, 442t, 465b, 485b, 492t and b, 505ct, 511t and cb, 516t, 534b.

Hugh Cowin: 449t, 450b, 479t, 485t, 486b, 489b, 496b, 501t and ct, 505cb, 512b, 514t, 516b,

De Agostini 16t, 17c and b, 18c, 20c and b, 21t, 22b, 24c, 30c, 32c, 33t, 38c, 39b, 41b, 42t and c, 43b, 45t, 48c, 50c and b, 52c, 58t, 59b, 61b, 62t, 63b, 64t, 65b, 66, 67c, 69t, 70t, 73b, 76b, 78b, 80c, 81t, 82t and b, 83b, 85t and c, 86cb, 87c, 90t, 91t, 92cb, 94c, 95t, 96t and cb, 97c and b, 99t, 100c, 112t and b, 113b, 114, 115t and c, 116t, 117t and b, 118cb and b, 119b, 120t and c, 122c, 123b, 130t and b, 131t and b, 132b, 133 all, 134t and c, 135c, 136t andb, 137cb and b, 138c, 139c, 140t and b, 141t, 142t, c and cb, 144all, 145ct and b, 146t, ct and cb, 147all, 148b, 149 all, 150c and b, 151c and b, 152t and cb, 153 c and b, 154t and c, 155cb and b, 157t and c, 158b, 159b, 160cb, 161c, 162t and b, 163t, 165all, 166both, 167ct, cb and b, 168cb and ct, 170b, 171t, cb and b, 172t, ct and cb, 173b, 174all, 175all, 176t andb, 179t and b, 180t, 181t, ct and cb, 182t and c, 183ct, cb and b, 184t, ct and cb, 185t, 186t, ct and cb, 187b, 188c, 189t and b, 190ct, 191b, 192t and ct, 193c and b, 194all, 195both, 197c, 198b, 200c, 201b, 202both, 203b, 205t, 207c, 211b, 212both, 213b, 214t, 216t, 220t and c, 224b, 225t, 227c and b, 229t, c and b, 230t and c, 231t, 232t, 234c and b, 235t, 236c, 237 all, 238t and c, 239t and b, 240cb and b, 241all, 242t and b, 243t andct, 245ct and cb, 246t and c, 247 all, 248t and ct, 249b, 250t and cb, 251 c and b, 253t, ct andcb, 254c and b, 255all, 256 all, 257t, 258 c and b, 259t, ct and cb, 260b, 262t, ct and b, 263b, 264c and b, 265t, 266t, 267t and c, 268c and b, 269ct and cb, 270t, 271ct, cb and b, 273all, 274t, cb and b, 275t and c, 277cb and b, 278t and b, 279ct and b, 281all, 282t and b, 283t and c, 284c and b, 285t, ct and cb, 286t, cb and b, 287t, 288t, 289both, 290all, 291 c and b, 294t, 295ct and b, 296, 297t and cb, 298c and b, 299t, ct, and b, 300b, 303, 304t and c, 305t, ct and b, 306ct and b, 307b, 308, 309c, 310t, 311, 312t, 313ct, cb and b, 314t and ct, 315, 316t, cb and b, 317t, 318t, 319c and b, 320, 321t, cb and b, 322t and c, 323b, 324t and c, 325c and b, 326t, 327t and b, 328b, 329cb, 330t and b, 331b, 332t and b, 333t, 334 ct, cb and b, 335, 336t and c, 337t and b, 338, 339t, 341c and b, 343t and c, 345, 346ct, 350c and b, 351t and c, 361, 362t and b, 364t, 365b, 366b, 367t and b, 368, 369ct and b, 370t and b, 371t, 372b, 374t and c, 375c, 376b, 377, 378t, 380, 381t and b, 382t and b, 383t, 384c, 385, 386, 387b, 388t, 389t, 390t and c, 391b, 393t, 396c, 398ct, 399t, 400, 402b, 403t and c, 404b, 408t, 414b, 416t and c, 417t, 419c, 420b, 422b, 424t, 425c and b, 435b, 436cb and b, 440c and b,441c, 443t, 445t, 446t, 448b, 449b, 450c, 451t and c, 452c and b, 453, 454c, 457c and b, 459t, 460t, 462t and c, 465t, 466b,467c and b, 468, 470t, 471t and ct, 472c, 473t, 475t, 476c, 477t, 478c and b, 479b, 482t, 483t, 487b, 493b, 508b, 513b, 515t, 521c and b, 524c, 532b and c, 533t and b.

Bob Garwood: 394t, 395b, 397c, 399c and b, 418b, 419b, 420c, 480t.

Tony Gibbons:16c and b, 17t, 18t, 19, 20t, 22t and c, 23b, 24t and b, 25, 28, 29t, 30b, 31t, 32b, 33b, 34, 35t, 36, 37t and c, 38b, 39t and c, 40t, 41t and c, 42b, 43t, 45b, 46, 47, 48t, 49, 50t, 51t and c, 52t, 53, 54, 55, 58b, 59c, 60c, 62b 64c, 65t and c, 67t, 68c, 69c and b, 70c and b, 71, 73t, 74 both, 75t, 77all, 78t and c, 79all, 80b, 81b, 82c, 83t, ct and cb, 84t, 87t and b, 88 t and c, 89t and b, 92t, 93t, 94 t and b, 96ct, 98t and ct, 99ct, cb and b, 100t, 101, 102, 103, 104t and b, 105b and c, 106all, 107c and b, 108t, cb and b, 109c and b, 110cb and b, 111t and c, 116c, 117c, 118ct, 121t and b, 122b, 128t and b, 129 t and b, 131cb, 132c, 135t, 136c, 139b, 140c, 143t, 145cb, 146b, 151t, 152ct, 154b, 155t, 156c and b, 158t, 160b, 161t and b, 162c, 163ct andb, 167t, 168b, 169c, 170t, 171ct, 173t, 178all, 180b, 183t, 184b, 185c, 186b, 187c, 189c, 190t, cb and b, 191t, 192b, 193t, 197t and b, 198c, 199t, 200b, 201t, 203t and c, 204b, 206t, 207t, 208t and c, 209b, 211c, 213t, 214b, 215t, 217c, 219b, 220b, 221c, 225c, 227b, 229t, 231b, 235c and b, 244c, 245b, 249c, 251t, 252t, 253b, 263c, 264t, 265c, 267b, 269b, 270c, 272b, 274ct, 275b, 276t, 280t, 283b, 285b, 294b, 295t, 302c, 318b, 322b, 329b, 332c, 336b, 340b, 346t and b, 349t, 357c, 359c, 360c, 362c, 369t, 370c, 373t, 375t, 378b, 382c, 383ct, 384b, 389b, 391c, 394b, 395c, 396t and b, 398cb, 401t, 403b, 405t and c, 406b, 407b, 408ct and cb, 410b, 412t and b, 415t and b, 421, 423, 424c, 425t, 434b, 437cb, 495t and b, 498b, 501b, 511ct, 534t.

MARS: 358t, 491ct, 507t.

Mary Evans Picture Library: 14, 15, 26, 27, 29, 30t, 38t, 56, 57, 68b, 75cb, 88b, 92ct, 95b, 96b, 107t, 108ct, 118t, 120b, 207b, 221b.

National Maritime Museum 35c and b, 44t, 48b, 51b, 52b, 59t, 63t, 67b, 68t, 72, 75ct, 76t, 80t, 84b, 85b, 86t, ct and b, 89c, 90b, 91c, 92b, 93c, 98cb and b, 100b, 104c, 105t, 110t and ct, 113c, 116b, 128c, 129c, 138t and b, 139t, 152b, 155ct, 163cb, 177t, 192cb, 196t, 199b, 200t, 204 t and c, 205b, 208b, 209c, 210b, 219c, 221t, 226b, 268t, 300c, 305cb, 317c, 329ct, 331t, 337c, 342b, 413t, 180c, 182b, 188t.

Popperfoto: 31, 131tc, 141b, 142b, 156t, 164b, 172b, 176c, 187t, 191c, 301b, 344t, 500c.

Royal Caribbean International: 127, 218b, 219t.

Guy Smith / Mainline Design: 313t, 342c, 356b, 381c, 397t, 406t, 408b, 411b, 412ct, 420t, 429t and c, 430t, 431t, 432cb and b, 438c, 440t, 441b, 445c, 457t, 461b, 465c, 469c, 471cb and b, 476b, 480b, 485t and b, 489c, 494c and b, 495c, 496ct, 498t and c, 504t, 506b, 512t, 517t, 518b, 520t, 526t, 528c.

Smithsonian Institution: 64b.

TRH Pictures 21b, 60b, 61t, 75b, 91b, 93b, 97t, 109t, 111b, 112c, 113t, 115b, 121c, 122t, 132t, 135b, 137ct, 143b, 148t, 150t, 158c, 159c, 160t and c, 164t, 169t, 177b, 185b, 188b, 196c and b, 201c, 205c, 206b, 210t, 215b, 217b, 222, 223, 224t and c, 230b, 231c, 232b, 233t and c, 234t, 236t and b, 238b, 239c, 240t and ct, 242c, 243b and cb, 244t and b, 245t, 246b, 248cb and b, 249t, 250ct and b, 254t, 257c and b, 258t, 259b, 260t, 261all, 262cb, 265b, 269t, 270b, 271t, 272t, 276ct, cb and b, 277t and ct, 278c, 279t, 280c and b, 282c, 284t, 286ct, 287c and b, 288c and b, 291t and b, 292, 293, 294c, 295cb, 297ct and b, 298t, 299cb, 300t, 301t and c, 302t and b, 304b, 306t and cb, 307t and c, 309t and b, 310c and b, 312c and b, 314cb and b, 316ct, 317b, 318c, 319t, 321ct, 323t, 324b, 325t, 326b, 327c, 328t, 329t, 333c and b, 334t, 339b, 340t,ct, and cb, 341t, 342t, 343b, 344b, 346cb, 347b and t, 348, 349ct, cb and b, 350t, 351b, 352b, t and c, 353, 354, 355, 356c, 357t, 358ct and b, 359t, 360b, 363, 364t and b, 365c, 366c, 367c, 369cb, 371b, 372t, 373c and b, 374b, 375b, 376c and t, 378c, 379t and b, 384t, 387t, 392t, b and c, 393c, 395t, 397b, 398t and b, 401c and b, 405b, 409c, 410t, 411t, 412cb, 413b, 414t, 415c, 417c, 418t and c, 422t, 424b, 426, 427, 428c and b, 430t and cb, 431c and b, 432ct, 433, 435t and c, 437b, 438t, 439c, 440t, 442b, 443c and b, 444, 446c and b, 448t and c, 451b, 452t, 455, 456, 458, 459c and b, 460b, 461t and c, 462b, 463c and b, 464b, 466t, 469t and b, 470c and b, 472b, 473b, 474t and c, 475c and b, 476t, 477c and b, 478t, 480ct and cb, 481, 482b, 483b, 484c, 486t, 487c, 488t, 493t and ct, 494t, 497, 499, 500b, 502t, 503, 505t and b, 506t, 507b, 508c, 509, 510b, 511b, 512c, 513t and c, 514b, 516c, 517c, 518t and c, 519, 520b, 522b, 523, 524t, 525, 526c and b, 527b, 528t, 529t, 530, 531c and b, 532t, 533c, 534ct and cb.

Leo Van Ginderen: 153t, 159t, 168t, 169b, 211t, 218t, 428t, 430ct, 434t and c, 436ct, 437t, 438b, 439t and b, 442c, 445b, 447b, 449c, 450t, 454b, 464t and c, 467t, 472t, 474b, 489t, 490, 491t and cb, 492c, 500t, 501cb, 504c, 507c, 510t and c, 515b, 517b, 522t, 524b, 528b, 531t.

Wherry Yacht Charter: 173.